LUKE

PREACHING THE WORD
Edited by R. Kent Hughes

Genesis | R. Kent Hughes
Exodus | Philip Graham Ryken
Leviticus | Kenneth A. Mathews
Numbers | Iain M. Duguid
Deuteronomy | Ajith Fernando
Joshua | David Jackman
1 Samuel | John Woodhouse
Proverbs | Raymond C. Ortlund Jr.
Ecclesiastes | Philip Graham Ryken
Song of Solomon | Douglas Sean O'Donnell
Isaiah | Raymond C. Ortlund Jr.
Jeremiah and Lamentations | Philip Graham Ryken
Daniel | Rodney D. Stortz
Matthew | Douglas Sean O'Donnell
Mark | R. Kent Hughes
John | R. Kent Hughes
Romans | R. Kent Hughes
2 Corinthians | R. Kent Hughes
Galatians | Todd Wilson
Ephesians | R. Kent Hughes
Philippians, Colossians, and Philemon | R. Kent Hughes
1–2 Thessalonians | James H. Grant Jr.
1–2 Timothy and Titus | R. Kent Hughes and Bryan Chapell
Hebrews | R. Kent Hughes
James | R. Kent Hughes
1–2 Peter and Jude | David R. Helm
1–3 John | David L. Allen
Revelation | James M. Hamilton Jr.
The Sermon on the Mount | R. Kent Hughes

PRESCHING the WORD

LUKE

That You May Know *the* Truth

R. KENT HUGHES

WHEATON, ILLINOIS

Luke

Published by Crossway
1300 Crescent Street
Wheaton, Illinois 60187

Cover design: John McGrath, Simplicated Studio

Cover image: Adam Greene, illustrator

First printing 2015

Printed in the United States of America

All emphases in Scripture quotations have been added by the author.

Hardcover: 978-1-4335-3830-8
PDF ISBN: 978-1-4335-3831-5
Mobipocket ISBN: 978-1-4335-3832-2
ePub ISBN: 978-1-4335-3833-9

Library of Congress Cataloging-in-Publication Data

Hughes, R. Kent.
Luke : that you may know the truth / R. Kent Hughes. – Revised edition.
pages cm. – (Preaching the word)
Previously published as two separate volumes.
Includes bibliographical references and index.
ISBN 978-1-4335-3834-6 (hc)
1. Bible. Luke.–Commentaries. I. Title.
BS2595.53.H84 2013
226.4'07–dc23 2013031284

Crossway is a publishing ministry of Good News Publishers.

VP 24 23 22 21 20 19 18 17 16 15 14
15 14 13 12 11 10 9 8 7 6 5 4 3 2 1

To my former colleagues
David Helm and Jon Dennis,
founding pastors of
Holy Trinity Church, Hyde Park, Chicago

"Good news of great joy . . . for all the people."

LUKE 2:10

*"For the Son of Man came to seek
and to save the lost."*

LUKE 19:10

Contents

Acknowledgments

A hundred-plus expositions from one preacher may look to be a solo effort, but far from it. They are the products of many hearts and minds. My first thanks goes to Mrs. Sharon Fritz, my administrative assistant and researcher, who not only produces the manuscripts, but locates sources and substantiates footnotes from their primary origins if possible. Also, deep thanks to Herb Carlburg who has given the manuscripts further scrutiny, especially as to their Biblical veracity and clarity. And, as always, more thanks to Ted Griffin who has edited all the volumes of the Preaching the Word series. Not only is Ted a fine editor, but a lover of Biblical exposition.

A Word to Those Who Preach the Word

There are times when I am preaching that I have especially sensed the pleasure of God. I usually become aware of it through the unnatural silence. The ever-present coughing ceases and the pews stop creaking, bringing an almost physical quiet to the sanctuary—through which my words sail like arrows. I experience a heightened eloquence, so that the cadence and volume of my voice intensify the truth I am preaching.

There is nothing quite like it—the Holy Spirit filling one's sails, the sense of his pleasure, and the awareness that something is happening among one's hearers. This experience is, of course, not unique, for thousands of preachers have similar experiences, even greater ones.

What has happened when this takes place? How do we account for this sense of his smile? The answer for me has come from the ancient rhetorical categories of *logos*, *ethos*, and *pathos*.

The first reason for his smile is the *logos*—in terms of preaching, God's Word. This means that as we stand before God's people to proclaim his Word, we have done our homework. We have exegeted the passage, mined the significance of its words in their context, and applied sound hermeneutical principles in interpreting the text so that we understand what its words meant to its hearers. And it means that we have labored long until we can express in a sentence what the theme of the text is—so that our outline springs from the text. Then our preparation will be such that as we preach, we will not be preaching our own thoughts about God's Word, but God's actual Word, his *logos*. This is fundamental to pleasing him in preaching.

The second element in knowing God's smile in preaching is *ethos*—what you are as a person. There is a danger endemic to preaching, which is having your hands and heart cauterized by holy things. Phillips Brooks illustrated it by the analogy of a train conductor who comes to believe that he has been to the places he announces because of his long and loud heralding of them. And that is why Brooks insisted that preaching must be "the bringing of truth through personality." Though we can never *perfectly* embody the truth we preach, we must be subject to it, long for it, and make it as much a part of our ethos as possible. As the Puritan William Ames said, "Next to the Scriptures, nothing makes a sermon more to pierce, than when it comes out of the inward affection of the heart without any affectation." When a preacher's ethos backs up his *logos*, there will be the pleasure of God.

Last, there is *pathos*—personal passion and conviction. David Hume, the Scottish philosopher and skeptic, was once challenged as he was seen going to hear George Whitefield preach: "I thought you do not believe in the gospel." Hume replied, "I don't, but *he does*." Just so! When a preacher believes what he preaches, there will be passion. And this belief and requisite passion will know the smile of God.

The pleasure of God is a matter of *logos* (the Word), *ethos* (what you are), and *pathos* (your passion). As you *preach the Word* may you experience his smile—the Holy Spirit in your sails!

R. Kent Hughes
Wheaton, Illinois

1

An Orderly Account

LUKE 1:1–4

LOUIS MACNEICE WROTE regarding his reading of ancient literature:

> And how one can imagine oneself among them
> I do not know;
> It was all so unimaginably different
> And all so long ago.

His rhyme expressed a valid concern. We might feel the same about the ancient gospel, except for the blessed fact that there are four Gospel accounts. One of them was the painstaking work of Luke, a historian, theologian, and physician, who has given us one of the finest pieces of historical writing in all of ancient literature.

Interestingly, no one knows anything of Luke's origin. He was definitely nonapostolic, and he was a Gentile (cf. Colossians 4:11,14). By his own admission he was not an eyewitness to the story he records in his brilliant account (Luke 1:2). But Luke was well educated and cultured, and a physician to boot. Though we don't know the details of his conversion, he apparently reached Christian maturity before coming under Paul's influence. He became an intimate acquaintance of Paul, as the so-called "we sections" in Acts attest (16:10–17; 20:5; 21:18; 27:1—28:16). Very possibly he is the anonymous brother "who is famous among all the churches for his preaching of the gospel" in 2 Corinthians 8:18.[1] This certainly accords with his humble, self-effacing manner in keeping himself in the background of both Luke and Acts.

Luke stayed with Paul during his second imprisonment, right to the end. Shortly before his martyrdom Paul wrote to Timothy, "Luke alone is with me" (2 Timothy 4:11). What happened to Luke after the Apostle's martyrdom is a secret of history. However, Luke seems to have written his Gospel during the early sixties.[2]

It is by far the longest of the Gospels, and it contains many extras that are not included in the other three Gospels—to begin with, the entire content of the first two chapters, which detail the advent of Christ beginning with the histories of Zechariah and Elizabeth, then the annunciation to Mary, culminating in the nativity. We can thank Luke for the stories of Zacchaeus, the penitent thief, the two disciples on the road to Emmaus, and the famous parables of the Pharisee and the publican, the rich man and Lazarus, and the prodigal son.

Luke has given us an invaluable gift—the most extensive and varied of the Gospels, as well as the most artistically constructed and the most beautifully reasoned and written. We will now consider this man of God as a *historian*, *theologian*, *physician*, and *musician*.

Luke the Historian (vv. 1–4)

Luke presented himself as historian in a long Greek sentence that is considered to be the best-styled sentence in the entire New Testament.[3] He thus shouted to the ancient world that he was writing about history that must not be ignored.

Luke's Historical Precedents

Luke began by citing others' earlier work as laying a foundation for what he was about to do. "Many," he said, "have undertaken to compile a narrative of the things that have been accomplished among us" (v. 1). His attempt at gospel history was not something totally new but bore similarity to previous works unknown to us today, except for the Gospel of Mark.

These earlier accounts were characterized by orderliness that was undoubtedly a considerable help to Luke. They were based on the testimony of people who were there, as Luke made clear in his next phrase (v. 2): "Just as those who from the beginning were eyewitnesses and ministers of the word have delivered them to us."

The earlier accounts had come from people who had seen with their own eyes the sacred events that began with the ministry of John the Baptist (cf. 1 John 1:1). These eyewitnesses ultimately became "ministers of the word"—that is, preachers of the gospel.[4] They were not detached observers but men vitally involved with the Word they preached.

Luke wanted his readers to understand that his history of Jesus came from the best, most authentic written and oral sources. Luke's work was grounded in solid historiography and many reliable sources.

Luke's Qualification as Historian

Not only was his historiography extensive, but he met the basic qualification of a historian—thorough research—as the opening phrase of verse 3 indicates: "It seemed good to me also, having followed all things closely for some time past. . . ." Luke had spent time tracking down each detail, tracing everything thoroughly. The result was a spectacularly accurate history.

One of the famous stories of New Testament scholarship recounts the early skepticism of the famous Sir William Ramsay regarding Luke's history, and how the facts completely changed his mind so that he eventually wrote: "Luke's history is unsurpassed in regard to its trust-worthiness."[5]

Dr. Luke had crossed all his t's and dotted his i's, down to the smallest details, such as the tricky nomenclature of the officials mentioned in Acts.

Luke's Task as Historian

Because Luke saw his task as historian as far more than a chronological listing of the facts, he added, "It seemed good to me also . . . to write an orderly account for you, most excellent Theophilus" (v. 3). What he meant by "orderly account" was a systematic arrangement grouped around themes he wished to emphasize. The facts were never altered, but the way he grouped and juxtaposed them, his artistic and logical arrangement, was meant to pierce the reader's heart. Luke took great pains to present the gospel with maximum power. This, of course, was done under the guidance of the Holy Spirit. The result was a compelling story—especially when it is read and studied in sequence.

Luke's Purpose as Historian

Finally, Luke's forthright purpose in writing the history was moral, because he told Theophilus, "That you may have certainty concerning the things you have been taught" (v. 4). The word "certainty" appears last (for emphasis) in the long Greek sentence that comprises verses 1–4. Luke believed that the proper telling of the story of Jesus would certainly produce belief in its truth. In a word, Luke believed in the power of the gospel!

What a motivation to read and study the Gospel of Luke! The solid historiography from which Luke had drawn his painstaking research, his subtly arranged account, and his moral purpose of bringing certain faith will change lives through the power of the Holy Spirit. The power of Jesus' story is inexhaustible!

Luke the Theologian

Luke was not only an accomplished historian, he was also a skilled theologian. We have already touched on this by noting his careful arrangement of his materials to emphasize his theology. For example, Luke selected exactly ten stories for the birth and infancy narratives in chapters 1, 2. Five deal with events before Christ's birth, and five are postbirth. Further, there are special pairings of the events within each quintet—all for a purpose.

Prominent among the great theological emphases in Luke is *love*. Matthew's keynote is royalty, Mark's is power, and in Luke it is love. Love uniquely shines through in saying after saying and parable after parable in this Gospel.

The offer of *salvation* for all is far more prominent in Luke than in the other Gospels. The word is not even used in Matthew and Mark and appears only once in John. But Luke employs it five times, as well as using "to save" more than any other Gospel. The angel announcing the birth of "a Savior" said the good news was for "all the people" (2:10, 11). Samaritans find grace and give it. Simeon sings about "light . . . to the Gentiles" (2:32). Jesus heals non-Israelites. The mission of the seventy has reference to the Gentiles.

Luke records Jesus' repeated references to his coming death and gives profound detail concerning both the passion and *the cross*. Simeon's prophecy (2:34, 35) refers to the coming passion. The ox is a traditional symbol for the Gospel of Luke because it is a sacrificial animal. Luke lifts high the cross.

The Gospel opens with repeated references to *the Holy Spirit*: the baby John filled with the Spirit in his mother's womb (1:15), Elizabeth and Zechariah filled with the Spirit (1:41, 67), the Holy Spirit coming upon Simeon (2:25–27), Jesus' conception by the Spirit (1:35), the Spirit descending like a dove upon Jesus when he was baptized (3:22), the Spirit leading him into the wilderness (4:1). Thus the Holy Spirit was emphasized, culminating in his descent at Pentecost in Acts 2.

So Luke the theologian teaches us great truths through story. Those who study Luke cannot remain the same.

Luke the Physician

Luke was a medical doctor. In fact, Paul called him "the beloved physician" (Colossians 4:14). But this was not because he excelled in the healing arts. It is rather because he was a lover of people, a man who could submit his ego and desires to the service of others. As already mentioned, some believe he was "the brother who is famous among all the churches for his preaching of the gospel" in 2 Corinthians 8:18. Luke was a doctor of souls!

He delighted in mentioning *individuals*: Zechariah and Elizabeth, Mary and Martha, Zacchaeus, Cleopas, the woman who anointed Jesus' feet. Jesus' parables in the Gospel of Matthew center on the kingdom, but those in Luke stress people.

Luke's Gospel transcends the first century's neglect of *women*. We hear their names more there than in any other Gospel: Mary, Elizabeth, Anna, Martha, her sister Mary, Mary Magdalene, Joanna, Susanna, the widow of Nain, the widow who gave all she had, the daughters of Jerusalem, the women in Jesus' parables.

We see Luke's heart for *babies and children* in the stories of the infancy of John and Jesus. Luke gives us the only information about Jesus' boyhood. He also speaks of various individuals' only sons or only daughters.

Luke also shows himself powerfully disposed to *the poor*. He portrays Jesus as coming to preach the gospel to the poor and blessing the poor. The shepherds were poor. Joseph and Mary made an offering of the poor at Jesus' birth. Luke cared about the poor. He also repeatedly warned about the dangers of riches. The parables he recorded repeatedly return to these themes: the rich fool, the unjust steward, the rich man who ignored the beggar Lazarus, the rich young ruler, the widow's mite.

Luke was a tender doctor of souls. His ethos will touch and penetrate ours, and we will be sweeter and more tender as we give our souls to the study of his Gospel.

Luke the Musician

Luke's Gospel is a singing Gospel. It resounds with the music of praise to God. Early on we find the *Magnificat* (1:46–55), the *Benedictus* (1:68–79), the *Nunc Dimittis* (2:29–32), and the *Gloria* (2:14). The verb *rejoice* is found in Luke more than in any other book in the New Testament. Likewise *joy* occurs regularly. There is joy in Zacchaeus' receiving Jesus. There is joy on earth in the finding of the lost sheep and the lost coin, and there is joy in Heaven when lost sinners are found. The Gospel ends just as it began—with rejoicing.

Luke the *historian* will make you certain about the Gospel. Luke the *theologian* will touch you with God's love and grace. Luke the *physician* will help you to love people. Luke the *musician* will set your heart to singing.

May God guide and enlighten our hearts as we study this magnificent portion of his holy Word!

2

The Annunciation of John

LUKE 1:5–25

THE CLOSING LINES of Luke's first chapter describe the birth of Jesus with a haunting metaphor—"The Sunrise from on high" (1:78 NASB). The night before that sunrise had been long and dark. But the faithful, bright flashes of hope from God's Word assured them that one day the night would end. Malachi had assured those who loved God that "the sun of righteousness shall rise with healing in its wings. You shall go out leaping like calves from the stall" (Malachi 4:2). Isaiah had promised that before "the glory of the LORD shall be revealed," there would come "a voice [crying]: 'In the wilderness prepare the way of the LORD; make straight in the desert a highway for our God'" (Isaiah 40:5, 3). Malachi spoke similarly as he penned the final words of the Old Testament: "Behold, I will send you Elijah the prophet before the great and awesome day of the LORD comes" (Malachi 4:5).

When Luke wrote his Gospel, more than four hundred years had passed since Malachi's time without a word of prophecy or any sign of a prophet of God. But the long darkness was about to experience sunrise.[1] Great plans, laid in eternal ages past, now began to activate. Angels scurried around busily preparing for the dawn. The focus of the activity would be Herod's great temple, which Josephus dramatically described as a building that

> wanted nothing that could astound either mind or eye. For, being covered on all sides with massive plates of gold, the sun was no sooner up than it radiated so fiery a flash that persons straining to look at it were compelled to avert their eyes, as from the solar rays. To approaching strangers it appeared from a distance like a snow-clad mountain; for all that was not overlaid with gold was of purest white.[2]

This shimmering grandeur housed the heartbeat of Jewish piety, and some who had attached themselves to the temple were anxiously awaiting the sunrise (cf. Luke 2:25–29).

A Supernatural Appearance (vv. 1–12)

The Dramatis Personae

Luke introduces us to two major players—an exemplary couple named Zechariah and Elizabeth who had received the grace of God in large measure.

> In the days of Herod, king of Judea, there was a priest named Zechariah, of the division of Abijah. And he had a wife from the daughters of Aaron, and her name was Elizabeth. And they were both righteous before God, walking blamelessly in all the commandments and statutes of the Lord. But they had no child, because Elizabeth was barren, and both were advanced in years. (vv. 5–7)

Zechariah was an ordinary country priest, one of an estimated eight thousand living in Palestine at the time.[3] The priests were divided according to an arrangement first instituted one thousand years earlier under King David and reconstituted as twenty-four divisions after the Babylonian captivity.[4] Each division numbered about three hundred priests. Zechariah's division, the eighth division of Abijah, served for two one-week periods per year, as did the others. Fifty-six priests were chosen by lot to participate each day.[5]

The name Zechariah was a popular priestly name that meant "The Lord has remembered," and in his case it would prove dramatically prophetic. Elizabeth was also of priestly descent, and she had the same name as Aaron's wife, a preferred name for a priest's wife. Significantly, her name pointed to the promise keeping of God. Both Zechariah and Elizabeth were "righteous before God" (v. 6), beautiful people in God's sight. This does not mean they were sinless, but their lives conformed to God's Law, as the rest of verse 6 emphasizes. They were magnificent flowers in the Jewish religious system garden.

Their house surely enjoyed the happiness that comes to homes where both husband and wife are righteous, except for one thing—the couple had not been able to have children. In any culture infertility is an aching disappointment, and for some an almost unbearable stress. But the burden cannot be compared to that borne by childless women in ancient Hebrew culture because barrenness was considered a disgrace, even a punishment. For example, Hagar looked down on Sarah when Hagar conceived but Sarah remained barren (Genesis 16:4). Leah referred to her former barrenness as "affliction" (Genesis 29:32). Infertile Hannah wept bitterly (1 Samuel 1:5–8). Barrenness even carried a moral stigma because in Jewish thinking it was not the fate of the righteous (see, for example, Leviticus 20:20, 21). So Elizabeth had undoubtedly suffered smug reproach. She called her barrenness her "reproach" (v. 25).

The text says the two were "advanced in years" (v. 7). Nature's planned obsolescence had taken its course, and there was no hope. They had never heard of Hippocrates, but he had put it perfectly: "A man, when his growth is over, is dry and cold." The fountains of maternity were dry. The spotted, worn hands of this righteous couple would never hold a child of their own.

The Occasion

They did not know that dawn was about to break.

> Now while he was serving as priest before God when his division was on duty, according to the custom of the priesthood, he was chosen by lot to enter the temple of the Lord and burn incense. And the whole multitude of the people were praying outside at the hour of incense. (vv. 8–10)

The *Mishnah* states that before each of the two daily services, four sets of lots were used to determine the participants (*Yoma* 2:1–5). In this case the incense lot finally fell to Zechariah, and in an instant he was at the apex of his personal history. The honor of offering incense was the grandest event in all his earthly existence. Many priests never had the privilege, and no priest was allowed to offer it more than once.

Zechariah's adrenaline began to flow, and with it came the alert attention that notes every detail. What joy he would have in telling Elizabeth.

Zechariah was serving God with his cohorts in the heart of the gleaming temple, in the Court of the Priests, where the sacrifice was to be made. Outside, in the Court of Israel, faithful worshipers were praying. Then came the moment to step into the Holy Place. Before him rose the richly embroidered curtain of the Holy of Holies, resplendent with cherubim woven in scarlet, blue, purple, and gold. To his left was the table of showbread. Directly in front of him was the horned golden altar of incense (Exodus 30:1–10; 37:25–29). To his right stood the golden candlestick. Zechariah purified the altar and waited joyously for the signal to offer the incense so that, as it were, the sacrifices went up to God wrapped in the sweet incense of prayer.

The Encounter

His heart soared upward with the curling fragrance. But suddenly it spasmed in divine arrest because "there appeared to him an angel of the Lord standing on the right side of the altar of incense. And Zechariah was troubled when he saw him, and fear fell upon him" (vv. 11, 12). To the right between the altar and the candlestick was a supernatural being. There is no indication whether the angel was in the conventional image of man or whether it assumed a dramatic form, perhaps like the pyrotechnic display of the angel who appeared to Manoah (Judges 13:19–22). But we do know that the angel's appearance was dramatic because of the extreme fear that fell upon Zechariah.

This "angel of the Lord" was none other than Gabriel, who had appeared in Babylon over five thousand years before (cf. Luke 1:19 and Daniel 8:16). There is divinely intended parallelism in these appearances.[6] Gabriel appeared to Daniel at the time of the evening sacrifice (Daniel 9:20, 21), and now Gabriel appears to Zechariah at the time of sacrifice, which was probably the evening sacrifice.[7] Daniel described his fearful response by saying, "I fell into a deep sleep with my face to the ground" (Daniel 8:17), and Zechariah matched his terror (v. 12). Daniel was temporarily rendered speechless, as would be Zechariah (cf. Daniel 10:15 and Luke 1:20, 22). Daniel's encounter and vision had to do with the revelation of future messianic times, and Zechariah's encounter with Gabriel signaled the dawn of messianic times.

Luke the theologian was perfectly aware of these parallels and artistically drew them out under the inspiration of the Holy Spirit. Some critical scholars have even seen an allusion to the seventy weeks of Daniel 9:24 in the explicit and implicit chronology of Jesus' infancy. There are six months (180 days) between the announcements of John's and Jesus' coming births. Mary's pregnancy took nine months (270 days). And there were forty days from Jesus' birth to his presentation in the temple (cf. Leviticus 12:1–4). 180 + 270 + 40 = 490 days, or seventy weeks. This is, of course, a highly tenuous view. But what is certain is that the prophetic eastern sky had assumed a predawn glow, and in a moment messianic fulfillment would light the Jewish landscape.

A Prophecy Given (vv. 13–20)

Stricken Zechariah needed comfort. "But the angel said to him, 'Do not be afraid, Zechariah, for your prayer has been heard'" (v. 13a). The verb tense used here seems to refer to the prayer Zechariah had just uttered as he offered incense. Therefore, some think that he had been praying for a son. But given his incomprehension and unbelief at being told he would have a son, it is more probable that he was praying for the redemption of Israel. He would never have dreamed that his having a son would be the beginning of the answer.[8]

Whatever the case, Gabriel spoke, and prophecy, which had ceased at the close of Old Testament times, occurred for the first time in four hundred years.

A Son Is Promised

Gabriel's opening line is a bombshell for Zechariah: "Your wife Elizabeth will bear you a son, and you shall call his name John" (v. 13b). John, *Yohanan*, means "God has been gracious" or "God has shown favor." The logic of the name is clear: a prayer had just been offered for grace or favor, and that prayer was heard. A son will be born and is to be named "God has been gracious."[9] Aged Elizabeth will experience a maternal spring. A gracious gift will come from her dry womb.

The Son's Character

Once the subject of the prophecy is stated, awesome Gabriel begins a joyous description of the son.

"And you will have joy and gladness, and many will rejoice at his birth, for he will be great before the Lord" (vv. 14, 15a). Both the personal delight of his parents and the public joy he would bring would come because of his inner greatness of soul. Samuel's prophetic declaration that "the LORD sees not as man sees: man looks on the outward appearance, but the LORD looks on the heart" (1 Samuel 16:7b) had stood for one thousand years. The Baptist would have a great heart. Jesus would later say of him, "Truly, I say to you, among those born of women there has arisen no one greater than John the Baptist" (Matthew 11:11a; cf. Luke 7:28). Next to Christ, Zechariah and Elizabeth's son would develop a soul second to none, not even Abraham, Joseph, or Daniel. What a perpetual joy he would be to his old parents.

The Son's Spiritual Formation

Gabriel then revealed what would go into their son's spiritual development: "He must not drink wine or strong drink" (v. 15b). Gabriel was saying that John would be a Nazirite, a man set apart by ascetic rigors to be especially devoted to God (cf. Numbers 6:1–21). From birth he would be prepared for special service to God through spiritual disciplines—he would never take strong drink, cut his hair, or touch a dead body. Thus, his inner life would bear powerful testimony to the world.

"And he will be filled with the Holy Spirit, even from his mother's womb" (v. 15c). John's fullness would not be found in what ordinarily fills people, but in the gift of the Spirit. Because he was a Nazirite, the Lord's Spirit would fill him instead of the drink he had foregone. The filling would be prenatal—"even from his mother's womb." Joseph Fitzmyer and John Nolland have shown that the grammar plus the context (1:41) demand the meaning "while still in the womb."[10]

Nolland aptly remarks, "Such total invasion by the Spirit of God is unprecedented."[11] Indeed it was! John's filling was prophetic of the filling of the Holy Spirit that would be the hallmark of all who are in Christ. Astounding internal and external forces would effect John's spiritual formation. What an extraordinary son was coming to "righteous" Zechariah and Elizabeth!

The Son's Ministry

Gabriel then prophesied the effects of their son-to-be's ministry: "And he will turn many of the children of Israel to the Lord their God, and he will go before him in the spirit and power of Elijah, to turn the hearts of the fathers to the children, and the disobedient to the wisdom of the just, to make ready for the Lord a people prepared" (vv. 16, 17). Gabriel quoted in part the final two verses of the Old Testament, Malachi 4:5, 6, to summarize John's earthly ministry: "'Behold, I will send you Elijah the prophet before the great and awesome day of the LORD comes. And he will turn the hearts of fathers to their children and the hearts of children to their fathers, lest I come and strike the land with a decree of utter destruction.'" The prophet Elijah had denounced the apostasy of his own people. He had withstood the pagan prophets of Baal. God rained down fire from Heaven on his behalf. The Baptist would minister in the same spirit and power. Jesus said of him:

> "Elijah does come, and he will restore all things. But I tell you that Elijah has already come, and they did not recognize him, but did to him whatever they pleased. So also the Son of Man will certainly suffer at their hands." Then the disciples understood that he was speaking to them of John the Baptist. (Matthew 17:11–13; cf. Mark 9:13)

John's ministry would so affect the hearts of his people that it would revolutionize the way they lived in their homes, turning "the hearts of fathers to their children." Fathers (parents) would awaken to their parental responsibilities. They would avoid the failures of Eli and Samuel and David. This marks the preaching of the gospel today as well. Regenerated hearts produce reprioritized lives, and families are redeemed. People are made ready for the Lord.

Picture old Zechariah. He is serving in the heart of the temple. The sacred ambience overwhelms him. The light from the flickering golden candlestick reveals the richly embroidered hues of the cherubim on the veil before the Holy of Holies. The golden altar of incense glistens in the light. The aroma of worship swirls about him. It is the grandest day of his life. Zechariah prays for the redemption of his people—and a supernatural being is there! Cardiac terror! Then the being speaks, promising a son whose name evokes the favor of God. He prophesies regarding the son's *character*, his *spiritual formation*, and his *ministry*, invoking the final lines of the Old Testament as his son's script.

Zechariah's Response

It may have seemed like the world had stopped spinning as Gabriel silently awaited Zechariah's answer. Sadly, Zechariah responded with woeful disbelief as he asked the angel, "How shall I know this? For I am an old man, and my wife is advanced in years" (v. 18).

Zechariah should not have doubted, for several reasons. 1) He was well acquainted with the Scriptures and knew about the divine interventions in the births of Isaac and Samson and Samuel. He should have concluded that since God had done it before, he could do it again. 2) Zechariah was a priest, not an atheist. He was a man of God and thus was noted for his piety and faith, a "righteous" man. 3) He was offering prayer in the temple on the most important day of his life. Moreover, the offering of incense symbolized petition for corporate Israel. As part of the community of faith, he should have had a bigger view of God. 4) He was confronted by a being he knew to be supernatural (thus his terror). So he knew the message was from God.

Yet Zechariah disbelieved! This was serious, because in his doubt he implicitly denied the power that would be so central to the gospel—namely, the power of resurrection. If God could not give Zechariah's wife Elizabeth the power to conceive, how could he raise Jesus' body from the tomb? The priest's unbelief was unknowingly subversive to the entire gospel.[12] The coming of "the sunrise . . . from on high" (1:78) would do no one any good apart from faith. The messianic age demands belief!

Gabriel's Declaration

Gabriel reacted decisively to Zechariah's doubt.

> And the angel answered him, "I am Gabriel. I stand in the presence of God, and I was sent to speak to you and to bring you this good news. And behold,

> you will be silent and unable to speak until the day that these things take place, because you did not believe my words, which will be fulfilled in their time." (vv. 19, 20)

Perhaps Gabriel's self-revelation reminded Zechariah of Daniel's prompt acceptance of Gabriel's word and by contrast showed Zechariah the shabbiness of his own unbelief. Gabriel's emphatic "I stand in the presence of God" was meant to shame the priest, as was his emphasis on Zechariah's rejection of "good news." The penalty for the man's unbelief was well fitted to the offense, for Zechariah's tongue, which had uttered unbelief, was struck speechless. The aged priest would have nine months of silence—plenty of time to reflect on the situation.

The Prophecy's Results (vv. 21–25)

Zechariah Stricken

It did not take long for a priest to offer incense, and normally the priest came out quickly to lead in blessing the people (*M. Tamid* 7:2). The throng wondered at the delay and undoubtedly became restless. When Zechariah finally emerged, he could not pronounce the blessing, for he was mute. The word used here can mean both mute and deaf, and 1:62 indicates that Zechariah's friends "made signs" to communicate with him, thus implying that he was deaf, confined to his own silent world.[13]

Zechariah was an upright man whose life was characterized by faith. His failure on this occasion was an aberration. And the judgment was not merely punitive but gloriously remedial. The fact that he was deaf and mute confirmed Gabriel's promise to him. And he knew that his condition was not permanent, but only until the birth of the child.

Elizabeth Conceives

Zechariah had so much to tell dear Elizabeth. Communicating what had happened was excruciating, but Zechariah succeeded. And in fulfillment of God's promise, Elizabeth conceived. Her old body experienced maternal bloom, and they were both ecstatic with excitement. "'Thus the Lord has done for me in the days when he looked on me, to take away my reproach among people'" (v. 25).

Though the true Sunrise would not come until the birth of Jesus, from this point on there was a glow in their lives. Their faith grew and grew and grew. In six months they would host the young mother-to-be of the Son of God and even nurture her faith. They would hear her sing the *Magnificat*.

And speechless Zechariah would one day sing his song of faith—the *Benedictus*. What stupendous spiritual events were on the horizon—leading up to the birth of Messiah so he could later die for our sins and give us eternal life! The truth of this message is as sure as the words of Gabriel to Zechariah.

Jesus' words are penetratingly clear: "'Truly, truly, I say to you, whoever hears my word and believes him who sent me has eternal life. He does not come into judgment, but has passed from death to life'" (John 5:24). "Then they said to him, 'What must we do, to be doing the works of God?' Jesus answered them, 'This is the work of God, that you believe in him whom he has sent'" (John 6:28, 29).

3

The Annunciation of Christ

LUKE 1:26–38

WITHOUT A DOUBT we could spend our lives searching the literature of the world for a story as beautiful as that of the nativity and never find it. The narrative of Christ's birth is especially piercing because it is true, being firmly fixed in history with an actual place and real people. It began for Christ's mother with the annunciation, which in itself is a story of singular beauty and wonder firmly situated in human life.

The setting for the annunciation drew amazement from first-century Jewish readers because Gabriel ignored Judea, the heartland of God's work through the centuries, and came to Galilee, a land that was the subject of abiding Jewish contempt because of its mongrelized population. Even more, the angel not only bypassed Judea for Galilee, but the city of Jerusalem for the village of Nazareth. Nazareth was a "nonplace." It was not even mentioned in the Old Testament or in Josephus's writings or in the rabbinical writings (either talmudic or midrashic). It wasn't until 1962 that a pre-Christian mention of Nazareth was found at Caesarea Maritima.[1] The later prominence of the town is a result of the Christian gospel. Nazareth, a shoddy, corrupt halfway stop between the port cities of Tyre and Sidon, was overrun by Gentiles and Roman soldiers. When guileless, straight-talking Nathaniel mentioned Nazareth, he said, "Can anything good come out of Nazareth?" implying that it was miserably corrupt (John 1:46). By consensus, Nazareth was not much.

Of course, in skipping Judea and Jerusalem, Gabriel also ignored the temple, the most holy place in Israel, and entered the lowly home of Mary, which certainly was not much.

In the world's eyes Mary herself was not of much account either. She was too young to know much of the world or to have accomplished anything.

According to the Apocryphal Gospel of the Birth of Mary, she was only fourteen; and the History of Joseph the Carpenter states that she was only twelve.[2] No less a scholar than Raymond Brown, author of the massive and definitive *The Birth of the Messiah*, argues for the younger age.[3] She was at most a young teenager. As with all poor peasant girls, she was illiterate, her knowledge of the Scriptures being limited to what she had memorized at home and heard in the synagogue.

From all indicators, her life would not be extraordinary. She would marry humbly, give birth to numerous poor children, never travel farther than a few miles from home, and one day die like thousands of others before her—a nobody in a nothing town in the middle of nowhere.

As we probe this beautiful text of the annunciation we cannot miss an inescapable fact: *the greatest news ever proclaimed in Israel came to the humblest of its people!* Mary said exactly that in her *Magnificat* when she sang, "My soul magnifies the Lord, and my spirit rejoices in God my Savior, for he has looked on the humble estate of his servant" (1:46–48a).

Nine months later, on Christmas Day, it was to poor, humble shepherd outcasts that the angels chorused their annunciation: "Glory to God in the highest, and on earth peace among those with whom he is pleased" (Luke 2:14). Whenever we consider those to whom the good news came, we must recite a list punctuated by the words "poor" and "humble." Martin Luther remarked, "He might have gone to Jerusalem and picked out Caiaphas's daughter, who was fair, rich, clad in gold embroidered raiment and attended by a retinue of maids in waiting. But God preferred a lowly maid from a mean town."[4] And if the incarnation happened today, it would be the same. The Lord would not be born in Jerusalem or Rome or Geneva or Canterbury, but on the ordinary streets of some nameless town.

As we study the annunciation, we must accept the essential spiritual fact of the incarnation and the gospel: the Lord comes to *needy* people—those who realize that without him they cannot make it—those who acknowledge their weakness and spiritual lack. The incarnation, salvation, resurrection, and *Christmas* are not for the proud and self-sufficient.

As we follow the course of the annunciation, we will catch the pulse of the virgin's heart because *Mary is a model for those who experience the birth of the Savior in their lives.*

Gabriel's Approach (vv. 26–29)

In considering Gabriel's approach to Mary, we must remember that he had made an appearance to Zechariah, the father of John the Baptist, six months earlier, striking Zechariah speechless (1:5–23)—a condition that remained until his son was born. Zechariah's encounter had been very similar to Gabriel's terrifying appearance to the prophet Daniel five hundred years before when the result was the same—Daniel too fell mute.

Meeting Gabriel could be very intimidating, to say the least! Now as he comes to Mary, we can reasonably suppose that his appearance was not as awesome as with Daniel and Zechariah, for she would likely have been frightened out of her senses. However, he probably also did not come looking like everyone else—in button-down collar and wingtips. Mary needed to see that he was indeed an angel. Perhaps he turned up his rheostat so he glowed like a summer firefly, or perhaps he stood with his feet just off the ground. However it was, verses 26–28 describe the encounter:

> In the sixth month the angel Gabriel was sent from God to a city of Galilee named Nazareth, to a virgin betrothed to a man whose name was Joseph, of the house of David. And the virgin's name was Mary. And he came to her and said, "Greetings, O favored one, the Lord is with you!"

Remember, Mary was somewhere between the ages of twelve and fourteen. She was unread and inexperienced. She was not cosmopolitan. She did not own a TV. She did not have a computer. Knowing this, how do you suppose she felt? I think Mary felt like fainting! Probably she thought, *This can't be real! I have to sit down.* We can be sure that Gabriel's buoyant greeting—"Greetings, O favored one, the Lord is with you!"—was most necessary.

What did Gabriel mean by this famous greeting? Certainly not the *Douai Version's* "Hail Mary full of grace" derived from the Latin Vulgate's *"Ave, gratia pleta."* Raymond Brown, the acknowledged dean of Catholic New Testament scholars, agrees, saying that "full of grace" is too strong a rendering, for if Luke wanted to say this, he would have used the phrase he employed in Acts 6:8 when he described Stephen as "full of grace."[5]

Brown notes that the Vulgate's faulty translation gave rise to the medieval idea that "Mary had every gift, not only spiritual but secular, even above those given to angels,"[6] thus giving rise to the idea of Mary being a dispenser of grace, resulting in prayers being offered to her. The ultimate extension of this thinking came on December 8, 1854, when Pius IX declared the doctrine of the Immaculate Conception, teaching that "From the first moment of her conception, the Blessed Virgin Mary was, by the singular grace and privilege of Almighty God, and in view of the merits of Jesus Christ, Savior of mankind, kept free from stain of original sin."[7] That doctrine is a sad, totally unjustified distortion. Mary would have been scandalized at the thought. Karl

Barth aptly responds, "Can such a figure meet with worse misunderstanding than that which happened to her in the Catholic church?"[8]

But at the same time, the Virgin Mary is in fact the most blessed of women, and therefore "the Blessed Virgin Mary" is a fitting designation for her. The title springs naturally from Mary's own self-bestowed beatitude in her *Magnificat*: "From now on all generations will call me blessed" (1:48). Mary was the only woman of the billions who have inhabited our planet who was chosen to carry and nurse God's Son. For that we must call her "blessed." "Hers . . . was the face that unto Christ had most resemblance."[9] The Savior bore some of her human features—Jesus' face could be seen in hers. Think of it. She is blessed indeed. Just because others have thought *too much* of her, we must not imagine that our Lord is pleased when we think *too little* of her. We, as part of the subsequent Christian generations, are to call her "blessed."

Gabriel's salutation, "Greetings, O favored one, the Lord is with you," was a dual declaration. First, Mary was the recipient of special divine favor. She was specially graced. Her humble estate and matching humility of soul made her the ideal receptor of God's greatest favor. As such, Luther praised her: "O Mary, you are blessed. You have a gracious God. No woman has ever lived on earth to whom God has shown such grace. You are the crown of them all."[10] God bypassed Judea, Jerusalem, and the temple and came to a despised country, a despised town, and a humble woman.

The second part of her being divinely favored is Gabriel's declaration, "The Lord is with you!" This unconventional phrase declares the dynamic power of God's presence, which runs like a golden thread in the lives of great saints in Old Testament history. And in Mary it reaches its glorious culmination.[11] The Lord was *with* her.

So Gabriel's dual declaration to Mary is one of God's special *favor* and his special *presence*. It is a stupendous declaration and certainly justifies the translation some scholars give to Gabriel's initial word "Greetings" as "Rejoice"—which is the literal sense.[12] "Rejoice, you who are highly favored! The Lord is with you."

Mary's response to Gabriel's greeting reveals another of her blessed heart's qualities: "But she was greatly troubled at the saying, and tried to discern what sort of greeting this might be" (v. 29). The literal sense is that she *kept* pondering the meaning of the greeting. Whatever Gabriel's glorious form was like, Mary was able to get past it to his greeting, upon which she meditated as she sought understanding.

This is a truly remarkable picture. Young and inexperienced as she was, Mary was not a flighty, shallow "young thing." She was reflective and meditative. It is said that contemplation is not a psychological trick but a theological grace. Mary had this grace. She stood on the ascent of the mount of grace and meditated upon what the angel's message meant *for* her and what it would require *from* her.

Mary's example has a practical relevance for our frenetic, uncontemplative age. Those who experience the birth of the Savior in their lives are those who take the time to ponder God's Word to them. "I will meditate on your precepts" (Psalm 119:78). We need such hearts today.

When the poet Southey was telling an old Quaker lady how he learned Portuguese grammar while he washed, and something else while he dressed, and how he gleaned in another field while he breakfasted and so on, filling his day utterly, she said quietly, "And when does thee think?"[13] That is the perfect question for us. When do we contemplate the condition of our lives, meditate on God's Word, and focus upon the course and destiny of where we are headed in light of God's revelation? At Christmastime, when we most consider the opening chapters of Luke, and at all other times too, we need to "center-down," to use the old Quaker term, and ponder the things that really count—perhaps even to be "greatly troubled," as was the blessed virgin, to be serious before God and devote ourselves again and again fully to his will.

Let all mortal flesh keep silent,
And with fear and trembling stand;
Ponder nothing earthly minded,
For with blessing in His hand
Christ our God to earth descendeth,
Our full homage to demand.

Liturgy of St. James (fifth century)

Gabriel's Annunciation (vv. 30–34)

Thus far Gabriel had told the virgin nothing of his mission. But now came the annunciation itself, and the initial words were shocking: "And the angel said to her, 'Do not be afraid, Mary, for you have found favor with God. And behold, you will conceive in your womb and bear a son, and you shall call his name Jesus'" (vv. 30, 31). Mary was told that she would have a baby boy, and she was commanded to name him Jesus. This news was a thunderbolt!

It is doubtful at this point that she fully understood. *Jesus* was a common name that meant "savior," but she could hardly have grasped its full impact. However, as Gabriel continued the annunciation—"He will be great and will be called the Son of the Most High" (v. 32a)—the impact must have been staggering. The child would be God's Son!

Gabriel went on to explain, "And the Lord God will give to him the throne of his father David, and he will reign over the house of Jacob forever, and of his kingdom there will be no end" (vv. 32b, 33). Mary was hearing that she would mother the long-awaited Messiah, and she got the idea! Gabriel's words were a free interpretation of 2 Samuel 7:8–16, a foundational messianic prophecy called "the Davidic Covenant." The Qumran texts reveal that this was indeed the way the Jews understood that prophecy.[14] No doubt Mary had heard those very lines in the synagogue readings and knew of their messianic implications.

She understood the gist of the angel's announcement: "You are going to become *pregnant*; you are going to call your son's name *Salvation*, he is going to be the *Son of God*, and he will be *the Messiah*." What an earful! What an incredible heartful!

Humble, reflective Mary thought about it—and understood. Then she asked the logical question: "How will this be, since I am a virgin?" (v. 34)—literally, "How can this be since I have not known a man sexually?" Mary was not disbelieving—she was simply asking for enlightenment. The question was biological: "God, how are you going to do this?"

Again, she is a spiritual model for all who experience the birth of the Savior in their lives because this is a believing question. It is the question that all those who know Jesus have asked: "God, how is it possible?" Do you have this blessed inquisitiveness? Have you asked, "God, how can I experience the life of Jesus within me?"

This is a life-giving question because it requires an examination of the significance of Christ's atoning work on the cross and how its cleansing benefits come to us by faith. The mysteries of the new birth must also be contemplated—the work of the Holy Spirit, what it means to be "in Christ" and "a new creation," and much more. Such "how can this be?" contemplations often serve as a prelude to knowing Christ.

Gabriel's Explanation (vv. 35–38)

The answer Mary received marvelously foreshadowed God's personal answer to us: "And the angel answered her, 'The Holy Spirit will come upon you, and the power of the Most High will overshadow you; therefore the child to be born will be called holy—the Son of God'" (v. 35). What is described here? Certainly not a sexual union (mating) with divinity, as some have argued. Nothing so crude is suggested here. All leading scholars agree that there are no sexual overtones whatsoever.[15] The word "overshadow" gives us the proper understanding because it is used in the Greek Old Testament to describe *God's presence* in the sanctuary and in the New Testament for his overshadowing *presence* at the transfiguration where the cloud of glory overshadowed our Lord and his apostles.

While it was not a sexual experience, it was surely a conscious experience—something Mary could feel. How could anyone have the Holy Spirit come upon him or her and be overshadowed as in the temple or on the Mount of Transfiguration and not know it? Perhaps it was in the very moment of Gabriel's statement that she was overshadowed. Or perhaps it was after the angel left and she stood there in awed silence. At any rate Mary understood the awesome significance of what she had heard, and that is one of the things that held her so faithful during the tumultuous months and years that followed.

Whether we choose to believe it or not is one thing, but we cannot deny that what was described by Gabriel is nothing less than the virgin birth of Christ.

Those of us who have experienced the birth of Christ within us have also experienced the presence of God and the miraculous life-giving work of the Holy Spirit as he has come upon us, bestowing life within. Jesus said, "That which is born of the Spirit is spirit" (John 3:6). Paul likewise said, "For in one Spirit we were all baptized into one body" (1 Corinthians 12:13). And if the Spirit has come upon us and has given us new life, we *know* it! "The Spirit himself bears witness with our spirit that we are children of God" (Romans 8:16).

This is one of the wonders Christ offers each one of us—new life from above—something we cannot do for ourselves—something palpable and living and growing—something we can know for sure!

Gabriel's mission now complete, he left Mary with a sign: "And behold, your relative Elizabeth in her old age has also conceived a son, and this is the sixth month with her who was called barren" (v. 36). Elizabeth's miraculous pregnancy in old age had been hidden from Mary by Elizabeth's having spent the last six months in seclusion in the hill country. This amazing news about Elizabeth and Mary's ensuing time with the elderly, godly woman would prove a great help to the young virgin.

Finally, Gabriel's parting words said it all as he proclaimed, "For nothing will be impossible with God" (v. 37)—literally, "For not impossible will be every word with God." This is an allusion to the Lord's words to barren Sarah confirming that she would bear Isaac in her old age (Genesis 18:14; cf. Job 42:2; Zechariah 8:6). God would fulfill his word! Nothing is too hard for God! It is as simple as that.

Mary instinctively knew her story would be questioned. Indeed, Joseph himself first doubted it (Matthew 1:19). She knew that the death penalty was prescribed for adultery (though it was no longer carried out). New Testament history records that Jesus' enemies on more than one occasion implied that he was illegitimate. In light of these daunting realities, consider Mary's eternally worthy response: "'Behold, I am the servant of the Lord; let it be to me according to your word.' And the angel departed from her" (v. 38). She could have said, "Gabriel, thanks but no thanks. Count this girl out." But not Mary, for she made a habit of submitting to God in everything.

For Luke the theologian, Mary is a fine example of belief and discipleship. She is a model Christian. Her obedience made her at the same time the *mother* and a *disciple* of Christ (cf. 8:19–21; 11:27, 28). She would wait in prayer with the faithful disciples after Jesus' ascension for the giving of the Holy Spirit (Acts 1:14). As a model for those who experience the birth of Christ in their lives, she has one word for them: *submission*. We cannot experience Christ and his ongoing power without totally surrendering ourselves to him.

Have you ever said, and can you now say, "I am the Lord's servant. May it be to me as you have said"? These are words that bring God's blessing. This is the way Jesus taught us to pray: "Your will be done, on earth as it is in heaven" (Matthew 6:10)—"Father, let your will be done right here, just as it is in Heaven itself."

Is your life submitted to God like Mary's was? You can say, "Let it be to me according to your word" through angry, clenched lips, but that was not Mary's tone. It is also possible to say it in a funereal tone of resignation and defeat that goes best with the cloying smell of flowers. Or you can say it with joy and expectancy: "Let it be to me according to your word! Conquer me, Lord! I am yours!"

If you can say that, you, like Mary, are blessed among the inhabitants of this earth. Do you need to say it now?

Closing Reflections

The annunciation story is ours because of the wonderful heart of the Virgin Mary.

She was humble and poor in spirit. She was not self-sufficient. This posture of her heart made her open to the grace of God, so that Gabriel could say, "Greetings, O favored one, the Lord is with you!" For this she was and is called blessed.

Mary's reflective, meditative nature made her open to the Word and work of God. She was not superficial. Because of this she was and is called blessed.

Mary was believing regarding God's power. She wondered about the mechanics of God's grace but knew he could do as promised. Because of this she was and is called blessed.

Finally, she gave herself in profound submission to God: "Mary said, 'Behold, I am the servant of the Lord; let it be to me according to your word'" (v. 38a). For this she was and is called blessed.

If Christ is in us, so that we are God's children, then Mary's heart is our model for discipleship.

We must cultivate a *humble* heart, an ongoing poverty of spirit that is not only open to God's grace, but desperately longs for it (cf. Matthew 5:3–6).

We must also intentionally nurture a *reflective* heart that meditates on God's Word (cf. Psalm 1).

Next, we must have *believing* hearts modeled on that dynamic certainty of Mary's heart, a *future* certitude ("Now faith is the assurance of things hoped for") and a *visual* certitude ("the conviction of things not seen" [Hebrews 11:1]).

Finally, we must have *submissive* hearts: "I am the servant of the Lord; let it be to me according to your word" (v. 38a).

> Lord, make me according to thy heart.
>
> Brother Lawrence

4

The Visitation

LUKE 1:39–55

THE ANGEL GABRIEL'S ANNUNCIATION declared the astounding facts of the incarnation. The Virgin Mary's young heart showcased the characteristics essential for all who would experience the birth of Christ in their lives. She was a living beatitude, and her soul was a blessed model for all who desire to cultivate the life of Christ in their hearts.

What further astounds us is her tender age. Joachim Jeremias, the master New Testament scholar, categorically states: "The usual age for a girl's betrothal was between twelve and twelve and a half."[1] This, coupled with the custom that after betrothal the bride would live with her family for a year before formal transferal to the groom's home, meant that Mary was just beyond puberty and that she had not even attained her adult height and figure. This is offensive to our modern, Western sensibilities. Nevertheless, a twelve- to fourteen-year-old girl was not only chosen to be the virgin mother of our Lord, but to model a godly heart and verbalize sublime spiritual realities that have challenged the greatest of saints.

Mary, despite her young age, sharing with the rest of humanity the *imago Dei*, had immense spiritual capacity. Though she was illiterate, she understood deep theological realities, as her *Magnificat* would soon attest. Though Mary was so young, the world sings of her amazing obedience. The church must never make the mistake of minimizing or patronizing its youth. Children must be taken seriously. Teenagers must be intelligently challenged. The church must invest deeply in the spiritual nurture and discipling of its young.

Mary Journeys (v. 39)

We take up Mary's story with her immediate decision to visit her aged, barren relative Elizabeth, who, as Gabriel had just revealed to Mary, was pregnant and six months along (v. 36). Her pregnancy was miraculous, but we must never confuse how vastly different it was from the miracle occurring within Mary. Barren Elizabeth was not a virgin, and Zechariah was the natural father of her child. Nevertheless, what a surge of joy swept through Mary as she heard the shocking good news about the miracle in Elizabeth's womb, for it bore parallel testimony to God's power.

Luke reports Mary's response matter-of-factly: "In those days Mary arose and went with haste into the hill country, to a town in Judah" (v. 39). Mary made hasty arrangements with her parents (did she tell them? we do not know) and rushed the 80 to 100 miles south to the countryside of Judea, a three- or four-day journey.[2] Her haste indicates eagerness.[3] She could not wait to get there. There were no leisurely teenaged conversations along the way. As she hurried along, she thought long and deep of their crossed destinies, as she and Elizabeth were both in miraculous pregnancy. And then she was there, unannounced, silhouetted in the old couple's doorway.

There was a strong human joy in the meeting of these two expectant mothers—one in the flower of youth, the other's bloom long gone. These two were to become innocent coconspirators, soul-sisters in the divine plot to save the lost. They would share their hearts as few humans ever have. Through their birthing pain, sweat, and blood, and their mothering too, the world would receive its greatest blessing.

John Leaps (vv. 40, 41)

The meeting was appropriately dramatic. Verses 40, 41 tell us, "She entered the house of Zechariah and greeted Elizabeth. And when Elizabeth heard the greeting of Mary, the baby leaped in her womb." Elizabeth explained what happened in her response (v. 44): "When the sound of your greeting came to my ears, the baby in my womb leaped for joy." The sense here is that before Elizabeth herself could return the greeting, the child in her womb leapt. John responded before Elizabeth did.[4]

Only a mother can relate to the sensation described here because more than a prenatal kick or turn, it was a leap, an upward vault. The word translated "leaped" here is used to describe skipping or leaping, as of sheep in the field.[5]

Why did Elizabeth's baby react in this way? The answer is twofold. First, there was a prophet in her womb, and this was his first prophecy. John the Baptist's ministry was beginning three months before his birth. The Holy Spirit, with whom he was filled before birth, prompted his inner vault (1:15). John's joyous leap was lived out in life some thirty years later when he compared his prophetic joy in announcing Christ with that of a friend of the groom at his wedding, saying, "The friend of the bridegroom, who stands and hears him, rejoices greatly at the bridegroom's voice. Therefore this joy of mine is now complete" (John 3:29).

Second, John leapt because he was overcome with the emotion of joy. The more exact sense is that he "leaped with delight."[6] Do not miss the point: this fetus, yet to see the light of the world, experienced the emotion of joyous delight. This is incontrovertible testimony to the prebirth personhood of John the Baptist. John was then about nine inches long and weighed about one and a half pounds. He looked like a perfect miniature newborn. His skin was translucent. He had fingerprints and toe prints. Sometimes he opened his eyes for brief periods and gazed into the liquid darkness of the womb.

If John could have spoken, he might have quoted Job: "Did you not pour me out like milk and curdle me like cheese? You clothed me with skin and flesh, and knit me together with bones and sinews" (Job 10:10, 11). As a fetus of six months, John was an emotional being. He had the capacity to be filled with the Spirit. He was so overcome that he leapt for joy. This is a sobering revelation for anyone who countenances abortion, but especially for Christians.

But there is more. Mary had already conceived. She was three or four days pregnant. Jesus was a zygote, and when Jesus, a zygote in the womb of his mother, entered the room, John the Baptist, a six-month-old fetus in Elizabeth's womb, leapt for joy. And Elizabeth addressed Mary in the present tense as "the mother of my Lord" (v. 43).

In view of all this, I pose this question: If young Mary had gotten an abortion, what would she have aborted—a potential human being or the person of the eternal Son of God?[7] Only one answer is possible.

I write these words with compassion, realizing that some readers, no doubt, have had abortions. Perhaps it was in ignorance, before knowing the Scriptures and coming to Christ. Or perhaps it was because of fear, or economic stress, or the pressures of a boyfriend or family. Whatever the reason, if you turn to Christ, God's grace is big enough to bring you forgiveness. Perhaps others were believers, and because you did not sin in ignorance, your sin is more grievous. Nevertheless, God's grace is still sufficient. Whatever our pasts, we are now all under the light of God's Word, and our responsibility to accept God's love and grace and to protect unborn life is immense.

Framed in light,
Mary sings through the doorway.
Elizabeth's six month joy
jumps, a palpable greeting,
a hidden first encounter
between son and Son.
And my heart turns over
when I meet Jesus
in you.

Luci Shaw

Elizabeth Prophesies (vv. 42–45)

As John vaulted in his mother's womb, Elizabeth underwent an elevation of soul, an inner expansion of her human spirit, as the prophetic Spirit seized her. She then saluted Mary as the mother of the Lord: "She exclaimed with a loud cry, 'Blessed are you among women, and blessed is the fruit of your womb!'" (v. 42). Under the inspiration of the Holy Spirit, Elizabeth affirmed Mary's wonderful secret with a double blessing. She blessed Mary's coming maternity with a Semitic superlative.[8] Mary was blessed among women, and the just-conceived son in her womb was likewise blessed. The virgin's heart surely soared.

Mary's heart elevated even further with the next prophetic line—"And why is this granted to me that the mother of my Lord should come to me?" (v. 43)—because it vocalized Elizabeth's recognition that Jesus was the Messiah ("my Lord" is a conscious allusion to the opening line of the messianic Psalm 110, "The LORD says to *my Lord*").[9] The sense of Elizabeth's inspired question is, "Why is this granted to me that the mother of my Lord (the Messiah) should come to me?"

How young Mary must have taken heart at old Elizabeth's shouts. Here was one who without any explanation immediately understood her secret and celebrated it by pronouncing a double blessing and affirming that Mary indeed carried the Lord and Messiah in her womb!

Elizabeth concluded her cries with a formal beatitude (v. 45).[10] To catch the sense here, we must understand that Zechariah, who was deaf and mute because he had disbelieved Gabriel, was standing in amazed silence at Elizabeth's side. Elizabeth's piercing beatitude played off Zechariah's failure to believe: "'Blessed is she who believed that there would be a fulfillment of what was spoken to her from the Lord.'" The Holy Spirit celebrated Mary's *faith* as she believed and submitted to God's will and so become the mother of God's Son.

Mary Believes (vv. 46–55)

Ponder for a moment Mary's faith. To grasp it, we must understand that faith is more than intellectual belief. Faith is belief plus trust. Understanding this, we can discern a pattern in Mary's celebrated faith. First, she intellectually *believed* what Gabriel said. She believed that the virgin birth was possible and would happen. Mary did not doubt. Second, she *trusted* her whole life to God's promise. Third, this trust produced a passivity, a negation of all activity, in which she *submitted* to God—"Let it be to me according to your word." And fourth, out of that passivity sprang energized *activity* as she immediately obeyed God's Word—"and went with haste into the hill country, to a town in Judah."

Mary, the mother of Christ, modeled faith for the church, the faith that realized the birth of Christ in her life and fostered her discipleship. Saving faith is belief plus trust that issues in a proper passivity,[11] leading to total dependence on Christ and then flaming into activity and producing a life of service. Pondering four key words will bring grace to your soul.

Belief. Do you believe without qualification or reservation that Jesus is God? Do you likewise believe that he died on the cross for your sins and paid for them with his blood? Do you believe he was physically resurrected and has ascended to the right hand of God? Do you believe that you are a sinner and that your only hope is in Christ?

Trust. If you believe the above, have you trusted him alone—have you rested everything on him for your salvation? Saving faith is *belief* plus *trust.* Are you reclining on the finished work of Christ?

Passivity. True faith issues in a profound passivity, a calm reliance. You stop seeking God's approval or response through your works. "For by grace you have been saved through faith. And this is not your own doing; it is the gift of God, not a result of works, so that no one may boast" (Ephesians 2:8, 9).

Activity. Faith works. It results in a life of service and discipleship.

Belief plus *trust* that issues in God-dependent *passivity* and a life of *activity*—do you have this saving faith?

God Cares

As we have moved through the account, virtually every line has added another stroke of beauty to Mary's portrait. But there is something else of immense beauty here, and that is God's care for Mary in giving her Elizabeth. Young Mary could share Gabriel's words, but she could not be expected to fully understand or articulate the mystery. And even if she could, who would have believed her? Would you, without the aid of divine revelation? Of course not.

But Elizabeth did! She had been prepared by her priestly husband Zechariah's dramatic experience with Gabriel and her own divinely wrought pregnancy. Also, during the last six months, Zechariah, despite his handicap, had certainly communicated relevant Scriptures to her, and this plus their isolation in the hills had fostered thoughtful meditation. Elizabeth's profound belief in what had happened in Mary's womb—her double blessing of Mary—her acknowledgment that Mary was carrying the Lord—her beatitude regarding Mary's faith—what a tender balm this all was to Mary's soul! God had given young Mary a godly woman as her closest friend and confidante during this formative time in her life.

Think of the mutual encouragement and fellowship that was theirs. Both were miraculously expecting. Elizabeth was well past the nausea that likely lay ahead for Mary. They became sisters in experience as well as in soul. Both their unborn babies had been announced by the same angel, Gabriel. Both their unborn sons had mutually fulfilling prophecies made regarding them. John would "make ready for the Lord a people prepared" (1:17). Imagine the women's exchange. They speculated over what the Scriptures meant. They prayed together. They talked about birth and babies. Encouragement flowed between them.

At such times reality is like a dream come true. Grandmotherly Elizabeth great with child, age lines erased by pregnancy's spring, stood beside the girl-virgin, ministering to her.

> Veined hand locked
> with smooth.
> Close breaths.
> Resonance
> of soul.

Life was filled with expectancy, much as it is for those who first experience the new life of Christ within.

Closing Reflections

The visitation is flesh-and-blood history about God's care for the Virgin Mary. It is about how God directed her to a community of faith in the humble home of Zechariah and Elizabeth, where she was linked with people of mutual belief, mutual experiences, and mutual hope. The visitation records how Mary's life within was affirmed, and how her faith was confirmed, celebrated, and strengthened. It is at the level of history that the visitation must first be approached. God took care of Mary.

At the same time, there are practical insights here for all who would know the birth of Christ in their lives. There is wisdom about real faith—that it is *belief* plus *trust* that eventuates in telltale *passivity* and *activity*. The visitation also instructs us in the necessity of a community of faith (the church) if we are to see Christ grow in our lives.

Like Mary, we must fly to the church because there we find people like Zechariah and Elizabeth who share a *mutual faith*, believing the same things. Mary's faith, as great as it was, would very likely have faltered had it not been for the fellowship of Elizabeth. Therefore, we must purposely place ourselves deep within the fellowship of those who also believe God's Word. Christians will naturally experience a mutual elevation of faith in the *credo*, the "I believes" of the Church.

Like Mary, we must make a priority of being with those who share the *mutual experience* of miraculous new life within. The resonance of soul that comes from such mutual experience universally empowers all believers.

And like Mary we must hurry to the community of faith because there we experience elevation through our *mutual hope* in the ultimate fulfillment of our own new birth, as the apostle John so memorably explained: "Beloved, we are God's children now, and what we will be has not yet appeared; but we know that when he appears we shall be like him, because we shall see him as he is. And everyone who thus hopes in him purifies himself as he is pure" (1 John 3:2, 3).

5

The *Magnificat*, Part 1

LUKE 1:46–50

UNBORN JOHN HAD SOARED for joy in the watery darkness of Elizabeth's womb as he responded to the presence of the unborn Christ in Mary. His glad leap was prophetic of his life's mission in heralding Jesus as God's Son and Messiah. Before baby John had settled, Elizabeth, also filled with the Holy Spirit, shouted her prophetic cry, celebrating the divine person in Mary's womb with a tumult of multiple blessings.

In stunning silence Mary and Elizabeth regarded one another, and then Mary with majestic calm began to sing the first song of the incarnation. Others would follow: the *Benedictus* of Zechariah, the angels' *Gloria in altissimus*, and the *Nunc Dimittis* of Simeon. But this song, the *Magnificat*, is the first and the greatest.

Predictably, due to its greatness some critics have howled that the song could not have been sung by young Mary because it is too theological, too packed with Old Testament allusions, too carefully structured, too poetic, too subtle, too finished! They theorize variously that Luke borrowed from existing canticles that praised the saving actions of God in Israel's history. Some think that the antecedents of this piece were Maccabean hymns of oppressed Jews, or Qumran hymnody, or even Jewish Christian hymns that were developed *after* Christ's birth by the suffering church.[1]

On the contrary, the *Magnificat* is a brilliantly woven tapestry of Scripture (there are specific parallels to the song of Hannah, and every line has a counterpart in or allusion to the Old Testament), though the critics are right about one thing—it is sublimely theological.

We must not forget, as the critics apparently have, that every young Israelite knew by heart the principal songs of Hannah and Deborah and David and sang them customarily on feast days. It is not at all unlikely that newly pregnant Mary would have brooded over the story of Hannah's conception of Samuel during her three- or four-day journey to see Elizabeth. So what would be more likely than that she would frame her song in forms so familiar to her—especially Hannah's hymn? It must also be remembered that Mary was inspired by the Holy Spirit. Her experience was like the prophets of old, as the apostle Peter described it:

> Knowing this first of all, that no prophecy of Scripture comes from someone's own interpretation. For no prophecy was ever produced by the will of man, but men spoke from God as they were carried along by the Holy Spirit. (2 Peter 1:20, 21)

Mary's mind was full of Scripture and sacred phraseology from what she had heard both in the synagogue and at home. So when the Holy Spirit came upon her, he took what she had and wove it into this hallowed tapestry. The *Magnificat* was a poignant, profound divine/human composition, nothing less.

Mary's Elevation of Soul (vv. 46, 47)

Mary began her song by giving unforgettable expression to the elevation of her soul: "My soul magnifies the Lord, and my spirit rejoices in God my Savior" (vv. 46, 47). The opening words, "My soul magnifies the Lord," are even more expressive of her elevation when rendered literally: "My soul *makes great* the Lord" or "My soul *enlarges* the Lord." The Latin translation's famous phrase *Magnificat anima mea Dominum*, "My soul magnifies the Lord," also matches the wording of our text.

Of course, God cannot be made any bigger, but he can be enlarged in one's life (in one's "soul" or "spirit," as Mary put it). We magnify or enlarge God when we take into our thinking some new aspect of his greatness. For example, when we meditate for the first time on the magnificent texts of creation, perhaps Colossians 1:15–18, John 1:1–3, or Hebrews 1:1–3, our thoughts regarding God are enlarged. Likewise, meditation on Christ's death and atonement in the Gospel accounts will expand our theological knowledge. The fuller our knowledge of his greatness, the greater our ability to enlarge him.

Mary, after the annunciation by Gabriel and her visitation with Elizabeth, had begun to think bigger and grander thoughts than ever before: "A God who could do what he did in my womb—what must he be able to do in the womb of the universe?" Her soul enlarged the Lord, and her mouth poured forth greater thoughts than ever before.

What a wonder this is when it happens to us. Christ is born in our lives, his life courses through us, and we naturally begin to think greater thoughts of God than were ever before possible. And as these soaring thoughts come to our lips, we enlarge the Lord.

There is another aspect to the growth of the *Magnificat* in our lives: it consists not only in enlarging the Lord with our minds and then our lips, but in doing so with the passion of our whole being. This is emphasized here in Mary's opening line by the Hebrew poetic device of parallelism (expressing the same thought in two different ways). First Mary says, "My soul magnifies the Lord," and second, "my spirit rejoices in God my Savior." "Soul" and "spirit" simply refer to the inner self, the I.[2] This combination is a powerful, emotive way of saying, "My total self, all that I am, magnifies and praises the Lord."

This is highly significant because when Jesus began his ministry he proclaimed, "But the hour is coming, and is now here, when the true worshipers will worship the Father in spirit and truth, for the Father is seeking such people to worship him. God is spirit, and those who worship him must worship in spirit and truth" (John 4:23, 24). By worshiping "in spirit" Jesus means the inner human spirit (small *s*), the inner person. God seeks people whose entire human spirits are engaged in worship. The Holy Scriptures record the supreme example of this in Mary of Bethany's breaking a priceless vial of perfume and anointing Jesus' head and feet, then wiping them with her hair. The divine pleasure in this rings yet today in Jesus' words, "She has done a beautiful thing to me" (Mark 14:6). Her entire human spirit, her total self, was given over to the passionate worship of the Lord Jesus Christ.

Similarly, one thousand years earlier, King David had danced before the ark of the Lord, totally absorbed in worship (2 Samuel 6:16). David pledged in the Psalms, "My heart is steadfast, O God! I will sing and make melody with all my being!" (Psalm 108:1).

Magnifying the Lord, making great the Lord with our entire spirit and soul—that is what God desires in our lives today. Charles Spurgeon understood this, as his own experience of complete enjoyment testified: "I like, sometimes, to leave off praying and singing, and to sit still, and just gaze upward till my inmost soul has seen my Lord; then I say, 'He is inexpressively lovely; yea he is altogether lovely.'"[3]

This is also what God desires in our corporate worship. Congregational worship makes possible an intensity of magnification that does not occur as readily in individual worship. On the tragic level, a mob tends to descend to a much deeper level of cruelty than individuals would by themselves. The appreciation and enjoyment of an informed group of music lovers at a symphony is more intense than that of a single listener at home. In a similar way corporate worship provides a context where holy passion is joyously elevated and God's Word comes to hearts with unique power. Martin Luther spoke of this when he confided, "At home in my own house there is no warmth or vigor in me but in the church when the multitude is gathered together, a fire is kindled in my heart and it breaks its way through."[4]

Mary has set the standard for all who would experience the birth of Christ: "My soul magnifies the Lord, and my spirit rejoices in God my Savior."

Personal Reasons for the *Magnificat* (vv. 48–50)

Following her opening celebration, Mary recited her very personal reasons for her holy magnification of the Lord.

Mary's Humble Estate (v. 48)

Mary's first reason was a direct allusion to the petition of barren Hannah when Hannah wept bitterly, as recorded in 1 Samuel 1:11: "O LORD of hosts, if you will indeed look on the affliction of your servant" (the translation in the Septuagint, meaning "humble state," is the same word Luke uses).[5] Mary says, "For he has looked on the humble estate of his servant" (v. 48a). Mary's "humble estate" was not her personal childlessness, as had been Hannah's, but rather the nation of Israel's childlessness as it awaited the birth of a messianic deliverer (cf. Isaiah 9:6).[6] "Humble estate" acknowledged that neither she nor her people could do anything to bring about their deliverance. In heart Mary was like Hannah of old, who humbly cast herself upon God as the only one who could help.

Here we are again brought face-to-face with the principle that Christ comes to those who realize their need, who know they cannot save themselves. Humble, disenfranchised, Mary was a nobody from a nonplace.

The inaugural words of her son's public ministry would come some thirty years later in Nazareth one Sabbath when the presiding rabbi gave Jesus the scroll of Isaiah, which Jesus then opened to 61:1, 2 and read:

> "The Spirit of the Lord is upon me,
> because he has anointed me
> to proclaim good news to the poor.

> He has sent me to proclaim liberty to the captives
> and recovering of sight to the blind,
> to set at liberty those who are oppressed,
> to proclaim the year of the Lord's favor."
>
> And he rolled up the scroll and gave it back to the attendant and sat down. And the eyes of all in the synagogue were fixed on him. And he began to say to them, "Today this Scripture has been fulfilled in your hearing." (Luke 4:18–21)

Similarly, the startling opening words of the Sermon on the Mount were: "Blessed are the poor in spirit, for theirs is the kingdom of heaven. Blessed are those who mourn, for they shall be comforted. Blessed are the meek, for they shall inherit the earth" (Matthew 5:3–5).

The eternal truth is: "The Lord is near to the brokenhearted and saves the crushed in spirit" (Psalm 34:18).

Aurelius Augustinus, better known as St. Augustine, considered by many to be the greatest theologian of the church, understood this implicitly and wrote: "For those who would learn God's ways, humility is the first thing, humility is the second, and humility is the third."

The necessity of humility is a common thread in the nativity accounts and in much of Scripture elsewhere, for Christ comes to the lowly. He does not come to major department stores' Christmas mechanized windows. He does not appear on televised Christmas specials, or sit on the lead float of the Rose Parade, or ride in stretch limos with the rich and famous. He was born to an ordinary young woman in a peasant town in an obscure country.

Is this negative teaching? Not at all. It is divinely positive because, unlike riches and position, the grace of humility, the divine favor that comes to those acknowledging conscious spiritual need, is available to us all—specifically, to "the brokenhearted and . . . the crushed in spirit." All may have this gift of God if they are aware of their humble state.

Mary's Blessedness (v. 48)

Mary celebrated the Lord because he met her in her humble state, and then she continued on in her song to give a further exultant reason for magnifying God. "For behold, from now on," she said, "all generations will call me blessed" (v. 48b). Lest we imagine any hubris here, we must keep in mind that Mary had just pronounced her "humble estate." What we have here is a statement of wonder that all future generations will pronounce beatitudes over her name, until the end of the world. What a mind-boggling revelation to this young teenager! Hers is the most popular name in the Western world. It has "blessed" or an apt parallel attached to it more than any other name.

She was and is "blessed." There were certainly times when Mary could be seen in God's Son—in the line of his smile, the mold of his forehead, his walk, his accent, his colloquialisms. Mary must always be blessed and honored, though not worshiped.

But hear this: if we are Christians, if Jesus is truly born in us, we too will be called blessed, far beyond earth's history. Jesus himself tells us: "Then the King will say to those on his right, 'Come, you who are blessed by my Father, inherit the kingdom prepared for you from the foundation of the world'" (Matthew 25:34). And again, "*Blessed* and holy is the one who shares in the first resurrection!" (Revelation 20:6).

And if this is not enough, we will actually bear a resemblance to Jesus: "Beloved, we are God's children now, and what we will be has not yet appeared; but we know that when he appears we shall be like him, because we shall see him as he is" (1 John 3:2). But our resemblance will not be genetic. We will have, not his walk or the shape of his eyes, but his "spiritual DNA"—his character, his purity, his heart. This is the ultimate blessedness!

Brothers and sisters, just as it was fitting for Mary to praise God for her future fame, it is right and proper to magnify our Savior for our eternal blessedness and our eternal fame with God. Christians as diverse as Thomas Aquinas and John Milton have understood this implicitly and rejoiced.[7] Let us too magnify the Lord!

Mary's Divine Celebration (vv. 49, 50)

In the last personal reason Mary gives for her *Magnificat*, she sings of three divine perfections of God—his *power*, his *holiness*, and his eternal *mercy*: "For he who is mighty has done great things for me, and holy is his name. And his mercy is for those who fear him from generation to generation" (vv. 49, 50).

Power. Mary had experienced God's power at conception when "the power of the Most High overshadow[ed]" her (1:35). Prophetically, the one Mary carried in her womb was identified in Isaiah 9:6 by the second of his four messianic titles as "Mighty God" (*El Gibbor,* "mighty hero God"), for Jesus would engage in mighty heroics and, ultimately, resurrection power. Mary's confession of God here as "he who is mighty" *(ho dynatos)* is in anticipation of the gospel principle, "What is impossible [*adynatos*] with man is possible with God" (18:27).

God does the impossible! He makes dry wombs conceive, he removes hearts of stone and replaces them with living hearts, he raises the dead. This is why we chorus with Paul:

> I am not ashamed of the gospel, for it is the power of God for salvation to everyone who believes, to the Jew first and also to the Greek. For in it the righteousness of God is revealed from faith for faith, as it is written, "The righteous shall live by faith." (Romans 1:16, 17)

Holiness. Mary was the first to know that the Son she bore would be "holy" because Gabriel had carefully instructed her in this (1:35). Thus she praised God, saying, "Holy is his name." God's holiness more than any other attribute describes his essence. That is why the angels intone the *Tris hagion*: "Holy, holy, holy!" Mary's experience of conception had given her a fresh, bracing revelation of the Divine Being. So it is with us when we experience Christ. Regeneration ignites our understanding of God's holiness. The Spirit informs us of his purity and holy splendor, and our hearts bow before him in adoration.

Mercy. The final perfection is God's mercy: "And his mercy is for those who fear him from generation to generation" (v. 50). Mary recognized that God's "mercy" (gracious faithfulness)[8] will extend to all generations. Mercy characterizes God's dealings with his people. Ultimately God's mercy will transcend time. As John Donne so beautifully said: "God's mercy hath no relation to time, no limitation in time. . . . Whom God loves He loves to the end; and not only to their end, to their death, but to His end; and His end is, that He might love them still." There are three divine perfections of which Mary sings—power, holiness, and mercy—but it is mercy that brings them to bear on God's own.

Closing Reflections

The reasons Mary magnified the Lord are these:

First, he took note of her and came to her in her "humble estate." God met her in her helplessness and weakness. This is how God comes to us as well. "Blessed are the poor in spirit, for theirs is the kingdom of heaven" (Matthew 5:3). "The LORD is near to the brokenhearted and saves the crushed in spirit" (Psalm 34:18).

For this we gladly magnify the Lord!

Second, Mary enlarged the Lord because "all generations will call [her] blessed" (v. 48). As believers, this is our destiny and eternal beatitude as well. "Blessed and holy is the one who shares in the first resurrection!" (Revelation 20:6).

For this we gladly magnify the Lord!

Last, Mary magnified the Lord because of her experience of his perfections—namely, his power, holiness, and mercy as she experienced Christ within. These are also ours when Christ is born within us.

For this we gladly magnify the Lord!

God is seeking hearts like Mary's, children who magnify him, who enlarge him in their souls and on their lips, with the passion of their entire beings.

And Mary said: "My soul magnifies the Lord, and my spirit rejoices in God my Savior."

Let us follow her heart!

6

The *Magnificat*, Part 2

LUKE 1:51–55

IN THE SECOND HALF OF THE *Magnificat*, Mary moves from naming *personal* reasons for her magnifying the Lord to giving *prophetic* reasons for making him great. The movement is quite natural—like riding a ship up to a wave's crest.[1] You begin down in the dark trough, but as the wave swells, you ride upward to its bright crest, where you can look across the surrounding waves to the rimming horizon, intermittent islands, and distant landfall.

Mary's soul was carried upward as she sang of her *personal* reasons for enlarging the Lord. Then from the crest of the wave her soul reached toward the horizons of the world as she sang of the *prophetic* reasons for magnifying the Lord. The change from personal to prophetic was quite natural because the principles with which God deals with individual souls are the same principles as those that guide his dealings with the world. Mary saw in the microcosm of her own life how God had dealt and would deal with the world in macrocosm—and she sang to him in praise because of those great reasons.

As we study the second half of the *Magnificat*, we will note that her prophecy was all in the past tense: "He has shown . . . he has scattered . . . he has brought down . . . exalted . . . he has filled . . . he has sent . . . He has helped." This is the prophetic past tense (aorist), which views the future work of God as so sure that it is presented as past and accomplished.[2] Prophets often foretold the future with the past tense—for example, Isaiah when he prophesied of the captivity of Babylon as an accomplished fact (Isaiah 14:4–7, 12–15). Mary's use of the prophetic past tense was historically informed, for she cast an eye back to what God had done in the past, then projected what she had seen into the future as an eschatological effect of the work of the Son who was to be born to her. This section of the *Magnificat* is *historic/prophetic*.

The theme of this second half of Mary's song is the mighty reversals her Messiah-Son would bring to life: 1) a *moral* reversal, 2) a *social* reversal, and 3) a *material/spiritual* reversal.[3]

Moral Reversal (v. 51)

As Mary began, she looked backward and forward, as historian and prophetess, and spoke regarding the moral reversal her Son would bring: "He has shown strength with his arm; he has scattered the proud in the thoughts of their hearts" (v. 51). "The proud" whom Mary referenced were literally the ones showing themselves preeminent. They were the strutting proud, the arrogant, the conceited. They were proud first in "the thoughts of their hearts" as they inwardly plotted and schemed to perpetrate their arrogance.

History

Numerous examples from Israel's history were known to Mary in the likes of Pharaoh, Haman, and Absalom. Perhaps the most insufferable of these, and possibly the one Mary had in mind, was Nebuchadnezzar, a man who could strut while sitting down—a man imperially proud in his inmost thoughts. Nebuchadnezzar was so self-absorbed that, though he had been warned in a dream interpreted by Daniel about a coming personal fall if he did not renounce his sins, he still could not control his ego. "At the end of twelve months he was walking on the roof of the royal palace of Babylon, and the king answered and said, 'Is not this great Babylon, which I have built by my mighty power as a royal residence and for the glory of my majesty?'" (Daniel 4:29, 30).

This incredibly conceited ruler called down the mighty arm of God upon himself, and Nebuchadnezzar's mind snapped. He descended to all fours, snorting and bulling his way among his courtiers. Like any good beast of the field, he cast off the royal robes his servants attempted to apply. His only interest was foraging in the vegetation of the palace grounds. Nebuchadnezzar's hair and beard grew long so that it fell over him like eagles' feathers, and his nails, as a result of the grubbing, toughened and grew thick like talons.

Technically, he had a rare mental disease called *boanthropy* from the combination of two Latin words—*bos*, which means cow or bull, and *anthropos,* meaning man. The symptoms of boanthropy are pronounced antisocial tendencies and the preference for a diet of water and handfuls of grass. Typically the patient is discriminating about the plants he ingests and can drift in and out of reality.[4] It is very likely that Nebuchadnezzar wandered in and out of his animal-like state, to his recurring chagrin. Perhaps he was sometimes in a helpless netherland of humiliation—aware of his absurdity but unable to regain his right mind. It is also conceivable that toward the end he experienced periods of increased lucidness and began to reflect on his folly.

In any event, after seven years the king came to his senses, and he officially recorded:

> At the end of the days I, Nebuchadnezzar, lifted my eyes to heaven, and my reason returned to me, and I blessed the Most High, and praised and honored him who lives forever,
>
> for his dominion is an everlasting dominion,
> and his kingdom endures from generation to generation;
> all the inhabitants of the earth are accounted as nothing,
> and he does according to his will among the host of heaven
> and among the inhabitants of the earth;
> and none can stay his hand
> or say to him, "What have you done?" (Daniel 4:34, 35)

His concluding observation was, "And those who walk in pride he is able to humble" (Daniel 4:37). Thus, a historical retrospect sharpens the force of Mary's prophecy—"He has shown strength with his arm; he has scattered the proud in the thoughts of their hearts."

Prophecy

Mary's words here are words of prophecy about the moral reversal brought about by the birth, life, death, and resurrection of Christ, who would scatter "the proud." We see glimpses of this in the subsequent annals of history. Prideful Herod Agrippa stood in his splendid royal robes before an admiring audience, enjoying their blasphemous praise—"The voice of a god, and not of a man!" But Luke tells us, "Immediately an angel of the Lord struck him down, because he did not give God the glory, and he was eaten by worms and breathed his last" (Acts 12:22, 23). Napoleon had his proud Austerlitz, but then came Russia and Waterloo. Hitler had his Anschluss, but a few years later D-Day. And today the grand sculptured heads of Lenin and Stalin lie in junkyards. The days of arrogant men echo amid the crash of falling thrones.

But most of all, Mary sang of the final reversal and reckoning that awaits the proud because of Christ's work. The Son she bore would later state categorically to the hypocritical religious leaders of his day, "Whoever exalts himself will be humbled, and whoever humbles himself will be exalted" (Matthew 23:12). Twice the New Testament records: "'God opposes the proud, but gives grace to the humble'" (James 4:6; 1 Peter 5:5; both quoting Proverbs 3:34). Those who possess an imagined sense of moral superiority because of their position in life—who are "proud in the thoughts of their hearts" because of their wealth or education or privilege or elite status or ease—who suppose their station is due to some inward spiritual excellence—are in for a rude awakening, because the arm of God (his ineluctable power) will be loosed against them. And if they do not repent and turn to God, their fate is a done deal just as it has been in the past—"He has shown strength with his arm; he has scattered the proud in the thoughts of their hearts." It has happened before, and God has not changed.

This is sobering news if in our heart of hearts we cherish thoughts of our moral excellence, if arrogantly we imagine that our good fortune in life is somehow due to an innate superiority.

Social Reversal (v. 52)

The next line in Mary's song sings of an exchange of positions, a social reversal: "He has brought down the mighty from their thrones and exalted those of humble estate" (v. 52).

History

Among the great acts of hubris in Biblical history was Belshazzar's feast in Babylon, the details of which may have laid the foundation for Mary's prophetic language in verse 52. Belshazzar's massive arrogance displayed itself in three ways. First, the armies of the Medes and the Persians had devoured the civilized world and were camped at the gates of Babylon, but Belshazzar chose to feast. He engaged in such arrogant royal thumbing of the nose at his enemies because he believed that Babylon's gates were impregnable and they had years of supplies stored away in case of a long siege. Second, during the feast drunken Belshazzar engaged in ritual blasphemy when he ordered that the gold and silver goblets that had been taken from the Jewish temple in Jerusalem be brought forth so they could drink toasts from them to the Babylonian gods. And third, Belshazzar did all of this though he had the example and written testimony of his humbled father Nebuchadnezzar at hand. Arrogant, conceited, overconfident of his own superiority and safety, Belshazzar was about to suffer disgrace and defeat.

The feast became a debauched, orgiastic affair. Sacred vessels clattered on the floor, soon red with wine and spittle and vomit, as roar after roar went up as idol after idol was praised using Jehovah's sacred vessels. But then the reveling gave way to deadly silence punctuated by terror-stricken moans when a bodiless hand wrote solemn words of judgment on the plaster wall. The effect was dramatic. "Then the king's color changed, and his thoughts alarmed him; his limbs gave way, and his knees knocked together" (Daniel 5:6). Or as the King James Version literally renders it, "The joints of his loins were loosed, and his knees smote one against another." One minute Belshazzar was leading defiant, blasphemous cheers, the next he was a wobbling, fainting coward.

Perhaps his fear was even heightened because no one could interpret the terrifying inscription. Daniel was summoned and easily, fearlessly translated the strange message, ending with the foreboding words, "Your kingdom is divided and given to the Medes and Persians" (Daniel 5:28). Daniel was then appointed the "the third ruler in the kingdom" (Daniel 5:29), and "that very night Belshazzar the Chaldean king was killed. And Darius the Mede received the kingdom" (Daniel 5:30, 31).

The ancient historians Xenophon and Herodotus fill in the details, revealing that during the siege crews had worked each night to divert part of the Euphrates, and that on the very night of the profligate banquet they succeeded and their armies waded into the city. So successful was the tactic that they took Babylon without a fight. Furthermore, if Xenophon is correct, the invading troops captured and killed Belshazzar in the very hall where the condemning handwriting appeared (October 11 or 12, 539 BC). Significantly, the new king, Darius, retained Daniel in power, with an eye to making him chief administrator of the kingdom. Thus we see that Mary's lyrics, "He has brought down the mighty from their thrones and exalted those of humble estate," had spectacular historical precedent in the fall of proud Belshazzar and the elevation of humble Daniel. We could also mention Joseph's ascendancy in Egypt and the victory of humble Mordecai over proud Haman.

Prophecy

These and other historical precedents were prophetic of the gospel's mighty reversals in bringing about the descent of the haughty and the ascent of the humble. Jesus himself is an example *nonpareil* because his willing humiliation in the incarnation and on the cross resulted in his being lifted up. As Paul wrote:

> Therefore God has highly exalted him and bestowed on him the name that is above every name, so that at the name of Jesus every knee should bow, in heaven and on earth and under the earth, and every tongue confess that Jesus Christ is Lord, to the glory of God the Father. (Philippians 2:9–11)

The gospel lifts up the humble and casts down the proud, effecting a mighty reversal. From this we understand that life is not always as it appears. Spiritually, down is up, and up is down!

This great truth too is a done deal, an accomplished fact that will be fully played out in the final judgment. The principle is so certain that Mary sang in the past tense: "He has *brought down* the mighty from their thrones and *exalted* those of humble estate." It will indeed be "the meek" who "inherit the earth" (Matthew 5:5). This is why Peter solemnly advises, "Humble yourselves, therefore, under the mighty hand of God so that at the proper time he may exalt you" (1 Peter 5:6). Prepare for the reversal!

Material/Spiritual Reversal (v. 53)

Next Mary sang of a material/spiritual reversal: "He has filled the hungry with good things, and the rich he has sent away empty" (v. 53). Here Mary must not be credited with purely spiritual (or spiritualized) views, nor discredited with purely material ones.[5] There is a correlation, though of course it is not absolute.

History

The Old Testament history to which Mary glanced back records the connection between one's material and spiritual state. For example, the song of Hannah, which Mary had been meditating upon, says, "The Lord makes poor and makes rich; he brings low and he exalts. He raises up the poor from the dust; he lifts the needy from the ash heap to make them sit with princes and inherit a seat of honor" (1 Samuel 2:7, 8). Mary's statement "He has filled the hungry with good things" is derived from Psalm 107:9, "For he satisfies the longing soul, and the hungry soul he fills with good things." Generally those in physical, material need are more likely to sense their spiritual need than are the rich and satisfied (though not always).

The Old Testament encourages spiritual hunger:

> O God, you are my God; earnestly I seek you;
>   my soul thirsts for you;
> my flesh faints for you,
>   as in a dry and weary land where there is no water. (Psalm 63:1)

> As a deer pants for flowing streams,
> so pants my soul for you, O God.
> My soul thirsts for God,
> for the living God.
> When shall I come and appear before God? (Psalm 42:1, 2)
>
> Open your mouth wide, and I will fill it. (Psalm 81:10)
>
> Blessed are those . . .
> who seek him with their whole heart. (Psalm 119:2)
>
> My soul longs for your salvation. (Psalm 119:81)

Spiritual hunger is the Old Testament prescription for spiritual health.

Prophecy

Mary's eye on history gave her perspective for a prophetic vision that was so sure, she stated it as past fact—"*He has filled* the hungry with good things, and the rich *he has sent* away empty." Those who are full and therefore imagine they, in themselves, are sufficient are in fact desperately needy. As the Spirit later explained to the Laodicean Christians,

> You say, I am rich, I have prospered, and I need nothing, not realizing that you are wretched, pitiable, poor, blind, and naked. I counsel you to buy from me gold refined by fire, so that you may be rich, and white garments so that you may clothe yourself and the shame of your nakedness may not be seen, and salve to anoint your eyes, so that you may see. (Revelation 3:17, 18)

How tragic is the damning effect of self-sufficiency! The rich young ruler missed Christ altogether not just because he would not get rid of his things to follow Jesus, but simply because he was not hungry enough! Desire for the material had dulled a budding spiritual appetite—and the rich man was sent away empty!

In contrast, consider the hungry in the Gospels: young Mary, aged Simeon and Anna, the fishermen, the tax-gatherer, the prostitute with seven devils, and many others—desperately hungry people who were sent away eternally full. Indeed, Mary's Son would make spiritual hunger the fourth pillar of his great sermon: "Blessed are those who [continually] hunger and thirst for righteousness, for they shall be satisfied" (Matthew 5:6). Jesus calls his people to a desperate hunger.

The divine reward for such hunger and thirst is complete satisfaction, as so many Scriptures attest. "But whoever drinks of the water that I will give him will never be thirsty again. The water that I will give him will become in him a spring of water welling up to eternal life" (John 4:14). "Jesus said to them, 'I am the bread of life; whoever comes to me shall not hunger, and whoever believes in me shall never thirst'" (John 6:35). Mary's prophetic past tense set God's promise of satisfaction in eternal concrete—"He has filled the hungry with good things." The filling is not only for now, but for eternity. The image of a divine feast was used more than once by Jesus to illustrate the satisfactions of the kingdom. On one occasion he told his disciples, "I assign to you, as my Father assigned to me, a kingdom, that you may eat and drink at my table in my kingdom" (22:29, 30). That will be eternal satisfaction!

No doubt we have sometimes wondered why so many people who have the opportunity to know Christ never benefit from his grace. The answer is, they make no serious effort to do so. To them, it seems like too much work. They don't have the time to spare. There are more important things like their favorite sports teams or the theater or golf. Having no hunger, they are "sent away empty."

As Christians, we must realize that our spiritual hunger is a "blessed" state, according to Christ in his Sermon on the Mount. It works like this: we hunger spiritually and are then filled and become supremely satisfied. The satisfaction then makes way for a deeper spiritual hunger, a further filling and blessed satisfaction. And so it goes on in sublime paradox: hunger—filling—satisfaction, hunger—filling—satisfaction. We become more and more full of Christ. St. Bernard of Clairvaux understood the hungry/full paradox and gave it memorable expression:

> We taste Thee, O Thou living Bread,
> And long to feast upon Thee still;
> We drink of Thee, the Fountainhead
> And thirst our souls from Thee to fill.

Eternal Mercy (vv. 54, 55)

Finally, Mary looked back on God's covenant promise to Israel first stated in Genesis 12:3 ("And in you all the families of the earth shall be blessed"; cf. Genesis 17:19; 22:18; 26:3, 4; 28:13, 14)—and then sang of its fulfillment in the prophetic past tense: "He has helped his servant Israel, in remembrance of his mercy, as he spoke to our fathers, to Abraham and to his offspring forever." God's covenant is a "done deal." The remarkable thing is that as Christians, we are the spiritual seed of Abraham (his descendants) through faith (cf. Romans 4:9–12, 18–22). As such, his covenant mercy extends to us forever and forever. His mercy is an accomplished fact.

Thus Mary's song ends on an eternal note of mercy.

Closing Reflections

All that is in Mary, her soul and her spirit, was given over to passionately magnifying the Lord. Her personal reasons were sublime, and as Christians we magnify the Lord for the same reasons. 1) The divine condescension as he met her in her "humble estate" (1:48)—she could do nothing to effect her own or Israel's deliverance; 2) his divine blessing, so that she is called "blessed" (1:48) for all generations, even as those who have Christ within are blessed for eternity; 3) and his divine excellencies—that is, his power, holiness, and mercy that were brought to bear upon Mary's life and upon all who know Christ.

Then, at the crest of the wave, as she looked across history, she sang prophetically of the mighty reversals her Son would bring to the world:

- The *moral* reversals, as Christ would scatter the mini-Nebuchadnezzars, those "proud in the thoughts of their hearts," who imagine that their status or good fortune is due to their superiority.
- The *social* reversals, as petty Belshazzars would be put down and humble Daniels brought up, for "He has brought down the mighty from their thrones and exalted those of humble estate."
- The *spiritual* reversals—"He has filled the hungry with good things, and the rich he has sent away empty." Those who know their need can be filled with Christ.
- Eternal *mercy*, a song of his covenant faithfulness, which goes on forever and ever.

Jesus has turned the world on its head. Morally, he scatters the proud. Socially, he lifts the humble. And spiritually, he fills the hungry with good things.

Therefore, let us magnify the Lord!

7

The Birth of John

LUKE 1:56–66

ACCOUNTS OF THE EVENTS surrounding the births of great persons can be both fascinating and enlightening. This is no exception with John the Baptist, forerunner of the Messiah.

John's Genesis (vv. 56–58)

Luke indicates that after Mary went to visit Elizabeth, she stayed there for the remaining three months of the old woman's pregnancy. So Mary was likely present at the birth of John. Commentators suggest that Mary's presence is not recorded because Luke rounds off the account by describing her return home before going on to the story of John's birth.[1]

If Mary was present, she witnessed an event of singular joy. Elizabeth, in the autumn of her life, experienced the spring rhythm of labor and birth. In a sublimely poignant moment, loving hands (perhaps the hands of the Virgin herself) placed Elizabeth's son in her arms. No doubt the godly mother recalled the joy of another aged mother, Sarah, the matriarch of Israel, who at the birth of her son Isaac (which literally means "he laughs"), said, "God has made laughter for me; everyone who hears will laugh over me" (Genesis 21:6). Sarah laughed, Abraham laughed, and mirth filled the tents of his people. Elizabeth too laughed aloud and wept for joy. Zechariah laughed silently as tears coursed down his gray beard. Their laughter, mixed with their son's cries, rang across the hillside of Judea.

Luke further tells us that Elizabeth's "neighbors and relatives heard that the Lord had shown great mercy to her, and they rejoiced with her" (v. 58). At first they were incredulous because they had not known that Elizabeth was pregnant. The secret had been well kept by mute Zechariah and the Virgin.

But when the neighbors came and saw radiant Elizabeth calmly nursing her son, "they rejoiced with her," perfectly fulfilling Gabriel's earlier words: "You will have joy and gladness, and many will rejoice at his birth" (1:14).

The joy of John's birth anticipated the cosmic joy of the coming birth of Christ—"good news of great joy . . . for all the people" (2:10). Today joy is the telltale experience of every soul who believes the good news of the gospel.

Circumcision (vv. 59a–63)

Genesis 17:12 records God's specifying to Abraham that all Hebrew males were to be circumcised eight days after birth. This in turn was taken up and formalized in the Mosaic Law (Leviticus 12:3). So on the eighth day all of Zechariah's and Elizabeth's relatives came for the happy occasion, just as we would take every measure possible to be present at a similar ceremony for the firstborn of an aged relative.

The circumcision would mark the boy with the sign of the covenant and incorporate him into Israel (Genesis 17:11; Joshua 5:2–9). Circumcision obligated him to live under the commands of the Law (Galatians 3:5) and to share in the blessings promised to God's people. Sometimes circumcisions were performed by women (cf. Exodus 4:25; see also the extra-Biblical book of 1 Maccabees, 1:60), but normally they were done by the head of the house, in this case silent, joyous Zechariah. The fulfillment of this rite on the eighth day (v. 59) gave John impeccable Jewish credentials (cf. 2:21; Philippians 3:5) so necessary for the forerunner of the Messiah. The baby cried in pain as Zechariah's trembling hand cleansed the bloody knife, and there were cheers all around.

Naming (vv. 59b–63)

Luke continues, "And they would have called him Zechariah after his father" (v. 59b). The literal sense is, "they [the relatives] were calling," or possibly, "they were trying to call him by the name of his father Zechariah." The relatives assumed that the boy would be "little Zechariah"—"big Zech and little Zech."[2] That was a nice thought, but a wrong one because Luke informs us that "his mother answered, 'No; he shall be called John'" (v. 60). She was firm, almost fierce. Raymond Brown translates this, "No you don't. He is to be called John!"[3]

The relatives were, of course, unaware that the angel Gabriel had specified that the boy be named John and that Zechariah had written it out for Elizabeth, and, further, that upon Mary's arrival the two women had hardly passed a day without mentioning the divinely given names of the sons they were carrying. Not understanding, the relatives persisted.

> And they said to her, "None of your relatives is called by this name." And they made signs to his father, inquiring what he wanted him to be called. And he asked for a writing tablet and wrote, "His name is John." And they all wondered. (vv. 61–63)

It is difficult for us to appreciate what a jolt this was to the family, because in that culture children were *always* named after someone in the family. The double vehemence of the old couple was truly shocking. "John," *Yohanan*, which means "the Lord has given grace," was a most fitting name for the child's calling as forerunner of the Savior. But there is more to this because by giving the boy a nonfamily name, God was indicating that his mission and power would come from outside the natural order. Who he was could not be explained by his being the child of his parents. The name *John* was meant to stir their spiritual imaginations.

Praise (v. 64)

The neighbors and relatives had already been jarred, but there was more to come: "And immediately his [Zechariah's] mouth was opened and his tongue loosed, and he spoke, blessing God" (v. 64). Zechariah's original disbelief in Gabriel's promise of a son had been replaced by faith when, in fulfillment of Gabriel's judgment, he became mute. His faith was further strengthened when Elizabeth conceived. Now Zechariah's faith produced obedience as he doggedly insisted that his son be named John. The combination of Zechariah's faith and obedience effected the loosing of his tongue!

Significantly, Zechariah's initial words did not include his son's name but were an outpouring of praise to God. Think of the spiritual voltage here! Zechariah has endured nine months of speechless frustration, and during the last three a young woman kept talking and asking questions by making signs to him, and he could only respond by scribbling answers on his writing pad. Now all that pent-up frustration poured out in loud, emotional praise. In this way he foreshadowed the future God-glorifying ministry of his son.

Response (vv. 65, 66)

All this brought about a fresh state of spiritual health within that whole area. "And fear came on all their neighbors. And all these things were talked about through all the hill country of Judea" (v. 65). They experienced a healthy "fear" in the presence of divine activity. They could sense God was at work, and an exhilarating reverence coursed through their souls. This resulted in ongoing spiritual conversations—an eminently healthy state.

Luke concludes his description by saying, "And all who heard them laid them up in their hearts, saying, 'What then will this child be?' For the hand of the Lord was with him" (v. 66). These words are essentially identical to those used to describe Mary's treasuring the shepherds' words and pondering them in her heart (2:19; cf. 3:15).

Spiritual reflection, a wise and spiritually healthy state, is rare in our unthinking age of sound bytes and limited attention spans and a hurried pace. The flashing stoplights, the elevator music, the shifting images, the ads, the vacuous conversation about where we are going and what we are buying keeps our minds too busy to reflect on more important matters. Years ago C. S. Lewis captured this idea when, in his famous *Screwtape Letters*, he described one of the charges of the junior devil, Screwtape, as he sat reading in the British museum and began to reflect on spiritual questions. Before he could ponder too long, Screwtape got him out onto the museum steps and back to "real life"—the passing buses and the shouts of boys selling papers.[4] It is a great privilege to treasure spiritual truth and ponder it in our hearts, and then to ask the right questions about who we are and who God is.

On this occasion the big question was, "What then will this child be?" That question, mulled over and considered further in the years to come, would open many to grace because John would become the greatest witness the world had ever known. The question sets the stage for Zechariah's song, the *Benedictus*, which will be the subject of our next chapter. But the question also invites reflection within the broader context of the Gospels.

John the Baptist—A Biographical Review

The Scriptures devote only one sentence to John's upbringing, and it is found in 1:80 after the conclusion of Zechariah's song: "And the child grew and became strong in spirit, and he was in the wilderness until the day of his public appearance to Israel." John spent years in the desert until AD 27 when he received his call during the priesthood of Annas and Caiaphas (3:2). Then John burst onto the scene as a bigger-than-life Old Testament prophet.

John's Character

Style. Mark's Gospel provides a visual introduction to John the Baptist: "Now John was clothed with camel's hair and wore a leather belt around his waist and ate locusts and wild honey" (Mark 1:6). Though John was not making a fashion statement, the way he dressed was a powerful prophetic statement—he dressed in carefully calculated radical prophetic chic. His camel's-hair robe was the kind worn by the very poor, and his belt, unlike the fancy belts so popular in those days, was a simple leather thong. Neither was there anything *haute* about his cuisine. His idea of eating out was to catch a few grasshoppers for locusts *alfresco*, and then visit the local beehive for dessert.

John knew exactly what he was doing, because he deliberately assumed the dress and style of the ancient prophet Elijah the Tishbite, who called his people to national repentance (cf. 2 Kings 1:8). John's dress and lifestyle were a protest against the godlessness and self-serving materialism of his day—a call to separate oneself from the surrounding sinful culture, to repent, and to live a life focused upon God. Even John's chosen context, the desert, was meant to emphasize this, because it was to the wilderness that ancient Israel came when they left Egypt. The people's coming out to John in the wilderness was a subtle acknowledgment of Israel's disobedience and rebellion and a demonstration of their desire to begin again—to follow God. The silhouette of John on the desert landscape was a potent call to repentance.

Courage. What was beautiful about John is that his preaching matched his profile. He was absolutely fearless in his proclamation of the message, just as his prophetic garb portrayed. John rebuked the Pharisees, saying, "You brood of vipers! Who warned you to flee from the wrath to come?" (3:7; cf. Matthew 3:7, 8). He gave the common people bold, practical instruction regarding giving: "Whoever has two tunics is to share with him who has none, and whoever has food is to do likewise" (3:11). He directed the tax-gatherers to be fair (3:13). He warned the Roman soldiers to be content and not act high-handedly (3:14). Indeed, John was as fearless as he looked!

Humility. Though steely and assertive, John was also self-forgetting and humble. Later, when Jesus' star began to rise and John's ministry was being eclipsed, John's disciples came to him in alarm. But John's response was impeccable: "A person cannot receive even one thing unless it is given him from heaven. . . . I am not the Christ" (John 3:27, 28). John then explained that his relation to Jesus was like that of a joyous friend of the bridegroom, concluding with the immortal words, "He must increase, but I must decrease" (John 3:30). John was a man of sublime downward mobility of heart, just as his humble apparel suggested.

Integrity. A modern proverb wisely says:

> To be persuasive,
> We must be believable.
> To be believable,
> We must be credible.
> To be credible,
> We must be truthful.

To his great credit, John fully embodied his message of repentance and holiness. His whole life had been divinely groomed to produce authenticity. He had been filled with the Holy Spirit while yet in Elizabeth's womb. He was a Nazirite from birth, never touching a dead body or consuming strong drink, never cutting his hair—all signs of his radical commitment and special separation to God's work.

Bishop William Quail alluded to this same principle of authenticity by commenting, "Preaching is the art of making a sermon and delivering it? Why no, that is not preaching. Preaching is the art of making a preacher and delivering that!"[5] John the Baptist embodied his message. In this sense he *was* the message! Others could have said the same things, but to no avail. The fact that his words saturated his being and oozed from his life—the fact that they were true in him—gave him immense power. Similarly, nothing will give God's Word greater impact than its being true in us and being lived and proclaimed by a totally sincere heart.

Passion. John's integrity was matched by his ethos. He lived out the essence of Charles Kingsley's striking words:

> Be earnest, earnest, earnest—
> Mad if thou wilt;
> Do what thou dost as if the
> Stake were Heaven,
> And that thy last deed before
> The Judgment Day.[6]

When he stood before the people in the wasteland, lean, gaunt, solitary, John preached with fire. Like Elijah of old, and Jesus and Paul too, he wept. God used everything about him (his style, his courage, his humility, his integrity, his passion) to reach the multitudes. The result? "And all the country of Judea and all Jerusalem were going out to him" (Mark 1:5). Some say that as many as three hundred thousand came out to John to hear the word of God and to be baptized, publicly repenting of their sin and putting themselves at God's disposal.

John's Message

John's preaching centered on the complementary subjects of sin and repentance, two essential facets of the gospel of Jesus Christ.

Sin. Church history has demonstrated again and again that the importance of preaching about the terrible reality and consequences of sin has to be repeatedly recaptured by the church. In this last century Scotland's greatest preacher, Alexander Whyte, had to do just that. While on a holiday, as he was walking on the highlands brooding over his ministry, a thought came to him that he believed to be the voice of God. The message was:

> "Go on, and flinch not! Go back and boldly finish the work that has been given you to do. Speak out and fear not. Make them, at any cost, to see themselves in God's Holy Law as in a glass. Do you that, for no one else will do it. No one else will so risk his life and his reputation as to do it; and you have not much of either left to risk. Go home and spend what is left of your life in your appointed task of showing My people their sin and their need of My salvation." . . . I know quite well that some of you think me little short of a monomaniac about sin, but I am not the first that has been so thought of and so spoken about. I am in good company, and I am content to be in it.[7]

Whyte was in excellent company indeed! When the people came to John, he first sat them down and preached about their sin. Imagine the scene. Hundreds, and later at the height of John's ministry, thousands, seated along the Jordan, listening as John named their sins, called for justice, and warned of judgment.

What a gift John gave his people by preaching on sin and judgment. This is too often neglected today. In some quarters the gospel is preached as the way to the good life and upward mobility, but that is not the message we have been given to proclaim. Preaching the true gospel is an inestimable privilege and responsibility, because without an understanding of the depth of our sin, the incarnation and the atoning death of Christ make no sense. If we do not see ourselves as radically sinful and totally lost, the cross makes no sense at all. But if we are lost, and in fact dead in our sins, the cross makes all the difference, for it is our only hope. When men and women are awakened to the depth of their sin and the fact of certain judgment, the gospel becomes the best news in the world! The bad news about us makes way for the good news of Christ. In fact, there is no good news apart from the bad news.

Repentance. The second thing we should notice is that John's preaching was for a baptism of repentance for the forgiveness of sin. This does not mean that baptism saves, but that it demonstrates a heart repentance that always accompanies saving faith—the salvation that comes only through the grace of God. John's baptism was later superseded by Christ's baptism of the Holy Spirit (3:16). Nevertheless, John's preaching coupled the conviction of sin with the moral necessity of repentance—a volitional turning away from sin. This is impossible apart from the grace of God, but it indicates true regeneration. Those who are born again repent, and one evidence of their regeneration is ongoing repentance.

Closing Reflections

Notwithstanding the *ordo salutis*, the order of salvation, when the gospel is preached today it must include both the preaching of sin and judgment and also the necessity of a faith that leads to repentance. No one receives Christ unless he or she is convicted of his or her sins and is willing to turn away from them. Both acts are gifts from God. For the non-Christian, an increased awareness of personal sin and fear of judgment, coupled with a growing desire to repent, may mean that grace is imminent. If one has come to this blessed state, the next step is to humbly trust Jesus Christ alone for salvation.

Such preaching is full of grace for Christians as well. The awareness of one's sin is a gracious awareness because it invites ongoing repentance and conformity to Christ.

William Beveridge put this perfectly for his day and ours:

> I cannot pray, except I sin;
> I cannot preach, but I sin;
> I cannot administer, nor receive the holy sacrament, but I sin.
> My very repentance needs to be repented of;
> And the tears I shed need washing in the blood of Christ.

8

The *Benedictus*

LUKE 1:67–79

THE NIGHT BEFORE the sunrise of Jesus' birth had been long and dark. According to the Scriptures the people of Israel had been "sit[ting] in darkness and in the shadow of death"—like a caravan lost in a desert at night and fearing for their lives (v. 79; cf. Isaiah 9:2). The faithful remnant knew the messianic sunrise would come because the prophet Malachi had memorably promised in the concluding lines of the Old Testament that "the sun of righteousness shall rise with healing in its wings. You shall go out leaping like calves from the stall" (Malachi 4:2). So despite over four hundred long years of darkness, the people were looking for the sunrise.

There had been recent glimmers of light indicating that dawn was imminent—Gabriel's annunciation of John to Zechariah, Gabriel's annunciation of Jesus to Mary, the meeting of the two pregnant mothers and Elizabeth's loud, joyful prophecy, Mary's *Magnificat*, the birth of John the Baptist. These momentary flashes were signs that steady rays of messianic sunlight would soon shine from the horizon.

Now, with the birth of John, a faint glow was almost perceptible. Zechariah circumcised his son, and the people asked, "What then will this child be?" (1:66).

Old Zechariah, speechless for nine months because of unbelief, then responded in faithful obedience, his tongue was loosed, and he gave the final song before the sunrise. Luke introduces it by saying, "And his father Zechariah was filled with the Holy Spirit and prophesied" (v. 67). Zechariah stood as the mouthpiece of God, a divine soloist. His words were God's words. Like Mary's song, his too was filled with Scripture. Zechariah's entire priestly life had drawn nourishment from the Holy Scriptures, and now he sang almost entirely in Old Testament phraseology. Some scholars have detected as many as thirty-three possible allusions and quotations from the Old Testament in this brief, rapturous song.[1]

This hymn has traditionally been called the *Benedictus* because the opening expression—"Blessed be the Lord God of Israel" (v. 68a) was rendered in the Vulgate, "*Benedictus Dominus Deus Israel*." The title captures the sense of the song quite well because it is a song of benediction and praise for how God had worked to bring about the messianic sunrise in the coming birth of Christ. It is most significant, in light of the fact that Jesus would be a descendant of King David, that David used the same phrase, "Blessed be the Lord, the God of Israel," when he installed his son Solomon as his successor and king (1 Kings 1:48). The first son of David and the ultimate Son of David were celebrated with identical praise to God.

This song before the sunrise is an ecstatic chain of praise from beginning to end—first, praise to God for keeping his promise to David (the Davidic Covenant); second, praise to God for keeping his promise to Abraham (the Abrahamic Covenant); third, praise to God for keeping his promise to Zechariah in giving him his son John, the forerunner; fourth, praise to God for the coming of "the sunrise." This systematic, intensely theological heaping of praise will draw any soul upward if it will make the effort to do so.

Praise for Fulfillment of the Davidic Covenant (vv. 68–71)

The so-called Davidic Covenant was simply God's promise (or covenant) to David that he would be succeeded by his son Solomon, who would build the temple, and that an ultimate greater successor would establish his throne forever. The covenant was delivered by the prophet Nathan to David when David was at the height of his power and had expressed his desire to build a temple for God. The covenant reads:

> The Lord declares to you that the Lord will make you a house. When your days are fulfilled and you lie down with your fathers, I will raise up your offspring after you, who shall come from your body, and I will establish his kingdom. He shall build a house for my name, and I will establish the throne of his kingdom forever. (2 Samuel 7:11b–13)

The great promise of an enduring kingdom and king fired the hopes of the faithful in Israel, and they looked longingly for the great coming ruler of the house of David.

Isaiah gave immortal expression to this great hope:

> For to us a child is born,
> to us a son is given;
> and the government shall be upon his shoulder,
> and his name shall be called
> Wonderful Counselor, Mighty God,
> Everlasting Father, Prince of Peace.
> Of the increase of his government and of peace
> there will be no end,
> on the throne of David and over his kingdom,
> to establish it and to uphold it
> with justice and with righteousness
> from this time forth and forevermore. (Isaiah 9:6, 7)

In the first movement of his song, Zechariah sang of this great person as "a horn of salvation." Note that he sang, as did Mary, in the prophetic past tense, so that what he sang about was "as good as done."

> Blessed be the Lord God of Israel,
> for he has visited and redeemed his people
> and has raised up a horn of salvation for us
> in the house of his servant David,
> as he spoke by the mouth of his holy prophets from of old,
> that we should be saved from our enemies
> and from the hand of all who hate us. (vv. 68–71)

The metaphor "horn" is derived from an animal's horns, especially that of a buffalo or ox, symbolizing strength and power (cf. Deuteronomy 33:17). The lifting up of the horn in the Old Testament refers to an animal tossing its horns in a display of power (cf. Psalm 148:14), and the language behind the phrase "raised up a horn" appears to suggest the same idea.[2] African hunters of the Cape buffalo tell us that when one of those great animals scuffs the ground and begins to rhythmically swing its horns back and forth, it is preparing for a deadly charge. An animal's horn is its weapon for defense and vengeance, and also its ornament of beauty. The Davidic horn would be "raised up" in a mighty display of power in the birth of Jesus—"a horn of salvation for us in the house of his servant David" (v. 69).

This awesome horn's ministry would be twofold. First, in *redemption* as he ransoms his people with his own blood. Note that the passion narrative occupies a large section at the end of Luke's Gospel and that, correspondingly, the ox (a symbol of sacrifice and atonement) has always been the symbol of

Luke. Second, the horn would bring *deliverance* from all earthly enemies in the final return of Christ (Revelation 19:1–16).

So we see that Zechariah's song celebrates the majestic, tossing horn of the Davidic Savior, Jesus, who would effect a mighty deliverance—"He . . . has raised up a horn of salvation for us in the house of his servant David."

Today this mighty "horn of salvation" is able "to save to the uttermost those who draw near to God through him" (Hebrews 7:25). Whoever we are, whatever we have done, no matter how heinous our sin—whether it is murder, infidelity, perversion, betrayal, embezzlement, lying, jealousy, hateful gossip, or whatever—Christ, the "horn of salvation," can save us completely and eternally. We must therefore take the greatest pride in the gospel, "for it is the power of God for salvation to everyone who believes, to the Jew first and also to the Greek" (Romans 1:16).

Praise for Fulfillment of the Abrahamic Covenant (vv. 72–75)

Zechariah's praise for God's fulfilling the Davidic Covenant through Christ naturally moved next to the Abrahamic Covenant because the promise to David rested upon the original promise to Abraham. The Abrahamic Covenant was first expressed when God promised Abraham, when he was yet childless, that he would make a great nation of him and that all the peoples of the earth would be blessed through him (Genesis 12:1–3).

On a subsequent occasion when God reiterated the promise, emphasizing that Abraham's offspring would be like the stars, Abraham "believed the Lord, and he counted it to him as righteousness" (Genesis 15:6). God was so pleased with Abraham's faith that on that night, when the sun had set, God himself appeared as "a smoking fire pot and a flaming torch [and] passed between these pieces" (Genesis 15:17), signifying that his promise was unconditional and that he (God) would be torn asunder like those pieces if he failed to keep his promises.

Yet, as great as this affirmation of the covenant was, a greater affirmation was to come when God *swore* to Abraham that he would keep his covenant—and that is what Zechariah referenced in his song:

> To show the mercy promised to our fathers
>   and to remember his holy covenant,
> the oath that he swore to our father Abraham, to grant us
>   that we, being delivered from the hand of our enemies,
> might serve him without fear,
>   in holiness and righteousness before him all our days." (vv. 72–75)

The oath took place after Abraham's unequaled display of obedience in his willingness to sacrifice Isaac through whom the promise of a great nation was to be fulfilled. After God stopped Abraham's hand in midair, God made an unparalleled oath:

> By myself I have sworn, declares the LORD, because you have done this and have not withheld your son, your only son, I will surely bless you, and I will surely multiply your offspring as the stars of heaven and as the sand that is on the seashore. And your offspring shall possess the gate of his enemies, and in your offspring shall all the nations of the earth be blessed, because you have obeyed my voice. (Genesis 22:16–18)

God was so pleased with Abraham's obedience that he swore by himself—something he had never done before and has not done since!

From Zechariah's inspired perspective, the effect of this great oath, as fulfilled through the coming of Christ, would not only be deliverance from enemies, but the enablement to "serve him without fear, in holiness and righteousness before him all our days" (vv. 74, 75). Certainly this is what Christ does for the believing heart—he liberates it so it can serve. Mary became the first servant of the new age of grace when she said, "I am the servant of the Lord; let it be to me according to your word" (1:38). Indeed, this is the precise call of the gospel age: "I appeal to you therefore, brothers, by the mercies of God, to present your bodies as a living sacrifice, holy and acceptable to God, which is your spiritual worship" (Romans 12:1).

Joyous service is a hallmark of lives where the Son has risen. Christianity not only delivers us, but infuses our lives with purpose. This is no small boon in a world where so many culture shapers teach that life is meaningless.

Praise for John (vv. 76, 77)

Zechariah was experiencing once-in-a-lifetime elevation of soul, and as his eyes fell to his newborn son, he sang of the part he would play in the new day: "And you, child, will be called the prophet of the Most High; for you will go before the Lord to prepare his ways, to give knowledge of salvation to his people in the forgiveness of their sins" (vv. 76, 77).

We cannot overstate Zechariah's emotion here. There had been no prophet among the Jews for four centuries. Zechariah had just recovered his voice, and he was using it to praise and prophesy. His baby boy was the focus of divine revelation. Surely Zechariah's words were not calm utterances. They came in a halting, tremulous voice as he struggled to gain composure.

In addition to citing John's functions as prophet and forerunner, Zechariah's words focused on the depth of John's ministry. He would "give knowledge of salvation to his people." This would not be theoretical knowledge, but personal knowledge of the inward experience of salvation as the result of a divine gift. Furthermore, the salvation that John would preach would consist of "the forgiveness of their sins." [3] John would bypass ritualistic religion and go right to the heart of spiritual life.

John's ministry, of course, anticipated the work of the coming spiritual Sonrise. Intimate knowledge of the divine gift of salvation is part of the New Testament legacy. "He came to his own, and his own people did not receive him. But to all who did receive him, who believed in his name, he gave the right to become children of God" (John 1:11, 12). This *intimacy with God* is extraordinary, like that between a child and a parent. The apostle John would later say, "I write these things to you who believe in the name of the Son of God that you may know that you have eternal life" (1 John 5:13).

Salvation also involves *the assurance of the forgiveness of sins*. We see this in Jesus' very name as ordered by the angel: "She will bear a son, and you shall call his name Jesus, for he will save his people from their sins" (Matthew 1:21). Jesus said of his own blood, "This is my blood of the covenant, which is poured out for many for the forgiveness of sins" (Matthew 26:28). This was the apostolic gospel as Peter and others preached it: "To him all the prophets bear witness that everyone who believes in him receives forgiveness of sins through his name" (Acts 10:43). Thus our assurance is, "If we confess our sins, he is faithful and just to forgive us our sins and to cleanse us from all unrighteousness" (1 John 1:9).

What incredible things Zechariah sang regarding his son! True knowledge of salvation and the forgiveness of sins would come from his ministry as people heard him preach and turned to God.

This is what the gospel offers—the only real forgiveness of sins in the universe—authentic forgiveness. Those who have experienced it can testify that there is nothing like it. It is complete and penetrates to the very depths of the human soul. The initial experience of divine forgiveness is often described as having a cosmic weight lifted from one's shoulders. The "knowledge of salvation" is not only *objective* but inward and *subjective*—"The Spirit himself bears witness with our spirit that we are children of God" (Romans 8:16).

Praise for the Rising Son (vv. 78, 79)

Zechariah ended his song with praise for the imminent rising of the sun—"Because of the tender mercy of our God, whereby the sunrise shall visit us from on high to give light to those who sit in darkness and in the shadow of death, to guide our feet into the way of peace" (vv. 78, 79).

Israel is portrayed here as a caravan that has lost its way and has been overtaken by night. It is stranded in utter darkness in a lonely, howling expanse of wilderness. The sky is lowering, and there is no starlight. It is (as the Greek literally says) "sitting in darkness." This is a moving picture of lethargy—oppressive, dark torpor—entropy—despair—hopelessness. They are helpless, just as Isaiah described it: "The people who walked in darkness . . . who dwelt in a land of deep darkness" (Isaiah 9:2).

But then a faint change is seen in the east. The sky is no longer black but blue. Their eyes move to the west, and in the darkness forms take shape, at first metallic and dull. Then comes just a wisp of color. As their eyes switch back to the east, the cobalt blue turns to royal blue and a long line of pink rims the horizon. The sun is up! They are quickly on their feet, exchanging smiles, rubbing hands, and beginning to cheer.

This is what we have here. The word "sunrise" was rendered in the Old English versions as "dayspring" (the day springing up) and in today's versions is given variously as "the first light of Heaven" (PHILLIPS), "the morning sun from heaven" (NEB), and "the Sunrise from on high" (NASB). All give the idea of the cosmic appearance of Christ as the light of the world.

He is the fulfillment of Malachi 4:2, "But for you who fear my name, the sun of righteousness shall rise with healing in its wings. You shall go out leaping like calves from the stall." Jesus is the "morning star [who] rises in [our] hearts" (2 Peter 1:19). He is "the root and the descendant of David, the bright morning star" (Revelation 22:16). Jesus said of himself, "I am the light of the world. Whoever follows me will not walk in darkness, but will have the light of life" (John 8:12). "Jesus took with him Peter and James and John, and led them up a high mountain by themselves. And he was transfigured before them, and his clothes became radiant, intensely white, as no one on earth could bleach them" (Mark 9:2, 3). Jesus told his followers, "Then the righteous will shine like the sun in the kingdom of their Father" (Matthew 13:43).

Closing Reflections

When Jesus rises in our lives, gone is "the shadow of death." We pass from death to life. Even more, in the light he is able "to guide our feet into the way of peace"—his *shalom*. This is more than the absence of conflict. It is wholeness and completeness, the sum of all that we require for conscious well-being. It is his gift to us. Jesus said, "Peace I leave with you; my peace

I give to you. Not as the world gives do I give to you. Let not your hearts be troubled, neither let them be afraid" (John 14:27). Those who experience the healing wholeness of God's peace "go out leaping like calves from the stall"—heels in the air, free and complete.

- Has "the sunrise . . . from on high" filled your life?
- Do you have the "knowledge of salvation"?
- Is Christ your mighty "horn of salvation"?
- Are you assured of "the forgiveness of . . . sins"?
- Have you been delivered from "the shadow of death"?
- Are you able to "serve him without fear"?
- Are your feet treading "the way of peace"?

If not, you need the Sunrise—you need the Christ who came to die for you—you need the spiritual realities of Luke 2, the birth of Jesus within you!

9

The Birth of Christ

LUKE 2:1–20

THE OPENING WORDS of this famous section of Scripture provide the setting for this, the greatest of all stories, by informing us that Caesar Augustus (Octavian) was ruler of "all the world"—"all the inhabited earth" (NASB). The ancient historians tell us that Caesar Augustus was the great-nephew of Julius Caesar and was a born fighter who clawed his way to power by defeating Antony and Cleopatra and then, through the considerable genius and force of his person, gave the empire a solidness that was to endure for centuries.

He was the first Caesar to be called "Augustus" when the Roman Senate voted to give him that title. Augustus means "holy" or "revered," and up to that time the title was reserved exclusively for the gods.[1] It was under Augustus' rule that decisive strides were taken toward making the Caesars gods. In fact, at about the same time Luke was writing these words, some of the Greek cities in Asia Minor adopted Caesar's birthday, September 23, as the first day of the New Year, hailing him as "savior." An inscription at Halicarnassus (birthplace of the famous Herodotus) even called him "savior of the whole world."[2]

Historian John Buchan records that when Caesar Augustus died, men actually "comforted themselves, reflecting that Augustus was a god, and that gods do not die."[3] So the world had at its helm a self-proclaimed, widely accepted god and savior. Luke, the historian and theologian, wants us to see this as the tableau for understanding the coming of the real Savior. The contrast could not be greater.

Inside Rome, in the Forum, the doors of the Temple of War had been closed for ten years and would remain closed for thirty more. To memorialize the peace, the famous monument *Ara Pacis Augustae* propagandizing Augustus's peace had been erected.[4] Rome and Augustus had bludgeoned every foe into submission. There was "peace," but it was a dark peace—a Hitler's peace—and no man or woman or boy or girl could say a word against it without fearfully looking over his or her shoulder.

Caesar Augustus's relentless arm stretched out to squeeze its tribute even in a tiny village at the far end of the Mediterranean. Thus it came about that a village carpenter and his expectant teenage bride were forced to travel to his hometown to be registered for taxation. It was a miserable journey. Mary was full term, which forced a slow, rolling gait as she walked those eighty miles. Perhaps, if she was fortunate, she had borrowed an animal to carry her. But whatever their situation, she traveled in the dust and cold of winter, bearing the distressing knowledge that she might have her first baby far from home, from her mother, and from nearly everyone who cared about her.

Seen through everyday logic, Joseph and Mary were insignificant nobodies from a nothing town. They were peasants. They were poor, uneducated, of no account. But she understood who she was and who God was. Early on, after Mary learned she was pregnant with "the Son of the Most High" (1:32) and met Elizabeth, she sang her great *Magnificat*, beginning with the words, "My soul magnifies the Lord, and my spirit rejoices in God my Savior, for he has looked on the humble estate of his servant" (1:46–48a). And toward the end of her song she said of her son, "He has shown strength with his arm; he has scattered the proud in the thoughts of their hearts; he has brought down the mighty from their thrones and exalted those of humble estate" (vv. 51, 52).

Joseph and Mary capsulized the mystery of grace—the King does not come to the proud and powerful but to the poor and powerless. As it is so often in life, things were not as they seemed to the world around them, because humble Mary and Joseph were the adoptive father and birth mother of the King of kings. Seven hundred years earlier, the prophet Micah had prophesied, "But you, O Bethlehem Ephrathah, who are too little to be among the clans of Judah [such an inconsequential little town!], from you shall come forth for me one who is to be ruler in Israel" (Micah 5:2). And now the poor couple's forced journey to Bethlehem to pay taxes would set the stage for the fulfillment of that messianic prophecy. They appeared to be helpless pawns caught in the movements of secular history, but every move was under the hand of Almighty God. The Messiah would indeed be born in tiny, insignificant Bethlehem! As the Virgin traveled, her steady beating heart, hidden from the world, kept time with the busily thumping heart of God.

> The Creator had woven Himself
> a robe of virgin flesh.[5]

The baby Mary carried was not a Caesar, a man who would become a god, but a far greater wonder—the true God who had become a man!

The Incarnation (vv. 6, 7)

The journey left Mary increasingly weary as she trod those dusty miles to the south, and when she and Joseph arrived in Bethlehem they were exhausted—especially Mary. Then the pains began. Perhaps at first young Mary was not sure it was her time and did not say anything to Joseph. But when there was no doubt that it was the real thing, she told him—probably with tears. Remember, she was only thirteen or fourteen years old.

We are all familiar with the haunting simplicity of Luke's description of the birth: "And while they were there, the time came for her to give birth. And she gave birth to her firstborn son" (vv. 6, 7a).

In Bethlehem the accommodations for travelers were primitive. The eastern inn was the crudest of arrangements. Typically it was a series of stalls built on the inside of an enclosure and opening onto a common yard where the animals were kept. All the innkeeper provided was fodder for the animals and a fire on which to cook. On that cold day when the expectant parents arrived, nothing at all was available, not even one of those crude stalls. And despite the urgency, no one would make room for them. So it was probably in the common courtyard where the travelers' animals were tethered that Mary gave birth to Jesus, with only Joseph attending her. Joseph probably wept as much as Mary did. Seeing her pain, the stinking barnyard, their poverty, people's indifference, the humiliation, and the sense of utter helplessness, feeling shame at not being able to provide for young Mary on the night of her travail—all that would make a man either curse or cry.

If we imagine that Jesus was born in a freshly swept, county fair stable, we miss the whole point. It was wretched—scandalous! There was sweat and pain and blood and cries as Mary reached up to the heavens for help. The earth was cold and hard. The smell of birth mixed with the stench of manure and acrid straw made a contemptible bouquet. Trembling carpenter's hands, clumsy with fear, grasped God's Son slippery with blood—the baby's limbs waving helplessly as if falling through space—his face grimacing as he gasped in the cold and his cry pierced the night.[6]

My mother groaned, my father wept.
Into the dangerous world I leapt.[7]

It was clearly a leap down—as if the Son of God rose from his splendor, stood poised at the rim of the universe irradiating light, and dove headlong, speeding through the stars over the Milky Way to earth's galaxy, finally past Arcturus, where he plunged into a huddle of animals. Nothing could be lower.

Luke finishes the picture in verse 7: "She . . . wrapped him in swaddling cloths and laid him in a manger, because there was no place for them in the inn." Mary counted his fingers, and the couple wiped him clean as best they could by firelight. Mary wrapped each of his little arms and legs with strips of cloth—mummy-like. No one helped her. She laid him in a feeding trough.

No child born into the world that day seemed to have lower prospects. The Son of God was born into the world not as a prince but as a pauper. We must never forget that this is where Christianity began, and where it always begins—with a sense of need, a graced sense of one's insufficiency. Christ, himself setting the example, comes to the needy. He is born only in those who are "poor in spirit."

The incarnation provides a marvelous paradigm for Christ's work in our lives. Every Advent season, and hopefully at other times as well, we are brought again to the wonder of the incarnation. See the swaddled Jesus, lying in the feeding trough in the stable, the birthplace of common livestock. Look long and hard with all your mind and all your heart. From early times the paradox of the incarnation has given birth to mind-boggling expressions. St. Augustine said of the infant Jesus:

Unspeakably wise,
He is wisely speechless.[8]

Lancelot Andrewes, who crafted much of the beautiful English of the Old Testament in the King James Version, preaching before King James on Christmas Day 1608, picked up on Augustine's idea and described Christ in the manger as:

the word without a word.[9]

He is in his person the Word of God!

Luci Shaw, in her beautiful poem "Mary's Song," says:

> Quiet he lies
> whose vigor hurled
> a universe. He sleeps
> whose eyelids have not closed before.[10]

The one who asked Job, "Where were you when I laid the foundation of the earth? Tell me, if you have understanding . . . when I made clouds its garment and thick darkness its swaddling band" (Job 38:4, 9) now himself lay wrapped in swaddling clothes.

The wonder of the incarnation! The omnipotent, omnipresent, omniscient God became a baby!

The Meaning (vv. 8–14)

Real Humanity

The great historic doctrine of the church is that the Son of God became a real man—not just someone who only appeared to be a man. When he was born, God the Son placed the exercise of his all-powerfulness and all-presence and all-knowingness under the direction of God the Father. He did not give up those attributes, but he submitted their exercise in his life to the Father's discretion. Though he was sinless, he had a real human body, mind, and emotions—complete with their inherent human weaknesses.

As a real baby in the cradle he watched his tiny clenched fist in uncomprehending fascination, just like any other baby. He did not feign babyhood. He did not say to himself, "You all think I am a prearticulate baby discovering I have a hand. Actually, I am God admiring my brilliant invention. I am your Creator, and I understand every word you are saying." Not at all. He was not pretending. This was not a postnatal spoof. He was a baby!

Reaching for analogies helpful in understanding the incarnation, some have likened Christ before the incarnation to

> a symphony, in all of its complexity and power—magnificence carried over a grand expanse. But when he became human he became a folk tune, simple and shortened. In this he lost nothing of his Godhead, his eternal character, his attributes, absolute purity, and changeless excellence.[11]

He was still the symphony (the eternal Son), but as a folk tune (a real man) he fully entered the human situation in a way that all could understand. John the apostle put it this way: "The Word became flesh and dwelt among us, and we have seen his glory, glory as of the only Son from the Father, full of grace and truth. . . . No one has ever seen God; the only God, who is at the

Father's side, he has made him known" (John 1:14, 18). The symphony/folk tune analogy is elegant and helpful, but its weakness is that no symphony is infinite. But in the incarnation, the infinite God both became finite man and remained infinite God.

This mystery is beyond earthly analogy or understanding. Truly human, the Son subjected himself to his own creation and its physical laws, its ups and downs. He would experience the development of human reason and language. He would be taught things he did not know. He walked like a baby before he walked like a man. He thought and talked like a baby before he thought and talked like a man. The growing pains of the Son of God were just as real for him as they were for us. As Harold Best explains: "The only difference was that Jesus did his learning, growing, and maturing sinlessly and perfectly, but this does not mean he was an instant learner."[12] He had to learn to be a carpenter from his earthly father, Joseph. Jesus Christ lived with a human body, mind, and soul with *all* their limitations, except for sin.

He really did it. It really did happen. Paul was right: "Great indeed, we confess, is the mystery of godliness: He was manifested in the flesh . . ." (1 Timothy 3:16). The implications of this reality are stupendous at Christmastime and year-round.

Divine Sympathy

Consider the implication of Christ's astounding capacity for sympathy and understanding. His instrument, so to speak, was the same as ours. It is a fact that if you have two in-tune pianos in the same room and a note is struck on one, the same note will gently respond on the other, though not touched by another person's hand. This is called "sympathetic resonance."

Christ's instrument, his humanity, was like ours in every way, except that he had no sin. And when a chord is struck in the weakness of our human instrument, it resonates in his! There is no note of human experience that does not play in Christ's as well. "For we do not have a high priest who is unable to sympathize with our weaknesses" (Hebrews 4:15). He has an unequaled capacity for sympathy. It goes far beyond intellectual understanding. Jesus does not just imagine how his children feel—he *feels* it!

We are all sometimes under incredible pressure. We may feel that no one understands, much less cares. But the truth is, any note we play (whether a melody or a dirge, or a minor key, or a discordant note) has sympathetic resonance in the heart of Jesus Christ. This is a supreme glory of the incarnation. All glory to God! Do you need sympathy? With Christ there is understanding.

The story began to move quickly as Christ's birth was announced. Shepherds were the first to hear. "And in the same region there were shepherds out in the field, keeping watch over their flock by night. And an angel of the Lord appeared to them, and the glory of the Lord shone around them, and they were filled with great fear" (vv. 8, 9). The shepherds on that wintry night were naturally huddled close to their fire, while icy constellations swept by overhead. Suddenly, as if a star had burst, glorious light overpowered the night, and an honored angel stepped forth as the shepherds recoiled in great fear despite his reassuring words.

That the message came to shepherds first, and not to the high and mighty, reminds us that God comes to the needy, the poor in spirit. Shepherds were despised by the "good," respectable people of that day. According to the *Mishnah*, shepherds were under a ban. They were regarded as thieves.[13] The only people lower than shepherds at that particular time in Jewish history were lepers. Scholars speculate that the only reason the flocks were so close in was because these men were keeping the sacrificial animals for the temple.

God comes only to those who sense their need. He does not come to the self-sufficient. The gospel is for those who know they need Jesus!

> For consider your calling, brothers: not many of you were wise according to worldly standards, not many were powerful, not many were of noble birth. But God chose what is foolish in the world to shame the wise; God chose what is weak in the world to shame the strong; God chose what is low and despised in the world, even things that are not, to bring to nothing things that are, so that no human being might boast in the presence of God. (1 Corinthians 1:26–29)

Wonderful Savior

The words of the angel, spoken not only for the shepherds but for all of us, were wonderful, for they promised a Savior: "Fear not, for behold, I bring you good news of great joy that will be for all the people. For unto you is born this day in the city of David *a Savior*, who is Christ the Lord" (vv. 10, 11). It was because of Christ's incarnation and his perfect identification with humanity—his taking on our nature, though without sin—that he could save us. He became "perfect" in regard to temptation by suffering temptation as a real man and putting the tempter to flight (Hebrews 5:8, 9; cf. Matthew 4:1–11). As a real man he became a perfect surrogate for us so he could take our sins upon himself, become sin for us (2 Corinthians 5:21), and die an atoning death for us. As Peter explained: "He himself bore our sins in his body on the tree, that we might die to sin and live to righteousness" (1 Peter 2:24).

Whatever our situation, he can deliver us. The angel said that the "good news" was "for all the people." Whoever you are, he can deliver you, help you, save you. "Because he continues forever . . . he is able to save to the uttermost those who draw near to God through him, since he always lives to make intercession for them" (Hebrews 7:24, 25).

After the angel's marvelous words—"Fear not, for behold, I bring you good news of great joy that will be for all the people. For unto you is born this day in the city of David a Savior, who is Christ the Lord" (vv. 10, 11)—something truly wonderful occurred: "And suddenly there was with the angel a multitude of the heavenly host praising God and saying, 'Glory to God in the highest, and on earth peace among those with whom he is pleased!'" (vv. 13, 14). A heavenly flash and suddenly the bewildered shepherds were surrounded by angels!

"A multitude" refers to not 50, not 150, not 1,500—but heavenly hosts beyond count. I think every one of God's angels was there because this was the most amazing event that had ever happened in the entire universe. I think the heavenly host stretched from horizon to horizon, obscuring the winter constellations. I like to imagine that they radiated golds, pinks, electric blue, hyacinth, and ultraviolet—maybe some were even sparkling. Milton imagined them in serried ranks:

> The helmed cherubim
> And sworded seraphim,
> In glittering ranks with wings displayed. . . .
> The stars with deep amaze
> Stand fixed in steadfast gaze.[14]

And when they lifted their voices to God, it was in cosmic stereo. They were announcing the long-awaited "sunrise . . . from on high" (1:78)—star music! Job tells us that at the creation of the world, "the morning stars [angels] sang together and all the sons of God shouted for joy" (Job 38:7). Now the angels again joined voices at the greatest creation of all—the birth of the God-man—the perfect sympathizer and Savior.

How we all would like to have been there—to be a fly on the ear of one of the shepherds' sheep. But actually, though the choir in Heaven played a major role, we on earth have the best part because we are the ones who receive God's grace. God became a *man*, not an angel. God redeemed *us*, not angels. Ours is the best part, and we will praise God for it for all eternity.

The Christmas message of this passage should make us sing year-round. The substance of the angels' song is instructive. It was first upward as they glorified God in "the highest" heavens, and then it was outward as it pronounced "on earth peace among those with whom he is pleased!"—peace, wholeness, well-being for those who have been favored by God's grace.

Has God worked in your heart? Are you the object of his good pleasure? Then you have a song to sing, for the best part is yours.

The Effect (vv. 15–20)

Soon the angels departed, the glory that lit the countryside faded, the constellations reappeared, and the shepherds were alone. But they allowed no grass to grow under their feet.

> When the angels went away from them into heaven, the shepherds said to one another, "Let us go over to Bethlehem and see this thing that has happened, which the Lord has made known to us." And they went with haste and found Mary and Joseph, and the baby lying in a manger. And when they saw it, they made known the saying that had been told them concerning this child. And all who heard it wondered at what the shepherds told them. But Mary treasured up all these things, pondering them in her heart. And the shepherds returned, glorifying and praising God for all they had heard and seen, as it had been told them. (vv. 15–20)

The shepherds were perhaps camped about a mile from the inn, and they certainly took off running, leaping the low Judean fences and entering the enclosure wide-eyed and panting. They searched the stalls around the perimeter of the enclosure and quickly found the new mother and her baby among the animals. Immediately they began to announce the good news, telling all who would listen about the angels and this wonderful birth. When they left, they continued glorifying and praising God for all they had experienced.

It is not enough to hear about Jesus. It is not enough to peek in the manger and say, "Oh, how nice. What a lovely scene. It gives me such good feelings." The truth is, even if Christ were born in Bethlehem a thousand times but not within you, you would be eternally lost. The Christ who was born into the world must be born in your heart. Religious sentiment, even at Christmastime, without the living Christ is a yellow brick road to darkness.

The Holy Spirit included this story in the Holy Scriptures so we would not miss the point: the real Savior of the world was not Caesar Augustus, nor will it be any great world leader. The Savior of the world is Jesus, the Son of God who came to earth veiled in Mary's flesh, was born in human flesh, lived in the flesh, died in the flesh, was resurrected in that flesh, and now lives in the same glorified flesh at the right hand of the Father.

The incarnation was real.

Christ's identification was complete.

His understanding and sympathy are real because he had the same type of physical body we have, and still does.

His complete identification means he can save you, whatever your situation.

That baby, God's Son, demands our complete allegiance.

He really did come into the world, and because of this, he really can come into your heart.

Let us lay our lives before him because:

> In this world of sin,
> Where meek souls will
> Receive him still
> The dear Christ enters in.
>
> Phillips Brooks

10

The *Nunc Dimittis*

LUKE 2:21–40

IMAGINE THAT A WEEK has passed since the first Christmas, when the angels filled the skies over the fields of Bethlehem as they announced Christ's birth to the amazed shepherds, who then ran, leaping the low fences, to see their newborn Savior King lying in a manger.

Young Mary had hardly recovered from giving birth, and the mental tapes of the miraculous events were set on constant replay: the forced journey to Bethlehem, their frantic search for a place to give birth, her labor under the stars, Joseph anxiously standing beside her in the night air.

> What is this flesh I purchased with my pains,
> This fallen star my milk sustains,
> This love that makes my heart's blood stop
> Or strikes a sudden chill into my bones
> And bids my hair stand up?[1]

Unlike the later millions who would nod to the memory of Christmas only briefly once a year, this couple would live their entire lives in the unfolding mystery of the incarnation.

The beautiful events recorded in Luke 2:21–40 were given to Mary and Joseph to deepen and confirm the significance of the incarnation in their minds—and ultimately in the thoughts of the faithful through the centuries. Specifically, the events associated with their baby's circumcision brought them profound meditation as they pondered the meaning of their son's birth. These same events can help make the dazzling wonder of the incarnation a year-long experience for us.

The Circumcision (v. 21)

Luke describes Christ's circumcision in a single concise sentence: "And at the end of eight days, when he was circumcised, he was called Jesus, the name given by the angel before he was conceived in the womb" (v. 21). It was important that Christ be circumcised, for circumcision was commanded in Genesis 17 for all males who would be a part of Abraham's household. Without it Jesus could not have identified with his people even though he was of pure Hebrew blood.

However, the matter of greatest significance at his circumcision was that he was officially named Jesus, which means "Jehovah is salvation." This is essential to understanding the incarnation, though sadly, in this secularized age, the average person on the street has no idea what *Jesus* means. But for those of us who know him, the name is both a claim and a promise, and that is why it is so often on our lips. "Jesus, O how sweet the name."

The origin of the name reveals something that makes it even more precious. Jesus is the Greek rendering of the Hebrew word *Joshua*, the name of the great man who succeeded Moses and led Israel into the promised land. Originally, however, Joshua's name wasn't Joshua but Hoshea, which means "salvation." But because of his faith and leadership in believing that the promised land could be conquered, as Numbers 13:16 records, "And Moses called Hoshea the son of Nun Joshua." And as we know, he became Israel's greatest general.[2] Joshua (or Jesus) not only means "Jehovah is salvation" but suggests deliverance. It carries the idea of our being delivered by heroic action from the bondage of sin (cf. Isaiah 9:6, "Mighty God"). The name *Jesus* shouts to the world the heroics of the incarnation and the cross.

Now consider this: both Mary and Joseph had been told *separately* by an angel to name the child Jesus. The angel said to Joseph, "She will bear a son, and you shall call his name Jesus, for he will save his people from their sins" (Matthew 1:21). Gabriel's announcement to Mary was similar: "You will conceive in your womb and bear a son, and you shall call his name Jesus" (Luke 1:31).

Certainly Mary and Joseph had often discussed this, both before their son's birth and during the week since, but when the time for circumcision came, and Joseph uttered the divinely given name, the sense of the moment must have overwhelmed them. "This child shall be called 'Jehovah is salvation.' This child, our baby, is salvation!" How about that for a birth memory! Certainly this was a topic of conversation time and time again. Mary would say to Joseph, "Tell me again," and he would recite the details of his encounter with the angel in his dream. Then he would ask the same of Mary, and she would describe Gabriel and reverently describe his announcement of the name of all names—"Jesus."

"Jesus—Jehovah is salvation—he is my deliverance." If this is not part of your mind-set, perhaps you have not yet come to know Jesus. As John Newton said so well:

> How sweet the name of Jesus sounds
> In a believer's ear!

The Christmas name was followed by the knife and the sharp cry of the Son of God and the blood of his circumcision as he fully identified with God's covenant people.

> Alas, how soon our sin
> Sore doth begin
> His Infancy to seize![3]

The post-Christmas events were the rites of Mary's purification and the couple's presentation of their baby in the temple, which took place about a month later. They reveal the kind of people to whom Christ comes.

The Purification (vv. 22–24)

The poverty of Jesus' parents was obvious, considering the humble offering they made for Mary's purification in obedience to the Law:

> And when the time came for their purification according to the Law of Moses, they brought him up to Jerusalem to present him to the Lord (as it is written in the Law of the Lord, "Every male who first opens the womb shall be called holy to the Lord") and to offer a sacrifice according to what is said in the Law of the Lord, "a pair of turtledoves, or two young pigeons." (vv. 22–24)

That they offered a poor woman's offering is clear from Leviticus 12:6–8, which stipulates that the purification offering must be a yearling lamb for a burnt offering and a pigeon or dove for a sin offering. However, "And if she cannot afford a lamb, then she shall take two turtledoves or two pigeons, one for a burnt offering and the other for a sin offering. And the priest shall make atonement for her, and she shall be clean" (Leviticus 12:8). Mary and Joseph's humble offering was a public declaration of their poverty.

So here we again see that Christianity began and always begins with a spirit of need—spiritual destitution. This was the persistent refrain of Christ's life. We heard it in Mary's *Magnificat*: "For he has looked on the humble estate of his servant" (1:48). The angels' revelation to the outcast shepherds, rather than to the high and mighty of Israel, sang of this as well. The wretched circumstances of Christ's birth echoed the refrain.

> The LORD is near to the brokenhearted
> and saves the crushed in spirit. (Psalm 34:18)

God did not and does not come to the self-sufficient. This is a truth that we must remind ourselves of again and again. Christianity wrongly understood gives some an illusive sense of personal spiritual adequacy. Even the born again can wrongly turn spiritual advances into prideful self-sufficiency—a sense that one has arrived. We must continually guard against this within ourselves. Our only adequacy is in Christ (cf. 2 Corinthians 3:5)!

The Presentation (vv. 25–38)

While Mary and Joseph were in the temple, they met two other Israelites whose lives exemplified godliness and faith. Their names were Simeon and Anna. Verse 25 introduces Simeon: "Now there was a man in Jerusalem, whose name was Simeon, and this man was righteous and devout, waiting for the consolation of Israel, and the Holy Spirit was upon him." We meet Anna in verses 36, 37: "And there was a prophetess, Anna, the daughter of Phanuel, of the tribe of Asher. She was advanced in years, having lived with her husband seven years from when she was a virgin, and then as a widow until she was eighty-four. She did not depart from the temple, worshiping with fasting and prayer night and day."

Simeon and Anna embodied all that was good in Israelite piety. To those who follow Christ, their similarities are wonderfully encouraging. First, both were *aged*. New Testament scholars R. E. Brown and I. H. Marshall believe the text says that Anna was a widow for eighty-four years, and that depending upon what age she was married, she was probably 103 to 105 years old.[4] Though Simeon's age is not given, the text suggests that he also was advanced in years. Their stooped profiles announced their age to all who approached. Up-close onlookers observed their age-spotted hands and the translucent skin around veined eyes but also saw evidence of souls that were young and growing.

Both were also *devoted to God*. Simeon is called "righteous and devout" (v. 25), meaning that he behaved well toward people and also was careful about his religious duties and his service for God.[5] And Anna "did not depart from the temple, worshiping with fasting and prayer night and day" (v. 37). Whenever the doors were open, she was there. She was a woman of rare piety.

Both were *prophets*. Anna is called "a prophetess" (v. 36), and Simeon's song is itself a prophecy.

Both were *filled with expectancy*. Simeon is described as a man "waiting for the consolation of Israel" (v. 25). The word used here for "consolation" appears in verbal forms in the Greek Old Testament translation of Isaiah in verses that refer to the Messiah, such as 40:1, "Comfort, comfort my people," and 66:13, "As one whom his mother comforts, so I will comfort you; you shall be comforted in Jerusalem." Messianic expectation had impacted the lives of Simeon and Anna, and they shared the same electric joy. Anna joined Simeon right after his prophetic song and "began to give thanks to God and to speak of him to all who were waiting for the redemption of Jerusalem" (v. 38). Anna was Simeon's cocelebrant of the consolation of Israel. They *believed* when few others truly believed in Christ's coming. They never gave up but kept trusting and looking. What an example they are even for us today!

Simeon and Anna represented all who saw that their only hope was in the mercy and grace of God. Along with the poor carpenter and his wife and the outcast shepherds, they were flesh-and-blood examples of those to whom Christ comes. They personified the paradox of being profoundly empty and profoundly full—"Blessed are those who hunger and thirst for righteousness, for they shall be satisfied" (Matthew 5:6). They longed for the righteousness and consolation that would come only through the Messiah. They came to God's house hungry, and they received as few others have in the history of the world.

Lives like these are rare. Such longing is not in vogue today. The ideal modern-day man sees himself as fulfilling Hemingway's line, "You're the completest man I've ever known." He needs nothing, no one, not even God—or so he thinks. We need to ask God to show us our insufficiency. What grace would come to us if we dared to pray for a greater sense of our spiritual need!

There is yet another facet to Simeon's beautiful soul. "And it had been revealed to him by the Holy Spirit that he would not see death before he had seen the Lord's Christ" (v. 26). Simeon had received an oracle from God, making it clear that though he was aged, he would not leave this life without seeing the Lord's Messiah. How long had he been waiting? Days—months—years? We do not know. But we can imagine his settled assurance and joyous anticipation as he daily came to the temple looking, reflecting, and sometimes asking himself, "Is this the One? There is a likely couple! Maybe this is him!" And then, one grand day, "And he came in the Spirit into the temple, and when the parents brought in the child Jesus, to do for him according to the custom of the Law, he took him up in his arms and blessed God" (vv. 27, 28).

With trembling arms Simeon lifted the fat, dimpled baby from the startled virgin, and for a moment the world ceased to turn. The man of God was, as the early church called him, *Theodoches*—God-receiver!

Simeon's Song (vv. 29–32)

As he held the baby Jesus, he began to praise God in song, and his song laid down for Mary and Joseph (and for us) the purpose of the Christ Child. "Lord, now you are letting your servant depart [*Nunc dimittis*, as the famous Latin has it] in peace, according to your word" (v. 29).

With the baby in his arms, secure in God's presence, Simeon experienced a profound peace of soul. And well he should have. After all, he held in his hands the "Prince of Peace" (prophesied in Isaiah 9:6), the one of whom the angels sang, "Glory to God in the highest, and on earth peace among those with whom he is pleased!" (2:14). God's favor rested upon Simeon. He was ready to die, for that is what "depart" means.[6] He was ready to go home to be with his God forever.

Simeon's reason was clear: "For my eyes have seen your salvation" (v. 30). The baby Jesus was and is God's salvation. Moreover, he did not say, "My eyes have seen *part* of your salvation!" Christ is totally sufficient. He is all we need!

True peace comes only when we, like Simeon, understand that salvation is Jesus Christ plus nothing—and rest our souls in him alone.

The salvation of which Simeon sang is universal in its offer—"that you have prepared in the presence of all peoples, a light for revelation to the Gentiles, and for glory to your people Israel" (vv. 31, 32). This is especially significant for Gentiles (the majority of the world's population). We were sung about in the Jewish temple by a prophet as he held the Messiah in his arms! Jesus is our "light" in this dark world, he is our salvation, and he is at the same time the "glory [of] . . . Israel." Christ, a light to Gentiles, is the full realization of Israel's glory.

Simeon surely held the baby tightly. It would have been impossible for him to do otherwise given his ecstasy. He looked at Jesus—and looked—and looked again. His heart, overflowing with joy at the coming of the Redeemer and the fulfillment of God's personal promise to him, soared even beyond his song.

To receive salvation, all one has to do is to take Jesus in his or her arms as Lord. Verse 33 tells us, "And his father and his mother marveled at what was said about him." Surely that amazement impressed every syllable, every instant upon their minds, confirming what had previously been shown to them. May we share their profound amazement and hold every word close to our hearts.

Simeon's Revelation (vv. 34, 35)

The encounter closes with Simeon turning to Mary and Joseph (Anna was also present; cf. verse 38) and addressing them directly, especially Mary: "And Simeon blessed them and said to Mary his mother, 'Behold, this child is appointed for the fall and rising of many in Israel, and for a sign that is opposed (and a sword will pierce through your own soul also), so that thoughts from many hearts may be revealed'" (vv. 34, 35). These words are meant for all of us, though the mention of the sword piercing Mary's soul was for her alone.

This prophecy would become very important to Mary. In her *Magnificat* she sang of how the future generations would call her "blessed." But here she learns that the future will also bring great sorrow. That future would include the family's flight to Egypt, her Son's being misunderstood and rejected, the terrible events of Passion Week, and watching her Son die on the cross.

> Hanging all torn she sees; and in His woes
> And pains; her pangs and throes.[7]

A great sword would go right through this mother's soul! The most honored woman of all would know great pain.

The rest of Simeon's prophetic words apply to all of us. Simeon's assertion that "This child is appointed for the fall and rising of many" (v. 34a) reveals the necessary experience of all who come to Christ, for we must bow in humiliation and poverty of spirit before we can rise to new life in Christ. When we see our inadequacy, we are ready for God's grace.

Truly Jesus has been "a sign that is opposed . . . so that thoughts from many hearts may be revealed" (vv. 34b, 35a). When people truly encounter Christ, their inner thoughts (that is, their evil thoughts) are seen for what they are. Apart from God's merciful intervention, people naturally oppose him.[8] But Christ reveals what our inner lives are really like. Human goodness is seen as filthy rags. Unable or unwilling to handle the truth, we naturally oppose Christ's work. But when we fall before him in humiliation, we receive grace and new life. Jesus always knocks us down so he can pick us up.

Closing Reflections

Imagine the thoughts that must have gone through Mary and Joseph's minds.

Their baby, "Jehovah is salvation," was and is a mighty deliverer. He delivers us through the heroics of the incarnation and the cross. This should give us Christmas joy year-round.

He comes to the needy—those who realize that he is their only hope (consider Mary and Joseph, the shepherds, Simeon and Anna). Truly "He has filled the hungry with good things, and the rich he has sent away empty" (1:53). Today it is those with a perpetual sense of spiritual need and spiritual hunger who live in the wonder of the incarnation.

Jesus Christ is the whole of salvation, not part of it. This realization brings peace.

We come to new life as he aggressively brings us to the end of ourselves and then raises us to new life.

Such reflections on the spiritual life will help us experience Christ day by day.

11

"Favor with God and Man"

LUKE 2:41–52

LUKE BEGINS THIS SECTION by informing us that "his parents went to Jerusalem every year at the Feast of the Passover. And when he was twelve years old, they went up according to custom" (vv. 41, 42). The Hebrew Scriptures, in three separate places, called for the mandatory attendance of all males age thirteen and above at the feasts of Passover, Pentecost, and Tabernacles (cf. Exodus 23:14–17; 34:23; Deuteronomy 16:16). But no such requirement was made of women, though godly women such as Hannah had been attending Passover for centuries (cf. 1 Samuel 2:19). Thus the multiple pilgrimages of Joseph and Mary together testify to their deep piety and devotion.

Passover had become a family event observed along with others from Nazareth (the word translated "group" in verse 44 was used to describe a traveling party or caravan).[1] The large number in the caravan provided safety as they passed through the hostile area of Samaria, and also added to their camaraderie.

We do not know if this was Jesus' first trip to Passover. Very likely he had been before. But his presence now as a twelve-year-old was significant because in another year, as a thirteen-year-old, Jesus would officially become a "son of the commandment," a full member of the synagogue (cf. *Mishnah*, Niddah 5:6), similar to the modern custom of *bar mitzvah*. Because of this, the *Mishnah* suggests that fathers should exercise their boys in the observance of the Passover "one year or two years before [they are of age]" (Yoma 8:4). So twelve-year-old Jesus, brimming with energy and excitement, was brought along to observe and learn as much as he could about the heart of Israel's religious life.

When the jostling, merry throng passed through the gates of the holy city, a grand sight met Jesus' twelve-year-old eyes. Some two hundred thousand pilgrims packed out the walled city. Every available space was rented, and in lieu of rent cheerful hosts were given the hides of sheep sacrificed by their guests. Merchants who had come in advance lined the streets displaying their wares, and beggars stationed themselves strategically by the city's ancient gates. The most intense activity was at the sheep stalls, where pilgrims bartered for sheep and goats to sacrifice at the temple.

When the sun rose on Passover, intense activity filled the encampments, the homes, and especially the temple. A full contingent of priests (twenty-four divisions instead of the customary one) attended the temple. Their first task of the day was to take the leaven that had been gathered by candlelight from each home and ceremonially burn it. Next they prepared for the ritual slaughtering of the Passover lambs. By midday all work stopped, and a holy air of anticipation rested over Jerusalem.

At about three o'clock the sacrifice began. We may well surmise that Joseph and his relatives, in preparation for Jesus' manhood, took preadolescent Jesus into the temple with them so he could observe the sacrifice. If so, as the gates of the temple court closed behind the vast group of worshipers, he heard a ram's horn sound and saw Joseph, in concert with hundreds of other worshipers, slaughter his family's lamb. The priests, standing in two long rows, caught the blood in gold and silver basins, then doused it against the base of the altar. Levites sang the Hallel Psalms (113—118) above the din as Jesus' father dressed his lamb and, before leaving, slung the animal, wrapped in its own skin, over his shoulder and departed with his young son in tow.

At home, the lamb was roasted on a pomegranate spit and eaten after sundown by the whole family. In the flickering amber light of a candle-decked room, the meal was joyfully consumed according to Passover liturgy with interspersed hand washings, prayers, and Hallel Psalms. At the conclusion the son (perhaps young Jesus was given the privilege) asked the father the ceremonial question, "Why is this night different from all other nights?" (*Mishnah*, Pesahim x.4), and his father responded with a moving review of Israel's deliverance from Egypt.

The night ended late, with many people returning to the streets for more celebration. Others went back to the temple mount to await the opening of the doors at midnight for further worship and prayer.[2]

When young Jesus finally went to sleep, the dazzling images of Passover undoubtedly danced in his awakening human soul. And that was not all. Jesus' devout family stayed for a whole week in Jerusalem, as the Greek tells us ("the days were completed"[3])—and so their twelve-year-old had the run of the old city, especially the temple. Jesus spent those seven days in "holy delight."[4] Every rite spoke volumes to his soul. His nimble mind connected Scripture with Scripture and then with life. His heavenly Father revealed more and more of the mystery of who Jesus really was.

Searching for Jesus (vv. 43–45)

The week flew by for Jesus. He had been in the heavenlies. His young mind was completely absorbed with the Passover and the temple and the Torah. He could not get enough. So much so that "when the feast was ended, as they were returning, the boy Jesus stayed behind in Jerusalem. His parents did not know it" (v. 43). They did not know that Jesus was not with them because when traveling en masse children often joined another part of the group, perhaps to be with some cousins or friends. Besides, Jesus' deportment had never caused them any concern. So it is understandable that they did not miss Jesus.

Nevertheless, there is a centuries-old question here: was Jesus a disobedient child? Some think so. As the argument goes, Jesus must certainly have known when the caravan was leaving. He was bright. He knew the time of day. But he was so caught up in the excitement of Passover and the temple that he couldn't resist staying behind—like a little boy who wants to join the circus. So Jesus was deliberately disobedient, it is said.

Others disagree, and for good reasons. The most important of these is that Jesus was without sin—*he never sinned*. As Jesus later asked his detractors, "Which one of you convicts me of sin?" (John 8:46). He also claimed, "I always do the things that are pleasing to [the Father]" (John 8:29). The corpus of the New Testament rests on his sinless perfection. The writer of Hebrews describes him as having been "tempted as we are, yet without sin" (Hebrews 4:15), and again as "holy, innocent, unstained, separated from sinners" (Hebrews 7:26). Peter extolled his sinlessness by saying, "He committed no sin, neither was deceit found in his mouth" (1 Peter 2:22). John categorically said, "and in him there is no sin" (1 John 3:5). Paul affirmed that Christ "knew no sin" (2 Corinthians 5:21). To say Jesus sinned by being a disobedient son contradicts Christ's words and all of Scripture.

The explanation for Jesus' behavior here rests, I believe, in the genuineness of his incarnation and his growing awareness of who he was. Accepting the incarnation at face value means that Jesus was genuinely a twelve-year-old. Though fully God, he was also human. Choosing not to avail himself of all the prerogatives of deity, he learned in the same way we do. As a child he had to learn that two plus two equals four, and as a twelve-year-old he was still learning about every part of life—including faith and relationships. As a twelve-year-old, he did not have the fine-tuned social awareness he would have at age thirty.

The point is, he was capable of *unknowingly* causing his parents distress; but as a sinless being, he was incapable of *knowingly* doing it. Here Jesus unknowingly brought anxiety to Joseph and Mary. Moreover, he unintentionally caused his parents to worry because his twelve-year-old mind was totally absorbed with the massive spiritual realization of his identity as the Messiah that had come to him that week. The combination of his authentic adolescence and the immensely absorbing revelation regarding his own person so occupied his mind that he did not imagine that staying in the temple would cause anyone alarm. Jesus did not sin in any of this. The sinless twelve-year-old Son of God was simply following the logic of the massive spiritual revelation of that week.

Regardless, he threw a major scare into his parents' fainting hearts. "Supposing him to be in the group they went a day's journey, but then they began to search for him among their relatives and acquaintances, and when they did not find him, they returned to Jerusalem, searching for him" (vv. 44, 45). If you have ever lost a child at a shopping mall or a ballpark or wherever, you know the scare that can cause you—the palpitating heart, the frantic searching, the calling out in ever more shrill tones, the sprinting from person to person, feeling so frightened, angry, or embarrassed. As Joseph and Mary questioned the caravan, they hoped for the best but feared the worst.

Jesus Found (vv. 46, 47)

Jesus was missing a total of three days. The first day the holy child's parents were unaware as they traveled away from Jerusalem, the second day was given to hurrying back to Jerusalem, and the third day they found him. "After three days they found him in the temple, sitting among the teachers, listening to them and asking them questions. And all who heard him were amazed at his understanding and his answers" (vv. 46, 47). Since Mary and Joseph found Jesus together, we know this was in the outer courts or porticoes of the temple, because women were not permitted in the inner chambers. There they found their twelve-year-old smack in the middle of the teachers. Amazingly, he was asking insightful questions, he understood the religious dialogue, and his answers were brilliant. All were "amazed"—literally, "struck" with his comprehension and exchange.

Jesus' extraordinary performance has inspired an apocryphal writer to see him as exercising omniscience on this occasion. The second-century

Gospel of Thomas portrayed Jesus as starting out with the caravan for home, but then slipping away and returning to the temple, where his parents later found him sitting in the midst of the doctors, listening and asking questions. "And all men paid heed to him and marveled how that being a young child he put to silence the elders and teachers of the people, expounding the heads of the law and the parables of the prophets."[5] A later Arabic Gospel portrays Jesus as instructing the astronomers in the mysteries of the universe and explaining the secrets of metaphysics to the philosophers.[6]

But Jesus was not exercising omniscience, and neither was he giving the teachers a lesson—"No, Dr. Isaac, you have it all wrong! The correct exegesis is. . . ." It is not even necessary to see Jesus as a genius here, though he may have been. Rather, twelve-year-old Jesus was *sinless*, *intelligent*, *well studied* in the Scriptures, and *illuminated* by his Father in Heaven. Though Jesus was not exercising omniscience, his knowledge was certainly informed by Heaven, and the depth of his participation was stunning.

Family Talk (vv. 48–52)

The Parents' Response

Though Mary and Joseph were peasants, they were not put off by the *literati* or their son's startling display.[7] "And when his parents saw him, they were astonished. And his mother said to him, 'Son, why have you treated us so? Behold, your father and I have been searching for you in great distress'" (v. 48). This reproach came from hurt feelings. Mary's words "Your father and I have been searching for you" are literally, "Suffering pain we are searching for you."[8] We can easily understand Mary's motherly concern and her reasons for reprimanding her son in front of such distinguished company. She obviously considered him to have sinned.

Jesus' Response

But Mary's divine twelve-year-old did not see it that way at all. And the answer he gave in the form of a question gives us the earliest recorded words of Jesus. As we might expect, they had great theological importance. His response was in fact a gentle question: "Why were you looking for me? Did you not know that I must be in my Father's house?" (v. 49).

Jesus called the temple where he stood his "Father's house," and in doing so he asserted that God was his Father and that he stood in unique relationship to God—that he had a relationship to God that no other human has ever had. There is no parallel in the Old Testament for the phrase "my Father" in speaking of God. Rather, some equivalent was used.[9]

As a twelve-year-old, one year before becoming "a son of the commandment," Jesus had come to understand that he had a unique relationship with God the Father, one far deeper and more profound than any that had ever been known before. Namely, he now knew that he was the Son of God—the Messiah—God become man. Eighteen years later, when Jesus began his public ministry, his awareness of God as his Father would become a trademark of his ministry. To catch the idea of how radical this self-understanding was, we need to understand that in the huge library of the Old Testament's thirty-nine books, God is only referred to as Father fourteen times—and then rather impersonally. In those fourteen references "Father" is always used in reference to the nation, not to individuals. God was referred to as Abraham's Father, but Abraham did not speak of God as "my Father." But when Jesus came on the scene, he addressed God as his Father and never used any other term. In all his prayers he addressed God as Father. The Gospels record his using "Father" more than sixty times in reference to God.

This was a watershed experience for the twelve-year-old. The awareness of his divine paternity was explicit in the very first of his recorded words in all of Scripture. This awareness was announced in the Jewish temple, the very heart of Israel's faith. And these words are part of the infancy narrative that began in the temple (cf. 1:5–25) and now ends in the temple. What is the point? *Jesus is God's Son! God is his Father!* One year before officially entering manhood, Jesus knew who he was—and that realization would open like a flower and become evident to the whole world eighteen years later.

Profound Obedience

How did Mary and Joseph react to all this? "And they did not understand the saying that he spoke to them" (v. 50). Despite her great humility and faith, it would take years for Mary to finally put it all together. But the divine twelve-year-old understood, and his understanding of his divine position produced an unexpected and amazing phenomenon: *human obedience*. "And he went down with them and came to Nazareth and was submissive to them. And his mother treasured up all these things in her heart" (v. 51). Literally, "And he was obeying them," a phrase expressing continuous obedience. This sums up the subsequent life of Jesus until his baptism.

Jesus' awareness that he was the divine Son, and that God was his Father, was the awareness that undergirded his human obedience to Joseph and Mary. Because he knew who he was, he could profoundly obey.

A Favored Life (v. 52)

What was the result of Jesus' amazing filial obedience? "And Jesus increased in wisdom and in stature and in favor with God and man" (v. 52). This is a picture of perfect development. The word translated "favor" is the Greek word *charis* ("grace"). He was graced in his relationship with God and graced in his relationship with men. Favor characterized his vertical and horizontal relationships.

Closing Reflections

There is an ocean of wisdom here for all of us who have been born again in Christ and now call God our Father.

An obedient, submissive inner spirit is a key to experiencing proper spiritual growth—growth in favor with God and with men. When we submit our lives to God in Scriptural terms, saying, "Here I am! Send me" (Isaiah 6:8) or presenting our bodies as "a living sacrifice" (Romans 12:1), God's favor rests upon us. Then our vertical obedience brings the fullness of the Holy Spirit and the impulse to "submit to one another out of reverence for Christ" (Ephesians 5:21). This inevitably brings favor with our brothers and sisters in Christ.

But there is more, for such Christians will also submit themselves to serving a lost world for the advancement of the gospel and the glory of Christ. Thus such lives often grow in favor with men. As Christ himself demonstrated, submission is the key to ongoing grace and favor with Heaven and earth.

Also, *an obedient, submissive inner spirit like Christ's comes from knowing who we are*. Jesus understood that he was the Son of God and that God was his Father, and that awareness produced profound submission to God and man. In our case, our union with Christ makes God our Father too, just as the apostle John exclaimed: "Beloved, we are God's children now" (1 John 3:2). The awareness of being a child of God makes us want to obey him and empowers us to submit ourselves to others for his glory.

Do you know who you are? Do you really know?

If so, then you can submit yourself to God and men.

And if you do that, you are walking in the way of grace!

12

John's Baptism

LUKE 3:1–14

SILENCE SHROUDS the first thirty years of the lives of Jesus and John, except for the brief glimpse of Jesus during his brilliant visit to the temple in his twelfth year. What we know of those shrouded years must be deduced from their birth narratives and the attendant prophecies.

In the case of John we know that at six months in his mother's womb he "leaped" at the sound of the virgin's voice (1:41), and thus John the Baptist's prophetic ministry actually began three months before his birth! We also know that he was "filled with the Holy Spirit, even from his mother's womb" (1:15) John was totally invaded by the Spirit before birth and through his whole life.[1] The fact that he never partook of "wine or strong drink" (1:15) indicates that he was a Nazirite from birth and the beneficiary of elite spiritual disciplines. These dynamic spiritual forces would promote an unparalleled spiritual formation in John over three full decades.

Doctor Luke tells us in the final verse of chapter 1 that "the child grew and became strong in spirit, and he was in the wilderness until the day of his public appearance to Israel" (v. 80). The reference is to his human spirit, which developed massive convictions and character and the passion needed to prepare the way for the promised Messiah. Whether his aged parents died early, thus facilitating or causing John's solitary existence, we do not know. But out in the country, alone with God, his great prophetic personality was established.

As Luke the historian prepares us for John's dramatic appearance, he names no less than seven historical figures to establish the date and context of John's ministry:

> In the fifteenth year of the reign of Tiberius Caesar, Pontius Pilate being governor of Judea, and Herod being tetrarch of Galilee, and his brother Philip tetrarch of the region of Ituraea and Trachonitis, and Lysanias tetrarch of Abilene, during the high priesthood of Annas and Caiaphas, the word of God came to John the son of Zechariah in the wilderness. (vv. 1, 2)

Together the names indicate that John began his public ministry about AD 27–29.[2] Even more, they establish the dark political ambience of the Roman/Palestinian governance. All the civil names given here evoke wickedness and intrigue: Tiberius—Pilate—Herod—Philip—Lysanias. The religious names—Annas and Caiaphas—similarly project a degenerate priesthood. Annas had been priest from AD 6–15 and then was followed by his four sons in succession, and eventually by his son-in-law Caiaphas.[3] The mention of their priesthood as one indicates a serpentine nepotism and an evil concentration of power.

It was against this backdrop of political and religious darkness that "the word of God came to John the son of Zechariah in the wilderness" (v. 2). This was a classic prophetic call, because similar language was used for the calls of such great figures as Isaiah and Jeremiah (cf. Isaiah 38:4; Jeremiah 1:1, 2; 13:3). So John strode full blown onto the Jewish landscape dressed in calculated radical prophetic garb, long flowing hair, and a robe of camel's hair, girded about with a leather thong. The mere appearance of John in the desert was a call to repentance.

John's Preaching: A Preparatory Baptism (vv. 3–6)

Luke introduces John's ministry with a concise sentence: "And he went into all the region around the Jordan, proclaiming a baptism of repentance for the forgiveness of sins" (v. 3). This does not mean that baptism brings forgiveness of sins. In point of fact, John's baptism followed each person's repentance and was a sign of it. John called his people to repent (turn away from their sins), and the subsequent acceptance of his baptism was an indication that they had done so. There was no power in his baptism.

Even the Jewish historian Josephus understood this, as he explained regarding John and his baptism:

> He was a good man and had exhorted the Jews to lead righteous lives, to practice justice towards their fellows and piety towards God, and so doing to join in baptism. In his view this was a necessary preliminary if baptism was to be acceptable to God. They must not employ it to gain pardon for whatever sins they committed, but as a consecration of the body implying that the soul was already thoroughly cleansed by right behaviour.[4]

Thus, the proper view of John's ministry is to see him full of the Spirit and preaching with such effect that multitudes visibly fell under conviction, resulting in many repenting of their sins and then asking for John's baptism.

There is also no suggestion here that repentance is a human work that merits the forgiveness of God. There is no hint of the idea that if we repent, God will look favorably upon us. John's ministry is consonant with Paul's teaching in Ephesians 2 that we were all "dead" in our transgressions and sins, utterly helpless to bring about our own salvation (Ephesians 2:1), that we are saved by grace, not by works (Ephesians 2:8, 9), and that as his children we have been "created in Christ Jesus for good works" (Ephesians 2:10). John's ministry was entirely due to the work of the Holy Spirit as he preached in the Spirit's power to God's covenant people. The Holy Spirit convicted them, and the Holy Spirit gave them the grace to believe John's message and repent. Baptism was a sign of the Spirit-given grace of repentance.

It is important for us to see the close connection between repentance and forgiveness, because while no amount of repentance can ever merit forgiveness in the sight of God, without repentance no soul will ever be saved. Repentance is the telltale mark of the grace of God at work in our lives. Saving faith and true repentance are always found together. Saved souls are repentant souls.

This truth has an immensely practical implication: if you think you are saved but do not have a repentant spirit, you are perhaps not saved at all. If there are sins of which you refuse to repent and in fact, if truth be known, are becoming more and more comfortable with, it is possible that you are not a child of God. (I am not referring to a person who is struggling with sin and often losing but really desires victory, but rather to the person who has no desire to repent.) Scripture and my own experience have taught me that an ongoing spirit of repentance—repenting not only of overt sins, but of unbelief, negative attitudes, self-centeredness, moral omissions—is not only a sign of salvation but is a necessity for spiritual health.

John preached "a baptism of repentance for the forgiveness of sins" with incredible power, thousands responded, and, as Luke notes, the ancient prophecy of Isaiah 40:3–5 was fulfilled:

> The voice of one crying in the wilderness:
> "Prepare the way of the Lord,
>   make his paths straight.
> Every valley shall be filled,
>   and every mountain and hill shall be made low,
> and the crooked shall become straight,

and the rough places shall become level ways,
and all flesh shall see the salvation of God." (vv. 4–6)

This prophecy reflects the widespread custom that when an eminent ruler was about to visit a city, the citizens would construct a smooth, broad road so he could enter the city with due pomp and dignity. A modern equivalent is the *Champs Elysees* in Paris, first used with great effect by Napoleon and his armies. But Isaiah's vision was far grander. The highway was not simply a grand entrance to a city, but a great thoroughfare through a mountainous wilderness. He saw mountains flattened and valleys filled in so that a broad superhighway could be made ready for the Messiah-King.

The point we must not miss is this: the great highway John was building was one of *repentance*. The Baptist was saying, "Mend not your roads, but your lives."[5] To put it in terms of American geography, repentance removes the obstacles, flattens the Sierras, and fills in the Death Valleys in our lives, so that Christ has full access. Repentance invites the fullness of God. In fact, when God's people live repentantly, it also opens the way for the world to know him. Note again the final line of Isaiah's words: "And all flesh shall see the salvation of God" (v. 6b; cf. 2:30–32). If the evangelical church today would repent of its individual and corporate sins—its materialism, its insularity, its lovelessness—a highway would be forged to a lost world, and many would repent and come to Christ.

As already mentioned, John's preaching brought a vast response as multitudes came out to the Jordan Valley for baptism. John was surely gratified by this, but he was not entirely pleased. He sensed that some were insincere, and some were even hardened hypocrites. Some had simply come to see the show. Some were religious groupies who just wanted to be part of the scene. Some who were more calculating had undergone baptism so their friends would think well of them or perhaps so business connections would be cemented.

It is no different today, when some people attend evangelical churches, "receive Christ," "repent," and are baptized for similar insufficient reasons. One of the most extreme cases I know of comes from 1986 and the bloodiest shootout in the FBI's history, when two agents were killed and three wounded. Their main assailant was William Matix, a self-proclaimed born-again Christian who regularly attended a Baptist church where he often gave his testimony. Just a month before the shootout he had been profiled as a fine family man in *Christian Home Life*, an evangelical family magazine. All the while, Matix was committing numerous robberies of banks and armored cars.[6]

Repentance, professions of faith, church attendance, and good standing in conservative, Bible-believing fellowships do not necessarily prove much—as John knew in his own situation. So John wisely became very directive in his preaching.

John's Preaching: An Authentic Baptism (vv. 7–14)

John became stridently *eschatological*—that is, he warned the multitudes of the great final judgment:

> He said therefore to the crowds that came out to be baptized by him, "You brood of vipers! Who warned you to flee from the wrath to come? Bear fruits in keeping with repentance. And do not begin to say to yourselves, 'We have Abraham as our father.' For I tell you, God is able from these stones to raise up children for Abraham. Even now the axe is laid to the root of the trees. Every tree therefore that does not bear good fruit is cut down and thrown into the fire." (vv. 7–9)

In characterizing his hearers as "vipers," he was saying they were like snakes fleeing a brush fire, trying to escape but having no intention of allowing their evil natures to be changed. John's language was also meant to convey the repulsive nature of their hypocritical smugness.

His advice to "Bear fruits in keeping with repentance" (v. 8a) went right to the heart of the problem. Jesus would later issue a further warning in his sermon on the Mount:

> You will recognize them by their fruits. Are grapes gathered from thornbushes, or figs from thistles? So, every healthy tree bears good fruit, but the diseased tree bears bad fruit. A healthy tree cannot bear bad fruit, nor can a diseased tree bear good fruit. Every tree that does not bear good fruit is cut down and thrown into the fire. Thus you will recognize them by their fruits. Not everyone who says to me, "Lord, Lord," will enter the kingdom of heaven, but the one who does the will of my Father who is in heaven. (Matthew 7:16–21)

True repentance first produces the fruit of *character*: "love, joy, peace, patience, kindness, goodness, faithfulness, gentleness, [and] self-control" (Galatians 5:22, 23). Then it produces the fruit of *action*.

Since some of these religious serpents were depending upon their ethnic privileges, John said, "And do not begin to say to yourselves, 'We have Abraham as our father.' For I tell you, God is able from these stones to raise up children for Abraham" (v. 8b). They thought that since they were Jews, they would surely enjoy the blessing of the Abrahamic Covenant. They blatantly rested on the merits of godly Abraham whose blood coursed through their veins. God certainly would not break his covenant—he needed them to be its recipients! But John in effect said, "Don't think God won't have a people to bless if he cuts you off. He can create children out of the stones if he wishes" (cf. John 8:31–47; Romans 4:16–25; Galatians 3:29).

John struck a mighty blow at the common delusion that connection with righteous people will save our souls. Thousands in every age have believed that association with the godly will make them acceptable with God. But faith in blood ties or church membership has led whole generations to destruction. Those in the church, where so many are related to someone who works in Christian service, are especially susceptible to such deception. But all a prominent name will get you, apart from God's grace, is greater judgment. Aaron Burr was the grandson of Jonathan Edwards!

John attempted to drive his eschatological warning home with a chilling vision: "Even now the axe is laid to the root of the trees. Every tree therefore that does not bear good fruit is cut down and thrown into the fire" (v. 9). The gleaming blade of a sharpened ax lies on the ground beside the root of those whose lives have no good fruit. The judgment that is about to fall is anything but superficial. It means radical severance and destruction.

What a terrible warning this is to those who have only a façade of belief, repentance, and goodness. Sadly, it is all too easy to fool pastors or family members or friends. In fact, the church is instructed *not* to attempt to root out the false believer. In Jesus' Parable of the Tares we read:

> So the servants said to him, "Then do you want us to go and gather them?" But he said, "No, lest in gathering the weeds you root up the wheat along with them. Let both grow together until the harvest, and at harvest time I will tell the reapers, Gather the weeds first and bind them in bundles to be burned, but gather the wheat into my barn." (Matthew 13:28–30)

One thing is sure—no one can fool God!

Thank God, John's prophetic heart was not controlled by a desire for popularity. He was free from the fear of offending others. Such directness is not in vogue today. Rather, many of God's people seldom mention sin, refrain from anything even remotely condemning, and speak obliquely. The approved method today is to flatter unconverted people, to preach on sins that are not characteristically theirs. But God's Word points us to a different path: "Woe to you, when all people speak well of you, for so their fathers did to the false prophets" (6:26). "For am I now seeking the approval of man, or of God? Or am I trying to please man? If I were still trying to please man,

I would not be a servant of Christ" (Galatians 1:10). To be charitable when Christ is not, to be silent when Christ speaks, is "positive treachery to men's souls."[7]

John's eschatological charge indeed chilled some souls. They realized they had not truly repented. They saw they had no authentic Spirit-derived fruit. They saw that their thoughts, their desires, their actions had no roots in the faith they professed with their lips. Convicted of their failings, the crowd asked, "What then shall we do?" (v. 10).

John's answer is somewhat surprising. We might have expected that he would ask them to do something *penitential* ("Go do four good acts to the orphans in your town") or *ecclesiastical* ("Commit yourself to your local synagogue") or perhaps *devotional* ("Pray through the Psalms"). But significantly, John's advice was *ethical*. He asked them to change how they treated their fellow human beings.

It is not uncommon for people who do not know Christ to perform elevated ethical deeds in an attempt to prove the authenticity of their "Christianity." They may take up a just social cause, then present it as evidence of their spiritual life—"I am pro-life—therefore I am a Christian," or "I am an advocate for the poor—this proves my Christianity." A real danger comes with spiritual presumption stemming from exemplary ethical performance. However, it is also true that if you are truly regenerate and repentant, your faith will most surely affect *how you treat others*, especially those who are closest to you—your family, your business associates, your employees, and those in need. If there is no change in your personal ethics, no elevation of your concern and care for others, you may be self-deceived about your salvation.

John also gives specific *ethical* advice to three groups—private citizens, tax collectors, and soldiers:

> And he answered them, "Whoever has two tunics is to share with him who has none, and whoever has food is to do likewise." Tax collectors also came to be baptized and said to him, "Teacher, what shall we do?" And he said to them, "Collect no more than you are authorized to do." Soldiers also asked him, "And we, what shall we do?" And he said to them, "Do not extort money from anyone by threats or by false accusation, and be content with your wages." (vv. 11–14)

It is significant that all three sections of advice have to do with money and material possessions. Private citizens are to share with others, tax collectors are not to take more than is proper, and soldiers are not to extort money.

The Holy Spirit through John is telling us that the way we hold on to money and material things in relationship to others is a good indicator of the authenticity and health of our spiritual lives. Therefore, we must understand that high among the observable fruit that is "in keeping with repentance" (v. 8) is a giving, generous spirit.

Do we want to have an accurate evaluation of the state of our spirituality? Here are some Biblical tests:

Are we *generous* with our possessions? Do we share our homes, our cars, our clothing, our food with others—joyfully? Or are we loath to share? Do we always push for more and then grasp it tightly?

Do we enjoy *giving* to family, friends, and, more significantly, those in need? Do we give regularly and sacrificially to the Lord? If you are a Christian but do not give regularly to the Lord, if you are tight, if you find it difficult to give to God, you are in spiritual trouble, and possibly you are not even a Christian at all! We must each do regular self-checks, including me!

One of the reasons healthy Christians like to give to their church and to others is because they are indwelt with the Spirit of Christ, who gave himself for us and said, "It is more blessed to give than to receive" (Acts 20:35).

Closing Reflections

Those today who have repented and whose lives are an inviting highway for the Lord give of their resources, substance, and time to others.

Moreover, they live in a constant Holy-Spirit-directed spirit of repentance. They repent of lovelessness, impatience, meanness, harshness, prejudice, jealousy, hatred, unbelief, prayerlessness, coldness, selfishness, and much more.

These people live in the refreshing air of the forgiveness of sins. They are guilt free. They are clear-eyed. Their countenances are an invitation to all mankind to tread the highway of God's salvation.

13

Messiah's Baptism

LUKE 3:15–20

DR. MARTYN LLOYD-JONES, arguably the most powerful preacher of the twentieth century, once described the stunning personal experience of the Holy Spirit's empowering his preaching on an unforgettable occasion: "Never, do I think, have I been so conscious of the Power of the Word and the Gale of the Spirit. It is exceedingly difficult to go on living after such an experience, especially difficult to go on preaching."[1] Lloyd-Jones described what all true preachers know: it is one thing to preach the Word—it is quite another to preach in the power of the Holy Spirit. And those who heard and knew the Doctor do not doubt a word of his testimony. His grandson, Christopher Catherwood, writes:

> The one thing he prayed for, the one thing he relied on, the one thing he waited for and the one thing above all else and beyond most other preachers of his generation which thousands felt under his preaching was the unction, or anointing, of the Holy Spirit.[2]

A preacher acquaintance told me of visiting London and attending Westminster Chapel where he sat under the Doctor's mighty ministry. As he listened, he was so elevated in the contemplation of spiritual things that he was momentarily unaware that Lloyd-Jones had finished preaching!

This, of course, is something of what the hearers of John the Baptist experienced, perhaps to an even greater degree because John was filled with the Spirit before birth, groomed by the Spirit for thirty years, and then launched by the Spirit to prepare the way for the Lord. In Jesus' own words, there was no one greater than John the Baptist (Luke 7:28; Matthew 11:11).

We need to keep this in mind when we read his preaching (for example, in Luke 3:7–14) because his great eschatological and ethical challenges were delivered in the mighty rush of the Holy Spirit's power. John almost surely felt it difficult to go on living after such an experience, as did some of his thousands of hearers who were cut to the quick and came to passionate repentance.

Because of this we should not be surprised when we read in verse 15 that "the people were in expectation, and all were questioning in their hearts concerning John, whether he might be the Christ." We must remember that their messianic expectations were hazy. All John's hearers knew was that they were looking for an anointed agent of the Lord who would bring about the restoration of Israel and the triumph of God's dominion. They did not know, for example, that the Messiah's name would be Jesus. So even though John was announcing the Messiah's coming, it is not surprising that they wondered if John was the Christ.

Such success and adulation would have been a seductive temptation to a lesser man—as has been the case with many preachers in our own day. But not so with John, because the text indicates that he went on to affirm the immeasurable superiority of the One who was coming and the likewise immeasurable superiority of Christ's ministry. John's preaching was supremely Christological because he mightily lifted up Christ, as we shall see in verses 15–20.

What the Holy Spirit did through the Baptist is, of course, what the Spirit always does. As Jesus would later say, "He will not speak on his own authority, but whatever he hears he will speak, and he will declare to you the things that are to come. He will glorify me" (John 16:13b, 14a). I once heard E. V. Hill, the pastor of Mount Zion Missionary Baptist Church in Los Angeles, tell of the ministry of an elderly woman in his church whom they all called "1800" because no one knew how old she was. Now, 1800 was hard on unsuspecting preachers because she would sit in the front row, and as soon as the preacher began she would say, "Get him up!" (referring to Christ). After a few minutes, if she did not think there was enough of Christ in the sermon, she would again shout, "Get him up!" If a preacher did not "Get him up!" he was in for a long, hard day! Here John the Baptist's response to misplaced adulation was to "get him up"—a noble task because it is the chief purpose for our existence.

Messiah's Superiority (v. 16a)

In response to the people's speculation that John was the Messiah, John solemnly affirmed the superiority of Christ's person: "I baptize you with water, but he who is mightier than I is coming, the strap of whose sandals I am not worthy to untie" (v. 16a). In Palestine teachers were held in such great respect by their disciples that they voluntarily acted as their teachers' slaves. A rabbinic saying, dated after Christ but very likely contemporary to Christ, stated that disciples ought to do everything for their masters that a slave does, except for one thing—untie his sandals.[3] That was simply too much to ask any Jew to do for another Jew. But John had it right in relationship to Christ. He affirmed that he was not worthy of doing the most personally degrading task for the Messiah.

The lesson here should be carefully taken to heart, because we can take the privileges of grace so for granted that we forget that we also are not worthy to get on our knees before him and touch his sandals. True, the Scriptures say, "Let us then with confidence draw near to the throne of grace" (Hebrews 4:16), inviting an open outpouring of the heart. But God's Word never encourages presumption or irreverence. We must never become *haoles* (in the original sense of the Hawaiian term)—we must not neglect reverence in our prayers.

John was the greatest of all men, he was having the greatest of all ministries to date, multitudes were at his feet, but he knew that he wasn't worthy to perform even the humblest act for Christ. If we aim to "get him up," we need to "get ourselves down."

Messiah's Superior Ministry (v. 16b)

The superiority of Jesus' person was matched by the superiority of his ministry, which John made so clear: "I baptize you with water. . . . He will baptize you with the Holy Spirit and fire" (v. 16). The superiority of Jesus' baptism is apparent: water baptism is *external*, while baptism with the Spirit and fire is *internal*. One can be water baptized without being baptized with the Holy Spirit, and vice versa. Water baptism can only wash the outside of a person. Baptism with the Spirit and fire cleanses the inside.

We should also carefully note that the language of the text (which couples Spirit and fire baptism with one preposition) makes it clear that all believers undergo both baptisms (Spirit and fire).[4] The baptisms are not separate but are complementary aspects of the same baptism, as Frederick Godet points out: "*The Spirit* and *fire* both denote the same divine principle."[5] So Spirit baptism and fire baptism are shades of the same inner baptism that occurs in all believers.

Spirit Baptism

The great classic text that at once describes and celebrates the believer's baptism in the Holy Spirit is 1 Corinthians 12:13: "For in one Spirit we were all baptized into one body—Jews or Greeks, slaves or free—and all were made to drink of one Spirit." This is a reference to the Spirit's work of initiating us into the Body of Christ, the experience of every believer ("we . . . all"). It happened to me when I was a 110-pound, immature eighth-grader. Of course, I had no idea of the incredible dynamics that had taken place. I had never even heard of the baptism of the Holy Spirit, but I was baptized indeed!

Now, forty years later, I can match my subjective realizations with the objective work that then took place in my soul. What does the Holy Spirit accomplish in us when he baptizes us into the Body of Christ? My own experience shared here is neither chronological nor comprehensive, but it is a basic summary of the divine work within us.

Regenerated. I was regenerated, born again. I was born "of the Spirit," as described in John 3:3–6. Though I was just a boy, I knew the experience was supernatural. My initial subjective experience of regeneration was twofold: first, a sense of being clean, and then a bounding experience of joy and well-being. And why not? Think of the massive transaction that had taken place. The metaphor of being born again is not overdrawn but is perfectly descriptive of the Holy Spirit's obstetrics. I had been delivered from darkness and brought into the light. I had come into a whole new world.

Indwelt. Next, I was indwelt by the Holy Spirit as Jesus had promised: "And I will ask the Father, and he will give you another Helper, to be with you forever, even the Spirit of truth, whom the world cannot receive, because it neither sees him nor knows him. You know him, for he dwells with you and will be in you" (John 14:16, 17). As a result, I lost my sense of aloneness, which had been profound, largely because my father had died when I was a preschooler. This was a continental divide in shaping my personality. I was given a new sense of paternity—God was my Father, and I was not an orphan in this world.

Sealed. What I did not know is that God had marked me with a seal, tagged me as his through the indwelling presence of the Holy Spirit, as Paul explained in Ephesians 1:13, 14: "In him you also, when you heard the word of truth . . . and believed in him, were sealed with the promised Holy Spirit, who is the guarantee of our inheritance." "The Spirit himself," says Paul in Romans 8:16, 17, "bears witness with our spirit that we are children of God, and if children, then heirs—heirs of God and fellow heirs with Christ." Thus the Spirit's seal not only assured me that I was his, it also gave me a sense of protection and security. Later in Ephesians the same word is used when Paul says that through the Holy Spirit we are "sealed for the day of redemption"

(Ephesians 4:30). The Holy Spirit had become my down payment, a deposit guaranteeing my inheritance.

Prayed for. Then, as a young boy who knew little of prayer and was in great need of intercession, the Holy Spirit himself began to pray for me! "Likewise the Spirit helps us in our weakness. For we do not know what to pray for as we ought, but the Spirit himself intercedes for us with groanings too deep for words. And he who searches hearts knows what is the mind of the Spirit, because the Spirit intercedes for the saints according to the will of God" (Romans 8:26, 27). The Holy Spirit has been praying for me for forty years! When I am in dark gloom, incapable of even forming a syllable, he prays for me in perfect accordance with the Father's will.

Enlightened. The night of my Spirit baptism, right there in the sour, gym-sock ambience of my sleeping bag, I took out my tiny Bible and read the passages recommended by my pastor (Romans 10:9, 10; John 1:12; Philippians 1:6), and, to borrow Charles Wesley's language, "The dungeon flamed with light." I understood God's Word, and it became alive within me. That which was before inscrutable now made sense to my enlightened soul.

Last but certainly not least, *the indwelling Holy Spirit began to put to death the deeds of the flesh in my life* (cf. Romans 8:13). That night the Spirit washed away my sins through the blood of Christ, and a lifelong process had begun in which the Spirit would relentlessly develop practical holiness within me.

As believers, "In one Spirit we were *all* baptized into one body." How transcendingly superior Jesus' baptism with the Spirit was to John's water-baptism. The former is not a mere washing of the skin but a washing and regeneration of the soul.

Fire Baptism

As we have seen, Spirit baptism and fire baptism refer to the same work. Fire represents the Spirit's ongoing work of purification and cleansing. Significantly, the Old Testament lists passages in which God's Spirit and fire do just that. Isaiah 4:4 speaks of cleansing Zion/Jerusalem with washing and fire. Malachi 3:1 describes the coming of John the Baptist by saying, "Behold, I send my messenger, and he will prepare the way before me." And then verse 2 speaks of Jesus' ultimate judgment in terms of washing and fire: "But who can endure the day of his coming, and who can stand when he appears? For he is like a refiner's fire and like fullers' soap." Of course, the lives of God's children do not undergo judgment. Rather, they are graciously refined by the fire of the Spirit in this life—blessed sanctification!

In ancient times refiners would heat the metal until it became liquid and then skim off the impurities, the dross. The refiner knew the metal was purified when the molten liquid mirrored back his own reflection. So it is with the Spirit's work in our lives. He melts our hearts, skims away the dross, allows us to cool into Christ's likeness, and then turns up the heat again.

> When through fiery trials thy pathway shall lie,
> My grace, all sufficient, shall be thy supply:
> The flame shall not hurt thee, I only design
> Thy dross to consume, and thy gold to refine.
>
> "How Firm a Foundation," *Rippon's Selection of Hymns* (1787)

How superior Jesus' baptism was to John's. Water only washes the surface, but fire melts the center. Spirit baptism makes all things new. God's Spirit regenerates, cleanses, indwells, prays for, illuminates, empowers, and sanctifies his children.

How appropriate it is for us to praise our Father and our Savior and our Spirit!

Messiah's Superior Judgment (v. 17)

John has lifted Jesus up as superior in his *person* and superior in his *baptism* and now presents him as superior in his final *judgment*: "His winnowing fork is in his hand, to clear his threshing floor and to gather the wheat into his barn, but the chaff he will burn with unquenchable fire" (v. 17).

Jesus' judgment is supremely *discriminating*. John himself did not know who the insincere were that pretended to come to him to repent. He threw the epithet "vipers" (3:7) at everyone in an attempt to smoke out the hypocrites.

But Christ suffers no lack of discernment. He knows the heart of every individual. The metaphorical setting here is that of a harvest. The grain is plucked, then brought to the threshing floor, where it is trodden by oxen. Jesus the harvester comes in, takes up the winnowing fork, and tosses the grain and chaff upward so the wind can blow the chaff aside. The real wheat is gathered safely in his barn, while the chaff is burned. Our Lord exercises perfect, unerring judgment.

The Baptist could not read a single mind, but Jesus reads every thought and weighs every motivation. As Peter said, "Lord, you know everything; you know that I love you" (John 21:17). Jesus, because he is infinitely superior, being fully God, knows all things. Positively this means he knows whether he has worked faith in our hearts, and thus none of us who are truly his will be lost. Every Spirit/fire-baptized child will be saved.

His judgment not only will be perfectly discerning but also *ultimate*. The Greek word for *unquenchable* ("unquenchable fire") is *asbestos*. "Unquenchable fire" is by definition eternal, ultimate judgment.

Jesus, who suffered the Father's wrath against sin on the cross, administers this judgment. The unregenerate often joke about it—for example, *Peter Pan* author James Barrie, who said, "Heaven for climate, hell for company." But divine judgment is no joke. We know from Jesus himself that Hell is everlasting. Jesus closed the Parable of the last judgment with the words, "Depart from me, you cursed, into the eternal fire prepared for the devil and his angels. . . . And these will go away into eternal punishment, but the righteous into eternal life" (Matthew 25:41, 46). Punishment is eternal in the same way that salvation is eternal.

We dare not harden our hearts to the terrible doom of the chaff—those headed for judgment in the next life. With awe we must lift up Christ, the righteous Judge, because at the name of Jesus every knee will "bow, in heaven and on earth and under the earth, and every tongue confess that Jesus Christ is Lord, to the glory of God the Father" (Philippians 2:10, 11).

We need to "get him up" now, for we will be getting him up for all eternity!

Closing Reflections

Luke closes this section with a minisummary of what lay ahead for John:

> So with many other exhortations he preached good news to the people. But Herod the tetrarch, who had been reproved by him for Herodias, his brother's wife, and for all the evil things that Herod had done, added this to them all, that he locked up John in prison. (vv. 18–20)

Interestingly, Luke calls John's preaching of judgment and repentance "good news." Judgment may not initially sound like good news. The "good news" of damnation? Nevertheless, it is an essential aspect of the gospel, because unless evil is perfectly and ultimately dealt with, there can be no good news. The bad news is part of the good news.

Note too that such preaching allows for no neutral response. Herod ultimately took John's life. People either "get Christ up" or put him down. There is no middle ground.

As John the Baptist proclaimed, Jesus Christ is superior in every way.

In his person, the Christ we worship is awesome. He is the Creator and Sustainer of the universe. He is perfectly holy and transcendent. He is the lover of our souls.

His baptism is no mere water rite. In it the Holy Spirit soaks and burns our souls. It is our souls' dreams come true as they are regenerated, forgiven, indwelt, sealed, prayed for, illuminated, and purified. Has he baptized you?

His judgment too is perfect and superior, because we do not have to be damned—he is willing to bring mercy into our hearts if we let him. Truth will prevail, and perfect, discriminating, unquestioned equity will reign.

> Oh, magnify the LORD with me,
> and let us exalt his name together! (Psalm 34:3)

14

The Sonship of Christ

LUKE 3:21–38

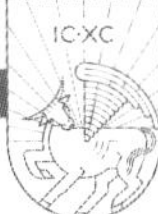

LUKE'S DESCRIPTION OF Jesus' baptism is sketchy. All he says is, "Now when all the people were baptized, and when Jesus also had been baptized . . ." (v. 21a). He gives no details of the location, or even the size of the crowd. Neither does he shed any light on the question of why Jesus was baptized. The baptism of John was a "baptism of repentance" (3:3), but Jesus, being sinless, clearly had no need of repentance and its accompanying rite.

We must turn to the other Gospels, especially Matthew, to get further details.

> Then Jesus came from Galilee to the Jordan to John, to be baptized by him. John would have prevented him, saying, "I need to be baptized by you, and do you come to me?" But Jesus answered him, "Let it be so now, for thus it is fitting for us to fulfill all righteousness." Then he consented. (Matthew 3:13–15)

Jesus was utterly righteous. Paul called him our "righteousness" (1 Corinthians 1:30). He had fulfilled all manner of righteousness from his youth up—moral righteousness, legal righteousness, spiritual righteousness. He was *sinless*. As such, he had no need to undergo John's baptism, but he did.

Why? Because as the embodiment of righteousness, he purposely *identified* with the righteous actions of his people. Jesus did not come to John to confess and repent of his own sins, of which he had none. He came to make himself one with those who did submit to the rite in order to fulfill all that the Law required.

Once John understood this, he acquiesced to Jesus' request for baptism, and Jesus Christ, outwardly appearing no different from the multitudes around him, was baptized in the Jordan River. From the crowd's perspective it was a routine baptism, but that was not the view from Heaven. In the next few moments, as Jesus ascended the banks of the Jordan (cf. Matthew 3:16, "went up from the water"), the three Persons of the Holy Trinity would celebrate the sonship of the incarnate Messiah.

The Divine Son of God (vv. 21, 22)

Significantly, Luke tells us this happened as Jesus "was praying." Certainly our Lord prayed without ceasing, but there were also times and places when and where he prayed publicly and more earnestly, and his baptism was one of them (cf. 6:12; 9:18, 28, 29; 11:1; 22:41). John the Baptist and alert onlookers, in an attitude of adoration, worship, and submission to and dependence upon the Father, observed Jesus in prayer. Three decades of incarnation—thirty winters of perfection—had seasoned his human soul, and being in fervent prayer he was now ready to go public as the only begotten Son of God.

It is clear in the Gospels that Jesus prayed passionately! What a lesson for prayerless people. Do we desire the blessings of the Holy Spirit—affirmation from God—power for ministry? Then we must pray. If fervent prayer was necessary for the eternal Son of God, how much more is it necessary for us?

According to verses 21b, 22, as he "was praying" three things happened 1) "the heavens were opened," 2) "the Holy Spirit descended on him in bodily form, like a dove," and 3) "a voice came from heaven, 'You are my beloved Son; with you I am well pleased.'"

Heaven Opens

Mark's parallel account gives us an additional peek at this drama of Heaven's opening: "And when he came up out of the water, immediately he saw the heavens being torn open" (Mark 1:10). Perhaps the scene was Cecil B. DeMille-like, with the clouds ripped in two as if great hands had divided them, producing an awesome glimpse of shining beings gliding about in God's presence. In any event, the skies above the Jordan were supernaturally sundered in a dramatic revelational motif known to God's special servants from Ezekiel to Stephen to Peter to John (cf. Ezekiel 1:1; John 1:51; Acts 7:56; 10:11; Revelation 19:11). We have reason to believe that the multitudes also saw the heavens open and were stunned (we think this because John the Baptist apparently saw everything, cf. John 1:29–34).

The Spirit Descends

With their eyes focused upward to the torn sky, the multitudes watched as "the Holy Spirit descended on him in bodily form, like a dove" (v. 22). The Holy Spirit made a visual, palpable descent. Matthew gives us Jesus' perspective: "He saw the Spirit of God descending like a dove and coming to rest on him" (Matthew 3:16). The Gospel of John supplies the Baptist's view: "I saw the Spirit descend from heaven like a dove, and it remained on him" (John 1:32). Thus, coming from the expanse beyond the sundered clouds the Holy Spirit circled downward, fluttering on the bodily wings of a dove and resting upon Jesus, signifying that the Holy Spirit had come upon him and would not depart.

There had never been anything like this in Biblical history—never! Also, never before had a dove been used to symbolize the Holy Spirit.[1] Why a dove? Though Jesus would baptize with the Holy Spirit and with fire (i.e., with purging and judgment), the gentleness of a dove suited the temper of Jesus' actual ministry of reconciliation.[2] Thomas Goodwin, the great Puritan theologian and president of Magdalen College, Oxford, explained:

> All apparitions that God at any time made of Himself, were not so much made to show to men what God is in Himself, as to show us how He is affected toward us, and to declare what effects he will work in us. . . . For a dove, you know, is the most meek and the most innocent of all birds; without gall, without talons, having no fierceness in it, expressing nothing but love and friendship to its mate in all its carriages, and mourning over its mate in all its distresses. And accordingly, a dove was a most fit emblem of the Spirit that was poured out upon our Saviour when He was just about to enter on the work of our salvation. For as sweetly as doves do converse with doves, so may every sinner and Christ converse together.[3]

To be sure, Jesus was, and is, a lion. His divine anger scorched the Pharisees, and he will return as a warrior to judge the earth (cf. Revelation 19:11–16). Nevertheless, his ministry was characteristically gentle. He said, "Learn from me, for I am gentle and lowly in heart" (Matthew 11:29). He also pronounced this beatitude: "Blessed are the gentle, for they shall inherit the earth" (Matthew 5:5 NASB). And the character of the Spirit he produces in us includes "gentleness" (Galatians 5:23). Jesus enjoined all of us to be as "innocent as doves" (Matthew 10:16).

How beautiful this is, and how inviting. The Holy Spirit flew down to Jesus, Jesus began his gentle ministry, and now he longs to continue his tender work in us.

The Father Speaks

The first two manifestations at Jesus' baptism were visual (the heavens opened, and the dove descended). The next confirmation was verbal: "And a voice came from heaven, 'You are my beloved Son; with you I am well pleased'" (v. 22b). We may well imagine that the Father's voice sounded like thunder because the voice of the Lord was often associated with a thunderclap (cf. Psalm 18:13; Isaiah 30:30, 31; Luke 9:35). Later rabbinical literature developed special language to describe God's awesome voice to man.[4]

The heavenly voice spliced together allusions to two remarkable messianic texts. The first, "You are my beloved Son," referenced verse 7 of the famous second Psalm, "You are my Son; today I have begotten you." The emphasis of Psalm 2 is on the Messiah's unique father/son relationship with God, which would be the basis for his kingly, messianic rule,[5] his *reigning messiahship*.

Luke deliberately showcases the radical dynamics of Jesus' unique sonship. Before Jesus was conceived, his mother was informed that he would be called "the Son of God" (1:35). As "Son of God" he had supernatural power and so could turn stones into bread or plunge off great precipices without harm (4:3, 9). The Father testified that the Son spoke on his behalf (9:35). As Son, Jesus dispensed the knowledge of God: "No one knows who the Son is except the Father, or who the Father is except the Son and anyone to whom the Son chooses to reveal him" (10:22).

So as Son he enjoyed a unique relationship, power, and authority. But the context of Psalm 2 emphasizes above all his kingly reign:

> The LORD said to me, "You are my Son; today I have begotten you. Ask of me, and I will make the nations your heritage, and the ends of the earth your possession. You shall break them with a rod of iron and dash them in pieces like a potter's vessel." Now therefore, O kings, be wise; be warned, O rulers of the earth. Serve the LORD with fear, and rejoice with trembling. Kiss the Son, lest he be angry, and you perish in the way, for his wrath is quickly kindled. Blessed are all who take refuge in him. (Psalm 2:7–12)

As a dove, his ministry was gentle, and as the eternal and incarnate Son he is uniquely related to the Father. Because he is King of kings and Lord of lords, his iron scepter will crush the raging nations. Those who are wise will bow to him: "Kiss the Son, lest he be angry, and you perish in the way" (v. 12).

The second Scriptural allusion, "with you I am well pleased," is a reference to Isaiah 42:1 and Jesus' *suffering messiahship*. That allusion clearly resides in a context of suffering:

> Behold my servant, whom I uphold,
> my chosen, in whom my soul delights;
> I have put my Spirit upon him;
> he will bring forth justice to the nations.
> He will not cry aloud or lift up his voice,
> or make it heard in the street;
> a bruised reed he will not break,
> and a faintly burning wick he will not quench;
> he will faithfully bring forth justice.
> He will not grow faint or be discouraged
> till he has established justice in the earth;
> and the coastlands wait for his law. (Isaiah 42:1–4)

This portrait is perhaps expressed most clearly in the atoning sufferings described in Isaiah 53, foreshadowing the cross.

Speaking of his suffering Son, the thunderous voice from heaven says, "With you I am well pleased." What exactly is he pleased with? First, in *retrospect* the Father is pleased with his Son's humble incarnation and his subsequent years of earthly conduct. For thirty years the Son had lived in humble circumstances in the seclusion of Nazareth. He had been the responsible head of a household, where everything he earned was needed at home. He had been a humble carpenter—the Mr. Fix-it of his backwoods village. Even after he began the great works of his ministry, he was still just a carpenter to the townsfolk. This "well pleased" his Father.

For thirty years his inner devotional life transcended the understanding and imagination of men. Three decades of unparalleled meditation, unparalleled prayer, and unparalleled communion with his Father and the Holy Spirit as he grew in his comprehension of who he was and what he was to do—this too "well pleased" his Father.

During these silent years the shaping of the second Adam was accomplished. Throughout infancy, childhood, adolescence, and on into manhood, Jesus grew from grace to grace, from holiness to holiness, in subjection and in love, without a single stain of sin—he was perfectly righteous. Jesus took his righteousness to the cross and there died in our place, the just for the unjust, "so that in him we might become the righteousness of God" (2 Corinthians 5:21). Now by faith we receive his righteousness as a gift. After thirty perfect years, the Father was "well pleased."

Secondly, the *prospect* of his Son's suffering atonement pleased the Father. As Isaiah 53 recounts the sufferings of Messiah, it makes the startling statement, "Yet it pleased the LORD to bruise him" (v. 10 KJV). The entire Trinity—Father, Son, and Holy Spirit—were pleased at the salvation Jesus Christ accomplished on the cross and on the occasion of Jesus' strategic baptism. It was the second person of the Godhead who came out of the waters in fervent prayer. It was the third person who descended in bodily form like a dove. It was the first person whose voice echoed, "You are my beloved Son; with you I am well pleased." The Holy Trinity rejoiced at the Jordan as they commemorated and celebrated the beginning of the official ministry of the Son of God.

There is something deeply comforting in all this. It demonstrates how powerfully God works for our redemption and also the mutual work of God the Father, God the Son, and God the Holy Spirit. All three persons are equally concerned for the deliverance of our souls. It is little wonder that Paul later confidently proclaimed, "I am not ashamed of the gospel, for it is the power of God for salvation to everyone who believes, to the Jew first and also to the Greek" (Romans 1:16). No person is too low for God to deliver. Someone may feel that his personal moral (or immoral) life is so bizarre that there is no hope. But the Holy Trinity disagrees. A man or woman, perhaps you, may be in such a relational quagmire that he or she feels utterly beyond understanding and grace. He or she is wrong! The gospel is the good news of a divinely wrought righteousness made available by faith through the power of God. The Trinity delights to save the "unsaveable." What cheer this brings to fallen sinners—to all of us! What hope is ours!

This is magnificent in itself, but Luke couples this celebration of the divine sonship of Jesus with the marvels of his human sonship. He does this by means of a genealogy.

The Human Son of God (vv. 23–38)

This genealogy might seem confusing, but Luke's intention becomes quite clear when we see the purpose of the genealogy. Before we consider that intent, it is important to note that on the surface the genealogy appears to be a genealogy of Joseph, just as in the Gospel of Matthew. However, there are great differences. For one thing, Luke's genealogy is given in reverse order. Matthew's extends up to Abraham. Luke's goes back to Adam and to God. Moreover, the genealogies in Luke and Matthew are almost completely different between Joseph and David (Matthew even lists Jacob as the father of Joseph, while Luke lists Heli as Joseph's father). However, between David and Abraham the genealogies agree.

Many ingenious solutions have been put forth, but the one that seems most likely is this: *Luke gives us the genealogy of Mary*. This would be the case if Mary had no brothers, because then her father Heli (in accordance with Biblical tradition) would have legally adopted Joseph as his own son and heir when Joseph married Mary. Apparently Matthew gives Joseph's ancestry by birth, while Luke gives it by adoption.[6] The introductory phrase, "Jesus . . . being the son (as was supposed) of Joseph," may allude to this situation, the implication being that Jesus was the son of Mary, whose genealogy then follows.

Be that as it may, the striking, central point of this genealogy is that it *terminates in God*. See the last entries in verse 38—"the son of Adam, the son of God." This ending is one-of-a-kind. There is no parallel in the Old Testament or in rabbinic texts for a genealogy to begin or end with the name of God.[7] Luke's ending the genealogy in this way shouts for attention. What Luke wants us to understand is that Adam was "the son of God" in the sense that all humans are the offspring of God, just as Paul told the Athenians: "'In him we live and move and have our being'; as even some of your own poets have said, 'For we are indeed his offspring'" (Acts 17:28). Therefore as the first man, Adam can be referred to as "the son of God." But Jesus, the eternal Son of God, has become part of the human family and its flawed sonship (flawed because of Adam's disobedience).[8]

The great thing about this is that Jesus exercises his perfect, eternal Sonship as he takes on Adam's (and our) flawed sonship—and therefore he can redeem it. Paul put it this way: "For as in Adam all die, so also in Christ shall all be made alive. . . . Thus it is written, 'The first man Adam became a living being'; the last Adam became a life-giving spirit" (1 Corinthians 15:22, 45). And again in Romans 5:17, "For if, because of one man's trespass, death reigned through that one man, much more will those who receive the abundance of grace and the free gift of righteousness reign in life through the one man Jesus Christ."

Closing Reflections

God's pleasure reverberates in those precious words, "You are my beloved Son; with you I am well pleased." He was pleased in retrospect because Jesus had lived thirty sinless years as "the righteousness of God." He was pleased at the prospect of Christ's atoning death. And he was pleased that the failed, flawed children of the first Adam would be redeemed by the blood of the flawless, triumphant second Adam.

Christ the Son of God
Became a son of Adam
That we sons of Adam
Might become sons of God.

Apart from the Son's work at Calvary, no one will ever hear God say, "You are my beloved Son; with you I am well pleased." God cannot say that to flawed humanity. However, "If anyone is in Christ, he is a new creation. The old has passed away; behold, the new has come" (2 Corinthians 5:17). Upon these new creations, God's sons and daughters, his pleasure abides!

15

The Temptation

LUKE 4:1–13

LUKE INTRODUCES the great temptation of Jesus with this sentence: "And Jesus, full of the Holy Spirit, returned from the Jordan and was led by the Spirit in the wilderness for forty days, being tempted by the devil" (vv. 1, 2a).

We must keep several things in mind if we are to understand this and the epic combat that follows. Most essential is the realness or completeness of the incarnation of Jesus. Many Christians do not understand this though they affirm that they believe it, because nestled in their understanding of the incarnation is the thought that though Christ had a human body, his mind was not completely that of a human. "How could God have a human mind and be God? Surely, the divine had to intrude." Such thinking is an unwitting version of the ancient heresy of *docetism*—that Christ only *seemed* to be a man.

But the Scriptures affirm otherwise. In the words of the writer of Hebrews, Christ "had to be made like his brothers in every respect" (Hebrews 2:17). Jesus did not merely resemble humankind in some qualities of humanity. Rather, "in every respect"—"in all things" (NASB) he was made like us. Christ's likeness was not simulated but absolute (cf. Philippians 2:7)—except that he had no sin (cf. Hebrews 4:15).

In actuality, when he became human he placed the exercise of his divine knowledge and power under the discretion of God the Father (cf. Philippians 2:5–11). So we understand that his human mind progressively acquired a divine awareness as his Father willed it. Jesus implicitly expressed this when he said, "Truly, truly, I say to you, the Son can do nothing of his own accord, but only what he sees the Father doing. For whatever the Father does, that the Son does likewise" (John 5:19), and again, "I do nothing on my own authority" (John 8:28).

At his temptation Jesus fully knew he was the Son of God, but he withstood the onslaughts of Satan as a real man, deriving his power to resist by depending upon God for strength. The temptations were real, and Jesus withstood them as a real man who was like us "in every respect." Significantly, the author of Hebrews concludes, "Because he himself has suffered when tempted, he is able to help those who are being tempted" (Hebrews 2:18). His help to us comes from the reality of the incarnation.

The next essential to be kept in mind is that Jesus' temptation was clearly arranged by the Holy Spirit for the purpose of concluding a two-part final preparation for Jesus' public ministry. The first part was *positive*—Jesus' baptism, at which "the Holy Spirit descended on him in bodily form, like a dove; and a voice came from heaven, 'You are my beloved Son; with you I am well pleased'" (3:22). At his baptism Jesus' soul danced with joy and anticipation.

The second purpose was *negative*—Jesus' temptation, during which he was made aware of the perils and errors he had to resist. As Frederick Godet said: "The temptation was the last act of His moral education; it gave Him an insight into all the ways in which His messianic work could be easily marred."[1] His temptation was the counterpart to his baptism. Heaven opened at one, and Hell yawned at the other, and both prepared Jesus to live as the victorious Son (cf. 3:22; 4:1, 3, 6, 9).

The final essential fact we must note if we are to understand the great temptation is that the Spirit led Jesus into the desert/wilderness where he spent forty days, an obvious parallel with Israel's forty-year sojourn during which (unlike Jesus) God's people repeatedly failed God. Evidently Jesus had reflected long and hard on their wilderness failures, because he answered Satan's temptations with three successive references to a brief section of Deuteronomy that makes reference to Israel's tests and failures (cf. Deuteronomy 8:3; 6:13, 16). These quotations from Deuteronomy hold the key to understanding Jesus' three temptations and his victory over them.

The wilderness setting was dramatic. The inhabited part of Judea perched on the backbone of southern Palestine. Between this inhabited hill country and the Dead Sea stretched a terrible wilderness called Jeshimon, which means "The Devastation."[2] Thus the backdrop for the temptation was a desolate, monotonous wasteland like that in the forlorn surrealism of a Dali painting—an anti-Eden. In the foreground sat the weary, forty-days-hungry Christ. Before him moved the resplendent figure of Satan, radiating power and promise—elegant evil. The first Adam fell to the gorgeous Serpent in the glories of Eden, and now the second Adam (cf. 3:38) faced Satan's alluring presence amid the barren desolation.

The First Temptation (vv. 3, 4)

The Devil Speaks

The jaws of Hell opened and, "The devil said to him, 'If you are the Son of God, command this stone to become bread'" (v. 3). In assessing this temptation we must note that this was a *real* temptation. Jesus' body was real, not docetic. He had been without food for six weeks, a characteristic time of crisis for such fasts. He felt like he was sinking, even dying, and a ravishing hunger convulsed him. Furthermore, because he was the Son of God and could invoke supernatural powers, the temptation was mighty. None of us has ever been tempted to turn stones into bread, because for us it is impossible. But Jesus could have done it in an instant, and his hunger screamed, "Do it!"

The temptation appeared innocent, but it was in fact a spiritual temptation to sin because as the incarnate Son, Christ had come to do the will of the Father and nothing else. He had followed the Father's will in obeying the Spirit's impulse to fast in the wilderness, and now in his hunger the Father had not seen fit to provide him with the needed food. So Christ was tempted to provide for his material needs apart from the will of the Father and, furthermore, to go outside the natural order to meet his needs, to momentarily suspend living like a real human.

Jesus Answers

But as Jesus reflected on his hungry plight, he recalled Exodus 16 and Deuteronomy 8, which record how Israel had been hungry (albeit not desperately hungry) and grumbled against the Lord for the stewpots of Egypt—and how God chose to meet their desires with quail and manna that he then supplied for forty years. The lesson to Jesus was obvious: God's provision of manna and quail proves that his power is not limited to providing ordinary bread. God can support his people with extraordinary means. He can even, if he so wishes, make man live by just speaking the word. So Jesus answered the devil with a quotation from Deuteronomy 8:3: "It is written, 'Man shall not live by bread alone'" (v. 4). In Deuteronomy the full quotation says, "Man does not live by bread alone, but man lives by every word that comes from the mouth of the LORD."

In essence, by alluding to Deuteronomy Jesus was saying, "I will not complain. Neither will I take matters into my own hands. My Father has not willed to immediately provide bread. But I will trust him and his word." In doing this Jesus demonstrated that no need would ever drive him to draw back from his humble human existence as a real man who lives by trusting God's Word. Perhaps Satan visibly recoiled when Jesus slapped him with God's Word. Clearly, he decided it was not wise to further pursue that line of thought.

This is spiritual dynamite! The temptation was real. Jesus was a real man. He was desperately famished. He knew he was the Son of God. He knew he could meet his need in a millisecond. But he was an obedient son, and the Father's word was his meat and drink. Jesus resisted the temptation without the benefit of his own omnipotence, showing himself to be the perfect obedient man. All glory to Jesus!

There is also personal wisdom here for us adopted sons and daughters of God. Our temptation may not be to turn stones into bread. The impossible does not tempt us. However, rather than trusting him, we regularly succumb to the temptation to go beyond the parameters of God's Word to satisfy our personal needs or desires. We are like Jacob. We attempt to help God give us our due, perhaps even engaging in "sanctified deception" (cf. Genesis 25—27).

We are too often overreachers. We promote ourselves because we are sure God will not do it. We scheme and plan for our well-being, assuming that God does not care or maybe does not know our needs. We refuse to live "by every word that comes from the mouth of the LORD." Jesus would later say:

> Therefore I tell you, do not be anxious about your life, what you will eat or what you will drink, nor about your body, what you will put on. Is not life more than food, and the body more than clothing? Look at the birds of the air: they neither sow nor reap nor gather into barns, and yet your heavenly Father feeds them. Are you not of more value than they? (Matthew 6:25, 26)

> Said the robin to the sparrow:
> "I should really like to know
> Why these anxious human beings
> Rush about and worry so."
> Said the sparrow to the robin:
> "Friend, I think that it must be
> That they have no heavenly Father,
> Such as cares for you and me."[3]

The Second Temptation (vv. 5–8)

The Devil Speaks

After our Lord's powerful affirmation from God's Word, the devil tried a different tactic:

> And the devil took him up and showed him all the kingdoms of the world in a moment of time, and said to him, "To you I will give all this authority and their glory, for it has been delivered to me, and I give it to whom I will. If you, then, will worship me, it will all be yours." (vv. 5–7)

Satan presented Christ with a fantasy-like vision of the world in which nations stood ready to abandon their idols and accept Christ as Lord. Jesus was made to hear the rustling of the world's flags flying in his honor. He could win the world without pain, the enemy promised—no weeping over Jerusalem, no crucifixion. The great countries of the world—Israel's elect nation, the mighty Roman Empire, and all the rest—would open their gates to their new king.

And it was Satan's to offer. He was not lying when he told Jesus, "For it has been delivered to me, and I give it to whom I will." To be sure, Satan had a limited, derived sovereignty, but it was in fact his. Jesus would three times call him "the ruler of this world" (John 12:31; 14:30; 16:11). Paul called him "the prince of the power of the air" (Ephesians 2:2) and "the god of this world" (2 Corinthians 4:4). So the devil's offer was legitimate.

But why would he make the offer? For the twisted satisfaction of seeing Christ recognize him as an authority that cannot be overcome but has to be reckoned with.[4] Perhaps Satan figured he would have that perverse satisfaction for eternity, no matter what judgment befell him.

The temptation was a powerful enticement. All the Master would have to do would be to acknowledge in worship the limited sovereignty Satan has been allowed to exercise on Planet Earth. The temptation was, again, to take the easy way to kingship, apart from God's will—to be a shortcut Savior. The choice juxtaposed infinite extremes—the long, cruel agony of the cross and the instant exaltation following a fleeting bow to the god of this world.

Of course, the effects of the fleeting bow would be disastrous. A breach with the Father, with whom the Son had known nothing but eternal intimacy; a slap at the Father's moral governance of the universe; a split second of idolatry that would eternally thunder through the universe; a shallow, fleeting political salvation instead of eternal soul salvation. No atonement. No real forgiveness. No righteousness.

Jesus Answers

Jesus drew himself up, faced the devil head on across the wild desolation, and quoted again from Deuteronomy (6:13), where Moses warned his people who were being attracted to idolatry, "It is written, 'You shall worship the Lord your God, and him only shall you serve'" (v. 8). There was to be no compromise in Jesus' ministry, no concessions to the power brokers of this world, no seeking improper ease, no idolatry. Again we must cry, all praise to Christ Jesus! We must not fall to the common error of supposing that the temptations that came to Jesus were somehow easy. They were excruciating. Jesus met them as a human totally dependent on the Father, not as a quasi man.

We do not have to look far to see the application to our own lives. The siren song of popular culture is to avoid pain and take the easy way, the path of least resistance. But God's Word still speaks truly: "All who desire to live a godly life in Christ Jesus will be persecuted" (2 Timothy 3:12). Jesus embraced the cross by refusing the easy way, and as his followers, he says, we must do the same: "If anyone would come after me, let him deny himself and take up his cross and follow me. For whoever would save his life will lose it, but whoever loses his life for my sake will find it" (Matthew 16:24, 25).

If we embrace the logic of Jesus' refusal to take the easy way, we will see that taking the path of least resistance, to follow comfortable expediency, is idolatry—it is worshiping a false God.

The Third Temptation (vv. 9–12)

In Jesus' final temptation on this occasion, the devil "took him to Jerusalem and set him on the pinnacle of the temple" (v. 9a). Very likely this was the point of the roof of the Royal Portico, which overlooked the ravine of the Kidron Valley, about a 450-foot drop. Josephus remarked that "if any looked down, his eyes would grow dizzy, not being able to reach to so vast a depth."[5] Whether the devil took Jesus there in a vision or in body, we do not know. But they stood there together, balanced on the southeast corner of the temple roof, the wind lifting their robes and wiggling their beards.

The Devil Speaks

Having seen Jesus vanquish the first two temptations by quoting Scripture, Satan now quotes it himself, for his own purposes: "If you are the Son of God, throw yourself down from here, for it is written, 'He will command his angels concerning you, to guard you,' and 'On their hands they will bear you up, lest you strike your foot against a stone'" (vv. 9–11). Attempting to stumble the Son of God by quoting Scripture to him—this was a very subtle ploy.

Psalm 91, from which the devil quoted, was a famous Wisdom Psalm that celebrated Jehovah's defense of the faithful, for whom he provides angelic protection. By urging Jesus to jump, Satan was trying to take advantage of Jesus' twice-voiced determination to trust and obey God's Word—"You are committed to obeying God's Word, so obey this!"

In addition, many Jews of that day expected prophets to do extraordinary feats (cf. Acts 5:35–37).[6] There may even have been a messianic overtone in Satan's challenge because a later Rabbinic saying read: "Our teachers have taught, when the King, the Messiah, reveals himself, he will come and stand on the roof of the Temple" (*Pesikta Rabbati*, 36).[7] Add to this the tendency of the godly to be attracted by the challenge to "step out in faith" and you can feel the tug of the temptation. In fact, refusal or even hesitancy in such situations could appear to be a lack of faith.[8]

It was a powerful, beguiling temptation. Satan was saying, in effect, "In the first temptations you have shown your trust in God's Word. You are a faithful man—Psalm 91 is you! This is what the people are looking for in a Messiah. You are a man of faith, aren't you? Just jump, and the whole world will see who you really are!" Really?

Jesus thought otherwise. He knew that he had no word from the Father directing him to leap off the temple. He again recognized that as God's Son he must never do anything in his own power, for that would be putting God to the test.

Jesus Answers

Jesus responded by again quoting from Deuteronomy, this time 6:16: "It is said, 'You shall not put the Lord your God to the test'" (v. 12). Even the very highest and best ends do not justify operating contrary to God's will. Years before, the Israelites tested God by complaining about his provision when God provided water by having Moses strike a rock. "And he called the name of the place Massah and Meribah, because of the quarreling of the people of Israel, and because they tested the LORD by saying, 'Is the LORD among us or not?'" (Exodus 17:7). Their disgraceful, faithless actions brought inevitable action by God.

The message is clear: do not attempt to force God to act.

Again all glory, honor, and praise go to Jesus for resisting the enemy's temptation, for living by "every word that comes from the mouth of the LORD."

This message is essential for us today. Willful swan dives test the LORD—diving into a marital relationship that does not have the approval of God's Word; misapplying Scripture with disastrous consequences, then crying out for God to catch us before we hit bottom; rationalizing a headstrong plunge by saying, "If this works, God will receive great glory. Just think of the souls that will be saved. God, you have to be in this—you just have to!" True, he specializes in picking up the pieces, but we must not test him through rationalized disobedience.

Closing Reflections

As the Son of God, *Jesus chose to live in absolute submission to the will of God in every temptation*. Jesus' sole desire was to do what the Father commanded him. Nothing less and nothing more.

If this is true for the Son of God, how much more is it true for us adopted children. Jesus would later say, "My food is to do the will of him who sent me and to accomplish his work" (John 4:34). We are to live on "every word that comes from the mouth of the LORD." We are to "worship the Lord [our] God, and him only shall [we] serve." We must never put our "Lord . . . to the test."

There is much wisdom here for us.

First, Jesus resisted these great temptations as a real man. "Because he himself has suffered when tempted, he is able to help those who are being tempted" (Hebrews 2:18). We can call upon Christ in times of temptation, for he is at our side. When Martin Luther was asked how he overcame the devil, he replied, "Well, when he comes knocking upon the door of my heart, and asks 'Who lives here?' the dear Lord Jesus goes to the door and says, 'Martin Luther used to live here, but he has moved out. Now I live here.'" When Christ fills our lives, Satan has no entrance.

Second, Jesus conquered temptation because he was "full of the Holy Spirit" and "led by the Spirit" (v. 1). The fullness of the Spirit produces the nine fruits of the Spirit, the seventh of which is "faithfulness" (Galatians 5:22, 23).

The third factor in fighting temptation involves being filled with God's Word. In response to each of the three temptations, Christ answered with Scripture (Deuteronomy 8:3; 6:13, 16). He knew the truth of, "I have stored up your word in my heart, that I might not sin against you" (Psalm 119:11). This is so because God's Word reveals God's mind, and God's mind cannot be subject to sin. So if we fill our hearts with his Word, sin and temptation cannot dominate us. We cannot live "by every word that comes from the mouth of the LORD" if we do not know the Word of God. We must follow Jesus' example and regularly meditate on God's Word.

> How firm a foundation,
> Ye saints of the Lord
> Is laid for your faith
> In His excellent Word!
>
> *Rippon's Selection of Hymns* (1787)

16

Jesus' Rejection

LUKE 4:14–30

MONDAY, APRIL 2, 1739, marked a signal event in the history of Christianity because it was on that day that John Wesley abandoned his reticence to preach outside the church and, at Kingswood Bristol, took to open-air evangelism. Wesley's decision brought him face-to-face with the common people and ignited a revival the likes of which England had never seen. Regarding that great day, Wesley wrote in his diary:

> At four in the afternoon I submitted to be more vile, and proclaimed in the highways the glad tidings of salvation, speaking from a little eminence in a ground adjoining to the city, to about three thousand people. The Scripture on which I spoke was this . . . "The Spirit of the Lord is upon me, because He hath anointed me to preach the gospel to the poor. He hath sent me to heal the brokenhearted; to preach deliverance to the captives and recovery of sight to the blind; to set at liberty them that are bruised, to proclaim the acceptable year of the Lord."[1]

Wesley had chosen his text with brilliant premeditation because it was the same Scripture with which Jesus introduced his ministry to the people of Nazareth. Subsequent history records that John Wesley lived out that text, bringing the gospel to the disenfranchised and needy masses of England. The following years also reveal that Wesley likewise experienced something of the rejection and ignominy that descended upon our Lord when he first brought God's message to his people.

Significantly, as we turn to Luke's account of the beginning of Jesus' ministry in 4:14–30, we must note that Luke could have devoted all of his report to chronicling the initial successes of Jesus in Galilee, which he only briefly summarizes in verses 14, 15: "And Jesus returned in the power of the

Spirit to Galilee, and a report about him went out through all the surrounding country. And he taught in their synagogues, being glorified by all." He could have surely spent several paragraphs, if not a whole book, on Jesus' "Galilean Springtime," as it has been called. But Luke the theologian chooses instead to give us the details of the story of the Savior's return to Nazareth, his preaching, and the quasi acceptance that turned to murderous rejection.

The reason Luke does this is that Jesus' infamous Nazareth experience dramatically reveals what the gospel is (and demands), why many people reject it, and why some receive it. The study of this text can truly be a spiritual eye-opener.

Jesus Accepted? (vv. 14–22)

Jesus returned to his hometown (v. 16) as somewhat of a celebrity. To those who might say, "Can anything good come out of Nazareth?" the locals could reply, "Here is something good!" Jesus had grown up there, and now all Galilee was praising him for his teaching and mighty works.

Jesus' Reception

"And he came to Nazareth, where he had been brought up. And as was his custom, he went to the synagogue on the Sabbath day, and he stood up to read" (v. 16). Because of the "hometown boy makes good" circumstances, we can assume that the building was packed. From the *Mishnah's* Megillah IV, which supplies numerous details about synagogue worship, we can trace the general flow of the service. There was the singing from Psalms 145—150, followed by the recitation of the *Shema*, which begins, "Hear, O Israel: The Lord our God, the Lord is one [*sema yisra'el 'adnay 'elhenu 'adnay 'ehad*]" (Deuteronomy 6:4–9; 11:13–21; Numbers 15:37–41). Next the Eighteen Benedictions, known as the *Tefillah*, were also recited aloud in succession. Then came the reading of Scripture. An officer went to the holy ark, took out the Torah scroll, removed its cloth covering, opened it to its designated place, and placed it on the table where it was read from by various attenders. The Torah was then returned to the ark, and a portion from the prophets, the *Haftarah*, was read. This was followed by a sermon. The service was closed with the Aaronic benediction, with the people pronouncing "Amen" at each of its divisions: "The Lord bless you and keep you" ("Amen"), "The Lord make his face to shine upon you and be gracious to you" ("Amen"), "The Lord turn his face toward you and give you peace" ("Amen") (cf. Numbers 6:24–26; *Mishnah Sotah*, XII.6).[2]

Very likely, before the service Jesus had been asked by the synagogue president to read the *Haftarah*, and Jesus had requested that it be a scroll of Isaiah.[3]

> And he stood up to read. And the scroll of the prophet Isaiah was given to him. He unrolled the scroll and found the place where it was written,
>
> The Spirit of the Lord is upon me,
> because he has anointed me
> to proclaim good news to the poor.
> He has sent me to proclaim liberty to the captives
> and recovering of sight to the blind,
> to set at liberty those who are oppressed,
> to proclaim the year of the Lord's favor. (vv. 16b–19)

The reading was a combination of Isaiah 61:1, 2 and 58:6 with a couple of lines left out, one of which was the final half of the last line, which adds, "and the day of vengeance of our God" (cf. Isaiah 61:2b).[4]

By omitting that last line, Jesus got their attention! All were silent and motionless. Then, records verse 20a, "He rolled up the scroll and gave it back to the attendant and sat down" (thus assuming the seated position of a preacher). "And the eyes of all in the synagogue were fixed on him. And he began to say to them, 'Today this Scripture has been fulfilled in your hearing'" (vv. 20b, 21). Jesus was obviously saying two things. First, the consolation of Israel promised long before by Isaiah found its ultimate expression in Jesus and his message. And second, while "the day of vengeance of our God" would come (Isaiah 61:2b), it was not being fulfilled on that day. What *was* being fulfilled that day was "the year [i.e., the season] of the Lord's favor."

Jesus' Sermon

This understood, we can examine Jesus' preaching. His arresting opening line, "Today this Scripture has been fulfilled in your hearing," was followed by an exposition of the four classes of people who would benefit from his ministry: the poor, the captives, the blind, and the oppressed. These categories powerfully portray the people to whom Christ came and whom he saves.

Jesus was "anointed . . . to proclaim good news to *the poor*." The word "poor" can cover poverty of every kind. But the emphasis here is on a conscious moral and spiritual poverty, which often is the lot of the financially poor. The rich are less likely to be aware of their spiritual poverty (cf. Revelation 3:14–22). The Greek word here (*ptochois*) is the same word Jesus used in the first beatitude, "Blessed are the poor in spirit, for theirs is the kingdom of heaven" (Matthew 5:3). Often the poor are especially open to receiving Jesus' teaching as good news because they realize their desperate spiritual straits.

Similarly, "*captives*" has a spiritual application because the word technically means prisoners of war.[5] No prisoners were attached to the congregation in Nazareth, but the word broadly includes many forms of spiritual bondage—bondage to money (cf. 19:1–10), bondage to Satan (cf. 8:26–39), bondage to guilt (cf. 7:41–50), bondage to sensuality, and bondage to hatred. To all in the prison house of sin, the truth about Jesus' ministry is:

> He breaks the power of cancelled sin,
> He sets the prisoner free;
> His blood can make the foulest clean;
> His blood availed for me.
>
> Charles Wesley (1739)

The next element that Christ's ministry offers is "recovering of sight to *the blind*," a mighty spiritual promise. In fact, Jesus used it again in explaining Paul's ministry to him: "But rise and stand upon your feet. . . . I am sending you to open their eyes, so that they may turn from darkness to light and from the power of Satan to God, that they may receive forgiveness of sins and a place among those who are sanctified by faith in me" (Acts 26:16–18).

Lastly, the root idea of "oppressed" is "broken in pieces" or "shattered" or "crushed." Jesus comes to those squashed by life's circumstances, who can see no way out, who find living itself an oppression—and he gives them freedom. Malcolm Muggeridge wrote, after coming to Christ in his later years, "All other freedoms, once won, soon turn into new servitude. Christ is the only liberator whose liberation lasts forever."

Can you imagine the exhilaration of hearing the Savior himself explain and apply his message in terms of the four metaphorical groupings of Isaiah 61? The congregation was enthralled. Such insight! Such logic! Such command of language! Luke says, "And all spoke well of him and marveled at the gracious words that were coming from his mouth" (v. 22a). They were captivated by the grace and charm of his words.

But that is as far as it went. They had all known him since he was a mere boy. They had known him as the nice little lad down the street, or a playmate, and later as "the carpenter." Their admiration apparently degenerated into cynicism: "Is not this Joseph's son?" (v. 22b). They admired his words, but they were totally unmoved and unaffected by their meaning. They did not see themselves in any of the metaphors, and did not want to. Within themselves they were saying, "We need to see some sign here. We need more than these pretty words."

Jesus had lived with them for thirty years. He could read them like a book. He didn't need his omniscience to know that he was in fact being rejected.

Jesus Rejected (vv. 23–30)

In response, Jesus assaulted their "acceptance" of him: "And he said to them, 'Doubtless you will quote to me this proverb, "Physician, heal yourself." What we have heard you did at Capernaum, do here in your hometown as well.' And he said, 'Truly, I say to you, no prophet is acceptable in his hometown'" (vv. 23, 24). Jesus said exactly what the pious worshipers, the good people of Nazareth, were thinking. "If he's a prophet, I'm Isaiah! How about a few tricks? It's not too much to ask of a real prophet. Blind? Poor? Captives? Oppressed? Who does he think he is?"

The fact is, they already had enough evidence to believe in him—the objective evidence of the miracles in Capernaum to which Jesus had alluded. All Galilee, which was only twenty-five by forty miles, was talking about what had happened. Their difficulty in accepting him did not come from the lack of objective evidence. As David Gooding writes:

> It was an irrational—or at least non-rational-instinctive, emotional bias. It would be difficult for them to overcome this emotional bias; but the difficulty was on their side not on his. They would have to recognize its existence, and overcome it, if ever they were going to be fair to the evidence.[7]

But the debate over evidence aside, Jesus went right to the heart of the matter, which was their spiritual self-sufficiency and pride. To make his point, he cited two famous Old Testament examples.

Elijah and the Widow

The first involved the prophet Elijah and a starving widow. "But in truth, I tell you," said Jesus, "there were many widows in Israel in the days of Elijah, when the heavens were shut up three years and six months, and a great famine came over all the land, and Elijah was sent to none of them but only to Zarephath, in the land of Sidon, to a woman who was a widow" (vv. 25, 26).

The story, recorded in 1 Kings 17:7–16, tells how Elijah encountered a woman gathering sticks to kindle a fire so she could bake a meal for her son and herself so, as she put it, "We may eat it and die" (v. 12). Elijah's response was surprising:

> Do not fear; go and do as you have said. But first make me a little cake of it and bring it to me, and afterward make something for yourself and your son. For thus says the LORD, the God of Israel, "The jar of flour shall not be spent, and the jug of oil shall not be empty, until the day that the LORD sends rain upon the earth." (vv. 13, 14)

Amazingly, the starving woman obeyed Elijah's strange words, and for as long as the famine endured, she had flour and oil. Why did she trust Elijah? If she had been like the people of Nazareth, she would have demanded a miracle first. But Elijah insisted that it be otherwise, and without any evidence this Gentile woman gave her last meal to him. Why? Very simply, she realized her absolute poverty and fatal lack of resources.[8] Perhaps if she had had a barrelful of flour when she met Elijah, she might have put her faith in her barrel rather than in God. Her blessing was that she was desperately poor, and she knew it.

The application to the congregation in Nazareth was obvious. If they wanted evidence that Jesus' claims to the poor, the blind, the captives, and the oppressed were true, all they had to do was trust him and there would be ample evidence. Of course, that was the problem, because in their own eyes they were not poor. They were the good, respectable, synagogue-attending, family-oriented, solid citizens of Nazareth. The comparison with the Gentile woman in Elijah's day was a massive insult.

Elisha and Naaman

If the people were insulted by the widow's story, the next example brought even greater anger. Jesus continued, "And there were many lepers in Israel in the time of the prophet Elisha, and none of them was cleansed, but only Naaman the Syrian" (v. 27). Naaman was the commander of the Syrian army and was sent by the king of Syria to be cured of leprosy. The Israelite king thought Syria was simply creating a pretext for war. But Elisha calmed him, directing that Naaman be sent to him. Upon Naaman's arrival, Elisha sent a messenger instructing him to go wash seven times in the Jordan and he would be cleansed.

> But Naaman was angry and went away, saying, "Behold, I thought that he would surely come out to me and stand and call upon the name of the LORD his God, and wave his hand over the place and cure the leper. Are not Abana and Pharpar, the rivers of Damascus, better than all the waters of Israel? Could I not wash in them and be clean?" So he turned and went away in a rage. (2 Kings 5:11, 12)

Why, then, did Naaman change his mind? Because his servants convinced him to, arguing that if he had been asked to do a great thing, something he could have been proud of, he would have done it. So why not do the humiliating thing and be cured?

The fine citizens of Nazareth had heard enough. It was bad enough to be told that they were poor and blind and captive and oppressed, but now to be told they were less spiritual and less wise than the *Gentiles*, both Naaman and the widow, was just too much! In fact, they did not even sit through the rest of the synagogue service—the Aaronic benediction and the Amens. Rather, "When they heard these things, all in the synagogue were filled with wrath. And they rose up and drove him out of the town and brought him to the brow of the hill on which their town was built, so that they could throw him down the cliff" (vv. 28, 29).

Think of it! They had seen Jesus grow from infancy to manhood. Even though they had never dreamed he was God, they certainly knew his character firsthand. They had never seen him do anything wrong. He had never lied, never disobeyed, never been unkind. In fact, he was the most loving, thoughtful, winsome person they had ever known. He was undoubtedly locally famous for his acts of mercy. He was the most lovely being they had ever encountered.

But when Jesus cut through their comfortable religious façade, they tried to lynch him—and on the Sabbath too! He would have been tossed off the cliff and then stoned had he not "pass[ed] through their midst" and gone away (v. 30). This was divine protection.

If there ever was proof of Paul's later dictum, "The mind that is set on the flesh is hostile to God" (Romans 8:7a), this was it!

Closing Reflections

Luke the theologian placed this story at the very beginning of his biography of the Messiah to show Theophilus, and all future readers, what the gospel is, to whom it comes, and the kinds of reception it is given. Sometimes it receives Galilean spring. Other times, especially when it comes to the religious, it brings a Nazarene winter.

Hear the gospel from Jesus' lips:

> The Spirit of the Lord is upon me,
> because he has anointed me
> to proclaim good news to the poor.
> He has sent me to proclaim liberty to the captives
> and recovering of sight to the blind,

> to set at liberty those who are oppressed,
> to proclaim the year of the Lord's favor. (vv. 18, 19)

But hear also the warning: "And there were many lepers in Israel in the time of the prophet Elisha, and none of them was cleansed, but only Naaman the Syrian" (v. 27). Naaman was saved because, knowing he was a leper and that there was no hope for him apart from God's grace, he trusted God. There are many lepers in the church today—and many starving widows. But they do not know they are spiritually poor, spiritually captive, spiritually blind, spiritually oppressed. Upright, religious, family-focused, they become furious at the thought that they need God's grace. Their enviable heritages and fine church traditions insulate them from their spiritual poverty. In effect, they cast Jesus out. Those most in need of mercy and grace often know it the least.

A large prestigious British church had three mission churches under its care. On the first Sunday of each new year all the members of the mission churches would come to the parent church for a combined Communion service. In those mission churches, located in the slums of a major city, were some outstanding cases of conversions—thieves, burglars, and others. But all knelt as brothers and sisters side by side at the Communion rail.

On one such occasion the pastor saw a former burglar kneeling beside a judge of the Supreme Court of England—the very judge who had sent him to jail where he had served seven years. After his release this burglar had been converted and became a Christian worker.

After the service, the judge was walking out with the pastor and said to him, "Did you notice who was kneeling beside me at the Communion rail this morning?" The two walked along in silence for a few more moments, and then the judge said, "What a miracle of grace." The pastor nodded in agreement. "A marvelous miracle of grace indeed." The judge then inquired, "But to whom do you refer?" "The former convict," the pastor answered. The judge said, "I was not referring to him. I was thinking of myself." The minister, surprised, replied, "You were thinking of yourself? I don't understand."

"You see," the judge went on, "it is not surprising that the burglar received God's grace when he left jail. He had nothing but a history of crime behind him, and when he understood Jesus could be his Savior, he knew there was salvation and hope and joy for him. And he knew how much he needed that help. But look at me—I was taught from earliest infancy to live as a gentleman, that my word was to be my bond, that I was to say my prayers, go to church, take Communion and so on. I went through Oxford, obtained my degrees, was called to the bar, and eventually became a judge. I was sure I was all I needed to be, though in fact I too was a sinner. Pastor, it was God's grace that drew me. It was God's grace that opened my heart to receive Christ. I'm the greater miracle."

All who bow to him, acknowledging their need and hopelessness, receive eternal life. Miracles of grace!

17

The Authority of Jesus

LUKE 4:31–37

WE ALL HAVE PICTURES in our minds of individuals who epitomize authority. Perhaps Winston Churchill, his jowls set like a bulldog as he faces the falling darkness of the Third Reich, or take-charge Vince Lombardi in black coat and hat as he instructs his quarterback Bart Starr, or perfectly coiffed Margaret Thatcher calmly addressing a noisy House of Commons, or confident General Norman Schwarzkopf, dressed in camouflage fatigues, pointer in hand, as he holds court on the strategy of war.

Each image is instructive and worthy of study. But for the Christian, the greatest study in authority is of course the incarnate Son of God, Jesus Christ. He is the fountain of all authority and the well from which all believers must draw for the proper use of authority in the church and in this fallen world.

Having recounted how Jesus' initial exercise of authority was murderously rejected by his hometown, Luke now describes another Sabbath in another town, Capernaum, where Jesus' authority was given full recognition.

Jesus' Authority in Teaching (vv. 31, 32)

"And he went down to Capernaum, a city of Galilee. And he was teaching them on the Sabbath, and they were astonished at his teaching, for his word possessed authority" (vv. 31, 32). Capernaum was a small town on the upper northwest shore of the Sea of Galilee, about two miles from where the Jordan flows into the lake. Jesus literally did go "down to Capernaum" because Nazareth was 1,200 feet above sea level and Capernaum some 686 feet below sea level.[1] It was a prosperous fishing town with a more varied population than Nazareth because it was closer to the Decapolis (an area comprised of ten cities). Capernaum became known as Jesus' own city (cf. Matthew 9:1). Those who visit Capernaum today can view the remains of a second-century synagogue, excavated in the 1920s, that may well have been built on the site of the original synagogue in which Jesus preached.[2]

Whatever the case, the congregation that gathered in the synagogue in Jesus' day was made up of humble townsfolk—fishermen, merchants, craftsmen, and laborers and their wives. As they participated in the psalms, the blessings, the prayers, and the reading of the Law and the Prophets, they eagerly awaited the sermon from the Nazarene who had been causing such a stir around Galilee. And they weren't disappointed. "They were astonished at his teaching" (v. 32a). The Greek word for "astonished" literally means "to strike with panic or shock."[3] They were "struck with amazement"[4]—thunderstruck in their souls! Jesus' preaching packed a powerful punch!

Why? Because "his word possessed authority" (v. 32b), or as the parallel passage in Mark has it, "He taught them as one who had authority, and not as the scribes" (Mark 1:22). This was always the way Jesus taught. The apostle Matthew confirms this: "And when Jesus finished these sayings [the Sermon on the Mount], the crowds were astonished at his teaching, for he was teaching them as one who had authority, and not as their scribes" (Matthew 7:28, 29). Their teachers, mostly Pharisees, were in bondage to quotation marks—they loved to quote authorities. For example, R. Elieser affirmed in the *Talmud*: "Nor have I ever in my life said a thing which I did not hear from my teachers." The same was said of R. Johanan b. Zakkai: "He never in his life said anything which he had not heard from his teachers" (T B *Sukkah,* 28a).[5] Thus their teaching was a chain of references: "R. Hillel says . . . But also R. Isaac says. . . ." It was secondhand theology—labyrinthine, petty, legalistic, joyless, boring, and weightless.

But when Jesus spoke, it was just the opposite. There were few quotation marks. His style was, "You have heard that it was said. . . . But I say to you" (cf. Matthew 5:21, 22, 27, 28). He preached God's Word, not just *about* God's Word. His preaching of the Law and the Prophets was clear and simple, as it has been with all true preachers of the Word. In contrast, consider the godtalk of contemporary theologian J. J. Altizer:

> Insofar as an eschatological epiphany of Christ can occur only in conjunction with a realization in total experience of the kinetic process of self-negation, we should expect that epiphany to occur in the heart of darkness, for only the universal triumph of the Antichrist can provide an arena for the total manifestation of Christ.[6]

Significantly, Altizer's words came from his book *The Gospel of Christian Atheism*—definitely not a gospel tract!

Once Harry Ironside was greeted by a visitor who said he had enjoyed the service, although he did not think Ironside was a great preacher. Ironside replied, "I know I'm not a great preacher. But what was it about my preaching that brought you to that conclusion?" The man answered, "I understood everything you said." This was an unwitting confession of one of the reasons for Ironside's greatness. Jesus too, when he preached the Word, was clear and painfully direct in his application, as we see again and again in the Gospels. The conclusion in Capernaum was that he taught them as one who had authority. If we had been there, we too would have been thunderstruck!

Jesus' preaching was not only *clear* but *convicting* because the "Holy Spirit descended on him" at his baptism (3:22), and because he was "full of the Holy Spirit" when he returned from the Jordan (4:1), and because when he began to preach he proclaimed, "The Spirit of the Lord is upon me" (4:18; cf. Isaiah 61:1). Jesus' listeners in Capernaum were convicted by his words. As Amy Carmichael, the great missionary, said, "If you have never been hurt by a word from God, it is probable that you have never heard God speak."[7] The people were shocked, thunderstruck, sublimely hurt. Jesus' teaching was authoritative because he proclaimed God's Word clearly and with conviction. We ought to pray for such divine hurt!

We dare not miss the point here: as Jesus went forth to war against the forces of evil, he staked everything on the authority of the written Word. He defeated Satan and his temptations in the desert by quoting God's Word, and in his ministry at large it became his mainstay. Isaiah 61 was the basis of his first sermon. The Sermon on the Mount was an exposition of the Law. Even after his resurrection, "Beginning with Moses and all the Prophets, he interpreted to them in all the Scriptures the things concerning himself" (24:27). Jesus ministered the Word!

If the church is to have any authority today, it must teach on the authority of God's holy Word. Paul's charge to Timothy comes to us all: "Do your best to present yourself to God as one approved, a worker who has no need to be ashamed, rightly handling the word of truth" (2 Timothy 2:15). A few paragraphs later Paul told Timothy what he was to do as a result of his hard study: "Preach the word" (2 Timothy 4:2). In our day when postmodern culture is not interested in reasoned doctrine but only on feelings, the church must stand on God's Word. Otherwise it has no authority.

Jesus' Authority in Power (vv. 33–37)

The Challenge

We do not know when the opposition came or who the opposer was, but as the thunderstruck people sat soaking in Jesus' teaching, "In the synagogue there was a man who had the spirit of an unclean demon, and he cried out with a loud voice, 'Ha! What have you to do with us, Jesus of Nazareth? Have you come to destroy us? I know who you are—the Holy One of God'" (vv. 33, 34). One of Satan's lesser minions had entered into the person of one of the synagogue attenders. This man had "the spirit of an unclean demon" that very likely affected both his mind and body.[8] As a fallen spirit, it was utterly evil and unredeemable. Like Milton's Satan it had irrevocably said, "Evil be thou my good."

As such, unable to bear the presence of Christ, it writhed in the presence of Jesus' holiness. As foul things scurry from the light when you lift a stone, evil spirits, lovers of darkness, recoil from the light of Christ. James declared that demons "believe—and shudder!" (*phrissousin*—literally, they bristle like a frightened cat [James 2:19]).

The hushed silence of the synagogue as the listeners sat motionless listening to Jesus was shattered by the possessed man's shrieks—"Ha! What have you to do with us, Jesus of Nazareth?" "Ha!" expresses displeasure, and the question "What have you to do with us?" literally means "What do we have in common?" It is a rhetorical question meaning, "Don't meddle with me"[9] or "Leave me alone."[10] The evil spirit wanted Jesus to go away.

The next phrase, also stated as a question—"Have you come to destroy us?"—is really a shout of defiance: "You have come to destroy us!" It was an instinctive cry of dread. The demon knew Jesus would destroy or eternally condemn him someday—perhaps today. Then came the final dramatic cry: "I know who you are—the Holy One of God." The demon was not trying to ingratiate itself with Christ but was frantically attempting to bring the Lord under his power. It was widely believed at that time that "the exact knowledge of the other's name brought mastery or control over him."[11] This was a desperate, ill-informed attempt to subdue Christ.

From this encounter we know without doubt that whenever the authority of Christ, the Son of God, is invoked in preaching or teaching, there will be a violent confrontation with the evil spirits who possess men's souls and rule (and ruin) their lives. This is what evangelists experience as they minister around the globe—and will continue to experience as long as they hold Christ high. Likewise, those who oppose pornography, abortion, and other moral evils of our day will encounter supernatural opposition in the days and years to come. The foul creatures of Hell do not like to be challenged.

The Exorcism

Self-proclaimed exorcists in Jesus' day engaged in weird, bizarre practices. For example, a ring would be placed under the subject's nose, the exorcist would recite a lengthy spell, and there would be a staged splash in a nearby basin of water—by the unlucky demon, of course![12] But Jesus engaged in no such hocus-pocus. Very likely there was total silence for a moment in that synagogue by the sea. Perhaps the lapping of the water could be heard. Surely some of those in the congregation could hear their heart beat more rapidly than normal. Then Jesus spoke sternly: "'Be silent [literally, "be muzzled"] and come out of him!' And when the demon had thrown him down in their midst, he came out of him, having done him no harm" (v. 35). Some probably wondered if the victim was dying as he rolled around on the floor. Instead he stood whole, delivered, and joyous.

The Response

"And they were all amazed and said to one another, 'What is this word? For with authority and power he commands the unclean spirits, and they come out!'" (v. 36). Indeed, what teaching! What authority and power! Jesus' authority came, of course, from who he was, the "Holy One of God," as even the demon had confessed, though not for the right reasons. But Jesus' authority was also a result of his victory over Satan in the wilderness (4:1–13). One little word had felled Satan there, and now it was the same with the unclean spirit.

Today the victory and authority of Christ are even more established, for Satan was defeated at the cross. Of this Paul says:

> And you, who were dead in your trespasses and the uncircumcision of your flesh, God made alive together with him, having forgiven us all our trespasses, by canceling the record of debt that stood against us with its legal demands. This he set aside, nailing it to the cross. He disarmed the rulers and authorities and put them to open shame, by triumphing over them in him. (Colossians 2:13–15)

Jesus has disarmed the enemy! The enemy's doom is sealed! Dr. Donald Grey Barnhouse once saw a small child playing with a toy balloon. When the balloon had no air in it, it was a small thing that could be hidden in the palm of the youngster's hand. But when it was blown up, it was a frightening thing with a devilish face on its side. The child kept blowing and blowing until the face was quite large. Suddenly the balloon exploded, and all the child held in his hand was a handful of rubber, with the distorted face reduced to virtually nothing. The child attempted to stretch out the face, but it had lost its power to frighten.

As Barnhouse reflected on this, he thought about what happened to Satan when Christ died. The devil and his principalities had been filled with pretensions, but Christ disarmed them and made a show of them—a public example. "We can thank God," wrote Dr. Barnhouse, "that Satan was effectively put to open shame, exposed publicly. His overblown balloon burst, leaving him nothing but the messy remains of his grinning pretensions."[13] Amen!

Jesus' authority has been established by his Word and his power. The Scriptures are explicit about his authority (note the relationship of authority with each of the following): he has authority to *teach* (Matthew 7:29; Mark 1:22, 27; Luke 4:32); to *exorcise* (Matthew 8:28–34; 9:1–8; Mark 1:23–27; Luke 4:35, 36); to *heal* (Matthew 8:1–17; 12:15, 16; Mark 1:29–34; Luke 4:38–41); to *forgive* (Matthew 9:2–8; Mark 2:3–12; Luke 5:18–26; cf. Psalm 103:3); to *judge* (John 5:27; 17:2); to *give life* (John 10:28; 17:2); to *empower* (Matthew 28:18–20).

All authority and power has been given to Jesus in Heaven and on earth. What picture might best portray Jesus' authority? Perhaps one of him standing with one foot in our galaxy and the other in the next galaxy, 100,000 light-years away—or, better, straddling the entire universe. All authority everywhere is his!

Closing Reflections

In light of all this, there is hope for the worst of us. Someone may seem to have the hardest heart possible—impenetrable, irredeemable—and the proudest will—bloodied, unbowed, unbroken, condemned. Yet there is great hope for that person, for Christ can free him or her from the evil that has him or her in bondage. If that person will bow to the authority of the Word and person of Jesus Christ, he or she will be saved, and the Savior's power will come as a healing balm.

18

Kingdom Authority

LUKE 4:38–44

JESUS' MESSAGE from the very first was "the good news of the kingdom of God" (v. 43). That storied day in Nazareth when he took up the scroll of Isaiah and read, "The Spirit of the Lord is upon me, because he has anointed me to proclaim good news to the poor," he was preaching the kingdom of God. His emphasis on the poor, the captives, the blind, and the oppressed was an implicit summary of the humble spiritual state of those to whom the kingdom comes. But Jesus' insistence upon this sense of spiritual inadequacy so enraged the self-satisfied Nazareth congregation that they attempted to kill him.

Happily, the synagogue attenders in Capernaum had a different response. Instead of being scandalized by his kingdom teaching, they were amazed at his authority. Able to work in this congenial climate, he showed his authority and power by delivering a poor man from an evil spirit. There is grim poetry here because the foul spirit (notwithstanding his hatred of Jesus) confessed who Jesus was—"the Holy One of God"—a confession that Jesus' hometown would not make.

In Capernaum the mighty kingdom power of Jesus showed itself and then began to move out in ever-widening circles—first to those closest to him, then to the townspeople, and then to the nation and, implicitly, to the world.

Kingdom Authority and Those Closest to Him (vv. 38, 39)

It was customary for synagogues to conduct a midmorning service and for the Sabbath meal to be served right after synagogue at the sixth hour (noon). So Jesus was invited to the home of his soon-to-be-disciple Simon

Peter: "An he arose and left the synagogue and entered Simon's house. Now Simon's mother-in-law was ill with a high fever, and they appealed to him on her behalf" (v. 38). Luke the physician literally tells us that the poor woman was "seized by a great fever." She was not dying, but she probably felt like it. We have all experienced such a high fever, when we feel like molecules of air are assaulting our bodies, with each molecule hitting us at about 100,000 miles per hour! When we are in the grip of a fever, brushing our teeth can seem as daunting as climbing Mount Everest. Peter's mother-in-law may have prepared the meal, but someone else would have to serve it.

Unable to attend the synagogue with the others, she was languishing amid a tangle of blankets. Then "they appealed to [Jesus] on her behalf. And he stood over her and rebuked the fever, and it left her, and immediately she rose and began to serve them" (v. 39). The word translated "rebuked" was the same one Jesus used when he sternly commanded the demon to come out of the man at the synagogue. One second the woman lay flattened out with fever, and the next she was cheerfully setting the meal on the table! All were astounded. I can imagine big old Peter smacking his lips as he ate heartily and bragged on his mother-in-law, the guests hanging on Jesus' every word, eyes turning in wonder from the happy hostess to Jesus and back.

The healing had been instant and complete! And the woman's healing enabled her to serve. As the subsequent church has reflected on this over the years, it has rightly seen a living example of what Christ wants to do in believers' lives. The measure of a Christian is not how many servants he has, but how many he serves. Christ's kingdom authority ought to enrich our private domestic circle as well as our corporate fellowship.

The memorable meal would never be forgotten. As family and friends lingered around the table, the shadows lengthened and the sun began to settle, signaling the Sabbath's end.

Kingdom Authority and the Townspeople (vv. 40, 41)

"Now when the sun was setting, all those who had any who were sick with various diseases brought them to him, and he laid his hands on every one of them and healed them" (v. 40). Word of the synagogue miracle quickly went to every home in Capernaum, and the city's ill were brought to Jesus in joyous anticipation. Suffering masses gathered at Peter's door as the western glow of the receding sun passed the horizon. Every manner of disease was there—consumption, raging fevers, cancer, degenerative diseases (MS, diabetes, rickets)—the crippled, the palsied, the blind. Some had to be carried. Many moaned in their distress.

Extra candles were lit, and in the flickering light Jesus healed "every one." This was a wholesale healing, purposely indiscriminate. At other times Jesus would heal some but not others, but on this unique occasion all who came were made whole. Perhaps even some who were demonized were healed against their own will. This was an unrestrained display of raw kingdom power. The night vibrated with healing wholeness.

Luke is most careful to tell us that "*he laid his hands on every one of them* and healed them." Hands-on healing was most unusual, for such a practice was unknown in the Old Testament and rabbinical literature.[1] Jesus' method, radically new, was symbolic of the outflow of divine power. Moreover, here it conveyed divine tenderness to the needy. Every single person that evening felt the touch of the Master's hand.

At this signal time in the outpouring of Christ's power, all history was meant to see that his kingdom authority is not an impersonal force. It is unequaled power to be sure, but it was personally and lovingly administered in Jesus' tender hands.

That was a poignant, memorable night. However, it was not without a hint of tragedy. Those who are ill of body know what they need and will go to great lengths to receive it. But sadly, people who will break their necks to get to Jesus the *physician* will scarcely move to reach Jesus the *Redeemer*. As Alexander Maclaren said: "Offer men the smaller gifts, and they will run over one another in their scramble for them; but offer them the highest, and they will scarcely hold out a languid hand to take them."[2]

Since some of the illnesses Jesus encountered were caused by evil spirits, Luke adds, "And demons also came out of many, crying, 'You are the Son of God!' But he rebuked them and would not allow them to speak, because they knew that he was the Christ" (v. 41). The demons' repeated shouts, "You are the Son of God!" were not confessions, but rather futile attempts to exercise mastery over Christ by showing that they knew his name. Jesus silenced them with a simple rebuke, just as he had done with the unclean spirit in the synagogue (v. 35) and in Peter's home when he rebuked the fever (v. 39). Jesus exercised his power with the ease of omnipotence. Just a word.

This is important because Scripture teaches that we are at war with a mighty enemy: "For we do not wrestle against flesh and blood, but against the rulers, against the authorities, against the cosmic powers over this present darkness, against the spiritual forces of evil in the heavenly places" (Ephesians 6:12). Our spiritual enemies are not petty officials. The designation of their leaders as "rulers," "authorities," "cosmic powers," and "spiritual forces of evil" indicates that they form a vast, organized hierarchy. The word translated "cosmic powers," or "world rulers" (RSV), is *kosmokratoras* or, in a recognizable English rendering, *cosmocrats*, referring to high-ranking angels. We face a great demonic enemy with a defined and disciplined chain of command. The evil we wrestle against is not the feeble Satan of folklore in command of a gang of winged possums! It is a great organized army of personal, evil beings.

But we need not fear—Jesus confronts the enemy in cosmic combat, and his powerful word is all that is needed for victory.

> But lo, his doom is sure;
> One little word shall fell him.

Nothing can stand against Christ and his kingdom!

Kingdom Authority and the Nation (vv. 42–44)

There was hardly a sick person left in Capernaum, except perhaps the most hardened cynic. Many, no doubt, had spent the whole night luxuriating in their newfound health—testing renewed appendages, running their hands over newly smooth skin, clutching a healthy infant, feeling good for the first time in years. So we are not surprised at what we read next: "An when it was day, he departed and went into a desolate place. And the people sought him and came to him, and would have kept him from leaving them" (v. 42). There is no mention of force here, but some very likely were thinking of it. The prospect of a town where everyone, old and young alike, is healthy—what a thought!

Neither are we surprised at Jesus' response: "But he said to them, 'I must preach the good news of the kingdom of God to the other towns as well; for I was sent for this purpose.' And he was preaching in the synagogues of Judea" (v. 43, 44).

This is the first mention of "the kingdom of God" in the Gospel of Luke, a phrase that will occur thirty-one more times in that book. It means "Jesus' activity in bringing salvation to men and the sphere which is thereby created."[3] The kingdom had a *past* manifestation because God has always been sovereign, as Psalm 24:1 attests: "The earth is the LORD's and the fullness thereof, the world and those who dwell therein." And past saints are identified in Luke's Gospel as part of the kingdom: "In that place there will be weeping and gnashing of teeth, when you see Abraham and Isaac and Jacob and all the prophets in the kingdom of God but you yourselves cast out" (13:28). The kingdom of God was also *present* with Christ and is *present* in the lives of his spiritual children, as Jesus explained: "The kingdom of God is in the midst of you" (17:21). Lastly, of course, the kingdom is *future* (cf. 11:2; 13:28, 29; 19:11; 21:31).

Closing Reflections

Luke gives us in chapters 4, 5 of his Gospel a cosmically authoritative Christ who has come with "the good news of the kingdom of God." The range of his authority stretches language and imagination. As we seek to grasp it, the Christ of the Andes, that towering statue, comes to mind. But that is far too small. We could picture Christ standing with his feet planted on twin peaks of the Rockies and towering another 14,000 feet above them. But that doesn't do it either. How about one foot planted in the Atlantic and the other in the Pacific, so that his shoulders extend 6,000 miles above the earth? Insufficient. We come closer to "seeing" his authority if we think of him straddling the one hundred thousand million galaxies of the universe and holding them together even as the universe expands, though even that does not capture the full picture. One thing we know for sure—"all authority in heaven and on earth" is Christ's (Matthew 28:18)!

Wherever Christ went, the kingdom went. When men and women come to him in faith, the kingdom enters their hearts. All true believers are part of the kingdom to come.

How should we respond to these massive spiritual realities? The answer is given by Christ himself in the second petition of the Lord's Prayer: "Your kingdom come" (11:2). If this is prayed in its fullest dimension, Christ's kingdom authority will be properly exalted. When we pray "Your kingdom come," we pray for the final and ultimate establishment of his reign, the great moment beyond earth's history when all evil will be judged and eliminated, when God's children will dwell in his holy presence and all will be "righteousness and peace and joy in the Holy Spirit" (Romans 14:17). In this sense our prayers ought to have an almost martial ring: "Your kingdom come—Maranatha!—Come, O Lord!"

Furthermore, praying "Your kingdom come" involves a commitment to do God's will. Matthew's record of the Lord's Prayer expands this phrase: "Your kingdom come, your will be done, on earth as it is in heaven" (Matthew 6:10). To pray "Your kingdom come" is to pray for the bending of our wills in profound obedience to his. It is a commitment to consciously submit everything to his authority.

This is not a prayer for people who want to stay the way they are. When we pray like this, we hand ourselves over to the grace of God so that he may do as he pleases in our lives—"Your kingdom come in my life. Use me in your kingdom!"

While it is easy to pray for the future eschatological kingdom and rule of Christ, it is quite another thing to pray for his present kingdom rule in our hearts. This is especially difficult for us moderns, for our culture has fostered a rebellious "submit to no one" spirit. Marriages fall apart because spouses have never submitted to anything or anyone unless they wanted to. Children are taught to question authority. Students reject teachers' authority. Employees chafe under the authority of employers. And so it goes with citizens in regard to laws and government, and with believers in regard to the church.

Add to this the modern antiauthority malaise, the uniquely American worship of independence and individualism, the "Don't tread on me," "Security by Smith and Wesson" attitude, and we have a potent recipe for a profound inability to truly submit to any authority, even that of Christ himself. This is why so many moderns have no kingdom power. You cannot enjoy a kingdom unless you are submitted to the king.

Have you ever officially submitted everything to the rule of Christ? Your will—your future—your ambitions—your longings—your vocation—your spouse—your children—your independence—your heart? Why not do it now?

Your kingdom come, Lord Jesus!

19

Calling Fishermen

LUKE 5:1–11

I LIKE TO FISH. For me there are few things more exhilarating than the crisp morning air (a tad cooler than the summer water), the rising fragrance of a healthy lake, and the slow lapping of the yet unchurned surface. Few things fill me with more pleasant anticipation than the sun's eastern rays lighting the mossy mysteries below and the voices of fellow fishermen echoing across the water. My wife gave me a T-shirt that says it all: *I fish, therefore I am*. If Descartes were a fisherman, this is surely what he would have written—*Piscare ergo sum*. When I send birthday cards to my brother, who is also a fisherman, I always sign them, "May all your fishes come true." So I have a good feel for the opening verses of Luke 5:

> On one occasion, while the crowd was pressing in on him to hear the word of God, he was standing by the lake of Gennesaret, and he saw two boats by the lake, but the fishermen had gone out of them and were washing their nets. Getting into one of the boats, which was Simon's, he asked him to put out a little from the land. And he sat down and taught the people from the boat. (vv. 1–3)

Peter, his brother Andrew (cf. Mark 1:16), and his partners James and John had spent the night fishing with dragnets. It was backbreaking work because it involved laying out a great net in a semicircle, encompassing over 100 feet, drawing it in hand-over-hand, then repeating the procedure again and again. It was hard work that only strong men could perform.

The group had sweat through the night without as much as a fish. So at dawn they beached their boats, ate breakfast, and under the warming sun engaged in the tedious and necessary process of washing, mending, and arranging their nets for drying. Once dry, they would be folded and placed back in the boats for the coming night.

On this particular day, the monotony was broken by the presence of a large crowd pressing around Jesus "to hear the word of God" (v. 1). Jesus was preaching "the good news of the kingdom of God" (4:43). His preaching with characteristic authority and power drew a packed crowd. So Jesus asked if he could use Simon Peter's boat as a floating pulpit, and Peter and Jesus and probably Andrew too anchored the boat a few yards from shore, where Jesus resumed his teaching, his voice carrying effectively over the waters to all gathered on the shore.

Fishing for a Carpenter (vv. 4–7)

We do not know how much attention Peter was paying to Jesus' message. Possibly he was spacing out because of the long night's work and was now sitting motionless in the warm sun.

The Divine Request

Whatever the case, Jesus soon had Peter's full attention. "And when he had finished speaking, he said to Simon, 'Put out into the deep and let down your nets for a catch.' And Simon answered, 'Master, we toiled all night and took nothing! But at your word I will let down the nets'" (vv. 4, 5). It was a demanding request, to say the least. Jesus was asking a man who had not slept all night, who had spent the night examining empty meshes, to beach the boat, load a thousand pounds of wet nets, row out to deep water, and circle around while setting the net—all at midday! Besides, what right did Jesus, a carpenter from Nazareth, have to ask an expert Galilean fisherman who had spent his life on the lake to do his bidding?

If you have ever fished with a professional guide, you will realize how outrageous Jesus' request was, humanly speaking. Professional fishermen know that 100 percent of the fish are in 10 percent of the water, and they definitely know where the percentages lie. I have been out with guides and caught my limit when no other fish were caught on the lake because professional fishermen know fish and how to find them.

I do not know how you respond at such times, but when someone offers me advice on a subject upon which I feel knowledgeable and competent (and I sense they are inexperienced in it), my concentration slackens. Imagine saying to star NBA forward Scottie Pippen, "Scottie, I don't play basketball. In fact, I've never played the game. But if you'll do as I say, you'll win the game tonight, guaranteed. Interested?"

So we can sympathize with Peter's expressed reticence—and enjoy his obedience. He had seen what Jesus had done in the local synagogue and in his own home. He had witnessed Jesus' toiling through the night as he performed a wholesale healing of all the sick in Capernaum who came to him. So now, being sure of what Jesus wanted, he responded, "But at your word I will let down the nets" (v. 5b).

What an example this is for you and me! Jesus' word comes, and it is demanding. We have some initial reticence. But we are sure he is the one who is speaking, and there is no doubt about what he wants, so we do it. And we are not sorry.

The Divine Catch

If Peter was yawning and rubbing his eyes as he dropped the nets over the side, he was soon shocked into being wide awake: "And when they had done this, they enclosed a large number of fish, and their nets were breaking. They signaled to their partners in the other boat to come and help them. And they came and filled both the boats, so that they began to sink" (vv. 6, 7). Peter could hardly hang on to his dragnet as an incredible catch of fish filled the nets and the boat was pulled toward the fish. Frantically, he nodded to his friends on shore, and a second boat was quickly launched. As they harvested their catch, the two boats, each seven and a half feet wide and over twenty-seven feet long,[1] filled to the gunwales and began sinking. Several tons of fish were hauled ashore that day amid the roar of the delighted crowds. All their fishes had come true!

It was a raw outpouring of power—a massive nature miracle. The onlookers saw that the fish of the sea were as obedient to Jesus' will as the frogs and flies and locusts were to Yahweh in Egypt centuries earlier.

Called by a Carpenter (vv. 8–11)

Sublime trauma fell on Peter's amazed soul: "But when Simon Peter saw it, he fell down at Jesus' knees, saying, 'Depart from me, for I am a sinful man, O Lord.' For he and all who were with him were astonished at the catch of fish that they had taken, and so also were James and John, sons of Zebedee, who were partners with Simon" (vv. 8–10a). Peter had been brought *personally* into the sphere of Jesus' mighty kingdom power. As we have noted, this was not his first exposure to Christ's kingdom authority, but this time Jesus ministered in Peter's personal universe—his sea, his boat, his nets—and so the significance came to him as never before.

An Awareness of Jesus

A series of thoughts flashed through the fisherman's mind like lightning. He saw that Jesus belonged to a sphere to which he did not belong. "Here was the Lord of fish and fishermen, the Lord of nature, the Lord of men and of their daily work."[2] If at this point Peter did not fully understand that Jesus was the Christ, he did at least understand that the divine presence was in Christ—and thus he called him "Lord." Peter knew he was in some way in the presence of God.

An Awareness of Sin

Peter was also overcome with an awareness of his own sinfulness. In moral agony he fell at Jesus' knees crying, "Depart from me, for I am a sinful man, O Lord." Faced with Christ's authority and power, his soul flooded with a sense of his own evil and hollowness, and with a trembling realization of the personal consequences of his sin.

This is the proper response to God. When Isaiah "saw the Lord sitting upon a throne, high and lifted up" (Isaiah 6:1), his first thought was not adoration but fear. He felt such moral trauma in respect to his own sin that he cried, "Woe is me!" (Isaiah 6:5). Job had much the same experience: "I had heard of you by the hearing of the ear, but now my eye sees you; therefore I despise myself, and repent in dust and ashes" (Job 42:5, 6). And John would write in the book of Revelation, "When I saw him, I fell at his feet as though dead" (Revelation 1:17). This response to Jesus is a great grace, because moral agony, an inner writhing over one's sin, is a necessary prelude to the grace of forgiveness. Peter was in the spiritual posture of Isaiah 61—poor, imprisoned, blind, oppressed (cf. 4:18). He was blessed because he mourned over his sin (cf. Matthew 5:4). He was a child of the kingdom.

In moral agony in Christ's presence, at this early stage of his spiritual development, Peter, feeling unworthy and not understanding what he was saying, asked Jesus to go away. But as Peter grew in his knowledge of and experience with God, his consciousness of sin drove him to God. John 21 provides the most dramatic instance of this. After the Resurrection Peter, deeply anguished over his denials of Christ, went back up to Galilee and in the calm of his old haunts decided to go fishing—perhaps to clear his head and sort things out. He and his old friends fished the night away without success.

Early in the morning Jesus stood on the shore, but the disciples did not realize that it was Jesus. He called out to them, "Children, do you have any fish?" "No," they answered. He said, "Cast the net on the right side of the boat, and you will find some." When they did, they were unable to haul the net in because of the large number of fish. Then the disciple whom Jesus loved said to Peter, "It is the Lord!" When Simon Peter heard that it was the Lord, he put on his outer garment, for he was stripped for work, and threw himself into the sea (John 21:4–7).

Peter stood before Jesus, his beard dripping, breathless from his plunge and charge to shore. Peter dashed to Jesus because he knew himself for what he was (all fleshly presumption was gone—he knew he was a weak, frail sinner) and also because he knew so much better now who Jesus was.

The more we know of our sin, and the more we know of Jesus, the more we will run to him! He, and only he, has made a sacrifice for our iniquities, taking all our sin away. He and only he can forgive. He and only he can give life. He and only he can put our lives together. Do you know you are a sinner? Do you see who Jesus really is? Then run to him.

An Awareness of Mission

Notwithstanding Peter's imperfect perceptions on that day as recorded in Luke 5, he had much of it right: the divine presence was indeed before him, and he knew himself to be a great sinner. His cry—"Depart from me, for I am a sinful man, O Lord"—showed his humility.

And Jesus responded with a prophetic call: "And Jesus said to Simon, 'Do not be afraid; from now on you will be catching men'" (v. 10b). There is an exquisite nuance here: "catching men" is a combination of two Greek words—*zoos* ("alive") and *agrein* ("catch, hunt)." [3] The exact sense is to "catch alive"—"from now on you will catch men alive." Catching men not for death but for life would be Peter's mission.[4]

Of course, this was famously fulfilled in Peter's life. Luke records in Acts that when Peter preached at Pentecost, "So those who received his word were baptized, and there were added that day about three thousand souls" (Acts 2:41), and a short time later when he was arraigned before the Sanhedrin his catch had grown to five thousand (Acts 4:3, 4). Throughout Peter's life the number grew and grew and grew.

"Catching men for life"—what a glorious description of gospel ministry.

Our family had a particularly joyous experience of this sort some years ago when our daughter Holly began kindergarten. We were delighted when she became one of Mrs. Smith's kindergartners. Susie Smith was known as "the best." She was a tall woman in her midthirties who was unusually graced with what the French call the *joie de vivre*. Mrs. Smith brimmed with joyous enthusiasm about life and teaching. And she loved her students. Mrs. Smith's smile and the warm cheer of her voice soothed the anxieties of students and parents alike. This winsomeness along with her wholesome enthusiasm and creativity made her a master teacher. And our shy little Holly loved Mrs. Smith.

As Holly, nurturing soul that she was even then, walked home from school or tended her menagerie (a parrot, a cockatiel, a white rat, and some turtles), she often thought of Mrs. Smith and how nice it would be if she would come to church—and especially if she would come to know Jesus. So every Friday Holly's guileless big brown eyes engaged Mrs. Smith's as she asked, "Mrs. Smith, will you come to church this Sunday?" And every Friday Mrs. Smith answered, "Well, maybe." This was followed every Monday, as Susie Smith tells it, by our disappointed daughter saying, "Mrs. Smith, you didn't come." At last it simply became too much for Holly's poor teacher to face, so she promised to come to church.

And Susie Smith did come to church, and she came again and again and again, for she had a deep unrequited spiritual need that was only met when she came to faith in Christ. She was "caught alive." Susie became a good friend and a vibrant Christian, bringing her vitality and élan to the work of Christ.

Today Susie Smith, though confined to a wheelchair by MS, still flashes that same sparkle because over twenty years ago she was "caught alive."

Closing Reflections

Peter and his partners, standing in their two boats overflowing with gasping fish, immediately caught the implication of Jesus' display of kingdom power and his kingdom call. Luke concludes this section by saying, "And when they had brought their boats to land, they left everything and followed him" (v. 11). "Followed" is a heavily freighted expression signifying the deepest inward attachment.[5]

This is the logic of the kingdom—and it applies to all of us who claim to be children of the King. Jesus calls his people to diverse vocations, but all are to devote their lives to catching men and women alive. This is to be our perpetual vocation.

20

Healed Indeed

LUKE 5:12–16

IN BIBLICAL TIMES the rare deliverances from leprosy were certified by an elaborate and uniquely joyful ceremony that extended over eight full days in fulfillment of the directives of Leviticus 14. It began when a priest met the would-be celebrant outside the camp and verified that he actually was healed. Then, still outside the camp, two birds were presented along with some cedar wood, scarlet yarn, and hyssop. One of the birds was killed in a clay pot (so that none of its blood was lost). This was done above fresh water (symbolic of cleansing). Next the live bird, along with the wood, yarn, and hyssop, was dipped in the blood, and blood was sprinkled upon the leper seven times as he was pronounced "clean." This initial ceremony concluded with the live bird being released in the open fields to wing its way to freedom (Leviticus 14:1–7). As a result, the blood-sprinkled person could once again join the community. This foreshadowed the effect of Christ's blood, which reconciles man to God and makes it possible for the sinner to join the household of faith.

After the bird's release the cleansed man washed his clothing, shaved the hair from his body, bathed, and entered the camp, where he, his family, and friends rejoiced for seven days (Leviticus 14:8, 9). On the seventh day his head, eyebrows, and beard were shaved, and he again bathed, so that, like a newborn, he was ready to enter a new phase of his existence.[1]

On the eighth day the former leper offered three unblemished lambs as a guilt offering, a sin offering, and a burnt offering. The guilt offering was not an atoning sacrifice but a restitution for the offerings and sacrifices he was unable to make while a leper.[2] His restitution and fresh commitment were then dramatically emphasized when the priest took some of the blood and smeared it on the offerer's right ear, thumb, and toe, then coated each smear with a second anointing of oil, thereby symbolizing that the man would listen to God's voice, use his hands for God's glory, and walk in God's ways. Fittingly, his shaved head was then anointed with the remaining oil (Leviticus 14:12–18; cf. Exodus 30:23–25). Finally, having thus declared the leper to be in the Lord's service, the priest made atonement for him with sin, burnt, and cereal offerings, the last being a joyous expression of gratitude (Leviticus 14:19, 20).

Imagine the joy of the healed man and his family—and the communal celebration that accompanied that great eighth day. It was as if a resurrection had taken place. Very likely there was feasting and singing long into the night.

For us Christians, the Old Testament's description of these ancient ceremonies elicits incredible joy not only because the Scriptures speak of Christ (cf. 24:27; John 5:39), but also because this elaborate ritual specifically speaks of the atonement through Christ and his power to deliver. This is precisely what Jesus' healing of the leper in Luke 5 is all about.

Needing the Healing Touch (v. 12)

The poor man who came to Jesus was desperately ill. Dr. Luke describes him as "full of leprosy." By this we understand that the disease had run its course. None of us needs a detailed description of the poor man's loathsome appearance. If you have seen one picture of someone full of leprosy, it is enough.

What is important to understand is that leprosy, or Hansen's disease as it is better known today (named after the man who diagnosed its cause), is not a rotting infection as was once commonly thought, nor are the sufferer's outward physical deformities horribly disfigured by the disease. In recent years the research of Dr. Paul Brand and others has proven that the disfigurement associated with Hansen's disease comes solely because the body's warning system of pain is destroyed. The disease brings numbness to the extremities as well as to the ears, eyes, and nose. The devastation that follows comes from incidents such as reaching into a charcoal fire to retrieve a dropped potato, or washing one's face with scalding water, or gripping a tool so tightly that the hands become traumatized and eventually stumplike.[3] In third-world countries vermin sometimes chew on sleeping lepers without the lepers even knowing it. Dr. Brand, after performing corrective surgery on a leper, would send a cat home with him as normal postoperative procedure. Dr. Brand calls the disease a "painless hell." The poor man in Luke had not been able to feel for years, and his body, mutilated from head to foot, was foul and rotting.

The Leper an Outcast

In Israel the lot of a leper was summed up in Leviticus 13:45, 46: "The leprous person who has the disease shall wear torn clothes and let the hair of his head hang loose, and he shall cover his upper lip and cry out, 'Unclean, unclean.' He shall remain unclean as long as he has the disease. He is unclean. He shall live alone. His dwelling shall be outside the camp." We can hardly imagine the humiliation and isolation of a leper's life. He was ostracized from society because it was thought at that time that leprosy was highly contagious (which it is not). Moreover, for the sake of the ritual purity of the community, whenever he came in range of the normal population, he had to assume a disheveled appearance and cry, "Unclean, unclean." Think about how you would feel shouting this while entering a grocery store or a mall, and the pervasive sense of worthlessness and despair you would experience. Lepers were typically beggars because there was no way they could support themselves. Sometimes their families deposited food in remote places. They customarily lived in bands—fellow outcasts (cf. 2 Kings 7:3; Luke 17:12).

By Jesus' time, rabbinical teaching, with its minute strictures, had made matters even worse. If a leper even stuck his head inside a house, the house was pronounced unclean. It was illegal to greet a leper. Lepers had to remain at least 100 cubits away if they were upwind, and four cubits if downwind. Josephus, the Jewish historian, summed it up by saying that lepers were treated "as if they were, in effect, dead men"[4]—dead men walking. Indeed, to the rabbis the cure of a leper was as difficult as raising a person from the dead.[5]

The Leper a Symbol of Sin

If this were not bad enough, it was also thought that those who had leprosy had contracted the disease because of some great personal sin. People assumed this erroneous conclusion because in past history people such as Miriam, Gehazi, and Uzziah had been judged with leprosy (cf. Numbers 12: 6–10; 2 Kings 5:25–27; 2 Chronicles 26:19 respectively).

Despite these misunderstandings, the plight of the leper did in fact illustrate the effects of sin, even though the leper was not any more sinful than anyone else. R. C. Trench, a great Greek scholar and the inspiration for and first editor of the monumental *Oxford English Dictionary*, recognized this, saying that though the leper was not worse or guiltier than his fellow Jews, nevertheless he was a parable of sin—an "outward and visible sign of innermost spiritual corruption."[6] The leper is a physical illustration of ourselves apart from the cleansing work of Christ. Sin has invaded all our faculties. Sin's leprosy runs from the soles of our feet to the crown of our heads, so that we are wholly unclean (cf. Isaiah 1:6). This is the state in which we were born and in which we naturally live. Spiritually, without Christ, we are dead long before the grave—"dead in . . . trespasses and sins" (Ephesians 2:1). If we could see ourselves with spiritual eyes as we are apart from Christ, we would know that we are walking dead trying to cover ourselves with filthy rags.

Obtaining the Healing Touch (v. 12)

Significantly, Matthew's account (8:1–4) places Jesus' encounter with the leper immediately after the Sermon on the Mount, when Jesus was descending the mountainside. No doubt the din of the multitude was considerable. But above it, with increasing clarity, was heard the faint, "Unclean, unclean." As if the prow of a boat were moving through the throng, the leper steadily made his way to Jesus as the people fell back, fearing contamination. Perhaps some cursed him, but he kept coming until he stood almost in front of Jesus. The Master was face-to-face with a foul, decaying leper who "fell on his face and begged him, 'Lord, if you will, you can make me clean'" (v. 12; note that the phrase is exactly the same in Matthew and Mark).

Awareness of Sin

The effect of his leprosy upon him was such that he did not ask, "Lord, if you are willing, you can *heal* me," but rather, "you can make me *clean*." Here we see the first and fundamental qualification for coming to Jesus—an awareness of one's condition. The poor man not only said he was unclean—he *knew* he was unclean. If he had had any illusions of wholeness, all he had to do was hold the remainder of his hand before his eyes and they vanished in an ugly moment. He knew he was hopeless, that there was nothing he could do to help himself. Everyone else had probably given up on him too. His many years of illness undoubtedly meant that some in his family had stopped praying for him. In this way he epitomized the blessed spiritual awareness found in the opening Beatitude: "Blessed are the poor in spirit, for theirs is the kingdom of heaven. Blessed are those who mourn, for they shall be comforted" (Matthew 5:3, 4).

The pitiful refrain "Unclean, unclean" had shaped the leper's whole psyche. He was a beggar indeed. He truly believed there was nothing within him commendable to God. Thus he was in the perfect posture to receive grace.

God does not come to the self-sufficient, those who think they have no need or imagine they can make it on their own. He comes to the empty in spirit, those who mourn their condition. If you would come to Christ, this is the way you must come—saying, "Unclean, unclean." In fact, if you come saying, "Only partly unclean" or "I'm 25 percent clean" or "I'm 10 percent clean," he will not receive you. This is the great tragedy of the comfortable today—we cannot accept that we are not acceptable. That is why the gospel is such an offense!

Worshipful Submission

"And when he saw Jesus, he fell on his face and begged him. . . ." Matthew's parallel description says the leper "knelt before him" (Matthew 8:2), and the basic meaning of "knelt" in early Greek literature was "to kiss," as in kissing the earth as one lay prostrate to the gods. In the Greek translation of the Old Testament, this word was used to translate the Hebrew word for "bowing down."[7] The humble leper put his whole soul into worship as he lay prostrate before Christ. He worshipfully submitted to Christ as the only possible source of his healing.

Christ's healing touch doesn't come in response to a casual, irreverent acknowledgment. It comes as we bow before him in the realization that he is our *only* hope.

Real Faith

The third factor in obtaining the healing touch of Christ is faith. "And when he saw Jesus, he fell on his face and begged him, 'Lord, if you will, you can make me clean.'" The Greek tense in the parallel passage in the Gospel of Mark indicates that he repeated this several times (Mark 1:40). What a poignant picture—the leper, still prostrate, repeating in the hoarse voice typical of those with advanced leprosy, "Lord, if you will, you can make me clean—Lord, if you will, you can make me clean—Lord, if you will, you can make me clean." No doubt he had heard of Jesus' miraculous power and, listening to him, that day came to the conclusion that Christ was omnipotent. But what is more significant is that the leper said, "You can make me clean." He probably did not have a great theological understanding, but he was pragmatic: "If he can do it for others, he can do it for me."

Sin controls people through two opposing lies. The first is, we are not sinners—nothing is wrong with us. The second is, we are sinners, but we are so bad that we are beyond help. Over the years in my pastoral ministry I have talked to a number of people who felt this way. They have recited their sins to me with the naive supposition that I would be shocked. The fact is, I *cannot* be shocked! I have heard it all, and I can say that Christ is sufficient for all. One man told me, "I'm such scum. How could he ever forgive me?" He does not say that now because he has experienced forgiveness. All of us have offended a perfectly holy God, but none of us is beyond God's love and Christ's redemption.

The leper knelt flat on his face before Christ in humble prostration. He was fully aware of his hopeless, leprous condition, and yet he believed Christ could heal him.

Experiencing the Healing Touch (v. 13)

The Touch

As the leper lay at Jesus' feet, Jesus looked on him as no one else had before. According to Mark's Gospel, Christ was "moved with pity" (Mark 1:41), indicating that Jesus was so touched by what he saw that he had a visceral reaction. Then came the height of the encounter: "And Jesus stretched out his hand and touched him" (v. 13). Perhaps it had been twenty or even thirty years since the leper had been touched by a nonleprous hand. Perhaps he was a father who had once known the embrace of his children and his wife, but for years he had not known even one touch. How he must have longed for such a touch. I once counseled a lonely man who had no family that cared about him. He belonged to no church. He said he had his hair cut once a week just so someone would touch him in a caring way. Imagine that leper's longing for a touch or a caress.

People avoided lepers, but Christ "touched" him. As Bishop Westcott says, the word "expresses more than superficial contact."[8] It is often translated, "to take hold of." Jesus, at the very least, placed his hand firmly on the leper. We cannot attempt to adequately describe the ecstasy that coursed through the leper's body. The onlookers were shocked, the disciples were shocked, and Jesus was now ceremonially unclean, but the leper felt loved.

Why did Jesus do this? The Savior wanted the leper to *feel* his willingness and sympathy. The touch said, "I am with you, I understand, I love you." But there was also an overshadowing theological reason: the touch of Christ's pure hand on the rotting leper is a parable of the incarnation and the cross. Jesus took on flesh, became sin for us, and gave us his purity. "For our sake he made him to be sin who knew no sin, so that in him we might become the righteousness of God" (2 Corinthians 5:21). Jesus laid hold of our flesh. He touched us and healed us. As we see Jesus bent over the prostrate sufferer, his holy hand resting on the decaying flesh of the foul-smelling leper, we see what he did for us.

The Healing

Luke concludes, "And Jesus stretched out his hand and touched him, saying, 'I will; be clean.' And immediately the leprosy left him" (v. 13). The healing was sudden and complete. The man's feet—toeless, ulcerated stubs—were suddenly whole, too large for his shrunken sandals. The knobs on his hands grew fingers before his very eyes. Back came his hair, eyebrows, eyelashes. His skin was supple and soft. The amazement of the multitude must have been audible. This is what Jesus Christ can do for individuals today in a split second of belief. The healing of Christ in salvation from sin is instantaneous and complete ("the blood of Jesus his Son cleanses us from all sin," 1 John 1:7).

Verifying the Healing Touch (v. 14)

"And he charged him to tell no one, but 'go and show yourself to the priest, and make an offering for your cleansing, as Moses commanded, for a proof to them.'" Some have been mystified by Jesus' immediate command to the healed leper—it seems unreasonable. Why did Jesus make this command?

Some Practical Reasons

There were some very down-to-earth reasons, such as the possibility that the priestly establishment, having heard that Jesus performed the healing, would refuse to acknowledge it, or that the ex-leper would in all the excitement forget to go through the ceremony or would forget the immensity of what had just happened.

A Prophetic Reason

But the biggest reason by far was prophetic, because this miracle was a massive witness to the leadership of Israel that the Messianic Age had come. The Jews expected the ravages of sin to be removed in the time of messianic salvation.[9] Indeed, Jesus would allude to this later in his message to John the Baptist about who he was (cf. 7:22).

The grand message was that messianic times had arrived—indeed, the Messiah was here. Many in Israel had leprosy in the time of Elisha the prophet, yet only Naaman was cleansed (cf. 4:27). But now one greater than Elisha had come. Jesus had the authority to heal the ravages of sin!

A Celebration Reason

Consider the eight days of ritual verification and celebration that followed—the inspection, the cedar and scarlet yarn and the hyssop, the blood-dipped bird winging heavenward, the sprinklings, the washings, the guilt offering, the three great sacrifices, the anointings of the healed leper's ear, hand, and foot—his whole life, the final atoning offerings. What a witness of grace to the religious establishment—eight joyous days right in front of their eyes!

Jesus heals leprosy, but even more he heals leprosy of the soul—he forgives sin and makes all new.

Concluding Reflections

We learn valuable lessons from the healing of this leper. Anyone wanting Christ's spiritual healing must put these lessons to work in his or her own life.

We must come to Christ with a deep *awareness of sin*. Do we acknowledge that we are sinners and that we have nothing in ourselves to commend us to God? Do we mourn our sins? If so, we are ready for Christ's healing touch.

We must bow before him in *humble reverence*—submit to him as our only hope and tell God that if he does not save us, we will be lost.

We must believe he can make us clean. Do you believe? "He himself bore [your name's] sins in his body on the tree, that [your name] might die to sin and live to righteousness. By his wounds [your name] ha[s] been healed" (1 Peter 2:24).

21

Healing and Faith

LUKE 5:17–26

BEFORE PUBLIC EVENTS such as debates and athletic contests, the air is charged and everyone just knows that "something is going to happen." That feeling is equivalent to what backpackers sometimes experience when caught on a high mountain during a brewing storm. They see the hair of their fellow hikers stand straight out from their heads, and the metal frames of their packs glow with an eerie neon blue light called St. Elmo's fire. The air is so charged with electricity that a lightning strike is imminent. For the hiker this is a signal to discard his pack and take cover.

Luke 5:17 gives us such a feeling: "On one of those days, as he was teaching, Pharisees and teachers of the law were sitting there, who had come from every village of Galilee and Judea and from Jerusalem. And the power of the Lord was with him to heal" (v. 17). There was power in the air, a spiritual St. Elmo's fire. Mark adds in his account, "And many were gathered together, so that there was no more room, not even at the door" (Mark 2:2).

The tension on this occasion came from two presences. First, there were the Pharisees and teachers of the Law, who had come from every tiny village of Galilee and Judea and even from Jerusalem—a broad-based investigative committee united in its eagerness to find something wrong with the young rabbi. The committee got to sit down, for they were people of honored rank (cf. Mark 2:6). Squeezed around them stood the curious populace. The other presence was, of course, Jesus, who sat across from them as he calmly preached about the kingdom. The more perceptive onlookers felt involuntary rushes of adrenaline, evidenced by goose bumps and moist palms. The atmosphere crackled. The room was charged.

Believing Jesus Can Heal (vv. 18, 19)

Suddenly, in the midst of the expectant crowd, a disturbance began: "And behold, some men were bringing on a bed a man who was paralyzed, and they were seeking to bring him in and lay him before Jesus, but finding no way to bring him in, because of the crowd, they went up on the roof and let him down with his bed through the tiles[1] into the midst before Jesus" (vv. 18, 19).

Comparing Luke's account with Mark 2:3, we see four men bearing a litter on which lay a paralytic, prone and helpless. As they approached the fringe of the dense crowd, their attempts to get through met with impassive rebuffs. After comforting their friend as they conferred with one another, they picked up the litter and circled around the crowd to the side of the house where there was likely an outside stairway leading up to the house's flat roof. Or perhaps they ascended a neighbor's stairs and stepped across to the roof of the crowded house. However it happened, after some hauling and lifting they had their friend on the roof, where they paused to catch their breath.

The four then proceeded to tear a hole in the roof! The typical roof of that day consisted of timbers laid parallel to each other about two or three feet apart. Sticks were closely laid crosswise upon the timbers, and the structure was padded with reeds, thistles, and twigs. The whole thing was overlaid with about a foot of earth, which was packed down to minimize leakage. All told, the roof was about two feet thick. During the spring, grass flourished on these primitive roofs. So the paralytic's friends had their work cut out for them—they were performing a mini excavation.

Those inside the house first heard shoveling and then, with increasing distinctness, the voices of the four men as they tore the thatch away and removed the roofing from between the beams. Debris began to fall upon those inside, and then a crack of light widened to the size of a man. Words were exchanged between those inside and those on the roof. Then a warning came from above, and the paralytic's bed was lowered on ropes.

What a photo op! Above, the light streaming past them in dusty beams, were four sweaty, impish, determined faces. Below were Pharisees and teachers of the Law shaking dirt from their robes. And in between was the paralytic and the Prince. This Capernaum caper would go down in history.

Love

How those four loved their friend! Their love overcame daunting obstacles. They would not be put off by the unyielding crowd. Because of their love they temporarily "vandalized" another's property to achieve their end. They ignored the judgments of those around them. Perhaps the paralyzed man was a beloved brother or uncle or father. Or maybe he was simply a neighbor with whom they had grown up.

One thing is certain: they cared about him, and their love was the first reason for the deliverance he was about to experience. This is how it was and is with God too, for God so loved the world that he made the ultimate sacrifice for us (cf. John 3:16). He dug, so to speak, through the roof of the world and lowered his Son down so Jesus could die for our sins.

The same holds true for missionaries. Their love for God produces a love for people and ultimately the inconvenience of moving into another culture despite the risk of being misunderstood. They may live in a difficult area where medical care is primitive and they are unappreciated. Nothing but immense love would sustain this.

In our own lives, our family and friends will very likely not know the healing touch of Christ unless we have the kind of love that rips open roofs. If we truly love those around us, we will pray regularly and fervently for their salvation. We will risk being judged as fools in our efforts to win them to Christ. If we are not praying, if we are not prying open any roofs, do we really love them?

Conviction

Coupled with the four friends' love was the conviction (shared by the paralytic) that Jesus was the only hope the man had. Similarly, Peter boldly declared, "And there is salvation in no one else, for there is no other name under heaven given among men by which we must be saved" (Acts 4:12). This is why Paul passionately wrote, "I have great sorrow and unceasing anguish in my heart. For I could wish that I myself were accursed and cut off from Christ for the sake of my brothers, my kinsmen according to the flesh. They are Israelites . . ." (Romans 9:2–4a). When a Christian believes Jesus is the only way, he or she will go to great lengths to encourage his or her friends to come to Jesus.

Do we truly believe this, or do we merely say it as an evangelical *shibboleth* (cf. Judges 12:4–7)? The importance of the conviction that Jesus is the only way cannot be overstated. It is the key to removing roofs—to missions—to evangelism—to the gospel itself.

Faith

Along with their love and conviction, the four friends had great faith. There is no way they would have gone to such outrageous extremes if they did not believe that Jesus could and would heal their friend. They all possessed faith's dynamic certitude (cf. Hebrews 11:1). A wavering faith would have opted out when they began digging up the roof, if not sooner. "Ah, man, this is embarrassing. You'll have to finish without me." Determined to bring their friend to Jesus, confident he would help the invalid, the faithful quartet worked on.

Their faith was *persistent*. Once they had their friend on the stretcher, there was no stopping them. None of them said, "The crowd is too big. I guess this isn't the Lord's will." Instead they started climbing! Jesus lauded such action when he said, "From the days of John the Baptist until now the kingdom of heaven has suffered violence, and the violent take it by force" (Matthew 11:12). When the four tore through the roof, they took the kingdom with determined force. Such graced violence is the key for the church making the impact it should.

Their faith was *creative*. Some who were standing idly by and saw the four's success probably thought, "Why didn't I think of that?" Perhaps they did not love as much or believe as passionately as the four friends. A faith that truly believes Christ is the only way will be inventive. This is the genius behind the Quito radio station HCJB, which sits directly on the equator at 10,000 feet and broadcasts the gospel to virtually the entire globe seven days a week, twenty-four hours a day. The almost legendary creativity of that ministry springs from the passionate, driving conviction that Christ is the only hope for the world. If you really love your neighbors, you will find a way to bring them to the love of Christ.

Their faith was *sacrificial*. Someone would have to repair the roof, and that would require time, labor, and expense. A faith that brings Christ's power to the world must always be willing to pay the price. Few Christians have influenced the church more in their time than did Francis and Edith Schaeffer. But there was a cost. Schaeffer wrote in *The Church at the End of the 20th Century*:

> In about the first three years of L'Abri [Francis Schaeffer's Christian fellowship group] all our wedding presents were wiped out. Our sheets were torn. Holes were burned in our rugs. Drugs came into our place. People vomited on our rugs. . . . Sure it is a danger to your family, and you must be careful. But have you ever risked it?[2]

The Schaeffers risked it because they believed Christ was the only answer.

So we see in the lives of the four stretcher-bearers how Christ's power is unleashed in the world—through *love*, through *conviction*, and through *faith*.

Do we truly love our families, our neighbors, our colleagues? Do we believe Christ is the only way? Where is our persistence, our creativity, our sacrifice?

Believing Jesus Cannot Forgive (vv. 20–23)

The real paralytics that day were the Pharisees and teachers of the Law. In marked contrast to the four stretcher-bearers, they were just "sitting there" (v. 17). As religious leaders charged with the care of their people, they should have been directing traffic to Jesus. Or at least when the roof parted, they should have reached up to receive the poor cripple. But instead of love they showed indifference. Instead of faith they issued criticism. Both attitudes hinder faith and healing.

Of course, Jesus knew exactly what was going on. So he decided to use this charged moment as the sun's rays lit the dusty air above the newly arrived paralytic. Knowing that the religious officials were looking for something to pin on him, he gave it to them, or so they thought. "And when he saw their faith, he said, 'Man, your sins are forgiven you'" (v. 20). This was a calculatedly provocative statement.

From an uninformed perspective Jesus' statement seems cruel. Here is a wretched paralytic, hopeful of healing, whose friends have assaulted Heaven to find him a cure, and Jesus merely says, "Man, your sins are forgiven you." He says nothing, does nothing about the man's desperate physical state. The paralytic's hopes may have deflated like a punctured balloon.

From the Pharisees' perspective, Jesus' pronouncement was blatant blasphemy, because only God can forgive sin. Thus Jesus was claiming to be equal with God. Such an assault on the holy name was punishable with death (cf. Leviticus 24:10, 11, 14–16, 23).[3] An expression of perverse satisfaction spread among the Pharisees and the teachers of the Law as they "began to question, saying, 'Who is this who speaks blasphemies? Who can forgive sins but God alone?'" (v. 21).

Why did Jesus do this? First, despite the man's physical distress, his greatest need by far was forgiveness of sin. What folly to obtain bodily wholeness, only to go into eternity without Christ. Forgiveness was a far greater work, for it cost Jesus his life. Jesus met the greatest need first, and forever. Perhaps despite his disappointment the paralytic felt a lift from his soul.

Second, the man may well have been a paralytic due to the guilt of some real or imagined sin. Physical impairments sometimes have a moral base. Whatever the situation, Jesus' words were a prelude to full healing.

Third, Jesus pronounced forgiveness so he could confront his detractors with the implications of the healing he was about to perform. Verses 22, 23 reveal his logic: "When Jesus perceived their thoughts, he answered them, 'Why do you question in your hearts? Which is easier, to say, "Your sins are forgiven you," or to say, "Rise and walk"?'" The Pharisees would naturally think forgiving sins would be easier because no one could verify it, and that the healing would be harder because it would be subject to objective verification. So Jesus put a lock on his spiritual logic by verifying the *moral* miracle of forgiveness by the *physical* miracle of healing.

Jesus' Authority to Forgive Substantiated (vv. 24–26)

Out of that electric atmosphere lightning struck:

> "But that you may know that the Son of Man has authority on earth to forgive sins"—he said to the man who was paralyzed—"I say to you, rise, pick up your bed and go home." And immediately he rose up before them and picked up what he had been lying on and went home, glorifying God. And amazement seized them all, and they glorified God and were filled with awe, saying, "We have seen extraordinary things today." (vv. 24–26)

The paralytic was on his feet, radiant in the dusty shafts of light, his bed on his shoulder, and he began striding around praising God. The delighted crowd oohed and aahed. The Pharisees and company frowned. Spurgeon wrote:

> I think I see him! He sets one foot down to God's glory, he plants the other to the same note, he walks to God's glory . . . he carries his bed to God's glory, he moves his whole body to the glory of God, he speaks, he shouts, he sings, he leaps to the glory of God.[4]

Maybe the paralytic and his friends danced down the street while the crowd clapped in rhythm. Certainly he had reason to dance. As he went home, he bore something far more impressive than his bed—a clean heart, the greatest miracle of all—and so no guilt, no bitterness, no tension. Someday his newly restored limbs would wither. But he would remain perpetually new because within his soul there was now a spring of everlasting life (cf. John 4:14).

This is what Luke the theologian has been building toward in his carefully arranged chain of stories. From the beginning of Christ's public ministry in 4:14–30, when Jesus' authority was rejected in Nazareth, the events have repeatedly demonstrated his authority to heal and to order away evil spirits (cf. 4:32–36, 41). When he used his authority to call the disciples to be fishers of men, the subject of sin was introduced as Peter cried, "Depart from me, for I am a sinful man, O Lord" (5:8). Next he healed a leper, doing away with a disease that illustrated the ravages of sin (5:12–15). Now he forgives the paralytic's sins, declaring that "the Son of Man has authority on earth to forgive sins" (v. 24; cf. Matthew 9:6; Mark 2:10). And in the following text he will show his authority to call sinners to follow him (5:27–32).

Thus the great point of this dynamic narrative is that Jesus has authority to forgive sins. His authority began with the incarnation when he genuinely became one of us, except for sin. His authority became evident in his leading a *sinless* life, so that he could honestly say, "Which one of you convicts me of sin?" (John 8:46) and "I always do the things that are pleasing to him [the Father]" (John 8:29). His authority rang from the cross where he became our *atonement*. "For our sake he made him to be sin who knew no sin, so that in him we might become the righteousness of God" (2 Corinthians 5:21; cf. Galatians 3:10–13). His authority to forgive sin abides because of his eternal *priesthood*: "He holds his priesthood permanently, because he continues forever. Consequently, he is able to save to the uttermost those who draw near to God through him, since he always lives to make intercession for them" (Hebrews 7:24, 25). The Greek word translated "uttermost" combines the idea of *completeness* with the idea of *eternality*—"for all time" (RSV). Christ has given us a complete, absolute, total, eternal salvation![5] Salvation is entirely Christ's work, from beginning to end.

Whoever a man (or woman) is, whatever he has done, no matter how heinous his sin—whether murder, infidelity, perversion, child abuse, betrayal, embezzlement, lying, jealousy, hateful gossip, or whatever—Christ can save him completely and eternally. This is the gospel, the good news. This is why we shout with Paul, "I am not ashamed of the gospel, for it is the power of God for salvation to everyone who believes, to the Jew first and also to the Greek" (Romans 1:16).

The Lord can do anything he wants. He can heal any disease he pleases. But the greatest miracle, the only one that is eternal, is the forgiveness of sin. Has he ever said to you, "Your sins are forgiven you" (v. 20)?

Closing Reflections

As we noted earlier, Luke says of this event, "And the power of the Lord was with him to heal" (v. 17). That power was unleashed by the *love*, *conviction*, and *faith* of the paralytic's four friends. We must love those around us so much that we will tear through roofs for their sakes. We must have the conviction that Jesus is the only way. We must believe that he can and will heal those who come to him.

To those longing to be healed, do you believe Jesus is the only way? Do you believe he can and will heal you? If so, hear Jesus' words now: "I am the way, and the truth, and the life. No one comes to the Father except through me" (John 14:6).

22

Calling Sinners

LUKE 5:27–32

BEFORE COMING TO CHRIST everyone has a spiritual need, though some have a greater awareness than others of the effects of sin in their lives. Sometimes the sense of need develops as we encounter difficult straits in our life—once-held morals fall, unhealthy appetites dominate us, our marriage falters, our family suffers, or our career sours. Guilt begins to choke us. Equilibrium, well-being, and peace become aching memories. Life becomes desolate—we have "no hope and [are] without God in the world" (Ephesians 2:12). But thankfully, sometimes this sense of need drives a person into the arms of Christ.

> Naked, come to Thee for dress:
> Helpless, look to Thee for grace.

Meeting Christ brings a peace previously unknown. "Peace I leave with you," says Jesus, "my peace I give to you" (John 14:27). The soul then has a sense of rest and well-being it has never known, even in the best of times. Getting to know Christ better and better through his Word brings us divine wisdom for living (James 1:5), a wisdom that slows down or reverses the destructive patterns in our lives. We experience new stability, self-control, and discipline.

While it is true that much of the ravages of sin cannot be undone (such as the finalities of divorce and remarriage), we can develop personal qualities that enhance the capacity for friendship and intimacy. Rightly related to God, Christians experience increasing fellowship with each other (cf. 1 John 1:3). Strong friendships ensue. Marriages become stronger, and families more nurturing. Through the Biblical virtues of integrity, honesty, hard work, and prudence, God's people become pillars in their churches and communities. But unfortunately, Christians also sometimes become adept at maintaining a façade of spirituality that does not necessarily match what is going on within them. No one swears. Everyone is well mannered. Biblical metaphors effortlessly flow through conversations. Being good, externally, becomes second nature. Everyone seems so "together." There are few evident needs, and those that do exist are skillfully disguised. But underneath . . .

It is too easy for Christian believers to forget that they are sinners—yes, justified, but still, in themselves, weak and vulnerable. "We all stumble in many ways" (James 3:2). The sinners are out there—not in the church. Church becomes an elite club that few on the outside want to join, even if they could.

The radical regenerating work of Christ sours when redeemed people lose sight of their continuing need—when they forget that though their eternal future is secure, in their daily walk they are frail and needy. The church can easily become a self-righteous subculture with no room or sympathy for "sinners."

This is a real danger to the evangelical church. We have been gloriously saved. We are hardworking. We are spiritually and perhaps materially prosperous. Many of us have few discernible needs. But are we seeing ourselves as we really are? Jesus' warning to the Laodicean church may apply to us: "You say, I am rich, I have prospered, and I need nothing, not realizing that you are wretched, pitiable, poor, blind, and naked" (Revelation 3:17).

Jesus' calling of Levi speaks to this very issue, and a study of it can help us assess ourselves and know what to do.

Levi's Call (vv. 27, 28)

Levi was a tax collector for the Roman government. The Romans collected their taxes through a system called "tax farming." They assessed a district a fixed tax figure and then sold the right to collect taxes to the highest bidder. The buyer then had to hand over the assessed figure at the end of the year and could keep whatever he gathered above that amount. Such a system invited extortion. The potential for abuse was further aided by both the primitive record keeping and the limited means of communication in the ancient world, both of which made it difficult for people to verify when they were being exploited or to appeal it.

There were two categories of taxes. *Fixed taxes* left little room for extortion. These included the poll tax, which all men and women paid simply because they were alive, the ground tax, which required one tenth of all grain, wine, and oil, and the income tax (1 percent of earnings).[1]

It was the second area of taxes—namely, *duties and tolls*—that allowed the tax collectors to rob others. The people paid separate taxes for using roads and for docking in harbors, and also import and export duties, and even a sales tax on certain items. There was even a cart tax, in which each wheel was taxed![2]

The system was a breeding ground for graft and exploitation. A tax collector could stop anyone on the road, make him unpack his bundles, and charge just about anything his larcenous heart desired. If the traveler could not pay, the tax collector would offer to loan him money at an exorbitant rate. Such men were skilled extortionists. The *Talmud* classified them as robbers (Sanhedrin 25b). Not surprisingly, they often allied themselves with thugs and enforcers—the scum of Jewish society. So rare was honesty in the profession that a Roman writer remarked in amazement that he once saw a monument to an honest tax collector![3]

Jewish tax collectors were easily the most hated men in Hebrew society—despicable, rich vermin. They were classed with "extortioners, [the] unjust, adulterers" (18:11), with prostitutes (Matthew 21:32), and with pagan Gentiles (Matthew 18:17). They were not only hated for their robbery, but also because they were lackeys of the Romans. Tax collectors could not serve as witnesses in court and were excommunicated from the synagogues.[4] Low-life Levi and his friends were the lowest of the lowest.

Understanding how much Levi was loathed, we can appreciate the drama in the opening description of his encounter with Jesus: "After this he went out and saw a tax collector named Levi, sitting at the tax booth" (v. 27). They very likely had seen each other before as Levi had stood at the fringes of various crowds listening to Jesus. Perhaps they had even talked privately about spiritual matters. But now Jesus stopped and took a good look at Levi (the word "saw," according to Abbott-Smith, means "careful and deliberate vision which interprets . . . its object"[5]). Such a contemplative look from Jesus probably made Levi nervously wonder, "What does Jesus want from me?"

The answer came like a bolt of lightning: "And he said to him, 'Follow me.' And leaving everything, he rose and followed him" (vv. 27, 28). This does not mean that he never again returned to set his affairs straight. But what Luke stresses is that he made a decisive break with his old life (indicated by the aorist participle in the Greek) and followed Jesus—literally, "was following him" (imperfect indicative)—as a continuous pattern of life.[6] In doing this Levi made a substantial sacrifice because he was wealthy. There were some quiet heroics here because, unlike the fishermen who had followed Jesus, he could not go back to his old job if things did not work out.[7]

And, indeed, Levi did follow Christ for the rest of his life, for this Levi is none other than Matthew the Gospel writer (cf. Matthew 9:9; 10:2, 3). Whether he was named Matthew when Jesus first called him, we do not know. Many think that just as Simon was named Peter ("the rock") by the Lord, so Levi was likewise tagged Matthew ("gift of God"). If so, this was divine poetry, because this covetous rip-off artist would become, as his name suggested, a gift of God to his people.

This was utterly amazing, because of all the people in Capernaum, Levi was the most publicly unacceptable candidate for discipleship. Jesus sought out the man no one else wanted, the one who some wished would come under God's most severe judgment. This is one of the glories of Jesus' ministry. And this is what Luke has been building toward in his Gospel arrangement—Jesus' healing the impossibly disfigured leper (thus demonstrating his power to heal the ravages of sin), then his pronouncement to those gathered around the paralytic that "the Son of Man has authority on earth to forgive sins" (5:24), and now this. Jesus offers real forgiveness for real guilt!

We also learn from this that Jesus sees what we can become even while we are lost in our sins. Christ saw in the disfigured life of Levi (tax collector) a Matthew (writer, evangelist, collector of souls). He sees sinners, with all their moral deformity, through his ultimate artist's eye. "For we are his workmanship, created in Christ Jesus for good works" (Ephesians 2:10). No matter how scarred and ugly a sinner's life may be, Christ can make it into something beautiful for God. He has devoted his life to it!

Levi's Banquet (v. 29)

Evidently Levi had no regrets about giving up everything to follow Jesus. He even hosted his own good-bye party: "And Levi made him a great feast in his house, and there was a large company of tax collectors and others reclining at table with them" (v. 29). Levi had the means to do it big, and he did. The large crowd would have required extra servants and a substantial outlay of money, but that was fine with Levi. They feasted in the traditional arrangement and posture, reclining on their left sides, fully enjoying the cuisine and libations of Palestine. Levi's reasons for the big bash relate to our own experience as believers.

Levi hosted the feast, not for selfish reasons, but as a celebration of what had happened to him. Feasting is for laughter and merriment (Ecclesiastes

10:19). The ex-tax collector regarded the change in his life as an occasion for rejoicing, as indeed it was. Nothing is a greater occasion for rejoicing than conversion! Bishop Ryle had it right when he said:

> It is a far more important event than being married, or coming of age, or being made a nobleman, or receiving a great fortune. It is the birth of an immortal soul! It is the rescue of a sinner from hell! It is a passage from death to life! It is being made a king and priest for evermore! It is being provided for, both in time and eternity! It is adoption into the noblest and richest of all families, the family of God![8]

Coming to know Christ is a great reason to party!

Levi also put on the banquet for Jesus, for the Savior was the guest of honor. Without him there would have been no celebration. The desire to honor God is the natural reflex of the soul that has received the divine touch. Jesus was everything to Levi (Matthew)!

The retired tax collector also hosted the feast for his friends' sake. The soul that has received God's grace does not want to go to Heaven alone.[9] This is the way it was with Andrew too, as the apostle John records: "He first found his own brother Simon and said to him, 'We have found the Messiah'" (John 1:41). Remember too the Samaritan woman's invitation: "Come, see a man who told me all that I ever did. Can this be the Christ?" (John 4:29). Levi knew that if his needy friends would meet Jesus and hear his words, they would be moved and perhaps follow him. Levi's changed heart longed for this.

As courses were served, cups were filled and refilled, and the lamps burnt low, Jesus engaged needy souls in conversation, and Levi's satisfaction swelled.

Jesus Criticized (v. 30)

The Pharisees and the teachers of the Law did not share Levi's joy. Of course, they had not been invited to the party, but they had gotten a full report. Some may have even watched the proceedings, unseen, through an open window. The Pharisees were the separatists of contemporary Jewish culture. From such Old Testament passages as Leviticus 10:10 ("You are to distinguish between the holy and the common, and between the unclean and the clean"), they developed the idea of "salvation by segregation."[10] They were deadly serious about their lifestyle, which had strict rules about ceremonial purity in regard to places, objects, people, and food. Their legalistic mind-set had no room for parties like the one Levi threw for Jesus.

Aghast at the motley gathering, they came, not to Jesus, but to his followers: "And the Pharisees and their scribes grumbled at his disciples, saying, 'Why do you eat and drink with tax collectors and sinners?'" (v. 30). The coupling of tax collectors with "sinners" took their indictment beyond Jews, who had some hope if they repented, to Gentiles, who were characterized as lawless, godless, and hopeless.[11] In their view, Jesus had defiled himself by consorting with the collective Hebrew and Gentile scum of Galilee. His eating with them indicated friendship and full acceptance.[12]

It never occurred to the Pharisees and the teachers of the Law that their lack of concern for sinners and their cavalier mercilessness had distanced them from God. These experts had the Scriptures, but they had failed to truly read them. For example, when the prophet Micah stated the Lord's case against Israel in the sixth chapter of his prophecy, he concluded by asking, "And what does the LORD require of you but to do justice, and to love kindness, and to walk humbly with your God?" (Micah 6:8). From Micah's perspective, the Pharisees' lack of concern for others indicated that they were completely out of sync with the heart of God.

The parallel account of Levi's calling in Matthew 9:13 records an extra line from Jesus: "Go and learn what this means, 'I desire mercy, and not sacrifice.'" This is a reference to Hosea 6:6 where Hosea, like Micah, condemns Israel for its attention to ceremony without caring for others. The whole of Hosea 6:6 reads, "For I desire steadfast love and not sacrifice, the knowledge of God rather than burnt offerings." Evidently Hosea's words were immensely important to Jesus. They lay at the heart of his mission. He had come to call those who knew they were sinners, not those who thought they were righteous.

Those who did not care about sinners were not only out of accord with Christ but were separate from him. Their mercilessness was a sign of their unregenerate hearts. The truth of Hosea 6:6 meant so much to Jesus that he apparently referenced it again in the Sermon on the Mount: "Blessed are the merciful, for they shall receive mercy" (Matthew 5:7). Superficial religious observance of rites and rituals without love and mercy for needy sinners means nothing (cf. Amos 5:21–24).

The Pharisees had religiously taken themselves right out of their faith. They had all the civilities. Their conversation was a collage of Scriptures and holy allusions. They never swore. They kept their homes in order. They regularly attended synagogue. They were "good people." They had no apparent need.

Does this ever happen to Christians? In the eighteenth century the Church of England had become so elitist and inhospitable to the common man that in 1739 John Wesley had to take to graveyards and fields to preach the gospel. We have poignant accounts of his preaching to thirty thousand coal miners at dawn in the fields, and the resulting saving power of the gospel evidenced by tears streaming white trails down coal-darkened faces. Wesley was no schismatic, but because there was no room in the established church for the common people, he reluctantly founded the Methodist-Episcopal Church. Tragically, a mere one hundred years later Methodist William Booth noticed that the poorest and most degraded were never in church.

Richard Collier in his history of the Salvation Army, *The General Next to God*, describes Booth's experience:

> Broad Street congregation never forgot that electric Sunday in 1846: the gas jets, dancing on whitewashed wall, the Minister, the Rev. Samuel Dunn, seated comfortably on his red plush throne, a concord of voices swelling into the evening's fourth hymn:
>
> Foul I to the fountain fly;
> Wash me, Savior, or I die.
>
> The chapel's outer door suddenly shattered open, engulfing a white scarf of fog. In its wake came a shuffling shabby contingent of men and women, wilting nervously under the stony stares of mill-managers, shop-keepers and their well-dressed wives. In their rear, afire with zeal, marched "Wilful Will" Booth, cannily blocking the efforts of the more reluctant to turn back. To his dismay the Rev. Dunn saw that young Booth was actually ushering his charges, none of whose clothes would have raised five shillings in his own pawnshop, into the very best seats; pewholders' seats, facing the pulpit. . . .
>
> This was unprecedented, for the poor, if they came to chapel, entered by another door, to be segregated on benches without backs or cushions, behind a partition which screened off the pulpit. . . .
>
> Oblivious of the mounting atmosphere, Booth joined full-throatedly in the service—even, he later admitted, hoping this devotion to duty might rate special commendation. All too soon he learned the unpalatable truth: since Wesley's day, Methodism had become "respectable."[13]

This experience, followed by many similar rejections by the "good people" in the church, led to William and Catherine Booth's expulsion by the Methodists and fourteen years of poverty before founding the Salvation Army.

We too must beware—we can be "Christianized" right out of our Christianity. We can become a club—an elite society that has all the right externals but has forgotten to show mercy to the lost.

We must never forget that we are sinners, and that each of us can honestly say, "*I* am the foremost" (cf. 1 Timothy 1:15). We dare not forget that people without Christ are lost sinners, "having no hope and without God in the world . . . dead in [their] trespasses and sins" (Ephesians 2:12, 1). We must keep preaching the gospel to a lost world, inviting sinners to come to Christ and into his church. Following Christ requires getting our hands dirty, believing Jesus' words, "Those who are well have no need of a physician, but those who are sick. I have not come to call the righteous but sinners to repentance" (vv. 31, 32). He did not come to call self-righteous people like the Pharisees. Christ has given us his righteousness, but we are not intrinsically, in ourselves, righteous (cf. 2 Corinthians 5:21; 1 Corinthians 1:30; Philippians 3:9). *Christ* is our salvation and our life!

Sinners without Christ have only one hope—Jesus. They must look nowhere but to him. If you have not come to Christ but are now hearing his call, will you come to him today?

> Nothing in my hand I bring,
> Simply to the cross I cling.

23

The New and the Old

LUKE 5:33–39

THE GREAT BANQUET THAT LEVI, the tax collector, hosted for his friends and for Jesus offended the conventional religious establishment. They were appalled at the collection of "sinners," the lowlife Jewish and Gentile flotsam of Galilee (cf. 5:30). Interestingly, the Pharisees and other critics were right in one sense—Levi's friends were indeed sinners, spiritual lepers in whom iniquity had run its course. If the spiritual reality could have been translated into physical terms, it would have been a macabre feast—leprous stubs thrusting the banquet's fare into gaping, featureless faces. It was truly a gathering of the living dead (cf. Ephesians 2:1–3).The good people of Galilee too were taken aback that these spiritual lepers were celebrating. And the Lord's explanation that "Those who are well have no need of a physician, but those who are sick" carried no weight with his horrified critics. They could not fathom his disciples' participation in the shocking event, or their generally joyous approach to life, which seemed to exclude fasting.

So at an opportune time, egged on by the Pharisees' evil intentions, some of John the Baptist's disciples approached Jesus (cf. Matthew 9:14; Mark 2:18). As Luke recounts it, "And they said to him, 'The disciples of John fast often and offer prayers, and so do the disciples of the Pharisees, but yours eat and drink'" (v. 33). If we wonder why John the Baptist's disciples would put forth such a biting accusation, we must remember that John himself was an ascetic who lived a barren lifestyle and whose message called for mourning and repentance. John came as the ultimate and final prophet of the old covenant to prepare the way for the new covenant of the Messiah. His style was that of an Old Testament seer, a style that his followers naturally adopted.

What they were seeing at Levi's house did not seem to mesh with what they had been taught.

Also, fasting was a conventional practice of Old Testament religion. Though fasting was only commanded once in the entire Old Testament, and then only implicitly in connection with the Day of Atonement (cf. Leviticus 16:24–31), its practice became widespread. In many situations, fasting was quite proper, as, for example, when the Jews mourned the genocidal edict of Xerxes (Esther 4:1–3), or when the prophet Joel called Israel to a repentant fast (Joel 1:13, 14; cf. Isaiah 58:6–9; 1 Kings 21:27). But along with these appropriate uses came abuses, like those who supposed that their fasting brought a self-achieved holiness, a works-righteousness, despite the fact that the prophets warned against such thinking (cf. Isaiah 58:3–5; Jeremiah 14:12).

Predictably, by Jesus' time the Pharisees had decreed that godly people fast twice a week (on the second and fifth days of the week—Mondays and Thursdays).[1] For them fasting meant mourning.[2] Some Pharisees viewed it as a sacrifice, a mournful offering of one's own flesh to God, that would gain God's attention. The overall effect of this was to view true religion as solemn, joyless, and gloomy. Therefore, when fasting the Pharisees tried to look as forlorn as possible. Some actually whitened their faces to effect an emaciated look, refused to wash, and wore their clothes in shoddy disarray.[3] The supposition was that you could not be spiritual unless you were uncomfortable. Spirituality, they thought, consists of doing things you do not want to do, and refraining from the things you want to do.

We have our parallels today, like the preacher's voice—dolefully addressing God with tomb-like tones that better fit a Stephen King novel than a gospel proclamation. Erma Bombeck wrote about sitting in church one Sunday when a small child turned around and began to smile at the people behind her. When her mother noticed, she told her daughter in a stage whisper, "Stop that grinning—you're in church," gave her a swat, and said, "That's better!" Bombeck concluded that some people come to church looking like they have just read the will of their rich aunt only to learn that she left everything to her pet hamster!

I once knew a man who believed Christians should always be solemn. He was a young believer, full of zeal, but not knowing how to keep things in perspective, he would go off on self-righteous tangents. On one particular occasion he noted that never once in Scripture does it say Jesus smiled or laughed—and therefore Christians should not smile. Never mind that arguments from silence are patently dangerous. Never mind the repeated smiling wit of Christ. I can still see my friend sitting in church with his wife and a few like-minded friends—righteous but sober, holy but unsmiling.

The issue behind all of this is the relationship between the old covenant (the Law of Moses) and the new covenant (the gospel of Christ). Jesus was about to give his critics a dynamic three-part answer.

A Relational Answer (vv. 34, 35)

The Presence

Jesus answered those who criticized the eating, drinking, and joyous demeanor of his disciples by asking, "Can you make wedding guests fast while the bridegroom is with them?" (v. 34). The explanation was divinely bold and packed with meaning for his Jewish listeners. A newly married Jewish couple did not honeymoon but stayed home for a week-long open house during which there was continual feasting and celebrating. The bride and groom were treated like king and queen that week (sometimes they even wore crowns). They were attended by chosen friends known as "guests of the bridegroom," which means literally, "sons of the bridal chamber." These wedding guests were exempted from all fasting through a rabbinical ruling that said, "All in attendance on the bridegroom are relieved of all religious observances which would lessen their joy."[4]

Jesus asserted that his presence justified a feast, and that his followers had the joyous privilege of a perpetual wedding party. In such exalted circumstances it is wrong, if not downright impossible, to mourn. Jesus' disciples experienced temporary unhappiness when they saw their own sin or failed him. But being in the presence of Jesus brought them relentless joy.

Jesus was a joyous person who "for the joy that was set before him endured the cross" (Hebrews 12:2). His sinless human personality radiated joy. He was love incarnate, and people felt his love. Jesus cared, and his disciples knew it. His presence evoked a sense of security and well-being. Jesus was also holy, and to be in the presence of perfect transcendent purity made his followers aware of their sin. But his presence was also a bath to the soul, for he forgives sin. Further, Jesus was truth, without the slightest deception. And Jesus was power. Lepers were completely cleansed at his word, and stormy seas became calm. Jesus brought genuine release from real guilt, liberation from bondage. As they followed him, his disciples awoke each day with bounding hope. They found life to be a continual feast in the presence of Jesus.

There would indeed come a time when the disciples would fast, as Jesus explained: "The days will come when the bridegroom is taken away from them, and then they will fast in those days" (v. 35). That happened at the cross, but their sorrow gave way to the joy of the resurrection, the ascension, Christ's being seated at the right hand of God, and the coming of the Holy Spirit (cf. John 16:19–21). Luke 5:33–39 touches directly on this matter.

The Temple

Here we see an exquisite truth about Christ's presence that, when understood, will make our souls sing. The temple in the Old Testament represented the presence of God among his people. The temple with its sacrificial system provided the setting and means for God to bring people into relationship with himself.

But when we read the New Testament, one thing is clear: a new temple has already come into existence, and it is none other than Jesus Christ himself. John describes it like this: "And the Word became flesh and dwelt among us" (John 1:14). The literal translation of the Greek is, "and *tabernacled* among us." Jesus is like the tabernacle in the wilderness. His life and sacrifice provided the place and means to bring people into relationship with God. Jesus is the temple—God dwelling with us (cf. Matthew 1:23). Jesus referred to his own body as the temple when he said, "Destroy this temple, and in three days I will raise it up" (John 2:19). And as we know, his temple was resurrected! Jesus is the temple!

Stupendous as this is, there is even more: those indwelt by Christ become temples.

> So then you are no longer strangers and aliens, but you are fellow citizens with the saints and members of the household of God, built on the foundation of the apostles and prophets, Christ Jesus himself being the cornerstone, in whom the whole structure, being joined together, grows into a holy temple in the Lord. In him you also are being built together into a dwelling place for God by the Spirit. (Ephesians 2:19–22)

Astounding! The great temple of Israel was superseded by an even greater temple, Christ himself. And by virtue of his indwelling us, we are temples! We are in relationship with God, and he is present in us! "Do you not know that you are God's temple and that God's Spirit dwells in you?" (1 Corinthians 3:16). "For we are the temple of the living God; as God said, 'I will make my dwelling among them and walk among them, and I will be their God, and they shall be my people'" (2 Corinthians 6:16).

The vast temple theology of the Old Testament is fulfilled in Christ: "And I heard a loud voice from the throne saying, 'Behold, the dwelling place of God is with man. He will dwell with them, and they will be his people, and God himself will be with them as their God'" (Revelation 21:3). No wonder Jesus is called "the Alpha and Omega"—"the first and the last"—"the beginning and the end." Christ is all in all—he is everything!

This is why knowing Christ is a perpetual celebration, a perpetual feast, and why joy is the inevitable emotion of the fullness of the Holy Spirit (cf. Galatians 5:22). This is why the first Franciscans were reproved for laughing in the church. They couldn't help it because they were so happy. This is why the first Methodists set the songs of Zion to dance music. This is why the early preacher Uke jumped for joy.[5] This is why Charles Simeon was able to watch a converted prisoner stand on the gallows and for a half hour joyfully declare his faith, after which "He then commended his soul into the hands of Jesus and launched into eternity without a doubt, without a sigh."[6] This is why Martin Luther said, "A Christian should and must be a cheerful person. If he isn't, the devil is tempting him."[7]

The bridegroom is with us, and we are the bride (cf. Ephesians 5:23–27)! Because he is the bridegroom of our soul, life is a celebration.

Parabolic Answers (vv. 36–38)

Christ now turned from the fundamental relational answer to twin parabolic explanations.

Garments

"He also told them a parable: 'No one tears a piece from a new garment and puts it on an old garment. If he does, he will tear the new, and the piece from the new will not match the old'" (v. 36). Judaism, as good as it was, had become an old, worn-out garment. It could not be patched with a few things taken from Christ's gospel. Paul and Barnabas understood this (cf. Acts 15; Galatians 4:3–5; Philippians 3:2–14). But some compromised, causing great difficulties (cf. Acts 15—the Judaizers; Galatians 2:11–21—Peter's lapse). The gospel of the new covenant is simply too dynamic for the old covenant structures.

Wineskins

Jesus sealed the point with another, even more apt illustration: "And no one puts new wine into old wineskins. If he does, the new wine will burst the skins and it will be spilled, and the skins will be destroyed. But new wine must be put into fresh wineskins" (vv. 37, 38). In ancient cultures, the skins of goats were stripped off as nearly whole as possible and partly tanned, so they could be filled with new wine. Their natural elasticity and strength would allow the fermenting new wine to expand. However, if new wine was put into old wineskins, their brittle, inflexible condition would cause them to burst, and both wine and wineskins would be lost.

Christ produces an expanding joy in the hearts of his own. The new wine of life cannot be restrained by old, unyielding structures.

Shortly after the Armistice of World War I, Dr. Donald Grey Barnhouse visited the battlefields of Belgium. In the first year of the war, the area around the city of Mons had been the scene of a great British retreat. In the last year of the war it was the scene of a great German retreat. For miles to the west of the city, the roads were lined with artillery, tanks, trucks, and other equipment of war that the enemy had abandoned in their hasty flight.

It was a lovely spring day. The sun was shining, and not a breath of wind was blowing. As Barnhouse walked along examining the German war equipment, he noticed that leaves were falling from the great trees arching above the road. He brushed at a leaf that had blown against his breast, and it caught in the belt of his uniform. As he removed it, he pressed it in his fingers, and it disintegrated. He looked up curiously and saw several other leaves falling from the trees. It was not autumn. There was no wind to blow them off. These leaves were seemingly falling without cause.

Then he realized that the most potent force of all was causing them to fall: it was spring. The sap was beginning to run, and the buds were pushing from within. From down beneath the dark earth, roots were sending life along trunk, branch, and twig until that life expelled every bit of deadness that remained from the previous year. It was, as a great Scottish preacher termed it, "the expulsive power of a new affection."[8]

When Christ fills our lives, the swelling life within expands us beyond our imagining. The inner life expels unneeded qualities and fills every aspect of life. Once Christ takes up residence in our lives, every aspect of our being—from our intellect to our emotions to our will—undergoes change. And Christ keeps increasing our spiritual capacity, so that we will always be able to hold more of his fullness. The more we receive, the more we are able to receive.

Jesus brings a superior *relationship* in that he is the temple, the focus and means for fellowship with God. Everything the old temple did, he does better. And when he indwells us, wonder of wonders, we become temples.

This in turn produces a perpetual *joy*. We are not only friends of the bridegroom—we are the bride.

A new dynamic infuses us, so that old structures cannot hold us. Our spiritual capacity has immense possibilities, and we experience a spiritual *fullness* we could not have imagined.

Incredibly, some people are uninterested in any of this. How can this be?

A Proverbial Answer (v. 39)

Jesus then shared a wry proverb, saying, "And no one after drinking old wine desires new, for he says, 'The old is good'" (v. 39). Many people who have not tasted the new are determined never to try it, because they imagine that what they have is "good." They will not even taste the new for sake of comparison. What arrogance, what stubbornness, what folly!

God still gives sinners an incredible offer: the presence of Christ—boundless joy—fullness of soul. The condition? The realization that their old life is not adequate, and the acceptance that Christ is everything—that he is the *Lamb* of God who fulfilled all that the sacrificial system pointed to—that he is the *temple*, the presence of God and the means of a relationship with him—that he is the *bridegroom*, the source of unending joy.

Understanding this, resting all our hopes on him, believing that he is God, that he died for us, that he has made us his bride, that he will be with us forever, and that he is our only hope—this is life!

24

The Lord of the Sabbath

LUKE 6:1–11

SUBSEQUENT TO LUKE'S RECORDING the beginning of Jesus' public ministry and his rejection by his hometown, the Gospel writer has carefully spotlighted seven events that pointed directly to Christ's authority. There will be nine in all, including the present text and the following section, which concludes with the exercise of Jesus' authority in calling the twelve disciples (6:12–16). The authority motif is essential because it heralds Jesus' authority to heal and deliver (4:36), forgive sins (5:24), and call people to himself (6:12–16).

Another motif that flashes gloriously from the opening events of Christ's ministry is that of mercy. His early public words, quoting Isaiah 61:1, 2, were a manifesto of mercy:

> The Spirit of the Lord is upon me,
> because he has anointed me
> to proclaim good news to the poor.
> He has sent me to proclaim liberty to the captives
> and recovering of sight to the blind,
> to set at liberty those who are oppressed,
> to proclaim the year of the Lord's favor. (4:18, 19)

This declaration of mercy was followed by acts of mercy. Jesus immediately healed a demonized man in Capernaum (4:31–37). That same night he tenderly laid his hands on each individual who came to him for healing (4:38–41). After calling Peter, James, and John, he encountered a man covered with leprosy and astonished the onlookers by compassionately placing his hand on the man's leprous body and healing him (5:12–16). Next, he healed a paralytic, mercifully forgiving his sins though he did not ask for that (5:17–26). Then came Levi's banquet, a veritable feast of mercy, because there the spotless Son of God sat down with sinners (5:27–31). At that feast, in answer to the Pharisees' questioning about his associating with sinners, he reminded them of Hosea 6:6, "Go and learn what this means, 'I desire mercy, and not sacrifice'" (Matthew 9:13).

Mercy was at the heart of Jesus' ministry. Hosea 6:6 in its entirety reads, "For I desire steadfast love and not sacrifice, the knowledge of God rather than burnt offerings." Hosea's message to the northern kingdom was that sacrifices and burnt offerings in themselves held no weight with God. What pleased God was a heart devoted to him and a life characterized by loving mercy. Such is inseparable from real faith.

Amos, another eighth-century BC prophet to the northern kingdom, was even more explicit.

> For I know how many are your transgressions and how great are your sins—you who afflict the righteous, who take a bribe, and turn aside the needy in the gate. . . . I hate, I despise your feasts, and I take no delight in your solemn assemblies. Even though you offer me your burnt offerings and grain offerings, I will not accept them; and the peace offerings of your fattened animals, I will not look upon them. Take away from me the noise of your songs; to the melody of your harps I will not listen. But let justice roll down like waters, and righteousness like an ever-flowing stream. (5:12, 21–24)

Religious observance that does not look out for the plight of the needy (i.e., religion without mercy) is unacceptable.

Micah, a contemporary of Hosea and Amos who prophesied to the southern kingdom, gave this truth its most famous expression: "And what does the LORD require of you but to do justice, and to love kindness, and to walk humbly with your God?" (Micah 6:8).

Finally, on the eve of the southern kingdom's Babylonian captivity, Jeremiah urged Shallum, son of King Josiah, to recall the example of his righteous father:

> Do you think you are a king
>   because you compete in cedar?
> Did not your father eat and drink
>   and do justice and righteousness?
>   Then it was well with him.
> He judged the cause of the poor and needy;
>   then it was well.
> Is not this to know me?
>   declares the LORD. (Jeremiah 22:15, 16)

Indisputably, mercy is a sure sign of knowing God and living a life that pleases him.

Such God-pleasing mercy is manifested in one's *social ethics* and in one's *spiritual ethics*. Socially, authentic believers care about the welfare of others. One of the great New Testament expressions of this comes from the apostle John's first epistle: "If anyone has the world's goods and sees his brother in need, yet closes his heart against him, how does God's love abide in him?" (1 John 3:17). Some Christians, uneasy with this material test of spiritual reality, ignore it, but in so doing, they imperil their souls' health.

Spiritually, true believers care intensely about the eternal destiny of others.

> The Pharisees . . . said to his disciples, "Why does your teacher eat with tax collectors and sinners?" But when he heard it, he said, "Those who are well have no need of a physician, but those who are sick. Go and learn what this means, 'I desire mercy, and not sacrifice.' For I came not to call the righteous, but sinners." (Matthew 9:11–13)

True Christians long for God's mercy to come to sinners. True Christians do evangelism!

It was precisely here that Jesus' detractors showed their true colors because they did not care about others' needs, physical or spiritual. And in Luke 6 their attempts to guard the Sabbath further demonstrated just how pathetically impoverished they were. Jesus has just described how the fermenting wine of the new covenant cannot be held in the calcified wineskin of the old covenant, and the subject of Sabbath observance is a logical extension of that discussion.

A Clash over Sustenance (vv. 1–5)

The Occasion

"On a Sabbath, while he was going through the grainfields, his disciples plucked and ate some heads of grain, rubbing them in their hands" (v. 1). The Jewish legal code contained a gracious provision for the hungry that allowed for a person to handpick fruit or grain for personal consumption: "If you go into your neighbor's vineyard, you may eat your fill of grapes, as many as you wish, but you shall not put any in your bag. If you go into your neighbor's standing grain, you may pluck the ears with your hand, but you shall not put a sickle to your neighbor's standing grain" (Deuteronomy 23:24, 25). So the disciples were not guilty of pillaging someone's field. The rub was that they picked the corn on the Sabbath, a day on which the fourth commandment specifically prohibited work:

> Six days you shall labor, and do all your work, but the seventh day is a Sabbath to the LORD your God. On it you shall not do any work, you, or your son, or your daughter, your male servant, or your female servant, or your livestock, or the sojourner who is within your gates. (Exodus 20:9, 10)

Over time the Jewish leaders had developed a series of thirty-nine clarifications of work, exotic legalisms, with each category capable of endless subdivision. The *Mishnah* explicitly listed as three of its thirty-nine categories "reaping . . . threshing, winnowing" (M. Shabbath, 7.2). Jesus' disciples *reaped* when they "plucked . . . some heads of grain" and *threshed* and *winnowed* when they "rub[bed] them in their hands." And when they began to eat the kernels, they prepared food on the Sabbath. The Pharisees were outraged—"Why are you doing what is not lawful to do on the Sabbath?" (v. 2). They thought they had Jesus and company dead to rights in a flagrant breaking of divine law. Their jaws flexed with firmness, and a flush of satisfaction lit their pious faces. They were sure they had Jesus trapped.

Lessons

They had no hint of the double slam dunk that was coming. It is never wise to go one-on-one with Jesus!

First, Jesus cited Old Testament precedent:

> Have you not read what David did when he was hungry, he and those who were with him: how he entered the house of God and took and ate the bread of the Presence, which is not lawful for any but the priests to eat, and also gave it to those with him? (vv. 3, 4)

"The bread of the Presence" consisted of twelve loaves of unleavened bread (Josephus, *Antiquities* 3.6.6) that were arranged in two rows of six on a table of gold (Leviticus 24:5, 6). Each Sabbath the old loaves were removed and replaced with fresh ones (24:8). It was referred to as "the bread of the Presence" (literally, "the bread of the face") (cf. Exodus 25:30; 35:13; 39:36) because it was placed in the presence of God. The placing of the bread in God's official presence symbolized the fact that God was the *source* of Israel's strength and nourishment and reminded them of their *dependence* upon God for everything, physical and spiritual.[1] The bread was ceremonially holy and could only be eaten by Aaronic priests at the conclusion of its seven-day display (Leviticus 24:9).

In the incident Jesus cited, David was a desperate, famished refugee fleeing from the wrath of Saul. His men were starving, and he begged the priest Ahimelech for bread. The priest replied that there was none, save the consecrated "bread of the Presence" that had been removed from sacred display. Ahimelech asked if David and his men were ceremonially clean. David answered yes and was given the bread. David dashed off with the bread, and he and his mighty men enjoyed a hidden feast (1 Samuel 21:1–6).

We see here the divine principle that human need must not be subjected to cold legalism—that God desires "mercy, and not sacrifice." We know Jesus made this painfully clear to the Pharisees because in Matthew's parallel account we see that he again referenced Hosea 6:6: "I tell you, something greater than the temple is here. And if you had known what this means, 'I desire mercy, and not sacrifice,' you would not have condemned the guiltless" (Matthew 12:6, 7). In other words, "If you had understood Hosea 6:6—that God desires merciful, compassionate actions rather than ritual observance—you would not have condemned my innocent disciples for plucking some grain on the Sabbath. Wake up, men! A thousand years ago Ahimelech, priest of Nob, understood and lived out this principle, using not raw grain, but consecrated bread, to feed the hungry. How much more are my disciples justified? You are ignorant of your Bible. You need to show mercy." Jesus' powerful Biblical reasoning put them off balance like the first pump of a double slam dunk.

The second lesson was a stupendous theological declaration: "And he said to them, 'The Son of Man is lord of the Sabbath'" (v. 5). That was a staggering claim because the Sabbath was a divine institution thundered down from Mount Sinai by God himself. Jesus' words asserted that he was greater than the Sabbath, for *lordship declares supremacy*. As such, Jesus Christ is greater than David. If David could override the Law without blame, how much more could the greater Son of David—Messiah himself—do so?

Extending the implications of Jesus' being "lord of the Sabbath," there is a sense in which he *is* the Sabbath because he supplies in his person everything the Sabbath was meant to give—peace, rest, restoration, communion. The writer of Hebrews makes a very subtle application of Jesus' Sabbath power by first noting that whereas the original Joshua failed to bring rest to his people, the ultimate Joshua (Jesus) would do so. His conclusion thrills our souls: "So then, there remains a Sabbath rest for the people of God, for whoever has entered God's rest has also rested from his works as God did from his" (Hebrews 4:9, 10).

Jesus has come to mercifully meet the needs of his people. On that Sabbath he broke religious convention in order to mercifully deal with his disciples' hunger. As "lord of the Sabbath" he shows mercy and meets our deepest spiritual needs—regeneration, renewal, peace, rest.

A Clash over Healing (vv. 6–11)

The Occasion

Luke has made his point, but he wants to make it even more convincingly, so he recounts another more dramatic Sabbath clash:

> On another Sabbath, he entered the synagogue and was teaching, and a man was there whose right hand was withered. And the scribes and the Pharisees watched him, to see whether he would heal on the Sabbath, so that they might find a reason to accuse him. (vv. 6, 7)

There is outrageous irony here as determined religious men sinisterly watch Jesus' every move to see if he will show kindness and heal the man, *so they can charge Jesus with sin*. These Pharisees were utterly unmerciful and utterly lost. Jesus gave this truth sobering expression when he said, "Blessed are the merciful, for they shall receive mercy" (Matthew 5:7). Put another way, a merciful spirit is a sign of having received mercy, while an unmerciful spirit is a sign of not having experienced mercy. No matter how religious you are, if you do not care about the welfare of others, if you have no concern about the salvation of the lost, you are lost! Do not soften this, because Jesus never did.

The Lesson

Jesus knew what the leering Pharisees were thinking, so he had the man get up and stand literally "in the middle" (v. 8). The afflicted man was on center stage, his dried-up hand hanging uselessly at his right side. "And Jesus said to them, 'I ask you, is it lawful on the Sabbath to do good or to do harm, to save life or to destroy it?'" (v. 9). In God's view, a refusal to do good is to do evil—"good omitted is evil committed" (Godet).[2] There is no neutral ground. To refuse to "save life" is to "destroy it."[3] To refuse to show mercy is a declaration of one's own damnation.

What is so astounding is that these Pharisees, self-proclaimed lovers of the Law, did not see that their lack of concern for their fellow Israelite was substantive proof that they did not keep the Law. Later in Luke the keeping of the Law, and eternal life itself, was conditioned on loving God with everything in you, and your neighbor as yourself (cf. Luke 10:25–28). In the economy of Heaven the two loves condition and define the other. As John writes, "He who does not love his brother whom he has seen cannot love God whom he has not seen" (1 John 4:20). The Pharisees were not lovers of God. They were spiritual felons, massive breakers of the Law, sons of Satan (cf. John 8:42–44). The truth of God's Word is relentless: only the merciful will receive mercy.

Jesus apparently paused after posing his question because Luke says that he was "looking around at them all" (v. 10). The synagogue undoubtedly became silent as a tomb as his eyes moved from face to face. Then Jesus said to the man, "'Stretch out your hand.' And he did so, and his hand was restored" (v. 10). The man had literally "a dry hand," shriveled and atrophied, but as he extended it toward Jesus, it inflated to normalcy like a new balloon. The fingers flexed and extended before the man's unblinking, ever-widening eyes.

Now Jesus' critics would certainly believe, would they not? After all, the healing took place just a few inches in front of their noses. This would be a day of grace for the Pharisees! Wishful thinking! "But they were filled with fury and discussed with one another what they might do to Jesus" (v. 11). The other Gospels tell us they actually plotted to kill him (cf. Matthew 12:14; Mark 3:6). Literally, "they were filled with madness." The Greek in Luke—*anoia*—actually describes a state of unthinking or thoughtlessness[4]—the absence of mind.

The self-righteous mind is not interested in mercy. It is not even interested in truth. Rather, it is interested in observance. In this case, their corporate minds united in a determination to prevent Jesus from doing any more acts of mercy because his methods did not fit with their religion. How sad!

Closing Reflections

Does Christianity really make a difference? Is there a difference between card-carrying, Bible-believing Christians and their culture in situations needing mercy? According to some pollsters and social commentators, Christians are prime candidates for intolerance. However, this was statistically put to the test in 1983 in a book entitled *The Religious Factor in Australian Life*. Part of the survey asked people about their attitudes toward various groups—people with criminal records, emotionally unstable people, people of a different race, members of minority religions, students, people in sects or cults, left-wing extremists, immigrants/foreign workers, never-married mothers, unemployed persons, heavy drinkers, aborigines, people with large families, homosexuals.

The answers were analyzed according to various religious groupings, and an "index of tolerance" was created. Can you guess who was most tolerant? Not liberals, not Catholics, not evangelicals, but *conservative fundamentalists*, by a significant margin. Those with no religion came in last.[5] So much for the pundits.

The fact is, true faith produces mercy. It is no surprise that the abolitionist movement was rooted in evangelical Christianity, led by Christians such as William Wilberforce. The same is true for the roots of modern social concern, with the likes of Lord Shaftesbury and William Booth. Likewise, the elevation of women and the protection and care of children sprang from the concern of followers of Jesus Christ.

Of course, mercy or compassion does not make one a Christian. Nevertheless, true faith produces a merciful heart. True Christians are compassionate to the needy—the poor, the immigrants, the cultural outcasts, unstable people, alcoholics, drug addicts, prisoners, AIDS victims. And Christians care about sinners. They witness to them about the love of Jesus Christ and win them to him.

Dynamic mercy in all its dimensions is nothing less than the life of Christ in us. Such a life is costly. It is inconvenient. It raises tension. It brings conflict. It is humbling. It is countercultural. But it is our calling, for God says, "I desire steadfast love and not sacrifice, the knowledge of God rather than burnt offerings" (Hosea 6:6).

25

Authority to Call

LUKE 6:12–16

THE THEME OF Jesus' authority is written large over chapters four through six of Luke, extending through the present text, where it culminates. Beginning in 4:6, 7 Satan offers Jesus an easy way to authority and victory, saying, "To you I will give all this authority and their [the kingdoms of the world] glory, for it has been delivered to me, and I give it to whom I will. If you, then, will worship me, it will all be yours." Next in 4:28, 29, after Jesus' initial exercise of authoritative teaching, Luke describes his horrifying rejection: "When they heard these things, all in the synagogue were filled with wrath. And they rose up and drove him out of the town and brought him to the brow of the hill on which their town was built, so that they could throw him down the cliff."

Undaunted, Jesus went to Capernaum, where his authority was then recognized. Luke records in 4:32, "They were astonished at his teaching, for his word possessed authority." And again in verse 36, "And they were all amazed and said to one another, 'What is this word? For with authority and power he commands the unclean spirits, and they come out!'"

Following this, Luke links a series of episodes that explicitly demonstrate Jesus' authority. In 4:38–44 we see Jesus laboring into the night healing and rebuking both demons and illnesses. Then in 5:1–11 his authority is showcased in his calling Peter, James, and John to fish for men. In 5:12–16 his dramatic healing of the man full of leprosy demonstrated his authority and ability to eradicate the effects of sin. In 5:17–26 Jesus coupled his healing of the paralytic with the sovereign declaration of his authority to forgive sins (v. 24): "'But that you may know that the Son of Man has authority on earth to forgive sins'—he said to the man who was paralyzed—'I say to you, rise, pick up your bed and go home.'"

This is followed in verses 27–32 by an assertion of authority in his calling of the arch-sinner Levi to become his follower. The authority motif carries on in Jesus' claim that he is the divine bridegroom and the implicit giver of new wine in verses 33–39. Then in chapter 6 Jesus made a dramatic declaration of his authority in verse 5 by proclaiming, "The Son of Man is lord of the Sabbath."

Now in verses 12–16 the authority theme peaks in Jesus' calling of the twelve apostles. This was an act of momentous importance for the nation Israel and for the church. *Twelve* apostles were named in implicit reference to their call to minister to the twelve tribes of Israel. Ultimately their names would be preserved in the very architecture of Heaven (cf. Revelation 21:14). The call of the Twelve affords us an opportunity to reflect on where and how Jesus got his authority, and the effect of his authority upon the lives of his followers.

A Dependent Authority (v. 12)

His Dependent Prayer

We begin by seeing that Jesus' authority was rooted in prayer: "In these days he went out to the mountain to pray, and all night he continued in prayer to God" (v. 12). It was Jesus' custom to get away by himself to pray. Luke gives us other clear examples of this. Earlier, after spending a good part of the night laying his healing hands on the populace of Capernaum, "And when it was day, he departed and went into a desolate place" (4:42). Similarly, amid the busyness that came from ministering to large crowds after his healing of the leper, Luke states, "He would withdraw to desolate places and pray" (5:16). Jesus understood that if he was going to save people, it was necessary to get away for private prayer.

But what is even more arresting here is that "all night he continued in prayer"—the entire night! If he began after sundown at, say, 8:00 p.m. and prayed until sunup (6:00 a.m.), he spent ten hours in focused prayer (the Greek word translated "all night he continued" expresses persevering energy).[1] As Jesus prayed on the mountainside, the moon ran its nocturnal course, the night's temperature modulated with the hours, and morning dew dampened his robes.

Why Jesus' lengthy engagement with the Father? Because he had huge decisions to make regarding who should comprise the Twelve. Jesus was a human being just like us, except that he was without sin. And though he was God, he placed the exercise of his attributes (his omniscience, for example) at the discretion of the Father. Thus he did not possess all knowledge, and his unaided knowledge was not sufficient to know whom to choose. Moreover, Jesus had numerous disciples, so it is conceivable that during some of those ten hours he presented them individually to his Father, so the nod would be given to those who were to become the Twelve. Three years later, at the end of his life, Jesus would lift the Twelve to God in prayer saying, "I have manifested your name to the people whom you gave me out of the world. Yours they were, and you gave them to me, and they have kept your word" (John 17:6).

Prayer was everything to Jesus. Through dependent prayer Jesus lived a life of flawless perfection, so that he could say, "I do nothing on my own authority, but speak just as the Father taught me. And he who sent me is with me. He has not left me alone, for I always do the things that are pleasing to him" (John 8:28, 29).

Though Jesus was the eternal Son, though he created everything, though he is the Alpha and Omega, though everything is moving toward and will culminate in him, he could not live his human life apart from dependent prayer.

Our Dependent Prayer

The spiritual logic is inescapable. If the eternal Son of God could not function as Jesus without dependent prayer, how much more is it essential for us adopted sons and daughters. What folly if we frame our lives with prayer as window dressing but do not really pray. What arrogance to understand Jesus' necessity but reject it for ourselves! Too often we engage not in *dependent* prayer but in *obligatory or routine* prayer. Jesus didn't say, "Apart from me you can do *something*." Rather, he said, "Apart from me you can do *nothing*" (John 15:5). This is the logic of a living church—the logic of spiritual power and true spirituality.

Effectual Authority (vv. 13–16)

Divine Choice

When the sun came up, Jesus knew the Father's will. So he acted with decisive authority: "And when day came, he called his disciples and chose from them twelve, whom he named apostles" (v. 13).

This was sovereign election.[2] None of the Twelve had sought this appointment. They were divinely chosen. In fact, in the tumultuous years that followed, they could comfort themselves that Jesus, not they, was responsible for the choice. Their number matched that of the tribes of Israel. They would be sent out as Messiah's official emissaries to the nation, and as such they would have special power and authority (cf. 9:1–2). After Pentecost they would become official witnesses and leaders of the new community of the Christian church (cf. Acts 1:8, 22). Some of them would become inspired writers of the New Testament.

We do not know the order in which Jesus called out their names. Luke's list begins with Peter and ends with Judas Iscariot, as do all the other lists in Scripture, though the order otherwise varies (cf. Matthew 10:2–4; Mark 3:16–19; and Acts 1:13, which does not mention Judas Iscariot as he had taken his own life). The list in Luke reads: "Simon, whom he named Peter, and Andrew his brother, and James and John, and Philip, and Bartholomew, and Matthew, and Thomas, and James the son of Alphaeus, and Simon who was called the Zealot, and Judas the son of James, and Judas Iscariot, who became a traitor" (vv. 14–16).

Today every name in this list has a notable ring, even the least known such as Bartholomew or Jude ("Judas the son of James"). But when Jesus chose them they were all unknown. This was the original "No Name Offense." All except Judas Iscariot were Galileans, "country boys." Four were fishermen. One was a hated tax-gatherer. Not one of them was famous or rich or noble or well connected. Not one of them was a scribe or a priest or an elder or a ruler of the people. They were, as their detractors labeled them, "uneducated, common men" (Acts 4:13). All were poor.[3]

Effectual Call

Yet they formed the nucleus of a band that conquered the ancient world with grace. And when we get to Heaven this ordinary, no-name bunch will actually find their names emblazoned on the twelve foundations of the new Jerusalem (with Matthias's name in place of Judas Iscariot's—cf. Acts 1:26): There were "on the east three gates, on the north three gates, on the south three gates, and on the west three gates. And the wall of the city had twelve foundations, and on them were the twelve names of the twelve apostles of the Lamb" (Revelation 21:13, 14). When God calls ordinary men and women to serve him, his call is always effectual, regardless of their apparent abilities or lack of them.

When God's call came to Gideon, he objected because of his ordinariness. "And [Gideon] said to him, 'Please, Lord, how can I save Israel? Behold, my clan is the weakest in Manasseh, and I am the least in my father's house'" (Judges 6:15). This was the kind of man God could use. Gideon would have to depend on the Lord—and depend he did! Since the Midianite host was "like locusts in abundance" (Judges 7:12), Gideon naturally recruited a vast army of some 32,000 so he could match them strength for strength. It would have been crazy to do otherwise. But "The LORD said to Gideon, 'The people with you are too many for me to give the Midianites into their hand, lest Israel boast over me, saying, "My own hand has saved me"'" (Judges 7:2).

Instead of allowing Gideon to increase the army, the Lord decreased it. First, all who were afraid were allowed to depart, reducing the army by 22,000. Then the 10,000 who remained were ordered to drink water from the river, and only the 300 who drank from their hands were retained.

From a military standpoint, the proper odds for launching an attack are three soldiers to one—in your favor, of course. When Gideon amassed 32,000 troops, the odds were four soldiers to one, *in the enemy's favor*. When Israel was reduced to 10,000, the odds became forty-five to one. And at 300, they were 750 to one!

From ground level this was insane—especially when the 300 went forth to battle armed only with trumpets and pitchers. But it was during this conscious renunciation of natural power—this profound dependence upon God—that God was pleased to work, and humble Gideon led his people to a mighty victory.

One of the supreme glories of God's call is that our weakness is the opportunity for his power—*our ordinariness makes room for his extraordinariness*. This was gloriously true in the case of Moses (Exodus 2, 4), David (1 Samuel 16, 17), and Jeremiah (Jeremiah 1). One of my most treasured quotations is the following, from Oswald Chambers:

> God can achieve his purpose either through the absence of human power and resources, or the abandonment of reliance on them. All through history God has chosen and used nobodies, because their unusual dependence on him made possible the unique display of his power and grace. He chose and used somebodies only when they renounced dependence on their natural abilities and resources.[4]

I cherish Chambers's beautiful statement not only because it well summarizes my own experience, but because it has been consistently confirmed by the history of the church and is, as we have seen, powerfully verified by Scripture. Chambers's words ought to be vastly encouraging because most of us are ordinary. As Abraham Lincoln said, "God must have liked ordinary people because he made so many of them!" At the same time, Chambers's words should also encourage those who are unusually gifted, because even the most gifted do not have within themselves the abilities to succeed in God's calling.

The great "apostle come lately," Paul, had a profound grasp of this truth. Originally he was wealthy, privileged, and connected, but when he came to Christ he renounced all dependence upon human capacity. His original name Saul (after the proud Benjaminite king) became Paul, *Paulos*, "small." Big Saul voluntarily became Small Paul!

Paul's writings powerfully substantiate that man's ordinariness, even his weakness, provide ready ground for God's extraordinary power. In discussing his own apostolic ministry, Paul made this unforgettable observation: "But we have this treasure in jars of clay, to show that the surpassing power belongs to God and not to us" (2 Corinthians 4:7). Paul summarized the secret of his ministry by referring to the ancient custom of hiding priceless treasure in common earthen, clay pots beneath the earth. The "treasure" was the gospel, and "jars of clay" a penetrating metaphor for frail humanity. The glorious gospel is committed to common, frail human beings so that the immensity of the power will be seen as God's and not man's! Clearly then, an awareness of one's weakness, one's ordinariness, can be an asset in gospel ministry, for such a recognition keeps us dependent upon the power of God. Conversely, if we think too much of our extraordinary gifts, we can be tempted to rely upon natural gifts to achieve supernatural ends. The full-blown expression of this principle is found in 2 Corinthians 12: 9, 10:

> But he said to me, "My grace is sufficient for you, for my power is made perfect in weakness." Therefore I will boast all the more gladly of my weaknesses, so that the power of Christ may rest upon me. For the sake of Christ, then, I am content with weaknesses. . . . For when I am weak, then I am strong.

We need to embrace this paradox, for the men and women God has used have always lived with the reality that they are clay. When they saw Jesus Christ, they became unconscious of all they used to call their wisdom and strength. Rather than focusing on their weaknesses, they made it their business to rely on him. From this flowed the surpassing greatness of his power.

Closing Reflections

Jesus' vast authority while here on earth was a dependent authority—he lived a life of dependent prayer. But his incarnation and death were followed by his glorious resurrection and ascension.

> Therefore God has highly exalted him and bestowed on him the name that is above every name, so that at the name of Jesus every knee should bow, in heaven and on earth and under the earth, and every tongue confess that Jesus Christ is Lord, to the glory of God the Father. (Philippians 2:9–11)

The exercise of his all-power, all-presence, and all-knowledge is at his sovereign discretion. How dare we live in anything but humble, prayerful dependence upon him who was our model while here on earth and who is now our intercessor and sovereign Lord. The logic of spirituality demands a life of dependent prayer.

Jesus' authority is eternally effectual. He sovereignly called twelve nobodies whose names will be forever written on the foundation stones of the New Jerusalem (except for Judas Iscariot, who was replaced by Matthias). And when he chooses nobodies like us, he writes our names in the eternal Book of Life (cf. Revelation 20:15).

As it was with the apostles, the calls to ministry that come to each of us are also endowed with the power to live out the call. Our ordinariness is the occasion for his extraordinariness, our weakness for his power.

Because all authority in Heaven and on earth are his, nothing makes sense except absolute submission to his will and a humble, prayerful dependence in every part of our lives.

26

The Sermon on the Level

LUKE 6:17–26

WHEN THE RISING SUN ENDED Jesus' night-long prayer, he knew the names of those who would be the Twelve. So the Lord immediately summoned his disciples, who by then had become a considerable number, and announced the twelve names to the throng. We surmise that Jesus further instructed his followers about the meaning of his sovereign choice, perhaps answering some questions and calming some fears.

Then, with the sun standing higher, Jesus initiated a signal public event. "And he came down with them and stood on a level place, with a great crowd of his disciples and a great multitude of people from all Judea and Jerusalem and the seacoast of Tyre and Sidon, who came to hear him and to be healed of their diseases" (vv. 17, 18a). The vast assembly would naturally have fallen into concentric arcs. Close about Jesus were the Twelve, self-consciously aware of their new status. Around them gathered a larger contingent of disciples, learners ready to assist in any way. Beyond them ranged a rich mixture of humanity that had come some distance to see and hear Jesus, from the port cities in the northwest and from the southern hamlets of Judea as well as from the great city of Jerusalem. This was the first time the Twelve stood with Jesus in a public, official capacity. The air was charged with dramatic tension.

No one would be disappointed. "And those who were troubled with unclean spirits were cured. And all the crowd sought to touch him, for power came out from him and healed them all" (vv. 18b, 19). Jesus evidently allowed healing to result in those who merely touched him, as he did at certain other times (cf. Matthew 9:20). The press of the people must have become frantic, taxing the energies of the Twelve and their friends. Yet Jesus' healing power was not the centerpiece of the day. Rather, it was the prelude to something far greater—namely, the Sermon on the Plain, literally "on a level place" (v. 17)—what I like to call "The Sermon on the Level" because Jesus dramatically leveled with the Twelve and their colleagues.

The sermon takes up the remainder of Luke 6 and is similar to the Sermon on the Mount (Matthew 5—7). Because of this, some think the same sermon is given in both accounts. This is possible, but as Leon Morris explains, "Preachers usually make use of the same or different matter in different sermons, especially if they speak without a written script. This habit of preachers seems a better explanation of the combination of resemblances and differences than extensive editorial activity."[1]

In accord with this explanation, there are substantial differences between the sermon we find in Luke and Matthew's sermons. Matthew devotes three long chapters to Jesus' sermon, Luke only one. Matthew records nine beatitudes, Luke four. Luke's beatitudes do not focus on the positives as do some of Matthew's—"blessed are the pure in heart" and so on. The sermon in Luke only includes the negatives such as poverty and hunger. Also, the woes that follow Luke's beatitudes have no parallel in Matthew's sermon. And Luke's beatitudes are given in the more personal second person (you) rather than in Matthew's third person (they). Lastly, the language that Luke records is much more stark and physical than Matthew's account. For example, Matthew says, "Blessed are the *poor in spirit,*" while Luke simply says, "Blessed are you who are *poor*." So I conclude that Luke presents a separate sermon, preached on a separate occasion, with a distinct theological intention.

Notice that the sermon is introduced in verse 20 with the phrase, "He lifted up his eyes on his disciples, and said," which clearly indicates that the sermon was specifically for his personal followers—the Twelve and the disciples. It was not directed to the crowds, though they were welcome to listen. The direct second person plural, "Blessed are you," addresses his disciples. Thus we have here a profile of what a disciple is to be—poor, hungry, sorrowful, rejected.

This is radical preaching. Luke's beatitudes are four spiritual H-bombs, concentrated theological epigrams that detonate with increasing effect, blowing away shallow talk of discipleship and thereby calling for true commitment.

As we look at these bombshells, we will examine the blessings and their parallel woes together.

The Blessing of Poverty (vv. 20, 24)

Jesus begins with the aggressive assertion that poverty is blessed: "And he lifted up his eyes on his disciples, and said: 'Blessed are you who are poor, for yours is the kingdom of God'" (v. 20), adding shortly afterward, "But woe to you who are rich, for you have received your consolation" (v. 24). For the meaning of these powerful statements we must turn to the Old Testament because Jesus dramatically stated a principle rooted there. Though the Old Testament does not see poverty per se as a blessing, Proverbs 30:8, 9 does says it can be a curse or a blessing: "Give me neither poverty nor riches; feed me with the food that is needful for me, lest I be full and deny you and say, 'Who is the LORD?' or lest I be poor and steal and profane the name of my God." Elsewhere Proverbs says, "The blessing of the LORD makes rich, and he adds no sorrow with it" (Proverbs 10:22).

Historically we know that God at times gave wealth to Israel as a blessing. When he delivered his people from Egypt, he blessed them with the Egyptians' willing plunder (cf. Exodus 12:35, 36), and then he brought them to a land "flowing with milk and honey" (numerous Scriptures—for example, Exodus 33:3). By the time of King David and King Solomon, national wealth was seen as a sign of divine blessing (cf. 1 Chronicles 29:13–16).

In addition to the Old Testament evidence, human experience teaches us that being poor is a miserable situation. Anyone who has known genuine poverty will testify that it is a humiliating experience. If money is power, then the poor are powerless, and their powerlessness is regularly exploited. Ask any of the world's poverty-stricken if it is a blessed state and see what they say.

Nevertheless, there were blessed poor in Old Testament times—after the fall of the nation when God's people were carried into exile in Babylon. They were the dispossessed, exiled poor. (Of course, not all of the exiles remained poor in Babylon. Some managed to do very well for themselves, but only by *compromising*. Those who sold out to Babylonian culture, who adopted their way of life, were able to become quite wealthy. And when it came time to return to build the fallen walls, they did not want to go, whereas the uncompromised poor did.)

This brings us back to the most prominent Old Testament quotation thus far in Luke's Gospel—Isaiah 61:1, 2, with which Jesus began his public ministry. Its opening line reads, "The Spirit of the Lord is upon me, because he has anointed me to proclaim good news to the poor" (Luke 4:18a). The poor in Isaiah 61 were the exiled people of Israel who had not compromised with their pagan conquerors. They knew they could not deliver themselves. They longed for the Messiah and his salvation.

Though several hundred years had passed by the time of Jesus, Israel still was suffering from a succession of foreign warlords—Persians, Greeks, and now Romans. And there were still uncompromised "poor" who longed for the fulfillment of Isaiah's promise. The Virgin Mary was in their line, and after Gabriel's visit she sang to Elizabeth, "My soul magnifies the Lord, and my spirit rejoices in God my Savior, for he has looked on the humble estate of his servant" (1:46–48). Two prime examples of the "poor" that Luke spotlights were Simeon and Anna. "Simeon . . . [was] waiting for the consolation of Israel" (2:25), and Anna "did not depart from the temple, worshiping with fasting and prayer night and day" (2:37). These two had no attachment to the riches and possessions of this world. They longed for the kingdom of God.

Significantly, when Jesus came, he gave the poor good news and established his kingdom by becoming poor himself. His life as an itinerant preacher was singularly poor. Jesus said of his life, "Foxes have holes, and birds of the air have nests, but the Son of Man has nowhere to lay his head" (9:58). Paul said of him, "For you know the grace of our Lord Jesus Christ, that though he was rich, yet for your sake he became poor, so that you by his poverty might become rich" (2 Corinthians 8:9; cf. Philippians 2: 5–11).

We should not be surprised that Jesus' teaching is so full of this idea. Jesus' disciples are generally poor (though God does sometimes grant them material riches). His disciples do not compromise with fallen culture. Their belief system is firmly rooted in Christ and his divine Word. They believe that Jesus Christ is the only hope of the world, that he is the only way to the Father. They stand true in their relationships and in their public conduct. Whatever wealth they have does not come through ethical compromise or the adoption of "everybody is doing it" business practices. They do not love money. They do not hold their earnings tightly, for they have given everything to Jesus. They know he is their only hope—he is their life.

Thus they live under his blessing. "Blessed are you who are poor," says Jesus as he looks directly at his disciples. They have his approval, his smile—*The Applause of Heaven*, as Max Lucado has so beautifully put it.

This is cause for deep reflection, especially for those of us who are comfortably ensconced in a prosperous culture.

- We rich are constantly assaulted with the temptation to rely on riches. Can we not rely upon them and yet have them?

- We rich are dulled to our need by our plenty. Can we have plenty and feel our need?
- We rich tend to be proud of what we have done, to take credit for our comforts. Can we live a humble life?

These are hard questions that we must each answer for ourselves. Let us not ignore Jesus' words: "Blessed are you who are poor, for yours is the kingdom of God."

The Blessing of Hunger (vv. 21a, 25a)

Jesus' word bomb leaves his disciples reeling and the onlookers in shock, but before they can adjust, another bomb comes flying: "Blessed are you who are hungry now, for you shall be satisfied" (v. 21a), and shortly afterward, "Woe to you who are full now, for you shall be hungry" (v. 25a). Again, the Old Testament does not directly equate blessing with physical hunger. But it does commend a different kind of hunger. Two eloquent passages in the Psalms give *spiritual* hunger lyric expression: "As a deer pants for flowing streams, so pants my soul for you, O God. My soul thirsts for God, for the living God. When shall I come and appear before God?" (Psalm 42:1, 2). And, "O God, you are my God; earnestly I seek you; my soul thirsts for you; my flesh faints for you, as in a dry and weary land where there is no water" (Psalm 63:1).

David's imagery is passionate. His soul thirsts. His spiritual longing is like a bodily ache. Life apart from God is desiccated. But on the flipside, God has promised Israel, "You will seek me and find me, when you seek me with all your heart" (Jeremiah 29:13).

With his coming, Christ became the source of all satisfaction. Jesus told the woman at the well, "Everyone who drinks of this water will be thirsty again, but whoever drinks of the water that I will give him will never be thirsty again. The water that I will give him will become in him a spring of water welling up to eternal life" (John 4:13, 14). He cried out in the temple, "If anyone thirsts, let him come to me and drink. Whoever believes in me, as the Scripture has said, 'Out of his heart will flow rivers of living water'" (John 7:37, 38). He had also said, "I am the bread of life; whoever comes to me shall not hunger, and whoever believes in me shall never thirst" (John 6:35).

So Jesus blesses spiritual hunger—"Blessed are you who are hungry now, for you shall be satisfied." The promise is at once eternal and temporal, because we can know both hunger and satisfaction in this world.

Someone left a plate of brownies in my church office. I resisted temptation (for a minute or two) and then poured myself a cup of coffee and retreated to my study, brownie in hand. When I bit in, I tasted an exquisite brownie and I was completely satisfied—for about ten minutes. Then I began to hunger for more! So I ate another one, with the same effect. It was a sublime cycle: hunger—satisfaction—hunger—satisfaction.

Paul knew the blessing of such a paradox. He wrote to Timothy in satisfaction, "I know whom I have believed" (2 Timothy 1:12). Yet to the Philippians he expressed a profound hunger for Christ—"that I may know him and the power of his resurrection, and may share his sufferings, becoming like him in his death" (Philippians 3:10).

The key is to keep on hungering, as Kierkegaard taught with this story:

> A duck was flying with his flock in the springtime northward across Europe. During the flight he came down in a Danish barnyard where there were tame ducks. He enjoyed some of their corn. He stayed, for an hour, then for a day, then for a week, then for a month, and finally, because he relished the good fare and the safety of the barnyard, he stayed all summer. But one autumn day when the flock of wild ducks were winging their way southward again, they passed over the barnyard, and their mate heard their cries. He was stirred with a strange thrill of joy and delight, and with a great flapping of wings he rose in the air to join his old comrades in their flight. But he found that his good fare had made him so soft and heavy that he could rise no higher than the eaves of the barn. So he dropped back again to the barnyard, and said to himself, "Oh well, my life is safe here and the food is good." Every spring and autumn when he heard the wild ducks calling, his eyes would gleam for a moment and he would begin to flap his wings. But finally the day came when the wild ducks flew over him and uttered their cry, but he paid not the slightest attention to them.[2]

May we never be domesticated! May we never become so well fed that we never hunger for "the things that are above" (Colossians 3:1, 2).

The Blessing of Sorrow (vv. 21b, 25b)

Before the debris could settle, Jesus' next sentence rocked the landscape: "Blessed are you who weep now, for you shall laugh. . . . Woe to you who laugh now, for you shall mourn and weep" (vv. 21b, 25b). The latter statement was not an attack on laughter. Jesus does not mean, "Blessed are grim, cheerless Christians," though some believers have apparently interpreted it this way. The Victorian preacher Charles Spurgeon once remarked that some preachers he had known appeared to have their neckties twisted around their souls.[3] Robert Louis Stevenson must have known some preachers like that because he once wrote in his diary, "I've been to church today and am not depressed." Christ certainly is not pronouncing a beatitude on a forlorn disposition.

Actually, humor and laughter are good and necessary for the believer. Solomon says that "a joyful heart is good medicine" (Proverbs 17:22). Abraham Lincoln said, "If I did not laugh, I would die." The need for laughter in the church was underlined by missionary statesman Oswald Sanders with these questions:

> Should we not see that lines of laughter about the eyes are just as much marks of faith as are the lines of care and seriousness? Is laughter pagan? We have already allowed too much that is good to be lost to the church and cast many pearls before swine. A church is in a bad way when it banishes laughter from the sanctuary and leaves it to the cabaret, the nightclub, and the toastmasters.[4]

What Jesus assaulted is the superficial, shallow mirth that characterizes the world—the inability to weep at the right things, and the ability to laugh at the wrong things.

Simeon and Anna were classic examples of the ideal mourners—those whom Jesus commended because they "weep now." Theirs was a life of perpetual mourning until the day Jesus was brought into the temple. Simeon was "waiting for the consolation of Israel"—the removal of mourning because of the arrival of the Messiah (2:25). And Anna "did not depart from the temple, worshiping with fasting and prayer night and day" (2:37). She was occupied in holy mourning. Both of these godly individuals were mourning for the condition of Israel and were praying for her restoration and consolation.

Jesus himself mourned for Israel. Isaiah prophesied that he would be "a man of sorrows, and acquainted with grief" (Isaiah 53:3). And while on earth in body Jesus wailed mournfully, "O Jerusalem, Jerusalem, the city that kills the prophets and stones those who are sent to it! How often would I have gathered your children together as a hen gathers her brood under her wings, and you were not willing!" (13:34). "And when he drew near and saw the city, he wept over it, saying, 'Would that you, even you, had known on this day the things that make for peace! But now they are hidden from your eyes'" (19:41, 42). Jesus was both the ultimate mourner and the ultimate consolation of Israel.

Simeon and Anna were in the minority. Many, especially the Sadducees and tax collectors, liked life as it was. But Simeon and Anna wanted change—not political change, but the spiritual newness of the kingdom of God. When

Simeon held the baby Jesus, he sang, "Lord, now you are letting your servant depart in peace, according to your word; for my eyes have seen your salvation" (2:29, 30). His laughter filled the universe and still echoes today.

We are called to weep over lost souls, over people who will go into eternal darkness without Christ. We are to weep over the world's misery, over the injustice that falls on so many helpless people, over the unfairness that victimizes the weak, over child abuse, over battered women, over adultery, over divorce, over betrayals, over rejection, over loneliness, over those who now laugh but who, unless they turn to Christ, will suffer God's condemnation forever.

We weep now but look forward to the eternal joy that will be ours in Heaven because of the death and resurrection of Jesus Christ.

The Blessing of Rejection (vv. 22, 26)

Jesus' final detonation was a shocker: "Blessed are you when people hate you and when they exclude you and revile you and spurn your name as evil, on account of the Son of Man! . . .Woe to you, when all people speak well of you, for so their fathers did to the false prophets" (vv. 22, 26). Notice that this beatitude does not say, "Blessed are you when people hate you and when they exclude you and revile you and spurn your name as evil, period," though, unfortunately, this is the way it is sometimes interpreted. Those who read it like this delude themselves into thinking that any time they experience conflict they are bearing the reproach of Christ.

Joseph Bayly's satire *The Gospel Blimp* humorously portrays this fallacy. In Bayly's tale, some believers in a small town, eager to share their faith, begin using a gospel blimp, then pilot it back and forth across town, dragging Scripture banners and dropping tracts ("gospel bombs") into backyards. At first the townspeople put up with the intrusion, but their tolerance changes to hostility when the blimp's owners install a loudspeaker and begin assaulting the people with gospel broadcasts. The locals have had enough, and the local newspaper runs an editorial:

> For some weeks now our metropolis has been treated to the spectacle of a blimp with an advertising sign attached at the rear. This sign does not plug cigarettes or a bottled beverage, but the religious beliefs of a particular group in our midst. The people of our city are notably broad-minded, and they have good-naturedly submitted to this attempt to proselytize. But last night a new refinement (some would say debasement) was introduced. We refer, of course, to the airborne sound truck, the invader of our privacy, that raucous destroyer of communal peace.[5]

That night the gospel blimp is sabotaged, an act that the Christians see as "persecution." Sad but true, Christians are often persecuted not for their Christianity, but for their lack of it. Sometimes they simply have unpleasing personalities. They are rude, insensitive, thoughtless—piously obnoxious. Some are rejected because they are discerned as proud and judgmental. Others are disliked because they are lazy and irresponsible. Either arrogance or incompetence mixed with piety is sure to bring rejection.

Christ's words must be read carefully: "Blessed are you when people hate you and when they exclude you and revile you and spurn your name as evil, *on account of the Son of Man!*" (v. 22). The fact is, everyone who lives like Jesus will be persecuted. Jesus stated in John 15:20, "Remember the word that I said to you: 'A servant is not greater than his master.' If they persecuted me, they will also persecute you." Since the wind was in Jesus' face, it will be in the faces of his followers as well.

Paul advised Timothy, "Indeed, all who desire to live a godly life in Christ Jesus will be persecuted" (2 Timothy 3:12). Paul also warned the Thessalonians, "For you yourselves know that we are destined for this [trials]. For when we were with you, we kept telling you beforehand that we were to suffer affliction, just as it has come to pass, and just as you know" (1 Thessalonians 3:3, 4). Likewise, he and Barnabas told the Christians in Antioch and elsewhere, "Through many tribulations we must enter the kingdom of God" (Acts 14:22). Few people in our time have understood and expressed this better than Dietrich Bonhoeffer:

> Suffering, then, is the badge of true discipleship. The disciple is not above his master . . . that is why Luther reckoned suffering among the marks of the true church, and one of the memoranda drawn up in preparation for the Augsburg Confession similarly defines the church as the community of those "who are persecuted and martyred for the Gospel's sake." . . . Discipleship means allegiance to the suffering Christ, and it is therefore not at all surprising that Christians should be called upon to suffer. In fact, it is a joy and a token of His grace.[6]

During a stressful time in Charles Spurgeon's life when he was depressed by criticism, his wife took a sheet of paper, printed the eight Beatitudes on it in large, old English script, and tacked it to the ceiling over his bed. She wanted the reality to saturate his mind morning and evening: *everyone who lives righteously will be persecuted.*

On the flipside, Jesus tells us, "Woe to you, when all people speak well of you." This cannot happen to a Christian apart from some sacrifice of principle. Yes, we should be well thought of by "outsiders" (1 Timothy 3:7), but that is different from universal popularity. If we are acceptable and popular with people who live according to the spirit of the present evil age, we may in fact belong to that evil age and thus share in its judgment. The desire for popularity can become a self-focused spiritual anesthetic.

A person who is persecuted because of Christ is truly alive. There is an old saying: "Even a dead dog can swim with the tide." To swim against the tide you must be alive and kicking. Being yes-men and yes-women of ungodly culture means drifting with the dead.

Are we *hated* for Christ? Have we been *excluded* for Christ? Do we suffer *insult* for Christ? Are we *rejected* because of Christ? Then we are blessed with special benefits of grace from him.

Closing Reflections

> Blessed are you who are poor, for yours is the kingdom of God.
> Blessed are you who are hungry now, for you shall be satisfied.
> Blessed are you who weep now, for you shall laugh.
> Blessed are you when people hate you and when they exclude you and revile you and spurn your name as evil, on account of the Son of Man! (vv. 20–22)

True disciples, though poor, hungry, weeping, and rejected, are "blessed."
Are we his followers?
Are we his disciples?

27

Supernatural Love

LUKE 6:27–36

THE LONG-TIME TALK SHOW HOST Phil Donahue makes a grievous assertion in his best-selling autobiography, *Donahue, My Own Story,* actually indicting God the Father for sending his Son, and not himself, to the cross. Donahue reasons:

> If God the Father is so all-loving, why didn't He come down and go to Calvary? Then Jesus could have said, "This is My Father in whom I am well-pleased." How could an all-knowing, all-loving God allow His Son to be murdered on a cross in order that He might redeem my sins?[1]

Donahue's charge is not new. It is an ancient blasphemy that falls short in several ways. Most seriously, it displays an ignorance of the doctrine of the Trinity. The Holy Trinity (Father, Son, and Holy Spirit) is not comprised of three separate Gods but is one God in three persons. Jesus is God, the Spirit is God, and the Father is God. And they are coeternal and coequal—possessing a dynamic unity of thought and purpose in which there is no disagreement. Therefore, the decision that the Son be sent to die for our sins was a decision of the Father, Son, and Holy Spirit, not of the Father only. We must understand from their dynamic ontological union (their union of being) that the sending of the Son was an ultimate Trinitarian gift—a gift of mutually costly love. Jesus' pain was the Father's and the Spirit's as well.

This understanding is what makes the opening line of John 3:16 throb in our souls: "For God so loved the world, that he gave his only Son." The Father could make no greater or more costly sacrifice, not even the sending of himself. The unqualified statement of Holy Scripture is that "God is love"

(1 John 4:8, 16). That is why he could send his Son to be murdered on a cross to redeem my sins.

When Jesus came, he was the love of God incarnate. If we wish to understand God's love, we must look at the revolutionary love of Jesus. The Old Testament taught that we must love our neighbors as ourselves (cf. Leviticus 19:18). Indeed, Jesus said that one could fulfill the whole Law if he could just love God with all his heart, and his neighbor as himself (cf. Matthew 22:34–40). But Jesus went even farther, for he not only loved his neighbors as himself, but his *enemies* as himself.

We see this in the upper room when, after washing the disciples' feet, he lovingly reached out to Judas, whose heart was set on murderous betrayal (cf. John 13:18–30). Jesus began reaching for Judas' soul by quoting Psalm 41:9, "He who ate my bread has lifted his heel against me" (John 13:18), a reference to Ahithophel who betrayed David and then committed suicide. The reference with its tragic end was meant to draw Judas back, as well as to fortify Jesus' other disciples. Evidently the Savior's voice broke with emotion as he further explained what he meant, because John 13:21 records, "After saying these things, Jesus was troubled in his spirit, and testified, 'Truly, truly, I say to you, one of you will betray me.'" His emotion was not for himself, but over the loss of Judas and the yawning abyss that awaited him. Then came the summit of Jesus' attempted rapprochement as amid the disciples' self-questionings he dipped a morsel of food and gave it to Judas. In the Palestinian culture, to lift a morsel from the table, dip it in the common dish, and then offer it to another was a gesture of special friendship (cf. Ruth 2:14). Jesus' gesture said in effect, "Judas, I know what you are up to. But here is my friendship. Here is my loving heart. All you have to do is take it." But poor Judas slammed the door shut. As a consequence, "It was night" (John 13:30)—eternal night for Judas' soul.

In that awesome event Jesus dramatized his new law of love—the call to love one's enemies. There had never been anything like it. Jesus capsulized this in the famous "as I have loved you" statement of John 13:34: "A new commandment I give to you, that you love one another: just as I have loved you, you also are to love one another." In retrospect, the disciples would see that this love command was explained by Jesus' washing their feet and then reaching out to his enemy. This is the church's new law for dealing with each other, and even with one's enemies, which is exactly what Jesus did in the next few hours when he hung on the cross with his arms stretched wide as if to embrace the world, as he died for the "ungodly," for "sinners," for his "enemies," as we see in Romans 5:

> For while we were still weak, at the right time Christ died for the ungodly. (v. 6)

> But God shows his love for us in that while we were still sinners, Christ died for us. (v. 8)

> For if while we were enemies we were reconciled to God by the death of his Son, much more, now that we are reconciled, shall we be saved by his life. (v. 10)

Jesus loved us not only when we were indifferent to him, but when we were actual enemies of his holiness and grace.

As we see in 6:27–36, at the beginning of his ministry, with the newly called Twelve standing before him, Jesus announced a new law, calling his followers to love as he loves. This is an impossible call apart from Christ. But it comes with full force to us if we are his followers.

Part of the Sermon on the Plain, this new love ethic was announced to the disciples while their spiritual landscape was still rocking from the four bombshell beatitudes that pronounced blessing on poverty, hunger, sorrow, and rejection. The context was explosively radical.

The New Love Ethic Declared (vv. 27–31)

Looking his disciples right in the eye, Jesus declared the new ethic: "But I say to you who hear, Love your enemies, do good to those who hate you, bless those who curse you, pray for those who abuse you" (vv. 27, 28). These four terse commands demand an altogether unnatural love.

There were several words for *love* in the Greek language. Jesus did not here command *storge*, natural affection. He did not command *eros*, romantic love. He did not command *philia*, the love of friendship. He demanded *agape* love.[2] Such a love is not motivated by the merit of the one who is loved. The other loves come quite naturally. For example, you can fall into *eros*. But *agape* love supersedes natural inclinations and often exists in spite of them. It is a deliberate love, rooted in the will—a love by choice. "Love [*agape*] is a deep, continuous, growing and ever-renewing activity of the will superintended by the Holy Spirit" (Mike Mason).[3] *Agape* love says, "I will love this person because, by God's grace, I choose to love this person."

This call to ascend to the unnatural heights of *agape* in loving our enemies is defined by Jesus' commands in this passage.

- *Unnatural deeds*: "Do good to those who hate you" (v. 27b). Imagine someone who hates you—then think of doing something nice to him or her. This is an unnatural exercise, to be sure, but it can and must be done.
- *Unnatural words*: "Bless those who curse you" (v. 28a; cf. Romans 12:14; 1 Corinthians 4:12; 1 Peter 3:9). This idea has no antecedents in Biblical literature.[4] The Essenes, in fact, were encouraged to curse those who did not join them (1 QS 2:2–17).[5] Incredible—someone pours vile abuse on you, and you respond with a heartfelt blessing!
- *Unnatural prayers:* "Pray for those who abuse you" (v. 28b). Praise God—it is impossible to truly pray for someone and hate them at the same time.

The command to love our enemies is a call to unnatural deeds, unnatural words, unnatural prayer. It is a command for *supernatural love*. Is there any hope for us? Can we possibly do this? Yes, as we shall see.

This unnatural love calls for Jesus' followers to exercise an unconventional love:

> To one who strikes you on the cheek, offer the other also, and from one who takes away your cloak do not withhold your tunic either. Give to everyone who begs from you, and from one who takes away your goods do not demand them back. And as you wish that others would do to you, do so to them. (vv. 29–31)

Conventional responses to such indignities took two basic patterns. The raw pagan response was to pay such actions back tenfold—"You slap me, I'll break your neck"—"You take my shirt, I'll chop off your hand." Many people today feel the same way. The ancient Hebrew response was a vast improvement. It was *lex talionis*, the law of retaliation, limiting retaliation to an equitable penalty—"life for life, eye for eye, tooth for tooth, hand for hand, foot for foot, burn for burn, wound for wound, stripe for stripe" (Exodus 21:23–25; cf. Leviticus 24:20; Deuteronomy 19:21). This is a civilized principle that, if followed, would help restore fairness to our litigious society.

But Jesus went far beyond these conventions in his call to turn the other cheek and give to all who ask! Is Jesus thus abrogating all exercise of personal defense and the right to private property? No. Rather, he is demanding a loving attitude that is not vengeful but is generous and giving. The slap to one's face probably refers to an insulting blow by someone who takes exception to the disciples' allegiance to Christ.[6] In such a situation the disciple is not to retaliate. Similarly, in reference to one's possessions, it is one's spirit or attitude that is important. As Leon Morris explains: "If Christians took this one absolutely literally there would soon be a class of saintly paupers, owning nothing, and another of prosperous idlers and thieves. It is not this that Jesus is seeking, but a readiness among his followers to give and give and give."[7] Love for possessions should never keep a Christian from giving. Love must be ready to give everything or have it taken away if need be. Love must decide when to give and when to withhold our possessions.

This is supraconventional to say the least! Its ultimate expression is the so-called Golden Rule: "As you wish that others would do to you, do so to them" (v. 31). Significantly, almost all pre-Christian formulations of this rule are negative—"Do *not* do to others what you would *not* want done to you"—though there are a few obscure positive formulations (cf. T. Naph. 1; 2 En. 61:1).[8] But it is significant that Jesus commands his followers to engage in the positive act of doing to others what they would like done to them. "*This* is how you are to treat all people, regardless of how they treat you. This is how you are to treat your enemies!" Is this unnatural, unconventional *agape* love possible? Can anyone today live on this level? With God's help, yes.

After the collapse of the Berlin Wall in 1989, no person in all of East Germany was more despised than the former Communist dictator Erich Honecher. He had been stripped of all his offices. Even the Communist Party rejected him. Kicked out of his villa, the new government refused him and his wife new housing. The Honechers were homeless and destitute.

Enter pastor Uwe Holmer, director of a Christian help center north of Berlin. Made aware of the Honechers' straits, Pastor Holmer felt it would be wrong to give them a room meant for even needier people. So the pastor and his family decided to take the former dictator into their own home!

Erich Honecher's wife, Margot, had ruled the East German educational system for twenty-six years. Eight of Pastor Holmer's ten children had been turned down for higher education due to Mrs. Honecher's policies, which discriminated against Christians. Now the Holmers were caring for their personal enemy—the most hated man in Germany.[9] This was so unnatural, so unconventional, so supernaturally sublime, so Christlike.

By the grace of God, the Holmers loved their enemies, did them good, blessed them, and prayed for them. They turned the other cheek. They gave their enemies their coat (their own home). They did to the Honechers what they would have wished the Honechers would do to them.

The New Love Ethic Explained (vv. 32–36)

Jesus went on to explain his new ethic by contrasting it with the reciprocal ethic of sinners.

First of all, *there is no credit for natural love.*

> If you love those who love you, what benefit is that to you? For even sinners love those who love them. And if you do good to those who do good to you, what benefit is that to you? For even sinners do the same. And if you lend to those from whom you expect to receive, what credit is that to you? Even sinners lend to sinners, to get back the same amount. (vv. 32–34)

Those in the Cosa Nostra love those who love them. Grown men kiss each other on both cheeks. They do "good" to those who do them right. They lend—big time. Of course, they expect to be paid in full! But the ethic of Jesus Christ goes way beyond any of this.

Jesus discourages any self-congratulation for reciprocal morality. We love people who love us. Big deal! So did Hitler and Stalin. There is simply no credit for natural love.

There is eternal credit for the new love. "But love your enemies, and do good, and lend, expecting nothing in return, and your reward will be great, and you will be sons of the Most High, for he is kind to the ungrateful and the evil" (v. 35). Jesus gives two emphases to the "reward" he promises.

First, it will be "great"—literally, "much"—and Jesus meant what he said. Are we mercenary or selfish if we love our enemies with an eye to great reward? No. As C. S. Lewis once pointed out, a man is mercenary who would marry for money, but if he marries for love, he is not. Why? Marriage is the proper reward of love.[10] Similarly, love for God and others has a proper reward, which is God himself (cf. Romans 2:7; 2 Corinthians 6:16b–18; Revelation 21:7).

Second, as a fitting corollary Jesus adds, "And you will be sons of the Most High, for he is kind to the ungrateful and the evil." To become "sons of the Most High" is the Hebrew way of saying we will be like the Most High, like God himself. Therefore, to love one's enemies is to be like Christ and like the Father. When the Holmer family took in Eric and Margot Honecher, they were like Christ. When we do good to our enemies, we are like Christ. When we bless those who curse us, we are like Christ. When we pray for those who abuse us, we are like Christ. And that likeness *is* our reward.

The great question is, how can any of us ever live up to this ethic—how can we in fact love our enemies? In ourselves, this is impossible. No one can love his enemy by an unaided act of the will. But praise God, through new birth in Christ we become partakers of his divine nature (2 Peter 1:4). This does not mean that we become God, but that his divine nature is at work within us. Christ's love that reached out to poor Judas has come to us. His love for sinners is ours. The key to Christ's moral teaching is Christ in us! Our ethic is radically Christocentric!

Closing Reflections

Several years ago one of my wife's friends took a missionary furlough with her husband and family after an unusually tiring stint of service. She had been looking forward to this time with great anticipation. For the first time she was going to have a place of her own, a new, large townhouse-styled apartment with a patio. She is very creative and made the patio the focus of her decoration.

After a few months some new neighbors moved in. The best word to describe them would be *coarse*. There was loud music day and night along with a constant flow of obscenities. They urinated in the front yard in broad daylight. They totally disrupted her peace. She could see nothing good in them.

She asked the Lord to help her be more loving, but all she got back was disgust and rejection. The crisis came when she returned home to discover that her neighbors' children had sprayed orange paint all over her beautiful patio—the walls, the floors—everything! She was distraught and furious. She tried to pray but found herself crying out, "I cannot love them. I hate them!"

Knowing she had to deal with the sin in her heart, she began to converse with the Lord in her inner being, and a Scripture came to mind: "And above all these put on love, which binds everything together in perfect harmony" (Colossians 3:14). In her heart she questioned, "Lord, how do I put on love?" The only way she could picture it was like putting on a coat. So that is what she determined to do—she chose to wrap herself in the love of God! As a result she began to experience a deeper life of Christ within her.

She made a list of what she would do if she really loved her exasperating neighbors, then did what she had listed. She baked cookies, she offered to babysit for free, she invited the mother over for coffee—and the most beautiful thing happened! She began to know and understand them. She began to see that they were living under tremendous pressures. She began to love her "enemies." She did good to them. She lent to them without expecting anything back.

The day came when they moved—and she wept! An unnatural, unconventional love had captured her heart—a supernatural love—the love of Jesus.

If we consider ourselves to be true followers of Christ, this love is our call. We are to love our enemies—to truly love them.

Are there some whom you hate, and do you, through some perverse twist, imagine that your hate is justified? If so, you are in trouble, for Christ is not ruling your life.

Are you doing good to those who hate you, or evil? If Christ is ruling your heart, it will be good.

Are you blessing those who curse you? If not, Christ is not on the throne of your heart.

Are you praying for those who mistreat you? If so, you are like Jesus.

This is an impossible life. It is unnatural. It is unconventional. It is—supernatural!

28

The Spirit of the Disciple

LUKE 6:37–42

ALL OF US HAVE PEOPLE WE ADMIRE, those we consider models for our lives. And most of us, at some time in our development, have attempted to copy our heroes. Many boys copy the way a great batter steps into the batter's box—how he hikes up his belt, taps each cleat with his bat, spits through his teeth exactly sixteen inches to the left of the third base line, and then steps into the box, cracks his neck, brushes the bill of his hat with his left hand, and assumes his stance. Some girls imitate the wardrobe of a much admired older girl—her casual panache, her poise, her walk. Young preachers often copy their heroes too. During the ascendancy of Billy Graham, it was common to hear "preacher boys," Bible draped over left hand, right index finger punctuating the air, imitate his southern lilt—"The Bible says. . . ."

The problem with this, as the great preacher Phillips Brooks pointed out long ago, is that the perception of the copyist is blind. Not understanding the real source of the power he so admires, he imitates some visible characteristics and repeats them over and over in a futile attempt to capture the greatness of his hero.[1] In reality, one will never become a great preacher by copying the cadences of Billy Graham, or a major leaguer by chewing tobacco, or a beautiful woman by changing nail polish. Spiritually, as Brooks rightly observes:

> If you really reverence a great man, if you look up to and rejoice in his good work, if you truly honor him, you will get at his spirit, and doing that you will cease to imitate his outside ways. You insult a man when you try to catch his power by moving your arms or shaping your sentences like his, but you honor him when you try to love truth and do God's will the better for the love and faithfulness which you see in him.[2]

That is what this section of Jesus' sermon is about—the spirit of discipleship—the disposition and spirituality of a devoted follower of Christ. The exhortation that Christ gives to his disciples in verses 37–42 goes beyond externals to the very heart of discipleship. No mere outward imitation here, but true Christianity from the inside out.

A Magnanimous Disposition (vv. 37, 38)

Magnanimous is a beautiful old word, but not a word used in everyday conversation. It comes from the Latin *magnus* ("great") and *animus* ("spirit")—great spirited, great souled. It describes a lofty spirit that is generous and forgiving.[3] This is precisely the kind of person the Lord commands his disciples to be:

> Judge not, and you will not be judged; condemn not, and you will not be condemned; forgive, and you will be forgiven; give, and it will be given to you. Good measure, pressed down, shaken together, running over, will be put into your lap. For with the measure you use it will be measured back to you. (vv. 37, 38)

Jesus' disciples are to be accepting, forgiving, and giving.

An Accepting Disposition

Jesus calls for an accepting disposition by two negative, mutually defining charges: "Judge not, and you will not be judged; condemn not, and you will not be condemned." These are some of the most misunderstood and misapplied verses in the Bible. Today they serve as the *Magna Carta* of much of American religion. Some people do not know a single Bible verse—they might not even know there is an Old and New Testament. But let them feel the slightest disapproval and the *King James* comes forth: "Judge not, and ye shall not be judged."

Americans love this verse because judging someone else is thought to be the most heinous of crimes. Never mind that they are lifting the verse out of its context and are ignoring other Scriptures that call for Christians to judge and even at times condemn sin. For example, here in this same sermon Christ calls his disciples to judge people by their fruits (6:43–45). Later, the Apostle Paul would challenge the Corinthians to make moral judgments, arguing, "Do you not know that the saints will judge the world?" (1 Corinthians 6:2; cf. 5:9–13). Christ's followers are to have a highly cultivated sense of right and wrong and to make subtle moral judgments. Christ's exhortation "judge not" contains no suggestion of moral flabbiness or an abdication of moral responsibility.

What Jesus *is* disallowing is a judgmental, condemning disposition, what Frederick Godet has described as "the tendency to place our faculty of moral appreciation at the service of natural malignity, or more simply still: judging for the pleasure of judging."[4] Jesus prohibits censoriousness and judgmentalism.

Judgmentalism is an unwitting revelation of one's own soul, because people rush to condemn their own sins in others. An example of this occurred in the life of King David after his adultery with Bathsheba and the murder of her husband Uriah. Nathan the prophet visited David and told the unsuspecting king the tale of a rich man who took a poor man's beloved pet sheep and slaughtered it to feed his guests. Horrified, David responded, "'As the LORD lives, the man who has done this deserves to die, and he shall restore the lamb fourfold, because he did this thing, and because he had no pity.' Nathan said to David, 'You are the man!'" (2 Samuel 12:5–7). David, though guilty of a far greater sin, was blind to his own condition even while he was enraged at the same sin in another. So it goes. The greedy delight to condemn greed in others. The ambitious charge others with self-ambition. Liars love to call others liars. Somehow judgmental people imagine they will lessen their guilt by judging their sins in others.

Furthermore, judgmentalism is merciless. It attaches motives to actions that have never been there. It sees others in the worst light. It pompously assumes the place of God (which is unwittingly to invite God's wrath). Judgmentalism is at best a sign of spiritual cancer, and at its worst a sign of spiritual death. This is why Jesus tells us that judgmental people will be judged and condemning people will be condemned. Martin Luther, preaching to the people of Wittenberg in 1523, said of this very text:

> Dost thou publish his sins, then truly thou art not a child of your merciful Father; for otherwise thou wouldst be also as he, merciful. It is certainly true that we cannot show as great mercy to our neighbor, as God has to us; but it is the true work of the devil that we do the very opposite of mercy, which is a sure sign that there is not a grain of mercy in us.[5]

Are you judgmental and condemning? Does this describe your favorite indoor sport? Take heed because then you are certainly not a disciple—and maybe not even a Christian. A merciful father has merciful children.

A Forgiving Disposition

Jesus couples his demand for an accepting (nonjudgmental) disposition with the demand for a forgiving disposition: "Forgive, and you will be forgiven."

Jesus is not implying that a person can become forgiven for his sins by forgiving others—that would be salvation through our own merit. Rather, his command is grounded on the fact that when God's grace saves a person, it changes him or her. A forgiving disposition is evidence that that person has been forgiven.

This is why only a Christian can truly pray the Lord's Prayer, especially the fifth petition: "Forgive us our debts, as we also have forgiven our debtors" (Matthew 6:12). As Thomas Watson, the great Puritan, observed: "A man can as well go to hell for not forgiving as for not believing."[6] To pray it without the willingness to forgive is to petition your own death warrant. Jesus made this absolutely clear in the two lines that follow the Lord's Prayer: "For if you forgive others their trespasses, your heavenly Father will also forgive you, but if you do not forgive others their trespasses, neither will your Father forgive your trespasses" (Matthew 6:14, 15).

True Christians can and do forgive. This is not to say that they do not struggle with forgiving, or that they are free from battles with bitterness or hatred, or that they are never so hurt and in such emotional shock that they are unable to respond with forgiveness, but it is to say that they work at forgiving and ultimately do forgive.

Jesus' disciples consistently have forgiving dispositions. W. E. Sangster, the beloved pastor of London's Westminster Central Hall during the 1940s and 1950s, wrote:

> It was Christmas time in my home. One of my guests had come a couple of days early and saw me sending off the last of my Christmas cards. He was startled to see a certain name and address. "Surely, you are not sending a greeting card to him," he said.
>
> "Why not?" I asked.
>
> "But you remember," he began, "eighteen months ago . . ."
>
> I remembered then, the thing the man had publicly said about me, but I remembered also resolving at the time with God's help, that I had remembered to forget. And God had "made" me forget!
>
> I posted the card.[7]

A forgiving disposition is at the heart of discipleship.

A Giving Disposition

Jesus links his calls for an accepting and a forgiving disposition with a command for a giving disposition: "Give, and it will be given to you. Good measure, pressed down, shaken together, running over, will be put into your lap. For with the measure you use it will be measured back to you" (v. 38). God will be no man's debtor—no matter how much we give him, he gives us more! Jesus' illustration of this is sumptuous. The grain is pressed down into the measure so that it will hold as much as possible. Next it is shaken together to make it fill every possible space. And then, not content with this full measure, the grain is piled above the rim so that it cannot be contained by the measure and spills over into the robes of one's lap.[8] This is the overflowing abundance of God's love and grace as we follow him!

This is universally true, whether it be the Christian businessman H. P. Crowell, founder of Quaker Oats, who said, "For over forty years I have given sixty to seventy percent of my income to God. But I have never gotten ahead of Him! He has always been ahead of me!"[9] or a humble, giving missionary who never made more than a poverty wage. Jesus said, "Truly, I say to you, there is no one who has left house or brothers or sisters or mother or father or children or lands, for my sake and for the gospel, who will not receive a hundredfold now in this time, houses and brothers and sisters and mothers and children and lands . . ." (Mark 10:29, 30; cf. Luke 18:29, 30). The principle of the overflowing measure applies to all givers great and small.

The point is, while some Christians may give and some may not, true disciples give. They give and give and give. Jesus' disciples are big souled, magnanimous. Beneath the externals, in their spirit, Jesus' disciples are accepting, forgiving, and giving. The reason they are like this is because Jesus was this way. He was *accepting*. Though he was and is Judge of the universe, he never exposed others' sins without also offering mercy—he never delighted in pointing to men's failings. He did at times pronounce judgments. He condemned people who refused to repent. But there never was a hint of the judgmentalism he urged us to avoid. Further, he was *forgiving*. As he hung between the thieves, freshly crucified, he prayed, "Father, forgive them, for they know not what they do" (23:34). He was also *giving*. "For you know the grace of our Lord Jesus Christ, that though he was rich, yet for your sake he became poor, so that you by his poverty might become rich" (2 Corinthians 8:9). And like him, his disciples are great souled. This is the very heart of discipleship.

A Life-Imparting Vision (vv. 39, 40)

By definition Jesus' disciples are to be disciple makers. This is what the Great Commission is all about (cf. Matthew 28:19, 20). So Jesus next instructed the Twelve (and us) in the subtleties of how spiritual life is imparted from person to person. He did so through two brief parabolic examples.

Spiritual Sight

"He also told them a parable: 'Can a blind man lead a blind man? Will they not both fall into a pit?'" (v. 39). The image was proverbial and widespread in ancient literature, Biblical and secular. The blind leading the blind suggests to my mind an Ingmar Bergman landscape—an extended desert plain across which stumble the blind hand-in-hand, their eyeless sockets unaware of a yawning chasm. The disciple must see, if he is to grow in grace himself and if he is to help others do the same. The better his vision, the better disciple he will be.

He sees through the illumination of the Holy Spirit, for the Spirit guides him "into all the truth" (John 16:13).

He prays for the spiritual vision of both himself and his charges. He prays along with Paul that fellow believers would have "the eyes of [their] hearts enlightened, that [they] may know what is the hope to which he has called [them], what are the riches of his glorious inheritance in the saints, and what is the immeasurable greatness of his power toward us who believe" (Ephesians 1:18, 19).

To maintain his spiritual vision, he meditates on the Word, avowing, "Your word is a lamp to my feet and a light to my path" (Psalm 119:105). God's Word opens his eyes and illumines his thinking. It gives him wisdom for living. His experience is like that of the psalmist:

> Your commandment makes me wiser than my enemies,
>   for it is ever with me.
> I have more understanding than all my teachers,
>   for your testimonies are my meditation.
> I understand more than the aged,
>   for I keep your precepts.
> I hold back my feet from every evil way,
>   in order to keep your word. (Psalm 119:98–101)

The Bible is an education in itself. That is why an uneducated believer like John Bunyan could write a book that has continued to astound the whole world. This is why many godly grandparents, who did not have the educational and professional advantages their children have enjoyed since the 1940s, lived wiser, better-balanced lives.

Prayer, the study of God's Word, and the illumination of the Holy Spirit enable the Christian to see. Great disciples possess great sight.

Spiritual Example

"A disciple is not above his teacher, but everyone when he is fully trained will be like his teacher" (v. 40). In Jesus' time one's teacher was everything because there were no libraries or other resources for the student. For one to claim to be above his teacher would have been the height of arrogance.[10]

To say a disciple is "like his teacher" was Jesus' way of saying that the lives of his disciples had to model spirituality. What we are in our lives, our disciples will become. There are few things more important for the discipler than the authenticity of his life. His subtle faults often become great flaws in his disciples. But it is also true that his virtues will sometimes blossom in his followers beyond his grandest dreams.

Next to God's Word, few things influence others more than the authenticity of someone else's life. Bishop Quail once said, "Preaching is the art of making a preacher and delivering that." It is the same with discipleship.

A Carefully Examined Life (vv. 41, 42)

Jesus' concern for the spiritual quality of his disciples' lives naturally moved to his call to examine their lives:

> Why do you see the speck that is in your brother's eye, but do not notice the log that is in your own eye? How can you say to your brother, "Brother, let me take out the speck that is in your eye," when you yourself do not see the log that is in your own eye? You hypocrite, first take the log out of your own eye, and then you will see clearly to take out the speck that is in your brother's eye. (vv. 41, 42)

The image is humorous. Similar to a Marx Brothers sketch, one brother approaches another uninvited to help him remove the speck in the second man's eye. But the log in the first brother's own eye keeps getting in the way.

Such hypocrites are not helpful, to say the least! The helpful disciple is the one who has submitted his life to the searchlight of God's Word, and thus his spiritual vision is not clouded with sin. He has confessed his sin, the specks and logs are gone, and thus he sees his brother's needs clearly.

Closing Reflections

Most of us have our spiritual heroes, the disciples we would like to become like. Granted, some imitation can be helpful—attending the schools they attended, reading the books they read, studying like they study, reading the Bible the way they do, praying like they pray, perhaps even dressing and walking and speaking the way they do. But if we really want to be what they are, we must get at their spirit, not just the externals.

The spirit of Jesus' disciples was, first, a magnanimous disposition—a disposition that was accepting, forgiving, and giving. They also understood that the quality of their inner lives was key to discipleship. And finally they asked God to search their lives. "Search me, O God, and know my heart! Try me and know my thoughts! And see if there be any grievous way in me, and lead me in the way everlasting!" (Psalm 139:23, 24).

May such a spirit be ours!

29

Checking the Fruit

LUKE 6:43–45

THE PRECEDING SECTION of Jesus' sermon began with what I have called America's favorite verse, "Judge not, and you will not be judged" (v. 37a). Often misused to put off others' criticisms or concerns, this statement lifted from its context does great harm. If one can make no moral judgments, there can be no morality. One of my sons once stayed in a Florida hotel during spring break, and some collegians in the adjacent room were doing some "heavy partying." As my son stepped from his room wearing his college sweatshirt, one of the partyers also stepped into the hall. Spotting my son's college sweatshirt, the other young man said, "Columbia Bible College. That's cool! Judge not lest ye be judged—that's what I believe."

Jesus' words do not forbid making moral judgments but rather condemn judgmentalism—a particularly grievous sin, especially if you are on the receiving end. Judgmentalism is particularly maddening because it puts you on the defensive when you have done nothing wrong. Any explanation sounds to the judge like defensive guilt—"methinks he doth protest too much." You simply cannot win in such a situation.

As we noted previously, judgmental people are often *blind to their own sins but quick to see them in others*. Judgmentalism is also intrinsically *self-righteous and self-superior*. The proud Pharisees seemed to imagine themselves atop Mount Sinai, above the rest of the *hoi polloi*, judging them with their petty legalisms.

Further, judgmentalism is *self-exculpating*. Its adherents unconsciously imagine that condemning one's sins in someone else will somehow lessen one's own guilt. It is a fact of modern history that the world's most oppressive, totalitarian regimes regularly unite in their condemnation of the policies of other nations.

Judgmentalism is *intrinsically hypocritical*. People often do the same things for which they judge others. In Romans 2:21–24 Paul indicts his fellow Jews for such hypocrisy:

> You then who teach others, do you not teach yourself? While you preach against stealing, do you steal? You who say that one must not commit adultery, do you commit adultery? You who abhor idols, do you rob temples? You who boast in the law dishonor God by breaking the law. For, as it is written, "The name of God is blasphemed among the Gentiles because of you."

Paul's fellow countrymen did not practice what they preached. Even worse, they hypocritically judged others. Note the opening verses of the chapter:

> Therefore you have no excuse, O man, every one of you who judges. For in passing judgment on another you condemn yourself, because you, the judge, practice the very same things. We know that the judgment of God rightly falls on those who practice such things. Do you suppose, O man—you who judge those who practice such things and yet do them yourself—that you will escape the judgment of God? (Romans 2:1–3)

The point is not that we should never make moral judgments, but that we should not do so if we are doing the same things we are judging. Judgmentalism is a hypocrite's favorite pastime. Judgmental people tend to be guilty of the sin they so readily judge.

Judgmentalism is *trivializing*. It views inconsequential things, which may or may not be sinful, as of major importance. In a letter sent to the American Tract Society in 1853, the writer rightly scolded ATS for condemning social dancing and horse racing but not slavery because, and there he quoted ATS, "On no subject, probably, are evangelical Christians more at variance than slavery."[1] This kind of trivializing condemns smoking but not gossip, drinking but not greed, social dancing but not slavery.

Lastly, judgmentalism is *merciless*. Whereas love "believes all things" (1 Corinthians 13:7), the judgmental person disbelieves all things. He presumes the worst. He reads evil into the most innocent actions. He impugns motives. He refuses to give others the benefit of the doubt. Judgmentalism is the opposite of the magnanimous, big-souled person. A judgmental person is certainly not a true disciple or follower of Christ and might not be a Christian at all.

In the present section of his sermon Jesus calls his disciples to a lifestyle of judgment—discerning, subtle, moral judgment! We must not forget that the opening line of this sermon, verse 20, indicates that the sermon was directed to the disciples, not to the crowd. Therefore, being able to judge is an essential part of discipleship and leadership. Jesus' disciples must be able to exercise moral discernment and to make necessary Biblical judgments. Big-souled disciples are to be skillful judges. Jesus makes this clear by giving a horticultural and then a human example.

A Commendation of Judgment (vv. 43–45)

Jesus begins with a horticultural axiom: "For no good tree bears bad fruit, nor again does a bad tree bear good fruit" (v. 43). In contemporary terms, bad apples do not come from good trees, and good apples do not come from bad trees. The Savior then states a principle of horticultural judgment: "For each tree is known by its own fruit. For figs are not gathered from thornbushes, nor are grapes picked from a bramble bush" (v. 44). Empirical evidence makes it possible to give a very accurate analysis of what kind of tree it is and its condition.

This being the case, the human axiom is easily understandable: "The good person out of the good treasure of his heart produces good, and the evil person out of his evil treasure produces evil" (v. 45a). The inner disposition determines the kind of fruit that comes from one's life. One can attempt an external veneer of goodness, but the truth will become known through one's words and deeds. Significantly, Jesus emphasizes here that the mouth is what provides the primary empirical evidence of the state of one's soul: "For out of the abundance of the heart his mouth speaks" (v. 45b).

It is a particularly sweet fact that Christ changes our speech habits. Bethan Lloyd-Jones, the wife of the venerable Welsh preacher Martyn Lloyd-Jones, tells in her *Memories of Sandfields* her recollections of ministry in Wales and of the remarkable conversion of a foul-mouthed man. His speech was so blasphemous and filthy that even his toughest acquaintances were sickened by him, so that he was almost always left to drink by himself. After meeting Christ, he found that he could not speak without swearing. The words poured forth before he could even think. He was sickened himself by the filth. But deliverance came. He was dressing for work and could not locate his socks. Instinctively, he shouted to his wife, "I can't find my _____ socks! Where are the _____ things?" As his words echoed back, sorrow gripped him, and he fell back on his bed and cried aloud, "O Lord, cleanse my tongue. Lord, I can't ask for a pair of socks without swearing.

Please have mercy on me and give me a clean tongue." Lying there, he knew something had happened. From that day on no foul or blasphemous word ever came from his lips.[2]

With most believers, the problem may not have been so embarrassingly obvious and the cure not so dramatic. Nevertheless, the Spirit of Christ changes one's speech. If there is no outer change, there has been no inner change. As the apostle James put it, "If anyone thinks he is religious and does not bridle his tongue but deceives his heart, this person's religion is worthless" (James 1:26). True faith changes our speech.

The tongue—the things we say—reveals what is in our heart. One's words are the most direct communication of the inward being. When a man's conversation is ungodly, his heart is graceless and unconverted. If his speech is carnal, he is carnal. If it is worldly, he is worldly. If it is godless, he is godless. If it is profane, he is profane. If it is mean, he is mean.

We must resist the temptation of regarding our good words as "typically me" and our many bad words as "not really being me at all."[3] Jesus' warning is unavoidable: "For out of the abundance of the heart his mouth speaks" (v. 45b). When Christ ultimately judges us, he will judge our words. On another occasion, when the Pharisees had blasphemed Jesus, he reused the language of the present sermon and ended with a chilling note:

> Either make the tree good and its fruit good, or make the tree bad and its fruit bad, for the tree is known by its fruit. You brood of vipers! How can you speak good, when you are evil? For out of the abundance of the heart the mouth speaks. The good person out of his good treasure brings forth good, and the evil person out of his evil treasure brings forth evil. I tell you, on the day of judgment people will give account for every careless word they speak, for by your words you will be justified, and by your words you will be condemned. (Matthew 12:33–37)

Here, in this world, Jesus' disciples are called to judge men's words. One's doctrine, morals, and heart can be judged by one's words. Disciples make it their business to judge all things by God's grace. The big-souled disciple is continually judging but perpetually nonjudgmental.

The Characteristics of Judgment

This brings us to an aside suggested by Jesus' words in our text but fully covered in the body of Scripture—*how to judge*. In considering this we must distinguish between *making* a judgment and *offering* a judgment. We will provide five suggestions for making judgment and three for offering judgment.

How to Make Judgments

Humbly, by being aware of and owning our own sinfulness and frailty. Christians do not believe or employ the autosuggestive delusion of Emile Coué, "Every day, in every way, I'm growing better and better." God's grace may have wrought some degree of growth, but we know what we are apart from Christ's redemption—sinners saved by grace. We know that our own "heart is deceitful above all things" (Jeremiah 17:9). Like David, we know our transgressions (Psalm 51:3). Understanding that we are thoroughly fallible, we attempt to make responsible judgments with humility lest we fall.

Prayerfully. Anyone who would make a judgment apart from humble prayer is engaging in folly. There must be prayerful confession of one's own sins, as James says: "Confess your sins to one another and pray for one another, that you may be healed" (James 5:16). Those who would judge must fervently pray for themselves and those they judge.

Biblically. Judgment must be according to the revelation of God's Word. Paul told Timothy, "All Scripture is breathed out by God and profitable for teaching, for reproof, for correction, and for training in righteousness, that the man of God may be complete, equipped for every good work" (2 Timothy 3:16, 17). The moral revelation of God's Word must inform our whole life. Because the Scriptures are explicitly clear in defining sin, judgment can be made on most matters with humble confidence. For example, we know that sexual immorality is sin, greed is sin, stealing is sin, drunkenness is sin, slander is sin, selfishness is sin (cf. 1 Corinthians 6:9, 10). At the same time there are less certain matters of faith and conscience regarding which we should judge no man. But the Scriptures are also clear as to how to handle these matters:

> As for the one who is weak in faith, welcome him, but not to quarrel over opinions. One person believes he may eat anything, while the weak person eats only vegetables. Let not the one who eats despise the one who abstains, and let not the one who abstains pass judgment on the one who eats, for God has welcomed him. Who are you to pass judgment on the servant of another? It is before his own master that he stands or falls. (Romans 14:1–4; cf. vv. 22, 23)

Lovingly. A fundamental difference between judgment and judgmentalism is love. *Judgmentalism* is rooted in ill will, while *judgment* has the best interests of the other person in mind. Judging others must be an act of love for God and his moral revelation, and also an act of love for the sinner, giving him the truth for his ultimate good.

Mercifully. Mercifulness is at the very core of Jesus' thinking, as evidenced by his twice referencing Hosea 6:6, "I desire steadfast love and not sacrifice" (cf. Matthew 9:13; 12:7). That principle is a guiding thought in this very sermon: "Be merciful, even as your Father is merciful" (v. 36). Often judgment degenerates to judgmentalism because a harsh, unmerciful spirit takes over. Love "does not rejoice at wrongdoing" (1 Corinthians 13:6), and neither does mercy.

If judgment is made humbly, prayerfully, Biblically, lovingly, and mercifully, it will be a reflection of Jesus. And the one who makes such judgments will be a faithful disciple.

How to Offer Judgment

Exemplarily. R. C. Sproul tells a story about one of the leading golfers on the professional tour who was invited to play in a foursome with Gerald Ford, then President of the United States, Jack Nicklaus, and Billy Graham. The golfer was especially in awe of playing with Ford and Graham (he had played frequently with Nicklaus before). After the round of golf was finished, one of the other pros came up to the golfer and asked, "Hey, what was it like playing with the President and with Billy Graham?" The pro unleashed a torrent of cursing and in a disgusted manner said, "I don't need Billy Graham stuffing religion down my throat." With that he turned on his heel and stormed off, heading for the practice tee.

His friend followed the angry pro to the practice tee, where the pro took out his driver and started to beat some balls in fury. His neck was crimson. His friend said nothing but just sat on a bench and watched. After a few minutes the anger of the pro was spent, and he settled down. His friend said quietly, "Was Billy a little rough on you out there?" The pro heaved an embarrassed sigh and said, "No, he didn't even mention religion. I just had a bad round."[4]

The most exalted way to offer judgment is by your life! Billy Graham had not said a condemning word—he had offered no sideward glance to make the pro feel uncomfortable. The judgment came from Billy's well-known commitment to God, from his personal holiness, even from his joy.

Privately. There are times for judgment to be offered publicly, but it must begin personally and privately. All too often one's judgment of another is shared with others (as a prayer request of course!) and the judged person is the last to hear about it. But Jesus says, "Go and tell him his fault, between you and him alone" (Matthew 18:15). And Jesus' way is the best way!

Gently and constructively. On this point the Scriptures give explicit guidance: "Brothers, if anyone is caught in any transgression, you who are spiritual should restore him in a spirit of gentleness. Keep watch on yourself, lest you too be tempted. Bear one another's burdens, and so fulfill the law of Christ" (Galatians 6:1, 2). Offering judgment is to be a display of gentle strength. One must also be willing to be a part of the solution. If you feel "led" to offer judgment but do not feel led to offer your help, you had best remain quiet.

The Necessity of Judgment

Christians who are correctly following Christ do not succumb to judgmentalism and its evil pathology. The aisles of Christ's church have run deep with the blood of innocents who have been gored by the self-righteous, self-exculpating, hypocritical, trivializing, merciless onslaught of judgmental Christians. Judgmentalism has given secular culture its most damning caricature of Christianity.

At the same time, Christians must not succumb to America's favorite battering ram—"Judge not, and ye shall not be judged." We must not discard our confidence in the moral standards of God's Word!

For one thing, disciples must make *doctrinal judgments*. The refusal to do so—to judge a belief as Biblical or un-Biblical, to call heresy what it is—is one of the reasons why in many places the church is sick and even dead. The Reformation's doctrine of the perspicacity of Scripture (that it is plain to the understanding) still applies. God's Word is unchained. You can read it and judge the doctrinal assertions you hear or read. You must do so, for the spiritual health of your own soul and of those around you!

Disciples must make *moral judgments*. The Bible is clear about most matters of sin. As Mark Twain said, "It's not what I don't understand about the Bible that bothers me; it's what I do understand." The more difficult, less revealed situations are matters of personal conscience and faith, and Romans 14 tells us how to navigate in such waters. But you can and must judge clear sin as sin, regardless of what the relativists say. It is your moral duty.

Disciples make *heart judgments*. Jesus has given us the principle, "The good person out of the good treasure of his heart produces good, and the evil person out of his evil treasure produces evil, for out of the abundance of the heart his mouth speaks" (v. 45). There is nothing inscrutable in this process. Without discernment in these matters the church cannot choose its leaders. Disciples must be capable of sensible, subtle, careful judgment. This is God's will.

Refusing to be steamrolled by America's favorite misapplication of Christ's "judge not" command, we can be confident in God's Word and in our calling. "Do you not know that we are to judge angels? How much more, then, matters pertaining to this life!" (1 Corinthians 6:3).

Closing Reflections

This crazy world seems to have only one absolute—that truth is absolutely relative. But in actuality Jesus is the moral gyroscope who keeps his people on course and standing upright.

The Judge of all humankind will render perfect judgment. Best of all, recognizing our hopelessness and certain condemnation, he underwent judgment for our sins. He is not only the Judge, but the judged! Now he offers us forgiveness for our sins and enables us to live a godly life in an upside-down world. "For our sake he made him to be sin who knew no sin, so that in him we might become the righteousness of God" (2 Corinthians 5:21).

Praise God!

30

Doing His Word

LUKE 6:46–49

PASTOR SCOTT WILLIS and his wife, Janet, had no inkling of what awaited them when they and the youngest six of their nine children piled into their minivan, buckled up, and left their home on Chicago's south side for Wisconsin. It would turn out to be a day of excruciating pain and horror. While driving north on Interstate 94 in Milwaukee, the van ran over a large piece of metal that punctured the gas tank, turning the van into a raging furnace. By the time the van stopped and the parents fell out, their children were hopelessly trapped as their mother screamed, "No! No! No!"

One could suppose that for the Willises, God had never been so far away. Yet, at a news conference the burned, bandaged couple, still in physical pain, gave witness to God's grace. Janet said that when she looked back toward the van and began screaming, Scott touched her shoulder. "He said, 'Janet, this is what we've been prepared for.' And he was right. He said, 'Janet, it was quick and they're with the Lord,' and he was right." In their shared hospital room they comforted themselves by watching videos of their children, reading passages from God's Word, and talking openly about what had happened.

The Willises' living testimony amid the tears and heartache is inspiring. "I know God has purposes and God has reasons," says Scott. "God has demonstrated His love to us and our family. There's no question in our mind that God is good, and we praise Him in all things." "It's His right," agrees Janet. "We belong to Him. My children belong to Him. He's the giver and taker of life and He sustains us."[1]

Storms have fallen on the Willises' home, floods of sorrow have roared at its foundations, the thunderclouds still bring pain, but their house stands and will stand! The supreme reason for all the world to see is, they are God's children, and they have built their lives upon his holy Word.

It is possible to claim to be a disciple of Christ and yet not be a doer of the Word. This is the clear implication of the question with which Jesus opens the conclusion of his Sermon on the Plain: "Why do you call me 'Lord, Lord,' and not do what I tell you?" (v. 46). "Lord" is the language of the disciple. Saying it twice—"Lord, Lord"—is an intense affirmation of allegiance. But ironically Jesus had followers (self-appointed or perhaps self-deluded "wanna-be" disciples) who did not do what he said, who did not make a habit of obedience.

So Jesus both warned them and instructed them regarding what to do. The warning is pictured in the extreme differences of two houses, one that stands and one that totally collapses. Jesus presented no middle ground. The structures of our lives will stand or fall depending on what we do with Christ's Word.

In verse 47 Jesus says, "Everyone who comes to me and hears my words and does them, I will show you what he is like. . . ." Faithful disciples are those who keep coming, hearing, and doing Jesus' words, as the three Greek participles in this sentence literally read. These three words, especially the latter two, are the key to authentic discipleship and to a life that stands amid the storms like those that Scott and Janet Willis have endured.

Authentic Discipleship (v. 47)

Coming

True discipleship must always begin with coming to Christ ("comes to me"). We must remember that when Jesus preached this sermon, his audience stood in widening concentric arcs. Closest stood the freshly chosen Twelve. Around them spread "a great crowd of his disciples" and beyond them "a great multitude of people" from all various areas (v. 17). The large group of disciples were doing the right thing—they had come to hear the Word of God. They were doing what they could to experience authentic discipleship.

Today the church's preaching of the Word supplies this setting, and a person can approach Christ when he attends corporate worship with Christ's Body and hears his Word preached. There are no churchless disciples.

Hearing

Coming to Christ then enables hearing—"and hears my words." Some in the vast crowd did not hear what he said, not because he was inaudible, but because they were not listening.

Today many church attenders listen to God's Word the way they listen to a flight attendant explain an aircraft's safety features—totally tuned out. That little talk has to be one of the worst jobs on any flight. The moment the flight attendant begins, he/she endures a ritual of frequent-flyer rejection. The shades go down in the passengers' eyes, the newspapers go up, the headphones go on. One flight attendant, exasperated by the inattention, altered the wording to, "When the mask drops down, place it over your navel and continue to breathe normally"—and no one noticed!

True hearing requires several disciplines.

Listening, so essential, is a skill that has been severely impaired by modern culture's glut of words. Billions of words are spoken every second, and sometimes it seems like they are assaulting us mercilessly through TV, radio, and the multiple conversations around us. We are a distracted people. Also, the visual media, with their video bytes and quick scene or topic changes, have reduced our attention spans. In addition, the postmodern mind, which responds so readily to self-directed, subjective, feeling-oriented messages, has difficulty following the reasoned arguments of Scripture. Even worse, many people who attend church regularly simply do not want to hear God's Word. "For the time is coming when people will not endure sound teaching, but having itching ears they will accumulate for themselves teachers to suit their own passions, and will turn away from listening to the truth and wander off into myths" (2 Timothy 4:3, 4).

For these various reasons listening is not in vogue and is, at best, difficult, making congregations look like the 6:30 a.m. flight to Cleveland. Listening requires discipline. Listening is work! What can we do to become and be good hearers of the Word in church?

Pray—for the preacher and for yourself. *Come prepared to listen*, understanding that listening is work. The will to concentrate is fundamental. We cannot listen to God's Word the way we watch TV—kicked back with a bag of chips in hand or pleasant daydreams occupying our minds. *Keep your Bible open to the sermon text* and turn to the other passages that are cited. *Take notes*. One of the curious by-products of the Great Awakening in America was a sudden interest in shorthand. It was not unusual to see men and women, quill pens in hand, carrying portable inkwells as they hurried to a preaching service on the village green. The same thing had happened in Scotland under similar circumstances.[2] Revived hearts lead to scribbling hands.

True hearing of the Word also requires *reflection and application*. This is no easy task either, because ours is a nonreflective age. Perhaps you have had the experience, while sitting quietly thinking, of having someone ask if you're "all right." The apex of hearing is application—discerning what it means to me and what I ought to do. This was impressed on me one day when a member of my pastoral staff burst into my office and enthusiastically shared seven resolutions he had written in response to the Word he had heard preached that week.[3] We all need to follow that example.

Doing

The first aspect of discipleship is coming to Christ, the next is hearing his words, and the final is doing his word—"and does them."

A young Korean man traveled a great distance to the home of the missionary who had led him to Christ, then announced his reason for the visit: "I have been memorizing some verses of the Bible, and I want to quote them to you."

The missionary listened as the young man recited without error the entire Sermon on the Mount. He commended the young man for the remarkable feat of memory. Then, being a good missionary, he cautioned the young man to not only "say" the Scriptures but to practice them. The man responded, "Oh, that *is* the way I learned them. I tried to memorize them, but they wouldn't stick, so I made a plan. First I would learn a verse. Then I would do it to a neighbor. After that, I found that I could remember it."[4]

That young Korean was an authentic disciple whether he knew it or not. He had come to Christ, he had heard Christ's words, and he had done them. It is in the doing that authentic discipleship is fully achieved.

Every time we truly hear the Word and are authentically moved, we must resolve to act upon it. Most of the time the resolution will not be dramatic or grand, but what seems to be some small action. Perhaps it will be a note written, an adjustment at work, an apology, a gift, a few words of witness, a commitment, a kind word, a subtle change in attitude. But the key is, do it! Do not procrastinate or you will forget it. And when you do it, you will be stepping into true discipleship. Each step will become more natural and a little easier.

When Jesus called into question the discipleship of the large crowd of self-professed disciples by saying, "Why do you call me 'Lord, Lord,' and not do what I tell you?" he was referring to their disobedience to the sermon he was then preaching. "Why do you call me 'Lord, Lord,' and neglect to do what I have just now been calling you to do?" True disciples obey Christ, including this very sermon—the sermon preached on the plain. What does this involve—what are we to do in light of what Jesus said in this remarkable sermon?

An unearthly perspective. Disciples listen to, reflect upon, and put into practice the unearthly perspective of verses 20–26 with its strange blessings and woes regarding being rich, wellfed, joyful, and accepted. The disciple examines his life. Perhaps he holds too tightly to riches. Perhaps the fact that all speak well of him means he has shied away from bearing witness for Christ. So he resolves to stand firm for Christ. He obeys the Word—and his life detonates brightly for the Master across the secular landscape.

Is Jesus calling you in this way? Then be a disciple and do it!

An unearthly love. Disciples hear and put into practice the unearthly love so eloquently described in verses 27–36. They hear the call to unnatural love—to "Love your enemies, do good to those who hate you, bless those who curse you, pray for those who abuse you" (vv. 27, 28)—"And as you wish that others would do to you, do so to them" (v. 31). This is terribly unnatural and wonderfully supernatural. Jesus calls you to do something good for someone who hates you, to offer a blessing to one who curses you, to pray for your abuser. With his help, you can do it! That is what his disciples do.

An unearthly mercy. Disciples hear and put into practice the unearthly mercy enjoined in verses 37–42. They are nonjudgmental and *accepting*—"Judge not, and you will not be judged" (v. 37). They are careful to clear up their own act first. They are *forgiving*—"Forgive, and you will be forgiven" (v. 37b). They are *giving*—"Give, and it will be given to you" (vv. 37b, 38a). This kind of mercy puts their hearts in sync with that of Jesus. Do you need to do some accepting, some forgiving, some giving? It is the only way to be Christ's disciple.

An unearthly discernment. Disciples hear and put into practice the unearthly discernment Jesus commended in verses 43–45. They reject a judgmental attitude but willingly embrace the hard work of moral judgment because they know that "The good person out of the good treasure of his heart produces good, and the evil person out of his evil treasure produces evil, for out of the abundance of the heart his mouth speaks" (v. 45). Relying on God's Word, they courageously make doctrinal and moral judgments. This is the task of a disciple.

Authentic disciples call Jesus "Lord" and hear and do what he says.

Authentic Disciples Stand (vv. 48, 49)

How do such disciples fare in life? Jesus answers, "He is like a man building a house, who dug deep and laid the foundation on the rock. And when a flood arose, the stream broke against that house and could not shake it, because it had been well built" (v. 48).

> When through the deep waters
> I call thee to go,
> The rivers of sorrow
> Shall not overflow;
> For I will be with thee,
> Thy troubles to bless,
> And sanctify to thee
> Thy deepest distress.
>
> Rippon's Selection of Hymns (1787)

Disciples who hear God's Word (who pay attention to it, reflect upon it, and apply it) and then do it will stand! Because of the broad life application of these principles as hearers and doers of the Word, Scott and Janet Willis still stand. The reason "they derive strength from reciting passages from the Bible," as the *Chicago Tribune* reported, is that they have been, and are, not merely hearers of the Word but authentic *hearers and doers*. They have endeavored to do God's Word. That is the only reason they could give glory to God in their darkest hour. This is the only way any of us can stand.

Glorious as this is, there is something even more significant here. As Leon Morris explains:

> When the final test comes at judgment day it is the foundation on which our lives are built that matters (cf. 1 Corinthians 3:11f). The words certainly have an application to the storms of this life. The person with a good foundation is not easily upset by life's difficulties; but it is the supreme final test that is specially in mind.[5]

Doers of the Word will endure the fires of judgment and reign eternally with Jesus Christ! That thought brings us great joy!

Closing Reflections

Hearing or not hearing—doing the Word or not doing the Word—is decisive for this life and for the life to come. Jesus concludes, "But the one who hears and does not do them is like a man who built a house on the ground without a foundation. When the stream broke against it, immediately it fell, and the ruin of that house was great" (v. 49).

Are you a hearer? Do you really listen? Or are you a drowsy commuter to nowhere? Honestly, what is your practice—what is mine? If you are not a good listener, covenant to become one now. Then do the Word! Do the love. Do the mercy. Do the faith.

Only two houses are being built—those with foundations and those without. Which house is yours? What about those around you? Where must one begin? The same place where Scott and Janet Willis began years ago—with belief in Christ. As Jesus made so clear when "they said to him, 'What must we do, to be doing the works of God?' Jesus answered them, 'This is the work of God, that you believe in him whom he has sent'" (John 6:28, 29).

31

Viewing Faith

LUKE 7:1–10

PROFESSIONAL MOUNTAIN CLIMBER Royal Robbins, writing for *Sports Illustrated*, described the one great essential of the sport. It is not physical strength or having the safest and best equipment, or even proper training, but the ability to see things as they really are. Robbins writes:

> If we are keenly alert and aware of the rock and what we are doing on it, if we are honest with ourselves and our capabilities and weaknesses, if we avoid committing ourselves beyond what we know is safe, then we will climb safely. For climbing is an exercise in reality. He who sees it clearly is on safe ground, regardless of his experience or skill. But he who sees reality as he would like it to be, may have his illusions rudely stripped from his eyes when the ground comes up fast.

Actually, mountain climber Robbins has given masterful expression to a crucial life principle. Wise people resist seeing life as they would like to see it. They are honest with themselves regarding their capabilities and weaknesses.

This universal principle applies to every area of life. But nowhere is it more essential than in matters of faith, because *real faith is an exercise in reality*. The present text about a centurion's faith takes us inside true faith and shows us how and what faith sees. It presents us with the flawed perspective of the centurion's friends (vv. 3–5), then the enlightened perspective of the centurion himself (vv. 6, 7a), and finally Jesus' divine perspective (vv. 7b–10).

This takes place immediately after the naming of the Twelve and Jesus' great Sermon on the Plain, which he ended by challenging his hearers to put what he had been preaching into practice. The apostles and many of the disciples were present because Jesus wanted them to learn something from *a Gentile's faith!* This story conveys universal insights into faith that are applicable to everyone, Jews and Gentiles.

The setting, given in verses 1, 2, is rather ordinary: "After he had finished all his sayings in the hearing of the people, he entered Capernaum. Now a centurion had a servant who was sick and at the point of death, who was highly valued by him" (vv. 1, 2). Centurions were commonplace in the Roman Empire. They were equivalent in rank to a modern-day army captain and normally commanded one hundred soldiers. Death, too, was commonplace in the ancient world. Normal life expectancy did not approach what we would consider to be midlife. But there is something extraordinary in the centurion's concern for his servant. The Greek word translated "highly valued" means the servant was honored by the centurion.[1] The centurion considered his manservant more than a valuable tool. He cared for him as a person, evidence of the soldier's gracious soul.

The Jews' Perspective (vv. 3–5)

But what is really extraordinary is that this Gentile, a captain in the occupying army, asked *Jewish elders* to ask Jesus for help—and the elders went eagerly! Clearly this centurion was no ordinary Gentile. The synagogue leaders were not given to running errands for anyone, much less a Gentile soldier.

As to what they thought of him, there can be no doubt: "And when they came to Jesus, they pleaded with him earnestly, saying, 'He is worthy to have you do this for him, for he loves our nation, and he is the one who built us our synagogue'" (vv. 4, 5). The centurion, of course, could have been deceiving them with his generosity because the Romans would sometimes support local religion when it was to their advantage. As the historian Gibbon wrote: "The various modes of religion which prevailed in the Roman world were all considered by the people as equally true; by the philosopher as equally false; *and by the magistrate as equally useful*."[2] But this centurion was apparently no such cynic. He was not a mere contributor to the synagogue fund—he built the whole place![3]

Evidently his pagan creed had become worn, and the lofty monotheism of Judaism magnetized his soul. The elders' assertion that "he loves our nation" was true and probably indicates that he was, in the language of the day, a "God-fearer"—that is, someone who accepted the Jewish God but declined to become a proselyte to Judaism (cf. Acts 10:2; 16:14).[4]

The elders had it right. The centurion was certainly a lover of Israel and a benefactor of her people. But their insistence that he was "worthy" to have Jesus heal his servant was their own spin. It certainly was not his (cf. vv. 6, 7)! To some extent this is excusable. The elders were understandably generous in their assessment. But their rationale was patently *external*—"He loves our nation, and he is the one who built us our synagogue"—*not internal*, "He is humble and meek and godly." They lauded the centurion for the kind of works with which people today think they can earn Heaven. Build a Gothic cathedral, solicit public donations with a promise that donors' names will appear on a published subscribers list, and the money will roll in! The Bible, in both Testaments, teaches that a plea of worthiness is totally unsustainable before God.

The elders presented such a surface argument for Jesus' involvement because that was the way they were accustomed to analyzing their own lives—by externals. Unfortunately, in spiritual matters seeing falsely is worse than being blind. The blind at least know they cannot see. But the surface seer thinks he sees.

Before the seventeenth century, when people looked at a lake or a pond or a glass of water, they judged it clean if they could see through it. But in 1674 the Dutchman Leeuwenhoek filled a glass vial with water, began curiously looking at it through his newly acquired microscope lens, and saw, as he quaintly put it, "very many small animalcules." He then examined a drop of water and jotted down his findings:

> I now saw very plainly that these were little eels, or worms, lying all huddled up together and wriggling; just as if you saw, with the naked eye, a whole tubful of very little eels and water, with the eels a-squirming among one another: and the whole water seemed to be alive with these multifarious animalcules.[5]

When we turn the magnifying glass of God's Word onto what is inside us, we find a whole universe of squirming critters and realize our own unworthiness. As a prophet said six hundred years before Jesus, "The heart is deceitful above all things, and desperately sick; who can understand it?" (Jeremiah 17:9).

The Centurion's Perspective (vv. 6, 7a)

Jesus, always on the alert for hearts that were turned toward him, "went with them" (v. 6). During the interlude, the centurion had evidently had second thoughts, realizing that a devout Jew might have scruples about entering a house of a Gentile, just as Peter would later express to Cornelius (cf. Acts 10:28; 11:2, 3; see also *Mishnah*, Oholot 18:7). So the Roman officer dispensed a delegation of friends to meet Jesus. It is also possible that word had gotten back to him as to how he had been misrepresented by the elders as worthy of Jesus' action.

Whatever the case, "the centurion sent friends, saying to him, 'Lord, do not trouble yourself, for I am not worthy to have you come under my roof. Therefore I did not presume to come to you" (vv. 6b, 7a). In the words and behavior of this centurion we can discern the elements of spiritual humility and unworthiness.

Seeing Oneself

This man had obviously seen himself as he really was. He had a wholesome consciousness of his own sin. Once we see ourselves as we are and take into account not only our actions, but our corrupt tendencies, foul thoughts, pampered sensualities, baseness, and meanness, much of which has never come to the surface, we will avoid ever saying or even imagining, "I am worthy."

The great problem for most non-Christians, and even many Christians, is that they are strangers to themselves. They look at the errors of others through a microscope and see all the wriggling animalcules, but they look at their own sins through the wrong end of a telescope and fail to spot the foul creatures bumping in the dark.[6] They live with an unwholesome, unconsciousness of their own sin.

Modern culture (including the church) distances itself from terrible sinners. We imagine that the John Gacys, Jeffrey Dahmers, and Ted Bundys are really not part of the human race, but are monsters, something we could never be. Gacy, appearing to the community as a child-loving clown, is from another planet, we think. But the truth is, such persons are people just like us who have surrendered to the evil impulses that are within all humanity. We have all had monstrous thoughts in our souls. Perhaps we have not thought of dining on another's flesh, but we have held on to our own social cannibalisms, sadisms, and verbal homicides.

The fact is, no one is in a position to understand Christ and Christianity who is not acquainted with his own evil nature. C. S. Lewis, writing to a friend, told how the writings of the great Scottish preacher Alexander Whyte had brought him face-to-face with a characteristic of Puritanism he had almost forgotten. "For him," says Lewis, "the one essential symptom of the regenerate life is a permanently horrified perception of one's natural and (it seems) unalterable corruption. The true Christian's nostril is to be continually attentive to the inner cesspool."[7] Lewis understood that there is a wholesome, in fact essential, consciousness of sin.

But we must also remember that while Christianity that ignores sin becomes sick, Christianity that sees very little but sin is a type of slavery. It has forgotten grace. We are not to go around lisping like Donald Duck in the old cartoon, "I'm a despicable person. I'm a despicable person." Yes, we are sinful and worthless, but we also bear the *imago Dei*, and by God's grace some of us may become a St. Francis or a Corrie ten Boom or a Rachel Saint.

No Biblically-informed, Spirit-filled Christian should ever look self-righteously upon an unbeliever, because the believer understands his own humanity and heart—his proneness to wander. Jesus is on our side. He does not just love and help people who think they are worthy. "But God shows his love for us in that while we were still sinners, Christ died for us" (Romans 5:8).

Seeing Christ

There is a sublime side to the centurion's spiritual posture—he saw and understood the implications of Jesus' power—he recognized that Jesus is the Son of God. This is amazing. Jesus was a Jewish Galilean peasant, and the centurion was a Gentile, a man of wealth and some local eminence. Yet the Roman officer not only regarded himself as undeserving of having Jesus come under his roof, but even unworthy of meeting Jesus in the street. What humility! The centurion apparently realized that one who has power over life and death, who can heal with a word, must be divine. And if Christ was divine, then he, a Gentile sinner, was unworthy to meet him.

The passage we have been studying reveals two essential components of Christian faith—knowing who Christ is, and knowing who we are. Do you know who and what you are? Do you know and believe that you are unworthy? Do you know that "we have all become like one who is unclean, and all our righteous deeds are like a polluted garment" (Isaiah 64:6)? Even more important, do you know who Jesus is?

Jesus' Perspective (vv. 7b–10)

The centurion now showed his faith through his words: "But say the word, and let my servant be healed. For I too am a man set under authority, with soldiers under me: and I say to one, 'Go,' and he goes; and to another, 'Come,' and he comes; and to my servant, 'Do this,' and he does it" (vv. 7b, 8). The centurion understood that Jesus can heal up close as much as he can heal from a distance.

Up to now the centurion's faith had produced a flurry of activity. A delegation of elders had gone to Jesus. Jesus had approached his home. A second delegation of friends had met Jesus, expressing the centurion's faith. But now the officer's faith rested. He knew his own limitations and unworthiness, and he knew who Christ was. He believed that Christ could heal his servant. His faith had found a resting place.

What was Jesus' perspective on the centurion's words? "When Jesus heard these things, he marveled at him, and turning to the crowd that followed him, said, 'I tell you, not even in Israel have I found such faith'" (v. 9). Only twice in Scripture was Jesus said to marvel or be amazed at something. The other time was when he began his public ministry in his hometown of Nazareth, and his fellow Jews rejected him: "He marveled because of their unbelief" (Mark 6:6; cf. Luke 4:14–30).

What could be more terrible than to amaze the Son of God with one's lack of faith? But what could be more wonderful than to amaze him with one's faith? This centurion had *amazing faith!*

Why was Jesus so amazed?

The man's background. He was an uncircumcised Gentile, raised without the benefits of the covenant, without the glorious synagogue tradition, without the Scriptures that were the lot of every Jewish child raised in a devout home (cf. Deuteronomy 6:4–9). Yet he had faith!

The man's occupation. He was a soldier, an instrument of the oppressive pagan establishment. As an officer, he wielded considerable power. He was not the kind to naturally come to Christ in humble, amazing faith. But he did!

The man's wealth. Riches are not a spiritual advantage, because they foster a this-world attachment. Jesus later said, "How difficult it is for those who have wealth to enter the kingdom of God! For it is easier for a camel to go through the eye of a needle than for a rich person to enter the kingdom of God" (18:24, 25). But, by the mercy of God, this centurion, this unusually rich soldier, had gone through the eye of a needle. Amazing!

The man's certainty. The certitude of his faith was expressed in stark simplicity: "But say the word, and let my servant be healed" (v. 7b). This was the dynamic dual certainty of faith given in Hebrews 11:1—future certainty: "Now faith is the assurance of things hoped for"—and also visual certainty: "the conviction of things not seen." The Roman saw Christ's invisible spiritual power, and he saw his servant as being made whole by Christ's word. Amazing! His faith was like that of Noah and Abraham and Moses.

Here, for all to see, are the fundamental perspectives of a faith that pleases God—it sees itself, and it sees God. Such faith is transcultural—it is the same for Jews and Gentiles. And it transcends time—it is a spiritual reality then and now.

Closing Reflections

Faith is an exercise in reality. He who sees clearly, and not merely as he would like to see, is on safe ground.

Do you see yourself as deserving Christ's grace, as the elders saw the centurion? Do you inwardly think that because you are a lover of the church, and even more, a giver of your money you are worthy of God's care? Have you secretly internalized others' good opinions of yourself, so that despite the persistent teaching of God's Word that salvation comes through faith and is a gift of God, you imagine that you will somehow make it into the kingdom by your personal virtue? Do you see Christians who glibly talk about their salvation but do not measure up in their walk, and then reason that because your life is better than theirs, you certainly will make it to Heaven?

If so, you are not seeing reality. You must face the truth—apart from the grace of God, your heart is desperately evil. Self is at the center of your universe, and therefore darkness reigns within. The reality is that you, like the centurion, are not worthy. No one is. All your acts of supposed righteousness will not cut it with God. Your only hope is the love and grace of Christ!

Furthermore, do you see Jesus for who he is? As your God?

> He is the image of the invisible God, the firstborn of all creation. For by him all things were created, in heaven and on earth, visible and invisible, whether thrones or dominions or rulers or authorities—all things were created through him and for him. And he is before all things, and in him all things hold together. And he is the head of the body, the church. He is the beginning, the firstborn from the dead, that in everything he might be preeminent. (Colossians 1:15–18)

Do you see him as your Savior?

> For in him [Jesus] all the fullness of God was pleased to dwell, and through him to reconcile to himself all things, whether on earth or in heaven, making peace by the blood of his cross. (Colossians 1:19, 20)

Do you see Jesus as your hope?

> For the Lord himself will descend from heaven with a cry of command, with the voice of an archangel, and with the sound of the trumpet of God. And the dead in Christ will rise first. Then we who are alive, who are left, will be caught up together with them in the clouds to meet the Lord in the air, and so we will always be with the Lord. (1 Thessalonians 4:16, 17)

Biblical faith is an exercise in reality—true seeing. Do you see yourself as you are? Do you see Christ as he is? If so, you see with the eyes of faith.

32

Jesus Raises a Widow's Son

LUKE 7:11–17

JOSEPH BAYLY knew what the loss of a child was like. In fact, he and his wife MaryLou lost three sons—one at eighteen days, after surgery; another at five years, with leukemia; the third at eighteen years, after a sledding accident. So when Joe Bayly wrote about the death of a child, people listened. Here is part of what he had to say:

> Of all deaths, that of a child is most unnatural and hardest to bear. In Carl Jung's words, it is "a period placed before the end of the sentence," sometimes when the sentence has hardly begun. We expect the old to die. The separation is always difficult, but it comes as no surprise. But the child, the youth? Life lies ahead, with its beauty, its wonder, its potential. Death is a cruel thief when it strikes down the young. The suffering that usually precedes death is another reason childhood death is so hard for parents to bear. Children were made for fun and laughter, for sunshine, not for pain. And they have a child's heightened consciousness rather than the ability to cope with suffering that comes with maturity. They also lack the "kind amnesia of senility." In a way that is different from any other human relationship, a child is bone of his parents' bone, flesh of their flesh. When a child dies, part of the parents is buried. . . . I met a man who was in his seventies. During our first ten minutes together, he brought the faded photograph of a child out of his wallet—his child, who had died almost fifty years before.[1]

The death of a child is certainly one of the greatest agonies possible in this life—a burying of a part of oneself, a period before the end of a sentence, the death of a future. It is a burden that all parents fear. Such untimely pain was the emotional context of Jesus' next ministry event.

Jesus Encounters Death (vv. 11, 12)

> Soon afterward he went to a town called Nain, and his disciples and a great crowd went with him. As he drew near to the gate of the town, behold, a man who had died was being carried out, the only son of his mother, and she was a widow, and a considerable crowd from the town was with her. (vv. 11, 12)

A public sorrow. The town of Nain was about twenty-five miles from Capernaum, a day's journey. So it was probably in the late afternoon that Jesus and his band of disciples encountered an unexpected public display of sorrow at the city gate. A funeral bier (an open coffin), preceded by the pathetic figure of a woman, stood directly in Jesus' path. The coffin was surrounded by professional mourners who were leading a large, wailing crowd with flutes, cymbals, and frenzied cries.[2] The cries were especially deafening because of the loud mourning associated with the death of an only child.[3]

A private sorrow. The wretched figure of the woman, without the company of a husband or, as far as we can tell, children, communicated in an instant to Jesus and his followers the depth of the tragedy. The tear-drenched woman was a widow, and the pale young corpse was her only son. The large crowd posed an ironic contrast to her actual state. She was alone in this world—without a provider or protector. Tomorrow she would awake by herself, brokenhearted, without the sustaining footfall and sounds of her beloved son.

There is something poignant in the tragic woman's silhouette because, given what is about to take place and the declarations to be made, she is a fit figure for the hurting soul to whom Christ ministers.

Jesus' Compassions (v. 13)

As the bereaved woman stumbled toward the burial ground, she had no hint of the miracle awaiting her.

Jesus' Heart

"And when the Lord saw her, he had compassion on her" (v. 13). Jesus' heart went out to her in unmitigated compassion. Luke uses the strongest word possible here to describe Jesus' pity. The root word from which it comes refers to what is inside (the heart, liver, lungs), the viscera.[4] It describes an emotion that has a physical effect. Jesus felt for her.

We should note that this was typical of Jesus. Later, at a similar occasion, when Jesus observed Mary and Martha weeping for Lazarus, "he was deeply moved in his spirit and greatly troubled" (John 11:33). The word translated "was deeply moved" comes from an ancient word describing a horse's snorting.[5] It indicates that the Lord let out an involuntary gasp—the breath just went out of him. E. V. Rieu comments, "He gave way to such distress of spirit as made his body tremble." Jesus felt for the two sisters so much that he had a physical reaction. And his convulsive feeling gave way to tears (v. 35). When he saw the widow of Nain, Jesus was again inwardly convulsed with compassion.

> In ev'ry pang that rends the heart,
> The man of sorrows has a part.[6]

Jesus' extraordinary compassion was grounded in his sinlessness and selflessness. Whereas our sin and self-focus inhibit our ability to care, Jesus' sinless self-forgetfulness allowed the full exercise of his sympathy and pity.

From this we infer, gladly, that Jesus has a heart that is big enough for our sorrows. His compassion, his empathy, is real. "His mercies never come to an end; they are new every morning; great is your faithfulness" (Lamentations 3:22, 23). You may have such an immense hurt that you cannot even voice it. Perhaps your trauma has left you inarticulate. But he understands completely and sympathetically. Not hindered by personal limitations, his immense heart goes out to you.

Jesus' Words

Not only did Jesus' heart go out to the poor widow, but also his soothing words: "Do not weep" (v. 13b). Now, he was not telling her to suppress her emotion—"OK, chin up. Don't be a baby." Rather, he was expressing genuine care for her and was hinting at the miracle about to occur. Moved by her tears, he gave her the gentle imperative, "Do not go on crying" as a prelude to what he was about to do.

Jesus Raises the Dead (vv. 14, 15)

The Touch

Touching a coffin meant sure pollution according to the ceremonial laws of the Old Testament (cf. Numbers 19:11, 16), but Jesus knew that the Law required mercy above sacrifice (cf. Hosea 6:6). So Jesus took charge: "Then he came up and touched the bier, and the bearers stood still" (v. 14a). His silent touch stopped everything, forcing a riveting silence. Life and death stood face-to-face. The scene is parabolic of Jesus' mission to arrest death and swallow it up in victory (cf. 1 Corinthians 15:54, 55).

The Command

The silence was broken by Jesus' simple command, "Young man, I say to you, arise" (v. 14b). Significantly, when performing lesser miracles Jesus would sometimes enjoin specific actions along with the healing. The actions were spiritually instructive. But when it came to resurrections, he used only his word (cf. Mark 5:41; Luke 8:54; John 11:43). Clearly, he wanted everyone to see that resurrection power rests in him!

Notice too that when he spoke to the boy's cold corpse, the boy heard him. The young man was dead in body, but he was fully alive somewhere! For we humans, death is only death of the body. The human spirit lives on.

Obedience

The young man heard the voice of Christ and obeyed (as must every deceased human in its own time): "And the dead man sat up and began to speak, and Jesus gave him to his mother" (v. 15). The gray, cold clay of his face flushed with color, his fixed, dilated eyes twitched and focused on the blue sky, he blinked, he sat up in his shroud—and he began to talk. Perhaps his words were mundane—"Mother, you sure look tired. I'm hungry. Who are these people?" Or perhaps it was gloriously exalted.

At any rate, the crowd fell back, and some began to shriek. There was a universal rush of adrenaline. Here and there incredulous voices began to praise God. And his mother? There were still tears, but her wet eyes radiated heavenly light and overwhelming joy as she embraced her only son.

This is a picture of our future as well.

> For the Lord himself will descend from heaven with a cry of command, with the voice of an archangel, and with the sound of the trumpet of God. And the dead in Christ will rise first. Then we who are alive, who are left, will be caught up together with them in the clouds to meet the Lord in the air, and so we will always be with the Lord. Therefore encourage one another with these words. (1 Thessalonians 4:16–18)

The voice that raised that poor, babbling young man from his coffin will be trumpeted into the depths of the sea, into the roots of the mountains, into the diffuse dust and lost molecules of God's physically dead children—and all who know Christ will hear it!

Joe and MaryLou Bayly will see Jesus whole! And the entire Bayly clan—mother, father, Danny, John, Joe Jr., Deborah, Tim, David, Nathan, and their own children—will be given to one another. The six small coffins of the children of Scott and Janet Willis will not be able to hold their eternally young bodies as they fly into the embrace of their parents in the presence of Jesus. What a reunion that will be! And best of all, we will all be face-to-face with Jesus Christ, our Savior!

We will all hear his voice. "Get up, Billy! Get up, Jessica! Get up, Brian! It's resurrection morning!"

Our Awesome Jesus (vv. 16, 17)

As heart-stopping as the resurrection of the widow's only son was, there was a further revelation in this event for Jesus' Jewish audience. Over five hundred years earlier the prophet Elijah had gone to another small town (Zarephath), just as Jesus went to Nain. There he met a widow at the gate of the town, just as Jesus did at Nain. The widow had an only son who became ill and died, as had happened in Nain. The highlight of the story goes like this:

> And he [Elijah] said to her, "Give me your son." And he took him from her arms and carried him up into the upper chamber where he lodged, and laid him on his own bed. And he cried to the LORD, "O LORD my God, have you brought calamity even upon the widow with whom I sojourn, by killing her son?" Then he stretched himself upon the child three times and cried to the LORD, "O LORD my God, let this child's life come into him again." And the LORD listened to the voice of Elijah. And the life of the child came into him again, and he revived. And Elijah took the child and brought him down from the upper chamber into the house and delivered him to his mother. And Elijah said, "See, your son lives." And the woman said to Elijah, "Now I know that you are a man of God, and that the word of the LORD in your mouth is truth." (1 Kings 17:19–24)

Jesus, at the Father's direction, sovereignly performed a miracle that nearly duplicated Elijah's. The language of Luke's account is conclusive because 7:15, which records that Jesus "gave him to his mother," is identical in Greek to 1 Kings 17:23, "delivered him to his mother" (Septuagint).[7]

Not only is the language identical, but the results are similar. There the widow became convinced that Elijah was "a man of God" (a prophet) and that he spoke God's Word. Here, after Jesus' miracle we read, "Fear seized them all, and they glorified God, saying, 'A great prophet has arisen among us!' and 'God has visited his people!'" (v. 16).

Jesus was much more than a great prophet. But ascribing such a title to him was the best the townspeople could do without further revelation. It was a spontaneous chorus of realization that messianic times had fallen on them. Their chorus that "God has visited his people" is similar to what Zechariah had sung in the birth narratives: "Blessed be the Lord God of Israel, for he has visited and redeemed his people" (1:68).[8]

So Jesus had come in Elijah-like power, except for one huge difference: Elijah had to stretch himself over the boy three times while crying to God for help (cf. 1 Kings 17:20–22), but Jesus had only to speak the word.

Closing Reflections

How awesome Jesus is!

Awesome Compassion

George Eliot wrote: "If we had a keen vision and feeling of all ordinary human life, it would be like hearing the grass grow and the squirrel's heart beat, and we should die of that roar that lies on the other side of silence."[9] It is true, wherever we are in this world, that on the other side of the silence of the people around us a vast roar exists. If we could hear it, the burden would kill us. But Christ's compassion and redeeming power are sufficient for every need.

There are grieving souls who mourn not only death but the loss of a relationship. There are rejected men, women, and children who feel worthless. There are the betrayed who are so wounded they fear they can never trust again. There are the depressed for whom a single positive thought is an impossibility.

The hurts and failures of this world are burdens that cannot be borne by anyone except Jesus. But he hears the pain of every voice, and his heart goes out to us, his children, with deep compassion. Are you afflicted and hurting? Jesus hurts with you!

Awesome Power

Not only does he have awesome compassion—he has awesome power to minister to our deepest needs. All he has to do is say "Get up!" and all the dead will rise. The same power is available for us in every trial we encounter.

Further, his power is mediated by his wisdom. He will not do everything we ask, but he will do what is best for our well-being and for his glory. He will bring his mercy and compassion to bear on the points of pain and need in our lives. He will bring healing. He will bring life.

"Fear seized them all, and they glorified God, saying, 'A great prophet has arisen among us!' and God has visited his people!'" (v. 16).

God has come to help us! Amen!

33

The Mystery of Unbelief

LUKE 7:18–35

AS JESUS' MINISTRY EXPANDED, that of John the Baptist suffered literal confinement. Straight-shooting John was in prison because he had the moral courage to condemn Herod's marriage to Herodias, Herod's one-time sister-in-law (cf. 3:19, 20). John was incarcerated in the dungeon of Machaerus, the desert fortress-palace perched on a desolate high ridge by the Dead Sea, where today the remains of the castle's dungeons can still be seen, complete with iron hooks. A more desolate, formidable place is difficult to imagine. And it was there that John's head would be given to Herodias (cf. Mark 6:21–29).

As John languished at Machaerus, he became increasingly perplexed by the reports he heard of Jesus' ministry because they didn't jibe with the twofold prophecy he had preached about what Jesus would do (3:16, 17). On the one hand, Jesus' marvelous miracles fit well with John's prophecy regarding the great work of the Holy Spirit. But in regard to his prophecy of judgment, that Jesus would "burn . . . the chaff . . . with unquenchable fire," nothing had happened. The Romans were still in firm control. Their lackeys, including Herod and Herodias, were living in comfort. The religious establishment was just as arrogant and self-righteous as ever. And John, sitting in prison, was getting no help from Jesus as far as he could see. Disappointed and puzzled, John sent messengers to Jesus asking, "Are you the one who is to come, or shall we look for another?" (v. 20).

Jesus Validates His Ministry (vv. 21–23)

Jesus' Answer

Jesus responded with a heart-stopping, eye-popping display of spiritual power: "In that hour he healed many people of diseases and plagues and evil spirits, and on many who were blind he bestowed sight" (v. 21). He produced a riot of healing, leading to unrestrained joy. Restored eyes beheld the blue Palestinian sky and the faces of family members, and both the healed and their loved ones whooped for joy. Newly restored minds engaged in noisy worship.

For the second part of the answer, Jesus informed the messengers that his actions were fulfilling messianic prophecies given in Isaiah: "And he answered them, 'Go and tell John what you have seen and heard: the blind receive their sight, the lame walk, lepers are cleansed, and the deaf hear, the dead are raised up, the poor have good news preached to them'" (v. 22). At least four separate Isaiah texts were alluded to in Jesus' answer—26:19; 29:18ff.; 35:5ff.; and 61:1, the last of which was earlier quoted by Jesus when he began his ministry (cf. 4:18, 19).

Jesus sent John's messengers back to him with overwhelming *empirical* and *Scriptural* evidence that massive messianic power was flowing through him. This was an awesome validation.

But significantly, Jesus offered no explanation as to why fiery judgment had been withheld, nor did he offer any encouragement that John would be delivered from prison.

Jesus' Blessing

The only hint of encouragement was in the form of a beatitude that Jesus derived from Isaiah 8:14, 15, "And blessed is the one who is not offended by me" (v. 23). The sense is: "John, you and anyone else like you will be blessed if you do not fall away because of your disappointment with the way I choose to work."[1] And John took heart and remained steadfast to the end.

John is not the only one who ever felt puzzled, even disappointed with Jesus. Many today say that they cannot believe in Jesus if spiritual salvation is his main interest rather than political or economic salvation. I have seen people who professed to be Christians fall away when they did not get the marriage partner they hoped for, or the healing, or the prosperity they felt ought to be part of their lives. So today, as much as ever (perhaps even more so in our self-focused, contemporary culture), we need to live out this beatitude: "And blessed is the one who is not offended by me."

Jesus Validates John's Ministry (vv. 24–28)

After sending John the Baptist's disciples back to him with such a challenging answer, Jesus evidently sensed that some who had heard his words might wrongly begin to depreciate John's ministry, a situation the Savior would not let go unchecked.

> When John's messengers had gone, Jesus began to speak to the crowds concerning John: "What did you go out into the wilderness to see? A reed shaken by the wind? What then did you go out to see? A man dressed in soft clothing? Behold, those who are dressed in splendid clothing and live in luxury are in kings' courts. What then did you go out to see? A prophet? Yes, I tell you, and more than a prophet. This is he of whom it is written, 'Behold, I send my messenger before your face, who will prepare your way before you.'" (vv. 24–27)

A reed swaying in the wind was metaphorical for an easygoing person.[2] That did not describe John! In keeping with his unyielding stance, John rejected "soft" clothing. He preferred prophetic chic—a camel's-hair coat, leather belt, and so on. There were no palaces for him. His life was gloriously alfresco. No one owned him but God. He kowtowed to no one.

He was "more than a prophet" because he fulfilled the prophecy of Malachi 3:1 as the messenger sent to prepare the way for the Messiah. The angel Gabriel had referred to the Malachi passage when he announced John's birth to his father Zechariah (1:17), Zechariah referenced the text again in his song after John's circumcision (1:76), and now Jesus cites it of him as well (v. 27).

John the Baptist was one great man, as Jesus attested: "I tell you, among those born of women none is greater than John" (v. 28a). John was the greatest man who ever lived, except of course for the God-man himself, Jesus. The qualification—"yet the one who is least in the kingdom of God is greater than he" (v. 28b)—does not diminish the fact of John's greatness. The kingdom must be superior to its announcement. The people of the kingdom must be superior to its announcer. A position in the kingdom must be greater than that of its herald (though, of course, John was also a member of the kingdom). So kingdom membership aside, John and his ministry were the greatest—greater than that of Abraham, Moses, or Elijah. This divine validation set the stage for the ultimate revelation of the human condition, which would be seen in the people's response.

The People's Response to the Validations (vv. 29, 30)

For our instruction, Luke parenthetically recorded opposite responses:

> (When all the people heard this, and the tax collectors too, they declared God just, having been baptized with the baptism of John, but the Pharisees and the lawyers rejected the purpose of God for themselves, not having been baptized by him.) (vv. 29, 30)

The common people, including the outcasts, agreed with Jesus' pronouncements regarding his and John's ministries—"They declared God just." Literally, they "justified God."[3] On the other hand, the leaders, those who knew all the ins and outs of the Law, rejected what was said, acknowledging that it might apply to others but not to them.[4]

The explicit reason for people's either receiving Jesus' word or rejecting it was whether or not they had been "baptized with the baptism of John." John's baptism had become a spiritual continental divide in Israel. John's baptism required confession and repentance of one's sins, and one's willingness or unwillingness to do so made all the difference. Earlier Luke wrote of John's ministry: "He went into all the region around the Jordan, proclaiming a baptism of repentance for the forgiveness of sins" (3:3). Mark records in his parallel description:

> John appeared, baptizing in the wilderness and proclaiming a baptism of repentance for the forgiveness of sins. And all the country of Judea and all Jerusalem were going out to him and were being baptized by him in the river Jordan, confessing their sins. (Mark 1:4, 5)

When the common people heard John thunder, "You brood of vipers! Who warned you to flee from the wrath to come? Bear fruits in keeping with repentance. And do not begin to say to yourselves, 'We have Abraham as our father'" (3:7, 8), many were convicted of the truth of John's teaching and saw their need. They knew they were sinners deserving God's wrath. So they hurried out to the Jordan to confess their sins and be baptized.

But Pharisees and lawyers, who prided themselves on their keeping of the Law and were content to rest their hope of salvation on their merits, refrained from the humiliation of baptism. Of course, they would never have claimed to keep the Law perfectly but rather, sufficiently. They were sure that at the final judgment their shortcomings would be overlooked by their benign Judge. Therefore, they considered John's insistence that God would not overlook their shortcomings, that they must repent and be baptized, as extreme and grotesque.[5]

What so dulled the hearts of Israel's leaders that they would not repent?

Familiarity. There was certainly a professional familiarity with religious observance among the establishment. In regard to religious familiarity, C. S. Lewis wrote to a friend, "Someone has said, 'None are so unholy as those whose hands are cauterised with holy things;' sacred things may become profane by becoming matters of the job. . . . I've always been glad myself that Theology is not the thing I earn my living by."[6]

There is a grave danger in ritual familiarity with holy matters, even if you are not a professional. It is all too easy to go spiritually brain dead when the prelude begins, to "say" prayers rather than pray them, to use the cadence of a confession as a rhythmic anesthetic, to mindlessly mouth the words of great hymns and gospel songs, to nod off during the sermon, to glibly mouth evangelical creeds—and then imagine that we're really spiritual.

Shallowness. Because the enemy works hard to keep churchgoers from thinking too deeply about sin, there is a pervasive shallowness of thought about the human condition. The Puritan theologian John Owen wrote, "He that hath slight thoughts of sin never had great thoughts of God."[7] Contemplation of God brings reflection on sin, and reflection on sin brings contemplation of God.

Evangelicals' ignorance of what the Scriptures say about sin makes them vulnerable to shallow doctrine. For example, one best-selling Christian author says, "Reformation theology failed to make clear that the core of sin is a lack of self-esteem."[8] He adds that salvation "means to be permanently lifted from sin . . . and shame to self-esteem and its God-glorifying human need-meeting, constructive and creative consequences."[9] Thus thousands of his naive readers imagine that sin is thinking ill of oneself rather than being an inward evil. Such reduction of basic Biblical theology is deadly.

Ignorance of the radical nature of sin has also allowed the cultural blurring of good and evil to invade Christian thinking. Films like *Batman* make dualism acceptable and cool. "Good" people like Batman have sexual affairs with evil people like Catwoman. Light and darkness become one! The movie's director, Tim Burton, said as much in a *Chicago Tribune* interview: "Batman and Catwoman are drawn toward one another—good/bad, bad/good, that kind of a thing. And she's wearing black and he's wearing black, and she has a whip, and it sounds like a pretty good weekend to *me*."[10] Sadly, many Christians uncritically watch such films, unaware that moral discernment is being replaced with a shallow, gray, relativistic fog—ancient Manichaeism.

Self-righteousness. A shallow or forgotten understanding of sin is a road to self-righteousness. Like the man who came to the preacher after the sermon and said, "I can't swallow what you say about depravity." Fortunately, the preacher had his wits and responded, "That's all right—it's already within you!" Self-righteousness leaves people sitting in their pews hearing preaching but never being moved to do anything in response.

Sin's grip. Many things dull our hearts, but perhaps the greatest of them all is the grip of the sin to which we give ourselves. The celebrated philosopher Mortimer Adler hesitated to become a Christian precisely because he knew what it would entail. Writes Adler:

> That's a great gulf between the mind and the heart. I was on the edge of becoming a Christian several times, but didn't do it. I said that if one is born a Christian, one can be light-hearted about living up to Christianity, but if one converts by a clear conscious act of will, one had better be prepared to live a truly Christian life. So you ask yourself, are you prepared to give up all your vices and the weaknesses of the flesh?[11]

It is imperative that we recognize what is within us. We must not be dulled by familiarity, or shallow, un-Biblical thinking, or self-righteousness, or sin's grip. The solemn fact is, if we do not understand our need, nothing will move us, whether it be the preaching of John or even Jesus' atoning death on the cross.

God's Word is precise in its estimation of every person who has ever lived:

- *Heart*: "As it is written: 'None is righteous, no, not one.'"
- *Words*: "Their throat is an open grave; they use their tongues to deceive." "The venom of asps is under their lips." "Their mouth is full of curses and bitterness."
- *Deeds*: "Their feet are swift to shed blood; in their paths are ruin and misery, and the way of peace they have not known."
- *Conclusion*: "There is no fear of God before their eyes" (Romans 3:10–18).

Jesus Profiles His Rejectors (vv. 31–35)

Having described the spiritual problem of the Pharisees and legal experts, Jesus went on to depict the perversity of his detractors:

> To what then shall I compare the people of this generation, and what are they like? They are like children sitting in the marketplace and calling to one another,
>
> "We played the flute for you, and you did not dance;
> we sang a dirge, and you did not weep."
>
> For John the Baptist has come eating no bread and drinking no wine, and you say, "He has a demon." The Son of Man has come eating and drinking, and you say, "Look at him! A glutton and a drunkard, a friend of tax collectors and sinners!" (vv. 31–34)

Jesus quoted a couplet that children shouted to one another when they would not join in games with the others, putting it in the mouths of the

Pharisees and lawyers who had directed it at ascetic John and joyful Jesus.[12] First they complained that John did not dance: "We played the flute for you, and you did not dance." Then they complained that Jesus did not weep: "We sang a dirge, and you did not weep." There was simply no way to please the religious establishment because imbedded in its self-righteous sufficiency was a deep dislike for heavenly wisdom.

They demonized John: "For John the Baptist has come eating no bread and drinking no wine, and you say, 'He has a demon'" (v. 33). His asceticism and insistence upon repentance was evidence of a deranged mind, they said. Then they scandalized Jesus: "The Son of Man has come eating and drinking, and you say, 'Look at him! A glutton and a drunkard, a friend of tax collectors and sinners!'" (v. 34). This was a scathing rejection because the description resembles that of the unruly son in Deuteronomy 21:20, 21 who had to be stoned. They were calling Jesus a sinner and apostate.[13]

Such perversity! And sadly, their tribe lives on. Some will find fault no matter what. "You're too serious. Lighten up!" "You're too 'Pollyanna.' Get real!" One sermon is "too doctrinal," and the next one is "too illiterate." The church is "too gushy and sentimental." Then it is "too condemning." Christians are "too dull," or they are "too frivolous." Ultimately such people want God to dance to their tune. Nothing will please the heart that feels no sin.

But what a grace it is to feel your need. What a grace it is to stand still as you mourn your sins with a dirge, confessing them to God and repenting—and then to dance to the music of Heaven's free grace.

Closing Reflections

The analysis (the spiritual autopsy) of the unbelieving religious establishment that Jesus offered in verses 31–34 was gloomy indeed. But verse 35 brings a smile: "Yet wisdom is justified by all her children." The divine wisdom that Jesus sent to John has been vindicated in the experience of her children.

Personally I know that the messages of John and Jesus are true because of what Jesus has done in my life. My experience of real forgiveness from real guilt perpetually testifies to my soul. The life of Christ within me animates all my waking moments. My interaction with the Word of God testifies that it is divine.

Divine wisdom has undoubtedly been proved right by your experience too. And the outworking of God's wisdom in your life is a powerful and tantalizing testimony to a cynical world.

Many unbelievers have seen the truth in the lives of their Christian friends. Because divine wisdom has been "justified by all her children," men and women must abandon any delusions of self-sufficiency or innate goodness. They must stop looking for a god small enough to allow them to pretend that their imperfect righteousness is okay. They must stop looking for a salvation that is small enough to be earned.

34

Forgiven Much

LUKE 7:36–50

WE DO NOT KNOW exactly why Simon the Pharisee invited Jesus to dine in his home. Perhaps because Jesus had preached in the synagogue, and it was considered a meritorious act to invite traveling rabbis to a Sabbath meal.[1] No doubt Simon also had other reasons. Perhaps he was curious. Maybe he liked to boast about the celebrities he knew. It is even possible that he had some spiritual interest, because in Jesus' time there were small study groups called *haberim* that held common meals for the purpose of religious study.[2]

Whatever the reason for Simon's inviting Jesus to dine with him, they were overlaid with a nasty animosity, for Simon purposely omitted the common courtesies accorded any honored dinner guest. Normally the host placed his hand on the guest's shoulder and gave him the kiss of peace. But this was not done for Jesus. Customarily a guest's sandals were removed and his feet were washed when he entered or while he reclined at the table, thus removing the dust of the street and refreshing him. Jesus' feet were left embarrassingly dirty. Dinner guests were also anointed with a touch of olive oil. But there was no such kindness for Jesus.

Simon treated Jesus with callous, calculated contempt. He carefully avoided every custom that would make the Lord feel at home. And all the guests and onlookers knew it as they took their places around the table.

In that day the homes of well-to-do people were built around central courtyards in which formal meals were served. The guests reclined on the left elbow on low-lying couches, eating with the right hand. One's feet would extend away from the table, in keeping with the belief that the feet were unclean and offensive by nature. At such occasions the doors of the home were kept open, and the uninvited townspeople were free to wander in to observe the conversation. Typically there was a great deal of coming and going by the onlookers.[3]

So, many people, in addition to Simon's dinner guests, were aware that Jesus had been slighted as his grimy feet extended behind for all to see. Though Jesus was perfectly at ease, the conversation was strained.

What do you say to your guest whom you have so insulted? "How was your walk over here? . . . A bit dusty you say? . . . Yes, I suppose we could do with a wash—er, some rain, I mean!"

Everyone sensed that a lively exchange was imminent. But no one expected what followed. It began with a chorus of murmurs as a woman emerged from the shadows and silently stood behind the feet of Jesus.

Jesus Anointed (vv. 36–38)

> And behold, a woman of the city, who was a sinner, when she learned that he was reclining at table in the Pharisee's house, brought an alabaster flask of ointment, and standing behind him at his feet, weeping, she began to wet his feet with her tears and wiped them with the hair of her head and kissed his feet and anointed them with the ointment. (vv. 37, 38)

Our English translation gives us a sense of the onlookers' shock with the opening phrase: "And behold, a woman." The shock was due primarily to the woman's being "a sinner" (v. 37). This term allows two possibilities. One is that she was married to a prominent sinner, and the other is that she was a prostitute. The latter seems apparent from Simon's revulsion at her actually touching Jesus, as recorded in verse 39. This is the view of most commentators, older and modern.[4]

As the notorious woman remained bent over the Lord's feet, the murmurs gave way to an embarrassing silence. Not only was she in an obvious state of emotional agitation, but to be in the Pharisee's house at all was a grave breach of social decorum. Her damp, quivering hands clasped a small, thin-necked alabaster vial of concentrated ointment with which she obviously intended to anoint Jesus' feet.

She was there because of gratitude. Somewhere, somehow, possibly through a public sermon or maybe through a private, unrecorded conversation, Jesus' words had gone to her heart, and she had turned to him and so found forgiveness. Her joy, coupled with the sorrow of seeing Jesus so disgracefully treated by Simon, thrust her forward to do him honor, disregarding the rejection and opprobrium that were sure to come her way.

She was at his feet with her ointment, about to anoint the Savior's feet, when everything went wrong! Her tears began to fall like raindrops in the dust, streaking his soiled feet. She had not meant for this to happen! And she had no towel. So the poor woman did the best she could by unloosing her long hair and wiping clean the Master's feet. This was socially unacceptable, because a woman was to loosen her hair only in the presence of her husband. The *Talmud* says that a woman could be divorced for letting down her hair in the presence of another man.[5] So grave was the offense that the rabbis put a woman's loosening her hair and uncovering her breasts in the same category.[6] The guests and the onlookers were in intense shock.

But the woman kept on anointing the Lord's feet. The aroma filled the courtyard. Then she repeatedly kissed his feet. The Greek verb means "to kiss again and again." The woman was a self-forgetful mess—crying unashamedly, her nose runny with weeping, her hair stringy with the muddy mixture of dirt and tears.

I would be embarrassed if I saw such a display. Yet, though it was clearly passionate, it was not erotic. It was a beautiful and fully proper outpouring of love by a redeemed soul. Slaves were assigned to attend the feet of others, but she washed his feet at her own command. It was an act of desperately joyous humility.

This dear woman loved Jesus! And she was in the spring of spiritual health. C. S. Lewis once wrote to a little girl, "If you continue to love Jesus, nothing much can go wrong with you, and I hope you may always do so."[7] Here we have a grown woman, with far more experience in life than the little girl, most of which she would rather forget—but she loved Jesus. Despite her sad past, she was brimming with spiritual life!

Consider her tears. This woman had been living with intense guilt. Having broken the seventh commandment, she was guilty, and her culture let her know it wherever she went. But now her guilt was gone—and the crushing burden had been lifted from her shoulders! So she wept. She had been given a virgin heart. She felt pure, washed. Her life had been one of constant rejection, but now she was accepted by God. Her tears were tears of both ongoing repentance and ongoing joy.

Consider her hair. It was her womanly glory, but she loosed it to wipe the Savior's feet. Her comeliness was devoted to Jesus' glory. She was his servant, and his glory was her first priority.

Consider her kisses. They were acts of pure adoration. Here was a sinner's expression like the heart of the Virgin Mary—"My soul magnifies the Lord, and my spirit rejoices in God my Savior, for he has looked on the humble estate of his servant" (1:46–48). Here was a woman who loved Christ! What an example for all of us!

But above all, consider Jesus Christ! He was not put off by the woman's fleshly sins. When she came to him, she sensed nothing of the judgmentalism of the self-righteous. Jesus did not have the conventional moralism that condemns *outward* sins while ignoring *inward* sins. Jesus freely received and redeemed her as she came to him in faith and repentance.

The good news is, Jesus, our Creator and Redeemer, has not changed (cf. Hebrews 13:8). The one who loved and forgave her loves and forgives us!

Up to this point, not a word has been spoken. No one has addressed the woman. There has been nothing said by anyone in the room. That was about to change.

The Exchange (vv. 39–50)

The drama naturally switches from the woman to the response of Simon, Jesus' host. Simon's thoughts were filled with indignant judgmentalism—"If this man were a prophet, he would have known who and what sort of woman this is who is touching him, for she is a sinner" (v. 39). Just how utterly contemptuous Simon's thoughts were is revealed by the word he uses for the woman's touching Jesus. Kenneth Bailey, one-time chairman of the Biblical Department of the New Eaton School of Theology, Beirut, says:

> The word "to touch" in biblical language is used on occasion for sexual intercourse (Genesis 20:6; Proverbs 6:29; 1 Corinthians 7:1). Obviously this is not intended here, but Simon's use of this word in this context has clear sexual overtones. He is affirming that in his opinion it is all very improper and Jesus (if he were a prophet) would know who she was and would (of course) refuse this attention from *such* a woman.[8]

Simon's righteousness was the kind that would prefer that Jesus kick the repentant woman away, back to her sin and misery. What an indictment of Simon this actually was. He saw the woman perform an act of repentance and devotion and called her a "sinner"! Simon, the moralist, had an arctic heart, a permafrost of the soul—Dante's Cocytus: Hell frozen over. He had a heart without grace.

In reality, of course, Jesus knew precisely what was going on in the woman's heart—and in Simon's heart too. So the Lord decided to teach him a few things with a little parable:

> And Jesus answering said to him, "Simon, I have something to say to you." And he answered, "Say it, Teacher." "A certain moneylender had two debtors. One owed five hundred denarii, and the other fifty. When they could

> not pay, he cancelled the debt of both. Now which of them will love him more?" (vv. 40–42)

Their Common Debt

The debtors in this miniparable are, of course, metaphorical for sinners. Both men have considerable debts because a denarius was equivalent to one day's wage for a common working man. Quite simply, it would take fifty working days to eliminate the one man's debt, and five hundred for the other! These were incredible debts considering that average wages were barely sufficient for survival. What Jesus was saying was that according to conventional, outward morality, the woman was a "five hundred sinner" and Simon a "fifty sinner." Outwardly she was ten times as sinful. "Yes, Simon, you are a whole lot better than this prostitute. She's dirty. Her innocence has been defiled innumerable times. She has been wallowing in sin. But you, with your rigid morality, have kept yourself from those things. Go ahead, give yourself some credit."

Of course, the penetrating point is that they were both sinners. One had ten times the volume of outward sin, but they were both guilty inside. The "high-class" moralist had the same problem as the "low-class" prostitute. Simon apparently did not have the slightest understanding of this and is thus a good representative of thousands of religious sinners who have lived and died in the succeeding years.

The great supporter of the eighteenth-century ministries of John Wesley and George Whitefield, the Countess of Huntingdon, once invited a duchess to hear Whitefield preach and received this amazing written reply:

> It is monstrous to be told, that you have a heart as sinful as the common wretches that crawl on the earth. This is highly offensive and insulting; and I cannot but wonder that your Ladyship should relish any sentiments so much at variance with high rank and good breeding.[9]

Only a twitty duchess, raised in the insular, racist, upper class of old England, would say such a thing. But thousands have used such thinking to avoid applying Christ's teaching to themselves—"Good people just don't need that kind of religion. Grace is for big-time sinners, not for people like me. I don't need it!"

Their Common Insolvency

But such people are so wrong. Jesus' point is not only that both Simon the moralist and the prostitute were debtors/sinners, but that both were equally insolvent. If you are unable to pay, it does not matter how great the debt is. You are insolvent, period! And that is the condition of the whole human race. "For all have sinned and fall short of the glory of God" (Romans 3:23). This doesn't mean that men and women cannot improve themselves or their character to some extent, but rather that they cannot wipe out their status as debtors—sinners.

What we all must understand is that the condition for being forgiven is to realize that we are broke and insolvent, whether we are accomplished moralists or accomplished sinners. This is *the* problem—people keep trying to persuade God to accept the currency of their own making. Some submit the currency of *integrity*. "God, I work with compulsive liars. The only honest man I know is myself. Surely I'm acceptable." Others would argue that their *domestic* currency ought to make it. "In this X-rated world, my life is a wholesome G. I'm faithful to my wife. I love her and my children. I am a good husband, father, and son. I reckon that's all I'll need!" *Social* currency is a favorite too. "I am truly color-blind. My money (lots of it!) goes to the needy. I volunteer at the crisis pregnancy center. I really do care. The world needs more people like me, and so does Heaven." *Church* currency is perhaps the biggest delusion. "I *live* at church. My goodness will surely be accepted."

God does recognize these things, but nevertheless we are all debtors. Regardless of our individual morality, we are all broke. The woman realized that she could never pay what she owed—so God paid it all.

This is what the cross is all about. No one could ever achieve the holy perfection necessary to stand before God. Sin infects every area of our lives, no matter how "good" we are. Perfect, sinless (debt-free, wealthy) Jesus chose to die, the perfect for the imperfect, so we could have life. Simon the Pharisee was blinded to his need by his self-righteousness. But the woman was illumined to her need by her sin.

It is only by God's mercy that we are aware of our sin.

Their Love

In verses 42, 43 our Lord asked Simon, "Now which of them will love him more?" Simon didn't realize all the implications of what Jesus said, but he realized enough to see that he was trapped, so he grudgingly answered, "The one, I suppose, for whom he cancelled the larger debt." Those who have been forgiven the most love the most! Some of the greatest sinners have made the greatest saints!

St. Augustine is the greatest classic example. As a seventeen-year-old student he acquired a live-in girlfriend who shared his bed for a decade and bore him an illegitimate son. At the age of twenty-three Augustine authored a book with a title that today sounds very modern—*On the Beautiful and the Fit*. But then, through the prayers of his mother, he came to see his sin, was converted, and became Augustine of Hippo, the greatest theologian of the early church.

Similarly, John Newton, author of the great hymn "Amazing Grace," had once been a debauchee and a slave trader.

Some people whom we would not touch with a ten-foot pole, if they met Christ, would put us to shame with their fervent love. *Such people love much because they have been forgiven much—and they cannot get over it.*

However, this does not mean that unless one falls into the depths of sin, he or she cannot love God deeply. What is necessary is a *consciousness of sin*. The depth and passion of our personal Christianity depends on how clearly we see our personal guilt—and then our forgiveness in Christ.

Why do many Christians show so little love for Christ? Because they have never truly seen what great sinners they are, and then how sure, sweet, and complete Christ's forgiveness is. Such people, though believers, treat the Lord very much the way Simon had treated Jesus.

> Then turning toward the woman he said to Simon, "Do you see this woman? I entered your house; you gave me no water for my feet, but she has wet my feet with her tears and wiped them with her hair. You gave me no kiss, but from the time I came in she has not ceased to kiss my feet. You did not anoint my head with oil, but she has anointed my feet with ointment." (vv. 44–46)

When Jesus touches some people's lives, they do the minimum in return. They seem to have no water for his feet or oil for his head. The kisses are grudging, if there are any at all. There is no impulse from the heart. They do their "religious duties" (what a miserable phrase), but there is no soul in it.

They need to really see the sin that lies within—and the more-than-sufficient grace of God. They need to know what they really are. As a great American evangelist used to say, "Oh, how hard it is to find sinners; I would go any distance to find a sinner who recognizes his need."[10] Nowhere is the vastness of the need of every human being (whether a moralist or a blatant sinner) more plainly stated than in the second chapter of Ephesians:

> And you were dead in the trespasses and sins in which you once walked, following the course of this world, following the prince of the power of the air, the spirit that is now at work in the sons of disobedience—among whom we all once lived in the passions of our flesh, carrying out the desires

> of the body and the mind, and were by nature children of wrath, like the rest of mankind. (vv. 1–3)

All people apart from Christ (the best and the worst of us) are dead in their transgressions and sins. The dead *ipso facto* cannot help themselves. You can play "Reveille" in the Arlington National Cemetery for a whole year, but you will get no response from the dead. A pastor friend of mine once told me that when he was working in a mortuary (while attending college and seminary), one night he walked into the darkened chapel and saw an eerie sight—an open casket at the front of the chapel with a body lying in it. He crept slowly to the casket, then slowly elevated himself so he could see the tip of the corpse's nose, then shouted, "Boo!" It did not move an eyelash! Of course not—the guy was dead!

The "good" and the "bad" in their spiritual deadness all follow the ways of the world, are captive to the world, the flesh, and the devil, and are objects of God's wrath.

We Christians, who have the life of Christ within us (cf. Galatians 2:20), need to be regularly reminded of the inclination to sin that also lives within us and that will flourish if we fail to tend our souls. I have been a believer for more than forty years, and I know how easy it is to be dulled as to what I really am. We need to learn from Paul: "The saying is trustworthy and deserving of full acceptance, that Christ Jesus came into the world to save sinners, of whom I am the foremost" (1 Timothy 1:15). St. Francis understood this too: "There is nowhere a more wretched and miserable sinner than I."

Paul the worst of sinners? St. Francis the most wretched and miserable of sinners? Really? Yes! This is not pious self-effacement. The more these men walked with Christ, the more sensitized they became to the tasteless, colorless, odorless carbon monoxide of inner sin. They knew they could make such holy pronouncements one moment and a few minutes later succumb to the vileness of burning envy or judgmentalism or unrighteous thinking.

Their greatness, their spiritual health, rested upon the knowledge that they were sinners in need of the constant grace of God. This is true of all of us. Do not succumb to the self-righteous delusion that God's grace has been so effectual in your life that you don't need it anymore.

Closing Reflections

Jesus' concluding remarks are also enlightening: "'Therefore I tell you, her sins, which are many, are forgiven—for she loved much. But he who is forgiven little, loves little.' And he said to her, 'Your sins are forgiven'"

(vv. 47, 48). The thought is not that her great love for Christ earned her forgiveness. Such a sense is impossible and goes against the entire context. *The Jerusalem Bible* brings out the meaning of Jesus' words: "For this reason I tell you that her sins, her many sins, must have been forgiven, or she would not have shown such great love." Her passionate display of love was a result of Jesus' forgiveness. We should all be people who love much! We should all show a deep love for Jesus, whether we are shy or extroverted, dispassionate or passionate. Such love is the telltale sign of real faith!

What a scene Luke gives us! The woman is still kneeling before Jesus. Her hair is hanging unattractively, and the tears are still flowing. She loves Jesus. In contrast, Simon's jaw is set. He has no love for Christ, or for the poor woman. Thus he is graceless.

Like the woman, unlike Simon, forgiven people love God and God's people. Those who are forgiven much, love much.

> We love because he first loved us. If anyone says, "I love God," and hates his brother, he is a liar; for he who does not love his brother whom he has seen cannot love God whom he has not seen. And this commandment we have from him: whoever loves God must also love his brother. (1 John 4:19–21)

Do I, do you, really love him? This is the unfailing test of our faith. Is our love for him growing? This is a sure indicator of our spiritual health.

How beautiful Jesus is. He is pure, utterly sinless, holy, perfect. Yet this sinful woman sensed from him, not condemnation, but forgiveness and acceptance that freed her to pour her love upon him. This is the way Christ receives all sinners who come to him.

How beautiful the woman is, for she has been forgiven. Though her sins were as scarlet, she is now pure as snow (cf. Isaiah 1:18). And she *feels* the freedom and joy of her forgiveness. If you understand the gospel, you understand what has happened inside her. Oh, does she love! She is like the woman who said, "If Christ saves me, he shall never hear the end of it!" And today, though she has been dead two thousand years, she loves him even more and is still worshiping him.

Do we love him like that?

> Thou, Thou, my Jesus after me
> Didst reach Thine arms out dying,
> For my sake sufferedst nails and lance,
> Mocked and marred countenance,
> Sorrows passing number

> Sweat and care and cumber,
> Yea and death, and this for me,
> And Thou couldest see me sinning:
> Then I, why should not I love Thee;
> Jesus so much in love with me?[11]

Do we truly love him?

Do we see our weakness? Do we realize how much we need our Savior's presence and enablement? Do we understand the danger of the carbon monoxide within?

Do you want to come to him for salvation or restoration or strengthening? If so, hear Jesus' words to you now: "Come to me, all who labor and are heavy laden, and I will give you rest. Take my yoke upon you, and learn from me, for I am gentle and lowly in heart, and you will find rest for your souls" (Matthew 11:28, 29).

35

Listen to the Word

LUKE 8:1–21

JESUS' MIRACLE-STREWN Galilean ministry began to attract a considerable entourage. At the core were the Twelve. Around them was a large contingent of devoted followers, generally spoken of as disciples (cf. 6:13), and along with them a band of women who gave of their own means to support the ministry. Jesus' human anonymity was gone forever.

Whole towns emptied to see the miracle worker and hear his unique message. The parallel account in Mark 4 adds that "a very large crowd gathered about him, so that he got into a boat and sat in it on the sea, and the whole crowd was beside the sea on the land" (v. 1). Some believe this crowd was the greatest yet in his ministry. A vast heterogeneous assembly sat in a great arc on the rising shore, facing Christ, who was seated as a teaching rabbi, while the sea gently lapped the shore.

It was an impressive scene. But, as we have come to expect, Jesus was not impressed. Today, too, large crowds do not mean that God's work is being done. Virtually any church in our country could be packed out every Sunday night if "worship" ended with a raffle for a luxury car. Mustang and Corvette Nights would always be well attended, especially by the under-thirty-five crowd, and Jaguar Nights would be standing room only, with the over-fifty group filling the front rows. People of the world love a gospel that is "good news" as they define it.

But Jesus was concerned about his vast audience. He knew that many had not come to hear his word but to sample it, to see what was going on. Indeed, some had no spiritual interest whatsoever. In fact, some by their repeated hearing but not believing were becoming hardened to the gospel.

So Jesus delivered a brilliant parable that, if understood and applied, would open his hearers to undreamed-of blessing.

The Parable of the Soils/Hearts (vv. 5–10)

Jesus' earthly story with a heavenly meaning drew on a rich agricultural image with which his hearers were all familiar—a man with a seed bag tied to his waist, walking his field and rhythmically casting the seed. "Seed" was a proper and powerful symbol of the Word of God springing to life. Within every seed there is almost infinite potential for life, and God's Word is seed *par excellence* because it can sprout forth in eternal life! The "sower" is, of course, Christ and anyone else who puts forth God's Word, whether in preaching or personal conversation. The "soil" represents the varying conditions of the human hearts on which the seed is tossed.

As the sower casts his seed, some falls on the path, and the birds flutter down and steal it away. He casts again, and it lands on rocky soil, where it quickly sprouts, only to wilt in the Palestinian sun. The sower throws seed in another direction, and it falls among thorns, where it is choked, and growth is strangled. Other seed is tossed onto good soil, where it marvelously multiplies one hundred times! End of parable.

Then Jesus called out, "He who has ears to hear, let him hear" (v. 8). Jesus was the Word incarnate, God's ultimate communication. His every fiber longed for his hearers to comprehend his spoken words that day.

But sadly, not everyone had ears to hear. Some understood, but many were perplexed. Even some of Jesus' followers were in the dark. Verse 9 tells us that they began asking him about the parable, and Jesus responded with one of his famous "hard sayings": "To you it has been given to know the secrets of the kingdom of God, but for others they are in parables, so that 'seeing they may not see, and hearing they may not understand'" (v. 10).

What did Jesus' mysterious pronouncement mean? The sixth chapter of Isaiah sheds some light on this because Jesus' words allude to it. There we find the record of Isaiah's great encounter with God in the temple: "In the year that King Uzziah died I saw the Lord sitting upon a throne, high and lifted up; and the train of his robe filled the temple" (Isaiah 6:1). The result of this holy confrontation was Isaiah's call and his acceptance: "And I heard the voice of the Lord saying, 'Whom shall I send, and who will go for us?' Then I said, 'Here I am! Send me'" (v. 8).

This is then followed by the oddest commission ever given to a prophet (at least it appears that way on the surface) because Isaiah is told to charge the people not to understand and thus to make their hearts hard:

Go, and say to this people:

> "Keep on hearing, but do not understand;
> keep on seeing, but do not perceive."
> Make the heart of this people dull,
>   and their ears heavy,
>   and blind their eyes;
> lest they see with their eyes,
>   and hear with their ears,
> and understand with their hearts,
>   and turn and be healed. (Isaiah 6:9, 10)

How did Isaiah obey this strange commission? Certainly not by preaching with obscure expressions and complex reasoning. On the contrary, Isaiah's preaching was plain, systematic, and reasoned. In fact, "the sophisticates of his day scorned him as fit only to conduct a kindergarten."[1] They disdained him, saying, "To whom will he teach knowledge, and to whom will he explain the message? Those who are weaned from the milk, those taken from the breast? For it is precept upon precept, precept upon precept, line upon line, line upon line, here a little, there a little" (Isaiah 28: 9, 10).

So Isaiah fulfilled his commission to blind and harden the people by clearly preaching the truth, and when they rejected it he preached it again in the clearest form possible, so that their repeated rejections effected an increased hardness of heart. Some hearts were so hardened that they went beyond the point of response.

Further light on what Jesus means in Luke is provided by the parallel account of the sower in Matthew 13:12, 13, which also references Isaiah 6: "For to the one who has, more will be given, and he will have an abundance, but from the one who has not, even what he has will be taken away. This is why I speak to them in parables, because seeing they do not see, and hearing they do not hear, nor do they understand." In essence Jesus was saying that the condition of one's heart determines whether there is any receptivity to the truth. Many people, especially the religious leaders, had heard straightforward teaching from Jesus that they rejected, and thus ultimately the truth would be taken away from them. Those who receive truth and act upon it will receive more. But those who reject truth will ultimately lose the little they have. The parables were full of truth, but for truth-rejecting people, they became increasingly inscrutable.

This principle has parallels in other areas of life. Physically, if we fail to exercise a muscle, we will one day lose its use. If we fail to use our intellectual powers, the time will come when we will not be able to summon their full powers. The principle in hearing God's Word, then, is "Use it or lose it," or more exactly, *"Do it or lose it!"*

This is by no means an easy task. The first step of listening is hard enough. I have great sympathy for Eutychus, the young man described in Acts 20 who fell asleep while Paul was preaching and unfortunately was sitting on the sill of a third-floor window, from which he fell to his death. Though he was then healed by Paul, I feel sorry for Eutychus on several counts. First, he fell asleep listening to the Apostle Paul! Second, because of the unhappy results. And third, because Luke was there to write down the whole embarrassing account!

There is one thing I am sure of after thirty years in the ministry: on any given Sunday some are in danger of falling asleep in church. You would be amazed at what the pastors can see. I have seen people fall asleep and bump their heads on the pew in front of them. I have been sitting on the platform when one of my associates dozed off and dropped his hymnal. I have heard people awaken with a snort. In one congregation a young man slept in the front row every Sunday. Before I could get through the introduction, his eyes closed, his head tilted, and he was gone. The most memorable instance, however, was the Sunday both he and his wife fell asleep with their heads propped against one another. I have heard a preacher tell of an elder who fell asleep, and when his wife nudged him during the service, he stood and pronounced the benediction!

I have great sympathy for those who have trouble staying awake in church. Some work such trying schedules that when they sit down, it is the first time they have relaxed all week. Others are sometimes the victims of medication. Sometimes the sermon is, I have to admit, boring.

Falling asleep in church really does not concern me. It can happen for any number of reasons, both good and bad. What *does* concern me are the thousands who warm a pew every Lord's Day with their bodies awake but their souls asleep. Some churchgoers pay more attention to television commercials than to the Word of God.

But God's Word demands more than listening—it demands *doing*. If we consider ourselves believers, we must determine to always respond to God's truth as we read it or hear it from another believer or from the pulpit. An excellent spiritual discipline is to respond to God's truth with action, be it ever so small. "Do it or lose it!"—our response brings certain vengeance or certain blessing.

Alone with his followers (cf. Mark 4:10), after his sobering pronouncements, Jesus graciously explained the parable. Essentially there were, and are, four kinds of hearts that hear God's Word: hard hearts, shallow hearts, infested hearts, and good hearts. All four hearts were present in the large crowd that listened to Jesus that day, and they are present in every large assembly of the church today. Jesus wanted his hearers to truly listen. This is a divine *cri de coeur*, a cry of the heart, to us today.

The Parable Explained (vv. 11–15)

Hard Hearts

The Lord began by explaining about the seed cast along the path: "Now the parable is this: The seed is the word of God. The ones along the path are those who have heard; then the devil comes and takes away the word from their hearts, so that they may not believe and be saved" (vv. 11, 12). The farmers' fields in ancient Palestine were long, narrow, often serpentine strips divided by paths that became beaten as hard as pavement by the feet, hooves, and wheels of those who used them.[2] The seeds merely bounced on these paths and were swept back and forth by the winds of nature and commerce.

These hard, beaten paths are emblematic of some people who hear God's Word. The footfalls of their own busy comings and goings and the incessant traffic of life have so hardened them that nothing in God's truth stirs them. If the thought regarding where they came from or where they are going even occurs to them, they dismiss it as "too hard." The same method is applied to Scripture's declarations about death and eternity—"Headache stuff!" "Sin? Everybody does it. So why should I be concerned?"

Life for many is no more than a sports page and a beer, or a fishing pole, or a movie magazine and an hour at the beauty shop, or a spin in the car. There may be no obvious major sin, but there is no interest in God or his Word either. Life is crowded with other things.

> Into this world to eat and to sleep,
> And to know no reason why he was born.
> Save to consume the corn,
> Devour the cattle, flock and fish,
> And leave behind an empty dish.

Some of the hard-hearted may be more sophisticated. They have drunk freely from a loose set of attitudes and ideas known as modernity. They are not interested in God's Word because they don't believe objective truth can be known. They worship technology's brilliance and substitute it for God. They rarely ever pursue the logical end of their presuppositions. They may be hostile, but very often they are simply uninterested. Their hearts are as hard as nails and dulled of all feeling by the busyness of life. As the truth bounces on the hardened surface of their lives, Satan comes with a fluttering, chirping interest—some busy excitement perhaps, maybe some gossip—and flies away with the life-giving seed.

This ground needs to be broken up. Most often, the plowing that is needed is some pain or stress or trial to soften the hardness of men's lives to the seed of God's truth. This is how grace came to many of us. Difficulties made us quit our spirit-dulling busyness, and then the Word of God fell powerfully into the broken ground of our lives. Hard hearts need to be plowed by sorrow and disappointment so God's Word can take root.

Shallow Hearts

Next our Lord explained about the seed sown on rock: "And the ones on the rock are those who, when they hear the word, receive it with joy. But these have no root; they believe for a while, and in time of testing fall away" (v. 13). In Palestine much of the land is a thin two- or three-inch veneer of soil over limestone bedrock. When seed fell there, the warm sun quickly heated the seed in the shallow soil, so that the seed sprouted with feverish growth. But then the sun continued to beat down, the seed's roots hit bedrock, and it withered and died. The same phenomenon occurs in the quick death of grass on the shallow shoulders of expressways.

I have seen this withering effect take its tragic toll in a number of lives over the years. On one occasion I saw a young man make a dazzling profession of Christ. In a few weeks he was speaking boldly everywhere, dominating testimony meetings, reproving older Christians for their coldness. But then he broke his leg, cursed God and his people for his condition, attempted vindictive litigation on an innocent property owner, and abruptly fell away from following Christ.

In retrospect, the problem was apparently that he had had a shallow emotional response to Christ that never truly penetrated his heart. When affliction came, there was immediate rejection, and the greening ceased. I am convinced that this is what makes so many enemies of the faith what they are. Too many have emotionally tasted something of God's power, but not true conversion—"half-Christians," we might say. Falling away, they become bitter and jaundiced—and remain terribly lost.

Affliction, like the sun, brings growth to roots in good soil but withers all shallow profession of faith. Helmut Thielicke, one of the great minds and personalities of evangelical Christianity, aptly comments:

> There is nothing more cheering than transformed Christian people and there is nothing more disintegrating than people who have been merely "brushed" by Christianity, people who have been sown with a thousand seeds but in whose lives there is no depth and no rootage. Therefore, they fall when the first whirlwind comes along. It is the half-Christians who always flop in the face of the first catastrophe that happens, because their dry intellectuality and their superficial emotionalism do not stand the test. So even that which they think they have is taken away from them. This is the wood from which the anti-Christians too are cut. They are almost always former half-Christians. A person who lets Jesus only halfway into his heart is far poorer than a one hundred percent worldling.[3]

Certainly authentic faith involves great emotion. An emotionless faith is crippled and may be bogus. But true faith puts down deep sustaining roots in the mind and the will.

Half-Christians have had an emotional response to God's Word, a temporary greening of the soul. Perhaps some well-meaning but ill-advised person told them, "Now you're a Christian. Don't let anyone tell you otherwise." But their faith shriveled when hard times came. There was no real life, and their soul still needs to come to Christ.

Infested Hearts

Next Jesus explained the image of the sower casting his seed among the thorns: "And as for what fell among the thorns, they are those who hear, but as they go on their way they are choked by the cares and riches and pleasures of life, and their fruit does not mature" (v. 14). When the seed is sown on this soil, then watered and germinated, the entrenched thorns also sprout and grow with a virulent violence, choking out the seed before it can produce fruit.

The thorns, Jesus explained, represented "the cares and riches and pleasures of life." This is a divided heart, infested by irreconcilable loyalties. This heart makes gestures toward Christ, but life's "cares" draw it back, leaving no room for authentic spiritual concern. Life's "riches and pleasures" lure the soul away from life in Christ. "Keeping up with the Joneses"—buying things we do not need to impress people we do not like with money we do not have—endangers our soul.

This is a lost heart. A heart that is overcome with a love for "riches and pleasures" is *not* a believing heart. As Jesus explained in the Sermon on the Mount, "No one can serve two masters, for either he will hate the one and love the other, or he will be devoted to the one and despise the other. You cannot serve God and money" (Matthew 6:24). Many begin well, and it looks like they are believers, but love for the world and worries over the things and pleasures of this life strangle all vestiges of life from their souls. Those with such a heart need to be honest with themselves for their soul's sake.

Good Hearts

Finally there is the good soil in which the seed brings forth fruit. Jesus said, "As for that in the good soil, they are those who, hearing the word, hold it fast in an honest and good heart, and bear fruit with patience" (v. 15). The seed of God's Word does not bounce off the hard surface of this heart. Neither does it temporarily flourish in the shallow soil of emotion, only to shrivel under adversity. Nor is it divided by its competing desires and thus strangled. Rather, it is a heart that allows God's Word to take deep root within it. It then produces a harvest of good character: "But the fruit of the Spirit is love, joy, peace, patience, kindness, goodness, faithfulness, gentleness, self-control" (Galatians 5:22, 23). This is followed by a bounty of good works as the heart is remade by Jesus Christ (cf. Ephesians 2:10).

This great parable gives us insight into what goes on with those who sit under the Word. There is no doubt as to what true hearing is—it is a heart that hears and does God's Word. To further share Christ's passion that we understand this, Luke links two brief supporting paragraphs to the parable.

The Lamp (vv. 16–18)

The first is the miniparable of the lamp:

> No one after lighting a lamp covers it with a jar or puts it under a bed, but puts it on a stand, so that those who enter may see the light. For nothing is hidden that will not be made manifest, nor is anything secret that will not be known and come to light. (vv. 16, 17)

Jesus depicts his followers, who hear and receive the Word, as lamps. His point is that they must let the light that is in them shine forth to illumine others.[4] They must shine the light in such a way that people will receive it and thus be prepared for judgment day when all will be revealed. This makes their present listening to the Word crucial. Jesus climaxes the parable by saying: "Take care then how you hear, for to the one who has, more will be given, and from the one who has not, even what he thinks that he has will be taken away" (v. 18). This is the same teaching as in Isaiah 6, which Jesus referenced earlier. *Do it or lose it!* Hearing the Word always involves doing. Humanly speaking, the spread of the light of the gospel in this world is dependent upon Jesus' hearers doing his Word. Happily, the more they do it, the more light they will receive.

Jesus' "Family" (vv. 19–21)

> Then his mother and his brothers came to him, but they could not reach him because of the crowd. And he was told, "Your mother and your brothers are standing outside, desiring to see you." But he answered them, "My mother and my brothers are those who hear the word of God and do it." (vv. 19–21)

You and I are Jesus' family if we *hear* and *do* his Word. This is the key to intimacy with God. We have the most intimate relationship with him if we hear and do his Word.

Hearing the Word

Whatever the condition of our heart, whether it be hard, shallow, infested, or good, we must listen with all we have to God's Word when it is read privately and proclaimed publicly.

Concerning listening to preaching, the example of the martyr Dietrich Bonhoeffer has helped me personally. Bonhoeffer ran an underground seminary for theological students during the oppressive years of Nazi Germany. He was a very intelligent man who possessed immense critical capabilities. But in his homiletics classes as he listened to his students preaching, he always set aside his pencil and listened intently with his Bible open before him—no matter how poor the sermon was. He believed that the preaching of God's Word ought to be attended as if he were listening to the very voice of God. That is how I try to listen too—always looking to the text, always engaged, always thinking, always praying. Jesus has called us to be sure we really hear the Word of God.

Doing the Word

But hearing is worthless if it does not result in doing. Attention to God's Word must be coupled with a willingness to do it, or the truth of it will fade.

Has God's Word impressed on you that you must forgive? Then do it!

Has God's Word impressed on you that you must confess a wrongdoing? Do it!

Has God's Word impressed on you that you must apologize? So do it!

Has God's Word impressed on you that you must speak the truth regardless of the consequences? Then do it!

Has God's Word impressed on you that you must discontinue a certain practice? Do it!

Has God's Word impressed on you that you must make a gift? Do it!

Has God's Word impressed on you that you must bear witness to an acquaintance? Do it today if you can!

Has God's Word impressed on you that you must leave all to serve him? Do it!

Or if you realize that you are a soil other than the good soil, repent and believe without delay! Ask God to put eternal life in your soul today and to produce the fruit of the Spirit abundantly in your life.

36

Lord of Creation

LUKE 8:22–25

THE *EDMUND FITZGERALD* was built in 1958 as hull number 301 at the Great Lakes Engineering Works at River Rouge, Michigan. More than ten thousand people watched as the vessel slid into the water on June 8, 1958. Possessing an overall length of 729 feet, she and her sister ship, the *Arthur B. Homer*, became the largest carriers on the Great Lakes.[1]

On November 10, 1975, after seventeen years on the lakes, the *Edmund Fitzgerald*, having left Duluth, found herself in the worst storm to hit Lake Superior in more than thirty years. Gale winds were being clocked at 70 knots (80.5 miles per hour), and gusts were reaching an incredible 96 miles per hour. Waves were running thirty feet high. Men on the lake later recalled how the wind in the rigging sounded like "dozens of air raid sirens, all going at once." The waves pounding on the ships were, in their words, like "a hundred wrecking balls" all banging on the steel plates of the hulls.[2] Mountainous waves crashed over the freighter, rolling 600 feet along the deck.

Shortly after seven o'clock in the looming darkness the *Edmund Fitzgerald*'s long hull bent, then bent further, then snapped like a broken bone. Her two great pieces foundered momentarily and began their tragic descent some 500 feet, settling 170 feet apart on Lake Superior's bottom. Some say that the breakup happened in ten seconds. One instant she was plowing through waves as high as a three-story building, the next she was gone.[3]

Many of us remember the wreck of the *Edmund Fitzgerald* from the driving beat of Gordon Lightfoot's guitar:

> With a load of iron ore 26,000 tons or more
> Than the *Edmund Fitzgerald* weighed empty

> That good ship and true was a bone to be chewed
> When the gales of November came early.[4]

It is a fact that inland waters, especially fresh waters, possess a unique treachery. Fresh waters do not have the even rhythms of the great seas. Waves are often nonrhythmic and contradictory. Inland lakes are more vulnerable to geography because instead of surrounding land like the oceans are, they are surrounded by varying topography. Thus they are subject to quick temperature inversions and violent changes of weather. Also, their smaller size instills a false sense of safety.

Though the Sea of Galilee is only five miles wide and thirteen miles long, its perils are considerable, due to the unique geography. The sea itself is an incredible distance below sea level, and it is surrounded by imposing mountains gouged with deep ravines. These ravines serve as gigantic funnels that bring winds whirling down upon the lake without notice. These gales are often strengthened by a thermal buildup in the extremely low valley that sucks the cold air violently downward.

The Crisis (vv. 22, 23)

Such or similar conditions were coming to a peak unbeknownst to the apostolic band when at the end of the day Jesus directed his disciples to sail to the other side of the lake (cf. Mark 4:35). It had been a long day of ministry that began with confrontations and continued amid the press of immense crowds. So as the shadows lengthened Jesus moved to the stern of the boat, where he wearily reclined and soon fell into a deep sleep. The disciples hoisted sail and began the five-mile trip across the lake followed by a flotilla of admirers in their boats.

It must have made a beautiful scene as they moved slowly across the calm sea with their patched sails backlit by the rising stars—when suddenly they were blasted with a terrific storm. As Luke has it, "A windstorm [literally, "a hurricane of wind"][5] came down on the lake, and they were filling with water and were in danger" (v. 23). Matthew uses the word *seismos* (literally, "earthquake") to describe the storm (8:24). It was as though the lake was being shaken. As the ship reeled, dark mountains of water on port and starboard rose and washed over the boat. Anyone who has been in a storm and has felt the stern plunge like an elevator in the trough of a rising, welling mountain of green, and then shoot toward the sky like a monster roller coaster, can imagine their misery.

A Divine Storm

Though the disciples had no way to know it during those terrible moments, that miserable storm was a divinely appointed vehicle to teach them about God and his power in their lives. This choreography of Heaven was essential for their spiritual development. This is a vital principle of spiritual life: *Without difficulties, without trials, without stresses, and even failures, we would never grow to be what we should become.* Storms are part of the process of spiritual growth. Some experienced believers believe that every spiritual truth, everything that has enhanced their existence, has come through affliction. They are largely right, as these anonymous words express:

> I asked the Lord that I might grow
> In faith and love and every grace,
> Might more of His salvation know,
> And seek more earnestly His face.
> 'Twas He who taught me thus to pray,
> And He I trust has answered prayer;
> But it has been in such a way
> As almost drove me to despair.[6]

Storms are God's way of bringing us into deeper grace.

Without adversity, we would be insufferably self-centered, proud, flat-dimensioned, empty people. This is why Ruth Graham has prayed for herself:

> Dear God, let me soar in the face of the wind: up . . . through cold or the storm with wings to endure. Let the silver rain wash all the dust from my wings. Let me soar as He soars . . . let it lift me. . . . Let it buffet and drive me, but, God, let it lift.[7]

The storm was a spiritual step up for the disciples, though they did not know it. Perhaps such a storm is raging in your life. You are so buffeted that you wonder if you are going to make it. Perhaps a relationship is foundering and about to sink, or the buffeting may be stress in your job, or some terrible disease. Your storm may be an errant child. Whatever the trial, you think you may be drowning.

But in the midst of the fury and confusion, if you will ask God to meet you in your deepest distress, you can and will ride those afflictions to new heights. Such an act of trust will become an epiphany on the landscape of your life.

Divine Slumber

As the storm continued with all its pounding violence, with the sails in rags and everything awash, what was Jesus doing? "He was in the stern, asleep on the cushion" (Mark 4:38). This was almost as remarkable as the storm! The Lord was fast asleep on hard boards that only great weariness could make comfortable. And he remained asleep despite the howling wind and the wet spray. He was utterly, totally exhausted! But this was also the sleep of a heart fully trusting God the Father.

We see here a remarkable insight into the incarnation. Though in a moment Jesus would calm the storm with an extraordinary display of power, he first slept in a weary body. In this grand display the opposites of weakness and omnipotence did not clash but coalesced in a harmony too magnificent to be the product of human imagination.

Of course, to the disciples Christ seemed to be unaware of their plight. We know that in the incarnation Christ chose to always live in conscious dependence upon the Father. Therefore, he could sleep a real sleep, knowing that the Father would awaken him to do his will. Nevertheless, their perception of Christ's (God's) apparent obliviousness to their misery pictures how we often feel during life's storms. Does he know or care? As Gordon Lightfoot put it:

> Does anyone know where the love of God goes
> When the waves turn the minutes into hours?

So often we mistakenly conclude that we are alone—that no one, not even God, knows what is happening and how we are feeling. "The Bible says he knows when a sparrow falls to the ground. Perhaps he's so busy counting the millions of sparrows that he's forgotten me!" How wrong we are! God knows every wave that falls on us. He knows the rate of our hearts while the waves fall, our respiration, the innermost thoughts in our minds, our emotions, even our dreams. In actuality that tiny boat bearing Christ and his own was the object of the most minute heavenly attention—and would have been even if it had sunk!

The Calm (v. 24)

The storm was necessary for the disciples' spiritual development, and so was the ensuing calm that was about to come.

The Disciples' Fear

Frantic, "They went and woke him, saying, 'Master, Master, we are perishing!'" (v. 24). They were afraid that all of them, including Jesus, would die. They thought that everything, including his great kingdom promises, would be lost. Though they had been with the Master for some time and had seen numerous miracles and had listened intently to his preaching and teaching, though they had even seen him raise the dead, they thought everything was going down with the boat.

They were so wrong, and so are we when we panic during trials! Jesus has demonstrated his power over and over in our lives, but in the midst of difficulty we imagine that all is lost. Will we ever learn?

Jesus' Calm

Perhaps they shook the Master by his shoulder. Whatever they did, they accomplished with their urgent plea what the storm could not do—they woke Jesus up! There is perhaps some gentle irony here. The storm did not disturb the Master, but the unbelief of his disciples did. "And he awoke," says Luke, "and rebuked the wind and the raging waves, and they ceased, and there was a calm" (v. 24b). Mark's account is more graphic: "And he awoke and rebuked the wind and said to the sea, 'Peace! Be still!' [literally, "Be muzzled!"]. And the wind ceased, and there was a great calm" (Mark 4:39). The tense indicates that the wind immediately stopped. In fact, all three Gospels speak of a sudden calm.[8] There was an eerie silence, as if a great hand had brushed away the wind and pressed down the sea.

What a way to get their attention! There were undoubtedly some deep gulps. This was a real learning experience.

Questions (v. 25)

Jesus' Question

Jesus' voice now rang across the calm. "He said to them, 'Where is your faith?'" (v. 25a). At first his question-rebuke might seem harsh. Their fear was so natural. After all, they *were* going down, and Jesus *was* asleep! But though their fear was natural, they had little excuse for their lack of faith. They had seen the centurion's servant healed and the Nain widow's son raised from the dead. Even more, they had been with Jesus night and day for three years. They had observed his perfect character and soaked up his divine words. But in their fear they had abandoned all spiritual logic. How like us—except that we have even less excuse. Fear comes, and all the reasons for trust depart—all our past experience, all the knowledge God has given us.

The Disciples' Question and Reasoning

But now, as they rode the flat sea, their logic returned, and so, "They were afraid, and they marveled, saying to one another, 'Who then is this, that he commands even winds and water, and they obey him?'" (v. 25b).

They knew their Old Testament Scriptures, which taught that God controls the seas. Psalm 107:24–30 was a precise parallel of what they had just seen:

> They saw the deeds of the LORD,
> his wondrous works in the deep.
> For he commanded and raised the stormy wind,
> which lifted up the waves of the sea.
> They mounted up to heaven; they went down to the depths;
> their courage melted away in their evil plight;
> they reeled and staggered like drunken men
> and were at their wits' end.
> Then they cried to the LORD in their trouble,
> and he delivered them from their distress.
> He made the storm be still,
> and the waves of the sea were hushed.
> Then they were glad that the waters were quiet,
> and he brought them to their desired haven.

Likewise, Psalm 65:7 refers to God as the one "who stills the roaring of the seas, the roaring of their waves." Psalm 89:9 addresses God directly: "You rule the raging of the sea; when its waves rise, you still them."

The disciples knew that Jehovah could still the seas by his word alone. Psalm 104:7 exults, "At your rebuke [the waters] fled; at the sound of your thunder they took to flight." Psalm 106:9 describes God's deliverance of Israel from Egypt: "He rebuked the Red Sea, and it became dry." All waters flow and cease to flow at God's simple command. Logic demands, therefore, that Jesus must be the Creator, God. The disciples' understanding of Christ suddenly shot right out of the universe!

This is, of course, the unified testimony of the entire New Testament. The Gospels through Revelation bear delightful testimony as to who Christ is.

- In the beginning was the Word, and the Word was with God, and the Word was God. He was in the beginning with God. All things were made through him, and without him was not any thing made that was made. (John 1:1–3)
- Yet for us there is one God, the Father, from whom are all things and for whom we exist, and one Lord, Jesus Christ, through whom are all things and through whom we exist. (1 Corinthians 8:6)
- For by him all things were created, in heaven and on earth, visible and invisible, whether thrones or dominions or rulers or authorities—all things were created through him and for him. And he is before all things, and in him all things hold together. (Colossians 1:16, 17)

- Long ago, at many times and in many ways, God spoke to our fathers by the prophets, but in these last days he has spoken to us by his Son, whom he appointed the heir of all things, through whom also he created the world. He is the radiance of the glory of God and the exact imprint of his nature, and he upholds the universe by the word of his power. After making purification for sins, he sat down at the right hand of the Majesty on high. (Hebrews 1:1–3)
- Worthy are you, our Lord and God, to receive glory and honor and power, for you created all things, and by your will they existed and were created. (Revelation 4:11)

So the logic of Jesus calming the sea with a mere word was not wasted on the disciples. Jesus is *Creator*, *Sustainer*, and *Goal* of the universe. Cambridge physicist Stephen Hawking, who has been called "the most brilliant theoretical physicist since Einstein," says in his best-selling *A Brief History of Time* that our galaxy is an average-sized spiral galaxy that looks to other galaxies like a swirl in a pastry roll and that it is over 100,000 light-years across[9]—about six hundred trillion miles. He says, "We now know that our galaxy is only one of some hundred thousand million that can be seen using modern telescopes, each galaxy itself containing some hundred thousand million stars."[10] It is commonly held that the average distance between these hundred thousand million galaxies (each six hundred trillion miles across and containing one hundred thousand million stars) is three million light-years!

In addition, the work of Edwin Hubble, based on the Doppler effect, has shown that all red-spectrumed galaxies are moving away from us—and that nearly all are red. Thus, the universe is constantly expanding.[11] Some estimates say that the most distant galaxy is eight billion light-years away—and is racing away at two hundred million miles an hour.

We have recited all this to emphasize the stupendous creative power of Christ. He created everything in the hundred thousand million galaxies of the universe. He created the vast, cold emptiness that flickers with explosive energy—the quasars, those torches that shine with thousands of times the light of whole galaxies.

He also created every atom—those submicroscopic solar systems with their whimsically named quarks (from James Joyce's *Three Quarks for Master Mark*) and leptons (the same Greek word used for the widow's mite) and electrons and neutrinos ("little neutral ones")—all of which have no measurable size.

If you could somehow travel at one hundred times the speed of light past countless yellow-orange stars to the edge of the galaxy and swoop down to the fiery glow that is located a few hundred light-years below the plane of the Milky Way, and there examine the host of young stars among the gas and dust, and there witness a star birth—everything you would see would be sustained by the same Christ who calms the seas.

In fact, though it appears to astronomers that our galaxies are "like rafts on a cosmic river, streaming toward the unknown,"[12] actually everything is moving toward consummation in Christ, for "all things were created through him and for him" (Colossians 1:16), and he is the "Alpha and the Omega" (Revelation 1:8).

Closing Reflections

The fact that Christ is the Creator, Sustainer, and Goal of everything brings us to the ultimate grand logic: he can meet every need we will have in this life or in the world to come. Also, because Jesus is Lord of the universe, nothing happens by accident. Though we may die if he does not return (for all of us are *Edmund Fitzgerald*s, "bones to be chewed"), we are in his omnipotent, loving hand, and he will take care of us—always.

> And we know that for those who love God all things work together for good, for those who are called according to his purpose. For those whom he foreknew he also predestined to be conformed to the image of his Son, in order that he might be the firstborn among many brothers. And those whom he predestined he also called, and those whom he called he also justified, and those whom he justified he also glorified. What then shall we say to these things? If God is for us, who can be against us? He who did not spare his own Son but gave him up for us all, how will he not also with him graciously give us all things? Who shall bring any charge against God's elect? It is God who justifies. Who is to condemn? Christ Jesus is the one who died—more than that, who was raised—who is at the right hand of God, who indeed is interceding for us. Who shall separate us from the love of Christ? Shall tribulation, or distress, or persecution, or famine, or nakedness, or danger, or sword? As it is written, "For your sake we are being killed all the day long; we are regarded as sheep to be slaughtered." No, in all these things we are more than conquerors through him who loved us. For I am sure that neither death nor life, nor angels nor rulers, nor things present nor things to come, nor powers, nor height nor depth, nor anything else in all creation, will be able to separate us from the love of God in Christ Jesus our Lord. (Romans 8:28–39)

37

Lord of All

LUKE 8:26–39

C. S. LEWIS WROTE:

> There are two equal and opposite errors into which our race can fall about the devils. One is to disbelieve in their existence. The other is to believe, and to feel an excessive and unhealthy interest in them. They themselves are equally pleased by both errors and hail a materialist and magician with the same delight.[1]

Kenneth Woodward is a disbeliever and has written in *Newsweek* that he regards the idea of a devil as merely a "trivial personification . . . hardly adequate to symbolize the mystery of evil."[2] This no doubt has given the devil some perverse joy.

On the other hand, there are believers who go overboard in their fascination with the devil and evil spirits, giving them equal delight. Several years ago in the suburbs of one of our major cities a promising spiritual renewal took place among a number of professional families—doctors, lawyers, and business executives. This gave birth to a joyous, thriving Bible study group. Many of their friends came to Christ. Marriages were enriched, families restored, and the church infused with new life. But some of the leadership became overly fascinated with the subject of spiritual warfare and, forgetting to keep their central focus on Christ, became self-styled experts in demons and exorcisms. Matters clearly got out of hand when one night they became convinced there were demons in the dining room chandelier and ended the "Bible study" by disassembling the light fixture so each could take a part of it and bury it in a different section of the city. One morning soon afterward some of this group's children were seen by neighbors running down the street shouting, "The devil is going to get us! The devil is going to get us!" Checking on the unusual situation, the neighbors found the group's women in a backyard hacking a rosewood chest to pieces to dispose of supposed demons.

If Satan cannot pull you down with disbelief, he will just as happily push you overboard with an obsession about him.

The story of the Gerasene demoniac in Luke 8 affirms the Biblical reality of Satan and his fallen evil host, but it does not encourage an unhealthy fascination. We see here Satan's *modus operandi* and purpose, but also, more importantly, Jesus' power and his ability to end and heal the harm that the devil and his servants have done. The opening lines of the passage reveal that Christ's encounter with the demoniac took place the morning after his calming of the great night storm on the Sea of Galilee. The region of the Gerasenes, directly across the lake from a purely Jewish area, was an unsavory place according to Jewish thinking because Gentiles and Jews commingled there. After his confrontation with nature's storm, Jesus would now confront an equally violent storm in human nature.

Confrontation (vv. 26–29)

This encounter is pathetic and heart wrenching because the afflicted man was an actual human being. Our text says he "had demons" (v. 27), but the literal translation is "demonized"—that is, under the influence of one or more evil spirits. Demonization can vary in degree of influence. Here it was extreme.

> Then they sailed to the country of the Gerasenes, which is opposite Galilee. When Jesus had stepped out on land, there met him a man from the city who had demons. For a long time he had worn no clothes, and he had not lived in a house but among the tombs. (vv. 26, 27)

Gross Possession

In verse 29 Luke describes the demon as an "unclean spirit." Typically, those under the sway of demons descend to filthy living, both physically and morally. It is not at all incidental that the rise of occultism and Satanism in recent years has been accompanied by increasing drug abuse, pornography, and obscenity. This man lived "among the tombs," rock-hewn caverns furnished with dead men's bones and carpeted with filth and vermin. The local townspeople had attempted to restrain him, but with terrifying herculean strength he had broken the fetters that bound him. He was uncontrollable and dangerous (cf. v. 29).

According to Mark's account, his wretchedness worked from the inside out, because at intervals during night and day he would let out a howl, then gash himself with jagged rocks in an obvious attempt to drive out the evil spirits (cf. Mark 5:5). This poor, naked man was a mass of bleeding lacerations, scabs, infections, and scar tissue, living in a delirium of pain and masochistic displeasure. The man was wild, naked, unkempt, and ill, and as a result all were against him. Little children fled at his approach.

In his lucid moments he surely realized how repulsive, unloved, and unwelcome he was. He was dehumanized, animalized, marginalized, and both frightening and fearful. What incredible misery!

Civilized Possession

Of course, not all demonization is so blatantly gross. Second Corinthians 11:14, 15 tells us: "Satan disguises himself as an angel of light. So it is no surprise if his servants, also, disguise themselves as servants of righteousness." Demon-controlled men and women can appear utterly conventional. They can even be spiritual leaders in the Christian community. I myself have known some whose bondage to evil was uncovered. At the same time, we must not foolishly think that human beings must be demonized in order to descend to the degradation of the Gerasene demoniac. Sin is endemic to the human situation. "Each person is tempted . . . by his own desire" (James 1:14). We are all fully capable of evil and degeneration.

Imago Dei

Nevertheless, demons do drive men and women to the depths of degeneration. Why? Because Satan and his minions hate God, and they will attack him any way they can through his created beings. Humankind was created in the image of God—"So God created man in his own image, in the image of God he created him; male and female he created them" (Genesis 1:27). Men and women bring glory to God by showing forth his image in their character and lives. Satan hates this and so seeks to distort and destroy the image of God in man. As the eminent New Testament scholar Werner Foerster explicitly says:

> In most of the stories of possession, what is at issue is not merely sickness but a destruction and distortion of the divine likeness of man according to creation. The center of personality, the volitional and active ego, is inspired by alien powers which seek to ruin man.[3]

Tertullian was right when he said, "The glory of God is a man fully alive," and thus the degeneration of man—the distortion of the divine image through sin—is a direct attack on the glory of God. We must recognize that anything that is degrading and animalizing to humans is in line with Satan's plan, be it an attitude, a habit, an addiction, a sexual practice, or a mental preoccupation.

As Christians, we must do everything we can, through Jesus Christ and the power of the Holy Spirit, to allow the manifestation of the image of God in our lives. Kate B. Wilkinson's prayer/hymn (1925) is an admirable yearning:

> May the mind of Christ my Savior
> Live in me from day to day,
> By His love and pow'r controlling
> All I do and say.

Confrontation on this occasion was inevitable. "When he saw Jesus, he cried out and fell down before him and said with a loud voice, 'What have you to do with me, Jesus, Son of the Most High God? I beg you, do not torment me.' For he had commanded the unclean spirit to come out of the man" (vv. 28, 29a). Jesus and his disciples beached the storm-battered boat, made it secure, and found themselves face-to-face with the disheveled man. The next thing they knew they were assaulted by the naked, screaming demoniac. First came his scream, then his falling at Jesus' feet, and, third, his shouted question. The scream (probably more of a howl) made the disciples' skin crawl, and then he shouted at the top of his voice, "What have you to do with me, Jesus, Son of the Most High God? I beg you, do not torment me." Behind this question was the popular belief that one could control or dominate another through the use of his/her name.[4] The man did not use Jesus' name as a confession of his deity but in a frantic attempt to control him, followed by the urgent plea that Jesus not harm him.

Exorcism (vv. 30–36)

Jesus stood firm, addressing the spirit within the man: "'What is your name?' And he said, 'Legion,' for many demons had entered him" (v. 30). This was a chilling admission. A Roman legion consisted of 6,000 foot soldiers as well as 120 horsemen and technical personnel. To the Jewish mind, "Legion" brought an image of great numbers, efficient organization, and relentless strength. A host of evil spirits leered at Christ through the poor man's wild eyes. It was time for Jesus' power to be seen in a most unforgettable way.

Luke supplies the details in verses 31–33:

> And they begged him not to command them to depart into the abyss. Now a large herd of pigs was feeding there on the hillside, and they begged him to let them enter these. So he gave them permission. Then the demons came out of the man and entered the pigs, and the herd rushed down the steep bank into the lake and drowned.

The Greek tense here graphically pictures the disappearance of pig after pig into the sea. Why did Jesus allow the demons to enter the swine? The presence of two thousand swine indicates big business. It may very well be that the swineherders were compromising Jews who saw a great profit in selling pork (unclean to Jews) to the Gentile market on the eastern side of the lake. If this was so, Jesus was taking a swipe at their secularization and materialism.

In the process, the pigs became vehicles of judgment to the unsuspecting demons who pled to be cast into the animals. The swine stampeded unexpectedly, due to the shock of demonization, blindly charging into the lake to rid themselves of their new guests. Thus these demons were disembodied and, some prominent scholars think, confined to the Abyss to await final judgment.[5]

The dramatic end of the swine also gave powerful visual testimony to the ex-demoniac that he had been delivered. For the rest of his life he would tell about this with all the relish of an Eastern storyteller. It would never be forgotten.

Jesus' Power

The dramatic destruction of the pigs, coupled with what happened to the man, formed a stupendous display of Christ's power, as we see in verses 34, 35:

> When the herdsmen saw what had happened, they fled and told it in the city and in the country. Then people went out to see what had happened, and they came to Jesus and found the man from whom the demons had gone, sitting at the feet of Jesus, clothed and in his right mind, and they were afraid.

The man was "sitting at the feet of Jesus" instead of roaming aimlessly among the tombs. He was "clothed" instead of naked. He was "in his right mind" (literally, sound in mind, and thus self-controlled). He was alert, laughing, and even devout. What a testimony to the power of Jesus Christ! His contest with the demons, despite all its seriousness, was almost farcical.[6] With a word, the illegitimate swine plunged to their death, and the demons were howling their misery in an incorporeal existence in the Abyss.

The night before, a single word from Jesus had flattened the raging sea. Now in the morning light, a veritable spiritual storm was again hushed with a single word. Only God could do this. The disciples' appreciation for and understanding of Christ flamed ever brighter. Jesus could do anything!

Healed!

Jesus had undone Satan's work. He restored his image in the life of the profoundly spiritually disfigured man. The ex-demoniac was now rational, controlled, at peace, and in communion with God. This is utterly amazing when we think of his previous wretched, loathsome existence. Such transformation is impossible except through God.

Perhaps you have descended so deeply into sin and the scars are so profound that you have given up on ever being made whole. You may even be demonized. You may think I am incredibly naive, that I live in some cloistered ivory tower. If we were to meet face-to-face perhaps you would tell me, "You do not know the grip that sin has on me. You cannot imagine the things I have done. You can't feel my hopelessness."

Having been charged with the care of souls, after counseling needy persons in all kinds of situations and having studied what the Scriptures say about the human heart, I have no naivete about the human condition. But I have full confidence in the transforming power of Jesus Christ. I have seen the naked clothed and in their right mind.

Are you deeply scarred? Do you have filthy habits—perhaps a mouth that is totally out of control? Your speech is lethal and has left deep cuts and wounds upon your nearest and dearest. Or perhaps it is dirty and unbridled because it reveals exactly what is within you.

Or perhaps you are dishonest. You were a deceptive child, and now you lie implicitly to your spouse. You are a liar in the business world, in the community, maybe even at church. Dishonesty is a way of life.

Or maybe your scar is sexual, whether heterosexual or homosexual, and you feel that your life is disfigured beyond help. Not so! Jesus who calmed the stormy seas also calms the storm-tossed soul. And he can do it with a word.

> Or do you not know that the unrighteous will not inherit the kingdom of God? Do not be deceived: neither the sexually immoral, nor idolaters, nor adulterers, nor men who practice homosexuality, nor thieves, nor the greedy, nor drunkards, nor revilers, nor swindlers will inherit the kingdom of God. And such were some of you. But you were washed, you were sanctified, you were justified in the name of the Lord Jesus Christ and by the Spirit of our God. (1 Corinthians 6:9–11)

If you have received Christ as your Savior, all has changed! Jesus spoke the word, and your raging soul was healed!

If you have not yet experienced this, today can be the day!

Epilogue (vv. 35b–39)

This story has an epilogue that is almost as instructive as the miracle itself. And for some people, it may be more so. The epilogue first highlights the Gerasenes and then the ex-demoniac.

The Gerasenes

What was the response of the Gerasenes to the exorcism and healing? Did they rejoice? Was there a revival? Hardly! Luke says, "And they were afraid. And those who had seen it told them how the demon-possessed man had been healed. Then all the people of the surrounding country of the Gerasenes asked him to depart from them, for they were seized with great fear. So he got into the boat and returned" (vv. 35b–37). Their fear would have been fine if it was the healthy, reflexive fear that comes from being in the presence of the supernatural. The disciples reacted in fear and amazement when Jesus calmed the storm (v. 25), and some of the Gerasenes may have begun with such proper fears.

Perhaps they agreed that a great miracle had been wrought in the life of the demoniac, and they were happy for him. But as they reflected on such spiritual power, they feared that it might require something of them. So they decided it would be best for Jesus to go away.

This fear took a very specific form—it was the fear of economic loss. Hogs were big business on the east side of the lake. Two thousand hogs is a lot of bacon. A massive business, by Palestine's ancient standards, had been felled in one blow. Clearly, if Christ stuck around, it would not be business as usual.

There is something frightening about one whose healings come at the expense of others' prosperity, even if the prosperity is illicit. Furthermore, the moral edge to Jesus' ministry made the people uncomfortable. Jesus was scary. The Gerasenes, a practical lot, preferred pigs to people, the profits from swine to the salvation of souls.

> Rabbi, begone! Thy powers
> Bring loss to us and ours.
> Our ways are not as Thine.
> Thou lovest men, we—swine.
> Oh, get you hence, Omnipotence,

And take this fool of Thine!
His soul? What care we for his soul?
What good to us that Thou hast made him whole,
Since we have lost our swine?[7]

John Oxenham

What do we value most today? Far more people than we imagine turn their backs on Christ or ask him to go away because they fear he will disrupt their lives. Is this the way you think? If so, be careful because Jesus, the Savior of the world, "got into the boat and returned" (v. 37b). And he does so today as well.

The Demoniac

The delivered man made a stark contrast to the others: "The man from whom the demons had gone begged that he might be with him, but Jesus sent him away, saying, 'Return to your home, and declare how much God has done for you.' And he went away, proclaiming throughout the whole city how much Jesus had done for him" (vv. 38, 39). Understandably, the man pleaded with Jesus to let him go with him. Conscious of his weaknesses and filled with grateful love, he wanted to stay with Jesus. But the Lord turned him down, and that denial made it possible for him to be an effective witness "throughout the whole city."

Some years ago an ophthalmologist, just fresh from college, opened his own business. Without friends, without money, and without patrons, he became discouraged, until one day he encountered a blind man. Looking into his eyes, he said, "Why don't you have your eyesight restored? Come to my office in the morning." The blind man went. When an operation was performed and proved successful, the patient said, "I haven't got a penny in the world. I can't pay you." "Oh, yes," said the doctor, "you can pay me, and I expect you to do so! There is just one thing I want you to do, and it is very easy. Tell everybody you see that you were blind, and tell them who it was that healed you." That is what the ex-demoniac did. He heralded the news in Decapolis (The Ten Cities), "and everyone marveled" (Mark 5:20).

This story is part of a trilogy of true tales about Christ's power. In our last study we saw Christ's power over *nature* as he calmed the storm. In this one we saw his power over *evil* in delivering the demonized man. In our next study we will see his power over *death and sickness*. The point is, he can deliver you from anything if you will come to him—not only from a miserable past, but from present sins—your hatreds, your prejudices, your loathings.

He can not only save your soul, but can restore your proper love for your spouse, your parents, your children.

Unless you do what the Gerasenes did: they sent him away. Tell him to leave you alone, and he will. And if you tell him enough, there will come a time when the opportunity for repentance will be gone.

If you have not already done so, turn to Christ for salvation. Come to Christ for healing. If he is speaking to you, you must respond now, for this may be the last time.

38

Providential Arrangement

LUKE 8:40–56

ONE TUESDAY MORNING I checked my wife, Barbara, into a hospital for a common surgical procedure, then sat in the lobby to wait. As I was reading a *Chicago Tribune*, I was cheerfully greeted by Susie Luchs, who had become a friend of my wife's niece when they had worked together several years earlier in the hospital's lab. We chatted for a few minutes, and Susie said she would drop by Barbara's room the next day for a visit.

I did not know then that Susie had gotten up that morning feeling angry and abandoned by God because of constant pain associated with an infertility problem. I also did not know that she normally did not come to the area where I was sitting in the hospital that morning, but had done so to use a nearby ATM.

At 10:00 a.m. the surgeon met with my oldest daughter, Holly, and me and cheerfully told us that everything was fine, Barbara would be in recovery for an hour and a half, and then we could see her. I decided to go home and do a few chores, and we agreed to see Barbara together later. But when I returned, I was met by my worried daughter who informed me they had taken my wife back to surgery, which would take about "fifteen minutes." Those "fifteen minutes" became another five anxious hours. (All told, I did not see my wife for ten and a half hours.) When the surgeons finally met with us, they told us an artery had been nicked during the original surgery and my wife had lost a liter and a half of blood. In fact, she had almost died during surgery.

Thus began a very long, dark night. As the nurses repeatedly changed the dressings it became increasingly apparent that her bleeding was not stopping, and consequently she kept getting weaker. At 1:30 a.m. the next morning I called Susan Fullerton, my associate pastor's wife, for prayer. I got more than I asked for when the entire church staff arrived within the hour along with several of our friends. They stayed and prayed with us for several hours.

Nevertheless, Barbara continued to decline. Her hemoglobin, which was 14 when she began surgery, hit 4.9. She was without almost two-thirds of her body's blood! Her heart was racing at about 140 beats per minute in an attempt to keep what little blood she had circulating. And she kept bleeding.

A hematologist was called in and also a kidney specialist. As Barbara, surrounded by busy attendants, was being moved to ICU, Susie Luchs came in with some magazines for Barbara. Realizing she had walked in on a family crisis, she felt like she should not be there. But before leaving she heard Pastor Larry Fullerton tell Barbara's brother and his wife, "You need to encourage her. She thinks she's going to die—something about her blood not clotting."

Susie suddenly remembered doing a blood test years ago on Barbara's niece and showing the results to a hematologist who then warned the niece that if she ever suffered trauma such as a car accident, she could bleed to death due to a rare blood disorder she had. So Susie now ran to the lab, switched on her computer, called up Barbara's niece's records, compared them with Barbara's workup, and found the same pathology that her niece had had. Susie contacted the doctor, who called the hematologist with the remedy—cryoprecipitate. As soon as the cure began to be administered, the hemorrhage began to slow down.

Later that afternoon Susie visited ICU, and when Barbara saw her, Barbara mumbled to the nurse, "Do you know who this is? This is the girl who saved my life! Do you know what happened?"

"Didn't somebody accidentally stumble across something?"

"Accidentally?" my wife protested and fell back asleep.

Not only had God done something marvelous for my wife and our family but for Susie, reminding her that he is in charge of life's complexities. If God could help Barbara, he could also take care of her fertility problems. She could trust him to do the right thing.

But this story is not about Barbara Hughes or Susie Luchs—it is a story about God. What happened to my wife and to Susie Luchs is an empirically verifiable miracle of divine providence. Think about it:

- Years ago two bored young lab technicians ran tests on each other, and one learned that the other had a rare clotting disorder. The one with the disorder is my wife's niece, who now lives on the East Coast.

- On the day of Barbara's surgery, the other technician, Susie Luchs, decided to go to a part of the hospital she does not normally go to, saw me, and we discussed Barbara.
- Susie wanted to see Barbara the next day, but was too busy to go to her room until her lunch break. Thus Susie arrived at just the right time to hear a revealing conversation about Barbara's blood not clotting properly.
- Susie remembered those tests from years before, thus coming up with the missing key for my wife's recovery.

Susie saved my wife's life, and she may have saved some of my family's lives in the future, because later tests revealed that Barbara's brother and our daughter Heather have the same genetic disorder.

But was it Susie who saved Barbara? No. God did! (And if he had chosen not to do so, he would have been just as loving and just as good.)

How awesome God is. He is to be praised above all else. He is adequate in life and death. We can trust God and his glorious providence.

The word *providence* comes from two Latin words—*pro* (before) and *video* (to see). Thus, when we speak of God's providence we are referring to his seeing all things before, his sovereign arrangement of all things.

Luke 8:40–56 gives us a wonderful portrait of this aspect of God's character and grace. That text is about God's sovereign power in the healing of a woman's hemorrhage and then the raising of a young girl from death. These displays of God's sovereign healing power juxtapose two contrasting situations in life, sharing only desperation and fledgling faith.

On the one hand it focuses on a woman who had been suffering from a disastrous hemorrhage for twelve years. The hemorrhage had rendered her ceremonially unclean according to the directives of Leviticus 15:19–30, which meant that she was a transmitter of uncleanness to all who came in contact with her—or even what she touched. She was forbidden to have sexual relations (cf. Leviticus 18:19). If she had been married, she was likely now divorced from her husband. She was ostracized from normal society and barred from worship in the temple and the like.[1]

Her situation had driven her to pursue medical help, and as Mark's parallel account says, she "had suffered much under many physicians" (Mark 5:26). The *Talmud* lists no less than eleven cures for this specific illness. Some were potions, but others were superstitious folly. For example, "Take of the gum of Alexandria the weight of a small silver coin; of alum the same; of crocus the same. Let them be bruised together, and given in wine to the woman that has an issue of blood. If this does not benefit take of Persian onions three pints; boil them in wine, and give her to drink, and say 'Arise from thy flux.' If this does not cure her, set her in a place where two ways meet, and let her hold a cup of wine in her right hand, and let some one come behind and frighten her, and say, 'Arise from thy flux.'"[2]

Very likely this woman had tried some of these remedies, but to no avail. Mark says she "had spent all that she had, and was no better but rather grew worse" (Mark 5:26). The poor woman was broke, cut off from home, society, and religion, and in declining health. She could not have been or felt any lower.

In marked contrast was the prominent family of Jairus, "a ruler of the synagogue" (v. 41). As such, he would select those who would preach, read the Scripture, and lead in prayer.[3] He was a man of substantial prestige. But he was in equally desperate need, for his twelve-year-old daughter lay dying. She was his "only daughter" (v. 42), his joy—and now that sweet life was about to be snuffed out. We parents would do anything to save our children, and Jairus undoubtedly thought, like any loving parent, "Take my life, not hers."

Here we have two desperate representations of life: one well-off, the other poor; one accepted, the other excluded; one familial, the other alone. But both were beyond human help. For twelve years the girl and the woman had led such different lives, but now adversity had bound their souls together unawares, and they would both be recipients of God's life-giving power.

Here we see God's providence and power interfacing with fledgling, imperfect faith. This is a story about a man, his daughter, and a woman—but really it is a story about God.

Jesus and Jairus (vv. 40–42)

Jesus had left the shores of Capernaum to escape the crowds and in the interval had calmed a raging storm and delivered a man from the grasp of a legion of demons. As he returned, a vast crowd swarmed the shore to greet him and to see what other miracles he might do. It was a dangerous, jostling, noisy crowd, but it was silenced momentarily by an extraordinary spectacle. Prostrated before Jesus was the leader of the synagogue, and he was pleading with Jesus to come with him and heal his dying daughter.

Jairus had not been known to be friendly toward Jesus. Jesus was an outsider and had even been accused of heresy by other synagogues. And his previous use of the Capernaum synagogue had proven controversial. This obeisance to Jesus was indeed amazing!

But we must not suppose that Jairus had become a devotee of Jesus or that he was a man of faith. The fact was, he was desperate. He had heard of Jesus' miracles (maybe had even seen some) and possibly had met some who had been healed. He was not sure about Jesus, but Jesus was his only chance. Thus his bare flicker of faith left him prostrate before the Savior. Jairus was like so many who have come to Christ. It was not his love for Christ that brought him—it was not what he hoped to do for Christ—it was his desperation, and a glimmer of hope. Despair is commonly the prelude to grace.

Jairus' incipient faith would bring great rewards, especially as Jesus developed it in his providential ordering of events.

Jesus and the Woman (vv. 43–48)

Luke's account implies that Jesus immediately set out with Jairus—with no hesitation. Jesus quickly responds to all who sincerely call on him. But "as Jesus went, the people pressed around him" (v. 42b). It must have been excruciating for Jairus as he and Jesus were slowed down like a modern ambulance in heavy traffic. The crowd meant no ill. It was simply that no one wanted to miss anything.

Then, to Jairus' awful dismay, everything came to a halt, for there was another desperate person there that day, an unknown woman with a hemorrhage: "And there was a woman who had had a discharge of blood for twelve years, and though she had spent all her living on physicians, she could not be healed by anyone. She came up behind him and touched the fringe of his garment, and immediately her discharge of blood ceased" (vv. 43, 44).

The poor woman had done her best to escape notice. The religious people in the crowd would have been angry had they known she was mingling with them and infecting them with uncleanness. But she found it was easier to get close to Jesus in the press of the crowd. She was undoubtedly humiliated by her illness and wanted anonymity but took a risk because she was desperate.

Probably she, like so many in her day, believed that sometimes the garments or even the shadow of the godly could bring healing. So as Jesus passed by, she reached out and momentarily closed her trembling hand around the edge of his cloak, or perhaps one of its four tassels (cf. Numbers 15:37–40). And in a vivid moment that lives in her eternal memory, she felt healing course through her body, and she knew she was whole!

Jesus realized that his healing power had gone forth (in fact, he had willed it). "Jesus said, 'Who was it that touched me?' When all denied it, Peter [undoubtedly opening his mouth to change feet] said, 'Master, the crowds surround you and are pressing in on you!'" (v. 45). Peter thought Christ was being irrational or even foolish. "But Jesus said, 'Someone touched me, for I perceive that power has gone out from me'" (v. 46).

How poor Jairus must have chafed at this interruption. Precious time was being wasted while his little daughter's life was slipping away. "Come on, Jesus. My daughter is dying, and you're worried about someone in this rude crowd touching you?" But Jesus' providential plan had greater things on tap—not only for the woman but for Jairus and his family.

The woman's heart was throbbing with joy and fear, her eyes tearing. Christ was calling her to stand before the throng, for her sake and for Jairus', though she did not know it. Would he take away her cure because she had disobeyed the Law? What would the people think of her? What would they do to her? The woman's faith was at its core an ignorant faith. She had sought a magical cure, as if Jesus was so charged with healing that anyone who touched him would get zapped with health. Her faith was uninformed, superstitious, presumptuous, and imperfect, but it was real. And Christ honored her fledgling faith.

God does the same thing today. Beginning faith is often uninformed and mixed with errors and misconceptions about, for example, Christ's person, the Trinity, the atonement, grace/works, or the Scriptures. But foggy understandings are often the true beginning of an authentic, informed trust in God. We can take courage in the fact that we do not have to have everything figured out doctrinally in order to possess a faith that pleases God. Certainly we must believe that Christ is God and that he died for our sins. We must rest everything on that. But true faith is not the sole property of the spiritually elite or those with the most Christian education.

The woman's faith was not only ignorant but also unconsciously selfish. She wanted health, but she did not especially care about the Healer. This is common with beginning faith. We come to him because of some problem—we reach out in stumbling faith amid the press of the crowd. But recognizing a genuine yearning and trust, he touches us with his love.

As Augustine said:

> Flesh presses,
> Faith touches.

In a sea of a million hands, Christ will see the one that is raised in faith. Are you sensing within you the stirrings of faith? By God's grace, move toward him. It will not go unnoticed by the Master.

The other thing we see here is that Christ instructs real faith, even when it is imperfect. After Christ had coaxed the trembling woman forth and she made her confession (v. 47), he said, "Daughter, your faith has made you well; go in peace" (v. 48). He was gentle toward her. This is the only woman he ever called "daughter" in the whole Bible. His explanation that her faith had healed her informed her that it was not her superstition, not some kind of magic, but her faith that put her in touch with God. Moreover, in establishing a personal relationship with her, he demonstrated that we cannot be saved by the power of Christ without coming into relationship with Christ as a person.[4]

How beautiful our Lord is! By calling her forth, he announced her healing to her whole world. She was no longer unclean. She could visit others' homes, the synagogue, and even the temple.

This desperate woman represents humanity—all of us. We are ill. We have spent our money for things that do not work. But when Christ comes to us, we need to touch him by faith. We must not fear that he will not respond. We must not fear that we are too ignorant. We must not fear that we are too selfish.

We should fear only one thing—that we will let him pass without responding in faith and reaching out to him.

Jesus and the Little Girl (vv. 49–56)

Jairus had not for a second forgotten his daughter, but he had been elevated by Christ's compassion to the suffering woman. His fledgling faith had been informed by what he had seen, though he could not process very much of it. But his hope was soaring for his daughter.

Then came the shock: "While [Jesus] was still speaking, someone from the ruler's house came and said, 'Your daughter is dead; do not trouble the Teacher any more'" (v. 49). In a terrible instant the growing flame of Jairus' hope was quenched. But with equal quickness it was inflamed and elevated: "Jesus on hearing this answered him, 'Do not fear; only believe, and she will be well'" (v. 50).

We must not miss the providential arrangement here. Jairus came to Jesus with an uninformed, wishful, quasi-belief that Jesus could heal his daughter. That belief had been enlightened and elevated through Jesus' exchange with the woman. But now Christ challenged Jairus not merely to believe in him for a healing but for his daughter's resurrection from the dead! Did he believe? Certainly! Otherwise he and Jesus and the three disciples would never have returned to his home and entered the room of his daughter, where she lay mouth open, eyes half open, pupils still and dilated, her color gone.

Luke tells us that Jesus said to the mourners, "'Do not weep, for she is not dead but sleeping.' And they laughed at him, knowing that she was dead" (vv. 52, 53). Jesus was interpreting death from God's viewpoint. True death—eternal death—is separation of the soul from God, not the soul from the body. Her dead body was asleep, but Jesus would bring it back to life.

"But taking her by the hand he called, saying, 'Child, arise.' And her spirit returned, and she got up at once. And he directed that something should be given her to eat" (vv. 54, 55). Can you hear the words as they fall on the child's cold, dull ears? Can you see her eyes blink, dilate, flutter into focus? The first thing she saw was the face of Jesus! And then the wet faces of her mother and father, then the astonished faces of three thunderous disciples.

The whole story is a vast tale of divine providence—a desperate father, a dying girl, a desperate woman, a delayed Jesus, a believing woman, a dead girl, a living girl, a believing man. The choreography of Heaven is awesome!

This is the capstone to a trio of episodes meant to teach us the comprehensive power of Jesus. Amid the towering walls of water on a storm-tossed sea, Jesus cried out, "Be muzzled!"—and the sea instantly lay flat. Confronted with a pathetically demonized man, the spirits pled with Jesus not to send them to the Abyss. But he did with a word—first through the swine, and then to the eternal pit. He is the God of nature and supernature. But he is also the God of timing and space, of all providence, and in the healing of the woman and the raising of a child we see him initiating and elevating human faith.

Jesus can do anything! He is sovereign! Nothing is too great for him. He can save your soul! He can restore your life! He can supply your most desperate need!

39

Earliest Apostolic Ministry

LUKE 9:1–9

DURING WORLD WAR II battles in the Pacific, a sailor in a United States submarine was stricken with acute appendicitis and was near death. The nearest surgeon was thousands of miles away. The sailor's friend, Pharmacist Mate Wheller Lipes, watched his temperature rise to 106 degrees. The man's only hope was an operation. So Lipes said to his stricken buddy, "I have watched doctors do this operation. I think I can do it. What do you say?" The sailor consented.

In the wardroom the patient was stretched out on a table beneath a floodlight. The mate and assisting officers, dressed in reversed pajama tops, masked their faces with gauze. The crew stood by the diving planes to keep the ship steady. The cook boiled water for sterilizing. A tea strainer served as an antiseptic cone. A broken-handled scalpel was the operating instrument. Alcohol drained from the torpedoes was the antiseptic. Bent tablespoons kept the muscles open.

After cutting through the layers of muscle, the mate took twenty minutes to find the appendix. Two and a half hours later, the last catgut stitch was sewn just as the last drop of ether gave out. Thirteen days later the sailor was back at work.[1]

It was a great accomplishment, greater than the appendectomies done by surgeons. Not because it was better, for it was not, but because an unskilled shipmate performed the surgery.

This story helps us understand an enigmatic promise Jesus made to his disciples shortly before he left the earth, when he said in the upper room, "Truly, truly, I say to you, whoever believes in me will also do the works that I do; and greater works than these will he do, because I am going to the Father" (John 14:12). Thus the apostles, the church, and we Christians today can do greater works than Jesus, not because they are greater works, but because of who we are—frail, sinful human instruments empowered by the Holy Spirit.

Luke 9:1–9 describes the apostles' pre-Pentecost taste of the miraculous ministering power, the "greater works," that would characterize their ministry after Christ was gone. It was a dress rehearsal for the post-Pentecost gospel ministry of the Twelve,[2] and as such it reveals the principles of gospel ministry necessary to fulfill Christ's greater commission (cf. 24:46, 47). It came at the end of Jesus' Galilean ministry, when he brought the Twelve together and sent them on a brief preaching tour, effectively completing Galilee's "season of grace."[3] Some of the specific directives were applicable for the tour only, but the principles are universal.

Empowerment (v. 1)

Luke explicitly records the apostles' empowerment for ministry: "And he called the twelve together and gave them power and authority over all demons and to cure diseases" (v. 1). "Power" here denotes capacity, energy, force. "Authority" is the right to use it. In a solemn instant the apostles were endowed with both, and that must have been a heady experience. Life provides fleeting experiences of power. It may begin for a toddler when he first gets his little hands on the remote control to the family television. Suddenly he can turn the world on and off—make adults appear and disappear. In fact, with that little black box in hand, he seems to control the whole household. Power!

Or do you remember the day you passed your driver's test, sat alone behind the wheel of the family car, turned the ignition key, and felt the engine come to life? You felt like you were in control! Or consider the thrill of turning the key in the corporate suite.

But this is all kindergarten when compared to the rush the apostles experienced when given "power and authority over all demons and to cure diseases." This was Jesus' power. They possessed the power of the sender.[4] The immediate context leaves no doubt as to the range of their power. They had ability to deliver people's souls from demons just as Jesus had done with the demoniac in the region of the Gerasenes, sending foul spirits to the Abyss and rendering the man "clothed and in his right mind" (8:35). They possessed the power to heal human bodies as Jesus had just done with the woman with the hemorrhage. Such power! Kingdom power. God's power. This was even more remarkable because of who they were.

Imagine what it must have been like for them when they heard evil spirits cry out to them begging for mercy. Or think what it would be like to heal terminal disease. To touch a feverish child who becomes instantly well while still in its frantic parents' arms, or to see a leper metamorphosed to wholeness, or to see a cripple skip with jubilation. How unutterably glorious!

Heady? Possibly. It is conceivable that some could become puffed up and think, "I'm a spiritual ICBM. I can kill disease and evil." But that is not how they saw it, because they humbly knew their power was derived from Christ himself. It was humbling to think that God would actually use them in such a way.

The Message (v. 2)

Besides, their extraordinary powers were only handmaidens of something far better, namely, their message—"And he sent them out to proclaim the kingdom of God and to heal" (v. 2). Their real work was not to heal the sick and cast out demons, as thrilling as that was. That was incidental. Their greatest work was to preach the kingdom of God.

What did they preach? The coming creation of a land that would be the territory of a kingdom? No, though there is an ultimate territorial aspect. Did they preach a coming time period? Partly, because there is a future culmination of the kingdom. Even today, as then, we pray, "Thy kingdom come."

But these aspects notwithstanding, the great emphasis of their preaching was that *the kingdom had come*. Jesus would later say, "But if it is by the finger of God that I cast out demons, then the kingdom of God has come upon you" (11:20). Kingdom power indicates the presence of the kingdom. Luke also records that in answer to the Pharisees' question about when the kingdom of God would come, he replied, "The kingdom of God is not coming in ways that can be observed, nor will they say, 'Look, here it is!' or 'There!' for behold, the kingdom of God is in the midst of you" (17:20, 21).

The grand truth is, the kingdom of God is the reign of God, the sovereignty of God. The apostles were to preach the kingdom of God and its nearness to all. They were to tell men and women that they were under it and could come into it. They were to tell them that its benefits were available if they turned to God. They preached that God reigns.

Notice in verse 6 that it is called "preaching the gospel"—"And they departed and went through the villages, preaching the gospel [i.e., the good news of the kingdom of God] and healing everywhere." Though their preaching surely had a prophetic edge and called for repentance, as Mark's account emphasizes (Mark 6:12), it was largely positive preaching—good news.[5]

And for any Jew the arrival of the kingdom was surely good news. "Good news! The kingdom has come. Good news! It is yours if you accept it."

The Approach (vv. 3–6)

The disciples' positive power and positive message were enhanced by the unique ministerial approach that Jesus demanded of them. "And he said to them, 'Take nothing for your journey, no staff, nor bag, nor bread, nor money; and do not have two tunics. And whatever house you enter, stay there, and from there depart. And wherever they do not receive you, when you leave that town shake off the dust from your feet as a testimony against them'" (vv. 3–5).

Luggage

That they were to travel light is an understatement. They went beyond light to nothing! Incidentally, on a subsequent mission Jesus commanded his followers to take a purse (cf. 22:35–38). So we are to understand that the instructions in Luke 9 were not literally meant for all who would preach the gospel in every age. The reason Jesus ordered them to travel light was to avoid looking like other false missionaries in the ancient world who made personal profit from their preaching.[6]

Jesus also wanted the Twelve to learn to trust him for everything. Faith in him was to be the foundation of their ministry. Significantly, at the Last Supper when he asked them if they lacked anything when he sent them out, they answered, "Nothing" (22:35).

Today many ministries suffer from having too much. The apostolic church could say, "I have no silver and gold, but what I do have I give to you. In the name of Jesus Christ of Nazareth, rise up and walk!" (Acts 3:6). Today much of the professing church can say neither.

Lodging

There was also to be no hotel hopping for the Twelve—"And whatever house you enter, stay there, and from there depart" (v. 4). They were not to seek better quarters but to be content. In terms of our day, if there was no hot tub or air-conditioned doghouse, they had to stay anyway. The English Church of the eighteenth and nineteenth centuries referred to pastorates as "livings" of so many pounds per year and became scandalized by fat country parsons who were authorities on hunting dogs and the vintages in their cellars but knew little of their Bibles.

Comfort seekers have never done anything for Christ and his kingdom. A committed life is an uncomfortable life. It sometimes is a tired life too because it will put itself out for others. It is often inconvenient, even taken advantage of.

Reception

Finally, should there be a hostile reception, Jesus ordered his disciples to "shake off the dust from your feet as a testimony against them" (v. 5). Does this suggest a short-fused, hostile approach to spreading the gospel? Not at all! Rather, it was a dramatically gracious warning to those who rejected the kingdom message. It was customary for pious Jews who had traveled abroad to carefully shake the dust of alien lands from their feet and clothing. This act dissociated them from the pollution of those pagan lands and the judgment that was to come upon them. The same action by the apostles symbolically declared a hostile Jewish village to be pagan or Gentile-like. It was a merciful prophetic act designed to make the people think deeply about their spiritual condition.[7] This ceremonial act undoubtedly made a strong impression on people and brought some to grace.

Today there are times when the church must shake the dust from its shoes and declare that rejection of Christ puts one in eternal peril. There are times to dissociate ourselves from sinful society and to do what we can to help them see the danger of their chosen path.

Jesus' directions to the Twelve were designed to bring about massive ministerial effects. The tandem gift of authority and power got everyone's attention by delivering the people's souls from demons and their bodies from disease. This was proof that the kingdom of God had come to them. Their message was "the kingdom of God"—that is, the sovereign reign of God. And the massive apostolic power and the enchanting good news of the kingdom were borne home by the apostles' radical ministry approach, symbolizing the greatest urgency. They preached with only the shirts on their backs. They gave no thought as to where they would lay their heads. They dramatically portrayed judgment on any who rejected the gospel. Everything they said and did emphasized the urgency of the huge claims of their message. And their ministry, by Christ's own definition, was a greater ministry because they were such rude, fallible instruments.

The Effect (vv. 7–9)

What was the effect of the divinely orchestrated apostolic ministry? Luke artfully tells us through the eyes of Herod: "Now Herod the tetrarch heard about all that was happening, and he was perplexed, because it was said by some that John had been raised from the dead, by some that Elijah had appeared, and by others that one of the prophets of old had risen" (vv. 7, 8). The people thought Jesus was a resurrected prophet, possibly the recently murdered John, or the long-dead Elijah who was understood as having to return to inaugurate the age to come (cf. Malachi 4:5), or one of the ancient prophets like Isaiah, Jeremiah, or Ezekiel resurrected.

So Herod, and in effect the entire populace of Galilee, had begun to ask the big question of who Jesus was: "Herod said, 'John I beheaded, but who is this about whom I hear such things?' And he sought to see him" (v. 9). When John the Baptist was living, Herod was interested in questions of morality and the prophetic eccentricities (as he viewed them) of the strange seer. But now his questions were about the person of Jesus. "Who exactly was he? Was he just one more prophet or holy man? Or was he really some kind of invasion from the world beyond?"[8]

This is where all apostolic preaching ultimately went—to the person of Jesus Christ. The people wondered who he was and where he came from. Had they been invaded from Heaven? Their perplexity set the stage for the great truth that would become so evident after Jesus' death and resurrection—this was God's Son sent from Heaven!

Closing Reflections

If this then was the effect of the apostles' preaching in the days before the resurrection of Christ, it certainly should be the effect of all preaching since Pentecost. We are failing miserably in our task if our preaching gives people the impression that the kingdom of God is mainly concerned with promoting a way of life, that it is a message of how Christ can improve your marriage or finances or sex life or parenting. The kingdom, of course, does affect such things. But our preaching fails if it does not bring people to see that the crucial question is who Jesus is and that he is coming in glory to judge the living and the dead.

Our preaching must not be anthropocentric (man-centered), and it must not even stop at being theocentric (God-centered)—it must be radically Christocentric! In this respect we must understand that all of Scripture, the Old Testament as well as the New, speak of Christ.

- Luke 24:27. After the Resurrection, Christ appeared incognito to two disciples on the road to Emmaus where Luke tells us, "And beginning with Moses and all the Prophets, he interpreted to them in all the Scriptures the things concerning himself." If only we could have been there as he began in Genesis and moved through the Pentateuch, then the historical books and the Psalms and the prophets, explaining what it all said about himself. Our hearts would have burned too.

- Luke 24:45, 46. Later that day, "He opened their minds to understand the Scriptures, and said to them, 'Thus it is written, that the Christ should suffer and on the third day rise from the dead.'"
- Acts 26:22, 23. Such preaching was at the heart of Paul's apostolic preaching too, as his defense before Agrippa makes so clear: "To this day I have had the help that comes from God, and so I stand here testifying both to small and great, saying nothing but what the prophets and Moses said would come to pass: that the Christ must suffer and that, by being the first to rise from the dead, he would proclaim light both to our people and to the Gentiles." Christ was so much the center of apostolic ministry that Paul told the Corinthians, "For I decided to know nothing among you except Jesus Christ and him crucified" (1 Corinthians 2:2).

The gospel is Jesus! Thus Paul says toward the conclusion of 1 Corinthians, "For I delivered to you as of first importance what I also received: that Christ died for our sins in accordance with the Scriptures, that he was buried, that he was raised on the third day in accordance with the Scriptures" (1 Corinthians 15:3, 4).

When Christ is preached like this, there is a sense in which God's people do greater works than he did while on earth, because though it is an incredibly great work for Christ to regenerate and save a sin-sick soul, it is an even greater work when he does it through the preaching of his frail church. What grace! What privilege! Praise him!

40

The Sufficiency of Christ

LUKE 9:10–17

THE FEEDING OF THE five thousand is a major turning point in Jesus' life because in Luke, and also in the other three Gospels, it marks the apex and conclusion of Jesus' Galilean ministry. Here Galilee's privileged opportunity, its season of grace, concludes. From here Jesus' ministry would move to the coastal cities of Tyre, Sidon, and Caesarea Philippi, and then to the Transjordan, and finally down to Judea and Jerusalem. The feeding of the five thousand is also crucial in Luke's account because it immediately follows Herod's question about Jesus: "Who is this about whom I hear such things?" (v. 9). This great miracle is a primary revelation of the person of Christ and, as we will see, a dramatization of his vast sufficiency.

Luke's brief introduction to the context of the miracle in verses 10, 11 gives us little more than the bare facts. Mark's account is more graphic, telling us that when the Twelve returned from their preaching mission, "The apostles returned to Jesus and told him all that they had done and taught. And he said to them, 'Come away by yourselves to a desolate place and rest a while.' For many were coming and going, and they had no leisure even to eat" (Mark 6:30, 31). Evidently by the time their reports ended, and probably even during their telling, the apostles were being "peopled to death" by those who had experienced their great ministries. The press was so great that they could not find time for a snack! This was wonderful but also draining on the exhausted Twelve. Ministry can be like that. As the ditty goes:

> Mary had a little lamb,
> 'Twas given her to keep,
> But then it joined the local church,
> And died for lack of sleep!

At any rate, the disciples needed some time to themselves. So Jesus prescribed a retreat on the north side of the lake. Luke reveals that they withdrew to Bethsaida (v. 10), at the top of the lake near where the Jordan empties into the Sea of Galilee. The retreat was apparently in the general vicinity of Bethsaida because Luke says it was "a desolate place" (v. 12), as does Mark (Mark 6:32).[1] There in that isolated spot they would be refreshed, but not in the way they expected.

It was about four miles to Bethsaida by direct sail and about eight miles by foot. So when the people saw the apostles set sail toward Bethsaida, the young and the strong began to charge north along the edge of the lake. Hundreds more from the lakeshore hamlets probably joined them, calling out to their friends to come along, so that finally thousands converged on the apostles' retreat site in noisy, jostling expectation. Mark reveals, "Now many saw them going and recognized them, and they ran there on foot from all the towns and got there ahead of them" (Mark 6:33). So much for some time away. "Welcome to Church Camp: Activities from dawn to dusk."

Very likely there was some dismay on the apostles' part, even resentment. But not so with the Master, as Luke reports: "He welcomed them and spoke to them of the kingdom of God and cured those who had need of healing" (v. 11b). He preached at great length (as the Greek suggests) on the same positive kingdom theme that the apostles had been preaching. Using Old Testament exposition, original parables, and brilliant reason, he heralded the kingdom, the sovereign reign of God. He called them to kingdom living, kingdom ethics (cf. 6:20ff.), and humility and repentance. The kingdom was theirs for the taking! He invited them to enter that kingdom and did miracles to confirm that the kingdom had come (cf. 11:20).

> The full bloom
> of Galilean Spring.
> Hearts were
> joyous captives
> of the King.

Hunger (Human Need) (v. 12)

Jesus had been ministering for hours. The shadows were lengthening eastward, and Jesus' profile lay long on the plain. It was spring (cf. Mark 6:39; John 6:4), probably mid-April, and the sun sets at about 6:00 at that time of year in Palestine. So perhaps it was around 4:30, and the people were beginning to get hungry. "Now the day began to wear away, and the twelve came and said to him, 'Send the crowd away to go into the surrounding villages and countryside to find lodging and get provisions, for we are here in a desolate place'" (v. 12).

This was more than advice or suggestion. It was impertinence—they were telling Christ what to do. Possibly their heady experience of power in their preaching tour had made them think they could give Jesus orders. The impertinence was understandable and forgivable, but it demonstrated just how inadequate their ideas still were of the person of Christ. They had been with him for over a year and had seen repeated miracles. Regardless of the situation, they had never seen him unable to meet the need. Yet, though they had witnessed many miracles, it never occurred to them that Christ would do another one this time.

How like us they were. We remain dull to Christ and his ways, though he has provided for us a thousand times. Jesus does a miracle for us, and yet not much later we find ourselves in a tight spot, and not only do we think God is not adequate for our needs, but we have the cheek to try to tell him what to do!

Oh, if only we could keep the vast sufficiency of Christ before us!

> Yesterday, God helped me,
> Today He'll do the same.
> How long will this continue?
> Forever—praise his name.

May God deliver us from our souls' sinful amnesia!

Miracle (Divine Provision) (vv. 13–16)

Luke's narrative has set the stage for an explosive revelation of Christ and his adequacy.

Jesus now set his disciples up with a calculated rejoinder: "But he said to them, 'You give them something to eat.' They said, 'We have no more than five loaves and two fish—unless we are to go and buy food for all these people.' For there were about five thousand men" (vv. 13, 14a). Jesus' instruction was meant to bring their helplessness and human inability to the forefront. The "you" is emphatic and a command[2]—"Give to them, *you*, to eat!" Jesus was being graciously aggressive. Just how ludicrously inadequate they and their resources were is captured in John's account: "Philip answered him, 'Two hundred denarii worth of bread would not be enough for each of them to get a little.' One of his disciples, Andrew, Simon Peter's brother, said to him, 'There is a boy here who has five barley loaves and two fish, but what are they for so many?'" (John 6:7–9).

There is precious insight here as to how God seeks to bring us to maturity. Sometimes he calls us to hard tasks just so we will find out how inadequate we are. As Alexander Maclaren said:

> It is often our (God-given) duty to attempt tasks to which we are conspicuously inadequate, in the confidence that He who gives them has laid them on us to drive us to Himself, and there to find sufficiency. The best preparation of His servants for their work in the world is the discovery that their own stores are small.[3]

When we understand that it is our responsibility to feed the multitude and tell him, "We don't have the resources," we are ready for his empowerment!

Jesus' brilliant rejoinder not only highlighted their inadequacy, it also pointed them to his divine sufficiency. In saying, "You give them something to eat," Jesus was alluding to 2 Kings 4:42–44, the account of Elisha's commanding his servant to feed a hundred men with twenty loaves of bread and the miraculous provision of God:

> A man came from Baal-shalishah, bringing the man of God bread of the firstfruits, twenty loaves of barley and fresh ears of grain in his sack. And Elisha said, "Give to the men, that they may eat." But his servant said, "How can I set this before a hundred men?" So he repeated, "Give them to the men, that they may eat, for thus says the LORD, 'They shall eat and have some left.'" So he set it before them. And they ate and had some left, according to the word of the LORD.

The parallels between this story of divine provision in the Old Testament and the gigantic miracle about to take place establish beyond dispute that Jesus wields the power of Jehovah God. He is *the* Provider.

Jesus' instructions also recall another comparison, especially explicit in John's Gospel—namely, that he is a second Moses and also greater than Moses, one whom Moses himself foreshadowed. The place where the great crowd sat down was "a desolate place" (cf. Mark 6:32; literally, "a desert place"), parallel to the wilderness in which Moses performed his miracles. It was in the wilderness that God provided "manna . . . bread from heaven" (John 6:31, 58; cf. Exodus 16; Numbers 11). In John 6 the miracle of the bread and fish was followed by Jesus' Bread of Life Discourse, in which he repeatedly proclaimed himself to be the bread of Heaven and of life. Finally, the orderliness of the people in seated regimentation before receiving the bread was reminiscent of the Mosaic camp in the wilderness (cf. Mark 6:40).

The impact of all of this as the miracle unfolded was to put forth the divinity and transcending sufficiency of Jesus Christ! He was more than a second Elisha or a second Moses. He was the Provider.

Now came the actual miracle of the feeding of the five thousand: "And taking the five loaves and the two fish, he looked up to heaven and said a blessing over them. Then he broke the loaves and gave them to the disciples to set before the crowd" (v. 16).

Jesus was in their midst, and around him were the twelve apostles. Jesus lifted his eyes to Heaven and probably gave the traditional blessing that is preserved in the *Mishnah*: "Blessed be you, O Lord our God, king of the world, who causes bread to come forth from the earth" (Berakcot 6:1).[4] This was followed by a thunderous five-thousand-voiced "Amen."

After he broke the bread and fishes into pieces, he "gave" (literally "kept giving," imperfect tense) them to the disciples. Jesus kept producing the bread and fish in his hands by the supernatural power of God.[5] "The pieces grew under his touch, and the disciples always found his hands full when they came back with their own empty."[6] Jesus kept creating tons of barley cakes and fish between the palms of his hands. This was creation power!

Think of this in the flow of Luke. Jesus is the *Lord of nature*, so that the raging sea calms at his command (8:22–25). He is the *Lord of supernature*, casting out evil spirits, again with a word (8:26–39). He is the *Lord of providence*, ordering the tapestry of life (its times, its meetings) to accomplish his will (8:40–56). He is the *Lord of life* as he restores a woman's health (8:40–48) and the *Lord of death* as he raises a young girl to life (8:49–56).

Now here he is the *Lord of creation*. This miracle was not *ex nihilo* (out of nothing), but it might as well have been, because material creation flowed from his hands just as the universe itself had. "For by him all things were created, in heaven and on earth, visible and invisible, whether thrones or dominions or rulers or authorities—all things were created through him and for him. And he is before all things, and in him all things hold together" (Colossians 1:16, 17).

All of this answers the question, "Who is this about whom I hear such things?" (v. 9). He is the King who has come and will come. His is the kingdom that has come and will come!

How ought we respond to all this?

> And whenever the living creatures give glory and honor and thanks to him who is seated on the throne, who lives forever and ever, the twenty-four

> elders fall down before him who is seated on the throne and worship him who lives forever and ever. They cast their crowns before the throne, saying,
>
> "Worthy are you, our Lord and God,
> to receive glory and honor and power,
> for you created all things,
> and by your will they existed and were created."
> (Revelation 4:9–11)

Satisfaction (Human Contentment) (v. 17)

"And they all ate and were satisfied. And what was left over was picked up, twelve baskets of broken pieces" (v. 17). Jesus provided more food than five thousand hungry men plus women and children could eat—basket loads extra. One can imagine them, as dusk falls, overcome with sleepy satisfaction—ready for a snooze under the stars.

The grand point of all of this is the utter sufficiency of Christ for all the needs of life.

Provision for Salvation

That provision begins with spiritual life and salvation. John's account of this miracle says, "Now the Passover, the feast of the Jews, was at hand" (John 6:4). Thus many among the crowd were Passover pilgrims. Significantly, it was just after the Passover some fourteen hundred years earlier, when Israel entered the promised land under Joshua, that the manna ceased (cf. Joshua 5:10–12). Now, just before Passover, the Lord miraculously supplied bread. Certainly the Passover and its ultimate significance (that he would be the Passover lamb slain for our sins) was on his mind.[7] His death would make him available to all as the bread of life. Therefore, this great miracle speaks first and foremost of the sufficiency of Christ's life for our salvation.

His atoning death on the cross is sufficient to save from sin all who come to him. This is why Paul would triumphantly write, "I am not ashamed of the gospel, for it is the power of God for salvation to everyone who believes, to the Jew first and also to the Greek" (Romans 1:16). No matter what we have done, no matter how pathological our sin, Christ is sufficient.

Provision for Living

Finally, the utter satisfaction given to the people through the miracle of Christ's supply means that he is sufficient for any need in life. Again Paul would exult, "He who did not spare his own Son but gave him up for us all, how will he not also with him graciously give us all things?" (Romans 8:32).

There is nothing Jesus will not do to enhance your ultimate well-being and satisfaction. He will withhold nothing from you that is good for you. The Savior is sufficient for anything you face—whether it be bereavement, a broken heart, loneliness, rejection, or depression.

The supreme sufficiency of Christ is the message that caps his great Galilean ministry. If you want to see who he is, see his hands giving birth to the bread that satisfies. He is bigger than anything, even the universe.

Yesterday, God helped me,
Today He'll do the same.
How long will this continue?
Forever—praise his name.

41

"Who Do You Say That I Am?"

LUKE 9:18–27

THE GREAT QUESTION Luke has set before his readers is: Who is Jesus? And he has done it with remarkable premeditation and skill. The first phrasing of the question came from Herod the tetrarch in response to the people's speculations: "Herod said, 'John I beheaded, but who is this about whom I hear such things?'" (9:9). This was implicitly answered by Christ's feeding of the five thousand with five loaves and two fish. Literally tons of barley cakes and fish came from his hands (cf. v. 16). Who is Jesus? Lord of creation!

Luke then skips over seven important events in Christ's life (recorded in Mark's Gospel, 6:45—8:26) before presenting the question a second time, thus eliciting the disciples' famous confession of who Jesus is. The question will be further answered by the subsequent section, which records Jesus' transfiguration.

Why is there such a pronounced emphasis as to who Jesus is in Luke? Because Jesus' Galilean ministry was over, and he now resolutely set his sights on Jerusalem, where he would be betrayed and flogged and would endure the bloody cross (cf. 9:51). In sum, because of the coming crises it was imperative that the apostles understand and confess who Jesus is.

Jesus clearly saw their confession as vitally important because he preceded it with prayer. Jesus had prayed at his baptism and before choosing the Twelve, and he would do so as a prelude to his transfiguration, and he prayed now as well (cf. Mark 3:12–15; 9:28). Very likely he prayed for guidance in asking just the right question, so his disciples' dense minds would be enlightened and their weakness would turn to steadfastness.

The Messiah (vv. 18–22)

Jesus began with a query about the opinions of others: "Now it happened that as he was praying alone, the disciples were with him. And he asked them, 'Who do the crowds say that I am?' And they answered, 'John the Baptist. But others say, Elijah, and others, that one of the prophets of old has risen'" (vv. 18, 19). The average Hebrew on the street thought Christ was excellent. They were impressed with his prophetic character but didn't have the slightest idea that he was the Messiah. Their best guess was that he was a prophet. Significantly, their guess was tinged with the supernatural because they thought he might be an Old Testament prophet come back to life. But they did not understand that he was the divine deliverer, the Messiah, and their miss was as good as a mile. Their stunted grasp of the person of Christ shows the variety of opinions that have existed about him despite his impeccable life, death, and resurrection.

Prophet. The millions who embrace Islam believe Jesus was a prophet, the greatest of prophets, but definitely not God. Their miss has eternal consequences—eternal death instead of eternal life.

Fiction. Some believe the old liberal heresy that Jesus is a product of wishful thinking or imagination. Fellow liberal Albert Schweitzer summarized their folly in his famous book *The Quest for the Historical Jesus*:

> The Jesus of Nazareth who came forward publicly as the Messiah, who preached the ethic of the Kingdom of God, who founded the Kingdom of Heaven upon earth, and died to give His work its final consecration, never had any existence. He is a figure designed by rationalism, endowed with life by liberalism, and clothed by modern theology in an historical garb.[1]

Interestingly, today the deconstructionist scholars of the Jesus Seminar have moved increasingly toward this old view.

Moral teacher. Perhaps the most prevalent view is that Jesus was a good man, even the best of men, and a great moral teacher. Millions hold this view despite the brilliant debunking given it by Thomas Aquinas, and more recently by C. S. Lewis, who wrote:

> I am trying here to prevent anyone saying the really foolish thing that people often say about Him: "I'm ready to accept Jesus as a great moral teacher, but I don't accept His claim to be God." That is the one thing we must not say. A man who was merely a man and said the sort of things Jesus said would not be a great moral teacher. He would either be a lunatic—on a level with the man who says he is a poached egg—or else he would be the Devil of Hell. You must make your choice. Either this man was, and is, the

> Son of God: or else a madman or something worse. You can shut Him up for a fool, you can spit at Him and kill Him as a demon; or you can fall at His feet and call Him Lord and God. But let us not come with any patronizing nonsense about His being a great human teacher. He has not left that open to us. He did not intend to.[2]

History and experience reveal that one might be able to pass any test on what Jesus said and believed, and have read every major work on Christology from St. Augustine to St. Anselm to John Calvin to B. B. Warfield to Carl Henry to John Stott—and still have it wrong!

On this occasion (as always) Jesus knew exactly what he was doing, because by getting the disciples to rehearse what the general populace was saying, he prepared them to make a confession that contradicted and surpassed the people's ideas. "Then he said to them, 'But who do you say that I am?'" (v. 20a).

Very likely there was a pause because they did not answer in unison as before, even though they all knew the answer. Predictably, Peter spoke with the confession, "The Christ of God" (v. 20b).

Christ is the Greek rendering of the Hebrew title *Messiah* and means "Anointed One." Peter's confession showed that the disciples had come to believe that Jesus was the Anointed One Israel had been waiting for from the time of David—a superhuman being who would overthrow Israel's enemies, regather God's earthly people from the four corners of the world, and make Jerusalem the center of the world, establishing the perfect reign of God on earth. Peter and the disciples did not understand all the ramifications of the Messiah's coming, but they had the big picture.[3] Peter was the only one who said it, but they all nodded and murmured their assent. Jesus was their long-awaited, God-given hope of salvation, their deliverer.

What we think about Jesus is everything. Acceptance or rejection of him makes all the difference. We must understand that he is Messiah, God's Son who came to us in human flesh and was crucified, buried, and raised from the dead, thus paying the full penalty for our sins. Now he reigns in Heaven, and one day he will judge every human who has ever lived. To be there with him, we must believe this—we must rest our lives on it.

"Who do *you* say that I am?" We each need to be ready with an answer to this most important question. One man going through customs, when asked for the hundredth time that day, "Do you have anything to declare?" answered, "Yes, I do. I declare that Jesus Christ is the Son of God." The official, taken aback, responded, "Well, I declare!"

"Who do you say that I am?" is a question every person must personally answer and believe for himself or herself.

But there is more. The exchange was full of surprises. No one would have expected Peter's great confession to be followed by a warning to keep it quiet. But Jesus "strictly charged and commanded them to tell this to no one" (v. 21). To have heralded throughout Palestine that Jesus was the Messiah could easily have incited a political movement staffed with loyal but unregenerate people. The word translated "strictly charged" is normally translated "rebuke." Jesus was very firm in his insistence that they keep quiet.

The disciples, and especially Peter, no doubt felt deflated by the prohibition, and would feel even more so when they heard Jesus' wholly unexpected revelation that "The Son of Man must suffer many things and be rejected by the elders and chief priests and scribes, and be killed, and on the third day be raised" (v. 22). Having history's perspective, we understand what Jesus was saying. But to the disciples this was a dark, inscrutable message.

Jesus, "the Son of Man" (a title that would become increasingly associated with humiliation and rejection), would "suffer many things and be rejected by the elders and chief priests and scribes." The three groups making up the Sanhedrin would later officially examine him and reject him like a counterfeit coin.[4] The Messiah would even be killed! This prophecy was so completely foreign to the disciples' concept of Messiah that when he died they were disoriented and devastated. They had heard him predict it but had never accepted it as fact. It just did not fit in with their picture of what the Messiah would be and do. Jesus mentioned his resurrection here also, but that event was incomprehensible to the disciples until after it occurred.

The scenario Jesus described was the precise opposite of their expectations. They knew he was indeed the Messiah, but his words were nonsensical to them at that time.

Though the Twelve did not know it, confessing Christ always requires embracing a suffering Savior. On this side of the cross, having the advantage of chronicled history, it is perhaps easier for us to accept the necessity of his suffering and dying for us. We were so thoroughly lost in our sins that only his atoning sacrifice could deliver us. Therefore we cling to the gory cross. In fact, we glory in it (cf. Galatians 6:14)!

In the cross of Christ I glory,
Tow'ring o'er the wrecks of time;
All the light of sacred story
Gathers round its head sublime.

John Bowring (1825)

The Disciples (vv. 23–27)

When we confess Christ, we embrace his dying on the cross for us. But we also accept the reality of a cross for ourselves.

The Necessity of the Cross

Apparently using no transition, Jesus next informed his disciples they too would have to carry a cross: "And he said to all, 'If anyone would come after me, let him deny himself and take up his cross daily and follow me'" (v. 23). This call to a crucified life demands a willingness to pour out one's life for Christ. The biography *The Shadow of the Almighty* records a beautiful prayer uttered by Jim Elliot:

> Father, take my life, yea, my blood if Thou wilt, and consume it with Thine enveloping fire. I would not save it, for it is not mine to save. Have it, Lord, have it all. Pour out my life as an oblation for the world. Blood is only of value as it flows before Thine altar.[5]

Young Jim Elliot went on to willingly shoulder his cross in missionary service, literally sealing it with his own blood at the hands of primitive spearmen deep in the jungles of Ecuador.

Living for Christ requires self-denial. This begins when we voluntarily abdicate the throne of our lives—when we radically renounce self-centeredness. A crucified Savior is not well served by self-pleasing, self-indulging people.

What are our crosses? They are not simply trials or hardships. Some think of a nutty boss or an unfair teacher or a bossy mother-in-law as a "cross." But they are not. Neither can we properly call an illness or a handicap a cross.

A cross results from specifically walking in Christ's steps, embracing his life. It comes from bearing disdain because we are following the narrow way of Jesus Christ, "the way, and the truth, and the life" (John 14:6). It comes from living out the business and sexual ethics of Christ in the marketplace, the community, the family, the world. It comes from standing true in difficult circumstances for the sake of the gospel.

Our crosses come from and are proportionate to our dedication to Christ. Difficulties do not indicate cross bearing, though difficulties *for Christ's sake* do. Do we have any difficulties because we are closely following Christ?

The Logic of the Cross

The necessity of the cross leads us to its logic: "For whoever would save his life will lose it, but whoever loses his life for my sake will save it" (v. 24). How dissonant this sounds in today's Christian culture. As James Davidson Hunter pointed out in his landmark study *Evangelicalism: The Coming Generation*, fascination with the self and with our own ways of seeing things has become a well-established cultural feature of evangelicalism.[6] Self-focus is part of the modern evangelical identity! This is why increasing numbers of evangelical Christians care little about the glory of God or reaching out to a lost world. For them Christianity exists to enhance their lives, their marriages, their bank accounts, their prestige. But to bear a cross, to pay a price for standing for Christ—no thanks.

But Jesus' words reveal the only way to life. To hug self is ruinous. But if we give ourselves to him, he will give us life and make us the persons we were meant to be. Losers are keepers.

Jesus went on to say, "For what does it profit a man if he gains the whole world and loses or forfeits himself?" (v. 25). To exalt the bank account or professional prestige or impressive possessions over the life of the soul is tragic folly.

One hundred and eighty years after the death of Charlemagne, about the year 1000, officials of the Emperor Otho opened the great king's tomb, where in addition to incredible treasures they saw an amazing sight—the skeletal remains of King Charlemagne seated on a throne, his crown still on his skull, a copy of the Gospels lying in his lap with his bony finger resting on the text, "For what does it profit a man if he gains the whole world and loses or forfeits himself?"

One might think that the teaching of Holy Scripture and the repeated examples of history, such as Charlemagne's, would convince modern men and women that keepers are losers. Not so! Consider the case of Somerset Maugham, the most famous author of the 1930s. He was an accomplished novelist, playwright, and short story writer. His novel *Of Human Bondage* is a classic. His play *The Constant Wife* has gone through thousands of stagings. He was a man who lived for his own refined tastes, comfort, and sensualities. In 1965, at the age of ninety-one, he was still a fabulously rich man, although he had not written a word in years. He still received over three hundred fan letters a week. But what had life brought W. Somerset Maugham? What did he have of lasting value? The *London Times* quoted his nephew, Robin Maugham:

> I looked round the drawing room at the immensely valuable furniture and pictures and objects that Willie's success had enabled him to acquire. I remembered that the villa itself, and the wonderful garden I could see through the windows—a fabulous setting on the edge of the Mediterranean—were worth £600,000.
>
> Willie had 11 servants, including his cook, Annette, who was the envy of all the other millionaires on the Riviera. He dined off silver plates, waited on by Marius, his butler, and Henri, his footman. But it no longer meant anything to him.
>
> The following afternoon I found Willie reclining on a sofa, peering through his spectacles at a Bible which had very large print. He looked horribly wizened and his face was grim.
>
> "I've been reading the Bible you gave me. . . . And I've come across the quotation, 'What shall it profit a man if he gain the whole world and lose his own soul?' I must tell you, my dear Robin, that the text used to hang opposite my bed when I was a child. . . . Of course, it's all a lot of bunk but the thought is quite interesting all the same."

Robin Maugham goes on to describe an empty, bitter old man who repeatedly cried in terror, "Go away! I'm not ready. . . . I'm not dead yet. . . . I'm not dead yet, I tell you. . . ."[7] He was a man who had gained the whole world but lost his own soul, a keeper who lost.

On the other hand, there are losers who are ultimately keepers. My wife, Barbara, and I once visited friends, John and Lorraine Winston, who were missionaries in France for many years. As we sat in their rooftop apartment overlooking seminary grounds, John told us that life there had not been easy. They were sometimes pushed to their limits. Lorraine nodded her assent. "But," he continued, "I have lived the best life. It has been challenging, exciting, and fulfilling. I wouldn't change a thing. I have no regrets."

Losers are keepers!

Closing Reflections

Jesus ended his comments by challenging his followers to confess him because those who do so will be affirmed by him in the judgment and because the kingdom of God would touch many of their lives before their death (which in fact it did in the transfiguration, the resurrection, and the ascension and at Pentecost).

> For whoever is ashamed of me and of my words, of him will the Son of Man be ashamed when he comes in his glory and the glory of the Father and of the holy angels. But I tell you truly, there are some standing here who will not taste death until they see the kingdom of God. (vv. 26, 27)

Who do *you* say Jesus is? Is he a fraud? Is he only a prophet? Is he merely a great moral teacher? Or is he the Messiah, God's Son, the Savior and King?

If you confess him as Christ, you must cling to his bloody cross as your only hope, and you must take up your own cross as you deny yourself and follow him. Do you do this? If so, you have made a good confession.

42

Christ Transfigured

LUKE 9:28–36

LUKE'S ACCOUNT OF the transfiguration of Christ, deeply rooted in the Old Testament, invites us to enjoy a Biblical feast. We will first partake of Old Testament glory, then taste the choice morsels of its New Testament counterparts. Only then can we properly dine upon the centerpiece of the feast, the Lamb of God. This meal becomes increasingly delicious the longer we feed upon it.

The Old Testament

The Old Testament first course serves up the *Shekinah* glory, the visible presence of God in a luminous cloud.

Pillar of Glory

Israel first saw this when they left Egypt and headed for the Red Sea. "And the LORD went before them by day in a pillar of cloud to lead them along the way, and by night in a pillar of fire to give them light, that they might travel by day and by night" (Exodus 13:21). God palpably demonstrated his presence by a pillar-shaped cloud that radiated a fiery luminosity upon the setting of the sun. It was spectacular, to say the least!

Moses and God's Glory

The most intimate encounter with this glorious cloud in the Old Testament was experienced by Moses when he received the Law on stone tablets for the second time (Exodus 33, 34). Originally Moses had dashed the stone tablets to pieces when he found Israel worshiping a golden calf (cf. Exodus 32:19). Afterward Moses, profoundly discouraged, would regularly go into "the tent of meeting" to seek God, and the pillar of cloud would come down and stand at the entrance of the tent (cf. Exodus 33:7–11). On one occasion Moses prayed, "Please show me your glory"—and God did (Exodus 33:18). As Exodus 33, 34 recounts the story, Moses again chiseled out two stone tablets and ascended high on Sinai, where the Lord came down in the cloud.

God then closeted Moses in a cleft in the rock, covered with the divine hand, and the dazzling glory of God passed by while the voice of God proclaimed his own goodness (cf. Exodus 33:19–23; 34:5–7). When God's luminous presence had passed by, the divine hand was lifted, and Moses saw the Lord's back (cf. 33:23). Moses saw the afterglow of God's presence.

Smitten, Moses remained there forty days without eating or drinking as he inscribed the Law as God dictated it (cf. Exodus 34:28). When Moses descended Sinai holding the two tablets, he was unaware that his face was radiant with God's glory (cf. Exodus 34:29–35).

Tabernacle Glory

Of course, Moses' radiance soon began to fade, and in time God created two successive physical repositories for his glory. The first was the tabernacle, a tent so minutely prescribed in Exodus that every fiber, texture, color, and shape was made according to a divine blueprint that God told to Moses. The glories of the tabernacle conclude the book of Exodus, with the *Shekinah* glory, in the heart of the pillar, hovering over the tent: "Then the cloud covered the tent of meeting, and the glory of the LORD filled the tabernacle. And Moses was not able to enter the tent of meeting because the cloud settled on it, and the glory of the LORD filled the tabernacle" (Exodus 40:34, 35). The glory lodged in the heart of the tabernacle, the Holy of Holies, where Aaron entered only once a year with the blood of the Passover lamb.

Temple Glory

As the centuries passed, the tabernacle was lovingly assembled and reassembled by the Kohathites, Gershonites, and Merarites and transported from place to place in the wilderness and during the wars for Canaan and then the settlement. The time finally came for Solomon's great temple to be built. Second Chronicles tells us:

> As soon as Solomon finished his prayer, fire came down from heaven and consumed the burnt offering and the sacrifices, and the glory of the LORD filled the temple. And the priests could not enter the house of the LORD, because the glory of the LORD filled the LORD's house. When all the people of Israel saw the fire come down and the glory of the LORD on the temple, they

> bowed down with their faces to the ground on the pavement and worshiped and gave thanks to the LORD, saying, "For he is good, for his steadfast love endures forever." (2 Chronicles 7:1–3; cf. 1 Kings 8:10, 11)

As Solomon lifted his arms to Heaven, he prayed, "But will God indeed dwell on the earth? Behold, heaven and the highest heaven cannot contain you; how much less this house that I have built!" (1 Kings 8:27). Solomon knew that God could not be contained by the universe, but he also knew his glory was there—luminous and good in its moral beauty.

Ichabod—No Glory

But Israel's history sadly reveals that men came to use the temple to glorify themselves rather than God. The tragic irony is that this began with Solomon himself, as we see in the reaction of the queen of Sheba to the magnificence of the temple:

> And when the queen of Sheba had seen the wisdom of Solomon, the house that he had built, the food of his table, the seating of his officials, and the attendance of his servants, and their clothing, his cupbearers, and their clothing, and his burnt offerings that he offered at the house of the LORD, there was no more breath in her. And she said to the king, "The report was true that I heard in my own land of your words and of your wisdom, but I did not believe the reports until I came and my own eyes had seen it. And behold, half the greatness of your wisdom was not told me; you surpass the report that I heard." (2 Chronicles 9:3–6)

The temple, created to be a house where God's glory was manifested, had degenerated into a prop for human glory.

Over the years, despite some bright spots, the slide continued until some four hundred years later seventy elders of the house of Israel assembled in the temple—each in front of his own painted idol and each offering incense to it (cf. Ezekiel 8:7–16). The very walls of the temple had been painted with "every form of creeping things and loathsome beasts, and all the idols of the house of Israel" (Ezekiel 8:10). The glory was about to leave the temple!

Ezekiel's vision in chapter 10 records that unforgettable departure. Four awesome cherubim (angels of God's presence) assembled on the south side of the temple. Each had four faces and four wings, so they could move in any direction without turning. Beneath each angel there was a turning wheel completely filled with eyes (Ezekiel 10:12). These were called "the whirling wheels" (Ezekiel 10:13). In the expanse above the angels was something that looked like a throne of sapphire (Ezekiel 10:1).

As the cherubim took their places on the temple's south side, the *Shekinah* glory filled the inner court, then rose above the cherubim engulfing the sapphire throne (Ezekiel 10:3). Then the glory moved to the door of the temple's threshold, filling everything with "the brightness of the glory of the LORD" (Ezekiel 10:4). The roar of the cherubim's wings was "like the voice of God Almighty when he speaks" (Ezekiel 10:5).

"Then," as Ezekiel tells it,

> The glory of the LORD went out from the threshold of the house, and stood over the cherubim. And the cherubim lifted up their wings and mounted up from the earth before my eyes as they went out, with the wheels beside them. And they stood at the entrance of the east gate of the house of the LORD, and the glory of the God of Israel was over them. (Ezekiel 10:18, 19)

As Ezekiel's eyes moved upward, he saw the four spinning wheels rotating ominously, and over them the four winged cherubim suspended, their wings drumming the air like colossal hummingbirds, and above them floated the dazzling glory of God. The glory was moving slowly away to the east and upward from the city where it had lingered above the Mount of Olives—and then it was gone (cf. Ezekiel 11:23)! Ichabod!—the glory had departed (cf. 1 Samuel 4:19–22). For the next six hundred years, though the temple was destroyed and rebuilt and rebuilt again, and though godly men and women came and went, the glory was not seen once!

New Testament Glory

Now we come to the delicacies of the New Testament, especially as they are presented in Luke's Gospel. On a cold winter's night the trembling hands of a carpenter, wet with the blood of birth, held his steaming son in the starlight. "And in the same region there were shepherds out in the field, keeping watch over their flock by night. And an angel of the Lord appeared to them, and the glory of the Lord shone around them, and they were filled with great fear" (2:8, 9). The glory had returned in the person of Jesus Christ and was reflected in the panorama of an announcing angel!

As the shepherds cowered under the dazzling radiance, a vast company of magnificent angels in festal array outshone the winter constellations. They were "praising God and saying, 'Glory to God in the highest . . .'" (2:13, 14). Ichabod ("the glory has departed") was replaced by the "glory as of the only Son from the Father, full of grace and truth" (John 1:14).

There were flashes of his glory at the advent. But during the next thirty years, as the Son quietly approached his *bar mitzvah* and grew into the full maturity of his manhood, the glory was veiled. Even after he began his public ministry there was no manifestation of the *Shekinah* glory. But as his ministry progressed there was an intensifying revelation of who he was. Luke 8, 9 successively shows him as the Lord of *nature* calming the storm, Lord of *supernature* casting out a legion of demons, Lord of *life* healing the sick and raising the dead, Lord of *creation* feeding the five thousand, and the *Messiah of God* as announced in Peter's great confession.

Peter's confession—"The Christ of God" (v. 20b)—answering Jesus' question, "But who do you say that I am?" (9:20) was supremely wonderful. But Jesus' enigmatic warning—"The Son of Man must suffer many things and be rejected by the elders and chief priests and scribes, and be killed, and on the third day be raised" (9:22)—filled them with confusion, as did his hard words about their having to bear crosses themselves (cf. 9:23–26). But at the transfiguration of Christ his self-revelation would peak—and with it, his disciples' encouragement.

Transfiguration (vv. 28, 29)

This revelation was given only to the inner circle of disciples—to Peter who had made the confession, and to John and James, "Sons of Thunder" (cf. Mark 3:17). It came a week later,[1] when Jesus invited the three to go up on the mountain with him to get away and pray. There, Luke tells us, "As he was praying, the appearance of his face was altered, and his clothing became dazzling white" (v. 29).

What a spectacle! Jesus was framed by a thousand summer stars, and "his clothing became dazzling white" ("white" here is *leukos*—the grand apocalyptic color, the color representative of what is beyond; cf. Revelation 2:17; 6:2; 20:11). Jesus' glorified body illuminated his clothing, so that it appeared to share in the transformation. Not only that, but Matthew records that "his face shone like the sun" (Matthew 17:2). Overhead were the Bear and Pleiades, but Jesus was shining like a star himself.

When as a young father I used to light the fireworks on the Fourth of July for my family, there were two views I enjoyed. The fireworks themselves pouring forth a fountain of sparks, and the faces of my children, eyes wide with delight and expectancy, their skin reflecting the changing hues of the fireworks. I liked the latter the most!

Jesus saw his own glory illuminating the faces of his awestruck inner ring of disciples—his very image dancing white in their wide eyes. Mark says Jesus "was transfigured"—more literally, "metamorphosed" (Mark 9:2).[2] For a brief moment the veil of his humanity was lifted, and his true essence was allowed to shine through. The glory that was always in the depths of his being rose to the surface that one time in his earthly life. This was both a glance back into his prehuman glory and a look forward into his future glory!

Peter, James, and John were meant to hold onto this during the difficult days to come—it was to be their solace and a reason for hope in the darkness. The crucifixion would eclipse their vision momentarily but not permanently. John, for example, would later write, "We have seen his glory, glory as of the only Son from the Father" (John 1:14)

Conversation (vv. 30, 31)

Superterrestrials

As Jesus stood radiating light, "two men were talking with him, Moses and Elijah, who appeared in glory and spoke of his departure, which he was about to accomplish at Jerusalem" (vv. 30, 31). Why Elijah and Moses? Why not Isaiah and Jeremiah, or Daniel and Joseph? There are several reasons. Both these men had previously conversed with God on mountaintops—Moses on Mount Sinai (Exodus 31:18) and Elijah on Mount Horeb, another name for Sinai (1 Kings 19:8ff.). They both had been shown God's glory. Both also had famous departures from this earth. Moses died on Mount Nebo, after which God buried him in a grave known only to himself. Elijah was taken up alive in a chariot of fire. Both were expected to return again at the end of the age (concerning Elijah, cf. 1:17; 9:8, 19; concerning Moses cf. Deuteronomy 18:15, 18). Moses was the great lawgiver, and Elijah was the great prophet. Moses was the founder of Israel's religious economy, and Elijah was the restorer of it. Together they were a powerful summary of the entire Old Testament economy.

Supertalk

What were Jesus and these superterrestrials talking about? Specifically, "his departure [literally "his exodus"], which he was about to accomplish at Jerusalem" (v. 31). They were talking about his impending death, resurrection, and ascension to the right hand of God—the ultimate exodus![3] The Greek tense indicates that this was an extended conversation. Moses and Elijah, the chief representatives of the Law and the Prophets, were carrying on a conversation with Jesus, who himself said, "Do not think that I have come to abolish the Law or the Prophets; I have not come to abolish them but to fulfill them" (Matthew 5:17). They were talking with the fulfillment of everything their lives represented!

What an amazing conversation that must have been! Peter, James, and John probably missed much of it due to their drowsiness and ignorance. But it must have become apparent that death and resurrection were part of the divine plan as Jesus had early explained (cf. 9:22). Jesus was the fulfillment of everything toward which the Law pointed. He fulfilled what the sacrificial system had taught and promised. He fulfilled the Decalogue (cf. Matthew 5:17ff.). He fulfilled every messianic prophecy—everything toward which their religion and history had been moving.

What an amazing sight! Luminous, dazzling Jesus is talking to Moses who had been dead over fourteen hundred years and to Elijah who had been gone for about nine hundred. And they are talking about his exodus—his imminent death for our sins.

Institutionalization? (vv. 32, 33)

If there ever was a time for silence, this was it. But Peter was a man who could always find something to say when nothing could or should be said.

> Now Peter and those who were with him were heavy with sleep, but when they became fully awake they saw his glory and the two men who stood with him. And as the men were parting from him, Peter said to Jesus, "Master, it is good that we are here. Let us make three tents, one for you and one for Moses and one for Elijah"—not knowing what he said. (vv. 32, 33)

What was Peter thinking? Perhaps it was just a courteous reflex. Maybe he wanted to make thatched booths for his heavenly visitors, so he, James, and John could wait on them. Certainly in Jewish thinking such booths were joyous symbols.[4] Others think it was a simple attempt to prolong the amazing conversation.[5] However, had Jesus complied, Peter's unfortunate suggestion would have placed all three figures on the same level, not to mention that it would have impeded the plan for salvation, planned from eternity. Peter was confused at best.

Jesus chose not to answer. But an unforgettable answer was in the air.

Revelation (vv. 34, 35)

Shekinah Glory

It had been six hundred years since anyone in Israel had seen the *Shekinah* glory. But "As he [Peter] was saying these things, a cloud came and overshadowed them, and they were afraid as they entered the cloud" (v. 34). The disciples were terrified as Jesus, Moses, and Elijah were enveloped by a "bright cloud" (cf. Matthew 17:5).[6]

It was the *Shekinah*! It is reasonable to imagine that from below any who happened to look up that night saw it—the mountain was capped with the divine incandescence. Peter, James, and John saw up close and personal the cloud that not even Moses was allowed to intimately view in Old Testament times. But now Jesus was with them, and so they could gaze upon the *Shekinah* glory.

Think of it! This was the pillar of the exodus (Exodus 13:21). This was the cloud that passed by Moses as God covered him in the cleft of the rock with his hand, so that Moses only saw the afterglow (Exodus 33:18–23). This was the cloud that covered the newly finished tent of meeting and so filled the new tabernacle with God's glory that Moses could not enter it (Exodus 40:35). It was the same cloud that filled Solomon's temple on dedication day so that the priests could not enter (1 Kings 8:10, 11; 2 Chronicles 7:1). It was the same glory that Ezekiel saw rise from between the cherubim and move to the threshold of the temple because of Israel's apostasy (Ezekiel 8:4; 9:3) and then slowly, hesitatingly move over the east gate of the temple where it hovered (Ezekiel 10:4, 18, 19), finally rising to be seen no more from the Mount of Olives (11:22–25).

Jesus is the glory! On the mount of transfiguration his face was shining like the sun—his body was dazzling white. This was the one who would pray on the night of his death, "And now, Father, glorify me in your own presence with the glory that I had with you before the world existed" (John 17:5). Everything signified by the pillar of fire is fulfilled in Jesus. Jesus *was* the pillar—he *was* the cloud. He is the glory of God today.

The cloud is also a prophecy. In the future, in death, believers will meet the risen Christ in the incandescent clouds to be with him forever (1 Thessalonians 4:17, 18). Peter, James, and John were to put their arms around this blessed experience and pull it within themselves. So must we! It is our hope. First Thessalonians 4:17b says that the same Lord is going to return in a cloud of glory, and that those who die before are going to rise up and meet him in the air (v. 16), and that the living are going to meet him in the air too (v. 17)—in that great cloud of glory. Someday *we* are going to be in that cloud! The *Shekinah* glory is going to surround us!

Words from Above

Amid the glory, "A voice came out of the cloud, saying, 'This is my Son, my Chosen One; listen to him!'" (v. 35). This was the voice of the Father, who said almost the same thing at Jesus' baptism (cf. 3:22). These words are not the groggy recollection of sleep-deprived disciples. As Peter said:

> For we did not follow cleverly devised myths when we made known to you the power and coming of our Lord Jesus Christ, but we were eyewitnesses of his majesty. For when he received honor and glory from God the Father, and the voice was borne to him by the Majestic Glory, "This is my beloved Son, with whom I am well pleased," we ourselves heard this very voice borne from heaven, for we were with him on the holy mountain. (2 Peter 1:16–18)

The command from God is emphatic—"Listen to him!" Jesus is a far greater authority than Moses or Elijah. The Law and the Prophets were only partial expressions, but here is the final statement, so "listen to him!" As the writer of Hebrews so perfectly put it in the opening lines of his letter, "Long ago, at many times and in many ways, God spoke to our fathers by the prophets, but in these last days he has spoken to us by his Son" (Hebrews 1:1, 2).

Given who he is, everything depends on listening to Jesus. "Listen to him!"

- Jesus said to him, "I am the way, and the truth, and the life. No one comes to the Father except through me" (John 14:6).
- On the last day of the feast, the great day, Jesus stood up and cried out, "If anyone thirsts, let him come to me and drink" (John 7:37).
- Come to me, all who labor and are heavy laden, and I will give you rest. Take my yoke upon you, and learn from me, for I am gentle and lowly in heart, and you will find rest for your souls. For my yoke is easy, and my burden is light (Matthew 11:28–30).

Luke concludes the account by saying, "And when the voice had spoken, Jesus was found alone. And they kept silent and told no one in those days anything of what they had seen" (v. 36). "Jesus . . . alone" means that Jesus is the focus of everything. Jesus is the focus of the Old Testament (cf. 24:27). Jesus is the focus of history (cf. Colossians 1:1 5–18). Jesus is the focus of eternity (cf. Revelation 4:11; 5:6–14). Jesus is everything!

Closing Reflections

Some months later, toward the very end of Jesus' life, as the cross loomed ever larger, he was in Jerusalem for the Feast of Tabernacles. It was the end of the festival, and the previous night an unforgettable ceremony, the illumination of the temple, had taken place before four massive golden candelabra topped with huge torches. The candelabra were as tall as the highest walls of the temple. At the top of these candelabra were mounted great bowls that held sixty-five liters of oil. There was a ladder for each candelabrum, and when evening came, healthy young priests would light the protruding wicks.

Eyewitnesses said that the huge flames that leapt from these torches illuminated not only the temple but much of Jerusalem.

The *Mishnah* tells us: "Men of piety and good works used to dance before [the candelabra] with burning torches in their hands singing songs and praises and countless Levites played on harps, lyres, cymbals, and trumpets and instruments of music."[7] The exotic rite celebrated the great pillar of fire (the glorious cloud of God's presence) that led the Israelites during their sojourn in the wilderness, spread its fiery billows over the tabernacle, and later engulfed the temple.

In the temple treasury the following morning, with the charred torches still in place, Jesus lifted his voice above the crowd and proclaimed, "I am the light of the world" (John 8:12a). There could scarcely be a more emphatic way to announce one of the supreme truths of his existence. Christ was saying in effect, "The pillar of fire that came between you and the Egyptians, the cloud that guided you by day in the wilderness and illumined the night and enveloped the tabernacle, the glorious cloud that filled Solomon's temple, was me! I am the light of the world. Whoever follows me will not walk in darkness, but will have the light of life" (John 8:12).

Jesus is the *Shekinah* glory! He is the light of life. If we do not have him, we are in darkness. He is the Savior of the world. If we are without him, we are lost. He is our only hope.

Do you have the light of life?

43

Christ's Majesty Below

LUKE 9:37–45

ON THE MOUNT OF TRANSFIGURATION Peter, James, and John had seen the greatest revelation of God's majestic glory ever granted to humankind. On the heights of Palestine, under the light of the Milky Way, they had witnessed Jesus' divine essence gloriously shining through his body. They saw Moses and Elijah, Israel's preeminent lawgiver and foremost prophet, both dead for many centuries, speaking with Jesus. They had seen the luminous cloud of the *Shekinah* glory envelop Jesus, Moses, and Elijah. And they heard the voice of God the Father speak from the cloud: "This is my Son, my Chosen One; listen to him!" (9:35). This stunning experience marked the three for life and eternity.

Years later Peter gave this eloquent retrospect regarding the experience:

> For we did not follow cleverly devised myths when we made known to you the power and coming of our Lord Jesus Christ, but we were eyewitnesses of his majesty. For when he received honor and glory from God the Father, and the voice was borne to him by the Majestic Glory, "This is my beloved Son, with whom I am well pleased," we ourselves heard this very voice borne from heaven, for we were with him on the holy mountain. (2 Peter 1:16–18)

The vision never faded but remained an anchor for his soul. The same thing will happen to us if we let the wild, explosive Scriptural teaching regarding God's glory enter our souls.

A Desperate Dilemma (vv. 37–41)

It is significant that though Peter and his friends would like to have stayed on the mountain, they dutifully followed Christ down the slopes the next day, back into the turmoil of regular life. The contrast was divinely intentional and most dramatic.

Luke the Editor

Dr. Luke, theologian and historian, wanted us to see a contrast here—they had seen Christ's glory *above* but would now also see his glory *below* in the dark world. So Luke edited Mark's extended account to emphasize this contrast, cutting it down to less than half its original size. He trimmed off Mark's recording of Jesus' words about the coming of Elijah and the suffering of the Son of Man (cf. Mark 9:11–13) in order to tighten the connection between what happened on the mountain and what happened below.[1]

Luke also chopped off Mark's account of the stimulating discussion as to why the disciples could not cast out demons (cf. Mark 9:28, 29; Matthew 17:19, 20). He also omitted what Jesus says about the necessity of faith to do such works (cf. Mark 9:23; Matthew 17:20).

Finally, having edited the story, Luke added a summary line about the crowd's response that the other Gospels do not include: "And all were astonished at the majesty of God" (v. 43). The significance of this is readily apparent when we understand that the Greek word translated "majesty" is the same word Peter used in his retrospect on the transfiguration, describing it as "his majesty" (2 Peter 1:16; cf. v. 17, "the Majestic Glory"). Peter saw Jesus' transfiguration and called it "his majesty"; the crowds saw Jesus exorcise a boy and were struck with "the majesty of God" (v. 43).

Luke wants us to consider the majesty *above* and the majesty *below* together, for both belonged to Christ. As I. H. Marshall writes: "What was visible only to the chosen three on the mountain is here visible to a greater number."[2]

Luke's Revised Version

Keeping the majesty connection in mind, we will now examine Luke's "revised" version.

What a conversation the three disciples must have had as they bounced down the slopes. It was likely all theology—questions about the relationship of Elijah and the Messiah, the sequence of events, the resurrection (cf. Mark 9:9–13). They did not understand it all, but Peter and the "Sons of Thunder" were exhilarated. But their reverie was quickly shattered when they arrived at ground level and came face-to-face with demonic powers:

> On the next day, when they had come down from the mountain, a great crowd met him [Jesus]. And behold, a man from the crowd cried out,

> "Teacher, I beg you to look at my son, for he is my only child. And behold, a spirit seizes him, and he suddenly cries out. It convulses him so that he foams at the mouth, and shatters him, and will hardly leave him. And I begged your disciples to cast it out, but they could not." (vv. 37–40)

It was a desperate scene. The disciples had attempted an exorcism but failed. Mark's Gospel indicates that a heated argument was in progress with the teachers of the Law (cf. Mark 9:14, 15), and the lawyers were on the attack. Out of the tumult rose a pathetic voice with a heart-rending plea: "Teacher, I beg you to look at my son, for he is my only child." The Greek verb translated "look at" is the same verb Mary used in the *Magnificat* in reference to God's compassion[3]—"Look with mercy, Lord!"

When we piece the Gospel descriptions together, we get a heartbreaking picture. When the demon seizes the boy (Mark 9:18; Luke 9:39), the child screams (Luke 9:39). The spirit throws him to the ground in convulsions so that he foams at the mouth (Luke 9:39). He grinds his teeth and becomes stiff as a board (Mark 9:18). Many times he had been cast into fire or water by the evil spirit (Matthew 17:15), and he is covered with scars. Even worse, the spirit has made him deaf and dumb (Mark 9:25). The poor boy lives an aquarium-like existence. He can see what is going on around his pathetic body, but he cannot hear or speak. His father concludes here in Luke, "It . . . shatters him, and will hardly leave him" (v. 39)—literally, "it is crushing him together."[4]

How utterly awful! And the disciples had been powerless to do anything about it despite the man's pathetic begging. Why was this so? They had done such feats before—actually, just a few days previously—during their Galilean ministry (cf. 9:1–6). Why not now? The answer lies in the opening phrase of Jesus' dismayed, emotional response in verse 41: "O faithless and twisted generation, how long am I to be with you and bear with you? Bring your son here." Frederick Godet, the French commentator, has suggested that Jesus' exasperated response may have been partially due to his wonderful night of prayer and communion on the mount of transfiguration: "He feels himself a stranger in the midst of unbelief. . . . The holy enjoyment of the night before, as it were, made him homesick."[5]

Unbelief

Whatever caused Jesus' emotion to swell, it is clear that the root of the apostles' powerlessness was their unbelief. Their failure was not because they did not try. They did their very best, no doubt repeatedly, probably using previously successful formulas. Their problem was, they had subtly moved from trust in God to faith in the process, which is to say faith in themselves. They had cast out demons before—certainly they could do it again. This is evidenced by their lack of prayer, as Jesus briefly notes in Mark's account (cf. Mark 9:28, 29). True prayer is an act of faith. And vital, authentic faith, believing, exists only in a life of perpetual, dependent prayer. Significantly, their unbelief and prayerlessness developed in just over a week! How quickly we drift! Jesus' indictment was a blanket indictment of the "faithless . . . generation" he ministered to and of the disciples who had begun to depend on themselves and not on God.

Perversity

Further insight into their condition comes from the other word Jesus used in his indictment: "twisted"—"O faithless and twisted generation." This is a calculated reference to Deuteronomy 32, the famous Song of Moses, which every synagogue-attending Jew knew well. The same Greek word translated here as "twisted" was used in the Greek version of Deuteronomy 32:5, 20 ("a crooked and twisted generation . . . I will hide my face from them; I will see what their end will be, for they are a perverse generation, children in whom is no faithfulness"), and every adult hearer surely recognized this at once.

In Moses' time the people had become twisted, bent, and perverted as a result of their lack of faith and their departure from God. Such crookedness always accompanies unbelief.

A Living Parable (vv. 42, 43a)

The situation with the enslaved, convulsing boy and his distraught father presented an eloquent parable of God the Father's dismay at seeing his sons and daughters turned away from him toward false religion, so that they became perverse and crooked in heart.[6] Thus Jesus' plaintive words are a universal cry of God over his errant children: "O faithless and twisted generation, how long am I to . . . bear with you?"

Jesus next gave the answer for wandering souls engaged in unbelief and perversity: "Bring your son here"—that is, for healing. Thus they would see a fresh revelation of the majesty of God that would in turn produce faith, obedience, and worship in their souls.

What happened is more than a parable—it is a real-life example of the difference Jesus Christ can make: "While he [the boy] was coming, the demon threw him to the ground and convulsed him" (v. 42a). Mark says, "He fell on the ground and rolled about, foaming at the mouth" (Mark 9:20b). The tenses are continuous, a terrible picture. Think how the boy's father felt seeing his maimed, scarred son wallowing in the dirt, mutely staring up through terror-filled eyes. But consider too Jesus' heart—the most compassionate person who ever lived. When he sees his wandering, crooked children, he cares more than we can imagine.

The next sentence speaks volumes: "But Jesus rebuked the unclean spirit and healed the boy, and gave him back to his father" (v. 42b). How infinite is the competence of Jesus! The boy was not half healed but was made completely whole. The Lord restored the boy's mind, hearing, speech, body, boyhood, and hope—and he gave him faith. Further, he "gave him back to his father." Can you hear the people's cheers as they praised God?

Now comes Luke's unique summary verse: "And all were astonished at the majesty of God" (v. 43a). The magnificent splendor of God seen the day before on the mountain was now apparent to the people below.[7] The glory of God and his awesome compassion was shown through his works of power and deliverance.

And his majesty is all around us today! It is seen in the thirty-something couple delivered from their unbelief and idolatries and perversities. It is showcased in a recently divorced woman whose life was a crooked, tangled mess but who has received the touch of Christ and has been transformed. It is visible in the man marvelously set free from his addiction to alcohol and who is once again a loving father and husband.

We all need firsthand observations of his majesty as seen in the healing of lives—ours and others. Personal and corporate worship takes us onto the mount of transfiguration where we see Jesus shine, and evangelism brings the *Shekinah* glory down into dark valleys where needy souls suffer under the cruelty of sin. This in turn reminds us of the incomparable wonders of God's grace and encourages further obedience and worship.

Whenever one is born anew by God's Spirit, that person becomes a partaker of the glory both now and ultimately at Christ's return. The light of Christ dwells within. Jesus says to us, "Let your light shine before others, so that they may see your good works and give glory to your Father who is in heaven" (Matthew 5:16). "Good works" (literally, "beautiful works"), possible only as we allow God to work in our hearts, reflect his moral splendor. Exodus 34 tells us that Moses' face glowed from being in God's presence and that he put a veil over his face so the people could not see the glory passing away (cf. Exodus 34:29–35). But today believers possess a glory that is unveiled in Christ.

> But when one turns to the Lord, the veil is removed. Now the Lord is the Spirit, and where the Spirit of the Lord is, there is freedom. And we all, with unveiled face, beholding the glory of the Lord, are being transformed into the same image from one degree of glory to another. For this comes from the Lord who is the Spirit. (2 Corinthians 3:16–18)

As we grow in Christ, as he possesses more and more of our life, his glory will shine forth, and we will shine like stars in the universe. Philippians 2:15, the only New Testament text besides Luke 9:41 that references the idea of the crooked generation in Deuteronomy 32:5, 20, combines all these themes exquisitely: "That you may be blameless and innocent, children of God without blemish in the midst of a crooked and twisted generation, among whom you shine as lights in the world."

Believers, stellar torches in this perverse world, fulfill Daniel's end-time prophecy: "And those who are wise shall shine like the brightness of the sky above; and those who turn many to righteousness, like the stars forever and ever" (Daniel 12:3).

And ultimately we will be citizens of a heavenly city that needs no lights.

> The throne of God and of the Lamb will be in [the city], and his servants will worship him. They will see his face, and his name will be on their foreheads. And night will be no more. They will need no light of lamp or sun, for the Lord God will be their light, and they will reign forever and ever. (Revelation 22:3–5)

Majesty to Come (vv. 43b–45)

"But while they were all marveling at everything he was doing, Jesus said to his disciples, 'Let these words sink into your ears: The Son of Man is about to be delivered into the hands of men.' But they did not understand this saying, and it was concealed from them, so that they might not perceive it. And they were afraid to ask him about this saying" (vv. 43b–45).

They were afraid to ask because they were beginning to realize that the ominous destiny facing Jesus had implications for their lives too. The parallel account in Matthew (17:23), rather than citing fear, says they were "greatly distressed" by Jesus' prediction.[8] So apparently they were afraid of hearing something that would make them feel sad (cf. 9:23, 24).

In contrast, the Lord of glory, the veritable *Shekinah* who manifests the majesty of God above and below, embraced the cross, willingly suffering the penalty of sin in our place and for our sake. As Paul exclaimed, "Far be it from me to boast except in the cross of our Lord Jesus Christ" (Galatians

6:14). Wherever the Lord went, whether onto the mount of transfiguration or down to the troubled world below or onto Calvary's tree, he did the Father's will perfectly and displayed his glory.

> For Thy blest Cross
> Which doth for all atone,
> Creation's praises
> Rise before Thy throne.
> Lift high the Cross,
> The love of Christ proclaim,
> Till all the world
> Adore his sacred name.
>
> G. W. Kitchen and M. R. Newbolt (1916)

Glory to his name!

44

True Greatness

LUKE 9:46–50

CHARLES COLSON WRITES:

> I vividly recall a glimpse . . . from my White House days. One brisk December night as I accompanied the president from the Oval Office in the West Wing of the White House to the Residence, Mr. Nixon was musing about what people wanted in their leaders. He slowed a moment, looking into the distance across the South Lawn, and said, "The people really want a leader a little bigger than themselves, don't they, Chuck?" I agreed. "I mean someone like de Gaulle," he continued. "There's a certain aloofness, a power that's exuded by great men that people feel and want to follow."

That, of course, was before Colson's humbling at Watergate and his subsequent encounter with Christ, because Colson goes on:

> Jesus Christ exhibited none of this self-conscious aloofness. He served others first; He spoke to those to whom no one spoke; He dined with the lowest members of society; He touched the untouchables. He had no throne, no crown, no bevy of servants or armored guards. A borrowed manger and a borrowed tomb framed His earthly life.
>
> Kings and presidents and prime ministers surround themselves with minions who rush ahead, swing the doors wide, and stand at attention as they wait for the great to pass. Jesus said that He Himself stands at the door and knocks, patiently waiting to enter our lives.[1]

Colson is absolutely right. True greatness is the antithesis of pride and exclusivity. Yet many churchgoers, and indeed many Christians, do not know this—as evidenced by the strutting leaders they choose to follow, and even more, the pride and narrowness that characterize their own lives and to which they actually aspire. Today in some quarters of organized Christianity, the church simply does not believe Jesus' words.

Why are things so upside-down? Consider the difference between dogs and cats. The master pets a dog, and the dog wags its tail and thinks, "He must be God." The master pets his cat, and the cat purrs, shuts its eyes, and thinks to itself, "I must be God." After God has graciously reached down to us, there is a perverse human tendency to think like the cat!

Think about it. As Christians, we began well as humble, needy sinners who received the free grace and mercy of God. Like the dog, God was everything to us, and we gladly worshiped him. But as time went by, the regrettable feline pathology began to shrink the recognition of grace in our hearts. The Christian life produces some positive changes within us. We become kinder people, our language changes, and destructive habits disappear. But those changes can become an unwitting source of pride. We may not think, "I must be God," but we do silently imagine, "I must be pretty good." We become proud of our apparent sanctification, our knowledge of the Bible, our evangelical routines. After all, we understand the mysteries of grace, while the unregenerate dolts around us have no clue. We become proud of our spirituality.

This condition is typically very interior, but it has a telltale aroma, and others can smell it, especially those outside the church. Sometimes it is an acrid air of condescension or subtle, smiling hostility, or aloofness, or clubbish exclusivity, or doubt about God's blessing on all who are not in the approved circle. This stench has kept multitudes away from the church and, more important, a knowledge of Christ.

An Appalling Argument (vv. 46–48)

Such wrong thinking even assaulted the ministry of Jesus. We read in verse 46, "An argument arose among them [the disciples] as to which of them was the greatest." God's gracious hand had reached down to them all in their humble circumstances. They had been called, taught, gifted for ministry, and used—and they began to think, "I must be something special. In fact, I—well, I'm the greatest!" They started staring each other down like chest-bumping basketball players at playoff time.

What brought the Twelve to such a point? The flow of Luke's story provides some answers. In 6:12–16 we saw that it was only after an entire night of prayer that Jesus named the Twelve. They were a special lot. No doubt about that. Then chapters 6—8 show the Twelve as being privy to the most intimate teaching and displays of Jesus' power. And at the beginning of chapter 9 we read of their being commissioned and then going out to minister with amazing power (9:1–6). They enjoyed elite status, thanks to the grace of God. And for three, it even went further when Peter, James, and John were taken up with Jesus to pray and saw Jesus transfigured (9:28–36)—what Peter called "the Majestic Glory" (2 Peter 1:17). Incredible privilege!

But when the three came down with Jesus, they discovered that their nine colleagues had been unable to heal a demonically afflicted boy (9:40). After Jesus' subsequent healing of the boy and ominous words about the end being imminent, jealous tempers flared. The apostles argued their personal claims to primacy and put down the claims of the others. No doubt some were more aggressive than others. "Peter, the only reason you were on the mount with Jesus is because he doesn't dare let you out of his sight." It was an ugly scene. Pride is the sin we cannot see in ourselves and yet so detest in others. There was a lot of loathing going on.

The Answer of an Object Lesson

Jesus did not directly hear the argument but either saw it from a distance or deduced it from the way they were acting. So he used an object lesson to help them see their erroneous thinking. "But Jesus, knowing the reasoning of their hearts, took a child and put him by his side and said to them, 'Whoever receives this child in my name receives me, and whoever receives me receives him who sent me'" (vv. 47, 48).

Though loved and cherished, a child was the smallest and most powerless individual in Hebrew culture. The *Talmud* regarded spending time with children to be a waste of time. One rabbi wrote: "Morning sleep, midday wine, chattering with children and tarrying in places where men of the common people assemble, destroy a man" (Ab. 3,10:R. Dosa b. Archinos).[2] Keeping company with children added nothing to a man, it was said. Later in Luke (18:15) we see that the disciples considered Jesus too important to receive children and attempted to send them away. The disciples undoubtedly thought (in line with their culture) that greatness is determined by the company one keeps—the great associate with the great and deal with matters of great significance, and children are not great or significant.[3] So Peter, James, and John probably argued for their greatness based on their meeting with Jesus, Moses, and Elijah at the transfiguration.

Seeking to break through the disciples' selfish ambitions, Jesus presented them with two opposite figures—himself who was everything to them, and a child who was nothing to them. Jesus then issued the challenge, "Whoever receives this child in my name receives me." Jesus was not saying that his disciples (or anyone else) would find him through being nice to children. But he was saying that how they related to a child (and by implication all who are lowly) would indicate whether they were related to him and to God the Father. Jesus' followers welcome the lowly, thus demonstrating that they have received him. And all who welcome Jesus welcome God the Father also. Greatness is not merely the possession of those who associate with the great. Rather, it is a gift of God to those who receive and serve the lowly.

The Answer of a Maxim

Jesus capped his argument with a concisely stated principle: "For he who is least among you all is the one who is great" (v. 48b). The one who is the greatest among Jesus' disciples is not the one who can boast of the greatest or most prominent relationships, but the disciple who is prepared to identify with the lowly, to receive them, and to minister Christ's kindness to them.[4]

Some Christians do not know any insignificant or weak members of society, much less have a relationship with them. Are we reaching out to and serving the poor, those who speak little English, international students, the mentally handicapped, ex-offenders, those struggling to leave their immorality behind? If all or nearly all our friends are the "great"—the well-off, the educated, the accomplished, the comfortable—we are not the men and women our Master wants us to be.

A Narrow Exclusion (vv. 49, 50)

Jesus' words to the disciples were piercing and deflating, and tender-souled John was convicted regarding something that had been bothering him. Being a "son of thunder," he voiced it: "Master, we saw someone casting out demons in your name, and we tried to stop him, because he does not follow with us" (v. 49). During their Galilean ministry, John and company had encountered a successful freelance exorcist. Apparently that man had not been called in the same way Jesus had called them (cf. 6:12–16), he had not been commissioned as they had (cf. 9:1–6), he had not been privileged to receive the instruction and have the experiences of the Twelve. So they "tried to stop him" but to no avail.

Significantly, their sin here had the same root as their preceding sin—namely, their sinful pride about being privileged disciples. They considered exorcism to be their exclusive ministry. As St. John of the Cross put it: "As far as envy is concerned, many experience displeasure when they see others in possession of spiritual goods. They feel sensibly hurt because others surpass them on this road. . . ."[5]

This sin tarnishes so much of professional ministry. John Claypool recalled in his 1979 Yale lecture on preaching that even while in seminary he experienced sinful competitiveness, and his experience in ministry was blatantly so. He writes:

> I can still recall going to state and national conventions in our denomination and coming home feeling drained and unclean, because most of the conversation in the hotel rooms and the halls was characterized either by envy of those who were doing well or scarcely concealed delight for those who were doing poorly. For did that not mean that someone was about to fall, and thus create an opening higher up the ladder?[6]

The problem is not only ministerial but congregational. How do we feel when others ascend to positions of responsibility and we do not? Or when someone surpasses us in our ability to lead or teach? Or if someone is honored where we would like to be honored? Even more telling, how do we feel when we become aware of such a person's being humbled? Self-importance is a cancerous sin.

The Answer of Prohibition and Aphorism

Jesus' answer to John was both a prohibition ("Do not stop him") and a principle ("For the one who is not against you is for you") (v. 50). He desires his followers to have an open heart, not an exclusive heart. Let's be like Jesus!

When Joshua rushed to Moses to warn him that some elders named Eldad and Medad were preaching and thus stealing some of Moses' prominence, Moses gave the big-hearted reply, "Are you jealous for my sake? Would that all the LORD's people were prophets, that the LORD would put his Spirit on them!" (Numbers 11:29).

While in "the slammer" in Rome, Paul learned that rival preachers were seizing the opportunity for self-promotion. His noble response? "What then? Only that in every way, whether in pretense or in truth, Christ is proclaimed, and in that I rejoice" (Philippians 1:18). Or consider Jonathan, next in line to be king according to human reason, but who "made a covenant with David, because he loved him as his own soul" and committed his life to making him king (1 Samuel 18:1–4). Or John the Baptist who responded to Jesus' ascendance by saying, "A person cannot receive even one thing unless it is given him from heaven. . . . He must increase, but I must decrease" (John 3:27–30).

To put aside personal hopes for success and to surrender to God's plans is the way of jubilant worship, obedient service, and utter freedom.

Closing Reflections

As believers, we have all experienced God's reaching down to us in grace. In that sense we are all special.

But we must never move from seeing the riches of his grace to saying, "I must be extraordinary. Aren't I something!" May our sinful hearts not pervert God's grace into a source of pride. Imagined greatness is a dangerous delusion.

The truly great person is one who consorts with the lowly, for Christ's sake and with his love. The truly great rarely reside in prominent pulpits. The truly great are rarely honored. They are hidden. They are among the anonymous. They stand with the weak.

The truly great rejoice in the elevation of others. They glory in others' growth, success, and honor.

45

Demands of the Road

LUKE 9:51–62

WE COME TO A MAJOR TURNING POINT in Luke's Gospel at this point because beginning here and continuing for ten lengthy chapters—right up to the Triumphal Entry (19:28–44)—Jesus is on the road. Luke alludes to this fact at least ten times (for example, 9:51–57; 10:1; 11:53; 13:22, 33; 17:11; 18:31, 35; 19:1). But it is easy to lose sight of this because Luke does not note the journey's geographical progress. So as readers, we must consciously remind ourselves that Jesus is on the road.

If we do this, we will get the proper feel for what is going on—Jerusalem now looms large in the Savior's thoughts. He will soon walk through everything involved in his being "taken up" (v. 51)—that is, his betrayal, passion, death, resurrection, and ascension. The walls of Jerusalem, the city of destiny, rise ominously over all that follows, standing taller with each event from here to the middle of chapter 19.

"When the days drew near for him to be taken up, he set his face to go to Jerusalem." The raw literalness of Luke's words communicate Jesus' intensity—"he stiffened face to go to Jerusalem."[1] Jesus has determined that nothing will stop him. Divine grit marks these chapters.

Of course, the Twelve and Jesus' other followers were short on steel. Some, like Peter, thought they had it but overestimated themselves. They did not understand Jesus' simplest warnings. For example, right after the transfiguration Jesus had said:

> "Let these words sink into your ears: The Son of Man is about to be delivered into the hands of men." But they did not understand this saying, and it was concealed from them, so that they might not perceive it. And they were afraid to ask him about this saying. (9:44, 45)

Jesus then proceeded to educate his would-be followers on the demands of the road—lessons on what it takes to effectively follow Jesus. As such, they are fiercely radical—scary really, even discouraging. We must resist the temptation to tame them, to make them more reasonable, to make them say what we want. The first demand is implicit and reasonable, but the following three explicit demands are increasingly stringent.

Mercy Demanded (vv. 51–56)

The first demand sprang from the experience of rejection. Luke tells us that as Jesus began his journey, "He sent messengers ahead of him, who went and entered a village of the Samaritans, to make preparations for him. But the people did not receive him, because his face was set toward Jerusalem" (vv. 52, 53). Samaria was the most direct route south to Jerusalem. Because of the large entourage that had begun to follow Jesus, an advance party was sent to make necessary arrangements in Samaria, where they were rejected.

The rejection was not at all surprising. The mutual hatred between the Jews and the Samaritans went back for centuries, when the Samaritans intermarried with their Assyrian conquerors. The Jews considered them racial half-breeds and religious apostates. So the Samaritans responded by calling the Jews apostates—full blooded but apostate. The Samaritans set up a rival temple on Mount Gerizim (later destroyed by the Jews), published their own edition of the Pentateuch, and established a rival liturgy. The Jews responded by publicly cursing the Samaritans in the synagogues and praying daily that they might not enter eternal life.[2] During New Testament times some Samaritans managed to sneak into the Jerusalem temple where they strewed some human bones.[3] This made both the Jews and Samaritans regret that life was so short—there was so much to hate and so little time!

So it is not at all surprising that "When his disciples James and John saw it, they said, 'Lord, do you want us to tell fire to come down from heaven and consume them?'" (v. 54). James and John, "Sons of Thunder" (Mark 3:17), were deadly serious. They were not naive, and they were not joking. They believed Jesus was an Elijah-like Messiah, and thus Elijah's life was a precedent for what should happen now. They remembered 2 Kings 1:1–14, which records how the apostate king Ahaziah twice sent soldiers to take Elijah and how twice the prophet said, "If I am a man of God, let fire come down from heaven and consume you and your fifty" (2 Kings 1:10, 12)—and it did! The two disciples' memory was good, but what they failed to understand was that though Ahaziah was rejecting God, the Samaritans were not, but were simply returning the rejection of the Jews. The situations were not the same.

Also, in their rush to call for God's judgment the apostles had chosen to ignore Jesus' example and teaching. Luke 6 reveals that both had heard Jesus say, "But I say to you who hear, Love your enemies, do good to those who hate you, bless those who curse you, pray for those who abuse you" (6:27, 28). Indeed, the ethic of the kingdom was mercy: "Blessed are the merciful, for they shall receive mercy" (Matthew 5:7). And they had seen it fleshed out in Jesus' life in a thousand ways. Thus, Jesus' response was appropriate: "But he turned and rebuked them. And they went on to another village" (vv. 55, 56).

Those on the road with Jesus, those who would pretend to share in his ministry, must be merciful. There is no room for the preacher who by his fierce preaching on Hell betrays a sick wish that people would end up there. "Turn or burn! And I hope you do!" If we are on the road with Jesus, we must be compassionate and forgiving, like him.

The merciful have received mercy, and therefore are merciful and will receive more mercy. A merciful spirit is essential for all who want to be on the road with the Son of God.

Commitment Demanded (vv. 57–62)

Jesus insisted that following him does not mean merely imitating him, but entering the very conditions of his life. He paired mercy with an astonishing call to commitment because it was his loving mercy and commitment that kept him on the road, that led him to fully obey the Father's will even though it meant giving his life.

Jesus was now explicitly didactic in providing three explosive sayings about commitment that detonated with increasing power.

Hardships

As they began to travel along the road, one of the group glibly announced, "I will follow you wherever you go" (v. 57). Words like this, easily spoken, reveal ignorance and inexperience. I remember a chorus we used to sing in my high-school days.

> I have decided to follow Jesus
> I have decided to follow Jesus
> I have decided to follow Jesus
> No turning back
> No turning back.

I like the words. But sometimes I think the airy tune is inappropriate. It might be all right for Dorothy and the Tin Man as they skip along the Yellow Brick Road to Oz! But for followers of Christ, something martial might better fit the words.

Jesus knew that following him would be no stroll in the park and that such a blithe declaration of commitment would never make it. So he sharply countered, "Foxes have holes, and birds of the air have nests, but the Son of Man has nowhere to lay his head" (v. 58). The fact is, Jesus sometimes did have a place to lay his head before and after this saying. He had enjoyed Peter's home in Capernaum and later would find respite and refreshment in the Bethany home of Mary, Martha, and Lazarus. He also had told his disciples:

> Truly, I say to you, there is no one who has left house or brothers or sisters or mother or father or children or lands, for my sake and for the gospel, who will not receive a hundredfold now in this time, houses and brothers and sisters and mothers and children and lands, with persecutions, and in the age to come eternal life. (Mark 10:29, 30)

So what did Jesus mean by his strong assertion? He meant that at times those who followed him would literally be homeless, that they would undergo immense discomfort. But more, Jesus was saying that if you walk with him, you will sense that the world is not your home. There will be dissonance, discomfort, unease, and rejection. He was saying that to follow him, one must embrace a life of discomfort.

No one who commits to following Christ, and does so, lives a life of ease. No one. If your Christianity has not brought discomfort to your life, something is wrong. A committed heart knows the discomfort of loving difficult people, the discomfort of giving until it hurts, the discomfort of putting oneself out for the ministry of Christ and his church, the discomfort of a life out of step with modern culture, the discomfort of being disliked, the occasional sense of having nowhere to lay your head. But Christ's rewards far outvalue anything lost by following him.

Urgency

The next exchange, this time at Jesus' instigation, raised the call to commitment even higher:

> To another he said, "Follow me." But he said, "Lord, let me first go and bury my father." And Jesus said to him, "Leave the dead to bury their own dead. But as for you, go and proclaim the kingdom of God." (vv. 59, 60)

Here Jesus seems to contradict the Decalogue and his own teaching, as well as the teaching of the rabbis. The Decalogue's fifth commandment says, "Honor your father and your mother" (Exodus 20:12). This includes at the very least showing them respect, giving them consideration by remembering them, engaging in acts of kindness toward them, and making provision for their welfare. In fact, Jesus had excoriated the religious leaders of his day for neglecting their parents' needs by the practice of *Corban*, which meant saying to one's parents, "What you would have gained from me is given to God" (literally, *Corban*) (Matthew 15:5). In other words, "I've dedicated all my money to God, so I can't help you." Jesus condemned this ethical sleight-of-hand, saying, "And why do you break the commandment of God for the sake of your tradition? For God commanded, 'Honor your father and your mother'" (Matthew 15:3, 4). Therefore, any neglect of parents is a grievous break of the fifth commandment.

In reference to honoring parents in death, the rabbis had created a mass of protective measures. Burial of the dead was considered a religious duty that took precedence over all others, including the study of the Law. They wrote: "He who is confronted by a dead relative is freed from reciting the Shema, from the Eighteen Benedictions, and from all the commandments stated in the Torah" (b. Ber. 31a.).[4] To assist in the burial of a nonrelative was a work that received great reward from God, and the burial of a father was a religious duty of the utmost importance.[5] So how could Jesus tell a would-be follower to neglect the burial of his dead father?

The answer is, the man did not say his father was dead, but only, "Let me first go and bury my father." If his father had indeed died, the man would not have been on the road with Jesus, but at home tending to the details and the service. Apparently the would-be disciple's father was getting elderly, and the man was asking Jesus' permission to delay following him until his father died. The request revealed that he had no concept of the urgency and importance of the task to which Jesus was calling him.

Jesus' famous answer, far from being a hard-hearted rejoinder, exalted the importance and urgency of his call: "Leave the dead to bury their own dead. But as for you, go and proclaim the kingdom of God" (v. 60). That is, "Let the spiritually dead bury the physically dead." The implication was that as a man alive to God, with the call of God upon him, he must do the greater thing—"proclaim the kingdom of God."[6] To neglect this would ultimately mean being false to his father's deepest need.[7]

If you are really on the road with Jesus, life is filled with intense urgency.

We have the words of life. Life is short. There is so little time, and we have such good news to proclaim far and wide!

Focus

A third man on the road now offered his services to Jesus with his own interposed condition: "Yet another said, 'I will follow you, Lord, but let me first say farewell to those at my home'" (v. 61). The request was minor, and it had Biblical precedent—again in the life of Elijah. When Elijah saw Elisha plowing behind his oxen, approached him, and threw his cloak over him, indicating his call to discipleship, Elisha accepted but begged to go kiss his father and mother good-bye first, saying, "And then I will follow you." And Elijah permitted him to go (cf. 1 Kings 19:19–21). Jesus was aware of the Old Testament story, so he answered with plowing imagery: "No one who puts his hand to the plow and looks back is fit for the kingdom of God" (v. 62). There would be time later for good-byes. But a disciple must not condition his commitment to even the most proper of obligations. The call must come first and must remain the focus of one's life.

It was proverbial in ancient culture that one could not look back while plowing and drive a straight furrow (Hesiod, *Works and Days*, 443).[8] Those who pine after what they left behind, who are always remembering the comforts of home and hearth, who dream about how life might have been if they had not stepped onto the road with Jesus, who keep looking in the rearview mirror, will not do well on Jesus' road.

William W. Borden was the heir of a wealthy Chicago family. In 1904 and 1905, at the age of eighteen, he traveled around the world. This was followed by a brilliant education at Yale and then Princeton Seminary, where he committed his life to seek to win the Muslims in China to Christ. Before he left, Borden gave away some $500,000 (equivalent to $10,000,000 in the 1990s) and served at the age of twenty-three as a trustee of Moody Bible Institute. In 1913, in his twenty-sixth year, he left for Egypt and never looked back. It was the final year of his life, because in Cairo he contracted cerebral meningitis. As he lay dying, he scribbled this note: "No reserve, no retreat, no regrets." That is the kind of attitude Christ was calling for in Luke 9.

Closing Reflections

What do we need to travel along the road with Jesus? Tender mercy and steely commitment. The only fire we wish to fall on those who have not welcomed Jesus are the fires of the Holy Spirit—fires of regeneration and new life. Jesus demands that we be merciful if we are to walk with him, that we be tenderhearted, compassionate, forgiving. We will want the best for our enemies if we have a heart like his.

Besides mercy we will have a commitment that accepts hardships and cultivates a sense of urgency in preaching the gospel. The dead can bury the dead. But the living must preach the gospel while they can. We will focus on Christ's plans for us, not on mourning the past.

46

Proper Joy

LUKE 10:1–20

WHEN D. L. MOODY returned from his triumphant British campaign in 1875 at the age of thirty-eight, he had reached unparalleled eminence. Many wondered how he would now fare. The answer came quickly when he held a month of meetings in Brooklyn with overflow crowds. One evening alone the *New York Herald* estimated that as many as twenty thousand were turned away. The press acknowledged that Moody "has held in silent attention and deeply moved, some of the largest assemblies that any speaker has addressed in America."[1]

When he next ministered in Philadelphia (from November 1875 to January 1876) in the disused freight depot of the Pennsylvania Railroad, some twelve thousand people would fill the hall an hour and a half ahead of time. Traveling to Princeton for a day of meetings, he received such a reception that he exclaimed, "I have not seen anything in America that pleased me like what I have seen at Princeton. They have got a Holy Ghost revival there. The president of the college told me that he had never seen anything like it at Princeton."[2]

Next came a three-month campaign in New York, where his lay committee (including such members as the famous financiers Pierpont Morgan and Cornelius Vanderbilt Jr.) had done a brilliant job of organization. Moody leased P. T. Barnum's "Great Roman Hippodrome" (where Madison Square Garden now stands), gathered a choir of a thousand, and after a half hour of singing stepped onto the platform. According to James M. Gray:

> He seemed to cover the space between the door and the pulpit in one step! . . . Mr. Moody was a meteor. He was at the little railing in front, his hand raised, our heads bowed in prayer and we were all saying "Amen" almost

> before we knew it. How lithe, springy, buoyant he was. How full of life and spirit![3]

Moody's story is one of the great ministerial success stories. It is a story of much joy.

The Seventy's Joyful Success (vv. 1–17)

Luke 10 recounts a ministry that culminated in joy and success. However, there was not one preacher but seventy (or seventy-two, depending on which translation or early manuscript you go by; the *English Standard Version* says "seventy-two," but I personally prefer the "seventy" reading). Like D. L. Moody when he first began, there were no big names here. But unlike Moody, they have remained anonymous to this day. They were on the road with Jesus when he unexpectedly commissioned them to a temporary ministry of going to the places where Jesus would go and preparing the people to receive Jesus' message of the kingdom. Scholars agree that the number seventy or (seventy-two) is, among other things, a reference to the seventy Gentile nations of the world listed in Genesis 10.[4] Thus they were pioneers, precursors, taking the good news to the larger world.

Drawing from their implicit obedience to Jesus' directions in Luke 10, we can piece together a pretty good picture of the scene. Adrenaline kept surging through the seventy eager followers of Jesus—recurrent holy goose bumps! They had been singled out in a manner similar to what had happened to the twelve apostles and were given a like task (cf. 9:1–6). Though their mission and abilities were similar, their role was temporary. Nevertheless, they were endowed with stupendous authority, and Jesus concluded their commissioning by saying, "The one who hears you hears me, and the one who rejects you rejects me, and the one who rejects me rejects him who sent me" (v. 16). They were to be the mouth of God.

Some may have initially felt, like Moses, that they were not eloquent—"slow of speech and of tongue" (Exodus 4:10). Perhaps they then recalled God's rebuke: "Who has made man's mouth? Who makes him mute, or deaf, or seeing, or blind? Is it not I, the Lord? Now therefore go, and I will be with your mouth and teach you what you shall speak" (Exodus 4:11, 12). Others may have at first felt too inexperienced, like a child who is asked to perform some task for which he is simply not ready. God's words to Jeremiah were their answer: "Do not say, 'I am only a youth'; for to all to whom I send you, you shall go, and whatever I command you, you shall speak. Do not be afraid of them, for I am with you" (Jeremiah 1:7, 8).

So they left in pairs, stopping periodically as Jesus had commanded, to beg the Lord of the harvest to send workers into his field. And as is so often the case, they were sometimes the answers to their own prayers. Barefooted, without cash or purse or weapon, the disciples were absolutely defenseless—and spectacularly dependent upon God. One might have expected them to be hesitant, but that was not their demeanor. They were so absorbed in their task, so focused on carrying out Jesus' will, that his command, "greet no one on the road" came naturally (v. 4). They had no time for chitchat. They were on a mission.

Some made it no farther than the first door, because when they declared "Peace be to this house!" (v. 5), the occupants received it. Because the home was open to Christ and his kingdom, they received the peace of God's presence and saving work. A pervasive air of wholeness and completeness—*shalom*—settled on that house. The pair repeatedly sat at table with the family, joyously expounding on the good news and the Messiah, Jesus. They sat under the smile of God (cf. Numbers 6:24–26).

Others, when they were welcomed into towns, began to heal the sick. The stimulating gift of God's power energized them for long days and nights of ministry. And to their abiding surprise, even the demons obeyed them. With power they proclaimed, "The kingdom of God has come near to you" (v. 9).

But some of the seventy were rejected. As Jesus had directed, they acted out the parable of rejection before the whole town, removing the dust from their feet. The town was foreign soil to God. With deep sadness they pronounced prophetic woes on the town. "For if the mighty works done in you had been done in Tyre and Sidon, they would have repented long ago, sitting in sackcloth and ashes. But it will be more bearable in the judgment for Tyre and Sidon than for you" (vv. 13, 14). They were actually the voice of God—"The one who hears you hears me, and the one who rejects you rejects me, and the one who rejects me rejects him who sent me" (v. 16).

What a time their return and rendezvous must have been! Seventy excited Hebrews, each with a score of amazing stories to tell. Everyone was so fresh, so full of life. They chorused with joy, "Lord, even the demons are subject to us in your name!" (v. 17). Their joy was reasonable. Their joy was understandable. Their joy was right—as far as it went.

Jesus' Perspective on the Seventy's Joy (vv. 18–20)

Jesus himself celebrated their ministry: "I saw Satan fall like lightning from heaven. Behold, I have given you authority to tread on serpents and scorpions, and over all the power of the enemy, and nothing shall hurt you"

(vv. 18, 19). "Lightning" graphically depicts a power of dazzling brilliance that is suddenly snuffed out.[5] Jesus had seen Satan snuffed out by the powerful works of his followers! His power even enabled them to "tread on serpents and scorpions," Biblical symbols of evil. This was something to rejoice in. It was a proper joy, as was Moody's nineteen hundred years later.

At the same time, Jesus moderated his followers' joy: "Nevertheless, do not rejoice in this, that the spirits are subject to you, but rejoice that your names are written in heaven" (v. 20). He was not saying they should not rejoice in spiritual power, but that there is a *primary* rejoicing, a rejoicing that takes precedence over it—namely, that their names were inscribed in God's book in Heaven.

In considering our own lives, there may be some to whom God has given many gifts. He may have given you influence in the church or power among people. Perhaps your gifts and influence have been used in many ways to thwart Satan and encourage the godly. Is this wrong? Should you not be joyful? Of course you should! We ought to be grateful for the gifts, influence, and success God has granted us. But there is a better joy—the joy that our "names are written in heaven."

A Joy That Needs Moderating

We must keep the joy of ministerial gifts, power, and success in right perspective because they can so easily foster pride. President Woodrow Wilson was the son of a Presbyterian clergyman and thus had many opportunities to observe ministers up close. He said of Henry Van Dyke, the gifted Presbyterian preacher and poet, "Henry Van Dyke is the only man I know who can strut sitting down!"[6] Virtually any person who is blessed with a spiritual gift, whether preaching or evangelism or pastoral counseling, and has had long success at it can begin to think it is because of some innate superiority.

Next, giftedness and success are not necessarily the signs of true grace. Judas preached the gospel and was an officer among the twelve apostles, but he was also "the son of perdition" (John 17:12 KJV)—a lost soul. Listen to Jesus' warning to his followers:

> Not everyone who says to me, "Lord, Lord," will enter the kingdom of heaven, but the one who does the will of my Father who is in heaven. On that day many will say to me, "Lord, Lord, did we not prophesy in your name, and cast out demons in your name, and do many mighty works in your name?" And then will I declare to them, "I never knew you; depart from me, you workers of lawlessness." (Matthew 7:21–23)

During my second year in seminary, an unusually gifted man won the senior preaching award and was published by a prominent Christian publisher within a year. Faculty and students all agreed that he was immensely gifted for ministry. How shaken we were a few years later when he renounced Christ. Billy Graham's coevangelist in his earliest days was mightily gifted and hugely successful—and today does not embrace the faith. Do not rejoice in your power and success—rejoice in your salvation!

Another reason we must resist placing our joy in our spiritual prowess is that giftedness does not indicate spiritual superiority. Some inarticulate people's prayers have been a thousand times more useful to the church than my preaching. Some who are illiterate reflect the heart of Christ more closely and more powerfully than seminary graduates.

Furthermore, joy in spiritual accomplishment must be moderated because it is not intrinsically abiding. If we place all our joy in the fact that the spirits submit to us, what will happen when they do not? What if Jesus sends us where there is no response to our giftedness? What will happen to us when successes are few and far between?

For all these reasons we must not base our joy on the devils that have been conquered, the crowds gathered, or the souls saved. Rather, we should derive our joy from the Lord's approval and directives.

A Joy That Needs Exalting

Again, Jesus said, "But rejoice that your names are written in heaven" (v. 20). Praise God—this is the joy in which we can indulge to the fullest, because it is the one in which *every believer* may lavish his or her soul. We can rejoice that our name is "written in heaven" because God chose to write it there. It was not the choice of a man or an angel. It was and is God's sovereign choice. We are citizens of the heavenly Jerusalem, those "who are enrolled in heaven" (Hebrews 12:23). We are children of Heaven by God's choice!

We rejoice that our names are written in Heaven because at the end we will see Jesus—as the Apostle Paul said, "Absent from the body, and . . . present with the Lord" (2 Corinthians 5:8 KJV; cf. Philippians 1:21–23).

We rejoice that our names are inscribed above because we will one day be transformed, as John explained: "Beloved, we are God's children now, and what we will be has not yet appeared; but we know that when he appears we shall be like him, because we shall see him as he is" (1 John 3:2; cf. Philippians 3:20, 21).

We rejoice that our names are written in Heaven because there "an eternal weight of glory beyond all comparison" (2 Corinthians 4:17) awaits us.

We rejoice that our names are penned in Heaven because we are thus "fellow heirs with Christ" (Romans 8:17)! How did our names ever get listed in the will along with his? The same divine hand that wrote our names in the Book of Life above put us in the will! What grace this is!

Closing Reflections

If we desire this joy, we must make sure we know Christ. There can be no rejoicing if our names are not written in Heaven.

And as believers we can cultivate our joy by meditating on the fact that our names are written in Heaven. He knows us. He looks on us and regards us as his treasures. We are not our own—we are bought with a price. We are his, and he is ours!

If you are rich, do not rejoice in your wealth, because your riches will fly away. Instead rejoice that your name is written in Heaven. If you are a person of learning, thank God for it and use it to his glory. But do not make it your source of joy. Rather, rejoice that your name is written in Heaven. Do you have a position of leadership in Christ's church? Thank God and glorify him in it. But rejoice first that your name is in the Book of Life. Do you have great gifts? Are you a meteor among many stars? Has God used you? Is he using you now? Fine. But rejoice first and foremost in this: your name is written in Heaven. As Dwight Moody said the Christmas before his death: "To see his star is good, but to see his face is better."[7]

47

The Praise and Blessing of Revelation

LUKE 10:21–24

BEFORE ETA LINNEMANN became a Christian, she was an esteemed New Testament scholar and theologian. Her educational credentials were impeccable. She had studied under the masters of form criticism, Rudolf Bultmann and Ernst Fuchs, and had become part of the elite in the practice of the historical-critical method. Her first book became a best-seller. She became professor of theology at Braunschweig Technical University. After writing her *Habilitationschrift*, the equivalent to a second doctoral dissertation, she was awarded the honorary title of Professor of New Testament in Theology at Philips University, Marburg and was then inducted into the Society for New Testament Studies.

But as her star was rising, she began to reflect on her critical methodology and came to the conclusion that her "scientific work on the biblical text" and her lectures were not grasping spiritual truth. She saw that she was serving a theological philosophy rooted in agnosticism.

The brilliant Dr. Eta Linnemann became profoundly disillusioned and drifted into addictions to alcohol and TV to dull her misery. But when she was at her very lowest, she experienced grace. In her own words:

> At that point God led me to vibrant Christians who knew Jesus personally as their Lord and Savior. I heard their testimonies as they reported what God had done in their lives. Finally God himself spoke to my heart by means of a Christian brother's words. By God's grace and love I entrusted my life to Jesus. He immediately took my life into his saving grasp and began to transform it radically. My destructive addictions were replaced by

> a hunger and thirst for his Word and for fellowship with Christians. I was able to recognize sin clearly as sin rather than merely make excuses for it as was my previous habit. I can still remember the delicious joy I felt when for the first time black was once more black and white was once more white; the two ceased to pool together as indistinguishable gray.[1]

Dr. Linnemann goes on to conclude her written testimony by saying:

> By God's grace I experienced Jesus as the one whose name is above all names. I was permitted to realize that Jesus *is* God's Son, born of a virgin. He *is* the Messiah and the Son of Man; such titles were not merely conferred on him as the result of human deliberation. I recognized, first mentally, but then in a vital, experiential way, that Holy Scripture is inspired. . . . That is why I say "No!" to historical-critical theology. I regard everything that I taught and wrote before I entrusted my life to Jesus as refuse. I wish to use this opportunity to mention that I have pitched my two books *Gleichnisse Jesu* . . . and *Studien zur Passionsgeschichte*, along with my contributions to journals, anthologies, and *Festschriften.* Whatever of these writings I had in my possession I threw into the trash with my own hands in 1978. I ask you sincerely to do the same thing with any of them you may have on your own bookshelf.[2]

Today Eta Linnemann serves God at a Bible institute in Indonesia.

Jesus' Joyous Prayer (vv. 21, 22)

Praise for Revelation to the Least

The experience of Eta Linnemann illustrates the pointed and disconcerting words of Jesus by which he lauded his Father for hiding his revelation from the likes of the learned Dr. Linnemann before she turned to Christ: "In that same hour he [Jesus] rejoiced in the Holy Spirit and said, 'I thank you, Father, Lord of heaven and earth, that you have hidden these things from the wise and understanding and revealed them to little children; yes, Father, for such was your gracious will'" (v. 21). Jesus was happy about the exclusion of the wise and learned. There is a mystery here that deserves our careful attention.

"The wise and understanding" were the Christ-rejecting religious establishment of Jesus' day, and the "little children" in this context were the seventy disciples—the unlearned fishermen, publicans, and common people who had just returned from a successful preaching ministry for Jesus. "Little children" (literally, "infants") describes those who are childlike and unspoiled by learning, who have listened to Jesus because they haven't presumed to be wise.[3] They are the humble who are open to being helped and enlightened.[4] For these Jesus offers praise for God's revelation to them. But in respect to the scribes, Pharisees, priests, and elders of Israel, the Eta Linnemanns of this world, those who were "wise and understanding" in their own eyes, Jesus praised the Father for his hiddenness. Jesus says the same thing today.

> For consider your calling, brothers: not many of you were wise according to worldly standards, not many were powerful, not many were of noble birth. But God chose what is foolish in the world to shame the wise; God chose what is weak in the world to shame the strong; God chose what is low and despised in the world, even things that are not, to bring to nothing things that are, so that no human being might boast in the presence of God. (1 Corinthians 1:26–29)

When you came to Christ, were you among the wise of your culture? Were you a person of influence? Were you part of a blue-blooded family? Few of us were.

God is pleased to reveal himself to "little children" with all their needs and deficiencies—those who are humble and teachable—those who are not wise in their own eyes. This is not to say that some persons are more deserving of God's grace than others. All people are sinners and merit nothing but judgment. The point is, the wisdom of the world makes people proud and increases their resistance to the gospel.

It is natural for those who see themselves as learned and wise to imagine that they have moral superiority—to assume that others have a far greater distance to go in coming to God—to think that their privilege proves God's approval. This kind of thinking can also create a delusion of salvation by comparison, a pharisaic delusion.

> Two men went up into the temple to pray, one a Pharisee and the other a tax collector. The Pharisee, standing by himself, prayed thus: "God, I thank you that I am not like other men, extortioners, unjust, adulterers, or even like this tax collector. I fast twice a week; I give tithes of all that I get." (Luke 18:10–12)

The secularized form of this delusion is found in the common rationalism, "I'm not perfect, but I'm certainly better than . . ."

Close to this errant thinking is the equally delusive thought of salvation by association. Some dismissed Jesus by asking, "Have any of the authorities or the Pharisees believed in him?" (John 7:48). "Certainly," they thought, "if Jesus is what he says he is, 'the good people' will believe in him. But look at those who follow him—the simple, common folk. If he was for real, people of substance would be at his side."

But the biggest self-deception by far for "the wise and understanding" is the idea that their superior knowledge gives them a spiritual advantage. Indeed, knowledge of God's Word is a good thing. The problem is, many fall into learned ignorance. That was Eta Linnemann's problem, as she explained:

> Historical-critical theology is hindered by ignorance, since the theologian generally is only aware of those small parts of the Bible which he regularly studies in keeping with the widespread tendency to specialize. As a rule he knows numerous books that deal with his area of interest, but he does not know his Bible.[5]

In Jesus' day the Pharisees saw the Bible through legalism's blinders, the scribes through technical blinders, and the Sadducees through philosophical blinders. We each need to see and hear God's Word clearly.

Was Jesus promoting ignorance as a virtue? No. God does not love ignorance—he simply hates conceit. A virtuous man may be ignorant, but ignorance is not a virtue. "Love of God is immeasurably more important than knowledge of God. But if a man loves God, knowing a little about Him, he should love God more from knowing more about Him, because every new thing known about God is a new reason for loving Him."[6]

Openness to God is always a virtue—whether we are learned or ignorant. God delights to reveal himself to those who are willing to open their lives to him—people like the desperate, empty Eta Linnemann.

Praise for Revelation through Himself

Having praised God for revealing himself to children, Jesus now praises the Father for making him the source of revelation: "All things[7] have been handed over to me by my Father, and no one knows who the Son is except the Father, or who the Father is except the Son and anyone to whom the Son chooses to reveal him" (v. 22). Jesus is the source of revelation because *only God knows God*, here as Father and Son. No father can know my sons as I do, because I am their father and I raised them under my roof. And no man can know me as my sons do. For better or for worse, and often to my dismay, they can read me like a book. I may be able to fool others with an ecclesiastical smile and pastoral affectations, but I cannot fool them. Such subjective, intimate knowledge can only come in a long-term domestic setting.

My father-son analogy reaches high but falls galaxies short of that to which it points—the eternal, mutual, exclusive intimacy of the Godhead.

Jesus says, "No one knows . . . who the Father is except the Son." Only God knows God, and this knowledge makes him the sovereign, sole dispenser of revelation.

> Long ago, at many times and in many ways, God spoke to our fathers by the prophets, but in these last days he has spoken to us by his Son, whom he appointed the heir of all things, through whom also he created the world. He is the radiance of the glory of God and the exact imprint of his nature. (Hebrews 1:1–3)

> And the Word became flesh and dwelt among us, and we have seen his glory, glory as of the only Son from the Father, full of grace and truth. . . . No one has ever seen God; the only God, who is at the Father's side, he has made him known. (John 1:14, 18)

What is God like? Exactly as Jesus revealed him.[8]

Jesus is the sovereign dispenser of the knowledge of God the Father to "anyone to whom the Son chooses to reveal him." No one will see who God or Jesus is unless he reveals him. So when unbelievers tell us they cannot see the beauty of the gospel, we are not surprised. The Word of God radiates light, but it cannot be seen unless a person's eye is opened by God.[9]

This makes Jesus *everything* in salvation. He is Revealer, Redeemer, Savior, and Keeper. He is everything now and forever.

> To him who sits on the throne and to the Lamb be blessing and honor and glory and might forever and ever! (Revelation 5:13)

Jesus' Joy

There is further eternal spiritual beauty here: Jesus is exploding with joy over what he has been declaring in prayer. Luke introduced Jesus' prayer at the beginning of verse 21 noting that "in that same hour he rejoiced in the Holy Spirit. . . ." Significantly, though Jesus no doubt rejoiced often, this is the only place in the New Testament where it specifically says he did so. Not only that, but Luke uses the same word that Mary used when she rejoiced in song over her pregnancy—"And my spirit rejoices in God my Savior" (1:47). So joyous is the word that Moffat's translation says he "thrilled with joy." Here we are given a glimpse of the inner feelings of God incarnate!

Note the twofold source of his bounding joy. First, his truth did not go to the privileged yet self-sufficient, "the wise and understanding," but rather to "little children" (v. 21), those like his disciples who were humble and open to him. When Jesus saw a few poor men and women receiving the glad tidings of salvation, his heart was refreshed and charged with joy. "For consider your calling, brothers: not many of you were wise according to worldly standards, not many were powerful, not many were of noble birth" (1 Corinthians 1:26). But "to all who did receive him, who believed in his name, he gave the right to become children of God" (John 1:12).

Second, Jesus rejoiced at being the revealer of the Father. "No one knows who the Son is except the Father, or who the Father is except the Son and anyone to whom the Son chooses to reveal him" (v. 22). We believe not because we were good, not because we were open, not because we were humble, but because Jesus opened our eyes. All glory to his name!

His Joyous Blessing (vv. 23, 24)

Knowing Christ because he has revealed himself to us, we are blessed, and the beatitude that Jesus pronounced upon his disciples rests upon us: "Then turning to the disciples he said privately, 'Blessed are the eyes that see what you see! For I tell you that many prophets and kings desired to see what you see, and did not see it, and to hear what you hear, and did not hear it'" (vv. 23, 24). The preparatory centuries had come to an end. Demons were subject to the disciples—"I saw Satan fall . . . from heaven" (10:18). And soon, at the cross, they would see the power of Satan dealt with in an even greater way. Soon too Jesus would be resurrected and received up to glory, where he reigns until his return in glory for those whose names are "written in heaven" (10:20).

The difference between what the prophets and kings saw and what we see (v. 24) is "the difference of twilight and noonday, of winter and summer, of the mind of a child and the mind of a full grown man" (Bishop Ryle).[10]

"Blessed are the eyes that see what you see!" (v. 23).

48

"But a Samaritan . . ."

LUKE 10:25–37

HISTORICAL STUDY HAS REVEALED that Karl Marx, the self-proclaimed defender of the working-class proletariat, never truly knew or had a friendship with a single member of the proletariat. So far as researchers know, he never set foot in a mill or a factory or a mine or any other industrial workplace in his whole life.[1] Living a self-conscious, Bohemian, intellectual lifestyle he knew poverty, but he always kept company with middle-class intellectuals like himself. When he and Friedrich Engels created the Communist League, and again when they formed the International, he made sure that working-class socialists were eliminated from any positions of influence.[2]

It is also clear that for all his endeavors to be the social benefactor of humankind, he disliked people and continuously fought with members of his family. Marx lived his life in an atmosphere of verbal violence, quarreling with everyone with whom he associated for any length of time.[3] He worked hard at becoming middle-class, *bourgeois*. Thanks to Engels, Marx spent the last two decades of his life in comfortable middle-class homes, and for the last ten years he never had fewer than two servants![4]

Actually, there was one working-class person in Marx's life—his wife's maid, by whom he fathered a son, which he publicly denied. That was too bad because his son Henry Frederich Demuth (his maid's last name) became one of the real proletariat. After being foster-raised by a working-class family, he spent his life working at King's Cross and Hackney as a member of the engineer's union.[5]

What is the point of all this? All humans find it difficult to live up to what we espouse intellectually. Further, so often those who are the loudest proclaimers of certain ideas are the biggest affront to those same ideas. And finally, it is not uncommon to love the idea that you love people and are their benefactor rather than to actually love people themselves. Historian Paul Johnson, from whose book *Intellectuals* I obtained the above information about Karl Marx, has shown this to be the case in the lives of numerous intellectuals who have presumed to refashion the world through their unaided intelligence[6]—people like Jean-Jacques Rousseau and Henrik Ibsen and Bertolt Brecht and Bertrand Russell and Jean-Paul Sartre.

Love for people, or the lack of it, reveals the quality and effectiveness of the philosophy we hold. And from a Biblical perspective our love for people is even more revealing, because it actually indicates the authenticity and health of our relationship with God. The two divisions of the Ten Commandments teach this explicitly. The first division, the first four commandments, all demand and enhance our love for God and are summed up in the *Shema*: "Hear, O Israel: The LORD our God, the LORD is one. You shall love the LORD your God with all your heart and with all your soul and with all your might" (Deuteronomy 6:4, 5). The concluding six commandments, the second table of the Law, all demand that we love others and are capsulized in the words of Leviticus 19:18: "You shall love your neighbor as yourself." The spiritual logic is clear: you must first love God with all that is in you, and if you do, you will be able to love others as you love yourself. Love for God produces love for people.

Turning this spiritual logic on its head, we are able to discern one's love for God by the existence of a love for others. Love for God is difficult to see, but love for people is subject to relational verification. Significantly, Paul, writing to the Galatians, quoted Leviticus 19:18 as shorthand for keeping the whole law: "The whole law is fulfilled in one word: 'You shall love your neighbor as yourself'" (Galatians 5:14). Does this mean we can earn salvation by being a good neighbor? No. We can only love our neighbor as ourselves if we love God with all that is in us and allow him to work in our hearts. No philosophy can do that, not even the best religious philosophy.

Eternal Life? (vv. 25–29)

A Calculated Question

"And behold, a lawyer stood up to put him to the test, saying, 'Teacher, what shall I do to inherit eternal life?'" (v. 25). The questioner was a lawyer and therefore one of "the wise and understanding" of whom Jesus had only recently said, "I thank you, Father, Lord of heaven and earth, that you have hidden these things from the wise and understanding and revealed them to little children; yes, Father, for such was your gracious will" (10:21). The lawyer was one of those who were sure they had the truth. The childlike openness that Jesus so prized could not be found in them. Luke mentions that he "stood up," indicating that Jesus and his hearers were seated as he taught. The lawyer's standing was an assertive gesture to "test" Jesus. He had an agenda, an ulterior motive.

In reality the lawyer already knew the answer to his question. Even more, he knew the answer that Jesus would give because Jesus had previously voiced that answer in a different situation when he combined the *Shema* with Leviticus 19:18 (cf. Mark 12:28–31), and he had almost certainly expressed it other times as well.[7] As T. W. Manson said, "Great teachers constantly repeat themselves."[8]

Counterquestion

Jesus, knowing the lawyer knew the answer, countered, "'What is written in the Law? How do you read it?' And he answered, 'You shall love the Lord your God with all your heart and with all your soul and with all your strength and with all your mind [Deuteronomy 6:4, 5], and your neighbor as yourself [Leviticus 19:18].' And he answered him, 'You have answered correctly; do this, and you will live'" (vv. 26–28). The lawyer looked foolish, having been made to answer his own question and then being kindly told to practice the answer he had just preached. How embarrassing!

An Impulsive Question

The lawyer was flustered and wanted to save face. "But he, desiring to justify himself, said to Jesus, 'And who is my neighbor?'" (v. 29). His response itself was deeply telling. He obviously had been thinking about the breadth that is implicit in the demand to love others as oneself. *Certainly it must be restricted to Israel, and even further to those who are of character*, he thought to himself. "We can't love everyone! Where do you draw the line? What about tyrants? What about blasphemers? Really, Jesus, who is my neighbor?" His questioning was reasonable enough. But it also shows that "wise and understanding" as he was, he was not completely tracking with Jesus.

The Parable (vv. 30–35)

So Jesus told him a story, the opening lines of which could come from our city paper if the names of the places were changed. "Jesus replied, 'A man was going down from Jerusalem to Jericho, and he fell among robbers, who stripped him and beat him and departed, leaving him half dead'" (v. 30). If you have ever seen anyone so beaten, you know the picture—chipped teeth, blackened eyes, hair matted down with dried blood.

Some years ago CBS anchorman and reporter Hugh Rudd was mugged outside his New York City apartment complex. He lay conscious, eyes open, but unable to move. All he could do was moan and mumble, though he was quite lucid. Rudd lay from 2:30 until dawn at the doorstep, watching life pass by. Returning theatergoers walked past him into the building. The milkman came and left. No one even stopped to see what was wrong—despite his pathetic attempts to ask for help. His experience was as old as history.

A Priest

The first person to discover the poor man on the Jericho road was a member of the cloth: "Now by chance a priest was going down that road, and when he saw him he passed by on the other side" (v. 31). Jericho was one of the main country spots where priests lived. So the priest was likely returning from performing holy service in the temple. If the man lying on the roadside was dead and the priest touched him, the priest would be ceremonially defiled (cf. Leviticus 21:1ff.). So rather than risk defilement, he passed by on the far side of the road. To preserve legal cleanliness, he heartlessly transgressed the entire second table of the Law. Oh, was he pure!

A Levite

"So likewise a Levite, when he came to the place and saw him, passed by on the other side" (v. 32). Levites were not as high ranking as priests, though they were highly privileged. They were the temple liturgists. They oversaw the temple cultus and services. The language of the text gives the sense that he actually went up close to the man to see him, and then passed by on the other side.[9]

As Jesus told the story, the lawyer and his hearers were expecting something other than what they got. They expected the threefold rhythm of the Semitic story form to reveal that an Israelite layman came by and helped the man. Many people were unhappy with the clergy, and they expected Jesus to say that an average good-guy Jew came along and showed the clergy up. That would be a slap at the establishment, but many, perhaps most, would applaud it.

The Samaritan

No one expected Jesus to finish the story the way he did: "But a Samaritan, as he journeyed, came to where he was, and when he saw him, he had compassion" (v. 33). A Samaritan? Not long before, James and John had urged the Lord to call down fire from Heaven to destroy some inhospitable Samaritans (cf. 9:54). The hatred between Judea and Samaria went back over four hundred years and centered around racial purity, because while the Jews had kept their purity during the Babylonian captivity, the Samaritans had lost theirs by intermarrying with Assyrian invaders. In the Jews' eyes the Samaritans were compromising mongrels. Also, the Samaritans had built a rival temple on Mount Gerizim only to have it destroyed by the Jews in Maccabean times.

So in Jesus' day the hatred was ingrained and utterly implacable. The rabbis said, "Let no man eat the bread of the Cuthites (Samaritans), for he who eats their bread is as he who eats swine's flesh." The ultimate insult came in the arsenic-laced Jewish prayer that concluded, "And do not remember the Cuthites in the Resurrection." Add to this the fact that in Jesus' day some Jewish travelers had been murdered in Samaria and that some Samaritans had defiled the temple with human bones and you can begin to imagine the shock of Jesus' introducing a Samaritan not as a villain but as a hero! Indeed, if the Jew in the story were not half dead, he would probably push away the loathsome Samaritan.[10]

But the hated Samaritan's pity and compassion was extraordinary:

> He went to him and bound up his wounds, pouring on oil and wine. Then he set him on his own animal and brought him to an inn and took care of him. And the next day he took out two denarii and gave them to the innkeeper, saying, "Take care of him, and whatever more you spend, I will repay you when I come back." (vv. 34, 35)

How beautiful this was! The Samaritan applied ancient first aid, humbly gave his donkey to the Jew and walked alongside, gave the innkeeper two silver coins (enough for twenty-four days' food), and promised to pay the whole bill when he returned.[11] Instead of being the battered Jew's worst nightmare, he was his best dream!

The driving power of Jesus' parable can only be felt in light of the pervasive influence of the *Shema*—the command to love God with the totality of one's being. It was recited every morning and every night by every faithful Israelite. The priest and the Levite in the story had intoned it that morning before they bypassed the half-dead fellow Jew, and they said it again at sunset. Their neglect of their neighbor was sandwiched between pious declarations of their love for God. Do we ever do the same?

The moral (or actually, immoral) dissonance roared, and the lawyer who had asked the question could hear it loud and clear. He was not a secular lawyer. He knew the Mosaic Law, the Torah. His forehead displayed a phylactery (a small, black calfskin box that contained the words of the *Shema*)—symbolic obedience to the challenge immediately following the *Shema*:

> And these words that I command you today shall be on your heart. You shall teach them diligently to your children, and shall talk of them when you sit in your house, and when you walk by the way, and when you lie down, and when you rise. You shall bind them as a sign on your hand, and they shall be as frontlets between your eyes. (Deuteronomy 6:6–8)

His very appearance was a statement that he was devoted to loving God and fulfilling the Law, at least the first half of it. So he could feel the dissonance in the parable. Jesus' radical teaching, which included loving one's neighbor as oneself (Leviticus 19:18), made perfect sense since such neighbor love fulfilled the second half of the Law. But Jesus' parable made it painfully clear that the lawyer fell short.

A Closing Question (vv. 36, 37)

Jesus presented a pinpoint application in his closing question: "'Which of these three, do you think, proved to be a neighbor to the man who fell among the robbers?' He said, 'The one who showed him mercy.' And Jesus said to him, 'You go, and do likewise'" (vv. 36, 37). The hated Samaritan—not the priest or the Levite (and by implication, not the question-asking lawyer)—the *Samaritan* was the keeper of the Law. He loved those who came his way as himself, and this showed that he loved God with all his heart.

Jesus' command, "You go, and do likewise" was the answer to the lawyer's question—the only answer. But it was an impossible one—unless one truly loves God with heart, soul, body, and mind, which will happen if we let him make our heart what he meant it to be.

Closing Reflections

This story is an important one for us. We evangelicals have our phylacteries too—and not only bumper stickers and T-shirts either. We claim to actually know Christ. We claim that Christ is in us and that we are in him. We claim that, though residing in a spiritually dead world, we are regenerated, born again, alive. We wear it on our foreheads, and some of us wear it on our sleeves. We claim to have Christ (the only person who ever fully loved God with all his being, and his neighbor as himself) in our hearts. But as we have seen in the parable, if we really do have Christ within us, we will be loving and merciful to our neighbors, those we meet along the road of life.

Jesus put this epigrammatically in the Sermon on the Mount so it would be easy to remember: "Blessed are the merciful, for they shall receive mercy" (Matthew 5:7). He was not saying that one can merit God's mercy by performing acts of mercy, but rather that those who are truly God's children, and as such are objects of his mercy, will themselves be merciful and so will receive mercy in the end. Showing mercy to one's neighbor is evidence of having received mercy.

Scripture's call to love our neighbors as ourselves gives us a way of testing our relationship with God. It delivers us from an infatuation with the idea that we are lovers of God when we are not. Rousseau's claim to be a lover of humanity was given the lie by his fathering and abandoning four illegitimate children. Marx's claims to be a benefactor of the proletariat was shown to be bogus by his elite bourgeois preferences and manners. Ibsen's claim to want the betterment of women in his play *The Dollhouse* was shown vacuous by his vicious hatred of women. Our relationship with fellow human beings validates or invalidates our claims to know and love God.

This is not a call to perfection. Only Jesus totally loved God and his neighbor as himself. Only Jesus was consistently merciful to everyone who came his way. But it is a call to consider whether in our relationships there is evidence that we love God. Are we merciful? Are we truly compassionate with others? If we characteristically pass by those who are in distress—physical, economic, social—we are probably not Christians. Are we forgiving? If not, we are very likely outside grace and yet unforgiven (cf. Matthew 6:14, 15).

How we live with others is shorthand for how we are related to God. May self-examination drive us to grace!

49

Choosing the Better

LUKE 10:38–42

THERE WAS A TENDENCY in the patristic church to regard Martha as symbolic of the active life and Mary as representative of the contemplative life, and that tendency persists today in some circles.[1] In such discussions Martha is unfairly put down, and Mary is exalted as an example of quietism and even monasticism. This is entirely wrong. As the eminent Catholic Biblical scholar Joseph Fitzmyer explains: "To read this episode as a commendation of contemplative life over against active life is to allegorize it beyond recognition and to introduce a distinction that was born only of later preoccupations."[2] The story of Mary and Martha is actually about the necessity of the priority of the Word of God in a life of active service for the Master. In fact, the teachings of Jesus were dramatically actualized in both women's lives. Both are women of excellence and noble character.

A Loving Home (v. 38)

Together Martha and Mary and their brother Lazarus provided a lovely home in Bethany that Jesus, the Son of Man who according to his own words had "nowhere to lay his head" (9:58), found irresistible. Jesus loved to be with this family (cf. John 11:5). "Now as they went on their way, Jesus entered a village. And a woman named Martha welcomed him into her house" (v. 38). Martha and her sister and brother were devoted followers of Jesus. They had heard him preach the word of the kingdom, had believed, and now loved him devotedly.

When Martha saw Jesus approaching, she likely thought to herself, *The Master is here—he probably needs a good dinner.* Perhaps she saw his weariness, and her domestic instincts went into action. She lived out Paul's dictum before he even thought of it: "Contribute to the needs of the saints and seek to show hospitality" (Romans 12:13). She had the gift of hospitality big time! She used her gift to serve others, as a "good steward of God's varied grace" (1 Peter 4:10). What a beautiful, nurturing soul she was.

Martha's prodigious energies were focused on the Master's comfort. The guest room was straightened. Off to market she went to select the best produce and the needed foods for the entree. Back at home she scrubbed, baked, and prepared the table. Everything must segue properly. The side dish must be warm. Only such and such a vintage would do. She was a whirlwind.

What Martha missed in all of her busyness was the sense of the ominous mystery that lay ahead. She did not realize that a light meal and more time to hear Jesus' words would have been more appropriate.

Loving Sisters (vv. 39, 40)

Mary

Martha's sister was better tuned in: "She had a sister called Mary, who sat at the Lord's feet and listened to his teaching" (v. 39). Judaism did not forbid women to be instructed in the Torah (Ned. 35b.; SBT, p107n.), but it was unheard of for a rabbi to allow a woman to sit at his feet.[3] Later rabbinic tradition includes quotations such as: "May the words of the Torah be burned, they should not be handed over to women" (j. Sota, 10a, 8), and "The man who teaches his daughter the Torah teaches her extravagance" (Sota, 3,4; cf. B. Sota, 21b.).[4] Clearly, Jesus rejected such un-Biblical, regressive attitudes outright.

Mary's posture expressed a desire to learn. Here is the point that is so crucial to understanding what this story is all about: Mary was listening intently to the Word of God through the lips of Jesus. She was an intense learner. So often she is sentimentally portrayed in terms of her subjective adoration or her passionate worship of Jesus. There is such awe with any disciple. But the telling point is her rapt attention to the Word. This is extraordinary to say the least!

Martha

As Mary was soaking up the Word, her big sister was getting frustrated: "But Martha was distracted with much serving" (v. 40a.). The sense of "distracted" here is "to be pulled away" or "dragged away." The implication is that Martha desperately wanted to hear Jesus herself, to be at his feet, but she was pulled away by her duties.[5] Flitting about with her busy preparations, she inevitably caught bits and snatches of Jesus' words, and she was drawn to hear more. But the burden of the beautiful meal kept dragging her back into the kitchen. How she wanted to be at Jesus' feet! But she told herself that true devotion is practical and that she must put her duty before her desires.

So this good woman, one of Jesus' most devoted and perceptive disciples (as we shall see), this excellent woman *smoldered.* She was angry at Mary for being so selfish, and she was also mad at Jesus for allowing it to go on. She focused "if looks could kill" glares upon Mary and let out some pained sighs as she fussed over the table and loudly banged pots in the kitchen. She was a Type A, and she knew it. She was verbal. She was blunt. People always knew where they stood with her. Nothing like a little scolding to get the troops in order! So "she went up to him and said, 'Lord, do you not care that my sister has left me to serve alone? Tell her then to help me'" (v. 40b). Today she'd say: "Lord, my sister's a flake, and you're part of the problem too. Tell her to get her sweet self in here!" In her self-righteous ire she reproached not only her sister, but the One for whom she was so lovingly preparing a meal—the Master, God's Son.

Martha did not realize that at that critical time in Jesus' life he would have preferred her company over her service—and that he regarded her fellowship with him as more important than serving him a meal. Her sense of priorities was skewed.[6] Given where Jesus was on the road to Jerusalem, some things were more important than a good meal. But Martha was so sure that what she was doing was what Christ most needed and wanted. We are like that. It is so natural to think that Jesus needs our work and that he cannot do without us. The preacher wonders what would become of the church without him (and perhaps the people dream of what it would be like without him!). The elder thinks that if he were removed, the whole place would crumble. The evangelist imagines that no one would be converted if he were to retire. How self-deceived we tend to be. A fly on the wall of the church might as well imagine that everything going on below him is dependent upon his presence and would cease if he flew away![7]

Certainly we should take our responsibilities seriously. But to think Christ needs us and that we are indispensable to his program—the thought is preposterous! God doesn't need me or you to do his work. It is only by his grace that we can serve him, and he can do quite well without us. To be sure, we ought to take our work seriously, but not ourselves. We ruin our service when we overestimate our importance.

Martha attempted to force Mary to serve Christ her way. She wanted Mary away from Jesus' feet and in the kitchen with her, because in her estimation what she was doing was more important. Such tunnel vision is common. Our responsibility, our means of service, is deemed to be everything by us. Since we teach Sunday school, and it is such a fruitful field, and since more teachers are needed, anyone who is not involved is—well, wrong! It is so natural to think this way about one's involvement in the youth program or missions or pet ethical concerns. We assume everyone should be committed to the same Christian cause to which we are committed. If others were good Christians, they would certainly live like us. If they were together spiritually, they would be doing what we are doing. Martha's attitude, unchecked, can destroy the inner soul of service.

Martha's self-appointed responsibilities distracted her from what mattered most. So it is with us. The self-imposed necessities of ministry smother us, and serving becomes drudgery.

Loving Correction (vv. 41, 42)

Poor seething Martha! Her perspective was so wrong. How embarrassed she would feel in retrospect for having scolded her sister—and Jesus to boot! But Jesus loved her and, affectionately repeating her name, chided her: "'Martha, Martha, you are anxious and troubled about many things, but one thing is necessary. Mary has chosen the good portion, which will not be taken away from her'" (vv. 41, 42).

This is a powerful statement. The "one thing" that is "necessary," "the good portion," is listening to the Word of God. The highest priority for those who would be activists for God is listening to his Word. Jesus informs Martha that the Word will not be taken away from Mary.

Jesus here provides wisdom for all who are serving Christ in various callings. It is all too common, and too easy, for our service to Christ to drag us away from his Word. Ironic as it may be, this is an epidemic among preachers of the Word. Ministers of the gospel often admit that the Word is not at the center of either their devotion or their ministries. The reason is, they are too busy serving Christ. Youth pastors, missionaries, executives of Christian organizations, and church leaders often admit to this syndrome. The programs and the unending needs are so pressing that reading and hearing the Word of God is neglected.

There is a tendency for people who are wound tight like Martha to give everything to their particular area of calling or interest (be it evangelism, the protection of the unborn, administration, marriage and family, care for the poor, or whatever) and to allow that interest to so dominate their lives that they have little time to let God's Word speak to them. Without the benefit of the Word, they adopt a mind-set of narrowness, judgmentalism, or fault finding. And eventually the creativity and vitality they once gave to their area of ministry sours. They have unwittingly lost the "one thing," "the good portion" that Christ promised would not be taken from Mary. They have lost the "integrating center which makes possible a singleness of vision"[8] and action.

Life is short. We need to choose very deliberately. Life does not automatically arrange itself into proper priorities. Amid a thousand other duties we must make sitting at Jesus' feet the "one thing"—"the good portion"—the primary focus of our hearts and lives. Mary's choice was: "good in sickness and good in health,—good in youth and good in age,—good in adversity and good in prosperity,—good in life and good in death—good in time and good in eternity."[9]

Closing Reflections

But we must note that this was also Martha's choice. Like Mary, she chose "the good portion," the "necessary" thing, for the rest of her days. How do we know? Because the truth of Jesus' teaching was dramatically actualized in her faith and confession in coming months.[10]

Martha's Confession

The later occasion was the death of the sisters' beloved brother, Lazarus. Lazarus had died during Jesus' delay before coming to his bedside. Martha heard that Jesus was approaching, so leaving her grieving sister in the house, she went out to meet him. She was the same Martha—verbal, blunt, and to the point:

> Martha said to Jesus, "Lord, if you had been here, my brother would not have died. But even now I know that whatever you ask from God, God will give you." Jesus said to her, "Your brother will rise again." Martha said to him, "I know that he will rise again in the resurrection on the last day." Jesus said to her, "I am the resurrection and the life. Whoever believes in me, though he die, yet shall he live, and everyone who lives and believes in me shall never die. Do you believe this?" She said to him, "Yes, Lord; I believe that you are the Christ, the Son of God, who is coming into the world." (John 11:21–27)

Martha is the author and verbalizer of one of the two great confessions of Christ in the New Testament. The other is Peter's in Matthew 16:16, to which Christ responded:

> Blessed are you, Simon Bar-Jonah! For flesh and blood has not revealed this to you, but my Father who is in heaven. And I tell you, you are Peter, and on this rock I will build my church, and the gates of hell shall not prevail against it. I will give you the keys of the kingdom of heaven, and whatever you bind on earth shall be bound in heaven, and whatever you loose on earth shall be loosed in heaven. (Matthew 16:17–19)

Peter's confession, the substance of what he said, became the rock on which the church was built. And in John 11 Martha's confession was almost word-for-word like Peter's except for the final phrase. Peter confessed, "You are the Christ, the Son of the living God" (Matthew 16:16). Martha confessed, "You are the Christ, the Son of God, who is coming into the world" (John 11:27). How did Martha come to this? She had chosen the "one thing." She sat with Mary at Jesus' feet. She was an avid hearer of the Word. And the church was built on the granite of such confession. We should never, ever disdain Martha.

Mary's Anointing

Mary, of course, kept to the "one thing" as an ardent hearer of the words of Jesus. And some time later, "Six days before the Passover, Jesus therefore came to Bethany, where Lazarus was, whom Jesus had raised from the dead. So they gave a dinner for him there. Martha served, and Lazarus was one of those reclining with him at table" (John 12:1, 2). We must not assume that Martha was doing all the work again. Mary was probably helping when without warning she approached Jesus carrying an alabaster jar of very expensive perfume (very likely a family heirloom). She poured a generous portion on Jesus' head, anointing him, and then poured the rest of the contents on his feet—humbly, worshipfully wiping his feet with her hair.

This was an intensely fervent expression of devotion, as fervent as any found anywhere in sacred Scripture! And it was costly, equal to a year's wages, perhaps as much as $35,000 in terms of today's economy.

Why this sacrifice? Why this grand act of worship? The answer came from Jesus' lips when he answered Mary's critics: "Leave her alone, so that she may keep it for the day of my burial" (John 12:7). Mary, sitting intently at Jesus' feet, understood what even the apostles had missed. Though Jesus had repeatedly spoken plainly of his death, the disciples just could not accept it. The concept of a suffering Messiah did not coincide with their expectations of One who would deliver them from Roman oppression. But Mary, listening to Jesus' words more carefully, understood that he would die. So she anointed him for burial.

The insight of these two sisters—evidenced in Martha's grand confession and in Mary's grand anointing of Jesus—came from the fact that they had given themselves to "one thing"—"the good portion"—listening to the Word of God.

This does not call us to a monastery but to action rooted in God's Word. We must hear the Word by actually listening when it is preached and by reading it for ourselves, hearing Christ's voice and doing his bidding.

Billy Graham once told a story about the Word-centeredness of his father-in-law, Dr. Nelson Bell. When Bell served as the single doctor for a four-hundred-bed hospital in China, he made it a point

> to rise every morning at four-thirty and spend two to three hours in Bible reading. He didn't use that time to read commentaries or write; he didn't do his correspondence or any of his other work. He just read the Scriptures every morning, and he was a walking Bible encyclopedia. People wondered at the holiness and the greatness in his life.[11]

Nelson Bell was an astounding activist whose life was shaped and empowered by "one thing"—the Word of God.

The church is full of Type A's—hard-driving, ministry-minded people. The question is, in your heart are you holding to that which is "the good portion," the integrating center that gives vision and purpose to all your serving?

50

Teach Us to Pray, Part 1

LUKE 11:1–4

THE LORD'S PRAYER has been, and remains, the greatest prayer of the church. The church's best minds have consistently treated it so and have used it to preach countless sermons on prayer and basic Christian doctrine. In the early church such notables as Origen, Gregory of Nyssa, Tertullian, Cyril of Jerusalem, and Cyprian published expositions of the Lord's Prayer. Later the greatest of the ancient theologians, Augustine, followed suit. The poet Dante devoted the eleventh canto of his *Purgatorio* to the Lord's Prayer. Meister Eckhart, the medieval Dominican mystic and theologian, used the categories of the Lord's Prayer to sum up scholastic theology. Martin Luther preached a volume of exposition on the Lord's Prayer. And the famous Westminster Catechism of the Presbyterian churches bases its last nine questions on the Lord's Prayer.[1] Millions of hours of intense study have been devoted to these verses by centuries of successive genius.

The Lord's Prayer—An Overview

The Disciples' Prayer

This great prayer has been called the Lord's Prayer for almost two thousand years. So it would be futile to attempt to change its name, though actually the best title would be "the Disciples' Prayer" because that is what it is. Luke is explicit about this: "Now Jesus was praying in a certain place, and when he finished, one of his disciples said to him, 'Lord, teach us to pray, as John taught his disciples'" (v. 1). Jewish religious leaders and their followers customarily had their distinctive prayers. John the Baptist had his own style of recommended prayers, though none of his prayers exist today.[2] Jesus' followers wanted a disciples' prayer from him as well, and he granted their request.

Strictly speaking, Jesus' recommended prayer is one that he, being sinless, could never fully pray because the last part includes a request for forgiveness—"Forgive us our sins, for we ourselves forgive everyone who is indebted to us" (v. 4). But the prayer's five petitions are absolutely perfect for every disciple of Christ, man or woman, who has ever lived. Every Christian who claims to have any seriousness about prayer will gladly receive Jesus' instructions—"when you pray" (v. 2).

A Different Prayer

Study of Jesus' prayer in Luke 11 reveals that it is a different Lord's Prayer than in Matthew's Gospel. The familiar rhythms and comfortable cadences of the prayer in Matthew 6 are not found here. Also, the prayer in Luke lacks two petitions that are included in Matthew. "Your kingdom come" is not followed by "your will be done," and the final petition ("lead us not into temptation") is not followed by "but deliver us from evil." Jesus clearly taught his disciples about prayer more than once. Also, the lines from Matthew are implicit in Luke's shorter form. That is, when one prays, "Your kingdom come," he or she is implicitly praying, "Your will be done," and likewise, "Lead us not into temptation" implies a desire for deliverance from it. The variations in the Lord's Prayers come naturally from Jesus' desire to teach a *pattern* for prayer rather than a rigid insistence on form.[3]

Some people who live in the mountains of Colorado rarely "see" the incredible scenery that occupies their every glance. Meanwhile, flatlanders travel a thousand miles just to view the mountains' beauty for a few days—and they really see it! Those who have been dulled to beauty need to see things in a new way. Have we really seen or heard the Lord's Prayer? Perhaps we need to see it anew—not so much to discover new truth, but to see the old truth for what it is. Then we will be delivered from merely "saying" the Lord's Prayer.

The Structure of the Prayer

Despite the differences, the prayer in Luke has the same structure as that in Matthew. The first part is *vertical* and has to do with God. Here in Luke the first two petitions successively—for God's name and God's kingdom—are vertical and God centered. The second part is *horizontal* and has to do with us. In this section of the prayer we see three requests—for "our daily bread," "our sins," and our "temptation."

We are not enslaved to the structure or obligated to always follow it, as for example when Peter cried out, "Lord, save me" when he began to sink

(Matthew 14:30). If he had begun first with "Our Father in heaven, hallowed be your name, your kingdom come . . ." he would have been blowing bubbles before he got to the point! But at the same time, the structure and logic of this prayer are valuable for all disciples. Are we followers of Christ? If so, what follows must inform and shape our everyday prayer life.

Vertical Prayer (v. 2)

"Father"

Jesus' opening word of instruction was, to say the least, explosive. "And he said to them, 'When you pray, say: "Father . . ."'" (v. 2a). The unadorned address "Father" is even more jarring than the longer opening of Matthew's version, "Our Father which art in heaven" (KJV), because the word "Father" by itself doesn't have the cosmic distance implicit in the phrase "which art in heaven."

That God should be personally addressed as "Father" may not seem out of the ordinary to those of us who frequent the church and pray the Lord's Prayer, but it was revolutionary in Jesus' day. The writers of the Old Testament certainly believed in the Fatherhood of God, but they saw it mainly in terms of a sovereign Creator-Father to whom they owed their existence. In fact, God is only referred to as "Father" fourteen times in the huge corpus of the Old Testament's thirty-nine books—and then rather impersonally. In those fourteen occurrences, the term was always used with reference to the nation, and not to individuals. God was spoken of as Israel's Father, but Abraham, for example, did not speak of God as "my Father."

The Jews were so focused on the sovereignty and transcendence of God that they were careful never to repeat his covenant name and invented the word *Jehovah* (a combination of two separate names of God) to use instead. The distance from God was well guarded.

But when Jesus came on the scene, he addressed God only as "Father." *All* his prayers address God as Father. The Gospels record his using *Father* more than sixty times in reference to God. So striking is this that some scholars maintain that this word *Father* dramatically captures the difference between the Old and New Testaments. No one had ever in the entire history of Israel spoken and prayed like Jesus. No one!

Abba

But there is more—the word Jesus used for Father was not a formal word. It was the common Aramaic word with which a child would address his father—"*Abba*." The great German New Testament scholar Joachim Jeremias, perhaps the most respected New Testament scholar of his generation, has argued convincingly that *Abba* was the original word on Jesus' lips here in the Lord's Prayer and, indeed, in all of his prayers in the New Testament—with the exception of Matthew 27:46 when he cried out from the cross, "My God, my God, why have you forsaken me?" But there Jesus was quoting Psalm 22:1. Jesus reverted to *Abba* with the final words before his death: "Father, into your hands I commit my spirit!" (Luke 23:46, quoting Psalm 31:5).

The word *Abba* was also the word Jesus regularly used to address his earthly father, Joseph, from the time Jesus was a baby until Joseph's death. Everyone used the word, but as the careful examination of other literature of the time shows, it was never used for God—under any circumstances. *Abba* meant something like "Daddy"—but with a more reverent touch than we use it. The best rendering is "Dearest Father."

To the traditional Jew, Jesus' prayer was shocking. Think of it. God was referred to only fourteen times in the Old Testament as *Father*, and then it was as the corporate Father of Israel—never as an individual or personal Father. But when his disciples asked him for instruction on how to pray, Jesus enjoined them to begin by calling God their Father, their Abba! As Jeremias says:

> In the Lord's Prayer Jesus authorizes His disciples to repeat the word *Abba* after Him. He gives them a share in His sonship and empowers them, as His disciples, to speak with their heavenly Father in just such a familiar, trusting way as a child would with his father.[4]

When we say *Abba* today in our prayers, as we sometimes do, we are making the same sound that actually fell from Jesus' lips and the lips of his incredulous disciples. Jesus transformed the relationship with God from a distant, corporate experience into an intimate, one-to-one bond, and he taught his disciples to pray with the same intimacy. He wants us to do the same.

We are to pray, "Father"—"*Abba*"—"Dearest Father." This is to be the foundational awareness of all our prayers. Does this awareness fuel our prayer life? Is a sense of God's intimate Fatherhood profound and growing in our souls?

Sincerely addressing God as *Abba* (Dearest Father) is not only an indication of spiritual health but is a mark of the authenticity of our faith. Paul tells us in Galatians 4:6, "Because you are sons, God has sent the Spirit of his Son into our hearts, crying, 'Abba! Father!'" Romans 8:15, 16 says the same thing: "but you have received the Spirit of adoption as sons, by whom we cry, 'Abba! Father!' The Spirit himself bears witness with our spirit that we are children of God." True believers are propelled to say this.

This is precisely what happened to me when I came to faith during the summer before my freshman year in high school. Before that I had a vague theological idea of the universal paternity of God as the Creator of all humanity. His Fatherhood was there, but it was not personal. But at my conversion God became warm and personal, and "Dear Father" was the constant refrain of my soul. I knew God, and I knew he was my Father! This realization is one of the primary works of the Holy Spirit. He keeps enhancing this "Spirit of adoption as sons" in us and increasingly integrates it into our lives.

Calling God *Father* brings sweetness to our souls. When I greet or say good-bye to my sons, I prefer to say "son" rather than use their names—"Son, it's great to see you"—"Have a good day, son." And my sons and daughters never address me as Kent, but as Dad, Daddy, or Father. This is the language of affection.

Father, *Dad*, and *Dearest Father* are expressions of security too. When I was a young father and my children were very small, my younger son once hid on top of the refrigerator. As I walked by, he suddenly dove off the refrigerator onto my back. I did not see him coming—he just tackled me and held on. And I held him and kept him from falling. Carey was sure that if he jumped in the direction of his father, he would certainly be safe. It never occurred to him that I would not catch him. That is the way it is with our *Abba*, our heavenly Father. He gives us a great sense of security and confidence—he assures us that we belong to him and that he will never forget or abandon us.

"Father"—the sweetness of that name—its air of connectedness and intimacy, the sense of affection and security, an upward rush of a sense of paternity—ought to be present in every disciple's prayer. The first disciples may have had trouble bringing themselves to say *Abba* at first, but it quickly became the joyful lyric of their souls. "When you pray, say: 'Father'"—*Abba*. How sweet this is!

"Your Name"

Amid the aura and upward rush of our sense of divine paternity, we are to pray for God's name—"'hallowed be your name'" (v. 2b). As I have researched names for baby dedications (so I can express a wish over the child's name), I have discovered that all names have meanings, no exceptions. I have also found that nearly all name meanings are positive, and most are beautiful.

The rest can be a problem and sometimes call for "homiletical creativity." For example, say a baby's name is Lena ("temptress") Cameron ("crooked nose"). I might say, "Lena Cameron, may your senses direct you through the winding paths of life, and may you tempt others to good!"

Actually, today names are often not much more than convenient labels by which to identify people. Some of us think about what a name means when we name our children but are usually more concerned that the name be euphonious or honor some relative. But for the Jews, names were considered to indicate character. And this especially applied to the name of God. Psalm 20:7 says, "Some trust in chariots and some in horses, but we trust in the name [the character] of the Lord our God." For the Jew, God's name referred to the reality of the essence and nature of God.

What name is prominent here in the Lord's Prayer? "Father"—"*Abba*." "Father, hallowed be your name." The name that we ask to be hallowed is *Abba* or Father. This is revolutionary. Certainly God's name as Creator (*Elohim*) and his covenant name (*Jehovah*), as well as his many other names, are to be hallowed. But the emphasis here is on his name as Father. This is especially what we pray for.

What does it mean to "hallow" God's name? The word means "to set apart as holy"—"to consider holy"—"to treat as holy." The best alternative term is "to reverence." "Hallowed" means "May you be given that unique reverence that your character and nature as Father demand." St. Chrysostom had the same idea when he said it included the idea of honor, and Calvin agreed, saying it called for the greatest veneration.[5]

We are to pray first for divine action—"God, may your essence as *Abba* be reverenced." Certainly the Son worked to fulfill this: "O righteous Father, even though the world does not know you, I know you, and these know that you have sent me. I made known to them your name, and I will continue to make it known" (John 17:25, 26a). We too should pray that the amazing revelation of God's divine paternity over his children be hallowed.

This prayer is, of course, implicitly a prayer concerning the quality of our own lives. Luther, in his *Greater Catechism*, asked: "How is it [God's Name] hallowed amongst us?" Answer: "When our life and doctrine are truly Christian." Again, Jesus is our great example. As the cross drew near, he prayed, "Father, glorify your name" (John 12:28)—and he knew what this meant in terms of his own commitment—it meant his dying for our sins.

How do we hallow his name as Father? With our lips, both privately and publicly. He is our Father. His name is never to be misused, as the third commandment so specifically insists (cf. Exodus 20:7). We must reverence our *Abba* with our lips. This in turn elevates and substantiates our love for him. Verbal reverence to God's name is of greatest importance for our souls and his glory.

Of course, we also hallow his name by our actions—as we live lives that show we really do honor our heavenly Father. The sweetness of that relationship (our connectedness, security, and true affection for God)—the aroma of our relationship with our *Abba*—should waft out to those around us. We ought to manifest the beautiful loyalty of a child toward his father in our devotion to God the Father.

"Your Kingdom"

The second and concluding vertical petition is, "'Your kingdom come'" (v. 2c). The tense of the verb "come" refers to a decisive time in the future when the kingdom will come once and for all—an event that will happen only once.[6] This is the second advent of Christ, when he will return, judge the world, and set up his eternal kingdom. This idea is so strong in the Greek that Tertullian changed the order of the prayer, placing "Your will be done, on earth as it is in heaven" (Matthew 6:10) before "Your kingdom come." He reasoned that once the kingdom comes, there will be no need to pray, "Your will be done"—everyone will be doing it!

Tertullian's reasoning was wrong, but he did accurately understand that "Your kingdom come" is a prayer for the final kingdom when, under Christ's rule, our evil hearts will be pure, our deceit, distrust, and shame banished, our asylums and penitentiaries gone, and all conversation and behavior done to the glory of God.

Some may say that such thinking is utopian, and in the general sense of the word they may be right. But it is not utopian in the strict sense, because as the *Oxford English Dictionary* tells us, *utopia* comes from the Greek *ou* ("not") and *topos* ("a place") and means "not a place," signifying an impossible dream. The coming advent of the kingdom of God is no impossibility. It is as sure as any established fact of history. In it our dreams will come true!

But the kingdom's coming is to be a centerpiece in every disciple's prayers today—the center of this present life, for Jesus brought the kingdom with him. Later in Luke he says of himself, "The kingdom of God is in the midst of you" (17:21). So it is future but also present. How did Christ bring the kingdom? Primarily by bringing men and women into obedience to the Father's will. This is the meaning of "Your kingdom come" in Luke 11, because the immediately following and parallel words in Matthew 6:10

are, "Your will be done, on earth as it is in heaven." Those who are in God's kingdom strive to do God's will.

When we see this, the kingdom becomes a very personal thing for several reasons. First, although my will wants to go its own way, being in the kingdom means my will is redirected to God's will. This is what repentance means. Jesus was continually saying, "Repent, for the kingdom of heaven is at hand" (Matthew 4:17; cf. Mark 1:14, 15). To pray "Your kingdom come" is to repent and live a life characterized by obedience.

Second, this prayer demands commitment. Jesus was very emphatic when he said, "No one who puts his hand to the plow and looks back is fit for the kingdom of God" (9:62). The kingdom of God is for those who have decided to follow him and who do not keep longingly looking back. To pray "Your kingdom come" is to commit ourselves to keep following him.

Third, the kingdom is therefore to be pursued above all else. As Jesus said, "But seek first the kingdom of God and his righteousness, and all these things will be added to you" (Matthew 6:33). This destroys any idea of easygoing, armchair Christianity. We cannot pray the Lord's Prayer with folded hands. To pray "Your kingdom come" is to pursue it.

Closing Reflections

The Disciples' Prayer begins with a vertical rush that focuses on the miracle of divine paternity. It cries out for God's name—*Abba*—to be hallowed in all its amazing, enticing sweetness. It is a prayer too for the Father's kingdom to come. But we are not to pray fatalistically or passively but to align our whole life under Christ's kingdom rule.

Unlike such terms as *omnipotence* and *omniscience*—words that have the feel of computer software—*Abba* calls us to the most intimate terms with God. There is nothing like this in any of the world's great religions. Jesus' call to address God as Dearest Father abounds with relationship, intimacy, security. It is ineffably sweet.

What a privilege is ours—to hallow God's name in this world. If his nature as *Abba* drenches our everyday life, we will embody God's good news to an orphaned world.

Disciples of Christ naturally plead for the kingdom where all will be at rest under his paternity. But their prayers are not hollow because they make a habit of repenting and living under the Father's will now—joyous kingdom living.

This is the *upward* section of the Disciples' Prayer.

51

Teach Us to Pray, Part 2

LUKE 11:3, 4

THE LORD'S PRAYER (or, more accurately, the Disciples' Prayer) supplies Jesus' disciples with the architecture of prayer. It first lays out its vertical dimensions. All prayer must be infused with a revolutionary awareness of our divine paternity—"When you pray, say: 'Father'"—"*Abba*"—"Dearest Father." This sweet sense of paternity provides the foundation for prayer with two requests that focus on God. The first is, "hallowed be your name" *as Father*. The second upward request is, "your kingdom come." This is both a prayer for the advent of the final kingdom and a commitment to kingdom living now—to lives of continual repentance and obedience.

Following these vertical dimensions comes the horizontal architecture of prayer, prayer for those things that Christ's disciples need—namely, bread, forgiveness, and strength when facing temptation.

Bread (v. 3)

The initial petition appears simple enough: "Give us each day our daily bread." But there is a richness here that makes the request sublime. It has to do with the word translated "daily," which appears in Greek literature only here and in Matthew's version of the Lord's Prayer.[1] Homer did not use it. Other ancients did not use it. Only in these two New Testament texts is it found in literature.

Today scholars tell us that the word can indicate either "today's bread" or "tomorrow's bread." Such groundbreaking New Testament scholars as Joachim Jeremias and Ernst Lohmeyer, taking their hint from St. Jerome who found in *The Gospel of the Nazareans* the Hebrew word *mahar,* "tomorrow," as a translation of this Greek word, have concluded that the meaning is "tomorrow." Thus, the literal reading is, "Our bread of tomorrow give us today."[2] This translation can be found in *Moffatt's Version* and in the margins of the *Revised Standard Version*, the *New English Bible*, and the *English Standard Version*.

This understanding allows for a dynamic interpretation that includes both our physical needs and our ultimate spiritual needs. As to physical needs, prayed in the morning, this is a prayer for the needs of the day. And prayed in the evening, it is a prayer for the needs of the next day. So "give us each day our bread of tomorrow" is a prayer for God to meet our daily physical needs. However, praying for tomorrow's bread also requests that God meet our needs with the bread of the ultimate tomorrow—the bread of eternity—as we shall see.

Material Bread

It is significant that the initial thing Christ instructs us to pray for when we pray for ourselves is "our daily bread"—our material needs. Notice that we are invited to pray for bread, not dessert. We are not to use the Nieman Marcus catalog as our daily devotional guide. One of the sweet realities of our prayer life is that God cares about the simple, day-to-day needs of life. He cares whether his children are warm, fed, and housed. He is concerned for our well-being, including those things necessary to maintain a whole, happy family.

What Christ is saying here is immensely freeing. We do not have to achieve some lofty spiritual plane, above the material and mundane, before we can offer requests to God. We are not instructed to bring only the "big things" to God but can bring our everyday requests—a coat, shoes, a car, books, a vacation, exercise, a bicycle, groceries, a tricycle, a doll. God meets us where we are and therein lies a glimpse of his loving greatness. When we come to our Father with everyday needs, even so-called "little things," we are glorifying him.

This leads to a parallel truth conveyed in Jesus' instructing his disciples to ask for "daily bread"—dependence upon the Father. No other line in the Lord's Prayer so directly challenges the times in which we live. The average person worries too much about achieving financial security. There is nothing wrong with planning for future rainy days, but it is wrong to allow such a goal to consume us. For some a fitting obituary would be, "He died financially secure and independent with no need of anything or anyone, even God!" This is a spiritual tragedy. Jesus is telling us, whether rich or poor, that God wants us to depend upon him daily. He wants us to pray for our daily material needs, and he wants us to thank him daily—"Give us each day our daily bread."

Spiritual Bread

"Give us each day our daily bread" is also a request for the spiritual bread characteristic of the eternal state. I believe this dual interpretation is justified for several reasons. First, the petition literally reads, "Give us this day our bread for tomorrow," thus pointing to the future state. Second, the three preceding petitions of the Lord's Prayer (combining Matthew and Luke) all ultimately refer to the final eternal state, when God's *name* is once and for all hallowed, his *kingdom* comes, and his *will* is perpetually done. Therefore, it follows that the bread of tomorrow is also eternal. Third, Jesus used only one symbol to describe the eternal state for believers, and he used it many times—a great, joyous feast.[3] Surely this is where the bread of Heaven will be served. So in three ways we see that when Jesus bids us to pray for the bread of tomorrow, he is inviting us to pray for the bread of eternity today.

Here in the Lord's Prayer Jesus tells us that through prayer we can stretch out our hands, grasp the glorious bread of eternity, and feast upon it. The ultimate bread is, of course, Christ. Jesus himself said, "I am the living bread that came down from heaven. If anyone eats of this bread, he will live forever. And the bread that I will give for the life of the world is my flesh" (John 6:51). And we respond:

> By Thee the souls of men are fed
> With gifts of grace supernal:
> Thou, who dost give us earthly bread,
> Give us the bread eternal.

Forgiveness (v. 4a)

Robert Louis Stevenson in his *Picturesque Notes of Edinburgh* tells the story of two unmarried sisters who shared a single room. As people are apt to do who live in close quarters, the sisters had a falling out, which Stevenson says was "on some point of controversial divinity"—in other words, they disagreed over some aspect of theology. The controversy was so bitter that they never spoke again to one another. There were no words, either kind or spiteful. Just silence.

One would think they would have separated, but whether because of lack of means or of the innate Scottish fear of scandal, they continued to keep house together in the single room. They drew a chalk line across the floor to separate their two domains, even dividing the doorway and the fireplace, so each could go in and out and do her cooking without stepping into the territory of the other. For years they coexisted in hateful silence. And at night, each went to bed listening to the heavy breathing of her enemy.[4]

Thus the two sisters (ostensibly daughters of the church who cared about theology) continued the rest of their miserable lives. No doubt when they attended church they "said" the Lord's Prayer, but they obviously never truly prayed it, for that would have meant their reconciliation. How could they truly pray "Our Father" and remain estranged? Or "Give *us* each day *our* daily bread"? Or "Forgive us *our* sins, for *we* ourselves forgive everyone who is indebted to *us*"? "Forgive us . . . for we ourselves forgive." There is no way they could have remained bitter and unforgiving if they truly prayed those words.

The parallel phrase in Matthew's version says essentially the same thing: "'Forgive us our debts (= sins), as we also have forgiven our debtors (= those who sin against us)'" (Matthew 6:12). This suggests that forgiveness must be fulfilled as a condition before we can ask God for forgiveness. And Luke's use of the present tense expresses a continual spirit of forgiveness in the hearts of those who ask for forgiveness.[5] The two passages are not contradictory. Jesus stated it both ways to dynamically express the truth that a heart that asks for God's forgiveness must be a heart that has forgiven and continues to forgive.

This is an unavoidable New Testament truth. St. Augustine called Matthew's version "the terrible petition" because if we pray "Forgive us our debts, as *we* also have forgiven our debtors" with an unforgiving heart, we are actually asking God *not* to forgive us. Listen to the New Testament.

> For if you forgive others their trespasses, your heavenly Father will also forgive you, but if you do not forgive others their trespasses, neither will your Father forgive your trespasses. (Matthew 6:14, 15)

> Blessed are the merciful, for they shall receive mercy. (Matthew 5:7)

> For judgment is without mercy to one who has shown no mercy. Mercy triumphs over judgment. (James 2:13)

> Then his master summoned him and said to him, "You wicked servant! I forgave you all that debt because you pleaded with me. And should not you have had mercy on your fellow servant, as I had mercy on you?" And in anger his master delivered him to the jailers, until he should pay all his debt. So also my heavenly Father will do to every one of you, if you do not forgive your brother from your heart. (Matthew 18:32–35)

The Scriptures are so conclusive on this matter that the Puritan Thomas Watson said, "A man can as well go to hell for not forgiving as for not believing."[6] And the nineteenth-century preacher Charles Spurgeon said, "Unless you have forgiven others, you read your own death-warrant when you repeat the Lord's Prayer."[7]

True believers forgive and are forgiving. That does not mean they do not wrestle with forgiveness. It does not mean that forgiveness comes naturally to real Christians. Many Christians' bitterness and hatred recur even though they have forgiven the offender. It is hard to maintain a forgiving spirit. But actually the struggle is evidence of God's grace in the believer's heart, because otherwise he or she would just give in to the hatred. The warning here is for those who claim to be Christian but *will not* forgive and have no desire to do so.

The question is, is this forgiveness petition in the Lord's Prayer a curse or a blessing? Are our most tightly held possessions our grudges? Do we pride ourselves on the fact that we never forgive? If so, we are probably not believers in Christ at all.

How good God is to put it this way. It requires no elaborate reasoning process to determine where we are—no special knowledge. All it requires is honesty. Is God's grace at work in your heart? This fifth petition of the Lord's Prayer is indeed "a terrible petition" but also a gracious one. It cuts through all the evangelical jargon and monitors our spiritual health. Are we healthy, forgiving people?

The importance of being forgiving cannot be overstressed. We do this for the health of *our own souls*. Bitterness causes innumerable ailments—emotional, physical, spiritual—within us. We do it for the health of the *church*. The church is weak and defeated because of refused forgiveness among its children. We do it for the sake of the *world*. The world has not yet discovered what Christ is like. But it can, if we will truly forgive.

Do you need to forgive your spouse? Covenant to do it right now. Have you been unwilling to forgive your parents? Promise God right now that you will do it. Have you forgiven your employer who wronged you? You need to do it now—and you can, with Christ's help. Do you have a grudge against your last church? Its pastor, its elders? Forgive today!

Forgiveness should mean more to you than your daily bread.

Temptation (v. 4b)

The final petition in Luke's version of the Lord's Prayer—"and lead us not into temptation"—has been subject to much misunderstanding. Some have thought it reveals that God is the prime mover behind all temptations. But that is utterly false. James, the Lord's brother, makes this perfectly clear: "Let no one say when he is tempted, 'I am being tempted by God,' for God cannot be tempted with evil, and he himself tempts no one" (James 1:13).

Others have thought nearly the opposite—that if Christians will truly pray this prayer, God will miraculously lead them away from *all* temptation. However, continual temptation has been the experience of all the apostles and all the saints, without exception. All of life is full of temptation.

The Greek word used here can mean temptation (enticement to engage in sin) or trial, testing. Here the meaning is temptation that, if yielded to, will lead us into sin.

It is important to note that temptation is actually good for us. It molded the life and ministry of the Lord Jesus Christ himself. His ministry began with his epic temptations in the wilderness as Satan came at him with a subtly contrived psycho-spiritual attack. Jesus withstood it all and, with those temptations conquered, went on to live a peerless life. Then, some three and a half years later, toward the end of his life he again triumphed over temptation in the garden of Gethsemane when he conquered the impulse to flee from the cross. The writer of Hebrews bears testimony to the molding effect of these and other sufferings: "For it was fitting that he, for whom and by whom all things exist, in bringing many sons to glory, should make the founder of their salvation perfect through suffering" (Hebrews 2:10).

If temptations helped shape the life and ministry of Christ, how much more they must do so for us. Temptation, when resisted, develops our moral character. "Temptation is not so much the penalty of manhood as it is the glory of manhood. It is that by which a man is made an athlete of God."[8] Temptation conquered knits the fibers of our souls into muscular cords. That is why the Scriptures urge the long view: "Count it all joy, my brothers, when you meet trials of various kinds, for you know that the testing of your faith produces steadfastness" (James 1:2, 3). That is why today we count among the great Christians of our time such people as Dietrich Bonhoeffer, Corrie ten Boom, and Alexander Solzhenitsyn. Their great trials knit together the moral fiber of their souls.

Jesus' recommended prayer regarding temptation is not that we be delivered from all temptation, for temptation, trials, and testing are necessary for the health of our souls. The proper prayer asks God to deliver us from overpowering temptations, recognizing that we are liable to fold under such enticement and assault.

The operative inner quality here is a humble awareness of our weakness. The very best person is, at his or her best, vulnerable and stumbles easily apart from God's gracious provision of strength. And we are never so vulnerable as when we think we are past a certain temptation. The strongest believers are sure that they cannot stand apart from the grace of God—those who doubt their ability to withstand temptation—those who plead, "Lead us not into temptation that is beyond our capacity to withstand."

Closing Reflections

What should be the horizontal architecture of our prayer lives? Jesus has made that most clear.

He wants his disciples to consciously depend upon him for their most basic needs. No need is too mundane or small. He glorifies himself by supplying what we need. But there is more, because this "bread of tomorrow" also refers to Christ himself—the bread we will feast on forever. "We can live without food, we can live without water. We can even live without air. But we cannot live without Jesus the bread of life" (adapted from Charles Malik).[9] "Give us the bread of tomorrow."

Further, having been forgiven by Christ, let us be forgiving people who daily seek the forgiveness of Christ. This is a call for daily examination, daily confession, and daily petition.

Let us also humbly pray that the Father will lead us away from any temptation that is too much for us. Let us embrace his testing, for it builds the fiber of our souls, but let us plead for deliverance from temptations that would prevail.

52

Teach Us to Pray, Part 3

LUKE 11:5–13

JESUS BEGAN TEACHING HIS DISCIPLES how to pray by giving the architecture of prayer. First, he gave the *foundation*: "When you pray, say: 'Father.'" Then he supplied two *vertical* petitions of prayer: "Hallowed be your name" and "Your kingdom come." Third, he laid out the *horizontal* structures of prayer with three petitions: "Give us each day our daily bread"—"Forgive us our sins, for we ourselves forgive everyone who is indebted to us"—"And lead us not into temptation."

The Lord's Prayer, with its five petitions here in Luke and the six in Matthew, is a divine outline for prayer. To use it rigidly is to be reductionist. Rather, it is meant to shape a life of expansive prayer with dynamic upward and outward dimensions that inform and include all of life.

Persistence (vv. 5–10)

As beautiful as the outline is, it still leaves some questions unanswered regarding how to pray, questions having to do with the expectancy and attitudes with which Jesus' followers ought to pray. So Jesus tells a parable to address these concerns:

> And he said to them, "Which of you who has a friend will go to him at midnight and say to him, 'Friend, lend me three loaves, for a friend of mine has arrived on a journey, and I have nothing to set before him'; and he will answer from within, 'Do not bother me; the door is now shut, and my children are with me in bed. I cannot get up and give you anything'? I tell you, though he will not get up and give him anything because he is his

> friend, yet because of his impudence he will rise and give him whatever he needs." (vv. 5–8)

This animated parable speaks volumes to the present day.

Shamelessness

The story begins with friends—say, a fellow pastor from my church and myself. Let's call him Larry. It is the middle of the night, and an old friend who has been serving the Lord in Kabul, Afghanistan arrives at Larry's home unexpectedly. The kids have eaten everything in the house, and all the stores are closed. In the past their unannounced friend had shown wonderful hospitality to their family, and now the visiting friend is exhausted, famished, and hoping for a return favor.

Larry, good man that he is, slips out the door, slides into the station wagon, and heads for the Hughes home, his friends of almost twenty years, who always have a full refrigerator because "he's the rich senior pastor."

Meanwhile, at the Hughes residence, after an exhausting day occupied with family activities, we have all gone to bed early, including the eleven grandchildren who are sleeping over. The door has been locked and the chain bolted, and we have been asleep for hours. My wife is comatose, and I am sawing logs.

When the doorbell rings, I just think it is part of my dream. But the bell keeps ringing, interspersed with determined knocks. I stumble out of bed, lift the window, look down from the second story on Larry's bald head, and whisper, "Man, it's almost one, and the children are all asleep here with us. Go away! I don't care if the mayor of Kabul is in your house. I'm not opening the door. Go ask somebody else!"

But Larry shamelessly keeps knocking and calling out, "I won't go away until you open the door and give me some food for my guest." When I do not answer, he gets even louder. Soon the neighbors' lights on all sides are on, so I stumble from the room, stepping across the slumbering little bodies, then down the steps, open the cupboard, grab some Doritos, throw them out to Larry, and he is on his way.

Utterly outrageous! But in ancient cultures such behavior was even more bizarre. The oriental sense of responsibility for a guest was legendary. The request here for three loaves of bread reflects this. One loaf is often more than enough to eat, but three loaves were not uncommon with Middle-Eastern hospitality.[1] Bread was essential not only for its own nutritional value but as something with which to eat the rest of the meal. The guest would break off bite-sized pieces of bread and use them to dip into the entrees. The borrower was out of bread but knew that his friend's wife had freshly baked bread. So he would not take no for an answer from his comfortably tucked-in friend.

The revealing word in this story is "impudence"—literally "shamelessness." "Yet because of his *shamelessness* he will rise and give him whatever he needs" (v. 8). Shamelessness generally does not describe a good quality. But it can be bad or good depending on the circumstances. If there are good reasons to feel shame, shamelessness is a bad thing. But if one's cause is good, shameless insistence is good.[2] Here, in light of the legendary commitment of the ancient Palestinians to hospitality, the shamelessness of the man's insistence is to be praised. The shameless carrying-on at the doorstep of his sleeping friend was admirable. This was good, excellent shamelessness.

What Jesus was saying here is, if a grouchy friend can be forced by his friend's shameless insistence to give what he ought, how much more will our loving God respond to our shameless petitioning for what we need. May we have a proper shamelessness as we pray through Jesus' design for prayer—the Disciples' Prayer! Knowing God cares, knowing that we are praying according to his standards and purposes, we can be bold!

A Confidence That Does Not Quit

Building upon the parable, Jesus next commanded a confident persistence: "And I tell you, ask, and it will be given to you; seek, and you will find; knock, and it will be opened to you. For everyone who asks receives, and the one who seeks finds, and to the one who knocks it will be opened" (vv. 9, 10). This, in light of its context, tells us how we ought to pray the structure of the Lord's Prayer. The Lord's language is unusually compelling because the three verbs—"ask," "seek," "knock"—indicate an ascending intensity.

"Ask" implies requesting assistance for a conscious need. We realize our lack and thus ask for help. The word also suggests humility in asking, for it is commonly used of one making a request of a superior.

"Seek" denotes asking but adds action. The idea is not just to express our need, but to get up and look around for help. It involves effort.

"Knock" includes asking plus acting plus persevering—like someone who keeps pounding on a closed door.

The stacking of these words is extremely forceful, and the fact that they are present imperatives gives them even more punch. The text actually reads: "*Keep on asking*, and it will be given to you; *keep on seeking*, and you will find; *keep on knocking*, and it will be opened to you." The man in this picture just will not stop knocking!

Does Jesus' call to persistence in prayer make prayer a meritorious work? The answer is clearly no, because what Jesus is calling for here has to do with heart attitude, not mere religious routine. For example, if today we pray, "Your kingdom come," and then tomorrow forget to ask, and keep forgetting to ask for the next year, it is obvious that the coming of his kingdom is not very important to us. As G. B. Caird notes in his *Gospel of Saint Luke*, "God does not have to be waked or cajoled into giving us what we need—many gifts he bestows on the ungodly and ungrateful; but his choicest blessings are reserved for those who will value them and who show their appreciation by asking until they receive."[3]

Persistence is an indication of our soul's confidence. Jesus says, "It *will* be given . . . you *will* find . . . and it *will* be opened." Those who "ask," "seek," and "knock" are people who believe God will answer. Their prayers are not works, but acts of faith—not ritual but reliance.[4]

The door opens not because hands are bruised, but because pounding hands value what Jesus directs his followers to pray for and because they believe he will answer. This is the way the Son of God prayed, as for example when he spent the whole night on the mountain in prayer before choosing his disciples (6:12–16) and in the garden of Gethsemane, where during his asking, seeking, and knocking "his sweat became like great drops of blood falling down to the ground" (22:44).

In the increasing intensity of "ask," "seek," "knock," Jesus is calling us to passionate prayer. Consider Jacob as he wrestled with the angel at Jabbok. What a storm of spiritual intensity broke on God's throne that night! Jacob's passion pulled his body apart, and he, limping, became Israel—"he strives with God" (Genesis 32:22–32).

When Hannah pled with God concerning her barrenness, so great was her passion that the priest Eli "said to her, 'How long will you go on being drunk? Put your wine away from you.' But Hannah answered, 'No, my lord, I am a woman troubled in spirit. I have drunk neither wine nor strong drink, but I have been pouring out my soul before the LORD'" (1 Samuel 1:14, 15). And God responded to Hannah's passionate prayer by giving her a godly son.

Ezra, the restorer of Israel, says, "At the evening sacrifice I rose from my fasting, with my garment and my cloak torn, and fell upon my knees and spread out my hands to the LORD my God" (Ezra 9:5, 6a). So it was also with his cohort Nehemiah, who prayed and wept over Israel's fallen walls (Nehemiah 1:4ff.).

Then, in the age of the gospel, came passionate Paul: "I could wish that I myself were accursed and cut off from Christ for the sake of my brothers, my kinsmen according to the flesh" (Romans 9:3). Consider also his disciple Epaphras, of whom Paul told the Colossians, "[He is] always struggling on your behalf in his prayers" (Colossians 4:12). Or the widow who wore the judge out with her petitions (18:1–5), picturing the value of persevering prayer. But the greatest example is Christ himself, who "offered up prayers and supplications, with loud cries and tears, to him who was able to save him from death" (Hebrews 5:7).

> Prayer is the soul's sincere desire
> Uttered or unexpressed—
> The motion of a hidden fire
> That kindles in the breast.[5]

"Ask," "seek," "knock" is the hidden fire of the heart that believes God will answer and values what he gives.

Paternity (vv. 11–13)

As Jesus closes his instruction on prayer, he reintroduces the subject of paternity with which he began when he said, "When you pray, say: 'Father'" (v. 2). He begins with a grotesque example: "What father among you, if his son asks for a fish, will instead of a fish give him a serpent; or if he asks for an egg, will give him a scorpion?" (vv. 11, 12). This sounds like something from Edgar Allan Poe or Stephen King. "Daddy, may I have a fish for lunch?" "Sure, son. Here you go." The boy trustingly grasps what his father gives him, only to find to his horror that he is holding a writhing serpent! "Daddy, I'm hungry. Give me an egg to eat." As the boy raises it toward his lips, a scorpion uncoils its arching, venomous tail. *Bon appetit!* That would be the paternity of Hell.

Not even a Mafia don, or a Hitler, or any run-of-the-mill sinful father (as we all are) would dream of such treachery. Granted, some fathers are incredibly cruel, but they are clearly exceptions. Fathers love their children! And despite our sinfulness, we enjoy giving good gifts to our children. Usually, if they ask for a fish, we take them fishing. If they ask for an egg, we make them an omelette.

The absurd picture of such grotesque paternity prepares us for a divine paternity. Jesus is arguing from the less to the greater. "If you then, who are evil, know how to give good gifts to your children, how much more will the heavenly Father give the Holy Spirit to those who ask him!" (v. 13). We, sinful shortcomings and all, go to great lengths to give good gifts to our children. We moderns work extra hours and scrimp and save so we can give nice gifts to our children at birthdays and holidays. How much more is this true of our perfect Father in Heaven! He has never given any of his children anything but the best. "He who did not spare his own Son but gave him up for us all, how will he not also with him graciously give us all things?" (Romans 8:32). He has given us so much, including the magnificent gift of his Holy Spirit.

The high point of the exalted structure of the Lord's Prayer, with its magnificent vertical and horizontal dimensions, is the gift of the Holy Spirit, who came upon Jesus' disciples just as he promised. God had promised through the prophet Ezekiel, "I will give you a new heart, and a new spirit I will put within you. And I will remove the heart of stone from your flesh and give you a heart of flesh. And I will put my Spirit within you, and cause you to walk in my statutes and be careful to obey my rules" (Ezekiel 36:26, 27). Joel also had said:

> And it shall come to pass afterward,
> that I will pour out my Spirit on all flesh;
> your sons and your daughters shall prophesy,
> your old men shall dream dreams,
> and your young men shall see visions.
> Even on the male and female servants
> in those days I will pour out my Spirit. . . .

> And it shall come to pass that everyone who calls on the name of the LORD shall be saved. For in Mount Zion and in Jerusalem there shall be those who escape, as the LORD has said, and among the survivors shall be those whom the LORD calls. (Joel 2:28, 29, 32)

At Pentecost these dreamlike prophecies were fulfilled. Believers no longer had to pray to receive the Holy Spirit (cf. 1 Corinthians 12:13; Ephesians 1:13). Nevertheless, we still pray for the work of the Holy Spirit in our lives: "I do not cease to give thanks for you, remembering you in my prayers, that the God of our Lord Jesus Christ, the Father of glory, may give you the Spirit of wisdom and of revelation in the knowledge of him" (Ephesians 1:16, 17; cf. 3:14–21). In all our praying, the greatest gift is the fullness of the Holy Spirit.

Closing Reflections

With this we come to the end of the Lord's instruction on prayer. How are we to pray the sublime architecture of the Lord's Prayer? How are we to pray for his name? His kingdom? Our bread? Our sins? Our temptations?

Because what we pray for through the petitions of the Lord's Prayer are so right, we are to pray shamelessly. God always delights to hear our petitions.

We are also to pray persistently—to keep on asking, seeking, and knocking. Our bruised hands display our confidence that he will answer.

Like Jacob and Hannah and Ezra and Nehemiah and Paul and Epaphras and, most of all, Jesus himself, we are also to pray passionately.

We also should pray expectantly. As we begin the Lord's Prayer with an upward rush of confidence in our heavenly Father, our *Abba*, we expect the Father's perfect gifts through the Holy Spirit. We expect everything he gives us to be good—and it is! What a blessed people we are!

53

Merciful Reasonings

LUKE 11:14–28

TO BE TWENTY-FIVE or thirty-five or forty-five or sixty-five and not have uttered a word for years—what must that have been like? Especially in a culture where only a few could read or write. The ability to verbally communicate with others is part of normal everyday life. Not having that, if the poor man in Luke 11 could not write (and very likely he could not), his needs and his feelings could only be conveyed by a frustrating combination of facial expressions, body language, gestures, and sounds that probably he alone could understand. There were times when he might have felt like a prisoner within his own body. And that feeling was not unfounded because his tongue was chained by a demonic spirit that satisfied its perverse pleasure by keeping him inarticulate. To bc tongueless was one thing, but to have one's tongue chained by palpable evil was much worse.

A Miracle Denied (vv. 14–16)

The Exorcism

But suddenly as the mute man stood before Jesus, "[Jesus] was casting out" the demon. The man could feel it. His tongue was free, and he spoke. With increasingly joyous volume he praised his deliverer. "Thank you, Master! Hallelujah! I can speak! Praise God! Thank you, Jesus! Hosanna!" Seeing this, "the people marveled." They had grown accustomed to the man's muteness and had not imagined his situation would ever change. Everyone knew it was a miracle, though Jesus' enemies found a way to mix in some bitter with the sweet.

The Slander

Unbelief loves to undermine clear evidence of God's love and power, in this case in the form of slander. "But some of them said, 'He casts out demons by Beelzebul, the prince of demons'" (v. 15). Ugly lies! "Beelzebul" had become in Hebrew culture an alternative name for Satan. In Ugaritic texts the name Beezeboul meant "Baal the prince." But in the Old Testament (2 Kings 1:2, 3, 6, 16) the name is rendered "Baal-zebub," meaning "Lord of the flies." It was a deliberate distortion to deprecate the pagan god. The Septuagint translates this, "Baal, the fly-God" (see also Josephus, *Antiquities* 9.2,1,19).[1] "Beelzebul" was, and is, a fitting name for Satan, but a monstrous slander when used for Christ. The hearts of the Pharisees and scribes were so hard that they said in essence, "Yes, Jesus has done a miracle, but only because he is in league with Satan, the Lord of the flies, the God of dung and carrion." It was a calculated blasphemy of immense perversity.

Not all were as inflammatory in their rejection of Christ, some displaying a moderated expression of disbelief: "Others, to test him, kept seeking from him a sign from heaven" (v. 16). They wanted a cosmic miracle, perhaps like the turning back of the sun (cf. 2 Kings 20:8–11) or manna from Heaven (cf. Exodus 16:4; John 6:30, 31). This was moderated slander but slander nevertheless, and its root was entrenched wickedness—"This generation is an evil generation. It seeks for a sign" (11:29).

Eternal Danger

The religious establishment's rejection of Christ was so insulting and so outrageous that humanly speaking he could have been tempted to simply turn away without a word. It is not easy to answer religious fools. But they were standing on the edge of the Abyss, and Christ cared about their souls' peril. As David Gooding puts it:

> God's finger was touching them; God was speaking to them. What they had just witnessed was a direct, unambiguous, demonstration of the Holy Spirit. Now they must make life's ultimate judgment; and they were at the point of making a decision which once deliberately made would be irreversible and would make deliverance forever impossible. Reject the Holy Spirit, call Ultimate Good evil, call Truth himself . . . a lie, and God himself has no further evidence left, nothing further left to say. . . . God himself is reduced to silence.[2]

They were tottering on the edge of an eternity of judgment. But merciful Jesus would not let them go on without explaining to them exactly what they were doing. He was not going to let them suppose that reason was on their side. He was going to show them that to reject him, they would have to shelve their religious sensibilities and common sense, and "knowingly and deliberately they must call black that which in every other context and circumstance of life they would have called white."[3] So in verses 17–22 Jesus mercifully reasons with his enemies, and in verses 23–26 he likewise mercifully warns them.

The Logic of Mercy (vv. 17–22)

Jesus' detractors had accused him of being in cahoots with Satan in this miracle. For the sake of argument, let's grant them a thread of plausibility. Suppose Satan here allowed one of his demons, who was holding a man mute, to be cast out by Jesus, so that Jesus would gain credibility, thus enabling Satan and Jesus together to win Israel to Jesus, a false Messiah. What if they accepted a little loss (one demonized man set free) in order to take many more captives (those who witnessed the miracle). That may sound plausible, but . . .

But what is implausible, and indeed impossible, is that Jesus' *entire* ministry could be devoted to casting out demons and that he could at the same time be in league with Satan. Luke alone records at least ten instances of healing, and four of them explicitly involve exorcisms—on one occasion, wholesale exorcisms:

> Now when the sun was setting, all those who had any who were sick with various diseases brought them to him, and he laid his hands on every one of them and healed them. And demons also came out of many, crying, "You are the Son of God!" But he rebuked them and would not allow them to speak, because they knew that he was the Christ. (4:40, 41; cf. 4:3, 9; 8:26–39; 9:37–45)

We must conclude in the light of Jesus' wholesale ongoing attack on Satan and the astounding morality of his kingdom preaching that it was impossible for an evil league between Savior and Satan to exist. Jesus' detractors stood on shaky logic, and Jesus mercifully reasoned with them with two parable-like utterances.

A Kingdom Divided

The first word picture Jesus gave was that of a divided kingdom:

> But [Jesus], knowing their thoughts, said to them, "Every kingdom divided against itself is laid waste, and a divided household falls. And if Satan also

> is divided against himself, how will his kingdom stand? For you say that I cast out demons by Beelzebul." (vv. 17, 18)

No kingdom, no house, no army, no business, no team, no movement can survive an internal war. Impossible! Take, for instance, the case of the 1986 peace march that began in Los Angeles only to stall in Barstow, about 120 miles out of LA, where about half of the twelve hundred disgruntled marchers went home. Soon the remaining personnel polarized over those who were real walkers and those who rode in vehicles. Civil war broke out! They even fought over a dress code. Finally they decided to hold an election but disagreed over who could vote, ultimately allowing even children to vote. Then the election was declared invalid. Many ended the peace march not speaking to each other.[4] "Every kingdom divided against itself is laid waste." There was no way Jesus and Satan could be marching together.

Jesus then went on to ask a telling question: "And if I cast out demons by Beelzebul, by whom do your sons cast them out? Therefore they will be your judges" (v. 19). Jewish contemporaries did indeed perform exorcisms (cf. Acts 19:13, 14; cf. Josephus, *Antiquities* 8.2, 5), and most people believed they did it by the power of God. Were they on Satan's team too? Were all who cast out demons in league with Satan? Absurd!

The final thrust of the miniparable drove the point home: "But if it is by the finger of God that I cast out demons, then the kingdom of God has come upon you" (v. 20). This allusion to "the finger of God" calls to mind the Scriptural account of Moses delivering Egypt by repeated displays of supernatural power, so that Pharaoh's own magicians warned him, "This is the finger of God" (Exodus 8:19). Jesus had the same delivering power, and he did it with the same ease. The inescapable conclusion? The power of God that enabled Christ to cast out demons was proof positive of the presence of the kingdom of God.

Instead of slandering Jesus, those men should have sought his forgiveness. *Think, scribes and Pharisees, think—your life is at stake!*

The Strong Man Bound

The other parable-like description Jesus used was that of a strong man overpowered: "When a strong man, fully armed, guards his own palace, his goods are safe; but when one stronger than he attacks him and overcomes him, he takes away his armor in which he trusted and divides his spoil" (vv. 21, 22). The picture is not of a palace but of a well-armed castle (the word "palace" is literally "courtyard").[5] This strong lord is concerned with maintaining the security of his estate. Being a strong man with substantial local power, his possessions are very secure—until someone stronger attacks. The strong man, the well-armed lord, is Satan. His possessions are people such as the poor mute man. The stronger man who attacks is Jesus. Conclusion: the very fact that Christ had delivered the mute man from Satan's clutches was evidence that he was not on Satan's side. Rather, he was and is the devil's super-powerful enemy. Jesus defeated Satan in order to deliver the man.

Think, you scribes and Pharisees, think—do not call white black, for to do so is to risk eternal loss.

Jesus' Further Warnings (vv. 23–26)

Others in the crowd (decent people that they were) were certainly against spiritual oppression and demon possession, and they did not appreciate the inflammatory "Beelzebul" accusations thrown at Christ. Nevertheless, they felt no need to openly align their lives with Christ. They wanted to remain neutral, perhaps until some cosmic sign convinced them to believe.

No Middle Road

But Jesus did not grant them that luxury, aggressively declaring, "Whoever is not with me is against me, and whoever does not gather with me scatters" (v. 23). If you are not for Jesus, you are against him. Given the massive claims of Jesus, neutrality is a self-deceiving ruse. His claims are so great that protestations of neutrality are in fact declarations of disbelief. Further, no one's life is neutral in its effects. If you are not part of the gathering process, your life is destructive, no matter how many philanthropies you claim.

Spiritual realities have not changed: Every man, every woman, is either for Christ or against him.

In Harm's Way

As the chill of his words settled in, Jesus related a grim story:

> When the unclean spirit has gone out of a person, it passes through waterless places seeking rest, and finding none it says, 'I will return to my house from which I came.' And when it comes, it finds the house swept and put in order. Then it goes and brings seven other spirits more evil than itself, and they enter and dwell there. And the last state of that person is worse than the first. (vv. 24–26)

It is not clear whether the evil spirit leaves the man in search of a better abode or is exorcised. In any event, its journey through desolate places turns up no suitable place to rest. So it returns to its previous abode, like the "night hag" (*Lilith*) of Isaiah to its resting-place (Isaiah 34:14 RSV). Meanwhile, its former victim has swept clean his inner life and reordered it so that the space is even more inviting. The returning demon is overjoyed at what it finds and seeks out seven other foul spirits so they can all settle down in demonic community to feast on the poor man's soul. "And the last state of that person is worse than the first."

Jesus is saying to his religious hearers that self-reformation without regeneration and the indwelling of God the Holy Spirit is fatal. Temporary moral reformation is inadequate. Anyone who purges evil but puts nothing in its place is in grave moral danger. This emphasizes the utter danger in today's postmodern world, with its profound inwardness and focus upon self, employing techniques and technologies that leave a house swept clean and in apparent order *and yet empty*. If a man or woman is empty and without God, any sin, any perversion, is possible. A vacuum has to be filled with something. And if it is not the Spirit of God, there is no telling what it will be.

This contrasts sharply with the sweetness of Jesus' words during his final days here on earth, when he stood on the last day of the Feast of Tabernacles and cried out, "If anyone thirsts, let him come to me and drink. Whoever believes in me, as the Scripture has said, 'Out of his heart will flow rivers of living water'" (John 7:37b, 38).

Jesus' *reasoning* in answering those who credited his power to Satan was overpowering. A kingdom divided cannot stand—it takes one stronger than the strong to rescue the victim of sin. Jesus' *warnings* also cut to the quick. There is no neutrality possible regarding him. We are either with him or against him. Reformation without regeneration is an empty affair, leaving one open to demonic community.

The Possibility of Mercy (vv. 27, 28)

The scene was overpowering. No one was smiling, neither Jesus nor his antagonists. Then, "As he said these things, a woman in the crowd raised her voice and said to him, 'Blessed is the womb that bore you, and the breasts at which you nursed!' But he said, 'Blessed rather are those who hear the word of God and keep it!'" (vv. 27, 28). The woman did not know it, but Jesus knew that her blessing coincided with the beatitude that Mary his mother had given herself in the *Magnificat*: "From now on all generations will call me blessed; for he who is mighty has done great things for me, and holy is his name" (1:48, 49). Indeed, his mother was the most blessed of women. She was great in her humility: "For he has looked on the humble estate of his servant" (1:48). She was great in her submission: "'I am the servant of the Lord; let it be to me according to your word'" (1:38). She bore under her steady heart the racing heart of God. The woman was so prophetically right: "Blessed is the womb that bore you, and the breasts at which you nursed!"

And Jesus did not disagree. Margaret Thrall has shown from the Greek that the sense of Jesus' response is, "Yes, but blessed rather are those who hear the word of God and obey it."[6] Jesus liked what the woman said. He did not reprove her speech but *improved* it. He said in effect, "What you have said is right, but there is a higher truth: she was blessed who bore me, but more surely blessed are those who hear the Word of God and keep it."

Mary was blessed because she heard the Word of God and obeyed it, and this beatitude rests on all who do the same. It rested on some in that sober crowd who heard Jesus' reasonings and warnings, those who opened their empty souls to Jesus, who became part of his army. His blessing has rested on thousands since.

This puts the highest blessing of God within reach of us all. There are only two steps to blessedness: to *hear* the Word of God and to *obey* it. We need to listen to the Word with reverence. We must hear it with understanding and know what it means. Then we must do what it says.

Jesus said that hearing the Word of God and keeping it is a higher blessing than Mary's blessing in giving birth to Jesus. This is the key to all blessings in this life and in Heaven beyond.

How this cut through the dark objections to Jesus. The woman's cry above the slander of the Pharisees and the murmurings of the crowd was brave and right. Jesus had mercifully reasoned with them and mercifully warned them and now gave them a merciful possibility that tugged at their souls.

54

Light for Hard Hearts

LUKE 11:29–36

JUST PRIOR TO THE EVENTS and pronouncements in this passage, Jesus had been dealing with hard hearts, hearts so calloused that, though they were eyewitnesses to the exorcism and healing of a mute victim of Satan, they dismissed the miracle out of hand by attributing Jesus' power to "Beelzebul, the prince of demons" (11:15) and then by asking for "a sign from heaven" (11:16). In response to the first dismissal, Jesus mercifully reasoned with them, demonstrating the illogical folly of their thinking (vv. 17–22), then gave them a chilling warning followed by a warm appeal (vv. 23–28).

Now he took up their less strident but nonetheless hard-hearted request for a miraculous sign. In doing so he called to their remembrance two famous occurrences in their history when Gentiles responded to the Word—the amazing cases of Jonah and the Queen of Sheba.

In the former, Jonah, upon receiving the divine call to go to Nineveh and preach against it, did just the opposite, hopping a ship to Tarshish, a port at the other end of the then known world. We are familiar with the story—the heaving sea, the terrified sailors, Jonah's being tossed overboard and inhaled by a monstrous fish. In his watery tomb he was swept down to the "roots of the mountains" as he described it (Jonah 2:6). There he repented. "Out of the belly of Sheol I cried, and you heard my voice," sang Jonah (Jonah 2:2). After his change of heart Jonah found himself exploding back into daylight as the fish coughed him onto a sandy beach. The pagan Ninevites gave credence to his message when he related the miraculous way God changed his mind about preaching to them. His very experience made him a sign to the Ninevites,[1] and all Nineveh repented. Amazing!

The other incredible account, that of the Queen of Sheba, is recorded in

1 Kings 10:1–13 and 2 Chronicles 9:1–12. In her own land of Sheba (southern Arabia, modern Yemen), months away by caravan, the queen had "heard of the fame of Solomon concerning the name of the LORD" (1 Kings 10:1). So, employing a vast retinue at immense cost, she made the long, dangerous journey to see Solomon.

> The report was true that I heard in my own land of your words and of your wisdom, but I did not believe the reports until I came and my own eyes had seen it. And behold, the half was not told me. Your wisdom and prosperity surpass the report that I heard. Happy are your men! Happy are your servants, who continually stand before you and hear your wisdom! Blessed be the LORD your God, who has delighted in you and set you on the throne of Israel! Because the LORD loved Israel forever, he has made you king, that you may execute justice and righteousness. (1 Kings 10:6–9)

The Queen of Sheba had gone through considerable discomfort and danger to hear Solomon—and she praised the God of Israel for her encounter.

A Sign for Hard Hearts (vv. 29–32)

With the Jonah/Queen of Sheba background in mind, we will look at Jesus' response to those who asked for a sign: "When the crowds were increasing, he began to say, 'This generation is an evil generation. It seeks for a sign, but no sign will be given to it except the sign of Jonah. For as Jonah became a sign to the people of Nineveh, so will the Son of Man be to this generation'" (vv. 29, 30).

The Great Sign

Jesus declared that he would be like Jonah to them—that was the sign. How was this so? Obviously both Jonah and Jesus were preachers of righteousness and repentance. But the deeper significance of "the sign of Jonah" is in Jonah's putative *death*, *burial*, and *resurrection* when he was tossed to his apparent death in the sea, entombed in the fish, and then delivered up alive![2] The rhythm of Jonah's seeming death experience was literally fulfilled in Jesus' death on the cross at the hands of the Romans, his burial by Joseph and Nicodemus, and his glorious resurrection. That is exactly what Jesus said according to Matthew's account: "For just as Jonah was three days and three nights in the belly of the great fish, so will the Son of Man be three days and three nights in the heart of the earth" (Matthew 12:40).

The great and grand sign that Jesus gives to all, and especially those who think they need miraculous signs in order to believe, is the miracle of his atoning death, burial, and triumphant resurrection. This is the gospel. This is apostolic preaching. Paul capsulized it by writing: "For I delivered to you as of first importance what I also received: that Christ died for our sins in accordance with the Scriptures, that he was buried, that he was raised on the third day in accordance with the Scriptures" (1 Corinthians 15:3, 4). We again see here the glorious threefold rhythm of Christ's *death*, *burial*, and *resurrection* on the third day.

There is much-needed instruction and correction here for segments of Christianity that have gone headlong in pursuit of miraculous signs and wonders. It is imperative that we recognize that miraculous signs do not *ipso facto* guarantee that one will believe. This is both implicit and explicit in Luke 11. Verse 16 records that "Others, to test him, kept seeking from him a sign from heaven." These were people who did not want to believe. They were maliciously testing Christ. That is why he indicted them here in verse 29 by saying, "This generation is an evil generation. It seeks for a sign." Ten million signs and wonders would not make the world turn to Christ. Belief is a choice, an act of the will, not a convincing of the intellect.

Second, the ultimate sign is "the sign of Jonah," because it makes *Christ everything*. Jesus was not interested in giving signs abstracted from his person.[3] He *is* the sign. He is the gospel.

Queen of Sheba: A Great Judgment

Jesus then explained that the sign would lead to greater judgment: "The queen of the South will rise up at the judgment with the men of this generation and condemn them, for she came from the ends of the earth to hear the wisdom of Solomon, and behold, something greater than Solomon is here" (v. 31).

Solomon at his zenith was the wisest man ever. The more we understand his proverbs, the more we are in awe. We thrill at the prologue to the book of Proverbs, which ends with the epigram, "The fear of the LORD is the beginning of knowledge; fools despise wisdom and instruction" (Proverbs 1:7). And yet in Jesus, one "greater than Solomon is here." Jesus *is* wisdom. Paul refers to him as "Christ Jesus, who became to us wisdom from God" (1 Corinthians 1:30). Paul also describes him as "Christ, in whom are hidden all the treasures of wisdom and knowledge" (Colossians 2:2b, 3). Regarding this Alexander Maclaren remarked:

> In Christ, as in a great storehouse, lie all the riches of spiritual wisdom, the massive ingots of solid gold which when coined into creeds and doctrines

> are the wealth of the Church. All which we can know concerning God and man, concerning sin and righteousness and duty, concerning another life, is in Him Who is the home and deep mine where truth is stored. . . . The central fact of the universe and the perfect encyclopaedia of all moral and spiritual truth is Christ, the Incarnate Word, the Lamb slain, the ascended King.[4]

Solomon's wisdom was derived, but Christ is himself wisdom!

Thus at the judgment the Queen of Sheba will rise as their accuser, because though Solomon was far inferior to Christ, she left throne and palace and risked the dangers of a thousand miles just to hear what he had to say. These men in the presence of the Son, God's Wisdom, thought he was not much—and said so. Some even rejected him. How great will be their judgment!

Jonah: Even Greater Judgment

Jesus went on to say, "The men of Nineveh will rise up at the judgment with this generation and condemn it, for they repented at the preaching of Jonah, and behold, something greater than Jonah is here" (v. 32). Jonah's preaching was simple and to the point, and the Ninevites, despite their untaught Gentile consciences, responded. Jesus' preaching too was plain and was laced with unmatched eloquence besides—yet the learned scribes and Pharisees did not repent. Oh, the accusations the Ninevites will bring against these people!

We must not try to escape the weight of these words. Our advantage is immense. We have explicit accounts of the death, burial, and resurrection of Christ from the four evangelists. We have the Pauline, Petrine, and Johannine corpus of New Testament writings and the rest of the New Testament too. We have the reasoning and living of two thousand years of church history. We have the Holy Spirit's work around and in us. How great our responsibility to be open to the light, to believe in Jesus Christ, and to follow him faithfully and courageously!

The Challenge to All Hearts (vv. 33–36)

Jesus' teaching now took on very broad application as he employed similitudes, short parable-like utterances, to drive home the message that we must make every effort to open ourselves to the light of his revelation. It is all too easy to become hardened to the sign of Jonah, gospel-hardened by hearing the Word of God so much.

A little girl was sitting in her first Good Friday service, and the epic story of the crucifixion was beautifully read. She heard about Judas' betrayal of Jesus. She heard about Peter's denial. She listened to Pilate's cross-examination of Jesus. She pictured the crown of thorns and felt the beating of the soldiers. Then came the words, "And there they crucified him." The little girl began to weep and buried her head in her mother's lap. Her sad voice could be heard throughout the auditorium as she sobbed, "Why did they do it? Why did they do it?"[5]

Lifelong familiarity with the rhythms of the gospel can dull us to its trembling realities, so that we listen to it with the same vitality with which we read the weather report. We need to be more like that little girl, again.

Jesus' Lamp

Jesus began this section by describing the effect of his own gospel preaching: "No one after lighting a lamp puts it in a cellar or under a basket, but on a stand, so that those who enter may see the light" (v. 33). The truth of his preaching is evident and must not be hidden. The light of Jesus is meant to be placed in a prominent place in the house so that it gives light to everyone.

The preceding context makes it plain that Jesus' preaching, his Word, is the light.

Our Lamps

But the second similitude is more difficult because it represents the human eye as the lamp of the body, and our eyes, strictly speaking, do not generate light. "Your eye is the lamp of your body. When your eye is healthy, your whole body is full of light, but when it is bad, your body is full of darkness" (v. 34). Jesus means that the eye is the lamp of the body because it lets light in, allowing the mind and interior faculties to comprehend, assimilate, and respond to what the light reveals. If one's eyes are good, everything can function as it should. But if they are defective, the body is, as it were, "full of darkness." Everything is adversely affected.[6]

Jesus is here speaking metaphorically of our spiritual perception. If our spiritual eye is "healthy"—literally "single" or simple, open, uncomplicated by sin—it will admit the light that Jesus shines on it, and our interior being will be illuminated. Listen to Jonathan Edwards describe his experience as a young man alone with his Bible on the banks of the Hudson:

> I had then, and at other times, the greatest delight in the Holy Scriptures of any book whatsoever. Oftentimes in reading it every word seemed to touch my heart. I felt a harmony between something in my heart, and those

> sweet and powerful words. I seemed often to see so much light exhibited by every sentence, and such a refreshing food communicated, that I could not get along in reading; often dwelling long on one sentence, to see the wonders contained in it; and yet almost every sentence seemed to be full of wonders.[7]

This is the way a healthy heart reads and hears God's Word. Paul expressed this in his admonition, "Let the word of Christ dwell in you richly, teaching and admonishing one another in all wisdom, singing psalms and hymns and spiritual songs, with thankfulness in your hearts to God" (Colossians 3:16).

What power do our eyes have? If they are bad, the outcome is disastrous, for we thus blind ourselves to the Word. But if they are good, eternity fills our souls.

The Challenge

We need to hear and heed Jesus' challenge: "Be careful lest the light in you be darkness" (v. 35). Jesus' "Be careful" puts the ball squarely in our court. It is up to us. And because he demands that we do this, we can do it. Where must we begin?

We must be men and women of *prayer*. We must see to it that we *confess our sins* and ask God to keep our eyes clear. Jesus' contemporaries could not see his radiant light and were missing "the sign of Jonah" because of a developed state. Surface confession had brought them to ignore the inconsistencies in their hearts. They had squelched their burning consciences until they were desensitized. If the light is to shine in our souls there must be regular confession, followed by passionately asking God to flood our eyes with light.

There must also be *contemplation*. We must "be careful" to make time to be alone so we can meditate and engage in healthy introspection. We must honestly ask ourselves, "Is the light in me actually darkness?" We must make every effort to see to it that it is not.

We also need to *read the Word of God* with expectancy, asking God to shine his light upon us. It may be that the proliferation and availability of the Word of God has dulled us to the urgency of obeying it. During the French Revolution some Christians were crammed into a dungeon where once a day for a few moments, as the sun stood at a particular angle, one of the prisoners who had a Bible would be hoisted on others' shoulders to a sunlit crack, where he would study the Scriptures. When the light dimmed, he would be lowered down, and his friends would say, "Now tell us what you read while you were in the light."[8] We ought to give quality time and full concentration to the light of God's Word.

The Queen of Sheba would turn green with envy at our spiritual privilege. And our message is not from a bedraggled prophet fresh from a whale's belly, but from Jesus who burst from the grave and gives resurrection life.

We must each "be careful lest the light in [us] be darkness."

55

"Woe to You Pharisees"

LUKE 11:37–44

WITHOUT THE BENEFIT OF historical hindsight, one could naively suppose that the Pharisees would follow Jesus. They were not upper class, like the Sadducees, but came from the common people, as did Jesus. They were committed to holy living. The very name *Pharisee* means "the separate ones." They were thought to be holy men, the true community of Israel.[1] When a man became a Pharisee, he first endured a probationary period up to a year in length, during which time he had to prove his ability to keep the rituals of the Law.

Many of the Pharisees were scribes, experts in the Law who so revered it that they hedged it in with extra protective laws. As the *Mishnah* says, "Tradition is a fence around the Law" (Aboth 3.14). They loved the Law, God's Word. Full entrance into the Pharisaic community came, after a probationary period, when a man pledged to observe all the laws regarding purity and tithes.[2] The Pharisees drew a hard line between themselves and the masses, who did not keep the Law as meticulously. The conflict between the Pharisees and the masses was largely due to the people's neglect of tithing.[3]

The Pharisees were exemplary. Tragically, however, their spiritual eyes had become bad (11:34). They had become darkened by pride and greed, so that the very light within them had become an appalling darkness (cf. 11:35). So deep was the darkness that these fastidiously religious idealists became Jesus' bitterest enemies.

Jesus had just warned the people against the danger of spiritual light becoming darkness within them, and a Pharisee's inviting Jesus to join him for lunch immediately afterward was not accidental or congenial—there was a hidden malevolence behind it. And Jesus knew it. "While Jesus was speaking, a Pharisee asked him to dine with him, so he went in and reclined at table. The Pharisee was astonished to see that he did not first wash before dinner" (vv. 37, 38). The omission of ritual washing was a premeditated, calculated affront on Jesus' part. The *Mishnah* records what the ritual hand washing was like.[4] This cleansing had to be perfect to be effective.

> The hands are susceptible to uncleanness, and they are rendered clean [by the pouring over them of water] up to the wrist. Thus if a man had poured the first water up to the wrist and the second water beyond the wrist, and the water flowed back to the hand, the hand becomes clean; but if he poured both the first water and the second beyond the wrist, and the water flowed back to the hand, the hand remains unclean. If he poured the first water over the one hand alone and then bethought himself and poured the second water over the one hand, his one hand [alone] is clean. If he had poured the water over the one hand and rubbed it on the other, it becomes unclean; but if he rubbed it on his head or on the wall [to dry it] it remains clean. (Yadaim 2.3)

Hand washing was important to the Pharisees, to say the least. So Jesus' declining to engage in this ritual was an in-your-face move. Jesus was on the offensive. And when Jesus' host indicated his surprise, Jesus launched into an accusatory speech:

> And the Lord said to him, "Now you Pharisees cleanse the outside of the cup and of the dish, but inside you are full of greed and wickedness. You fools! Did not he who made the outside make the inside also? But give as alms those things that are within, and behold, everything is clean for you." (vv. 39–41)

Seeing their hands still damp from the ritual cleansing, Jesus assailed their externalism. Outwardly their rituals portrayed them as generous and holy, but inwardly they were "full of greed and wickedness."

The defining sin of these tithing, alms-giving Pharisees was love of money, greed, and that is still a telltale sin among even the most religious today. Love of money assaults the most idealistic, including preachers and missionaries. Consider the Scottish clergyman who took his wife out to dinner for their annual night out. Both ordered steak. The wife started eating hers at top speed, but the preacher left his untouched. "Something wrong with the steak, sir?" asked the waiter. "No, no, I'm just waiting for my wife's teeth."[5]

Our degree of attachment to money and possessions is an unfailing indicator of the health of our souls. The Pharisees' hearts were the exact antithesis of what their external religiosity portrayed. We too must beware.

Jesus then cited the ultimate sobering reality that God *knows*: "You fools! Did not he who made the outside make the inside also?" (v. 40). Jesus' appeal was similar to his response on a similar occasion: "You hypocrites! Well did Isaiah prophesy of you, when he said: 'This people honors me with their lips, but their heart is far from me; in vain do they worship me, teaching as doctrines the commandments of men'" (Matthew 15:7–9, quoting Isaiah 29:13). Their external lip service was at odds with their internal heart reality. Their freshly washed hands contradicted their unwashed hearts.

Perhaps on this occasion damp hands receded under the table as Jesus challenged them. In verse 41 we read, "But give as alms those things that are within, and behold, everything is clean for you." That is, give away your greed and wickedness, get rid of your sin, and everything will be clean for you—the outside and the inside. This is Jesus' perpetual call to the Pharisees and indeed to all of us.

This is the dynamic behind Jesus' three mournful woes to the Pharisees (vv. 42–44) and then the three to the experts in the law (vv. 45–52). He wants radical spiritual reality in his people.

Woeful Giving (v. 42)

Jesus' initial woe fell hard on the Pharisees' famous, much-ballyhooed giving of the tithe: "Woe to you Pharisees! For you tithe mint and rue and every herb, and neglect justice and the love of God. These you ought to have done, without neglecting the others" (v. 42).

The Pharisees tithed, which is more than can be said for most of the professing church today. So we must admire their legalistic commitment. No sincere Pharisee ever knowingly gave less than his legal obligation. Synagogues that had a good sprinkling of Pharisees prospered. They were such givers that they even gave a tenth of their necessary household spices—one mint leaf out of every ten. They even went beyond what was required. For example, the *Mishnah* states that "Rue, goosefoot, purslane, hill-coriander, celery and meadow-eruca are exempt from Tithes" (Shebiith 9:1)—yet they tithed them anyway! Pharisees were legendary tithers, and they disdained the *hoi polloi* of the Jewish masses precisely because they did not tithe. Most preachers would not mind a few such givers—"Come to my church, all you Pharisees and heavy-laden givers, and you shall find rest for your checkbooks!"

The Pharisees were great tithers, but they were inward failures, as Jesus' words made so clear: "For you . . . neglect justice and the love of God." The fact is, they were Scrooges toward the needy—the stranger, the fatherless, the widow. They perpetuated the sin of their forefathers who loved ritual performance but neglected justice. The prophet Micah stated:

> He has told you, O man, what is good;
> and what does the LORD require of you
> but to do justice, and to love kindness,
> and to walk humbly with your God? (Micah 6:8)

Similarly, Amos said:

> I hate, I despise your feasts,
> and I take no delight in your solemn assemblies.
> Even though you offer me your burnt offerings and grain offerings,
> I will not accept them;
> and the peace offerings of your fattened animals,
> I will not look upon them.
> Take away from me the noise of your songs;
> to the melody of your harps I will not listen.
> But let justice roll down like waters,
> and righteousness like an ever-flowing stream. (Amos 5:21–24)

The Pharisees had calculated their tithing down to the decimal point, and they never missed a leaf. But when someone came to them with a personal material need, they responded like stingy characters from a Dickens novel. And Jesus could not tolerate this.

> High Heaven rejects the lore
> Of nicely calculated less and more.
>
> William Wordsworth [6]

Why? Because when you do not personally care and give aid to others, you do not really love God. Listen to the apostle John on this: "If anyone has the world's goods and sees his brother in need, yet closes his heart against him, how does God's love abide in him? Little children, let us not love in word or talk but in deed and in truth" (1 John 3:17, 18).

In an age of religious Scrooges, the great Samuel Johnson commented of Boswell:

> He frequently gave all the silver in his pocket to the poor, who watched him, between his house and the tavern where he dined. He walked the streets at all hours, and said he was never robbed for the rogues knew he had little money, nor had the appearance of having much.[7]

We dare not live under the collectivist delusion of those Christians who reason, "I gave at the church. Sorry I can't help you." We are to be generous to all in need. Jesus was clear on this: "These you ought to have done [loving God and loving others by ministering to their needs], without neglecting the others [tithing]." Our Savior wants us to live "both and"—to tithe and to be personally generous.

Woeful Pride (v. 43)

Jesus had minced no words with the Pharisees. Perhaps the just-washed hands now had sweaty palms. Now Jesus had more to say: "Woe to you Pharisees! For you love the best seat in the synagogues and greetings in the marketplaces" (v. 43).

The most important seats in the synagogues were those in front, facing the congregation.[8] The Pharisees loved to be seen by all, in their religious finery. There they could look pensive as the Law was read and beatific as the Psalms were sung. During the homily they could assume various postures and facial expressions to communicate their approval or restraint. And out on the street, well, the more elaborate the greetings the better. "Ah, Rabbi Eliesar, glorious doctor of the Torah, repository of Solomonic epigrams, son of Amos, son of Saul, son of. . . ."

The principal folly here was that their pride left no room for the God they so meticulously served. In fact, it left no room for real faith. On another occasion Jesus put this truth to the Pharisees in the form of a question. "How can you believe, when you receive glory from one another and do not seek the glory that comes from the only God?" (John 5:44). To pursue the adulation and praise of men is to despise the praise of God. You cannot seek both.

Vacuous religiosity is found in every age. Charles Spurgeon, the Victorian preacher, told his students:

> Theodore Hook once stepped up to a gentleman who was parading the street with great pomposity, and said to him, "Sir, are you not a person of great importance?" and one has felt half inclined to do the same with certain brethren of the cloth. I know brethren who, from head to foot, in garb, tone, manner, necktie, and boots, are so utterly *parsonic* that no particle of manhood is visible. One young sprig of divinity must needs go through the streets in a gown, and another of the High Church order has recorded it in the newspapers with much complacency that he traversed Switzerland and Italy, wearing in all places his biretta; few boys would have been so proud of a fool's cap.[9]

In Spurgeon's day there were bedecked, preening preachers like those you might find in an E. M. Forster novel. They really existed.

And they are still around today! A seminary friend of mine was asked to preach the Easter sunrise service at the Hollywood Bowl. When he met with the planning committee, they asked, "Where can the helicopter pick you up?" He answered that there was not enough room on his street for a helicopter to land. "But," they responded, "the man who spoke last year *had* to have a helicopter." My friend declined. Then he was offered a police escort. He imagined how his neighbors would "appreciate" him at 3:00 a.m. leaving in his Volvo escorted by motorcycles and squad cars with flashing lights. He insisted he could get there on his own. On Easter morning, as he stood behind the platform, he noticed another participant dressed in T-shirt and Levis. After all, this was LA. But as the service was about to begin, the same man put on a robe of multiple pastels that would have made the Queen of Sheba blush. Yes, some strutting ecclesiastical peacocks love seats in helicopters and grand Easter entrances to dramatize their humble proclamation of the resurrection—characters right out of a Kurt Vonnegut novel.

I have in my files a flyer advertising an "All-Star Worship Band." If there ever was an oxymoron, that is it. What would Jesus say about focusing on human stars while we "worship"?

The examples are endless, such as the missionary who handed me his business card with all his degrees and titles printed on the reverse side—some twenty of them—followed by additional honors and professional associations. But it becomes far more subtle than all that. It is easy to feed inwardly on sitting in honored seats and receiving exaggerated greetings with a benign, grandfatherly smile, even protesting such excesses but swelling with pride within.

Jesus grieves over all this. "Woe" is an expression of regret, not vindictiveness. "Woe to you. . . . For you love the best seat in the synagogues and greetings in the marketplaces."

The Woeful Effect (v. 44)

The third woe to the Pharisees has a terminal ring to it: "Woe to you! For you are like unmarked graves, and people walk over them without knowing it" (v. 44). Graves, repositories of the remains of the dead, were ceremonially defiling (cf. Numbers 19:11–22; Leviticus 21:1–4, 11). Because of this, they were clearly marked. Otherwise, a pilgrim, perhaps on his way to the temple, could step unaware on a grave, be defiled, then defile the temple (cf. Numbers 19:13). That is why Matthew mentions the yearly whitewashing of graves before Passover (cf. 23:27).

So we have a gruesome irony here. The Pharisees, so concerned about external religion, were actually sources of spiritual contamination to unsuspecting Israelites. They were unclean, full of dead men's bones, so to speak. And they were monstrously deceptive. Their external posturing drew unsuspecting people to them, then ruined them. They were spiritual Typhoid Marys—diseased, defiling, infecting, polluting.

In Francois Mauriac's novel *Viper's Tangle,* the narrator speaks of the damning effect that professing Christians had on their grandfather: "That does not alter the fact that, except in the case of Grandmother, our principles remained separate from our lives. Our thought, our desires, our actions struck no roots in that faith to which we adhered with our lips."[10]

In the same way, the internal, real lives of the Pharisees did not resonate with what they professed. They were filled with greed, stingy hardheartedness, pride, and hubris. The point is, all of us inevitably communicate what we are. We can externally do all the right religious things, right down to tithing our basil and garlic off our pasta, but we will ultimately impart what is within. The people around us will see the artificiality, the affectedness, the elitism, the anger, the hostility, the hatred, the suspicion, the sourness, the inner blasphemies. We leave our fingerprints on each other's souls, for Christ or for unbelief.

Therefore it is imperative that our thoughts, our desires, our actions have roots in the faith we confess with our lips.

Closing Reflections

How can we do this? "But rather give what is inside as alms and you will find everything is clean for you" (v. 41, literal translation). If you are a believer, the change in your life was wrought by the Holy Spirit—he washed the inside of the cup. And now you must perpetually give everything that is within you as alms. There must be ongoing inspection in the light of God's Word, regular confession, and constant petition for the Spirit's power to enable you to live a pure life.

If you do not have true faith, do not attempt external reform. That will never produce love for God and humankind. You must open your heart to his grace and give him your old heart as an alm. Then he will make you a new person through Christ, and you will find everything is clean!

56

"Woe to You Lawyers"

LUKE 11:45–52

JESUS HAD PUMMELED the Pharisees with three power-packed woes. They came with the force of two left jabs and a thunderous right. A left—*smack!* "You are tightwad tithers, cheap hypocrites." Another left—*smack!* "You are puffed-up lovers of places and prominence—vain clerical frauds." And then the right—*pow!* "And to top it off, you are unmarked graves, spiritually diseased, spreading your defilement to all who come your way."

These well-aimed spiritual punches left the Pharisees reeling and their lawyer friends perplexed and off balance. So "One of the lawyers answered him, 'Teacher, in saying these things you insult us also'" (v. 45). If there ever was a case of leading with the chin, this was it. The scribe or lawyer might as well have said, "Hit me!" The Lord then delivered three more powerful blows or woes. *Whack!* "Here's one for overloading the people with un-Biblical burdens." *Whack!* "And here's another for memorializing the dead prophets." *Smash!* "And this is for depriving my people of the Word."

All six woes were mighty punches, but the second three were subtly different from the first trio. This was because though the Pharisees and lawyers were cohorts, they were different. The Pharisees were *religionists*, members of a religious party that enforced the legal code. The lawyers, scribes, or experts in the Law (the three terms are interchangeable) were the *codifiers* of the Law, the people who built hedges around it by encrusting it with myriads of extra regulations. Jesus' woes to the Pharisees were swipes at their hypocritical religious practices, whereas the woes that fell on the lawyers had to do with the way they abused the Torah, God's Word.

We find in these last three woes the divine assessment and judgment upon those who pervert the Word of God. This is a very solemn theme.

Again, while Jesus' woes were fiercely aggressive, they were not damnations, but rather sorrowful groans over the destiny of those who will not heed God's Word.

Woeful Overloading (v. 46)

Jesus' initial punch went right to the heart of the issue: "Woe to you lawyers also! For you load people with burdens hard to bear" (v. 46a). The lawyers ladened the people with laws manufactured from the sacred text and designed to provide a protective crust for the Law. Eventually this crust became no less than six thousand laws—a smothering incrustation!

Among the most notorious of these laws were those created to protect the fourth commandment ("Remember the Sabbath day, to keep it holy. Six days you shall labor, and do all your work, but the seventh day is a Sabbath to the LORD your God. On it you shall not do any work," Exodus 20:8–10a). To ensure that no work was performed on the Sabbath, the *Mishnah* listed thirty-nine classifications of labor, with each category capable of endless subdivision (M. Shabbath 7:2). For example, one of the thirty-nine categories forbade the carrying of burdens on the Sabbath and hedged it with minute prohibitions for every occasion. This section declared that anything equal to or heavier than a dried fig was a burden. So it was permissible to carry something that weighed less than a dried fig on the Sabbath. But if one inadvertently put it down and then picked it up, he would be counted as doubling the weight and thus breaking the Sabbath!

The *Mishnah* also specified that there were permissible ways to carry burdens. On the Sabbath if a man carries a burden

> in his right hand or in his left hand, in his bosom or on his shoulder, he is culpable; for this last was the manner of carrying of the sons of Kohath. If [he took it out] on the back of his hand or with his foot or with his mouth or with his elbow, or in his ear or in his hair or in his wallet [carried] mouth downwards, or between his wallet and his shirt, or in the hem of his shirt, or in his shoe or in his sandal, he is not culpable since he has not taken it out after the fashion of them that take out [a burden]. (M. Shabbath 10:3)

These and other petty regulations were made even more burdensome by the rabbinical reasoning stating that while it was a serious matter to offend the Mosaic Law that was sometimes hard to understand, it was an even greater offense to offend against the scribal interpretations that made everything so clear (M. Sanhedrin 11:3)! Thus life had become impossible for the average Israelite in Jesus' day. Oppressive religion took the spring from his footsteps.

And to make matters worse, the creators of these laws did not care about the heavy burden they had created. "And you yourselves do not touch the burdens with one of your fingers" (v. 46b). If the scribal lawyers truly believed their extra laws were beneficial, they should have given the people encouragement and support in shouldering the load. Instead they were inclined to despise the ordinary people who found it difficult to understand the lawyers' religious demands, let alone keep them.

Jesus' initial woe to the experts in the Law echoes tellingly down through the corridors of the last twenty centuries and rightly falls on us today. We must beware of all expressions of Christianity that place tradition on an equal footing with the Scriptures. Their accretions invariably obscure the Word and place un-Biblical regulations on their followers. And the problem is not only "out there"—it is also often found in evangelical churches where gurus and their new systems are continually embraced as having the key to effective Christian living. We must ever beware of anything that separates us from primary exposure to God's Word and anything that encrusts God's Word, no matter how appealingly it is packaged or marketed.

When Jesus later said, "Come to me, all who labor and are heavy laden, and I will give you rest. Take my yoke upon you, and learn from me, for I am gentle and lowly in heart, and you will find rest for your souls. For my yoke is easy, and my burden is light" (Matthew 11:28–30), he was issuing an invitation to people who were loaded down with the traditions and additions of the scribes and Pharisees. In point of fact, those who come to Christ do take on a burden, but the "burden is light" because it is the proper burden for every soul. What about the scribes' many additions? No soul was ever meant to bear them.

Rather than such a burden, we are to give ourselves to the reading and study of the Word of God.

> His delight is in the law of the LORD,
> and on his law he meditates day and night.
> He is like a tree
> planted by streams of water
> that yields its fruit in its season,
> and its leaf does not wither.
> In all that he does, he prospers. (Psalm 1:2, 3)

It is a woeful thing to have the Word taken away by human encrustations, no matter how well intended.

Woeful Memorializing (vv. 47–51)

The immensity of Jesus' indictment left the lawyers off balance, their minds reeling futilely for rejoinders. Then came the next blow, which at first hearing seems rather unfair: "Woe to you! For you build the tombs of the prophets whom your fathers killed. So you are witnesses and you consent to the deeds of your fathers, for they killed them, and you build their tombs" (vv. 47, 48). Why does Jesus rebuke them for building tombs for past prophets whom they admired? Or perhaps they built the tombs as public declarations that their forefathers' murders of the prophets were wrong and to distance themselves from their deeds. So why would Jesus say that their building tombs for the prophets was a testimony that they approved of their murder? Was he being unfair?

Yes, the scribes and their cohorts built tombs to celebrate the dead prophets. But as the following context about their murderous treatment of present prophets shows, their building of tombs for ancient martyrs was an unwitting celebration of those murders! The true sense of Jesus' words is: "They killed the prophets: you make sure they are dead."[1] Or "You build great tombs to insure that the prophets will never return to trouble the living."[2] Jesus charged them with completing the work of those who killed the prophets. They were in partnership with the prophet killers. This hurt big time, like a punch on the nose.

They were also Word killers because the essential function of a prophet is to deliver God's Word—"Thus says the Lord . . ." These "lawyers," who ostensibly loved the Word so much that they gave their lives to its study and preservation, were actually murderers of the Word—they made it impossible for the people to hear the Word of the Lord. Their actions then and in the near future would show them for what they were. Jesus made a prophecy[3] about this in the next verse when he said: "Therefore also the Wisdom of God said, 'I will send them prophets and apostles, some of whom they will kill and persecute'" (v. 49). The way they would treat the prophets and apostles associated with Jesus would prove what kind of men the scribes really were. The punch vibrated with a sweeping declaration of their immense guilt:

> So that the blood of all the prophets, shed from the foundation of the world, may be charged against this generation, from the blood of Abel to the blood of Zechariah,[4] who perished between the altar and the sanctuary. Yes, I tell you, it will be required of this generation. (vv. 50, 51)

Would Jesus' own generation, a single generation, be judged for the accumulated blood of all the prophets slain in multiple millennia before they were born? That is in fact what Jesus said. But why did he say this?

Jesus' contemporaries comprised the most privileged of all generations in Israel's history. They possessed the accumulated witness of all the prophets. God had sent them the greatest prophet ever—John the Baptist. And then he sent the Messiah himself—the Word of God preaching the Word! Along with him came the Christian apostles who lived out the exhortation to "Preach the word" (2 Timothy 4:2). The apostolic preaching of the cross was a more glorious statement of the gospel than any previous generation had ever heard. And when Jesus' generation rejected it, they demonstrated that they were partners with their forefathers in killing the prophets. Indeed, they were far more guilty than their ancestors because they rejected the Word preached by greater prophets and apostles.

This was a lethal punch! "You experts in the Law, you legal wordsmiths, you self-appointed interpreters and keepers of the Word, are in fact Word-killers! And you will be held responsible for it all." They would answer at the final judgment. But between then and that final day, so all could see this principle at work, judgment fell on Jerusalem in AD 70 and again in 135 when the temple was destroyed, and the people deported, and Jerusalem became a Gentile city (cf. 21:20–24; 1 Thessalonians 2:14–16).

We will all answer at the judgment. If their responsibility was great, how much more is ours who have the entire corpus of the Word of God (both the Old and New Testaments) and have had the preaching of that same Word for the last two thousand years. We Americans love to avoid responsibility. As Will Rogers once remarked: "There are two eras in American history—the passing of the buffalo and the passing of the buck." Or as a more contemporary "person" put it—Calvin to Hobbes: "Nothing I do is my fault. . . . I love the culture of victimhood." To which Hobbes sagely replies, "One of us needs to stick his head in a bucket of ice water." We need to keep our minds and hearts in the Word as obedient children.

Woeful Deprivation (v. 52)

Our Lord's final swipe at the experts in the Law was perhaps the most telling of all: "Woe to you lawyers! For you have taken away the key of knowledge. You did not enter yourselves, and you hindered those who were entering" (v. 52). They had taken "the key of knowledge," the Scriptures, away from the average people through their scribal encrustations. Sadly, the experts in the Law were outside the kingdom and had made it immeasurably more difficult for others to find entrance as well.

This woe falls heavily upon those of us who are professional clergy. Pastors must make sure that they keep the Word, "the key of knowledge," before their people. We must take care that we preach the Word and not succumb to merely preaching about the Word. We must be like Paul who said, "I became a minister [of the church] according to the stewardship from God that was given to me for you, to make the word of God fully known" (Colossians 1:25). The opening of God's Word was at the heart of Paul's passion for ministry, and the same should drive us. We have all had the experience of hearing a text read and waiting in anticipation for its exposition, only to have the preacher depart from it never to return. Many of us have also listened to a preacher do a series of sermons that, regardless of the text used, all ended up sounding nearly the same because he coated every sermon with his favorite texts. Other sermons remain in the parameters of the text, even quoting it occasionally, but never really deal with the text in either the broader context of the book or in the immediate context. There has been little thinking, no rigor, and little work put into such a message. It does not take God's Word seriously.

Preaching is not exposition if it views the text through the lens of a personal agenda—say, a patriotic lens or a therapeutic lens or a social lens—so that one's sermons, regardless of text, are characterized by, for example, political chauvinism or a repeated emphasis on wellness or a narrowly defined social issue. We must free the Word from our scribal accretions, be they ever so evangelical, and let God's Word say what it says.

God's Word to preachers is: "Do your best to present yourself to God as one approved, a worker who has no need to be ashamed, rightly handling the word of truth" (2 Timothy 2:15). And, "I charge you in the presence of God and of Christ Jesus, who is to judge the living and the dead, and by his appearing and his kingdom: preach the word; be ready in season and out of season" (2 Timothy 4:1, 2).

There is also a warning here for the nonclergy—see to it that you do not take "the key of knowledge" away from yourselves. I am an incorrigible bibliophile with a library of perhaps six thousand books, but I am convinced that we must not allow books about the Book to so encrust our lives that the Word of God is effectively nullified. For example, there are thousands of books on marriage and family (Barbara and I wrote one of them). But if they become our sole fare, we may end up seeing child discipline in John 3:16 or gender roles in passages about the great tribulation!

Even in serious Bible study, we must maintain the necessary focus. The eminent Karl Barth gave this advice:

> The Bible is like a love-letter . . . and should be read in the same way. If the letter is written in a foreign language, the lover will need to decipher

> it with the aid of a dictionary, but he will regard the toil of translation as an irritating delay to the reading of the letter, a necessary evil, and he will certainly not imagine that he is reading the letter while he is still translating it. Therefore, "If thou art a learned man, then take care lest with all thy erudite reading (which is not reading God's Word) thou forgettest perchance to read God's Word."[5]

We need to be very careful to be people that give primary exposure to God's Word—in the pulpit and in our personal lives. We must be people primarily of one Book. We must be John Bunyans. If there is one goal I would like to reach through long years of ministry, it is to form a group of people who know when they hear the Word preached and who know when they do not hear it preached—people who are discerning. I would like to leave behind a legacy of people who read many books but who are people of one Book. If that happens, the future will be very bright.

Closing Reflections

The Lord Jesus rained mighty blows upon the experts in the Law, but they were gracious woes. Their shocking and uncompromising ferocity was an attempt to get their hearers' attention. Jesus wants us to be people of the Word. That was his concern through the entire conflict.

> As he said these things, a woman in the crowd raised her voice and said to him, "Blessed is the womb that bore you, and the breasts at which you nursed!" But he said, "Blessed rather are those who hear the word of God and keep it!" (11:27, 28)

> The queen of the South will rise up at the judgment with the men of this generation and condemn them, for she came from the ends of the earth to hear the wisdom of Solomon, and behold, something greater than Solomon is here. (11:31)

> Therefore be careful lest the light in you be darkness. (11:35)

57

Confessing Christ

LUKE 11:53—12:12

BECAUSE THE INCIDENT that sparked Jesus' woeful warnings happened at the beginning of the meal, most of the participants probably left their food untouched. If the event had taken place today, the dessert of choice would have been generous amounts of Tums or Rolaids! To say that the Pharisees and lawyers were upset would be an understatement. They were enraged! "As he went away from there, the scribes and the Pharisees began to press him hard and to provoke him to speak about many things, lying in wait for him, to catch him in something he might say" (11:53, 54). The establishment would hunt Jesus like a wild animal. They had had enough!

At the same time Jesus' notoriety was drawing vast, dangerously enthusiastic throngs. The press of the people was so great that Luke says they were actually "trampling one another" (12:1a). The combination of the Pharisees' terrifying pursuit of Jesus and the jostling, unruly crowd made it dangerous to associate with Jesus. This mounting pressure had the effect of making some of the disciples less than open about their relationship with Jesus. Some hid their allegiance, succumbing to disgraceful and ultimately untenable spiritual hypocrisy. Some even denied him.

In the midst of the rising confusion, Jesus "began to [speak] to his disciples first" (v. 1b). He addressed his own, but those nearby in the pressing crowd also heard what he said and passed it on to the rest.[1] He gave his followers a sequence of forceful reasons why they should maintain their bold, public confession of him. The reasons still hold today with undiminished force.

A Good Confession and Full Disclosure (vv. 1–3)

As he began, Jesus was most direct: "Beware of the leaven of the Pharisees, which is hypocrisy" (v. 1c). Hypocrisy means playing a part, engaging in pretense. It demands conscious insincerity. It is a character sin, a moral deficiency. And it comes naturally to every one of us. Sir Arthur Conan Doyle of Sherlock Holmes fame used to playfully tell a bogus tale about how he sent a telegram to each of twelve friends, all men of great virtue, reputation, and considerable position in society. The message simply said: "Fly at once, all is discovered." Within twenty-four hours, Doyle says, all twelve had left the country! This is playful but penetrating humor, as some uneasy smiles may attest.

The Pharisees' hypocrisy lay in their elaborate ritual piety that served as a veneer for their sinful, contaminated, and contaminating souls. But the pretense of the disciples had a different twist. For them it meant downplaying the level of their commitment to Christ. Hypocrisy always functions on the principle of corruption: it sours the dough with which it is mixed, causing a swelling ferment. It works slowly but inflates the human spirit with swelling rot.

"Beware," says Jesus to his disciples, "of the leaven of the Pharisees, which is hypocrisy." Why? "Nothing is covered up that will not be revealed, or hidden that will not be known. Therefore whatever you have said in the dark shall be heard in the light, and what you have whispered in private rooms shall be proclaimed on the housetops" (vv. 2, 3). Full disclosure will come on judgment day. Everything will be revealed, and the disclosure will be ruthless. The things whispered invisibly in the dark will be shouted in full light from the rooftops. The limitless capacities of divine omniscience assure perfect exposure of hypocrisy.

Jesus was warning them to avoid exposure at the judgment by owning up to what they really were then and by letting God make their lives pleasing to him.

A Good Confession and Fear (vv. 4–7)

Proper Fear

Jesus knew that the pretense of some of his followers who had succumbed to hypocrisy came from fear of what the Pharisees and their comrades would do to them. So he went on: "I tell you, my friends, do not fear those who kill the body, and after that have nothing more that they can do. But I will warn you whom to fear: fear him who, after he has killed, has authority to cast into hell. Yes, I tell you, fear him!" (vv. 4, 5). In other words, fear God. A proper fear of God will free us from improper fears of men.

When Martin Luther first stood before the Diet at Worms, John Eck, the Archbishop of Trier, asked him, "Martin Luther, do you recant of the heresies in your writings? . . . Do you defend them all, or do you care to reject a part?" Luther gave the quiet answer, "This touches God and His word. This affects the salvation of souls. Of this Christ said, 'He who denies me before men, him will I deny before the Father.' To say too little or too much would be dangerous. I beg you, give me time to think it over."[2]

Luther asked for twenty-four hours to consider the situation. Eck and the whole assembly were amazed. How could the supreme intellectual leader of this movement ask for more time to think? Was he succumbing to fear? Roland Bainton, the great Lutheran historian, answers, "Anyone who recalls Luther's tremors at his first Mass will scarcely so interpret this hesitation. Just as then he wished to flee from the altar, so now he was too terrified before God to give answer to the emperor."[3]

That night Luther and his colleagues passionately called out to God in now-celebrated prayers. With the rising of the sun another, larger hall was chosen, and it was so crowded that scarcely anyone except the emperor could sit. Eck spoke long and eloquently in the flickering candlelight, concluding, "I ask you, Martin—answer candidly and without horns—do you or do you not repudiate your books and the errors which they contain?"[4]

Luther *contra mundum* spoke, and his voice rang. He spoke first in German and then in Latin:

> Since then Your Majesty and your lordships desire a simple reply, I will answer without horns and without teeth. Unless I am convicted by Scripture and plain reason—I do not accept the authority of popes and councils, for they have contradicted each other—my conscience is captive to the Word of God. I cannot and I will not recant anything, for to go against conscience is neither right nor safe. God help me. Amen.[5]

At that towering moment Luther's massive fear of God freed him from the smaller fear of men!

When the Scottish reformer John Knox was lowered to his grave, it was declared: "Here lies one who feared God so much that he never feared the face of man."[6]

Fear of God is desperately needed in today's church. Wise Solomon concluded his prologue to the book of Proverbs by declaring, "The fear of the LORD is the beginning of knowledge" (Proverbs 1:7). Solomon saw this as the key to all living—and it is. Believing this implicitly, Joseph Bayly defined fear of God by saying:

> "Awe: Emotion in which dread, veneration, and wonder are variously mingled, as: (a) a profound and humbly fearful reverence inspired by deity or by something sacred or mysterious; (b) wondering reverence tinged with fear inspired by the sublime" (*Webster's*). Biblical use: "Let all the earth fear the LORD; Let all the inhabitants of the world stand in awe of Him." (Psalm 33:8 NASB)

Then he added: "*Awe* was damaged in the churches, destroyed by the electronic church. Awe has been replaced by good feelings toward oneself and God, by a happy-face image of God."[7]

How we need this wholesome fear that Jesus commended to his disciples. We need Moses' fear before the burning bush when with trembling hands he removed his sandals and "hid his face, for he was afraid to look at God" (Exodus 3:6). We need Isaiah's fear who cried out, "Woe is me! For I am lost; for I am a man of unclean lips, and . . . my eyes have seen the King, the LORD of hosts!" (Isaiah 6:5). He then rose to gallantly answer, "Here I am! Send me" (Isaiah 6:8). We need a fear like Luther's—the grand liberating fear of God! It is a liberating day when we see God's awesome purity and holiness and our own sin and finiteness—and tremble before God as earth's fears flee.

Secure Fear

Actually, the fear of the Lord is a secure fear, as is indicated by Jesus' immediate enlargement: "Are not five sparrows sold for two pennies? And not one of them is forgotten before God. Why, even the hairs of your head are all numbered. Fear not; you are of more value than many sparrows" (vv. 6, 7). Matthew's parallel account (Matthew 10:29) tells us that two sparrows were sold for a penny. So evidently when two cents' worth were bought, one was thrown in for nothing. But not one of the sparrows (even the freebie) was forgotten by God.

Medical scientists have computed that a blond person has about 145,000 hairs, a dark-haired person 120,000, and a redhead 90,000.[8] God knows how much hair we began with, how much hair we have, and how much will remain at the end of our days. His caring knowledge of us is intimate and detailed.

Jesus urged his followers to consider their comparative value—"Fear not; you are of more value than many sparrows." We are made in the *imago*

Dei, we are the apex of his created order, and we are the objects of his redemption—he gave his life for us. "He who did not spare his own Son but gave him up for us all, how will he not also with him graciously give us all things?" (Romans 8:32). God knows at every moment exactly what is happening to us. "If God's unrestricted providence extends to such minutiae, will it not be concerned also with the disciples of the heaven-sent mouthpiece of God?"[9]

His eye is on the sparrow
And he watches over me.

A Good Confession and an Eternal Choice (vv. 8–10)

Jesus issued two warnings in order to urge his followers to confess him. First, "I tell you, everyone who acknowledges me before men, the Son of Man also will acknowledge before the angels of God, but the one who denies me before men will be denied before the angels of God" (vv. 8, 9).

According to Paul, the inception of authentic faith in Christ involves verbal confession of him: "If you confess with your mouth that Jesus is Lord and believe in your heart that God raised him from the dead, you will be saved. For with the heart one believes and is justified, and with the mouth one confesses and is saved" (Romans 10:9, 10). True faith always moves from the heart to the lips. On the other hand, a lack of desire to confess Christ before others is a warning alarm—do we really have faith? An unwillingness to bear witness may mean we have fooled ourselves—we are not truly children of God.

This is a great concern to Jesus. He said, after Peter's great confession, "Whoever is ashamed of me and of my words, of him will the Son of Man be ashamed when he comes in his glory and the glory of the Father and of the holy angels" (9:26). And the one who gave himself for us says it here again. We must confess him—always!

Jesus' famous and often misunderstood second warning was about blasphemy: "And everyone who speaks a word against the Son of Man will be forgiven, but the one who blasphemes against the Holy Spirit will not be forgiven" (v. 10). What is blasphemy against the Holy Spirit? Helpfully, we know from Matthew and Mark and from an earlier passage in Luke that Jesus made this declaration after the scribes and Pharisees had attributed his cures to Beelzebul, the prince of devils (Matthew 12:31, 32; Mark 3:28, 29; Luke 11:14–26). In other words, they attributed the mighty work of the Holy Spirit to Satan. Jesus said there is no forgiveness for this.

On this occasion Jesus introduced the thought with the assertion that sins against him can be forgiven. This does not mean that such sins are a small thing (see the preceding verses). But sin against his august person can be forgiven. Some blaspheme Christ but then repent—their blasphemy is not their final word. Many blasphemers have been saved. But those who blaspheme the Holy Spirit by attributing his work and witness to Satan are damned. This blasphemy is not so much a matter of blasphemous language but of a conscious, persistent, wicked rejection of the Spirit's witness.[10] It is a setting of the mind against the Spirit of God.[11]

These words were meant to bring a sobering shock to the hearts of those who had been toning down their confession in hopes of escaping the impending trouble. Those with true faith would hear the wake-up call and continue their good confession.

A Good Confession and Divine Help (vv. 11, 12)

Having given these chilling warnings regarding blasphemy against the Spirit, Jesus wanted his followers to embrace the great positive fact that the Holy Spirit is the believer's Helper: "And when they bring you before the synagogues and the rulers and the authorities, do not be anxious about how you should defend yourself or what you should say, for the Holy Spirit will teach you in that very hour what you ought to say" (vv. 11, 12). This text does not excuse a lack of preparation by preachers or Sunday school teachers. One woman told me that her father found preaching "easy"—he never prepared—"the Lord always gave him something to say." Of course, that was in church after church after church! This is not an invitation to neglect preparation and study—it is a promise of divine provision for embattled servants of Christ who find themselves in troublesome situations for his sake. People like the fisherman Peter, who was hauled in before seventy learned doctors of Israel, the Sanhedrin, for healing a cripple in the name of Jesus:

> Then Peter, filled with the Holy Spirit, said to them, "Rulers of the people and elders, if we are being examined today concerning a good deed done to a crippled man, by what means this man has been healed, let it be known to all of you and to all the people of Israel that by the name of Jesus Christ of Nazareth, whom you crucified, whom God raised from the dead—by him this man is standing before you well. This Jesus is the stone that was rejected by you, the builders, which has become the cornerstone. And there is salvation in no one else, for there is no other name under heaven given among men by which we must be saved." Now when they saw the boldness of Peter and John, and perceived that they were uneducated, common men,

> they were astonished. And they recognized that they had been with Jesus. (Acts 4:8–13)

The same phenomenon can be seen in erudite Paul's life when his answers exceeded his considerable abilities before Felix and Festus and Agrippa (cf. Acts 24—26).

Jesus' followers are to be "prepared to make a defense to anyone who asks you for a reason for the hope that is in you" (1 Peter 3:15). But they also face situations they can never prepare for, and the Spirit's astounding grace will sustain them in those situations.

Closing Reflections

Perhaps time pressures or the uncongenial atmosphere of your workaday world or your student world or your social world have made you less than candid about your allegiance to Jesus. Perhaps you see yourself as being in his "secret service." Perhaps you have bought into trite rationalizations such as "I witness with my actions—I don't need to put it into words" or "My faith is a very personal thing." What a tragedy!

Of course we must witness with our actions. And of course we must not share Christ insensitively or rudely or use the pretext of the gospel to work out our unresolved aggressions. But we should consistently and joyfully confess Christ whenever possible—over a business luncheon when a prize account is at stake, to a teacher who holds our academic future in his hands, to an acquaintance who holds the keys to our social acceptance.

If we are professing Christians but do not confess Christ openly, (1) we are hypocrites, and our fermenting insincerity will be ruthlessly proclaimed at the judgment. Or (2) we lack the proper fear of God. We do not see who he is and who we are because if we feared him as we ought, we would not fear to tell men who he is. (3) We also have forgotten our immense worth and the incredible care he gives us, especially as we confess him. Or (4) we have forgotten that to deny him is to be denied in Heaven. Or (5) we do not truly believe the Spirit will help us confess Jesus. But that is his task, and he never fails!

58

The Rich Fool

LUKE 12:13–21

A STORY THAT MY college English professor related to the freshman English class sounded like it had been scripted by Tennessee Williams, but it was her own real-life drama. She and her five sisters had grown up in a small Midwestern town during the Depression where her father, despite the difficulties of the time, rose to become a successful banker. She had gone off to a university, but her sisters stayed close to home, married, and settled down. She likewise married and taught on the West Coast.

When her aging father died, she and her husband hurried home for the funeral. As they comforted her poor mother, they noticed in mute amazement that everything in the house had been tagged by the other sisters with their names—Judy's, Margaret's, Annie's. She and her husband were appalled but said nothing.

The table was set, and dinner was served amid mounting tension and awkward conversation. There were long periods of acrimonious silence. Then her husband stood, stepped behind their mother's chair, and said, "Everyone's tagged what they want. We're placing our tag on what we want." And he placed his hands on their poor mother's shoulders.

Greed is always ugly. Covetousness can turn a family's mutual mourning into an orgy of hatred.

The Would-Be Fool (vv. 13–15)

"Someone in the crowd said to him, 'Teacher, tell my brother to divide the inheritance with me'" (v. 13). The demand here came from an anonymous individual who was so obsessed with getting what he considered his rightful portion of the family inheritance that he rudely accosted Jesus right after

Jesus' passionate call to confess him before men. His interjection was out of sync and disruptive. He didn't ask Jesus for a reasoned decision regarding the fairness of his claim but just demanded, "Tell my brother to divide the inheritance with me."

Jesus didn't like his impertinence at all because he addressed him as "man," as if he were a stranger[1]—"Man, who made me a judge or arbitrator over you?" (v. 14). Jesus would not be drawn into settling domestic accounts. He was not interested in being a divine judge in a "People's Court." One day, of course, he will be the ultimate judge and arbitrator when he returns to judge the quick and the dead, but that was not his task during his three years of earthly ministry. Besides, getting one's legal fair share is not a good thing if one is motivated by a covetous spirit, and Jesus sensed such a spirit here.

A Warning

So Jesus issued a warning, which applies to us all: "Take care, and be on your guard against all covetousness" (v. 15a). The word translated "covetousness" here means the lust to have more than one's fair share, a boundless grasping after more. It describes one who lives in perpetual transgression of the tenth commandment (Exodus 20:17). The book of Proverbs views greed as the dividing line between righteous and evil people: "All day long he [the sluggard] craves and craves, but the righteous gives and does not hold back" (Proverbs 21:26). The Apostle Paul repeatedly condemned greed: "But sexual immorality and all impurity or covetousness must not even be named among you, as is proper among saints" (Ephesians 5:3). To the Ephesian elders he proclaimed, "I coveted no one's silver or gold or apparel" (Acts 20:33). He exhorted the Colossians, "Put to death therefore what is earthly in you: sexual immorality, impurity, passion, evil desire, and covetousness, which is idolatry" (Colossians 3:5).

Jesus specifically warned the "wanna-be" inheritor—in reality, the would-be fool—about material greed. Such a pursuit is a dead-end road. The Bible is clear: "He who loves money will not be satisfied with money, nor he who loves wealth with his income; this also is vanity" (Ecclesiastes 5:10). And as Paul said, "The love of money is a root of all kinds of evils" (1 Timothy 6:10). "Be on your guard against all covetousness." Guard yourself against the lust for more and more money, against coveting your neighbor's clothing, his house, his car, his wife, his education, his position, his children. We must heed the divine warning against "all covetousness."

A Principle

Jesus crowned his warning with a life-giving principle: "One's life does not consist in the abundance of his possessions" (v. 15b).

I grew up in the 1950s, graduating from high school in 1959. I remember my friend Richard Smith's '57 Chevy with idolatrous accuracy. Richard lived three doors down the street from me and was four years older than the rest of us. That Chevy was so beautiful—Campbell's Soup red—its fins sided with a gorgeous swath of etched chrome—its dual exhausts rumbling with that big Chevy V8—white angora-covered dice hanging from the rearview mirror. And Richard made such a cool profile behind the wheel—his perfect flattop haircut, his arm hung nonchalantly over the wheel, his imperial nod as he floated by. After school in the spring when my buddies and I played baseball in the street, Richard Smith would drive home from work, his fine Chevrolet gleaming, and we stood aside reverently as he passed by.

I was sure that life consisted, if not in the "abundance of . . . possessions," at least in one possession—a 1957 Chevrolet Bel Aire coupe! If I owned one of those, I would be significant, important, and certainly cool.

At age fifteen my soul bought into the great materialistic delusion that grips many souls their entire three score and ten years—right to the grave. Flattopped adolescents in '57 Chevys become graying old men in European coupes. Life for them is about an abundance of possessions. Designer clothing to effect the impression of originality and brilliance, significant architecture to house a shrinking frame, imposing porticoes to impress one's guests with one's importance, and a coffin that demonstrates that you knew how to live!

The greedy person lives as if the most important things of life are assured when they have amassed the superfluous. But Jesus said, "One's life does not consist in the abundance of his possessions." Material excess will never make one alive or happy or fulfilled. It is perhaps understandable to be fooled when you are fifteen. But at fifty, or seventy-five? How utterly foolish!

The Rich Fool (vv. 16–21)

Jesus then told the would-be fool, and all who would listen, a parable about a rich fool. "The land of a rich man produced plentifully," he began (v. 16). The rich man was a farmer, but he represents all human beings who are seduced by "all [kinds of] covetousness," whether statesmen or craftsmen or peasants or lawyers or nurses or doctors or secretaries or professors or mechanics or students.[2] He had come by his wealth honestly, like so many of us. He did not cheat to get his fields, he did not devour widows' homes, he was not an abuser of employees. And God had blessed him materially—just the right amount of rain and sun, no disease or pestilence—and huge yields. He was a success in everyone's eyes. New respect came his way. But unknowingly he, like some of us, was in great danger.

Foolish Reasoning

Having a false sense of security because of his financial success, he fell prey to some foolish reasoning: "He thought to himself, 'What shall I do, for I have nowhere to store my crops?' And he said, 'I will do this: I will tear down my barns and build larger ones, and there I will store all my grain and my goods'" (vv. 17, 18). Building new barns was logical and prudent. It was a good idea. But the danger lay in what was missing. There was no thought of sharing, and no thought of stewardship. There was no thought for the poor, the ill, and the naked who were all around him. The language in verses 17–19 reveals an ingrained selfishness. In the Greek the personal pronoun "my" occurs four times and "I" eight times.[3] He was completely self-absorbed. That is why he reached the fateful conclusion, "And I will say to my soul, 'Soul, you have ample goods laid up for many years; relax, eat, drink, be merry'" (v. 19).

This is the only place in the Bible where retirement is spoken of, and here it is in the context of disapproval. Of course, the Bible recognizes aging and slowing down. But retiring to a life of self-indulgence finds no favor with God.

The problem with this man's retirement package is that it was a ticket to hedonism. In the Scriptures, to "eat, drink, be merry" is a description of dissipation (cf. 1 Corinthians 15:32; Ecclesiastes 8:15; Isaiah 22:13). A retirement that lives for self is un-Biblical and immoral. If the rich man had survived that night, he would have gone on to live a life of bored hedonism and perhaps would have ended up like the despairing young woman, exhausted by pleasure, who when told she should simply stop, responded with relief, "You mean I don't have to do what I want to do?"[4]

Hedonism aside, the glaring fault of this foolish man was that he was living as if there was no God. "The fool says in his heart, 'There is no God'" (Psalm 14:1). The man had no fear of God, the grand, liberating fear that Jesus commended in 12:4, 5. And since "the fear of the LORD is the beginning of knowledge" and "wisdom" (Proverbs 1:7; 9:10), he was singularly unequipped for living. This successful man had arrived without ever thinking where his life was heading. He was a parable of modern man.

Moderns do not like to think, and they especially do not like to think metaphysically. A man's thoughts about life are disquieting, so he switches the channel. The thoughts begin again, so he pours a second and third drink. The disquiet creeps in again, and he calls a friend to chat. Again thoughts about life assail him, so he gets out the hunting rifle and polishes it. Nothing like "real life" to clear the mind.

Like so many, this rich man was like an old tree—he was dead inside, even while displaying the vestiges of life.

> And because we know we have breath in our mouth and think we have
> thought in our head,
> We shall assume that we are alive, whereas we are really dead. . . .
> The Lamp of our Youth will be utterly out, but we shall subsist on the
> smell of it,
> And whatever we do, we shall fold our hands and suck our gums and
> think well of it.
> Yes, we shall be perfectly pleased with our work,
> And that is the perfectest Hell of it!
>
> Rudyard Kipling[5]

Wisdom's Answer

"But God said to him, 'Fool! This night your soul is required of you, and the things you have prepared, whose will they be?'" (v. 20). God called him a "fool."

He was a fool because life is short. A sensible person will choose what is best for the long run. He will consider what will be best for him between his twenty-thousandth year and his seventy-thousandth year, not just his three score and ten. The man was a fool because he did not reckon with the fragility of life. This is understandable when you are a child, but when you are thirty, or fifty, or seventy and you live as if what is now will always be, you are a fool and will, Jesus said with certainty, not receive "the things you have prepared."

Closing Reflections

Jesus, the wisdom of God, says to us all: "So is the one who lays up treasure for himself and is not rich toward God" (v. 21). So often the rich, like the wealthy farmer, are lovers of money but are not rich toward God. Indeed, that is precisely why they are rich—every dream and every waking moment is filled with dollar signs. They are greedy. They amass money the old-fashioned way—they hoard it! And very often the rich are not rich toward God because they have built their fortune by taking it from others.

But there are also rich (and poor too) who are "rich toward God" because they use what God has given them for others. The Scriptures celebrate such people—the well-to-do centurion who built a synagogue for God's people—the hospitable home of Mary, Martha, and Lazarus where Jesus found respite—the well-connected women who supported Jesus' ministry. All these wealthy people were rich toward God. The way to become rich toward God is to invest in Christ's church and in the lives of his people.

We can enlarge our savings and build huge accounts to hold it all. We can plan our retirement so we will have nothing to do but change positions in the sun. We can plan our menus for the twilight years so that nothing but the finest cuisine crosses our lips. We can live as if this is all of life. We can laugh our way to the grave—only to discover at the end that we have nothing and are in God's eyes fools.

Or we can be rich toward God because we gave and gave and gave. How are your investments—your heavenly portfolio? Where are your riches? Are you rich toward God?

The domestic concern that elicited the parable suggests a particular warning regarding an overweening demand to get our "fair share." It is so much better to take less than our fair share or to give it away. Squabbling over an inheritance is not worth it. Many, in retrospect, would pay hundreds of thousands of dollars to forego the miseries that came as a result of insisting on their rightful portion. As Christians, we can and should avoid such deadly errors.

The key to all of this is not the adoption of a particular lifestyle, but to give and give and give and give. Because to do so is to invest and invest and invest and invest—to become "rich toward God."

59

Not to Worry

LUKE 12:22–34

THE PRECEDING PARABLE about the folly of the rich fool's greed is intimately connected with the following text, which deals with worry. "Greed can never get enough, worry is afraid it may not have enough."[1] Worry is the emotional reward of material preoccupation.

Don't Worry! (vv. 22, 23)

Jesus understood that worry about the things of life could undo a disciple's career. "And he said to his disciples, 'Therefore I tell you, do not be anxious about your life, what you will eat, nor about your body, what you will put on. For life is more than food, and the body more than clothing'" (vv. 22, 23). Those who chose to be on the road with Jesus necessarily lived on the edge in respect to their food and clothing. If a disciple worried about breakfast, and then when breakfast was provided, thought, *Whew! That's over. Now where will lunch come from?* that disciple would soon become neutralized and spiritually ineffective.

There is a broad application of this truth to all would-be disciples of Jesus in today's culture, because modern culture is neurotic about food, drink, and clothing. TV ads feed our neuroses with alluring images of lithe legs in jeans and painted lips ecstatically downing chips and prunes and libations. Perhaps nothing does this better than airline magazines with their sumptuous beaux arts ads for champagne, antiques, carpets, watches, and "esoteric shopping sprees in Rome." Every product imaginable for the body is promoted—how to tan it, massage it, pamper it, clothe it, drug it, and stimulate it.

Modern culture addresses worries we did not know we had, worries that neutralize our discipleship. But Jesus commands us not to worry about life.

"For life is more than food, and the body more than clothing" (v. 23). We must reject the popular reductionist view of life that claims we are just bodies that need to be fed, watered, clothed, and serviced—putting us on the same level as plants and animals and reducing "God" to our needs. Life is more than a good meal and a new outfit. And it is certainly more than worrying about these things.

Don't Worry about Food (vv. 24–26)

Consider the Birds

Concerning food, Jesus said, "Consider the ravens: they neither sow nor reap, they have neither storehouse nor barn, and yet God feeds them" (v. 24a). The ravens and their little brothers the crows were and are everywhere, in every nation of the world. They are in fact scavengers and in Biblical times were considered unclean (cf. Leviticus 11:15). These insolent, squawking birds know nothing of the prudential habits of a farmer (note the farm language here: "sow . . . reap . . . storehouse . . . barn"), "and yet God feeds them." This does not mean that Jesus' followers are not to work, for in other places the Scriptures employ other animals as examples of hard work. Jesus was merely holding up a common bird that lives according to its God-given capabilities and function and showing that God provides for it.

Consider Yourself

Jesus says in effect, "Consider the birds and then consider yourself"—"Of how much more value are you than the birds!" (v. 24b). We are much more valuable than a bunch of rascally crows, and God will take care of us.

> Said the Robin to the Sparrow,
> "I should really like to know
> Why these anxious human beings
> Rush about and worry so."
> Said the Sparrow to the Robin,
> "Friend, I think that it must be
> They have no Heavenly Father,
> Such as cares for you and me."
>
> Author unknown

Well said. But the actual truth is even more compelling because birds, in the full sense, do not have a heavenly Father. Only we, his children, can call him Father because we bear his image (cf. Genesis 1:26, 27). And because of this, we are more mysterious and complex than anything the Hubble telescope will ever see. We are even more enduring than any young star. And if we know him, we have double paternity. He is our Father-Creator and our Father-Regenerator. So why should we ever worry? Worry insults God and defies reality.

Worry's Absurdity

"And which of you by being anxious can add a single hour to his span of life? If then you are not able to do as small a thing as that, why are you anxious about the rest?" (vv. 25, 26). In truth, worry shortens life and desolates what is left. Kierkegaard said, "No Grand Inquisitor has in readiness such terrible tortures as anxiety."

> Worriers feel every blow
> That never falls
> And they cry over things
> They will never lose.

Worriers fear, worriers suffer, worriers wither and twist and die. Worry takes a terrible toll, and we see it every day—the stammer in midsentence, the distractedness, the missed appointment, the wasted hour in front of the television, the second pack of cigarettes. Worry is not a moral virtue in a disciple of Christ. Worry is not something to be proud of. It is a desiccator, a shriveler.

Don't Worry about Clothing (vv. 27, 28)

Consider the Flowers

Jesus now introduces a second focus: "Consider the lilies, how they grow: they neither toil nor spin, yet I tell you, even Solomon in all his glory was not arrayed like one of these" (v. 27). Most see "lilies" here as referring to the various bright flowers that dot the Palestinian fields in the spring—the scarlet anemone, the Easter daisy, the autumn crocus, the poppies. A bee's-eye view of any of these reveals ravishing beauty, and the tiniest flowers are often the most ornate in their textures and colors. We adorn our walls with their botanic prints. The great American artist Georgia O'Keefe has entranced the world with her sensuous paintings of such flowers. Indeed, Solomon's robes were paupers' rags in comparison.

Is this hyperbole? Not at all! It is certain truth from the lips of the God-man Jesus who picked the flowers of the field, sniffed their fragrance, and looked joyfully at their beauty. The flowers existed without concern or worry, though they were only passing ornaments of the field.

> The grass withers, the flower fades
> when the breath of the LORD blows on it. (Isaiah 40:7)

Consider Yourself

So in light of their magnificent, transitory adornment, Jesus' logic is, "If God so clothes the grass, which is alive in the field today, and tomorrow is thrown into the oven, how much more will he clothe you, O you of little faith!" (v. 28). His followers are not only citizens of earth but of eternity. They are not temporary but eternal. God will certainly see to it that his own are properly clothed.

The "how much more" phrase is a huge argument as to why we are not to worry. Luther quaintly said of the lesson of the flowers: "It seems . . . that the flowers stand there and make us blush and become our teachers. Thank you, flowers, you who are to be devoured by the cows! God has exalted you very highly, that you become our masters and teachers."[2] We are to consider the flowers, then consider ourselves. If we persist in worry, it is because we are "of little faith"—we do not believe God's Word. It is as simple as that! We do not believe he is in control. We do not believe he is capable of taking care of us. We do not believe what his Word tells us about his love and care for his own. Disbelief is the midwife of worry.

A Don't and a Do (vv. 29–32)

Don't!

Jesus again reiterated his command not to worry, with a slight variation: "And do not seek what you are to eat and what you are to drink, nor be worried. For all the nations of the world seek after these things, and your Father knows that you need them" (vv. 29, 30). Worry is intrinsically useless, and especially so for Christians because God knows what we need.

When Lincoln was on his way to Washington to be inaugurated, he spent some time in New York with Horace Greeley and told him an anecdote that was meant to be an answer to the question everybody was asking him: Are we really going to have a civil war? In his circuit-riding days Lincoln and his companions, riding to the next session of court, had crossed many swollen rivers on one particular journey, but the formidable Fox River was still ahead of them. They said one to another, "If these streams give us so much trouble, how shall we get over the Fox River?" When darkness fell, they stopped for the night at a log tavern, where they fell in with the Methodist presiding elder of the district who rode through the country in all kinds of weather and knew all about the Fox River. They gathered about him and asked him about the present state of the river. "Oh, yes," replied the circuit rider, "I know all about the Fox River. I have crossed it often and understand it well. But I have one fixed rule with regard to the Fox River—*I never cross it till I reach it*."[3]

Worry projects the worst: the Fox becomes the mighty Mississippi at flood stage. The worrier is perpetually going unfed and unclothed. Worry loads the present with the weight of the future. And when you load the troubles you are *anticipating* upon the troubles you are presently *experiencing*, you give yourself an impossible burden. As George MacDonald wisely put it: "No man ever sank under the burden of the day. It is when tomorrow's burden is added to the burden of today, that the weight is more than a man can bear." Jesus said just that in his summary statement of the parallel passage in Matthew: "Therefore do not be anxious about tomorrow, for tomorrow will be anxious for itself. Sufficient for the day is its own trouble" (Matthew 6:34).

Obsessive worry about food and clothing is actually pagan. "For all the nations of the world seek after these things," said Jesus (v. 30). We are not to worry. We are to live like Christians, trusting God to take care of us!

Do!

The power to live above worry is found in the famous positive command that Jesus gave next: "Instead, seek his kingdom, and these things will be added to you" (v. 31). The meaning of this remarkable command and promise has suffered unconscionable twisting from evangelical Christians who have wrenched it from its context and used it to justify an overemphasis on material luxury. I once saw an expensive ski boat with Matthew 6:33 emblazoned on the hull. The driver was announcing to the world that he had his ski boat because God was first in his life.

The license plate of a large luxury car I once saw parked in a church parking lot read "TITHE." No one could mistake the message: "I give to God, and God has given this to me. If you gave like I do, you would have one too."

The context of Jesus' promise both here and in Matthew is not about luxuries but life's essentials—food and clothing. We Americans all have many luxuries, but to imagine that we have them because we have sought God's kingdom is a wicked delusion. If that were the case, a Mafia don's luxuries would be the result of his spiritual priorities!

The transcending point of "Seek his kingdom, and these things will be added to you" is that one's liberation from worry about the things of life comes from "seek[ing] his kingdom." Those who make the kingdom of God their foremost aim have no need to worry about life's essentials. If we seek the development of his rule in our lives and the lives of others through the gospel, if we pray and work to this end as good disciples, we need not and will not worry! One's commitment to the kingdom is the key to a life liberated from worry and anxiety.

In point of fact, Jesus' followers already have the kingdom: "Fear not, little flock, for it is your Father's good pleasure to give you the kingdom" (v. 32). The benefits are ours already, and they ought to liberate us from fear and worry about material things—and will loosen the grip of possessions upon us too.

Give (vv. 33, 34)

Jesus concluded his teaching by exhorting his followers to a life of *giving* as the crowning liberation from worry over things.

Divest

He told his disciples to "Sell your possessions, and give to the needy. Provide yourselves with moneybags that do not grow old, with a treasure in the heavens that does not fail, where no thief approaches and no moth destroys" (v. 33). The disciples were on the road with Jesus and, like Jesus himself, had no place to lay their heads (cf. 9:58). Jesus had left his trade behind, and so had they. They were ex-fishermen and craftsmen for the most part. Their giving away of virtually everything they had had liberated them to go anywhere Jesus went.

There are times when Christ calls believers to give up everything, to totally disengage from their old lives to follow him. Barbara and I have some friends who did this as newlyweds. The young bride was concerned about her husband's languid spiritual life. He was a professor at the University of Minnesota and was quite content to do nothing with his faith—even attend church. So she prayed fervently for his soul but got more than she bargained for when he came home and said:

> I've been reading the Bible where it says, "Sell your possessions and give to the poor. Provide purses for yourselves that will not wear out, a treasure in heaven that will not be exhausted, where no thief comes near and no moth destroys" (v. 33), and I think we should do it!

Then she really started praying! Though this was a radical step, they did it. They sold everything except a few changes of clothing, bought a double sleeping bag, and hit the road for Jesus. They eventually ended up in Albuquerque where they were mightily used to evangelize the sixties generation. Today they own a home and live very conventionally, but they are characterized by constant ministry and reaching out to others.

All of us are called to divest ourselves. For a few it may be like the couple just mentioned—on the road with Jesus and his disciples. For others, it means to loosen your grip on your possessions, to hold everything loosely, to share what you have, to use your possessions to serve others, and to give—"Provide yourselves with moneybags that do not grow old, with a treasure in the heavens that does not fail, where no thief approaches and no moth destroys" (v. 33). Heavenly treasure will endure—heavenly purses will never spring holes. Such is the treasure that a generous lifestyle stores up.

We are to be generous with everything—our money, our homes, our possessions, our luxuries, our time, our lives. Everything we have must be committed to Christ. If you have never done it before, pray through all you have, giving everything to God, especially your most treasured possessions. Put everything at his feet, so he can use it as he desires.

Invest

Jesus concluded with impeccable logic, "For where your treasure is, there will your heart be also" (v. 34). Heart and treasure always go together. Your heart, the center of your being, is where your valuables, your energies, your time, all the things you value most, are.

Where is your heart? In your barns and storehouses? In a Swiss bank account? On the golf course? In your home? In your kitchen? In your yard? In your wardrobe? In your car?

Or is it in Heaven? In your church? In the inner city? In the poor? In Africa or China or South America or the islands of the sea?

If it is there, you have no worries!

60

Be Ready

LUKE 12:35–48

ARNOLD T. OLSON WROTE:

> Ever since the first days of the Christian church, evangelicals have been "looking for that blessed hope, and the glorious appearing of the great God and our Savior Jesus Christ." They may have disagreed as to its timing and to the events on the eschatological calendar. They may have differed as to a pre-tribulation or post-tribulation rapture—the pre- or post- or non-millennial coming. They may have been divided as to a literal rebirth of Israel. However, all are agreed that the final solution to the problems of this world is in the hands of the King of kings who will someday make the kingdoms of this world his very own.[1]

This agreement regarding the sure return of Jesus Christ to judge the living and the dead comes from the overwhelming evidence of Scripture. There are 260 chapters in the New Testament, and Christ's return is mentioned no less than 318 times in those chapters. Statistically, one verse in twenty-five mentions the Lord's return. The only books that don't mention the second advent are Galatians (which is focused on refuting the Judaizers) and the tiny letters of 2 and 3 John.[2]

Jesus himself spoke often of his return. He followed up his challenge to take up his cross and follow him by warning, "Whoever is ashamed of me and of my words in this adulterous and sinful generation, of him will the Son of Man also be ashamed when he comes in the glory of his Father with the holy angels" (Mark 8:38). Later, in the Olivet Discourse, he announced, "And then they will see the Son of Man coming in clouds with great power and glory. And then he will send out the angels and gather his elect from the four winds, from the ends of the earth to the ends of heaven"

(Mark 13:26, 27). In the upper room on the eve of his death he promised, "And if I go and prepare a place for you, I will come again and will take you to myself, that where I am you may be also" (John 14:3).

Paul's letters abound with references to Jesus' return. For example, he encouraged the Philippians by saying, "But our citizenship is in heaven, and from it we await a Savior, the Lord Jesus Christ, who will transform our lowly body to be like his glorious body, by the power that enables him even to subject all things to himself" (Philippians 3:20, 21). He later told the Thessalonians:

> For the Lord himself will descend from heaven with a cry of command, with the voice of an archangel, and with the sound of the trumpet of God. And the dead in Christ will rise first. Then we who are alive, who are left, will be caught up together with them in the clouds to meet the Lord in the air, and so we will always be with the Lord. Therefore encourage one another with these words. (1 Thessalonians 4:16–18)

The apostle John begins the book of Revelation with the warning, "Behold, he is coming with the clouds, and every eye will see him, even those who pierced him, and all tribes of the earth will wail on account of him. . . . 'I am the Alpha and the Omega,' says the Lord God, 'who is and who was and who is to come, the Almighty'" (Revelation 1:7, 8).

The Scriptures shout that Christ is coming again. Peter called this a "living hope" (1 Peter 1:3). And Paul termed it "our blessed hope, the appearing of the glory of our great God and Savior Jesus Christ" (Titus 2:13). How perfectly sweet this is!

At this point in the Gospel of Luke, we find the first extended teachings on the second coming as Jesus warned his followers to be ready. The positioning of this warning in the flow of Luke's context is very natural and revealing. By recounting the parable of the rich fool, Jesus warned against material greed. He followed this with the exalted warning not to worry over material things. And now Christ challenged his hearers to be ready for his return. Jesus saw readiness for his return as the antidote to greed and worry.

How to Be Ready (vv. 35–40)

Like a Faithful Servant

Jesus recommended a manner of readiness like that of faithful, devoted servants: "Stay dressed for action and keep your lamps burning, and be like men who are waiting for their master to come home from the wedding feast, so that they may open the door to him at once when he comes and knocks" (vv. 35, 36).

A Hebrew wedding celebration could last several days, so that the time of a master's return could be anyone's guess. But the uncertainty did not put off these excellent servants. Though it was late at night, they were "dressed for action." That is, they not only remained fully clothed in daytime wear, but they had their waists girded, with their long robes tucked under their belts, making it possible for them to move quickly to the door. They were prepared.

The night was also kept bright because they vigilantly replenished the oil in their lamps and trimmed the wicks for maximum light. They were awake and alert. These servants were remarkable. They did not give in to fatigue, they displayed no irritable grouchiness, they did not have an "attitude." Rather, they kept a bright house and bare legs so they could spring up to give their master a joyous reception.

That is how Jesus' followers are to wait for him. It is not to be a passive, lethargic wait but one filled with active service, continual preparation, and joyous anticipation.

What a lovely scene greeted the returning master. Warm light streamed from the windows, breathless, smiling, eager servants bearing shining lamps gathered at the door, and no doubt there was a choice nocturnal snack on the table (my revisionist mind imagines peanut butter cookies and milk). "Welcome home, master! We're all so glad you're back. Here, give us your robe. Sit down. Let us wash your feet. You must be so tired."

This was lovely indeed. But even better was what happened to the servants! Jesus went on: "Blessed are those servants whom the master finds awake when he comes. Truly, I say to you, he will dress himself for service and have them recline at table, and he will come and serve them" (v. 37). The master was so moved by their faithfulness that instead of sitting down at the table, he dressed himself to wait on them (the same word in Greek as when the servants were "dressed for action"), made them recline around the table, and served them! What joy is portrayed in this night feast! The girded, bare-legged master setting dishes before his servants, refilling their cups, happy—even uproarious—conversation floating from the well-lit house.

Several months later in the upper room in Jerusalem, when the Lord stripped himself and wrapped a towel about his waist and washed the feet of the Twelve (cf. John 13:1–17), they were witnesses to an action that was both *symbolic* of his work in the incarnation and *prophetic* of the messianic meal at the inauguration of the kingdom—the wedding supper of the Lamb. At that meal "people will come from east and west, and from north and south, and recline at table in the kingdom of God. And behold, some are last who will be first, and some are first who will be last" (13:29, 30). The future celebration is described in Revelation in unstinted terms:

> Then I heard what seemed to be the voice of a great multitude, like the roar of many waters and like the sound of mighty peals of thunder, crying out,
>
> "Hallelujah!
> For the Lord our God
>   the Almighty reigns.
> Let us rejoice and exult
>   and give him the glory,
> for the marriage of the Lamb has come,
>   and his Bride has made herself ready;
> it was granted her to clothe herself
>   with fine linen, bright and pure"—
>
> for the fine linen is the righteous deeds of the saints.
>
> And the angel said to me, "Write this: Blessed are those who are invited to the marriage supper of the Lamb." (Revelation 19:6–9)

That passage helps us understand Jesus' words in verse 38: "If he comes in the second watch, or in the third, and finds them awake, blessed are those servants!" (v. 38). Those who have had to wait until the second watch (10:00 p.m. to 2:00 a.m.) or third watch (2:00 a.m. to 6:00 a.m.)[3]—the world's very last time period before the return of Christ—are nevertheless blessed!

We will be blessed if we are "awake"—that is, serving and ready to serve—dressed for action, the lights on. Why? Because we are going to sit down at the feast of feasts as guests of the King of kings. Eternity is no sterile, plastic, nickel-plated existence. It is a sumptuous feast. It is laughter. It is jubilation and intimate fellowship eternally!

Those who are ready for Christ's return are not lolling around lethargically, nor are they sitting on the church steps dressed in white robes. They are alive and active, serving Christ. Are you ready?

Like a Wise Homeowner

The other analogy Jesus employed to urge readiness for his return was that of a wise homeowner: "But know this, that if the master of the house had known at what hour the thief was coming, he would not have left his house to be broken into. You also must be ready, for the Son of Man is coming at an hour you do not expect" (vv. 39, 40).

Among all the sayings of Jesus, there are none that are more clearly evidenced in the writings of the apostles. Paul wrote, "For you yourselves are fully aware that the day of the Lord will come like a thief in the night. While people are saying, 'There is peace and security,' then sudden destruction will come upon them as labor pains come upon a pregnant woman, and they will not escape. But you are not in darkness, brothers, for that day to surprise you like a thief" (1 Thessalonians 5:2–4).

Peter used similar language: "But the day of the Lord will come like a thief, and then the heavens will pass away with a roar, and the heavenly bodies will be burned up and dissolved, and the earth and the works that are done on it will be exposed" (2 Peter 3:10).

The risen Lord himself said, "Remember, then, what you received and heard. Keep it, and repent. If you will not wake up, I will come like a thief, and you will not know at what hour I will come against you" (Revelation 3:3). And, "Behold, I am coming like a thief! Blessed is the one who stays awake, keeping his garments on, that he may not go about naked and be seen exposed!" (Revelation 16:15).

The celebrated Scottish preacher of the last century, Robert Murray McCheyne of Dundee, who exercised so much influence during his brief twenty-nine years, used to ask groups of pastors the question, "Do you think the Lord is coming tonight?" The preachers would quietly respond, "No." Then McCheyne would counter with a quote from our text, "The Son of Man is coming at an hour you do not expect" (v. 40). It was a trick question and a bit unfair because to say that this day, out of the three-quarters of a million since the resurrection, is the day is quite bold. On the other hand, we live 750,000 days closer to the return, and indeed Christ's return will always be on a statistically improbable day, when the world doesn't expect him. There is a sense in which humbly saying, "I don't think he will come back tonight" increases the likelihood that it will be tonight, though of course no one knows when he will return.

The point is, Jesus' return will be unexpected, like a thief in the night, and the world will not be prepared! The networks will not be prepared, the world's leaders will not be prepared, the false religions will not be prepared, and most of the church will not be prepared. But the faithful will be ready because they will see the signs of the times (12:54–59; 21:25–36). They will be ready because they have obeyed the Word and wait "for our blessed hope, the appearing of the glory of our great God and Savior Jesus Christ" (Titus 2:13). They will be ready because their sleeves are rolled up and the lights are on as they labor for Christ.

Jesus could come today, and perhaps he will!

The Consequences of One's State of Readiness (vv. 41–48)

This was electrifying teaching, and the disciples' minds were reeling at the implications. So Peter asked a question they were all thinking: "Lord, are you telling this parable for us or for all?" (v. 41). Jesus' subsequent answer revealed that the parable was for the Twelve—and then for others who would subsequently exercise authority over God's people.

Reward for Wise and Faithful Servants

The Lord said reward would be given to the ready, the wise, and the faithful:

> Who then is the faithful and wise manager, whom his master will set over his household, to give them their portion of food at the proper time? Blessed is that servant whom his master will find so doing when he comes. Truly, I say to you, he will set him over all his possessions. (vv. 42–44)

In simplest English, the servant of Christ who has been faithful in his *temporary* earthly responsibilities will at Christ's return be given vast *permanent* authority in the eternal state. This principle is again highlighted in the parable of the ten minas in 19:15–17:

> When he returned, having received the kingdom, he ordered these servants to whom he had given the money to be called to him, that he might know what they had gained by doing business. The first came before him, saying, "Lord, your mina has made ten minas more." And he said to him, "Well done, good servant! Because you have been faithful in a very little, you shall have authority over ten cities."

As to the nature of the enlarged eternal authority, we do not know exactly what that means. But we can be sure it will be joyous, because to do his bidding will be the delectable food and drink of the redeemed.

I am reminded of the earthly servanthood of John Broadus, the faithful president of Southern Baptist Seminary during the Civil War. At war's end the seminary had four professors and seven students, and one of those was blind. Only the blind student took Broadus's course on preaching. Under such circumstances, many teachers would have been tempted to give less than their best. But not Dr. Broadus, who gave painstaking care to every lecture. Those magnificent lectures became the substance for the most famous and influential of all books on homiletics in American history, *The Preparation and Delivery of Sermons*. Broadus's authority was increased because he was a faithful servant. But that is only the beginning of the story. The final story is being written now, as Broadus serves Christ in the final estate.

Punishment for Foolish and Unfaithful Servants

Of course, not all servants are faithful and wise, so Jesus addressed their plight as well:

> But if that servant says to himself, "My master is delayed in coming," and begins to beat the male and female servants, and to eat and drink and get drunk, the master of that servant will come on a day when he does not expect him and at an hour he does not know, and will cut him in pieces and put him with the unfaithful. (vv. 45, 46)

The "servant" here has not simply been lazy or indolent but monstrously unfaithful—a drunken glutton who beats not only men but women—an abuser of both divine trust and human life. His life is a grotesque perversion. When the master (Jesus) returns, the cruel servant suffers a grisly end, and Christ pronounces him to be "unfaithful."

Those in Christian leadership may profess what they will. They can use every Christian cliché, hold the Bible like Billy Graham and say "The Bible says," build a following in wide Christian circles, but if that man or woman consistently behaves in an unchristian way, he or she is not a true believer. Paul told the Ephesians: "For you may be sure of this, that everyone who is sexually immoral or impure, or who is covetous (that is, an idolater), has no inheritance in the kingdom of Christ and God. Let no one deceive you with empty words, for because of these things the wrath of God comes upon the sons of disobedience. Therefore do not become partners with them" (Ephesians 5:5–7). And listen to the apostle John: "By this it is evident who are the children of God, and who are the children of the devil: whoever does not practice righteousness is not of God, nor is the one who does not love his brother" (1 John 3:10).

Everything will be revealed when Jesus returns, so we must make sure our life matches our profession. Everything will be put right, and the truth will be known at last! There will be justice on earth.

Just Punishment

Jesus tells us that ultimate justice will be exquisitely meted out: "And that servant who knew his master's will but did not get ready or act according to his will, will receive a severe beating. But the one who did not know, and did what deserved a beating, will receive a light beating" (vv. 47, 48). Some people by virtue of their greater knowledge, age, experience, and influence in the church will suffer far greater penalty for the same sin than an ignorant person will. James rightly warned, "Not many of you should become teachers, my brothers, for you know that we who teach will be judged with greater strictness" (James 3:1). Equity at the end of this unfair world is a delectable thought. Praise God that he is such a judge that nothing will get by him. Praise him for his fairness. And, of course, praise him for his grace—our only hope.

A Just Proverb

Jesus summed it all up in a famous proverb: "Everyone to whom much was given, of him much will be required, and from him to whom they entrusted much, they will demand the more" (v. 48b). We have so much. We have the word of the Old Testament, the word of the prophets, the word of the covenants. We have the word of the New Testament, the revelation of the incarnation, the gospel of grace, the life and teachings of Jesus, the apostolic witness and teaching. We have two thousand years of the church's testimony. We have abundant preaching. We have Christian education. We have thousands of books. We have a wealth of opportunities. Consequently, much is required of us!

Closing Reflections

The thrust of Jesus' message can be summed up in two words: *Get ready!* His return is as sure as his incarnation. The second advent of Christ is as sure as the first advent. He will come when least expected. CNN will not expect it. Wall Street will have no hint. The nations will have no clue. The world's religions disbelieve it. To these, he is coming like a thief in the night! Revelation closes with Jesus' promise, "Surely I am coming soon." And we say with the people of God, "Amen. Come, Lord Jesus!" (Revelation 22:20).

How can we be ready?

By living a *godly life* that reflects the abundant truth God has given us. "For the grace of God has appeared, bringing salvation for all people, training us to renounce ungodliness and worldly passions, and to live self-controlled, upright, and godly lives in the present age, waiting for our blessed hope, the appearing of the glory of our great God and Savior Jesus Christ" (Titus 2:11–13).

By *joyful service*. "Stay dressed for action and keep your lamps burning, and be like men who are waiting for their master to come home from the wedding feast, so that they may open the door to him at once when he comes and knocks" (vv. 35, 36).

Roll up your sleeves, turn the lights on, get ready—Jesus is coming soon!

61

Reality Check

LUKE 12:49–53

WE READ EARLY IN Luke's Gospel that John the Baptist's preparation for the coming Christ was so popularly successful that some people wondered if he was the Christ, which prompted him to explain, "I baptize you with water, but he who is mightier than I is coming, the strap of whose sandals I am not worthy to untie. He will baptize you with the Holy Spirit and fire" (3:16).

John's careful denial that he was the Christ emphasized his own inferiority to Jesus and the superiority of Jesus' baptism. John's water baptism was external, while Jesus' baptism of the Spirit and fire would be internal. It would cleanse the inside of believing humanity. Believers would be baptized "with the Holy Spirit and fire" because the regenerating work of the Holy Spirit would involve the fire-like work of purification. And those who would refuse Christ would undergo the fire of Christ's judgment, as John further explained: "His winnowing fork is in his hand, to clear his threshing floor and to gather the wheat into his barn, but the chaff he will burn with unquenchable fire" (3:17). Therefore, we are given to understand from the very first that Jesus' ministry would be fiery—first, as a purifying baptism of believers, and, second, as a consuming judgment upon unbelievers.

Now, toward the end of Luke 12, as Jesus and his disciples approached Jerusalem, and the cross loomed larger and larger, so that it filled Jesus' mental horizon, our Lord paused to reflect on the fiery realities the cross would unleash upon him and his followers. His reflections were a precross reality check. Jesus bared his feelings, his innermost heart, and revealed some harsh realities. It was good for the disciples, and it is good for his followers today, to see these realities because we are always in good shape when we see things as they are. The trouble comes when we see reality as we wish it would be, not as it is.

Precross Realities for Jesus (vv. 49, 50)

Jesus' Longing

The reality for Jesus was that the prophesied fire had not fallen, but he so longed for it—"I came to cast fire on the earth, and would that it were already kindled!" (v. 49). He longed for the time when he would baptize his followers "with the Holy Spirit and fire" (3:16).

Through this baptism, all who believed in him would be *regenerated*, born of the Spirit, made eternally alive as eternal sons and daughters of God (cf. John 1:12, 13; 3:3–6)—and he longed for that. They would be *indwelt* by the Holy Spirit, the Counselor, the Spirit of truth—and he longed for that. They would no longer be alone (cf. John 14:16, 17)—and he longed for that. They would be *sealed* with the Holy Spirit as a down payment insuring their eternal inheritance. They would enjoy eternal life *now* (cf. Ephesians 1:13, 14; 4:30)—and he longed for that. They would be *sanctified*, made holy by the Spirit's fiery work of internal soul purification. He would melt their hearts, so to speak, and skim away the impure dross from their souls so they could mirror his holy image—and he longed for that. And ultimately their lives would be *ignited*, they would become incendiary. Pentecostal fire would flame from their lives, the Spirit of burning would rest above their willing heads, and the fire would spread—and he longed for that.

How Jesus longed for the baptism of "the Holy Spirit and fire"—the regeneration, indwelling, sealing, sanctification, and igniting of his people. How he longed for judgment to fall too—to take up the "winnowing fork . . . in his hand, to clear his threshing floor and to gather the wheat into his barn, but the chaff he will burn with unquenchable fire" (3:17)—to at last bring justice and equity to the earth. This was the real longing of Jesus' heart. These are not Luke's imagined words. These are the words of Jesus, the *verbum mentis* of his mind and heart—"I came to cast fire on the earth, and would that it were already kindled!" This is how Jesus felt before the Passion and the cross.

Jesus' Distress

The daunting reality for Jesus was that he first had to be immersed in death before the things for which he longed could happen. "I have a baptism to be baptized with, and how great is my distress until it is accomplished!" (v. 50).

I. H. Marshall says the exact idea here is: "How I am totally governed by this until it be finally accomplished!"[1] With perfect candor Jesus described the impatient misery that drenched his soul. He wanted to get the ordeal over with. The thought of it dominated him—"how great is my distress until it is accomplished!"

What made the waiting so terrible was that he knew exactly what his baptism entailed. The artful butchery and prolonged torture were not what distressed him, but rather the necessity of his taking on the raw sewage of our sins—so that he, in effect, would choke and drown in it and become the same (cf. 2 Corinthians 5:21). Here is where the cross lifts Christ and Christianity high above all other religions. Frederick Buechner writes:

> Buddha sits enthroned beneath the Bo-tree in the lotus position. His lips are faintly parted in the smile of one who has passed beyond every power in earth or heaven to touch him. "He who loves fifty has fifty woes, he who loves ten has ten woes, he who loves none has no woes," he has said. His eyes are closed.[2]

But the Holy Trinity mandates and lives out a boundless love. "For God so loved the world, that he gave his only Son, that whoever believes in him should not perish but have eternal life" (John 3:16). He who loves the world takes on the world's woes!

Jesus stood before his disciples, eyes wide open, and said, "I have a baptism to be baptized with, and how great is my distress until it is accomplished!" A short time later, eyes wide open, having made the triumphal entrance into Jerusalem, he said, "Now is my soul troubled. And what shall I say? 'Father, save me from this hour'? But for this purpose I have come to this hour. Father, glorify your name" (John 12:27, 28a). And in the garden he prayed, "'Father, if you are willing, remove this cup from me. Nevertheless, not my will, but yours, be done.' And there appeared to him an angel from heaven, strengthening him. And being in an agony he prayed more earnestly; and his sweat became like great drops of blood falling down to the ground" (22:42–44). And on the cross, having become sin for us, he called out with a loud voice, "Father, into your hands I commit my spirit!" (23:46). Then his eyes closed. The difference is this: Buddha's eyes close to shut out the world. Christ's close having taken it in.

How exalted our Savior was in his precross reality check. He longed to bring fire on the earth. He wished that the fire was kindled. But he had first to undergo the baptism of death on the cross, immersed in our sins. And he could not wait to get it done! Jesus charged headlong to the cross. Jesus raced to save us.

Precross Realities for Jesus' Disciples (vv. 51–53)

Having shared the facts about his precross longing and distress, Jesus laid out a sobering reality for his disciples:

> Do you think that I have come to give peace on earth? No, I tell you, but rather division. For from now on in one house there will be five divided, three against two and two against three. They will be divided, father against son and son against father, mother against daughter and daughter against mother, mother-in-law against her daughter-in-law and daughter-in-law against mother-in-law. (vv. 51–53)

Division

The division Jesus described is of the most heartbreaking kind. A family of five (father, mother, daughter, son, and daughter-in-law) will be torn apart by appalling enmity. The prophetic nature of Jesus' words were emphasized by lines borrowed from Micah 7:6, which prophesied coming hostility between the younger generation and the old. But this is worse. The division is mutual and goes every generational direction.

Jesus' intent in proclaiming that he came to bring division was both to shock and to inform his followers. The shocking effect came easily because peace, not division, had been the grand theme of his coming, especially as described by Luke. At the nativity the angels praised God saying, "Glory to God in the highest, and on earth peace among those with whom he is pleased!" (2:14). This was a reference to the coming "Prince of Peace" (Isaiah 9:6). It was also a conscious fulfillment of Zechariah's song about how his son John the Baptist would pave the way for the Messiah, "the sunrise"—"to give light to those who sit in darkness and in the shadow of death, to guide our feet into the way of peace" (1:78, 79). Twice when Jesus healed people, the disciples heard him say, "Go in peace" (7:50; 8:48). When he sent his disciples out two by two to preach, he instructed them to say, "Peace be to this house!" as they walked in the door (10:5).

But now Jesus said, "Do you think that I have come to give peace on earth? No, I tell you, but rather division." The Twelve were shocked. He definitely had their attention.

But this was and is reality. The very mention of Jesus' name sundered ancient Judaism, giving his words exquisite fulfillment. During the first four hundred years of the Roman Empire, his name could land one in jail, or worse.

To the world religions, the name Jesus has been strident and invasive. During the last seventy years, allegiance to Jesus could land one in a Chinese prison. Islam is at war with the Christ of the Scriptures. Just ask a convert! Even the American media are generally hostile to personal reference to Jesus Christ. Charles Colson writes that he regularly encounters interviewers who suggest

> just before we go on the air, that we steer away from religious topics. "Some people take offense, you know," said one. Another advised me it was against station policy to discuss religion on the air. Others say nothing; once we begin they simply steer the questions to the comparatively safer ground of prisons, criminal justice, or politics. They usually appear aghast when I bring the answers back to my experiences with Jesus Christ.[3]

In fact, one major US daily, as a matter of policy, will not print the two words *Jesus Christ* together because, the editor says, that represents an editorial judgment.[4] Such attitudes are commonplace today.

The name of Jesus Christ always produces some type of painful division, even in the most personal of relationships. His words, "I am the way, and the truth, and the life. No one comes to the Father except through me" (John 14:6) are offensive to a pluralistic society. Jesus did not come to tell people that all paths lead to God. He did not come to tell people that what you believe does not matter. Jesus did not believe that all people are good, or espouse the perfectibility of humanity. Jesus did not say you can do whatever you want as long as you do not hurt anyone else. His ethics are radical. He demands careful obedience and costly loyalty. And not everyone is willing to pay the price or to accept those who do.

If you attempt to follow Christ, you will experience division. It is also true, of course, that many Christians suffer not because they follow Jesus, but because they are judgmental, boorish, pious buffoons. But it is also a fact that "all who desire to live a godly life in Christ Jesus will be persecuted" (2 Timothy 3:12). And sometimes the division and persecution come from those we love the most. That is a fact.

Peace

Of course, division is only half the story. Jesus also brings peace with God—the ground and foundation of all peace. John Wesley was so right when he said, "Oh what a pearl . . . is the lowest degree of peace with God. It is worth selling everything to receive it."

Jesus gives us his peace. This is not something from a package. It is not a philosophical abstraction. It is *his own personal peace*. "Peace I leave with you; *my peace* I give to you. Not as the world gives do I give to you" (John 14:27). He gives us the peace he had for thirty-three years amid turmoil and rejections, even on the cross. He shares with us the peace that is now his in glory. This is not a dream. This is reality!

He also gives us *peace with his own people*, other believers. As Paul put it, "He came and preached peace to you who were far off and peace to those who were near. For through him we both have access in one Spirit to the Father" (Ephesians 2:17, 18). Jesus prayed for his people's mutual peace—"that they may all be one, just as you, Father, are in me, and I in you" (John 17:21).

How sweet this is—peace with God, then Christ's own personal peace in our hearts, and then peace with each other.

Closing Reflections

Jesus longed to bring "fire on the earth," to baptize his own "with the Holy Spirit and fire" (3:16), so they would be regenerated, indwelt, sealed, and sanctified, and so judgment would be set in motion for the world. To this end he had to be baptized in death, a fact that dominated and distressed him until it was done. He ran to the cross to save us.

As a result the realities for us are immense. There is dissonance and division in this world, but there is also peace with God, the peace of Jesus, and peace with each other.

He gave his all. He sank in death's waters that we might have his fire and his peace. We owe everything to his blood.

62

Settle Up!

LUKE 12:54–59

LUKE 9:51 TELLS US, "When the days drew near for him to be taken up, he set his face to go to Jerusalem." From that point until the events recorded at the end of chapter 12, the single upright post of the cross (the *crux simplex*) and the crossbar (the *patebulum*) grew ominously on Jesus' horizon, and the warnings to his followers became more ominous. He had just warned his disciples to get ready because wrenching division was coming. Now he turned to the crowd (those who were neither disciples nor committed followers but curious onlookers) and gave them a gracious wake-up call. We catch the feel of this passage if we imagine Jesus trudging toward the walls of Jerusalem, then halting and turning to face the curious crowd.

Heavy Weather (vv. 54–56)

Earth's Weather

He began by lightly referencing the weather, but it quickly became apparent that he was talking about something more. "He also said to the crowds, 'When you see a cloud rising in the west, you say at once, "A shower is coming." And so it happens. And when you see the south wind blowing, you say, "There will be scorching heat," and it happens'" (vv. 54, 55). Even today you can hear Tel Aviv radio say, "Today will be a scorcher. Southerly breezes are blowing up from the Arabian desert." And rain has always come from the west in Palestine. First Kings 17, 18 records how, due to Ahab's wicked leadership of Israel, God judged the land with a terrible drought that eventuated in Elijah's famous conflict and victory over the priests of Baal on Mt. Carmel. After that victory, Elijah knelt on Mt. Carmel, bent down to the ground, put his face between his knees, and prayed. Six times he paused from prayer and sent his servant to look west toward the sea, and six times the servant returned saying, "There is nothing" (1 Kings 18:43). But on the seventh time the servant reported, "Behold, a little cloud like a man's hand is rising from the sea" (1 Kings 18:44). And Elijah knew his prayer was answered, as anyone raised in Palestine would.

> And he [Elijah] said, "Go up, say to Ahab, 'Prepare your chariot and go down, lest the rain stop you.'" And in a little while the heavens grew black with clouds and wind, and there was a great rain. And Ahab rode and went to Jezreel. And the hand of the LORD was on Elijah, and he gathered up his garment and ran before Ahab to the entrance of Jezreel. (1 Kings 18:44b–46)

No Jew needed NBC weatherman Willard Scott or any local forecaster to tell him what was coming. They all understood the weather patterns.

Cosmic Weather

At that point some may have thought, *That's me. Anyone who's the least bit observant can figure the weather. It's easy*. But the next word from Jesus' mouth was, "You hypocrites! You know how to interpret the appearance of earth and sky, but why do you not know how to interpret the present time?" (v. 56). Jesus indicted them for their hypocrisy because they didn't apply the same shrewdness to the winds and currents of his messianic ministry.[1] They could read earthly weather, but they neglected to read the cosmic weather—the signs of the moral and spiritual storm that was blowing in. The signs that a great spiritual thunderstorm was brewing were there for all to see, if they would just open their souls' eyes.

First, there was the sheer weight of *Jesus' person*. There was not a hint of pride or lust or jealousy in Jesus. His ethical conduct was blameless. There were no attitudinal sins. He was without fault, and his sizzling perfection dominated every encounter. His words were unlike any ever heard. His knowledge of Scripture, his reason, his originality (consider the parables), his insight and wisdom were unparalleled. No one ever had spoken like him!

His astounding deeds were done in public for all to see, including healings, raisings of the dead, nature miracles, and exorcisms. He had said, "But if it is by the finger of God that I cast out demons, then the kingdom of God has come upon you" (11:20). Never had there been such a display of power.

His messianic persona was there for all to see. Indeed, his disciples knew and preached that he was "the Christ of God" (9:20). The massive force of his person, his words, his deeds, and his messianic assertions confronted all who met him.

Second, they had the testimony of *history*. They had the record of their people's tragic repeated historical cycles in dealing with the prophets: 1) the prophets preached righteousness, 2) the people rejected their message, 3) divine judgment fell. How could they ignore the repeated cycles of Israel's persecution and rejection of the prophets, followed by God's judgment in the form of exile? Could they not see the relevance of that history to their choice of whether or not to believe and follow Jesus Christ, the Messiah?

Third, *the mounting rejection of Christ* should have forewarned them of what was to come. The final verses of chapter 11 record, "The scribes and the Pharisees began to press him hard and to provoke him to speak about many things, lying in wait for him, to catch him in something he might say" (11:53, 54). And they eventually succeeded and had Jesus impaled in the darkness outside the city.

Why were they so good at reading earth's winds and such failures at reading the spiritual winds that were beginning to howl? Why were they so shrewd in earthly matters and such dunces in spiritual matters? Why this hypocrisy—this pretense that they did not know what was happening?

They did not want to discern the cosmic events, and in fact were unwilling to try. If they had paid half as much attention to the spiritual winds that were blowing as they did to Palestine's meteorological patterns, they would have understood what was happening and would have prepared themselves.

Today too many people pay far more attention to what is blowing in from the west than they do to the cosmic winds that are determining their future. That is why at least a brief weather summary is placed on the front page of the newspaper, but the religion section is buried in an obscure subsection.

In Jesus' day the cycle repeated, bringing terrible judgment on Israel. After the cross Israel was given time to repent, but when there was no national repentance, the wrath of God fell. Jerusalem fell by the sword, crosses covered the hills like grim forests, and the people were deported to all the nations. The city was trampled upon by the Gentiles (cf. 21:24).

What about us? Do we plan our lives around the weather but ignore the cosmic zephyrs? Peter said that most people do.

> I am stirring up your sincere mind by way of reminder . . . knowing this first of all, that scoffers will come in the last days with scoffing, following their own sinful desires. They will say, "Where is the promise of his coming? For ever since the fathers fell asleep, all things are continuing as they were from the beginning of creation." For they deliberately overlook this fact,

> that the heavens existed long ago, and the earth was formed out of water and through water by the word of God, and that by means of these the world that then existed was deluged with water and perished. But by the same word the heavens and earth that now exist are stored up for fire, being kept until the day of judgment and destruction of the ungodly. (2 Peter 3:1–7)

The winds are there if we are willing to observe them, and they portend a firestorm of judgment, a fact most people prefer to ignore or deny. Thus we have a world culture that, despite the church's witness, rejects the good news that Christ died for their sins and was resurrected on the third day, calls good evil and evil good, worships money, glorifies perversions, makes heroes of its villains, segregates and marginalizes the poor, kills unwanted children, and worships self as the measure of all things.

I believe heavy weather is surely coming, and coming soon. The storm warnings are out.

Being Prepared (vv. 57–59)

Having issued the warning, Jesus next gave the crowd (and us!) some advice about how to prepare for judgment:

> And why do you not judge for yourselves what is right? As you go with your accuser before the magistrate, make an effort to settle with him on the way, lest he drag you to the judge, and the judge hand you over to the officer, and the officer put you in prison. I tell you, you will never get out until you have paid the very last penny. (vv. 57–59)

This miniparable presumes that all of us are guilty and are heading for judgment. The only sensible thing to do is try to settle out of court before the judgment, where the verdict can only be guilty and we will have to pay the ultimate price.

This is a gospel call! We need to wake up to the spiritual reality that we are all sinners before God—to see for ourselves what is right. I remember well a lovely woman who could not at first accept the idea that she was a sinner. Her daughter had come to Christ as a student during my youth pastor years and had asked me to talk to her mother. The woman bristled and said, "I'm no sinner!" I assured her that she was. The conversation was long and frustrating—until it became clear that "sinner" for her meant committing a heinous sin such as murder. It was then that we began to make progress that eventuated in her coming to Christ a few years later.

That lovely lady was indeed a vile sinner, as was the pastor who was sharing the gospel with her. She came to understand that in her soul she was ungodly. She came to understand that she was an enemy of God in her heart of hearts (cf. Romans 5:6–10). Actually the full depth of her awareness came after she became a Christian, because the Holy Spirit continues to convict us of sin, righteousness, and judgment (cf. John 16:8–11).

The truth is, the greatest saints knew they were sinners. Paul told Timothy, "The saying is trustworthy and deserving of full acceptance, that Christ Jesus came into the world to save sinners, of whom I am the foremost" (1 Timothy 1:15). This was not disingenuous, pious, "I'm worse than you" rhetoric. This was how Paul, the magisterial theologian, regarded himself—even as a regenerated man.

Martin Luther expressed this in a famous Latin phrase, *simul justus et peccator*—"at the same time justified and a sinner"—because he knew that though he had been given righteousness from God by faith, he still sinned. This understanding led Luther to cast himself upon God in desperate dependence. The Puritans thought the same way, and it drove them to constant reliance on God's grace. The Scriptures speak of such a state as a blessing: "Blessed are those who mourn [over their sins], for they shall be comforted" (Matthew 5:4). Graced people mourn their sins. The lost do not acknowledge their guilt.

Those who heed Jesus' little parable know they are guilty sinners—they have judged for themselves "what is right." They know the wrath of God abides on their souls (cf. John 3:18, 36). So as they are going to court where they will surely be found guilty, they wisely seek to settle out of court. Jesus' call to all of us is to settle things in this life so that our lives will not come to the court of final judgment, where it will be too late to find salvation.

Elsewhere Jesus tells us simply and straightforwardly how this can be done: "Truly, truly, I say to you, whoever hears my word and believes him who sent me has eternal life. He does not come into judgment, but has passed from death to life" (John 5:24). Those who truly believe never come into court, because their case is settled and they have already passed from death to life.[2]

Closing Reflections

Jesus has told us that if we can read the earth's weather, we should also read the cosmic or spiritual weather. And the spiritual winds that are blowing tell us that judgment is coming, and maybe very soon. It may be a national judgment or a localized judgment, or it may be the great "Day of the Lord"—the final judgment and disposition of life. Or judgment may be brought into the present by our personal death.

In any event, the storm of judgment awaits the unbelieving, unrepentant soul. So, to use Jesus' words, "Why do you not judge for yourselves what is right? As you go with your accuser before the magistrate, make an effort to settle with him on the way" (vv. 57, 58a).

Charles Colson tells about the night he came to understand that he was a sinner on his way to judgment. Colson writes:

> That night when I . . . sat alone in my car, my own sin—not just dirty politics, but the hatred and evil so deep within me—was thrust before my eyes, forcefully and painfully. For the first time in my life, I felt unclean, and worst of all, I could not escape. In those moments of clarity I found myself driven irresistibly into the arms of the living God.[3]

If you have not yet come to Christ, do you want to settle up with him now? Do you want eternal life? Do you want to believe? Hear this:

> "The word is near you, in your mouth and in your heart" (that is, the word of faith that we proclaim); because, if you confess with your mouth that Jesus is Lord and believe in your heart that God raised him from the dead, you will be saved. For with the heart one believes and is justified, and with the mouth one confesses and is saved. (Romans 10:8–10)

Settle now, on the way, for Jesus is coming to judge the world!

63

Repentance Time!

LUKE 13:1–9

A PULPIT COMMITTEE has been defined as a group of people in search of a man who will be "totally fearless and uncompromising as he tells them exactly what they want to hear!"[1] Actually there is some truth in this because church people, like most people, naturally prefer comfort to challenge and encouragement to correction.

The fact is, Jesus' very own preaching would not please some congregations because he was certainly not in the habit of telling people what they wanted to hear. Take, for example, the context immediately preceding chapter 13, where he told his hearers he had come to bring "fire on the earth" (12:49) and division instead of peace (12:51–53), then indicted them as "hypocrites" who would not apply the same interest and energy to reading the spiritual weather that they apply to understanding earth's weather (12:54–56).

Stuart Briscoe has imagined the kind of conversation that could have taken place at a family meal time after that.

> "Well, Dad, what did you think of the sermon?"
>
> "I was insulted!"
>
> "Why? What did he say to insult you?"
>
> "He said that if I was interested in weather forecasting that proved I was a hypocrite."
>
> "Oh come off it, Dad, he didn't say anything of the sort. What he actually said was that if you take the time to become an expert in reading the skies so that you can predict the weather but won't take time to become an expert in spiritual matters when you profess to be spiritual then you are being inconsistent!"
>
> "Well, I don't think he has any right to judge people like that and I won't be going back to listen to him again. In fact, I'm going to see if

> something can't be done to get him silenced. We don't need that kind of talk around here."[2]

Jesus simply was not in the habit of telling people what they wanted to hear. And as Luke further reveals in chapter 13, the Master became even more aggressive. And people, except for the most committed, did not like it. And yet everyone needed to hear what Jesus had to say. And the same goes for us today.

Repentance: The Necessity (vv. 1–5)

A Galilean Atrocity

Jesus' teaching heated up when some of his listeners brought up a recent atrocity: "There were some present at that very time who told him about the Galileans whose blood Pilate had mingled with their sacrifices" (v. 1). As best we can reconstruct the bloodshed, this took place in the temple at Passover, because that was the only time laymen, Galilean or otherwise, were involved in the slaughter of animal sacrifices.[3] So the victims were Galilean pilgrims offering Passover sacrifices in the temple. Evidently Pilate thought they were guilty of sedition and had his soldiers fall upon them when they least expected. In the ensuing melee human blood mixed with lambs' blood in an appalling bouquet.

Everyone knew of the event, but the reason it was mentioned to Jesus is that it was generally believed that victims of calamities and misfortunes were guilty of extraordinary sins that they had kept hidden. A famous example of this kind of thinking is found in John 9:1, 2: "As he [Jesus] passed by, he saw a man blind from birth. And his disciples asked him, 'Rabbi, who sinned, this man or his parents, that he was born blind?'" It was obvious to them that the man's misfortune was due to someone's sin. Similarly, Job's "comforters" earned their ironic title by expounding repeatedly on this theme, beginning in Job 4:7 with the question, "Remember: who that was innocent ever perished? Or where were the upright cut off?" (cf. 8:4, 20; 22:5; also Exodus 20:5; Psalm 1:4; 37:20).

This was an attractive way to think about life for those who had been spared adversity. Their goodness, their moral superiority, had spared them! It was all so very neat, and so self-satisfying. "Come on, Jesus, expound on the moral inadequacies of those Galileans who met such scandalous deaths, so we can further sanctify our souls."

Jesus refused to play their game. Instead he answered with the ruthless truth, "Do you think that these Galileans were worse sinners than all the other Galileans, because they suffered in this way? No, I tell you; but unless you repent, you will all likewise perish" (vv. 2, 3). Jesus was not denying that sin sometimes brings tragedy, because it does (cf. Matthew 9:2). But he flatly refused the idea that *all* tragedy is due to the sins of its victims. In fact, he emphatically answered those who wondered about whose sin caused the man's blindness by saying, "It was not that this man sinned, or his parents" (John 9:3a). This speaks to the misguided tendency of so many ill-informed Christians who heap imagined guilt upon themselves for the calamities that have befallen their children or other loved ones. We must accept reality. Death happens. Tragedies come to all. Sometimes unthinkable things befall the most godly and committed.

One lazy Sunday afternoon in Papua New Guinea, Wycliffe missionaries Walt and Vonnie Steinkraus were resting alongside their daughters Kerry and Kathy when their world came to an abrupt end. At precisely 3:00 p.m. a half-mile-wide section of the mountain on the opposite side of the river from their village broke off and buried them. They may never even have heard the sound. In a world full of vacant hillsides, in a world full of reprobates, in a world with too few missionaries, the Steinkrauses disappeared under a mountain. Was it because of their sin? No! Jesus settled the issue—not all tragedy or crisis is due to one's own sins.

Judean Accidents

Jesus strengthened the impact of his point by citing another incident: "Or those eighteen on whom the tower in Siloam fell and killed them: do you think that they were worse offenders than all the others who lived in Jerusalem? No, I tell you; but unless you repent, you will all likewise perish" (vv. 4, 5). Many believe that the tower stood at the juncture of the south and east walls of Jerusalem and may have fallen during the construction of an aqueduct from the reservoir of Siloam to improve the water supply.[4] Some of Jesus' listeners could have argued that the Galileans had "asked for" such tragedy from Pilate due to their political activity and thus were morally culpable, but no one could say the same about the random deaths from the collapse of the tower of Siloam.[5]

Jesus wanted to be sure he got his point across. "Do you think that these Galileans were worse sinners than all the other Galileans, because they suffered in this way? . . . Or those eighteen on whom the tower in Siloam fell and killed them: do you think that they were worse offenders than all the others who lived in Jerusalem?" His answer was emphatic. "No, I tell you . . . No, I tell you." Jesus could not have put it more forcefully. Those who died were run-of-the-mill sinners like the rest of us.

Jesus assumed and taught the universality of sin, and of death as its consequence.[6] We are all sinners. Sure, there are differences between us sinners, but they are only differences of degree—we all "fall short of the glory of God" (Romans 3:23). We are all guilty. We all deserve death.

What Repentance Is Not

When death comes, we will all perish unless we have repented. The context here is the final judgment.[7] *Repentance* is a much misunderstood word. Some people think "repentance is an emotional experience enjoyed by strange people who like to cry in public."[8] This caricature involves well-trained men who lead their fellow Christians to weep and wail their way back to God. There is more to repentance than manipulated or even genuine remorse.

Another well-traveled caricature identifies repentance with the ritual of penance, which begins with an obligatory "confession," followed by the mechanical carrying out of ordered exercises as a means of making restitution or paying the price of our sin in some sense.

Neither of these caricatures is true repentance. Repentance begins with a change of the mind, but not in the contemporary sense of changing one's mind only to change it again. It is a change of mind that brings a change of actions. It is both *intellectual* and *volitional*—and then, though not necessarily, *emotional*. Repentance is a real turnaround of one's life in respect to sinful conduct.

Repentance must happen in our souls, or we will perish in the judgment. If Jesus has not changed your conduct, and if he is not continuing to change your conduct, you are very likely not a Christian. Repentance is the style of true Christianity! Repentance is not an option.

Evidence: The Necessity (vv. 6–9)

To make sure no one misunderstood, Jesus issued a brief parable:

> A man had a fig tree planted in his vineyard, and he came seeking fruit on it and found none. And he said to the vinedresser, "Look, for three years now I have come seeking fruit on this fig tree, and I find none. Cut it down. Why should it use up the ground?" And he answered him, "Sir, let it alone this year also, until I dig around it and put on manure. Then if it should bear fruit next year, well and good; but if not, you can cut it down." (vv. 6–9)

The parable rests on three symbolisms not readily apparent to the precross crowd of onlookers (who only understood it as a challenge to bear spiritual fruit or be judged). The symbols became apparent to the apostolic church after the death and resurrection of Christ. The *fig tree* represents Israel, as it sometimes did in the Old Testament (cf. Jeremiah 24:1–10; Hosea 9:10; Micah 7:1).[9] Jesus' hearers, and us by virtue of our desire to follow him, were to examine themselves through the metaphor of the fig tree. The *owner* is emblematic of God the Father, and the *caretaker* represents Christ. They are in concert, but, without interrupting their harmony, the owner argues from the logic of righteousness, while the caretaker reasons from the logic of mercy.

The Owner

The wishes of the owner of the vineyard are perfectly reasonable. Three years earlier he had a fig tree planted on a sunny slope in the fertile ground of his vineyard. As expected, it rose above the garden with the whole sky to itself. Its large dense leaves blocked out the sun from the grapes below, and it drew precious nourishment from the soil. This was expected and acceptable because of the fruit it promised. Excellent care was given to it by the caretaker. But after one, then two, then three years there was no fruit! So the owner's common sense commanded, "Cut it down. Why should it use up the ground?" (v. 7). The useless tree was taking up precious space and exhausting the soil. It must go.

The Caretaker

But the caretaker pleaded for one last opportunity for the tree: "'Sir, let it alone this year also, until I dig around it and put on manure. Then if it should bear fruit next year, well and good; but if not, you can cut it down'" (vv. 8, 9). This is astonishing mercy and grace. Astonishing because it means that the Lord of the universe, who transcends, sustains, and maintains the vast cosmos (cf. Colossians 1:15–17), gives us an extended period of grace during which he painstakingly does what he can to bring forth the fruit of repentance. Such mercy is awesome!

The great Puritan John Bunyan, a man who lived close to the earth, saw that the caretaker's promise to "dig around it" indicated that its root structure was perhaps earthbound. Bunyan addressed the tree in one of his sermons: "Barren fig-tree! See how the Lord Jesus, by these very words, suggesteth the cause of thy fruitless soul. The things of this world lie too close to thy heart; the earth with its things has bound up thy roots; thou art an earth-bound soul."[10]

Then Bunyan has Jesus, the caretaker, address the owner—the Father: "Lord, I will loosen his roots; I will dig up this earth, I will lay his roots bare. My hand shall be upon him by sickness, by disappointments, by cross providences. I will dig about him until he stands shaking and tottering, until he be ready to fall."[11]

Bunyan goes on to explain:

> Thus, I say, deals the Lord Jesus ofttimes with the barren professor; He diggeth about him, He smiteth one blow at his heart, another blow at his lusts, a third at his pleasures, a fourth at his comforts, another at his self-conceitedness: thus He diggeth about him. This is the way to take bad earth from the roots, and to loosen his roots from the earth. Barren fig-tree! see here the care, the love, the labor, and way, which the Lord Jesus, the Dresser of the vineyard, is fair to take with thee, if haply thou mayest be made fruitful.[12]

Oh, the astonishing mercy and grace of God! He digs to free us, pounds on us through life's ups and downs, pries at our earthly attachments, so we might become fruitful.

Has Jesus been digging around the roots of your earthbound soul with inexplicable providences in your relationships or your profession or your family that have left you reeling? The object of these shakings is that you might become fruitful. Astonishing mercy!

The caretaker's other stated method is to fertilize your soul with the Word and the Spirit. Month after month he applies the hearty, life-giving nourishment of the gospel to your soul. He sends the Spirit to minister his Word. He brings to memory failures and sins and great needs. Has the Word been coming to you? Has the Spirit been stirring your soul? Then the time has come, as Bunyan would say, to "suck in the Gospel" and bear fruit—"love, joy, peace, patience, kindness, goodness, faithfulness, gentleness, self-control" (Galatians 5:22, 23)—and then engage in a fruitful life of obedience and service.

Closing Reflections

If the Lord does not return while we are here on earth, we are all going to die. Some of us will live more than three score or four score years. Some of us will die much sooner due to weakness, illness, trauma, or violence.

> It is no secret, and never has been. Many things have been hidden from the minds of men, but it has always been made entirely clear that they are going to die. The day is coming when all our earthly possessions will be swept away, including our ability to enjoy and even perceive them, and our very flesh will be required of us. The earth will close over our skins and they will be like a brown, crumbling leaf that blows away and vanishes.[13]

That day is coming sooner than we think, and if we do not repent in this life, we will perish. Truly the wrath of God abides on the unbelieving, unrepentant heart (cf. John 3:18).

Repentance is nothing less than a radically changed life, a life that has intellectually and volitionally turned from sin. The fruits of such a life are first inward and then outward for all to see as beautiful works (Matthew 5:16, original Greek). Is your life changed and changing? Is there fruit?

The mere fact that you are alive is due to the grace of God, especially if there is no fruit in your life. The message is: *do not presume on the grace of God*. He is looking for fruit. If he does not find it, you may be cut down!

64

Straightened on the Sabbath

LUKE 13:10–21

DURING OUR 1987 SABBATICAL IN CAMBRIDGE, England, my wife, Barbara, and I worshiped at "the Round Church," shorthand for The Church of the Holy Sepulcher. The Round was built in 1107 as a prayer chapel for knights on the way to the Crusades. Its circular design was modeled on the Church of the Holy Sepulcher in Jerusalem. The Round is small, seating perhaps two hundred worshipers on tiny, low-cut pews.

We enjoyed the evangelical services at the Round, but I was always miserably uncomfortable by the end of Sunday morning. So I asked one of the members why the pews were so small, and I was told that in the mid-nineteenth century the church's vicar was a dwarf, and on one occasion when Queen Victoria visited the church he gave her a great fright when he stepped from behind a pew. So thence all the pews were shortened so the Queen would never be frightened again!

Luke 13 tells of a woman who was short by reason of a crippling infirmity and Jesus' healing her—a great miracle but done on the wrong day, according to some. This confrontation would provide a demonstration of God's kingdom.

The Kingdom of God

According to Luke, a short woman visited the synagogue on what turned out to be Jesus' final recorded ministry in such a place. Her shortness was not due to her inherited stature but to a crippling disease that left her bent over. The consensus of modern opinion is that she was suffering from an affliction called *spondylitis deformans*, causing the bones of her spine to fuse into a rigid mass. There is no suggestion that the woman was demon-possessed (no demon was subsequently cast out), though she had come under the attack of an evil spirit eighteen years before that bound her up like a hobbled animal. She lived in a posture of forced humility, her face always toward the dust of the earth, unless she wrenched sideways and peered upward like an awkward animal. She seemed to sink lower and lower as the weight of years pressed upon her. Her gait was a lunging shuffle. "She walked about as if she were searching for a grave."[1] At times she probably wished she could find one. And yet this woman's spiritual focus was upward. She was evidently a regular worshipper at the synagogue, for no one took special note of her. Due to her infirmity it would have been much easier to stay at home, but to her credit she sought the solace of worship and the Word.

The Kingdom Manifested

On that Sabbath when the woman shuffled in and slowly took her place, no one took notice except Jesus: "When Jesus saw her, he called her over and said to her, 'Woman, you are freed from your disability.' And he laid his hands on her, and immediately she was made straight, and she glorified God" (vv. 12, 13). The woman saw loving resolve in Jesus' eyes. This was because he was the only man who ever perfectly fulfilled the two tables of the Law. Vertically, he loved God with all his heart. Horizontally, he loved his neighbor as he loved himself. He loved this daughter of Abraham as he loved his own body (cf. Ephesians 5:28–30).

In response, the poor woman rose to his beckoning and dottered forward until, eyes rolled upward, she could see him standing above her. "Woman," he said, "you are [permanently, Greek perfect tense] freed from your disability." She heard the words, but she did not move. The bent woman was not only bound by body but by habit. Still doubled, she felt his gentle hands urge her upward, and as she attempted to rise, she straightened to her full height—graceful, head erect. The people gasped. Exclamations came from all corners.

The immediacy of the healed woman's praise revealed her previously and presently devout heart. Thanksgiving naturally erupts from a prayerful heart. No reporter could have written all her praise down because she spoke not only in words but with her eyes, her hands, her upright body, her rising soul. She was in those moments the most eloquent woman in the universe.[2]

This was a divine display of kingdom power. Jesus' ministry had begun in the synagogue in Nazareth when he took the scroll of Isaiah and read:

> The Spirit of the Lord is upon me,
> because he has anointed me
> to proclaim good news to the poor.
> He has sent me to proclaim liberty to the captives
> and recovering of sight to the blind,
> to set at liberty those who are oppressed,
> to proclaim the year of the Lord's favor. (4:18, 19)

This was followed by lavish displays of power—healing miracles, exorcisms, nature miracles, and the gifting of his disciples to do wonders (cf. 10:1–20). Now, at his final recorded visit to a synagogue, he set this poor woman free—creating a memorable bookend to his opening words of ministry.

This healing was a taste of the kingdom power that Christ has worked throughout history. Jesus sees us in our need and, even more significant, our deepest inward deformities. If we could see others as Jesus sees them, we would see dead people staring with fixed, dilated eyes, indistinguishable on the outside from the truly alive. We would see the blind man and the maimed. But when Jesus says, "You are freed," glazed eyes would flicker open with redeeming light, and lives twisted by sin would stand straight and erect. All glory to God!

The Kingdom Rejected

Sadly, not everyone accepts God's kingdom rule. Consider the synagogue president on that day: "But the ruler of the synagogue, indignant because Jesus had healed on the Sabbath, said to the people, 'There are six days in which work ought to be done. Come on those days and be healed, and not on the Sabbath day'" (v. 14).

What a slab of ecclesiastical granite! He had no heart to pity the poor bent woman's plight, no eye for the beauty of Christ's compassion, no soul to rejoice with the woman's deliverance, no ear for the music of her praise.

He was a chickenhearted religious snob. He did not lower himself to address Jesus directly but turned to the people: "There are six days in which work ought to be done. Come on those days and be healed, and not on the Sabbath day." His heart was pumping great amounts of formaldehyde. He breathed arsenic. He fancied that he was a lover of the Law and its protector. However, his lack of love for the woman showed that he did not love his neighbor as himself, indicating that he did not love God. The cold synagogue leader was about to be "iced" by Jesus.

The Kingdom Defended

Jesus and his contemporaries lived amid a sea of regulations that allowed for the care of livestock on the Sabbath. Rabbinical regulations were very kind to dumb animals, assuring that they could be led out to eat and be watered (cf. M. Shab. 5:1–4; 7:2; 15:1–2; and M. Erub. 2:1–4). A few lines from the *Mishnah's* Shabbath 5:1–4 give the idea:

> 5:1 With what [burdens] may cattle go out [on the Sabbath] and with what may they not go out? The camel may go out with its curb, the female camel with its nose-ring, the Libyan ass with its bridle, the horse with its chain, and all beasts which wear a chain may go out with a chain and be led by the chain; and these things may be sprinkled and immersed without being removed.
>
> 2. The ass may go out with its saddle-cloth if this was fastened on [before the Sabbath]. . . . R. Judah says: Goats may go out [with their udders] bound up if this is to keep them dry, but not if it serves to collect the milk.
>
> 3. And with what may they not go out? A camel may not go out with a rag hung to its tail or with fore and hind legs bound together, or with hoof tied to thigh. So, too, is it with all other cattle. . . .
>
> 4. The ass may not go out with its saddle-cloth if this was not fastened on [before the Sabbath], or with a bell even though it is plugged, or with the ladder-yoke round its neck, or with its leg-strap. . . . R. Eleazar b. Azariah's cow used to go out with the strap between its horns, which was not with the consent of the Sages.[3]

In light of these regulations regarding the care of animals on the Sabbath, the synagogue ruler had led with his chin, and Jesus responded.

> You hypocrites! Does not each of you on the Sabbath untie his ox or his donkey from the manger and lead it away to water it? And ought not this woman, a daughter of Abraham whom Satan bound for eighteen years, be loosed from this bond on the Sabbath day? (vv. 15, 16).

This was an unanswerable indictment using the canons of Jewish logic *qal wa- hōmer*, arguing from the light to the heavy. Jesus' protest "You hypocrites!" castigated the ruler and everyone who was thinking like him. The effect of Jesus' perfect answer was immediate and open for all to see: "As he said these things, all his adversaries were put to shame, and all the people rejoiced at all the glorious things that were done by him" (v. 17). The crowds were with Jesus on this day. The synagogue ruler slumped away, the woman paced about upright, praising God, and the crowd rejoiced. Kingdom power filled the air!

Kingdom Victory (vv. 18–21)

With the healing of the woman, Jesus had demonstrated the ongoing victory of the kingdom despite the opposition of men and of Satan. Now he used the occasion to instruct them concerning the growth of the kingdom through two tiny parables or similes:

> He said therefore, "What is the kingdom of God like? And to what shall I compare it? It is like a grain of mustard seed that a man took and sowed in his garden, and it grew and became a tree, and the birds of the air made nests in its branches." And again he said, "To what shall I compare the kingdom of God? It is like leaven that a woman took and hid in three measures of flour, until it was all leavened." (vv. 18–21)

These growth parables, as they have been called, have been subject to overinterpretation. This was especially true in the nineteenth century when it was commonly taught that the gospel would keep spreading until the world was Christianized and the kingdom was ushered in.

For example, toward the end of that century Sidney Gulick wrote a book entitled *The Growth of the Kingdom of God*. The book's argument was that Christianity is inexorably spreading and will ultimately take over the world—so why not convert now? Gulick reasoned, as James Montgomery Boice summarizes:

> The Christian powers have increased the territory under their rule from about 7% of the surface of the world in 1600 to 82% in 1893, while the non-Christian powers have receded from about 93% to about 18% during the same period. At present the Protestant nations alone rule about twice as much territory as all the non-Christian nations combined. He added, "During the [first] ninety years of the religious history of the United States more persons have come under the direct influence of the Christian Church than during the first thousand years of Christianity in all lands combined."[4]

Christianity is going to take over, so get on the bandwagon!

Those who imagine that the kingdom can be brought in by the preaching of the gospel neglect the teaching of the mystery parables of Matthew 13, such as "the sower" (Matthew 13:3–23) and "the weeds" (Matthew 13:24–30), which demonstrate that the church and its rule will be neither universal nor perfect.

What really put an end to such un-Biblical (though noble) dreams were the great wars—and sins—of the so-called "Christian nations." In 1945 Helmut Thielicke, the eminent theologian and preacher of the University of

Hamburg, stood before his congregation in the choir loft of his church, which had been reduced to ruins by the air raids, and spoke these words:

> We must not think of it as a gradual Christianization of the world which will increasingly eliminate evil. Such dreams and delusions, which may have been plausible enough in more peaceful times, have vanished in the terrors of our man-made misery. The nineteenth century, which brought forth a number of these dreams and dreamers, strikes us today as being an age of unsuspecting children.[5]

> Who can utter the word [progress] today without getting a flat taste in his mouth? Who can still believe today that we are developing toward a state in which the kingdom of God reigns in the world of nations, in culture, and in the life of the individual? The earth has been plowed too deep by the curse of war, the streams of blood and tears have swollen all too terribly, injustice and bestiality have become all too cruel and obvious for us to consider such dreams to be anything but bubbles and froth.[6]

Pessimism? I do not think so! The Biblical realism in these two parables does not teach triumphalism (the view that one religion will displace all others), but rather the effective growth of the church and the authentic transforming power of Christ's gospel.

Seed Power

"The kingdom of God . . . is like a grain of mustard seed that a man took and sowed in his garden, and it grew and became a tree, and the birds of the air made nests in its branches" (vv. 18, 19). The tiny mustard seed (so small it is almost invisible to the eye) produces a veritable "tree" capable of housing many birds. Likewise, the kingdom, which began so insignificantly, has grown immensely so that it has a huge effect on the world, and it will continue to do so until Christ returns. The kingdom will reach all nations.

Yeast Power

"[The kingdom of God] is like leaven that a woman took and hid in three measures of flour, until it was all leavened" (v. 21). Yeast or leaven works silently and unseen—from the inside—but it affects everything. It wields incredible transforming power.

We see from these parables that the kingdom of God will go out to all the nations, and its effect will be vast and profound. The crippled woman stretching to her full height, standing tall, giving praise to God—that is what the kingdom does. It works individually—a life here, a life there—transforming men and women—creating lovers of God who spread the good news.

I do not hold to the triumphalist delusion that we will bring about a Christian nation, much less a Christian world. I reject the political delusion that the liberal church succumbed to in the 1950s when it embraced political means to bring in the kingdom. But at the same time kingdom power is immense, because gospel yeast truly transforms lives, and transformed lives preserve society.

This is the power of the kingdom of God. Jesus sees us as we are. He sees the blindness and twistedness. And he has the power to say, "You are freed."

His hands are outstretched to each of us and to everyone around us today.

65

The Narrow Door

LUKE 13:22–30

AT A CONVOCATION I ATTENDED to proclaim the year of ministers in Cambridge, Massachusetts, one of the plenary speakers, Alistair Begg, shared a heartening encounter he had experienced as he was preparing his message. He had risen early and found a restaurant next to Harvard Yard where he planned to apply some "finishing touches." As he worked, he watched Cambridge wake up, and the restaurant filled up with a variety of weird and wonderful people. Some had slept in the street. Others were apparently regulars. He was out of his element. The university culture was overwhelming, and he felt insignificant. And he began to muse about his insignificance and how foolish the gospel seemed in such a setting. He was feeling small.

But two things that happened encouraged him. When a sparrow landed on his table *inside* the restaurant, he thought of Christ's words about sparrows. Then he looked across the aisle and saw an Asian girl intently reading what appeared to be a Bible. He watched further and saw that she was indeed studying the Scriptures. So he asked, "I see that you are reading the Bible. Are you a Christian?" She smiled and replied, "Oh yes. I've found the narrow way."

Her answer was remarkable. Neither he nor I in all our years in ministry had ever heard anyone answer like that. In the ensuing conversation she explained that she had come from Korea to study at Harvard, and she was the only Christian in her family. Here was a young Christian woman 10,000 miles away from her Buddhist home (with its three million gods, the antithesis of "the narrow way") in the midst of Harvard's aggressive pluralism (which tolerates everything except the narrowness of the gospel) who so profoundly understood her Christian faith that she expressed it with unabashed acumen as "the narrow way."

As you would expect, my friend Alistair Begg was encouraged that morning to preach the Word—which he did with great effect. This young student understood and had appropriated a kingdom truth that is glossed over by so many, especially if they live in a congenial Christian subculture—namely, the entrance into God's kingdom is narrow.

Jesus' setting forth of this truth on the road to Jerusalem was in response to a question from an unnamed person in the crowd: "Lord, will those who are saved be few?" (v. 23). It was a smug, self-complacent question because the general understanding among the Jews was that all Jews except the very worst would be saved. The *Mishnah* was explicit about this:

> All Israelites have a share in the world to come, for it is written, *Thy people also shall be all righteous, they shall inherit the land for ever; the branch of my planting, the work of my hands that I may be glorified.* And these are they that have no share in the world to come: he that says that there is no resurrection of the dead prescribed in the Law, and [he that says] that the Law is not from Heaven, and an Epicurean. (Sanhedrin 10.1)[1]

So when the question rang from the crowd, the hearers expected Jesus to affirm that all Jews would make it through the pearly gates, unless they had committed especially grievous sins like the rebellion of Korah or that of Absalom. They also thought all Gentiles would be excluded from the kingdom except for a few proselytes who followed the examples of Rahab and Ruth. The question was a presumptive query meant to solidify Jewish feelings of religious superiority.

A Narrow Door (v. 24)

Jesus' regard for the question can be seen in his response, because he really did not answer it but responded with a command: "Strive to enter through the narrow door. For many, I tell you, will seek to enter and will not be able" (v. 24).

The Many

Jesus' words assaulted their complacency. "Many [of you Jews] . . . will seek to enter and will not be able." "Many," not "some"—implying that a majority of his hearers would not make it! The Jews' complacency had drawn a stinging slap, and an uneasiness spread through their hearts.

Jews in Jesus' day felt privileged to be part of the covenant community. They had the Law, the prophets, the temple. So they assumed salvation was a given. This was fatal thinking. Paul later attacked such presumption in his letter to the Romans:

> But if you call yourself a Jew and rely on the law and boast in God and know his will and approve what is excellent, because you are instructed from the law; and if you are sure that you yourself are a guide to the blind, a light to those who are in darkness, an instructor of the foolish, a teacher of children, having in the law the embodiment of knowledge and truth—you then who teach others, do you not teach yourself? (Romans 2:17–21)

Jesus' point was, your Jewish privilege had better make a difference or it is all for nothing. Sadly, *many* did not have personal faith in Christ and so were lost.

Jesus sustained this warning in his kingdom parables—for example, in the parable of the soils when the seed fell on three of the four soils in vain. Only the fourth soil yielded believers. The parable of the soils taught that many professing "believers" would be lost (cf. 8:1–15). Likewise, in the parable of the sheep and the goats, the great flock will be divided, and a large contingent of goats will be sent off to eternal punishment (Matthew 25:31–46). Privileged presumption characterizes many of the lost in this parable.

Presumption of salvation through privilege continues to delude multitudes in the professing church today. And Jesus' "many . . . will seek to enter and will not be able" applies with the same urgency. Jesus does not want to inject false fears into our minds, but he does want us to examine our lives so we will be sure to take the narrow way.

The Narrow Door

Jesus represented the way of salvation as "the narrow door." This image suggests the moral posture of the person who would strive to enter the kingdom. I. H. Marshall notes that "the imagery is akin to that of a camel passing through the needle's eye, and suggests the difficulty of facing up to the demands of Jesus in self-denial."[2] The passage to Heaven is not through the great portal of a palace, but a narrow, low door through which one must humbly squeeze. And after entering, the road remains narrow, as Jesus explained when he preached at another time: "Enter by the narrow gate. For the gate is wide and the way is easy that leads to destruction, and those who enter by it are many. For the gate is narrow and the way is hard that leads to life, and those who find it are few" (Matthew 7:13, 14).

Few people are willing to assume the humble posture and to shed what is necessary to get through the gate, and few are willing to tread the narrow road.

The Agony

The Lord's call to "strive to enter" is the Greek word *agonizomai*, from which we get our word *agonize*. This is the kind of moral effort necessary to enter the kingdom. "We are not saved by effort, but we shall not believe without effort."[3]

In light of what is at stake (Heaven or Hell) and in light of the finality of eternity, we cannot strive too much to get through the narrow door. It must be sought with all that we are. The Word must be mined. Prayer ought to be perpetual.

> "Do not work for the food that perishes, but for the food that endures to eternal life, which the Son of Man will give to you. For on him God the Father has set his seal." Then they said to him, "What must we do, to be doing the works of God?" Jesus answered them, "This is the work of God, that you believe in him whom he has sent." (John 6:27–29)

We must agonize over being sure to enter the kingdom of God.

A Closed Door (vv. 25–27)

Closing

There is a time limit on the offer of salvation, as Jesus made so ominously clear: "When once the master of the house has risen and shut the door, and you begin to stand outside and to knock . . ." (v. 25a). The gate is open right now. The fact that you can read these words in your mortal flesh means that you can respond if you so wish. But when your body is gone, so will be the opportunity. "It is appointed for man to die once, and after that comes judgment" (Hebrews 9:27). Today you are alive. Therefore the door is still open, though it will not always be. "Now is the day of salvation" (2 Corinthians 6:2). If you do not yet know Christ, call to him today!

Slammed

Eventually the narrow door will be slammed shut by either death or the Lord's return, ushering in eternal tragedy for those who have not entered the kingdom. This fact was portrayed in the prophetic dialogue Jesus then shared:

> "Lord, open to us," then he will answer you, "I do not know where you come from." Then you will begin to say, "We ate and drank in your presence, and you taught in our streets." But he will say, "I tell you, I do not know where you come from. Depart from me, all you workers of evil!" (vv. 25b–27)

Two complementary things kept them out of the kingdom. First, they had *no personal relationship* with the Master. Twice Jesus issued a categorical denial of relationship: "I do not know where you come from." This is a total denial despite the fact that they argue, "We ate and drank in your presence, and you taught in our streets." None of the crowd could persuade Christ to say that their superficial knowledge of him had established a relationship. They were strangers.

Some today may argue that they have eaten and drunk with Christ at the Lord's Table, and they have heard his Word preached in his church. This is all very good, but it does not establish relationship, and some who have never missed the Lord's Table and the preaching of the Word will hear him say, "I do not know where you come from." If attendance in the Lord's house could save a soul, Caiaphas would be in glory. If hearing the Word was enough, Herod would be in Heaven.

Even engaging in ministry does not prove relationship. In the Sermon on the Mount, shortly after Jesus urged his hearers to enter through the narrow gate (Matthew 7:13, 14), he warned:

> Not everyone who says to me, "Lord, Lord," will enter the kingdom of heaven, but the one who does the will of my Father who is in heaven. On that day many will say to me, "Lord, Lord, did we not prophesy in your name, and cast out demons in your name, and do many mighty works in your name?" And then will I declare to them, "I never knew you; depart from me, you workers of lawlessness." (Mathew 7:21–23)

We may be preachers and have perhaps ministered to thousands. We may be Sunday school teachers and point many little ones to Christ. We may be missionaries and are held up as paragons of sacrifice, and yet end up as castaways. Why? Because mighty works do not save us, but only vital union with Christ through real faith.[4] So the burning question is, does Christ know you? *Are you in authentic relationship with him?*

The corollary question is, has the relationship with Christ that you claim to have turned you away from evil? Are you morally improved from God's point of view? Or will he say, "Depart from me, you worker of lawlessness"? The telling question is not a matter of ministry or standing in the church but of authentic righteousness.

A Closed Feast (vv. 28–30)

Surprise Exclusion

When Moses encountered God at the burning bush, God identified himself as "the God of your father, the God of Abraham, the God of Isaac, and the

God of Jacob" (Exodus 3:6). Those men were the progenitors of Israel and representatives of the greatest members of their race. So we can understand how horrifying Jesus' next sentence was to his hearers: "In that place there will be weeping and gnashing of teeth, when you see Abraham and Isaac and Jacob and all the prophets in the kingdom of God but you yourselves cast out" (v. 28). "Weeping" indicates sorrow, "gnashing of teeth" fierce rage. Many Israelites would be cast out of glorified Israel!

Surprise Inclusion

But there was more: "And people will come from east and west, and from north and south, and recline at table in the kingdom of God" (v. 29). Unbelieving Israel will be cast out, but believing Gentiles will sit down with the three patriarchs and the redeemed house of Israel. Because they belong to Christ they are, in Paul's words, "Abraham's offspring, heirs according to promise" (Galatians 3:29). And they will not only be there—they will be joyously feasting!

Eternal Reversal

Who will fellowship at the feast? Evidently the big three, and the prophets, and a bunch of no-name Gentiles, because Jesus concluded, "Behold, some are last who will be first, and some are first who will be last" (v. 30). Because of God's grace all will receive the same reward, as the parable of the workers in the vineyard makes so clear. The master paid those who worked an hour the same as those who worked all day, answering the day-long workers' objections by saying:

> "Friend, I am doing you no wrong. Did you not agree with me for a denarius? Take what belongs to you and go. I choose to give to this last worker as I give to you. Am I not allowed to do what I choose with what belongs to me? Or do you begrudge my generosity?" So the last will be first, and the first last. (Matthew 20:13–16)

Closing Reflections

Perhaps you have noticed that this "narrow door" text touches on one of Luke's grand themes—the universality of the gospel—the good news of salvation for all people, both Jews and Gentiles. Christ's words teach us that the kingdom is narrower than his Jewish hearers thought because they assumed that all Israel would automatically be included. But Jesus said that many of them would not make it through "the narrow door." The door's narrowness demanded humility. It demanded moral determination. Only those who are in relationship with God go through the door. Jesus later explained in his High Priestly prayer, "And this is eternal life, that they know you the only true God, and Jesus Christ whom you have sent" (John 17:3). This relationship with God delivered them from evildoing.

But here is the ultimate beauty—the narrowness of the kingdom has created a kingdom that is broader than we would ever have thought! This is because "the narrow way" is spiritual and not hereditary, because it is a relationship with God that comes by faith, because it makes men and women new from the inside out, and because it is all by grace.

Consequently, there is hope for you and me. There is hope for all Jews and Gentiles. There is hope for a Korean girl from a family of Buddhists. There is hope for a Hebrew of the Hebrews. There is hope for every shade of suburbanite and city dweller. The narrow way is wide open to all.

Have you entered it? If not, Jesus says, "Strive to enter through the narrow door." It is not too late!

66

Mourning for the City

LUKE 13:31–35

LUKE LEAVES US IN no doubt about the Pharisees' dislike for Jesus. Jesus' pronouncement of six woes, three on the Pharisees and three on their friends the scribes as recorded in chapter 11, rendered them implacable enemies. As a result, "The scribes and the Pharisees began to press him hard and to provoke him to speak about many things, lying in wait for him, to catch him in something he might say" (11:53, 54). They wanted to get Jesus!

And Jesus did nothing to soften their ire. In fact, he immediately warned his disciples, "Beware of the leaven of the Pharisees, which is hypocrisy" (12:1). In Jesus' estimation they were swollen carriers of hypocrisy who passed on their poison to their followers.

So when some Pharisees came to Jesus with what appeared to be friendly advice ("Get away from here, for Herod wants to kill you," v. 31), Jesus was not fooled. He was the gentle Lamb of God, but even a lamb is suspicious of wolves when they feign concern for its safety. Jesus knew there was collusion between his enemies. Herod had already been politically damaged by his murder of John the Baptist, and he did not want another such blotch on his record. So he used the Pharisees to pass on the threat to Jesus, hoping he would be frightened into going south to Judea. And the Pharisees liked Herod's ploy because if Jesus could be manipulated into traveling to Judea, he would fall to the powerful Sanhedrin.

Jesus' Message to His Enemies (vv. 32, 33)

Their malevolent intentions were ultra clear to Jesus, and he replied to Herod and then to the Pharisees in perfectly crafted parallel answers.

To Herod

"And he said to them, 'Go and tell that fox, "Behold, I cast out demons and perform cures today and tomorrow, and the third day I finish my course"'" (v. 32). "Fox" was common parlance in Hebrew for a person with base cunning[1] and was used to designate someone as insignificant and worthless. It was an expression of utter contempt.[2] Significantly, Herod is the only individual whom Jesus is recorded as treating with contempt. Later when Jesus stood before Herod, the Master would say nothing to him at all, again showing contempt for him. As Leon Morris has remarked, "When Jesus has nothing to say to a man that man's position is hopeless."[3] Herod was a dead man in every way.

Jesus' disdain showed itself in his answer: "I cast out demons and perform cures [i.e., I will continue to do my normal ministry] today and tomorrow, and the third day I finish my course [i.e., I will carry on my ministry for a short time and then I will be finished]." To Herod this meant that Jesus would do what he set out to do at his own pace and his own schedule until he was finished, despite Herod's attempts at manipulation. But in the wider context of Luke, this was a cryptic reference to Jesus' death and resurrection being under divine control. King Jesus had addressed Herod, the petty monarch, with regal contempt and kingly confidence. This was sovereign premeditation! As the Master said on another occasion when he affirmed that he would lay down his life for his sheep, "No one takes it from me, but I lay it down of my own accord. I have authority to lay it down, and I have authority to take it up again" (John 10:18).

To the Pharisees

Having aggressively answered Herod, Jesus' corresponding answer to the Pharisees was even sharper: "Nevertheless, I must go on my way today and tomorrow and the day following, for it cannot be that a prophet should perish away from Jerusalem" (v. 33). What scathing irony! Jesus said in essence, "Jerusalem has the monopoly on killing the prophets, and on this highest occasion the city will not be deprived" (cf. 2 Chronicles 24:20–22; Jeremiah 26:20–23; 38:4–6). "It would never do for a prophet to perish except in Jerusalem!" If Herod or anybody else wanted to kill Jesus, he had better make plans to go to Jerusalem—because then, and only then, would he die.

What revealing strokes this adds to our portrait of Jesus. We see his human bravery. It would rightly be regarded as undue cruelty to a condemned criminal if each day he was moved a foot closer to the gallows. But this was Jesus' daily experience as he deliberately chose to go to Jerusalem. Jesus knew he was the Lamb who was to be sacrificed there. He was like an all-knowing Isaac who carried the wood of sacrifice and the knife on his back as he dutifully climbed the mountain knowing where and who was the offering.[4] Jesus was and is the hero of our souls.

We also see his extraordinary human spirit. The relentless terror of the cross daily loomed higher over his life, but his love for others drove him on. He was truly sympathetic with those who came to him, totally engaged when they spoke. He was tender with every need. He wore himself out ministering to others. And all the while he moved closer to his cosmic excruciation.

This is a marvelous still life of Jesus, the incarnate Son, the exalted Son, our Savior and Priest.

> In the days of his flesh, Jesus offered up prayers and supplications, with loud cries and tears, to him who was able to save him from death, and he was heard because of his reverence. Although he was a son, he learned obedience through what he suffered. And being made perfect, he became the source of eternal salvation to all who obey him, being designated by God a high priest after the order of Melchizedek. (Hebrews 5:7–10)

Jesus Message to His People (vv. 34, 35)

Jesus had answered Herod and the proud Pharisees with royal disdain and irony. And the mention of his death in Jerusalem turned his thoughts to his people, represented by Jerusalem (cf. Psalm 147:2; Galatians 4:26).

Jesus' Longing

So he gave out a pathetic soliloquy: "O Jerusalem, Jerusalem, the city that kills the prophets and stones those who are sent to it! How often would I have gathered your children together as a hen gathers her brood under her wings, and you were not willing!" (v. 34). Jesus expressed his desire for his people with a magnificent image, that of a mother bird brooding over her young in the nest. The emphasis on "her wings" reminds us of the first use of this image in Scripture in the Song of Moses when he celebrated God's care for Jacob (i.e., Israel):

> He found him in a desert land,
>   and in the howling waste of the wilderness;
> he encircled him, he cared for him,
>   he kept him as the apple of his eye.
> Like an eagle that stirs up its nest,

that flutters over its young,
spreading out its wings, catching them,
bearing them on its pinions. (Deuteronomy 32:10, 11)

The picture of an eagle spreading her vast wings in protection, and even scooping fallen chicks from the air and carrying them aloft to safety, is instructive and encouraging. This image was a favorite of the authors of the Psalms.

Keep me as the apple of your eye;
hide me in the shadow of your wings. (17:8)

How precious is your steadfast love, O God!
The children of mankind take refuge in the shadow of your wings. (36:7)

Be merciful to me, O God, be merciful to me,
for in you my soul takes refuge;
in the shadow of your wings I will take refuge,
till the storms of destruction pass by. (57:1)

Let me dwell in your tent forever!
Let me take refuge under the shelter of your wings! (61:4)

For you have been my help,
and in the shadow of your wings I will sing for joy. (63:7)

He will cover you with his pinions,
and under his wings you will find refuge;
his faithfulness is a shield and buckler. (91:4)

Tucked under his wings, one finds sustenance, warmth, and security. This is not a sentimental image. This is what Jesus longs to do for us. It is a metaphor divinely chosen to convey God's longing in Christ for his people. Have you allowed him to tuck you snugly under his wings?

I recall my initial experience of this as I began my teenage years. I think it was particularly monumental for me because my father died when I was four, leaving my brother and me in the care of three poor, struggling women—all widows—my mother, my grandmother, and my aunt. I can never once remember feeling sorry for myself, but I can often remember feeling alone, like I was in a universe by myself. But when I met Christ, that emptiness disappeared! I felt like I had come home to a warm house on a cold night. I was sheltered under his wings.

This metaphor poignantly expressed Jesus' heart cry for his people. But they were "not willing"! They were responsible for their aloneness and ultimate lostness. This is also true of us if we do not choose to be under the security of his wings.

Are you under his wings? Do you want to be? Will you come to him?

Jesus' Prophecy

Because his people refused to turn to him, Jesus gave this prophecy: "Behold, your house is forsaken" (v. 35a). Jerusalem, the center of the nation, was destroyed by the Romans in A.D. 68–70. The city was starved into submission before its desolation. According to Josephus, the roofs were thronged with famished women with babies in their arms, and the alleys were filled with corpses of the elderly. Children and young people swollen from starvation "roamed like phantoms through the market-places and collapsed wherever their doom overtook them." But there was no lamenting or wailing, because famine had strangled their emotions. Jerusalem could not bury all the bodies, so they were flung over the wall. The silence was broken only by the laughter of robbers stripping the bodies.[5]

But Christ's verdict on Jerusalem did not end with desolation. Judgment was not the final word. The Jews were to look farther into the future because Jesus concluded, "And I tell you, you will not see me until you say, 'Blessed is he who comes in the name of the Lord!'" (v. 35b). This quotation from Psalm 118:26 was properly quoted by Luke again in the mouths of Galilean pilgrims as they celebrated Jesus' Triumphal Entry into Jerusalem (cf. 19:38).

But there is a further messianic application because these words represent believing Israel's response to Christ at his second advent. When Christ returns, many in Israel will understand the words of many relevant Scriptures, including Isaiah 53:3–5:

> He was despised and rejected by men;
> a man of sorrows, and acquainted with grief;
> and as one from whom men hide their faces
> he was despised, and we esteemed him not.
>
> Surely he has borne our griefs
> and carried our sorrows;
> yet we esteemed him stricken,
> smitten by God, and afflicted.
> But he was pierced for our transgressions;
> he was crushed for our iniquities;

> upon him was the chastisement that brought us peace,
> and with his wounds we are healed.

They will believe, along with believing Gentiles.

Closing Reflections

The theme of 13:31–35 is that everything regarding salvation has to do with and is dependent upon Jesus' loving determination to die in Jerusalem for his people. Jesus would not be manipulated by Herod's threats into changing either his timetable or his destination. He contemptuously informed Herod that he would continue his ministry at his own pace until he finished his goal. Then with scathing irony he told the Pharisees that he would get to Jerusalem in his own good time, where he would die.

Jesus is the hero of our souls. He fully understood what lay ahead and faced it fully as every step took him closer to death. Jesus was determined to die for our sins. He would not be deterred. He died for us because he chose to do so.

This rocklike determination was grounded on his tender love. God incarnate tenderly longed to pull his people to himself, under his wings. This is what God wants to do and can do for you and for me.

Unwilling people are under his judgment. But the gospel goes out to them again and again and again. And those who respond will cry at the second advent, "Blessed is he who comes in the name of the Lord."

He has done everything. All you need to do is believe and be willing.

67

The Dinner Party, Part 1

LUKE 14:1–14

IT WAS A SETUP ALL THE WAY. The place had been carefully chosen—the home of a prominent Pharisee where he and his notable guests could observe Jesus firsthand and then bear unified testimony to any and every transgression. Also, the dinner party was scheduled on the Sabbath, a day that Jesus had reportedly violated on three separate occasions when he cast out demons and healed Simon Peter's mother (4:31–41), then healed a man with a withered hand (6:6–11), and most recently healed the bent woman (13:10–17). Further, most conveniently, a sick man was present—"a man . . . who had dropsy"—whose torso was pathetically swollen by the retention of body fluids in the stomach and chest cavities and connective tissues. Such swelling often indicates organ failure. The man was very sick, probably terminally ill.

A terrible snare had been set for Jesus, baited with misery that he would find irresistible. They thought they had Jesus trapped.

But Jesus confounded them with a single question: "Is it lawful to heal on the Sabbath, or not?" (v. 3). If they said yes, they would appear soft and hypocritical regarding the stringent measures they required for Sabbath observance. But if they said no, they could be accused of being inhumane and uncaring about human suffering. It was one thing for the Pharisees to condemn Jesus for healing on the Sabbath. It was quite another to take responsibility for denying recovery to a needy person.[1] Trapped, their only response was sulking silence.

"Then he took him and healed him and sent him away" (v. 4). This must have been an amazing spectacle because "healed" here means completely healed. The watery fluids dissipated, his organs healed, the swelling disappeared! But Luke gave little detail because he wanted his readers to focus on the utter entrapment of the Pharisees and scribes by Jesus.

Jesus' second question further sealed their lips: "And he said to them, 'Which of you, having a son or an ox that has fallen into a well on a Sabbath day, will not immediately pull him out?' And they could not reply to these things" (vv. 5, 6). Their Sabbath regulations allowed them to rescue their animals, as did the later *Mishnah* (Shabbath 18:3). So to forbid the deliverance of humans would have meant they treated their animals better than people.

The dinner party remained silent for a few moments, an uneasy, resentful quiet. For a few golden seconds humble, gentle Jesus rose high above his arrogant host and fellow guests.

Though they were leaders in Israel, the people at that dinner party were a lost bunch, tragically far from the kingdom. In their keeping of legalistic minutiae, they had completely missed the point of the Law—they neither loved God nor their neighbors. They were actually proud lovers of self and position. None of them would make it into the kingdom unless there was a radical change in their spiritual disposition.

So Jesus went after their souls. What we have in the extended record of this dinner party is brilliant lunchtime evangelism. We will study this in this and the next chapter of this book.

The Gospels reveal that our Lord was a close student of everyday life. Nothing escaped him regarding human nature and conduct. Perhaps he watched the seating of the party with a faint smile so as not to reveal his disapproval (just yet!). What he saw was scandalous and so revealing. What he witnessed was similar to what air travelers sometimes see today when their plane lands. The plane touches down, and the flight attendant reminds the passengers to check all their personal belongings and to remain seated until the seat belt sign is turned off. However, some passengers leap to their feet, grab their coats from the overhead compartments, and stumble down the swaying aisle to the front of the aircraft. Some may have a good reason, but most are simply being selfish.[2] Their behavior says, "I am the most important person in my life, and my 'firstness' will be asserted anytime I wish."

Jesus watched the elite dinner guests make their moves for the honored seats. Jesus saw some deft moves as certain guests, all elbows, slipped into the honored places on the surrounding couches. Earlier in his ministry Jesus had ridiculed the Pharisees for their love of place: "Woe to you Pharisees! For you love the best seat in the synagogues and greetings in the marketplaces" (11:43), but this group was unaware of what he thought, or they simply did not care.

The truth was there for all to see. The Pharisees and scribes, despite all their god-talk and religious posturing, were a selfish, self-seeking, ambitious lot. Selfishness always reduces the importance of others and enlarges the importance of one's own life. "I'm the greatest, so where is my seat?" "I'm superior, and this place reflects my worth!" They assumed that if they did not get the chief seats, the meal, regardless of how good the fare or the fellowship was, would be a bummer. It was important that they be seen in a worthy place.

Their sin was intensely spiritual. Human honor gave them a sense of substance and reality. Human recognition told them they were superior to their fellows. And if that was true, they were also of greater value before God. The same illusion is rampant today. Salvation by recognition. Eternal life through temporal significance. Immortality through notoriety.

The dinner party was a dinner of the damned, as the final verse of the section indicates (v. 24). Jesus does not wish that on anyone.

How to Be a Dinner Guest (vv. 7–11)

Jesus began with some seemingly prosaic advice drawn from an old proverb: "Do not put yourself forward in the king's presence or stand in the place of the great, for it is better to be told, 'Come up here,' than to be put lower in the presence of a noble" (Proverbs 25:6, 7).

How Not to Seat Yourself

First Jesus gave some common-sense advice to the guests on what not to do:

> When you are invited by someone to a wedding feast, do not sit down in a place of honor, lest someone more distinguished than you be invited by him, and he who invited you both will come and say to you, "Give your place to this person," and then you will begin with shame to take the lowest place. (vv. 8, 9)

This is an outrageous sketch. The guest arrives early, surveys the dinner arrangements, chooses the most prominent place in the room, and ceremoniously seats himself. He loves it! All eyes are upon him at the front of the table. The seeming adulation makes him feel so good about himself. He imagines what excellent, respectful thoughts the others must be thinking about him. What a meal! Everything tastes so good!

Is it his imagination? All the guests' eyes seem to be staring at him. This is even better than he had hoped. Then he feels a presence hovering nearby. He looks up—the host is asking him to move so a distinguished personage can have his seat. Instantly he feels hot, flushed. He rises perspiring and slinks to an obscure seat. Everyone's eyes are still on him, unfortunately, and there is nowhere to hide. Pride has made him an absurd little man. Spiritually "he is an outrageous freak, a cardboard figure on stilts . . . blown away by the winds of reality."[3]

How to Seat Yourself

Jesus went on with his common-sense advice, now giving the proper way to be seated: "But when you are invited, go and sit in the lowest place, so that when your host comes he may say to you, 'Friend, move up higher.' Then you will be honored in the presence of all who sit at table with you" (v. 10). Hundreds of years later this was still standardized Hebrew common sense. The fifth-century *Leviticus Rabbah I* recommends: "Stay two or three seats below your place and sit until they say to you, 'Go (farther) up.' Do not begin by going up because (then) they may say to you, 'Go down.' It is better that they should say to you 'Go up, go up,' than that they should say to you, 'Go down, go down.'"[4] This was good practical advice.

But there is more here than social wisdom. Our Lord was not concerned that his hearers merely learn to take the lower seat so they would avoid embarrassment and then achieve high human honor when they were ostentatiously ushered from the lowest seat to the highest. Neither was he teaching the Pharisees and scribes to put on a staged humility, so they would be greatly honored above their peers. Jesus hated the pride that pretends to be humble. Rather, he was imparting an eternal spiritual principle that will be evident in the end when everything is made right.

An Axiom of the Kingdom

Jesus stated this as an immutable law, an axiom of the kingdom: "For everyone who exalts himself will be humbled, and he who humbles himself will be exalted" (v. 11). Mary, the pregnant mother of Jesus, testified that this axiom was at the very heart of Jesus' kingdom work when she used the same key words "exalt" and "humble" in the *Magnificat*—"he has brought down the mighty from their thrones and exalted those of humble estate" (1:52). This is what God in Christ does. Humbling the proud and exalting the humble is an essential kingdom principle and work. Here in 14:11 "will be humbled" and "will be exalted" are what New Testament scholars call theological passives[5]—it is God who humbles the proud and exalts the humble. It is his personal work, and he will see to it.

The Pharisees' and scribes' undignified scramble for the most honored seats identified pride as a particularly damning sin of the religious. Jesus made the same point in 18:9–14, in the contrast between the Pharisee who prayed, "God, I thank you that I am not like other men . . . or even like this tax collector" and the tax collector who prayed, "God, be merciful to me, a sinner!" Jesus concluded on that occasion, "I tell you, this man went down to his house justified, rather than the other. For everyone who exalts himself will be humbled, but the one who humbles himself will be exalted" (18:14).

Jesus used this axiom again in reference to the scribes and Pharisees as a prelude to his seven woes against them in Matthew 23:12, 13: "Whoever exalts himself will be humbled, and whoever humbles himself will be exalted. But woe to you, scribes and Pharisees, hypocrites! For you shut the kingdom of heaven in people's faces. For you neither enter yourselves nor allow those who would enter to go in."

Jesus' axiom is equally penetrating and appropriate today—because it is not believed! Washington, D.C. doesn't believe it, despite its nods to the likes of Billy Graham and Mother Teresa. The Democratic and Republican Parties do not believe it. Listen to the campaign rhetoric. Professional athletes do not believe it. Business executives do not believe it. Has Wall Street ever advertised executive positions as especially available to the humble and lowly of heart? The high church does not believe it either, with its penchant for vestments, sedan chairs, and miters. Neither does the low church with its shiny designer suits, coiffed hairdos, and telethons.

Do we believe it? The truth is, we are sometimes ambivalent. We subscribe to the axiom in principle. We loathe the proud climbing in others. But we do it too, only we are far more subtle. The trick is to get into the prominent seat without appearing to try, to get there all the while protesting, to decry it in others while we ourselves subtly pursue it.

God help us all! And he will, and does. "'God opposes the proud but gives grace to the humble.' Humble yourselves, therefore, under the mighty hand of God so that at the proper time he may exalt you" (1 Peter 5:5, 6).

How to Be a Dinner Host (vv. 12–14)

Having given advice to the honor-seeking dinner guests, Jesus next focused his observations and advice upon the host and his guest list.

Who Not to Invite

"He said also to the man who had invited him, 'When you give a dinner or a banquet, do not invite your friends or your brothers or your relatives or rich neighbors, lest they also invite you in return and you be repaid'" (v. 12). Jesus was not, as it might first sound, discouraging normal hospitality with family and friends and loved ones. He regularly accepted invitations to such gatherings—for example, with Lazarus and his wonderful sisters where he was refreshed (cf. 10:38–42).

What Jesus is against is limiting our guest list to family members and friends who can repay us with a reciprocal dinner. He forbids what makes up so much of elite modern social life—an endless round of giving and getting in return—the social *quid pro quo*.

The penetrating point Jesus is leading to is that one's social ethics show whether one is a member of the kingdom of God. Elitism indicates a selfish, proud, shriveled soul. Reciprocation as a primary goal is the product of an immense self-focus. If we do not reach out to others who cannot benefit us (and we should not limit this to dinners), we must ask ourselves if we are true believers.

Whom to Invite

Jesus went on to be very specific about the proper guest list: "But when you give a feast, invite the poor, the crippled, the lame, the blind, and you will be blessed, because they cannot repay you. For you will be repaid at the resurrection of the just" (vv. 13, 14). This is the first mention of the resurrection in Luke's Gospel, though it is regularly assumed in Luke (cf. 9:24; 10:14; 12:5; 13:27, 28). The payoff to the generous host is immense—he will be resurrected as one of the righteous at the end of the age. And he is "blessed" now. His reward was long ago prophesied by Daniel: "And many of those who sleep in the dust of the earth shall awake, some to everlasting life, and some to shame and everlasting contempt. And those who are wise shall shine like the brightness of the sky above; and those who turn many to righteousness, like the stars forever and ever" (Daniel 12:2, 3). He will shine forever in the kingdom of God!

Closing Reflections

The scribes and Pharisees tried to trap Jesus that Sabbath day. But with two penetrating questions he reduced them to frustrated silence. Then over the table he mercifully reached out to those proud, social-climbing status seekers, undressing their concealed, half-forgotten motives and laying them out on the dinner table.

The guests rushed for honor, but "everyone who exalts himself will be humbled, and he who humbles himself will be exalted" (v. 11). Unless they repented, they would be humbled and lost. The host's reciprocal pay-me-back hospitality revealed an immensely selfish heart that would suffer loss at the resurrection.

They all presumed to be in the kingdom but were in fact lost. Jesus was saying that how we live reveals the authenticity or absence of our faith. A proud, me-first lifestyle (no matter how deftly hidden) indicates we are not part of the kingdom. A selfish *quid pro quo* social life is not a kingdom life.

True members of the kingdom love God and are learning to love their neighbors as themselves (Leviticus 19:18).

68

The Dinner Party, Part 2

LUKE 14:15–24

JESUS WAS IN THE MIDST OF A Sabbath dinner party that had grown quite intense. The party became tension-filled from the moment Jesus stepped through the door because the religious leaders "were watching him carefully" (14:1). They had been invited to the dinner for just that purpose. And the tension escalated when he healed a man of dropsy (edema in modern medical terminology), then silenced his would-be critics with a deft question and an allusion to their own rabbinical practice of rescuing mere animals but not people on the Sabbath. As if that were not enough, Jesus went on to criticize both the guests and the host—the guests for seeking the seats of honor, and the host for inviting only those who could return the favor. Everyone in the room had been deliberately insulted by Jesus.

It is reasonable to imagine that in the silence no one was eating the sumptuous fare. The party was becoming a disaster. The host and his friends were silently enduring a theological meltdown. They were mortified.

A quick-tongued guest then attempted to save the day with a pious exclamation. "When one of those who reclined at table with him heard these things, he said to him, 'Blessed is everyone who will eat bread in the kingdom of God!'" (v. 15). The man's words no doubt had a feigned earnestness to them. The exclamation sounded good—but it was insincere. Its pious language evoked everyone's assent and a momentary hope of escaping Jesus' onslaught. The man's statement mirrored the religious leaders' corporate confidence. In essence it meant, "Blessed are the likes of us who will eat at the feast in the kingdom of God." "Amen! Well said! Now pass the condiments . . ."

But their confidence was misleading, and Jesus could not let the exclamation pass—for their souls' sake. He knew that in their inmost being there was little desire for God's kingdom, pious declarations aside. So there at the Sabbath feast, with the religious leaders at the table, Jesus delivered the parable of the great banquet to expose the true motivations and desires of the religious establishment. Jesus' tale issues a warning to every pious heart.

The Invitation (vv. 16–20)

Invitations Extended

> But [Jesus] said to him, "A man once gave a great banquet and invited many. And at the time for the banquet he sent his servant to say to those who had been invited, 'Come, for everything is now ready.'" (vv. 16, 17)

A man of immense means extended an invitation to his friends to attend "a great banquet," the greatness of which would have derived from two things—a large list of names and an extensive menu of culinary delights and libations. This was a feast no one would wish to miss. This "great banquet" pictured the ultimate kingdom banquet, the supper of the Lamb (cf. 13:28, 29; 22:16; Revelation 19:9). Using the symbol of a feast for Heaven is of immense spiritual significance because it suggests eternal satisfaction. Even in this world, a banquet is much more than a means of satisfying physical hunger—it is more than eating.

As David Gooding has explained, "The metaphor of feasting, as distinct from merely eating a meal assures us that no true potential appetite, desire, or longing given us by God will prove to have been a deception, but all will be granted their richest and most sublime fulfillment."[1] The "great banquet" is a lavish, sumptuous image of the kingdom of Heaven that will be exceeded by its reality—joyous satisfaction! And, of course, the ultimate convener and host will be Christ himself.

The custom of invitation in Jesus' time involved two invitations that can be traced back to the Book of Esther (cf. 5:8; 6:14) and extended well into the fifth century A.D. when the Midrash on Lamentations said of the men of Jerusalem, "None of them would attend a banquet unless he was invited twice" (4:2).[2] Therefore, when a prominent banquet was given, invitations were first sent out announcing the time of the upcoming meal, and the guests indicated their acceptance. Then on the day of the banquet a servant was sent out to reinvite the invited guests.[3] To accept the first invitation but decline the second was an unconscionable insult.

Regrets Returned

And yet in Jesus' parable those who had accepted the first invitation unanimously begged off with lame excuses.

Century 21 excuse. "But they all alike began to make excuses. The first said to him, 'I have bought a field, and I must go out and see it. Please have me excused'" (v. 18). Some excuse! Who would ever purchase land in his town without looking it over? Besides, the field was not going to run away! But at least he was courteous and couched his excuse as a matter of duty—"I must go out and see it." But it was still just an excuse.

Bovine excuse. The second excuse was less courteous: "Another said, 'I have bought five yoke of oxen, and I go to examine them. Please have me excused'" (v. 19). He did not argue duty but simply said, "I go to examine them." But the excuse was transparently flimsy. No one would buy ten oxen (20,000 pounds of livestock) without knowing their capabilities.

Nuptial excuse. The third excuse was terse and rude: "And another said, 'I have married a wife, and therefore I cannot come'" (v. 20). This one may have even cited Scripture (Deuteronomy 24:5), but he used it wrongly because that text exempts the newly married from duties, specifically the military, but not from parties.

The first two excuses had to do with material possessions, and the third with affections. Possessions and affections cover virtually every reason by which men and women give their regrets to the kingdom.

Furthermore, the basic thinking behind their regrets reveals humankind's universal rejection of the kingdom. It is obvious that their refusal to come to the feast was contrary to sound reason. The decision to forgo a sumptuous feast prepared for you and your friends, to forgo the joy and laughter and satisfactions offered in order to visit your properties or your farm machinery, or even to be with your new wife, does not make good sense. They will all be there when you return. Your new wife might even be glad for a break from your wonderful presence!

Jesus offers the kingdom, a perpetual feast of peace, a feast of help, guidance, friendship, rest, victory over self, control of passions, supremacy over circumstances—a feast of joy, tranquillity, deathlessness, Heaven opened, immeasurable hope—*salvation.* Yet people turn their backs on this feast, preferring a visit with their possessions and affections.

Jesus' parable does not demean our possessions (our fields and oxen) or our affections (our loved ones). These are all legitimate. We certainly ought to check out our land, try our oxen, give pleasure to our loved ones. In fact, the more a man lives upon the feast that is in Christ, the more fit he will be for all these other enjoyments. The field will be better tended, the oxen better utilized, and his wife more tenderly and sacredly loved. But if our possessions and affections are so preferred that they become excuses to turn down Christ's feast, our thinking is absurd and our souls in danger.

The real reason the three invitees offered their lame excuses was that they really did not want to go to the feast. Their excuses that, in their minds, made attendance at the feast impossible would have evaporated if they really wanted to be there. In today's terms, if they were offered front-row seats at the NBA Championships, or a box seat to hear "The Three Tenors" (Pavarotti, Domingo, and Carreras), or a week's fly fishing on the Madison, or a week's shopping in Paris, they would have found someone to tend the field, the oxen, and, yes, even the home. Make no mistake, the real reason people turn away from the eternal feast is that they do not want to be there. They have no appetite for higher things.

It is easy to make general applications, but this text is talking about us and our preferences. We need to ask ourselves whether we like our car more than we like God. If Christ's banquet and a large worldly estate were spread before us as options, would we rather have the estate?

Why is it that when Christ offers forgiveness, peace, eternal life, and an eternal feast, so few respond? Why is it that people do not want the kingdom? It is because their thinking is skewed. They do not think rightly about the eternal. In the depths of their hearts they do not want God.

The religious leaders in Christ's day acted as if they wanted the kingdom, but in fact they did not. What a tragedy! The hardest people to reach are those who say, "Blessed is everyone who will eat bread in the kingdom of God!" (v. 15), who bow toward God's Word but are unwilling to come to the feast.

Successive Invitations (vv. 21–23)

Luke does not tell us how those at the dinner party responded to Jesus' parable. Some of them must have seen where the story was going—that they cared little for God's kingdom despite their affirmation to be kingdom seekers.

Outcasts Invited

Likely few or none of them were ready for the next turn in the tale—namely, the kingdom offered to outcasts. "So the servant came and reported these things to his master. Then the master of the house became angry and said to his servant, 'Go out quickly to the streets and lanes of the city, and bring in the poor and crippled and blind and lame'" (v. 21).

Historically, from the time of the giving of the Law, the physically blemished were barred from full participation in worship (cf. Leviticus 21:17–23). The rule had been rigorously stressed in the Qumran community (cf. I Q Sa 2:5ff. CD 13:4–7).[4] Of course, their disabilities also forced many into poverty, making them ragged outcasts. But now the sumptuous feast, the lavishly appointed tables, and the endless entrees of exquisite cuisine were set before many who could not even see it all—blind beggars. The lame and crippled hobbled to the tables, their eager eyes reflecting the bountiful feast. Pitiful rags draped from bent limbs as they eased awkwardly into place. Amazing!

This is, of course, what the gospel does. Listen to the lines of Vachal Lindsey's poem "General William Booth Enters Heaven":

> Walking lepers followed, rank on rank,
> Lurching bravoes from the ditches dank . . .
> Vermin-eaten saints with mouldy breath,
> Unwashed legions from the ways of death—
> Drabs and vixens in a flash made whole!
> Gone was the weasel-head, the snout, the jowl;
> Sages and sibyls now, and athletes clean,
> Rulers of empires, and of forests green![5]

In Jesus' parable, the subclasses of society, those of less noble standing, were called to the table. But the great banquet still had many unfilled spaces.

Gentiles Invited

So the servant approached his master. "'Sir,' the servant said, 'what you commanded has been done, and still there is room.' And the master said to the servant, 'Go out to the highways and hedges and compel people to come in, that my house may be filled'" (vv. 22, 23). This is a prophetic reference to the Gentiles who would soon be invited into the kingdom through faith in Christ (cf. Acts 13:46; 18:6; 28:23–28). The Apostle Paul's heart would be aflame with his gospel mission to the Gentiles.

Historically, the phrase "compel people to come in" (literally, "force them to enter") has been abused, as, for example, by the leaders of the Inquisition. But the point of it is that outcasts, Gentiles, and the poor would need some convincing in order to overcome their natural reticence. The servant was not to take no for an answer. The feast must be filled. No seat can be left empty.

And so it will be in the eternal state. When all the seats are filled by Jews and Gentiles, many (or most!) of whom are poor, crippled, blind, and lame, the feast will begin. What rejoicing there will be!

> Then I heard what seemed to be the voice of a great multitude, like the roar of many waters and like the sound of mighty peals of thunder, crying out,
>
> "Hallelujah!
> For the Lord our God
> the Almighty reigns.
> Let us rejoice and exult
> and give him the glory,
> for the marriage of the Lamb has come,
> and his Bride has made herself ready;
> it was granted her to clothe herself
> with fine linen, bright and pure"—
>
> for the fine linen is the righteous deeds of the saints.
>
> And the angel said to me, "Write this: Blessed are those who are invited to the marriage supper of the Lamb." And he said to me, "These are the true words of God." (Revelation 19:6–9)

Closing Reflections

Presuming that silence still prevailed at the dinner party, Jesus' final words must have settled with a pall over the guests: "'For I tell you, none of those men who were invited shall taste my banquet'" (v. 24). This was an extremely personal confrontation. They were the original invitees, but *not one* would be admitted to the messianic meal unless there was a response of repentance. At that moment every soul in that room except Jesus was lost! Those custodians of the Law, those leaders of Israel, were doomed to judgment!

They had received two invitations to the messianic banquet. The first had come through the Law, the Prophets, and the Writings. They had answered yes. Of course they would not miss the banquet, whenever it would come. Just send the customary second invitation and they would be there for the feast. It was a conventional yes, but it was not from the heart. They actually loved their fields and their oxen and their homes far more than they loved God. They preferred their possessions and affections to Heaven. They loved the world first! And now that Jesus the Messiah had come with the second invitation to the feast, they would have none of it.

All their religious posturing was so empty. "Blessed is everyone who will eat bread in the kingdom of God!" was pious jargon. Their kingdom longing was bogus. Their true longing was for worldly comfort. There was such urgency in Christ's method here. He was combative because he ached for their repentance. They must hear and do his Word to avoid judgment.

The question for Jesus' hearers and us is, do we really want to attend the feast? Or are other things more important? Our portfolios? Our cars? Our homes?

It has cost Jesus everything to prepare the feast—pain, tears, flesh, and blood. Now he invites us to come and drink the blood he has shed and to eat the bread that cost him everything.

69

Being a Disciple

LUKE 14:25–35

ANNIE DILLARD, in her essay *An Expedition to the Pole*, describes the ill-fated Franklin expedition that perished because its preparations were adapted to the posh conditions of the Royal Navy officers' clubs in England rather than to the harsh realities of the Arctic.

> In 1845, Sir John Franklin and 138 officers and men embarked from England to find the northwest passage across the high Canadian Arctic to the Pacific Ocean. They sailed in two three-masted barques. Each sailing vessel carried an auxiliary steam engine and a twelve-day supply of coal for the entire projected two or three years' voyage. Instead of additional coal, according to L.P. Kirwan, each ship made room for a 1,200-volume library, "a hand-organ, playing fifty tunes," china place settings for officers and men, cut-glass wine goblets, and sterling silver flatware. The officers' sterling silver knives, forks and spoons were particularly interesting. The silver was of ornate Victorian design, very heavy at the handles and richly patterned. Engraved on the handles were the individual officers' initials and family crests. The expedition carried no special clothing for the Arctic, only the uniforms of Her Majesty's Navy.
>
> The ships set out in high dudgeon, amid enormous glory and fanfare. . . . Two months later a British whaling captain met the two barques in Lancaster Sound; he reported back to England on the high spirits of officers and men. He was the last European to see any of them alive.
>
> Years later, civilization learned that many groups of Inuit—Eskimos—had hazarded across tableaux involving various still-living or dead members of the Franklin expedition. Some had glimpsed, for instance, men pushing and pulling a wooden boat across the ice. Some had found, at a place called Starvation Cove, this boat, or a similar one, and the remains of the thirty-five men who had been dragging it. At Terror Bay the Inuit found a tent on the ice, and in it, thirty bodies. At Simpson Strait some Inuit had

> seen a very odd sight: The pack ice pierced by the three protruding wooden masts of a barque.
>
> For twenty years, search parties recovered skeletons from all over the frozen sea. . . . Accompanying one clump of frozen bodies . . . were place settings of sterling silver flatware engraved with officers' initials and family crests.
>
> Another search party found two skeletons in a boat on a sledge. They had hauled the boat sixty-five miles. With the two skeletons were some chocolate, some guns, some tea, and a great deal of table silver. Many miles south of these two was another skeleton, alone. This was a frozen officer. . . . The skeleton was in uniform: trousers and jacket "of fine blue cloth . . . edged with silk braid, with sleeves slashed and bearing five covered buttons each. Over this uniform the dead man had worn a blue greatcoat, with a black silk neckerchief." That was the Franklin expedition.[1]

Sir John Franklin and 138 men perished because they underestimated the requirements of Arctic exploration. They ignorantly imagined a pleasure cruise amid the comforts of their English officers' clubs. They exchanged necessities for luxuries, and their ignorance led to their deaths.

In 14:25–35 Jesus' life was set on going to Jerusalem, where he had determined to die. As he had explicitly said, "Nevertheless, I must go on my way today and tomorrow and the day following, for it cannot be that a prophet should perish away from Jerusalem" (13:33). A rough voyage lay ahead for Jesus and his followers.

But presently great multitudes were constantly around Jesus because of his kingdom preaching and power. In today's terms there were throngs of gapers, hangers-on with no commitment. And they conducted themselves as if they were on the way to a holiday feast. So Jesus gave them a reality check as he laid out in unforgettable terms the cost of being a disciple. The whole passage is a grand unity consisting of a brief introduction (v. 25), two parallel sayings on discipleship (vv. 26, 27), two parabolic sayings (vv. 28–33), and a memorable conclusion (vv. 34, 35). Jesus did for his followers what Sir John Franklin failed to do for his. Any would-be disciple who listened would understand that discipleship would cost him dearly, though the benefit of following Christ would make it all worthwhile.

The Cost of Discipleship (vv. 26, 27)

The Relational Cost

Jesus' opening declaration was a shocker: "If anyone comes to me and does not hate his own father and mother and wife and children and brothers and sisters, yes, and even his own life, he cannot be my disciple" (v. 26). Joseph

Ernest Renan, the nineteenth-century author of the blasphemous *The Life of Jesus*, seized this text to declare that Jesus was "trampling under foot everything that is human—blood and love and country . . . despising the healthy limits of man's nature . . . abolishing all natural ties."[2] In an effort to make Jesus appear monstrous, Renan ignored Jesus' regular use of startling, penetrating paradox to make his point. As the esteemed New Testament scholar Alfred Plummer pointed out, "Jesus, as often, states a principle in a startling way, and leaves his hearers to find out the qualifications" (cf. 6:29, 30; Matthew 19:12).[3] Jesus wanted his listeners to think.

Certainly, in the full light of the New Testament, Jesus was not demanding an unqualified hatred. He could not command, "Honor your father and your mother" (Mark 7:9–13) and demand that we also hate them. He could not command, "Husbands, love your wives, as Christ loved the church and gave himself up for her" (Ephesians 5:25) and then advise them to hate their spouses. Jesus, who so loved little children that "he took them in his arms and blessed them, laying his hands on them" (Mark 10:16) could not advise their parents to hate them. Neither could he advise his followers to "be reconciled to your brother" (Matthew 5:24) and then encourage brotherly hatred. How could he command, "Love your enemies" (Luke 6:27) and then call us to hate our friends? The truth is, in the Biblically recommended sense that we are to love our neighbor as ourselves (cf. Mark 12:32–34) and to love one another as Christ has loved us (cf. John 13:34, 35), we cannot love others too much! We can focus on our family too much, we can dote on our loved ones too much, but we cannot love them too much. Further, in the final clause Jesus recommended that each of his followers must hate "even his own life." Jesus could not be recommending a psychologically destructive loathing of existence. What Jesus was saying paradoxically was that our love for him must be so great and so pervasive that our natural love of self and family pales in comparison. We are to subordinate everything, even our own being, to our love and commitment to Christ. He is to be our first loyalty. All other relationships must take second place.

So with a harsh, enigmatic epigram, Jesus yanks us from our dreamworld. "Do you fancy yourself a disciple? Do you think you are going to follow me? Then you must love me so much that your love for your family seems like hatred in comparison! Hate your own life. Otherwise, don't pretend to be following me!" Jesus' words astonish us.

This is where so many of us fall short. In the secularized, antifamily culture of today, our family is at the center of our Christian ethic. And that is proper. But some of us love our wives, husbands, and children more than we love God. We miss the mark when we put their development athletically, intellectually, culturally, artistically, socially before their spiritual well-being. We fall short when we spend more time in the car in one day shuttling them to games and lessons than we do in a month in prayer for their souls. By comparison our lives reveal that we hate God and love our children disproportionately—and that we are not Jesus' disciples.

The paradox is that the proper way to love our children is to "hate" them because our greater love for God will enable us to love them with a greater love! Disciples are the best lovers of God and of family and friends. Disciples must always be ready to "hate"—to give second place to everything and everyone else. The relational cost of discipleship may seem harsh at first. But in right perspective and priority this focuses our lives and makes them richer and fuller. Accepting discipleship's costliness produces a sweet saltiness, as we will see.

The Sacrificial Cost

Jesus then cited the vast relational Calvary cost of discipleship: "Whoever does not bear his own cross and come after me cannot be my disciple" (v. 27). The cross is an instrument of execution. He is saying in effect, "He who does not hoist up his gallows or his electric chair and follow me cannot be my disciple." Discipleship is a series of deaths—perpetual dying. Disciples follow Christ on a path of self-denial. Disciples embrace suffering as a part of life. As Paul prayed, "I have suffered the loss of all things . . . that I may know him and the power of his resurrection, and may share his sufferings, becoming like him in his death, that by any means possible I may attain the resurrection from the dead" (Philippians 3:8–11).

The disciple's life is not easy. C. S Lewis had it right:

> The Christian way is different. . . . Christ says, "Give me all. I don't want so much of your time and so much of your money and so much of your work: I want you. I have not come to torment your natural self, but to kill it. No half-measures are any good. I don't want to cut off a branch here and a branch there, I want to have the whole tree down. I don't want to drill the tooth, or crown it, or stop it, but to have it out. Hand over the whole natural self, all the desires which you think innocent as well as the ones you think wicked—the whole outfit."[4]

Discipleship requires everything. There are no exceptions. No one has ever become a disciple of Christ and lived a life of ease! You can search the writings of the apostolic church and you will find no exception. You can check every writing and personal vignette during the first four hundred years of the church and you will find no disciple lounging on a bed of constant comfort. The same is true of the Dark Ages and the Renaissance and the Reformation and the five hundred years of intervening history. Discipleship calls for sacrifice.

Application

But in all this discomfort something beautiful emerges. The tandem challenges to pay the relational cost (to hate one's closest relationships and even one's own life in comparison with one's love for Christ) and to pay the sacrificial cost (to shoulder death and follow Jesus) begins to create a new disciple—a man or woman who is sharp and pungent—a salty Christian who brings tang and flavor to life. Everyone benefits, not the least of which is his "hated" family.

The Calculation of the Cost (vv. 28–33)

Having challenged his hearers about the cost of discipleship with two parallel sayings, Jesus now used twin parables of a tower and a war to encourage his followers to count the cost:

> For which of you, desiring to build a tower, does not first sit down and count the cost, whether he has enough to complete it? Otherwise, when he has laid a foundation and is not able to finish, all who see it begin to mock him, saying, "This man began to build and was not able to finish." Or what king, going out to encounter another king in war, will not sit down first and deliberate whether he is able with ten thousand to meet him who comes against him with twenty thousand? And if not, while the other is yet a great way off, he sends a delegation and asks for terms of peace. (vv. 28–32)

These little parables make essentially the same point but with slightly different emphases. The builder of the tower was free to build or not as he chose. The king was being invaded and had to make a quick choice.

But both parables emphasize the necessity of careful calculation—to "sit down," take some time, and compute it all out. This was where the Franklin expedition went awry. The upside was that their failure to calculate the cost paved the way for the success of future expeditions. In the following decade no less than thirty ships set out looking for traces of the Franklin expedition, all with increasingly careful calculations of what it would take to succeed. Ultimately they mapped the Arctic, found the Northwest Passage, and developed a technology that conquered the Arctic.

Virtually every accomplishment in life requires counting the cost. Do you want to be a great violinist? Jascha Jeifitz at age seventy-five had logged some 102,000 hours of practice! If you want to be an artist, remember that da Vinci's anatomically perfect sketches came only after incredible effort—on one occasion he drew a thousand hands! Do you want to be an Olympic champion lifter and set a world record? Your training lifts added together just might equal the weight of the Willis (formerly Sears) Tower!

Jesus says every would-be disciple must count the cost before he enters discipleship. And what is the cost? Every possession he has and everything he is—every corner of his life! "So therefore, any one of you who does not renounce all that he has cannot be my disciple" (v. 33). Joseph Fitzmyer's translation makes this so clear: "Similarly, then, every one of you who does not say goodbye to all he has cannot be a disciple of mine."[5]

When money or the things it can buy makes us hesitant about doing what we feel the Lord is calling us to do, we are the disciples of things, not of Christ. Would-be disciples need to think about it, then say, "Lord, all I have is yours."

One test of discipleship is what we are doing with our money. Regardless of our income, if we are not giving regularly and generously, we are not living as Christ's disciples. We cannot follow the Lord if he does not have our hearts, and as Jesus said, "Where your treasure is, there your heart will be also" (Matthew 6:21). Does he have your treasure? Then he has your heart. Does such a life of sacrifice sound monochromic and bland? Far from it! Such a life brims with gusto and zest.

Closing Reflections

Jesus concluded with the epigram, "Salt is good, but if salt has lost its taste, how shall its saltiness be restored? It is of no use either for the soil or for the manure pile. It is thrown away. He who has ears to hear, let him hear" (vv. 34, 35). Salt, sodium chloride, is a stable compound. Technically it cannot lose its saltiness. But it can be diluted when mixed with impurities, thus losing its saltiness.

The image of salt, coming here on the heels of the three conditions of discipleship ("hating" one's life and family, taking up the cross, and giving everything), expresses the willingness of the disciple to give his life totally to Jesus Christ. Even as salt can lose its saltiness, so commitment to Christ can deteriorate. If the saltiness is lost, the disciple is useless and fit for nothing but to be tossed out. He does not lose his salvation, but he bears no fruit for the Savior.

But the disciple who is dynamically committed to Jesus in respect to family, the cross, and money is a powerful agent of the kingdom! His life is delivered from insipid blandness. His presence is always felt. He seasons the life of family, friends, church, and society. His life brims with vitality. "Saline saints bring zest and gusto to life. Like salt, they bring out the best of the flavor of living."[6]

The cost of discipleship produces saltiness. Are we willing to pay the price?

70

"Rejoice with Me"

LUKE 15:1–10

WE KNOW WHY JESUS ATE WITH "tax collectors and sinners" (v. 1). He was concerned about their souls. They were lost, and he hoped to retrieve them. Jesus' own self-designation was "the good shepherd" (John 10:14), and he sought out lost sheep. And what better way to do it than in the relaxed, extended time that comes with sharing a meal, the apparent setting for this account.

We know, too, that the tax collectors and sinners were a scandalous bunch. For centuries before and after Christ, tax collectors were universally hated. Cicero insulted an opponent by saying that he must have imagined himself a tax-gatherer, "since you most thievishly ransacked every man's house, the warehouses and the ships, entangled men engaged in business with the most unjust decrees, terrified the merchants as they landed, and delayed their embarkation" (*In Vatin.* 5).[1] St. Chrysostom preached, "The tax-gatherer is the personification of licensed violence, of legal sin, of specious greed" (*Hom.* 2.4).[2]

In Jewish culture they were anathematized because they were turncoat Jews who had sold their souls to buy Roman tax-gathering franchises so they could prey on their fellow Jews. They were loathed in every way. Synagogues would not accept their alms. Their testimony was not received in Jewish courts. They were held to be worse than the heathen. As such, along with the "sinners" (those who were immoral or not living according to the establishment's strictures), they were in desperate need of redemption.

The only persons more scandalous in this account were "the Pharisees and the scribes" (v. 2), who could not have cared less about the sinners. The rabbinic commentary on Exodus 18:1 cites an old rule that "a person should not associate with the godless" and points out that the rabbis would not associate with such a person, even to teach him the Law *(Midrash Mek. Amalek* 3 on Exodus 18:1, 65a).[3] Not only did the Pharisees not care about the tax-collecting scum and their like—they were upset that Jesus cared, so that they were continually mumbling (imperfect tense), "This man receives sinners and eats with them" (v. 2). They put the worst interpretation on Jesus' ministry, ignoring his reaching out and preferring to view him as in secret sympathy with "sinners." This despite the fact that Jesus taught a far more demanding morality than the Pharisees, for example, in the Sermon on the Mount (cf. Matthew 5:48).

The scandal was that as leaders of Israel, these teachers of the Law were considered undershepherds of the Shepherd, God. But they were failing in their task, just as their fathers of old had done when Ezekiel prophesied against them. One wonders if some of them did not recall Ezekiel's prophecy, at least after hearing what Jesus was about to say. Listen to Ezekiel:

> The word of the LORD came to me: "Son of man, prophesy against the shepherds of Israel; prophesy, and say to them, even to the shepherds, Thus says the Lord GOD: Ah, shepherds of Israel who have been feeding yourselves! Should not shepherds feed the sheep?" (Ezekiel 34:1, 2)

> The weak you have not strengthened, the sick you have not healed, the injured you have not bound up, the strayed you have not brought back, the lost you have not sought. (Ezekiel 34:4)

> Thus says the Lord GOD, Behold, I am against the shepherds, and I will require my sheep at their hand and put a stop to their feeding the sheep. No longer shall the shepherds feed themselves. I will rescue my sheep from their mouths, that they may not be food for them. For thus says the Lord GOD: Behold, I, I myself will search for my sheep and will seek them out. As a shepherd seeks out his flock when he is among his sheep that have been scattered, so will I seek out my sheep, and I will rescue them from all places where they have been scattered on a day of clouds and thick darkness. (Ezekiel 34:10–12)

The thrust of Ezekiel's prophecy is clear: since the undershepherds of Israel had failed, God himself would shepherd and rescue the people.

How would God do this? The prophetic answer is so astounding and sweet: "I will set up over them one shepherd, my servant David, and he shall feed them: he shall feed them and be their shepherd. And I, the LORD, will be their God, and my servant David shall be prince among them. I am the LORD; I have spoken" (Ezekiel 34:23, 24). Who is this David? It's not King

David because at the time of Ezekiel's prophecy King David had been dead for over five hundred years. This David is none other than the ultimate son of David, the lion of David's tribe Judah, Jesus the son of David and Son of God. It was through Jesus the Good Shepherd that God the Father would shepherd his people!

The undershepherds could not care less, but the Shepherd could not care more. What a grand tableaux this is for the following parables in which Ezekiel's prophetic word was hammered home by the ultimate David.

These three coordinated parables—the lost sheep (vv. 4–7), the lost coin (vv. 8–10), and the lost son (vv. 11–32)—are, as I. H. Marshall has said, an "artistically constructed unit with a single theme"[4]—namely, God's joy when he finds a lost sinner. Jesus would later say of himself in 19:10, "The Son of Man came to seek and to save the lost," and that is what this passage is about. This section has been called "the heart of the Third Gospel" because here Luke's great theme of God's love and mercy for sinful human beings and his call for repentance and conversion come forth with full power.[5]

We will examine the first two parables in this chapter. Because their literary structure is the same—loss and search, then recovery and joy—we will simultaneously examine what each says on the subject.

Lost and Found (vv. 3, 4, 8)

The Loss

Both parables begin on the note of loss. A shepherd loses one of his flock ("What man of you, having a hundred sheep, if he has lost one of them . . . ," v. 4), and a woman loses a coin ("Or what woman, having ten silver coins, if she loses one coin . . . ," v. 8). The shepherd had a considerable flock of sheep. He was moderately well-off. On paper the loss of a single sheep would not affect his estate much. On the other hand, the loss of the coin was very serious to the woman, for she was apparently poor. The coin, a drachma, was about a day's subsistence wage for a laborer—no great amount,[6] but nevertheless a great loss for the woman.

The Search

Both the shepherd and the woman immediately began their search. He searched because he cared for his sheep, she because the coin was of great value to her. The good shepherd knows what a pitifully helpless animal he is seeking. Its instincts are virtually useless, and it is pathetically defenseless. The search is not a perfunctory, token search. He pours his energy into the task. He combs the valleys and peers from the hilltops, always calling and seeking. Ezekiel's prophecy is lived out: "I myself will search for my sheep" (Ezekiel 34:11). "I will rescue them from all places where they have been scattered" (Ezekiel 34:12). "I will seek the lost, and I will bring back the strayed, and I will bind up the injured, and I will strengthen the weak" (Ezekiel 34:16). "I will rescue my flock; they shall no longer be a prey" (Ezekiel 34:22). The search is relentless. The shepherd cannot allow himself to rest—the lost must be found!

The lost coin is of such value to the woman that she is a whirlwind of organized persistence. Ancient homes were traditionally windowless and dark. Since the only light came in through a low door, a lamp was always shining. Straw that normally covered the dirt floor was swept away, and she searched every nook and cranny. Nothing was left unturned as she searched upon her knees. She must find the coin!

I can relate to this because of an event very early in my memory. I was five years old. My mother had been widowed for a year, and she had taken my little brother and me to Los Angeles' famous Griffith Park for a picnic, where we got to play on the merry-go-round. Arriving home, my mother realized that her engagement ring was missing, and the last place she could remember seeing it was at the merry-go-round. Even as a boy of five, I felt her emotion as my mother spent Sunday morning on her hands and knees intermittently weeping and futilely combing the sand for her tiny engagement ring with the minuscule diamond. I know what the search for something precious is like.

Perhaps you have had the experience of becoming separated from a young child while in a large department store or sporting event or whatever. You look for the youngster frantically, feeling confident that the child is all right but also fearing the worst. And when the two of you are reunited, what joy!

Jesus was saying, as the parables turn out, that the shepherd and the woman together reveal his heart as he searches for the lost—his shepherd's *compassion* for lost souls, and the immense *value* he places on lost souls. The great Jewish New Testament scholar C. G. Montefiore said these parables were revolutionary because while the rabbis agreed that God would welcome a repentant sinner, the idea that God *seeks* sinners was a new insight.[7]

The Lord of the universe, who came as a seeking, suffering Savior, has come to us with the persistent will-not-be-denied love of the Holy Spirit. If we go up to the heavens, he is there; if we sleep in the deep, he is there; if we fly to the sun, he is there (cf. Psalm 139:8–10). We find him because he finds us. Pascal experienced this searching when he heard the Shepherd say,

"You would not be searching for me had I not already found you."[8] We long for him because he draws near.

The *Hound of Heaven* was relentless in his pursuit of poet Francis Thompson:

> I fled Him, down the nights and down the days;
> I fled Him, down the arches of the years;
> I fled Him, down the labyrinthine ways
> Of my own mind; and in the mist of tears
> I hid from Him, and under running laughter
> Up vistaed hopes I sped;
> And shot, precipitated,
> Adown titanic glooms of chasmed fears.
> From those strong feet that followed,
> Followed after.

This is every man's and every woman's experience who has come to Christ. He knows where we are. He knows his sheep by name. Listen to Thompson's final line save one:

> Ah, fondest, blindest, weakest
> I am He whom thou seekest![9]

He finds us through crumbling dreams. Dreams fall apart in two ways. One is by failing to achieve them—the marriage we wanted, the success we pursued, the perfect home. The other is by achieving our dreams but still finding a nagging emptiness. The effect is the same. A feeling of incompleteness. An underlying sense of loss. Alienation. And then comes a desire to find God and to be found. Are you seeking him? Then he is seeking you!

Recovery and Joy (vv. 5, 6, 9)

The two story lines are virtually identical in respect to the recovery and resulting joy. Of the shepherd we read, "And when he has found it, he lays it on his shoulders, rejoicing. And when he comes home, he calls together his friends and his neighbors, saying to them, 'Rejoice with me, for I have found my sheep that was lost'" (vv. 5, 6). And we read of the woman, "And when she has found it, she calls together her friends and neighbors, saying, 'Rejoice with me, for I have found the coin that I had lost'" (v. 9).

Carried Home

It is significant that the earliest existing statuary from the Western church dates from the third century, and it is a statue of the Good Shepherd bearing the recovered lamb on his shoulders. It is thought to have first come from the catacombs. The statue can be seen today in the Lateran Museum in Rome. Besides its Christian theme, one of the distinguishing features of this statue of the Good Shepherd is "the sweetness of His countenance."[10] Evidently the persecuted postapostolic church found immense comfort in the parable of the lost sheep. Jesus' delicate mention that "he lays it on his shoulders, rejoicing" pictures tender love. The lost sheep is more than a missing piece of livestock. He spies the lost sheep alive, races to it, picks it up, checks it over, plucks away some thorns, nuzzles it, joyfully hoists it high on his shoulders, and strides home!

The shepherd, of course, is our Savior, Jesus Christ. He takes lost, perishing sinners on his powerful shoulders and takes them to his own home. King David's ancient prayer is fulfilled in him: "Oh, save your people and bless your heritage! Be their shepherd and carry them forever" (Psalm 28:9). And the Lord has promised through Isaiah that he will continue to do so through all our earthly years: "Even to your old age I am he, and to gray hairs I will carry you. I have made, and I will bear; I will carry and will save" (Isaiah 46:4).

He began carrying us even while he was on the cross, where all our sins were laid on his omnipotent shoulders. As Philip Melanchthon, Martin Luther's right-hand man, said, "Inwoven in the text there is a sweet signification of the passion of Christ: He places upon his shoulders the sheep He has found, that is, He transfers to himself the burden of us."[11]

Has he found you and lifted you high on his shoulders? Has he borne your sins? "He himself bore our sins in his body on the tree, that we might die to sin and live to righteousness. By his wounds you have been healed. For you were straying like sheep, but have now returned to the Shepherd and Overseer of your souls" (1 Peter 2:24, 25). Has he tended to your wounds by applying the balm of his wounds to yours? Is he bearing you home to the place he has prepared for you? Are you allowing him to do that for you?

A Time to Celebrate

The woman's recovery of the coin is mentioned without details, but she and the shepherd have virtually identical responses. "She calls together her friends and neighbors, saying, 'Rejoice with me, for I have found the coin that I had lost'" (v. 9). "He calls together his friends and his neighbors, saying to them, 'Rejoice with me, for I have found my sheep that was lost'" (v. 6). Her friends entered laughing and embraced her for her good fortune while she danced with joyous excitement over the shining coin. And perhaps he received his friends with embraces and high fives as they joyously examined his once-lost lamb.

Eternal Joy (vv. 7, 10)

Now came the divine application: "Just so, I tell you, there will be more joy in heaven over one sinner who repents than over ninety-nine righteous persons who need no repentance" (v. 7). "Just so, I tell you, there is joy before the angels of God over one sinner who repents" (v. 10).

God rejoices in the presence of his angels when the lost are found! Sometimes the uninformed think of God as an immense, impassive sea where "The ocean of his being is neither torn by storms nor shimmers of light."[12] But this is not the God of Jesus' description. Here is a laughing, congratulating, hugging God. Observe too that he rejoices more over a newly found sinner than he does for the multitude already in his fold. There is an initial, lively joy that momentarily outshines settled joys—a greater joy over the safety of one who is in jeopardy than for what is secure—just as one rejoices more at the recovery of a sick child than at the health of one's family. Notice, too, that when God rejoices, Heaven (his angels) rejoice as well.

Why this heavenly rejoicing of God and his angels? It is because a sinner *repents*! He turns from sin. Her life changes. St. Bernard of Clairvaux wrote that "the tears of the repentant form the wine of angels."[13] What exquisite spiritual poetry! The angels drink the wine of the tears of sinners and rejoice.

I can say, on the authority of Christ's word, that if you are lost and he finds you, and you thus find him and repent, God and his angels will rejoice over you.

Closing Reflections

We all begin as lost sinners. "All we like sheep have gone astray; we have turned—every one—to his own way" (Isaiah 53:6). "'None is righteous, no, not one; no one understands; no one seeks for God'" (Romans 3:10, 11). But God searches us out. "With unhurrying chase and unperturbed pace, deliberate speed, majestic instancy" he tracks us down. Then he hoists us on his sovereign shoulders, made wide by the cross. We believe and repent, he bears our sins, and he bears us home as the constellations ring with divine joy.

> Amazing grace! How sweet the sound
> That saved a wretch like me!
> I once was lost, but now am found,
> Was blind, but now I see.
>
> "Amazing Grace" by John Newton

71

The Prodigal God

LUKE 15:11–32

THUS FAR MY FAVORITE DESCRIPTION of the greatness of God's love is that given by A. W. Tozer in his book *Knowledge of the Holy*: "Because God is *self-existent*, His love had no beginning; because He is *eternal*, His love can have no end; because He is *infinite*, it has no limit; because He is *holy*, it is the quintessence of all spotless purity; because He is *immense*, His love is an incomprehensibly vast, bottomless, shoreless sea."[1]

Other descriptions may surpass Tozer's, but I have not seen them. I rejoice when I sing "O the Deep, Deep Love of Jesus," which has an opening stanza that could well have inspired Tozer:

> O the deep, deep love of Jesus,
> Vast, unmeasured, boundless, free!
> Rolling as a mighty ocean
> In its fullness over me.
>
> Thomas J. Williams

Many of you probably feel similar emotions when you sing those words. The lines are so elevating and suggestive. There is one major problem, however. These beautiful descriptions are not particularly comprehensible or appealing to the average man or woman. The problem is that metaphors like "ocean" are abstract and impersonal, and unless you are really into Christianity, they will not mean much to you. Most people will better understand God's love through more personal illustrations expressed in terms of the closest, most intimate relationships—perhaps father-daughter or brother with brother. That is why we so often quote Psalm 103:13: "As a father shows compassion to his children, so the LORD shows compassion to those who fear him." Most people can relate to that.

This is precisely why the Lord has given us this remarkable tale in Luke 15—the story we commonly call the parable of the prodigal son—because a story illustrating love in the most fundamental of relationships will readily be understood by all. The parable could be called "the parable of the prodigal God" because the word *prodigal* can mean "extremely generous or lavish," and the story is primarily about the lavishness of God's love—that it is "an incomprehensibly vast, bottomless, shoreless sea." But the parable also gives us a unique opportunity to take our own spiritual temperature by observing how we relate to God's extravagant love through the characters of the two brothers. Where we stand depends on how well we are able to step into the skin of first the younger brother, and then the older.

The Younger Brother (vv. 11–24)

Sick of Home

The story begins with a young man who wanted to break away from the nest. Like thousands before and after, he had his "reasons" and was not shy about expressing them. He wanted to be his own man—his own boss. He was tired of what he felt was constant harping—"Do this! Do that! Take out the trash! Tidy your room before Dad sees it! Remember to put your robe in the wash! I've told you a million times to put the cap on the toothpaste!" Anything that came close to this drove him absolutely wild! Rudyard Kipling captured the idea in his poem "The Prodigal Son (Western Version)":

> My father glooms and advises me,
> My brother sulks and despises me,
> My mother catechises me,
> Till I want to go out and swear![2]

He longed for a life where he could get up when he wanted to, go where he wanted to, and return when he pleased. Life at home was claustrophobic.

He probably also reasoned that he was only going to be young once—and that under the present arrangement he would be "ancient" (probably thirty at least!) before he would be able to enjoy his wealth. And as he followed that train of thought, he minimized present joys and freedoms. Everything was lousy—even the food!

Familiar story, isn't it? Maybe even more relevant today after a couple of dark decades where the culture of victimhood has been so finely tuned.

In any event the father saw that further argument was useless, so he gave his young son his inheritance, knowing full well what the boy had in mind. To observers, the father's decision was crazy. But he knew this was the only way his son would learn—*if* he ever would.

So they parted—the father stooped in sadness, the young man feeling very smart and self-satisfied, his hot blood racing. Like Frank Sinatra, he said, "I did it my way."

The Prodigal Life

So he "took a journey into a far country, and there he squandered his property in reckless living" (v. 13). Very likely the squandering began with a new wardrobe. Today it might be a robe by Halston, a timepiece by Cartier, Gucci saddlebags. The young man had "taste." At least that is what everyone told him. He was surprised at how he was adored by all. His new manliness had done his personality good. Strangers laughed at his humor. People continually sought his company. The prodigal life was great!

Now he could buy anything—even other people. And he did. But after a while, though he was more popular than ever, life was not quite as exhilarating. There were new pleasures, but also deeper degradation. Even before his money ran low—even before famine came—there were times when he thought of home, but only as a passing thought.

Misery

Then came famine, and Jesus' explicit description of what happened must have made his Jewish hearers wince: "So he went and hired himself out to one of the citizens of that country . . ." (v. 15). Literally, he "glued" himself to a Gentile as a servant—a horrible humiliation for a Jew. He was a day laborer, the very lowest of servants. His master "sent him into his fields to feed pigs"—an unspeakable degradation for a Hebrew—a Jewish swineherd! Verse 16 frames the picture: "And he was longing to be fed with the pods that the pigs ate, and no one gave him anything." So there he was amid a sea of moving snouts and uncaring pigs' eyes. Just a few months before, everybody loved him. They said he had class. He was like a star rising in the heavens. Now no one would even give him a husk to chew on. He had sought freedom and thought he had found it, but now he was in virtual slavery.

A well-traveled outline of this parable goes like this: I. Sick of home, II. Sick, III. Homesick, IV. Home. At this point he was homesick.

> But when he came to himself, he said, "How many of my father's hired servants have more than enough bread, but I perish here with hunger! I will arise and go to my father, and I will say to him, 'Father, I have sinned against heaven and before you. I am no longer worthy to be called your son. Treat me as one of your hired servants.'" (vv. 17–19)

What a change! He had come to personify the opening lines of the Sermon on the Mount: poverty of spirit, mourning over sin, meekness, and desperate spiritual hunger (cf. Matthew 5:3–6).

His change of mind was not just because he was miserable—he was driven by unrelenting memories of home. He longed to be with his father.

He had forgotten much, but he had not forgotten his father's love. He reasoned that it was better to be a lowly servant in his father's house than to remain where he was. But he was not prepared for what awaited him!

The Prodigal Father (vv. 20–24)

What the son did not realize was that everything about him was burnt on his father's consciousness. Every feature had been treasured in his dear father's memory and wept over repeatedly, so that he would recognize his errant son anywhere. Even more, the father had been daily scanning the horizon for his lost son.

One powerful sentence tells the whole story: "And he arose and came to his father. But while he was still a long way off, his father saw him and felt compassion, and ran and embraced him and kissed him" (v. 20). Though covered with rags, something familiar in the son, perhaps his posture or gait, told the father this was his son. And immediately he "felt compassion." That is, he was so overcome that he had a physical reaction (his whole body ached and thrilled at once), and he "ran" (a very undignified thing for an old man) and literally "embraced him and kissed him" again and again and again (as the Greek tense demands).

The son then blurted out his well-rehearsed confession: "Father, I have sinned against heaven and before you. I am no longer worthy to be called your son" (v. 21). But his father cut him off before he could finish and cried out, "Bring quickly the best robe, and put it on him, and put a ring on his hand, and shoes on his feet. And bring the fattened calf and kill it, and let us eat and celebrate. For this my son was dead, and is alive again; he was lost, and is found" (vv. 22–24).

Then "they began to celebrate." The father had his servants bring out "the best robe"—a long, stately garment that reached to the feet, the kind worn by kings. Then a ring was thrust on the returned son's finger—symbolic of sonship. And finally new sandals were strapped to his callused feet. The father's slaves went barefoot—not his sons!

Here we must see that the real prodigal is the father, representing our heavenly Father, God himself. This is the parable of the prodigal God, who is infinite. He is a consuming fire! But when we turn to him, he is a God who comes running—to lavish his love upon us! This is the gospel—the good news of a prodigal God who rushes to meet sinners with his love!

No one is beyond his love. You cannot do anything that will keep him from kissing you and bestowing upon you the robe, the ring, and the sandals. Utter forgiveness is the only kind God gives.

There are only two qualifications for this forgiveness. First, we must see ourselves before we can see God. We must recognize that we are wayward sons if we are to see his love. If we know what we are, we can know his love. We must see ourselves in the lost son, and then we must come home.

The joy of the party described here is no exaggeration. But like all earthly illustrations of spiritual realities, it falls short. Jesus said, "There will be more joy in heaven over one sinner who repents than over ninety-nine righteous persons who need no repentance" (15:7). Tears of repentance are the wine of angels. This is uproarious heavenly joy, and it is real.

So is the gloom that came when the elder brother arrived. This is the difference between spring and winter. The candles dim and freeze. Ice drips from the chandeliers. The flowers wilt.

The Elder Brother (vv. 25–32)

He had been out in the field working—that was where he always seemed to be. As he came in he heard the unaccustomed sound of dancing and music. He summoned one of the servants, who of course told him the great news (v. 27). "Your brother has come," he replied, "and your father has killed the fattened calf, because he has received him back safe and sound." "Master! Isn't it wonderful! Your kid brother is home! He's showing a little wear and tear, but he's okay! Oh, I'm so happy to be the first to let you know!"

Rather than joining in the party, the elder brother was "angry" (v. 28). The word used here carries the idea of swelling, settled anger that rises like sap in a tree on a hot day. He was boiling! He absolutely "refused to go in." His father came out to him and encouraged him again and again to share the celebration, but the older son finally exploded.

> Look, these many years I have served you, and I never disobeyed your command, yet you never gave me a young goat, that I might celebrate with

> my friends. But when this son of yours came, who has devoured your property with prostitutes, you killed the fattened calf for him! (vv. 29, 30)

What does all this mean? It is possible for us elder brothers to leave the Father without leaving the farm. St. Augustine put it this way: "For it is not by our feet, nor by change of place, that we either turn from Thee or to Thee . . . in darkened affections, lies (the) distance from Thy face" (*Confessions*, I.28). The young son had been far from the father (in a distant country) because of sins of *passion*. But the elder son was separated from his father through sins of *attitude*. He was even farther away than his younger brother, and he had not even left the farm!

Now, the older son was not all bad. He was a good man in his community. He was a respectable, correct, exemplary, obedient, dutiful son. He was steady, dependable, industrious, and thrifty. He also had a high sense of moral rightness.

None of these things could be said about his younger brother. The older brother was good on the outside, but something was missing. This may be what the little boy had in mind when he prayed, "Dear God, make all bad people good, and all good people nice." Or as Mark Twain's adage has it: "He was a 'good man' in the worst sense of the word." The older son's heart was completely out of sync with that of his father. He did not share his father's loving heart. In fact, he was sorry his little brother had come home. He called him "this son of yours," not "this brother of mine." Why? Because somehow he had gotten it in his mind that his position was dependent upon performance, and rather than enjoying his position as Number One son, he worked to maintain and strengthen it. Rather than sharing his father's wide-ranging affection, he cared only about himself.

For similar reasons he did not share his father's joy. There were no festivals in his life, no music and dancing—only serious, tedious monotony and boring, mildewed piety. Inside he resented the current situation. "Look, these many years I have served you. . . ." Somehow in his thinking his father was a stern taskmaster. The elder brother was judgmental. He was too convinced of his own goodness, too attached to his own hardships, to understand his own brother. Self-righteous, he overstated his performance: "Look, these many years I have served you, and I never disobeyed your command" (v. 29). Never? He was convinced of his own goodness, and this assurance made improvement impossible.

Deep down inside he may even have wished he could blow it like his younger brother did and get away with it. No one had said his little brother was with prostitutes, and yet the elder son accused, "This son of yours came, who has devoured your property with prostitutes." This may be an unconscious confession of the older brother's voyeurism.

Too, he complained that no party had been given for him despite his faithfulness, but he never really took advantage of his daily opportunities for fellowship and rejoicing with his father.

Elder brothers are lethal. Imagine what would have happened if he had encountered his returning brother first. "So you've come back? Things didn't work out like you thought? Too bad! Listen, little brother, you aren't welcome here. You broke your poor father's heart. You've disgraced us all. You've only come back because your money has run out. If you still had some cash, you'd still be gone. At least have enough self-respect to come back when you have a job and get yourself cleaned up."

Kipling's poem imagines the prodigal son meeting his brother and then leaving as he says:

> I never was very refined, you see?
> (And it weighs on my brother's mind, you see)
> But there's no reproach among swine, d'you see,
> For being a bit of a swine.[3]

Do you wonder how older brothers get this way? It is very easy to forget what we were like before we came to the Father! As time passes we begin to imagine we are "good people" because we have avoided sins of passion—and all the while sins of attitude run rampant within us. We do not regard our jealousy, pride, and judgmentalism as sins. We call them faults or shortcomings. So we easily become critical, judgmental, and unloving. Our surface familiarity with holy things has rendered them dull, insipid, and boring.

Closing Reflections

Our story closes with the elder son standing face-to-face with his father, fists clenched, mouth twitching with uncontrolled rage. The father answers, "Son (literally, "my child"),[4] you are always with me, and all that is mine is yours" (v. 31). Then he repeated the language of his heart: "It was fitting to celebrate and be glad, for this your brother was dead, and is alive; he was lost, and is found."

This is the parable of the prodigal God—the lavishly loving God. Now those impersonal metaphors take on flesh.

O the deep, deep love of Jesus,
Vast, unmeasured, boundless, free!
Rolling as a mighty ocean
In its fullness over me.

"Because He is *immense*, His love is an incomprehensibly vast, bottomless, shoreless sea."

Our spiritual temperature is a highly personal matter. The main thing we must remember is that he who fails to recognize himself fails to recognize God. Are we in "a far country" like the younger brother because of our *passions*, or because of our *attitudes* like the older brother?

Let us hold close the Father's words: "Son," the father said, "you are always with me, and all that is mine is yours."

72

The Dishonest Manager

LUKE 16:1–15

ANITA SHARPE, writing in the April 5, 1996 edition of the *Wall Street Journal*, penned a penetrating article entitled "More Spiritual Leaders Preach the Virtue of Wealth." The opening line reads: "God has a new co-pilot: Midas." Her thesis is that the convergence of the conspicuous consumption of the 1980s and the more spiritual focus of the 1990s has produced a climate in which virtually every religious expression is preaching the spiritual virtue of wealth: Jews, charismatics, evangelicals, liberals, and New-Agers.

She reports that a large charismatic church in Seattle hosted a seminar led by conservative Jew Paul Zane Pilzer on the topic of his book *God Wants You to Be Rich*. The church's pastor is quoted as saying that the denomination's college uses *God Wants You to Be Rich* as a text: "It's a kind of foundation for our economics class." God supposedly wants every layperson, pastor, and missionary to be rich. Ms. Sharpe goes on to report on two Chicago churches, one evangelical and one liberal, that have had huge responses to seminars about money and the Bible.

She concludes her article with snippets from New-Age spokespersons such as Catherine Ponder of the Unity Church Worldwide who sponsors "prosperity dial-a-thought" and Deepak Chopra's best-selling *The Seven Laws of Spiritual Success*, which draws from the Bible, Khalil Gibran, Lao-tzu, and the Rig-Veda. New-Agers even have a retreat center devoted to success and affluence—the Little Horse Spa for the Spirit.

Many in our culture, from evangelicals to New-Agers, are doing their best to serve God and mammon. But as Christians we want to know what Jesus says about all this, and we find out in Luke's Gospel. We have heard him in the jolting woe of the Sermon on the Plain ("Woe to you who are rich, for you have received your consolation," 6:24) and in the pungent parable of the rich fool in 12:13–21. Now Jesus raised the issue again in the successive parables of the dishonest manager (16:1–13) and the rich man and Lazarus (16:19–31) and not much later in the account of the rich ruler (18:18–30), followed by the story of Zacchaeus who gave half his possessions to the poor (19:1–9). Jesus has indeed spoken on the issue!

On this occasion he began by telling his followers, through parable and specific lessons, what should be their (and our) attitude toward wealth and possessions.

The Parable (vv. 1–8a)

The parable is straightforward. There is nothing allegorical in it. It has no hidden meaning. It is the story of a dishonest household manager who has a terminal confrontation with his boss, engages in some serious reflection, and comes up with an ingenious solution.

The confrontation is a firing. If you have ever been fired, you know it leaves you with an empty feeling to say the least. It happened to me when I was a young teenager who was not performing to my boss's expectations. He said something like, "Your time with us is terminated," and I said "What's terminated?" In the following minutes he added to my vocabulary! I had a slow, low walk home.

In Jesus' tale, the terminated man was a scoundrel and wastrel, and he deserved what he got. His boss didn't waste any words: "What is this that I hear about you? Turn in the account of your management, for you can no longer be manager" (v. 2). In today's terms, "Give me all your records, and clean out your desk. You're outta here!" This is depressing, even if you are a crook.

Even if you are not given to deep thought, being sacked is cause for reflection, especially if you're thoroughly white collar with no calluses except on your elbow from "tipping a few." The thought of manual labor was unacceptable. And begging? The noncanonical book of Ecclesiasticus says, "It is better to die than to beg" (46:28b). The man's musings sound like a soliloquy from an opera: "What shall I do, since my master is taking the management away from me? I am not strong enough to dig, and I am ashamed to beg. I have decided what to do, so that when I am removed from management, people may receive me into their houses" (vv. 3, 4).

The solution that he dreamed up was pretty slick. You can see him high-fiving the air and shouting, "Yes!" In order to get the sense of just how clever this was, we must understand that it was illegal in Jewish culture to charge interest to fellow Jews (cf. Exodus 22:25; Leviticus 25:36; Deuteronomy

23:19). There was no such thing as principal and interest. So they would hide the business interest by hiding it in the loan, so that the principal included the interest. It was not unknown to charge as much as 100 percent interest on profitable commodities. The manager, according to common, accepted business practice, was making such usurious loans, just like everyone else.[1]

Thus the solution: "So, summoning his master's debtors one by one, he said to the first, 'How much do you owe my master?' He said, 'A hundred measures of oil.' He said to him, 'Take your bill, and sit down quickly and write fifty'" (vv. 5, 6). The truth is, the debtor actually only owed fifty measures of oil (about 400 gallons). The other fifty measures were the manager's commission.[2] The debt had been large (100 measures was the yield of 146 olive trees). Accordingly, the debt reduction was massive.

"Then he said to another, 'And how much do you owe?' He said, 'A hundred measures of wheat.' He said to him, 'Take your bill, and write eighty'" (v. 7). Here he wrote off a 20 percent commission on a less inflationary commodity.

The manager did this with each one of "his masters' debtors" (v. 5)—and every one of them thus became his debtor. So when the unemployed manager would show up over the years as he made his rounds, there would always be a room and a table set for him. What a rascal this creative crook was!

As the disciples listened, they were expecting to hear how the master cleverly extricated himself and gave the crook his due. Imagine their surprise, and I think laughter, when Jesus said, "The master commended the dishonest manager for his shrewdness" (v. 8a). He did not approve of what his ex-employee had done, but he certainly admired his foresight and astuteness. This was one smooth operator. He was so quick, so artful, so utterly cool in looking out for Number One.

Lessons to Be Learned (vv. 8b–13)

While the disciples were admiring the surprise turn in the story, Jesus turned it on them, perhaps with a smile himself: "For the sons of this world are more shrewd in dealing with their own generation than the sons of light" (v. 8b). The dishonest manager had faced reality. He refused to live with his head in the sand. If he did not do something fast, he would be out on the street. He used all his intelligence, wit, and energy to insure his earthly comfort. In contrast, "the sons of light" stand on the edge of eternity but lack the vision, foresight, and strength of will to do anything about it—especially in their relationships with others. If only Christians would give as much attention to the things that concern eternity as they do to their worldly business. . . .

If only we would be as spiritually shrewd as the corrupt manager was in temporal pursuits.

Lesson #1

Jesus went on, "I tell you, make friends for yourselves by means of unrighteous wealth, so that when it fails they may receive you into the eternal dwellings" (v. 9). The friends you have made with your worldly wealth will receive you into eternal dwellings.

Just who are these "friends" who will receive us into Heaven? Many scholars think this refers to God himself, because Jewish literature often referred to God in the divine plural ("they") to avoid using the name of God.[3] Others think "friends" refers to people who have been spiritually benefited by one's wealth. The word may include both God and redeemed humanity welcoming a newly departed and generous believer to glory. What a picture! God, his angels, and grateful souls—eternal friends, those who have heard the gospel because of one's giving—greeting and leading a faithful believer into the eternal tents. St. Ambrose said, "The bosoms of the poor, the houses of widows, the mouths of children are the barns which last forever."[4]

What is inescapably clear here is that our wealth and possessions are to be used to win eternal friends. This is the proper use of what we have. We must give generously of our money for the furtherance of the gospel. If we are not doing so, we are not making proper use of what God has given us and we are not enhancing eternal friendships. This is an intensely spiritual matter.

We must also use our possessions to gain eternal friends. It is not enough to give money—we must devote our personal belongings to making eternal friends as well. The mere giving of money can be so sanitized and insulating, but when we use our homes for others, so that our personal space is loaned to others, when we use our vacation homes to refresh others, or let others borrow our cars, then we have begun to touch upon what Christ says.

One thing is sure: our worldly wealth will go somewhere—we cannot hang on to it. One day our most precious things will fit in a hospital drawer. The only wealth that will endure is that which has been invested in others for the sake of Christ and his gospel.

Is our use of our money bringing us closer to God? Have we used our wealth and possessions to gain eternal friends?

Lesson #2

Jesus next taught that we must be trustworthy with money: "One who is faithful in a very little is also faithful in much, and one who is dishonest in a very little is also dishonest in much. If then you have not been faithful in the unrighteous wealth, who will entrust to you the true riches? And if you have not been faithful in that which is another's, who will give you that which is your own?" (vv. 10–12). Some neuter this text by confining it to the general principle of verse 10—namely, if you are faithful in small things, God will trust you with much. Of course, that principle is true, and it has been lived out millions of times among God's people. But verses 10–12 are a unit, and *Jesus is talking about money!* Verse 11 means that if you have not been faithful with money, "unrighteous wealth," God will not trust you with true spiritual riches—the care of souls, missions, evangelism, the oversight of his church.

Frankly, this is where many would-be Christian leaders fall short. They simply are not trustworthy with their money. For them, God is sovereign in everything but money. God needs "help" in financial matters, a little crossing of the line here and there. Second to sensuality, this is the greatest stumbling block of pastors. I was recently informed of a minister in a prominent church who was dismissed because he had not paid his income taxes for five years.

Again, some Christian leaders cultivate a public impression of generosity and magnanimity but give only a pittance, thus falling short in the integrity of stewardship. Jesus is clear: one must be trustworthy with money if he or she is to be trusted with spiritual riches. Jesus says it again, with a different twist: "And if you have not been faithful in that which is another's, who will give you that which is your own?" (v. 12). If you have not been trustworthy with the material possessions God has given you to manage, how can he give you eternal spiritual possessions of your own? We are merely stewards of our material wealth—God is the owner. Martin Luther lived with this perspective. He wrote:

> Therefore we must use all these things upon earth in no other way than as a guest who travels through the land and comes to a hotel where he must lodge overnight. He takes only food and lodging from the host, and he says not that the property of the host belongs to him. Just so should we also treat our temporal possessions, as if they were not ours, and enjoy only so much of them as we need to nourish the body and then help our neighbors with the balance. Thus the life of the Christian is only a lodging for the night, since we have here no continuing city, but must journey on to heaven, where the Father is.[5]

One's use of money and spirituality are inseparably bound together. The sooner we realize this and do something about it, the better for our souls.

Lesson #3

It is totally impossible to serve both God and money: "No servant can serve two masters, for either he will hate the one and love the other, or he will be devoted to the one and despise the other. You cannot serve God and money" (v. 13). This is radical. There is no middle ground. If we are devoted to money, we will "despise" God with our intellect and "hate" him with our emotions—the totality of our being.

New-Agers feel no tension about this because God, self, and money are all tied up together in one profound idolatry (cf. Colossians 3:5).[6] We Christians are the ones who feel the tension because duty pulls us in one direction and the pressures of daily life in the other.

A few words of qualification before we go on: we all go through times when a material focus is required—the purchase of a home, remodeling, redecorating, buying a car, the management of investments, etc. We live in a material world, which requires attention. Also, the possession of wealth, even great wealth, does not make one a materialist, though it dramatically increases the danger. Jesus said, "Where your treasure is, there your heart will be also" (Matthew 6:21). I have known rich people who lived very well but were not materialists. Furthermore, as a Ugandan friend observed of us Americans, "You are all wealthy." So the application is relevant to all of us.

Having said this, I am sure that while as a group we subscribe to the truth that we cannot serve God and mammon, we nevertheless attempt to do both. And we are good at it. Perhaps the best in the world. We are so good that we think we are serving only God.

But we are often failures. And we know it because of the way we talk about these things with our spouses and friends. What usually characterizes your husband-and-wife talks? Your house, shopping, a new car? What is it that you most want to talk about with your friends? "Have you seen my . . . ?" "Let me show you . . ." We all need to be on our guard in this area.

Closing Reflections

Jesus was so forthright in these lessons. Make friends through your use of money. Use your money to gain friendship with God and people so that both Heaven and redeemed humanity will welcome you home in eternity. Be faithful with money because if you are, God will entrust you with true spiritual riches. And remember, you cannot serve both God and money, period. Serve God only. Use your money to serve him.

The Lord calls us to be shrewd, to use all our mind, intellect, and will in the management of money, so that we will be welcomed above. What are we doing with our money? How shrewd and calculated are we with our wealth so we can make sure we are gaining eternal friends to welcome us to Heaven?

It must begin with giving. Dr. Carl F. H. Henry, the dean of evangelical theologians, was asked in a 1990 interview, "One of the major weaknesses, perhaps, of the Western church is our affluence. What kind of crippling effect has this had on the Western church and what can we do to remedy that?"

Dr. Henry answered:

> I don't think that God despises riches; in fact, He gives them to us. What He despises is the misuse of them, and He rewards stewardship. Even Christian missions owe a great debt to the consecrated and often sacrificial philanthropy of well-to-do Christian leaders. What we need to do is enlarge the vision and burden of those to whom God has given much so they understand that they have an opportunity that is rare in the history of Christianity to substantially advance the way of Christ.[7]

Our giving must be matched by the sharing of all we have for the well-being and refreshment of God's people and the proclamation of the gospel.

73

Rich Man, Poor Man

LUKE 16:19–31

THE APOSTLE JOHN issues this warning in his first letter: "If anyone has the world's goods and sees his brother in need, yet closes his heart against him, how does God's love abide in him?" (1 John 3:17).

James, the practical-minded brother of our Lord, asks a similar question: "If a brother or sister is poorly clothed and lacking in daily food, and one of you says to them, 'Go in peace, be warmed and filled,' without giving them the things needed for the body, what good is that?" (James 2:15, 16).

John does not see how it is possible to love God and not help one in material need. James questions the authenticity of the faith of one who does nothing to help another who has physical needs. In effect, both view uncaring, stingy people as lost despite their affirmations of faith in and love for God. And well they should, because that is what the Lord himself affirmed in the parable of Lazarus and the rich man. The preceding parable of the dishonest manager (vv. 1–15) addresses the proper *use* of money. This parable confronts the *abuse* of money, especially by the rich. It is a solemn warning.

But even more, it warns us about the dramatic reversals that can come after death and also the terrors of Hell. It exposes the subtle causes of the callous indifference that people within the worshiping community sometimes show to the poor. Jesus did his best to wipe the sneers off the faces of those who brushed aside his teaching in the parable of the dishonest manager (cf. v. 14) and in the process provided deep, sobering wisdom for the Church universal.

Lifestyles of the Rich and the Poor (vv. 19–23)

Earthly Lifestyles

He began by giving a gripping description of contrasting lifestyles.

First, that of a rich man: "There was a rich man who was clothed in purple and fine linen and who feasted sumptuously every day" (v. 19). "Lifestyles of the Rich and the Famous"! He lived like a king. Since purple was the color of royalty, he wore outer garments of imported Phoenician wool dyed by the purple of murex, a rare and expensive sea mussel. Next to his skin he wore byssus, an unusually fine linen from Egypt.[1] And at the center of his daily existence was a brilliant table, *haute cuisine* every day. This was Roman chic to the nth degree, even though he was a Jew.

In stark contrast, "At his gate was laid a poor man named Lazarus, covered with sores, who desired to be fed with what fell from the rich man's table. Moreover, even the dogs came and licked his sores" (vv. 20, 21). The beggar was so ill that he had to be "laid" (literally, "cast") at the rich man's gate. His illness and malnutrition left him covered with weeping ulcers. Assaulted with constant hunger, he would gladly have accepted the leftovers from the rich man's table. Lukan scholar John Nolland says that though the common view is that the dogs were wild, he believes they were dogs from the rich man's estate. "Instead of a servant coming with the fallen scraps, the dogs come from having consumed the scraps and continue their meal with the juices that ooze from the afflicted man's sores."[2] Be that as it may, the picture is of a man utterly neglected, helpless, and receiving more compassion from unclean dogs than from the rich man's house.

The wealthy man knew who the beggar was because he would later recognize him after both their deaths. Meanwhile, day by day as the man passed through his gate wearing his purple robes, his perfumed aroma collided with the beggar's stench. Occasionally their eyes met, but with no recognition and no feeling by the wealthy man. The beggar was simply part of the landscape—an unpleasant sight one had to endure. Soon the beggar would be gone.

Significantly, Lazarus' name (not to be confused with Lazarus of Bethany) meant "God has helped," appropriate in view of the divinely arranged outcome of his life. But while sitting at the rich man's gate, his name seemed to mock him.

How could the rich man, considering himself a son of Abraham and a blessed member of God's people, be so heartless? He certainly was not an atheist. He believed in God. He apparently was not a Sadducee (who denied the hereafter) because Jesus told this story to help Pharisees see themselves more clearly (cf. 16:14). His theology was probably orthodox. He would have affirmed the Torah and understood that after death came judgment.

So why his total lack of compassion? He did not take seriously Holy

Scripture, which he and the rest of his culture professed to believe.[3] God's word through the prophets was uniformly consistent about the necessity of mercy and compassion.

For I desire steadfast love and not sacrifice,
  the knowledge of God rather than burnt offerings. (Hosea 6:6)

This text was a pillar in Jesus' teaching as well. Twice he quoted it to show that mercy/compassion is far more important than legalistic performance of religious ritual (cf. Matthew 9:13; 12:7). Other Old Testament texts confirm this truth.

I hate, I despise your feasts,
  and I take no delight in your solemn assemblies.
Even though you offer me your burnt offerings and grain offerings,
  I will not accept them;
and the peace offerings of your fattened animals,
  I will not look upon them.
Take away from me the noise of your songs;
  to the melody of your harps I will not listen.
But let justice roll down like waters,
  and righteousness like an ever-flowing stream.

Did you bring to me sacrifices and offerings during the forty years in the wilderness, O house of Israel? You shall take up Sikkuth your king, and Kiyyun your star-god—your images that you made for yourselves, and I will send you into exile. (Amos 5:21–27)

"With what shall I come before the LORD,
  and bow myself before God on high?
Shall I come before him with burnt offerings,
  with calves a year old?
Will the LORD be pleased with thousands of rams,
  with ten thousands of rivers of oil?
Shall I give my firstborn for my transgression,
  the fruit of my body for the sin of my soul?"
He has told you, O man, what is good;
  and what does the LORD require of you
but to do justice, and to love kindness,
  and to walk humbly with your God? (Micah 6:6–8)

We cannot please God without having a merciful spirit!

As a Jew, the rich man knew the Ten Commandments. He knew that the last six prescribed how he ought to relate to people. He might not have summed it up like Jesus did ("Love your neighbor as yourself," Matthew 22:37–40; cf. Leviticus 19:18), but he understood the rightness of compassion from the Decalogue. He simply did not take the commandments seriously.

God gave us the Law and the Prophets to bring us face-to-face with our sin, impotence, and need. (See Paul's brilliant argument in Romans 7:7–14.) But the rich man never really thought about any of that.

A surface reading of this parable might indicate that the rich man missed salvation because he was not generous enough with his money. But that is not the case. The true reason for his damnation was his disregard for God's Word and his rejection of the Lord. He did not believe the Scriptures. And he certainly did not think his disregard would land him in Hell. To think that someone like him, living in such abundance, can miss Heaven! And yet, without Christ, such is the case.

Heavenly Lifestyles

Death sometimes brings a dramatic reversal of lifestyle. This happened first for Lazarus: "The poor man died and was carried by the angels to Abraham's side" (v. 22a). No one bothered to give the beggar's loathsome body a burial. It was probably tossed onto the trash heap in the Valley of Hinnom. Ignored by human beings, he was carried by heavenly beings to Abraham's bosom—a place of honor at a heavenly feast, where he reclined to the right of Abraham as they enjoyed intimate conversation (cf. John 13:23).[4]

Lazarus was in Abraham's bosom not because he was poor, but because though his name ("God has helped") had mocked him in life, he believed God's Word and trusted in him. He was at rest, serene, and eating his fill at the messianic table.

Then came the exodus of the man who loved purple: "The rich man also died and was buried, and in Hades, being in torment, he lifted up his eyes and saw Abraham far off and Lazarus at his side" (vv. 22b, 23). You can be sure he had an impressive funeral! *Everyone* was there and properly mourning. How marvelous his corpulent body looked in purple and byssus. He was then laid in a beautiful above-ground tomb. But that was not the end of the story.

Christ is not here indicating the geography or juxtaposition of Heaven and Hell—that they exist within view of each other and so on. This is a parable, not a historical account. At the most, it alludes to Hades as an intermediate state in which the dead await the final resurrection. As a parable, it is intended to teach principles, not to give an exhaustive picture of the afterlife. The rich man was in eternal torment. Massive eternal equity was underway.

The eternal state will be perfectly equitable for everyone, though some will experience incredible reversals.

The Rich Man's Plea to Abraham (vv. 24–31)

A Plea for Himself

The rich man then pathetically cried across the distance, pleading, "Father Abraham, have mercy on me, and send Lazarus to dip the end of his finger in water and cool my tongue, for I am in anguish in this flame" (v. 24). His plea asserted his kinship with "Father Abraham" (in fact, he calls him "father" three times in all; cf. vv. 27, 30). The rich man, so insensitive in this life, may even have thought he was in good standing with Father Abraham and so assumed he had the right to say what should happen next. "Send Lazarus [the beggar he let die] . . . and cool my tongue [the part of him that feasted during life on earth]." This was the end of his presumption and the beginning of his recompense. Fire is a punitive image. There is more than redress here—this is eternal punishment.

Note that Lazarus does not say a word in the entire parable. On earth he did not complain or blame God, and in Heaven he does not gloat or refuse to be an errand boy. There is a godly, regal silence.

Abraham does the answering: "Child, remember that you in your lifetime received your good things, and Lazarus in like manner bad things; but now he is comforted here, and you are in anguish" (v. 25). Abraham was actually quite tender in his response; he addressed the rich man as "child." He acknowledged hereditary kinship but rejected the man's spiritual right to share in the blessings. The rich man exemplified Jesus' woe in the Sermon on the Plain: "Woe to you who are rich, for you have received your consolation" (6:24). Jesus was not teaching that there will be an automatic reversal of roles in Heaven, but rather that his judgment will be equitable.

Abraham went on, "And besides all this, between us and you a great chasm has been fixed, in order that those who would pass from here to you may not be able, and none may cross from there to us" (v. 26). This "great chasm" (literally "yawning") is unbridgeable. No surge of human sympathy can reach across it. While in this world the rich man could have reached out to Lazarus at any time. But once in eternity the gulf was uncrossable.

A Plea for His Brothers

Now for the first time the man showed some interest in others: "Then I beg you, father, to send him [Lazarus] to my father's house—for I have five brothers—so that he may warn them, lest they also come into this place of torment" (vv. 27, 28). He figured that if Lazarus returned from the dead and gave an eyewitness account, his family would believe and so escape judgment.

But Father Abraham thought otherwise: "They have Moses and the Prophets; let them hear them" (v. 29). The patriarch said that those still alive on earth had the Word of God, and that is all they needed! If they would pay attention to that, as we noted earlier, they would heed the Scriptures' great teaching regarding mercy, would see they were to love their neighbors as themselves, would see they were sinful and impotent, and would turn to God for mercy. In light of Christ's ministry, if they read Moses and the Prophets they would begin to glimpse the need for a Messiah upon whom they could cast their souls.

Jesus later told the two disciples on the road to Emmaus, "'O foolish ones, and slow of heart to believe all that the prophets have spoken! Was it not necessary that the Christ should suffer these things and enter into his glory?' And beginning with Moses and all the Prophets, he interpreted to them in all the Scriptures the things concerning himself" (24:25–27). If the rich man's five brothers would give attention to God's Word, they would need nothing else.

But the rich man disagreed: "No, father Abraham, but if someone goes to them from the dead, they will repent" (v. 30). The rich man's insistence that if someone would return from the dead, his brothers would repent was a subtle way of excusing himself. He was implicitly arguing that he would have repented if a special messenger from the dead had come to him. He was saying that Moses and the Prophets, God's Word, was not enough.

This is exactly what our culture says today. "The Bible is not enough. The resurrection is not enough. We need special 'signs and wonders.' Then we will believe." How arrogant we humans are, daring to tell God what he must do if we are to believe. If God would just send ambassadors from the other side, great multitudes would believe. Would they? Jesus' parable shouts a resounding *no!*

Jesus himself came from the other side, and though some believed, many, like the rich man and his brothers, did not believe. Abraham concluded, "If they do not hear Moses and the Prophets, neither will they be convinced if someone should rise from the dead" (v. 31). Those who have hardened their hearts to God's Word refused Jesus even after he walked out of his own tomb. And it is still the same today.

Closing Reflections

What does this ancient parable have to say to us who live in the light of the cross and the resurrection? We too know from Moses and the Prophets that we must love God and love others as ourselves, that we are sinful and helpless to save ourselves, that Christ has suffered death and rose on the third day for our sins (cf. 24:46). We also have the witness of Christ who rose from the dead, was seen by his disciples and hundreds of witnesses, and ascended into Heaven. We have too the entire witness of the New Testament, which expounds Christ to us. The New Testament writings include the Sermon on the Mount and the multiple ethical teachings of the Epistles, which tell us how to live—even in regard to our use of riches.

As with the rich man, our use of our wealth in relation to the needs of our neighbors reveals our spiritual state. If we claim to be Christians (as the rich man claimed to be a son of Abraham), but our material wealth is amassed for our own pleasures, if we are not generous and compassionate in our use of wealth, if we hoard our money, if we only give what amounts to crumbs to others, then we do not truly believe God's Word. We are deluded, and a mighty reversal awaits us.

> But if anyone has the world's goods and sees his brother in need, yet closes his heart against him, how does God's love abide in him? (1 John 3:17)

> If a brother or sister is poorly clothed and lacking in daily food, and one of you says to them, "Go in peace, be warmed and filled," without giving them the things needed for the body, what good is that? (James 2:15, 16)

Are we Christians? Do we believe God's Word? Then our faith will affect the way we use our wealth, because money speaks!

74

Discipleship's Duties

LUKE 17:1–10

I HAVE OCCASIONALLY PRAYED with my pastoral colleagues, "Lord, if one of us here is headed for adultery, take him home now." And all my colleagues nod their verbal assent. The Scriptural rationale for this corporate prayer comes from the opening lines of Luke 17: "Temptations to sin are sure to come, but woe to the one through whom they come! It would be better for him if a millstone were hung around his neck and he were cast into the sea than that he should cause one of these little ones to sin" (vv. 1, 2). Jesus' opening words here are literally, "It is inevitable that stumbling blocks should come" (NASB)—that is, stumbling blocks that will alienate one from allegiance to Christ and lead back into sin.[1] Jesus on this occasion gave sound, practical teaching none of us can afford to ignore.

Watch Yourselves (vv. 1–3a)

The human condition makes stumbling blocks inevitable. The destructiveness of sin is seen throughout general culture. Intellectuals often directly assault Christian belief. Criminal offenders regularly lead others headlong into sin. The icons of pop culture lure multitudes away from truth and life. Even some within the religious culture of faith, pastors and teachers who engage in spiritual compromise, lay huge stumbling blocks before "little ones," people who are weak and vulnerable as they are being drawn to Christ.[2]

False doctrine is the primary stumbling block of these religious leaders, and it is not limited to rank heresy but sometimes takes the form of eccentric teaching, legalism, and doctrinal imbalance—all of which turn people away from simple faith in Jesus Christ. Nearly as bad as the stumbling block of false teaching is scandalous living.

A few summers ago Barbara and I were sharing the gospel with a French rail conductor between Geneva and Paris, and he said, "Are you like Jimmy Bakker?" He was kidding, but he knew the whole sordid story and viewed Christianity with skepticism as a result. Many thousands have been turned off by the actions of people who claim to be Christ's disciples. Untold havoc has come not only through sensuality but through callous, uncaring lifestyles like that of the rich man toward Lazarus, through snobbishness, racism, and classism, and through the goody-goody self-righteousness of some church people.

In this fallen world all these stumbling blocks will come. "But," says Jesus, "woe to the one through whom they come!" We must interpret this woe very carefully. Jesus did not say the woe upon the offender is that he will have a millstone tied around his neck and be tossed into the sea. Being cast into the sea is the way to escape the woe.[3] The woe is far worse.

It would be better to die (even a horrible death) than to cause a little one to stumble and ultimately incur the woe of which Jesus warns. Better for the disciple or leader or pastor to die than to teach errant doctrine. Better to die than to have a lifestyle that trips others. Better to die than to have attitudes that drive others away from Christ.

I must confess that I do not understand what woe could await a true believer who has scandalized others away from Jesus Christ that could make a horrible physical death preferable, but I believe what the Savior is saying. Maybe the woe is an official dressing down at the Judgment Seat of Christ, with shipwrecked "little ones" there as accusers. Such a one is "saved, but only as through fire" (1 Corinthians 3:15). Whatever Jesus meant, death now is better than the woe. And thus Jesus' warning, "Pay attention to yourselves!" (v. 3a) must be taken to heart. Watch your teaching. Watch your lifestyle. Watch your attitudes.

Forgive (vv. 3b, 4)

Closely linked with the responsibility of not causing others to stumble into sin is the responsibility to help them when they fall.

Responsible to Rebuke

"If your brother sins, rebuke him" (v. 3b). Here "brother" would mean fellow Christian,[4] though it may refer either to the brother whose sinful conduct is causing another to stumble, or to the little brother or sister who has stumbled back into sin. In either case the rebuke is to be serious and frank, but gentle.[5] There is no room for censoriousness. The mere possibility of enjoying rebuking another is a disqualification for the undertaking. Most of us tend to go the other way, however, by choosing to say nothing. We live in comfortable, culpable silence. But Jesus gives his followers no option—"If your brother sins, rebuke him."

Responsible to Forgive

The duty to rebuke is attached to the responsibility to forgive: "and if he repents, forgive him, and if he sins against you seven times in the day, and turns to you seven times, saying, 'I repent,' you must forgive him" (vv. 3c, 4). The duty to forgive becomes increasingly personal. "If your brother sins [against a "little one," or if a "little one" sins] . . . and if he repents, forgive him." Then, more personally, "If he sins against *you* seven times in the day, and turns to you seven times, saying, 'I repent,' you must forgive him." The idea is that after the initial rebuke and your granting forgiveness, if he again sins, and again sins, and so on, the matter becomes highly personal. His sin is increasingly against you.

But regardless of the personal nature of the offense and the repetition of the offense, if the other person repents, you are to forgive him. This forgiveness is, to cite the adjectives used by various commentators, "boundless," "total," "immeasurable," "limitless," "habitual." Jesus places the burden of responsibility on the person forgiving rather than on the person who is repenting. The benefit of the doubt goes entirely to the one being forgiven. This raises immense practical difficulties. What about hypocritical requests for forgiveness? What if the sins being repented of repeatedly hurt others? Obviously there are some qualifications. Nevertheless, "Jesus' teaching does identify in sharp contours what genuine forgiveness is all about"[6]—upon whom the burden lies and the extent of forgiveness. It is better to be willing to forgive seven times a day even though the "brother" is not sincere than to refuse to forgive a truly repentant soul and thus place a stumbling block in his way.

This is difficult stuff. We must rebuke sin, even though we do not want to; and we must forgive sin, even though we do not want to. But obedience in these matters is sublime, because to do so is to become more like God. He always stands against sin in perpetual rebuke, and yet he also delights to forgive repentant sinners. His forgiveness is limitless. Has not God forgiven each of us countless times? All with such a spirit have become like God.

Have Faith (vv. 5, 6)

Jesus laid terrible responsibilities upon his followers, and the apostles reeled under the impact of his demand.

The Essential Request

The disciples then chorused to the Lord, "Increase our faith!" (v. 5). They did not ask for more love and tolerance so they could forgive. Neither did they ask for more understanding. Instead they asked for faith so they could adequately rebuke and forgive others.

How were they able to make the connection between faith and the ability to forgive? They may have learned it on other occasions when Jesus said essentially the same thing, though in a different order. For example:

> Jesus answered them, "Have faith in God. Truly, I say to you, whoever says to this mountain, 'Be taken up and thrown into the sea,' and does not doubt in his heart, but believes that what he says will come to pass, it will be done for him. Therefore I tell you, whatever you ask in prayer, believe that you have received it, and it will be yours. And whenever you stand praying, forgive, if you have anything against anyone, so that your Father also who is in heaven may forgive you your trespasses." (Mark 11:22–25)

At that time the Lord began by saying, "Have faith in God." Then he explained the power of faith to do wonders, finally concluding with a call to forgive. This understanding lay behind their group prayer in our passage: "Increase our faith!" Their prayer declared their faith. It is by faith that we ask for faith.

Their cry, "Increase our faith!" though it indicated their faith, also confirmed they could not increase their own faith. They knew better than to proudly declare, "I resolve to believe more—I will accumulate more faith." They understood that faith is a gift. "For by grace you have been saved through faith. And this is not your own doing; it is the gift of God, not a result of works, so that no one may boast" (Ephesians 2:8, 9). They remembered the humble prayer of the father of the epileptic boy: "I do believe, help me in my unbelief" (Mark 9:24 NASB). Faith for life's challenges is a gift. They knew that greater faith only comes through prayer. They understood that we obtain God's power only through faith—and that forgiveness requires supernatural power. So they prayed for faith.

The grand narratives of the Old Testament teach us that people of faith have the ability to forgive. People of faith are forgivers.

Abraham, the father of the faithful, was a man of faith. And when the herdsmen of Lot quarreled with his herdsmen, Abraham did not quarrel but calmly gave Lot his choice. Abraham's faith fostered a forgiving spirit. Joseph, a man full of faith, forgave his brothers. Moses, when reviled by Miriam and Aaron, did not retaliate but meekly trusted God. And David stood over sleeping Saul as his comrades urged him to kill him and spared Saul's life because he trusted God.

If a man is truly great in faith, he will be gentle and forgiving.[7] The man or woman of faith enters a rest that produces a calm spirit, which keeps him or her from seeking revenge, readily extending forgiveness instead.

If we are having trouble forgiving, we need faith. We need to believe that God is in control, that he is not slumbering. We need to believe he loves us. We need to believe he will take care of us. We need to believe he is equitable. We need to pray "Increase my faith!"—then take the step and forgive.

The Sure Victory

Jesus liked their request for faith and replied, "If you had faith like a grain of mustard seed, you could say to this mulberry tree, 'Be uprooted and planted in the sea,' and it would obey you" (v. 6). This text is not about denuding forests and casting them into the sea. Apart from wholly apocryphal tales, you can search history's records and not find a single instance of this happening through someone's faith. Eastern languages are unusually vivid and visual.

Also, this proverbial expression must be interpreted in its context, which is forgiveness. Here is the idea: "You may say, 'As a tree takes hold of the earth by its roots, my ill temper is rooted in the very depth of my nature. I am constitutionally quick-tempered. From my very birth I have found it hard to forgive.' But if you have faith, you can say to that ill-tempered mulberry tree, 'Be uprooted and planted in the sea!'"[8]

If we find it impossible to forgive, we need to pray, "Increase our faith!" And he will do it, for he always answers a prayer that is according to his will. Then we can forgive and forgive and forgive—and our souls will be secure, gentle, and liberated.

Do Your Duty (vv. 7–10)

Given the immense requirements Jesus gave his disciple leaders—to not cause a little one to stumble, to rebuke those who sin, to extend unlimited forgiveness, to exercise immense faith—a disciple might presume that in so doing he or she merits divine favor.

Jesus explodes such thinking with a miniparable consisting of three rhetorical questions that are answered with a no, a yes, and a final no. The answers derive from the relationships of slaves and masters in the ancient world.

> Will any one of you who has a servant plowing or keeping sheep say to him when he has come in from the field, "Come at once and recline at table"? (v. 7)

No!

> Will he not rather say to him, "Prepare supper for me, and dress properly, and serve me while I eat and drink, and afterward you will eat and drink"? (v. 8)

Yes!

> Does he thank the servant because he did what was commanded? (v. 9)

No!

Then comes the wake-up application: "So you also, when you have done all that you were commanded, say, 'We are unworthy servants; we have only done what was our duty'" (v. 10).

Closing Reflections

Jesus meant that watching ourselves, rebuking, forgiving, believing is nothing extraordinary—this is the way we are supposed to live. And when we do it, we are at best "unworthy servants." Such a life is our duty. This life (extraordinary as it may be) is ordinary Christianity. Oh, that we could be extraordinarily ordinary!

This concluding parable reminds us of an earlier passage:

> Stay dressed for action and keep your lamps burning, and be like men who are waiting for their master to come home from the wedding feast, so that they may open the door to him at once when he comes and knocks. Blessed are those servants whom the master finds awake when he comes. Truly, I say to you, he will dress himself for service and have them recline at table, and he will come and serve them. (12:35–37)

On that occasion Jesus revealed what he will do for faithful, watchful servants. When the day is over, he will make them sit down, and he will wait on them. That is the kingdom feast.

But the little parable in Luke 17 makes such a thing seem incomprehensible. He was at that time warning his followers against pride and presumption.

The eternal marvel is that ultimately he will do for us what our earthly masters will never do. But everything is of grace. There is nothing we can claim. There is no ground for pride—only eternal praise.

75

The Tenth Leper

LUKE 17:11–19

ONE OF THE SCARCEST VIRTUES of the human race is gratitude. Alexander Whyte, the most eminent Scottish preacher of the nineteenth century, once visited an elderly parishioner who complained at length about everything and everyone. Finally, hat in hand, Whyte rose to bid her good-bye. His only comment was a phrase from Psalm 103:2, "And mind you, forget not all his benefits."[1] Thanklessness is not new to our time.

But it is also true today that never have people had so much and been so ungrateful. Consider the typical Ivy League sophomore. From birth he has lacked nothing. He has had loving, doting parents and grandparents, the best in medical care, music lessons, tennis lessons, family vacations, summer sailing school, trendy wardrobes, religious instruction, European educational experiences, special work experiences, distinctive cars, credit cards. Yet he is an angry, ungrateful, depressed "poor me." He appreciates nothing. He regards his family as a nuisance. He focuses on shortcomings and slights in his upbringing, holding on to grudges with a death-grip. It never occurs to him that some of his happy friends have had it rougher than he.

Ungratefulness, though it has always been endemic to the human soul, is flourishing throughout our culture—and it is cresting in Generation X.

And Christian culture is not immune. The contemporary diseases that afflict others attach to Christians as well, so that in some cases, apart from perfunctory prayers of thanks at meals, no one would ever know they are grateful people, much less recipients of divine healing grace. This ought not to be. Scripturally, thankless Christians are a contradiction in terms (Philippians 4:4; cf. Romans 1:21; 2 Timothy 3:2). The account of the ten lepers in Luke 17 addresses the question in a powerful way.

Mass Healing (vv. 11–14)

On the outskirts of an unnamed village on the borderlands of Samaria and Galilee, ten leprous men stood before Jesus in various stages of decay, their clothing torn in perpetual mourning, their skeletal heads uncovered, their lips unveiled as they warned others, "Unclean, unclean" (cf. Leviticus 13:45; Numbers 5:2; 12:10–12).

They looked as though they had climbed out of the graves. But they were alive, sensitive human beings, feeling souls living in the nether world of society's fringe while they rotted away. So from a safe distance they shouted the traditional plea, "Jesus, Master, have mercy on us" (v. 13). They were loud and persistent. "Have mercy on us!" "Master, have mercy!" "Mercy please!"

Once Jesus saw them, he immediately responded. However, this time there was no touch as he had previously given a leper. Neither was there the pronouncement, "Be clean" (cf. 5:13). He simply told them, leprous as they were, "Go and show yourselves to the priests" (v. 14a). The command was to do what a *cured leper* would do, following the regulations stipulated in Leviticus 14, which required examination by a priest. If they were cured, they would joyfully undergo an eight-day ceremony and then be reunited with their families.

Jesus' command required faith, and we surmise that not all the lepers were of the same mind. No ten people would be. Some were convinced they should go to the priest immediately. Others demurred. After all, it was a long way to the temple. If Jesus could heal them, why did he not just do it? What fools they would be if they tried to see a priest but were still leprous. On the other hand, they had everything to gain and very little to lose. The consensus was to give it a try.[2] So they set off at their stumbling lepers' pace.

"And as they went they were cleansed" (v. 14b). It was a mass healing! There were no mirrors to reflect the dramatic change, but they saw it in each other instantly. From cadaverous faces reemerged ears, noses, eyebrows, lashes, hairlines. Feet—toeless, ulcerated stubs—were suddenly whole, bursting shrunken sandals. Knobby appendages grew fingers. Barnacled skin became soft and supple. It was like ten new births. The dust of a wild celebration quickly began in the bright sunlight.

Solitary Thanks (vv. 15, 16)

Among those ten lepers was a Samaritan. Normally Jews had "no dealings with Samaritans" (John 4:9), and likewise Samaritans with Jews, but these men had been united by their common misery—nine Jews and one Samaritan in a suffering community.

And when the healing occurred, the Samaritan was seized with "an irresistible emotion of gratitude"[3] and, captive to this spontaneous gratitude, put off going to the temple to rush back to Jesus. The ceremonial clean bill of health could wait. His spiritual obligation overrode his ceremonial need. So the Samaritan and the Jews parted company.

The thankful Samaritan knew he had "two to thank—God and Jesus; he did not know that the two were one."[4]

First he said thank you to God: "Then one of them, when he saw that he was healed, turned back, praising God with a loud voice" (v. 15). Earlier he had loudly pled for healing, and now he was loud with his praise. The Greek for "loud voice" is recognizable to the English ear, for it is the two words from which we get *megaphone*, here reversed *phonēs megalēs*. He was mega-voiced in his praise to God.

Then he thanked Jesus: "He fell on his face at Jesus' feet, giving him thanks. Now he was a Samaritan" (v. 16). At the very least he recognized Jesus as an agent of God. More likely, he realized that Jesus was King.[5] The Samaritans were well acquainted with the messianic Scriptures, and this man saw Jesus in that light. He returned to Jesus with a heart giving glory to God and thanks to Jesus. He recognized God's power in Christ.

Sovereign Declaration (vv. 17–19)

Jesus' Questions

Jesus asked three closely coordinated questions, all freighted with amazement: "Were not ten cleansed? Where are the nine? Was no one found to return and give praise to God except this foreigner?" (vv. 17, 18). The questions were not rhetorical. The human Jesus (who had placed his omniscience at his Father's discretion) expected all ten to return, glorifying God, and then to receive the ultimate blessing he had prepared for them. Jesus was disappointed!

But evidently the other nine lepers were so caught up in their new wholeness that it did not occur to them to return to Jesus. This is understandable at one level. After all, Jesus had told them to show themselves to the priests. Of course they were thankful. How could they be otherwise? And they were deeply happy. And they were eager to get back into everyday life.

Are we sympathetic with their not returning to Jesus? There is a deadly problem here—God was not the center of their gratitude. Note Jesus' final question: "Was no one found to return and give praise to God except this foreigner?" (v. 18). Only the foreigner, the Samaritan, gave praise to God!

The other nine were so earthbound, so like the shrewd manager and the rich man of the preceding parables, that they missed the spiritual dimension altogether. Vague gratitude to divinity was not an adequate response to what had happened. Christ wanted their hearts! By failing to glorify God and returning to thank Jesus, they missed the greatest possible moment of their existence.

Jesus' Pronouncement

The account closes with Jesus' sovereign pronouncement to the Samaritan: "Rise and go your way; your faith has made you well" (v. 19). The Greek in the last part of verse 19 is literally, "Your faith has saved you." This is the studied opinion of the three most prominent Lukan scholars in the world, men of diverse traditions. I. H. Marshall, Senior Lecturer in New Testament Exegesis at the University of Aberdeen, writes, "His faith has been the means of his cure and his salvation."[6] Joseph A. Fitzmyer, a professor at Catholic University of America and a past president of the Society of Biblical Literature, translates unequivocally, "Your faith has brought you salvation."[7] And John Nolland of Trinity College Bristol writes, "But as much of a foreigner as he might be, this man is now sent off by Jesus as a person who has experienced the salvation that Jesus came to bring. None of the others, despite their new-found freedom from leprosy, receives this special blessing."[8]

We must let Jesus' declaration, "Your faith has saved you," have its deepest meaning. The fatal spiritual leprosy fell from the Samaritan's spirit. He received forgiveness, reconciliation, eternal life, and the removal of all alienation and distance between God and himself in place of his sin and moral sickness.[9] Jesus' words were clear: only the Samaritan who returned to praise God and offer thanksgiving to Christ himself had saving faith. Indeed, his gratitude and praise to God were signs of his saving faith.

Closing Reflections

There are eternal lessons here for us. Certainly we must understand that no one is saved by virtue of having a pleasant, optimistic, or thankful spirit. Jesus is not teaching salvation by disposition. But Jesus is teaching that where there is true faith there are profoundly thankful hearts.

Thanks to God

Praise to God the Father is at the heart of authentic faith.

> But thanks be to God, who gives us the victory through our Lord Jesus Christ. (1 Corinthians 15:57)

> But thanks be to God, who in Christ always leads us in triumphal procession, and through us spreads the fragrance of the knowledge of him everywhere. (2 Corinthians 2:14)
>
> Thanks be to God for his inexpressible gift! (2 Corinthians 9:15)
>
> With joy, giving thanks to the Father, who has qualified you to share in the inheritance of the saints in light. He has delivered us from the domain of darkness and transferred us to the kingdom of his beloved Son, in whom we have redemption, the forgiveness of sins. (Colossians 1:11b–14)
>
> And whatever you do, in word or deed, do everything in the name of the Lord Jesus, giving thanks to God the Father through him. (Colossians 3:17)

The New Testament is clear: believing hearts are hearts that praise and glorify God.

Thanks to Jesus Christ

Did you notice that in every one of these principal references to praising God, Jesus is the reason? As people of faith, our praise to God must be radically Christ centered. Saving faith does not vaguely give glory to God the Father. Hearts of faith are doxologically Christocentric. Near the end of the great book of Hebrews we hear the call, "Through him [Jesus] then let us continually offer up a sacrifice of praise to God, that is, the fruit of lips that acknowledge his name" (Hebrews 13:15).

We are to praise God through Jesus. This is true in this world and in eternity.

Charles Spurgeon was sharing the gospel with a very talkative woman who was beginning to understand the good news when she burst out: "Oh Mr. Spurgeon, if Christ saves me he will never hear the end of it!" She spoke beyond her understanding, because such praise will be the eternal occupation of the redeemed.

> And whenever the living creatures give glory and honor and thanks to him who is seated on the throne, who lives forever and ever, the twenty-four elders fall down before him who is seated on the throne and worship him who lives forever and ever. They cast their crowns before the throne, saying,
>
> "Worthy are you, our Lord and God,
> to receive glory and honor and power,
> for you created all things,
> and by your will they existed and were created." (Revelation 4:9–11)

> Then I looked, and I heard around the throne and the living creatures and the elders the voice of many angels, numbering myriads of myriads and thousands of thousands, saying with a loud voice,
>
> "Worthy is the Lamb who was slain,
> to receive power and wealth and wisdom and might
> and honor and glory and blessing!" (Revelation 5:11, 12)

The hearts of those who do not know Christ are ungrateful. Speaking of man's spiritual history, Paul reported, "For although they knew God, they did not honor him as God or give thanks to him" (Romans 1:21). His perspective on man's future matched his perspective on man's past: "But understand this, that in the last days there will come times of difficulty. For people will be lovers of self, lovers of money, proud, arrogant, abusive, disobedient to their parents, ungrateful, unholy" (2 Timothy 3:1, 2).

Many Generation X-ers, besides being ungrateful, are depressed. Interestingly, thankfulness and depression are mutually exclusive. It is impossible to lift one's heart in thankful praise to God and be depressed, too.

How beneficial grateful people are for themselves and for those around them. They are light in the darkness. And when their gratitude rings out to God through Jesus and for Jesus, Christ is powerfully proclaimed, and some in a dark, depressed, thankless culture begin to see a ray of light.

76

The Kingdom—Now and Not Yet

LUKE 17:20–37

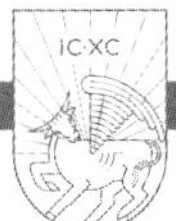

THE NEW TESTAMENT has a great deal to say about the kingdom of God. In fact, the Gospel of Luke alone has thirty occurrences of the phrase *the kingdom of God*. This is understandable because the New Testament is about the kingdom's King—Jesus Christ. But at the same time, the kingdom of God did not begin with the first advent of the Messiah. Rather, it is a reality that extends back to the beginning of Biblical revelation and courses through the entire Old Testament. In fact, it is the kingdom of God that gives the Old Testament its continuity.

We first see the kingdom in the garden of Eden, where Adam and Eve lived in willing obedience to God's rule. The fundamental definition of the kingdom of God is: *God's people, in God's place, under God's rule*.[1] That phrase perfectly describes the protokingdom, the final eschatological kingdom of God, and all the manifestations in between. As we know, in Eden the kingdom was destroyed by the sin of man, and the rest of the Bible is about the restoration of a people who are willing subjects of the perfect rule of God.

After Eden, we next see the kingdom memorably promised to Abraham in the so-called Abrahamic Covenant (Genesis 12:1–3), in which God promised that Abraham's descendants (God's people) would possess the promised land (God's place) and live under his authority (God's rule).[2] The historical process by which Israel came to enter the promised land (as temporary and flawed as their living under God's rule at that time was) was the sovereign, redemptive act of God as he rescued his people from captivity in Egypt—the blood of the Passover lamb.

The monarchy that later flowered under David and Solomon (as disappointing as it also was) imperfectly manifested the essential elements of God's kingdom as well.

The failure of Solomon's kingdom and the subsequent Babylonian Exile made it clear that the prophesies of the pre-exilic prophets (Isaiah, Jeremiah, and Ezekiel) were about a future great day when the perfect, everlasting kingdom of God will come. The post-exilic prophets prophesied about this eternal kingdom with uniform passion. In fact, the Old Testament ends on a note of promise and expectation of the coming of the kingdom.[3] This was followed by over four hundred years of prophetic silence between the Old and New Testaments. During that time a number of solutions were dreamed of. Perhaps the best known was that of the Pharisees, who sought a literal return of the Davidic Monarchy and the liberation of Israel from foreign oppression.

After the passing of those four dark centuries, the night skies over Palestine gave way to a great company of angels glorifying God for the incarnation of Jesus—Messiah! And thirty years later Jesus began to say, "The time is fulfilled, and the kingdom of God is at hand; repent and believe in the gospel" (Mark 1:15). The gospel is the bringing near of the kingdom. Jesus did not mean that the ultimate fulfillment had taken place, but that the kingdom was near in him. The book of Matthew repeatedly describes Jesus' ministry as "proclaiming the gospel of the kingdom" (Matthew 4:23; 9:35; cf. 24:14).

We can say that the kingdom came in Jesus Christ and will come in its fullness at Jesus' return.

The Who, What, and Why of the Kingdom

In Jesus Christ we find the kingdom of God. All that we know or need to know about God's kingdom is found in Christ.

The People

In Eden, Adam and Eve were the people of God. Significantly, Jesus, the Son of God, chose to come to earth as the last or second Adam (cf. Romans 5:18–21; 1 Corinthians 15:20–22, 45–49). Jesus identified himself with Adam's race at his baptism (3:21, 22). In the wilderness he overcame temptation (Adam had failed the same test), ultimately triumphing on the cross (Matthew 4:1–11; Mark 1:12, 13; Luke 4:1–13). Thus Paul could write, "For as by the one man's disobedience [Adam's] the many were made sinners, so by the one man's obedience [Jesus Christ's] the many will be made righteous" (Romans 5:19). The people of God come to him through Jesus!

Jesus also was and is the ultimate, perfect offspring of Abraham, as Paul wrote in Galatians: "Now the promises were made to Abraham and to his offspring. It does not say, 'And to offsprings,' referring to many, but referring to one, 'And to your offspring,' who is Christ" (Galatians 3:16). The offspring of Abraham *par excellence* is Christ. The promises of Abraham only have their fulfillment in and through Christ.

In addition to being the ultimate offspring of Abraham, Jesus was and is the ultimate son of King David (cf. 2 Samuel 7:14). As the King, Jesus embodies the whole people as their representative.

All these realities—Jesus as the last Adam, the one true offspring of Abraham, the true Israel, the promised son of King David—establish one glorious point: Jesus Christ is the head of a new race, the people of God! All who are "in Christ" are a new creation (2 Corinthians 5:17). They are the people of God. They are the people of the kingdom.

Place

In a significant sense Jesus also was and is the place of the kingdom of God. The Old Testament images of locality—the garden of Eden, the promised land, the city/Zion, the temple—all reach fulfillment in Christ, because in the New Testament the locality of the kingdom is Jesus Christ himself (cf. John 1:14; 2:21; Acts 13:34). Jesus replaced the temple, and thus those indwelt by Christ become the place of God's rule (cf. Galatians 2:20; Ephesians 3:17).[4]

Rule

Lastly, Jesus was and is himself the rule of God. In the incarnation he lived under the rule of God so perfectly that he could say, "I always do the things that are pleasing to him" (John 8:29). At the same time he was (and is) King, and he repeatedly exhibited kingdom powers (cf. Luke 8:1, 2; 9:1, 2; 11:20). And all who are in Christ live and serve under God's rule in their hearts.

So we see that the kingdom of God was at hand in Christ, for he was God's person, in God's place, under God's rule—and all those in him are God's people, in God's place, under God's rule. True Christianity, kingdom Christianity, is radically Christ centered. With the advent of Christ, the kingdom had drawn near.

The Now (vv. 20, 21)

Jesus now issued a question to the Pharisees, who were looking for the re-establishment of the old Davidic kingdom. Having been asked when the kingdom of God would come, Jesus replied, "The kingdom of God is not coming in ways that can be observed, nor will they say, 'Look, here it is!' or 'There!' for behold, the kingdom of God is in the midst of you" (vv. 20, 21).

The kingdom was standing in their midst in the person and work of Christ![5] The irony here was huge, because they were arrogantly and unknowingly asking the kingdom's King, indeed the King of kings, when his kingdom would come.

They thought that their careful, cultured expertise in observing every phenomenon would assure them of seeing the kingdom before others did. Significantly, Jesus had encouraged his followers to interpret the times:

> When you see a cloud rising in the west, you say at once, "A shower is coming." And so it happens. And when you see the south wind blowing, you say, "There will be scorching heat," and it happens. You hypocrites! You know how to interpret the appearance of earth and sky, but why do you not know how to interpret the present time? (12:54–56)

Jesus encouraged his people to read both the Scriptures and the times. But the Pharisees had the whole picture wrong. They thought the kingdom might have a localized beginning like, say, a political movement, so that they could say, "Here it is," or "There" (v. 21a). They were so blind—though the King himself was giving his kingdom message with kingdom power, they completely failed to recognize him.

Their problem was not due to any lack of signs. Jesus had done numerous miracles. But recognizing Jesus as Messiah, seeing the kingdom, was a matter of inner revelation and divine insight (cf. 10:21). Entering the kingdom of God was essentially an inner process of repentance in response to the invisible winds of the Holy Spirit. The Pharisees needed to concentrate less on the external form of the kingdom and more on its spiritual dimensions. They had missed the deeper levels of the Old Testament's teaching as to the people, place, and rule of God's kingdom.

This is a call (actually a warning) to us to be sure that we invite and submit to the lordship of Christ in every part of our lives. We must prayerfully ask God to build the radical kingdom ethics of the Sermon on the Mount into our lives. Above all, we must be radically Christ centered, for then we become the people of God, our hearts the place of God, and our lives examples of the rule of God.

The Not Yet (vv. 22–37)

Every Eye Will See

Having given the Pharisees more than enough to think about regarding the now of the kingdom, Jesus went on to offer advice, possibly private advice, to his disciples about the not yet of the kingdom:

> And he said to the disciples, "The days are coming when you will desire to see one of the days of the Son of Man, and you will not see it. And they will say to you, 'Look, there!' or 'Look, here!' Do not go out or follow them. For as the lightning flashes and lights up the sky from one side to the other, so will the Son of Man be in his day." (vv. 22–24)

Certainly the disciples would see the evidence of the resurrection, they would all watch Christ gloriously ascend to the right hand of the Father in a radiant cloud (Acts 1:9), but none would see any of the days surrounding his final advent. We are still waiting for his glorious appearing today.[6] But heavy waters awaited them all, and amid them they would long to see his return. And in their longing, they were not to be seduced by "prophecy experts" crying that they had seen Messiah.

His great appearing will be cosmic—like a thousand 24,000-mile-long lightning bolts simultaneously ringing the earth. All will see this—in the Middle East, across the steppes of Russia and into Siberia, in Asia, in China, in Australia, in Europe, in Africa, in the Americas, on all the world's islands, at the North and South Poles. No one will miss it!

Rejection First

But Jesus went on to graciously warn them that before any final appearing, there would be rejection. Before his glorious reign, there would be humiliation and suffering.

> But first he must suffer many things and be rejected by this generation. Just as it was in the days of Noah, so will it be in the days of the Son of Man. They were eating and drinking and marrying and being given in marriage, until the day when Noah entered the ark, and the flood came and destroyed them all. Likewise, just as it was in the days of Lot—they were eating and drinking, buying and selling, planting and building, but on the day when Lot went out from Sodom, fire and sulfur rained from heaven and destroyed them all—so will it be on the day when the Son of Man is revealed. (vv. 25–30)

That Jesus was to be "rejected" was prophesied repeatedly in the Old Testament (Isaiah 53:3; cf. Psalm 22). This was a necessary price for our salvation. And Jesus saying this here, as he did again after his resurrection, prepared the disciples to wait for the not yet (cf. Luke 24:25, 26).

This rejection of Christ will go on and on around the world until the end, as the two Old Testament illustrations from the days of Noah and Lot graphically depict. Both Noah and Lot were righteous men according to the New Testament, despite their faults (cf. 2 Peter 2:5, 7). Both escaped destruction—Noah because of his obedience (Hebrews 11:7), and Lot because angels induced him to leave Sodom (Genesis 19:16, 17). And both men lived in utterly depraved cultures.

But on this occasion Jesus made no mention of the righteousness of Noah and Lot or the sinfulness of their cultures. According to Jesus, people's problem was their regular everyday activities—"eating and drinking and marrying and being given in marriage . . . buying and selling, planting and building" (vv. 27, 28). It was not their sin, as great as it was, that damned them to destruction—it was their *indifference*. They were so preoccupied with normal life that they rarely had a thought above the mundane.

That is the way it will be at the end—"so will it be on the day when the Son of Man is revealed" (v. 30), and that is the way it is today!

Jesus' words describe many people's priority today—"eating and drinking and marrying and being given in marriage . . . buying and selling, planting and building." Better homes and cars, gardening, menus and feasts, friends, marriage, children are all good things. But many give such high consideration to these things that they even wonder whether they have a soul! They give no thought to their sin. They are shallow, complacent, comfortable—and lost.

Possessed by Possessions

As David Gooding observes:

> Some people are so taken up with material things, that Christ thinks it necessary to warn them that on the very day in which he will be revealed to execute the wrath of God on evil centres and conglomerations of human iniquity, they will be tempted to go back into the house or city to get their favourite possessions because they cannot imagine life without them. For the sake of things they will lose life itself (see 17:31–33).[7]

Lot's wife could not imagine existence without her possessions. Longing for what she was leaving behind, she lingered and so perished in the brimstone. "But Lot's wife, behind him, looked back, and she became a pillar of salt" (Genesis 19:26).

Jesus then issued a critical maxim: "Whoever seeks to preserve his life will lose it, but whoever loses his life will keep it" (v. 33; cf. 9:24, 25). On this occasion, Jesus was putting forth the need to let go of the world's possessions, so we can put our full trust in him. The constant hedging of one's life with things—home, investments, retirements—trying to keep one's life—is a sure way to lose it.

Jesus then explained that his coming and the ensuing judgment will be subtly discriminate and eternal. In all outward respects two people may appear the same as they share the same bed or work at the same mill. But one will be taken away to deliverance, while the other is left to destruction: "I tell you, in that night there will be two in one bed. One will be taken and the other left. There will be two women grinding together. One will be taken and the other left" (vv. 34, 35). There will be no mistakes, for omniscience will determine the separation. Outward appearance will count for nothing. God knows every heart!

Evidently the Lord's warning not to return to the city or to one's home when judgment comes led the disciples to imagine that the judgment might be focused on a particular place. So they asked, "Where, Lord?" (v. 37). And the Lord replied enigmatically, "Where the corpse is, there the vultures will gather" (v. 37). Judgment will fall on all humanity. Where there are spiritually dead, there will be judgment.

Closing Reflections

In this prophetic section Jesus has given the now and not yet of his kingdom. The truth is, though Jesus has been gone for over two thousand years, "the kingdom of God is in [our] midst"! If we have trusted him and are in Christ, we are his people, living in his place (Jesus the temple), living under his rule. We are children of thc kingdom.

Jesus, through his life, death, and resurrection, has won for us the riches of his glory. We have perfect acceptance with God in Christ. And even more, there is nothing that we will possess in glory that we do not now have in Christ.

Thus "the Christian lives in the tension of the *now* of living 'by faith' and the *not yet* of knowing the full reality of the kingdom 'by sight.'"[8] But we each have great assurance about the not yet because of the now in Christ. If we are his people, in his place, under his rule, we will look beyond the regular living of life to him, and we will hold loosely the things of this world.

Jesus Christ is everything. He is the maker and goal of all creation (Colossians 1:15–17). He is the source and goal of redemption (Colossians 1:18–20). He is the heir of all things (Romans 8:17). He is the focus of God's Word (Luke 24:25, 26, 45, 46). He is our person, our place, our rule. He is the King. He is our destiny. He gives us the kingdom.

77

Living in the Not Yet

LUKE 18:1–8

LIVING IN THE NOT YET of the kingdom, the period of time before Christ's return and the inauguration of the ultimate kingdom, is no easy task. This is because Christians also live in the now of the kingdom. Christ has come, and with him has come the kingdom, as he himself declared: "The kingdom of God is in [your] midst" (17:21). In his person came the kingdom, and those who believe in him and therefore are "in him" are members of the kingdom—the people of God, in the place of God, under the rule of God.

This creates relentless tension. To enjoy the now of the kingdom while living in the not yet makes us different from the rest of the world. We are seated with God "in the heavenly places in Christ Jesus" (Ephesians 2:6). God has "blessed us in Christ with every spiritual blessing in the heavenly places" (Ephesians 1:3). Both the seating and blessing are present realities. Therefore we are commanded to set our minds on the eternal, the not yet:

> If then you have been raised with Christ, seek the things that are above, where Christ is, seated at the right hand of God. Set your minds on things that are above, not on things that are on earth. For you have died, and your life is hidden with Christ in God. When Christ who is your life appears, then you also will appear with him in glory. (Colossians 3:1–4)

We are called to live out the radical ethics of the kingdom (cf. Matthew 5—7) while we wait for the King.

> For the grace of God has appeared, bringing salvation for all people, training us to renounce ungodliness and worldly passions, and to live self-controlled, upright, and godly lives in the present age, waiting for our blessed hope, the appearing of the glory of our great God and Savior Jesus Christ,

> who gave himself for us to redeem us from all lawlessness and to purify for himself a people for his own possession who are zealous for good works. (Titus 2:11–14)

So the tension for us in the not yet is vast. Jesus referred to this in his words just prior to the passage we will examine in this chapter: "The days are coming when you will desire to see one of the days of the Son of Man, and you will not see it" (17:22). This longing will stand in stark contrast to the casual neglect of busy culture: "Just as it was in the days of Noah, so will it be in the days of the Son of Man" (17:26, cf. v. 30).

Most people simply could not care less, and some even mock, as Peter warned: "Knowing this first of all, that scoffers will come in the last days with scoffing, following their own sinful desires. They will say, 'Where is the promise of his coming? For ever since the fathers fell asleep, all things are continuing as they were from the beginning of creation'" (2 Peter 3:3, 4). The not yet has been filled with persecution, and it has been especially so in our own bloody lifetimes. For the last two thousand years the question has been, how are we to live in the not yet as we await the return of Christ?

Jesus addressed this question with a parable found only in Luke: "And he told them a parable to the effect that they ought always to pray and not lose heart" (18:1). The parable's purpose was explicit. We do not have to guess at its central message (though there is much to unpack). Jesus' disciples are to continue praying until Jesus comes back. His people are not to give up on prayer.[1]

The Parable (vv. 2–5)

With a minimum of words, Jesus created indelible pictures of two very distinct people, a judge and a widow: "In a certain city there was a judge who neither feared God nor respected man. And there was a widow in that city who kept coming to him and saying, 'Give me justice against my adversary'" (vv. 2, 3).

Here Comes the Judge!

The judge admitted he did not fear God or care about men (v. 4). If he was a Jew, he was openly defying the primary qualification for judges—the fear of God. This qualification had been made famous when, after the death of Ahab, a chastened King Jehoshaphat took steps to restore order by appointing judges with these orders: "Consider what you do, for you judge not for man but for the LORD. He is with you in giving judgment. Now then, let the fear of the Lord be upon you. Be careful what you do, for there is no injustice with the Lord our God, or partiality or taking bribes" (2 Chronicles 19:6, 7). A fear of God is essential for a good judge.

Conversely, a judge with no fear of God recognizes no universal ethic outside his own self-interest, and his mistaken belief that he will never stand before God's bar relieves him of any burden to render just decisions. The judge in the parable was such a man. History's worst villains, disingenuous as they were, even Hitler and Stalin, professed love for humanity. But not this man. He was capable of anything except justice.

Here Comes the Widow!

Life had dealt the woman in the parable a bitter blow. Similarly, in the opening chapter of the book of Ruth when newly widowed Naomi returned from Moab to Bethlehem, she responded to her old friends' greetings by saying, "Do not call me Naomi; call me Mara, for the Almighty has dealt very bitterly with me. I went away full, and the Lord has brought me back empty. Why call me Naomi, when the Lord has testified against me and the Almighty has brought calamity upon me?" (Ruth 1:20, 21).

Widows were among the most defenseless in Hebrew society. The Old Testament refers to their being oppressed (cf. Malachi 3:5) and taken advantage of (cf. Exodus 22:22–24). They were often legal victims (cf. Isaiah 1:17, 23), and this was the case for this poor woman. Likely she was one of those later described in Luke as victims of men who "devour widows' houses" (20:47). The poor woman did not want vengeance—just restorative justice.

The options for obtaining redress or justice from a rogue judge like this were few—a bribe, a threat, or a pathetic plea, the latter being her only recourse. And plead she did! Every day she begged him to help her. The language leaves open the possibility of confrontation everywhere, not just in court. She pleaded with him in front of his colleagues, she confronted him on the street, she pestered him in the market, and she called out to him at his home. Her chances of redress were very slim with this godless, hardened, cynical man, but it was the only thing she could do. *The poor woman*, we think. *This evil judge is not going to budge. Sometimes there is no justice!*

Here Comes Justice!

For a time the judge remained unmoved, but eventually, despite his cynical resolution, "afterward he said to himself, 'Though I neither fear God nor respect man, yet because this widow keeps bothering me, I will give her justice, so that she will not beat me down by her continual coming'" (vv. 4, 5). The literal translation of "beat me down" ("blacken my eye") conveys even better his frustration. This was a boxing expression (cf. 1 Corinthians 9:27).[2]

Her persistence had been punching him out, probably in the sense of public embarrassment, giving his reputation or prominence a black eye. So suddenly there was justice! The old rogue judge had met his match.

The Lesson (vv. 6–8a)

> And the Lord said, "Hear what the unrighteous judge says. And will not God give justice to his elect, who cry to him day and night? Will he delay long over them? I tell you, he will give justice to them speedily." (vv. 6–8a)

This parable's lesson has often been greatly misunderstood, because most people think it teaches that feverish importunity (troublesome persistence) in prayer is a virtue. Untold numbers of sermons have wrongly used this text to teach that we must frantically beg God to answer our prayers. This is not the idea at all.

The parable of the unjust judge and the pestering widow is a parable of *contrast*. The clear lesson of the parable is that God is not like the judge, for God is good and gracious. And we are not like the nameless widow, for we are his chosen ones. So a distressed bugging of God is in fact inadequate prayer.

Our Just God

The judge was unloving, evil, ungracious, merciless, and unjust. But God is loving, good, gracious, merciful, and just. Moreover, whatever God is, he is infinitely. He is infinitely loving, infinitely gracious, infinitely merciful, and infinitely just. As A. W. Tozer wrote: "Just, when used of God is a name we give to the way God is, nothing more; and when God acts justly He is . . . simply acting like himself in every situation."[3]

In the parable the woman was an insignificant nobody. But in life, as Christians we are God's elect, his chosen ones, created in his image and redeemed by the Son of God. Because of who God is and who we are, there is no reason to frantically assault his door or nag him for a response. It was because the prophets of Baal were idolaters, deluded and worshiping a false concept of God, that they "called upon the name of Baal from morning until noon, saying, 'O Baal, answer us!'" (1 Kings 18:26). And that is why "at noon Elijah mocked them, saying, 'Cry aloud, for he is a god. Either he is musing, or he is relieving himself, or he is on a journey, or perhaps he is asleep and must be awakened.' And they cried aloud and cut themselves after their custom with swords and lances, until the blood gushed out upon them" (1 Kings 18:27, 28).

The Christian (actually sub-Christian) version of this parable is to imagine that our fervent prayers will begin to accumulate a meritorious critical mass that God cannot ignore. Such a view is idolatrous because it imagines that God is something like the unjust judge.

C. Samuel Storms poses some relevant questions in his book *Reaching God's Ear* that we can use to evaluate our prayer lives.

- Do we repeat a request because we think that the quality of a prayer is dependent on the quantity of words?
- Do we repeat a request because we think that God is ignorant and needs to be informed, or if not ignorant at least he is unconcerned and therefore needs to be aroused?
- Do we repeat our prayers because we believe that God is unwilling to answer and we must prevail upon him, somehow transforming a hard-hearted God into a compassionate and loving one?
- Do we repeat a petition because we think that God will be swayed in his decision by our putting on a show of zeal and piety, as if God cannot see through the thin veil of hypocrisy?[4]

Our Prayer Life

Does this mean we must never engage in importunate prayer, fervently beseeching God? Not at all. The teaching of the parable is that we must continue in our prayers, even when there seems to be no answer, because God, unlike the unjust judge, is loving, good, and gracious. We persist in prayer not because we have not yet gotten God's attention, but because we know he cares and will hear us.

The Apostle Paul engaged in such prayer when three times he pleaded with the Lord for the removal of his thorn in the flesh (cf. 2 Corinthians 12:7–9). These were three sustained, passionate times of intercession. Paul did not think that his repetitions were due to a defect in his faith—"Sorry, Lord, but I'm back. Please forgive my lack of faith! My prayers will be better this time." There was none of that. And in the end, the thorn was still there, but God gave him something better to go along with it—*more grace!*

There are times for importunate prayer—times when tragedy strikes or when critical decisions are at hand. But we know that God knows what we need before we ask, and we know that he hears us, and we know that he will answer.

God's Quick Answers

Through the centuries many believers have struggled with the seeming silence of God to their prayers. But here Jesus says that God answers all pleas for justice, and does so quickly: "And will not God give justice to his elect, who cry to him day and night? Will he delay long over them? I tell you, he will give justice to them speedily" (vv. 7, 8a).

How can this be? The next sentence Jesus spoke refers to his coming, which makes it clear that "speedily" does not mean "immediately."[5] The idea here is swiftly—that is, when God acts it will be quick or swift.[6] When we consider God's timing, we must keep in mind Peter's wisdom regarding God's promise: "But do not overlook this one fact, beloved, that with the Lord one day is as a thousand years, and a thousand years as one day. The Lord is not slow to fulfill his promise as some count slowness" (2 Peter 3:8, 9a). To the elect it may seem to be a long time until he answers, but afterwards they will realize that it was very short. Jesus' parable teaches the certainty of speedy action when it comes.[7]

But many are still discouraged by God's seeming silence. We need to learn that in the silence our loving God is answering, whether we see his working or not, for he delights to answer his children's prayers.

Sometimes the silence means that God's answer is a loving no. Perhaps we asked amiss, or though the request was good, a better way is coming. Far better for Paul than the removal of his thorn was God's sufficient grace, which was perfected in his weakness. This is why he could write, "By the grace of God I am what I am, and his grace toward me was not in vain. On the contrary, I worked harder than any of them, though it was not I, but the grace of God that is with me" (1 Corinthians 15:10).

Also, sometimes the silence means that God has a bigger answer in store than we could ever have dreamed of or asked for. As Oswald Chambers explained, "Some prayers are followed by silence because they are wrong, others because they are bigger than we can understand. It will be a wonderful moment for some of us when we stand before God and find that the prayers we clamoured for in early days and imagined were never answered, have been answered in the most amazing way, and that God's silence has been the sign of the answer."[8]

Further, sometimes the silence of God is meant to instill dependence upon him. In the case of Paul he was left with his thorn so that he would lean entirely upon God. We are so prone to independence that the granting of certain of our requests would lead us to self-sufficiency, pride, and independence. There can be no better way to cultivate a sense of dependence upon God than the need for persistent or determined prayer.

Sometimes the silence is a delay to allow our prayers to mature. If God had answered our prayers according to our schedule, our prayers would not have been honed by the Spirit for our greater good and his glory.

Closing Reflections

As we live in the not yet, longing for the return of the Son of Man, Jesus' closing question has the same force as it did in A.D. 33: "Nevertheless, when the Son of Man comes, will he find faith on earth?" (v. 8b). Jesus' question implies that such faith will not be found on earth unless his disciples learn that they "ought always to pray and not lose heart" (v. 1b).

Jesus was saying that continual prayer until he comes is not only the evidence of faith, but the means of building faith until his return. The God to whom we pray is not like the unjust judge who could only be badgered into responding, for our God is loving and gracious. And we are not like the nameless widow, for we are his chosen ones. Because of this, he delights to hear and quickly answer our prayers until he comes.

"When the Son of Man comes, will he find faith on earth?" Yes, he will, if we have learned to live a life of prayer in the not yet.

78

Two Ways to Pray

LUKE 18:9–14

THOSE WHO HAVE READ *War and Peace* or *Anna Karenina* or short stories like "How Much Land Does a Man Need?" agree that Leo Tolstoy was a great novelist. Some would say he is the greatest of novelists. His writings have a moral force to them, and much of what he says is personally helpful. Nevertheless, Tolstoy's morality was not God centered but self-centered. He defined God as "the desire for universal welfare"—and insofar as Tolstoy saw himself as embodying this desire, he was God. Having so defined God, he wrote in his diary, "Help, father, come and dwell within me. You already dwell within me. You are already 'me.'" Historian Paul Johnson writes, "There were times when Tolstoy seemed to think of himself as God's brother, indeed his elder brother."[1] Tolstoy once wrote:

> Read a work on the literary characterization of genius today, and this awoke in me the conviction that I am a remarkable man both as regards capacity and eagerness to work. I have not yet met a single man who was morally as good as I. . . . I do not remember an instance in my life when I was not attracted to what is good and was not ready to sacrifice anything to it.

He felt in his own soul "immeasurable grandeur."[2] Tolstoy saw himself as above the rest of humanity, as part of an apostolic succession of moral superiors that included the likes of Moses, Isaiah, Confucius, the early Greeks, Buddha, Socrates, Jesus, Pascal, and Spinoza.[3]

It could be said, borrowing from the opening words of our text, that Leo Tolstoy was confident of his own righteousness and looked down on everybody else. This was especially true of his later days when he adopted the prophetic chic of a peasant and promoted himself as a humble seer.

Further, it can be said that the parable in 18:9–14 is a perfect fit for Count Tolstoy.

But what about us? We have heard the parable of the Pharisee and the tax collector so often that it has become to us like a comfortable old slipper that *other* people wear. They wear it to their discomfort, and we enjoy seeing them wearing it! Actually, this parable paradoxically both fits our feet and pinches them.

The parable, like the preceding parable of the persistent widow, has to do with prayer. In the preceding parable we learned that persistence in prayer shows what we think of God—that we are confident that he is gracious and caring. In this parable we learn that our prayers unwittingly reveal what we think of ourselves.[4] Here Jesus gives two prayers—one by a Pharisee and one by a publican. One leads to Heaven, and one leads to Hell.

The parable of the Pharisee and the publican seems so simple that we often misread it, drawing ungrounded comfort to our souls instead of the gracious discomfort that God intended.

The Parable (vv. 10–13)

The story begins simply enough: "Two men went up into the temple to pray, one a Pharisee and the other a tax collector" (v. 10). The intended contrast is evident. Tax collectors were the scum of Jewish society, third-level lackeys of the Roman tax system. Rome imposed taxes on its conquered peoples, but the collection of those taxes was delegated to private Roman contractors (tax farmers), who then employed Jewish underlings to do the dirty work, their pay being whatever extra they could extort from their fellow Jews. Such tax collectors were considered monsters, and in fact some were. They were religious and political traitors to Hebrew society—utterly despicable. They were disallowed from public office and were barred from giving testimony in court. They were outcasts, untouchables.[5] In today's culture, the closest social equivalent would be drug pushers and pimps, those who prey on society, who make money off others' bodies and make a living of stealing from others.

On the other hand, the Pharisees had justly earned the reputation as, in Josephus' words, "a body of Jews known for surpassing the others in the observance of piety and exact interpretation of the laws" (*Jewish Wars* 1.5.2, 110). They were the most highly esteemed group in Jewish society. No Pharisee would ever sell out his people for gain. Like everyone else, they too were victims of the tax collectors. You could count on a Pharisee to love the Law and attempt to uphold it. What a contrast these two made when they went up the temple mount to pray. The mere thought of a publican praying was jarring in itself.

To read the parable properly through first-century Jewish eyes requires starting with a positive image and expectation for the Pharisee (he was the "good guy") and a negative expectation for the tax collector (the crook).

The Pharisee's Prayer

The Pharisee's prayer began well enough: "God, I thank you that I am not like other men, extortioners, unjust, adulterers, or even like this tax collector" (v. 11). He was appropriately grateful for what God had kept him from. He had stolen from no one. He had been faithful to his wife. It is appropriate to thank God for being able to avoid serious sin. To Jewish ears, the inclusion of "or even like this tax collector" seemed appropriate. "God, thanks for keeping me from falling into the kind of awful sin this man has fallen into."

Today we might word this prayer a little differently: "God, I thank you that I haven't fallen to what so many of my contemporaries have succumbed to—sensuality, dishonest business practices—the gutter life of so many of the unchurched."

We ought to be thankful for God's grace in our lives. "There, but for the grace of God, go I." Nevertheless, there is something wrong here. First, note the prominence in which the Pharisee placed himself. The contrasting position of the tax-gatherer in verse 13 suggests that the Pharisee moved to the front of the Court of Israel within the temple precincts.[6] The sense is that he came to the temple at the precise hour of prayer, entered the Court of Israel, and drew near to the altar of burnt offering. Then he stood erect, so all could see his substantial phylacteries (boxes on the forehead and wrists containing Scriptures), and began to pray.

Second, the prayer was loud enough for all in the court to hear. He was like the American preacher whose prayer was described as "the most eloquent prayer ever offered to a Boston audience."[7]

Third, his prayer was self-absorbed. The *Revised Standard Version* renders the literal sense of the Greek: "The Pharisee stood and prayed thus with himself" (literally, "to himself"). After his initial nod to God, his was essentially a self-congratulatory monologue disguised as a prayer. There are fives uses of the personal pronoun *I* implicit in the nominative case in the Greek: "I—I—I—I—I." He was stoned on self!

Fourth, our discomfort with his prayer peaks when he drags in the sleazy tax collector to draw attention to his own "mister-cleanness." His self-estimate rides on the exposure of the moral failures of others. Furthermore, he does not appear to care about the plight of the tax collector. The Pharisee has not been warmed by the love of God.[8] His ostensible claim to be a lover of God is shown to be false by his lack of love for his poor, pitiful, sinning neighbor.

Many professing Christians today make the same error as the self-righteous Pharisee. They thank God they are not living sinful lives. The prayer is "good" in a restricted sense. Such prayers begin well enough, thanking God for his saving grace that has changed their lives, but they regard the living out of their lifestyle as due to their own discipline and effort. They have made the grace of God into personal accomplishment. They began the Christian walk as Augustinians (understanding that everything is of God) but later began to live as Pelagians (living as if it were all due to their virtues). In the words of verse 9, such "trusted in themselves that they were righteous, and treated others with contempt" (literally, "utterly despised the rest"). Comparative side glances and lips pursed in disapproval reveal the terrible interior delusion that all is well with one's self-righteous soul.

A life that finds security in comparison is deluded. It is utterly un-Biblical in its understanding, so un-Paul-like, who concluded about himself while contemplating God's saving grace, "I know that nothing good dwells in me, that is, in my flesh" (Romans 7:18).

The Publican's Prayer

In contrast with the Pharisees' spiritual façade came the publican's pitiful prayer: "But the tax collector, standing far off, would not even lift up his eyes to heaven, but beat his breast, saying, 'God, be merciful to me, a sinner!'" (v. 13). The contrast is intense. Whereas the Pharisee stood in prominence, the tax-gatherer stood "far off," probably just a step within the confines of the Court of Israel. Whereas the Pharisee stood erect with eyes open to Heaven, the publican could not bring himself to lift up his head. Whereas the Pharisee confidently prayed, the tax collector sorrowed over what he was and what he had done (cf. 23:48). Like the Pharisee, the tax collector verbalized his prayer, but with a difference. It is one thing to publicly announce your virtues, and it is quite another to proclaim your sins.

The publican had no desire to compare himself with the other man but merely cried out, "God, be merciful to me, the sinner!" (NASB). Not *a* sinner, but *the* sinner. "I am everything people say I am, and more. I will not attempt to make myself look better by comparing myself with someone else. I am *the* sinner" (cf. 1 Timothy 1:15). This wayward son of Abraham had been excluded from the synagogue and ostracized from the godly, but he knew where to go and how to pray in his pitiful state. His plea, "Be merciful to me," is similar to the opening line of Psalm 51, the great penitential Psalm of David following his adultery and murder, where David repents and sings of God's forgiveness. The man's hope is that as God forgave the heinous sins of David, he would forgive his monstrous treacheries too. "God have mercy on me, God be propitiated to me the sinner"[9]—"Let your anger against my sin be removed." He knew that God's wrath was upon him. The merciful removal of God's anger was his only hope!

What opposites stood in the temple at the hour of prayer. Both the scum and the cream of Hebrew society. One infamous for his sins, the other famous for his righteous lifestyle. One lowly, the other self-assured.

> Two men went to pray; or rather say,
> One went to brag, the other to pray;
> One stands up close, and treads on high,
> Where th' other dare not send his eye.
> One nearer to the altar trod,
> The other to the altar's God.
>
> Source unknown[10]

The Declaration (v. 14)

Justified

Jesus declared the meaning of this unusual scene by saying, "I tell you, this man went down to his house justified, rather than the other" (v. 14a). The excellent Pharisee, with his wide phylacteries, strode from the temple confident in his righteousness—such a dramatic contrast with the spiritual unworthiness of the publican. He felt great! But having taken his stand on his own merits, the Pharisee left the temple unaccepted, unjustified, and under God's wrath.

But the publican, who had systematically made his money on the backs of his people, this traitor, this pariah, by having repented and having humbly cast himself on God's mercy, left the temple justified. Just like that his sins were gone. In a flash God's wrath was turned away. In an instant he had a new life.

The great Pauline doctrine of justification by faith has its roots here in the teaching of Jesus, and that is what Luke (Paul's sidekick) wants us to see. The doctrine was made possible by Jesus himself, as Paul would tell us: "But now the righteousness of God has been manifested apart from the law, although the Law and the Prophets bear witness to it—the righteousness of God through faith in Jesus Christ for all who believe" (Romans 3:21, 22a).

A Closing Maxim

Our Lord loved to close his parables with axioms that formally expressed fundamental moral laws of life,[11] and this time was no exception: "For everyone who exalts himself will be humbled, but the one who humbles himself will be exalted" (v. 14b). This principle is rooted in the Old Testament (cf. Ezekiel 21:26) and was repeated over and over again in Israel's history. It was restated at the very birth of Jesus when his mother sang in the *Magnificat*:

> My soul magnifies the Lord,
> and my spirit rejoices in God my Savior,
> for he has looked on the humble estate of his servant. . . .
> He has shown strength with his arm;
> he has scattered the proud in the thoughts of their hearts;
> he has brought down the mighty from their thrones
> and exalted those of humble estate. (1:46–48, 51, 52)

Jesus spoke truly: "For everyone who exalts himself will be humbled, but the one who humbles himself will be exalted" (v. 14b).

Life and eternity will present us with surprising turnarounds and eternal reversals.

Closing Reflections

This parable conveys penetrating wisdom: the spiritual posture with which we pray in our heart of hearts reveals whether we have been made righteous by God.

Though the unrighteous heart may never say it publicly, its prayers reveal to God that it is really depending upon itself for eternal life. Though lip service may be given to humility and repentance, they are not real. The unrighteous heart subtly sees itself as a partner in one's own salvation. One's own goodness (due perhaps to God's grace and one's use of it) is held dear as the real source of salvation. "Good people" will be okay, because they are not big-time "sinners," it is thought. Such a heart is in for a terrible surprise.

In contrast, the righteous heart is a heart that, whether just made righteous or having been justified decades earlier, says, "God, be merciful to me, the sinner" (v. 13b NASB). The righteous heart's only hope is in the blood and mercy of Jesus.

Do you pray like the Pharisee or like the tax-gatherer?

Eternity will tell.

79

Kingdom Entrance

LUKE 18:15–17

I THINK THAT IF I COULD TRAVEL at multiples of the speed of light, past countless yellow-orange stars, to the edge of the galaxy, then swoop down to the fiery glow located a few hundred light-years below the Milky Way, and if I could then slow down and observe, close up, new stars bursting forth from their foggy cocoons—in all my stellar journeys I would never see anything as wondrous as a baby's birth.

The stars of the universe are temporal, but a soul is eternal. When the stars melt, that soul will continue to exist. The height of the wonder of a baby's birth is that the tiny newborn is the apex of creation because he or she is created in the image of God (cf. Genesis 1:26, 27). Its soul has a delicate moral sensibility that can, through grace and regeneration, ultimately conform to the likeness of Jesus Christ. No angel can rival a human baby because no angel is created in the image of God.

Children are masterpieces from the hand of the triune God, and it is no surprise that the incarnate God-man was a lover of children. The New Testament sparkles with accounts of his love as he celebrates the delight of a mother on giving birth (John 16:21), the gentle love of a father who cuddles his children (11:7), the parental love that listens to a child's every request (11:11–13; cf. Matthew 7:9–11), and his use of children as spiritual examples, as for example when he said, "Whoever receives this child in my name receives me, and whoever receives me receives him who sent me. For he who is least among you all is the one who is great" (9:48).

Jesus Loves the Little Children

Many of Jesus' miracles involved children—the nobleman's little son (John 4:46–54), the demonized only son of the man at the foot of the Mount of Transfiguration (Mark 9:14–29), and Jairus' daughter, to whom Jesus tenderly said, "'Talitha cumi,' which means, 'Little girl, I say to you, arise'" (Mark 5:41). Jesus, as man and God, truly loved children, and we should too.

Children Are a Blessing

When my wife and I had our first child, we announced her birth with a joyous line from the psalmist's praise of children: "Children are a gift of the LORD" (Psalm 127:3 NASB). This is a concise expression of the age-old regard that God's covenant people had for children.

> Behold, children are a heritage from the LORD,
> the fruit of the womb a reward.
> Like arrows in the hand of a warrior
> are the children of one's youth.
> Blessed is the man
> who fills his quiver with them! (Psalm 127:3–5a)

These words are beautifully corrective in a culture that so often views children as an inconvenience.

Jesus Blesses Children

In Luke 18 we see that Jesus was a natural with children and that the parents' instincts were right in bringing "infants to him that he might touch them" (v. 15a; cf. 1:41, 44; 2:12, 16; Acts 7:19). Jesus' touch apparently involved the act of blessing. This was in keeping with a classic Jewish custom dating back to the time of the patriarch Israel (Jacob), who laid his hands upon the heads of Ephraim and Manasseh and blessed them (Genesis 48:14). Proud parents held out their precious children to Jesus, who took them in his arms where they snuggled close. Placing his hand on their warm, soft heads, lifting his eyes to Heaven, he pronounced a blessing. Jesus thoroughly enjoyed such scenes.

A number of cheerful families probably stood waiting, chatting, with little ones in arms and other children scurrying around. But the gaiety was about to cease abruptly. The disciples were having a few words with the people, and some were moving off. The Twelve apparently did not approve of the parents' bothering Jesus with their infants: "And when the disciples saw it, they rebuked them" (v. 15b).

The disciples' motivations are not entirely clear. At best they were protecting Jesus from what they deemed as interruptions or pressure. At worst they saw the situation as a waste of time. But whatever their motivation, Jesus used their intervention to give some of his most penetrating teaching and most often quoted words. He did not talk about his love for children (as beautiful as that was) or about parenting or about blessings or even about the spirituality of children (though there are some wonderful implicit insights that I have expounded in the parallel passage in Mark 10:13–16 in my Preaching the Word commentary on that Gospel).

Rather, he spoke about the kind of people who enter the kingdom of God. The encircling context leaves no doubt about this. In the preceding parable of the Pharisee and tax collector (18:9–14), we see that the tax collector got into the kingdom because he did not depend on self-righteousness as did the Pharisee, but cast himself upon God's mercy. Humble people are the kind of people who get into the kingdom. In the following story of the rich ruler (18:18–30), we will learn that the rich man will get into the kingdom only after divesting himself of dependence upon material wealth. The people who get into the kingdom do not trust in riches. And here between those two kingdom-entrance accounts, children are held up as symbols of the ideal entrants into the kingdom—models for all adults who hope to get into God's kingdom.

Jesus taught two things here. We enter the kingdom by *being* as a child and by *receiving* as a child.

Being As a Child (v. 16)

Jesus asserted the matter of being like a child in his response to his disciples' protest: "But Jesus called them to him, saying, 'Let the children come to me, and do not hinder them, for to such belongs the kingdom of God'" (v. 16). He did not say that the kingdom belongs to the children he was holding, but to "such [as these]"—those who are like the little ones.[1]

What is the quality of being of children, and especially those characterized as "infants" in the opening line of this passage? What is the ontological distinctive of a newborn? Helplessness! Jesus has in mind here the objective state that every child who has ever lived (regardless of race, culture, or background) has experienced—namely, *helpless dependence*. A newborn, naked, with flailing hands and feet lifted toward the sky, is a heart-wrenching profile of helplessness. And unlike any other creature, its helplessness extends for years. No child would survive its early years without the help of others.

Eduard Schweizer, Professor of New Testament at the University of Zurich, wrote:

> But this is the reason they are blessed—just because they [the little children] have nothing to show for themselves. They cannot count on any achievements of their own—their hands are empty like those of a beggar. Jesus enlarges the promise to include everyone. With an authority such as only God can claim, he promises the Kingdom to those whose faith resembles the empty hand of a beggar. Such faith is possible because they have no achievements of their own nor any conceptions of God which can intrude between them and God.[2]

Every child born into the world is absolutely, completely, totally, actually helpless. And so it is with every child who is born into the kingdom of God. Children of the kingdom enter it helpless. If Billy Graham enters the kingdom, it will not be because he has personally preached to more people than any man in history. It will not be because he has remained impeccable in his finances when so many have failed. It will not be because he has been a faithful husband. It will not be because, despite his fame, he has remained a humble, self-effacing, kind man. When Billy Graham enters the kingdom, it will be because he came to Christ as a helpless child. It will be because of God's undeserved kindness toward Billy's helplessness.

> Nothing in my hand I bring,
> Simply to Thy cross I cling;
> Naked, come to Thee for dress:
> Helpless, look to Thee for grace.

If you would enter the kingdom, this is the only way you can come.

Receiving As a Child (v. 17)

Jesus' teaching reached its climax in an authoritative declaration that moved from the requirement of *being* like a child to *receiving* as a child: "Truly, I say to you, whoever does not receive the kingdom of God like a child shall not enter it" (v. 17). What are the elements of such childlike receiving?

Unmitigated Trust

We see such trust in a baby who stands on his father's hand high over his dad's head—and smiles proudly. This may sometimes be misplaced trust, but it is nevertheless complete and sincere. Children trust others for everything—their food, their lodging, the arms of others who bear them about. Regarding trust in God, the child's ability to believe has never been wounded by wicked suggestion or burdened with superstition or perverted by falsehoods. These little ones are the opposite of the skeptical theologians whom Christ battled (cf. 5:21; 20:2). Those who receive the kingdom like a little child have the saving element of faith. They have belief plus trust. They believe in Jesus, but it is more than a mind-belief—they trust Jesus for everything to do with salvation and life.

> Truly, I say to you, whoever does not receive the kingdom of God like a child shall not enter it. (v. 17)

Untutored Humility

Children do not engage in the various forms of pride of adulthood. Unlike the Pharisees, little children are not proud of their virtues—"God, I thank you that I am not like other men, extortioners, unjust, adulterers, or even like this tax collector. I fast twice a week; I give tithes of all that I get" (18:11, 12). A child does not battle self-righteousness in coming to Christ—"Lord, I have been constant in my attendance for years. I have sat at the Lord's Table for half a century. I give a lot of money to missions." Self-righteousness is impossible in a child!

Further, a little child is free from the pride of knowledge. He has no learning, no degrees to pile up before the cross. Intellectual conceit is impossible. Children are teachable too. They receive the gospel without proposing amendments to it. They hold no "Jesus seminars"! Because children have not developed the pride of adulthood, they readily repent. Little ones will readily cry over a wrong done. Their unseared consciences have left their powerful moral instruments intact—and they are utterly miserable over their sins. Untutored humility leaves a young soul open to receiving the greatest of gifts.

Untarnished Receptivity

Children know how to receive a gift—they simply take it. At their first birthday, they are not sure what a gift is. As two-year-olds, if they have siblings, they understand well enough. And by the time they are three, they are really into receptivity! The wrapping paper flies! As David Gooding explains: "A little child takes its food, its parents' love and protection, because they are given, without beginning to think of whether it deserves them or whether it is important enough to merit such attention. So must we all receive God's kingdom and enter into it (see 18:17)."[3]

The soul that receives the kingdom is grace oriented. It is open to the unmerited favor of God.

Unabashed Love

Children easily return love for loving gifts. Enthusiastic hugs and kisses and multiple "Thanks" are showered on the giver. And spiritually, "We love because he first loved us" (1 John 4:19). Unabashed love is the province of those who receive the kingdom as little children.

Closing Reflections

A newborn is the apex of creation. But truth does not allow us to remain there. And those who have lived the proverbial "three score and ten years" are also the crown of God's creation. The universe is mortal, and we will all outlive her. Each of us has an eternal soul that can live forever and conform to the likeness of Christ.

We each have the potential of being an eternal son or daughter so graced that if we were to meet our future selves, we might want to fall before them. On the other hand, we also have the possibility of becoming a person of such spiritual disfigurement that we would flee if we met ourselves.[4] Our eternal potential depends upon whether we enter the kingdom or not. And kingdom entrance first depends on our coming to God as a child—in total helpless dependence.

> Not what these hands have done
> Can save this guilty soul;
> Not what this toiling flesh has borne
> Can make my spirit whole.
> Thy work alone, O Christ,
> To me can pardon speak;
> Thy power alone, O Son of God,
> Can this sore bondage break.
>
> Horatius Bonar, 1861

We must not think a child cannot come to God until he is like a man, but a man cannot come until he is like a child. We must grow down until we become like a child.[5]

Jesus' words are true: "Truly, truly, I say to you, unless one is born again he cannot see the kingdom of God" (John 3:3), and "Truly, I say to you, unless you turn and become like children, you will never enter the kingdom of heaven" (Matthew 18:3).

80

How Hard It Is for a Rich Man!

LUKE 18:18–30

JESUS' JARRING DECLARATION, "Truly, I say to you, whoever does not receive the kingdom of God like a child shall not enter it" (18:17) encapsulated the truth that essential to salvation is the recognition of one's total helplessness, coupled with a trusting faith in God. In contrast, the rich ruler in the passage we will now examine was the opposite of a helpless babe. "He was extremely rich" and had the clout that went with it (v. 23; cf. Matthew 19:22). He was powerful and affluent.

Evidently this ruler (probably a civil magistrate) had watched Jesus tenderly hold the little children, lift his eyes to Heaven, and pronounce individual blessings. And he was positively attracted to Jesus. He had also heard Jesus' enigmatic words about receiving the kingdom "like a child" and was further drawn to the Savior.

He then responded with an impressive question: "Good Teacher, what must I do to inherit eternal life?" (v. 18). The ruler was a sensitive man with unusual openness. Unlike the Pharisee who earlier had asked the same question (10:25), he was not testing Jesus. He truly wanted to know what to do. As we shall see, though he meticulously observed the Law, he evidently had found no assurance of eternal life. He assumed that some additional generous action, some great sacrifice, would secure his highest good. And he was willing to do it. He had always been able to pay for what he had in this life, and he was quite prepared to do so now. "Name the price! I'm ready to do whatever it takes!"

But there is a subtle negative here, because the ruler's question assumed that he had the inner power to do whatever was required and that he was intrinsically good. No doubt, he was "good" when compared to most men. The ruler indeed had a winsome spiritual attractiveness, but it was a two-edged sword.

Kingdom Probings (vv. 19–23)

Who Is Good?

In any event, his was an excellent question, and Jesus responded graciously: "Why do you call me good? No one is good except God alone" (v. 19). God's goodness is a persistent motif in the Old Testament. "Oh give thanks to the LORD, for he is good" (1 Chronicles 16:34). "Oh, taste and see that the LORD is good! Blessed is the man who takes refuge in him!" (Psalm 34:8). "The LORD is good, a stronghold in the day of trouble; he knows those who take refuge in him" (Nahum 1:7). God has an exclusive claim on goodness. No man can make such a claim in himself.

That is why in Jesus' day it was a breach in religious decorum to call Jesus "Good Teacher." There is not one example in the *Talmud* of a rabbi being addressed as "good."[1] So was the ruler's use of "good" casual, thoughtless flattery? Or was it simply "the poverty of his moral perception"?[2] Or was the ruler breaking decorum to voice what he sensed in his heart?

Whatever the answer is, Jesus used the occasion to do some metaphysical probing so the man would reflect upon his own soul. "Why do you call me good? No one is good except God alone" is a challenge to reflect on Jesus' ministry as it related to God as the only truly good person in existence. If the ruler could see this level of goodness in Jesus' ministry, he would realize that the kingdom of God was present.[3] "Think, man! If I am good, and if only God is good, then who am I, and what am I doing? Think!"

Are You Good?

Having pushed the goodness question, Jesus then focused upon the insufficient goodness of the ruler. Jesus did so by calling him to keep the second half of the Ten Commandments, the commandments that have to do with our social ethics, our duty to other people. "You know the commandments: 'Do not commit adultery, Do not murder, Do not steal, Do not bear false witness, Honor your father and mother'" (v. 20). Jesus knew that if the ruler would do some deep reflection here, he would see that he was totally unqualified for the kingdom he was seeking.

Tragically, the ruler missed the whole point: "And he said, 'All these I have kept from my youth'" (v. 21). There is a noble sincerity here, but also great moral ignorance. He really did think he had kept the Law. But he was ignorant of the commandments' spiritual meaning, so ignorant that he sincerely thought he had fulfilled all the commandments. He was like the pre-Christian, un-thought-through Apostle Paul, who in his initial understanding of the Law thought he was doing quite well. But when he seriously considered the tenth commandment ("You shall not covet . . . ," Exodus 20:17), he discovered the awful truth:

> Yet if it had not been for the law, I would not have known sin. For I would not have known what it is to covet if the law had not said, "You shall not covet." But sin, seizing an opportunity through the commandment, produced in me all kinds of covetousness. For apart from the law, sin lies dead. I was once alive apart from the law, but when the commandment came, sin came alive and I died. (Romans 7:7–9)

Spiritually illuminated, Paul saw that his entire interior life was filled with coveting. And when he tried to abstain from coveting, he did it all the more. The Law killed—it condemned him! Now he knew who he was, and he felt the sentence of death. Unchecked coveting precipitates the breaking of the second table of the Law, bringing evil acts of murder, adultery, theft, and lying.

Significantly, the rich ruler's problem was material covetousness,[4] and the Lord went after it. "When Jesus heard this, he said to him, 'One thing you still lack. Sell all that you have and distribute to the poor, and you will have treasure in heaven; and come, follow me.' But when he heard these things, he became very sad, for he was extremely rich" (vv. 22, 23). The rich man loved his possessions more than he loved God. His materialism indicated that he did not love his neighbor as he loved himself and therefore was not a keeper of the Law (cf. Galatians 5:14). He simply was not as good a man as he had thought.

Missionary poetess and mystic Amy Carmichael of Dohnavur described in her famous book *Things As They Are* sitting with a Hindu queen in her palace as the queen revealed her spiritual hunger. As the conversation developed, she kept pushing Miss Carmichael regarding what was necessary for salvation, and Amy attempted to deflect her, saying she should wait. But the queen was determined to hear it, so Amy read her a little of what Jesus says about it himself. In Amy Carmichael's words:

> She knew quite enough to understand and take in the force of the forceful words. She would not consent to be led gently on. "No, I must know it now," she said; and as verse by verse we read to her, her face settled sorrowfully. "So far must I follow, so far?" she said, "I cannot follow so far."[5]

It was not one text that put the queen off but the radical claims of the gospel upon her whole life.

That is, in effect, what the rich man said too—"I cannot follow so far." He was overcome with profound sadness because he had so much money, and he could not possibly bring himself to give it up. Dante referred to this as "The Great Refusal." It was from there that the man became a wandering star—lost, haunted by what might have been.

Jesus was not making a case for universal asceticism (giving up all wealth and living a life of conscious denial and negation). The Old Testament holds up some godly rich men (such as Abraham, Boaz, and Job) as examples, though Scripture constantly warns us about the greed of the rich. The apostolic father Tertullian was certainly right when he called it *irreligious* to scorn this wonderful world and to refuse to enjoy God's bounty and thank him for it. He said: "It was goodness, goodness, goodness that made it all."[6] We are right to enjoy it.

Neither was Jesus recommending poverty to his people, because poverty does not deliver one from the love of money. As George MacDonald said: "It is not the rich man only who is under the dominion of things; they too are slaves who, having no money, are unhappy for the lack of it. . . . The money the one has, the money the other would have, is in each the cause of an eternal stupidity."[7]

The fact is, wealth can be spiritually beneficial. It can teach us the hollowness of things, and if used for Christ it can enhance one's spiritual growth—a benefit that, sadly, too few experience. For the disciples, as they watched the rich young man trudge sadly away, this was a teachable moment—one that set the stage for a hard saying of Jesus.

Kingdom Declarations (vv. 24–30)

> Jesus, seeing that he had become sad, said, "How difficult it is for those who have wealth to enter the kingdom of God! For it is easier for a camel to go through the eye of a needle than for a rich person to enter the kingdom of God." Those who heard it said, "Then who can be saved?" (vv. 24–26)

We do our souls a disservice if we water down Jesus' words by imagining that "the eye of a needle" refers to a diminutive portal in the wall of Jerusalem that required one to stoop low to enter the city. There simply is no evidence for this. Likewise, there is no linguistic or cultural evidence for "camel" referring to a *kamel* rope. The *Babylonian Talmud* contains quotations regarding elephants passing through the eye of a needle—illustrations of impossibility. Jesus' reference to a camel, the largest beast in Palestine, being thrust through a needle's eye, humps and all, was readily understood as a humorous illustration of the impossible.[8]

> All things (e.g., a camel's journey through
> A needle's eye) are possible, it's true.
> But picture how the camel feels, squeezed out
> In one long bloody thread from tail to snout.[9]

Jesus categorically says it is impossible for a man or woman who *trusts* in riches to get into Heaven.

Mark's Gospel says the disciples were "amazed" at these words (Mark 10:24). Why? Because they believed in a kind of "prosperity gospel" taught by rabbis who used Old Testament passages to equate God's blessing with material prosperity and taught that the rich could build up future merit and reward for themselves by giving to the poor. To the Jewish mind it was inconceivable that riches could be a barrier to the kingdom.[10] Protestantism has frequently been afflicted with the same kind of errant thinking. Today we see this in the crass materialism of the "name it and claim it" school and similar embarrassments for the church in our day.

> Name it and claim it, that's what faith's about!
> You can have what you want if you just have no doubt.
> So make out your "wish list" and keep on believin'
> And you will find yourself perpetually receivin'.[11]

We need to hear what Jesus was really saying, and to hear it well: *wealth is a handicap!* We think the rich to be overprivileged. Jesus said they were underprivileged. At the end of the Sermon on the Mount Jesus warned: "Do not lay up for yourselves treasures on earth, where moth and rust destroy and where thieves break in and steal, but lay up for yourselves treasures in heaven, where neither moth nor rust destroys and where thieves do not break in and steal. For where your treasure is, there your heart will be also" (Matthew 6:19–21). He also said, "No servant can serve two masters, for either he will hate the one and love the other, or he will be devoted to the one and despise the other. You cannot serve God and money" (16:13). The parable of the rich man and Lazarus is a dramatic warning about this matter (16:19–31). The same is true of the parable of the rich fool (12:13–21).

There is a proper fear of being rich. There are disadvantages to having wealth—primarily what it can do to the soul. How easy it is for an earnest man or woman to become so attached to material riches that he or she forgets what is infinitely more important. Wealth can pervert one's values. We soon know the price of everything and the value of nothing.

Paul told Timothy, "As for the rich in this present age, charge them not to be haughty, nor to set their hopes on the uncertainty of riches" (1 Timothy 6:17). Pride, arrogance, insensitivity, indifference, harshness, self-satisfaction, worldliness, and other ungodly mind-sets feed on affluence. Most tragically, wealth can steel one against the indispensable requirement for entering the kingdom of God—*helpless dependence*. Jesus says to the Church, "For you say, I am rich, I have prospered, and I need nothing, not realizing that you are wretched, pitiable, poor, blind, and naked" (Revelation 3:17).

Closing Reflections

It would be easy to think that this applies only to the extra rich among us. But nearly all Americans are wealthy. We have everything we need and more. For most of the world, our debts, our problems, and even our payments would be welcome luxuries. So this passage has something to say to each of us. What we do with our wealth will determine the spiritual health of ourselves and our families. With prosperity comes great danger. Some militant idealists who at one time were living for Jesus have become hardened, self-focused materialists. We must beware.

What are we to do? First, we must divest ourselves of dependence on our wealth. We must make this a matter of prayer—not just once or once in a while, but regularly and frequently. Second, we must invest our wealth. That is, as our income rises, we must give to God's work in such a way that it affects our lifestyle, so there are some things we do not buy and some places we do not go because we have made a priority of giving to God.

Those who heard the camel-needle proverb asked in wonder, "'Then who can be saved?' But he said, 'What is impossible with man is possible with God'" (vv. 26, 27). Salvation is impossible for a rich man (and a poor man as well). The point is, anyone's salvation is a miracle. But this is especially evident of anyone snorting the cocaine of possessions and inhaling the delusion of financial power. But with God, the impossible is possible!

The seventh chapter of Hebrews says the ground of the miracle of salvation is Christ's sacrifice of himself for our sins (Hebrews 7:27) and the fact that he serves as a priest forever, praying for those he saves (Hebrews 7:25): "Consequently, he is able to save to the uttermost those who draw near to God through him, since he always lives to make intercession for them."

Complete, absolute, total, eternal salvation is ours because of the miraculous work of Jesus Christ.

Whoever we are, regardless of our boastings and our attachments, he can do the impossible in our hearts. For the rich or poor, the materialist or idealist, there is but one hope. Each must let go of possessions or passion or position or person and come to Christ. The rewards of so doing are stupendous.

> And Peter said, "See, we have left our homes and followed you." And he said to them, "Truly, I say to you, there is no one who has left house or wife or brothers or parents or children, for the sake of the kingdom of God, who will not receive many times more in this time, and in the age to come eternal life." (vv. 28–30)

I like Jesus' math. The rewards he promised are true in this world, as we know from our own experience of serving him. How much greater will be our experience in the next world!

I like Jesus' odds, so to speak. It is totally impossible for us to enter the kingdom of God, an impossibility that is intensified by wealth. The odds for all of us are zero. But with God, thanks to his grace, the odds are infinite.

> For by grace you have been saved through faith. And this is not your own doing; it is the gift of God, not a result of works, so that no one may boast. (Ephesians 2:8, 9)

81

Blind Sight

LUKE 18:31–43

"SON OF MAN" is a much-used New Testament name for Jesus. The Gospel of John employs it thirteen times, and it is found sixty-six times in the other Gospels.

Interestingly, "Son of Man" is not a name that others gave to Jesus, but a name he gave to himself. He derived it from the seventh chapter of Daniel, which records Daniel's vision of the sweep of world history graphically represented by a series of beasts eventuating in ultimate judgment presided over by the Ancient of Days, God the Father. The vision concludes with these words:

> I saw in the night visions, and behold, with the clouds of heaven there came one like a son of man, and he came to the Ancient of Days and was presented before him. And to him was given dominion and glory and a kingdom, that all peoples, nations, and languages should serve him; his dominion is an everlasting dominion, which shall not pass away, and his kingdom one that shall not be destroyed. (Daniel 7:13, 14)

God, the Ancient of Days, gives to another divine being, "one like a son of man," glory, sovereignty, worship, and everlasting dominion—an eternal kingdom.

Jesus, when he came to full messianic consciousness, said in effect, "I am *the* Son of Man. I am the eternal, sovereign King!" Jesus himself is responsible for the high Christology of the New Testament, first using the term "Son of Man" for himself at the healing of the paralytic in Capernaum: "But that you may know that the Son of Man has authority on earth to forgive sins . . . I say to you, rise, pick up your bed, and go home" (Mark 2:10, 11). He thus indicated that he was "consciously and creatively investing the title with deep Christological meaning, tantamount to sharing the prerogative of God."[1]

Jesus claimed to be the transcendent being of Daniel's vision and used "Son of Man" as a substitute for the personal pronoun "I" again and again. He especially used the term when he spoke of himself to his disciples. They heard the term many times.

We also know that Jesus regularly spoke of his coming death. For example, after Peter's great confession, Jesus explicitly said, "The Son of Man must suffer many things and be rejected by the elders and chief priests and scribes, and be killed, and on the third day be raised" (9:22).

Jesus was equally clear after he healed the boy with an evil spirit: "Let these words sink into your ears: The Son of Man is about to be delivered into the hands of men" (9:44).

And in Luke 18, as the Savior's journey to Jerusalem wound up and the end was only a few days away, we read, "And taking the twelve, he said to them, 'See, we are going up to Jerusalem, and everything that is written about the Son of Man by the prophets will be accomplished. For he will be delivered over to the Gentiles and will be mocked and shamefully treated and spit upon. And after flogging him, they will kill him, and on the third day he will rise'" (vv. 31–33). He could not have been more explicit about his being "the Son of Man" or more clear about his impending suffering, death, and resurrection.

But even so, the disciples just did not get it! Luke emphasizes this three times in verse 34: "But they understood none of these things. This saying was hidden from them, and they did not grasp what was said." Amazing! They had been with Jesus nearly three years night and day, and now Passion Week was almost on them, and they did not understand what was about to occur. Why? The big reason is that their minds simply did not have room for a suffering, dying Messiah (cf. 24:25–27, 44–46). The idea was theologically beyond their grasp. Only history and Christ himself would open their eyes, as Luke would record in his final chapter: "And their eyes were opened, and they recognized him" (24:31).

Today we have four supreme Gospel accounts, but our understanding still requires the work of the Holy Spirit. If you understand but do not truly understand, if the ideas are taking shape but you are not yet on the inside of the mystery, if you feel like a spiritual interloper, ask Christ to open "the eyes of your heart" (Ephesians 1:18).

The story of Christ's healing of the blind man stood in dramatic contrast with the incomprehension of the Twelve. Their spiritual blindness was reproved by the blind sight of a beggar. The story elucidates the genesis and flowering of a blind man's faith and is a treasure for all who would see.

The Blind Man (vv. 35–37)

"As he drew near to Jericho, a blind man was sitting by the roadside begging" (v. 35). Jesus' approach to Jericho was accompanied by a large crowd of his disciples and also numerous pilgrims making their way up to Jerusalem for Passover. It was customary for distinguished rabbis to travel with an entourage and to teach as they walked. So Jesus' passage was not unusual. Passing through Jericho compounded the crowding because the city was full of Levitical priests awaiting their turn to make a day's journey to the temple to serve. Virtually everyone had heard of Jesus and wanted to see him. Vincent Taylor, the venerable New Testament scholar, believed that Jesus' passage through Jericho bore the character of an ovation,[2] with some of the crowd hostile and others giving forth enthusiastic "Hosannas." Jericho, "the City of Roses," was alive.

The day had begun like any other day for the blind man. Waking up, he shook the straw from his shabby, torn garments, stretched, got to his feet, and began tapping his way along the familiar turns leading to the main gate of Jericho. Perhaps he was able to beg a crust of bread or two at some familiar stops along the way. Arriving at the gate he took his regular place with the other beggars, where he drew his greasy cloak tightly around him because, though it was spring, the sun had not yet dispelled the morning chill. As he sat there, just like so many days before, he listened to the city come to life—first a donkey loaded with melons for market, after that several women chatting as they bore pitchers toward the well, then the clomp of camels' hooves. Soon Jericho abounded with the sounds of life, and the blind man was intoning his beggar's cry.

Suddenly the blind man tensed and lifted his head, for his blind-sensitive ears heard the hubbub of a great crowd approaching. First came young boys running ahead with shrill cries, then more people hurrying past the gate talking excitedly. The blind man, brushed by a robe, reached out and asked what was happening.

The passersby, pulling away, called back, "Jesus of Nazareth is passing by" (v. 37). The geographical designation did not say anything about Jesus other than his hometown. But the word was out about him and his healing exploits. The blind man had likely heard first-person accounts from those who had heard Jesus or who had seen or even experienced his power. Messianic speculation was high among the Jews in the first century. Perhaps the blind man had heard that Jesus called himself "the Son of Man," that he had the right blood line, that he was from the tribe of Judah.

With amazing blind sight, the beggar came to the conclusion that Jesus must be the Messiah. His heart began to pound, and he was trembling, though the warm sun was now standing high. The crowd was passing. The blind man was jostled. Jesus would soon be gone. The man had to do something!

The Blind Man's Plea (vv. 38, 39)

"And he cried out, 'Jesus, Son of David, have mercy on me!' And those who were in front rebuked him, telling him to be silent. But he cried out all the more, 'Son of David, have mercy on me!'" (vv. 38, 39). It was impossible to press through the throng, but he made himself heard. He was crying pitifully, begging at the top of his lungs. He was desperate, frantic.

I remember doing something like this at the 1962 Rose Parade. UCLA was playing in the Rose Bowl, and as their float came by, I saw that an old high school friend was one of the Bruin cheerleaders. I began to shout, "Hey, Patti, it's me! Remember me? Kent Hughes!" And then I saw that all the Bruin cheerleaders, and people on both sides of Colorado Boulevard, were looking at me! Should I keep yelling or just shut up?

But the poor blind man's cries would have made my outburst look like a sedate conversation. The people around him tried to shush him—"You're making a scene." Some chided him—"Shut up, beggar!" But no way was the blind man going to shut up! "Jesus, Son of David, have mercy on me!" "Quiet, beggar." "Jesus, Son of David, have mercy on me!" "Will someone make him be quiet?" "Jesus, Son of David, have mercy on me!" He was beyond their control.

If we turn down the volume for a moment and reflect on what was implicit in this man's conduct, we see why his cries got him everything. He was full of blind sight.

Blind Sight about His Condition

The man knew he was blind and in perpetual darkness. He may have passed from the darkness of his mother's womb into the darkness of a sightless world. If so, he had never seen a tree wave its arms in the spring, or the blue of a summer sky, or the face of his mother or anyone else who loved him. There was no sight in his darkened eyeballs. He knew there was no hope for him apart from a divine miracle.

There is only one thing worse than blindness, and that is not knowing that you are blind. Multitudes are blind to their darkness, blind to their sin, blind to their destiny, blind to their hopelessness, spiritually out of touch.

Human reasoning says that every time a person sins, he or she will see more of his or her sin. But the opposite is true. Every time a man sins he makes himself more blind, less capable of realizing what sin is, less likely of realizing that he is a sinner. For unforgiven sinners, darkness and light are the same—their blindness makes it impossible to see.

What a grace it is to see reality, even when what we see is unpleasant or grotesque. Because when we see what we are, when we cannot escape the truth, when we are surrounded by darkness and know it, we will begin to ask for the light. The blind man's pitiful cry, "Have mercy on me" came from a profound self-understanding, and it brought grace into his soul. Christ rejoices to engage such reality.

Blind Sight about Jesus

The blind man voiced penetrating insight as to who Jesus is as he kept repeating, much to everyone's distress, "Son of David, have mercy on me!" That title was not geographical but theological—a blatant messianic assertion! It is, in fact, the only occurrence of this title in Luke's Gospel. The miseries of the Greek and then Roman domination had so inflamed the Old Testament hope that an ultimate "Son of David," a Messiah, would come and depose the Gentiles that during the first century "Son of David" was constantly used by the rabbis as a messianic designation.[3] They held that since the Messiah would come as the second David, he would sometimes simply be called "David."[4]

The pious Jew devoted lines in his daily prayers for the coming of a Messiah from David's race. In the Fourteenth Benediction of the Prayer of Eighteen Benedictions, according to the *Palestinian Record*, God is asked to have mercy "on the kingdom of the house of David, of the Messiah of thy righteousness."[5] The Habhinenu Prayer, which briefly summed up the most important prayer concerns, made prayers for "the sprouting forth of a horn of David, thy servant."[6] The first-century book *The Psalms of Solomon* (not to be confused with the Biblical Song of Songs) contains an extended messianic hymn describing the coming reign of the King, the anointed son of David.[7]

This blind man believed Jesus was the Messiah, and he was shouting it. It was dangerous to do so within the hearing of the Romans, but he did not care. He was sure Jesus could heal him. The blind had sight!

Someone once bluntly asked blind and deaf Helen Keller, "Isn't it terrible to be blind?" To which she responded, "Better to be blind and see with your heart, than to have two good eyes and see nothing." So it was with the blind man. Sometimes blindness has its benefits. He had a lot of time to think without visual distractions—time to develop the interior life and a contemplative spirit and to see with his heart. He thought about Christ and came to an exalted Biblical view of him, realizing his own darkness and need and who Jesus was.

Blind-Sighted Persistence

Next we see the man's amazing, passionate persistence. He rejected the crowd's control, shouting again and again, "Jesus, Son of David, have mercy on me!" Understanding something of who Jesus was and his own personal need, he kept saying this over and over, like a helpless infant. Only a few days earlier Jesus had said regarding children, "Truly, I say to you, whoever does not receive the kingdom of God like a child shall not enter it" (18:17). The man was coming to Jesus like a small child who is well aware of his helplessness and dependence.

The blind man's extreme sense of urgency reveals what should be in our souls. This is the meaning of Jesus' words, "The Law and the Prophets were until John; since then the good news of the kingdom of God is preached, and everyone forces his way into it" (16:16). Spiritual blessings belong to those who go for it. In the Old Testament the Lord instructed his people, "You will seek me and find me, when you seek me with all your heart" (Jeremiah 29:13). In the New Testament the Lord Jesus said, "Blessed are those who hunger and thirst for righteousness, for they shall be satisfied" (Matthew 5:6). Spiritual blessings do not go to the halfhearted but to those who want them above all else.

Helpless as he was, the blind man went for it, and God heard him.

Jesus' Response (vv. 40–43)

"And Jesus stopped and commanded him to be brought to him" (v. 40a). The final stop was Jerusalem, just seventeen miles away, but Jesus made time for this poor beggar. The Son stood still. On the one hand, nothing could have stopped Christ from finishing his mission—no opposition, no pleading by loving, ignorant friends, no protesting Peter. But the humble cry of a needy blind man stopped him—"Jesus, Son of David, have mercy on me!"

What a window into our Savior's heart! He is alive today doing in a far more exalted fashion the things he did while here on earth. Now in Heaven, he hears constant hosannas from the heavenly host and the Church. Yet he is instantly attentive to all our cries, even when a million of we beggars cry to him at the same time! The heart's cry of one in need is far sweeter to Christ than the shallow hallelujahs of the crowd. Are you hurting? Do you feel helpless? If so, understand that your plea will be sweetness to his ears.

Mark's Gospel adds, "Jesus stopped and said, 'Call him.' And they called the blind man, saying to him, 'Take heart. Get up; he is calling you.' And throwing off his cloak, he sprang up and came to Jesus" (Mark 10:49, 50). The instant the beggar heard Jesus' invitation, he stopped shouting, threw off his moth-eaten cloak (an extreme gesture for a blind man, who would normally keep his cloak where he could touch it), sprang to his feet, and stumbled with the help of others to Jesus.

Can you imagine his thrill? His heart was really pounding now. What a painting this would make. Face-to-face—Jesus with the most penetrating eyes ever, and the sightless sockets of the blind man framed by a countenance of ultimate expectation. This is the way to come to Jesus, and this is how he will respond!

"And when he came near, he [Jesus] asked him, 'What do you want me to do for you?'" (vv. 40, 41). Our Lord wanted the man to articulate his heart's desire, so he could strengthen the man's faith. The blind man knew *exactly* what he wanted. When we know our needs and can articulate them in prayer, what blessing follows! "And Jesus said to him, 'Recover your sight; your faith has made you well.' And immediately he recovered his sight and followed him, glorifying God. And all the people, when they saw it, gave praise to God" (vv. 42, 43).

On February 17, 1982 the *Chicago Sun-Times* carried a story originally printed in the *Los Angeles Times* about Anna Mae Pennica, a sixty-two-year-old woman who had been blind from birth. Mrs. Pennica had never seen the green of spring or the blue of a summer sky. Yet because she had grown up in a loving, supportive family, she never felt resentful about her handicap and always exuded a remarkably cheerful spirit.

Then in October 1981 Dr. Thomas Pettit of the Jules Stein Eye Institute of the University of California at Los Angeles performed surgery to remove the rare congenital cataracts from the lens of Mrs. Pennica's left eye—and she saw for the first time ever! The newspaper account does not record her initial response, but it does tell us that she discovered that everything was "so much bigger and brighter" than she had ever imagined. While she immediately recognized her husband and others she had known well, other acquaintances were taller or shorter, heavier or skinnier than she had pictured them.

Think how wonderful it must have been for Anna Mae Pennica when she looked for the first time at faces she had only felt, or when she saw the kaleidoscope of a Pacific sunset, or a tree waving its branches, or a bird in flight. The gift of physical sight is wonderful. And the miracle of seeing for the first time can hardly be described.

Imagine how it was for the blind beggar. Blind at the beginning of Christ's sentence, he was seeing at the end of it! No surgery! No bandages! No adjustment! Boom—sight! He saw human beings for the first time. He saw the gawking crowd. He saw "The City of Roses" hung with palm trees, and the hills of Moab off in the distance. But the thing he saw first was the face of Jesus.

Of this, Clarence Macartney wrote:

> And for you and me, too, that will be the greatest of all sights. When we awake from the dream men call life, when we put off the image of the earth and break the bonds of time and mortality, when the scales of time and sense have fallen from our eyes and the garment of corruption has been put off and when this mortality has put on immortality and this corruption has put on incorruption and we awaken in the everlasting morning, that will be the sight that will stir us and hold us.[8]

Jesus said to the gaping man, "Your faith has made you well." Christ had responded to the blind man's understanding of his own darkness, his penetrating assessment of Christ, and his persistence. But in the final analysis the miracle was all Christ's doing. Jesus came to the beggar, for he could not come to Jesus, and the Savior called forth his faith (cf. Ephesians 2:8, 9).

Scholars say Mark's Gospel preserves Bartimaeus' name (10:46) because he became a stalwart in the Jerusalem church. He followed Jesus, witnessing the Triumphal Entry on Palm Sunday, the horror of the crucifixion, and the joy of the resurrection. Talk about getting an eyeful.

Closing Reflections

What were the disciples meant to learn from this event? What are we to learn from the blind sight, the marvelous spiritual vision, of the blind beggar?

First, we must see our need. The man knew he was blind, and he articulated it—"Lord, let me recover my sight" (v. 41). Are you blind?—to your sin, your need of Christ? Or perhaps you are a Christian, but your sin has cauterized your eyes to what Christ is asking of you. Whatever, you need to ask the Holy Spirit to open the eyes of your heart.

Second, once you see your need, you need to see who Jesus is. He is "*the* Son of Man," the awesome, glorious sovereign whom all peoples and all nations will worship and whose kingdom and dominion will never end. He is the "Son of David," the deliverer who will fulfill everything King David foreshadowed. He is the Savior, Christ the King.

Third, you need to cry out, "Jesus, Son of David, have mercy on me!" Seeing your need, seeing who Jesus really is, now cry out in faith, "Have mercy on me!"

Do you see yourself? Do you see Jesus? Have you called out to him, "Jesus, Son of David, have mercy on me"?

Blind Bartimeus

As Jesus went into Jericho town,
'Twas darkness all from toe to crown,
About blind Bartimeus.
He said, "Our eyes are more than dim,
And so, of course, we don't see him,
But David's son can see us."
"Cry out, cry out, blind brother—cry;
Let not salvation dear go by.
Have mercy, Son of David."
Though they were blind, they both could hear—
They heard, and cried, and he drew near;
And so the blind were saved.
O Jesus Christ, I am deaf and blind;
Nothing comes through into my mind;
I only am not dumb;
Although I see thee not, nor hear,
I cry because thou may'st be near:
O son of Mary, come.
I feel a finger on mine ear;
A voice comes through the deafness drear:
"Be opened, senses dim!"
A hand is laid upon mine eyes;
I hear, and hearken, see, and rise—
'Tis He: I follow him.[9]

82

The Little Big Man

LUKE 19:1–10

CHARLES SPURGEON, the famed Victorian preacher who preached to a standing room only congregation of five thousand both Sunday morning and evening, also established a Pastor's College that exists to this day. A famous feature of the college experience was "the question oak," a large tree on Spurgeon's estate where, in good weather, students would gather on Friday afternoons to ask questions of Mr. Spurgeon and then deliver extemporaneous sermons. On one memorable occasion Spurgeon called on a student to give a message on Zacchaeus. The student rose and said: "Zacchaeus was of little stature, so am I. Zacchaeus was up a tree, so am I. Zacchaeus came down, so will I." And the student sat down as the students, led by Spurgeon, applauded.[1]

Zacchaeus' escapade makes for a fun story. The idea of a wee man perched like a bird in a tree (and being found out) is the stuff of humor and children's songs.

> Zacchaeus was a wee little man
> And a wee little man was he.
> He climbed up in a sycamore tree,
> For the Lord he wanted to see. . . .

We can have fun with this, but we must remember that the story occupies a very serious place in Luke's account of Jesus' life because it is Jesus' last personal encounter before his arrival in Jerusalem and the events leading to his death. All that remains is his telling of the parable of the ten minas and then the Triumphal Entry into Jerusalem. Significantly, the final line in the Zacchaeus story contains the summary line of the purpose of Jesus' ministry:

"For the Son of Man came to seek and to save the lost" (v. 10). Saving the lost is what Jesus is all about.

In this respect the salvation of Zacchaeus has telling spiritual connections to the two events that preceded it. The healing of the blind beggar—the deliverance there of a man lost in blindness and poverty—corresponds here to the deliverance of a man lost in wealth and corruption.[2] And its connection to the story before that, that of the rich ruler, is also clear because what is there stated is humanly impossible—namely, the salvation of a rich man ("For it is easier for a camel to go through the eye of a needle than for a rich person to enter the kingdom of God," 18:25). This impossibility now takes place in the salvation of rich little Zacchaeus.

Divine Overture (vv. 1–7)

If I had been casting for *Zacchaeus, the Movie* in the 1940s, I would have chosen diminutive Edward G. Robinson. Today I would choose Danny DeVito as the "Z-Man." Those shifty eyes, his swagger—the perfect little big man.

From a tax-collecting perspective, Zacchaeus had it made. Taxes were collected at three places inland—Capernaum, Jericho, and Jerusalem—and he had one of the big three.[3] Jericho had a commanding position at the crossing of the Jordan River and one of the prime approaches to Jerusalem. And Jericho was rich due to its great palm forests and balsam groves. As chief tax collector Zacchaeus was head of a tax-farming corporation with collectors who extorted the people, then paid him before he paid the Romans. He was the kingpin of the Jericho tax cartel and had the scruples of a modern-day crack dealer. He was filthy rich in the fullest sense of the term. Not a likely candidate for the kingdom!

And, of course, he was hated. In the eyes of his countrymen, his littleness was more than physical. He was a despised nobody. Some of the locals would have liked to see if they could put him through the eye of a needle—"squeezed out," as C. S. Lewis put it, "in one long bloody thread from tail to snout."[4]

Interior Initiative

No one would ever have guessed on that spring day that Zacchaeus would want to see Jesus. But as Luke says, "He was seeking to see who Jesus was" (v. 3a). Why? Perhaps he had heard of the conversion of Levi the tax collector, St. Matthew as we call him, who was now one of Jesus' followers (cf. 5:27–32). Perhaps he had even known Levi. Palestine was a small place, and tax collectors would have naturally hung out together. Because Jesus had ministered to Levi and others of his crowd, he had irked the religious establishment and was known as a friend of tax collectors and sinners. Jesus evidently had a soft spot for people like Zacchaeus.

It is also very likely that Zacchaeus had found his wealth and lifestyle unsatisfying. A sense of unease made every pleasure unfulfilling. Nothing lasted. This lack of satisfaction is what drew St. Augustine to Christ, as he wrote in retrospect to God: "You were always present, angry and merciful at once, strewing the pangs of bitterness over all my lawless pleasures to lead me on to look for others unallied with pain."[5] And again, "Your goad was thrusting at my heart, giving me no peace until the eye of my soul could discern you without mistake."[6] Like Augustine, Zacchaeus was drawn by the severe mercy of dissatisfaction.

Also, it is very probable that Zacchaeus was weary of being hated by his people. When people hassled him, he gave as good as he got, but he was miserable. The relentless contempt of his people left him desolate and alone.

Tired of his sad life, the restless little man determined to see Jesus, "but on account of the crowd he could not, because he was small in stature" (v. 3b). The crowd probably enjoyed boxing the little man out. "Sorry about the elbow, Zacchaeus, you're hard to see. Oh, that's your foot?"

Short or not, Zacchaeus had legs, and he used them: "So he ran on ahead and climbed up into a sycamore tree to see him, for he [Jesus] was about to pass that way" (v. 4). To be specific, it was a *ficus sycomorus*, a sturdy tree, some forty feet high, with a short trunk and wide branches. Very easy to climb.[7] The picture of the tiny, rejected man sitting alone, hidden in order to get a glimpse of Jesus, is very touching. He certainly did not want the crowd to know he was there. He had his dignity! He would get a private view of Jesus. The crowd would pass, and he would remain unseen, like an orphan peering through a lighted window on a dark cold night.

Exterior Initiative

But the interior-driven initiative of Zacchaeus was matched by the exterior initiative of Christ: "And when Jesus came to the place, he looked up and said to him, 'Zacchaeus, hurry and come down, for I must stay at your house today.' So he hurried and came down and received him joyfully" (vv. 5, 6). As the song goes:

> And as the Savior passed his way,
> He looked up in the tree.
> And he said, "Zacchaeus, you come down!

For I'm going to your house today,
For I'm going to your house today."

When Jesus stopped by the sycamore-fig tree, hidden Zacchaeus would have naturally tensed, maybe even experienced a quick sweat. And then sheer terror gripped his soul as Jesus (and the crowd) lifted his eyes. Zacchaeus braced himself to be a further spectacle of ridicule—especially when Jesus called him by name. But in Jesus' use of his personal name there was a hint of grace, because the same all-knowing eyes that earlier had seen Nathanael under a fig tree and discerned his guileless character now saw Zacchaeus and his guilty character, and Jesus called him, just as he had called Nathanael, to himself (cf. John 1:47–51). This was supernatural knowledge given to Jesus for that moment by the Father! And then, as Jesus invited himself to Zacchaeus' home, he did not say, "I would like to stay at your house," but "*I must stay*."[8] Jesus regarded his encounter with Zacchaeus as a divine mission. His seeking Zacchaeus was a work of sovereign grace.

What we begin to see at this point in the story is that Zacchaeus' seeking of Jesus and Jesus' seeking of Zacchaeus were both sovereign works of God. The crossing of their lives at the sycamore was a work of divine providence. This meeting was ordained before the foundation of the world (cf. Ephesians 1:4–6). The camel was about to go through the eye of a needle!

"So he hurried and came down and received him joyfully" (v. 6). The glad leap with which Zacchaeus left the tree, twigs and leaves flying, may have revealed to Zacchaeus himself, as it no doubt did to the bystanders, what it was that he had been dimly wishing for.[9] From here on, apart from the crowd's muttering, "He has gone in to be the guest of a man who is a sinner" (v. 7), there was only joy—Zacchaeus' and Jesus'.

Divine Transformation (v. 8)

To the crowd's amazement, off strode Jesus as the half-pint kingpin of the Jericho tax machine hurried alongside on his short legs. Jesus and his disciples would spend the night there according to Palestinian custom. And sometime during that stay, probably after much discussion and prayer, a little big man would formally stand and declare for all Jericho to hear, "Behold, Lord, the half of my goods I give to the poor. And if I have defrauded anyone of anything, I restore it fourfold" (v. 8).

A Big Divestment

For starters, Zacchaeus gave 50 percent of everything he had to the poor. This went far beyond the normal requirement of 20 percent of one's income.[10]

And then, from the remaining 50 percent he pledged to make restitution to the tune of four times the amount of what he had extorted. He had cheated many people, and now he placed his entire fortune in jeopardy to make things right. In effect, he lived out the command that had earlier caused the rich ruler so much grief: "Sell all that you have and distribute to the poor, and you will have treasure in heaven; and come, follow me" (18:22). He was walking through the eye of a needle and living to tell about it.

A Big Man

The little man had become a big one! Acceptance by God had given the tax collector what he had vainly sought through the accumulation of wealth—wholeness and satisfaction. The compulsive drive to make money was gone. He no longer needed his wealth. Instead of the passion to get, he now had a passion to give. He went into his house the littlest man in Jericho. He left the biggest man in town. All because of Jesus.

Divine Declaration (vv. 9, 10)

A Declaration to Zacchaeus

"And Jesus said to him, 'Today salvation has come to this house, since he also is a son of Abraham'" (v. 9). Zacchaeus had been saved, and the liberating joy of salvation was coursing through his soul. By faith Zacchaeus had become a true son of Abraham. He now shared the faith and works of Abraham (cf. John 8:39, 40; Romans 2:28, 29; 4:1–16; Galatians 3:13, 14).[11] In Jesus he had met the "horn of salvation" prophesied just before Jesus' birth, the one who would "give knowledge of salvation to his people in the forgiveness of their sins" (1:69, 77). Zacchaeus was a new man. That is why he gave away his fortune.

Nonbelievers are quick to criticize the gospel as sentimental and unpractical. But if it is impractical, it is our fault, not the gospel's. The demands of the gospel are intensely practical, and they include a reorientation to one's material possessions. One's grip on things is dramatically loosened.

In 6:24 Jesus says: "But woe to you who are rich, for you have received your consolation." Jesus pronounces this woe because in their self-sufficiency the rich can become the opposite of those to whom he came to preach the gospel. As he said at the onset of his public ministry, "The Spirit of the Lord is upon me, because he has anointed me to proclaim good news to the poor" (4:18).

Luke 12:20, 21 bears these solemn words to all who trust in riches: "But God said to him, 'Fool! This night your soul is required of you, and the things you have prepared, whose will they be?' So is the one who lays up treasure for himself and is not rich toward God."

And 16:13 records Jesus' material/spiritual axiom, "No servant can serve two masters, for either he will hate the one and love the other, or he will be devoted to the one and despise the other. You cannot serve God and money."

Luke 18:24, 25 records Jesus' response to the rich ruler: "How difficult it is for those who have wealth to enter the kingdom of God! For it is easier for a camel to go through the eye of a needle than for a rich person to enter the kingdom of God."

Jesus said over and over that it is useless to talk about loving him and trusting him and having the sweet assurance of forgiveness and the glorious hope of Heaven unless it makes a difference in our material attachments. Strong emotion, deep sweet feelings, and confidence in forgiveness are all very nice if they open our hands.

Jesus' repeated emphasis is that though generosity is not the means of redemption, it is an evidence of redemption. In fact, generosity and giving are pillars of discipleship. No one truly follows Christ who has not learned to give. The faithful church will proclaim this, not to serve itself, but to serve Christ and his people.

You may have reached a sticking point in your spiritual development, and you wonder why. You read your Bible, your language has changed, you are honest. But regular, generous giving? Well, you are not quite ready for that. Therefore, you do not keep growing in your soul.

Zacchaeus was ready because he was regenerated. He was ready because he was enlarged. The gospel makes little men big!

A Declaration to the World

The account of Zacchaeus' changed life ends with the great summary of Christ's mission: "For the Son of Man came to seek and to save the lost" (v. 10). From what others could see, Zacchaeus was beyond salvation. If you had lived in Jericho, you would have written him off too. He had turned his back on God's Word and his covenant people. He was a participant in Roman oppression, a traitor. He made his money off the backs of his own people, like a pimp. He loved money. His cartel was the cause of much injustice. He was the "baddest," smallest, meanest man in town.

Zacchaeus change? Impossible! Except for one thing—he was sought out by the Son of Man. "Son of Man"—the name for the majestic being of Daniel's vision to whom the Ancient of Days has given all dominion and authority (Daniel 7:13, 14). Jesus is an awesome God. "Son of Man" is also the name that prophesied the incarnation, because God the Son became a son of man—he took on human form. He is the transcendent God-man, coeternal with the Ancient of Days, who sought Zacchaeus and did the impossible. Camel-brained, dromedary-souled Zacchaeus passed through the eye of a needle not as a "long bloody thread from tail to snout," but because of the blood of Jesus, the Door (cf. John 10:9).

Salvation came to Zacchaeus because he was sought out. It was God who prompted his interior seeking. As Augustine said of God, "You follow close behind the fugitive and recall us to yourself in ways we cannot understand."[12] He makes us hungry. He causes the search. He compels us to come. At the end of C. S. Lewis's spiritual biography he writes:

> The words *compelle intrare,* compel them to come in, have been so abused by wicked men that we shudder at them; but, properly understood, they plumb the depth of the Divine mercy. The hardness of God is kinder than the softness of men, and His compulsion is our liberation.[13]

God orchestrated Zacchaeus' interior compulsion to seek Jesus, and the exterior crossing of their lives at the fig tree and Jesus' call were all divinely managed. Zacchaeus was caught because in his seeking he was sought.

> I sought the Lord, and afterward I knew
> He moved my heart to seek him, seeking me;
> It was not I that found, O Savior true;
> No, I was found of Thee.[14]

Closing Reflections

Is God seeking you? If so, you will know it by an interior unease. Nothing satisfies, and that goes for the most privileged delights. You are never really comfortable anymore. You lack wholeness. You lack a clear conscience. You lack peace. But understand this: "The hardness of God is kinder than the softness of man, and His compulsion is our liberation." Christ is seeking you.

And if that is so, you are at the sycamore-fig tree, and he is saying, "Come down. I want to dine with you. I want your soul. I have sought you. I am seeking you. I am the Son of Man. I am an awesome God. I died for you. Come down!"

You may say, "I'm too small. If you knew my heart, you wouldn't say that!" And he says, "I will give you a new heart, a big heart. Come to me."

Will you come?

83

The Parable of the Investment

LUKE 19:11–27

THE PARABLE JESUS GIVES HERE played off the "front page" political context of the times in which Jesus lived, specifically the events that had surrounded the ascension of the present Palestinian ruler, Archelaus, and his vain desire to be granted the title *king*. The Romans, under whom he served, avoided using the title *rex* (king) for their own rulers, but on occasion would allow one of their vassal rulers in the eastern provinces to be called such. Herod the Great, Archelaus' father, had been granted the title when, in league with the Romans, he defeated the Parthians and was then feasted by Mark Antony on "the first day of his reign" (Josephus, *Jewish War* 1.4,4 §284–485). That is why he is called "Herod the king" in the Bible (Matthew 2:3).

When King Herod died, his will gave Archelaus over half of his kingdom, but the title could not be passed on. And poor Archelaus' ego smarted. So it was that Archelaus assembled an entourage and departed for Rome to ask Caesar for the title. The group included his mother (Malthace), his friends (Poplas, Ptolemy, and Nicholas), and other family members (namely, Solome and her children and various nephews and sons-in-law of the late king (Josephus, *War*, 2.1 §14,15).

But to Archelaus' surprise, in Rome some of his family opposed his getting the title, even accusing him before Caesar. Then, even more surprising, a delegation of fifty Palestinians (amazingly Jews and Samaritans together) had also traveled to Rome to oppose him before Caesar. Solome's children accused him first (*War* 2.5 §26–32). And when the fifty Palestinians arrived, a huge confrontation took place in the lavish setting of the temple of the Palatine Apollo. The fifty were joined by eight thousand expatriate Jews living in Rome (*War* 2.6,1 §80–83). There, before Caesar and the vast throng, the Palestinians related that Archelaus had massacred some three thousand Jews at Passover, heaping the bodies in the temple, and then tortured others—all to prove he was as powerful as his father (*War* 2.6, 2 §84–89). And if this was not enough, they argued that he was inept, corrupt, and corrupting and was ruining a prosperous land (*Antiquities* 17. 11, 2 §304–315).

Caesar, after hearing both parties, dismissed the great assembly. A few days later he announced his decision, which satisfied no one. Josephus records: "He gave half the kingdom to Archelaus, with the title ethnarch, promising, moreover, to make him king, should he prove his deserts" (*War* 2.6, 3 §93–95). All returned to Palestine unhappy. And Archelaus never did "prove his deserts"—he never was called king.

All this scandal was tucked into the Palestinian/Jewish mind. It was part of their lore—"Archelaus the wanna-be." When Jesus proceeded to give the parable, he referenced this well-known story line. But his parable took a different turn than the Archelaus episode because it was not about a would-be-king but the true King. It was about Jesus himself.

Why did Jesus tell this parable? Messianic expectation (kingdom expectation) had reached a feverish pitch among his followers. "As they heard these things [the dialogue between Zacchaeus and Jesus], he proceeded to tell a parable, because he was near to Jerusalem, and because they supposed that the kingdom of God was to appear immediately" (v. 11). They believed the kingdom would come into existence at Jerusalem. As they neared the great city, mystic lines like those from Zechariah 14 raced through their minds:

> On that day his feet shall stand on the Mount of Olives . . . and the Mount of Olives shall be split in two from east to west. . . . Then the LORD my God will come, and all the holy ones with him. On that day there shall be no light, cold, or frost. . . . And the LORD will be king over all the earth. On that day the LORD will be one and his name one. (Zechariah 14:4, 5, 6, 9)

They were excited! Jerusalem was only seventeen miles away, and Passover was at hand. Crowds were thronging from Jericho up to the Holy City.

Jesus was the "Son of David." He could reestablish David's throne. And he was calling himself "the Son of Man," the awesome, divine being of Daniel 7. They had seen his supernatural power repeatedly, and now, with the seventeen-mile ascent to the Holy City rising before them, they looked for a mighty outbreak of his redemptive powers to overrun the old age and bring in the new. Their feverish kingdom expectancy was peaking!

Jesus' parable countered their expectations with an allegory of his own life that spoke of his incarnation, his investment in his followers, his rejection by his enemies, his crowning as King (through his death, resurrection and ascension), and finally his return to judge the world.

The opening line of the parable would have recalled Archelaus' folly: "A nobleman went into a far country to receive for himself a kingdom and then return" (v. 12). This was like a front-page banner headline. Jesus certainly had their attention. But this opening line really encapsulated Jesus' own life—from his incarnation to his final return. Of course, his hearers could not possibly understand it all then. But in retrospect they would see that the parable was about his kingship and what his being King meant to his followers and to the world.

The King-to-Be Delegates Responsibilities (vv. 13–15a)

Servants' Responsibilities

Before the nobleman departed to obtain his kingship, Jesus says, he gave his servants sums to invest: "Calling ten of his servants, he gave them ten minas, and said to them, 'Engage in business until I come'" (v. 13).

A mina was equal to about one hundred days' wages for a laborer—three months' salary.[1] Notice that he gave each of his servants the *same* amount, one mina each. Sometimes this parable has been confused with the parable of the talents (Matthew 25:14–30). But the parables are entirely different. There the talents represent *abilities* (one is given five talents of gold, another two, and another one). The very word *talent* (literally, a large sum of money) has been adopted into English as a synonym for ability, as in a "talented person." But here in Luke *mina* does not signify an ability but rather a *deposit* that is given to every Christian—namely, the gospel.

Every follower of Christ is a steward of the gospel. Paul repeatedly would speak of being "entrusted with the gospel" (1 Thessalonians 2:4; cf. 1 Timothy 1:11; 6:20; 2 Timothy 2:2). Each believer receives the same investment capital for his Christian life. "Joe Christian" receives the same as St. Paul and John Calvin and Billy Graham. We all have the good news of Jesus Christ and its marvelous effect in our lives.

And we all have the same command, to "Engage in business until I come." We must invest the investment Christ has made in us! We are to multiply our spiritual capital—invest the gospel—increase the yield of the good news of salvation through Christ! This is not a matter of gifts but of investment.

Enemies' Resistance

After Jesus vested his servants with the good news, his enemies attempted to thwart his kingship: "But his citizens hated him and sent a delegation after him, saying, 'We do not want this man to reign over us'" (v. 14). This resembles the Archelaus episode—except that Jesus is a righteous King and his enemies are evil. Oh, how the unbelieving have always hated him. Consider his infamous rejection before the crucifixion:

> Now it was the day of Preparation of the Passover. It was about the sixth hour. He said to the Jews, "Behold your King!" They cried out, "Away with him, away with him, crucify him!" Pilate said to them, "Shall I crucify your King?" The chief priests answered, "We have no king but Caesar." So he delivered him over to them to be crucified. (John 19:14–16)

> Pilate also wrote an inscription and put it on the cross. It read, "Jesus of Nazareth, the King of the Jews." Many of the Jews read this inscription, for the place where Jesus was crucified was near the city, and it was written in Aramaic, in Latin, and in Greek. So the chief priests of the Jews said to Pilate, "Do not write, 'The King of the Jews,' but rather, 'This man said, I am King of the Jews.'" Pilate answered, "What I have written I have written." (John 19:19–22)

He has again and again been rejected. The dark world rebels against everything for which he stands.

In the case of Archelaus the people were justified, though unsuccessful. We cannot transfer this aspect of the historical situation to Jesus' parable/allegory because Jesus is the perfect King and nothing can interfere with his kingship. "When he returned, having received the kingdom . . ." (v. 15a). He was declared King by his resurrection. He was received as King at his ascension. The closing lines of the Philippian hymn of the incarnation are relevant here:

> Therefore God has highly exalted him and bestowed on him the name that is above every name, so that at the name of Jesus every knee should bow, in heaven and on earth and under the earth, and every tongue confess that Jesus Christ is Lord, to the glory of God the Father. (Philippians 2:9–11)

The first phrase of verse 15 catapults us into the future: "when he returned." This is the second advent, the return of our great God and Savior Jesus Christ (cf. Titus 2:12, 13). He will then judge the living and the dead.

The New King Settles Accounts (vv. 15b–27)

At his return Jesus will settle accounts, first, with his servants on the basis of their investments, and then with his enemies who rejected his kingship.

Servants Addressed

The king reckoned first with his servants to whom he had invested the minas: "He ordered these servants to whom he had given the money to be called to him, that he might know what they had gained by doing business" (v. 15b). This represents the Judgment Seat of Christ, the judgment of believers: "For we must all appear before the judgment seat of Christ, so that each one may receive what is due for what he has done in the body, whether good or evil" (2 Corinthians 5:10).

The returned king then conducted interviews with huge importance:

> The first came before him, saying, "Lord, your mina has made ten minas more." And he said to him, "Well done, good servant! Because you have been faithful in a very little, you shall have authority over ten cities." And the second came, saying, "Lord, your mina has made five minas." And he said to him, "And you are to be over five cities." (vv. 16–19)

The first and second servants had gained 1,000 percent and 500 percent respectively on their investment. And they were humble about it, taking no credit for themselves. "Lord, your mina has made . . ." they both said.

Their rewards astound us. They got entire cities! They managed their investments well, and their rewards exceeded all expectation. But there was something far greater for them than being coregents, as Helmut Thielicke explains:

> The splendor of the cities committed to them will be far less important than the fact that now they are the viceroys of the Lord and therefore among those closest to him and thus will always have access to him and be able to speak to him and tarry in his presence at all times. Their reward is that in the end the Lord will receive them with honors, that they will be privileged to speak and to live with Jesus forever. For heaven does not consist in what we shall receive, whether this be white robes and heavenly crowns or ambrosia and nectar, but rather in what we shall become—namely, the companions of our King.[2]

The reward of Christ's faithful servants is an elevation of eternal intimacy with him. They will be his coregents, viceroys, and confidants. What joy! Happily, the eternal reward is not rest but responsibility as we work with Christ in unimaginably vast new spiritual enterprises.

What a sweet motivation to invest our gospel deposits! Listen to Peter in this vein: "If you practice these qualities you will never fall. For in this way there will be richly provided for you an entrance into the eternal kingdom of our Lord and Savior Jesus Christ" (2 Peter 1:10b, 11).

The Judgment Seat is not without its tragedy, however:

> Then another came, saying, "Lord, here is your mina, which I kept laid away in a handkerchief; for I was afraid of you, because you are a severe man. You take what you did not deposit, and reap what you did not sow." He said to him, "I will condemn you with your own words, you wicked servant! You knew that I was a severe man, taking what I did not deposit and reaping what I did not sow? Why then did you not put my money in the bank, and at my coming I might have collected it with interest?" (vv. 20–23)

The man made no investment. He simply stashed the mina (the gospel) away. His thoughts regarding his master were slanderous, not based on truth. He called him "a severe man," using the adjective *austeros* meaning "strict" or "exacting"—"a man who expects to get blood out of a stone"[3]—one who gets rich on the backs of others. I. H. Marshall comments: "The servant appears to have feared that he would get no return for his work: all the profit would have been taken by the master. At the same time, he may have feared that if he incurred a loss on the capital he would have to make it up to the master."[4]

This sorry Christian slanders God in his heart and hoards what he has received from Christ. He carefully folds it in a cloth and stores it away. He thinks, "I can't be active, but I can at least be a conservative. I can preserve the Christian tradition. I can submit to a church wedding and send my children to Sunday school. I can take a Christian point of view. I can wrap my religion in my handkerchief and conserve it."[5]

Such a disgraced believer will be judged.

> And he said to those who stood by, "Take the mina from him, and give it to the one who has the ten minas." And they said to him, 'Lord, he has ten minas!' "I tell you that to everyone who has, more will be given, but from the one who has not, even what he has will be taken away." (vv. 24–26)

This man's works are incinerated, though he himself is saved. As Paul said of a wood, hay, and straw kind of life, "If anyone's work is burned up, he will suffer loss, though he himself will be saved, but only as through fire" (1 Corinthians 3:15).

Every believer has been given the same gospel deposit to invest. Regardless of our abilities, if we invest it, we will receive rewards far beyond reason or measure. We will reign with Christ. We will be his confidants. We will be his coworkers in eternal enterprises. "I tell you that to everyone who has, more will be given, but from the one who has not [who has wrapped the gospel up and put it away], even what he has will be taken away" (v. 26).

Are we investing the gospel? Are we investing what he has done for us? Are we investing what he can do for others? This is not a question of giftedness but of faithfulness. Are we using what we have to invest in the ministry of the gospel? There are many specific applications of this question. Are we using our money to invest the good news? Jesus minced no words about this: "I tell you, make friends for yourselves by means of unrighteous wealth, so that when it fails they may receive you into the eternal dwellings" (16:9). Your money personally given to aid people in need or to promote evangelism and missions will win souls, eternal friends who will welcome you into Heaven! How do you spend your time? Your personal calendar tells all. Everyone can make massive investments in the matter of prayer, but few do. Do our mouths, the things we say, invest testimony and witness? There can never be such a thing as passive investment. Gospel investment requires action.

Enemies Addressed

The parable finishes with frightening severity: "But as for these enemies of mine, who did not want me to reign over them, bring them here and slaughter them before me" (v. 27). This is the future for all who reject Christ—an apocalyptic end. Christ, the Lamb-Lion, will slaughter his enemies at his return (cf. Revelation 14:9–11). This is what John saw as recorded in Revelation:

> Then I saw heaven opened, and behold, a white horse! The one sitting on it is called Faithful and True, and in righteousness he judges and makes war. His eyes are like a flame of fire, and on his head are many diadems, and he has a name written that no one knows but himself. He is clothed in a robe dipped in blood, and the name by which he is called is The Word of God. And the armies of heaven, arrayed in fine linen, white and pure, were following him on white horses. From his mouth comes a sharp sword with which to strike down the nations, and he will rule them with a rod of iron. He will tread the winepress of the fury of the wrath of God the Almighty. On his robe and on his thigh he has a name written, King of kings and Lord of lords. (Revelation 19:11–16)

We may be horrified by the fierceness of this passage, but beneath the terrifying imagery is a solemn fact: Jesus, coming into the world, forces every person to decide—and the decision is a matter of life and death.

The noble Son came, and before he went away to acquire his kingship two things happened. First, he gave a gospel deposit to every one of his followers. And second, his enemies attempted to deny his kingship. But through his death, resurrection, ascension, and glorification he substantiated his eternal position as King of kings and Lord of lords. And he will someday return.

To those who have invested his investment, there will be unthought-of rewards. To those who have hidden it, shame. To those who reject him, death.

We are at the final hour. The King is coming. How are our investments?

84

A New Kind of King

LUKE 19:28–44

ON DECEMBER 4, 1977 in Bangui, capital of the Central African Empire, the world press witnessed the coronation of his Imperial Majesty, Bokassa I. The price tag for that single event, designed and choreographed by French designer Olivier Brice, was $25 million.

At 10:10 a.m. that morning the blare of trumpets and the roll of drums announced the approach of His Majesty. The procession began with eight of Bokassa's twenty-nine official children parading down the royal carpet to their seats. They were followed by Jean Bedel Bokassa II, heir to the throne, dressed in a white admiral's uniform with gold braid. He was seated on a red pillow to the left of the throne. Catherine followed, the favorite of Bokassa's nine wives. She was wearing a $73,000 gown made by Lanvin of Paris, strewn with pearls she had picked out herself.

The emperor arrived in an imperial coach bedecked with gold eagles and drawn by six matched Anglo-Norman horses. When the Marine Band blared "The Sacred March of His Majesty, Emperor Bokassa I," His Highness strode forth, cloaked in a 32-pound robe decorated with 785,000 strewn pearls and gold embroidery. White gloves adorned his hands, pearl slippers his feet. On his brow he wore a gold crown of laurel wreaths like those worn by Roman consuls of old, a symbol of the favor of the gods. As the "Sacred March" came to a conclusion, Bokassa seated himself on his $2.5 million eagle throne, took his gold laurel wreath off, and, as Napoleon 173 years before had done, took his $2.5 million crown, which was topped with an 80-carat diamond, and placed it upon his own head. At 10:43 a.m., December 4, 1977, the twentieth century saw a new emperor.

Mercifully, Bokassa's reign was not as imposing as his coronation. Just two years later, while Bokassa was out of the country, the French engineered a successful coup. It came too late for many of his victims, among them two hundred children who had been executed because they complained about the expense of their school uniforms.

Bokassa did his best to establish an enduring kingdom but infamously failed. So it is with the kings and rulers of the earth. Try as they will, even though they cling tightly, when death comes they always lose their Reich, empires, and kingdoms. They leave it all behind!

But every Palm Sunday, and often at other times as well, we who know Christ rejoice because it was not so with the King of kings. He was a new kind of king—a king who operated from a different kind of principle. Luke's account of the Triumphal Entry of Christ can bring to our souls a kingdom touch, a regal understanding.

Jesus was at the end of a journey that had begun some nine months before when he purposefully began a zigzag journey first through Galilee, then Samaria, then Perea, and finally Judea. During this final journey he had ministered in at least thirty-five localities, timing the journey just right in order to end up in Jerusalem for Passover.[1]

Now it was Passover, and he was back in Bethany, on the outskirts of Jerusalem. Expectations were running high. Earlier he had raised Lazarus from the dead (John 11), and the sensational news of that event had spread around Jerusalem many times. The numbers of those watching his entourage had greatly enlarged. Mary had dramatically anointed Christ with an alabaster flask of immensely costly ointment, and Jesus had defended her extravagance, saying she was anointing him for burial (Matthew 26:10; Mark 14:6–9; John 12:7, 8). Throngs of Jews were coming out of Jerusalem to see Jesus and also to see Lazarus. And the religious leaders were counseling together as to how they might kill the Lord, because many were believing in him (Mark 14:10, 11; John 12:9–11).

There was unprecedented national tension in the Holy City. Would Jesus make a move? If so, when? And what would the authorities do then?

The King's Deliberate Preparation (vv. 29–34)

> When he drew near to Bethphage and Bethany, at the mount that is called Olivet, he sent two of the disciples, saying, "Go into the village in front of you, where on entering you will find a colt tied, on which no one has ever yet sat. Untie it and bring it here. If anyone asks you, 'Why are you untying it?' you shall say this: 'The Lord has need of it.'" So those who were sent went away and found it just as he had told them. And as they were untying

> the colt, its owners said to them, "Why are you untying the colt?" And they said, "The Lord has need of it." (vv. 29–34)

Bethphage was a little hamlet or district between Jerusalem and Bethany.[2] A traveler approaching Jerusalem from the east would come to Bethany about two miles out, then pass through Bethphage on the slope of the Mount of Olives on his way into Jerusalem.

On that celebrated day, the first Palm Sunday, Jesus was walking in front of his disciples when they came to the area of Bethphage on the ascent of the Mount of Olives (v. 29). From there he sent two of his disciples into the hamlet to procure an unridden donkey colt that they obtained by simply saying, "The Lord has need of it." As to how he knew it was there, the Scriptures are silent. Perhaps one of his disciples told him, or perhaps he used his omniscience through the power of the Holy Spirit. We surmise that the owners gave it to him because they had heard of his ministry—he was a respected rabbi with growing fame.

What we see here on Jesus' part is careful premeditation. He was carefully coordinating everything. The day and hour had been selected in eternity past. The timing was precise. The mode of his entry, a previously unridden donkey, was carefully chosen. Never before had Jesus done anything to promote a public demonstration. In fact, he had repeatedly withdrawn from the crowds if there was any hint of such a thing. But now he invited attention, even though that meant courting danger.

Why the choice of a young donkey? Because over five hundred years earlier Zechariah had prophesied that the Messiah would come riding on the foal of a donkey:

> Rejoice greatly, O daughter of Zion!
> Shout aloud, O daughter of Jerusalem!
> Behold, your king is coming to you;
> righteous and having salvation is he,
> humble and mounted on a donkey,
> on a colt, the foal of a donkey. (Zechariah 9:9; cf. Matthew 21:4, 5)

Jesus was unequivocally identifying himself as the Messiah. The choice of the donkey revealed his life and ministry in two ways. First, it identified him with kings in the royal line of David, and especially with David himself, because the donkey was regarded as a royal animal before and during David's reign. After David, the Hebrew kings and warriors switched to horses, and the donkey was considered unsuited to the dignity of kings.[3] But Jesus' identification with the emblem and with the specific prophecy was exact and perfectly revelatory of his position.

Second, the use of a donkey speaks of Jesus' inner spirit. As Zechariah (who lived long after David) said, Jesus was "humble and mounted on a donkey." This was Christ's intrinsic attitude in life. As Paul wrote to the Philippians, "Have this mind among yourselves, which is yours in Christ Jesus, who, though he was in the form of God, did not count equality with God a thing to be grasped" (Philippians 2:5, 6). The fact that the donkey was borrowed further enhanced this idea. There was a remarkable blending of Jesus' dignity and poverty in his instructions to the borrowers: "You shall say this: 'The Lord has need of it.'" He chose the donkey because it beautifully portrayed both his position as King and his character as servant.

Jesus was unlike any other king who ever lived. As Clarence Macartney so beautifully described it:

> How strange a contrast to the triumphal entry of ancient warriors and conquerors into the cities which they had taken! This time no wall broken down for entry; this time no garlanded hero standing in his war chariot, driving down the lane of cheering subjects past smoking altars, and followed by captive kings and princes in chains. Instead of that, just a meek and lowly man riding upon the foal of a donkey.[4]

We must keep ever before us that on the day Christ rode humbly into Jerusalem, the Jerusalem then dominated by Roman pomp and splendor, he was absolutely in control. He was in control the entire length of the Passion Week. The wheel of history did not crush him as Albert Schweitzer argued in *The Quest for the Historical Jesus*—Jesus was turning the wheel.[5]

The King's Triumphal Entry (vv. 35–40)

Having secured the donkey, the triumphal march began: "And they brought it to Jesus, and throwing their cloaks on the colt, they set Jesus on it. And as he rode along, they spread their cloaks on the road" (vv. 35, 36). Jesus was the center of attention! All eyes were focused on him. All homage was given to him. Not only did the exuberant followers place their clothing on the donkey as a saddle—they flung their garments to the ground as a gesture of reverence and indicating their willingness for him to take everything they had.

"As he was drawing near—already on the way down the Mount of Olives—the whole multitude of his disciples began to rejoice and praise God with a loud voice for all the mighty works that they had seen" (v. 37). As Jesus rode on up toward the ridge where "the way down" the Mount of

Olives began, fresh throngs from Bethany and Bethphage joined in, and the procession became proportionately exuberant. And when they reached the descent where they caught a glimpse of the southeastern corner of the city, great cheers rang out from the mountain.

In addition to praising God for all the miracles they had seen, the people kept repeating, "Blessed is the King who comes in the name of the Lord!" (v. 38). This is a line from the Hallel Psalms (Psalms 113—118), which were chanted at the end of the Passover Supper and at the Feast of Tabernacles. This particular line (from Psalm 118:26) had been changed and appropriated by the travelers as a way of greeting one another. In Psalm 118 it reads, "Blessed is *he* who comes in the name of the LORD." It was a beatitude addressed to the king as he approached the temple. This implicit kingly reference became explicit at Christ's triumphal entrance as the crowd modified it and shouted, "Blessed is *the King* who comes in the name of the Lord!"[6]

To this they added, "Peace in heaven and glory in the highest!" (v. 38), which naturally reminds us of another song of another multitude, the great host of angels who announced Christ's birth in 2:14: "Glory to God in the highest, and on earth peace among those with whom he is pleased!" The heavenly chorus sang of peace on *earth,* while the earthly throng now sang of peace in *Heaven.* They sang more than they knew, for peace on earth is dependent on peace in Heaven. In fact, it comes down from above. It is only when man finds peace with God that there is peace on earth.

The growing throng was caught in a corporate prophetic ecstasy as the long procession moved up the slope of the Mount of Olives, chanting:

> Blessed is the King who comes in the name of the Lord! Peace in heaven and glory in the highest! (v. 38)

Alfred Edersheim, the great Hebraist and scholar on the life of Jesus, believes that they were repeatedly met by pilgrims coming out of Jerusalem because the word of his coming had already reached there, so that with each new encounter there was renewed jubilation.[7]

The other Gospel accounts add to Luke's picture of joy. John 12:13 tells us, "They took branches of palm trees and went out to meet him, crying out, 'Hosanna! Blessed is he who comes in the name of the Lord, even the King of Israel!'" The palm branches represented their nationalistic desire to be delivered, for the palm had been the symbol on the coin of the second Maccabean revolt. "Hosanna" was an anticipatory cry that literally meant "Save" or "Save us" or perhaps "Lord, save him," similar to "God save the Queen."

The people viewed Jesus as their deliverer. And indeed he was. But not in the way they thought.

Our Lord was in control, and he was making a statement. The donkey he rode prophesied of his position as King and his character as servant—a burden bearer. The Hallel Psalm repeated on the people's lips, "Blessed is the King who comes in the name of the Lord," recalled his messianic character. This was his moment—a moment set before the foundations of the world.

Against this the Pharisees were predictably the counterpoint: "And some of the Pharisees in the crowd said to him, 'Teacher, rebuke your disciples'" (v. 39). Here it is difficult to discern the Pharisees' motive. Perhaps they were afraid the Romans would hear about the parade and squelch it with force, or perhaps they thought the adulation for Jesus was misplaced. Whatever their motivation, Christ shouted for all to hear, "I tell you, if these were silent, the very stones would cry out" (v. 40).

When we meditate upon Jesus' deliberate march into Jerusalem, a march that would seal his fate on the cross as the atonement for our sins, our hearts should praise him! But there is more to the picture, for as the little donkey bore Jesus down toward Jerusalem amid the repeated cheers, no one knew that amid the cheers would come tears—the King's tears.

The King's Tears (vv. 41–44)

"And when he drew near and saw the city, he wept over it" (v. 41). The road down to Jerusalem descended into a hollow, and the glimpse of the city was again withdrawn from the multitude because of the intervening ridge. But after a few moments the path mounted again, and in an instant the whole city burst into view![8]

With the panorama of Jerusalem before his eyes, the Savior began to weep—not with quiet tears as when he wept at the grave of Lazarus, whom he was going to resurrect, but with loud and deep lamentation.[9] There in the middle of the road, with the great city in full view, the stunned multitude heard the Savior of the world wail over Jerusalem! We must fix this picture in our eyes and hearts, for it will do us great good. This was a new kind of king.

His wailing was followed by a lamentation (vv. 42–44):

> Would that you, even you, had known on this day the things that make for peace! But now they are hidden from your eyes. For the days will come upon you, when your enemies will set up a barricade around you and sur-

> round you and hem you in on every side and tear you down to the ground, you and your children within you. And they will not leave one stone upon another in you, because you did not know the time of your visitation.

The Lord prophetically saw the proud, unrepentant Holy City as a pile of rubble wet with blood—and that is what later happened. Josephus tells us:

> Caesar had already commanded the entire city and the temple to be razed to the ground, leaving only the towers which projected higher than the others to stand, Phasel, Hippicus, and Mariamme, and that part of the wall which enclosed the city on the west. This was to be an encampment for the troops which would be left behind, and the towers were to reveal to posterity how great a city Jerusalem had been and what sort of fortifications Roman prowess had dominated. All the rest of the wall which encompassed the city the demolition teams leveled so that no one who would come there in the future would ever believe that the spot had been inhabited.[10]

The destruction was terrible when the city was stormed and the temple burned. Josephus records that the victorious Roman general "Titus threw his arms heavenward, uttered a groan, and called God to witness that this was not his doing."[11]

Jesus wept terribly over Jerusalem! This was and is the heart of a new kind of king. It is the heart of God. The body was human, but the heart was divine. This is how Jesus Christ and God the Father and the blessed Holy Spirit sorrow over hearts that miss their "day" and "the things that make for peace"—namely, repentance toward God and faith in the Lord Jesus Christ.

Will he weep over you?

> The son of God in tears
> The wondering angels see.
> Be thou astonished, O my soul,
> He shed those tears for thee.[12]

The tears of Christ measure the value of your soul!

Closing Reflections

The story of His Imperial Majesty Bokassa I is all too typical of earthly kings. It is all too true of us. We try to hold on to what we have. But the very best we can do is little better than a fleeting self-coronation.

However, Christ, the new kind of king, shows us how to live. The King came riding a lowly donkey. Therefore, "Have this mind among yourselves, which is yours in Christ Jesus, who, though he was in the form of God, did not count equality with God a thing to be grasped" (Philippians 2:5, 6). He came loving our fragmented world, and he wept over it. Those who want to reign in this life will do the same.

We celebrate a new kind of king. Because of him we can live a new kind of life!

85

Sovereign in His Temple

LUKE 19:45–48

THE TRIUMPHAL ENTRY and the cleansing of the temple were apparently one premeditated fabric, and Jesus orchestrated them both with an eye to Old Testament Scripture. We see this in the Triumphal Entry by his prescient knowledge of an unridden colt of a donkey in the next town, his regal assurance that its loan would be granted simply by saying, "The Lord has need of it" (19:34), and his royal ride into Jerusalem. This was a conscious demonstration that he was the Messiah-King prophesied in Zechariah 9:9.

The crowds understood this messianic act and began to chant lines from the Hallel Psalms (Psalms 113—118)—principally, "Blessed is the King who comes in the name of the Lord!" (19:38; cf. Psalm 118:26). Jesus had deliberately arranged everything. Even his weeping over Jerusalem was part of the Father's plan to reveal the heart of the King of kings. And this all happened at Passover—the chosen time for the Lamb to die.

We see the same divine control in the subsequent temple cleansing. The verse the throngs had been chanting to Jesus, "Blessed is the King who comes [*ho erchomenos*] in the name of the Lord," echoed the question that messengers from John the Baptist had earlier asked Jesus: "Are you the one who is to come. . . ?" (7:19). This question about his coming was generated from their knowledge of the famous prophecy of Malachi 3:1—"Behold, I send my messenger, and he will prepare the way before me. And the Lord whom you seek will suddenly come to his temple; and the messenger of the covenant in whom you delight, behold, he is coming, says the LORD of hosts." So we understand that the chant repeated by the joyous crowds was an answer to the messianic expectation of Malachi 3:1, which emphasized that the Lord would "*suddenly*" come to his temple.[1] And this is why Jesus, in conscious prophetic fulfillment, ended up in the temple.

Earlier, about the time of Jesus' bar mitzvah, when Jesus' searching parents found him in the temple, Jesus referred to it as his Father's house, saying, "Did you not know that I must be in my Father's house?" (2:49). Now Jesus established himself as sovereign in his Father's house. "These are the days of the Messiah's sovereignty in his temple."[2] And what is it that the King of the temple does? He purges it of worship abuse and, in doing so, prepares it for his own ministry of preaching and ultimately points to himself becoming the temple of his people. He was sovereignly in control of his every action and word.

Jesus Cleanses the Temple (vv. 45, 46)

Action

Luke describes Jesus' famous actions in a notably concise sentence: "And he entered the temple and began to drive out those who sold" (v. 45). The commercial abuse of God's house had grown out of worshipers' need to obtain unblemished animals for sacrifice (cf. Leviticus 1:3) and the annual requirement that every male Israelite pay a half-shekel temple tax (cf. Exodus 30:11–14 and M shekalim 1:3; 2:1, 4), which often necessitated changing money into the proper currency.

But apparently exorbitant charges were made by the money changers, and there was also a large traffic in livestock for the sacrifices, all at the worshipers' expense (cf. John 2:14). Records exist of transactions in which three thousand livestock were brought to the temple hill to be sold for offerings.[3] In Jesus' day the middlemen were under the control of the high priest Ananias, whom Josephus cynically called "the great procurer of money" (*Antiquities* 20.205).[4]

A huge religious scam had been going on for years in the temple, specifically in the Court of the Gentiles, the only place in the temple where a non-Jew could go to pray and meditate. So much for Gentile evangelism!

Suddenly in walks the Lion of the tribe of Judah. Malachi's prophetic "the Lord . . . will suddenly come to his temple" was fulfilled. Mark is more graphic than Luke:

> And they came to Jerusalem. And he entered the temple and began to drive out those who sold and those who bought in the temple, and he overturned the tables of the money-changers and the seats of those who sold pigeons. And he would not allow anyone to carry anything through the temple. (Mark 11:15, 16)

Have you ever seen a table flipped over? This is a violent act. And to top it off, Jesus halted the traffic of those who were using the Court of Gentiles as a shortcut—he "would not allow anyone to carry anything through the temple." So much for the one-sided "gentle Jesus, meek and mild."

Now, Jesus is indeed the meekest, gentlest person who ever lived. He himself said, truthfully, "I am gentle and lowly in heart" (Matthew 11:29), and also taught us, "Blessed are the meek, for they shall inherit the earth" (Matthew 5:5). But meekness is not weakness. It is, rather, strength under control. Meekness has the strength to not defend oneself (Jesus when he went to the cross, for example). But meekness will boldly defend others. And on this occasion Jesus struck out in defense of the holiness of God the Father.

Words

Jesus' mighty actions gave way to mighty prophetic words, contained in two brief quotations from the Old Testament. The first is from Isaiah 56:7: "It is written, 'My house shall be a house of prayer'" (v. 46a). In the context of Isaiah 56, the meaning is, "My house will be a house of prayer for all peoples."

This goes back first to the day Solomon dedicated the temple, as recorded in 1 Kings 8. On that day, amid great celebrating, the empty temple received the Ark of the Covenant into the Most Holy Place, and "when the priests came out of the Holy Place, a cloud filled the house of the Lord, so that the priests could not stand to minister because of the cloud, for the glory of the Lord filled the house of the Lord" (1 Kings 8:10, 11). After blessing the people, Solomon spread out his hands toward Heaven and offered his great dedicatory prayer, which toward the end included prayer for Gentiles/foreigners:

> Likewise, when a foreigner, who is not of your people Israel, comes from a far country for your name's sake (for they shall hear of your great name and your mighty hand, and of your outstretched arm), when he comes and prays toward this house, hear in heaven your dwelling place and do according to all for which the foreigner calls to you, in order that all the peoples of the earth may know your name and fear you, as do your people Israel, and that they may know that this house that I have built is called by your name. (1 Kings 8:41–43)

The temple was to be used for Gentile evangelism.

The words of Isaiah 56 sharing what God says about foreigners and the temple are enlightening: "Let not the foreigner who has joined himself to the Lord say, 'The Lord will surely separate me from his people'; and let not the eunuch say, 'Behold, I am a dry tree'" (Isaiah 56:3). No one is to be excluded from God's people by ancestry (the foreigner) or by defect (the eunuch). All will be received if they come in sincerity of heart. Isaiah concludes about such people:

> And the foreigners who join themselves to the LORD,
> to minister to him, to love the name of the LORD,
> and to be his servants,
> everyone who keeps the Sabbath and does not profane it,
> and holds fast my covenant—
> these I will bring to my holy mountain,
> and make them joyful in my house of prayer;
> their burnt offerings and their sacrifices
> will be accepted on my altar;
> for my house shall be called a house of prayer
> for all peoples. (Isaiah 56:6, 7)

Foreigners who bind themselves to the Lord by personal decision (cf. Ruth 1:16, 17; 2:11, 12; 2 Samuel 15:19–22) are received into deepest intimacy with him. Note the intimate progression in Isaiah 56—to the *place* where God is found ("my holy mountain"), to his *presence* ("my house of prayer"), to *acceptance* ("my altar").[5] This great welcome to foreigners was not a concession but a fulfillment of Solomon's prayer and what the Lord's house was always meant to be.

The scandal Jesus attacked and abolished by driving the corrupted clerics from the Court of the Gentiles and preaching, "My house shall be a house of prayer" was the exclusion of Gentiles from the grace of God. The reverse would soon be fully accomplished by the shed blood of Christ. Listen to Paul's glorious retrospect:

> Therefore remember that at one time you Gentiles in the flesh, called "the uncircumcision" by what is called the circumcision, which is made in the flesh by hands—remember that you were at that time separated from Christ, alienated from the commonwealth of Israel and strangers to the covenants of promise, having no hope and without God in the world. But now in Christ Jesus you who once were far off have been brought near by the blood of Christ. (Ephesians 2:11–13)

Jesus threw over the tables and drove out the perpetrators for two reasons: 1) the honor of his Father's name, and 2) the salvation of sinners. This is a glimpse of the zeal he has for our eternal souls!

Jesus' second brief quotation was from Jeremiah 7:11—"But you have made it a den of robbers" (v. 46b). This is a line from Jeremiah's famous temple speech that was a warning to the people of Israel who had embraced wickedness as a way of life but imagined that their being Israelites and possessing the temple would keep them safe. The prophet warned that destruction of the temple was coming.

To get the feel for this, we must imagine Jeremiah standing in front of the doors of Solomon's temple, with the huge freestanding pillars Jakin and Boaz (symbolizing God's power) on either side (cf. 1 Kings 7:15–22; 2 Chronicles 3:15–17). Jeremiah told approaching worshipers:

> Hear the word of the LORD, all you men of Judah who enter these gates to worship the LORD. Thus says the LORD of hosts, the God of Israel: Amend your ways and your deeds, and I will let you dwell in this place. Do not trust in these deceptive words: "This is the temple of the LORD, the temple of the LORD, the temple of the LORD." (Jeremiah 7:2b–4)

God's people must not think that confident musings like "This is the temple of the LORD. This is where God dwells" will save them if they do not repent. The prophet argued that safety was a delusion for those who had turned the temple into a robber's den:

> Will you steal, murder, commit adultery, swear falsely, make offerings to Baal, and go after other gods that you have not known, and then come and stand before me in this house, which is called by my name, and say, "We are delivered!"—only to go on doing all these abominations? Has this house, which is called by my name, become a den of robbers in your eyes? Behold, I myself have seen it, declares the LORD. (Jeremiah 7:9–11).

The robber-worshipers were standing in harm's way. In case they doubted it, he advised: "Go now to my place that was in Shiloh, where I made my name dwell at first, and see what I did to it because of the evil of my people Israel" (Jeremiah 7:12). Shiloh was where the tabernacle of God once was, but in Jeremiah's time it was completely obliterated![6]

So in his day Jesus graciously predicted the temple would be destroyed not only because it had failed to fulfill its function as a house of prayer, but because the people who worshiped there were corrupt. What fools we are if we imagine that our association with the things of God—thoughts like "This is the house of the LORD . . . These are God's people . . . This is the covenant community"—makes us safe. Paul's later warning to the Jews is a warning to every Christian:

> For no one is a Jew who is merely one outwardly, nor is circumcision outward and physical. But a Jew is one inwardly, and circumcision is a matter

> of the heart, by the Spirit, not by the letter. His praise is not from man but from God. (Romans 2:28, 29)

Jesus Appropriates the Temple (vv. 47, 48)

It was the hand of God the Father that enabled Jesus to cleanse the temple. What else would have kept the Roman garrison from intervening? We surmise that many of the people had for a long time been scandalized by the misuse of the temple. And it may be that the power brokers were given to such infighting that none could take charge and silence the meddlesome Messiah. Besides, outright opposition to Jesus might have been unpopular. But as we know, his enemies would finally find a way to do away with him, at least temporarily.

Whatever the reasons, what a glorious scene overtook the Court of the Gentiles. The tables were righted, but no money changed hands that day. The bawling livestock and fluttering birds were gone, and commerce ceased. For several days Jesus was sovereign in his Father's house. The temple was his.

The temple had had a significant place in the presentation of Jesus' messianic mission.[7] It had been in the Holy Place, next to the Holy of Holies, that the angel Gabriel announced the birth of the Messiah's forerunner, John the Baptist (1:11–20). It was in the courts of the temple that aged Simeon took baby Jesus in his arms and praised God (2:29–32). It was in the temple that Jesus first voiced his messianic consciousness: "Did you not know that I must be in my Father's house?" (2:49). It was on the highest point in the temple that Satan perversely tempted him to prematurely reveal his Messiahship (4:9).

And now, after cleansing the temple and purifying it, he possessed and taught there. As John Nolland suggests, "Jesus, in conscious fulfillment of Mal. 3:1–2, is coming as Lord to his temple to purge like a refiner's fire (notably in Luke, Jesus at this point 'takes possession' of the temple as the 'schoolroom' [perhaps royal chapel] where he teaches)."[8]

From here to the end of chapter 21 the temple is Jesus' pulpit, as we especially see in two passages. "And he was teaching daily in the temple. The chief priests and the scribes and the principal men of the people were seeking to destroy him, but they did not find anything they could do, for all the people were hanging on his words" (vv. 47, 48). "And every day he was teaching in the temple, but at night he went out and lodged on the mount called Olivet. And early in the morning all the people came to him in the temple to hear him" (21:37, 38).

His temporary appropriation of the temple and his exposition from within the temple's walls is one vast messianic act. His use of the temple was the last and ultimate glory of the temple, because it would be destroyed, just as Jesus would be destroyed, as Jesus later predicted to his disciples when they admired the temple: "As for these things that you see, the days will come when there will not be left here one stone upon another that will not be thrown down" (21:6). Sovereign in his Father's house, Jesus preached as prophet and judge.

Jesus Succeeds the Temple

Jesus would soon be rejected and ejected from the temple. He prophesied this even as he taught in the temple when he quoted an Old Testament passage concerning himself.

> The stone that the builders rejected
> has become the cornerstone. (20:17; cf. Psalm 118:22)

Jesus would become the cornerstone of God's temple, but not the temple of religious Judaism.

From the onset the temple had been the locus of God's dwelling amid his people, but Jesus' death and resurrection changed that. We see this when Jesus disputed with the Jews over his first cleansing of the temple early in his ministry, when he proposed as a sign of his authority, "Destroy this temple, and in three days I will raise it up" (John 2:19).

His opponents could only think of the bricks and mortar of Herod's temple. But John says he was referring to his own body, and his resurrection would give the disciples the key to what he meant (John 2:22).[9] So for the apostle John the true temple of God was the bodily presence of Jesus. John explains, "The Word became flesh and dwelt [made his dwelling] among us" (John 1:14). The literal Greek here is, "tabernacled among us." Jesus was the temple because he was God dwelling among us.[10]

Stephen, in his great sermon before the Sanhedrin prior to his stoning, spoke of the impermanence of both the tabernacle and the temple (Acts 7:44–47) and then declared, "Yet the Most High does not dwell in houses made by hands" (Acts 7:48).

For Paul, all believers become members of the heavenly temple by virtue of their importance in Christ—"In him you also are being built together into a dwelling place for God by the Spirit" (Ephesians 2:22, cf. Ephesians 2:14–21).

And Revelation 21:3 adds, "And I heard a loud voice from the throne saying, 'Behold, the dwelling place of God is with man. He will dwell with them, and they will be his people, and God himself will be with them as their God.'" Furthermore, "I saw no temple in the city, for its temple is the Lord God the Almighty and the Lamb. And the city has no need of sun or moon to shine on it, for the glory of God gives it light, and its lamp is the Lamb. By its light will the nations walk, and the kings of the earth will bring their glory into it" (Revelation 21:22–24).

Closing Reflections

Jesus, the Messiah and our Savior, is everything the temple with its gorgeous imagery and ascending sacrifices ever was or signified.

He is the *presence* of God. "For in him the whole fullness of deity dwells bodily" (Colossians 2:9). "He is the radiance of the glory of God and the exact imprint of his nature" (Hebrews 1:3a).

Himself God, he is the only *access* to God. "I am the way, and the truth, and the life. No one comes to the Father except through me" (John 14:6).

He is our *atoning sacrifice*. "He himself bore our sins in his body on the tree, that we might die to sin and live to righteousness. By his wounds you have been healed" (1 Peter 2:24).

He is our *mediator*. "We have this as a sure and steadfast anchor of the soul, a hope that enters into the inner place behind the curtain, where Jesus has gone as a forerunner on our behalf, having become a high priest forever after the order of Melchizedek" (Hebrews 6:19, 20).

He is our *standing*. "For I am sure that neither death nor life, nor angels nor rulers, nor things present nor things to come, nor powers, nor height nor depth, nor anything else in all creation, will be able to separate us from the love of God in Christ Jesus our Lord" (Romans 8:38, 39).

Jesus is everything! Jesus is everything! Jesus is everything! May this realization grow and grow until the reality bursts full in our hearts. He cleansed the temple for us. He commandeered the temple for us. He is the temple for us.

Jesus is everything!

86

The Authority of Jesus

LUKE 20:1–19

JESUS' ARRIVAL IN JERUSALEM was grounded upon two landmark displays of authority: first, his Triumphal Entry when he rode into Jerusalem on the colt of a donkey amid the joyous adulation of the crowds, and second, the cleansing of the temple when he drove out the money changers.

The Scriptural reality was then and still is that *the true temple* had come to the temple! Jesus' cleansing act signaled both the coming destruction of Herod's temple and Jesus' sovereign role as the temple of his people (cf. Revelation 21:22). Thus, for a few exalted days the temple sat in the temple and taught with marvelous authority, just as he had done from the very first when the people of Capernaum "were astonished at his teaching, for his word possessed authority" (4:32). Similarly, after the Sermon on the Mount, "the crowds were astonished at his teaching, for he was teaching them as one who had authority, and not as their scribes" (Matthew 7:28, 29).

Jesus' Authority Challenged (vv. 1–8)

Jesus' bold assertions would not go unchallenged. As soon as the chief priests, scribes, and elders (the principal elements of the Sanhedrin) could put their heads together, they swept down on Jesus. "One day, as Jesus was teaching the people in the temple and preaching the gospel, the chief priests and the scribes with the elders came up and said to him, 'Tell us by what authority you do these things, or who it is that gave you this authority.'" (vv. 1, 2).

Specifically, they wanted to know what authority lay behind his triumphal entry, the temple cleansing, and his right to teach. Derived authority was a major pillar in their system. The act of teaching was typically a tedious chain of authority citings—"R. Meir says . . . but R. Judah says . . . but R. Simeon also permits . . ." But Jesus did not teach this way. He *was* the authority! Moreover, they correctly assumed that no leader of Israel had been consulted about the propriety of Jesus' notorious activities, much less had given approval.

They hoped, therefore, that he would be forced to admit this and would thus begin to be discredited in the eyes of the people. Jesus saw the trap and with effortless brilliance put a counterquestion to them that they dared not answer:

> He answered them, "I also will ask you a question. Now tell me, was the baptism of John from heaven or from man?" And they discussed it with one another, saying, "If we say, 'From heaven,' he will say, 'Why did you not believe him?' But if we say, 'From man,' all the people will stone us to death, for they are convinced that John was a prophet." (vv. 3–6)

The problem was, John the Baptist was a popular hero. Vast throngs of people had received his baptism of repentance as they confessed their sins (cf. 3:3). But the leaders had refused. Earlier in this Gospel, Luke had explained:

> (When all the people heard this, and the tax collectors too, they declared God just, having been baptized with the baptism of John, but the Pharisees and the lawyers rejected the purpose of God for themselves, not having been baptized by him.) (7:29, 30)

Now, amid the throngs in the temple, it would not be healthy to deny that John's authority was from Heaven. But if they said his baptism was from Heaven, they would be admitting they had sinned in rejecting his baptism. Even worse, they would have to admit that Jesus was the Messiah because John had announced:

> Behold, the Lamb of God, who takes away the sin of the world! This is he of whom I said, "After me comes a man who ranks before me, because he was before me." I myself did not know him, but for this purpose I came baptizing with water, that he might be revealed to Israel." And John bore witness: "I saw the Spirit descend from heaven like a dove, and it remained on him. (John 1:29b–32; cf. Matthew 3:1–16; Luke 1:76; 3:16–18).

There was no way these leaders would even consider that Jesus was the Messiah. And as to their being sinners—no way! So, with Jesus' question hanging heavy, these self-assured, aristocratic know-it-alls became meekly agnostic: "So they answered that they did not know where it came from"

(v. 7). Liars! Cowards! If they truly believed Jesus was a fraud, it was their duty to tell the people, regardless of the personal cost. But to merely oppose him for self-centered reasons . . .

To these craven "leaders" Jesus said, "Neither will I tell you by what authority I do these things" (v. 8). This was another authoritative slam dunk by "gentle Jesus, meek and mild"—and in one of the temple courts!

Jesus' Parable on Rejected Authority (vv. 9–19)

It was not smart to go one on one with Jesus. It was not even smart to go ten on one or fifty on one with him. Team Sanhedrin was about to see some moves that would leave them speechless.

The first was a parable about rejected authority. Jesus' story employed an image that everyone readily understood—a vineyard representing Israel. Israel thought of itself as the vineyard of God, and a number of Scriptures make that allusion, including Psalm 80:8–16, Isaiah 27:2–5, Jeremiah 2:21, Ezekiel 19:10–14, and Hosea 10:1. But the most famous is the Song of the Vineyard in Isaiah 5:1–7. There Isaiah describes God's loving care for his vineyard ("The vineyard of the LORD of hosts is the house of Israel, and the men of Judah are his pleasant planting," v. 7a), his disappointment with the vineyard because it yielded only bad fruit, and finally his judgment of it—and his mourning over it.

The vineyard/Israel connection was so much a part of their national consciousness that the very temple in which Jesus was standing sported a richly carved grapevine, seventy cubits high, sculpted around the door that led from the porch to the Holy Place. The branches, tendrils, and leaves were of finest gold. The bunches of grapes hanging upon the golden limbs were costly jewels. Herod first placed the golden vine there, and rich and patriotic Jews would from time to time add to its embellishment. One contributed a new jeweled grape, another a leaf, and still another a cluster of the same precious materials. This vine had immense sacred meaning in the eyes of the Jews.[1]

Jesus had everyone's rapt attention and understanding as he began the parable of the vineyard keepers. But whereas Isaiah's Song of the Vineyard was about the failure of the vineyard, Jesus' parable would be about the failure of the *leaders* of the vineyard/Israel. And just to make sure they understood it, he made it an allegorized parable. The man = God the Father, the vineyard = Israel, the tenant farmers = Israel's leaders, the servants = the prophets, and the Son = Jesus.

Authority Entrusted

Jesus began easily enough: "A man planted a vineyard and let it out to tenants and went into another country for a long while" (v. 9b). Clearly, the meaning was that God established Israel as his vineyard, put it in charge of spiritual leaders (tenant farmers), and did not show his presence for a long time. The note that he was gone for "a long while" accounts for what took place. The longer God was gone, the more remote and powerless he seemed, and the tenant leaders began to assume that his absence was permanent.[2] An abusive attitude festered in the leaders that the vineyard/Israel was, in effect, their possession.

Authority Violated

With the passage of time, the leaders were capable of a terrible breach, which became apparent at harvesttime:

> When the time came, he sent a servant to the tenants, so that they would give him some of the fruit of the vineyard. But the tenants beat him and sent him away empty-handed. And he sent another servant. But they also beat and treated him shamefully, and sent him away empty-handed. And he sent yet a third. This one also they wounded and cast out. (vv. 10–12)

This triad of beatings summarizes Israel's wretched and uniform treatment of its prophets. Stephen, before his stoning, referenced this when he shouted to the Sanhedrin, "You stiff-necked people, uncircumcised in heart and ears, you always resist the Holy Spirit. As your fathers did, so do you. Which of the prophets did your fathers not persecute?" (Acts 7:51, 52a). Elijah was driven into the wilderness by the monarchy (1 Kings 19:1–5). Isaiah, according to tradition, was sawn asunder. Zechariah was stoned to death near the altar (2 Chronicles 24:21). John the Baptist was beheaded (Mark 6:14–29). The writer of Hebrews summarizes: "They were stoned, they were sawn in two, they were killed with the sword. They went about in skins of sheep and goats, destitute, afflicted, mistreated—of whom the world was not worthy—wandering about in deserts and mountains, and in dens and caves of the earth" (Hebrews 11:37, 38).

All this was done, said Jesus' parable, because Israel's leaders had become so sleekly successful and fat from the fruits of the vineyard and because they wanted to keep the bounty for themselves. God's prophets were such threats to the profitable status quo that they had to be removed.

Finally, the outrage in the parable peaks to the ultimate violence: "Then the owner of the vineyard said, 'What shall I do? I will send my beloved son;

perhaps they will respect him.' But when the tenants saw him, they said to themselves, 'This is the heir. Let us kill him, so that the inheritance may be ours.' And they threw him out of the vineyard and killed him" (vv. 13–15a).

The logic behind the homicide lay in the fact that it was possible for a tenant farmer to claim land for himself if the landlord was gone for three years, the presumption being that he had lost interest or was dead (M. *Baba Bathra* 3:1).[3] Possibly the appearance of the son gave them the notion that the father was dead and that if they killed the son, the vineyard would be theirs. The bottom line was, the leadership of Israel was portrayed (prophesied) as going as far as murder to maintain their authority.

And, of course, the son they would murder was Jesus. The father's soliloquy—"What shall I do? I will send my beloved son"—is a deliberate echo of God the Father's voice at Jesus' baptism: "You are my beloved Son" (3:22b). We must not miss the huge distinction that Jesus made between himself and the prophets and the religious leaders. The prophets were servants, but he was the Son. The leaders were tenants, but he was the heir and joint owner with the Father.[4] Their crime, which would take place within the week, was not just homicide but deicide—God-murder! Sovereign Jesus was the author of this death parable, his prophetic autobiography (cf. 9:21, 22). These are the temple's words in the temple.

This allegory is rooted in God's love. In the face of Israel's hard-heartedness, he persisted and persisted and persisted. One prophet after another was abused. "If I were God," cried Martin Luther, "and the world had treated me as it treated Him, I would kick the wretched thing to pieces." But instead of turning his back on the world, God continued sending servant after servant. Rebuffs, insults, beatings did not stop him. And finally he sent his Son. Spurgeon said, "If you reject him, he answers you with tears; if you wound him, he bleeds out cleansing; if you kill him, he dies to redeem; if you bury him, he rises again to bring resurrection. Jesus is love made manifest."[5]

Authorities Judged

But then there was also a terminal severity awaiting the unrepentant leaders. "What then will the owner of the vineyard do to them?" poses Jesus. The answer: "He will come and destroy those tenants and give the vineyard to others" (vv. 15b, 16a). This was partly realized in the national judgment that took place at the destruction of Jerusalem in A.D. 70. But the ultimate reference is to eternal judgment for Israel's leadership and the reassignment of leadership to a people who were mostly Gentile, as is recorded in the book of Acts.

There is eternal peril in resisting Christ's authority. The thought of this is probably not half as horrible to anyone who rejects Christ as it is to believers. Why? Because we believe it! The penalty of rejecting Jesus' authority is damnation, the wrath of the Lamb! Paul believed this, and he said in the context of the coming judgment, "Knowing the fear of the Lord, we persuade others" (2 Corinthians 5:11). Have you surrendered to Jesus' authority? Is he your Lord? Is this what your life says?

Jesus Cites Scriptures on Rejected Authority (vv. 16a–19)

Notwithstanding the crowd's wild enthusiasm and support for Jesus, the people could not imagine their chief priests, scribes, and elders (Team Sanhedrin) being displaced. "When they heard this, they said, 'Surely not!'" (v. 16b). In answer, Jesus took them to the Scriptures to show that the rejection of his authority, his subsequent exaltation, and judgment upon those who rejected him was clearly taught in the Old Testament. In each of the Scriptures he quoted, Jesus is the stone.

The Capstone

Nearly everyone recognized Psalm 118 as messianic, and that is why the Pharisees objected so strenuously when the crowd applied it to Jesus as he rode into Jerusalem as Zion's King. Luke 19:38, 39 records the people's quotation of Psalm 118:26 and the Pharisees' unhappy response: "'Blessed is the King who comes in the name of the Lord! Peace in heaven and glory in the highest!' And some of the Pharisees in the crowd said to him, 'Teacher, rebuke your disciples.'"

Now, after telling the parable, Jesus again directed them to Psalm 118, this time to verse 22 where the stone that becomes a capstone was understood to be the Messiah:[6] "But he looked directly at them and said, 'What then is this that is written: "The stone that the builders rejected has become the cornerstone"?'" (v. 17). The "builders" here were not stonemasons, but those who were the builders of Israel—the leaders of Israel.[7] "Builders" was a popular image for leaders in Jesus' day.[8] Psalm 118:22 prophesied that the leaders of Israel would reject the stone—the Messiah, Jesus, who subsequent to his rejection would become the capstone. Christ is the capstone in the eternal, spiritual temple of God.[9] He went from rejection to highest exaltation!

In the rejected stone becoming the capstone, we see Jesus symbolized in his rejection and crucifixion, but then through resurrection becoming the risen Lord. "Destroy this temple," Jesus had said, "and in three days I will raise it up" (John 2:19). Jesus is more than the key figure in God's new building—he is the building! Now that is authority!

The Judgment Stone

So authoritative is Jesus that he is the judgment stone for every person, culture, and nation of all history. Whether you fall on him or he falls on you, the result is the same—*destruction*: "Everyone who falls on that stone will be broken to pieces, and when it falls on anyone, it will crush him" (v. 18).

The first function of the stone (bringing disaster to those who fall over it) is derived from Isaiah 8:14, 15: "And he will become a sanctuary and a stone of offense and a rock of stumbling to both houses of Israel, a trap and a snare to the inhabitants of Jerusalem. And many shall stumble on it. They shall fall and be broken; they shall be snared and taken."

When Mary and Joseph brought baby Jesus into the temple for presentation, and aged Simeon scooped Jesus up in his arms, he knew not only that he had seen God's provision for salvation but also the stone of stumbling, because Luke records, "Simeon blessed them and said to Mary his mother, 'Behold, this child is appointed for the fall and rising of many in Israel, and for a sign that is opposed (and a sword will pierce through your own soul also), so that thoughts from many hearts may be revealed'" (2:34, 35). The falling is unbelief, rebellion against Jesus' authority, disbelief in his messianic work, rejection of his atoning work. God's Word says, "Everyone who falls on that stone will be broken to pieces," and therefore that truth is indisputable!

The corresponding function of the stone (falling on some in judgment—"when it falls on anyone, it will crush him") is derived from Daniel 2:34, which describes a supernaturally sculpted rock that smashes to pieces the statue of gold, silver, bronze, and clay (representative of the world's kingdoms) that Nebuchadnezzar saw in his dream.

> As you looked, a stone was cut out by no human hand, and it struck the image on its feet of iron and clay, and broke them in pieces. Then the iron, the clay, the bronze, the silver, and the gold, all together were broken in pieces, and became like the chaff of the summer threshing floors; and the wind carried them away, so that not a trace of them could be found. But the stone that struck the image became a great mountain and filled the whole earth. (Daniel 2:34, 35; cf. vv. 44, 45)

Our awesome, risen Lord will return as a great dreadnought to judge the world. And his authority cannot be ignored or avoided!

Our attitude toward Jesus is everything. We will either fall or rise according to our faith or lack of faith in him. If we fall over him, he will fall on us, bringing eternal destruction upon our souls.

Closing Reflections

Did Team Sanhedrin get the message? Oh yes! They recognized a spiritual slam dunk when they saw one. They understood the parable/allegory and understood its implications. They knew it threatened the giving of the vineyard/Israel to new leadership. They understood Jesus' application of some famous Old Testament passages.

They got it—but tragically they didn't believe it for a second. "The scribes and the chief priests sought to lay hands on him at that very hour, for they perceived that he had told this parable against them, but they feared the people" (v. 19). They set themselves to fulfill the parable to the letter—to throw him "out of the vineyard and [kill] him" (v. 15). Golgotha, where Jesus was crucified, was outside the city (cf. John 19:17; Hebrews 13:12, 13).

As the leaders of Israel stood in the temple, the great golden vine symbolizing Israel gleamed nearby in the light. Before them sat the Lord of the temple, the capstone to the entire structure. Around the temple spread the vineyard-clad slopes of Israel, pleading reinforcement for his words.

But despite all the reasons to believe they rejected him. Spiritually, they stepped into the gaping abyss below.

What about us? Jesus claims authority in every area of our lives.

Early in his ministry he displayed his *authority to forgive sin* when he said to the paralytic, "'But that you may know that the Son of Man has authority on earth to forgive sins'—he said to the man who was paralyzed—'I say to you, rise, pick up your bed and go home'" (5:24; cf. Matthew 9:6; Mark 2:10). He now forgives sin with ease because he bore the unfathomable burden of our sins on the cross.

He also has *authority to give spiritual life*. As John explained, "But to all who did receive him, who believed in his name, he gave the right [that is, authority] to become children of God, who were born, not of blood nor of the will of the flesh nor of the will of man, but of God" (John 1:12, 13).

He has *all authority*, and he passes it on to all who take his name to the world. Matthew's Gospel concludes, "And Jesus came and said to them, 'All authority in heaven and on earth has been given to me. Go therefore and make disciples of all nations, baptizing them in the name of the Father and of the Son and of the Holy Spirit, teaching them to observe all that I have commanded you. And behold, I am with you always, to the end of the age'" (Matthew 28:18–20). From the bottom of the sea to the end of the expanding universe, from the depth of Hell to the heights of Heaven, all authority belongs to Jesus!

What is Jesus to you? Is he an impediment? Or is he your Master? Your Lord? Your authority?

Are you rising or falling?

87

Caesar and God

LUKE 20:20–26

TWO OPPOSITE POWERS can bind people together. One is love, and the other is hatred. Of course, love is to be preferred by far. It is the glue of the Holy Trinity. It is God's ordained adhesive for the Church as well (cf. John 13:34, 35). Nevertheless, hatred, though fragmenting and destructive, serves as a diabolical superglue among otherwise diverse people.

Such was the case with the Pharisees and Herodians. There could hardly be two groups with such opposing outlooks. The Pharisees were nationalistic. They longed for the messianic kingdom and the overthrow of the Romans. The Herodians had sold themselves out to the Romans and served as their well-cared-for stooges. The Pharisees represented conservative Judaism, whereas the Herodians were liberal and syncretistic in their convictions. The Pharisees were (so to speak) right-wingers. The Herodians were left-wingers. The Pharisees represented cautious resistance to Rome, the Herodians wholesale accommodation. But they were cemented together by their mutual hatred for Jesus. The Pharisees hated him because he was disrupting their *religious* agenda, the Herodians because he threatened their *political* arrangements. They both wanted him dead.

Mark's parallel account about the conflict over Caesar and Christ reveals that through the auspices of the Sanhedrin these natural enemies were brought together and sent as spies to catch Jesus in his words (Mark 12:13). This was not the first time they had collaborated against Christ (cf. Mark 3:6). So as in the past, these natural enemies pumped their common venom back and forth in murderous solidarity. Jesus was a formidable opponent, they agreed. Look how he had just turned their questioning of his authority back on them with his counterquestion about the origin of John's baptism, a question that reduced them to helpless silence (20:1–8). Then he vilified them with the parable of the wicked vineyard keepers (20:9–16), and finally he assaulted them with his brilliant applications of messianic Old Testament Scriptures (20:17–19).

Yet, formidable as Jesus was, there had to be a way to defeat him. Approach after approach was suggested and tossed around. Very likely the deadly question regarding paying taxes to Caesar was concocted and kept ready for just the right moment.

An Attempted Entrapment (vv. 20–22)

They knew they would have to be extremely clever. Their deceit became an art form.

Opponents' Flattery

> So they watched him and sent spies, who pretended to be sincere, that they might catch him in something he said, so as to deliver him up to the authority and jurisdiction of the governor. So they asked him, "Teacher, we know that you speak and teach rightly, and show no partiality, but truly teach the way of God." (vv. 20, 21)

Their strategy was perfumed with flattery. Flattery is the reverse mirror-image of gossip. Gossip involves saying behind a person's back what you would never say to his face. Flattery is saying to a person's face what you would never say behind his back. How ingratiating their language was—like puffs from a perfume bottle: (squeeze) "Teacher, you're always right." (squeeze) "Preacher, you don't play favorites. You show us the true way." How sweet it seemed!

Like politicians, preachers are peculiarly susceptible to flattery. It is a professional titillation. A preacher, extravagantly flattered by a fawning parishioner, responds, "What you say is very kind, and of course, untrue. But tell me more about your thoughts . . ."

Of course, Jesus, *the* Preacher, smelled it for what it was—the stench of duplicity. Jesus well knew the wisdom of the Word: "A flattering mouth works ruin" (Proverbs 26:28). "A man who flatters his neighbor spreads a net for his feet" (Proverbs 29:5). "May the Lord cut off all flattering lips" (Psalm 12:3).

Jesus' Query

Jesus was ready for the question that followed their flattery: "Is it lawful for us to give tribute to Caesar, or not?" (v. 22). The question was meant to hang

Jesus over the dual horns of a dilemma, so he would impale himself on one or the other. The tax issue was explosive. When Jesus was a little boy, Roman taxation had been the cause of a serious revolt (cf. Josephus, *War* 2, 8, 1; *Antiquities* 18, 1, 1).[1] That revolt spawned the Zealot movement that would ultimately issue in the revolt of A.D. 70 and the destruction of Jerusalem.[2]

If Jesus answered "No, it is not right to give tribute to Caesar," he would be impaled on the horn of *arrest*. The Herodians would sprint to Pilate, and Jesus would be arrested as an insurrectionist and summarily executed. Rome tolerated diversity in religion but used cold steel to deal with political problems. But if Jesus answered, "Yes, it is right to give tribute to Caesar," he would be impaled on the horn of *alienation* from his people. The Pharisees would gleefully spread the message that he was a collaborationist, and the people would abandon him in disgust.

They were confident that they had him. They had imitated his brilliance by creating a dilemma question much like the one with which he had embarrassed them when he asked, "Now tell me, was the baptism of John from heaven or from man?" (20:3, 4). They had been bested then, but at least they were good learners. *Jesus, let's see you get out of this one!* they thought. His antagonists waited with bated breath—the Pharisees hoping for a yes they could herald to the nation, and the Herodians equally eager for a no that could be taken to the Romans. How delicious the prospect. How joyous their hatred!

An Astonishing Escape (vv. 23–26)

They could see no way Jesus could escape from this perfect dilemma.

The Coin

What followed was astonishing. "But he perceived their craftiness, and said to them, 'Show me a denarius'" (vv. 23, 24a). The denarius was a small silver coin weighing about 3.8 grams. One side bore the head of Caesar and the abbreviated inscription TI. CAESAR DIVI AVG. F. AVGVSTVS ("Tibirius Caesar, son of the divine Augustus, Augustus").[3] The denarius was the amount that had to be paid into the Roman fiscus (treasury) by all adult men and women just for the privilege of existing. It could only be paid with that coin bearing Caesar's image and inscription.

As our Lord regarded the coin, a hush fell upon the entire throng. The demand was sobering because for an upright Jew the image of Caesar on a coin was an abomination.[4] The inscription "divine Augustus" was considered a transgression of the second commandment against graven images (Exodus 20:4) and thus obvious blasphemy. Moreover, Jesus' asking that *they* show the coin implied that his upright detractors were carrying such a coin. The scene became very quiet indeed. His counterquestion broke the silence: "Whose likeness and inscription does it have?" (v. 24b). "Caesar's" (v. 25a) came the grudging reply. They had hoped to avoid using that name.

The Proverb

Jesus answered by creating a proverbial saying that has become one of the great "sound bites" of world history: "'Then render to Caesar the things that are Caesar's, and to God the things that are God's.' And they were not able in the presence of the people to catch him in what he said, but marveling at his answer they became silent" (vv. 25b, 26).

This was an astonishing answer then, just as it was in our day for a young American lawyer who saw it for the first time. Someone had given him a New Testament, and as he was reading it through he came to this account, which he read with great interest because he was involved in a similar type of legal dilemma. When he saw Jesus' answer, he was so astonished, he actually dropped his Bible, exclaiming, "That's the most amazing wisdom!"[5] The high hopes of those flattering, lying spies in Jesus' day fizzled to nothing. Now they were really silent.

The Abiding Demands of Jesus

Jesus' incredibly dexterous mind had given two answers, neither of which could be gainsaid.

A Transient Demand

They could not contest the first answer ("render to Caesar the things that are Caesar's") because ancient coins were actually understood to be the property of the person whose picture and inscription were on them. Who could object to giving to Caesar what was already his?

Today historians universally say that Jesus' words have been the single most influential political statement ever made. It has been decisive and determinative in shaping Western civilization. Paul's exposition of it in Romans 13:1–7 gave shape to the political world as we know it today (cf. 1 Peter 2:13–17).

Christ's words give the shape of the Christian's transient earthly allegiance: "Render to Caesar the things that are Caesar's." Implicit in Christ's teaching is that the state is a valid institution. Richard Halverson, past chaplain of the United States Senate, wrote:

> To be sure, men will abuse and misuse the institution of the State just as men because of sin have abused and misused every other institution in history including the Church of Jesus Christ; but this does not mean that the institution is bad or that it should be forsaken. It simply means that men are sinners and rebels in God's world, and this is the way they behave with good institutions. As a matter of fact, it is because of this very sin that there must be human government to maintain order in history until the final and ultimate rule of Jesus Christ is established. Human government is better than anarchy, and the Christian must recognize the "divine right" of the State.[6]

Jesus assumes the validity of the secular state and its demands, even when it is controlled by a man who thinks he is God. A poorly run state is better than no state at all. Not only is the state valid, but it also makes legitimate claims on our behavior. In Romans 13 Paul expands on Jesus' words, saying, "Let every person be subject to the governing authorities. For there is no authority except from God, and those that exist have been instituted by God" (Romans 13:1).

There are, of course, limits upon the authority of the state. There are also at least three situations in which a Christian must resist authority.

He or she must resist when asked to violate a command of God. The perfect example of this is found in Acts 4, 5, when the authorities arrested the disciples for preaching, summoned them before the Sanhedrin, and ordered them not to teach in the name of Jesus (cf. Acts 4:17–20). Of course, the disciples went right back to it and were arrested again. "'We strictly charged you not to teach in this name, yet here you have filled Jerusalem with your teaching, and you intend to bring this man's blood upon us.' But Peter and the apostles answered, 'We must obey God rather than men'" (Acts 5:28, 29). Our call to preach the gospel transcends the restrictions of government. The disciples went out and took up preaching where they had left off.

Christians must never violate a command of God, regardless of what the state says. This responsibility may take on very personal significance in these opening decades of what may be a hostile twenty-first century.

Christians must resist when asked to do an immoral act. The sexual significance of this is obvious and easiest to understand. But it also extends to ethical areas in which many are constantly asked to compromise—whether in the context of government service, business, home, community, or even church. Christians must never think it is all right to do something unethical, no matter how good the cause might seem or actually be!

Believers must never go against their Christian conscience to obey government. This may involve such diverse things as participation in questionable entertainment, working in institutions that perform abortions, or participating or not participating in war, as one's conscience dictates. It is imperative that Christians immerse themselves in God's Word so their consciences are radically Biblical.

But the main point is that, noting the exceptions just stated, Christians are called to a profound obedience to their government. Christians are to be markedly law abiding, even down to the traffic laws and paying taxes.

Our obedience is to be careful and prayerful. We must be like the conscience-stricken taxpayer who wrote the IRS, "Dear Sir, My conscience bothered me. Here is the $175 which I owe in back taxes." Then came a PS: "If my conscience still bothers me, I'll send the rest."

As Paul said to Timothy, "I urge that supplications, prayers, intercessions, and thanksgivings be made for all people, for kings and all who are in high positions, that we may lead a peaceful and quiet life, godly and dignified in every way" (1 Timothy 2:1, 2).

Our Lord says we must give to Caesar what is Caesar's. Are we doing so? Even more importantly, are we giving to God the things that are God's?

A Transcendent Demand

The utter brilliance of Jesus' statement detonates in its second half because by demanding that we are to give "to God the things that are God's," Jesus recognized only one God, thus transcending and obviating Caesar's claims to divinity. And because Jesus named God in the second half of the statement, the demands of God, the eternal ruler, subsume the petty reign of Caesar.

The famous New Testament scholar Adolf Deissmann of Heidelberg and Berlin put it this way: "That pregnant sentence does not present us with two equal magnitudes, Caesar and God: the second is clearly the superior of the first; the sense is, '"Render unto Caesar the things that are Caesar's; and *a fortiori*, unto God the things that are God's.'"[7]

Jesus put Caesar in his place, and again there was nothing that Jesus' enemies could do about it. On top of this, Jesus' demand to give "to God the things that are God's" implicitly declared God's claim to total ownership. The coin belonged to Caesar because it bore his image, and we are God's because we bear his image![8] "So God created man in his own image, in the image of God he created him; male and female he created them" (Genesis 1:27).

Jesus' Jewish listeners, with their mental listening habits, automatically made this connection. Every human is cast in the image of God, and the superscription on every human coin should remind us of God's ownership.

How do we bear God's image? In many beautiful ways, including our awareness of being. God said of himself, "I AM WHO I AM" (Exodus 3:14). This was a statement of his eternal existence. God had called Moses to return to Egypt to lead his people from bondage. Moses was terrified and objected. God answered, "I will be with you" (Exodus 3:12a). To which Moses asked, "If I come to the people of Israel and say to them, 'The God of your fathers has sent me to you,' and they ask me, 'What is his name?' what shall I say to them?" (Exodus 3:13). God then responded with one of the greatest revelations of sacred history: "'I AM WHO I AM.' And he said, 'Say this to the people of Israel, "I AM has sent me to you"'" (Exodus 3:14).

We cannot say, "I AM WHO I AM." We do not have an independent existence. But we alone in the order of things, created in the image of God, can and do say, "I am"—something no other earthly creature has ever thought, much less said. No turtle has ever said, "I am." No golden retriever has such a self-awareness.

Because we are in his image, we are aware of our being. We are also conscious that we are *eternal* beings. "He has put eternity into man's heart" (Ecclesiastes 3:11). Whoever is able to say to himself, "I am" will never know rest until he or she turns to God and says, "You are."

The fact that we bear his image also is evident in our moral sense, our awareness that there is right and wrong. We are able to perceive right, and we know that right is supreme. Even a distorted moral sense testifies to the image of God within us. The fact that we all bear the image of God means we are magnificent beings. The *imago Dei* is the basis for human dignity. The image of God in man means that we, though finite, are capable of immense things.

The fact that we are made in God's image is cause for the greatest optimism. "Because man is like God, it is possible for God to become like man."[9] That is, the incarnation rests on the fact that we were made in the image of God. Jesus, says the writer of the Hebrews, is "the exact imprint of his nature" (Hebrews 1:3), so that Jesus could say, "Whoever has seen me has seen the Father" (John 14:9). Yet, on the other hand, he was "made like his brothers in every respect" (Hebrews 2:17) except for sin that marred the divine image within them (Hebrews 4:15) because his image remained untarnished, perfect.

Because we all have been created in the image of God, because we are *persons* with a sense of existence and a sense of eternity and a sense of right and wrong, the incarnation of the second person of the Trinity was possible. The Person of God took on the person of man. Thus Jesus was able to deliver us.

And the final outcome of all this will be stupendous: "We shall be like him, because we shall see him as he is" (1 John 3:2). Paul writes of the effects of the resurrection: "As was the man of dust, so also are those who are of the dust, and as is the man of heaven, so also are those who are of heaven. Just as we have borne the image of the man of dust, we shall also bear the image of the man of heaven" (1 Corinthians 15:48, 49).

Closing Reflections

Christ's words suggest two questions for us. Whose image do we bear? The answer is self-evident: the image of God. The second question is, have we given "to God the things that are God's"? If (following the analogy of Caesar's due) we think God just wants our money, we are wrong. If we think it is our time and talents he asks for, we are wrong. If we think it is our nearest and dearest he wants, we are wrong.

He wants us! We must give God what is God's. We must give him our lives.

He will not settle for less than all. And if we resist him, we will not rest in this life.

> The souls that seek not God
> Fly thus, strangers and restless
> Through a drowned and lifeless world.[10]

Give to God what is God's. Give yourself!

> Christ, He requires still, wheresoe'er He comes,
> To feed, or lodge, to have the best of rooms:
> Give Him the choice; grant Him the nobler part
> Of all the house: the best of all's the heart.
>
> Robert Herrick (1591–1674)

88

Resurrection's Realities

LUKE 20:27–40

SEVERAL YEARS AGO the American Academy of Religion and the prestigious Society of Biblical Literature held joint meetings in Chicago. In one of the sessions Martin Marty, the Fairfax M. Cone Distinguished Service Professor of the History of Modern Christianity at the University of Chicago and the foremost authority and writer on religion in America, began his address to the more than four thousand attenders (representing a minimum of about twenty thousand years of PhD research) with these words: "Never in the history of Christianity has more brain power been assembled in one room—than when Jonathan Edwards sat alone in his study in Northampton!" The vast audience broke into loud laughter and applause. Martin Marty had cheerfully introduced healthy perspective to the august assembly and paid fair due to America's towering religious genius.

Some people are simply in a class by themselves. And never was this more true than with the God-man, Jesus. Jesus' sequential encounters with his religious enemies, the scribes and the Pharisees, as he taught in the temple were brilliant cases in point. His counterquestion "Now tell me, was the baptism of John from heaven or from man?" had rendered them embarrassingly agnostic—"They answered that they did not know where it came from" (20:3–8). Next, his deft exegesis and use of Old Testament texts about the messianic stone had established that he would be rejected, and then exalted, and would ultimately come in crushing judgment (cf. 20:17, 18). Then Jesus answered their deadly political question by asking for a coin and, after receiving a denarius bearing the image of Caesar, said, "Then render to Caesar the things that are Caesar's, and to God the things that are God's" (20:25).

So much for the attempts of the antagonistic scribes and Pharisees. Perhaps the Sadducees (v. 27) decided they would have to show their ignorant cronies how to put Jesus in his place.

The Sadducees had become a class unto themselves, based on their hereditary advantage as descendants of Zadok, those who had been granted the privilege of serving as priests after the return from the Babylonian captivity. These "Zadokites" formed the nucleus for the priesthood staffing the Jerusalem temple. During Jesus' time the Sadducees had a lock on the high-priestly line and were a tightly knit group of lay as well as priestly leaders.[1] Josephus described them as "well-to-do" (*Ant.* 13.10, 6 §298) and "men of the highest esteem" (*Ant.* 18.1, 4 §17). As such, they were thoroughly rooted in this world. The temple business of selling animals and exchanging money belonged to the Sadducees. Josephus said of the Sadducean high priest Ananias that he advanced in reputation because "he was able to supply them with money" (*Ant.* 20.205).

As a result the Sadducees had become thoroughgoing philosophical/theological materialists—a most convenient philosophy for the "haves." They did not believe in life after death, and they did not believe eternal judgment awaited anyone. Josephus explains, "As for the persistence of the soul, penalties in death's abode, and rewards, they do away with them" (*War* 2.8, 14 §165), and also, "the soul perishes along with the body" (*Ant.* 18. 1, 4 §16). This all produced a blatant denial of the resurrection. Later the Apostle Paul used this to divide his enemies when he stood before the Sanhedrin:

> Now when Paul perceived that one part were Sadducees and the other Pharisees, he cried out in the council, "Brothers, I am a Pharisee, a son of Pharisees. It is with respect to the hope and the resurrection of the dead that I am on trial." And when he had said this, a dissension arose between the Pharisees and the Sadducees, and the assembly was divided. For the Sadducees say that there is no resurrection, nor angel, nor spirit, but the Pharisees acknowledge them all. (Acts 23:6–8)

Swinburne's famous line, "That no life lives forever, That dead men rise up never" could have been written by a Sadducee. It was all so simple for the Sadducee—there was nothing beyond. In regard to practical living, they believed that God never intervened. They rejected divine providence, arguing that everything in life is up to man (*War* 2:164–165; *Ant.* 13.173).

The basis for their belief was a strict interpretation of the Torah (the Pentateuch), in which they claimed they could find no reference to resurrection. They rejected the resurrection witness of the non-Pentateuchal parts of the

Old Testament (for example, Job 19:26; Psalm 16:9–11; Isaiah 26:19) and remained closed-minded to any of the Pharisees' arguments to the contrary (cf. *Ant.* 13:297).

All in all, they were a tight little circle of mean-spirited, religious aristocrats—insular, patrician, heartless, philosophical materialists. Josephus says they were "indeed more heartless than any other of the Jews" (*Ant.* 18:17) and that "The Sadducees . . . are, even among themselves, rather boorish in their behavior, and in their intercourse with their peers are as rude as aliens" (*War* 2, 8.14).

Resurrection Ridiculed (vv. 27–33)

So the carbon-hearted, steel-souled, priestly elite approached Jesus, the country-bumpkin Galilean. It was time for the city boys to take charge. "Teacher, Moses wrote for us that if a man's brother dies, having a wife but no children, the man must take the widow and raise up offspring for his brother" (v. 28). At the core of their approach was the custom of levirate marriage that stipulated that if a man's married brother died childless, he must marry the widow (cf. Deuteronomy 25:5, 6). This was a custom that existed long before the Law, and its neglect created the scandal of Judah and Tamar (cf. Genesis 38:6–18). Levirate marriage also forms the background for the marriage of Ruth and Boaz (cf. Ruth 1:11–13; 4:1–22). Its purpose was to keep a family from dying out and to keep the family wealth intact.

Having introduced the levirate marriage regulation, the Sadducees then put forth a stock riddle they had used to embarrass and silence the resurrection-believing Pharisees. It granted, for argument's sake, their opponents' belief in resurrection after death: "Now there were seven brothers. The first took a wife, and died without children. And the second and the third took her, and likewise all seven left no children and died. Afterward the woman also died. In the resurrection, therefore, whose wife will the woman be? For the seven had her as wife" (vv. 29–33).

The argument was grotesque, the idea for which they may have borrowed from the apocryphal book of Tobit, which tells the bizarre story of a woman who married seven times only to have each husband strangled by a demon in the bedchamber on the wedding night (a kind of intertestamental Stephen King tale!—cf. Tobit 3:8, 15; 6:13; 7:11). However they came up with the idea, they now waited for Jesus' answer in leering confidence.

Assuming the presupposition that life in the resurrection is an exact counterpart to earthly life, the resurrected woman would be guilty of sevenfold incest—exponential and eternal carnality! Or if not, she must arbitrarily be designated the wife of one of the brothers. But which one? Or (and this is the answer the Sadducees hoped for) the entire notion of the resurrection must be absurd. As they waited in smug satisfaction, little did they suspect that they had met the supreme mind of the cosmos, the source of all truth.

Resurrection Defended (vv. 34–38)

A Theological Defense

The first part of Jesus' answer offered a corrective to the Sadducees' defective theology. Jesus' answer divided human existence into two ages, what he termed "this age" and "that age."

> And Jesus said to them, "The sons of this age marry and are given in marriage, but those who are considered worthy to attain to that age and to the resurrection from the dead neither marry nor are given in marriage, for they cannot die anymore, because they are equal to angels and are sons of God, being sons of the resurrection." (vv. 34–36)

No marriage in that age. Among the Jews of Jesus' day the resurrection was commonly understood to bring about an extension of the good life of this age in which one's delights would be multiplied.[2] This presumed continuity between this life and the next was not only wrong, but if unchecked could lead to tragic error—like that of the Mormons who believe that marriages sealed in the Mormon Temple are eternal.

In Mormon theology marriage becomes essential to one's development to becoming a god. Thus, if you in this life make good "celestial marriages" to multiple wives who in the next state produce many offspring, you will fill countless millions of worlds with your children as you ascend to divinity.[3] Oh, the tragedy of disregarding the words of Christ!

The fact that there is no marriage after the resurrection may be good news to some who have unhappy marriages, but if you are in love with your spouse and happy as I am, it seems sad. But the good news is, we will love each other more! We will be our sinless perfected selves at our ultimate best.

No death in that age. Marriage and procreation are of primary necessity in mortal, earthly life so human life can go on. But since there is no death in Heaven, marriage will be superseded. The quality of life is such in the coming age that death cannot touch it. No funeral knell will ever be heard in Heaven. There will be no gray hairs on the heads of immortals.

Exalted existence in that age. Jesus says three things about the immortality of the resurrected in verse 36: 1) "they are equal to angels," and 2) "they . . . are sons of God" and 3) "sons of the resurrection." These phrases are mutually descriptive of the eternal state of the redeemed—each phrase describes the other.

The first phrase ("they are equal to angels") is particularly revealing because it teaches us by comparison. We will be like the angels in beauty and strength. Our bodies will have powers of which we now have no conception. We will have an enlarged mental capacity and a greater spiritual range. We have been "sown in weakness" but will be "raised in power" (1 Corinthians 15:43).

Like the angels, our character will be faultless. The angels perfectly do God's will. We now pray, "Your will be done, on earth as it is in heaven," but there we will always do his will! There we will have no unrighteous desires, no covetous cravings, no proud thoughts, no depressions of spirit, no pulls of self-will, no inclinations to sin. Our habitual sins that afflict us so much will finally be gone.

Like the angels, we will perpetually worship God. They cast their crowns before him. Cherubim and seraphim veil their faces, but they all sing. And we will have even more than they to sing about because we have been redeemed.

> Never did angels taste above,
> Redeeming grace and dying love.[4]

We will have perpetual new songs. We will:

> Plunge into the Godhead's deepest sea,
> And bathe in his immensity.[5]

Joy will ever be our emotion because it is the emotion of Heaven. To be like angels is to be like God's children and children of the resurrection! Jesus obliterated the Sadducees' ridiculous theological notion of a crass earth-like continuity between this age and the next.

An Exegetical Defense

Jesus then added an exegetical corrective by going right to the heart of the Torah, where the Sadducees said the resurrection could not be found. The text is among the most famous in the Torah, the story of the burning bush, where God revealed himself to Moses and then commissioned him. Jesus said, "But that the dead are raised, even Moses showed, in the passage about the bush, where he calls the Lord the God of Abraham and the God of Isaac and the God of Jacob. Now he is not God of the dead, but of the living, for all live to him" (vv. 37, 38).

Jesus' logic was: God's statement (present tense), "I am the God of your father, the God of Abraham, the God of Isaac, and the God of Jacob" (Exodus 3:6) makes no sense if they are not presently alive. If someone comes to you and says, "I was your father's (or your mother's) friend," it may be because your parent is dead or there has been a change in their relationship. But if one comes to you and says, "I am your father's (or mother's) friend," that conveys two things: the existence of your parent and the ongoing relationship. So when God said, not "I was the God of Abraham, but I am," he was declaring not only Abraham's existence, but his ongoing relationship with him. To put it another way, if Abraham, Isaac, and Jacob are nothing but dust, God cannot now be their God! "Take that, Sadducees! It's right out of Book Two of the five books you claim to accept. Read your Scriptures! Do you get it, Sadducees?"

It was a powerful argument, and the logic is easy for us to appreciate. But Jesus' words actually conveyed something that was even more compelling to the ancient Hebrew mind. These three patriarchs—Abraham, Isaac, and Jacob—enjoyed a special covenant relationship with God that was so dynamic, so profound that it demanded a continued living relationship with God after death.[6]

The writer of Hebrews tells us the patriarchs knew that the covenant promises transcended earthly life and were eternal. Hebrews 11 says that Abraham "was looking forward to the city that has foundations, whose designer and builder is God. . . . These all died in faith, not having received the things promised, but having seen them and greeted them from afar, and having acknowledged that they were strangers and exiles on the earth" (Hebrews 11:10, 13). Verse 16 adds, "But as it is, they desire a better country, that is, a heavenly one." The eternal God does not covenant with temporal creatures who live only three score and ten years, then go out like a candle.[7]

Jesus' words were powerfully compelling to the Hebrew mind, and his concluding thrust, "He is not God of the dead, but of the living, for all live to him" (v. 38), must have caused a murmur in the crowd. If God is the God of the living, and since God said, long after the death of the patriarchs, that he is their God, then they must be alive, and *resurrection is coming!*

If the Sadducees had understood the nature of the miracle-working God of the Old Testament, they would not have doubted his power to raise the dead. There are numerous places in the Old Testament outside the Torah from which resurrection can clearly be understood.

> And many of those who sleep in the dust of the earth shall awake, some to everlasting life, and some to shame and everlasting contempt. And those

who are wise shall shine like the brightness of the sky above; and those who turn many to righteousness, like the stars forever and ever. (Daniel 12:2, 3)

Your dead shall live; their bodies shall rise.
You who dwell in the dust, awake and sing for joy!
For your dew is a dew of light,
and the earth will give birth to the dead. (Isaiah 26:19; cf. 25:8)

You guide me with your counsel,
and afterward you will receive me to glory.
(Psalm 73:24; cf. vv. 25–28)

Therefore my heart is glad, and my whole being rejoices;
my flesh also dwells secure.
For you will not abandon my soul to Sheol,
or let your holy one see corruption. (Psalm 16:9, 10)

For I know that my Redeemer lives,
and at the last he will stand upon the earth.
And after my skin has been thus destroyed,
yet in my flesh I shall see God,
whom I shall see for myself,
and my eyes shall behold, and not another.
My heart faints within me! (Job 19:25–27)

So the resurrection is clear in the Old Testament. But more specifically, the Torah itself bears evidence as well.

There is, of course, the creation account—God created everything *ex nihilo* and then specifically breathed life into the lifeless body of Adam (Genesis 2:7)—a protoresurrection.

Genesis 5:24 concludes, "Enoch walked with God, and he was not, for God took him." This is the language of rapture, not death. Nevertheless, it is a resurrection-like experience in which the mortal puts on the immortal (1 Corinthians 15:53).

When Abraham took Isaac up the mount to sacrifice him, he ordered his servant to "Stay here with the donkey; I and the boy will go over there and worship and come again to you" (Genesis 22:5). This implies belief in the resuscitating, if not resurrecting, power of God. The writer in Hebrews says that Abraham "considered that God was able even to raise him [Isaac] from the dead, from which, figuratively speaking, he did receive him back" (Hebrews 11:19).

Resurrection is in the Torah, and it rings out from the New Testament as well.

> For they cannot die anymore, because they are equal to angels and are sons of God, being sons of the resurrection. (v. 36)

> Now he is not God of the dead, but of the living, for all live to him. (v. 38)

> And he will send out his angels with a loud trumpet call, and they will gather his elect from the four winds, from one end of heaven to the other. (Matthew 24:31)

> Do not marvel at this, for an hour is coming when all who are in the tombs will hear his voice and come out. (John 5:28, 29)

> Jesus said to her, "I am the resurrection and the life. Whoever believes in me, though he die, yet shall he live." (John 11:25)

> So is it with the resurrection of the dead. What is sown is perishable; what is raised is imperishable. It is sown in dishonor; it is raised in glory. It is sown in weakness; it is raised in power. It is sown a natural body; it is raised a spiritual body. (1 Corinthians 15:42–44)

> For the Lord himself will descend from heaven with a cry of command, with the voice of an archangel, and with the sound of the trumpet of God. And the dead in Christ will rise first. Then we who are alive, who are left, will be caught up together with them in the clouds to meet the Lord in the air, and so we will always be with the Lord. Therefore encourage one another with these words. (1 Thessalonians 4:16–18)

Closing Reflections

Mark's parallel account says that Jesus commented during the dispute with the Sadducees, "Is this not the reason you are wrong, because you know neither the Scriptures nor the power of God?" (Mark 12:24). Truly the Sadducees did not know the Scriptures or God's power. What about us? Do we know the reality and relationship that the patriarchs perceived? If so, we can expect resurrection!

Knowing Christ, having an exchange of soul with him in New-Covenant terms, having a new heart (cf. Jeremiah 31:33; Hebrews 8:8–12), is a powerful argument for the life hereafter, and eventually resurrection. Something so real, so dynamic, so encompassing, so right, so energizing, so holy cannot end! The sense of resurrection is the signature of the regenerated soul!

Do you know the Scriptures? Do you know God's power? If so, he says, "I am your God," for he is not the God of the dead but of the living. And your soul bears his signature.

89

Son of David, David's Lord

LUKE 20:41–47

THE WESTMINSTER LARGER CATECHISM, a standard that has exercised considerable influence over the life of the Protestant church for centuries, states a principle rarely expressed in our age of relativism and fuzzy thinking—namely, that the same sin may be more terrible when committed by one person than another.

> Question 150.
> Are all transgressions of the law of God equally heinous in themselves, and in the sight of God?
> Answer.
> All transgressions of the law of God are not equally heinous; but some sins in themselves, and by reason of several aggravations are more heinous in the sight of God than others (cf. John 19:11; Ezekiel 8:6, 13, 15; 1 John 5:16; Psalm 78:17, 32, 56).
>
> Question 151.
> What are those aggravations that make some sins more heinous than others?

The Catechism gives a four-part answer that I will summarize.[1]

1. Some sins are more heinous than others due to the advantages of the offenders—"if they be of riper age, greater experience of grace, eminent for profession, gifts, place, office, guides to others, and whose example is likely to be followed by others" their sins are more terrible.
2. Some sins are more heinous than others due to the parties they directly offend. Blasphemy of God is heinous, but also sins "against any of the saints, particularly weak brethren, the souls of them, or any other, and the common good of all or many" are particularly heinous.

3. Some sins are more heinous than others due to the nature and quality of the sin—that is, if the sin is committed while fully knowing God's graces and requirements, and yet doing it anyway while admitting no reparation or fault.
4. Some sins are more heinous than others due to the "circumstances of time and place . . . if in public, or in the presence of others, who are thereby likely to be provoked or defiled."

From this we draw this sobering conclusion: sin committed by experienced Christians is greater than that of others because experienced Christians have 1) longer and therefore greater experiences of grace, 2) offend not only God, but in particular the souls of weaker brethren, 3) knowingly sin against God's requirements, and 4) defile others through the leadership roles that go to experienced Christians.

All this serves to emphasize that ministerial sins are particularly heinous. Sin in a pastor is more grievous and culpable than in those new to the faith. This is what in Jesus' day rendered the religious establishment (the scribes, Pharisees, and Sadducees) so terribly sinful and culpable. They had every advantage but chose sin. They defiled a whole nation. In Jesus' temple ministry as recorded in Luke these guilty leaders had repeatedly taken swings at Jesus—three to be exact. Jesus had brilliantly counterpunched—and they had stepped back (cf. v. 40). So now Jesus took the offensive, throwing a punch of his own and attacking them for two things—their disgraceful use of the Scriptures and their equally disgraceful lifestyle.

The Ignorance of the Teachers of the Law (vv. 41–44)

The specific objects of Jesus' counterattack were "the scribes," the Biblical scholars (20:39). One could always recognize a scribe because he wore a white linen robe with a long white fringe that reached to his feet. They were religious "power dressers"—ecclesiastical swans regally gliding among the mudhens of common humanity. Jeremias, the great New Testament authority, says in his book *Jerusalem in the Time of Jesus* that all the people rose respectfully when a scribe passed by, and that only tradesmen busy at their work were exempt. They were greeted respectfully as "Rabbi" ("my great one") or "Master" or "Father." When the wealthy gave feasts, scribes were considered necessary ornaments to adorn the meal. They were always given a place of honor, reclining to the right or left of the host. The teachers of the Law were honored above the aged, even above their own parents. When they came to the synagogue, they sat in the place of ultimate honor—facing the congregation with their backs against the chest holding the Torah, so all could see their pious visages.[2]

It was to these proud birds that Jesus now turned. His aggression and the subsequent exchange will tell us wonderful things about him and sobering things about his enemies—and as a result, much about ourselves.

Jesus went after the scribes by posing a theological puzzle that referenced their common belief, Scriptural teaching, and a logical question.

Common Belief

It was a commonly held belief that the Messiah would be a descendant of King David, and Jesus made reference to this in his opening question: "How can they say that the Christ is David's son?" (v. 41). There was no doubt that the Messiah would be a physical, hereditary descendant of David. Ample Scriptural evidence attested to this, like the famous words of Isaiah: "Of the increase of his government and of peace there will be no end, on the throne of David and over his kingdom" (Isaiah 9:7).[3] Luke's birth narratives assert Jesus' Davidic bloodline four separate times (1:27, 32, 69; 2:4). And Jesus received the title shouted from the lips of the blind Bartimaeus: "Jesus, Son of David, have mercy on me!" (18:38).

So there was no question about his Davidic descent. But what Jesus was referencing by his question was the unfortunately limited and earthbound conception of Messiah that was prevalent. The common view was that the son of David would be a gifted human leader who would bring in a new political kingdom like David of old. The problem was that the scribes had not read the messianic prophesies with spiritual eyes, because those prophecies demanded a suprahuman figure (cf. 2 Samuel 7:12–16).

Scriptural Teaching

After referencing the belief that Messiah must be in David's bloodline, Jesus called their attention to a radiant prophecy (Psalm 110, quoting the first verse) that indicated that Messiah must be suprahuman. "But [Jesus] said to them, 'How can they say that the Christ is David's son? For David himself says in the Book of Psalms, "The Lord said to my Lord, 'Sit at my right hand, until I make your enemies your footstool'"'" (vv. 41–43).

The person David refers to as "my Lord" is messianic, for the idiom used here for "my Lord" represents a way of speaking to or about a king.[4] He is David's Messiah-King, David's Lord. The Psalm's description of this king's mission makes it clear that he is Messiah.

Also, the opening two words of the Psalm ("The Lord") is literally "Yahweh"—"Yahweh says to my Lord [Messiah]: 'Sit at my right hand.'"

These insights help us see the full messianic understanding of Psalm 110:1–4:

> [Yahweh] says to my Lord [Messiah]:
> "Sit at my right hand,
> until I make your enemies your footstool."
>
> [Yahweh] sends forth from Zion
> your mighty [messianic] scepter.
> Rule [Messiah] in the midst of your enemies!
> Your people will offer themselves freely
> on the day of your power,
> in holy garments;
> from the womb of the morning,
> the dew of your youth will be yours.
> [Yahweh] has sworn
> and will not change his mind,
> "You [Messiah] are a priest forever
> after the order of Melchizedek."

Verse 4 asserts that Messiah will replace the old covenant's temporal Levitical priesthood with the eternal priesthood of Melchizedek. Thus the entire Psalm describes the Messiah as an eternal Priest-King.

The writers of the New Testament grasped this in a big way, making Psalm 110 one of the most quoted Old Testament texts. Verse 1 is not only quoted by Luke and the other Synoptists, but the writer of Hebrews says, "To which of the angels has he [God] ever said, 'Sit at my right hand until I make your enemies a footstool for your feet'?" (Hebrews 1:13). The apostle Peter referenced this Psalm in his great sermon at Pentecost: "For David did not ascend into the heavens, but he himself says, 'The Lord said to my Lord, "Sit at my right hand, until I make your enemies your footstool"'" (Acts 2:34–36).

Verse 4 is quoted prominently in Hebrews, where the writer says of Christ's eternal priesthood:

> And no one takes this honor for himself, but only when called by God, just as Aaron was.
>
> So also Christ did not exalt himself to be made a high priest, but was appointed by him who said to him,
>
> "You are my Son,
> today I have begotten you";

> as he says also in another place,
>
> > "You are a priest forever,
> > after the order of Melchizedek."
>
> In the days of his flesh, Jesus offered up prayers and supplications, with loud cries and tears, to him who was able to save him from death, and he was heard because of his reverence. Although he was a son, he learned obedience through what he suffered. And being made perfect, he became the source of eternal salvation to all who obey him, being designated by God a high priest after the order of Melchizedek. (Hebrews 5:4–10)

And again:

> This becomes even more evident when another priest arises in the likeness of Melchizedek, who has become a priest, not on the basis of a legal requirement concerning bodily descent, but by the power of an indestructible life. For it is witnessed of him, "You are a priest forever, after the order of Melchizedek." (Hebrews 7:15–17)
>
> And it was not without an oath. For those who formerly became priests were made such without an oath, but this one was made a priest with an oath by the one who said to him:
>
> > "The Lord has sworn
> > and will not change his mind,
> > 'You are a priest forever.'" (Hebrews 7:20, 21)

So we see that Psalm 110 was and is massively messianic.

A Logical Question

Jesus now asked a question based on two opposing realities: 1) the Messiah must be a son/descendant of David, and 2) King David called the Messiah his Lord. The question is: "David thus calls him Lord, so how is he his son?" (v. 44). Excellent question! Especially since in Hebrew patriarchal order it was beyond imagination that anyone would call his son Lord![5] The white-suited clergy had never thought of this. This was some puzzle.

What was the answer? There is no record in any of the Synoptic Gospels that Jesus bothered to explain it to the scribes that day. The answer lies in the two stages of Messiah's history. First, by birth he became the "son" of David. Second, by his death, resurrection, ascension, and position at God's right hand he reigns as David's "Lord." Peter gave the same answer at Pentecost:

> For David did not ascend into the heavens, but he himself says,
>
> "The Lord said to my Lord,
> 'Sit at my right hand,
> until I make your enemies your footstool.'"
>
> Let all the house of Israel therefore know for certain that God has made him both Lord and Christ, this Jesus whom you crucified. (Acts 2:34–36)

Jesus wanted to elevate their minds to a contemplation of the resurrection and its implications for Messiah as laid out in Psalm 110. In an exchange with these same teachers of the Law a day or two earlier, he had raised the resurrection idea with reference to the Old Testament's messianic stone prophecies, especially Psalm 118:22 ("The stone that the builders rejected has become the cornerstone," 20:17). And the immediate conflict with the Sadducees over the resurrection (20:27–40) was now apparently only a few minutes old.

It all would become so clear after his death, as Paul explained in his opening remarks to the Romans: "Concerning his Son, who was descended from David according to the flesh and was declared to be the Son of God in power according to the Spirit of holiness by his resurrection from the dead, Jesus Christ our Lord" (Romans 1:3, 4).

The problem with these scribes is that they had a studied ignorance of God's Word and a practiced inability to think beyond rabbinical traditions. They read the Word through a *political* lens that reduced the Messiah to a mere man on the analogy of David. We do the same with our lenses—an *economic* lens that turns every Scripture into advice for financial well-being, a *racial* lens that not too long ago edited out the Scriptural teaching on ethnic equality, a *feminist* lens that interprets and rejects the Scriptures as a tract for patriarchal dominance, a *postmodern* lens that subjectivizes Holy Scripture into "what it means to me." We all have our lenses, and our lenses blind us to the glory of God's Word. We must try to read God's Word for what it is. And we must humbly seek the Holy Spirit's help in bowing to what we read. The responsibility comes doubly upon teachers of the Word.

Today's evangelicals have abandoned "proof-texting" (i.e., lifting a text from its context to prove a doctrine), but now we are engaged in "text-proofing" (i.e., ignoring any text that does not fit our categories). This is wrong! A text is announced, the hearer sits back in anticipation, but disappointment sets in as the text is preached around, not engaged. Or pious evangelical themes are plucked that have nothing to do with the text. Or Biblical jargon anesthetizes the hearers.

We need to wake up. As William Willimon, Dean of the Chapel at Duke University, wrote in an article entitled "Been There, Preached That":

> Do you know how disillusioning it has been for me to realize that many of these self-proclaimed biblical preachers now sound more like liberal mainliners than liberal mainliners? . . . these "biblical preachers" were becoming "user friendly" and "inclusive," taking their homiletical cues from the "felt needs" of us "boomers" and "busters" rather than the excruciating demands of the Bible.
>
> I know why they do this. After all, we mainline-liberal-experiential-expressionists played this game before the conservative-evangelical-reformed-orthodox got there . . . reducing salvation to self-esteem, sin to maladjustment, church to group therapy, and Jesus to Dear Abby . . . is our chief means of perverting the biblical text.[6]

The Lifestyle of the Teachers of the Law (vv. 45–47)

With no answer being offered, Jesus went on to assault the scribes: "And in the hearing of all the people he said to his disciples, 'Beware of the scribes'" (vv. 45, 46a).

Their Pride

"[They] like to walk around in long robes, and love greetings in the marketplaces and the best seats in the synagogues and the places of honor at feasts" (v. 46b). Hearers could sense the disgust in Jesus' voice as he described his antagonists to their faces as gliding about in their resplendent power outfits, receiving the obeisance of the masses in the marketplace, sitting facing the congregation with other-world expressions on their faces, reading the Torah in sonorous Hebrew. Masters of ecclesiastical cant, they were proud lovers of self!

We have our Christian counterparts—always in a sweaty hurry, running from meeting to airport to news conference to talk shows—now pious, now good ole boys, now intellectuals. There is a mind-set that sees religious life as a kind of lordship—sitting in the honored seat, being the feted guest at luncheons, speaking at prominent gatherings, building monuments, collecting honoraria and titles. But watch out! As Joseph Bayly observed, "No person can foster the impression that he/she is great, then exalt a great God."[7]

Their Greed

"[They] devour widows' houses" (v. 47). They did this by taking payment from widows for legal aid even though such payments were prohibited, cheating inexperienced widows of their inheritance, living off the hospitality of lonely women, mismanaging widows' property who had dedicated themselves to service in the temple, and accepting money from the naive elderly in exchange for special prayer.[8]

Such clerics are everywhere. I remember one such preacher very clearly. I was wary from the beginning. I was put off by the gold chains he wore around his neck, and his satiny baby blue running suit, and his luxury car with the custom mint-green paint job and white leather landau top. His spiel matched his exterior. If any of us wanted things like his, it was "God's will." How so? Psalm 37:4 promises, "Delight yourself in the LORD, and he will give you the desires of your heart." If we were delighting in the Lord, we would have whatever we wanted! And by the way, all his desires were good because his old nature had died with Christ. Such thinking is mistaken and far astray from the true teachings of God's Word—an evangelical cover-up for greed.

Their Hypocrisy

When pride is paired with greed, prayers will be ostentatious—"and for a pretense make long prayers" (v. 47). Prayers like these are not from the heart, regardless of their length. Such intercessory offerings can come from the most eminent sources, like the archbishop who died of surprise when God answered him back!

Closing Reflections

Jesus ended his attack on the teachers with the deadly warning: "They will receive the greater condemnation" (v. 47b). The apostle James, the Lord's brother, wrote similarly, "Not many of you should become teachers, my brothers, for you know that we who teach will be judged with greater strictness" (James 3:1). If we claim to have a full knowledge of God's Word for his people, and further claim that we are charged to deliver it, we are more responsible to deliver it clearly and obey it. I, by virtue of my professed calling and study of God's Word and having had the privilege of receiving more knowledge of God's Word than many Christians, will undergo a stricter judgment. Increased responsibility means increased accountability.

Jesus, concluding the parable of the foolish manager, said, "Everyone to whom much was given, of him much will be required, and from him to whom they entrusted much, they will demand the more" (12:48). This is what the Westminster Confession has laid out with such precision in Question 151 concerning "The aggravations that make some sins more heinous than others." Are we of riper age and greater experience of grace? Have we served as guides to others? Have our sins not only offended God but caused weaker brethren to stumble? Have our sins had public effects and so scandalized others? If so, they are particularly grievous.

The solution for us all is to immerse ourselves in the truth of God's Word and to obey it. The truth the scribes missed, as they read God's Word through their *political* lens, was that the Messiah was and is much more than an earthly deliverer. He is indeed the Son of David. David's blood was in his veins. He is the second and greater David. But he is also Lord. He is the eternal King who resides at the right hand of God: "The LORD says to my Lord: 'Sit at my right hand, until I make your enemies your footstool'" (Psalm 110:1). He is also the eternal Priest, by divine oath: "The LORD has sworn and will not change his mind, 'You are a priest forever after the order of Melchizedek'" (Psalm 110:4).

> This makes Jesus the guarantor of a better covenant. The former priests were many in number, because they were prevented by death from continuing in office, but he holds his priesthood permanently, because he continues forever. Consequently, he is able to save to the uttermost those who draw near to God through him, since he always lives to make intercession for them. (Hebrews 7:22–25)

This is what God's Word teaches pure and simple. Jesus is supreme for salvation. And such a Savior demands a lifestyle that glorifies him. He demands everything—our status, all our wealth, all our prayer and devotion!

90

Money's Eloquence

LUKE 21:1–4

WHEN WLADZIU VALENTINO DIED, entrepreneurs leased the Los Angeles Convention Center to display the twenty-five thousand to thirty thousand objects left from his estate. This was an event for the well-heeled of LA. Why? Mr. Valentino was better known as Liberace. Thousands of people willingly paid six dollars each for the privilege of viewing the lavish remains of Liberace's materialism. This was followed by an auction at Christie's where another admission charge of ten dollars was levied in an attempt to lessen the size of the enthusiastic crowd. In a frenzied auction, a king's ransom was paid by the bejeweled crowd for the eight warehouses of Liberace's belongings.[1]

At that incredible event money literally spoke, as money was the only speech acknowledged by the auctioneer. It also spoke in other ways, for it eloquently revealed volumes about the heart of the deceased entertainer and the hearts of the competing bidders.

"Money speaks" is more than a cliché. It is an axiom of the heart. Jesus said, "For where your treasure is, there your heart will be also" (Matthew 6:21). During the last decade Americans spent over $180 billion dollars per year on gambling, fifteen times more than it gave to its churches.[2] That is a tragic declaration of the heart of this country. Money speaks!

Aware of this, the Lord chose the temple treasury for his departing shot at his detractors before leaving the temple for good. Money—giving—reveals the state of the heart as few other things can. Thus Jesus chose this setting to contrast the phony righteousness of the religious leaders, who "devour widows' houses and for a pretense make long prayers" (20:47), with true devotion to God as exemplified in the life of one poor widow.

"Jesus looked up and saw the rich putting their gifts into the offering box" (v. 1). The treasury where they placed their offerings consisted of thirteen brass treasure chests called trumpets because they were shaped like inverted horns, narrow at the top and enlarged at the bottom.[3] According to the *Mishnah*, each of the chests bore inscriptions designating what the offerings were for: "'New Shekel dues,' 'Old Shekel dues,' 'Bird offerings,' 'Young birds for the whole offering,' 'Wood,' 'Frankincense,' 'Gold for the Mercy-seat,' and, on six of them 'Freewill-offerings.'"[4]

Because of the Passover the treasury was a most busy place as both local inhabitants and pilgrims crowded past the thirteen *shopharoth* (chests) and inserted their offerings into the narrow brass mouths made shiny by the constant friction of worshipers' hands. Here amidst the noisy din Jesus could easily observe the givers without drawing attention to himself. Have you ever sat at an airport or a shopping mall and watched the people over your newspaper or coffee? Such times can be most intriguing.

Jesus was observant. He not only noted people's actions but assessed their motives. Neither the widow (the principal focus of Jesus' attention) nor the rest of the people had any idea they were being watched. We too are being watched in our least conscious moments. As George MacDonald said: "When we feel as if God is nowhere, He is watching over us with an eternal consciousness, above and beyond our every hope and fear" (cf. Psalm 139:1–6). What a staggering moment it is for a worshiping soul when one first awakes to this reality. Jesus really is watching us. As Hannah said in her prayer, the Lord is weighing our actions (1 Samuel 2:3). And later David prayed, "You discern my thoughts from afar" (Psalm 139:2). Every action is important, and every action is seen by the One to whom we will give account.

Jesus Observes (vv. 1, 2)

What did Jesus see as he watched the worshipers make their deposits? Initially he saw "the rich putting their gifts into the offering box" (v. 1). We should not assume that he disapproved of all the offerings of the wealthy. Very likely there were some who had noble motivations.

But Jesus also saw much that displeased him. Public giving, such as this setting required, promotes self-conscious ostentation—like the man who stood up in a meeting where they were taking subscriptions for donations and said, "I want to give $100—anonymously."[5] What would happen to our great national charities today without celebrity benefits, or published subscribers' lists, or bronze plaques, or pictures of donors holding three-foot-long checks or standing beside crippled children?

The huge Passover crowds and the public display made possible by the thirteen trumpets created an opportunity for outrageous preening and posturing. Imagine the hush that came over the crowd when a notable person approached, perhaps with an offering too heavy to carry himself, and the audible gasp as the shekels crashed into the brass trumpets. Can you see the pious countenances of the rich givers, their satisfied, restrained "see if you can top that" expressions?

The rich, fashionable religious world of Jerusalem and the Jewish *diaspora* paraded before Jesus' eyes. It was a world of souls in peril. The ability to give on a scale that is not possible for others can produce a delusion of superiority and spiritual safety—"I have done what others cannot—so my soul is superior and my eternity secure." Such people can develop a sense of intrinsic goodness, when in actuality they are evil.

But as Jesus watched, he noticed something that made his heart applaud: "He saw a poor widow put in two small copper coins" (v. 2). Jesus, and anyone else who happened to see her, knew she was a poverty-stricken widow because widows wore distinctive clothing, in her case undoubtedly worn and tattered. The life of widows in Biblical times was proverbially difficult.[6] This woman's beauty of soul makes us wonder where she lived and how, and what had been her suffering. Her offering was two coins, so small they were called *lepta* (literally, "peeled" or "fine," the idea being a tiny, thin coin).[7] The miniature *lepton* was worth only one four-hundredth of a shekel, or about one-eighth of a cent.[8] The two *lepta* represented barely anything—like today's pennies that most do not even bother to pick up.

She undoubtedly approached the trumpets quietly, almost stealthily, head bowed, hoping to draw no attention to herself. Though she did not know Jesus was watching, she knew God saw her, and that was who she came to please. Seen in the context of the grasping greed of the scribes who were devouring widows' houses, her gift unwittingly slammed the religious establishment.

Her motivation for such giving could only be love. There is no other explanation. She (not the religious leaders) was living out the *Shema*, loving God with all she was and had. When she slipped the two coins into the mouth of the "trumpet," they fell inaudibly against the shekels of the rich. The temple was, in effect, no richer, but she was immeasurably poorer, for she had given all!

J. A. Bengel, an early eighteenth-century commentator, beautifully noted that she gave "two—one of which the widow might have retained."[9] *She gave everything!* She was silently saying to God, "I love you. Here's my heart, my life. It's not much, but it's all I have."

The Passover crowd had been oohing and aahing over the generosity of the rich, and Jesus had remained unmoved. But when the widow passed by, though he sat still, inwardly he was on his feet applauding. This widow was a rare flower in a desert of official devotion, and her beauty made his heart rejoice.[10]

Jesus' Conclusions (vv. 3, 4)

"And he said, 'Truly, I tell you, this poor widow has put in more than all of them. For they all contributed out of their abundance, but she out of her poverty put in all she had to live on'" (vv. 3, 4). Jesus held in his hands the balance scales of eternity. On one side he emptied all the contents of the thirteen trumpets—the shekels, the denarii, the heavy gold and silver. On the other side he placed the two minuscule copper coins. And the massive load of the rich gave way to the eternal weight of the widow's tiny offerings.

John Calvin correctly saw Jesus' words as double edged, encouraging to those who have little, but a sobering exhortation to those with much. He remarks:

> The lesson is useful in two ways. The Lord encourages the poor, who appear to lack the means of doing well, not to doubt that they testify to their enthusiasm for Him even with a slender contribution. If they consecrate themselves, their offering which appears mean and trivial will be no less precious than if they had offered all the treasures of Croesus. On the other hand, those who have a richer supply and stand out for their large giving are told that it is not enough if their generosity far exceeds the commoners and the underprivileged, for with God it rates less for a rich man to give a moderate sum from a large mass, than for a poor man to exhaust himself in paying out something very small.[11]

Realizing that Jesus' commendation cuts both ways calls for some soul-searching observations.

First, *when it comes to giving, the posture of our hearts makes all the difference*. When I write a check to the IRS, that agency does not care at all about my heart's attitude. It does not care whether I give willingly or grudgingly, lovingly or hatefully, joyfully or sadly. All the IRS is interested in is the bottom line. Just pay up! Not so with the Lord! The world sees the quantity, but the Lord sees quality. "If I give away all I have, and if I deliver up my body to be burned, but have not love, I gain nothing" (1 Corinthians 13:3). But if I give a penny with the widow's heart, it is great gain to me and to God.

> Not what we give, but what we share,
> For the gift without the giver is bare;
> Who gives himself with his alms feeds three,
> Himself, his hungering neighbour, and Me.[12]

God weighs our motivations. This truth is either a terror or a comfort. Which way does it strike you?

Second, *giving that pleases God is giving that costs us*. We must give in such a way that we go without something we would like to hang on to—travels forgone, clothing and cars that wait another season, pleasures put off. Joseph Parker of City Temple made this unflinching declaration: "The gold of affluence which is given because it is not needed, God hurls to the bottomless pit; but the copper tinged with blood He lifts and kisses into the gold of eternity."[13]

Centuries earlier, King David said it all in response to Araunah the Jebusite's generous offer of his threshing floor as a site on which to build an altar to God, as well as the animals to sacrifice there. David answered, "No, but I will buy it from you for a price. I will not offer burnt offerings to the Lord my God that cost me nothing" (2 Samuel 24:24). Giving that costs us is giving that pleases God.

C. S. Lewis offers this sage advice:

> I do not believe one can settle how much we ought to give. I am afraid the only safe rule is to give more than we can spare. In other words, if our expenditure on comforts, luxuries, amusements, etc., is up to the standard common among those with the same income as our own, we are probably giving away too little. If our charities do not at all pinch or hamper us, I should say they are too small. There ought to be things we should like to do and cannot do because our charitable expenditure excludes them.[14]

Third, *God can do great things with tiny offerings*. Those two pennies (totaling together a quarter of a cent), given quietly with the widow's motive, have produced more for the kingdom in the intervening two thousand years than all the other gifts presented that Passover Week. Down through the ages those two little coins have been multiplied into billions and billions for God's work as humble people have been liberated to give from their little or their much. The Lord has converted those two coins into a perennial wealth of instruction and motivation for his Church.

If there is love and sacrifice on the part of the giver, there will be spiritual power in the gift. In this respect we can say that what the church needs is not larger gifts, but gifts given with the sacrificial attitude of the poor widow. Jesus meant to encourage all of us with his commendation of this godly woman.

Fourth, *at the Judgment, Christ will square his accounts*. There is no evidence that the woman ever knew what Jesus thought of her gift. There is no evidence that she ever became a prosperous woman in this life. In fact, since the final judgment and the ultimate bestowing of eternal rewards is still future for the whole Church, there is every possibility that she does not know to this very day what we know about her. The Judgment is going to reveal her work—the architecture of a beautiful soul adorned with gold, silver, and precious stones (cf. 1 Corinthians 3:11–14).

The memory of the widow's giving stayed with Jesus as he went from the temple to the judgment hall and to the Mount of Calvary. She, to use his words, "put in all she had to live on," and he gave all he had too, even his life! Someday he is going to say to her, "I saw what you did!" The crown of our widow-sister will be glorious!

Fifth, *God is sublimely "equal opportunity*." There is no advantage to the poor or the rich, to the unlettered or the educated, to the unknown or known in the matter of giving. Billy Graham has no advantage over the humblest believer, and vice versa. The questions are: How do we give? Grudgingly or willingly? Does our giving cost us anything? What will the Judgment reveal? What is our attitude when we are not being watched?

Closing Reflections

Is it possible for the Church to love and give like the widow? Has it ever done so? The history of the apostolic church answers with a resounding yes! Paul told the Corinthians:

> We want you to know, brothers, about the grace of God that has been given among the churches of Macedonia, for in a severe test of affliction, their abundance of joy and their extreme poverty have overflowed in a wealth of generosity on their part. For they gave according to their means, as I can testify, and beyond their means, of their own accord, begging us earnestly for the favor of taking part in the relief of the saints—and this, not as we expected, but they gave themselves first to the Lord and then by the will of God to us. (2 Corinthians 8:1–5)

God does not want our money. He wants us. And yet we cannot give ourselves to him apart from our money. It is true that money speaks. It tells us where our hearts are. What does our giving say about us?

Jesus sits across from the treasury of every church and watches. What does he see in your church? In your life?

91

The Olivet Discourse

LUKE 21:5–38

ACCORDING TO EARLE ELLIS, the venerable New Testament scholar, the so-called Olivet Discourse, recorded in the Gospels of Matthew, Mark, and Luke, "has been the subject of more scholarly debate than perhaps any other passage in the Gospels."[1] This is because of the rich nature of the prophetic language that Jesus used (virtually every verse has multiple allusions to both the Old Testament and to other Jewish apocalyptic literature), and because of the nature of prophecy itself—multiple fulfillments culminating in a final fulfillment. The fact is, we have yet to find a scholar who can perfectly unravel the knotty problems of the Olivet Discourse. Study of it requires a proper humility and a willingness to admit that we do not have all the answers. We must mind Chesterton's dictum: "It is only the fool who tries to get the heavens inside his head, and not unnaturally his head bursts. The wise man is content to get his head inside the heavens." In this chapter we will try the latter.

During the preceding days Jesus had made his triumphal entry into Jerusalem, cleansed the temple, and entered into several debates with the religious establishment that he repeatedly won. Then, by exalting the poor widow and her offering, he passed judgment on the religious leadership of Israel. Now Jesus left the temple for good. The cross awaited him. And the Olivet Discourse formed a fitting bridge to Jesus' final days. It was his final address, his farewell prophecy.

The occasion for the discourse was his disciples' admiration of the temple. "And while some were speaking of the temple, how it was adorned with noble stones and offerings, he said . . ." (v. 5). Mark's account is more specific: "And as he came out of the temple, one of his disciples said to him,

'Look, Teacher, what wonderful stones and what wonderful buildings!'" (Mark 13:1).

There was no hyperbole in this. The temple was considered one of the great wonders of the Roman world. It had been under reconstruction for forty-six years (cf. John 2:20) and was nearing completion, which would come in AD 63, a mere seven years before it was destroyed.[2] Its spectacular location on Mt. Moriah gave it an imposing dominance over ancient Jerusalem. From a distance it looked like a mountain of gold, because its nine massive gates[3] and because much of its exterior was plated with gold and silver and jeweled sculptures such as the famous grapevine bearing a cluster the size of a man. Josephus wrote:

> The exterior of the building wanted nothing that could astound either mind or eye. For, being covered on all sides with massive plates of gold, the sun was no sooner up than it radiated so fiery a flash that persons straining to look at it were compelled to avert their eyes, as from the solar rays. To approaching strangers it appeared from a distance like a snow-clad mountain; for all that was not overlaid with gold was of purest white. From its summit protruded sharp golden spikes to prevent birds from settling upon and polluting the roof. Some of the stones in the building were forty-five cubits in length, five in height and six in breadth.[4]
>
> The incredible size of the foundation's stones, almost the size of boxcars,[5] was breathtaking.

The temple was indeed a wonder. But if the disciples hoped to raise Jesus' spirit by their admiration, they failed. Jesus' unexpected response left them flabbergasted: "As for these things that you see, the days will come when there will not be left here one stone upon another that will not be thrown down" (v. 6). Jesus' words were tragically true. When Titus first conquered Jerusalem, he ordered that the temple be preserved, but it was gutted by a fire set by one of his soldiers. As a result, Titus "ordered the whole city and temple to be razed to the ground,"[6] a task especially carried out in respect to the temple as soldiers driven by avarice pulled the stones apart in an attempt to reclaim the melted gold.

Mark's Gospel tells us that the inner circle of disciples was so riveted by this astounding prophecy that they sought a private audience with Jesus that providentially took place on the Mount of Olives (Mark 13:3). Rising one hundred fifty feet higher than Jerusalem, the mountain afforded a dramatic view of the temple. So there, with the ivory and gold temple lying below them, the disciples asked Jesus the questions that precipitated the Olivet Discourse: "Teacher, when will these things be, and what will be the sign when these things are about to take place?" (v. 7). We need to keep this stunning scene and these questions before us as we proceed. What will be the *times* and the *signs* that will precede the destruction of the temple? We should also remember that it was on this very mount that the *Shekinah* glory had departed from the temple six hundred years before (Ezekiel 11:22–25). Also, it would be upon the Mount of Olives that the Lord would return (Zechariah 14:6).

Jesus would answer their questions, but some of his replies would go far beyond their initial inquiries, instructing his Church about his return. We will also see that Jesus was not interested in giving date-setting details but in encouraging his own to be steadfast and faithful until he returns. Jesus spoke pastorally.

The Period Prior to the Temple's Destruction (vv. 8–24)

Historical Insight and Perspective

Jesus began by giving them insight regarding the tumultuous events in history and life—namely, they were not to be deceived by false teachers or continued wars or catastrophes or cosmic signs into believing that the end had come.

- *False teachers:* "And he said, 'See that you are not led astray. For many will come in my name, saying, "I am he!" and, "The time is at hand!" Do not go after them'" (v. 8).
- *Wars:* "'And when you hear of wars and tumults, do not be terrified, for these things must first take place, but the end will not be at once.' Then he said to them, 'Nation will rise against nation, and kingdom against kingdom'" (vv. 9, 10).
- *Catastrophes:* "There will be great earthquakes, and in various places famines and pestilences" (v. 11a).
- *Cosmic signs:* "And there will be terrors and great signs from heaven" (v. 11b).

It is easy to think the end has arrived when we personally experience such things. But wars, for example, have always been with us. Will Durant wrote: "War is one of the constants of history, and has not diminished with civilization and democracy. In the last 3,421 years of recorded history only 268 have seen no war."[7] And that is not even taking into account unrecorded history! The Jews suffered from Rome's interior wars and the deadly internal struggles in Palestine.

When you or I are touched by war, it is so easy to think apocalyptically—"Surely the end of the world is here!" This is how the Russians felt in the Napoleonic wars, and how many believers felt in Germany in 1945.

This is all very natural, but sometimes our thinking becomes absurd, like one man who told me that the return of the Lord must be imminent because our national debt is out of hand. This is narcissistic, self-centered, money-clip eschatology!

It is tempting to regard natural catastrophes the same way. During the years between Christ's death and the destruction of the temple, there was a terrible earthquake in Laodicea, Vesuvius buried Pompeii, and there was a famine in Rome itself. These events did not mean the end of all things. Neither would it mean the end if California fell into the sea and you could sail to Hawaii from Las Vegas! But sadly, with the rise of every war and earthquake there comes an increase of false christs who say they have the answer.

Toss in "terrors and great signs from heaven" and people can be led into incredible absurdities. The convergence of Holy Week, the vernal equinox, a partial lunar eclipse, and the extraordinary Hale-Bopp comet lighting the night skies provided the architecture of apocalypse for the Heaven's Gate cult.[8]

We must never allow ourselves to interpret the tumultuous events of life as meaning it is all over. These things are the result of man's sin and will continue to the end of time. "See that you are not led astray," says Jesus (v. 8).

Personal Insight

Jesus then gave his followers further insight into what would befall them in the natural course of following him:

> But before all this they will lay their hands on you and persecute you, delivering you up to the synagogues and prisons, and you will be brought before kings and governors for my name's sake. This will be your opportunity to bear witness. Settle it therefore in your minds not to meditate beforehand how to answer, for I will give you a mouth and wisdom, which none of your adversaries will be able to withstand or contradict. You will be delivered up even by parents and brothers and relatives and friends, and some of you they will put to death. You will be hated by all for my name's sake. (vv. 12–17)

His disciples would face religious persecution—ironically, at the hands of the local Sanhedrins and synagogues that should have been havens for them. They would also suffer under the secular state and bear powerful witness. This persecution would mean their forced dispersion, and thus the gospel would be preached to the Gentiles, fulfilling prophecy.

Persecuted disciples would dazzle their interrogators with their wisdom—for example, Peter and John before the Sanhedrin (Acts 4:13), Stephen before the Sanhedrin (Acts 6:10; 7:2–54), Paul before Agrippa (Acts 25:13—26:32), and Martin Niemoller before Hitler.

They would also experience intense personal hatred. The radical commitment that the gospel demands can disrupt even the most natural and sacred human relationships, and still does. Announce your conversion in a Muslim country or in a hard-line Communist country and Jesus' words take on a terrible reality. Jesus said on another occasion:

> Do not think that I have come to bring peace to the earth. I have not come to bring peace, but a sword. For I have come to set a man against his father, and a daughter against her mother, and a daughter-in-law against her mother-in-law. And a person's enemies will be those of his own household. (Matthew 10:34–36)

In saying, "You will be hated by all," Jesus meant people in general. Christians sometimes receive favorable press, but they should never forget that the same media powers can quickly turn the world against them. Jesus said, "If the world hates you, know that it has hated me before it hated you. If you were of the world, the world would love you as its own; but because you are not of the world, but I chose you out of the world, therefore the world hates you" (John 15:18, 19). Any follower of Christ who follows his example will suffer persecution. But that person will also know, along with Paul, what it means to "share his sufferings" (Philippians 3:10), a state that Jesus said was "blessed" (Matthew 5:10, 11). Though some of Jesus' followers would die, Jesus told them, "But not a hair of your head will perish" (v. 18; cf. 12:4, 7; 1 Samuel 14:45; 2 Samuel 14:11; 1 Kings 1:52). This was the case for Stephen (Acts 7:54–60) and James the son of Zebedee (Acts 12:1, 2), because though their bodies died, their souls lived on in Heaven with God forever.

Jesus ended this part of his warning by saying, "By your endurance you will gain your lives" (v. 19). Rather than being blown away by persecution (religious, secular, or domestic), we are to persevere, to endure, to stand firm. The Christian life is not a sprint but a marathon. And by refusing to give up, we will continue to enjoy the eternal life we cannot lose. Over the years I have been repeatedly surprised by acquaintances who have dropped by the wayside. Jesus' warning is painfully relevant. Regardless of one's theological construct, a warning given by the apostle John must be taken to heart: "They went out from us, but they were not of us; for if they had been of us, they would have continued with us. But they went out, that it might become plain that they all are not of us" (1 John 2:19). True believers keep on going through thick and thin. We should pray that we will finish well.

That I should end before I finish or
Finish, but not well.
That I should stain your honor, shame your name,
Grieve your loving heart.
Few, they tell me, finish well. . . .
Lord, let me get home before dark.[9]

Eleventh-Hour Insight

Having imparted insight for living the "normal" Christian life in tumultuous times, Jesus gave insight for living in the eleventh hour before the temple's destruction. He began, "But when you see Jerusalem surrounded by armies, then know that its desolation has come near" (v. 20). To understand the word "desolation," we have to examine the parallel passage in Mark 13:14—"the abomination of desolation." This is a quotation from Daniel 9:27 and 11:31 that described a coming figure who would desecrate the temple and abolish the daily sacrifices there. It meant an abomination so detestable that it would cause the temple to be abandoned by the people of God and provoke desolation.

This had happened one hundred fifty years earlier when the Seleucid King Antiochus IV Epiphanes conquered Jerusalem and attempted to Hellenize the people, forbidding them to circumcise their children (1 Maccabees 1:60) or offer Levitical sacrifices (1 Maccabees 1:45), and forcing them to sacrifice swine (1 Maccabees 1:47). In the words of the writer of 1 Maccabees, "On the fifteenth day of Chislev [possibly December] in the one hundred and forty-fifth year, they erected a desolating sacrilege upon the altar of burnt offering" (1 Maccabees 1:54). It was a statue of Zeus and probably an image of Antiochus himself!

The sense of Jesus' warning in verse 20—"But when you see Jerusalem surrounded by armies, then know that its desolation has come near"—was: when the Roman legions begin to encircle the city, a new desolation is about to take place. His warning was to get out of the city before the encirclement was complete.

> Then let those who are in Judea flee to the mountains, and let those who are inside the city depart, and let not those who are out in the country enter it, for these are days of vengeance, to fulfill all that is written. Alas for women who are pregnant and for those who are nursing infants in those days! For there will be great distress upon the earth and wrath against this people. They will fall by the edge of the sword and be led captive among all nations, and Jerusalem will be trampled underfoot by the Gentiles, until the times of the Gentiles are fulfilled. (vv. 21–24)

The fourth-century historian Eusebius records that Christians gave heed to this warning:

> The people of the church in Jerusalem were commanded by an oracle given by revelation before the war to those in the city . . . to depart and dwell in one of the cities of Perea which they called Pella. To it those who believed on Christ migrated from Jerusalem, that when holy men had altogether deserted the royal capital of the Jews and the whole land of Judea, the judgment of God might at last overtake them for all their crimes against the Christ and his Apostles, and all that generation of the wicked be utterly blotted out from among men.[10]

Josephus describes the people as leaving the city "as swimmers deserting a sinking ship," an image that accords well with Jesus' command to leave everything behind.

The horror that Jesus predicted for Jerusalem came with the fall of the temple and is a matter of historical fact. The roofs were thronged with famished women with babes in arms, and the alleys with corpses of the elderly. Children and young people swollen from starvation "roamed like phantoms through the market-places and collapsed wherever their doom overtook them." But there was no lamenting or wailing, because famine had strangled their emotions. Jerusalem could not bury all the bodies, so they were flung over the wall. The silence was broken only by the laughter of robbers stripping the bodies.[11]

Though "the times of the Gentiles" began with Jesus' death when the veil of the temple was torn from top to bottom and with his subsequent resurrection, the symbol of this was the Gentiles' trampling Jerusalem when they destroyed the temple. According to Romans 11, this era is a time of evangelizing the Gentiles:

> A partial hardening has come upon Israel, until the fullness of the Gentiles has come in. And in this way all Israel will be saved, as it is written,
>
> "The Deliverer will come from Zion,
> he will banish ungodliness from Jacob";
> "and this will be my covenant with them
> when I take away their sins."
>
> As regards the gospel, they are enemies for your sake. But as regards election, they are beloved for the sake of their forefathers. For the gifts and the calling of God are irrevocable. (Romans 11:25b–29)

The times of the Gentiles will end with the return of Christ, and that was the subject to which Christ turned as he closed his Olivet Discourse.

Christ's Second Coming (vv. 25–33)

Portents of His Return

Perhaps Jesus lifted his eyes from the temple and looked beyond as he continued speaking:

> And there will be signs in sun and moon and stars, and on the earth distress of nations in perplexity because of the roaring of the sea and the waves, people fainting with fear and with foreboding of what is coming on the world. For the powers of the heavens will be shaken. And then they will see the Son of Man coming in a cloud with power and great glory. Now when these things begin to take place, straighten up and raise your heads, because your redemption is drawing near. (vv. 25–28)

Virtually everything Christ said here is from Old Testament material too vast to mine in one chapter or even in a whole book—passages like Joel 2:30, 31: "And I will show wonders in the heavens and on the earth, blood and fire and columns of smoke. The sun shall be turned to darkness, and the moon to blood, before the great and awesome day of the LORD comes" (cf. Isaiah 13:10; 34:4; Ezekiel 32:7; Haggai 2:6, 21; and in the New Testament, 2 Peter 3:10–13; Revelation 8:7–13). The end will feature unnatural disasters. Cosmic portents—quakes in the heavens, terrestrial catastrophes, tidal disturbances, chaos—all these are part of his final appearing. This is apocalyptic language for violent change in the natural order and in human life.[12] The result will be widespread despair and apprehension.

Then amid this universal confusion, Jesus will come in shining clouds of glory. He is the awesome "son of man" of Daniel 7:13, 14 to whom the Ancient of Days has given ultimate authority—"And to him was given dominion and glory and a kingdom, that all peoples, nations, and languages should serve him; his dominion is an everlasting dominion, which shall not pass away, and his kingdom one that shall not be destroyed" (Daniel 7:14). David Gooding writes:

> As surely as men standing in Jerusalem once saw him slowly descending the Mount of Olives and then ascending the opposite hill into the city, so surely shall the world one day see the Son of man descending the heavens. Not then shall he come as the meek and lowly: he shall come with power and great glory. Not then shall he come riding on an ass: he shall come in a cloud, the emblematic carriage of Deity. Not then shall he have to borrow

> a donkey: then his advance preparations shall be the roaring of the sea and the shaking of the powers of the heavens.[13]

> Lo, He comes with clouds descending
> Once for favored sinners slain;
> Thousand thousand saints attending
> Swell the triumph of His train:
> Alleluia! Alleluia!
> God appears on earth to reign.
>
> Charles Wesley

This is our dream—and it will be our reality! Jesus advises, "Now when these things begin to take place, straighten up and raise your heads, because your redemption is drawing near" (v. 28).

When will this happen?

The Time of the Second Coming

Regarding when, Jesus gave a miniparable:

> Look at the fig tree, and all the trees. As soon as they come out in leaf, you see for yourselves and know that the summer is already near. So also, when you see these things taking place, you know that the kingdom of God is near. Truly, I say to you, this generation will not pass away until all has taken place. Heaven and earth will pass away, but my words will not pass away. (vv. 29–33)

When the final cosmic portents happen, there will be no time. The generation of the end signs will see all this fulfilled.[14]

Jesus closed his prophecy with the declaration, "Heaven and earth will pass away, but my words will not pass away" (v. 33). Jesus placed his words on equal footing with the Old Testament Scriptures. Therefore we must understand that as surely as every word spoken by Jesus concerning the destruction of Jerusalem came true—that Jerusalem would be surrounded by armies—that they must flee the dreadful days—that they would otherwise be deported—that Jerusalem would be trampled by the Gentiles—that one stone would not be left on another—as surely as all of this took place, *just as sure is his second coming!* Every word will be fulfilled!

Advice Concerning Christ's Return

What is Jesus' advice to us in light of his second coming?

> But watch yourselves lest your hearts be weighed down with dissipation and drunkenness and cares of this life, and that day come upon you

> suddenly like a trap. For it will come upon all who dwell on the face of the whole earth. But stay awake at all times, praying that you may have strength to escape all these things that are going to take place, and to stand before the Son of Man. (vv. 34–36)

This call to vigilance is universal. It is meant for us today. Jesus issued the command from the Mount of Olives, the official site of his return. Will his coming be today, or in the next decade? Possibly . . .

We must not be numbed by all the earthbound, secular voices that say life will go on and on. It will not! All of life is moving toward him. "He is the image of the invisible God, the firstborn of all creation. For by him all things were created, in heaven and on earth, visible and invisible, whether thrones or dominions or rulers or authorities—all things were created through him and for him" (Colossians 1:15, 16).

We are to keep looking up. "For the grace of God has appeared . . . training us to renounce ungodliness and worldly passions, and to live self-controlled, upright, and godly lives in the present age, waiting for our blessed hope, the appearing of the glory of our great God and Savior Jesus Christ" (Titus 2:11–13). "Beloved, we are God's children now, and what we will be has not yet appeared; but we know that when he appears we shall be like him, because we shall see him as he is. And everyone who thus hopes in him purifies himself as he is pure" (1 John 3:2, 3).

Keep looking up!

92

The Night without a Morning

LUKE 22:1–6

> In my dream I was carried away to a great and high mountain where I saw that great city: the goal of all our hopes and desires, the end of our salvation, the Holy City of God, the New Jerusalem. Around the city, as around the earthly Jerusalem, there ran a wall great and high. There were twelve gates, north, south, east, and west; and every gate was a pearl, and at every gate stood one of the Great Angels. On the gates were written the names of the Twelve Tribes of the Children of Israel, from Reuben to Benjamin. The wall of the city stood upon twelve massive foundation stones, and on each stone was the name of one of the Twelve Apostles of the Lamb; and as I walked around the city, thrilling with joy and rapture at the glory and splendor of it, I read the names written upon the twelve stones—Peter, James, John, and all the others. But one name was missing. I looked in vain for that name, either on the twelve gates or on the twelve foundation stones—and that name was Judas.

So dreamed the celebrated Presbyterian preacher Clarence Edward Macartney in his *Great Nights of the Bible*.[1]

Luke now focuses on this missing name as a prelude to the Last Supper, from which Judas would step out into eternal darkness. We will look first at his tragic decision to betray Jesus as Luke recorded it, and then John's record of his exit into the night.

Judas' Tragic Decision (vv. 1–6)

Murderous Resolve

The authorities had hardened in their deadly determination to eliminate Jesus when he cleansed the temple and began to teach in its porticoes. "And he was teaching daily in the temple. The chief priests and the scribes and the principal men of the people were seeking to destroy him, but they did not find anything they could do, for all the people were hanging on his words" (19:47, 48). Any chance of a lessening of their murderous resolve disappeared when Jesus told the parable of the vineyard keepers in which he predicted they would kill him. Luke says, "The scribes and the chief priests sought to lay hands on him at that very hour, for they perceived that he had told this parable against them, but they feared the people" (20:19). Their hearts were cold granite.

The Jews' religious calendar added desperation to their deadly resolution: "Now the Feast of Unleavened Bread drew near, which is called the Passover. And the chief priests and the scribes were seeking how to put him to death, for they feared the people" (vv. 1, 2). The prospect of several hundred thousand pilgrims descending upon Jerusalem made it imperative that something be done lest Jesus influence them and garner an even bigger following. And the enemy of our souls had an idea he knew they would like.

"Then Satan entered into Judas called Iscariot, who was of the number of the twelve" (v. 3). An apostle became one with their devilish hearts! Of course, Satan had actively opposed Jesus throughout his ministry (cf. 4:33–37, 41; 8:26–38; 9:37–43; 10:18, 19; 11:14–28). But he was also especially active at what he discerned to be opportune times, such as his temptation of Christ in the wilderness at the beginning of our Lord's ministry (4:1–13). At that time, we read, "And when the devil had ended every temptation, he departed from him until an opportune time" (4:13). Now was the time for another major onslaught.

Luke's statement that "Satan entered into Judas" does not suggest demon possession as such but rather influence. The same idea was clearly stated by Peter to Ananias, the husband of Sapphira: "Ananias, why has Satan filled your heart to lie to the Holy Spirit?" (Acts 5:3). Ananias was under the sway of Satan. The apostle John also describes what happened to Judas in the upper room: "Then after he had taken the morsel, Satan entered into him" (John 13:27). Judas' heart was under the devil's influence. But on each occasion Satan could not have entered into Judas unless Judas opened the door.

Judas did this for money. When he had earlier objected to Mary's anointing Jesus with the expensive perfume, "He said this, not because he cared about the poor, but because he was a thief, and having charge of the moneybag he used to help himself to what was put into it" (John 12:6).

A Murderous Contract

"He [Judas] went away and conferred with the chief priests and officers how he might betray him to them. And they were glad, and agreed to give him money. So he consented and sought an opportunity to betray him to them in the absence of a crowd" (vv. 4–6). The blood money he accepted was the delight of the damned, the fellowship of Hell and eternal darkness.

It would all be so easy. As an insider, Judas knew Jesus' every move. He would choose a time when the crowds slept and Jesus was isolated. At such a time Jesus would be as vulnerable as a fawn among a pack of wild dogs. The religious leaders and their new coconspirator excitedly made preparations for the kill.

Jesus Reaches Out (John 13:18–30)

We turn now to John's account of the exchange between Jesus and Judas at the Last Supper. John's introduction sets the stage:

> Now before the Feast of the Passover, when Jesus knew that his hour had come to depart out of this world to the Father, having loved his own who were in the world, he loved them to the end. During supper, when the devil had already put it into the heart of Judas Iscariot, Simon's son, to betray him. . . . (John 13:1, 2)

Jesus knew what Judas was up to but, as with the other disciples, would show Judas that "he loved them to the end" as he reached out to his sinking soul.

Jesus Initiates

As we come to the dialogue of sorts between Jesus and Judas, the evening is rather late. Remarkable teaching has taken place. Perhaps Jesus lowered his voice and spoke with careful deliberation when he said, "I am not speaking of all of you; I know whom I have chosen. But the Scripture will be fulfilled, 'He who ate my bread has lifted his heel against me'" (John 13:18).

He was quoting Psalm 41:9—"Even my close friend in whom I trusted, who ate my bread, has lifted his heel against me." Tellingly, this is a reference to Ahithophel, King David's friend who so grievously betrayed him. As the Jewish commentator A. Cohen explains, "If the Psalm mirrors an incident in David's life, the faithless friend must have been Ahithophel."[2] The expression "has lifted his heel against me" describes the lifting of a horse's foot and delivering a deadly kick[3]—just as Judas was about to deliver. Jesus' correlation between Judas and Ahithophel would show brilliantly in retrospect, because Ahithophel's end was: "He set his house in order and hanged himself" (2 Samuel 17:23). Jesus was saying, "My friends, there is an Ahithophel in our midst, and he is reclining at this table, sharing my bread."

With the shocking truth out, Jesus continued, "'I am telling you this now, before it takes place, that when it does take place you may believe that I am he. Truly, truly, I say to you, whoever receives the one I send receives me, and whoever receives me receives the one who sent me.' After saying these things, Jesus was troubled in his spirit, and testified, 'Truly, truly, I say to you, one of you will betray me'" (John 13:19–21). The Master's voice must have given way. He apparently choked up, because "troubled" is the same word used by Jesus when he said, "Now is my soul troubled" as he contemplated his mission and death (John 12:27). His anguish was visible.[4]

All the disciples could see his emotion, but they did not guess it was over Judas. But Judas saw it all from a few feet away in the flickering candlelight. Perhaps his cold heart skipped a beat. But the murderous determination remained. Jesus was demonstrating a remarkable truth. On the eve of the cross, just a few hours before the nails would go into his body, Jesus' soul was troubled, not for himself, but for another. And not just for anyone, but for the one who was going to deliver him to death!

Thou, Thou my Jesus, after me
Didst reach Thine arms out dying,
For my sake sufferedst nails and lance,
Mocked and marred countenance,
Sorrows passing number
Sweat and care and cumber,
Yea and death, and this for me,
And Thou couldest see me sinning.

Francis Xavier, trans. Gerard Manley Hopkins
O Deus Ego Amo Te

Judas Ignores

The Eleven were in corporate shock—"The disciples looked at one another, uncertain of whom he spoke" (John 13:22). Matthew's Gospel records, "And they were very sorrowful and began to say to him one after another, 'Is it I, Lord?'" (Matthew 26:22). Judas, as he reclined close by Jesus, played the game, coolly mouthing the same question—"Is it I, Rabbi?"

No one had the slightest inkling that it was Judas. Again we see the Lord's loving heart because in a tight group like the Twelve, if Jesus had cast the slightest suspicion Judas' way, the other disciples would have been on him like a dog on a bone! In my family a raised eyebrow can mean ten pages single spaced! A pause or a voice inflection are letters written large. But

Jesus had revealed nothing of Judas' character because he was after Judas' soul. There was no hint of rejection, lest Judas turn away.

> Then I, why should not I love Thee:
> Jesus so much in love with me?
>
> Francis Xavier, trans. Gerard Manley Hopkins
> *O Deus Ego Amo Te*

Jesus Persists

The atmosphere of the upper room was charged with Jesus' persistence.

When Jesus washed the disciples' feet, he had lovingly taken each of Judas' feet in his hands. And in the process of washing Peter's feet, he had remarked to them all, "And you are clean, but not every one of you" (John 13:10). It was a loving arrow aimed at Judas' waning conscience. His words hurt Judas, but not enough.

The very seating arrangement bore the architecture of grace, because from left to right it was Judas, Jesus, and John, as evidenced by the private conversation going on between the three in John 13:25–28. As they reclined, Jesus' head was at Judas' breast, and John's head was at Jesus' breast too. Jesus had given Judas the left-hand side, the place of honor. It appears that Jesus probably said something like "Judas, I want to have a talk with you. Sit at the place of honor to my left tonight."[5]

> The disciples looked at one another, uncertain of whom he spoke. One of his disciples, whom Jesus loved, was reclining at table at Jesus' side, so Simon Peter motioned to him to ask Jesus of whom he was speaking. (John 13:22–24)

The intimate seating arrangement made this so easy. John had only to lean back a few inches and say, "Lord, who is it?" (John 13:25). To which Jesus quietly responded, "'It is he to whom I will give this morsel of bread when I have dipped it.' So when he had dipped the morsel, he gave it to Judas, the son of Simon Iscariot" (John 13:26).

The offer of the dipped morsel was both a rich, symbolic custom and a powerful, ultimate appeal. In Palestinian culture the act of the host's taking a morsel from the table, dipping it in the common dish, and offering it to another was a gesture of honor or friendship.[6] A thousand years before, when Boaz invited his future wife Ruth to come dine with him, he said, "'Come here, that you may eat of the bread and dip your piece of bread in the vinegar' . . . and he served her" (Ruth 2:14 NASB). Jesus was saying, as he extended the dipped bread, "Judas, here is my friendship. It's not too late." Judas took it but did not turn back to the Master. So the door slammed shut, and he locked it with his own hand.

Judas Departs (vv. 27–30)

Incredibly, Judas walked!

> Then after he had taken the morsel, Satan entered into him. Jesus said to him, 'What you are going to do, do quickly.' Now no one at the table knew why he said this to him. Some thought that, because Judas had the moneybag, Jesus was telling him, 'Buy what we need for the feast,' or that he should give something to the poor. So, after receiving the morsel of bread, he immediately went out. And it was night. (John 13:27–30)

For Judas, it was the night that would know no morning. How utterly alone he was. Judas skulked about and concealed himself as Jesus and his men crossed the Kidron and climbed toward Gethsemane. He had the information he needed. As he hurried through the dark streets to the chief priests and elders, his last glimpse of Jesus would be by torchlight as Jesus was taken away.

Matthew supplies further details of that night:[7]

> When morning came, all the chief priests and the elders of the people took counsel against Jesus to put him to death. And they bound him and led him away and delivered him over to Pilate the governor. Then when Judas, his betrayer, saw that Jesus was condemned, he changed his mind and brought back the thirty pieces of silver to the chief priests and the elders, saying, "I have sinned by betraying innocent blood." They said, "What is that to us? See to it yourself." And throwing down the pieces of silver into the temple, he departed, and he went and hanged himself. (Matthew 27:1–5)

Macartney again uses his imagination:

> The night is passing, but the day has not yet come. Far to the east, over the mountains of Moab, there is just the faintest intimation of the coming day. The huge walls of Jerusalem and the towers and pinnacles of the Temple are emerging from the shadows of the night. In the half darkness and half light I can make out a solitary figure coming down the winding road from the wall of Jerusalem towards the gorge of the Kidron. On the bridge over the brook he pauses for a moment and, turning, looks back towards the Holy City. Then he goes forward for a few paces and, again turning, halts and looks up towards the massive walls of the city. Again he turns, and this time he does not stop.

> Now I can see that in his hand he carries a rope. Up the slope of Olivet he comes and, entering in at the gate of Gethsemane, walks under the trees of the Garden. Seizing with his arms one of the low-branching limbs of a gnarled olive tree, he draws himself up into the tree. Perhaps he is the proprietor of this part of the Garden, and has come to gather the olives. But why with a rope? For a little he is lost to my view in the springtime foliage of the tree. Then . . . I see his body plummet down like a rock from the top of the tree. . . . And there it swings slowly to and fro.[8]

Jesus Loves (vv. 31–35)

Jesus Embraces Death

> When he [Judas] had gone out, Jesus said, "Now is the Son of Man glorified, and God is glorified in him. If God is glorified in him, God will also glorify him in himself, and glorify him at once. Little children, yet a little while I am with you. You will seek me, and just as I said to the Jews, so now I also say to you, 'Where I am going you cannot come.'" (John 13:31–33)

The paradox of divine governance leaps from the story. The religious establishment and Judas, empowered by Satan, were determined that Jesus should die. And Jesus, as an antidote to the world's rebellion, came to earth and Jerusalem determined to die. It was only the loving determination of God that made possible that which was determined by man.[9] "For God so loved the world, that he gave his only Son . . ." (John 3:16). Here is gospel love for those who are:

- *Ungodly:* "For while we were still weak, at the right time Christ died for the ungodly" (Romans 5:6).
- *Sinners:* "But God shows his love for us in that while we were still sinners, Christ died for us" (Romans 5:8).
- *Enemies:* "For if while we were enemies we were reconciled to God by the death of his Son, much more, now that we are reconciled, shall we be saved by his life" (Romans 5:10).

In Jesus' reaching out to Judas we see him loving an enemy, a sinner, and an ungodly man—and he does the same for each one of us. Through his atoning death on the cross Jesus did it all. There is hope for us amid our ungodly ways. There is deliverance for those who are caught in sin. There is reconciliation for the most hardened enemies of God.

Jesus Demands Love

Jesus then issued a revolutionary call: "A new commandment I give to you, that you love one another: just as I have loved you, you also are to love one another" (John 13:34). The beautiful and exalted old commandment of the Law called us to love our neighbors as we love ourselves (cf. Leviticus 19:18; Matthew 22:34–40; Mark 12:28–31). The new commandment calls us not only to love others with a self-loving love, but with the sacrificial love modeled by Jesus in his reaching out to Judas and on the cross when he reached out to us. We must give ourselves in loving others when they persist in their ungodliness and sin. We must love our enemies. We must give ourselves for them.

Closing Reflections

We are to love as Jesus loves.

In the incarnation he stripped himself of his glory so he could wash us clean. He is our servant-Savior.

Though we have raised our heel against him, though we have been Ahithophels, he offers his eternal friendship. He stretches his arms out on the cross to embrace us.

> O the deep, deep love of Jesus,
> Vast, unmeasured, boundless, free!
> Rolling as a mighty ocean,
> In its fulness over me. . . .
>
> S. Trevor Francis

93

The Last Supper, Part 1

LUKE 22:7–20

THE PASSOVER IN JESUS' DAY was a festival of immense scale and enthusiastic devotion.[1] Huge crowds descended on Jerusalem. Josephus' estimate of about three million is undoubtedly exaggerated. More probably the number of pilgrims was about two hundred thousand—a vast multitude given the size of the ancient city. Accommodations for sleeping and feasting were scarce. The only allowable rent for those who opened their homes were the hides of the Passover sheep slaughtered by their guests (T.B. *Yoma* 12a).

Long in advance of Passover, Jerusalem began to pulse with added commercial activity. Many of the pilgrims were merchants who arrived early to sell their wares (cf. Matthew 21:12ff.; John 2:13–16). Their cries filled the air as they hawked everything from jewelry to spices. Beggars clogged the principal gates. The major purchase of the week was a sacrificial sheep or goat, preferably a lamb. It was required that the people band together in groups of ten or more to eat the entire lamb at one sitting (T.B. *Pesahim* 64b).

The day of sacrifice was given entirely to festive preparations. A massive assembly of priests (twenty-four divisions instead of the customary single division) arrived at the temple early. Their first duty was to burn all the leaven that had been ceremonially collected by candlelight and spoon the preceding night (M. *Pesahim* 1–3). By noon all work ceased.

At midafternoon, 3:00 p.m., the ritual slaughtering began (M. *Pesahim* 5.1). This was completed in three huge shifts. When the first group entered in and the temple court was filled, the gates of the court were closed. A priest's shofar played a sustained blast, and the sacrifices began (M. *Pesahim* 5.5). The pilgrims approached two long rows of priests holding basins of silver and gold. Each Israelite slaughtered his own offering, and the priest caught the blood, which was then tossed at the base of the altar (M. *Pesahim* 5.5, 6). As the offerer left the temple, the slain lamb and its skin was draped over his shoulder (T.B. *Pesahim* 65b).

That evening the Passover was observed in a home or room reserved for the occasion. The lamb was roasted on a pomegranate spit (M. *Pesahim* 7.1). Inside, the company dressed in festive white and reclined at tables with the leader at the head.

In Jesus' time the celebration had added elements beyond the Old Testament's prescriptions. There was a seder, a set order of service (M. *Pesahim* 10.1–9). The celebrants reclined while they ate because they were no longer slaves (cf. Exodus 12:11). It was the host's duty to interpret each of the foods on the table as it related to their deliverance from Egypt. The bitter herbs recalled their bitter slavery. The stewed fruit, by its color and consistency, recalled the misery of making bricks for Pharaoh. The roasted lamb brought to their remembrance the lamb's blood applied to the doorposts, their eating of the lamb within their house, and the death angel's passing over them as it destroyed the firstborn of Egypt.

The celebration concluded late, but many people returned to the streets to continue celebrating. Others returned to the temple mount to await the reopening of the temple gates at midnight, so they could spend the rest of the evening in worship and prayer (cf. Josephus, *Antiquities* 18.2.2).

The Last Supper built upon the rich, full religious and social context of this great day in Israel.

The Passover (vv. 7–13)

"Then came the day of Unleavened Bread, on which the Passover lamb had to be sacrificed" (v. 7). Luke's mention of "the day of Unleavened bread" in conjunction with "Passover" fixes the date. The lamb was slain on Nisan 14 between 3:00 and 5:00 p.m. At 6:00 p.m., when the new day began for the Jews, Nisan 15, the Passover meal was eaten, thus also beginning the week of the Feast of Unleavened Bread (Nisan 15–21).[2]

Luke is also precise about Jesus' careful preparations:

> So Jesus sent Peter and John, saying, "Go and prepare the Passover for us, that we may eat it." They said to him, "Where will you have us prepare it?" He said to them, "Behold, when you have entered the city, a man carrying a jar of water will meet you. Follow him into the house that he enters and tell the master of the house, 'The Teacher says to you, Where is the guest room, where I may eat the Passover with my disciples?' And he will show you a large upper room furnished; prepare it there." (vv. 8–12)

The counterintelligence-like secrecy was due to the fact that Jesus was quite aware of Judas' intention to betray him at a time when he and the disciples were isolated. If Jesus had let it be known where the rendezvous and meal would occur, Judas would have informed on them, the meal would never have taken place, and the institution of the Lord's Supper would never have been given to the Church. So Jesus himself had prearranged the place and the secret signs by which Peter and John would find it. Women normally carried water jars, while men carried water in skins.[3] Thus their guide was easily recognizable.

Everything went like clockwork: "And they went and found it just as he had told them, and they prepared the Passover" (v. 13). The householder led them to a large room above his home that was "furnished"—literally, "spread," indicating that the couches were arranged and covered for the meal. Jesus' two most trusted disciples hurry off to purchase a lamb and all the trimmings for the feast, then stand in one of the three great sacrificial shifts at the temple, bear the lamb back to the house, present the skin to the owner, put the lamb roast on, with the falling dark light the candles, and wait for Jesus and the others.

From the onset of this near-final event we see that Jesus was in control of his destiny. He was not caught like a rag doll on the relentless gears of history. He was not done in by a satanic plot. Jesus would accomplish everything he set out to do—and on his own schedule.

The Last Supper (vv. 14–20)

As Peter and John sat waiting in the candlelight, extra hungry because of the aroma of the roasting lamb, the party arrived resplendent in white and took their places on the *triclinium*, the three couches arranged in a horseshoe around the table.

A Heart Revelation

The time had come. This was the hour—a critical moment in salvation history when Jesus would reveal his heart: "And when the hour came, he reclined at table, and the apostles with him. And he said to them, 'I have earnestly desired to eat this Passover with you before I suffer. For I tell you I will not eat it until it is fulfilled in the kingdom of God'" (vv. 14–16).

Jesus had an intense longing for this special time alone with his disciples at the eating of his last Passover meal. This is also why he had taken such elaborate preparations to insure that the meal be undisturbed. He was eager to teach them from that meal the most wonderful truths ever revealed. That meal would be transformed forever. Its celebration would become an acted parable of his life and death. Jesus would recoil at the reality of the cross but not from this!

His heart also swelled at the thought of the next time he would eat with his own beyond history. Jesus' heart traveled beyond the sorrow and death to reunion with them in lavish festal joy. These anticipated joys sustained him in this crucial hour. As the writer to the Hebrews put it, "who for the joy that was set before him endured the cross, despising the shame" (Hebrews 12:2). And the center of that joy is that his redeemed will sit with him at table in the kingdom.

Jesus also longed for the messianic banquet so magnificently described in the book of Revelation:

> Then I heard what seemed to be the voice of a great multitude, like the roar of many waters and like the sound of mighty peals of thunder, crying out,
>
> "Hallelujah!
> For the Lord our God
> the Almighty reigns.
> Let us rejoice and exult
> and give him the glory,
> for the marriage of the Lamb has come,
> and his Bride has made herself ready;
> it was granted her to clothe herself
> with fine linen, bright and pure"—
>
> for the fine linen is the righteous deeds of the saints.
>
> And the angel said to me, "Write this: Blessed are those who are invited to the marriage supper of the Lamb." And he said to me, "These are the true words of God." (Revelation 19:6–9; cf. Luke 13:29; 14:15)

Whenever we celebrate the Lord's Table, we should eat with an eye to the ultimate Communion. This is why Paul added, "For as often as you eat this bread and drink the cup, you proclaim the Lord's death until he comes" (1 Corinthians 11:26). The eagerness of our Savior's heart for this meal ought to set our hearts to racing. This is the heart of God!

A Cup of Communion

Unlike the other Gospels, which describe only one cup at the Last Supper, Luke mentions an additional cup before the traditional words of institution of the Lord's Supper. Most believe this was the first cup of the meal, which the Passover seder describes as taking place immediately after the opening prayers. But unlike the seder, in which the participants were directed to drink from their own cups, Jesus distributed the single cup among the disciples, emphasizing the *communal aspect* of the meal.[4] They were at a table of fellowship with one another—in communion. Thus from the onset Jesus emphasized the radical, mutual participatory nature of the Supper he was about to institute.

And again Jesus strongly emphasized the future communal hope of the messianic table: "For I tell you that from now on I will not drink of the fruit of the vine until the kingdom of God comes" (v. 18). A deep, eternal oneness awaits those who will dine at the ultimate table with Christ—a oneness that comes by virtue of our being in him.

The Lord's Supper (vv. 19, 20)

Now Jesus was ready to speak the famous words of institution. The words changed the meaning of two elements of the meal—the bread and the cup—charging them with surpassing significance.

The Bread

"And he took bread, and when he had given thanks, he broke it and gave it to them, saying, 'This is my body, which is given for you. Do this in remembrance of me'" (v. 19). The unleavened bread was equated in the seder with bread of affliction because it reminded them of their persecution in Egypt as mentioned in Deuteronomy 16:3: "You shall eat no leavened bread with it. Seven days you shall eat it with unleavened bread, the bread of affliction—for you came out of the land of Egypt in haste—that all the days of your life you may remember the day when you came out of the land of Egypt." This unleavened bread was now given greater significance—it represented Jesus' body and the affliction he would endure on the cross.

Jesus' statement was freighted with immense meaning.

"This is my body" meant that the unleavened bread *represents* his body. Jesus was not saying that the bread was literally his body, thereby teaching the Roman Catholic Church's doctrine of transubstantiation. Some medieval theologians pounded their fists as they quoted the Latin Vulgate (*hoc est corpus meum*—"This is my body") and argued that this is the plain sense of Christ's words.

But the Jews, with their prophetic legacy of parabolic acts and languages and their customary symbolic expression, understood that Christ was speaking *figuratively*—just as when he said "the field is the world" or "I am the door." To his hearers who saw him sitting there in his body holding a piece of bread, "This is my body" could not mean anything other than "This is a symbol of my body." They knew he was speaking figuratively.

"Given for you" speaks of the vicarious gift of himself on the cross for our sins—"Christ died for our sins in accordance with the Scriptures" (1 Corinthians 15:3).

"Do this in remembrance of me" calls for studied remembrance through the memorial (the bread) of what Christ has done for us.

Tragically (though we may think it is impossible), we are in constant danger of forgetting. The memorial of the bread is meant to graciously assault our fickle memories.

The Cup

Substantial time must have elapsed between the acts of institution because Luke says, "And likewise [Jesus took] the cup after they had eaten, saying, 'This cup that is poured out for you is the new covenant in my blood'" (v. 20). By calling the cup "the new covenant in my blood," Jesus was intentionally contrasting his atoning work (the shedding of his blood) with the Old Covenant's ocean of blood.

Exodus 24 gives the full account of the old covenant's inauguration. The Ten Commandments had already been delivered (Exodus 19, 20), and then the Book of the Covenant was read (Exodus 20:18—23:33), to which the people responded in one voice, "'All the words that the Lord has spoken we will do.' And Moses wrote down all the words of the Lord" (Exodus 24:3, 4). The next few verses complete the picture:

> And he sent young men of the people of Israel, who offered burnt offerings and sacrificed peace offerings of oxen to the Lord. And Moses took half of the blood and put it in basins, and half of the blood he threw against the altar. Then he took the Book of the Covenant and read it in the hearing of the people. And they said, "All that the Lord has spoken we will do, and we will be obedient." And Moses took the blood and threw it on the people and said, "Behold the blood of the covenant that the Lord has made with you in accordance with all these words." (Exodus 24:5–8)

From Exodus we understand that everything of significance was doused with blood—half on the altar and the other half on the people and the scroll. The altar, people, and book dripped with blood. It was not a pretty sight, except in its supreme symbolism. The old covenant was launched on a sea of blood for two reasons. First, to emphasize the seriousness of sin. Second, to teach that the payment for sin is death. The weakness of the old covenant was that it depended on man's keeping his pledge to obey the Law. The people promised, "All the words that the Lord has spoken we will do," and again, "All that the Lord has spoken we will do, and we will be obedient." But they couldn't—not even for a day!

So we come to the glory of the new covenant in Christ's blood—namely, the keeping of this promise, this covenant, is totally dependent on Christ. He does it all! Our salvation rests on the infinite ocean of his divine blood "that is poured out for you."

Closing Reflections

Historically, the idea of the new covenant was not new, but it was made possible by the body and blood of Christ. The cup that Jesus offered brimmed with Jeremiah 31:31–34, which prophesied the new covenant:

> Behold, the days are coming, declares the Lord, when I will make a new covenant with the house of Israel and the house of Judah, not like the covenant that I made with their fathers on the day when I took them by the hand to bring them out of the land of Egypt, my covenant that they broke, though I was their husband, declares the Lord. For this is the covenant that I will make with the house of Israel after those days, declares the Lord: I will put my law within them, and I will write it on their hearts. And I will be their God, and they shall be my people. And no longer shall each one teach his neighbor and each his brother, saying, 'Know the Lord,' for they shall all know me, from the least of them to the greatest, declares the Lord. For I will forgive their iniquity, and I will remember their sin no more.

This is the superior work of Jesus—superior, according to Jeremiah, in four ways.

A Superior Inwardness

"For this is the covenant that I will make with the house of Israel after those days, declares the Lord: I will put my law within them, and I will write it on their hearts" (Jeremiah 31:33a). The problem with the old covenant was, it was patently external. Its laws were written on stone (Exodus 32:15, 16). They provided no internal power to live them out. To be sure, there was great benefit in memorizing God's Word. But the writing on the heart was beyond the power of unaided man. Something far more radical was needed—a spiritual heart operation.

On one occasion Dr. Christian Barnard, the first surgeon ever to do a heart transplant, impulsively asked his patient, Dr. Philip Blaiberg, "Would you like to see your old heart?" On a subsequent evening,

> the men stood in a room of the Groote Schuur Hospital, in Johannesburg, South Africa. Dr. Barnard went up to a cupboard, took down a glass container and handed it to Dr. Blaiberg. Inside that container was Blaiberg's old heart. For a moment he stood there stunned into silence—the first man in history ever to hold his own heart in his hands. Finally he spoke and for ten minutes plied Dr. Barnard with technical questions. Then he turned to take a final look at the contents of the glass container, and said, 'So this is my old heart that caused me so much trouble.' He handed it back, turned away and left it forever.[5]

This, in essence, is what Christ does for us. He gives us a new heart. God has written his laws within us. He has made his people partakers of the divine nature (2 Peter 1:4). True, we still battle with our fleshly nature, but through baptism into Christ's Body, God's laws are no longer external and foreign but internal (cf. John 14:15–17; 16:12, 13; 1 Corinthians 12:13).

A Superior Relationship

"And I will be their God, and they shall be my people" (Jeremiah 31:33b). The Old Testament echoes this repeatedly, though it was only fulfilled in some of the hearers. But this is perfectly fulfilled in all who partake of the new covenant, through which believers actually become God's possession and possess God. "I will be their God" means he gives himself to us. And "they shall be my people" means he takes us to himself! When this happens, everything our complex nature can require is found in him.

Superior Knowledge

"And no longer shall each one teach his neighbor and each his brother, saying, 'Know the LORD,' for they shall all know me, from the least of them to the greatest" (Jeremiah 31:34a). The old covenant was corporately entered into by a nation, including many who did not know God personally. But those who experience the new covenant by faith in Jesus' blood come one by one as they are born into a relationship with God. Jesus defined eternal life by saying, "And this is eternal life, that they know you the only true God, and Jesus Christ whom you have sent" (John 17:3). Those who are partakers of the new covenant all know God, "from the least of them to the greatest." No one needs to say, "Know the LORD" to such persons, though at the same time this is a command and an invitation to a lost world.

Superior Forgiveness

"For I will forgive their iniquity, and I will remember their sin no more" (Jeremiah 31:34b). This is precisely what the old covenant could not do. Under the old covenant, sins were never completely forgiven because they were never truly forgotten. They were covered, awaiting and pointing to the true forgiveness through Christ's death. Some of us have phenomenal memories, but God never forgets anything. In fact, he cannot forget unless he wills to do so. And when sins are not remembered, "it is because His grace has determined to forgive them—not in spite of his holiness, but in harmony with it" (F. F. Bruce). The new covenant brings total forgiveness!

As the disciples reclined on the Passover while in the upper room, and the candles flickered lower and lower, they saw and heard the eager Savior of the world unlock the mystery of salvation, saying, "This is my body, which is given for you," and "This cup that is poured out for you is the new covenant in my blood."

Here is a salvation that is superior—and eternal.

94

The Last Supper, Part 2

LUKE 22:21–38

AT THE CONCLUSION of the Last Supper when, in the candlelit room amid his white-clad disciples, Jesus took the cup of wine in hand and said, "This cup that is poured out for you is the new covenant in my blood," it was one of the supreme moments of salvation history. In that single sentence Jesus declared that his soon-to-be shed blood would supersede the blood sacrifices of the old covenant.

Indeed, Jesus thus declared the all-surpassing superiority of the new covenant over the old. The blood of the old-covenant sacrifices could not atone for sin. Its animal sacrifices covered sin but could not remove it. As the writer of Hebrews so explicitly stated, "It is impossible for the blood of bulls and goats to take away sins" (Hebrews 10:4), and "Every priest stands daily at his service, offering repeatedly the same sacrifices, which can never take away sins" (Hebrews 10:11). Precisely because no dumb animal was competent to serve as a substitute for a human sinner, there was an unending repetition of sacrifices. And those repetitions bore constant testimony to their impotency.

But the blood of the new covenant, Jesus' blood, perfectly atoned for all the sins of those who would come to him and thus made possible the reality of the new covenant promised by Jeremiah:

> For this is the covenant that I will make with the house of Israel after those days, declares the LORD: I will put my law within them, and I will write it on their hearts. And I will be their God, and they shall be my people. And no longer shall each one teach his neighbor and each his brother, saying, "Know the LORD," for they shall all know me, from the least of them to the greatest, declares the LORD. For I will forgive their iniquity, and I will remember their sin no more. (Jeremiah 31:33, 34)

The cup Jesus held brimmed with the joyous wine of Jeremiah's new-covenant prophecy—a new heart, a new relationship, authentic forgiveness.

How much of this penetrated the disciples' understanding at that moment is impossible to determine. But it would become the center of their faith and hope!

Divine Disappointment (vv. 21–38)

We do know that the immediate conversation and conduct in the upper room revealed a pathetically shallow understanding and appropriation of Jesus' astounding revelation.

Betrayal

The scene was heart breaking because without a pause Jesus, cup evidently still in hand, said,

> "But behold, the hand of him who betrays me is with me on the table. For the Son of Man goes as it has been determined, but woe to that man by whom he is betrayed!" And they began to question one another, which of them it could be who was going to do this. (vv. 21–23)

If Luke is writing in chronological order, then Judas had just participated in his first (and last!) Communion. Jesus was not surprised. He knew of Judas' deadly bargain, and he knew that the Father had "determined" the way he would be delivered over to death. Nevertheless, the numbing reality that a man with whom he had shared his life day and night, who had seen his manner of life, who had heard him bare his soul, had become his enemy—this sickening reality bore down on Jesus. His "woe" for Judas was an alas over what awaited his betrayer. Amid the ensuing hubbub of questioning—"Surely it isn't me?"—there was the Savior's deep sadness.

Dissension

The holy solemnity of the institution of the Lord's Supper had dissipated in a moment—and with it the effect of his words about his body and blood—his life. Then the disciples began to argue about (of all things!) who was the greatest (v. 24). Amazing! They had been his constant companions for three years. They had seen him live a life of service. This self-promoting conversation was an outrageous slap in the Savior's face.

Jesus responded with sad irony: "The kings of the Gentiles exercise lordship over them, and those in authority over them are called benefactors"

(v. 25). The mentality of pagan lords was to domineer and practice overweening selfishness, all the while giving themselves pleasant titles like "Benefactor" or "Your Grace" or "Your Royal Munificence."

"But," says Jesus, "not so with you. Rather, let the greatest among you become as the youngest, and the leader as one who serves. For who is the greater, one who reclines at table or one who serves? Is it not the one who reclines at table? But I am among you as the one who serves" (vv. 26, 27). The phrase "one who serves" (used three times here) signifies the service of a table waiter,[1] those who were at that moment serving them, those who lived as Jesus had.

Actually, Jesus was far gentler than you and I would have been with such boneheads, because he ended the discussion by reminding them of the authority that awaited them in the kingdom: "You are those who have stayed with me in my trials, and I assign to you, as my Father assigned to me, a kingdom, that you may eat and drink at my table in my kingdom and sit on thrones judging the twelve tribes of Israel" (vv. 28–30). The disciples' future kingdom authority would not be like the delusive authority of earthly kings who practice dominance and demand lordship. Jesus' followers' rule would be like his rule—"as one who serves."

What dolts these disciples were in the upper room. Jesus was so close to the cross, and yet his most intimate followers were so far from him in spirit.[2] How disheartening this was for Jesus.

Failure

The Lord may have addressed Peter specifically because his voice overpowered the others in the quarrel:

> "Simon, Simon, behold, Satan demanded to have you, that he might sift you like wheat, but I have prayed for you that your faith may not fail. And when you have turned again, strengthen your brothers." Peter said to him, "Lord, I am ready to go with you both to prison and to death." Jesus said, "I tell you, Peter, the rooster will not crow this day, until you deny three times that you know me." (vv. 31–34)

This is a familiar story that we will take up in detail when we come to verses 54–62. But here we must notice that in the crumbling atmosphere of the upper room, one of Jesus' most trusted disciples, one of the inner circle, his most sanguine, enthusiastic supporter, vowed, "Lord, I am ready to go with you both to prison and to death." And yet this foremost disciple would succumb to cowardly denial and infamous failure.

The upper room, so festive with table and candles a few minutes before, was now dark and somber. The betrayer had gone out into the night, awaiting the right moment to trap Jesus. Shameful dissension had broken out over who was the greatest. And denial and failure was about to come from the most unlikely of apostles. What more could happen?

Dullness

Done with Peter, Jesus turned again to the whole group:

> "When I sent you out with no moneybag or knapsack or sandals, did you lack anything?" They said, "Nothing." He said to them, "But now let the one who has a moneybag take it, and likewise a knapsack. And let the one who has no sword sell his cloak and buy one. For I tell you that this Scripture must be fulfilled in me: 'And he was numbered with the transgressors.' For what is written about me has its fulfillment." (vv. 35–37)

Luke records two earlier occasions (9:3; 10:4) when Jesus sent his disciples out to preach the gospel of the kingdom having no provisions. And as Jesus suggested, they met with such receptiveness that their hearers provided everything they needed. But now, with his arrest, trial, and death imminent, Jesus knew that their ministry experience would change. Jesus quoted Isaiah 53:12 about himself—"And he was numbered with the transgressors"—because that is how he would be treated. In fact, he would be crucified between two thieves, two outlaws (cf. 23:32, 33). The reality for his disciples was that because they followed him, they too would be regarded as transgressors or outlaws.

They were to ponder his advice, "But now let the one who has a moneybag take it, and likewise a knapsack. And let the one who has no sword sell his cloak and buy one" (v. 36). The apostles, however, with a dullness we have seen before, focused on the specific mention of a sword without attempting to grapple with what that suggested—namely, the hostility that awaited them, and the necessity of making adequate provision.[3] The proof that Jesus was not suggesting his disciples arm themselves came later that evening when one of the disciples drew a sword in Gethsemane and cut off the ear of the servant of the high priest, to which Jesus responded, "No more of this!" and healed the man (cf. 22:50, 51).

In the upper room the disciples responded literally to his question saying, "Look, Lord, here are two swords" (with which they presumably thought they could hold off the Romans), and Jesus had had it. He replied, "It is enough," meaning as commentators variously explain, "That's enough of that,"[4] "Enough of that,"[5] "Enough of this kind of talk!"[6] As Marvin Pate explains, "So complete was the disciples' misunderstanding of His saying about the need to buy a sword, that he refused to explain it any more. We might colloquially render Jesus' words thus, 'I give up!'"[7]

Jesus had come to the upper room with such great anticipation. His opening words to his disciples were, "I have earnestly desired to eat this Passover with you before I suffer" (22:15). And during the Passover feast he fulfilled his desire by reinterpreting the bread and the cup to show that he is the ultimate Passover Lamb and that his blood established the new covenant long ago prophesied by Jeremiah.

All this majestic eagerness from Jesus even though he knew he was going to die! But then came Judas' betrayal, and the disciples' dissension, and Peter's denial, and their dullness. So Jesus finally exclaimed "Enough of this!"—the utterance of a broken heart.

If this was our first reading of the story, we might well think, "Is there any hope for such dunderheads?" We know there was and is because we are blockheads too—every bit as self-centered and presumptuous and dense and utterly sinful. What hope do we have for anything better?

Divine Enablement (vv. 37, 38)

The answer is magnificently tucked into Jesus' brief reference in verse 37 to Isaiah 53:12: "And he was numbered with the transgressors." Isaiah 53 is the messianic Servant Song that describes in detail the passion, death, and atonement of the Lamb of God. It is all about Christ. The further significance of this quotation is that this is the only verse from Isaiah 53 that Jesus expressly quoted. In addition, verse 12 is the final and the summary verse of Isaiah 53, providing us with a compact description of what Jesus did for his own.

The phrase "and was numbered with the transgressors" in Isaiah 53 is followed by two other phrases—"Yet he bore the sin of many" and "makes intercession for the transgressors." Together these three phrases give us the basis of all hope.

Identification

The phrase "And was numbered with the transgressors" was dramatically fulfilled when Jesus was hung on a cross between two outlaws. The Septuagint of Isaiah 53:12 has the sense, "and he was classed among the outlaws."[8] Here the joyful reality is that we too are transgressors/outlaws—and that on the cross he fully identified with us. On the cross the sinless Son of God became a transgressor, though he himself had broken no law. Consequently, we transgressors can find saving identification in him. He "was numbered with the transgressors"—praise his name forevermore!

Atonement

He not only identified with us in our sin, but he atoned for our sin, as the second phrase says—"Yet he bore the sin of many." Earlier in Isaiah 53 (vv. 4–6) we read:

> Surely he has borne our griefs and carried our sorrows; yet we esteemed him stricken, smitten by God, and afflicted. But he was pierced for our transgressions; he was crushed for our iniquities; upon him was the chastisement that brought us peace, and with his wounds we are healed. All we like sheep have gone astray; we have turned—every one—to his own way; and the LORD has laid on him the iniquity of us all.

Whereas it was "impossible for the blood of bulls and goats to take away sins" (Hebrews 10:4), Peter tells us, in referring to Isaiah 53, "He himself bore our sins in his body on the tree, that we might die to sin and live to righteousness. By his wounds you have been healed" (1 Peter 2:24).

> Full atonement can it be?
> Hallelujah! What a Savior!
>
> "Man of Sorrows, What a Name"
> Philip P. Bliss

Intercession

The final clause, "makes intercession for the transgressors," is the final element in the triad of hope. Jesus makes full identification with us transgressors, and then full atonement, and then caps it with full intercession for us outlaws. This is why Peter ultimately made a comeback. Satan had asked to sift Peter as wheat, hoping to dispose of the wheat and harvest the chaff. But Christ prayed for Peter, and through Peter's failure the chaff blew away and the wheat remained. Peter's vanity was sifted out, his misplaced self-confidence was sifted away, his presumption was sifted, his impulsive mouth was winnowed—and he became a great strength to his brothers and sisters in the early church.[9]

Jesus' intercession is at the root of the new covenant's superior power. The old covenant was administered by mortal priests who were themselves sinners. But Jesus is an eternal priest in the order of Melchizedek according to the eternal oath of God.

> The LORD has sworn
> and will not change his mind,
> "You are a priest forever
> after the order of Melchizedek." (Psalm 110:4)

This has untold implications for every believer. The writer of Hebrews gives it unforgettable expression: "But he holds his priesthood permanently, because he continues forever. Consequently, he is able to save to the uttermost those who draw near to God through him, since he always lives to make intercession for them" (Hebrews 7:24, 25). No matter what our sinful history might be, Christ can save us "to the uttermost" and eternally. This is the perpetual experience of all believers in every situation.

The reason he saves to the uttermost is that "he always lives to make intercession." Though we are finite, he is infinite. Though we are temporal, he is eternal. He prays with the ease of omniscience and omnipotence perfected through his own human suffering. He is praying for us right now!

Closing Reflections

The upper room discourse is beautiful and profound.

When Jesus held up the cup saying, "This cup that is poured out for you is the new covenant in my blood," he was declaring that he was and is the ground and originator of those amazing promises made in Jeremiah 31:33, 34. But Jesus is more than the originator of the new covenant. He is also its High Priest, as the writer of Hebrews made so clear when he quoted Jeremiah's new covenant promise in 8:8–12 and then concluded in 9:15a, "Therefore he [Christ] is the mediator of a new covenant, so that those who are called may receive the promised eternal inheritance."

This was and is the hope of those dull, self-centered, presumptuous, weak disciples in the upper room, and it is our hope as well. Jesus does it all. Jesus Christ the Lord is the originator and mediator of the new covenant. His promise and his priesthood do it all. There is hope for everyone!

95

Divine Dread

LUKE 22:39–46

THE LAST SUPPER closed as a vast disappointment to Jesus. The Messiah had come so eagerly to the upper room and had taken the Passover bread and cup and instituted the Last Supper—only to see the evening disintegrate. Judas left to betray him, the disciples fell to infighting, Jesus prophesied failure for Peter and the rest, and his final words were misunderstood due to the disciples' abysmal spiritual dullness. In dismay, Jesus despaired: "It is enough" (22:38).

Jesus' disappointment with the disciples carried over to Gethsemane because the succeeding passage begins with his giving them explicit instructions to pray (v. 40) and ends with him finding the Eleven asleep and again charging them to "Rise and pray that you may not enter into temptation" (v. 46). The disciples' failures frame a portrait of Jesus' garden prayer. Luke's picture of the event is briefer than the more detailed accounts of Gethsemane in Mark and Matthew. Those Gospels describe Jesus returning three times to find them sleeping and record his exasperated words to Peter. But Luke economizes the scene.

The reason for this stark abridgment is to intensify the focus on Jesus' relationship to his Father in prayer.[1] Here we are taken into Jesus' heart as never before. In Gethsemane we see a Jesus who has never before appeared in any of the Gospels. This is the *Sanctus Sanctorum* of Jesus' heart. It demands of us a profound reverence, almost a reticence, lest we get it wrong.

Up to now, Jesus has been absolutely fearless. We see this in the temptation in the wilderness at the beginning of his ministry. During those forty days face-to-face with Satan, Jesus remained totally unintimidated and immovable (4:1–13). Then, at the opening of his public ministry when his hometown people attempted to kill him, he eluded them with fearless aplomb (4:29, 30). Shortly after that, Jesus silenced a screaming demoniac with an unruffled "Be silent" (4:33–35). His preaching was fearless, as seen in the six scorching woes he delivered to the scribes and Pharisees (11:37–54). And toward the end, as he taught in the temple, his repeated conflicts with the authorities and his repeated slam dunks were all done with unintimidated composure.

Jesus was always in control and in full power, whether quieting a demon or calming a storm (8:22–25) or feeding a multitude (9:10–17). He fearlessly approached his own death. For example, after the transfiguration he said to his disciples, "Let these words sink into your ears: The Son of Man is about to be delivered into the hands of men" (9:44). A short time later, "When the days drew near for him to be taken up, he set his face to go to Jerusalem" (9:51). And just before ascending the hill to the Holy City, he said, "See, we are going up to Jerusalem, and everything that is written about the Son of Man by the prophets will be accomplished. For he will be delivered over to the Gentiles and will be mocked and shamefully treated and spit upon. And after flogging him, they will kill him, and on the third day he will rise" (18:31–33). Finally, in the upper room, he was fearless and eager to eat the Passover with his own—though he knew he was the Passover Lamb who would be devoured (22:14–16). Throughout the entire range of his tumultuous life Jesus knew no fear.

Jesus' Agony (vv. 43, 44 and Mark 14:33, 34)

However, in the garden there was an abrupt change, for Jesus was overcome with a fearful dread of death. Mark's parallel report says that he "began to be greatly distressed and troubled. And he said to them, 'My soul is very sorrowful, even to death'" (Mark 14:33, 34).

His expression "greatly distressed" bears the element of astonishment.[2] The King James Version carries this idea in its rendering, "sore amazed." Jesus' horrified astonishment at his imminent death evoked his pathetic self-revelation, "My soul is very sorrowful, even to death." It is hard for us to fathom this, but his fear of death could well have killed him![3]

Luke adds, "And there appeared to him an angel from heaven, strengthening him. And being in an agony he prayed more earnestly; and his sweat became like great drops of blood falling down to the ground" (vv. 43, 44). As Jesus poured out his heart, an angel strengthened him. And he was in such "agony" that his sweat fell like drops of blood from a running wound and splashed on the ground.[4] Jesus' body and soul were racked with fearful anguish at his impending death. Incredible fear!

Why this surprising fear? Others have faced death quite calmly. Socrates awaited death with indifference, if not anticipation. Consider the death of Joachim Murat, marshal of France and king of Naples under Napoleon who was sentenced and executed by his captors. As Gay Talese recounts it:

> On the day of his death he had a shock of his hair cut off and asked one of the officers to enclose it with a letter he had written to his wife, Napoleon's sister, and his children, who were then all living in Trieste. Then Murat took off his watch and gave it to the officer as a gift. But before he parted with the watch he removed from its lid a tiny carnelian on which was carved a portrait of his wife. Murat held this carnelian tightly in the palm of his hand as he followed the soldiers out to the courtyard, where they were preparing to kill him. The sergeant of the firing squad offered Murat a chair, but Murat said he wanted to die standing up. The sergeant offered to cover up his eyes with a cloth, but Murat said he wanted to die with his eyes open. "I do have one request," Murat then said. "I have commanded in many battles, and now I would like to give the word of command for the last time." The sergeant granted his wish. Murat then stood against the wall of the castle and called out in a loud voice: "Soldiers, form line." Six soldiers drew themselves up to within about ten feet of him. "Prepare arms—present." The soldiers pointed their muskets at him. "Aim at the heart, save the face," Murat said, with a little smile.
>
> And then, after he had held up his hand to look for the final time at the carnelian showing the portrait of his wife, he issued his final command—"Fire!"[5]

Many men and women alike have died brave, fearless deaths. So why such fear from Jesus? The learned pagan Celsus used this question as an argument against Christianity—how can one who is divine "mourn and lament and pray to escape the fear of death . . . ?" (*Contra Celsum* 2:24).[6]

The answer is: 1) Jesus knew that death is the "wages of sin" (Romans 6:23)—and that he would pay the total wages in full. 2) He also knew that death is a result of the judgment of God (cf. Romans 5:12)—and that he would bear that judgment. 3) He knew that he would become sin (cf. 2 Corinthians 5:21). 4) He knew that death would bring on him the wrath of God (cf. 1 John 2:2)—and that he would propitiate it to the full. That is why Jesus was filled with such unremitting dread. This is why he was so fearful. This is why he could well have died *before* the cross.

Jesus' Prayer (vv. 41, 42)

That fear was also the reason for his prayer, "Father, if you are willing, remove this cup from me. Nevertheless, not my will, but yours, be done" (v. 42).

"Father"

Jesus began with the expression "Father," which calls to mind his relationship with the One to whom he prayed, and also the character of that One. Though Jesus is God and is coeternal and coequal with God, he exists in relation to the Father as Son. They have always existed in eternal, perpetual, unbroken relationship (cf. John 1:1–3).

Jesus' invocation "Father" reminds us that God loves to give to his Son. The phrase (meant for all of God's children) "how much more will the heavenly Father give . . ." (11:13) exists for Christ in the "how much more" of eternal Sonship! The Father loves to give to his Son, just as earthly fathers delight to give to theirs. Jesus asked his Father who had never refused him. At the same time, his using the word "Father" invoked protection. As Philip Jensen has said, "Basically, prayer is offered *to* the Father, *through* the Spirit, *by* the Son—because it is the role of the Father to protect."[7] Thus this request went directly to the Father's heart. He would do anything to protect his Son. Jesus' use of "Father" also suggests submission. As he himself declared, "I always do the things that are pleasing to him" (John 8:29).

We must remind ourselves that this is a real prayer by a real man (notwithstanding his divinity). Jesus really prayed this way. He submissively appealed to his Father, who always gave him everything and loved to protect him here on earth. Jesus' prayer went like a dagger to the heart of the Father.

"If"

Jesus' words "if you are willing" addressed the disposition of his loving Father. Jesus was not praying to an impotent Father but the omnipotent Father, for whom all things are possible. Indeed, Jesus had declared regarding the rich ruler, "What is impossible with man is possible with God" (18:27). God can do anything! In fact, Isaiah records that on one occasion God had taken the cup of wrath that Judah had drunk and put it into the hands of their godless tormentors (cf. Isaiah 51:17–23, esp. v. 23). Perhaps God would do a similar thing for his Son! Perhaps there could be a later appointed "hour" (cf. Mark 14:35). Perhaps there could be some other "cup"—some other way.

Jesus' Gethsemane prayer testifies to the authenticity of the incarnation, that he was a real man (as well as truly God). As a man, Jesus had placed the exercise of his omniscience at the discretion of the Father. Jesus was genuinely saying that if there was any other way, he wanted the Father to use it. He was not seeking to disobey the will of God, but in his manhood he desired to not suffer the shame of the cross and all it entailed.

"Remove"

Jesus' plea to "remove this cup from me" was grounded in the fact of his absolute sinless purity, and the fact that the cup was filled with sin and wrath.[8] The cup was steaming with a brew that was so awful, so fearful, so dreadful, so unbearable, so appalling, so horrendous that Jesus' soul was revulsed and convulsed. How could he drink such filth? How could he bear his Father's wrath? Though in the upper room he had declared that "this cup that is poured out for you is the new covenant in my blood" (22:20) and thus embraced his own death on the cross so he could give them the blessings of the new covenant, he now recoiled at the personal horror he was about to endure.

"Nevertheless"

"Father, if there is any possible way out, please do it. Nevertheless, not my will, but yours, be done." Jesus was caught between two proper desires. It is proper and good to want to avoid death, alienation, and wrath. But it is also proper and best to want to do God's will, whatever the cost. Jesus chose the best!

And he did it all with complete sincerity. There was no ignorant devotion like that of Peter: "Lord, I am ready to go with you both to prison and to death" (22:33). Jesus knew what he was acceding to. As he sincerely prayed that the cup be taken from him if it was the Father's will, he just as sincerely prayed—though "every emotion in his heart, every fibre and cell in his flesh rose up against the prospect"[9]—"Nevertheless, not my will, but yours, be done." But "Your will be done!" was the cry of a conqueror because "whoever does the will of God abides forever" (1 John 2:17). Jesus wanted the Father's will more than anything!

Was Jesus' prayer heard? Yes, though his request was denied. The writer of Hebrews, apparently referring explicitly to Gethsemane, comments, "In the days of his flesh, Jesus offered up prayers and supplications, with loud cries and tears, to him who was able to save him from death, and he was heard because of his reverence" (Hebrews 5:7). His submission was, "Nevertheless, not my will, but yours, be done." That is the prayer God answers. Jesus' prayer was a prayer of great faith because he trusted the Father with everything. All true prayers of faith end with, "not my will, but yours, be done."

The Disciples' Failure (vv. 45, 46)

As we noted earlier, Jesus' victory was bordered on either side by the failure of the disciples. "And when he rose from prayer, he came to the disciples and found them sleeping for sorrow, and he said to them, 'Why are you sleeping? Rise and pray that you may not enter into temptation'" (vv. 45, 46). Jesus was ready for the culmination of his mission and would soon stand before Caiaphas, before the Sanhedrin, before Pilate, before Herod, before his executioners, doing his Father's will perfectly throughout. He was the paragon of fearless, loving strength.

But the disciples gave themselves to post-Passover sleep, brought on by their emotional exhaustion, and perhaps by their Passover feast. They had been so eager to fight God's war with man's weapons (22:38), but they now fumbled with a more essential weapon—prayer.[10] Their immediate failures would quickly be there for all to see—their silly use of the sword, their wholesale desertion, denial by the bravest of them.

Closing Reflections

We have seen the depths of Jesus' heart. What have we learned?[11]

Prayer

We have learned that prayer is more than content—it is a process of relationship with God. True, we often get things we ask for. But most of all, prayer gives us God himself, and he gives us increased faith and obedience besides. We also have seen the importance of praying, "not my will, but yours, be done." Expressing our desires in the context of submitting to God's will—God hears all such prayers!

We have learned, too, about the beauty of approaching God as our Father. "Father" signifies eternal relationship and protection by the one for whom all things are possible. "He who did not spare his own Son but gave him up for us all, how will he not also with him graciously give us all things?" (Romans 8:32).

Submission

We see how submission is lived out. Jesus submits to the authority of the Father though they are equal (cf. Ephesians 1:2; 1 Peter 1:2). Jesus has never deviated from the Father's will. He said, "I do nothing on my own authority, but speak just as the Father taught me. And he who sent me is with me. He has not left me alone, for I always do the things that are pleasing to him" (John 8:28, 29). Within the Godhead, this is, as Charles Williams noted, "a particular means of joy." He added, "The Son is co-equal with the Father, yet the Son is obedient to the Father. A thing so sweetly known in many relations of human love is, beyond imagination, present in the midmost secrets of heaven."[12] Our submission is our entrance into this sweet joy.

Temptation

Prayerful waiting is the secret of not succumbing to temptation. The Scriptures promise, "No temptation has overtaken you that is not common to man. God is faithful, and he will not let you be tempted beyond your ability, but with the temptation he will also provide the way of escape, that you may be able to endure it" (1 Corinthians 10:13). But so often we miss "the way of escape" because we are asleep!

Death

We see that real death is due to God's wrath for our sin. We learn the pain of sin as we observe Jesus' revulsion at becoming sin—his plea that if there is any other way, the cup be taken from him. We see the oneness of God assaulted by sin. As Luther said of the cross, "Mystery of mystery, God deserts God." We see the Son of God's blood-like sweat and listen as he wrestles with death and wrath. We hear Jesus' cry, "My God, my God, why have you forsaken me?"

Blasphemy

There in the garden the perfect omnipotent Father listened to his perfect Son's agonized pleading for an alternative way. And if there was any other way he would have done it. But since there was not, he willed his Son's death.

What a blasphemous affront to God to think that sin does not matter!

What an outrage to imagine that we are good enough for God to accept us!

What a cosmic affront to hold that there is any way apart from Jesus!

What a slur to say that God does not care about us!

We join St. John in amazement: "See what kind of love the Father has given to us, that we should be called children of God; and so we are. The reason why the world does not know us is that it did not know him" (1 John 3:1).

John's Gospel says it all: "For God so loved the world, that he gave his only Son, that whoever believes in him should not perish but have eternal life" (John 3:16).

96

"The Power of Darkness"

LUKE 22:47–53

TO SOME, Jesus' arrest in Gethsemane may look like his life had spun out of control.

H. G. Wells once said that the world is like a great stage production, directed and managed by God. As the curtain rises, the set is perfect, a treat to every eye. The characters are resplendent. Everything goes well until the leading man steps on the hem of the leading lady's gown, causing her to trip over a chair, which knocks over a lamp, which pushes a table into the wall, which in turn knocks over the scenery, which brings everything down on the heads of the actors. Meanwhile, behind the scenes God, the Producer, is running around, shouting orders, pulling strings, trying desperately to restore order from chaos. But, alas, he is unable to do so! Poor God! As Wells explains, he is a very little, limited God.[1]

Is that not what apparently had begun to happen in the upper room? The meal had peaked when Jesus held up his cup and declared, "This cup that is poured out for you is the new covenant in my blood" (22:20). The gleaming red wine sparkled with the ancient promise of a new heart and forgiveness of sins through his blood that was about to be shed for us.

But that evening Judas had refused Jesus' extended morsel of friendship and went out into the night that for him would know no morning. He had expected a different Messiah, a Messiah with a sword. He had looked for a revived Israel riding high on horses and camels as a dreadful army to slaughter the Romans. He had expected the Messiah to sit on the throne of David with the universe as a cushion under his feet. But now he would see Jesus (and himself) killed—"Huge teardrop on the cheek of night."[2]

Inside, the Eleven fell to infighting like children in a sandbox—egos puffed with imaginary greatness. Jesus quieted boasting Peter with an unbelieved prophecy of his denial. And the upper-room conversation ended with the disciples' stupid response, "Look, Lord, here are two swords." Dismayed, Jesus responded, "It is enough" (22:38).

Then, in the garden such fear gripped Jesus that he thought he might die of terror before the cross. A great sweat fell from his body like hot blood coursing to the ground as he asked God to find another way if possible. Apparently his well-laid plans had gone awry.

Albert Schweitzer, the famous turn-of-the century genius—a musician (Bach expert), medical doctor, radical theologian—believed this. In his landmark book *The Quest for the Historical Jesus* (1906), he claimed to have ended the century-long search for the historical Jesus. Here is his conclusion in one of the most celebrated paragraphs in historical-critical theology:

> There is silence all around. The Baptist appears, and cries: "Repent, for the Kingdom of Heaven is at hand." Soon after that comes Jesus, and in the knowledge that He is the coming Son of Man He lays hold of the wheel of the world to set it moving on that last revolution which is to bring all ordinary history to a close. It refuses to turn, and He throws Himself upon it. Then it does turn; and crushes Him. . . . The wheel rolls onward, and the mangled body of the one immeasurably great Man, who was strong enough to think of Himself as the spiritual ruler of mankind and to bend history to His purpose, is hanging upon it still. That is His victory and His reign.[3]

Schweitzer admired Jesus for his Bergsonian kind of life-force, as a strong man. Nevertheless he was, says Schweitzer, only a man whose mangled remains now flop like a rag doll on the wheel of the world.

Did the stage production get out of control? Is Jesus still hanging on the wheel of history? Further revelations from that night suggest otherwise.

Jesus' Control: Labeling Judas' Betrayal (vv. 47, 48)

When Jesus rose from prayer the last time and stood glistening with sweat in the starlight, he was a fearless pillar of determination and mastery. He knew Judas would soon come. And now he could see lights coming toward the garden. As he urged the disciples to pray—"Rise and pray that you may not enter into temptation" (22:46)—he could clearly see the quivering shadows and the flashing of bronze armor.

The Kiss of Judas

With Gethsemane over, Jesus was serene and in sublime control of all events, including his death. The approaching circumstances were no different, but he had perfect trust in his loving Father. "While he was still speaking, there came a crowd, and the man called Judas, one of the twelve, was leading them. He drew near to Jesus to kiss him, but Jesus said to him, 'Judas, would you betray the Son of Man with a kiss?'" (vv. 47, 48). Significantly, both Matthew and Mark describe the kiss. Mark says that Judas "went up to him at once and said, 'Rabbi!' And he kissed him" (Mark 14:45; cf. Matthew 26:49). At once Judas' heavy-breathed mouth was pressed to that of Jesus. But Luke deliberately does not give the details, since for him the event is too monstrous to describe.[4]

The Greek word translated "to kiss" is the same word for "to love" (*philein*). Thus we see the mocking horror of the gesture. This image of betrayal is one of the most powerful ever to grip the human imagination. It was a truly devilish, Mephistophelean act—a kiss from Hell.

The Love of Jesus

But despite the diabolical betrayal, Jesus reached out to Judas, much as he had done at the Last Supper. Though Satan's agent, Judas was still a lost soul, and Jesus always cares about lost souls. The question Jesus asked combined foreknowledge with an appeal for repentance: "Judas, would you betray the Son of Man with a kiss?" (v. 48). It was a poignant appeal. "Judas, how could you have chosen such a sign? Could you not have employed another way? Are you so dead, so beyond feeling, that you would use a kiss?" As the old preacher Alexander Maclaren put it, "Thus to the end Christ seeks to keep him from ruin, and with meek patience resents not indignity, but with majestic calmness sets before the miserable man the hideousness of his act."[5] In the middle of the night that would devour him, Jesus was not helplessly falling into the gears of history!

Jesus' Control: Neutralizing His Disciples' Impulsive Actions (vv. 49–51)

Those spiritually dull disciples still had their two swords among them, and as we might have guessed, one of them was in Peter's possession (cf. John 18:10). He was the one who had boasted earlier in the evening, "Lord, I am ready to go with you both to prison and to death" (22:33)—and he was serious.

Luke gives the literal blow-by-blow description: "And when those who were around him saw what would follow, they said, 'Lord, shall we strike with the sword?' And one of them struck the servant of the high priest and cut off his right ear" (vv. 49, 50). The question (probably Peter's) was not really a question because before Jesus could answer, out came Peter's *macharia* (the same word used for a Roman short sword), and with poor aim but great determination Peter whacked off the right ear of one of the high priest's servants. Lucky for the man that Peter's sport was fishing! Swords instantly gleamed blue under the night sky.

There was certainly no lack of heart on the part of Peter and company. Swordsmanship aside, Peter was a good man to have on your side. A soldier who served under George Washington, nicknamed "Mad" Anthony Wayne, is alleged to have told Washington, "General, I'll storm Hell if you lay the plans." The problem with Peter was that he did not listen to plans. He was more like the taxi driver who missed the directions and only heard the words "and hurry," so he took off at high speed in the opposite direction of the destination. When the passenger asked, "Do you know where you're going?" he answered, "No, sir! But we're going there very fast!"

Peter's move was pure stupidity. He was playing perfectly into the hands of the temple mob. Thanks to Peter's impulsive violence, the authorities could now claim they had received an anonymous tip that Jesus and his armed followers were preparing for some guerrilla action. And when challenged, Jesus' gang had attacked the authorities. Most of them had been killed, and the rest were on the run. And Jesus? He was just a political subversive. Good job, Peter!

Peter's blunder had yet another grievous implication because later Jesus was to tell Pilate, "My kingdom is not of this world. If my kingdom were of this world, my servants would have been fighting, that I might not be delivered over to the Jews. But my kingdom is not from the world" (John 18:36). Were it not for Jesus' immediate mending of Peter's errant swordwork, Jesus would not have been able to make this claim. Peter's courageous violence was at cross-purposes with the divine plan. "Peter's reaction was natural, the all-too-natural reaction of mere human nature, unprepared by prayer."[6] Peter's embarrassing *faux pas* would never have happened if he had heeded the Master's words, "Pray that you may not enter into temptation" (22:40). Our human nature, unprepared by prayer, gets us into much trouble.

There is also a corporate lesson here—whenever the church has taken up the sword, it regularly has demonstrated that it does not know how to wield it, and as often as not has struck the wrong man. The sword is rightfully within the province of the state (cf. Romans 13:1–7; 1 Peter 2:13, 14), not the church.

Amid the running blood and ringing swords Jesus called out, "No more of this!" (v. 51). Jesus' words froze the action. He then reached toward the gushing wound. "And he touched his ear and healed him." This was a breath-taking display of power. The man's right ear had been severed, cut clean off according to John 18:10. But now it was whole, and Malchus (named in John's Gospel) gingerly felt it with his bloody hand.

Cosmic power flashed bright under the stars at the tips of Jesus' fingers. Such mastery! Jesus at the very moment of his arrest, with blood on the ground and steel in the air, reached out to one of his enemies and healed him. Jesus is ever full of compassion. His act prophesied that his arrest and death would provide forgiveness and healing for those who would come to him. Is this a man being crushed on the wheel of the world?

Some feel that John identified the servant as Malchus because, as the early church held, he later became a Christian. In any event, Jesus controlled the circumstances of the arrest with majestic calm.

Jesus' Control: Defining His Arrest (vv. 52, 53)

Jesus certainly had their attention, and from that vantage he serenely defined the whole event.

The Defining Question

"Then Jesus said to the chief priests and officers of the temple and elders, who had come out against him, 'Have you come out as against a robber, with swords and clubs? When I was with you day after day in the temple, you did not lay hands on me'" (vv. 52, 53a). In the upper room Jesus had predicted that he would be classed with outlaws when he quoted Isaiah 53:12: "And he was numbered with the transgressors" (22:37).

There is beautiful irony here. They could have taken him anytime they wanted if they had not feared the people (cf. 19:47, 48). In point of fact, *they* were the lawless ones, and his challenge questioned the legality of his arrest. They came under the cloak of night like armed robbers, their conduct an implicit admission that they were outside the realm of justice. Jesus' question undressed his captors, exposing their naked guilt.

The Defining Statement

This done, he issued the defining statement: "But this is your hour, and the power of darkness" (v. 53b). The physical darkness of the night matched and covered the moral darkness reigning in their hearts. What Jesus called "your hour" was really three hours in one.

It was *earth's hour* in that it was the climactic moment when fallen human beings marshaled their forces against Jesus. Jesus, the light of the world, had come as the "sunrise . . . from on high to give light to those who sit in darkness and in the shadow of death" (1:78, 79). But the Jerusalem authorities refused the light and sat stubbornly in the darkness. Their spiritual eyes were not "healthy" but "bad," so that their entire beings were "full of darkness" (11:33, 34). As a result of their resolute darkness and their eminent murder of Jesus, darkness would fittingly come over the whole land from high noon to 3:00 p.m. on the day of the crucifixion (cf. 23:44). This was fallen earth's hour of dark infamy.

The "your hour" of earth was also *Hell's hour*. In fact, the very language describing the hour and "the power of darkness" is used in other places to describe the rule and dominion of Satan (cf. Ephesians 6:12; Colossians 1:13).[7] Earth's hour was Hell's hour because fallen humanity had become instruments in Satan's assault against Jesus. The devil, who after testing Jesus at the beginning of Jesus' ministry had left him for "an opportune time" (4:13), now had his hour! The earthbound Sanhedrin may have thought themselves free when they condemned Jesus to death, but they were slaves of impulses that came straight from Hell.

When all is said and done, however, "your hour," Earth's hour, which was also Hell's hour, was preeminently *Heaven's hour*. In the upper room Jesus began his great prayer by saying, "Father, the hour has come" (John 17:1)—that "hour" being the destined hour for the events of the cross. Here in Luke the Passover meal was introduced with, "When the hour came, he reclined at table, and the apostles with him" (22:14). Thus the "hour" for Jesus began with his self-giving at the Last Supper and culminated with his delivering his spirit into the hands of the Father.[8] The suffering and death of Christ came in Heaven's hour!

As earth's hour played out, Jesus' captors freely exercised their own sinful impulses in his ritual murder. But at the same time it was Hell's hour because they were acting as unwitting agents of Satan at his time of grand opportunity. But ultimately it was Heaven's hour because Satan was but an instrument in God's great plan for the salvation of the world. Satan was the unwitting stage manager for God, and every fall and humiliation he choreographed for Christ was actually a step toward our salvation. A very limited and little God? We think not.

Closing Reflections

Albert Schweitzer's words, though elegantly composed, are pitifully empty when set beside Luke's account:

Jesus glistened as a pillar of majestic calm under the swirling stars. He received the heavy-breathed mouth of Judas—and then, again, went after Judas' soul. Mark's language portrays the kiss as mockingly passionate, using the intensive form of *philien—kataphilien*—"to kiss fervently."[9] The careful scholar Cranfield sees it as a prolonged kiss.[10] The kiss dripped hatred, but Jesus went after his heart—"Judas, would you betray the Son of Man with a kiss?" The demons howled, but the angels sang! Earth's hour and Hell's hour were both subsumed in Heaven's hour, appointed before the foundation of the world. As Peter, so disgraced in that hour, would later proclaim at Pentecost:

> Men of Israel, hear these words: Jesus of Nazareth, a man attested to you by God with mighty works and wonders and signs that God did through him in your midst, as you yourselves know—this Jesus, delivered up according to the definite plan and foreknowledge of God, you crucified and killed by the hands of lawless men. (Acts 2:22, 23)

There was silence all around because this night was the necessary prelude to Christ's reign! There in the devouring darkness Jesus was victor.

And we share in that victory. A Savior who triumphs in his darkest hour can deliver his children from theirs. We can be sure, when our world spins out of control, that he is with us. We can be sure that the apparent evil we suffer will work out for our good and his glory. Joseph in his Egypt found it so. Paul in prison found it so. It is true for all of God's children.

> Who every grief hath known
> That wrings the human breast,
> And takes and bears them for His own,
> That all in Him may rest.
>
> Matthew Bridges, 1851

97

Peter's Plunge

LUKE 22:54–62

THE GOSPELS ARE FULL OF PETER! No disciple spoke as often as Peter. And of necessity our Lord addressed him more than any other of his followers. No disciple was reproved by Jesus as much or as strongly as Peter was, and he was the only disciple who thought it his duty to reprove Jesus! No disciple ever so boldly confessed and encouraged Christ—and none ever bothered our Lord more than Peter.

Peter was always talking—and his verbiage ranged from the ridiculous to the sublime. Sometimes he only opened his mouth to change feet, and at other times his words were immortal. Christ spoke words of approval and blessing to Peter, the like of which he never spoke to any other man. But at the same time, almost in the same breath, Jesus said sterner things to Peter than to any other of his twelve disciples, including Judas. All the Gospels testify to Peter's primacy. In each of the four lists of the apostles given in the Gospels the order of the names vary, but Peter's is always first and Judas' is always last.

Shortly after Peter's calling, when he observed the miracle of the great catch of fish, he cried, "Depart from me, for I am a sinful man, O Lord" (5:8). He was profoundly aware of his need. In answer to Christ's question as to who he was, Peter's immortal response was, "You are the Christ, the Son of the living God" (Matthew 16:16). And yet a few moments later when Christ spoke of the cross, Peter foolishly replied, "Far be it from you, Lord! This shall never happen to you" (Matthew 16:22). Foot-in-mouth disease again! On that stormy night on Tiberias, it was Peter who bravely called, "Lord, if it is you, command me to come to you on the water" (Matthew 14:28), then a few moments later cried, "Lord, save me" (Matthew 14:30).

It will always be to his credit that when the others abandoned Jesus, realizing he was not primarily a Savior of the material order but a spiritual Savior, and Jesus poignantly asked, "Do you want to go away as well?" Simon Peter answered him, "Lord, to whom shall we go? You have the words of eternal life" (John 6:67, 68). But it was also Peter who later on the Mount of Transfiguration, when Jesus shone like the sun, made the preposterous proposal, "Lord, it is good that we are here. If you wish, I will make three tents here, one for you and one for Moses and one for Elijah" (Matthew 17:4).

Later, in the upper room, John's account records Peter as saying, "You shall never wash my feet" (John 13:8). Then, hearing Jesus' explanation, he loudly reversed himself, saying, "Lord, not my feet only but also my hands and my head!" (John 13:9). Finally, after the Resurrection his unforgettable devotion was memorably expressed: "Lord, you know everything; you know that I love you" (John 21:17).

When I think of Peter, I imagine a broad-shouldered, loud, extroverted, assertive man who is always sweating. Lloyd Douglas's title *The Big Fisherman* captures him for me. He was a headstrong, unbridled hulk who was always getting into trouble and causing his Master plenty of the same. Sometimes we preachers use him as a homiletical whipping boy. It's great fun to portray "God's clod" slipping below the waters of Galilee! But we forget that none of us have ever walked on water!

Peter's sheer humanity makes him everyone's teacher. As Clarence Macartney so well explained: "His impulsive deeds, his frequent questions, his eager exclamations and confessions, the praise and honor and rebukes that were bestowed upon him, his sometimes manly and sometimes cowardly acts, his oaths, his bitter tears—all this makes Peter the great companion and the great instructor of his fellow men and his fellow Christians."[1] The night of his failure is perhaps the most instructive night of his life.

Peter's Presumption (22:31–34)

You will recall it was in the upper room, amid the din of the disciples' chest-thumping and bleating about who was the greatest, that Jesus unmasked Peter's presumption. Peter reacted to Jesus' prediction of his failure by saying, "Lord, I am ready to go with you both to prison and to death" (22:33). It was a wholly sincere presumption—"I'm telling you, Lord, that right now I can do this. I'm a strong man, and if I put my mind to it, that's it!" Peter meant it. He was no mere braggart. But it was dangerous presumption. Perhaps if angels were present, they winced and reflected, "Peter, you shouldn't have said that—at least not like you did. Proverbs 16:18, Peter—pride comes before a fall."

Alexander Whyte, the celebrated Scottish preacher, wrote: "Peter was born a supreme man. Nature herself, as we call her, had, with her ever-bountiful and original hands, stamped his [*sic*] supremacy upon Peter before he was born. And when he came to be a disciple of Jesus Christ he entered on, and continued to hold, that natural and aboriginal supremacy."[2]

We often see this kind of presumption in a naturally gifted athlete who finds it hard to listen to coaching advice because he feels no need. Sadly, the sidelines are strewn with has-beens who refused to learn from the wisdom of others and never developed the technique and understanding they needed. Perceived natural strength can be a disadvantage—especially in spiritual matters.

Peter's fateful presumption was also aided by his intense love for Jesus. How could he love Jesus so and conceive of disappointing him under any circumstance? Unthinkable! But Peter was also just plain naive. He did not understand the spiritual Everest before him. He figured all he needed were some strong legs and a good pair of sandals and he could scale any spiritual peak.

It was hard to get Peter to see reality, but the Lord was adamant: "I tell you, Peter, the rooster will not crow this day, until you deny three times that you know me" (22:34). Perhaps Peter sulked like a chastened puppy dog—"Just wait—I'll show everyone . . ."

Peter's Outburst (22:49–51)

When Peter had proclaimed that he would never desert the Lord, he was thinking, no doubt, of an attack by the Lord's enemies. And Peter made good on his vow, because when the armed detachment came, and Judas so obscenely bestowed his kiss of betrayal, out came Peter's sword. It was Peter against the world. Peter's swordsmanship may have been less than Zorro-like. But there is another explanation. Malchus may have been wearing the traditional helmet that left the ears exposed, and Peter caught him atop the head and took off an ear. Peter was playing for keeps! Though impulsive and angry, Peter was willing and ready to take on the enemy. He was a brave man. "Lord, I don't know about the rest of these 'men.' But at least you have me, and Judas and his friends are going to have to come through me. It's just you and me, Jesus . . . I'll lay down my life for you!" Peter saw red. His trembling sword would show no mercy. But Jesus' commanding voice rang louder than Peter's sword—"No more of this!" (22:51)—as he calmly restored the severed ear.

Angry confusion fell like a shroud on Peter. He had been rebuked when he expected praise. Then came the sickening humiliation of Jesus in shackles. The night faded to a monochrome, and his mind gave way to a jostled gray kaleidoscope as he stumbled down the mountain after Jesus—unappreciated, embarrassed, despairing. Peter's faltering stand foreshadowed his miserable plunge.

Peter's Fall (vv. 54–62)

"Then they seized him [Jesus] and led him away, bringing him into the high priest's house, and Peter was following at a distance. And when they had kindled a fire in the middle of the courtyard and sat down together, Peter sat down among them" (vv. 54, 55). In the dreary, damp chill of a spent night, Peter sat down amid the enemy. Matthew says that he sat down with the guards "to see the end" (Matthew 26:58). He was overwhelmed with cold, dark, listless depression.

Peter was in dangerous company. One of the servant girls of the high priest's household had been studying him. Perhaps the fire blazed up, revealing him more clearly, for Luke says, "Then a servant girl, seeing him as he sat in the light and looking closely at him, said, 'This man also was with him.' But he denied it, saying, 'Woman, I do not know him'" (vv. 56, 57). Peter's wording is similar to the Jewish ban formulas—"I have never known you."[3] But formal or not, it was a lie, a bald-faced denial.

At this time most of Christ's disciples had run off and abandoned him. Peter, to his eternal credit, had at least followed him. But in a foggy instant he had abandoned the battle. He gave the impression that if he was not one of the enemy, he was at most a mutual bystander. The lie had thrown its first coil about him, and it began to tighten.

Because it was cold, as Jesus' interrogation continued behind closed doors those in the courtyard stayed close to the fire. The conversation ranged from one subject to another—the Passover crowds, yesterday's fight at the barracks, the new dancing girl, this eccentric teacher from Galilee. Then came another accusation: "And a little later someone else saw him and said, 'You also are one of them.' But Peter said, 'Man, I am not'" (v. 58). Another serpent's coil slid about Peter. In his first lie he had denied knowing Jesus; in the second he denied being one of his disciples.

The coiled deception rested comfortably on Peter, imperceptibly tightening. "And after an interval of about an hour still another insisted, saying,

'Certainly this man also was with him, for he too is a Galilean.' But Peter said, 'Man, I do not know what you are talking about'" (vv. 59, 60a). Mark's parallel is more damning: "He began to invoke a curse on himself and to swear, 'I do not know this man of whom you speak'" (Mark 14:71). Curled lips, flashing teeth, vile shouts of denial.

It was the moment of truth. In the heat of his denial, Peter was oblivious to the shuffle of feet as Christ was being led out into the courtyard—and certainly he was not prepared for the excruciation of the next moment. Dr. Luke tells us: "And immediately, while he was still speaking, the rooster crowed. And the Lord turned and looked at Peter. And Peter remembered the saying of the Lord, how he had said to him, 'Before the rooster crows today, you will deny me three times.' And he went out and wept bitterly" (vv. 60b–62). Terrible providence! Christ paused and looked right into the soul of Peter, and the tears coursed down Peter's face like rain down a rock.

No one will ever know the hellish anguish that Peter went through during the next few hours and days! Something died inside Peter that night—Simon the natural man with all his self-assured presumption.

Peter's Preservation

The Lord was after nothing less than Peter's perfection. And this final terrible encounter with the Master reveals what saved the apostle.

Christ's Look

The cosmic pain that jolted Peter when their eyes met began the necessary process of remorse. Again he was "a sinful man," as he had earlier called himself after the miracle of the great catch of fish (5:8). But the knowledge of what he was in his heart was stripped of any rhetoric. Its raw meaning was there to stay, with all its sanctifying potential. But the Master's look did even more—it maintained the link between Peter's soul and Christ. It was a knowing look that said, "Peter, it is happening just as I told you. Now remember it all! Because I prophesied more than your fall as the rooster crowed."

Christ's Word

Christ's prophetic word in the upper room had foretold that Peter would be sifted by Satan's temptation (22:31), and the sifting process had shown that Peter was "mere chaff in the sieve of discernment."[4] Yet Christ was preserving him, so that only real wheat would remain. Peter was being made into a man of substance.

But there is more! Christ had said, "when you have turned again" (22:32), prophesying Peter's repentance. The message was clear: though through his denial he was a sinner *par excellence*, he would be granted repentance. And repent he would. Not only that, Jesus had said that when Peter turned back, he was to "strengthen [his] brothers." He would have a ministry—a strengthening ministry. The "sinful man" would actually become a pillar of the church.

Christ's Prayer

Of course, the grand redemptive power, the reason Peter had not been sifted into oblivion, the reason he repented and was restored, was Christ's prayer for him: "But I have prayed for you that your faith may not fail" (22:32a). When Peter was indulging in his post-supper snooze in Gethsemane, Jesus prayed for him. In fact, Jesus had been praying for him since the beginning of their relationship. We all need the prayers of others—godly parents and siblings and friends. But behind all those prayers are the prayers Christ offers for us (cf. Romans 8:34; Hebrews 7:25). Even if those who love you are gone, Christ keeps praying for you.

> Since then we have a great high priest who has passed through the heavens, Jesus, the Son of God, let us hold fast our confession. For we do not have a high priest who is unable to sympathize with our weaknesses, but one who in every respect has been tempted as we are, yet without sin. Let us then with confidence draw near to the throne of grace, that we may receive mercy and find grace to help in time of need. (Hebrews 4:14–16)

Peter's Perfection

All of this was meant by God to perfect Peter in the sense of maturing him. Of course, Peter never became perfect in this life. No one does! Evidence of his imperfections abound (cf. Galatians 2:11–14). Nevertheless, a massive perfecting took place in Peter in respect to his innate, fleshly presumption. From here on, the Scriptures record a different Peter.

A Fish Breakfast

Peter's formal restoration came on the shores of Galilee when, after recognizing Christ at the water's edge, he dove into the sea and came to sit wet around a charcoal fire with Christ (John 21). And there three times our Lord extracted an avowal of love, also commissioning the fallen apostle three times. After this Peter was never the same. Gone was the presumption. Gone was the arrogance. Gone was the independence. Gone was the self-reliance.

Pentecost

In their place was the power of God freely coursing through a broken, humble man—and it was awesome. Listen to the man who earlier cowered before a slave girl:

> Men of Israel, hear these words: Jesus of Nazareth, a man attested to you by God with mighty works and wonders and signs that God did through him in your midst, as you yourselves know—this Jesus, delivered up according to the definite plan and foreknowledge of God, you crucified and killed by the hands of lawless men. God raised him up, loosing the pangs of death, because it was not possible for him to be held by it. (Acts 2:22–24)

Fearless power!

Death

After Peter's restoration at Galilee, Jesus prophesied that Peter would die by crucifixion himself ("when you are old, you will stretch out your hands," John 21:18), using what became standard Christian language for martyrdom.[5] The Church Fathers used the term as referring to crucifixion.[6] There is significant support from tradition that Peter was indeed crucified—but upside down at his request because he deemed himself unworthy to die like Christ.

Closing Reflections

God excels at perfecting his saints. Delivering us from self-sufficiency is a major function of the ups and downs of this life. Paul besought the Lord three times to have a certain affliction removed, but God answered, "My grace is sufficient for you, for my power is made perfect in weakness." Paul then commented, "Therefore I will boast all the more gladly of my weaknesses, so that the power of Christ may rest upon me. For the sake of Christ, then, I am content with weaknesses, insults, hardships, persecutions, and calamities. For when I am weak, then I am strong" (2 Corinthians 12:9, 10).

Peter has been purposely portrayed by the Holy Spirit in Holy Scripture as a very human man to whom we can all relate. He is an archetype of those who have come to Christ in loving submission but with the passing of time have succumbed to independence and self-reliance. Peter is us! Peter's experience is our experience writ large on the pages of Holy Scripture so that we will not miss it.

As C. S. Lewis said in *Mere Christianity*:

Though our feelings come and go, His love for us does not. It is not wearied by our sins, or our indifference; and, therefore, it is quite relentless in its determination that we shall be cured of those sins, at whatever cost to us, at whatever cost to Him.[7]

He warned people to "count the cost" before becoming Christians. "Make no mistake," He says, "if you let me, I will make you perfect. The moment you put yourself in My hands, that is what you are in for. Nothing less, or other, than that. You have free will, and if you choose, you can push Me away. But if you do not push Me away, understand that I am going to see this job through. Whatever suffering it may cost you in your earthly life, whatever inconceivable purification it may cost you after death, whatever it costs Me, I will never rest, nor let you rest, until you are literally perfect—until my Father can say without reservation that He is well pleased with you, as He said He was well pleased with me. This I can do and will do. But I will not do anything less."[8]

98

Jesus' Religious Trial

LUKE 22:63–71

IT IS A FACT that a mob will descend to deeper levels of cruelty than the individuals within the mob normally would if acting alone. The tradition of lynch mobs testifies to the corporate cruelty of otherwise law-abiding citizens.

Luke here describes Jesus' becoming a victim of the corporate depravity of a bunch of bored guards. Jesus claimed to be a prophet, so how about a game of blindman's bluff with an interesting twist? "Now the men who were holding Jesus in custody were mocking him as they beat him. They also blindfolded him and kept asking him, 'Prophesy! Who is it that struck you?' And they said many other things against him, blaspheming him" (vv. 63–65). Let the games begin! The other Gospels add that, bare-knuckled, they punched and slapped and slugged Jesus left and right and also spit in his face (Matthew 26:67, 68; Mark 14:65).

Religion is always good for a joke among godless men, and especially for a self-proclaimed prophet. The grim irony was that their abuse fulfilled Jesus' own prophetic words: "He will be delivered over to the Gentiles and will be mocked and shamefully treated and spit upon. And after flogging him, they will kill him" (18:32, 33). The irony was further compounded because his prophetic powers had just been vindicated in the preceding event when Peter denied him three times, precisely as Jesus had predicted. Now the torture had begun, and Jesus stood in regal silence, dripping spittle and blood.

The religious establishment began to gloat. They had him at last. The populace of Jerusalem would soon awaken, but none would know what had transpired before Jesus was hustled off to the Roman authorities. "When day came, the assembly of the elders of the people gathered together, both chief priests and scribes. And they led him [Jesus] away to their council"

(v. 66). Torches were still flickering against the walls in the chilled judgment chamber as the light of dawn outlined the Mount of Olives. No doubt, it was a kangaroo-court Sanhedrin that glared at Jesus. Not all the members knew of the event, so some seats were empty. But, oh, their satisfaction as their disheveled, bloodied adversary stood before them. There they sat in concentric semicircles—a mess of beards, sly, sinister eyes, evil tongues. Their eyes were red with rage. Some shook with uncontrollable, delicious anticipation. They felt themselves in full control now.

But again they were deluded. Their hour of power when darkness reigned was in truth his hour of power (cf. 22:53). Jesus seized the occasion to again confirm who he was (with a formal declaration of his deity) before he died. Three of his divine titles were showcased before the Sanhedrin—namely, *Christ*, *Son of Man*, and *Son of God*. And it was done in such a way that they would only have themselves to blame for pulling the declaration out of him.

It was so fitting that the representative leaders of Israel, evil and truth-rejecting as they were, should hear at this crucial moment in salvation history the full assertion of Jesus' full deity.

The Christ (vv. 67, 68)

The Sanhedrin's opening question cut to the quick: "If you are the Christ, tell us" (v. 67). Luke's Gospel leaves us in no doubt that Jesus is the Christ, the Messiah. (The terms are synonymous. Both mean "anointed one." *Messiah* is the Hebrew word and *Christ* the Greek word.) The noun *Christ* is used as a title some twenty-five times in Luke.[1]

The earliest themes of Luke's Gospel, the birth narratives themselves, exude messianic identification for Jesus. Gabriel's annunciation to Mary makes it explicit, though he does not use the word *Messiah*: "And behold, you will conceive in your womb and bear a son, and you shall call his name Jesus. He will be great and will be called the Son of the Most High. And the Lord God will give to him the throne of his father David" (1:31, 32). Jesus would be the Messiah because only the Messiah could sit on David's throne. And when Jesus was born, the glory-dazzled shepherds heard the angel of the Lord say, "For unto you is born this day in the city of David a Savior, who is Christ the Lord" (2:11).

And when Jesus' parents presented him in the temple, the man who swept Jesus into his arms and sang the *Nunc Dimittis* is described in this way: "Now there was a man in Jerusalem, whose name was Simeon, and this man was righteous and devout, waiting for the consolation of Israel, and the

Holy Spirit was upon him. And it had been revealed to him by the Holy Spirit that he would not see death before he had seen the Lord's Christ" (2:25, 26).

Later when people were wondering if John the Baptist might be the Christ, he demurred, saying, "I baptize you with water, but he who is mightier than I is coming, the strap of whose sandals I am not worthy to untie. He will baptize you with the Holy Spirit and fire" (3:16). John saw Jesus as the Messiah.

And, of course, when Jesus asked Peter who he was, Peter answered, "The Christ of God" (9:20). Jesus himself attempted to get the religious authorities to understand that the Messiah must be divine by referencing Psalm 110:1 and asking them, "David thus calls him Lord, so how is he his son?" (20:44). So Luke explodes with the fact that Jesus is the Christ/Messiah.

But significantly, Jesus rarely asserted his messianic title and generally avoided the term *Messiah*, because the title was so politicized. In Jesus' day the title *Messiah* was not generally thought to be a divine title, but that of an anointed agent, descended from David's royal line, who would cast out the Romans and restore Israel. And that is what the people wanted. However, it was the one title that could get Jesus killed by the Romans because it smacked of rebellion. Rome could not care less if he claimed to be God. But Messiah? Watch out! So if the Sanhedrin could get Jesus to say it, he was a dead man!

Jesus, of course, knew he was a dead man, but he had some other assertions about himself he wanted to proclaim. So he gave them a non-answer: "If I tell you, you will not believe, and if I ask you, you will not answer" (vv. 67b, 68). Jesus saw that it was useless to answer them, for they had already decided to reject whatever he said. They were not truly interested in considering the matter. Furthermore, their earlier prevarications, when he had asked them about the origin of John's baptism, had demonstrated their dishonesty (cf. 20:1–8). Jesus' deft nonanswer was not a denial that he was the Messiah. In fact, he would openly embrace the fact that he was "the King of the Jews" before Pilate (23:3)—and that would be his epitaph over the cross. His nonanswer here indicated that he was Messiah, but it did not give them the words to hang him—yet!

The Son of Man (v. 69)

Jesus was and is Messiah/Christ, but he was a far greater Messiah than they ever dreamed, for he is also *the Son of Man*! And he let the Sanhedrin know it in no uncertain terms! "But from now on the Son of Man shall be seated at the right hand of the power of God" (v. 69).

Son of Man was Jesus' awesome title of choice. No one had given the title to him. Sometime in the process of Jesus' coming into his full messianic consciousness, Jesus read of the divine being in Daniel 7:13—"one like a son of man"—who came on the clouds of Heaven, and to whom the Ancient of Days gave "glory and a kingdom" and also "everlasting dominion" (Daniel 7:14), and he said, "This is me!" Jesus began to use *Son of Man* as a substitute for the personal pronoun "I." The Gospels have eighty-two instances of its use, mostly on the lips of Jesus. *Son of man* encapsulated how Jesus saw himself!

The term beautifully expressed two huge realities of his earthly life: 1) his human mortality, and 2) his heavenly existence. As to his humanity, that title perfectly expressed the incarnation and the paradox of his subjection to death. Immediately after Peter's confession that Jesus was "the Christ of God," Jesus said, "The Son of Man must suffer many things and be rejected by the elders and chief priests and scribes, and be killed, and on the third day be raised" (9:22; cf. 9:43b–45). As to his divinity, he was and is the awesome being to whom the Father gives everything. Upon his ascension, he declared, "All authority in heaven and on earth has been given to me" (Matthew 28:18)—a veritable bookend to the original bequeathal of "dominion and glory and a kingdom" to the Son of Man in Daniel 7:14.

Jesus' declaration to the Sanhedrin—"But from now on the Son of Man shall be seated at the right hand of the power of God" (v. 69)—was a prophecy of his heavenly exaltation as Messiah at the right hand of God that would begin with his resurrection and be consummated at his second coming (cf. Psalm 110:1; Luke 21:27; Acts 2:32–36). At the same time, it spoke of his exercising ultimate judgment. The Sanhedrin, those who were then judging him, would one day see him as their eternal judge.[2]

Indeed, Jesus is the Messiah, the King. But he is a Messiah before whom all politicized messiahs melt. He is "the Son of Man," and "His dominion is an everlasting dominion, which shall not pass away, and his kingdom one that shall not be destroyed" (Daniel 7:14). He sits at the right hand of God, and he is coming in the clouds to judge the world!

The Son of God (vv. 70–71)

Those members of the Sanhedrin who were Biblically literate caught the drift of Jesus' bold declaration, and their beards bristled and their eyes fired. The "son of man" of Daniel 7:13 was generally considered to be *divine!* So now all the assembly chorused, "Are you the Son of God, then?" (v. 70a), hoping to catch him in blasphemy.

As with the title *Messiah*, the term *Son of God* was Jesus' from the earliest chords of the birth narratives. In Gabriel's annunciation we hear it: "And behold, you will conceive in your womb and bear a son, and you shall call his name Jesus. He will be great and will be called the Son of the Most High" (1:31, 32a). At Jesus' baptism, "the Holy Spirit descended on him in bodily form, like a dove; and a voice came from heaven, 'You are my beloved Son; with you I am well pleased'" (3:22). Twice during Jesus' temptation in the wilderness, the devil attempted to create doubt by saying, "If you are the Son of God . . ." (4:3, 9). And at the transfiguration, as Jesus was enveloped in the *Shekinah* glory, "A voice came out of the cloud, saying, 'This is my Son, my Chosen One; listen to him!'" (9:35).

Notwithstanding the exalted nature of the titles *Messiah* and *Son of Man*, the supreme title of Jesus is *the Son of God*. That title describes the unique Father-Son relationship within the Trinity. To be the Son the way Jesus' incarnation was described by Gabriel is to be divine (cf. 1:35). The opening verses of John's Gospel describe the relationship as eternal equality: "In the beginning was the Word, and the Word was with God, and the Word was God. He was in the beginning with God" (John 1:1, 2). To be the Son of God is to be God!

Thus, in the next few hours when God "gave his only Son" (John 3:16), it was God the Son who was given for our sins. The atonement's sufficiency would come from the infinity of the eternal Son. Thus Jesus serenely answered, "You say that I am" (v. 70b). The Sanhedrin now had what they so wanted. "Then they said, 'What further testimony do we need? We have heard it ourselves from his own lips'" (v. 71). Perhaps a red-faced Levite flew from the Sanhedrin in an uproar, eager to announce to a crowd outside what had just transpired. "The High Priest is tearing his robes! The criminal just said he is the Son of God! The elders are on their feet ripping their garments and shouting, 'Death! Death!'"

Closing Reflections

Jesus demonstrated incredible mastery at his "religious" trial before the Sanhedrin. He said in effect, "If you're going to kill me, you're going to have to kill me for who I am—the Messiah, the Son of Man, the Son of God." Jesus had been toying with them. He had what *he* wanted!

We must never forget that on the night before Jesus died, he proclaimed to the world that he was *the Messiah*, the long-awaited descendant of David who would sit on the throne. Furthermore, what he proclaimed went far beyond their dreams. He was a suffering, atoning Messiah. After his death and resurrection he said, "O foolish ones, and slow of heart to believe all that the prophets have spoken! Was it not necessary that the Christ should suffer these things and enter into his glory?" (24:25). He died as Messiah-King with the declaration "Jesus of Nazareth, the King of the Jews" penned in three languages above his head so all the world would know that he is Messiah (John 19:19). His kingdom rule flows from the cross. And this same person who went into Heaven will return on the clouds to judge the world (cf. Acts 1:11; Revelation 19:11ff.).

We must never forget that on the night before Jesus died, he declared that he was *the Son of Man*. He saw himself riding in the clouds to the Ancient of Days and receiving everlasting dominion. The Son of Man is both human and divine. It was the Son of Man who was judged to be a criminal that early dawn. And he is the one who will come to judge, and the judges of that morning as well as the whole world will stand at his bar.

We must never forget that on the night before Jesus died, he proclaimed that he was *the Son of God*. God the Son bore our sins. And that is why we have such hope.

99

Herod before Jesus

LUKE 23:1–12

JESUS HAD JUST EMERGED at dawn from his religious trial before the Sanhedrin, where its enraged members had concluded that he must die. His admission that he was the Son of God, a blasphemous admission in their eyes, launched them into a murderous, robe-tearing rage. They would have killed him outright, but they lacked the political power to do so. The right to inflict capital punishment had been taken from them by the occupying Romans (cf. John 18:31).

A political trial under secular Roman authority and law was necessary. Thus came the most infamous trial in history, a weird, twisted thing that began before Pilate, the careerist Roman politician, then detoured to the tetrarch Herod, the half-Jew puppet ruler, and finally returned to Pilate where the awful judgment was rendered. The drama was exquisite—almost like a classic Greek play with its chorus and actors. The chorus was first the Sanhedrin howling for Jesus' death, then the multitudes crying, "Crucify him!" Jesus stood at center stage in serene mastery, and around him were the supporting actors Pilate and Herod, their decaying consciences creeping toward death. We will in this chapter consider Herod and Jesus. First, a little background.

John and Herod (Mark 6:14–25)

This Herod, Herod Antipas, is the one who along with his wife Herodias had come under fire by John the Baptist. Herodias was the daughter of Herod's half-brother Aristobulus and thus was Herod's niece. Furthermore, when he met her in Rome she was the wife of another of his half-brothers, Herod Philip, and was therefore his sister-in-law. But he nevertheless seduced her and persuaded her to leave Philip to become his wife. This was totally unallowable under Jewish law (cf. Leviticus 18:6, 16).

Straight-shooting John the Baptist had let the "liberated" royals both have it, charging, "It is not lawful for you to have your brother's wife" (Mark 6:18). So for very personal reasons, "Herodias had a grudge against him" (Mark 6:19). But it was mainly for political reasons that Herod arrested John and threw him in the dungeon of the desert fortress-palace of Machaerus, perched on a high ridge by the Dead Sea.[1] Here the Baptist and Herod resided below and above in dramatic antithesis. John was the man who kept his conscience and lost his head. Herod was the man who took John's head and lost his own conscience.

Conscience Stirred

As John languished in the dungeon, a wholly unexpected relationship developed with Herod. Mark records: "And Herodias had a grudge against him and wanted to put him to death. But she could not, for Herod feared John, knowing that he was a righteous and holy man, and he kept him safe. When he [Herod] heard him, he was greatly perplexed, and yet he heard him gladly" (Mark 6:19, 20). When the gorgeously robed tetrarch and hair-coated prophet met, there was confrontation. John held nothing back. As a result, though Herod held every advantage, he "feared John . . . and he kept him safe." Why? Because he considered him to be "a righteous and holy man." Goodness is terrifying to evil people. Someone has said, "The truth will make you free, but first it will make you miserable." The important point is, Herod's discomfiting fear was evidence that his conscience was stirred by John's words.

"When he [Herod] heard him, he was greatly perplexed, and yet he heard him gladly." What pleasure would there be for Herod in this? Why would bologna like the meat grinder? John must have been a breath of fresh air amid the debauchery and intrigues of the Hasmonean court. Herod may have felt inexplicably elevated by John's company. Perhaps he made even some attempts at self-reformation and did a good deed or two. We know that he returned again and again to take it on the chin from John, and then protected him. His conscience had been stirred.

Conscience Violated

Meanwhile, Herodias hated John and wanted to do him in, and "an opportunity came when Herod on his birthday gave a banquet for his nobles and military commanders and the leading men of Galilee" (Mark 6:21). Stag birthday parties were common to the Herodians,[2] and Herodias knew what to expect—a drinking crowd that would become increasingly sensual and nasty as the evening progressed, increasingly demanding "male entertainments." Presumably the evening was well along and the crowd sufficiently under the influence when she made her move, using her teenage daughter Salome. "When Herodias's daughter came in and danced, she pleased Herod and his guests" (Mark 6:22). Normally this dance would have been by the *hetarai*, the professional court dancers and prostitutes, but Herodias put forth her own daughter. The girl's sensuous, voluptuous dance, unheard of among women of rank, was a sensation.

Pleased, the wine-dazed tetrarch slurred, "Ask me for whatever you wish, and I will give it to you" (Mark 6:22). Then he promised her with an oath, consciously aping the style of the king to Queen Esther (Esther 5:3): "Whatever you ask me, I will give you, up to half of my kingdom" (Mark 6:23). You can imagine the cheers from the men—"All right, Herod"—and their rapt expectations. They began to mentally speculate on what she would ask. A pair of matched stallions? A pearled dress from Rome?

The trap was perfectly set. "And she went out and said to her mother, 'For what should I ask?' And she said, 'The head of John the Baptist.' And she came in immediately with haste to the king and asked, saying, 'I want you to give me at once the head of John the Baptist.'" Salome even added her own gruesome twist—"on a platter" (Mark 6:24, 25). Like mother, like daughter. The room was silent, and Herod was suddenly sober. This is what Salome wanted? That scheming Herodias!

"And the king was exceedingly sorry" (Mark 6:26). He was in genuine grief. The Greek word used here appears only one other time in the New Testament, to describe Jesus' pain in the garden of Gethsemane (Mark 14:34). For a moment at least Herod's conscience was mightily torn! His moral shudder was a sign of life. For an instant everything was possible, even his repentance.

But what would his friends think? The tribunes would carry news of his reneging back to Rome, and the whole Imperial Court would laugh at him. He could not have that. "And immediately the king sent an executioner with orders to bring John's head. He went and beheaded him in the prison and brought his head on a platter and gave it to the girl, and the girl gave it to her mother" (Mark 6:27, 28). What a tragedy! Herod's conscience had begun to speak, but he silenced it because of what he feared others would think, because of his reputation, his "honor." Now only gaping darkness awaited Herod.

Conscience Heard

Later, though John was dead, Jesus' ministry was flourishing. His dramatic miracles had galvanized the attention of the countryside. His disciples had gone out ministering in his power, and they too were healing many and casting out demons. Eventually word about Jesus crept into the palace: "King Herod heard of it, for Jesus' name had become known. Some said, 'John the Baptist has been raised from the dead. That is why these miraculous powers are at work in him.' But others said, 'He is Elijah.' And others said, 'He is a prophet, like one of the prophets of old.' But when Herod heard of it, he said, 'John, whom I beheaded, has been raised'" (Mark 6:14–16). The language here is graphic. The "I" is emphatic in the Greek: "I am the one—I did it!" The sense is that he said it again and again. He was worried!

We all do evils that we naturally put away from our conscience as if they never happened. We refuse to confess them to God or man. Then some hook tossed at random brings up a memory we mistakenly supposed was lost in the ocean of oblivion. Trivial incidents may awaken the suppressed conscience—a chance word, a sound, a scent, an expression on a face. Such an event is meant to call us to repentance and forgiveness.

That is what Herod's conscience was furtively doing. But there was no repentance, no radical turning, just a futile occult speculation that Jesus was somehow John returned from the dead. Herod was frightened into a paganistic spiritism that did not lead him to Christ. The tide was out, never to return.

Jesus and Pilate (Luke 23:1–7)

Now, after Jesus had been found guilty in a religious trial, the Sanhedrin frantically pushed for political judgment as they rushed Jesus over to Pilate and then, unexpectedly, to Herod. They leveled three political charges against him (vv. 1, 2). "Then the whole company of them arose and brought him before Pilate. And they began to accuse him, saying, 'We found this man misleading our nation.'" This was a bald-faced lie. There was not a hint of sedition in any of Jesus' teachings. They continued, "[He forbids] us to give tribute to Caesar"—another palpable lie. That was not what he meant when he said, "Then render to Caesar the things that are Caesar's, and to God the things that are God's" (20:25)—"and saying that he himself is Christ, a king." Though at the Triumphal Entry he had received the crowd's adulation ("Blessed is the King who comes in the name of the Lord!"—19:38), he had never himself made the claim, and certainly not in the politicized sense with which they were charging him.

And Pilate, the wily politician, saw through their spurious accusations. He was incredulous. "And Pilate asked him, 'Are you the King of the Jews?'" (v. 3a). To which Jesus answered obliquely, "You have said so" (v. 3b)—literally, "You say it"[3] or "It is you who say this!"—"The statement is yours, Pilate." Jesus was serenely casual—almost nonchalant. So Pilate rendered his initial verdict: "Then Pilate said to the chief priests and the crowds, 'I find no guilt in this man'" (v. 4). He could see that Jesus was harmless. "Case closed!"

And it should have ended there. "But they were urgent, saying, 'He stirs up the people, teaching throughout all Judea, from Galilee even to this place'" (v. 5). It was a frantic, indefinite charge. And Pilate could see the situation was becoming crazy. But their mention of "Galilee" gave him an idea. "When Pilate heard this, he asked whether the man was a Galilean. And when he learned that he belonged to Herod's jurisdiction, he sent him over to Herod, who was himself in Jerusalem at that time" (vv. 6, 7).

Will Rogers once said, "There have been two great eras in American history, the passing of the buffalo and the passing of the buck." Pilate passed the buck to Herod. It was Herod's shekel now.

Jesus and Herod (vv. 8–12)

Herod's Delight

Herod was thrilled but for the wrong reasons. "When Herod saw Jesus, he was very glad, for he had long desired to see him, because he had heard about him, and he was hoping to see some sign done by him" (v. 8). Herod had no spiritual interest whatsoever in seeing Jesus. For him it was show time. He was not even interested in seeing Jesus prove his claims by signs (cf. 11:16, 29). All he wanted was a spectacular show—a religious Houdini. Note too that his former spiritual interests had evaporated. There was now no fear. All he felt was a debauched delight in the anticipation of a few tricks. His murder of John had produced an incapacity to see anything in Jesus.

Jesus' Silence

Jesus gave no response to Herod whatsoever—"So he questioned him at some length, but he made no answer" (v. 9). The phrase "He questioned " is in the Greek imperfect tense, indicating that Herod conducted a lengthy interrogation. He was having fun!

Jesus was willing to reason with the scoundrel high priest Caiaphas, and even to prophesy to him (cf. 22:69, 70). Jesus conversed with Pilate and gave him great substance for thought (cf. 23:3; John 18:33–38). Jesus grieved over Judas as he tenderly reached out for his soul in the upper room. But this same Jesus maintained a dreadful silence before Herod. Herod's day of grace was already over! Herod had stifled his conscience long before, and now it could not respond.

Jesus' appalling silence was matched by Herod's appalling dismissal. He stood face-to-face with God the Son who is absolute righteousness and absolute goodness and saw nothing in him. Herod was so dead that he dressed God in a robe so he and his bodyguards could mock him (v. 11). He held God in contempt.

Closing Reflections

A great truth shouts for our attention in this story—*the conscience is perishable.*

Nonbelievers

It is possible for a human being to be so jaded that he or she can stand face-to-face with Christ and feel nothing. This is a real possibility for any nonbeliever. Most who descend to this level do not perform the outrages of Herod. Most do not verbalize their opposition. They are simply indifferent and feel nothing.

If you are not a believer, if you presently like to listen to God's Word, if you have a reverence and fear for God, do not be content to simply go on hearing his words—do what his words call you to do! If you go on hearing the gospel but neglect it, you invite a fog over your eyes that in time will shut out all the light. Respond now while the gospel impresses you, for a day may come when it no longer does.

The silence of Jesus is an extreme and dramatic warning not to trifle with holy things, not to suppress the private appeals and suggestions of the Holy Spirit. "Today, if you hear his voice, do not harden your hearts" (Psalm 95:7, 8).

Believers

While it is impossible for the conscience of a true believer to become dead, it can surely be weakened. Those who do not hold "a good conscience" can become shipwrecked like Hymenaeus and Alexander (1 Timothy 1:19, 20). Paul exhorted Timothy to maintain "a pure heart and a good conscience and a sincere faith" (1 Timothy 1:5). A good conscience is essential to spiritual vitality.

We must submit our conscience to the informing light of God's Word, and thus enlightened we must obey it. We cannot neglect any conviction of what we are to do without lowering the whole level of our character. If there is something we are doing or saying, if there is an attitude we ought to have, if Scripture and conscience are calling to us, we must hear and change. If we resist, the moral shudder may become less and less, and the Word of God dimmer and dimmer.

100

Pilate before Jesus

LUKE 23:13–25

THERE HAD BEEN long-standing unconcealed animosity between Pilate and Herod that was rooted in the political order of Palestine. Pilate administered the hard-fisted power of the Roman overlords. Herod was the puppet representative of the local Hasmonean dynasty. Herod liked to imagine he was more powerful than he really was, and he was given to face-saving rhetoric and petty ego maintenance. Thus the two had existed in mutual disdain.

But all that changed on the day Pilate sent Jesus to Herod for judgment: "And Herod and Pilate became friends with each other that very day, for before this they had been at enmity with each other" (23:12). Pilate had simply passed on a politically explosive "buck." But Herod took it as a sign of Pilate's respectful deference. And Herod's interview of Jesus produced the same conclusion as Pilate's regarding Jesus' innocence, despite the Jewish establishment's wild charges. The two men seem to have had a similar smoldering dislike for the Sanhedrin. So Jesus' trial occasioned a political rapprochement between them.

Twice Innocent (vv. 13–16)

Pilate, though very pleased with the new peace with Herod, was naturally disappointed with Herod's returning Jesus to him. But the return also bolstered his initial assessment of Jesus' innocence.

> Pilate then called together the chief priests and the rulers and the people, and said to them, "You brought me this man as one who was misleading the people. And after examining him before you, behold, I did not find this man guilty of any of your charges against him. Neither did Herod, for he sent him back to us. Look, nothing deserving death has been done by him." (vv. 13–15)

Pilate had initially listened to the charges against Jesus with a Roman legal ear and discerned that they were unfounded. Now Herod's Palestinian ear had heard the same charges and had come to the same conclusion. The agreement of such an unlikely pair about the political innocence of Jesus renders beyond doubt the absolute guiltlessness of Jesus.[1] In fact, Herod's cruel mockery of Jesus placed his judgment that Jesus was innocent beyond question. He did not like Jesus, yet still found him innocent. Pilate was rightly convinced of Jesus' innocence.

So Pilate voiced a decision calculated to save Jesus: "I will therefore punish and release him" (v. 16). Under Roman law a light beating was sometimes given along with a warning, so the accused would watch his behavior more carefully in the future.[2] Pilate was trying to appease Jesus' accusers, hoping that a lesser judicial act would quell their blood lust. At this point it had become dramatically apparent that Pilate (the thoroughly political man) was, surprisingly, truly trying to save Jesus. Evidently influences beyond the merely political were inwardly tugging at this Roman leader.

This is especially significant in that Pilate was not a sensitive man. Early on during his administration over Jerusalem he had caused a riot by his cavalier disregard of Jewish sensibilities regarding idolatry. His predecessors had always ordered the Roman soldiers to remove the images of Caesar from their standards when they marched into Jerusalem. But Pilate refused, causing an ugly riot. He only relented when the crowd prostrated themselves, baring their necks in a willingness to die rather than see the second commandment broken (cf. Josephus, *Antiquities*, III, 1; *War*, II, IX, 2, 3).

On another occasion Pilate raided the sacred Corban treasury of the temple (a treasury used only for service to God) to pay for the building of an aqueduct. Those who objected were beaten by plainclothes soldiers (cf. *Antiquities*, XVIII, III, 2; *War*, II, IX, 4). Then he provoked the Jews with another idolatry incident (cf. Philo, *Legatio ad Caium*, XXXVIII). And ultimately he would lose his position when he ordered his cavalry to attack Samaritans who were assembled at Mt. Gerazim in a religious quest (*Antiquities*, XXXVIII, IV, 1,2). The fourth-century historian Eusebius records that from then on life went so bad for Pilate, he eventually took his own life (*Ecclesiastical History*, II, VII). Pilate was almost pathologically insensitive and could be vicious when crossed.

So why this display of scruples in his initial handling of Jesus? There are several possible reasons. To begin with, Roman law prided itself on being evenhanded, just as we do with our statue of Justice blindfolded, holding up the scales of justice. And there simply was not clear evidence against Jesus.

Also, we must remember that Pilate's conscience, though seared, was not dead like that of Herod. Further, Pilate's repeated run-ins with the Jewish establishment had conditioned him to dislike their intrigues. So there were numerous reasons for Pilate's surprising scruples.

But there was also a very specific reason for his sustained attempts to save Jesus—namely, his wife's dream. St. Matthew tells us, "While he was sitting on the judgment seat, his wife sent word to him, 'Have nothing to do with that righteous man, for I have suffered much because of him today in a dream'" (Matthew 27:19).

We wish we knew more about her nightmare. Was it like Daniel's vision with one "like a son of man" coming to "the Ancient of Days" (Daniel 7:13)? Did accusing faces rise leering at her from dark seas? What words did she hear? How much did she know about Jesus before her dream? Did the knowledge ultimately bring her to God's grace? Her message to her husband was clear. "He's innocent, Pilate! Get out of this as fast as you can." And Pilate thought, "Yes, it's true. I know he is innocent." Pilate's thoughts had been momentarily turned toward the spiritual.

We also know that Pilate had begun to fear. According to John's Gospel, during the proceedings:

> The Jews answered him, "We have a law, and according to that law he ought to die because he has made himself the Son of God." When Pilate heard this statement, he was even more afraid. He entered his headquarters again and said to Jesus, "Where are you from?" But Jesus gave him no answer. So Pilate said to him, "You will not speak to me? Do you not know that I have authority to release you and authority to crucify you?" Jesus answered him, "You would have no authority over me at all unless it had been given you from above. Therefore he who delivered me over to you has the greater sin." (John 19:7–11)

So we have an inner profile of this politician's desire to save Jesus. He knew Jesus was innocent. Jesus' innocence had been corroborated by Herod. Pilate feared what might happen if he gave in. His wife's dream and the mention of Jesus being God's Son were unnerving. As a result of all this, his dying conscience lifted itself up off its bed in fear. He wanted to save Jesus!

The People's Will (vv. 18–20)

But the external climate had changed. The leaders were no longer alone in calling for Jesus' blood. The people agreed. "But they all cried out together, 'Away with this man, and release to us Barabbas'—a man who had been thrown into prison for an insurrection started in the city and for murder. Pilate addressed them once more, desiring to release Jesus, but they kept shouting, 'Crucify, crucify him!'" (vv. 18–21). Up to the present, the people had functioned as a buffer between Jesus and the murderous leaders of Jerusalem. Now they turned on him like wild dogs.

There was a tragic threefold irony in their turning.

The same voices that a week before had been strained in shouting, "Blessed is the King who comes in the name of the Lord!" (19:38) were now screaming, "Crucify him!" In both cases mob psychology had carried the day. And now, in their corporate blood lust, they were more violent than they would ever have been if acting alone.

Second, there was tragic irony in the fact that Barabbas embodied the seditious spirit of which Jesus was falsely accused.

Third, Barabbas means "son of the father." The people cried out for the release of one called "son of the father" and rejected the One who really is the Son of the Father!

A seemingly impossible reversal had taken place.

Thrice Innocent (vv. 22, 23)

Pilate had twice declared Jesus innocent. Now he made it three times: "A third time he said to them, 'Why, what evil has he done? I have found in him no guilt deserving death. I will therefore punish and release him'" (v. 22). There was no doubt of Jesus' innocence. So Pilate reasserted his futile intention to have Jesus whipped and released.

If we only had Luke's account and were reading it for the first time, we would naturally think there was still hope for Jesus. But there was not. John's Gospel tells us that Jesus' enemies now stooped to political blackmail: "From then on Pilate sought to release him, but the Jews cried out, 'If you release this man, you are not Caesar's friend. Everyone who makes himself a king opposes Caesar'" (John 19:12). This placed the ax at Pilate's political Achilles' heel. He could not risk allowing any threat to Rome—especially since his record in Palestine was notably sour. He noticed too that public opinion had changed: "But they were urgent, demanding with loud cries that he should be crucified. And their voices prevailed" (v. 23). Pilate could see a riot coming. That, too, he could not have.

Crucified Innocent (vv. 24, 25)

With this Pontius Pilate caved in: "So Pilate decided that their demand should be granted. He released the man who had been thrown into prison for insurrection and murder, for whom they asked, but he delivered Jesus over to their will" (vv. 24, 25).

How could he do this, having proclaimed three times the innocence of Jesus? Actually, it was easy because pagan Pilate was very much a modern man.

During Pilate's first encounter with Jesus, he had responded to Christ's assertion of truth by saying, as John's Gospel has it, "What is truth?" (John 18:38) and thus unwittingly anticipated the words of twentieth-century skepticism. Today's modernist heirs to Enlightenment relativism say in effect, "What is truth?" when they insist that truth is a matter of subjective opinion. The postmodernist says with a weary, world-worn tone, "What is truth?" because he or she does not believe truth exists.

Pilate embodied the skepticism that was fashionable among the educated, polished Romans of his day. His words were those of a man who considered himself too experienced in the ways of the world to imagine that truth exists. His words suggest that he felt superior to and liberated from the thoughts that trouble simpler people. He exuded the urbane skepticism of a man who doubted everything, distrusted everything, despised everything. He made light of truth. His attitude was weary and mournful, worldly wise and smilingly sarcastic. Pilate was indeed a stranger to truth. That is why Pilate gave in.

His decision produced an integrity deficit. As a Roman, he had a professional regard for justice, but no personal commitment to truth. Above all, Pilate was a careerist politician who always had a moistened index finger in the air to see which way the winds were blowing. Though he had withstood the Sanhedrin, he gave in when the tide of popular opinion cried for Jesus' crucifixion.

Pilate, despite his affected superiority, his bluster, and his occasional cruelties, was a weak man. He did not become such a man overnight. It happened incrementally as he repeatedly gave in on lesser issues. But when Pilate decided to execute Jesus, it was the weakest thing he would ever do.

Pilate's behavior shows us why so many moderns reject Jesus today. But at the same time he blows their cover. The terminology may be new (Kantian, post-Kantian, deconstructionist), but the problem is not new. The cop-out "What is truth?" is as old as the gospel itself. What folly to imagine a personal superiority with lazy, jargoned skepticism as so many do today. What a delusion to imagine that the way to go is best determined by consensus.

Jesus said, "I am the way, and the truth, and the life. No one comes to the Father except through me" (John 14:6). He backed up his claim by fulfilling the Old Testament Scriptures. He backed it up by living a perfect life. He backed it up by willingly dying on the cross for our sins. He backed it up by rising from the dead. And he still backs it up by giving life to all who come to him.

Closing Reflections

The trial of Jesus before Pilate unequivocally affirmed three times that Jesus was politically innocent, undeserving of death. This final court unwittingly declared what is theologically true of Jesus, that he was and is the spotless "Lamb of God, who takes away the sin of the world" (John 1:29). He is the fulfillment of what was symbolized by the millions of unblemished lambs slain under the old covenant.

Along with this, Pilate's substitution of innocent Jesus for Barabbas unwittingly symbolized the substitutionary death of Jesus. Barabbas, the one guilty of death, was pardoned, and Jesus, the innocent one, died in his place.[3]

This is the gospel—Jesus dying as a substitute on the cross for us. As our substitute, he took all our sins upon himself, then gave us his life and righteousness.

Jesus' gospel is so simple. He says, "It's my life for yours. It's my purity for your sin. Will you take it? There is no other way."

> And just as it is appointed for man to die once, and after that comes judgment, so Christ, having been offered once to bear the sins of many, will appear a second time, not to deal with sin but to save those who are eagerly waiting for him. (Hebrews 9:27, 28)

Perfect Jesus does it all!

101

The Cross of Christ

LUKE 23:26–34

THIS SECTION OF LUKE is about the road to the crucifixion. It was a winding road with surprises at several turns.

As we take up the *Via Dolorosa*, the "Road of Sorrows," we must understand that the Gospel accounts reveal that Jesus had already suffered greatly. In Gethsemane, as he contemplated becoming sin for us—that his righteous soul would absorb and deflect divine wrath—he said with astonished horror, "My soul is very sorrowful, even to death" (Mark 14:34). Reflection on the spiritual horrors that awaited him actually threatened to kill him.

At his religious trial under Caiaphas, Christ was struck in the face (cf. John 18:22, 23). Then he was subjected to a series of blows as the temple guards blindfolded him and taunted him to identify them as they passed by, striking him and spitting in his face (cf. Mark 14:65).

Near the conclusion of his political trial under Pilate, he was scourged (cf. Mark 15:15). Scourging was done with the dread *flagellum* whip, consisting of thongs plaited with pieces of bone and lead. Eusebius tells of martyrs who "were torn by scourges down to deep seated veins and arteries, so that the hidden contents of the recesses of their bodies, their entrails and organs, were exposed to sight" (*Ecclesiastical History*, IV, XV, 3–5). Josephus describes this in similar terms (*War,* II, XXI 5, VI, v. 3). The *flagellum* left Jesus with bone and cartilage showing. There was gruesome prophetic fulfillment in Jesus' very appearance: "His appearance was so marred, beyond human semblance, and his form beyond that of the children of mankind" (Isaiah 52:14).

Finally, the Roman soldiers presented him as the "Coming King." His brow bore the mocking crown of thorns. A faded purple robe, crimson with blood, hung dripping from his shoulders (cf. Mark 15:16–20). Bored with their fun, the soldiers put his own clothes on him and led him out to crucifixion.

The grim customs of the crucifixion march were well known to every Roman subject. Jesus was placed in the center of a *quarterion*, a company of four Roman soldiers. The *patibulum*, the crossbeam of the cross, weighing perhaps as much as one hundred pounds, was placed on his shoulders. As Jesus stumbled along the route to Golgotha, a soldier preceded him carrying a wooden placard whitened with chalk and bearing the darkened inscription of Jesus' crime: "Jesus of Nazareth, the King of the Jews" (John 19:19).[1] Jesus was led on the longest route possible, so cold fear would grip the populace as a deterrent to crime.[2]

Crucifixions were so common that the soldiers probably began the march with a sober, business-as-usual attitude. But there were to be some surprises that day that, in the light of redemption history, are eternally significant.

Surprises on the Way (vv. 26–31)

A Surprised Cyrenian

Jesus was a carpenter in the physical prime of his life. He was accustomed to heavy lifting. He knew how to put his shoulder to a task. Bearing the *patibulum*, however heavy, was well within his normal capacity. But Jesus had already undergone prolonged agony, and the final scourging had inflicted a horrible loss of blood and tissue. Thus with his arms extended wide, he began to reel like a wounded butterfly. The soldiers discerned that he would not make it to the site of execution, and that he might even die under the crossbeam while on the road. Indeed, the Gospels record that the soldiers would be surprised at the swiftness of Jesus' death once he was crucified (cf. Mark 15:44; John 19:33).[3]

What were they to do? The answer came to them in the form of one very surprised North African from the city of Cyrene in what is today Libya. The Cyrenian Jews had a synagogue in Jerusalem mentioned in the book of Acts (6:9). Christian preachers such as Lucius the Cyrenian were converts from the Cyrenian synagogue (cf. Acts 13:1).[4] Simon now involuntarily joined the procession: "And as they led him away, they seized one Simon of Cyrene, who was coming in from the country, and laid on him the cross, to carry it behind Jesus" (v. 26). As Jesus agonizingly put one foot in front of the other, humiliated Simon unhappily bore the crossbar.

Why do all the Synoptic Gospels mention this? First, Simon, bent under the weight of the cross and following in Christ's footsteps, is a dramatic image of what is necessary to be a disciple of Jesus. After Peter's confession that Jesus was the Messiah, Jesus made it clear that he would die at the hands of the Sanhedrin, and "He said to all, 'If anyone would come after me, let him deny himself and take up his cross daily and follow me'" (9:23). Later when his popularity was on the rise, he turned to the large crowd and said, "If anyone comes to me and does not hate his own father and mother and wife and children and brothers and sisters, yes, and even his own life, he cannot be my disciple. Whoever does not bear his own cross and come after me cannot be my disciple" (14:26, 27). So the bent silhouette of Simon from Cyrene trudging after Jesus made a striking profile for every disciple of the Savior. Jesus sovereignly created the symbol, even when he appeared most helpless. The image is sobering, because if we do not feel the weight of the cross, if there is no sacrifice, if there are no occasions of humiliation, we are not following Christ.

But Simon's image is also heartening for those who are following Christ. High among the grand examples of great English preachers stands Charles Simeon, the eighteenth- and nineteenth-century leader of the evangelical renewal of the Church of England. Simeon, amid great opposition, brought the Bible back to the pulpit of Holy Trinity Church, Cambridge. During his first decade of ministry, his wealthy parishioners actually chained their pews closed, so that any who came to hear Simeon had to sit in the aisles. Simeon not only outlasted them but preached there for fifty years. His twenty volumes of sermons, *Horae Homiliticae* (*Hours of Preaching*), modeled exposition for generations within the church. Simeon, over Friday evening tea, discipled many of the great missionaries and preachers of his day. His black Wedgewood teapot can still be seen on display at Holy Trinity.

Early on, young Simeon was mightily encouraged by this section of Luke as he felt the weight of his difficult ministry.

> "One day," he said, "when I was an object of much contempt and derision in the University, I strolled forth, buffeted and afflicted, taking my little Greek Testament in my hand. I prayed that God would comfort me with some cordial from His Word; and opening it, the first text which caught my eye was this: *They found a man of Cyrene, Simon by name; him they compelled to bear His cross*. Simon, you know, is the same name as Simeon. It was the very word I needed. What a privilege—to have the cross laid on me to bear it with Jesus! It was enough! I could leap and sing for joy! 'Lay it on me, Lord!' I cried; and henceforth I bound persecution as a wreath of glory round my brow."[5]

The bent image of Simon of Cyrene both sobers us and lifts us up!

But there is a second reason for the space given to Simon in Luke's account. Simon of Cyrene became a Christian and followed Christ. All three Synoptic Gospels give the impression that Simon was both unknown and coerced into carrying the crossbeam.[6] Yet Mark's Gospel lists the name of Simon's sons—"Alexander and Rufus" (Mark 15:21). Mark would not have named Simon's sons had he not subsequently come to know Simon. And why would he have gotten to know Simon unless Simon became a follower of Christ? This is the view of the cautious scholar Raymond Brown in his massive study *The Death of the Messiah*.[7]

Significantly, Mark's Gospel, which lists Simon's sons, was written to the church in Rome. And in Romans 16:13 Paul writes, "Greet Rufus, chosen in the Lord; also his mother, who has been a mother to me as well." Simon's family may well have ended up as pillars of the expatriate church in Rome!

What we have here is a huge surprise of sovereign grace during one of the most outwardly helpless moments of Christ's life. Simon of Cyrene happened upon the gruesome parade at the precise moment of Christ's extremity, was forced to carry the loathsome crossbeam, unwillingly saw every movement and heard every word of Jesus who staggered before him, observed the execution, and at some time during that day or the following days believed in Jesus Christ. Amazing grace!

Surprised Mourners

As Simon followed behind Jesus, "There followed him a great multitude of the people and of women who were mourning and lamenting for him" (v. 27). Jesus, faint and reeling, and Simon, stooped and steady, trudged along amid a steady din of loud female wails.

These women are not to be confused with his devoted followers who had traveled from Galilee and would stay with him to the bitter end (cf. 23:49). Rather, these were devout women of Jerusalem who had come to bewail the death of a young man, local women who regularly turned out to witness executions and provide opiates and drugs to ease the pain (*M. Sanhedrin* 43a).[8] Some were acting out the part of professional mourners as they literally "were beating themselves and bewailing him."[9] These daughters of Jerusalem were well-intentioned, sympathetic, kind souls.

But these good women, absorbed with their ritual wailing and self-pummeling, were in no way prepared for what was to happen as, incredibly, Jesus turned around, facing both them and Simon, and said, "Daughters of Jerusalem, do not weep for me, but weep for yourselves and for your children" (v. 28). The surprise was that the wretched prisoner, on the verge of a most torturous death, was thinking of them. Amazing grace! In doing so,

Jesus followed the Old Testament pattern of addressing women as representatives of the nation.[10] His surprising message to the devout in Israel was: "Do not weep for me, but weep for yourselves."

Jesus drove home his gracious warning with a terrifying prophecy and a terrifying proverb.

The prophecy: "For behold, the days are coming when they will say, 'Blessed are the barren and the wombs that never bore and the breasts that never nursed!' Then they will begin to say to the mountains, 'Fall on us,' and to the hills, 'Cover us'" (vv. 29, 30). The coming judgment would be so horrific that barrenness, normally held to be a reproach in Israel, would be counted a blessing. The coming judgment would be so unbearable that Israel would cry out with language used by ancient unfaithful Israel (Hosea 10:8), pleading for an earthquake to cause the mountains to fall on them and thus put them out of their misery.

The proverb: "For if they do these things when the wood is green, what will happen when it is dry?" (v. 31). Trees do not naturally burn when they are green, but they are highly flammable when dry. Righteous (green) Jesus was not a natural object of disaster. But the sinful (dry) nation was.[11] The how-much-more aspect of this proverb was terrible.

What was the underlying message of this prophecy and proverb? The very fact that Jesus warned the devout women (and thus devout Israel) indicated that not all who would experience the coming devastation deserved it. Not all Israel was hostile to Christ. Thus Jesus left open the possibility that God, who was in the process of redeeming Simon's heart, could also redeem the hearts of those who were lamenting what was being done to Jesus. This gloriously occurred through the New Testament church. It is also wonderfully true that many Christians were spared the holocaust of A.D. 70 because the Jewish persecutions drove them out of Jerusalem (cf. Eusebius, *Ecclesiastical History*, III.5.4).

Jesus' surprise prophecy to the daughters of Israel on the *Via Dolorosa* was an act of grace. It should encourage every hearer down through the centuries to this present day, this side of the final judgment, to turn to Jesus for grace and mercy.

> Weep, O my daughters, but grieve not for me;
> Weep for yourselves and your children;
> Shed bitter tears of mourning and pray.
> O pray *miserere, nostri Domine.*
>
> Edwin Cox

Have mercy on us, Lord!

Surprise at the Cross (vv. 32–34)

After delivering his gracious prophecy, Jesus turned and shuffled along the winding Road of Sorrows to the appointed place. Luke wastes no words: "Two others, who were criminals, were led away to be put to death with him. And when they came to the place that is called The Skull, there they crucified him, and the criminals, one on his right and one on his left" (vv. 32, 33).

At the *kranion*, the skull, some rounded hillock outside the city (cf. Leviticus 24:14; John 19:17; Hebrews 13:11–13), Simon the Cyrenian at last was allowed to cast the loathsome *patibulum* to the ground. Jesus was then thrown upon it, and spikes were driven through his hands. The crossbar was raised by the four soldiers with Jesus dangling from it and fastened to the *crux simplex,* a single standing post. Jesus' feet were nailed, probably with a single spike, to the post. Jesus began his agonized prayers as he struggled upward for breath and slumped downward again in exhaustion.

Two criminals, possibly members of Barabbas' band, were crucified on Jesus' right and left. The message was intentional—Jesus was a criminal among criminals. Unwittingly, the intentional disgrace fulfilled Jesus' upper-room prophecy in which he applied Isaiah 53:12, the final word of Isaiah 53, to himself: "For I tell you that this Scripture must be fulfilled in me: 'And he was numbered with the transgressors.' For what is written about me has its fulfillment" (22:37). Jesus fulfilled every line of Isaiah 53.

The cosmic trauma had begun. There never had been such pain as physical and spiritual evil now came against Jesus in terrible conjunction. Body and soul recoiled. The initial shock of crucifixion had rendered him paralyzed and quivering. Physical disbelief screamed from severed nerves. And even greater spiritual horror closed in—he would soon become sin.

But then came a startling surprise! Jesus, gazing upon the blood-spattered soldiers, said, "'Father, forgive them, for they know not what they do.' And they cast lots to divide his garments" (v. 34). Two things here require careful notice. First, the "them" in "forgive them" was for the Roman soldiers alone, who in all truthfulness did not know what they were doing. As David Gooding has remarked, "False sentiment must not lead us to extend the scope of the prayer beyond his intention."[12] Second, Jesus did not forgive the soldiers for their sins or sinful condition. He extended specific forgiveness for a specific sin. Nevertheless, the amazing initial (and enduring) reflex of Jesus' crucified heart was to forgive. This is amazing, astounding grace!

And for at least one of the soldiers, Jesus' prayer was not futile. Some hours later, when Jesus said, "Father, into your hands I commit my spirit"

(23:46), "the centurion saw what had taken place, [and] he praised God, saying, 'Certainly this man was innocent!'" (23:47). The crucifixion was for him the dawning of amazing grace.

Closing Reflections

The gracious surprises on the road to the cross amaze us. Simon the Cyrenian crossed Jesus' path in a moment in time and space that led to the saving of his soul and gave him a place in Biblical history. Unwillingly and unwittingly, he modeled the posture of all true disciples.

Next Jesus, shuffling along, his flesh flayed, trailing blood, on his way to cosmic agony, did a most surprising thing—he thought not of himself but of others when he told his mourners, "Daughters of Jerusalem, do not weep for me, but weep for yourselves and for your children" (v. 28). Jesus then used Holy Writ to urge their repentance.

Then, having just been impaled, he forgave the men who pierced him, for they did not know what they were doing.

Luke recorded three dazzling explosions of grace in Jesus' interaction with Simon of Cyrene, the daughters of Jerusalem, and the Roman soldiers. Jesus evangelized on the terrible road to the cross and even from the cross. These blazing flashes of grace are meant to grip our souls.

But here is the final surprise—he can and will save you if you have not yet come to him, no matter how deep you are in sin. And if you come to him, you will live in eternal amazement—perpetual, joyous surprise!

102

Jesus Saves

LUKE 23:35–43

THE PRESENCE OF crosses and crucifixes everywhere around us has served to desensitize us to the appalling horror of the cross. Often in our busy day-to-day lives we pass depictions of the crucifixion with barely a notice. But how would we respond to a painting or sculpture of a crucified dog or cat? I say this not to question our devotion because we are not shocked by the cross, but rather to cite the numbing effect of continual exposure to its obscene horror.

We would not be so cauterized if we had ever seen a real crucifixion, as had most adult inhabitants of the Roman Empire. Cultured Gentiles were so offended by the cross that they refrained as much as possible from even mentioning the word *cross*. Once when an upper-class Roman actor performed a mime depiction of the crucifixion of a robber chief, the writer Juvenal was so repulsed that a member of the patrician class would so debase himself, he said he hoped the actor would end up on a real cross![1]

The March 21, 1986 issue of the *Journal of the American Medical Association* recreated the horror with the most exhaustive medical review of Christ's crucifixion ever published in a medical journal, complete with anatomical illustrations. The authors detailed the pain of the *flagellum* as it tore into Christ's skeletal muscles, the pain produced by the weight of the body hanging from spikes that penetrated the medial nerves and tore at the tarsals, the gruesome respiratory agony, the cramping, the ensuing plural effusions, concluding that "Death by crucifixion was in every sense of the word excruciating, literally, 'out of the cross.'"[2] Their clinical assessment remarkably justifies C. S. Lewis's description and deductions in 1960:

> He creates the universe, already foreseeing—or should we say "seeing"? There are no tenses in God—the buzzing cloud of flies about the cross, the flayed back pressed against the uneven stake, the nails driven through the medial nerves, the repeated incipient suffocation as the body droops, the repeated torture of back and arms as it is time after time, for breath's sake hitched up. If I may dare the biological image, God is a "host" who deliberately creates His own parasites; causes us to be that we may exploit and "take advantage of" Him. Herein is love. This is the diagram of Love Himself, the inventor of all loves.[3]

The cross reveals the love of God as nothing else in the universe could! We must passionately weave this truth into the threads of our consciousness for our soul's health. We must never fall to the delusion of thinking that Jesus' physical suffering was not as great for him because he was God. He did it as a man, among men, in total (and exemplary) dependence upon the Father. His pain was alleviated by nothing. If anything, it was heightened by his mind's perfect health. And this says nothing of his ultimate pain as our sin bearer, which we will consider in the next chapter of this book. The cross reveals excruciating pain and excruciating love.

As we observe Jesus' regal conduct amid the mockery of the rulers, soldiers, and thieves, we see our Savior's incredible love. Luke 23:35–43 is not about a good thief but about the goodness and saving grace of Jesus Christ.

Mocking Leaders (v. 35)

Gazing up at the dripping gore, the Jewish leaders led the mockery amid a people who now stood mute and sympathetic.[4] "And the people stood by, watching, but the rulers scoffed at him, saying, 'He saved others; let him save himself, if he is the Christ of God, his Chosen One!'" (v. 35). The taunt was an unwitting echo of the cross-prophesying oracle of Psalm 22:6–8: "But I am a worm and not a man, scorned by mankind and despised by the people. All who see me mock me; they make mouths at me; they wag their heads; 'He trusts in the Lord; let him deliver him; let him rescue him, for he delights in him!'" Record of their heartless cynicism had existed for one thousand years before that day and still leaps from the Twenty-second Psalm two thousand years later.

The rulers admitted, at the foot of the cross, that "He saved others." That was an ironic admission. The evidence for his saving others was massive—the incredible healing of the paralytic in Capernaum, the restoration of sight to the blind man in Jericho, the raising of the widow's son and then Lazarus, the calming of the sea. But none of this carried any weight with them.

The only thing that would convince them, they inferred, would be a supernatural loosening from the nails that impaled him. If he had come floating down from the cross like a levitating spook—saving himself—they would have believed, they said. Then they would believe that he was "the Christ of God" of Peter's confession (cf. 9:20) and the chosen one of the transfiguration—"This is my Son, my Chosen One" (9:35).

The very fact that they had gotten him onto a cross settled it for them, for Deuteronomy 21:23 said, "A hanged man is cursed by God." This was the lowest humiliation—"even death on a cross" (Philippians 2:8). To Jews it was madness to suppose that anyone crucified could be God.

Of course, we know what they did not know. We know that in the Triumphal Entry, he came as King. But when he entered the city and the upper room, he came as a Passover lamb. Therefore, "To mock Christ as the rulers and elders did was sublimely misconceived: they might as well have mocked a literal Passover lamb because, while it saved others, it could not save itself" (Gooding).[5] How they howled their mockery. And what did Jesus say amid all this? Not a word.

Mocking Soldiers (vv. 36–38)

The five Roman soldiers, the *cruciari*, naturally followed suit: "The soldiers also mocked him, coming up and offering him sour wine and saying, 'If you are the King of the Jews, save yourself!' There was also an inscription over him, 'This is the King of the Jews'" (vv. 36–38). The inscription was Pilate's grim vengeance at the Jewish leaders for manipulating him into rendering his guilty verdict. It was boldly inscribed in three languages—Aramaic, Latin, and Greek, in effect making it a universal verdict and declaration of Christ's kingship. According to John's Gospel, the leaders pushed Pilate to change it to read "'This man said, I am King of the Jews.'" But Pilate answered with vengeful satisfaction, "What I have written I have written" (John 19:19–22).

In the minds of most of those at the scene, the title was laughably absurd, and the Roman soldiers decided to engage in some absurd theater of their own. They mockingly offered him a bitter cocktail[6] as a drink for a royal person, then repeated the logic of the Jews directly to Jesus' face: "If you are the King of the Jews, save yourself!" This was savage humor, especially remembering he had already prayed for the soldiers, "Father, forgive them, for they know not what they do" (23:34).

The apostle Peter would later record Jesus' regal silence as a fulfillment of Isaiah 53:9: "He committed no sin, neither was deceit found in his mouth. When he was reviled, he did not revile in return; when he suffered, he did not threaten, but continued entrusting himself to him who judges justly" (1 Peter 2:22, 23). Divine silence endured. To such blasphemy, Jesus had nothing to say.

Mocking Thieves (vv. 39–45)

Both Jews and pagans cackled their mockery in howling harmony over their tortured prey. But the chorus suddenly enlarged as the dying thieves joined in.

Hardened Criminals

Mark's Gospel reveals that "Those who were crucified with him also reviled him" (Mark 15:32). The men impaled on his right and left hitched themselves up, gathered in precious air, and exhaled abuse on Jesus in deadly blasphemy.

In Luke's account we learn that after a while one of the thieves fell silent, but the other continued his insults: "One of the criminals who were hanged railed at him, saying, 'Are you not the Christ? Save yourself and us!'" (v. 39). Bitter, bitter scorn. Some commentators suggest that this criminal had the Zealots' political outlook and that his contempt was fueled by Jesus' not being a politicized Messiah.[7] The poor man was dying for his earthbound politics. Tragically, he expressed no thought of God, no guilt, no repentance, no concern for forgiveness. And ominously he heard no word from Jesus, no argument, no warning, but only silence as he raged.

A Softened Criminal

Amid this a solo voice of spiritual sanity rang out from (of all people) the quieted thief! "But the other rebuked him, saying, 'Do you not fear God, since you are under the same sentence of condemnation? And we indeed justly, for we are receiving the due reward of our deeds; but this man has done nothing wrong'" (vv. 40, 41). Undoubtedly his silence had been brought on by a spiritual awakening. He had seen the meekness with which Jesus had let himself be led to punishment. Likely he had heard Jesus charge the mourning daughters of Jerusalem to weep for themselves. He had heard Jesus' prayer for his executioners. In that prayer Jesus had addressed God as Father, with an unheard-of intimacy. And most of all, there was an obvious contrast between the holiness of Jesus and his own crimes.

All this awakened in him a beautiful posture of grace. He knew he was a sinner—"And we indeed justly, for we are receiving the due reward of our deeds" (v. 41). He owned his own crucifixion as a just civil punishment. The thief likewise knew he had no merit to which he could appeal for Jesus' help. Such a clear awareness of sin is a profound advantage over most of humanity. Most people live in a foggy world of ambiguity and relativism, falling in love with the dark contours of their lives, convincing themselves their sins are noble and glorious—that their pride is "dignity," their unwillingness to forgive "character." No such haze clouded this man's soul.

He feared God—that is, God's just judgment of his sins. In those moments on the cross he had become profoundly humble. He had come to possess the bankruptcy of spirit that Jesus requires: "Blessed are the poor in spirit, for theirs is the kingdom of heaven" (Matthew 5:3). He knew he had nothing within himself to commend him to God.

In this spirit he turned to address Jesus who, he had concluded, was the Messiah, King of the coming kingdom.[8] "Jesus, remember me when you come into your kingdom" (v. 42). He did not say, "Remember my works." Neither did he say, "Remember that I aligned myself with you in your death." He said only, "Remember me." He asked for mercy. That is all any of us can ask for. The dying words of the devout astronomer Copernicus were: "I do not ask for the grace that you gave St. Paul; nor can I dare to ask for the grace that you granted to St. Peter; but, the mercy which you did show to the dying robber, that mercy, show to me."[9]

Jesus Saves!

The suffering Savior was no longer silent. "And he said to him, 'Truly, I say to you, today you will be with me in Paradise'" (v. 43). The word translated "Paradise," *paradeisos*, bore the root meaning of "garden." It came to represent the future bliss of God's people. It was understood as describing the intermediate resting place for the souls of the righteous dead prior to the great resurrection. The New Testament writers used it two other times as a symbol of Heaven and its bliss—once when Paul referred to his experience of being "caught up into paradise" where he heard inexpressible things (2 Corinthians 12:3, 4), and also in the book of Revelation as the location of the Tree of Life from which the overcomer may eat (Revelation 2:7).[10]

This was an astounding promise to the crucified criminal, made even more so by its immediacy. The thief had asked that he would be granted life at Jesus' appearing to establish the kingdom. Jesus' answer promised *immediate* entry into Paradise on the very day of the crucifixion! And to compound the astonishing immediacy, Jesus told the wretch, "Today you will be *with me*"—"You will be with me, close by me!"

Jesus gave the wretched thief life! The man hung writhing next to Jesus in mortal agony. He too was gasping for breath. The same severed nerves screamed. He moaned in agony. He was probably mocked too—for his deathbed conversion, his ridiculous faith in this helpless king—"Save you, you fool? He can't even save himself." The man hung with his own sins heavy upon him, and darkness covered the land. But in that darkness Jesus took the thief's sins upon himself, necessitating the cry, "My God, my God, why have you forsaken me?" The thief heard and watched Jesus die. Soon he too would be dead, but somehow he felt peace. The earth grew dimmer to his glazed eyes as a soldier approached to break his legs and hasten his death. He collapsed in suffocation. The spear was hardly a prick. At last his body hung relaxed.

Where was he then? Far away. Released from his agony and his sin. He was, as Alexander Maclaren so wonderfully expressed it, "a new star swimming into the firmament of heaven, a new face before the throne of God, another sinner redeemed from earth!"[11]

The thief's redemption dramatizes for us the immediate bliss of the departed. Sinners who cast themselves into the arms of Christ go into the presence of God—"away from the body and at home with the Lord" (2 Corinthians 5:8). Paradise Lost is reopened to us—a better paradise is flung wide open forever. And there the angels rejoice with us.

Closing Reflections

The old divines used to say about this text, "*One* alone was saved upon the Cross that none might despair; and only one, that none might presume."[12] The thief's redemption makes it clear that salvation does not come by works. It is all of grace (cf. Romans 11:6). To presume on our works is to be lost.

At the same time we must not despair. Are we caught in sin, perhaps sin so unspeakable that if others knew they would consider us a wretch or worse? Do we imagine we are beyond grace? If so, we are wrong. The only thing that will put us beyond hope is to be like the thief who rejected Christ. He died that day only to become one of the "wandering stars, for whom the gloom of utter darkness has been reserved forever" (Jude 13).

The thief's redemption assures us that it is never too late to turn to Christ. Samuel Johnson was fond of quoting a hopeful epitaph for those who despair. The image is that of a man being pitched to his death from horseback.

> Between the stirrup and the ground,
> I mercy ask'd, I mercy found.[13]

It is never too late—never!

The thief's reward was Heaven to its fullest—Paradise, face-to-face with Jesus. In Jesus' parable of the workers in the vineyard (Matthew 20:1–16), the workers who were hired for the last hour were paid the same as those who had labored all day. The landowner's response to the workers' complaint was, "'Take what belongs to you and go. I choose to give to this last worker as I give to you. Am I not allowed to do what I choose with what belongs to me? Or do you begrudge my generosity?' So the last will be first, and the first last" (Matthew 20:14–16).

My wife's father died a terrible death with emphysema. But at the eleventh hour he wonderfully repented and turned to Christ in faith. My wife and I came home to Wheaton, Illinois, to attend another funeral over which famed author Joe Bayly officiated. Joe read that parable and said, "Those that come last receive as much as the first!" Our hearts were elevated as we reflected on the grace of God that had come to my wife's dear father.

Luke's account of the cross is not about a good thief but about a sinful, wretched thief and a good Savior. It is about the fact that Jesus loved to forgive our sins:

> We have heard the joyful sound—
> Jesus saves! Jesus saves!
> Spread the tidings all around—
> Jesus saves! Jesus saves!
>
> Waft it on the rolling tide—
> Jesus saves! Jesus saves!
> Tell to sinners far and wide—
> Jesus saves! Jesus saves!
>
> "Jesus Saves" by Priscilla J. Owens

One Saturday morning Dr. Donald Grey Barnhouse was in his study working when the custodian came in and announced there was a man outside to see him, giving him the man's card. Dr. Barnhouse read the card, which indicated that the visitor was the captain of the *Mauritania*, the largest passenger vessel afloat.

When Dr. Barnhouse went out to meet the man, the captain said, "You have a very beautiful church here." Dr. Barnhouse replied, "We are grateful for all that was done by our faithful predecessors a hundred years ago." The captain said, "It is very much like the Basilica at Ravenna in Italy." Dr. Barnhouse responded, "Well, it is an architectural duplication. In fact, years ago they brought workmen from Italy, and the tessellated ceilings and the marble columns and the mosaics were all done by Italian workmen. But that's not what you came to talk about. You didn't come to talk about architecture, did you?"

The man said, "No. Twenty-three times a year I sail the Atlantic. When I come down the bank of Newfoundland, I hear your broadcast out of Boston. And as I came this week I thought to myself, 'I've got twenty-four hours in New York. I'm going to go down and see Dr. Barnhouse.' So I took a train, hoping perhaps I would be able to meet you, and here I am." Dr. Barnhouse was very straightforward as he said, "Sir, have you been born again?" The captain replied, "That is what I came to see you about."

By this time they had reached a chalkboard in the prayer room, and Dr. Barnhouse drew three crosses. Underneath the first one he wrote the word "in." Underneath the third he wrote the word "in." Underneath the middle cross he wrote the words, "not in." He said, "Do you understand what I mean when I say those men who died with Jesus had sin within them?" The captain thought and said, "Yes, I do. But Christ did not have sin within him." Then over the first cross and over the third cross Dr. Barnhouse wrote the word "on." He said, "Do you understand what that means?" The captain wrinkled his brow.

Dr. Barnhouse said, "Let me illustrate. Have you ever run through a red light?" "Yes." "Were you caught?" The man said, "no." "Well, in running that red light you had sin in you. If you would have been caught, you would have had sin on you. So here the thieves bear the penalty of God." Then he wrote another "on" over Jesus Christ and said, "The one thief's sins rested on Christ by virtue of his faith in Christ. The other man's sins remained upon him. Which one are you?"

The man was a very tall, distinguished man, and as he stood Dr. Barnhouse could see that he was fighting back tears. He said to Dr. Barnhouse, "By the grace of God, I am the first man." Dr. Barnhouse said, "You mean your sins are on Jesus?" He said, "Yes. God says my sins are on Jesus!" He shot out his hand and said, "That's what I came to find out!" Dr. Barnhouse invited him to lunch and shared with him further, and the man went back to New York a glowing Christian.[14]

All of us, like the thieves, have sin *in* us. But some of us have the penalty of sin resting on us, and others have by grace had it shifted over to Christ. Is your sin on you or on Christ in whom there is no sin? That is the great question.

103

Jesus Dies

LUKE 23:44–49

IT WAS THE CUSTOM for respected women in Jerusalem to humanely provide a narcotic drink to those condemned to death in order to ease their pain (T B *Sanhedrin* 43a).[1] This mercy was prompted by Proverbs 31:6, 7: "Give strong drink to the one who is perishing, and wine to those in bitter distress; let them drink and forget their poverty and remember their misery no more." When Jesus arrived at Golgotha, he was offered "wine mixed with myrrh," presumably by the daughters of Jerusalem (since this was a Jewish rather than a Roman custom), "but he did not take it" (Mark 15:23) because he determined to endure with full consciousness the bitter sufferings appointed for him.

Remember that he would have gladly escaped them if it were the Father's will: "Father, if you are willing, remove this cup from me. Nevertheless, not my will, but yours, be done" (22:42). But since it was not possible, he determined to drink the cup to its fullest. Jesus did *not* come to suffer as little as he could. Understanding this, John Henry Newman wrote:

> And as men are superior to brute animals, and are affected by pain more than they, by reason of the mind within them, which gives a substance to pain, such as it cannot have in the instance of brutes; so, in like manner, our Lord felt pain of the body, with an advertence and a consciousness, and therefore with a keenness and intensity, and with a unity of perception, which none of us can possibly fathom or compass, because His soul was so absolutely in His power, so simply free from the influence of distractions, so fully directed *upon* the pain, so utterly surrendered, so simply subjected to the suffering. And thus He may truly be said to have suffered the whole of His passion in every moment of it.[2]

The full significance of Newman's words lies not in the keenness and intensity of Jesus' physical sufferings, but in the unnumbed spiritual agony he endured as our sin-bearer. He suffered with an intensity that no other being could possibly suffer.

Death Comes (vv. 44–46)

The Darkness

Luke reveals, as do the other Synoptic Gospels, that Jesus' death was covered by darkness: "It was now about the sixth hour, and there was darkness over the whole land until the ninth hour" (v. 44). The sixth hour was twelve noon when the sun was at its zenith. Darkness engulfed the cross at midday and remained for three terrible hours. Most likely the darkness was localized, covering only the Holy City and the nearby countryside. Perhaps God used lowering clouds or a desert sirocco or a fog. Thirty-three years earlier there had been dazzling light in the night when Jesus was born. Now there was darkness at noontime as he died.

What did it mean? The Old Testament identified darkness as a cosmic sign of mourning. Amos had long before prophesied that there would be darkness at the time of the Day of the Lord, saying, "I will make the sun go down at noon and darken the earth in broad daylight . . . I will make it like the mourning for an only son . . ." (Amos 8:9, 10; cf. Zephaniah 1:15). The cross was draped in the mourning sackcloth of darkness.

The darkness also signified the reign of evil predicted by Jesus at his arrest when he said, "But this is your hour, and the power of darkness" (22:53). The demons bayed in apparent victory. Devilish music swirled in the darkness.

What was actually happening? In those three black hours, sin was poured upon Christ's soul until he became sin. This accords with the prophetic Scriptures:

> He was despised and rejected by men;
>   a man of sorrows, and acquainted with grief;
> and as one from whom men hide their faces
>   he was despised, and we esteemed him not.
>
> Surely he has borne our griefs
>   and carried our sorrows;
> yet we esteemed him stricken,
>   smitten by God, and afflicted.
> But he was pierced for our transgressions;

he was crushed for our iniquities;
upon him was the chastisement that brought us peace,
and with his wounds we are healed.
All we like sheep have gone astray;
we have turned—every one—to his own way;
and the LORD has laid on him
the iniquity of us all. (Isaiah 53:3–6)

Peter makes what happened very clear: "He himself bore our sins in his body on the tree, that we might die to sin and live to righteousness. By his wounds you have been healed" (1 Peter 2:24). Paul says that God "made him to be sin who knew no sin, so that in him we might become the righteousness of God" (2 Corinthians 5:21).

All analogies or explanations of what happened fall short, though they are helpful. Think of Christ's heart as a sea hemmed in by the mountains of our sin. Then imagine our sins coursing down from the mountains into his heart until all the mountains of evil slide into the sea. Or think back to the magnifying glass you played with as a child. If held under the sun's rays, it could start a fire. Remember how if you focused the white spot of its concentrated light on a leaf or a bug (only boys did this!) it would begin to burn. Our sins were focused on Christ on the cross, and he suffered the fiery wrath of God. On the cross Christ was robed in all that is heinous and hateful as the mass of our corruption poured over him. With horror Christ found his entire being to be sin in the Father's sight.

Wave after wave of our sin was poured over Christ's sinless soul. Again and again during those three hours his soul recoiled and convulsed as all our lies, infidelity, hatreds, jealousies, murders, and pride were poured upon his purity. "Christ redeemed us from the curse of the law by becoming a curse for us—for it is written, 'Cursed is everyone who is hanged on a tree'" (Galatians 3:13). Jesus was cursed as he became sin for us! Can you see him writhing like a serpent in the gloom (cf. John 3:14, 15)?

Jesus in full, lucid consciousness took on your sins and mine and bore them with a unity of understanding and pain that none can fathom. And he did it willingly, so that "we might become the righteousness of God" (2 Corinthians 5:21). There in the darkness our sins were imputed to Christ, and his righteousness has now been imputed to us who believe.

The Curtain

At the very end of the darkness another event occurred that Matthew 27:51 indicates was coincident with Jesus' death. The great curtain of the Holy of Holies was sundered: "And the curtain of the temple was torn in two" (v. 45b). This curtain was the grandest of the thirteen curtains in the temple. It was woven with expensive yarns from Babylon in blue, white, red, and purple with representations of cherubim. Its function was to block all eyes from and forbid access to the Holy of Holies except once a year when the high priest entered with blood offered for himself and the sins of the people (cf. Hebrews 9:7). But now, in the darkened heart of the temple, this great curtain (as thick as a man's hand) was slashed in two as if a great sword had sliced through it. This was a portentous omen of the coming destruction of the temple.[3] The judgment had begun.

But even more, it was a joyous sign of spiritual access. With the curtain sundered, the Ark of the Covenant, the blood-covered mercy seat, and the cherubim were momentarily opened to the world. That afternoon the way into God's presence opened to all. The writer of Hebrews exults:

> Therefore, brothers, since we have confidence to enter the holy places by the blood of Jesus, by the new and living way that he opened for us through the curtain, that is, through his flesh, and since we have a great priest over the house of God, let us draw near with a true heart in full assurance of faith. (Hebrews 10:19–22)

And again, "We have this as a sure and steadfast anchor of the soul, a hope that enters into the inner place behind the curtain, where Jesus has gone as a forerunner on our behalf" (Hebrews 6:19, 20). There was no longer a need for a priesthood, for all who are in Christ are "a royal priesthood" (1 Peter 2:9). Unlimited access would become the lot of every child of God.

The Prayer

The Gospels together reveal that under the cover of the remaining darkness, Jesus uttered three phrases: 1) the so-called cry of dereliction in which he quoted Psalm 22, "My God, my God, why have you forsaken me?" (Mark 15:34), 2) the penultimate expression "It is finished" *(Tetelestai)* (John 19:30), and 3) Jesus' very last word from the cross (recorded only here in Luke), "'Father, into your hands I commit my spirit!' And having said this he breathed his last" (v. 46). Though Luke was aware of the other sayings, he wanted his readers to focus on this final prayer at death.

"Into your hands I commit my spirit" was the traditional evening prayer that pious Jews offered before going to sleep.[4] Jesus chose to pray it at the moment he entered the ultimate sleep—death.

This prayer is a quotation from Psalm 31:5, a psalm in which David describes what has befallen him from his enemies (cf. Psalm 31:10, 12, 13), concluding with an assertion of confidence in God (cf. Psalm 31:22–24). When David prayed, "Into your hand I commit my spirit," he was asking to be preserved from death. But when Jesus, the ultimate son of David, prayed it, it was a prayer of trust in the Father at the moment of death.

When Jesus prayed this "good night" prayer, he prayed it as no other Jew had ever prayed it—because he added "Father" to the beginning—"Father [*Abba*], into your hands I commit my spirit!" It is a matter of Biblical and scholarly record that no one prayed this way until Jesus did so. The ascription of "Father" was revolutionary! "Father" framed Jesus' public ministry. It was the signature of his soul from first to last. It is the one recorded word of his youth: "Did you not know that I must be in my Father's house?" (2:49). It was the implicit title of the One who called to him from Heaven at his baptism: "You are my beloved Son" (3:22). "Father" was the opening word of the prayer he taught his followers to pray (11:2). It was the word he used to accept the cross: "Father, if you are willing, remove this cup from me. Nevertheless, not my will, but yours, be done" (22:42). It was the first word spoken from the cross: "Father, forgive them, for they know not what they do" (23:34). Now it was part of the last statement before his death. "Father" was the sustaining lyric of Jesus' life, and here at death it expressed his ineffable trust and peace at death.

This prayer lifted and personalized from Psalm 31 is beautiful. But we will miss its force unless we feel the triumph in which it came. Luke records that "Jesus, calling out with a loud voice, said, 'Father, into your hands I commit my spirit!' And having said this he breathed his last" (v. 46). It was a shout of victory!

This was no ordinary death by crucifixion. Normally the crucified, due to progressive weakening, fell unconscious and died feebly. But Jesus was in lucid control to the very last. He gave up his soul because he chose to do so, with a shout of confident victory.

And why not?

- He had refused to be drugged for the ordeal.
- He had remained, due to his superior Person, fully sensitized to all the suffering of the cross. He chose to suffer fully.
- Wave after wave of our transgressions poured onto him, so that his heart became the cesspool for our sin. Our iniquity focused upon him the infinite searing of a thousand suns. He became sin. He became a curse. He bore it all!

- He shouted the prophetic dereliction in fulfillment of all of Psalm 22. "My God, my God, why have you forsaken me?"
- He cried, "Finished!"—"It is finished and always will be finished" (perfect tense).
- And he shouted in the lifting gloom his own version of Psalm 31:5, "Father, into your hands I commit my spirit."

This is why we are able to sing, "Jesus saves." Only an infinite God-man could take the totality of our sins on himself and then give us his righteousness. "For our sake he [God] made him to be sin who knew no sin, so that in him we might become the righteousness of God" (2 Corinthians 5:21). This is the great exchange: his righteousness for our sin—our sin for his righteousness. How do we receive this? By faith.

> For I am not ashamed of the gospel, for it is the power of God for salvation to everyone who believes, to the Jew first and also to the Greek. For in it the righteousness of God is revealed from faith for faith, as it is written, "The righteous shall live by faith." (Romans 1:16, 17)

> The righteousness of God [comes] through faith in Jesus Christ for all who believe. (Romans 3:22)

So the question is, does your faith rest on Jesus alone?

Life Comes (vv. 47–49)

As death came to Jesus, life began to come to some who were there.

The Centurion

The centurion had supervised the cruel flagellation of Jesus. But he had also heard Jesus mercifully tell the daughters of Jerusalem not to weep for him but for themselves (v. 28). He had seen Jesus look at him and his cohorts and pray, "Father, forgive them, for they know not what they do" (v. 34). He had heard Jesus promise Paradise to one of the thieves crucified beside him (v. 43). He likely had stood close enough to the cross in the chilling darkness to make sure no foul play occurred and had sensed the cosmic portent of the eerie midnight day. He had heard the three triumphant cries and had seen the victorious calm with which Jesus gave up his life.

When Jesus expired, "The centurion . . . praised God, saying, 'Certainly this man was innocent [better, "just"][5]!'" (v. 47). This does not mean he was saved, but he had clearly become convinced of spiritual truth. He saw far deeper into Jesus than did his fellow Roman, Pontius Pilate, and was thus a likely candidate for conversion. Indeed, in Luke's other New Testament writing, the book of Acts, we see centurions like Cornelius who marvelously believe (cf. Acts 10). And it is in the story of Cornelius that stubborn Peter learns that "the gift of the Holy Spirit was poured out even on the Gentiles" (Acts 10:45).

Thus, in the centurion's declaration at the foot of the cross we see that Jesus' death was not only for Jews but also for Gentiles. Luke tells us in the beginning of his Gospel that the first person to address Jesus in Jerusalem after his birth was Simeon, who praised God and said, "For my eyes have seen your salvation that you have prepared in the presence of all peoples, a light for revelation to the Gentiles" (2:30–32a). And Luke tells us here at the end of his Gospel that the first one to speak of Jesus in Jerusalem after his death was the centurion who glorified God and, by confessing Jesus, became a proclaimer of the salvation possible for Gentiles.[6]

Countrymen

Luke also saw hope for Jesus' countrymen: "And all the crowds that had assembled for this spectacle, when they saw what had taken place, returned home beating their breasts" (v. 48). They, too, saw the righteousness of Jesus and went so far as to dramatically lament his death. Such an indication of guilt was a sure prelude to grace for some of them, as so beautifully happened in such volume at Pentecost (Acts 2).

Followers

Luke also mentions Jesus' desolated followers, the men and women who believed in him and "stood at a distance watching these things" (v. 49). They were the devastated faithful who would soon charge all over Zion with news of the resurrection.

Closing Reflections

A small boy was turning the pages of a book of religious art. When he came to a picture of the crucifixion he looked at it for a long time, and a sad look came to his face. Finally he said, "If God had been there, he wouldn't have let them do it."

So the crucifixion seems—until we understand what it really meant. Then we learn that God was there on the cross. We learn that he willed it. We learn that because of the cross, grace flashed in the lives of Simon the Cyrenian, the daughters of Jerusalem, the crucifying soldiers, the thief, the centurion—and thousands upon thousands since that day.

And we conclude:

> All this is from God, who through Christ reconciled us to himself and gave us the ministry of reconciliation; that is, in Christ God was reconciling the world to himself, not counting their trespasses against them, and entrusting to us the message of reconciliation. Therefore, we are ambassadors for Christ, God making his appeal through us. We implore you on behalf of Christ, be reconciled to God. For our sake he made him to be sin who knew no sin, so that in him we might become the righteousness of God. (2 Corinthians 5:18–21)

Have you been reconciled? "We implore you on behalf of Christ, be reconciled to God."

104

Jesus' Burial and Resurrection

LUKE 23:50—24:12

LUKE'S ACCOUNT OF Jesus' Passion sparkles with bursts of grace that detonated like fireworks in a night sky. On the way to the cross, grace flashed to Simon of Cyrene and then to the daughters of Jerusalem (23:26–31). On the cross grace burst over the Roman soldiers as Jesus forgave them (23:34) and then cascaded over the repentant thief as he was promised Paradise (23:40–43). Jesus' triumphant shout at the moment of his death, "Father, into your hands I commit my spirit!" (23:46), was followed with bright beams of grace—grace to the Gentiles, grace to his own people, and grace to his followers (23:47–49).

Of course, we see the fireworks above the cross because we have the retrospect of Luke's carefully written account and the other Gospels, which those present did not have. They saw no rockets burst in the sky over the cross. All they could see was encroaching darkness and gloom as Jesus slumped into unconsciousness on the dripping pillar.

None of Jesus' followers had even the slightest glimmer of hope. The only light that shone was the light of love and devotion in the lives of some of his followers such as Joseph of Arimathea and the women who had followed him from Galilee.

Of Joseph, Luke writes, "Now there was a man named Joseph, from the Jewish town of Arimathea. He was a member of the council, a good and righteous man, who had not consented to their decision and action; and he was looking for the kingdom of God" (vv. 50, 51). The site of Arimathea is generally thought to be the modern town of Rentis, just north of Jerusalem.[1] His local proximity and membership in the Sanhedrin had led him to have a new family tomb excavated near the Holy City. Apparently he was out of town when the Sanhedrin condemned Jesus because the deed was done by a unanimous vote to which he did not consent (cf. Mark 14:64; Luke 22:70, 71).

Or perhaps the trial had been hidden from him because he was out of sync with the Sanhedrin. John's Gospel tells us he was a secret disciple of Jesus (John 19:38). Indeed, Luke says here that he was a man of character—"a good and righteous man." As such, he fit the pattern of pious Jews mentioned at the beginning of Luke's Gospel whom God used, people like the parents of John the Baptist, Zechariah and his wife Elizabeth, who were "righteous before God" (1:6), and the aged Simeon in the temple who was not only an upright man but was "waiting for the consolation of Israel" (2:25), just as Joseph of Arimathea was "looking for the kingdom of God."[2] Wealthy Joseph of Arimathea humbly longed for the kingdom that Jesus preached—even though Jesus had said, "It is easier for a camel to go through the eye of a needle than for a rich person to enter the kingdom of God" (18:25).

What a shock it must have been to learn too late of Jesus' crucifixion. Joseph evidently decided he would be a secret disciple no more! "This man went to Pilate and asked for the body of Jesus. Then he took it down and wrapped it in a linen shroud and laid him in a tomb cut in stone, where no one had ever yet been laid. It was the day of Preparation, and the Sabbath was beginning" (vv. 52–54). Never mind the risk—there was no time to waste, for the Sabbath began at sunset (6:00 p.m.). Joseph went right to the top, asked for the Savior's corpse, quickly wrapped it in linen, put it in his own tomb (now everyone would know for sure where he stood), and went home to mourn the dark Sabbath night. He had no hope. His only consolation was that he had honored Christ.

Unlike Joseph of Arimathea, the women had been public followers of Jesus from his Galilean days, and they had witnessed the horrible event from a distance. Now they sadly applauded the Arimathean in their hearts. "The women who had come with him from Galilee followed and saw the tomb and how his body was laid. Then they returned and prepared spices and ointments. On the Sabbath they rested according to the commandment" (vv. 55, 56). The necessary haste of the burial had not allowed for all that was essential for a proper anointing. When the sun rose after the Sabbath, they would be ready. They probably slept little or none those two nights.

Like Joseph of Arimathea, they had no hope. Jesus' death was "not only an event, it was a state."[3] In death's grip, decay had begun its work on the body of Jesus, though it did not run its full course (cf. Acts 2:27; Psalm 16:10). Jesus was dead. All they could hope to do was to further honor his body.

Those who have imagined that Jesus actually did not die but was the major player in a hoax defy all logic. The unified testimony of all four Gospels points to the fact of Jesus' death, the impossibility of a freshly impaled man padding around Jerusalem making "ghost appearances," the psychological absurdity of his followers remaining loyal to such a hoax until death, and the impossibility of the greatest of moral teachers perpetrating a lie. If you believe these myths, you probably also believe that Elvis Presley is still alive.

Actually, some people do believe that Elvis did not die but has perpetrated "the Graceland Hoax"—this despite the fact that he was pronounced dead by several physicians, was autopsied and the cause of death determined, and was prepared for burial by two morticians, dressed by his wardrobe manager, made-up by his personal cosmetologist, his hair colored to jet black by the famous Larry Geller, and then viewed by his entire family before closing the seamless copper casket—all this from an article in *The American Funeral Director* appropriately entitled "Elvis Has Really Left the Building."[4]

Bewildered (vv. 1–3)

As we consider the state of the Galilean women, we must not let our knowledge of the glorious revelation that awaited them dull us to the dark sackcloth covering these women's souls. They were depressed, exhausted, mourning, with no hope whatsoever—and according to Mark, fretting over how they would get into the tomb (Mark 16:3). They did not expect anything except more sorrow. If you take flowers to the cemetery, do you expect to see an empty grave? And if you did see one, would it occur to you that the deceased had risen from the dead? Of course not! "But on the first day of the week, at early dawn, they went to the tomb, taking the spices they had prepared. And they found the stone rolled away from the tomb, but when they went in they did not find the body of the Lord Jesus" (vv. 1–3). Now they were definitely confused and bewildered! They apparently assumed Jesus' body had been stolen—that is what John tells us Mary Magdalene thought (cf. John 20:13). The empty tomb intensified their distress.

Rebuked (vv. 4, 5)

> While they were perplexed about this [NEB, "utterly at a loss"], behold, two men stood by them in dazzling apparel. And as they were frightened and bowed their faces to the ground. . . . (vv. 4, 5a)

The resplendent male figures were angels, and they cast an entirely new light on the matter. They radiated the splendor of God (the same words are used to describe shining garments on the Mount of Transfiguration—cf. 9:29). The women were overcome with fear and bowed down until their faces were on the ground as a sign of respect and perhaps avoidance of the bright light (cf. Acts 9:4).

While they bowed, one of the angels voiced the immortal rebuke, "Why do you seek the living among the dead?" (v. 5b). They were accused of coming to anoint a lifeless Jesus when they should have known he would rise from the dead. It was scandalous to look for Jesus in the grave. If you are looking for Elvis, the proper place is in Memphis in a Doric-style mausoleum with ornate brass and bronze fittings on marble, in his own vault in a massive seamless copper casket—"among the dead."[5] But if you are looking for Jesus in a similar environment, you have it all wrong.

All resurrection-denying churches look for Jesus "among the dead." They love the example of the dead Jesus. They preach his courage, his conviction, even his faith. Sentimentality fills their sermons with language about recurrent spring making hope eternal, about a butterfly discarding its chrysalis. But the R word is never used, except metaphorically.

Instructed (vv. 6–8)

The rebuke set the stage for the angels' proclamation of the joyous Easter message: "He is not here, but has risen" (v. 6a)—or more accurately, "He has been raised!" (theological passive).[6]

With the astounding truth ringing over their now uplifted faces, he called them to "'Remember how he told you, while he was still in Galilee, that the Son of Man must be delivered into the hands of sinful men and be crucified and on the third day rise.' And they remembered his words" (vv. 6b–8). The angel challenged them to remember the prophecies of his Passion that he had made back in Galilee. Those prophesies were explicit. Right after Peter's great confession of Christ, Jesus had said, "The Son of Man must suffer many things and be rejected by the elders and chief priests and scribes, and be killed, and on the third day be raised" (9:22; cf. Matthew 16:21). Also, immediately after the transfiguration, he said to his apostles, "'The Son of Man is going to be delivered into the hands of men, and they will kill him. And when he is killed, after three days he will rise.' But they did not understand the saying, and were afraid to ask him" (Mark 9:31, 32; cf. Matthew 17:22, 23).

The women did remember Jesus' words. But Jesus had often spoken metaphorically, and they had probably relegated his hard words to some such interpretation. But now the light began to come on. We do not know whether they immediately believed that he had risen, but shortly thereafter they became messengers of what they had seen and heard.

The great truth here for us is that the significance of the resurrection is inseparable from Jesus' prophetic word about his death and resurrection. It is the Word of God that makes sense of everything. The very structure of this final chapter of Luke makes this clear. Luke 24 recounts three episodes—first, the women's encounter with the angels at the empty tomb (vv. 1–12), second, the encounter on the road to Emmaus (vv. 13–35), and third, Jesus' appearance to his disciples in Jerusalem (vv. 36–49). Significantly, all three episodes are structured the same way: bewilderment, rebuke, instruction, and witness. And the instruction section in all three episodes consists of a call to *remember God's Word*. Here the women are told:

> "Remember how he told you, while he was still in Galilee, that the Son of Man must be delivered into the hands of sinful men and be crucified and on the third day rise." And they remembered his words. (vv. 6b–8)

And on the Emmaus road, Jesus chided:

> "O foolish ones, and slow of heart to believe all that the prophets have spoken! Was it not necessary that the Christ should suffer these things and enter into his glory?" And beginning with Moses and all the Prophets, he interpreted to them in all the Scriptures the things concerning himself. (24:25–27)

And then in Jerusalem, he instructed the whole apostolic band:

> "These are my words that I spoke to you while I was still with you, that everything written about me in the Law of Moses and the Prophets and the Psalms must be fulfilled." Then he opened their minds to understand the Scriptures, and said to them, "Thus it is written, that the Christ should suffer and on the third day rise from the dead." (24:44–46)

The prophetic word from Jesus and throughout the entire corpus of the Bible is central to the gospel. Jesus' atoning death is fully understood only in the light of the whole Word. His resurrection is only understandable in conjunction with his Word. In point of fact, those who had rejected the prophetic word rejected the resurrection, just as Jesus had taught they would: "'If they do not hear Moses and the Prophets, neither will they be convinced if someone should rise from the dead'" (16:31).

This means that we are to be people of the whole Book. We are to devour the Word! Our minds and hearts will begin to embrace the massive dimensions of Christ only through the light of the Scriptures—all of them.

Witnessing (vv. 9–22)

These great women had been bewildered, rebuked, and instructed, but now they would be witnesses! It is impossible to know how much the women really understood at this point, but they did bear testimony to what they had seen and heard: "And returning from the tomb they told all these things to the eleven and to all the rest. Now it was Mary Magdalene and Joanna and Mary the mother of James and the other women with them who told these things to the apostles" (vv. 9, 10). Here all the women are mentioned by name for the second time in Luke's Gospel. They were first named in 8:1–3 when they began their role, and now they were named at the culmination of that role.[7] They kept telling the good news to the Eleven over and over.

However, the "lordly males" were not impressed.[8] "[B]ut these words seemed to them an idle tale, and they did not believe them" (v. 11). They regarded the women's witness as female hysteria—"silly talk" (Abbot-Smith), "humbug" (Fitzmyer), "babbling" (Maclaren). *What dolts!* we might say. But we probably would have done the same thing or worse, given our own sin and dullness. Nevertheless, these were the apostles—the men over whom Jesus had prayed for an entire night before calling them (cf. 6:12, 13). Their faith would be the foundation of the Church. Jesus had explicitly told them numerous times about his death and resurrection. But now they dismissed the women's witness about an empty tomb and called the angels' words humbug.

Like so many of us, they had heard and not heard God's Word. They never bothered to think that Jesus meant exactly what he said. We need to remember that 98 percent of the Bible is intelligible. As Mark Twain once said, "It's not what I don't understand about the Bible that bothers me. It's what I do understand!" The apostles failed to put into practice what they did understand. Jesus had earlier prayed, "Sanctify them in the truth; your word is truth" (John 17:17). Our growth toward spiritual maturity begins by heeding the Word.

It is to Peter's credit that despite all their doubt, he checked things out: "But Peter rose and ran to the tomb; stooping and looking in, he saw the linen cloths by themselves; and he went home marveling at what had happened" (v. 12). Yet Peter's inspection led to wonder, not belief. He saw the empty tomb, but he was still miles away from an Easter faith. The Word was yet to take root. But when it did, he became a powerhouse. Listen to the explosive fireworks at Pentecost:

> Men of Israel, hear these words: Jesus of Nazareth, a man attested to you by God with mighty works and wonders and signs that God did through him in your midst, as you yourselves know—this Jesus, delivered up according to the definite plan and foreknowledge of God, you crucified and killed by the hands of lawless men. God raised him up, loosing the pangs of death, because it was not possible for him to be held by it. (Acts 2:22–24)

Closing Reflections

A grand truth that emerges from this story, as it does in none of the other Gospels, is that the disciples did not invent the resurrection story. At first, they neither understood it or believed it. None of the Gospels tells us how Jesus was resurrected because none of the Gospel authors saw it. How did they resist creatively imagining such a spellbinding story for the Church? They resisted because they were not myth makers but witnesses. In Alexander Maclaren's words, "The evidential value of the disciples' slowness to believe cannot be overrated."[9]

The only reasonable explanation for the apostles' devotion, even at the cost of their own death, is:

- They saw the empty tomb.
- They met their risen Lord.
- They came to believe the Word of God: "That Christ died for our sins *in accordance with the Scriptures*, that he was buried, that he was raised on the third day *in accordance with the Scriptures*" (1 Corinthians 15:3, 4).

105

Easter Fire

LUKE 24:13–35

IN THE LATE AFTERNOON when the darkness lifted from Golgotha and the sun was full upon him, Jesus cried out in triumph and breathed his last. But those gathered around the cross did not recognize his victory. As Christ hung motionless, the warm sun spread over his spilled blood. As those who had hoped in Jesus slowly trudged away from the scene, the icy fingers of death tightened about their hearts in chilling, numbing grief. Despairing hands prepared his cold body for burial and laid it in the tomb. So deep was their despair that no one possessed even the slightest thought of resurrection. When at dawn on the third day the women found the tomb empty, still no one suspected resurrection. It appears that they did not believe even after the angels announced he had risen. And when Peter inspected the empty tomb, instead of believing, he went away wondering.

Confusion (vv. 13–24)

Indeed, all those who had followed Christ were still in despair that afternoon, though they had heard bits and pieces about the empty tomb. As we pick up the story, two of them were on the road to a village named Emmaus, located a short distance from Jerusalem. One of them is identified as Cleopas (v. 18; cf. John 19:25—I believe the "Clopas" mentioned there is the "Cleopas" in Luke 24), a blood relative—Jesus' uncle, the brother of his father Joseph. The best guess as to who the other traveler was is that it was his wife Mary, as she is identified in John 19:25.[1] Uncle Cleopas and Aunt Mary, overcome with grief, were making the sad journey back to their lodging in Emmaus.

They were devastated. Their hope had been elevated by this nephew of theirs. They "had hoped that he was the one to redeem Israel" (v. 21).

But a "Messiah" who managed to get himself imprisoned and handed over to the Romans who then crucified him was a disappointing delusion. They had supported Jesus—and because of that their life had not been easy. Now they ached with grief and confusion. The Scriptures promised a Messiah, and they thought Jesus was the one, but Jesus did not deliver. They needed a word from God.

Did God care? Indeed he did! And our resurrected Lord understood perfectly the confusion in their hearts. Cleopas and Mary moved ever so slowly along the road to Emmaus. Others rushed past them, but they did not even notice. But the resurrected Christ knew not only their geographical location but the terrain of their souls. The omniscient Savior understood!

The word *omniscient* sounds so cosmic and cold, but Jesus' knowledge of his followers is tender and personal. As the Psalmist wrote, "You know when I sit down and when I rise up; you discern my thoughts from afar. You search out my path and my lying down and are acquainted with all my ways" (Psalm 139:2, 3). We may feel insignificant and alone, but when we see Jesus fresh from the cosmic trauma of death and resurrection monitoring the footsteps and heartbeats of a despairing couple, we know that we too are known and loved.

We do not know how Jesus positioned himself to intercept the couple, but he did manage to walk with them. They were apparently prevented from recognizing him. "And he said to them, 'What is this conversation that you are holding with each other as you walk?' And they stood still, looking sad. Then one of them, named Cleopas, answered him, 'Are you the only visitor to Jerusalem who does not know the things that have happened there in these days?' And he said to them, 'What things?'" (vv. 17–19a). Cleopas responded to Jesus' initial question with depressed, biting sarcasm. The irony was that he accused Jesus of not knowing what was going on, but they did not know who was talking with them and that the resurrection had in fact taken place.

Graciously seeking to enlighten them, our Lord would not be put off. His second question, "What things?" got them to express their confusion. Note that in verse 19 both of them spoke, and that they were definitely not possibility thinkers:

> And they said to him, "Concerning Jesus of Nazareth, a man who was a prophet mighty in deed and word before God and all the people, and how our chief priests and rulers delivered him up to be condemned to death, and crucified him. But we had hoped that he was the one to redeem Israel. Yes, and besides all this, it is now the third day since these things happened. Moreover, some women of our company amazed us. They were at the tomb

> early in the morning, and when they did not find his body, they came back saying that they had even seen a vision of angels, who said that he was alive. Some of those who were with us went to the tomb and found it just as the women had said, but him they did not see." (vv. 19b–24)

They were so depressed and so negative in their confusion that it was beyond their capacity to make the obvious connection. If you have ever been depressed or tried to help someone who is depressed, you know that such people are amazingly resourceful in finding reasons not to take comfort in anything you say to them. They are determined to hear everything as bad news. And that is exactly what these two did with the news of the empty tomb. To them, the empty tomb compounded the tragedy, for they thought someone had stolen the body, adding insult to injury. So the good news was bad news! Ironically, Cleopas mentioned that it had been three days since Jesus' death, not recalling that Jesus had said over and over before his Passion that he would be put to death and rise again on the third day (cf. 9:22; Mark 9:31; John 2:19).[2]

Cleopas had let it all out—his confusion, his depression, his disillusionment, his shrinking faith, his anger. And did Jesus reject him? Of course not. Jesus coaxed the couple to reveal their true thoughts, which were by and large their doubts. And when they did so, he answered. Our Lord honors spiritual honesty. For example, in the opening four verses of Habakkuk, the prophet used powerful, emotive language to honestly express his complaints and questions. And God answered his depressed prophet so wonderfully that Habakkuk experienced prophetic ecstasy:

> Though the fig tree should not blossom,
>   nor fruit be on the vines,
> the produce of the olive fail
>   and the fields yield no food,
> the flock be cut off from the fold
>   and there be no herd in the stalls,
> yet I will rejoice in the LORD;
>   I will take joy in the God of my salvation.
> GOD, the Lord, is my strength;
>   he makes my feet like the deer's;
>   he makes me tread on my high places. (Habakkuk 3:17–19)

Our Lord invites honesty from his people. This is not to suggest that we are called to trumpet our doubts to those around us, especially to the young and uninformed, but he wants us to tell him the truth. He knows anyway.

New Light (vv. 25–27)

Rebuke

Earlier that day when the women had been rebuked—"Why do you seek the living among the dead?" (24:5)—they knew they had been rebuked by supernatural beings. But now, when Christ rebuked Cleopas and Mary, they had no idea that it was Christ who was saying to them, "O foolish ones, and slow of heart to believe all that the prophets have spoken! Was it not necessary that the Christ should suffer these things and enter into his glory?" (vv. 25, 26). Certainly they believed the prophets, but just as certainly they did not believe all that the prophets had said. They had read and believed the prophets selectively as they embraced the Messiah-ruler passages, ignoring the passages that prophesied his sufferings. Foolish people! Slow of heart to believe! That was the rebuke from the King incognito.

Explanation

"And beginning with Moses and all the Prophets, he interpreted to them in all the Scriptures the things concerning himself" (v. 27). If there is anything that would make a preacher swell with envy, this is it! This was exegetical Heaven! The root idea of "interpreted" is the word from which we derive the word *hermeneutics*, the science of Bible interpretation.[3] The Word of God incarnate explained the written Word of God.

Moreover, "He interpreted to them in all the Scriptures the things concerning himself." We know from the Savior himself that the entire Old Testament points to him. He would say this again later that day (and even more explicitly) to the assembled apostles in Jerusalem:

> Then he said to them, "These are my words that I spoke to you while I was still with you, that everything written about me in the Law of Moses and the Prophets and the Psalms must be fulfilled." Then he opened their minds to understand the Scriptures, and said to them, "Thus it is written, that the Christ should suffer and on the third day rise from the dead." (24:44–46)

John's Gospel states that from the very onset of Jesus' ministry, he taught that he was central to the Old Testament. "You search the Scriptures," he told the Pharisees, "because you think that in them you have eternal life; and it is they that bear witness about me, yet you refuse to come to me that you may have life" (John 5:39, 40).

This understanding and conviction that the Old Testament corpus is about Christ informed and energized the Apostle Paul's preaching, as he explained before King Agrippa: "To this day I have had the help that comes from God, and so I stand here testifying both to small and great, saying nothing but what the prophets and Moses said would come to pass: that the Christ must suffer and that, by being the first to rise from the dead, he would proclaim light both to our people and to the Gentiles" (Acts 26:22, 23).

When Philip encountered the Ethiopian eunuch on the road, reading Isaiah 53:7, 8, and the eunuch asked who that passage was talking about, "Then Philip opened his mouth, and beginning with this Scripture he told him the good news about Jesus" (Acts 8:35). The prophet Isaiah preached Jesus!

And when Peter was preaching in the house of the Gentile Cornelius, his recorded sermon concluded with these words: "He [Jesus] commanded us to preach to the people and to testify that he is the one appointed by God to be judge of the living and the dead. To him all the prophets bear witness that everyone who believes in him receives forgiveness of sins through his name" (Acts 10:42, 43).

The apostles knew that the Old Testament preached Christ! Indeed, the Old Testament prophets themselves understood this and tried "inquiring what person or time the Spirit of Christ in them was indicating when he predicted the sufferings of Christ and the subsequent glories" (1 Peter 1:11; cf. 1 Peter 1:10–12).

The apostles' Christocentric/bibliocentric belief that the Old Testament is full of Christ was stated by the Apostle Paul in the epigram, "For all the promises of God find their Yes in him [Jesus]" (2 Corinthians 1:20). As the venerable Charles Hodge put it, "All that God had promised relative to the salvation of man met its full accomplishment in him. . . . Christ as regards the promises of God, was the yea, i.e. their affirmation and accomplishment."[4] Here in Luke, on Resurrection Day, Jesus taught that he is the divine "yes" to the Old Testament!

Certainly as "he interpreted to them in all the Scriptures the things concerning himself," he did not touch upon every text that alluded to him (they would never have gotten to Emmaus!), but he did interpretively include the whole of Scripture. What a gripping revelation to hear Christ interpret the sacrifice of Isaac in Genesis 22 as emblematic of his substitutionary atonement and even a prophetic hint of his resurrection (cf. Hebrews 11:17–19), or to hear Jesus, "the Lamb of God" (John 1:29), discourse on the messianic significance of the Passover lamb as it related to his suffering and death, his body and his blood (cf. 22:14–20).

Under Jesus' Emmaus tutelage, the various Old Testament sacrifices coursed with fresh insights on salvation. Possibly Jesus taught them on how the tabernacle and temple pointed to him—that indeed he is the temple (cf. 19:45—20:19; John 2:18–22; cf. also the eschatological reference to the Lamb as the temple in Revelation 21:22). Perhaps Jesus discoursed on some of the grand images that spoke of him, such as the manna and the bronze serpent. He must have taken them through Isaiah 53, showing as he did in the upper room that he was "numbered with the transgressors" (Isaiah 53:12; cf. Luke 22:37), and that the shape of chapter 53 prophesied how the Suffering Servant would die for our sins (Isaiah 53:1–9), then appear alive, triumphant, and reigning (Isaiah 53:10–12). Surely he unpacked Psalm 22, beginning with the words "My God, my God, why have you forsaken me?"—and then applied it to the cross.

The more Jesus opened the Word, the faster their pulses raced. The stranger had established that suffering and death were not obstacles to Jesus' being Messiah, and in fact made Jesus' claim to be Messiah more credible and compelling. The real Messiah had to suffer! Their confusion and depression melted like frost before the sun. The Scriptures were alive to the couple as never before.

What grief they would have been spared if they had only known and believed God's Word to begin with. If we find ourselves hurting and despairing and do not find that Scripture speaks to our condition, it is not because the Bible has failed us, but because we do not know it well enough. We cannot be profoundly comforted by that which we do not know. We need to study our Bible with an eye to our Savior, because everything to do with our salvation and *shalom* is "yes" in Christ.

Revelation

As the incognito Christ was expounding the Scriptures, the two had come to see the plausibility, and indeed the necessity, of the Passion and resurrection. Now they began to understand why the tomb was empty. I think they were divinely kept from recognizing Christ so they would base their understanding of the resurrection squarely on the Scripture and not on experience. A privileged experience such as this, if not grounded in the Word, runs the danger of becoming a privatized, eccentric interpretation. The couple on the road, however, were in no such danger. Their belief in the resurrection rested on the Scriptures before they saw Christ!

Arriving at their lodging, the couple strongly urged him to come in. The word carries the idea of force.[5] They insisted—and we can understand why.

As busy Mary finished preparing the evening meal, she called them to the table, and "When he was at table with them, he took the bread and blessed and broke it and gave it to them. And their eyes were opened, and they recognized him. And he vanished from their sight" (vv. 30, 31). Many believe that the moment of recognition came when, as he broke the bread, they saw his nail-pierced hands. That may well have been. The breaking of bread in Jesus' life, for example in the feeding of the five thousand and at the Passover table, was "an inimitable gesture of self-revelation."[6]

How they were jolted! Surprise, Cleopas! Surprise, Mary! Surprise, citizens of Emmaus! Surprise, world! *Christ is risen! He is risen indeed!*

That explosive moment was burned into their minds for eternity. And then he was gone. But their hearts were left with Easter fire: "They said to each other, 'Did not our hearts burn within us while he talked to us on the road, while he opened to us the Scriptures?'" (v. 32). Their winter of soul was gone forever. So it is when the Scriptures come alive in your soul with the centrality and reality of Jesus Christ. The great Frenchman Blaise Pascal must have been somewhere in the Emmaus latitudes on the memorable night of November 23, 1654, when he wrote in his journal the word "Fire" to describe the most memorable spiritual experience of his life. This glowing word was followed with the hurried scribble: "Joy, joy, joy, tears of joy," and then several inscriptions of the name "Jesus Christ" like signatures on a letter.[7]

Witnesses (vv. 33–35)

Two souls were left flaming in the dark at Emmaus. Jesus was gone, but they sensed his presence. Otherwise they would not have rushed from their table back to Jerusalem with their dynamic news. Sensible Palestinians did not travel lonely roads at night, for fear of thieves and muggers, but the two disciples could not keep their news to themselves.

"And they rose that same hour and returned to Jerusalem. And they found the eleven and those who were with them gathered together, saying, 'The Lord has risen indeed, and has appeared to Simon!' Then they told what had happened on the road, and how he was known to them in the breaking of the bread" (vv. 33–35). They would see Jesus again later that evening along with the rest of the apostolic band. But for now they were thrilled that Peter had seen Christ, and all were beginning to grasp the wonderful truth. This was the beginning of what would become the fellowship of burning hearts, a band that would bear potent witness of Christ to the entire known world.

Closing Reflections

This very moment Christ knows where we are. He knows the geography of our lives inside and out. He knows the temperature of our souls. He knows whether there is ice or fire. Whatever our state, his method is the same—to meet us where we are with his own person framed in the beautiful context of his Word.

The life-giving, energizing truth is that Christ suffered and died for our sins "in accordance with the Scriptures." And then, on the third day, he rose from the dead "in accordance with the Scriptures" (1 Corinthians 15:3, 4).

He is the Savior prophesied on Mt. Moriah, the atoning Lamb of the Passover, our tabernacle and temple (for he is our sacrifice and our priest), our manna/bread of heaven, the Suffering Servant who was "numbered with the transgressors," the Son who suffered separation from the Father for us when he bore our sins.

He delights to bring fire to cold hearts. We do not need more light—we need heat!

106

Easter Gospel and Mission

LUKE 24:36–49

A THREE-PANELED PRINTING is called a triptych. If you have seen one, it was probably in a museum or an ancient church, where they often resided on the altar and depicted three parallel scenes.

Luke 24 provides us with a resurrection triptych—three parallel scenes from Easter day. If the scenes were painted, the first panel would be a painting of the women in conversation with the angels at the empty tomb. The second scene would be of the two disciples on the Emmaus road, their hearts burning as they listened to Christ, unrecognized, explain the Old Testament Scriptures to them. And the third panel would be a painting of Jesus suddenly standing in the midst of his startled disciples on Easter evening. It is very likely that such a resurrection triptych can be found in numerous old cathedrals, because the three parallel scenes are so obvious in Luke 24.

From a literary point of view, Luke's resurrection triptych is particularly stunning because, as we have noted, all three scenes follow the same outline: first confusion, next rebuke, then instruction, and lastly witness.

As we take up the third and final scene we see confusion bordering on pandemonium. The Eleven had gathered behind closed doors in Jerusalem (cf. John 20:19), where the apostle Peter had amazed them by relating that he had personally seen the risen Lord. This was followed by the entrance of the couple from the Emmaus road with the report of their astounding encounter with Christ incognito, their burning hearts, and the grand moment of recognition when he broke the bread.

Confusion (vv. 36, 37)

"As they were talking about these things, Jesus himself stood among them, and said to them, 'Peace to you!' But they were startled and frightened and thought they saw a spirit" (vv. 36, 37). They had nodded in seeming acceptance of Peter's report, they continued nodding as they listened to the Emmaus report, but with the sudden appearance of Jesus they gasped, their eyes bulged, and their skin crawled as they saw what they took to be a ghostly apparition of Jesus. It was indeed Jesus' voice that greeted them—"Peace to you!" Peace on earth had been announced at the coming of Jesus (2:14), but they did not have much peace in their hearts—only scandalous disbelief. These handpicked apostles were as "foolish . . . and slow of heart" (24:25) and confused as the Emmaus disciples had been!

Rebuke (vv. 38–43)

Jesus' lordly rebuke took the form of a disappointed question, followed by an invitation for tactile examination: "And he said to them, 'Why are you troubled, and why do doubts arise in your hearts? See my hands and my feet, that it is I myself. Touch me, and see. For a spirit does not have flesh and bones as you see that I have.' And when he had said this, he showed them his hands and his feet" (vv. 38–40). After this, none could argue that they had seen a specter. They felt for themselves solid flesh over hard bones. Some even touched the open wounds. Jesus was physically there. It was his earthly body, but raised to a higher position. The materiality of his resurrection was a fact.

In moments the apostles' condition had become one of positive (rather than negative) disbelief: "And while they still disbelieved for joy and were marveling . . ." (v. 41a). They were in the wacky state of giddy disbelief—like football fans whose team just scored as time ran out to win the game. The literal Greek here reads, "They being unbelieving from joy and amazement." Jesus then delivered the final blow to their doubts: "He said to them, 'Have you anything here to eat?' They gave him a piece of broiled fish, and he took it and ate before them" (vv. 41b–43). This was not the only time Jesus did this. After the resurrection he appeared to them over a period of forty days and occasionally ate with them (cf. Acts 1:4). Peter told Cornelius, "God . . . made him to appear, not to all the people but to us who had been chosen by God as witnesses, who ate and drank with him after he rose from the dead" (Acts 10:40, 41).

After this, none of the Eleven ever again doubted the reality of the resurrection. In the following moments Jesus had their attention as perhaps he had never had it before. This was so appropriate because he proceeded to impart the eternal essentials of gospel and mission.

Instruction (vv. 44–47)

As Jesus proceeded to instruct them, we must note that the resurrection triptych, the three successive events of Easter day, all focused on God's Word for instruction. First, the angels at the tomb referred the women back to Christ's words: "'Remember how he told you, while he was still in Galilee, that the Son of Man must be delivered into the hands of sinful men and be crucified and on the third day rise.' And they remembered his words" (24:6b–8).

Next, Christ incognito chided the despondent couple on the Emmaus road: "'O foolish ones, and slow of heart to believe all that the prophets have spoken! Was it not necessary that the Christ should suffer these things and enter into his glory?' And beginning with Moses and all the Prophets, he interpreted to them in all the Scriptures the things concerning himself" (24:25–27).

And now, in the third event of the triptych in Jerusalem, he explained his Passion and resurrection in the dynamic context of Old Testament Scripture: "These are my words that I spoke to you while I was still with you, that everything written about me in the Law of Moses and the Prophets and the Psalms must be fulfilled" (v. 44). As Leon Morris has said, "The solemn division of Scripture into *the law of Moses and the prophets and the psalms* (the three divisions of the Hebrew Bible) indicates that there is no part of Scripture that does not bear its witness to Jesus."[1]

And again we must understand that one of the reasons Jesus taught them from Scripture was that he did not want them to rest their belief in his resurrection on their personal experience alone. He was not interested in their becoming an esoteric coterie, an elite group with a special knowledge of Christ. Resting their faith on a miracle was not sufficient. He wanted them to ground their experience of his resurrection on the massive testimony and perspective of Scripture. Tragically, one can actually believe in the resurrection and not believe in Christ—as Jesus had warned earlier in the parable of the rich man and Lazarus: "If they do not hear Moses and the Prophets, neither will they be convinced if someone should rise from the dead" (16:31). Jesus' passion and resurrection only make saving sense in the beautiful context of the Law, the Prophets, and the Psalms.

This encounter was undoubtedly the ultimate teachable moment in all history. Jesus would have seated himself, taking the traditional posture of a teacher, and as he gestured in the candlelit room his nail-pierced hands or wrists emphasized his points. No wandering minds here. No Eutychus nodding and falling off his perch!

His teaching was enhanced by divine illumination: "Then he opened their minds to understand the Scriptures" (v. 45). Though they had been his devoted followers, a spiritual veil had covered their understanding, so that on two occasions when he had foretold his death we read, "It was concealed from them, so that they might not perceive it. And they were afraid to ask him about this saying" (9:45), and again, "But they understood none of these things. This saying was hidden from them, and they did not grasp what was said" (18:34; cf. 2 Corinthians 3:13–16). But on Easter night the blinders were removed as the Holy Spirit opened their minds! What a dynamic combination—the Holy Scriptures illumined by the Holy Spirit. What they learned that night and in succeeding conversations during the forty days before Christ's ascension became the Biblical substance for the apostolic preaching of the gospel and their apostolic mission.

Gospel Instruction

First we read that Jesus instructed them about the gospel (i.e., Jesus' passion and resurrection) from the Old Testament: "[He] said to them, 'Thus it is written, that the Christ should suffer and on the third day rise from the dead'" (v. 46). From this we understand that the apostolic preaching of the gospel was always framed by the rich background of Old Testament exposition. Paul says exactly this in 1 Corinthians 15:1–4:

> Now I would remind you, brothers, of the gospel I preached to you, which you received, in which you stand, and by which you are being saved, if you hold fast to the word I preached to you—unless you believed in vain. For I delivered to you as of first importance what I also received: that Christ died for our sins in accordance with the Scriptures, *that he was buried, that he was raised on the third day* in accordance with the Scriptures.

From this, we must also understand that the gospel is only fully preached when set in the context of the Law, the Prophets, and the Psalms.

The Law? Where do we find the gospel of Christ in the Law? Most clearly, we see his sufferings in the great institutions and events of the Law. According to Exodus 24, the old covenant was launched on a sea of blood from sacrificial animals with which Moses doused the altar, the Book, and the people. In the following centuries oceans of blood flowed upon Jewish altars from suffering animals, effecting an external ceremonial cleansing of the offerers. These sacrifices pointed to and were fulfilled by the shed blood of Christ, as the writer of Hebrews so well explained:

> For if the blood of goats and bulls, and the sprinkling of defiled persons with the ashes of a heifer, sanctify for the purification of the flesh, how much more will the blood of Christ, who through the eternal Spirit offered himself without blemish to God, purify our conscience from dead works to serve the living God. (Hebrews 9:13, 14)

The daily sacrifices pointed to and begged for the ultimate atoning sacrifice of Christ.

In a similar way the Passover lamb of Exodus 12 prophesied of Christ's sufferings. Just before his death, while with his disciples in the upper room, Jesus made it very clear that he was the Passover lamb as he prepared to eat the Passover meal, saying, "I have earnestly desired to eat this Passover with you before I suffer. For I tell you I will not eat it until it is fulfilled in the kingdom of God" (22:15, 16). Jesus then fulfilled the Passover to the letter as a male in his prime without defect (cf. Exodus 12:5), who in the sacrificial process did not have any of his bones broken (cf. Exodus 12:46; John 19:36). And now, just as faith in the blood of the Passover lamb delivered the Israelites from death, so faith in Jesus' blood brings life. Christ is our Passover (cf. 1 Corinthians 5:7).

In this connection the entire tabernacle spoke of Christ, and the epicenter of the tabernacle (the mercy seat atop the Ark of the Covenant where the blood was sprinkled) pictured Christ's atoning/propitiating work. It is a fact that the New Testament word "propitiation" (*hilaskomai*) comes from the root word for mercy seat (*hilasterion*), so that the apostle John would explain of Christ, "He is the propitiation for our sins, and not for ours only but also for the sins of the whole world" (1 John 2:2). Paul similarly comments of Christ, "whom God displayed publicly as a propitiation in His blood" (Romans 3:25 NASB). Jesus is both the atoning place and the atoning blood for our sins.

Christ's sufferings are written huge in the Law. There is even a hint of the resurrection in the Law. Luke records in chapter 20 that Christ embarrassed the resurrection-denying Sadducees by showing them that Exodus 3:6, where God says, "I am the God of your father, the God of Abraham, the God of Isaac, and the God of Jacob," proves the idea of resurrection because God would not say "I am" (present tense) the God of those deceased patriarchs unless they were still living. Peter remembered this and alluded to it in his sermon in Acts 3:13, then went on to proclaim the resurrection: "You killed the Author of life, whom God raised from the dead" (Acts 3:15). Peter saw that the same resurrection power that raised the patriarchs to life after death raised Jesus, who was after all the author of life!

The Prophets? Where is the gospel found in the Prophets? The most explicit foretelling of Christ's sufferings in the prophetic Scriptures is in Isaiah 53, the text to which Christ directed his disciples in the upper room by referring to its final verse indicating that he himself "was numbered with the transgressors," thus directing their attention to the fact that every line of the chapter refers to him as the ultimate Suffering Servant. Isaiah 53 drips with Christ's Passion!

Not only do the prophets detail Christ's sufferings—they also speak of his resurrection occurring on the third day. In verse 46 Luke was apparently alluding to Hosea 6:2: "After two days he will revive us; on the third day he will raise us up, that we may live before him." That prophecy was given to sinful Israel, but there was nothing in their history to correspond to it—except that when Christ rose from the dead on the third day, he raised with himself believing Israel. The prophecy plainly points to Christ. Christ's body lay in the tomb for two days, and on the third day he rose again. Christ "was raised on the third day in accordance with the Scriptures" (1 Corinthians 15:4).

The Psalms? Indeed, the gospel was in the Law and the Prophets, and in the Psalms as well. Psalm 22 is the *locus classicus* as it gives a technical description of one dying of crucifixion before the cross was ever invented. But even more, it perfectly describes Jesus' experience, even to the detail of the soldiers gambling over his clothing (Psalm 22:18).

The Psalms also teach the resurrection, as Peter explained in his sermon at Pentecost when he quoted Psalm 16:8–11:

> For David says concerning him [i.e., Jesus],
>
> "I saw the Lord always before me,
> for he is at my right hand that I may not be shaken;
> therefore my heart was glad, and my tongue rejoiced;
> my flesh also will dwell in hope.
> For you will not abandon my soul to Hades,
> or let your Holy One see corruption.
> You have made known to me the paths of life;
> you will make me full of gladness with your presence."
> (Acts 2:25–28)

Then Peter explained that David did not fulfill the prophecy because he rotted in the grave. But Christ, the ultimate Son, did fulfill it because he rose before decomposition began:

> Brothers, I may say to you with confidence about the patriarch David that he both died and was buried, and his tomb is with us to this day. Being therefore a prophet, and knowing that God had sworn with an oath to him that he would set one of his descendants on his throne, he foresaw and spoke about the resurrection of the Christ, that he was not abandoned to Hades, nor did his flesh see corruption. This Jesus God raised up, and of that we all are witnesses. (Acts 2:29–32)

Thus along these lines Jesus is the theme of the entire body of Scripture. As the Law was opened, their hearts burned. As the Prophets came alive, the flames rose higher. And with the Psalms, their hearts became passionate, roaring furnaces. They became men of the gospel!

Mission Instruction

But it didn't stop there. Jesus also showed them that world mission was taught throughout the Scriptures.

The Law? The Law, the Torah, foretold this right at the origin of the Jewish nation when God said to Abram, "And I will make of you a great nation, and I will bless you and make your name great, so that you will be a blessing. I will bless those who bless you, and him who dishonors you I will curse, and in you all the families of the earth shall be blessed" (Genesis 12:2, 3; cf. 17:3–7). This was accomplished through his ultimate offspring, Jesus Christ, as Paul explained: "Now the promises were made to Abraham and to his offspring. It does not say, 'And to offsprings,' referring to many, but referring to one, 'And to your offspring,' who is Christ" (Galatians 3:16). So Christ is the heir and mediator of the promise made to Abraham. And the blessing goes out to the Gentiles as they come to Christ and are incorporated into his body: "And if you are Christ's, then you are Abraham's offspring, heirs according to promise" (Galatians 3:29). The nations of the earth are blessed with the spiritual riches of Abraham when believers preach Christ.

The Prophets? Mission is also found in the Prophets. In Acts 13 Paul and Barnabas explain why they are turning to the Gentiles, and they quote from Isaiah 49:6 (a passage citing the task first given to the servant-Messiah but that is now the responsibility of his followers): "For so the Lord has commanded us, saying, 'I have made you a light for the Gentiles, that you may bring salvation to the ends of the earth.'" And when the Gentiles heard this, they began rejoicing and glorifying the word of the Lord, and as many as were appointed to eternal life believed" (Acts 13:47, 48). All Christ's followers are charged to aid in bringing light to the Gentiles and salvation to the ends of the earth.

The Psalms? This is also the ancient message of the Psalms. Psalm 22, which so graphically describes Christ's sufferings, ends with a statement of mission: "All the ends of the earth shall remember and turn to the Lord, and all the families of the nations shall worship before you. For kingship belongs to the Lord, and he rules over the nations" (Psalm 22:27, 28; cf. the marvelous string of five Psalms that declare God's salvation to the Gentiles: Psalm 96, esp. vv. 1–3, 7, 10; 97, esp. vv. 1, 6; 98, esp. vv. 1–3; 99, esp. vv. 1–3; 100).

That Easter night, privately locked up with the Eleven, Jesus grounded gospel and mission in the Old Testament Scriptures. He showed that the Law, the Prophets, and the Psalms all taught his suffering, all taught his death, all taught his resurrection, all taught mission to the world beginning with Jerusalem, the very heartland of the Jewish faith, the place where the incarnate Son suffered, died, and rose again.

The gospel was and is for the world! We are to be gospel men and women who proclaim that "Christ died for our sins *in accordance with the Scriptures,* that he was buried, that he was raised on the third day *in accordance with the Scriptures*" (1 Corinthians 15:3, 4). Our message is not a philosophy. It is not even a way of life. It is the eternal good news based on historical events prophesied in the Old Testament and fulfilled by Jesus the Messiah. We are to preach Christ and him crucified.

And gospel people are to be mission people. The gospel demands that we share Christ everywhere, and that we use our time and resources to go to the nations. It is a matter of life and death. It is about the glory of God.

Witness (vv. 48, 49)

All three panels of the resurrection triptych conclude with witness. The women hurried from the empty tomb to share the good news with the Eleven (24:9, 10). The couple on the road marched back to Jerusalem to share what had happened along the way. And here Jesus made it formal: "You are witnesses of these things. And behold, I am sending the promise of my Father upon you. But stay in the city until you are clothed with power from on high" (vv. 48, 49). He was promising the Holy Spirit, a promise reiterated at his ascension: "But you will receive power when the Holy Spirit has come upon you, and you will be my witnesses in Jerusalem and in all Judea and Samaria, and to the end of the earth" (Acts 1:8).

And when the Spirit came, what power there was! The preaching of the gospel was not advanced by the mere recitation of what the Law, the Prophets, and the Psalms said about Jesus. Neither was it advanced by the declaration of the Scriptures' fulfillment in the death and resurrection of Jesus. The gospel was advanced when the messengers were empowered by the Holy Spirit, and the Holy Spirit was pleased to do his work of regeneration. As Paul testified to the Thessalonians, "Our gospel came to you not only in word, but also in power and in the Holy Spirit and with full conviction" (1 Thessalonians 1:5).

May we be gospel people, devoted to mission in the power and passionate conviction of the Holy Spirit!

107

Christ's Ascension

LUKE 24:50–53

IN THE PREVIOUS CHAPTER we noted that Luke 24 is a resurrection triptych, a three-paneled verbal painting of Easter Day. The first panel is the picture of the empty tomb before which the troubled women conversed with angels. The second shows two of Jesus' followers on the road, their hearts aflame as Jesus, unrecognized, instructed them about himself from the Scriptures. The third is of Jesus' sudden appearance that night amid his startled disciples. Now at the conclusion of Luke's Gospel, we see another marvelous picture—Christ rising in the clouds to Heaven.

The glorious ascension not only concludes the Gospel of Luke but provides a bridge to Luke's sequel, the Acts of the Apostles, which begins with the ascension. In fact, just as Luke addressed his Gospel to Theophilus saying, "It seemed good to me also . . . to write an orderly account for you, most excellent Theophilus" (1:3), he later began the book of Acts by saying, "In the first book, O Theophilus, I have dealt with all that Jesus began to do and teach, until the day when he was taken up, after he had given commands through the Holy Spirit to the apostles whom he had chosen" (Acts 1:1, 2). And in Acts he then greatly expanded on the brief description of the ascension with which he had concluded his Gospel.

We learn in Acts that the ascension did not immediately take place on Easter evening, but forty days later: "He presented himself alive to them after his suffering by many proofs, appearing to them during forty days and speaking about the kingdom of God" (Acts 1:3). We know that Jesus appeared to specific individuals on Easter Day—to Peter, to the two on the Emmaus road, and to Mary Magdalene (cf. 24:13–35; John 20:10–18). We know that he made appearances at the apostles' gatherings during the forty days, first on

Easter night (cf. 24:36ff., John 20:19–23), a week later to the disciples and Thomas (cf. John 20:24–29), and the third time to some disciples when they were fishing in Galilee (John 21:1, 14).

There were evidently other appearances over the forty days, as is apparent from Paul's summary in 1 Corinthians 15: "He appeared to Cephas, then to the twelve. Then he appeared to more than five hundred brothers at one time, most of whom are still alive, though some have fallen asleep. Then he appeared to James, then to all the apostles. Last of all, as to one untimely born, he appeared also to me" (1 Corinthians 15:5–8).

Luke also tells us in Acts that sometime during those forty days Jesus enlarged on the promise of the Holy Spirit that he had given Easter evening (cf. 24:49): "And while staying with them he ordered them not to depart from Jerusalem, but to wait for the promise of the Father, which, he said, 'you heard from me; for John baptized with water, but you will be baptized with the Holy Spirit not many days from now'" (Acts 1:4, 5). What grand days they were—multiple appearances, compounded learning, restoration, and simmering passions.

At the end of those forty days Jesus called the Eleven together on the Mount of Olives. There the apostolic band flamed with expectancy.

> So when they had come together, they asked him, "Lord, will you at this time restore the kingdom to Israel?" He said to them, "It is not for you to know times or seasons that the Father has fixed by his own authority. But you will receive power when the Holy Spirit has come upon you, and you will be my witnesses in Jerusalem and in all Judea and Samaria, and to the end of the earth." (Acts 1:6–8)

Such immense spiritual drama! Just before Jesus left earth, he gave the Church its enduring mission—to be done until his feet again touch down on the Mount of Olives (cf. Zechariah 14:4). Acts 1:8 is the key verse to the book of Acts. "Jerusalem"—"Judea and Samaria"—"the end of the earth"—this is the outline of Acts. It continues to be the mandate of the Church today.

The Ascension (Luke 24:50, 51; Acts 1:9–11)

Luke 24:50, 51 together with Acts 1:9 tell us what the Eleven saw at the ascension: "Then he led them out as far as Bethany, and lifting up his hands he blessed them. While he blessed them, he parted from them and was carried up into heaven" (Luke 24:50, 51). "And when he had said these things, as they were looking on, he was lifted up, and a cloud took him out of their sight" (Acts 1:9). The ascension began as Jesus lifted his hands like an Old

Testament priest and began blessing the apostles (cf. Leviticus 9:22 and the noncanonical Sirach 50:20ff.). As he continued to bless them, he ascended so that he was calling down the Father's favor as he moved away. The use of the imperfect tense in both Luke and Acts for "was carried up" (Luke 24:51) and "he was lifted up" (Acts 1:9) seems to indicate that he ascended slowly while raining down blessings.[1]

The cloud that "took" (Acts 1:9; literally, "received") him was the *Shekinah*, a visible representation of the pleasure and presence of God. This was the same luminous presence that Moses had encountered on Sinai when God covered him and he saw its afterglow. It was the same cloud that traveled before Israel by day and appeared as a pillar of fire at night. It was the cloud that lay over the tabernacle and filled the temple. It was the glorious cloud that Ezekiel saw depart over the east gate. It was the same shimmering presence that surrounded Jesus on the Mount of Transfiguration when his face shone forth like the sun.

The disciples remained transfixed as the *Shekinah* moved farther away. As the distance increased, their dazzled countenances began to fade, their sparkling eyes dimmed, and they could hear Jesus no more.

> And while they were gazing into heaven as he went, behold, two men stood by them in white robes, and said, "Men of Galilee, why do you stand looking into heaven? This Jesus, who was taken up from you into heaven, will come in the same way as you saw him go into heaven." (Acts 1:10, 11).

This was the exodus toward which the Gospel of Luke had so inexorably moved. In Luke 9 we read that during the transfiguration, amid the glorious splendor, Jesus had talked to Moses and Elijah about his "departure [Greek, *exodon*], which he was about to accomplish at Jerusalem" (9:31). Shortly after that discussion, "When the days drew near for him to be taken up, he set his face to go to Jerusalem" (9:51). Finally, before the Sanhedrin on the night of his crucifixion, he referred to the exaltation that would follow his ascension: "But from now on the Son of Man shall be seated at the right hand of the power of God" (22:69).[2]

Jesus' great exodus was now complete. And with his ascension, there also came an elevation of Jesus' ministry to new heights.

The Meaning of the Ascension

What is the significance of the ascension, and what does it mean to us? The answer begins in the Old Testament where the prophecies of Jesus' ascension are so instructively rooted (cf. Psalm 2:7–9; 8:6; 68:18; 110:1, 5; Daniel 7:13, 14).

Psalm 68:18 reads: "*You* ascended on high, leading a host of captives in *your* train and receiving gifts among men." In Ephesians 4:8 Paul quotes this as referring to Christ's ascension: "When *he* ascended on high *he* led a host of captives, and *he* gave gifts to men." Note that Paul, knowing this Psalm was about Jesus, freely changed the pronouns "you" to "he" (to make it clear that it prophetically referred to Christ) and pictured Christ as giving gifts to men instead of receiving gifts.

How are we to understand this? To begin with, Psalm 68, apart from its prophetic significance, celebrated the ascent of a Davidic king to Jerusalem after a victory. It likely refers to King David's festive procession with the ark to Jerusalem (cf. 2 Samuel 6:12) or commemorates David's earlier capture of Jerusalem (2 Samuel 5:6, 7). As such, it is a Psalm of huge celebration. The Psalm sees the victorious ascent to Jerusalem as the culmination of the journey begun when Israel left Egypt.

But since Jesus is both the son of David and the Lord of David, the Psalm is also a prophecy of a far greater ascension. Instead of merely being the record of an Old Testament ascension up Mount Zion to what would be the new temple of Jerusalem, Psalm 68 celebrates a messianic ascension from this world into God's Heaven, where the great King distributes the spoils of victory.[3] Thus Paul interprets it in this way:

> (In saying, "He ascended," what does it mean but that he had also descended into the lower regions, the earth? He who descended is the one who also ascended far above all the heavens, that he might fill all things.) And he gave the apostles, the prophets, the evangelists, the shepherds and teachers, to equip the saints for the work of ministry. (Ephesians 4:9–12a)

So we see that the ascension of Christ, his earthly exodus, meant two things to the apostolic church: first, Jesus' incredible exaltation, and second, Jesus' massive ministry to and through his people.

His Exaltation

Jesus was "carried up into heaven" (24:51). This is not a spatial description. His ascent cannot be described in terms of space and distance. The descent and ascent of the Son of God cannot be measured in miles or light-years. The created universe cannot hold God, as Solomon indicated when he prayed at the dedication of the temple, "Behold, heaven and the highest heaven cannot contain you; how much less this house that I have built!"

(1 Kings 8:27). Heaven is another sphere "where God is wholly experienced and known."[4]

Wherever this awesome sphere may be, we do know that Jesus was exalted at his ascension to the right hand of the Father: "So then the Lord Jesus, after he had spoken to them, was taken up into heaven and sat down at the right hand of God" (Mark 16:19). It is the place of ultimate power. Peter has described the resurrected, ascended Christ as the one "who has gone into heaven and is at the right hand of God, with angels, authorities, and powers having been subjected to him" (1 Peter 3:22). "Right hand" is a metaphor for all power. To see Jesus ascended in this way is to understand that he has been exalted to the highest position possible.

The night before he died Jesus prayed, "And now, Father, glorify me in your own presence with the glory that I had with you before the world existed" (John 17:5). That reglorification appears to be more glorious than his original glory—an acquired glory—a glory consequent on his earthly life and suffering. How can this be? How can one who is infinitely glorious become more glorious? The answer is suggested by the new name he received at his return to Heaven: "Therefore God has highly exalted him and bestowed on him the name that is above every name, so that at the name of Jesus every knee should bow, in heaven and on earth and under the earth, and every tongue confess that Jesus Christ is Lord, to the glory of God the Father" (Philippians 2:9–11).

The new name was "Jesus"—the name of his acquired humanity that he took in glorified bodily form to Heaven. Today our Lord has a greater glory as he reigns in his human body, beautified by those scars in the way an artist makes a figure more lovely than before by the marks of his tools. His infinite glory may not be improved, but it is "greater" in that angels and men have acquired a better understanding of it.

Our Exaltation

So we see that the incarnation was not something casual and fleeting but has permanent consequences in taking Christ's humanity to Heaven. Christ's humanity is in Heaven, and at his coming he will take the humanity that he has redeemed to be there with him.[5] Jesus has become "the firstfruits" of his people through his resurrection and ascension and therefore guarantees the final redemption of those in union with him (1 Corinthians 15:20, 23). As a result of their unity with Jesus, there is a sense in which believers have ascended into Heaven with him. Thus where the head is, there are the members (cf. Ephesians 1:20–22). Paul writes, "And [God] raised us up with him and seated us with him in the heavenly places in Christ Jesus" (Ephesians 2:6). The present exaltation of believers is a fact that will be seen fully at Christ's return. We have ascended with him, and we are to glory in it now!

His Ministry: Intercession

There is more. Jesus ascended into Heaven to begin his heavenly ministry as High Priest. Paul rejoiced at this, asking, "Who is to condemn? Christ Jesus is the one who died—more than that, who was raised—who is at the right hand of God, who indeed is interceding for us" (Romans 8:34). The writer of Hebrews likewise rejoiced:

> Since then we have a great high priest who has passed through the heavens, Jesus, the Son of God, let us hold fast our confession. For we do not have a high priest who is unable to sympathize with our weaknesses, but one who in every respect has been tempted as we are, yet without sin. Let us then with confidence draw near to the throne of grace, that we may receive mercy and find grace to help in time of need. (Hebrews 4:14–16)

The fact that his glorified earthly body is in Heaven is at the core of our comfort. There is no chord in our human experience that does not resonate with his.

> Our fellow-suff'rer yet retains
> A fellow-feeling of our pains;
> And still remembers in the skies
> His tears, his agonies, and cries.

Again the writer of Hebrews rejoiced, "We have this as a sure and steadfast anchor of the soul, a hope that enters into the inner place behind the curtain, where Jesus has gone as a forerunner on our behalf, having become a high priest forever after the order of Melchizedek" (Hebrews 6:19, 20). And again, "Consequently, he is able to save to the uttermost those who draw near to God through him, since he always lives to make intercession for them" (Hebrews 7:25). Oh, the comfort that comes to our souls because of the ascension of Christ!

His Ministry: The Spirit

Yet there is even more, because his ascension meant the sending of the Holy Spirit. In the upper room he said, "Nevertheless, I tell you the truth: it is to your advantage that I go away, for if I do not go away, the Helper will not come to you. But if I go, I will send him to you" (John 16:7). Christ ascended to Heaven so he could be nearer to his own. Imagine if he had chosen Jerusalem as his seat. Localized, he would have deprived every other place of his presence. But with the ascension all restrictions have been removed and he is our ever-present Christ.

His Ministry: Power

Jesus not only sends us the Holy Spirit, but he supplies power to his Church. At the Father's right hand all power is his. "Truly, truly, I say to you," said Jesus as he was about to promise the Spirit, "whoever believes in me will also do the works that I do; and greater works than these will he do, because I am going to the Father" (John 14:12). Not many days later, the disciples saw the truth of this at Pentecost. Jesus had ascended to Heaven and had given gifts to his people by his Spirit, then empowered them by his Spirit. The greatest of all works is the salvation of a soul, and soulwinning is a "greater work" considering the poor vessels God uses to preach his saving Word.

The ascension of our Lord to Heaven brought about:

- His superexaltation
- Our exaltation
- His intercession for us
- His presence with us
- His power through us

This is why the apostolic church confessed the ascension!

> Great indeed, we confess, is the mystery of godliness: He was manifested in the flesh, vindicated by the Spirit, seen by angels, proclaimed among the nations, believed on in the world, taken up in glory. (1 Timothy 3:16)

Closing Reflections

The ascension is part of the Apostles' Creed "The third day he rose again from the dead. He ascended into Heaven and sitteth. . . ." The immediate effect of Jesus' ascension upon his followers was twofold.

They worshiped. Luke concludes his Gospel, "And they worshiped him and returned to Jerusalem with great joy, and were continually in the temple blessing God" (vv. 52, 53). With the ascension all his disciples at last understood—and they bowed in awed adoration. This is where the gospel ought to leave us too—worshiping the ascended King.

They witnessed. Acts, Luke's sequel, records that their worship flowered into witness to the world. This is where the gospel ought to take us too—witnessing to a lost world.

Soli Deo gloria!

Notes

Chapter One: An Orderly Account

1. Philip Edgcumbe Hughes, *Paul's Second Epistle to the Corinthians* (Grand Rapids, MI: Eerdmans, 1962), p. 313: "[T]he balance of opinion is, if anything, in favour of the identification of Luke with the 'brother' to whom Paul here refers, and the strength of the tradition to this effect has also to be taken into account."

2. Leon Morris, *Luke* (Grand Rapids, MI: Eerdmans, 1974), pp. 24–28.

3. John Nolland, *Luke 1—9:20* (Dallas: Word, 1989), p. 14.

4. Joseph A. Fitzmyer, *The Gospel According to Luke I—IX* (Garden City, NY: Doubleday, 1981), p. 295.

5. Morris, p. 36, who quotes William Ramsay, *The Bearing of Present Discovery on the Trustworthiness of the New Testament,* p. 81.

Chapter Two: The Annunciation of John

1. David Gooding, *According to Luke: A New Exposition of the Third Gospel* (Leicester, UK: Inter-Varsity, 1987), pp. 33–34 supplies the preceding Scriptural arrangement of the darkness before the sunrise.

2. Josephus, *War*, V. 5. 3.

3. Joachim Jeremias, *Jerusalem in the Time of Jesus* (Philadelphia: Fortress, 1978), pp. 200–204.

4. Joseph A. Fitzmyer, *The Gospel According to Luke I—IX* (Garden City, NY: Doubleday, 1981), p. 322. Jeremias, *Jerusalem in the Time of Jesus*, p. 199, similarly writes:

> The division of the priesthood into twenty-four courses, each of which did service for one week in Jerusalem from sabbath to sabbath (CA 2. 108; Ant. 7. 365; Luke 1. 8)—for which reason they were called weekly courses—was the system prevailing at the time of Jesus.

5. M. *Yoma* 2:5; Jeremias, *Jerusalem in the Time of Jesus*, pp. 201–2.

6. John Nolland, *Luke 1—9:20* (Dallas: Word, 1989), p. 29.

7. Fitzmyer, *The Gospel According to Luke I—IX*, p. 324, explains:

> Parallels with Dan 9:21 otherwise found in the infancy narrative would suggest that it is the time of the evening offering that is to be understood here, since at that hour Gabriel appeared in Daniel 9. Acts 3:1 speaks of the ninth hour as the hour of prayer, i.e. about 3 p.m. Cf. Josephus *Ant.* 13, 10, 3.282.

8. Leon Morris, *Luke* (Grand Rapids, MI: Eerdmans, 1974), p. 76.

9. Nolland, *Luke 1—9:20*, pp. 29–30, writes:

> The name John . . . *Yohanan* means "God has been gracious," while the cognate . . . *tehinna* ("prayer for favor") is rendered by the LXX as *benaus;*

the word in Luke 1:13 for prayer. Thus the logical basis for the specified name is in the original Hebrew provided by the statement that the prayer for favor has been heard (Winter, NTS 1 [1954–55] 120; Laurentin, Bib 37 [1956] 441–42).

10. Fitzmyer, *The Gospel According to Luke I—IX,* p. 326, writes:

Even from his birth. Lit. "still from the womb of his mother." Ms. W reads rather *en koilia,* "While still in the womb." The substitution of prep. *en* for *ek* is an obvious correction smoothing out the relation between the prep. phrase and the adv. *eti,* "still." In the OT the phrase *ek/apo koilias mtros* can mean either "from birth on" (Isa 48:8; Ps 22:11) or "while still in the womb" (Judg 13:3–5; 16:17; Isa 44:2). That the latter is meant here is evident from 1:41. But the phrase is also used in a broad sense, meaning that John's whole existence will be graced. Later theological speculation will interpret it as the sanctification of John in his mother's womb (see 1:41; cf. DS 790).

11. Nolland, *Luke 1—9:20,* p. 31.
12. Gooding, *According to Luke: A New Exposition of the Third Gospel*, p. 35.
13. Nolland, *Luke 1—9:20*, p. 33 explains:

Silence descends on Zechariah at once, and he is not able to pronounce the blessing. Is the blessing here withheld delivered by Jesus in Luke 24:50–51 (R. E. Brown, *Birth,* 280)? . . . Zechariah could only communicate by body movements. [The word used] can mean both "mute" and "deaf," more often the latter. Probably both are implied here (cf. v 62).

Chapter Three: The Annunciation of Christ

1. Joseph A. Fitzmyer, *The Gospel According to Luke I—IX* (Garden City, NY: Doubleday, 1981), p. 343.
2. Merrill C. Tenney and Steven Barabas, eds., *The Zondervan Pictorial Encyclopedia of the Bible,* vol. 4 (Grand Rapids, MI: Zondervan, 1975), pp. 106–7.
3. Raymond E. Brown, *The Birth of the Messiah* (New York: Image/Doubleday, 1979), p. 304.
4. Roland Bainton, *The Martin Luther Christmas Book* (Philadelphia: Fortress, 1948), p. 22.
5. Fitzmyer, *The Gospel According to Luke I—IX,* p. 341, writes:

Mary as "the favored one," chosen to be the mother of him who will be hailed the Savior, Messiah, and Lord (2:11). This element of Mary's motherhood will appear again in the Lucan account (8:19–21; 11:27–28) and in Acts 1:14; her motherhood will serve the Lucan picture of Christian discipleship.

And still more important is Luke's portrayal of Mary as "the handmaid of the Lord" (1:38). Here Luke writes with hindsight, and foreshadows the way in which he will depict Mary in the Gospel proper, especially in 8:19–21, where she will be, along with his "brothers," among those "who hear the word of God and act on it." Here, Mary's enthusiastic response to

> the angel depicts her from the very beginning of the account as one who cooperates with God's plan of salvation. . . . For Luke, Mary is the model believer (see 1:45), pronounced blessed; and because she has been favored, she will be declared blessed by all generations (1:48). In Acts 1:14 she sits among the believers awaiting the promised Holy Spirit.

6. Brown, *The Birth of the Messiah*, pp. 326–27, referring to the famous medieval *Mariale Super Missus est.*

7. J. D. Douglas, ed., *The New International Dictionary of the Christian Church* (Grand Rapids, MI: Zondervan, 1978), pp. 500–1.

8. Karl Barth, *The Great Promise* (New York: Wisdom Library, a division of Philosophical Library, 1963), p. 20.

9. Alexander Whyte, *The Walk, Conversation and Character of Jesus Christ Our Lord* (Edinburgh: Oliphant, Anderson and Ferrier, 1905), p. 22.

10. Bainton, *The Martin Luther Christmas Book*, p. 21.

11. John Nolland, *Luke 1—9:20* (Dallas: Word, 1989), p. 50.

12. Ibid.

13. J. Oswald Sanders, *Spiritual Leadership* (Chicago: Moody, 1967), p. 101.

14. Brown, *The Birth of the Messiah*, pp. 310–11.

15. Nolland, *Luke 1—9:20*, p. 43; Fitzmyer, *The Gospel According to Luke*, pp. 337–38, 351; Brown, *The Birth of the Messiah*, p. 290; and I. H. Marshall, *The Gospel of Luke* (Grand Rapids, MI: Eerdmans, 1978), pp. 70–71.

Chapter Four: The Visitation

1. Joachim Jeremias, *Jerusalem in the Time of Jesus* (Philadelphia: Fortress, 1978), pp. 364–65.

2. I. H. Marshall, *The Gospel of Luke* (Grand Rapids, MI: Eerdmans, 1978), p. 80.

3. John Nolland, *Luke 1—9:20* (Dallas: Word, 1989), pp. 65–66.

4. Marshall, *The Gospel of Luke*, p. 80, explains:

> Even before Elizabeth herself could respond to Mary's words, the child in her womb leapt with joy, 1:46; 6:23. . . . Although it is said that an emotional experience of the mother can cause a movement of the fetus (Ellis, 76), it is more likely that a miraculous expression of the emotion of the unborn child is meant than that Elizabeth simply saw her own joy reflected in the unconscious movement of her child.

Similarly, Joseph Fitzmyer, *The Gospel According to Luke I—IX* (Garden City, NY: Doubleday, 1981), p. 353 writes:

> As Luke presents the scene, the mere utterance of Mary's greeting (which must be understood as not disclosing any information about the angelic revelation to her of Elizabeth's condition) causes the movement of the child.

5. Raymond E. Brown, *The Birth of the Messiah* (New York: Image/Doubleday, 1979), p. 44.

6. Fitzmyer, *The Gospel According to Luke I—IX*, pp. 363–65.

7. Robertson McQuilkin, *An Introduction to Biblical Ethics* (Wheaton, IL: Tyndale, 1989), p. 320.

8. Fitzmyer, *The Gospel According to Luke I—IX*, p. 364, explains:

> Luke uses here the Greek perf. pass. ptc. *eulogtos* for the condition of God's blessing or favor bestowed upon him/her. Used in the positive degree along with a prep. phrase *en gynaixin,* "among women," it is a Semitic way of expressing the superlative, "most blest" (see BDF 245. 3).

9. Brown, *The Birth of the Messiah*, p. 344, explains:

> The question in vs. 43, "Who am I that the mother of my Lord should come to me?," vocalizes Elizabeth's recognition that Jesus is the Messiah. Both in the Gospel (20:41–44) and in Acts 2:34 Luke uses Ps 110:1, "The LORD said to my Lord," to show that Jesus is the Messiah and Son of God; and Elizabeth is recognizing Mary as the mother of "my Lord," i.e., of the Messiah.
>
> See also Leon Morris, *Luke* (Grand Rapids, MI: Eerdmans, 1974), p. 83.

10. Fitzmyer, *The Gospel According to Luke I—IX*, p. 365, writes:

> In contrast to v. 42 above, where a double "blessing" was uttered (using *eulogmen*), Luke here introduces the first beatitude into his Gospel. The adj. is *makaria* (see Note on 6:20). It is uttered over Mary, whose faith stands in contrast to Zechariah's incredulity (1:20).

11. C. H. Dodd, *The Epistle of Paul to the Romans* (London: Hodder and Stoughton, 1960), p. 16, writes:

> Nor does it mean belief in a proposition, though doubtless intellectual beliefs are involved when we come to think it out. It is an act which is the negation of all activity, a moment of passivity out of which the strength for action comes, because on it God acts.

Chapter Five: The *Magnificat*, Part 1

1. Raymond E. Brown, *The Birth of the Messiah* (New York: Image/Doubleday, 1979), pp. 346–52.

2. Joseph Fitzmyer, *The Gospel According to Luke I—IX* (Garden City, NY: Doubleday, 1981), p. 366, writes:

> "My soul" is a Hebrew surrogate for "I" (see Gen 27:4, 25; Ps 34:3); in literary parallelism with "my spirit" (v. 47) it can be found in the LXX (Ps 77:3–4; cf. Job 12:10; Wisd 15:11). It would be a way of expressing what we call in English the "self." In 1 Sam 2:1 Hannah uses another parallelism with similar meaning, "my heart" and "my horn." "My spirit" is again a Hebrew surrogate for "I" (see Gen 6:3; Ps 143:4). If one were to substitute "my soul" for it, one would find a very close parallel to the first part of this verse in Ps 35:9, where the LXX has *he de psyche mou avalliasetai epi (or en) to kyrio,* "my soul shall delight in the Lord."

3. C. H. Spurgeon, *The Metropolitan Tabernacle Pulpit*, vol. 14 (Pasadena, TX: Pilgrim Publications, 1970), p. 202.

4. Robert G. Rayburn, *O Come Let Us Worship* (Grand Rapids, MI: Baker, 1984), pp. 29–30.

5. Fitzmyer, *The Gospel According to Luke I—IX*, p. 367:

> This part of the verse is a direct allusion to the vow of Hannah (1 Sam. 1:11), "If you have regard for the affliction (Hebrew *onî,* Greek *tapeinsis,* as in Gen 16:11; 29:32) of your handmaid. . . ." Luke too uses *tapeinsis* of Mary.

6. John Nolland, *Luke 1—9:20* (Dallas: Word, 1989), p. 75, explains:

> It is not that Mary has some personal and individual affliction; her affliction is simply that of God's people awaiting his saving intervention on their behalf. Hannah's affliction has been childlessness (1 Sam 1:11); for God's people it may be spoken of as the lack of that child who is to be the messianic deliverer (Isa 9:6).

7. C. S. Lewis, *The Weight of Glory and Other Addresses* (Grand Rapids, MI: Eerdmans, 1965), pp. 8–9, writes:

> When I began to look into this matter I was shocked to find such different Christians as Milton, Johnson and Thomas Aquinas taking heavenly glory quite frankly in the sense of fame or good report. But not fame conferred by our fellow creatures—fame with God, approval or (I might say) "appreciation" by God. And then, when I had thought it over, I saw that this view was scriptural; nothing can eliminate from the parable the divine accolade, "Well done, thou good and faithful servant." With that, a good deal of what I had been thinking all my life fell down like a house of cards.

8. I. H. Marshall, *The Gospel of Luke* (Grand Rapids, MI: Eerdmans, 1978), p. 83.

Chapter Six: The *Magnificat*, Part 2

1. H. P. Liddon, *The Magnificat* (London: Rivington's, 1889), p. 58, provides the analogy of the wave's crest.

2. Leon Morris, *Luke* (Grand Rapids, MI: Eerdmans, 1992), pp. 84–85, explains:

> The impression left by an English translation is that Mary continues to recite God's habitual actions. But we have a series of six aorist tenses in the Greek which are most unlikely to have this meaning. Mary may be looking back to specific occasions in the past when God has done the things she mentions. Ford takes this view and comments, "Only because the mighty Lord has done mighty things is there good news to tell, only because of the past tenses which speak of God's deeds is there a gospel to proclaim." Or Mary may be referring to acts still future but which have begun to be realized. It is perhaps more likely that she is looking forward in a spirit of prophecy and counting what God will do as so certain that it can be spoken of as accomplished (this is frequent in the Old Testament prophets).

3. William Barclay, *The Gospel of Luke* (Philadelphia: Westminster, 1956), pp. 9–10, suggests the homiletical outline.

4. Roland Kenneth Harrison, *Introduction to the Old Testament* (Grand Rapids, MI: Eerdmans, 1979), pp. 1116–17 provides a first-person description of the disease.

5. Alexander Maclaren, *Expositions of Holy Scriptures* (Grand Rapids, MI: Baker, 1971), p. 22.

Chapter Seven: The Birth of John

1. I. H. Marshall, *The Gospel of Luke* (Grand Rapids, MI: Eerdmans, 1978), p. 85, explains:

> "Although Mary was probably present at the birth of John, Luke rounds off this section of the story, which concerns her particularly, by describing her return home before going on to the story of John's birth." In addition to this literary argument favoring Mary's presence, there is a psychological factor—namely, that Mary would not have left Elizabeth just before the great moment. Because the women shared so much and because of their complementary destinies, it is unlikely they would part before the sacred juncture of John's birth.

2. Joseph A. Fitzmyer, *The Gospel According to Luke I–IX* (Garden City, NY: Doubleday, 1981), p. 380.

3. Raymond E. Brown, *The Birth of the Messiah* (New York: Image/Doubleday, 1979), p. 367.

4. C. S. Lewis, *Screwtape Letters* (London: Geoffrey Bles, 1942), pp. 12–14:

> Once he was in the street the battle was won. I showed him a newsboy shouting the midday paper, and a no. 73 bus going past, and before he reached the bottom of the steps I had got into him an unalterable conviction that, whatever odd ideas might come into a man's head when he was shut up alone with his books, a healthy dose of "real life" [by which he meant the bus and the newsboy] was enough to show him that all "that sort of thing" just couldn't be true.

5. Haddon Robinson, *Biblical Preaching* (Grand Rapids, MI: Baker, 1980), p. 24.

6. Elisabeth Elliot, *A Chance to Die, the Life and Legacy of Amy Carmichael* (Old Tappan, NJ: Revell, 1987), p. 13.

7. F. R. Webber, *A History of Preaching in Britain and America*, Part Two (Milwaukee: Northwestern, 1955), p. 470.

Chapter Eight: The *Benedictus*

1. Raymond E. Brown, *The Birth of the Messiah* (New York: Image/Doubleday, 1979), pp. 386–89.

2. Joseph A. Fitzmyer, *The Gospel According to Luke I—IX* (Garden City, NY: Doubleday, 1981), p. 383, explains:

> The figure is derived from an animal's horns, especially that of wild buffalo or oxen, which symbolize strength and power (see Deut 33:17). The lifting up of the horn in the OT refers to the animal's tossing of its horns

> in a display of might (see Ps 148:14). But in the Greek OT neither "horn" nor the "horn of salvation" occurs with the verb *egeirein,* "raise up," which may thus seem to be a mere synonym for other expressions used, such as *hypsoun, epairen,* "lift on high." But *egerein* is used of God's providential summoning into existence favored or anointed instruments of salvation for his people (see Judg 2:16,18; 3:9,15; cf. Acts 13:22).

3. I. H. Marshall, *The Gospel of Luke* (Grand Rapids, MI: Eerdmans, 1978), p. 93:

> The compound phrase is unparalleled, but the coupling of abstract nouns in this way was not without precedent (D. R. Jones*, 36). The knowledge described is not something imparted theoretically, but refers to the inward appropriation or experience of salvation as the result of a divine gift (IQS 11:15f.; cf. R. Bultmann, TDNT I, 706; J. Gnilka*, 234). The words ἐυ ἀφέσει ἁμαρτιῶυ αὐτῶυ should not be linked with δοῦναι (so Creed, 26), but with σωτηρίας, indicating that the salvation envisaged consists in the forgiveness of sins.

Chapter Nine: The Birth of Christ

1. T. Walter Wallbank, et al., eds., *Civilization Past & Present,* 5th ed. (Glenview, IL: Scott, Foresman, 1977), p.75.

2. Raymond E. Brown, *The Birth of the Messiah* (Garden City, NY: Image/Doubleday, 1979), p. 415, especially note 21, which says:

> Augustus himself refers to the *Ara Pacis* in his famous *Res Gestae* inscription. For the other inscriptions, see *Inscriptions of the British Museum,* #894; and *Inscriptiones Graecae ad Res Romanas Pertinentes,* ed. R. Cagnat (3 vols; Paris: Leroux, 1901–1927), III, #719. "Savior" was a frequent title for subsequent emperors. Josephus, *War* III ix 8; #459, tells how the Palestinian city of Tiberias opened its gates to Vespasian and received him as "savior."

3. John Buchan, *Augustus* (Boston: Houghton Mifflin, 1937), p. 346.

4. Brown, *The Birth of the Messiah*, p. 415.

5. Paraphrased from Pestle on the Incarnation (1584–654).

6. Steven Mosely, "When God was Made Vulnerable," *Moody Monthly*, December 1983, p. 25, provides the source of some of these phrases descriptive of Christ's birth.

7. Michael Mason, ed., *William Blake*, Oxford Authors Series, "Infant Sorrow," from "Songs of Innocence and Experience" (New York: Oxford University Press, 1988), p. 276.

8. *His Magazine*, December 1981, vol. 42, no. 3, on back inside cover.

9. *Great Sermons on the Birth of Christ,* comp. Wilbur M. Smith (Natick, MA: W.A. Wilde Co., 1963), p. 140.

10. Luci Shaw, *Listen to the Green* (Wheaton, IL: Harold Shaw, 1971), p. 66.

11. Harold M. Best, *Music Through the Eyes of Faith* (San Francisco: Harper, 1993), p. 33.

12. Ibid.

13. Gerhard Friedrich, ed., *Theological Dictionary of the New Testament*, vol. 6 (Grand Rapids, MI: Eerdmans, 1968), pp. 488–91.

14. John Milton, "On the Morning of Christ's Nativity" (XI, 12–14; 69–70; VI, 69–70).

Chapter Ten: The *Nunc Dimittis*

1. William Butler Yeats, "The Mother of God."

2. J. D. Douglas, ed., *The New Bible Dictionary* (Grand Rapids, MI: Eerdmans, 1962), p. 661, explains:

> Joshua ben Nun, grandson of Elishama chief of Ephraim (I Ch. vii. 27; Nu. i. 10), was called by his family *Hoshea'*, 'salvation' (Dt. xxxii. 44; transliterated *Oshea,* Nu. xiii. 8, AV); this name recurs in the tribe of Ephraim (see 1 Ch. xxvii. 20; *cf.* 2 Ki. xvii. 1; Ho. i. 1). Moses added the divine name, calling him *yehosua'*, normally rendered in English *Joshua.* The Gk. *Iesous* reflects the Aramaic contraction *Yesu'* (*cf.* Ne. iii. 19, *etc.*).

3. John Milton, "Upon the Circumcision."

4. Raymond E. Brown, *The Birth of the Messiah* (New York: Image/Doubleday, 1979), p. 442.

5. Leon Morris, *Luke, an Introduction and Commentary* (Grand Rapids, MI: n.p., 1988), p. 96.

6. Brown, *The Birth of the Messiah*, p. 439, explains that *apolyein*, "release, deliver" is a euphemism for "die," as in the LXX of Numbers 20:29, perhaps in the sense of being delivered from the troubles of life (Tobit 3:6,13).

7. James Hastings, ed., *The Speaker's Bible,* vol. 9 (Grand Rapids, MI: Baker, 1971), p. 163, attributes this line to Richard Crashaw.

8. Brown, *The Birth of the Messiah*, p. 441, says: "All thirteen uses of *dialogismos* in the NT are pejorative: bad thoughts, vain thoughts, doubting thoughts. The five other uses in Luke refer to thoughts hostile to Jesus or questioning him. The *dialogismoi* of 35b constitute a continuation of the *semeion antilegomenon*, the 'sign to be contradicted,' of 34d, for the contradiction is expressed in hostile thoughts."

Chapter Eleven: "Favor with God and Man"

1. Joseph A. Fitzmyer, *The Gospel According to Luke I—IX* (Garden City, NY: Doubleday, 1981), p. 441.

2. Geoffrey W. Bromiley, ed., *The International Standard Bible Encyclopedia,* vol. 3 (Grand Rapids, MI: Eerdmans, 1986), p. 677, provides most of the detail for the description of Passover.

3. I. H. Marshall, *The Gospel of Luke* (Grand Rapids, MI: Eerdmans, 1978), p. 127, explains:

> The two feasts of Passover and Unleavened Bread occupied a total of seven days (Ex. 12:15; Lv. 23:8; Dt. 16:3), and pilgrims were required to stay at least two days (SB II, 147f.). Jesus' parents piously fulfilled the prescribed periods. (This is implied by, 13:32; Acts 20:24; cf. Jos. *Ant.* 3:201.)

4. Frederick Louis Godet, *Commentary on the Gospel of Luke* (Grand Rapids, MI: Zondervan, reprinted from the 4th edition of the translation from the second French edition by E. W. Shalders, printed by T. and T. Clark in 1887), p. 146.

5. M. R. James, *The Apocryphal New Testament* (London: Oxford, 1980), p. 54.

6. Godet, *Commentary on the Gospel of Luke,* p. 148.

7. Fitzmyer, *The Gospel According to Luke I—IX,* p. 442, gives the literal rendering of verse 48a as "seeing him (they were startled)," explaining that Luke uses the strong verb *ekplessesthai*, "be struck out of oneself"; cf. 4:32; 9:43; Acts 13:12.

8. Ibid., p. 443.

9. Leon Morris, *Luke: An Introduction and Commentary* (Grand Rapids, MI: Baker, 1971), pp. 101–2, explains:

> The expression "my Father" is noteworthy and no parallel appears to be cited (the Jews added "in heaven" or used "our Father" or the like). The first recorded words of the Messiah are then a recognition of his being in the Father's house. There is a Jewish *midrash* which speaks of the Messiah as knowing God directly, without human assistance, a distinction shared only by Abraham, Job and Hezekiah (*Midrash Rabbah,* Numbers xiv. 2). But Luke is saying more than this. Jesus had a relationship to God shared by no other. Joseph and Mary did not understand this. They learnt what Jesus' Messiahship meant bit by bit.

Chapter Twelve: John's Baptism

1. Joseph A. Fitzmyer, *The Gospel According to Luke I—IX* (Garden City, NY: Doubleday, 1981), p. 326.

2. Leon Morris, *Luke* (Grand Rapids, MI: Eerdmans, 1974), p. 103.

3. Fitzmyer, *The Gospel According to Luke I—IX*, p. 458.

4. Josephus, *Antiquities* XVIII, 116–118.

5. William Barclay, *The Gospel of Luke* (Philadelphia: Westminster, 1956), p. 27.

6. *Chicago Tribune*, Monday, April 14, 1986, Section 1, p. 4.

7. J. C. Ryle, *Expository Thoughts on the Gospels: Luke,* vol. 1 (Cambridge, UK: James Clarke & Co. Ltd, 1976), p. 90.

Chapter Thirteen: Messiah's Baptism

1. Iain H. Murray, *D. Martyn Lloyd-Jones, The First Forty Years 1899–1939* (Carlisle, PA: Banner of Truth, 1981), p. 172.

2. Christopher Catherwood, ed., *Martyn Lloyd-Jones: Chosen by God* (Wheaton, IL: Crossway, 1986), p. 87.

3. Leon Morris, *Luke: An Introduction and Commentary* (Grand Rapids, MI: Baker, 1971), p. 109, referencing Strack-Billerbeck, vol. 1, p. 121.

4. Frederick Louis Godet, *Commentary on the Gospel of Luke* (Grand Rapids, MI: Zondervan, reprinted from the 4th edition of the translation from the second French edition by E. W. Shalders, printed by T. and T. Clark in 1887), p. 121.

5. Ibid., p. 180.

Chapter Fourteen: The Sonship of Christ

1. Joseph A. Fitzmyer, *The Gospel According to Luke I—IX* (Garden City, NY: Doubleday, 1981), p. 484.

2. John Nolland, *Luke 1—9:20* (Dallas: Word, 1989), pp. 161, 165.

3. Alexander Whyte, *The Walk, Conversation and Character of Jesus Christ Our Lord* (Edinburgh: Oliphant Anderson & Ferrier, 1905), p. 91.

4. Fitzmyer, *The Gospel According to Luke I—IX*, pp. 484–85 explains:

> The idea of the God of heaven speaking to his people is found in the OT (see e.g. Deut 4:10–12). The "voice" of the Lord was often associated with the thunder-clap (Isa 30:30–31; Ps 18:14), thus stressing its heavenly origin. This OT notion has been carried over into the NT; it occurs again in the Lucan writings (9:35; Acts 10:13,15; 11:7–9). In later rabbinical literature there developed the idea of the *bat gol,* "Daughter of a voice," to convey the echo of God speaking to mankind (see Str-B, 1. 125–34).

5. Nolland, *Luke 1—9:20*, p. 165.

6. Ibid., pp. 170–71:

> The most attractive of the harmonizing solutions is that proposed by Holzmeister (ZKT 47 [1923] 184–218) and cf. Nolle (Scr 2 [1947] 38–42). Holzmeister argues that Mary was an heiress (i.e., had no brothers) whose father Eli, in line with a biblical tradition concerned with the maintenance of the family line in cases where there was no male heir (Ezra 2:61 = Neh 7:63; Num 32:41 cf. 1 Chr 2:21–22, 34–35; Num 27:3–8), on the marriage of his daughter to Joseph, adopted Joseph as his own son. Matthew gives Joseph's ancestry by birth, Luke that by adoption.
>
> ώς ένομὶξετο, "as was reckoned, raises the question of what kind of reckoning was involved. If we link ή̓ν with του ΄Ηλί (see above) then the reckoning is the mistake of the uninformed who judge from the place of Jesus in Joseph's family when actually Jesus' descent is to be reckoned through Mary, or is only to be directly linked to God. For Johnson (*Biblical Genealogies,* 230) the reckoning casts its doubt over all the details of the genealogy to follow—Luke is not sure that it is historically accurate! But surely our points of departure for understanding Luke here are (i) the birth without human father anticipated in 1:34–35; but also (ii) the seriousness with which Luke takes the genealogy—continuing it as he does all the way to God at the creation. The reckoning will be that of legal standing (cf., Schurmann, 199): Jesus has the status of son and heir in the family of Joseph and thus a place in his genealogy (cf. 2:41, 48).

7. Fitzmyer, *The Gospel According to Luke I—IX*, p. 491.

8. Nolland, *Luke 1—9:20*, p. 173.

Chapter Fifteen: The Temptation

1. Frederick Louis Godet, *Commentary on the Gospel of Luke* (Grand Rapids, MI: Zondervan, reprinted from the 4th edition of the translation from the second French edition by E. W. Shalders, printed by T. and T. Clark in 1887), p. 224.

2. William Barclay, *The Gospel of Luke* (Philadelphia: Westminster, 1956), p. 38.

3. David Gooding, *According to Luke: A New Exposition of the Third Gospel* (Leicester, UK: Inter-Varsity, 1987), p. 70.

4. Joseph A. Fitzmyer, *The Gospel According to Luke I—IX* (Garden City, NY: Doubleday, 1981), p. 517.

5. Josephus, *Antiquities*, 15.11, 5; 412.

6. Ibid., 20.5, 1.97–98.

7. Gooding, *According to Luke: A New Exposition of the Third Gospel*, p. 80.

8. Ibid.

Chapter Sixteen: Jesus' Rejection

1. J. S. Simon, *John Wesley and the Religious Societies* (London: Epworth, 1921), p. 282.

2. Geoffrey W. Bromiley, ed., *The International Standard Bible Encyclopedia*, vol. 4 (Grand Rapids, MI: Eerdmans, 1986), pp. 682–83.

3. Joseph A. Fitzmyer, *The Gospel According to Luke I—IX* (Garden City, NY: Doubleday, 1981), pp. 531–32.

4. Ibid., p. 532, explains:

> The quotation from Second Isaiah is actually a conflation of 61:1a,b,d: 58:6d; 61:2a. Two phrases are omitted: 61:1c, "to heal the broken-hearted" (at the end of v. 18); and 61:2b, "the day of vengeance of our God" (at the end of v. 19). The omission of the former is of little consequence; but the latter is a deliberate suppression of a negative aspect of the Deutero-Isaian message. The "today" of v. 21 is not to be identified with a day of divine vengeance.

5. I. H. Marshall, *The Gospel of Luke* (Grand Rapids, MI: Eerdmans, 1978), p. 184.

6. Malcolm Muggeridge, *Jesus Rediscovered.*

7. David Gooding, *According to Luke: A New Exposition of the Third Gospel* (Leicester, UK: Inter-Varsity, 1987), p. 85.

8. Ibid., p. 87.

Chapter Seventeen: The Authority of Jesus

1. I. H. Marshall, *The Gospel of Luke* (Grand Rapids, MI: Eerdmans, 1978), p. 191.

2. Edward M. Blaiklock and R. K. Harrison, eds., *The New International Dictionary of Biblical Archaeology* (Grand Rapids, MI: Zondervan, 1983), pp. 118–19.

3. G. Abbott-Smith, *A Manual Greek Lexicon of the New Testament* (New York: Charles Scribner's Sons, n.d.), p. 141.

4. Max Zerwick and Mary Grosvenor, *A Grammatical Analysis of the Greek New Testament* (Rome: Biblical Institute Press, 1981), p. 187.

5. Rabbi Dr. I. Epstein, *The Babylonian Talmud Seder Mo'ed*, vol. 3 (London: Soncino, 1938), pp. 122–23.

6. Colin Brown, *Philosophy and Christian Faith* (Downers Grove, IL: Inter-Varsity, 1986), p. 219, quoting J. J. Altizer, *The Gospel of Christian Atheism*, p. 120.

7. Joseph T. Bayly, *Out of My Mind* (Grand Rapids, MI: Zondervan, 1993), pp. 188–89.

8. Leon Morris, *Luke* (Grand Rapids, MI: Eerdmans, 1974), p. 120.

9. Marshall, *The Gospel of Luke*, p. 193.

10. John Nolland, *Luke 1—9:20* (Dallas: Word, 1989), pp. 65–66.

11. William L. Lane, *The Gospel According to Mark* (Grand Rapids, MI: Eerdmans, 1975), p. 73. See also Marshall, *The Gospel of Luke*, p. 193.

12. William Barclay, *The Gospel of Luke* (Philadelphia: Westminster, 1956), p. 47, writes:

> The east was full of people who could exorcise demons. But their methods were weird and wonderful. An exorcist would put a ring under the afflicted person's nose. He would recite a long spell; and then all of a sudden there would be a splash in a basin of water which he had put near to hand—and the demon was out! A magical root called Bares was specially effective. When a man approached it, it shrank into the ground unless gripped, and to grip it was certain death. So the ground round it was dug away; a dog was tied to it; the struggles of the dog tore up the root; and when the root was torn up the dog died, as a substitute for a man. What a difference between all this hysterical paraphernalia and the calm single word of command of Jesus! It was the sheer authority which staggered them.

13. Donald Gray Barnhouse, *Let Me Illustrate* (Old Tappan, NJ: Revell, 1967), p. 280.

Chapter Eighteen: Kingdom Authority

1. I. H. Marshall, *The Gospel of Luke* (Grand Rapids, MI: Eerdmans, 1978), p. 196, explains:

> Healing by the laying on of hands was unknown in Judaism, except in IQapGen 20, 21, 22, 29 (E. Lohse, TDNT IX, 428), but is found in Hellenistic accounts of miraculous healings (ibid. 425). This does not mean that the stories of Jesus healing in this way must have originated in Hellenistic circles outside Palestine. There is no good reason why Jesus should not have followed a practice known in the pagan world and which was in any case familiar in Judaism as a means of conveying divine blessing. The act was symbolic of the flow of divine power from Jesus to the person healed; it should not be regarded as magical.

2. Alexander Maclaren, *Expositions of Holy Scriptures* (Grand Rapids, MI: Baker, 1971), pp. 100–1.

3. Marshall, *The Gospel of Luke*, p. 198.

Chapter Nineteen: Calling Fishermen

1. Geoffrey W. Bromiley, ed., *The International Standard Bible Encyclopedia*, vol. 4 (Grand Rapids, MI: Eerdmans, 1991), p. 484, says: "The remains of one such boat were discovered near Magdala in 1986. From the 1st cent. B.C. or 1st cent A.D., it is made of pine and measures 8.2 by 2.3m. (27 by 7 1/2 ft.) (W. G. Pippert, *Christianity Today*, 30 [May 16, 1986], 58."

2. David Gooding, *According to Luke: A New Exposition of the Third Gospel* (Leicester, UK: Inter-Varsity, 1987), p. 103.

3. Joseph A. Fitzmyer, *The Gospel According to Luke I—IX* (Garden City, NY: Doubleday, 1981), p. 568.

4. Leon Morris, *Luke: An Introduction and Commentary* (Grand Rapids, MI: Baker, 1971), p. 126.

5. Fitzmyer, *The Gospel According to Luke I—IX*, p. 569.

Chapter Twenty: Healed Indeed

1. R. K. Harrison, *Leviticus, an Introduction and Commentary* (Downers Grove, IL: InterVarsity, 1980), pp. 150–51.

2. Ibid., p. 151.

3. Philip Yancey, *Where Is God When It Hurts?* (Grand Rapids, MI: Zondervan, 1977), p. 32.

4. William Barclay, *The Gospel of Matthew*, vol. 2 (Philadelphia: Westminster, 1958), p. 301.

5. I. H. Marshall, *The Gospel of Luke* (Grand Rapids, MI: Eerdmans, 1978), p. 208, who cites *SB*, vol. 2, pp. 745–63.

6. Richard Chenevix Trench, *Notes on the Miracles of Our Lord* (Grand Rapids, MI: Baker, 1965), p. 135.

7. Colin Brown, *The New International Dictionary of New Testament Theology*, vol. 2 (Grand Rapids, MI: Zondervan, 1979), pp. 875–77.

8. John Nolland, *Luke 1—9:20* (Dallas: Word, 1989), p. 226., who references *SB*, vol. 1, pp. 693–96.

9. Ibid., p. 226.

Chapter Twenty-One: Healing and Faith

1. Geoffrey W. Bromiley, ed., *The International Standard Bible Encyclopedia*, vol. 2 (Grand Rapids, MI: Eerdmans, 1982), pp. 771–72, states:

> Smaller timbers as joists ("rafters," *rahîit*) were spaced out and covered in turn with brushwood; the final covering, being of mud mixed with chopped straw, was beaten and rolled. A tiny stone roller is found on every modern native roof, and is used to roll the mud into greater solidity every year on the advent of the first rains. Similar rollers have been found among the ancient remains throughout the country. Grass might grow temporarily on such roofs (Ps. 129:6; Isa. 37:27). "They let him down through the tiles [Gk. kéramos] with his couch into the midst before Jesus" (Lk. 5:19) refers to the breaking through of a roof similar to this.

2. Francis Schaeffer, *The Church at the End of the Twentieth Century* (Downers Grove, IL: InterVarsity, 1970), n.p.

3. Joseph A. Fitzmyer, *The Gospel According to Luke I—IX* (Garden City, NY: Doubleday, 1981), pp. 383–84.

4. Charles Spurgeon, *The Metropolitan Tabernacle Pulpit,* vol. 17 (Pasadena, TX: Pilgrim, 1971), p. 167.

5. Philip Edgcumbe Hughes, *A Commentary on the Epistle to the Hebrews* (Grand Rapids, MI: Eerdmans, 1977), p. 269.

Chapter Twenty-Two: Calling Sinners

1. William Lane, *The Gospel According to Mark* (Grand Rapids, MI: Eerdmans, 1975), p. 102.

2. William Barclay, *The Gospel of Luke* (Philadelphia: Westminster, 1956), p. 61.

3. Ibid., pp. 61–62.

4. Lane, *The Gospel According to Mark*, p. 102.

5. G. Abbott-Smith, *A Manual Greek Lexicon of the New Testament* (New York: Scribner's, n.d.), p. 203.

6. I. H. Marshall, *The Gospel of Luke* (Grand Rapids, MI: Eerdmans, 1978), p. 219.

7. Leon Morris, *Luke* (Grand Rapids, MI: Eerdmans, 1974), p. 131.

8. J. C. Ryle, *Expository Thoughts on the Gospels: Luke,* vol. 1 (Cambridge, UK: James Clarke & Co. Ltd., 1976), p. 149.

9. Ibid., pp. 149–50.

10. Joseph A. Fitzmyer, *The Gospel According to Luke I—IX* (Garden City, NY: Doubleday, 1981), p. 584.

11. Ibid., p. 591 states:

> But "sinners" should most likely be understood in a wider sense, referring to two groups: (a) Jews who fell short of Mosaic obligations (without restricting these to the Pharisaic interpretation), but who could repent and be reconciled to God, and (b) Gentiles, who were *a-nomoi* (Law-less) and *a-theoi* (God-less), often considered hopeless in Jewish apocalyptic literature (see J. Jeremias, ZNW 30 [1931] 293–300).

12. Morris, *Luke*, p. 132.

13. Richard Collier, *The General Next to God* (New York: E. P. Dutton, 1965), pp. 31–32.

Chapter Twenty-Three: The New and the Old

1. William Barclay, *The Gospel of Luke* (Philadelphia: Westminster, 1956), pp. 62–63.

2. Joseph A. Fitzmyer, *The Gospel According to Luke I—IX* (Garden City, NY: Doubleday, 1981), p. 598.

3. Barclay, *The Gospel of Luke*, p. 63.

4. William Barclay, *The Gospel of Mark* (Philadelphia: Westminster, 1956), p. 53.

5. W. E. Sangster, "Drunk and Mad," in Clyde E. Fant Jr. and William A. Pinson Jr., *Twenty Centuries of Great Preaching*, vol. 11, (Waco, TX: Word, 1971), pp. 341–42.

6. Hugh Evan Hopkins, *Charles Simeon* (Grand Rapids, MI: Eerdmans, 1977), p. 53.

7. D. A. Carson and John D. Woodbridge, *Letters Along the Way: A Novel of the Christian Life* (Wheaton, IL: Crossway, 1993), pp. 104–5.

8. Donald Grey Barnhouse, *Let Me Illustrate* (Old Tappan, NJ: Revell, 1967), p. 97.

Chapter Twenty-Four: The Lord of the Sabbath

1. Merrill C. Tenney, ed., *The Zondervan Pictorial Encyclopedia of the Bible*, vol. 5 (Grand Rapids, MI: Zondervan, 1975), p. 421.

2. Frederick Louis Godet, *Commentary on the Gospel of Luke* (Grand Rapids, MI: Zondervan, reprinted from the 4th edition of the translation from the second French edition by E. W. Shalders, printed by T. and T. Clark in 1887), p. 292.

3. E. Earle Ellis, *The Gospel of Luke* (Grand Rapids, MI: Eerdmans, 1974), p. 108.

4. Joseph A. Fitzmyer, *The Gospel According to Luke I—IX* (Garden City, NY: Doubleday, 1981), p. 611.

5. Philip D. Jensen and Tony Payne, *The Good Living Guide* (Sydney: St. Matthias Press, 1991), pp. 434–44.

Chapter Twenty-Five: Authority to Call

1. Frederick Louis Godet, *Commentary on the Gospel of Luke* (Grand Rapids, MI: Zondervan, reprinted from the 4th edition of the translation from the second French edition by E. W. Shalders, printed by T. and T. Clark in 1887), p. 299, explains:

> To pass the night in watching, is a word rarely used in Greek, and which in all the N.T. is only found here. The choice of this unusual term, as well as the analytical form (the imperf. with the participle), expresses the persevering energy of this vigil.

2. I. H. Marshall, *The Gospel of Luke* (Grand Rapids, MI: Eerdmans, 1978), p. 238, amplifies:

> The element of choice is brought out by the use of ἐκλέγομαι (9:35; 10:42; 14:7; cf. especially Acts 1:2, 24; 6:5; 15:7, 22, 25), a word used in the LXX of God's choice of his servants (cf. Nu. 16:5, 7).

3. J. C. Ryle, *Expository Thoughts on the Gospels: Luke,* vol. 1 (Cambridge, UK: James Clarke & Co. Ltd., 1976), pp. 172–73.

4. "Man's Weakness—God's Strength," *Missionary Crusader*, December 1964, p. 7.

Chapter Twenty-Six: The Sermon on the Level

1. Leon Morris, *Luke* (Grand Rapids, MI: Eerdmans, 1974), pp. 138–39.

2. Clarence McCartney, *Preaching Without Notes* (Grand Rapids, MI: Baker, 1976), pp. 56–57.

3. Charles Spurgeon, *Lectures to My Students* (Grand Rapids, MI: Zondervan, 1969), p. 166.

4. Oswald Sanders, *Spiritual Leadership* (Chicago, IL: Moody Press, 1967), p. 60.

5. Joseph Bayly, *The Gospel Blimp* (Richardson, TX: Windward Press, 1969), p. 32.

6. Dietrich Bonhoeffer, *The Cost of Discipleship* (New York: Macmillan, 1969), pp. 100–1.

Chapter Twenty-Seven: Supernatural Love

1. Phil Donahue, *Donahue, My Own Story* (New York: Simon & Schuster, 1979), p. 94.

2. Leon Morris, *Luke* (Grand Rapids, MI: Eerdmans, 1974), p. 142.

3. Mike Mason, *The Mystery of Marriage* (Portland: Multnomah, 1978), p. 99.

4. I. H. Marshall, *The Gospel of Luke* (Grand Rapids, MI: Eerdmans, 1978), p. 261.

5. Joseph Fitzmyer, *The Gospel According to Luke I—IX* (Garden City, NY: Doubleday, 1981), p. 638.

6. Ibid.

7. Leon Morris, *Luke*, p. 143; cf. Marshall, *The Gospel of Luke*, p. 261:

> It goes without saying that the examples and even the principles given by Jesus are not to be taken over-literally. If v. 29b were so taken, the issue would be nudism, a sufficient indication that it is a certain spirit that is being commended to our notice—not a regulation to be slavishly carried out. But this fact does not entitle us to evade the demand, which is here put forward in an extreme case. What Jesus here says is seriously, even if not literally, meant; and his followers have the task of manifesting the spirit of the injunction in the varied situations which arise in actual life (Manson, *Sayings,* 51).

8. Marshall, *The Gospel of Luke*, p. 262.

9. Reported by George Cowan to Campus Crusade at the U.S. Division Meeting Devotions, Thursday, March 22, 1990.

10. C. S. Lewis, *The Weight of Glory and Other Addresses* (Grand Rapids, MI: Eerdmans, 1965), p. 2, explains:

> We must not be troubled by unbelievers when they say that this promise of reward makes the Christian life a mercenary affair. There are different kinds of reward. There is the reward which has no natural connexion with the things you do to earn it, and is quite foreign to the desires that ought to accompany those things. Money is not the natural reward of love; that is why we call a man mercenary if he marries a woman for the sake of her money. But marriage is the proper reward for a real lover, and he is not mercenary for desiring it. A general who fights well in order to get a peerage is mercenary; a general who fights for victory is not, victory being the proper reward of battle as marriage is the proper reward of love. The proper rewards are not simply tacked on to the activity for which they are given, but are the activity itself in consummation.

Chapter Twenty-Eight: The Spirit of the Disciple

1. Phillips Brooks, *Lectures on Preaching* (Manchester, UK: James Robinson, 1899), p. 167.

2. Ibid., p. 169.

3. *Webster's Seventh New Collegiate Dictionary* (Springfield, MA: G. & C. Merriam, 1971), p. 508.

4. Frederick Louis Godet, *Commentary on the Gospel of Luke* (Grand Rapids, MI: Zondervan, reprinted from the 4th edition of the translation from the second French edition by E. W. Shalders, printed by T. and T. Clark in 1887), p. 328.

5. Nicholas Lenker, ed., *Sermons of Martin Luther*, vol. 4 (Grand Rapids, MI: Baker, 1983), p. 107.

6. I. D. E. Thomas, ed., *Puritan Quotations* (Chicago: Moody Press, 1975), p. 111.

7. Haddon Robinson, *Biblical Preaching* (Grand Rapids, MI: Baker, 1980), p. 150.

8. John Nolland, *Luke 1—9:20* (Dallas: Word, 1989), p. 301.

9. Stephen Olford, *The Grace of Giving* (Memphis: Encounter Ministries, 1972), p. 10.

10. Leon Morris, *Luke* (Grand Rapids, MI: Eerdmans, 1974), p. 147.

Chapter Twenty-Nine: Checking the Fruit

1. Timothy Bayly, *Out of My Mind: The Best of Joe Bayly* (Grand Rapids, MI: Zondervan, 1993), pp. 117–18.

2. Bethan Lloyd-Jones, *Memories of Sandfields* (Edinburgh: Banner of Truth, 1983), pp. 87–88.

3. David Gooding, *According to Luke: A New Exposition of the Third Gospel* (Leicester, UK: Inter-Varsity, 1987), p. 122.

4. R. C. Sproul, *The Holiness of God* (Wheaton, IL: Tyndale, 1985), pp. 91–93.

Chapter Thirty: Doing His Word

1. Michael A. Lev, "Couple Held on to God in Tragedy," *Chicago Tribune*, November 17, 1994, pp. 1, 18.

2. F. R. Webber, *A History of Preaching in Britain and America*, vol. 1 (Milwaukee: Northwestern, 1952), p. 329.

3. Resolutions by Marc Maillefer after sitting under preaching on 2 Timothy 4, November 15, 1994:

> 1) I resolve to teach our interns the Word of God regarding ministry, not just our philosophy, by opening up the Epistles like 1 and 2 Timothy and others, laying out a theology of pastoral ministry. 2) I resolve that my commitment to God and his authoritative Word would never bow to the coercion or power of any earthly establishment. "I would rather be an Amos on the carpet of Amaziah than Amaziah on the king's throne." 3) I resolve to remember that I am a weak vessel, and as such will endure the hardships of ministry, that I might carry the brandmarks of Jesus Christ and display his glory. 4) I resolve to seize every opportunity to herald the good news of Jesus Christ, seeking to win as many as possible. 5) I resolve to preach the Word, always ready to correct, rebuke, and encourage, refraining from the "itchy ear syndrome" of our day, working hard for the cause of Christ. 6) I resolve to remember that spiritual battles are to be fought with spiritual weapons, mainly prayer and the Word. 7) I resolve to be kind to the people God has called me to serve, realizing that my eloquence and cleverness will soon be forgotten, but kindness remains in the heart.

4. *Our Daily Bread* (Grand Rapids, MI: Radio Bible Class, March 1992), n.p.

5. Leon Morris, *Luke* (Grand Rapids, MI: Eerdmans, 1974), p. 148.

Chapter Thirty-One: Viewing Faith

1. I. H. Marshall, *The Gospel of Luke* (Grand Rapids, MI: Eerdmans, 1978), p. 279, explains:

> Luke adds that he was ἔυτιμος to his master, a word that here means "honoured, respected" (14:8; Phil. 2:29), rather than "precious, valuable" (1 Pet. 2:4, 5), and indicates why the centurion was so concerned over him; Luke's own concern for the inferior members of society is perhaps also reflected.

2. William Barclay, *The Gospel of Luke* (Philadelphia: Westminster, 1956), p. 83.
3. Marshall, *The Gospel of Luke*, p. 280 explains:

> The giving of contributions by gentiles towards the upkeep of synagogues is well attested: t. Meg. 3:5 (224) SB IV:1, 142f); cf. Creed, 101: W. Schrage, TDNT VII, 813f. That a gentile should have built the synagogue itself, however, is unusual. Possibly he was simply a large, or the main, benefactor.

4. E. Earle Ellis, *The Gospel of Luke* (Grand Rapids, MI: Eerdmans, 1974), p. 117.
5. Daniel J. Boorstin, *The Discoverers* (New York: Vintage, 1983), pp. 330–31.
6. Alexander Maclaren, *Expositions of Holy Scriptures* (Grand Rapids, MI: Baker, 1971), p. 143, who also supplies many of the thoughts in this section.
7. C. S. Lewis, *Letters to Malcolm: Chiefly on Prayer* (New York: Harcourt Brace Jovanovich, 1964), pp. 97–98.

Chapter Thirty-Two: Jesus Raises a Widow's Son

1. Joseph Bayly, *The View from a Hearse* (Elgin, IL: Cook, 1967), pp. 50–51.
2. Leon Morris, *Luke* (Grand Rapids, MI: Eerdmans, 1974), p. 153 explains:

> Luke does not mention professional mourners, but they would have been there: "Even the poorest in Israel should hire not less than two flutes and one wailing woman" (Ketuboth 4:4).

3. I. H. Marshall, *The Gospel of Luke* (Grand Rapids, MI: Eerdmans, 1978), p. 285, explains: "Mourning was all the greater for an only child (Je. 6:26; Am. 8:10; Zc. 12:10; cf. on mourning customs SB I, 521–523, 1047–1051)."
4. G. Abbott-Smith, *A Manual Greek Lexicon of the New Testament* (New York: Charles Scribner's Sons, n.d.), p. 414.
5. Ibid., p. 148.
6. William Barclay, *The Gospel of Luke* (Philadelphia: Westminster, 1956), p. 86.
7. Marshall, *The Gospel of Luke*, p. 286 explains: "The comment that Jesus gave him to his mother (cf. 9:42 diff. Mk.; 1 Ki. 17:23 LXX verbatim; 2 Ki. 4:36) serves to remind the readers of the Elisha typology and also to indicate the widow."
8. John Nolland, *Luke 1—9:20* (Dallas: Word, 1989), pp. 324–25, explains: "The language about a visitation by God echoes that of 1:68, 78, and fits well with the citation from Malachi at v 27. The terms here are thoroughly Jewish."
9. George Eliot, *Middlemarch* (Boston: Houghton Mifflin Company, 1956), p. 144.

Chapter Thirty-Three: The Mystery of Unbelief

1. I. H. Marshall, *The Gospel of Luke* (Grand Rapids, MI: Eerdmans, 1978), p. 292 explains:

> The saying thus refers to the possibility of a person not accepting Jesus as "the coming One" because he "stumbles" at the kind of things done or left undone by Jesus, and thinks that he should have behaved differently.

2. Ibid., p. 294.
3. Leon Morris, *Luke* (Grand Rapids, MI: Eerdmans, 1974), p. 158.
4. Marshall, *The Gospel of Luke*, p. 299.
5. David Gooding, *According to Luke: A New Exposition of the Third Gospel* (Leicester, UK: Inter-Varsity, 1987), p. 136.
6. Sheldon Vanauken, *A Severe Mercy* (San Francisco: Harper & Row, 1977), pp. 104–5.
7. D. A. Carson and John D. Woodbridge, *Letters Along the Way, a Novel of the Christian Life* (Wheaton, IL: Crossway, 1993), p. 16.
8. Robert Schuller, *Self Esteem, The New Reformation* (Waco, TX: Word, 1982), p. 98.
9. Ibid., p. 99.
10. *Chicago Tribune,* June 14, 1992, Section 13, pp. 4, 5.
11. Charles Colson, *Kingdoms in Conflict* (New York/Grand Rapids, MI: William Morrow/Zondervan, 1987), p. 71.
12. Marshall, *The Gospel of Luke*, pp. 300–1.
13. Ibid., p. 302.

Chapter Thirty-Four: Forgiven Much

1. Joachim Jeremias, *The Parables of Jesus* (London: SCM, 1955), p. 101.
2. Kenneth E. Bailey, *Poet and Peasant and Through Peasant Eyes* (Grand Rapids, MI: Eerdmans, 1980), p. 3.
3. Ibid., pp. 5, 7.
4. Alfred Plummer, *The Gospel According to St. Luke* (Edinburgh: T.&T. Clark, 1905), pp. 210–11; and Jeremias, *The Parables of Jesus*, p. 101.
5. Jeremias, *The Parables of Jesus*, p. 101–2. (See *Tos. Sota* 5,9; j. *Gitt.* 9,50d.)
6. Bailey, *Poet and Peasant and Through Peasant Eyes*, p. 9.
7. Clyde Kilby, ed., *A Mind Awake, an Anthology of C.S. Lewis* (New York: Harcourt, Brace & World, 1969), p. 123.
8. Bailey, *Poet and Peasant and Through Peasant Eyes*, p. 11.
9. Arnold A. Dallimore, *George Whitefield*, vol. 1 (Edinburgh: Banner of Truth, 1975), p. 132.
10. Harry Ironside, *Gospel of Luke* (New Jersey: Loizeaux, 1974), p. 229.
11. Charles L. Wallis, ed., *A Treasury of Poems for Worship and Devotion* (New York: Harper & Brothers, 1959), Gerard Manly Hopkins from St. Francis Xavier, "O Deus Ego Amo Te," pp. 98, 99.

Chapter Thirty-Five: Listen to the Word

1. J. A. Motyer, *The Prophecy of Isaiah* (Leicester, UK: Inter-Varsity, 1993), p. 79.

2. William Barclay, *The Gospel of Mark* (Philadelphia: Westminster, 1956), pp. 91–92.

3. Helmut Thielicke, *The Waiting Father* (New York: Harper and Row, 1975), p. 57.

4. Leon Morris, *Luke* (Grand Rapids, MI: Eerdmans, 1975), p. 168.

Chapter Thirty-Six: Lord of Creation

1. Frederick Stonehouse, *The Wreck of the Edmund Fitzgerald* (Au Train, MI: Avery Color Studios, 1989), p. 13.

2. Robert J. Hemming, *Gales of November: The Sinking of the Edmund Fitzgerald* (Chicago, IL: Contemporary, 1981), p. 2.

3. Ibid., p. xi.

4. Stonehouse, *The Wreck of the Edmund Fitzgerald*, p. 200.

5. Joseph A. Fitzmyer, *The Gospel According to Luke I—IX* (Garden City, NY: Doubleday, 1981), p. 729.

6. Quoted in Harry Ironside, *Lectures on the Book of Acts* (Neptune, NJ: Loizeaux, 1975), p. 457.

7. Ruth Graham, *Sitting by My Laughing Fire* (Waco, TX: Word, 1977), p. 26.

8. A. T. Robertson, *Word Pictures in the New Testament*, vol. 1 (Nashville: Broadman, 1930), p. 293.

9. Stephen W. Hawking, *A Brief History of Time* (New York: Bantam, 1990), p. 37.

10. Ibid.

11. Ibid., pp. 38–39.

12. Bradford A. Smith, "New Eyes on the Universe," *National Geographic*, January 1994, vol. 185, no. 1, p. 38.

Chapter Thirty-Seven: Lord of All

1. C. S. Lewis, *The Screwtape Letters* (London: Geoffrey Bles, 1942), p. 9.

2. Kenneth L. Woodward with David Gates, "Giving the Devil His Due," *Newsweek*, August 30, 1982, p. 74.

3. Gerhard Kittel, *Theological Dictionary of the New Testament*, vol. 2, trans. Geoffrey W. Bromiley (Grand Rapids, MI: Eerdmans, 1968), pp. 18–19.

4. Joseph A. Fitzmyer, *The Gospel According to Luke I—IX* (Garden City, NY: Doubleday, 1981), p. 738.

5. Ibid., p. 739.

6. Karl Barth, *Church Dogmatics*, vol. 4, *The Doctrine of Reconciliation*, Part 2 (Edinburgh: T. & T. Clark, 1985), p. 231, who says:

> We have only to think of the story of the demoniac in Mark 5. Someone has described it as a burlesque. And why not? For all its final seriousness what happens to evil in its confrontation with Jesus is grotesque and (if we like) farcical. In Luke 10:18, for example, it tumbles down from heaven, and in this story it can only ask for permission to go, itself unclean, into the herd of unclean swine, to plunge with them over the cliff into the lake and to be drowned, thus perishing finally from the world. If only the community

had let it rest at that, or learned again not merely to laugh, but genuinely to rejoice at this sign and what it so drastically signified!

7. V. Raymond Edman, *Storms and Starlight* (Wheaton, IL: Van Kampen, 1951), p. 124, who quotes John Oxenham, "Gadara, A.D. 31," from *Bees in Amber*.

Chapter Thirty-Eight: Providential Arrangement

1. Leon Morris, *Luke* (Grand Rapids, MI: Eerdmans, 1974), p. 174.

2. M. R. Vincent, *Word Studies in the New Testament* (Wilmington, DE: Associated Publishers and Authors, 1972), p. 103.

3. Morris, *Luke*, p. 173.

4. David Gooding, *According to Luke: A New Exposition of the Third Gospel* (Leicester, UK: Inter-Varsity, 1987), pp. 150–51.

Chapter Thirty-Nine: Earliest Apostolic Ministry

1. Donald Grey Barnhouse, *Let Me Illustrate* (Old Tappan, NJ: Revell, 1967), pp. 358–59.

2. John Nolland, *Luke 1—9:20* (Dallas: Word, 1989), p. 426.

3. Frederick Louis Godet, *Commentary on the Gospel of Luke* (Grand Rapids, MI: Zondervan, reprinted from the 4th edition of the translation from the second French edition by E. W. Shalers, printed by T. and T. Clark in 1887), p. 392.

4. E. Earle Ellis, *The Gospel of Luke* (Grand Rapids, MI: Eerdmans, 1974), p. 136.

5. I. H. Marshall, *The Gospel of Luke* (Grand Rapids, MI: Eerdmans, 1978), p. 350, explains:

> In Mk. the theme is not stated, but we are told that they preached that men should repent (Mk. 6:12). Luke has stressed the positive activity of preaching the good news (9:6) of the kingdom, although he himself often emphasizes repentance; the good news of the kingdom (cf. 4:16–21) precedes the call to repent.
>
> Joseph Fitzmyer, *The Gospel According to Luke I—IX* (Garden City, NY: Doubleday, 1981), p. 754 also explains, "Significantly, he avoids the Marcan *hina inetanosin,* 'that people may repent,' a notion that is otherwise dear to him; instead he uses *evangelizesthai*."

6. Marshall, *The Gospel of Luke*, pp. 350–51.

7. David Gooding, *According to Luke: A New Exposition of the Third Gospel* (Leicester, UK: Inter-Varsity, 1987), pp. 160–61.

8. Ibid.

Chapter Forty: The Sufficiency of Christ

1. I. H. Marshall, *The Gospel of Luke* (Grand Rapids, MI: Eerdmans, 1974), p. 358 explains:

> Bethsaida was a "new town" built by Herod Philip at the head of the lake (Jos. *Ant.* 18:28; *Bel.* 2:168). In Mk. 6:45 it is mentioned as the destination of the disciples after the feeding. Luke knew that the feeding took place in

the wilderness; he names Bethsaida as the nearest well-known town, and also to prepare the way for its mention in 10:13.

2. Joseph Fitzmyer, *The Gospel According to Luke I—IX* (Garden City, NY: Doubleday, 1981), p. 766.

3. Alexander Maclaren, *Expositions of the Holy Scriptures* (Grand Rapids, MI: Baker, 1971), p. 257.

4. Marshall, *The Gospel of Luke*, p. 362, who explains that the Greek word used here refers to a prayer of thanks for the bread.

5. C. Marvin Pate, *Luke* (Chicago: Moody, 1995), p. 205.

6. Maclaren, *Expositions of the Holy Scriptures*, p. 258

7. Alfred Edersheim, *The Life and Times of Jesus the Messiah* (Grand Rapids, MI: Eerdmans, 1967), p. 279 says:

> There is at least in our view, no doubt that thoughts of the Passover and the Holy Supper, of their commanding and mystic meaning, were present to the Saviour, and that it is in this light the miraculous feeding of the multitude must be considered, if we are in any measure to understand it.

Chapter Forty-One: "Who Do You Say That I Am?"

1. Albert Schweitzer, *The Quest for the Historical Jesus* (New York: Macmillan, 1959), p. 398.

2. C. S. Lewis, *Mere Christianity* (New York: Macmillan, 1976), pp. 55–56.

3. I. H. Marshall, *The Gospel of Luke* (Grand Rapids, MI: Eerdmans, 1978), pp. 366–67.

4. Leon Morris, *Luke* (Grand Rapids, MI: Eerdmans, 1974), pp. 185–86 explains:

> The word "rejected" seems to be a technical term for rejection after a careful legal scrutiny to see whether a candidate for office was qualified (see LSJ). It implies here that the hierarchy would consider Jesus' claims but decide against him. The one article in the expression of the elders and chief priests and scribes points to the fact that the three formed a single group in the Sanhedrin.

5. Elisabeth Elliot, *Shadow of the Almighty* (New York: Harper & Bros., 1958), pp. 55–56.

6. James Davidson Hunter, *Evangelicalism: The Coming Generation* (Chicago: University of Chicago Press, 1987), p. 69.

7. *The London Times,* April 9, 1978.

Chapter Forty-Two: Christ Transfigured

1. I. H. Marshall, *The Gospel of Luke* (Grand Rapids, MI: Eerdmans, 1978), p. 382, who explains regarding Mark's "six days" (9:2) and Luke's "eight days":

> The addition of ὡσεί may indicate that he is conscious of giving an approximation to Mark's figure. The view that the eighth day as the day of the new creation is meant (Grundmann, 192; Ellis, 142, 275f.) should be rejected: Luke never uses this phrase, except here.

Similarly, Joseph A. Fitzmyer, *The Gospel According to Luke I—IX* (Garden City, NY: Doubleday, 1981), p. 797: "The 'eight days' may be nothing more than a rounded-off way of saying, 'about a week.'"

2. Marshall, *The Gospel of Luke*, p. 383, explains:

> Luke has dropped Mark's verb μεταμορφόω (on which see J. Behm, TDNT IV, 755–759), probably because it could be misunderstood in a Hellenistic sense (although this was not intended by Mark).

3. Fitzmyer, *The Gospel According to Luke I—IX*, p. 800.
4. Ibid., p. 801.
5. Marshall, *The Gospel of Luke*, pp. 380, 387.
6. Ibid., p. 387, explains:

> But whom does the cloud cover? αὐτούς (par. Mt., diff. Mk αὐτοίς), can refer to Jesus and his companions and/or the three disciples. It is obvious that the former group is meant; the doubts concern the inclusion of the latter. In favour of the view that the cloud separated them from Jesus and his companions is the fact that the voice came from (ἐκ) the cloud; this seems in any case to be the view of Mark (A. Oepke, . . .). On the other hand, Luke's statement that they were afraid as they entered the cloud can mean that the disciples were afraid as they themselves entered it, in which case he has reinterpreted Mk (Schürmann, I, 561). But Luke's statement can equally well mean that the disciples were frightened as they saw the other (especially Jesus) disappear in the cloud, and there is no indication in the story that the disciples were to be taken into the presence of God.

7. *The Mishnah,* Sukkah 5:2–3, trans. Herbert Danby (London: Oxford University Press, 1974), p. 180.

Chapter Forty-Three: Christ's Majesty Below

1. I. H. Marshall, *The Gospel of Luke* (Grand Rapids, MI: Eerdmans, 1978), p. 389.
2. Ibid., p. 392.
3. Joseph A. Fitzmyer, *The Gospel According to Luke I—IX* (Garden City, NY: Doubleday, 1981), p. 808.
4. Ibid.
5. Frederick Louis Godet, *Commentary on the Gospel of Luke* (Grand Rapids, MI: Zondervan, reprinted from the 4th edition of the translation from the second French edition by Shalers, printed by T. and T. Clark in 1887), p. 435.
6. David Gooding, *According to Luke: A New Exposition of the Third Gospel* (Leicester, UK: Inter-Varsity, 1987), p. 172.
7. John Nolland, *Luke 1—9:20*, vol. 2 (Dallas: Word, 1993), p. 511.
8. Fitzmyer, *The Gospel According to Luke I—IX*, p. 814.

Chapter Forty-Four: True Greatness

1. Charles Colson, *Kingdoms in Conflict* (New York/Grand Rapids, MI: William Morrow/Zondervan, 1987), p. 85.

2. *Theological Dictionary of the New Testament*, vol. 5 (Grand Rapids, MI: Eerdmans, n.d.), p. 646.

3. John Nolland, *Luke 9:21—18:34*, vol. 3 (Dallas: Word, 1993), p. 519.

4. Ibid., p. 520.

5. Henry Fairlie, *The Seven Deadly Sins* (Notre Dame, IN: University of Notre Dame Press, 1979), p. 79.

6. John R. Claypool, *The Preaching Event* (Waco, TX: Word, 1980), p. 68.

Chapter Forty-Five: Demands of the Road

1. Joseph A. Fitzmyer, *The Gospel According to Luke I—IX* (Garden City, NY: Doubleday, 1978), p. 827.

2. W. O. E. Oesterley, *The Gospel Parables in the Light of Their Jewish Background* (New York: Macmillan, 1936), p. 162, writes:

> To the Jews the Samaritans were "strangers," and were regarded with supreme contempt; the scribes had an especial dislike for them. The Samaritans were publicly cursed in the synagogues; and a petition was daily offered up praying God that the Samaritans might not be partakers. The testimony of a Samaritan was inadmissible in Jewish courts.

3. Joachim Jeremias, *Jerusalem in the Time of Jesus* (Philadelphia: Fortress, 1969), p. 353.

4. John Nolland, *Luke 1—9:20* (Dallas: Word, 1989), p. 53.

5. I. H. Marshall, *The Gospel of Luke* (Grand Rapids, MI: Eerdmans, 1978), p. 411.

6. Fitzmyer, *The Gospel According to Luke I—IX*, p. 836, writes:

> Jesus' saying does not deny that his follower has a filial obligation, but the next part of it reveals that another consideration is in order. Hence, the sense should be: "Leave the (spiritually) dead to bury their (physically) dead."

7. David Gooding, *According to Luke: A New Exposition of the Third Gospel* (Leicester, UK: Inter-Varsity, 1987), p. 195.

8. Marshall, *The Gospel of Luke*, p. 412.

Chapter Forty-Six: Proper Joy

1. J. C. Pollock, *Moody: A Biographical Portrait of the Pacesetter in Modern Mass Evangelism* (New York: Macmillan, 1963), p. 181.

2. Ibid., p. 182.

3. Ibid., p. 184.

4. I. H. Marshall, *The Gospel of Luke* (Grand Rapids, MI: Eerdmans, 1978), p. 415; and E. Earle Ellis, *The Gospel of Luke* (Grand Rapids, MI: Eerdmans, 1974), pp. 155–56.

5. Frederick Louis Godet, *Commentary on the Gospel of Luke*, vol. 2 (Grand Rapids, MI: Zondervan, n.d.), p. 25.

6. Clarence Macartney, *The Making of a Minister* (Great Neck, NY: Channel, 1961), p. 123, writes:

> In that same conversation with Wilson at the Friars Club I heard him say of Henry Van Dyke, quoting, I think what someone else had said, that Van Dyke was the only man he had ever known who could "strut sitting down."

7. Pollock, *Moody,* p. 316.

Chapter Forty-Seven: The Praise and Blessing of Revelation

1. Eta Linnemann, *Historical Criticism of the Bible: Methodology or Ideology?*, trans. Robert W. Yarbrough (Grand Rapids, MI: Baker, 1990), p. 18.
2. Ibid., pp. 19–20.
3. I. H. Marshall, *The Gospel of Luke* (Grand Rapids, MI: Eerdmans, 1974), p. 434.
4. John Nolland, *Luke 9:21—18:34* (Dallas: Word, 1993), p. 57.
5. Eta Linnemann, *Historical Criticism of the Bible: Methodology or Ideology?*, p. 154.
6. This thought is attributed to Frank Sheed. Source unknown.
7. Joseph A. Fitzmyer, *The Gospel According to Luke I—IX* (Garden City, NY: Doubleday, 1981), p. 874, explains:

> Again, to what *panta* referred in the original saying is difficult to say. It might be thought to refer to the totality of cosmic power and sovereignty implied in the title "Lord of heaven and earth," with which Jesus has just hailed the Father, but it more likely refers to the knowledge of the mutual relation of himself and God, the content of the revelation gratuitously to be given.

8. Leon Morris, *Luke* (Grand Rapids, MI: Eerdmans, 1974), p. 204.
9. Charles Spurgeon, *The Metropolitan Tabernacle Pulpit,* vol. 26 (Pasadena, TX: Pilgrim, 1972), pp. 679–80.
10. J. C. Ryle, *Expository Thoughts on the Gospels: Luke,* vol. 1 (Cambridge, UK: James Clarke & Co. Ltd., 1976), p. 368.

Chapter Forty-Eight: "But a Samaritan . . ."

1. Paul Johnson, *Intellectuals* (New York: Harper & Row, 1988), p. 60.
2. Ibid., p. 61.
3. Ibid., pp. 70–71.
4. Ibid., p. 78.
5. Ibid., pp. 80–81 where Johnson writes:

> Lenchen was the only member of the working class that Marx ever knew at all well, his one real contact with the proletariat. Freddy might have been another, since he was brought up as a working-class lad and in 1888, when he was thirty-six, he got his coveted certificate as a qualified engineer-fitter. He spent virtually all his life in King's Cross and Hackney and was a regular member of the engineers' union. But Marx never knew him. They met only once, presumably when Freddy was coming up the outside steps from the kitchen, and he had no idea then that the revolutionary philosopher was his father. He died in January 1929, by which time Marx's vision of the dictatorship of the proletariat had taken concrete and terrifying shape, and Stalin—the ruler who achieved the absolute power for which Marx

had yearned—was just beginning his catastrophic assault on the Russian peasantry.

6. Ibid., pp. 151, 171, 258, 340.

7. Some have pointed out that in a couple of instances in extra-Biblical literature the sentiments of Deuteronomy 6:4, 5 and Leviticus 19:18 are combined. True, but they may well have been influenced by Christian teaching. Jesus was original and radical in his emphasis.

8. T. W. Manson, *The Sayings of Jesus* (London: SCM, 1957), p. 260, explains:

> But in the first century A.D. in Palestine the only way of publishing great thoughts was to go on repeating them in talk or sermons. It is thus quite possible, even probable, that when Jesus gave His famous answer to the scribe's question in the Marcan story, it was not the first time that He had expressed the whole duty of man by putting together those two texts. It must be emphasised that cases of this sort are not on all fours with the duplication of the miracles of feeding the multitude or with the two cleansings of the Temple. Great teachers constantly repeat themselves. We may therefore entertain the hypothesis that the lawyer in the Lucan story gives the reply (v. 27) which he already knows to represent the opinion of Jesus, and that he does so in order to raise the further question: Who is my neighbour?

9. I. H. Marshall, *The Gospel of Luke* (Grand Rapids, MI: Eerdmans, 1978), p. 451.

10. Ibid., p. 450, where Marshall explains: "Jews were forbidden to receive works of love from non-Jews (SB IV: 1, 537, 543f.)."

11. Joachim Jeremias, *Jerusalem in the Time of Jesus* (Philadelphia: Fortress, 1969), p. 123.

Chapter Forty-Nine: Choosing the Better

1. E. Earle Ellis, *The Gospel of Luke* (Grand Rapids, MI: Eerdmans, 1974), p. 162, explains:

> The patristic Church interpreted the passage to show the superiority of the contemplative over the "active" life. Similarly, some modern commentators think that the story illustrates, from Jesus' own example, the relative value of two kinds of ministry, "liturgy" and "diaconate." The apostles' choice in Acts (6:4) concurs with Christ's attitude here (cf. Gerhardsson, pp. 239ff.; B. Reicke, SE, pp. 212f.). However, Jesus rebukes Martha for diverting Mary from his word to less essential tasks. The issue is not two kinds of Christian service but religious busyness which distracts the Christian—preacher or layman—from the word of Christ upon which all effective service rests.

2. Joseph A. Fitzmyer, *The Gospel According to Luke, I–IX* (Garden City, NY: Doubleday, 1981), pp. 892–93.

3. Ellis, *The Gospel of Luke*, p. 162.

4. Geoffrey Bromiley, ed. and trans., *Theological Dictionary of the New Testament*, vol. 1 (Grand Rapids, MI: Eerdmans, 1968), pp. 781–82.

5. I. H. Marshall, *The Gospel of Luke* (Grand Rapids, MI: Eerdmans, 1974), p. 452.

6. David Gooding, *According to Luke: A New Exposition of the Third Gospel* (Leicester, UK: Inter-Varsity, 1987), p. 216.

7. Charles Spurgeon, *The Metropolitan Tabernacle Pulpit*, vol. 16 (Pasadena, TX: Pilgrim, 1970), p. 235, states: "Ah but a fly on St. Paul's Cathedral might as well imagine that all the traffic at his feet was regulated by his presence, and would cease should he remove."

8. John Nolland, *Luke 9:21—18:34*, vol. 2 (Dallas: 1993), p. 606.

9. J. C. Ryle, *Expository Thoughts on the Gospels: Luke,* vol. 1 (Cambridge, UK: James Clarke & Co. Ltd., 1976), p. 388.

10. Ellis, *The Gospel of Luke*, p. 161.

11. This was said by Billy Graham at the Congress on Discipleship and Evangelism (CODE '76), a gathering of 1,500 young people during the Greater San Diego Billy Graham Crusade, August 1976.

Chapter Fifty: Teach Us To Pray, Part 1

1. James M. Boice, *The Sermon on the Mount* (Grand Rapids, MI: Zondervan, 1972), p. 192.

2. I. H. Marshall, *The Gospel of Luke* (Grand Rapids, MI: Eerdmans, 1974), p. 456.

3. Leon Morris, *Luke* (Grand Rapids, MI: Eerdmans, 1974), p. 210.

4. Joachim Jeremias, *The Lord's Prayer* (Philadelphia: Fortress, 1980), p. 20.

5. William Barclay, *The Beatitudes and Lord's Prayer for Everyone* (New York: Harper & Row, 1964), p. 17.

6. Ernst Lohmeyer, *Our Father* (New York: Harper and Row, 1965), p. 104.

Chapter Fifty-One: Teach Us to Pray, Part 2

1. Joseph A. Fitzmyer, *The Gospel According to Luke, I–IX* (Garden City, NY: Doubleday, 1981), p. 904, explains:

> The word is not found with certainty in any extrabiblical text; it is often said to occur in a fifth-century A.D. papyrus (see F. Preisigke, *Sammelbuch griechischen Urkunden aus Agypten* [Strassburg: Trubner, 1915–1958], 1. 5224:20 *epiousi[ ],* supposedly = Latin *diaria,* "daily ration"), but the papyrus is no longer accessible for checking and the original publisher (A. Sayce) was notorious for his inaccuracy in reading and transcribing. See B. M. Metzger, "How Many Times," 52–54.

2. Joachim Jeremias, *The Lord's Prayer* (Philadelphia: Fortress, 1980), pp. 23–24. Also Ernst Lohmeyer, *Our Father* (New York: Harper and Row, 1965), pp. 134ff.

3. Lohmeyer, *Our Father*, p. 148, says:

> And this thought is further underlined by the fact that while in the Old Testament there are many vivid pictures which paint the glory of the final kingdom, in the words of Jesus there is only one, which is drawn many

> times, the picture of the marriage feast or the king's feast, of eating and drinking or reclining at table with the patriarchs in Abraham's bosom, and the pictures of harvest or sowing only serve to show the great context in which "our bread" is situated. One might almost say that from this point of view to pray for the coming of the kingdom and to pray "Give us our bread today" amounted to the same thing.

4. F. C. Cook, ed., *Speakers' Commentary* (New York: Scribner's, 1878–1896), p. 30.

5. I. H. Marshall, *The Gospel of Luke* (Grand Rapids, MI: Eerdmans, 1974), p. 461 writes:

> Luke's καί γάρ avoids the quid pro quo element that might be detected in Mount ὡς καί. He also has the verb in the present tense, expressing a continual readiness to forgive, while Matthew's perfect form suggests a condition that must be fulfilled before we can ask God to act (cf. Sir. 28:1–7; Mount 5:23f.; 6:14f.).

6. I. D. E. Thomas, ed., *Puritan Quotations* (Chicago: Moody, 1975), p. 111.

7. Charles Haddon Spurgeon, *The Metropolitan Tabernacle Pulpit,* vol. 2 (Pasadena, TX: Pilgrim, 1969), p. 694.

8. Thomas, *Puritan Quotations*, p. 111.

9. Charles Malik, *The Two Tasks* (Wheaton, IL: Crossway, 1980), p. 17. Malik said as he opened his address at the dedication of the Billy Graham Center in Wheaton, Illinois: "I speak to you as a Christian. Jesus Christ is my Lord and God and Savior and Song day and night. I can live without food, without drink, without sleep, without air, but I cannot live without Jesus."

Chapter Fifty-Two: Teach Us to Pray, Part 3

1. Kenneth E. Bailey, *Poet & Peasant and Through Peasant Eyes* (Grand Rapids, MI: Eerdmans, 1980), pp. 122–23.

2. David Gooding, *According to Luke: A New Exposition of the Third Gospel* (Leicester, UK: Inter-Varsity, 1987), p. 220.

3. Ibid., p. 910.

4. Joseph A. Fitzmyer, *The Gospel According to Luke, I–IX* (Garden City, NY: Doubleday, 1981), p. 912, explains:

> Because of his persistence. Lit. "Because of his shamelessness indeed," i.e. his importunity in begging and begging at this late hour of the night. It forces the one asked to be gift-ready. In this interpretation the *anaideia* is a quality of the petitioner. Some commentators have attempted to make it rather a quality of the neighbor roused from sleep: "he will fulfil the request because of his own shamelessness, namely, that which will be brought to light through his refusal" (A. Foridrichoosen, "Exegetisches," 40–43). But that interpretation fails because the *autou,* "his," that modifies *anaideia* has to be understood in the same sense as the *autou* with the preceding *philon,* "his friend," a reference to the begging neighbor.

5. George A. Buttrick, *The Parables of Jesus* (Grand Rapids, MI: Baker, 1979), p. 175, quoting James Montgomery, "What Is Prayer?"

Chapter Fifty-Three: Merciful Reasonings

1. Joseph A. Fitzmyer, *The Gospel According to Luke, I–IX* (Garden City, NY: Doubleday, 1981), p. 920.

2. David Gooding, *According to Luke: A New Exposition of the Third Gospel* (Leicester, UK: Inter-Varsity, 1987), pp. 223–24.

3. Ibid., p. 224.

4. *The Orange County Register*, July 6, 1986, pp. A1, A2.

5. Fitzmyer, *The Gospel According to Luke, I–IX*, p. 922.

6. Ibid., pp. 928–29 explains:

> Rather. The compound Greek particle *menoun* (used only four times in the NT and, against classical usage, at the head of a sentence) can have three different senses: (a) adversative, "nay, rather," "on the contrary": so commonly in classical Greek (Sophocles, *Ajaz* 1363; Aristophanes, *Eccl.* 1102) and in the NT (Rom 9:20; 10:18); this would mean that Jesus was rejecting the woman's blessing of his mother (it seems to be the sense advocated by T. W. Manson, I. H. Marshall, M. P. Scott, et al.). (b) affirmative, "indeed," expressive of agreement with what was said. See Phil 3:8. corrective, "yes, but rather," meaning that what was said is true as far as it goes (Plato, *Rep.* 489D). M.E. Thrall (*Greek Particles in the New Testament,* 34–35) points out that for Luke the first two uses are to be eliminated since, when he wants to express contradiction, he uses *ouchi, lego hymin* (12:51; 13:3, 5); and for affirmation he employs *nai* (7:26; 10:21; 11:51; 12:5). Hence, the last corrective sense is to be preferred. Cf. C.F.D. Moule, *Idiom Book,* 163–64.

Chapter Fifty-Four: Light for Hard Hearts

1. David Gooding, *According to Luke: A New Exposition of the Third Gospel* (Leicester, UK: Inter-Varsity, 1987), p. 228, explains: "It was the miraculous way in which Jonah arrived at Nineveh that gave force to his preaching and made him a sign to the Ninevites. It would similarly be Christ's death, burial and resurrection that made Christ God's ultimate sign to Israel (cf. Jn. 2:18–22)."

2. Leon Morris, *Luke* (Grand Rapids, MI: Eerdmans, 1974), p. 220, answers those who would limit the sign to Jonah's/Jesus' preaching:

> Many recent scholars think that the sign here is not the same as in Matthew, but a simple appeal to the fact that Jonah preached the authentic word of God and the Ninevites recognized the fact and repented. Similarly Jesus proclaimed the word of God and people ought to repent. One difficulty in the way of accepting this commonly held view is that of seeing in what sense preaching can properly be called a sign. A second is that Jesus does not speak of Jonah's and his own words as signs, but of Jonah and himself. In each case the sign is the person. A third is the use of the future tense. Jesus does not say that he is a sign, but that he will be a sign. This fits in with Matthew's account and also with the fact that John tells us that, when Jesus was asked for a sign on another occasion, he pointed forward to the

resurrection (Jn. 2:19). Jesus then makes it clear that when he gives a sign it will be one of his own choosing, not one given at the demand of an unbelieving generation.

3. Joachim Jeremias, "Ιωνᾶς," in *Theological Dictionary of the New Testament* (TDNT), ed. Gerhard Kittel, vol. 3 (Grand Rapids, MI: Eerdmans, 1968), p. 410 says:

> This is the only sign which will be given them. Materially, there is no discrepancy between the absolute refusal to give a sign (Mk. 8:11) and the intimation of the sign of Jonah. Both statements make it clear that God will not give any sign that is abstracted from the person of Jesus and that does not give offence.

4. Alexander Maclaren, *The Epistles of St. Paul to the Colossians and Philemon, The Exposition Bible* (New York: A.C. Armstrong, 1903), pp. 165–66.
5. William Barclay, *The Gospel of Luke* (Philadelphia: Westminster, 1956), p. 157.
6. Joseph A. Fitzmyer, *The Gospel According to Luke, I–IX* (Garden City, NY: Doubleday, 1981), p. 939.
7. Jonathan Edwards, *The Works of Jonathan Edwards* (Edinburgh: Banner of Truth, 1974), p. xiv.
8. *Focal Point*, vol. 6, no. 3.

Chapter Fifty-Five: "Woe to You Pharisees"

1. Joachim Jeremias, *Jerusalem in the Time of Jesus* (Philadelphia: Fortress, 1978), p. 246.
2. Ibid., p. 251.
3. Ibid., pp. 266–67.
4. William Barclay, *The Gospel of Luke* (Philadelphia: Westminster, 1956), p. 159.
5. Kingsley Amis, *Memoirs* (New York: Summit, 1991), p. 1.
6. William Wordsworth, *Ecclesiastical Sonnets*, Part 3, 43.
7. James Boswell, *The Life of Samuel Johnson* (London: Penguin, 1979), p. 151.
8. Leon Morris, *Luke* (Grand Rapids, MI: Eerdmans, 1974), p. 223.
9. Charles H. Spurgeon, *Lectures to My Students* (Grand Rapids, MI: Zondervan, 1969), pp. 166–67.
10. François Mauriac, *Viper's Tangle* (Garden City, NY: Image, 1957), pp. 198–99.

Chapter Fifty-Six: "Woe to You Lawyers"

1. John Nolland, *Luke 9:21—18:34*, vol. 2 (Dallas: Word, 1993), p. 667, who quotes T. W. Manson, *Sayings*, p. 101.
2. Joseph A. Fitzmyer, *The Gospel According to Luke, I–IX* (Garden City, NY: Doubleday, 1981), p. 952 who references G. B. Caird, *The Language and Imagery of the Bible* (Philadelphia: Westminster, 1980), p. 208.
3. C. Marvin Pate, *Luke* (Chicago: Moody, 1995), p. 260 explains:

> One answer is that wisdom is here understood in terms of the Old Testament preexistent figure of wisdom personified (cf. Prov. 8). This is true as

far as it goes, but in light of 7:35 we should probably go further and equate wisdom with Jesus Christ (cf. 1 Cor. 1:30; Col. 1:15–20).

4. I. H. Marshall, *The Gospel of Luke* (Grand Rapids, MI: Eerdmans, 1974), p. 506, where Marshall details the evidence as to which Zechariah is meant:

> Zechariah, the son of Jehoiada (2 Chronicles 24:20–22), or Zechariah son of Barachias (Matthew 23:35 and Josephus *War* 4:334–344). Either choice does not affect the point of the text.

5. T. H. L. Parker, *Karl Barth* (Grand Rapids, MI: Eerdmans, 1970), p. 42.

Chapter Fifty-Seven: Confessing Christ

1. I. H. Marshall, *The Gospel of Luke* (Grand Rapids, MI: Eerdmans, 1974), p. 511, explains:

> The situation is similar to that in the Sermon on the Plain and elsewhere (cf. 20:45) where teaching intended primarily for the disciples is given in the presence of the crowds who are thus taught what is involved in discipleship.

2. Roland Bainton, *Here I Stand* (New York: Times Mirror, n.d.), p. 141.
3. Ibid., p. 142.
4. Ibid., p. 144.
5. Ibid.
6. William Barclay, *The Gospel of Luke* (Philadelphia: Westminster, 1956), p. 164.
7. Timothy Bayly, *Out of My Mind: The Best of Joe Bayly* (Grand Rapids, MI: Zondervan, 1993), pp. 168–69.
8. Barclay, *The Gospel of Luke*, p. 165.
9. Joseph A. Fitzmyer, *The Gospel According to Luke, I–IX* (Garden City, NY: Doubleday, 1981), p. 958.
10. Leon Morris, *Luke* (Grand Rapids, MI: Eerdmans, 1974), pp. 230–31.
11. Fitzmyer, *The Gospel According to Luke, I–IX*, p. 964.

Chapter Fifty-Eight: The Rich Fool

1. Joseph A. Fitzmyer, *The Gospel According to Luke, I–IX* (Garden City, NY: Doubleday, 1981), p. 969. See also Leon Morris, *Luke* (Grand Rapids, MI: Eerdmans, 1974), p. 232.
2. Fitzmyer, *The Gospel According to Luke, I–IX*, p. 970.
3. Morris, *Luke*, p. 233.
4. Charles W. Colson, "The Enduring Revolution" (Speech, University of Chicago, Chicago, IL, September 2, 1993), p. 7.
5. Rudyard Kipling, "The Old Men."

Chapter Fifty-Nine: Not to Worry

1. Leon Morris, *Luke* (Grand Rapids, MI: Eerdmans, 1974), p. 223, who quotes W. F. Arndt.

2. John Nicholas Lenker, ed., *Sermons of Martin Luther*, vol. 5 (Grand Rapids, MI: Baker, 1983), p. 115.

3. Clarence Macartney, *Macartney's Illustrations* (New York: Abingdon Press, 1946), p. 415.

Chapter Sixty: Be Ready

1. James Montgomery Boice, *Foundations of the Christian Faith* (Downers Grove, IL: InterVarsity, 1986), p. 705.

2. Ibid.

3. Joseph Fitzmyer, *The Gospel According to Luke, I–IX* (Garden City, NY: Doubleday, 1981), p. 988 says:

> Reference may be made to the Roman custom of dividing the night (from 6 p.m. to 6 a.m.) into four equal periods (6–9,9–12,12–3,3–6) or "watches" (phylakai), when sentinels were posted (see Vegetius, De re mil. 3.8); or possibly to the Hellenistic and Jewish custom of three watches (6–10, 10–2, 2–6). See Judg 7:19. Josephus (Ant. 18. 9, 6 §356) speaks of the "fourth watch," but alludes to a three-watch night in J.W. 5. 12, 2 §510. Cf. Mark 13:35–36. Luke seems to reckon elsewhere with four watches. See Acts 12:4.

Chapter Sixty-One: Reality Check

1. I. H. Marshall, *The Gospel of Luke* (Grand Rapids, MI: Eerdmans, 1974), p. 547.

2. Frederick Buechner, *Now and Then* (San Francisco: Harper, 1983), pp. 53–54. I have modified the exact application to fit the text. Buechner's original reads,

> The difference seems to me this. The suffering that Buddha's eyes close out is the suffering of the world that Christ's eyes close in and hallow. It is an extraordinary difference, and even in a bare classroom in Exeter, New Hampshire, I think it was as apparent to everyone as it was to me that before you're done, you have to make a crucial and extraordinary choice.

3. Charles Colson, *Kingdoms in Conflict* (New York/Grand Rapids, MI: William Morrow/Zondervan, 1987), p. 215.

4. Ibid., p. 216.

Chapter Sixty-Two: Settle Up!

1. John Nolland, *Luke 9:21—18:34*, vol. 2 (Dallas: Word, 1993), pp. 712–13 writes:

> Jesus accuses the crowds of hypocrisy because they are not ready to apply the same shrewdness to the indicators contained in the unfolding of his own ministry (and perhaps also its precursor in the ministry of John). The events of "this [present] time" point just as reliably as any weather indicators to the coming day of answerability to God.

2. David Gooding, *According to Luke: A New Exposition of the Third Gospel* (Leicester, UK: Inter-Varsity, 1987), pp. 248–49.

3. Charles Colson, *Who Speaks for God?* (Wheaton, IL: Crossway, 1985), pp. 136–37.

Chapter Sixty-Three: Repentance Time!

1. D. Stuart Briscoe, *Patterns for Power* (Glendale, CA: Regal, 1979), p. 87.
2. Ibid., p. 89.
3. Joseph Fitzmyer, *The Gospel According to Luke, I–IX* (Garden City, NY: Doubleday, 1981), p. 1006.
4. I. H. Marshall, *The Gospel of Luke* (Grand Rapids, MI: Eerdmans, 1974), p. 554, explains:

> Σιλωάμ was the name of the reservoir associated with the water supply from Gihon to Jerusalem (Jn. 9:7, 11; Is. 8:6); it lay near the junction of the S and E walls, and the tower may have been part of the fortifications in this area (cf. Jos. Bel. 5:145; so SB II, 197; Finegan, 114f.). Pilate built an aqueduct to improve the water supply, and it is also possible that the tower (and its collapse) had something to do with this building operation (Jos. Bel. 2:175; Ant. 18:60).

5. John Nolland, *Luke 9:21—18:34*, vol. 2 (Dallas: Word, 1993), p. 719, explains:

> While in vv. 2–3 we were dealing with the act of a cruel leader and perhaps of people who "asked for it" by their political activity, now we are probably to think of an "act of God" falling randomly on those who just happen innocently to be present. The same judgments apply.

6. E. Earle Ellis, *The Gospel of Luke* (Grand Rapids, MI: Eerdmans, 1974), p. 185:

> In the Gospels Jesus does not speak to the question of original sin. However, in this saying he assumes the universality of sin and death as its consequence. In every death, whether an accident at "Siloam" or an execution by Pilate, the funeral bell "tolls for thee."

7. Fitzmyer, *The Gospel According to Luke, I–IX*, p. 1008.
8. Briscoe, *Patterns for Power*, p. 93, provides the following explanation of what repentance is not and is.
9. Fitzmyer, *The Gospel According to Luke, I–IX*, p. 1008.
10. John Bunyan, "The Barren Fig-Tree," in *Twenty Centuries of Great Preaching*, eds. Clyde E. Fant and William M. Pinson Jr., vol. 2 (Waco, TX: Word, 1976), p. 332.
11. Ibid., p. 333.
12. Ibid.
13. Ibid., p. 334.

Chapter Sixty-Four: Straightened on the Sabbath

1. Charles H. Spurgeon, *The Metropolitan Tabernacle Pulpit,* vol. 24 (Pasadena, TX: Pilgrim, 1972), p. 423.
2. Ibid., p. 431.

3. Herbert Danby, trans., *The Mishnah* (London: Oxford, 1974), pp. 103, 104.

4. Quoted by James Boice, *The Sermon on the Mount* (Grand Rapids, MI: Zondervan, 1972), p. 208.

5. Helmut Thielicke, *Our Heavenly Father* (Grand Rapids, MI: Baker, 1980), p. 60.

6. Ibid., p. 62.

Chapter Sixty-Five: The Narrow Door

1. Herbert Danby, trans., *The Mishnah* (London: Oxford, 1933), p. 397.

2. I. H. Marshall, *The Gospel of Luke* (Grand Rapids, MI: Eerdmans, 1974), p. 565.

3. Alexander Maclaren, *The Epistles of St. Paul to the Colossians and Philemon, The Exposition Bible* (New York: A.C. Armstrong, 1903), p. 9.

4. Charles H. Spurgeon, *The Metropolitan Tabernacle Pulpit,* vol. 8 (Pasadena, TX: Pilgrim, 1975), p. 582. The preceding two paragraphs have utilized Spurgeon's thoughts and phraseology.

Chapter Sixty-Six: Mourning for the City

1. I. H. Marshall, *The Gospel of Luke* (Grand Rapids, MI: Eerdmans, 1974), p. 571 explains:

> In rabbinic literature the fox was typical of low cunning (Ber. 6lb, citing R. Akiba; SBII, 200f), but it was also portrayed as an insignificant creature in comparison with the lion: "Be first in greeting every man; and be a tail to lions and not be a head to foxes" (P. Ab. 4:15).

2. Leon Morris, *Luke* (Grand Rapids, MI: Eerdmans, 1974), p. 249.

3. Ibid.

4. Alexander Maclaren, *The Epistles of St. Paul to the Colossians and Philemon, The Exposition Bible* (New York: A.C. Armstrong, 1902), p. 17, writes:

> And it was not another's eye, as a reverent modern painter has profoundly, and yet erroneously, shown us in his great work in our own city gallery—it was not a mother's eye that first saw the shadow of the Cross fall on her unconscious Son, but it was Himself that all through His earthly pilgrimage knew Himself to be the Lamb appointed for the sacrifice. This Isaac toiled up the hill, bearing the wood and the knife and knew where and who was the Offering.

5. Josephus, *War* V. 12. 3.

Chapter Sixty-Seven: The Dinner Party, Part 1

1. John Nolland, *Luke 1—9:20*, vol. 2 (Dallas: Word, 1993), p. 511.

2. D. Stuart Briscoe, *Patterns for Power* (Glendale, CA: Regal, 1979), pp. 111–12 expounds this illustration in charming detail.

3. George A. Buttrick, *The Parables of Jesus* (Grand Rapids, MI: Baker, 1979), p. 87.

4. Joseph A. Fitzmyer, *The Gospel According to Luke, I–IX* (Garden City, NY: Doubleday, 1981), p. 1047, quotes the Leviticus Rabbah and adds:

> A similar saying is recorded in Abot de Rabbi Nathan 25. See Str-B 1. 916. Are these rabbinical traditions possibly influenced by the early Christian tradition?

5. C. Marvin Pate, *Luke* (Chicago: Moody, 1995), p. 295.

Chapter Sixty-Eight: The Dinner Party, Part 2

1. David Gooding, *According to Luke: A New Exposition of the Third Gospel* (Leicester, UK: Inter-Varsity, 1987), p. 267.
2. Leon Morris, *Luke* (Grand Rapids, MI: Eerdmans, 1974), pp. 223, 255–56.
3. John Nolland, *Luke 9:21—18:34*, vol. 2 (Dallas: Word, 1993), p. 755.
4. E. Earle Ellis, *The Gospel of Luke* (Grand Rapids, MI: Eerdmans, 1974), p. 194.
5. Vachel Lindsay, *Collected Poems* (New York: Macmillan, rev. ed., 1945), pp. 123–25.

Chapter Sixty-Nine: Being a Disciple

1. Annie Dillard, *Teaching a Stone to Talk* (New York: Harper & Row, 1988), pp. 24–26.
2. George Buttrick, *The Parables of Jesus* (Grand Rapids, MI: Baker, 1979), p. 79.
3. Alfred Plummer, *The Gospel According to St. Luke* (Edinburgh: T. & T. Clark, 1905), p. 364.
4. C. S. Lewis, *Mere Christianity* (London: Fontana, 1955), pp. 163–64.
5. Joseph A. Fitzmyer, *The Gospel According to Luke, I–IX* (Garden City, NY: Doubleday, 1981), pp. 1059–66.
6. Lloyd Ogilvie, *Autobiography of God* (Glendale, CA: Regal, 1979), p. 157.

Chapter Seventy: "Rejoice with Me"

1. Richard Chenevix Trench, *Notes on the Parables of Our Lord* (London: SPCK, 1906), p. 373.
2. Ibid.
3. Joseph A. Fitzmyer, *The Gospel According to Luke, I–IX* (Garden City, NY: Doubleday, 1981), p. 1076.
4. I. H. Marshall, *The Gospel of Luke* (Grand Rapids, MI: Eerdmans, 1974), p. 597.
5. Fitzmyer, *The Gospel According to Luke, I–IX,* p. 1071.
6. E. Earle Ellis, *The Gospel of Luke* (Grand Rapids, MI: Eerdmans, 1974), p. 197, explains:

> I. Silver coin: a drachma. It was about 60 grains weight and was a (subsistence) day's wage for a labourer. Cf. Mt. 20:2; Rostovtzeff, I, 471; Jeremias, *Jerusalem*, pp. 9in, 111, 121f,; see on 15:29.

7. Leon Morris, *Luke* (Grand Rapids, MI: Eerdmans, 1974), p. 261.
8. Lloyd Ogilvie, *Autobiography of God* (Glendale, CA: Regal, 1979), p. 157.

9. Ibid., p. 34. The idea to use the opening lines of Francis Thompson's poem here, and then to juxtapose the penultimate lines, comes from Pastor Ogilvie's eloquent sermon.

10. Orazio Marucchi, *Manual of Christian Archaeology* (Paterson, NJ: St. Anthony Guild, 1935), pp. 338–39.

11. Trench, *Notes on the Parables of Our Lord*, p. 380.

12. George Buttrick, *The Parables of Jesus* (Grand Rapids, MI: Baker, 1979), p. 185.

13. Trench, *Notes on the Parables of Our Lord,* p. 391.

Chapter Seventy-One: The Prodigal God

1. A. W. Tozer, *The Knowledge of the Holy* (New York: Harper & Row, 1961), p. 105.

2. George A. Buttrick, *The Parables of Jesus* (Grand Rapids, MI: Baker, 1979), p. 196.

3. Ibid.

4. Joseph A. Fitzmyer, *The Gospel According to Luke, I–IX* (Garden City, NY: Doubleday, 1981), p. 1091.

Chapter Seventy-Two: The Dishonest Manager

1. Leon Morris, *Luke* (Grand Rapids, MI: Eerdmans, 1974), p. 269–70, who draws on the extensive research of J. D. M. Derrett, *Law in the New Testament* (London: n.p., 1970), pp. 48–77.

2. Joseph A. Fitzmeyer, *The Gospel According to Luke, I–IX* (Garden City, NY: Doubleday, 1981), p. 1101, explains:

> This does not mean a cancellation of half the debt or a falsification of accounts, *pace* J. Jeremias, *Parables*, 181. It means that the debtor actually owed the master only fifty jugs of oil, and that the other fifty were the manager's commission. The amount of interest (100%) seems exorbitant; it may be nothing more than the (fantastically) high figures used in parabolic stories (see J. Jeremias, *Parables*, 28, 181), but J. D. M. Derritt (*Law*, 69–72) has tried to show that the interest of 100% is not unknown (in Indian sources!).

3. E. Earle Ellis, *The Gospel of Luke* (Grand Rapids, MI: Eerdmans, 1974), p. 200, reasons:

> Probably God or the angels who, as God's agents, distribute punishment or reward. "They" frequently is used in rabbinic literature to avoid mentioning the name of God. Cf. 12:20, 48. Less likely, the reference may be to the persons helped by the "unrighteous mammon." Instead of accusing (cf. 11:31f.), they will be friendly witnesses at the last judgment. Similarly, Leon Morris, p. 273, explains: More probably we have a common Jewish use of the plural to mean "God" in accordance with a tendency to avoid use of the divine name (SB). It is God who receives people into heaven.

4. William Barclay, *The Gospel of Luke* (Philadelphia: Westminster, 1956), p. 216.

5. Martin Luther, *Commentary on Peter & Jude* (Grand Rapids, MI: Kregel, 1990), pp. 70–71.

6. Fitzmeyer, *The Gospel According to Luke, I–IX,* p. 1000.

7. Carl F. H. Henry, "Evangelical Courage in an Age of Darkness," *Tabletalk,* January 1990, p. 10.

Chapter Seventy-Three: Rich Man, Poor Man

1. Joseph A. Fitzmyer, *The Gospel According to Luke, I–IX* (Garden City, NY: Doubleday, 1981), pp. 1130–31.

2. John Nolland, *Luke 9:21—18:34*, vol. 2 (Dallas: Word, 1993), p. 829.

3. David Gooding, *According to Luke: A New Exposition of the Third Gospel* (Leicester, UK: Inter-Varsity, 1987), p. 276. He provides the likely theological profile of the rich man, and the assertion that "he had never really believed what he professed to believe."

4. Fitzmyer, *The Gospel According to Luke, I–IX*, p. 1132.

Chapter Seventy-Four: Discipleship's Duties

1. Joseph A. Fitzmeyer, *The Gospel According to Luke, I–IX* (Garden City, NY: Doubleday, 1981), p. 1138.

2. John Nolland, *Luke 9:21—18:34*, vol. 2 (Dallas: Word, 1993), p. 839.

3. G. Campbell Morgan, *The Gospel According to Luke* (New York: Revell, 1931), p. 194.

4. Nolland, *Luke 9:21—18:34*, vol. 2, p. 838, explains: "'Brother' will have originally meant 'fellow Jew,' but in Luke should probably be read as fellow Christian. To rebuke is, for Jesus, to challenge with a view to change all that is evil, inappropriate, or defective."

5. Fitzmeyer, *The Gospel According to Luke, I–IX,* p. 1140.

6. John Nolland, *Luke 9:21—18:34*, vol. 2, p. 839.

7. Charles Spurgeon, *Metropolitan Tabernacle Pulpit,* vol. 22 (Pasadena, TX: Pilgrim, 1971), pp. 371–72 develops the theme that great people of faith are forgivers.

8. Ibid., p. 574. The statement here is a paraphrase of Spurgeon's original:

> "Ah, my bad temper is rooted in me: as a sycamore tree takes hold of the earth by its roots, so an ill temper has gone into the very depth of my nature. I am constitutionally quick tempered. From my very birth I have found it hard to forgive." If thou have faith, my brother, thou canst say to that sycamore tree, or better still upas tree within thee, "Be thou plucked up by the roots."

Chapter Seventy-Five: The Tenth Leper

1. G. F. Barbour, *The Life of Alexander Whyte, D.D.* (London: Hodder & Stoughton, 1923), p. 365.

2. John Nolland, *Luke 9:21—18:34*, vol. 1 (Dallas: Word, 1993), p. 846.

3. Frederick Louis Godet, *Commentary on the Gospel of Luke* (Grand Rapids, MI: Zondervan, n.d.), p. 192.

4. Alexander Maclaren, *The Epistles of St. Paul to the Colossians and Philemon* (Grand Rapids, MI: Baker, 1974), p. 129.

5. Joseph A. Fitzmyer, *The Gospel According to Luke, I–IX* (Garden City, NY: Doubleday, 1981), p. 1155, explains:

> An act of prostration symbolizes his recognition of Jesus' status. W. Grundmann (*Evangelium nach Lukas,* 337) considers the act to be the homage due to a king: "He pays homage to him as to a king." It could also be a recognition of him as an agent of God.

6. I. H. Marshall, *The Gospel of Luke* (Grand Rapids, MI: Eerdmans, 1974), p. 652.

7. Fitzmyer, *The Gospel According to Luke, I–IX*, pp. 1148–56.

8. John Nolland, *Luke 9:21—18:34*, vol. 2, p. 848.

9. David Gooding, *According to Luke: A New Exposition of the Third Gospel* (Leicester, UK: Inter-Varsity, 1987), p. 288.

Chapter Seventy-Six: The Kingdom—Now and Not Yet

1. Graeme Goldsworthy, *Gospel and Kingdom* (New South Wales, Australia: Anzea, 1992), p. 47.

2. Ibid.

3. Ibid., p. 48.

4. Ibid., pp. 87–98.

5. E. Earle Ellis, *The Gospel of Luke* (Grand Rapids, MI: Eerdmans, 1974), p. 211.

6. Ibid., p. 211, where Ellis explains:

> More probably, (2) the plural is equivalent to "days" in verse 26 and to the singular "day" in verse 30. It may be a rabbinic idiom for the times of Messiah (SBK); or "one" *(mian)* may mean "first." In this context the phrase would refer to the *parousia.* To "see" the days of the Son of man, i.e., the *parousia,* is something different from "seeing" the kingdom of God. See notes on 9:9, 27.

7. David Gooding, *According to Luke: A New Exposition of the Third Gospel* (Leicester, UK: Inter-Varsity, 1987), pp. 291–92.

8. Goldsworthy, *Gospel and Kingdom*, p. 99.

Chapter Seventy-Seven: Living in the Not Yet

1. John Nolland, *Luke 9:21—18:34,* vol. 2 (Grand Rapids, MI: Eerdmans, 1978), p. 867, explains:

> Πάντοτε προσεύχεσθαι and μὴ εγκακεῖν mutually qualify one another's meaning. So the former takes the sense "always to keep on praying" (not "pray without ceasing" as the similar phrase in 1 Thess 5:17), and the latter means "not to give up" in the sense of not giving up on prayer and expresses the expectation that God will respond with vindication.
>
> See also Joseph A. Fitzmyer, *The Gospel According to Luke, I–IX* (Garden City, NY: Doubleday, 1981), p. 1178, and I. H. Marshall, *The*

Gospel of Luke (Grand Rapids, MI: Eerdmans, 1974), p. 671, for similar illuminating comments.

2. Fitzmyer, *The Gospel According to Luke, I–IX* p. 1179.

3. A. W. Tozer, *The Knowledge of the Holy* (New York: Harper & Row, 1961), p. 93.

4. C. Samuel Storms, *Reaching God's Ear* (Wheaton, IL: Tyndale, 1988), p. 145.

5. John Nolland, *Luke 9:21—18:34*, vol. 2, p. 871.

6. E. Earle Ellis, *The Gospel of Luke* (Grand Rapids, MI: Eerdmans, 1974), p. 213.

7. Leon Morris, *Luke* (Grand Rapids, MI: Eerdmans, 1974), p. 288.

8. Oswald Chambers, *Daily Thoughts for Disciples* (Fort Washington, PA: Christian Literature Crusade, 1976), p. 75.

Chapter Seventy-Eight: Two Ways to Pray

1. Paul Johnson, *Intellectuals* (New York: Harper & Row, 1988), p. 108.

2. Ibid., p. 107.

3. Ibid.

4. David Gooding, *According to Luke: A New Exposition of the Third Gospel* (Leicester, UK: Inter-Varsity, 1987), p. 293.

5. George Arthur Buttrick, ed., *The Interpreter's Dictionary of the Bible*, vol. 4 (New York: Abingdon, 1962), p. 522.

6. Joseph A. Fitzmyer, *The Gospel According to Luke, I–IX* (Garden City, NY: Doubleday, 1981), p. 1186.

7. William Barclay, *The Gospel of Luke* (Philadelphia: Westminster, 1956), p. 232.

8. John Nolland, *Luke 9:21—18:34*, vol. 2 (Dallas: Word, 1993), pp. 877–79.

9. Leon Morris, *Luke* (Grand Rapids, MI: Eerdmans, 1974), p. 290.

10. Neil R. Lightfoot, *Lessons from the Parables* (Grand Rapids, MI: Baker, 1965), p. 145.

11. Frederick Louis Godet, *Commentary on the Gospel of Luke* (Grand Rapids, MI: Zondervan, n.d.), p. 204.

Chapter Seventy-Nine: Kingdom Entrance

1. Joseph A. Fitzmeyer, *The Gospel According to Luke, X—XXIV* (Garden City, NY: Doubleday, 1985), p. 1194.

2. Eduard Schweizer, *The Good News According to Mark,* trans. Donald H. Madvig (Atlanta: John Knox, 1970), p. 207.

3. David Gooding, *According to Luke* (Grand Rapids, MI: Eerdmans, 1987), p. 295.

4. C. S. Lewis, *The Weight of Glory* (Grand Rapids, MI: Eerdmans, 1949), pp. 14–15, provides the original classic expression of this thought:

> It is a serious thing to live in a society of possible gods and goddesses, to remember that the dullest and most uninteresting person you talk to may one day be a creature which, if you saw it now, you would be strongly tempted to worship, or else a horror and a corruption such as you now meet, if at all, only in a nightmare. All day long we are, in some degree, helping

each other to one or other of these destinations. It is in the light of these overwhelming possibilities, it is with the awe and circumspection proper to them, that we should conduct all our dealings with one another, all friendships, all loves, all play, all politics. There are no ordinary people. You have never talked to a mere mortal. Nations, cultures, arts, civilization—these are mortal, and their life is to ours as the life of a gnat. But it is immortals whom we joke with, work with, marry, snub, and exploit—immortal horrors or everlasting splendours.

5. Charles H. Spurgeon, *The Metropolitan Tabernacle Pulpit,* vol. 24 (Pasadena, TX: Pilgrim, 1972), p. 581, from which the preceding thoughts and phraseology are adapted.

Chapter Eighty: How Hard It Is for a Rich Man!

1. Leon Morris, *Luke* (Grand Rapids, MI: Eerdmans, 1974), p. 292.
2. E. Earle Ellis, *The Gospel of Luke* (Grand Rapids, MI: Eerdmans, 1974), p. 218.
3. John Nolland, *Luke 9:21—18:34,* vol. 2 (Dallas: Word, 1993), p. 887.
4. Ellis, *The Gospel of Luke*, p. 218, writes: "Jesus puts his finger on the one commandment, unmentioned before (20), that the young man failed to keep. He was covetous. See on 16:14; 12:33f."
5. Amy Carmichael, *Things As They Are* (Old Tappan, NJ: Revell, 1903), p. 74.
6. James Hastings, ed., *The Spoken Bible*, vol. 8 (Grand Rapids, MI: Baker, 1974), p. 20.
7. Roland Hein, ed., *Creation in Christ* (Wheaton, IL: Harold Shaw, 1976), p. 128.
8. C. S. Lewis, *Poems* (New York: Harcourt Brace Jovanovich, 1964), p. 134.
9. Joseph Fitzmyer, *The Gospel According to Luke, I–IX* (Garden City, NY: Doubleday, 1981), p. 1204.
10. Morris, *Luke*, p. 274.
11. John G. Stackhouse, Jr., "The Gospel Song" (unpublished).

Chapter Eighty-One: Blind Sight

1. Walter A. Elwell, ed., *Evangelical Dictionary of Theology* (Grand Rapids, MI: Baker, 1984), p. 1035.
2. Vincent Taylor, *The Gospel According to St. Mark* (Grand Rapids, MI: Baker, 1981), p. 447.
3. Gerhard Kittel, ed. *Theological Dictionary of the New Testament* (TDNT), vol. 8 (Grand Rapids, MI: Eerdmans, n.d.), p. 481.
4. Ibid.
5. Ibid.
6. Ibid.
7. James H. Charlesworth, ed., *The Old Testament Pseudepigrapha*, vol. 2 (Garden City, NY: Doubleday, 1985), p. 639. See also pp. 665–69 for the messianic text of the psalm, chapter 17.
8. Clarence Macartney, *Great Interviews of Jesus* (New York: Abingdon-Cokesbury, 1944), p. 155.

9. George MacDonald, *The Disciple and Other Poems* (Eureka, CA: Sunrise Books, 1989), pp. 216–17.

Chapter Eighty-Two: The Little Big Man

1. Bob L. Ross, *A Pictorial Biography of C. H. Spurgeon* (Pasadena, TX: n.p., 1974.), pp. 85–88.

2. John Nolland, *Luke 9:21—18:34* (Dallas: Word, 1993), pp. 903, 907.

3. Gerhard Kittel, ed. *Theological Dictionary of the New Testament* (TDNT), vol. 8 (Grand Rapids, MI: Eerdmans, n.d.), p. 98.

4. C. S. Lewis, *Poems* (New York: Harcourt Brace Jovanovich, 1977), p. 134.

5. R. S. Pine-Coffin, trans., *Saint Augustine Confessions* (London: Penguin, 1961), bk. 2, 2, p. 44.

6. Ibid., bk. 7, 8, p. 144.

7. J. D. Douglas, ed., *The New Bible Dictionary* (Grand Rapids, MI: Eerdmans, 1962), p. 1294.

8. Leon Morris, *Luke* (Grand Rapids, MI: Eerdmans, 1988), p. 298.

9. Alexander Maclaren, *Expositions of Holy Scriptures* (Grand Rapids, MI: Eerdmans, 1974), p. 156.

10. I. H. Marshall, *The Gospel of Luke* (Grand Rapids, MI: Eerdmans, 1978), p. 698.

11. E. Earle Ellis, *The Gospel of Luke* (Grand Rapids, MI: Eerdmans, 1974), pp. 220–21 explains:

> The New Testament teaches that the kingdom of God and the "salvation" which it brings belong to the heirs of Abraham. In this regard Christianity is absolutely Jewish. But who is "a son of Abraham" (9)? Natural descent or religious adherence to the law was the qualification required by contemporary Judaism. In the eyes of the Christians the religious leaders had distorted the Old Testament teaching. The true heir, that is, the true Jew, is one who shares the faith and does the works of Abraham. This concept is rooted in such sayings of Jesus as the "teaching word" in this passage. Zacchaeus receives the kingdom message and with it the messianic "salvation." This shows that he is a son of Abraham.

12. Pine-Coffin, *Confessions*, bk. 4, 4, p. 75.

13. C. S. Lewis, *Surprised by Joy* (New York: Harcourt, Brace & World, n.d.), p. 229.

14. D. A. Carson and John D. Woodbridge, *Letters Along the Way* (Wheaton, IL: Crossway, 1993), p. 36.

Chapter Eighty-Three: The Parable of the Investment

1. Leon Morris, *Luke* (Grand Rapids, MI: Eerdmans, 1974), p. 306.

2. Helmut Thielicke, *The Waiting Father* (New York: Harper & Row, 1959), p. 143.

3. Morris, *Luke*, p. 301.

4. I. H. Marshall, *The Gospel of Luke* (Grand Rapids, MI: Eerdmans, 1974), p. 707.

5. Thielicke, *The Waiting Father*, p. 144.

Chapter Eighty-Four: A New Kind of King

1. Johnston M. Cheney, *The Life of Christ in Stereo* (Portland: Western Baptist Seminary Press, 1973), pp. 145–46.

2. I. H. Marshall, *The Gospel of Luke* (Grand Rapids, MI: Eerdmans, 1978), p. 711.

3. Merrill F. Unger, *Zechariah* (Grand Rapids, MI: Zondervan, 1972), pp. 163–64.

4. Clarence E. Macartney, *Salute Thy Soul* (New York: Abingdon, 1957), p. 80.

5. Albert Schweitzer, *The Quest for the Historical Jesus* (New York: Macmillan, 1959), pp. 370–71.

6. Marshall, *The Gospel of Luke*, p. 715.

7. Alfred Edersheim, *The Life and Times of Jesus the Messiah*, vol. 2 (Grand Rapids, MI: Eerdmans, 1967), pp. 366–67.

8. Ibid., p. 369.

9. Ibid.

10. Joseph A. Fitzmyer, *The Gospel According to Luke, I–IX* (Garden City, New York: Doubleday, 1985), p. 1259.

11. Macartney, *Salute Thy Soul,* p. 84.

12. G. Campbell Morgan, *The Gospel According to Luke* (Old Tappan, NJ: Revell, 1931), p. 221.

Chapter Eighty-Five: Sovereign in His Temple

1. Joseph A. Fitzmyer, *The Gospel According to Luke, I–IX* (Garden City, NY: Doubleday, 1981), p. 1246.

2. Frederick Louis Godet, *Commentary on the Gospel of Luke*, vol. 2 (Grand Rapids, MI: Zondervan), p. 233.

3. Joachim Jeremias, *Jerusalem in the Time of Jesus* (Philadelphia: Fortress, 1969), p. 49.

4. Ibid.

5. J. A. Motyer, *The Prophecy of Isaiah* (London: Inter-Varsity, 1993), p. 467.

6. Theo Laetsch, *Bible Commentary Jeremiah* (St. Louis: Concordia, 1965), p. 96.

7. E. Earle Ellis, *The Gospel of Luke* (Grand Rapids, MI: Eerdmans, 1974), p. 230.

8. John Nolland, *Luke 9:21—18:34*, vol. 2 (Dallas: Word, 1993), p. 935.

9. Graeme Goldsworthy, *Gospel and Kingdom* (NSW, Australia: Lancer, 1992), p. 95.

10. Ibid., p. 98.

Chapter Eighty-Six: The Authority of Jesus

1. James E. Rosscup, *Abiding in Christ* (Grand Rapids, MI: Zondervan, 1973), p. 28 quotes *Calmet's Dictionary,* p. 877.

2. John Nolland, *Luke 9:21—18:34*, vol. 2 (Dallas: Word, 1993), pp. 950–54.

3. Leon Morris, *Luke* (Grand Rapids, MI: Eerdmans, 1974), pp. 211–12.

4. David Gooding, *According to Luke: A New Exposition of the Third Gospel* (Leicester, UK: Inter-Varsity, 1987), p. 318.

5. Charles H. Spurgeon, "The Pleading of the Last Messenger," *The Metropolitan Tabernacle Pulpit*, vol. 33, sermon 1, 951, (Pasadena, TX: Pilgrim, 1975), p. 137.

6. E. Earle Ellis, *The Gospel of Luke* (Grand Rapids, MI: Eerdmans, 1974), p. 233, explains:

> stone: a frequently used "testimony" to Messiah from Ps. 118:22. In Palestinian Judaism the term was related to the messianic "servant." Cf. The Targum on Ps. 118:24; Zech. 3:8f; Walton III, 274 (Pss.), 114 (Zech.).

7. Nolland, *Luke 9:21—18:34*, p. 953.

8. Joseph Fitzmyer, *The Gospel According to Luke, I–IX* (Garden City, NY: Doubleday, 1981), p. 1283.

9. Ellis, *The Gospel of Luke*, p. 161.

Chapter Eighty-Seven: Caesar and God

1. E. Earle Ellis, *The Gospel of Luke* (Grand Rapids, MI: Eerdmans, 1974), p. 233.

2. John Nolland, *Luke 18:35—24:53* (Dallas: Word, 1993), p. 958, explains:

> There had clearly been rioting and rebellion at the time when, as a preliminary to incorporating it into the taxing structure of the empire, Quirinius conducted a major census in Palestine in A.D. 6–7 (see Josephus, *War* 2. 118; *Ant.* 18. 1–8). Josephus links the role of Judas the Galilean in this revolt with the emergence of the Zealot movement and its leadership in the final revolt that led to the downfall of Jerusalem in A.D. 70, but there is reason to be cautious about this connection.

3. Joseph Fitzmyer, *The Gospel According to Luke, I–IX* (Garden City, NY: Doubleday, 1981), p. 1296, explains:

> The silver denarius, weighing 3.8 grams, had been in use in the Roman world since 268 B.C. and continued to be used into the reign of L. Septimius Severus (A.D. 193–211). Denarii bore the head of Tabors and the inscription TI. CAESAR DIVI AVG. F. AVGVSTVS (Tabors Caesar, son of the divine Augustus, Augustus). See F. W. Madden, *Coins of the Jews* (London: Trübner; Boston: J. R. Osgood, 1881), 291–292; E. Stauffer, *Christ and the Caesars* (London: SCM, 1955), 112–113; IDB 1. 824

4. Ibid., p. 1291.

5. Ray C. Stedman, *Expository Studies in Mark 8–16: The Ruler Who Serves* (Waco, TX: Word, 1976), p. 114.

6. Richard Halverson, *Prologue to Prison* (Los Angeles: Cowman, 1964), p. 223.

7. Adolf Deissmann, *Light from the Ancient East* (New York: Hodder and Stoughton, 1911), p. 247.

8. Fitzmyer, *The Gospel According to Luke, I–IX,* p. 1293.

9. Alexander Maclaren, *Expositions of Holy Scriptures* (Grand Rapids, MI: Baker, 1971), p. 202.

10. Ibid.

Chapter Eighty-Eight: Resurrection's Realities

1. Joseph Fitzmyer, *The Gospel According to Luke, X–XXIV* (Garden City, NY: Doubleday, 1985), pp. 1302–3, explains:

> The Greek name *Saddoukaioi* is to be related to the Hebrew proper name *Sadõq*, "Zadok," which appears in Greek (with a double delta) in the LXX as Saddouk (2 Sam 8:17; Ezek 40:46; 43:19) and in Josephus as Saddok or Saddouk (depending on the mss., see *Ant.* 18. 1,1 § 4). The descendants of Zadok (*benê Sadôq*) were granted the privilege of officiating as priests in the Temple after the return from the Babylonian Captivity. These "Zadokites" formed the nucleus of the priesthood staffing the Jerusalem Temple. 1 Chr 5:30–35 [6:4–10E] traces the lineage of Zadok back to Eleazar, elder son of Aaron. Cf. Sir 51:12 (Hebrew; lacking in the Greek and Syriac versions). The Sadducees of first-century Palestine (B.C. and A.D.) were related to this Zadokite priestly line, but they had become a tightly closed circle, no longer exclusively a priestly group.

2. E. Earle Ellis, *The Gospel of Luke* (Grand Rapids, MI: Eerdmans, 1981), p. 235, writes: "Doubtless the argument was effective against the common view that resurrection life was merely an extension of the good life of this age. Cf. SBK I, 887ff. On Mt. 22:28; Enoch 10:17ff.; 1QS 4:7." Similarly John Nolland, *Luke 9:21—18:34* (Dallas: Word, 1993), p. 965, and Leon Morris, *Luke* (Grand Rapids, MI: Eerdmans, 1988), p. 317.

3. Anthony Al Hoekema, *The Four Major Cults* (Grand Rapids, MI: Eerdmans, 1963), pp. 11, 61, and Jan Karl Van Baalen, *The Chaos of Cults* (Grand Rapids, MI: Eerdmans, 1955), pp. 157–59.

4. Charles H. Spurgeon, *The Metropolitan Tabernacle Pulpit*, vol. 14 (Pasadena, TX: Pilgrim, 1970), p. 658.

5. Ibid., p. 657.

6. William L. Lane, *The Gospel According to Mark* (Grand Rapids, MI: Eerdmans, 1975), p. 430, summarizes the argument of French New Testament scholar F. Dreyfus, saying:

> If God has assumed the task of protecting the patriarchs from misfortune during the course of their life, but fails to deliver them from that supreme misfortune which marks the definitive and absolute check upon their hopes, his protection is of little value. But it is inconceivable that God would provide for the patriarchs some partial tokens of deliverance and leave the final word to death, of which all the misfortunes and sufferings of human existence are only a foretaste. If the death of the patriarchs is the last word of their history, there has been a breach of the promises of God guaranteed by the covenant, and of which the formula "the God of Abraham, of Isaac and of Jacob" is the symbol. It is in fidelity to his covenant that God will resurrect the dead.

7. C. H. Spurgeon, "Departed Saints Yet Living," *The Metropolitan Tabernacle Pulpit,* vol. 31, sermon 1, 863, (Pasadena, TX: Pilgrim, 1973), p. 546.

Chapter Eighty-Nine: Son of David, David's Lord

1. *The Westminster Standards,* "The Larger Catechism" (Philadelphia: Great Commission, n.d.), p. 61.

> Question 151.
> What are those aggravations that make some sins more heinous than others?
>
> 1. From the persons offending; if they be of riper age, greater experience of grace, eminent for profession, gifts, place, office, guides to others, and whose example is likely to be followed by others.
> 2. From the parties offended: if immediately against God, his attributes and worship; against Christ, and his grace; the Holy Spirit, his witness, and workings; against superiors, men of eminency, and such as we stand especially related and engaged unto; against any of the saints, particularly weak brethren, the souls of them, or any other, and the common good of all or many.
> 3. From the nature and quality of the offence; if it be against the express letter of the law, break many commandments, contain in it many sins; if not only conceived in the heart, but breaks forth in words and actions, scandalize others, and admit of no reparation; if against means, mercies, judgments, light of nature, conviction of conscience, public or private admonitions, censures of the church, civil punishments; and our prayers, purposes, promises, vows, covenants, and engagements to God or men. . . .
> 4. From circumstances of time and place . . . if in public, or in the presence of others, who are thereby likely to be provoked or defiled.

2. Joachim Jeremias, *Jerusalem in the Time of Jesus,* trans. F. H. and C. H. Cave (Philadelphia: Fortress, 1978), p. 244.

3. I. H. Marshall, *The Gospel of Luke* (Grand Rapids, MI: Eerdmans, 1974), p. 747, says:

> The scribal belief that the Messiah would be a son of David is based on such passages as 2 Sa. 7; Ps. 89:20–37; Is. 9:2–7; Je. 23:5f.; 33:14–18; Ezk. 34:23f.; Ez. 12:32; Shemoneh Esreh 14. "Son of David" is the regular title for the Messiah in rabbinic texts (e.g. Sanh. 981); cf. SB I, 11–14, 525, E. Lohse, TDNT VIII, 480–482; Burger, 16–24. Mars. 747.

4. John Nolland, *Luke 9:21—18:34,* vol. 2 (Dallas: Word, 1993), p. 973.

5. E. Earle Ellis, *The Gospel of Luke* (Grand Rapids, MI: Eerdmans, 1981), p. 237.

6. William H. Willimon, "Been There, Preached That," *Leadership*, Fall 1975, pp. 75ff.

7. Joseph T. Bayly, *Out of My Mind* (Grand Rapids, MI: Zondervan, 1993), p. 174.

8. Joseph Fitzmyer, *The Gospel According to Luke, X—XXIV* (Garden City, NY: Doubleday, 1985), p. 1318.

Chapter Ninety: Money's Eloquence

1. Rachael Field, "Art, Antiquities and Auction," *Pan Am Clipper*, vol. 18, no. 4, April 1988, p. 13.

2. *Psychology Today,* December 1986, p. 23, which quotes from Brad Edmondson, "The Demographics of Gambling," *American Demographics*, vol. 8, no. 7.

3. James Hastings, ed., *Dictionary of Christ and the Gospels*, vol. 2 (Grand Rapids, MI: Baker, 1973), p. 748.

4. *Mishnah*, Shekalim XI.5.

5. Ray C. Stedman, *Expository Studies in Mark 8–16: The Ruler Who Serves* (Waco, TX: Word, 1976), p. 130.

6. Merrill C. Tenney, ed., *The Zondervan Pictorial Encyclopedia of the Bible*, vol. 5 (Grand Rapids, MI: Zondervan, 1975), p. 928.

7. C. E. B. Cranfield, *The Gospel According to St. Mark* (Grand Rapids, MI: Baker, 1966), p. 386.

8. William L. Lane, *The Gospel According to Mark* (Grand Rapids, MI: Eerdmans, 1975), p. 442.

9. John Albert Bengel, *Bengel's New Testament Commentary*, vol. 1, trans. Charlton T. Lewis and Marvin R. Vincent (Grand Rapids, MI: Kregel, 1981), p. 362.

10. Frederick Louis Godet, *Commentary on the Gospel of Luke* (Grand Rapids, MI: Zondervan, n.d.), p. 256.

11. John Calvin, *A Harmony of the Gospels Matthew, Mark and Luke and the Epistles of James and Jude*, vol. 3, trans. A. W. Morrison (Grand Rapids, MI: Eerdmans, 1975), p. 72.

12. J. D. Jones, *The Greatest of These* (London: Hodder & Stoughton, 1925), p. 51.

13. G. Campbell Morgan, *The Gospel According to Luke* (New York: Revell, 1931), p. 235.

14. C. S. Lewis, *Mere Christianity* (New York: Macmillan, 1957), p. 67.

Chapter Ninety-One: The Olivet Discourse

1. E. Earle Ellis, *The Gospel of Luke* (Grand Rapids, MI: Eerdmans, 1981), p. 239.

2. Josephus, *War,* V.1–6; *Antiquities* XV.1–7.

3. Josephus, *War,* V.5. 3.

4. Ibid., V.5. 6.

5. Josephus, *Antiquities*, XV, 11. 3, says: "The temple was built of hard, white stones, each of which was about twenty-five cubits in length, eight in height and twelve in width."

6. Josephus, *War,* VII.1. 1.

7. Will and Ariel Durant, *The Lessons of History* (New York: Simon and Schuster, 1968), p. 81.

8. *TIME*, April 7, 1997, p. 31.

9. Robertson McQuilkin, "Let Me Get Home Before Dark." Used by permission.

10. Eusebius, *Ecclesiastical History*, III.5. 4.
11. Ibid., V.12. 3.
12. Leon Morris, *Luke* (Grand Rapids, MI: Eerdmans, 1974), p. 327, explains:

> In vivid apocalyptic imagery Jesus speaks of heavenly portents. It is not easy to see how literally the words are meant to be taken. Such language is often used in apocalyptic to denote sudden and violent change and the emergence of a new order.

13. David Gooding, *According to Luke: A New Exposition of the Third Gospel* (Leicester, UK: Inter-Varsity, 1987), p. 329.
14. Ellis, *The Gospel of Luke,* p . 247, explains:

> "This generation" in this passage is the "generation of the end-signs" (cf. Conzelmann, p. 105). It is identical with the "generation of the end time" to which Jesus spoke and which extends from the pre-resurrection mission to the parousia. The fact that it covers several (or several dozen) lifetimes is quite irrelevant. Luke especially wishes to stress this point in his opposition to the false, apocalyptic interpretation of Jesus' saying.

Chapter Ninety-Two: The Night without a Morning

1. Clarence Edward Macartney, *Great Nights of the Bible* (New York: Abingdon, 1953), pp. 85–86.
2. A. Cohen, *The Psalms* (London: Soncino, 1962), p. 127, comments:

> In particular one man whom he considered a close friend had proved traitorous. If the Psalm mirrors an incident in David's life, the faithless friend must have been Ahithophel, and the time of its composition the uprising of Absalom. "It is true that the narrative in 2 Samuel makes no reference to an illness such as is here described; but that narrative necessarily passes over many details. Such an illness would account for the remissness in attending to his official duties, which Absalom's words to the suitors for justice seem to imply (2 Sam. xv. 3). It would account also for the strange failure of David's natural courage which his flight from Jerusalem at the first outbreak of the rebellion appears to indicate" (K.).

3. H. C. Leupold, *Exposition of the Psalms* (Grand Rapids: Baker, 1974).
4. D. A. Carson, *The Gospel According to John* (Grand Rapids, MI: Eerdmans, 1991), p. 439–40.
5. William Barclay, *The Gospel of John*, vol. 2 (Philadelphia: Westminster, 1956), p. 169, explains:

> It is quite clear that Judas was in a position in which Jesus could speak to him privately without the others overhearing it. There is a kind of private conversation here going on between Jesus and Judas. Now if that be so there is only one place in which Judas could be sitting. He must have been sitting on Jesus' left, so that, just as John's head was in Jesus' breast, Jesus' head was in Judas' breast. And the revealing thing about that is that the place on the left of the host was the place of highest honour, kept for the most intimate friend. When that meal began, Jesus must have said to Judas:

"Judas, come and sit beside me to-night; I want specially to talk to you." The very inviting of Judas to that seat was an appeal.

6. Carson, *The Gospel According to John*, p. 474, is most helpful:

> Apparently Jesus' answer was given in quiet tones: vv. 27–30 make it clear that the other disciples did not know why Judas Iscariot left. Why "the disciple whom Jesus loved" did nothing is less clear, unless the momentous nature of Jesus' confidence left him temporarily paralyzed—the more so since Jesus himself was clearly taking no remedial action. The host at a feast (whose role is here filled by Jesus) might well dip into a common bowl and pull out a particularly tasty bit and pass it to a guest as a mark of honour or friendship. The word behind this piece of bread *(psomion),* used only here in the New Testament, means, literally, a morsel, and commonly referred to bread, though sometimes to meat. The Evangelist may well be thinking of an early point in the paschal meal when bitter herbs were dipped into a bowl of fruit puree, the haroset sauce of dates, raisins and sour wine. This "sop" Jesus passed to Judas Iscariot. That Jesus could pass it so easily suggests Judas was close by, possibly on his left, the place of honour.

7. William Hendrickson, *Exposition of the Gospel According to Matthew* (Grand Rapids, MI: Baker, 1973), p. 943 says:

> Exactly when it was that Judas was seized with remorse is not indicated, but the text leaves the impression that it was immediately after he knew that Jesus had been sentenced to death. He may have rushed to the chief priests and elders at the very moment when the procession was forming to lead Jesus to the praetorium.

8. Macartney, *Great Nights of the Bible*, pp. 86–87.

9. David Gooding, *According to Luke: A New Exposition of the Third Gospel* (Leicester, UK: Inter-Varsity, 1987), pp. 330–31.

Chapter Ninety-Three: The Last Supper, Part 1

1. Geoffrey W. Bromiley, ed., *The International Standard Bible Encyclopedia*, vol. 3 (Grand Rapids, MI: Eerdmans, 1986), p. 677. Most of the following description of the Passover is taken from the excellent article by Marvin R. Wilson.

2. C. Marvin Pate, *Luke* (Chicago: Moody, 1995), p. 418, where the writer adds:

> The eating of unleavened bread commemorated the haste with which the Jews in captivity in Egypt ate their bread before their Exodus. Because it takes time for leaven to cause bread to rise, the Jews ate unleavened bread, so that they could be ready for a quick escape from Pharaoh. The idea of unleavened bread later took on spiritual connotations—it represented the purging of sin from one's life (see 1 Cor. 5:7–8). To this day orthodox Jews celebrating Passover participate in a ceremony on *parasceve* in which, with candle and spoon, they find and remove any leaven present in the house.

3. Leon Morris, *Luke* (Grand Rapids, MI: Eerdmans, 1988), p. 332.

4. E. Earle Ellis, *The Gospel of Luke* (Grand Rapids, MI: Eerdmans, 1981), pp. 421–22.

5. John Blanchard, *The Truth for Life* (West Sussex, UK: H. E. Walker, Ltd., 1982), p. 231.

Chapter Ninety-Four: The Last Supper, Part 2

1. Leon Morris, *Luke* (Grand Rapids, MI: Eerdmans, 1988), p. 336.

2. Ibid.

3. John Nolland, *Luke 9:21—18:34* (Dallas: Word, 1993), p. 1078.

4. E. Earle Ellis, *The Gospel of Luke* (Grand Rapids, MI: Eerdmans, 1981), p. 257.

5. Joseph A. Fitzmyer, *The Gospel According to Luke, X—XXIV* (Garden City, NY: Doubleday, 1985), p. 1430.

6. Morris, *Luke,* p. 339.

7. C. Marvin Pate, *Luke* (Chicago: Moody, 1995), p. 432.

8. Fitzmyer, *The Gospel According to Luke, X—XXIV,* p. 1432.

9. Alexander Maclaren, *Expositions of Holy Scriptures* (Grand Rapids, MI: Baker, 1971), p. 246.

Chapter Ninety-Five: Divine Dread

1. Joseph A. Fitzmyer, *The Gospel According to Luke, X—XXIV* (Garden City, NY: Doubleday, 1985), pp. 1438–39 explains:

> The result is a stark abridgment of the Marcan account, one that centers on Jesus' relation to his Father much more than on his concern about the nonchalance of the uncomprehending disciples. As one might expect in the Gospel, the Lucan Jesus emphasizes the need for prayer in the lives of the disciples who are "following" him into the ordeal that is about to unfold. His double exhortation to them to pray forms a frame for his own prayer.

2. D. Edmond Hiebert, *Mark: A Portrait of a Servant* (Chicago: Moody, 1974), p. 358.

3. Vincent Taylor, *The Gospel According to St. Mark* (Grand Rapids, MI: Eerdmans, 1981), p. 553, comments: "The addition ἕως θανάγου denotes a sorrow which threatens life itself, cf. Swete, 342, 'a sorrow that well nigh kills.'"

4. Fitzmyer, *The Gospel According to Luke, X–XXIV*, p. 1444.

5. Gay Talese, *Unto the Sons* (New York: Alfred A. Knopf, 1992), pp. 179–80.

6. Raymond E. Brown, *The Death of the Messiah*, vol. 1 (New York: Doubleday, 1994), p. 218.

7. Philip Jensen, as transcribed from *Did Christ Have to Die?* A taped message delivered at College Church in Wheaton, Illinois, April 25, 1993.

8. Leon Morris, *Luke* (Grand Rapids, MI: Eerdmans, 1988), p. 348, explains of the cup:

> τούτο τό ποτήριου (for the order, diff. Mk., cf. 22:20) is a metaphor for the impending suffering of Jesus (cf. especially Is. 51:22; Mk. 10:38). It refers especially to the infliction of punishment associated with the wrath of

God (Pss. 11:6; 75:8; Is. 51:17; Je. 25:15, 17, 28; La. 4:21; Ezk. 23:31–33; Hab. 2:16).

9. David Gooding, *According to Luke: A New Exposition of the Third Gospel* (Leicester, UK: Inter-Varsity, 1987), p. 336.

10. E. Earle Ellis, *The Gospel of Luke* (Grand Rapids, MI: Eerdmans, 1981), p. 257.

11. Jensen, *Did Christ Have to Die?* Here many of the concluding applications are drawn from Rev. Jensen's masterful exposition.

12. Charles Williams, *The Descent of the Dove* (London: The Religious Book Club, 1939), pp. 39–40.

Chapter Ninety-Six: "The Power of Darkness"

1. D. James Kennedy, *Truths That Transform* (Old Tappan, NJ: Revell, 1974), p. 16.

2. Robert Atwan and Laurence Weider, eds., *Chapters into Verse,* vol. 2 (New York: Oxford, 1993), p. 191, which records the last line of Vassar Miller's poem "Judas."

3. Albert Schweitzer, *The Quest for the Historical Jesus* (New York: Macmillan, 1959), pp. 370–71.

4. Raymond E. Brown, *The Death of the Messiah,* vol. 1 (New York: Doubleday, 1994), p. 258.

5. Alexander Maclaren, *Expositions of Holy Scriptures* (Grand Rapids, MI: Baker, 1971), p. 252.

6. David Gooding, *According to Luke: A New Exposition of the Third Gospel* (Leicester, UK: Inter-Varsity, 1987), p. 336.

7. The comparisons are: Luke 22:53, ἡ ἐξοσια τοῦ σκότους Colossians 1:13, τῆς ἐξουσιας τοῦ σκότους; and Ephesians 6:12, τὰς ἐξουσσὶας πρὸς τοὺς κοσμοκράτορας τοῦ σκότους τούτου.

8. Brown, *The Death of the Messiah*, p. 293.

9. G. Abbott-Smith, *A Manual Greek Lexicon of the New Testament* (New York: Scribners, n.d.), p. 20.

10. C. E. B. Cranfield, *The Gospel According to St. Mark* (Cambridge, UK: Cambridge, 1983), p. 437.

Chapter Ninety-Seven: Peter's Plunge

1. Clarence Edward Macartney, *The Greatest Men of the Bible* (Nashville: Abingdon, 1980), p. 74.

2. Alexander Whyte, *Bible Characters*, vol. 2 (Grand Rapids, MI: Zondervan, 1967), p. 38.

3. Leon Morris, *Luke* (Grand Rapids, MI: Eerdmans, 1988), p. 482.

4. Joseph Fitzmyer, *The Gospel According to Luke, X—XXIV* (Garden City, NY: Doubleday, 1985), p. 1460.

5. Raymond E. Brown, *The Gospel of John*, vol. 2 (Garden City, NY: Doubleday, 1970), p. 1121.

6. J. H. Bernard, *The Gospel According to St. John*, vol. 2 (Edinburgh: T. & T. Clark, 1928), p. 709. Also C. K. Barrett, *The Gospel According to St. John* (London: S.P.C.K., 1975), p. 487.

7. C. S. Lewis, *Mere Christianity* (New York: Macmillan, 1960), p. 118.

8. Ibid., p. 172.

Chapter Ninety-Eight: Jesus' Religious Trial

1. Joseph Fitzmyer, *The Gospel According to Luke, I–IX* (Garden City, NY: Doubleday, 1981), p. 197.

2. Joseph Fitzmyer, *The Gospel According to Luke, I–IX* (Garden City, NY: Doubleday, 1981), p. 1467 explains: "If the title 'Son of Man' is intended to have a judicial connotation (so C. Colpe, *TDNT* 8. 435), as it seems to have in 11:30, then Jesus declares that as such he will turn out to be the judge of those who interrogate him now."

Chapter Ninety-Nine: Herod before Jesus

1. Josephus, *Antiquities*, Book XVIII, v. 2.

2. *Ibid.*, Book XIX, vii. 1.

3. Joseph Fitzmyer, *The Gospel According to Luke, X—XXIV* (Garden City, NY: Doubleday, 1985), p. 1475.

Chapter One Hundred: Pilate before Jesus

1. John Nolland, *Luke 18:35—24:53* (Dallas: Word, 1993), p. 1124, comments:

> In v 15 this action on the part of Herod will be taken up as evidence for Jesus' innocence of any major crime. For the Lukan reader, this evidence weighs yet more heavily because of the known hostility of Herod toward Jesus (13:31 and demonstrated here in the mockery of Jesus and toward his precursor, John (3:19–20).

2. I. H. Marshall, *The Gospel of Luke* (Grand Rapids, MI: Eerdmans, 1978), p. 859.

3. E. Earle Ellis, *The Gospel of Luke* (Grand Rapids, MI: Eerdmans, 1974), p. 264.

Chapter One Hundred One: The Cross of Christ

1. William L. Lane, *The Gospel According to Mark* (Grand Rapids, MI: Eerdmans, 1975), pp. 567–68 writes:

> On the way to the execution site a delinquent wore or had carried before him a wooden board whitened with chalk on which letters were written in ink or burned in specifying his crime. After the execution this summary statement was fastened to the cross above the head of the crucified (cf. Juvenal, *Satires* VI. 230; Pliny the Younger, *Epistles* VI). The notice attached to the cross on which the tortured body of Jesus hung bore, in black or red letters on the white ground, the inscription "King of the Jews."

2. Martin Hengel, *Crucifixion* (Philadelphia: Fortress, 1978), p. 50, explains: "Quintillian could therefore praise the crucifixion as a good work: in his view the crosses ought to be set on the busiest roads."

3. Raymond E. Brown, *The Death of the Messiah*, vol. 2 (New York: Doubleday, 1994), pp. 914–15.

4. Ibid., p. 915, provides helpful background:

> Certain details in the description of Simon need comment. He is identified as a Cyrenian, an unusual detail to invent if his role was not historical. Cyrene was the capital city of the North African district of Cyrenaica in the area of Libya. Josephus (*Against Apion* 2. 4; #44) reports that Ptolemy I Soter (ca. 300 BC), in order to solidify Egyptian hold on the cities of Libya, sent in Jews to settle. There was a Cyrenian synagogue in Jerusalem (Acts 6:9). Christian preachers from Cyrene appear in Acts 11:20; and Lucius the Cyrenian is mentioned alongside Simon Niger in Acts 13:1 as a Christian leader at Antioch. Thus there is no inherent implausibility that there could have been a Cyrenian Jew named Simon in Jerusalem at the time of Jesus' death and that he could have become a Christian.

5. F. W. Boreham, *A Casket of Cameos* (New York: Abingdon, 1924), pp. 234–35.

6. Brown, *The Death of the Messiah*, p. 914.

7. Ibid., pp. 915, 931, 932.

8. I. H. Marshall, *The Gospel of Luke* (Grand Rapids, MI: Eerdmans, 1978), p. 864.

9. Joseph Fitzmyer, *The Gospel According to Luke, I–IX* (Garden City, NY: Doubleday, 1985), p. 1497.

10. Brown, *The Death of the Messiah*, pp. 920–21, explains:

> Luke follows here an OT pattern of addressing females as representatives of the nation or the city in oracles of joy or woe: "Daughters of Israel" (II Sam 1:24); "Daughter Zion" (Zeph 3:14; Zech 9:9); and "Daughters of Jerusalem" (Song [Canticle] 2:7). Calling the women "Daughters of Jerusalem" is not pejorative, but it identifies their fate with that of the city.

11. John Nolland, *Luke 18:35—24:53* (Dallas: Word, 1993), p. 1139.

12. David Gooding, *According to Luke: A New Exposition of the Third Gospel* (Leicester, UK: Inter-Varsity, 1987), p. 342.

Chapter One Hundred Two: Jesus Saves

1. Martin Hengel, *Crucifixion* (Philadelphia: Fortress, 1978), p. 35.

2. William D. Edwards, MD, Wesley J. Gabol, MDiv, Floyd E. Josmar, MS, AMI, "On the Physical Death of Jesus Christ," *Journal of the American Medical Association*, 255, no. 11 (1986), pp. 1455–63.

3. C. S. Lewis, *The Four Loves* (New York: Harcourt, Brace, Jovanovich, 1960), p. 176.

4. John Nolland, *Luke 18:35—24:53* (Dallas: Word, 1993), pp. 1144–45.

5. David Gooding, *According to Luke: A New Exposition of the Third Gospel* (Leicester, UK: Inter-Varsity, 1987), p. 342.

6. Derek Kidner, *Psalms 1–72* (Downers Grove, IL: InterVarsity, 1972), p. 247.

7. I. H. Marshall, *The Gospel of Luke* (Grand Rapids, MI: Eerdmans, 1978), p. 871.

8. Ibid., p. 872, explains:

> The reference is to the parousia of Jesus as the Son of man as a future event associated with the raising of the dead. The criminal thus regards Jesus as more than a martyr; he implicitly confesses his faith that Jesus is the Messiah or Son of man.

9. Clarence Macartney, *The Making of a Minister* (Great Neck, NY: Channel, 1961), p. 224.

10. Marshall, *The Gospel of Luke*, pp. 872–73.

11. Alexander Maclaren, *Expositions of Holy Scriptures* (Grand Rapids, MI: Baker, 1971), pp. 316–17. In addition to the author's marvelous quotation I have also borrowed most of the thoughts that frame the quotations and put them in my own words.

12. Ibid., p. 318.

13. James Boswell, *The Life of Samuel Johnson* (London: Penguin, 1979), p. 299.

> Johnson. 'Sir, we are not to judge determinately of the state in which a man leaves this life. He may in a moment have repented effectually, and it is possible may have been accepted by God. There is in *Camden's Remains,* an epitaph upon a very wicked man, who was killed by a fall from his horse, in which he is supposed to say, "Between the stirrup and the ground, I mercy asked, I mercy found."

14. Donald Grey Barnhouse, *The Love Life* (Glendale, CA: Regal, 1974), pp. 270–73.

Chapter One Hundred Three: Jesus Dies

1. Rabbi Dr. I. Epstein, ed., *The Babylonian Talmud Seder Nezikin*, vol. 3 (London: Soncino, 1935), pp. 279–80, reads:

> When one is led out to execution, he is given a goblet of wine containing a grain of frankincense, in order to benumb his senses, for it is taught, Give strong drink unto him that is ready to perish, and wine unto the bitter in soul. And it has also been taught: The noble women in Jerusalem used to donate and bring it. If these did not donate it, who provided it?— As for that, it is certainly logical that it should be provided out of the public [funds]: since it is written, 'Give', [the implication is] of what is theirs. (7) Prov. XXXI,6.

2. John Henry Cardinal Newman, *The Kingdom Within (Discourses Addressed to Mixed Congregations)* (Denville, NJ: Dimension, 1984), pp. 328–29.

3. I. H. Marshall, *The Gospel of Luke* (Grand Rapids, MI: Eerdmans, 1978), pp. 873–75.

4. Ibid., p. 876.

5. Raymond E. Brown, *The Death of the Messiah,* vol. 2 (New York, Doubleday, 1994), pp. 1163–67.

6. Ibid., p. 1167.

Chapter One Hundred Four: Jesus' Burial and Resurrection

1. I. H. Marshall, *The Gospel of Luke* (Grand Rapids, MI: Eerdmans, 1974), p. 879: "'Αριμαθαία is mentioned only here and in the parallels. The site is generally identified with Ramathaim-zophim (1 Sa. 1:1), modern Rentis, just N of Jerusalem."

2. Raymond E. Brown, *The Death of the Messiah,* vol. 2 (New York: Doubleday, 1994), p. 1227.

3. E. Earle Ellis, *The Gospel of Luke* (Grand Rapids, MI: Eerdmans, 1974), p. 270.

4. Edward J. Defort, "Elvis Has Really Left the Building," *The American Funeral Director*, pp. 2–11.

5. Ibid., p. 9.

6. Joseph Fitzmyer, *The Gospel According to Luke, I–IX* (Garden City, NY: Doubleday, 1981), p. 1545.

7. John Nolland, *Luke 18:35—24:53* (Dallas: Word, 1993), p. 1139.

8. Leon Morris, *Luke* (Grand Rapids, MI: Eerdmans, 1988), p. 365.

9. Alexander Maclaren, *Expositions of Holy Scriptures* (Grand Rapids, MI: Baker, 1971), p. 322.

Chapter One Hundred Five: Easter Fire

1. I. H. Marshall, *The Gospel of Luke* (Grand Rapids, MI: Eerdmans, 1978), p. 894. Marshall says that if these identifications are correct, they were probably the parents of Simeon who would later become Bishop of Jerusalem as Eusebius suggested, HE 3:11, 32; 4:22.

2. J. I. Packer, "Walking to Emmaus with the Great Physician," *Christianity Today*, April 10, 1981, p. 22. Dr. Packer provides the ideas for the preceding paragraphs with what to do with the depressed person's determination to hear bad news.

3. Marshall, *The Gospel of Luke*, p. 897.

4. Charles Hodge, *A Commentary on 1 & 2 Corinthians* (Edinburgh: Banner of Truth, 1974), p. 398.

5. Marshall, *The Gospel of Luke,* p. 897.

6. David Gooding, *According to Luke* (Grand Rapids, MI: Eerdmans, 1987), p. 353.

7. James Hastings, ed., *The Speakers' Bible,* vol. 3 (Grand Rapids, MI: Baker, 1971), p. 268.

Chapter One Hundred Six: Easter Gospel and Mission

1. Leon Morris, *Luke* (Grand Rapids, MI: Eerdmans, 1988), p. 373.

Chapter One Hundred Seven: Christ's Ascension

1. Peter Toon, *The Ascension of Our Lord* (Nashville: Thomas Nelson, 1984), p. 6.

2. Joseph Fitzmyer, *The Gospel According to Luke, I–IX* (Garden City, NY: Doubleday, 1981), p. 1587, explains:

> This episode not only forms the end of the Lucan Gospel, but it is the climax of the whole latter part of it—from the crucial chap. 9 on. In 9:31 the transfigured Jesus converses with Moses and Elijah about his "departure" *(exodos),* which he is to complete in Jerusalem. Again, in 9:51 the reader learns about the days that were drawing near "when he was to be taken up to heaven." The *exodos,* which has been explained as "his entire transit to the Father" through death and resurrection "ending in the ascension" (p. 800), has now been achieved. The goal and destiny toward which the Lucan Jesus has been resolutely moving have now been reached. It is the status to which he referred in his answer to the Sanhedrin in 22:69, "From now on the Son of Man will be seated at the right hand of the power of God." Indeed, from the "glory" (v. 26) he has appeared to Simon (v. 34), to the two disciples at Emmaus (vv. 15–31), and finally to the Eleven and all the others in this literary unit (vv. 36–53).

3. Toon, *The Ascension of Our Lord*, p. 23.
4. Ibid., p. 5.
5. Leon Morris, *Luke* (Grand Rapids, MI: Eerdmans, 1988), p. 375, argues:

> The incarnation is not something casual and fleeting but a divine action with permanent consequences. And Moule argues that if the ascension means the taking of Christ's humanity into heaven, "it means that with it will be taken the humanity which He has redeemed—those who are Christ's, at His coming. It is a powerful expression of the redemption of this world, in contrast to mere escape from it."

Scripture Index

General Index

Index of Sermon Illustrations

C. S. Lewis on how Christ wants to kill self, so that we hand all of it to him, 560
How Charles Simeon, amidst his ministerial burdens, was encouraged when his eye fell on the story of Simon from Cyrene, 811

Dissatisfaction
Augustine on God's strewing bitterness over his pleasures, 657
Augustine on God's giving him no peace until his soul could discern him, 657
Augustine on how God follows us fugitives close behind, 661
C. S. Lewis: "The hardness of God is kinder than the softness of men . . . ," 661

Division
The peace march that broke up due to strife, 440

Dualism
How films like *Batman* conflate good and evil, promoting dualism, 279

Earnestness
Charles Kingsley's poem that begins "Be earnest, earnest, earnest," 72

Ego
Woodrow Wilson's remark about a man being the only one he knew who could strut while sitting down, 388
Spurgeon describes the vain dress of some Victorian preachers, 457–58
The preacher who had to have a helicopter in order to preach an Easter service, 458

Elitism
How Methodism, which originally ministered to the poor, became elitist and kicked out William Booth who then founded the Salvation Army, 193
Karl Marx never truly knew or had a friendship with a member of the proletariat, 397

Encouragement
How Charles Simeon, amidst his ministerial burdens, was encouraged when his eye fell on the story of Simon from Cyrene, 811

Envy
St. John of the Cross on how we come to envy others who are more spiritual than us, 374–75

Evangelism
John Wesley's momentous decision to be "more vile" and take the gospel to the open air, 143
Conversion of Mrs. Smith, 169–70
The ophthalmologist to the man for whom sight had been restored: "Tell everybody you see that you were blind, and tell them who it was who healed you," 318
James Davidson Hunter's research conclusion that modern evangelicals are fascinated with self, 350

Expectancy
St. Elmo's fire as a metaphor for relational tension, 179

Faith
More than intellectual belief, 45
How Edith and Francis Schaeffer's faith meant cost and sacrifice, 182
How Radio Station HCJB's belief that Christ is the only way has produced immense creativity, 182
The faith of the Willis family at the time of the loss of six children, 253
"We are not saved by effort, but we shall not believe without efforts" (Alexander Maclaren), 530

"I want to give $100—anonymously," 724
When we write a check to the IRS, it doesn't care at all about our heart's attitude, 726
Poem with line "For the gift without the giver is bare," 727
Joseph Parker on how God disregards "the gold of affluence which is given because it is not needed," 727
C. S. Lewis: "I am afraid the only safe way to give is to give more than we can spare . . . ," 727

Glorifying God
The old woman who would shout to the preacher "Get him [Jesus] up!" 118

God
John Owen: "He that hath slight thoughts of sin never had great thoughts of God," 279

God the Father
Poem that begins "Said the Robin to the Sparrow," 136, 484

God's Care
Poem: a dialogue between a sparrow and a robin that concludes, "They have no heavenly Father / Such as cares for you and me," 136, 484

God's Faithfulness
Poem "Yesterday, God helped me . . . ," 339

God's Pursuit of Sinners
Augustine on God's strewing bitterness over his pleasures, 567
Augustine on God's giving him no peace until his soul could discern him, 567
Francis Thompson's *Hound of Heaven*, 569
Augustine on how God follows us fugitives close behind, 661
C. S. Lewis: "The hardness of God is kinder than the softness of men . . . ," 661

Goodness
Little boy's prayer: "Dear God, make all bad people good, and all good people nice," 578
Mark Twain: "He was a 'good man' in the worst sense of the word," 578

The Gospel
John Wesley's momentous decision to be "more vile" and take the gospel to the open air, 143
The Asian Harvard student who said, "Oh yes. I've found the narrow way," 527

Government
U.S. Senate Chaplain Richard Halverson regarding human government as a divine institution, 701

Grace
The once self-righteous judge who rightly considered his salvation a greater miracle of grace than the salvation of a thief, 150–51
C. S. Lewis poem that ends, "But picture how the camel feels, squeezed out / In one long bloody thread from tail to snout," 641

Growth
Poem about asking God for growth, and God sending difficulty, 305
Ruth Graham's prayer that she soar on the wings of adversity, 305

Greed
The daughters who tagged their dead father's possessions for themselves while he lay in the funeral home, 477

Guilt
Calvin to Hobbes, "I love the culture of victimhood . . . ," 465

Arthur Conan Doyle's playful telegram: "Fly at once, all is discovered," 470
Chuck Colson's pre-salvation awareness of sin, 510
To the IRS: "If my conscience still bothers me, I'll send the rest," 702
Will Rogers: "There are two eras in American history—the passing of the buffalo and the passing of the buck," 465, 799

Happiness
Erma Bombeck's story of the woman who chastened her daughter: "Stop that grinning—you're in church," 196
The man who concluded that good Christians do not smile because the Scriptures never record that Christ smiled, 196
How the Franciscans laughed, the Methodists adopted dance music, preachers jumped for joy, 199

Hatred
Robert Louis Stevenson story about the sisters who because of a theological disagreement never spoke to each other again, though they lived together, 423

The Heart
St. Augustine: It is not our feet, but our darkened affections that distance us from God, 578

Heaven
C. S. Lewis explains that a desire for heavenly reward is not mercenary, 234
Vachal Lindsey poem "General William Booth Enters Heaven," 553

Hedonism
Hedonist's relief: "You mean I don't have to do what I want to do?" 480

Hell
James Barrie's flip comment: "Heaven for climate, hell for company," 123

Holy Spirit
Lloyd-Jones's unforgettable experiences of the Holy Spirit's power in preaching, 117
How Lloyd-Jones prayed for and relied upon the Holy Spirit's power for preaching, 117

Honesty
Royal Robbins on how mountain climbing is an exercise in reality, 261
A scientist's astonishment in 1674 when he looked through his primitive microscope at a drop of water, 263

Hope
"One alone was saved upon the Cross that none might despair; and only one, that none might presume," 822
Poem: "Between the stirrup and the ground, I mercy ask'd, I mercy found," 822

Humility
St. Augustine on humility as the first, second, and third thing, 53
John Wesley's momentous decision to be "more vile" and take the gospel to the open air, 143
President Nixon's mistaken belief that the people want proud, aloof leaders, 371
G. K. Chesterton: "It is only the fool who tries to get the heavens inside his head," 729
Copernicus's request to God for the mercy shown to the dying robber on the cross, 821

Hypocrisy
The "evangelical" bank robbers, 112
C. S. Lewis: "None are so unholy as those whose hands are cauterised with holy things . . . ," 278
Helmut Thielicke regarding "half-Christians" whose "faith" has no root, 298–99